THE
ANABASIS OF XENOPHON

EDITED WITH INTRODUCTION
AND COMMENTARY

BY

AUGUSTUS TABER MURRAY, PH. D.

Professor of Greek in the
Leland Stanford Junior University

SCOTT, FORESMAN AND COMPANY

CHICAGO   ATLANTA   DALLAS   NEW YORK

COPYRIGHT, 1914
BY
SCOTT, FORESMAN AND COMPANY
491.6

Printed in the United States of America

PREFACE

This edition of the Anabasis was undertaken with no other end in view than the production of a book which might prove interesting and helpful to the student of Greek in the early stages of his study, and a useful manual for the teacher. The text given follows Gemoll more closely than any other editor, but by no means all of his readings have been accepted. In general no real revision of the text has been undertaken. A very few excisions have been made, but for the most part square brackets have been used to designate words or phrases of doubtful authenticity. In passages in which the true reading is uncertain the needs of those for whom the book is intended have naturally led the editor to give a readable text.

The text of the entire *Anabasis* (seven books), is given. although the commentary covers only the four books commonly read. The interesting narrative of the later books is therefore available for sight translation, and the vocabulary has been made to cover all seven books, not the first four merely.

The vocabulary itself is condensed, and is meant to supply only what the student of Xenophon needs and can use. This is particularly true in the matter of etymologies, where a scientific treatment seems quite beyond the reach of the average student of Xenophon, and it is true also in the matter of verb forms.

Military matters occupy much less space in Introduction and Commentary than is the case in many editions, although enough information is given to enable the student to understand Xenophon's narrative; and as regards the grammatical element, which may seem to have been unduly emphasized, the editor has been guided by the desire to meet the needs both of those who teach syntax from the grammars, and of those who, like himself, prefer to teach it by illustration.

Hence references to the standard grammars are given (G for Goodwin, H for Hadley-Allen, B for Babbitt), while at the same time much syntactical information is included in the Commentary itself. Cross-references naturally abound, and these have been repeatedly checked off to ensure accuracy. References to the text are to chapter and line, unless the section mark (§) is given. In the Vocabulary, however, references are uniformly to sections.

The author has endeavored not to allow the stress laid upon grammar to prevent the student from feeling the charm of the story, or from becoming interested in Xenophon as writer and as man

A. T. MURRAY.

Chappaqua, New York.
October, 1913.

TABLE OF CONTENTS

	PAGE
PREFACE	iii

INTRODUCTION—

   I. Xenophon, His Life, Character, and Writings..... vii

  II. Persia to the Time of Cyrus the Younger........ xvii

 III. Cyrus and His Expedition.....................xxiii

 IV. Miscellaneous xliv

TEXT AND COMMENTARY................................ 1

VOCABULARY

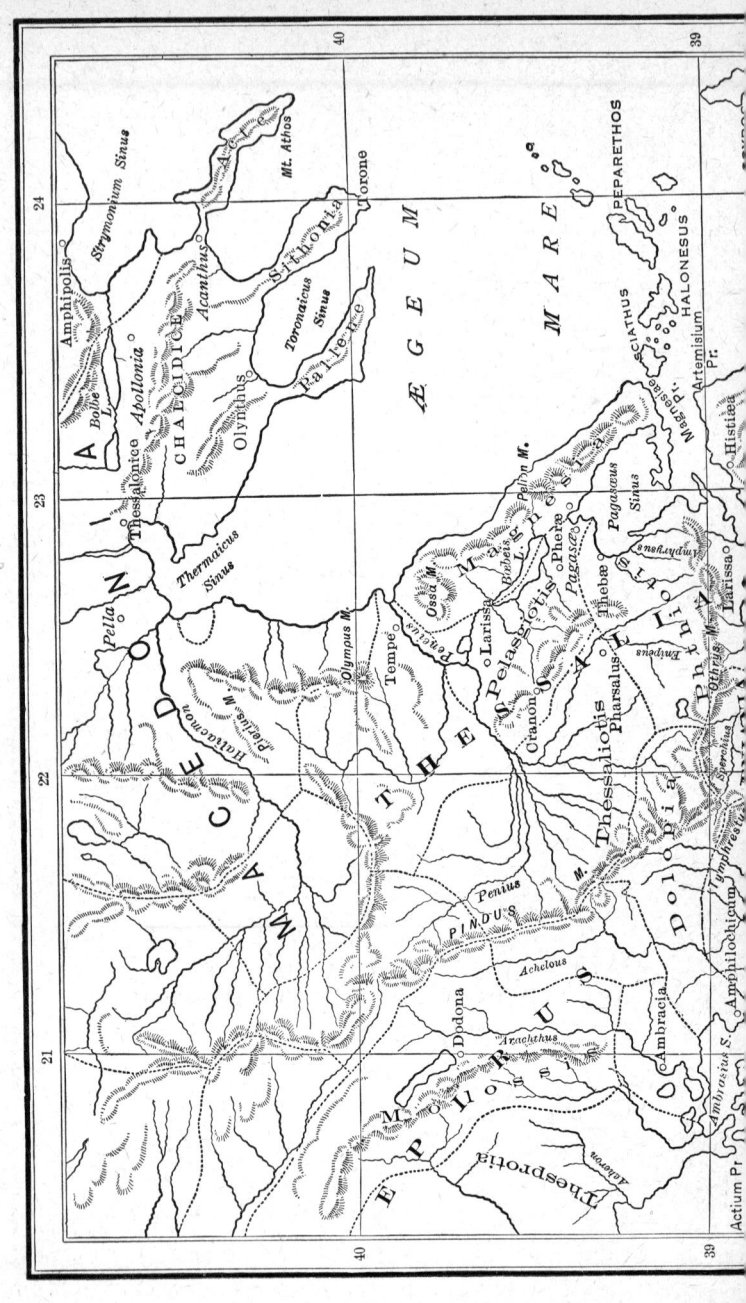

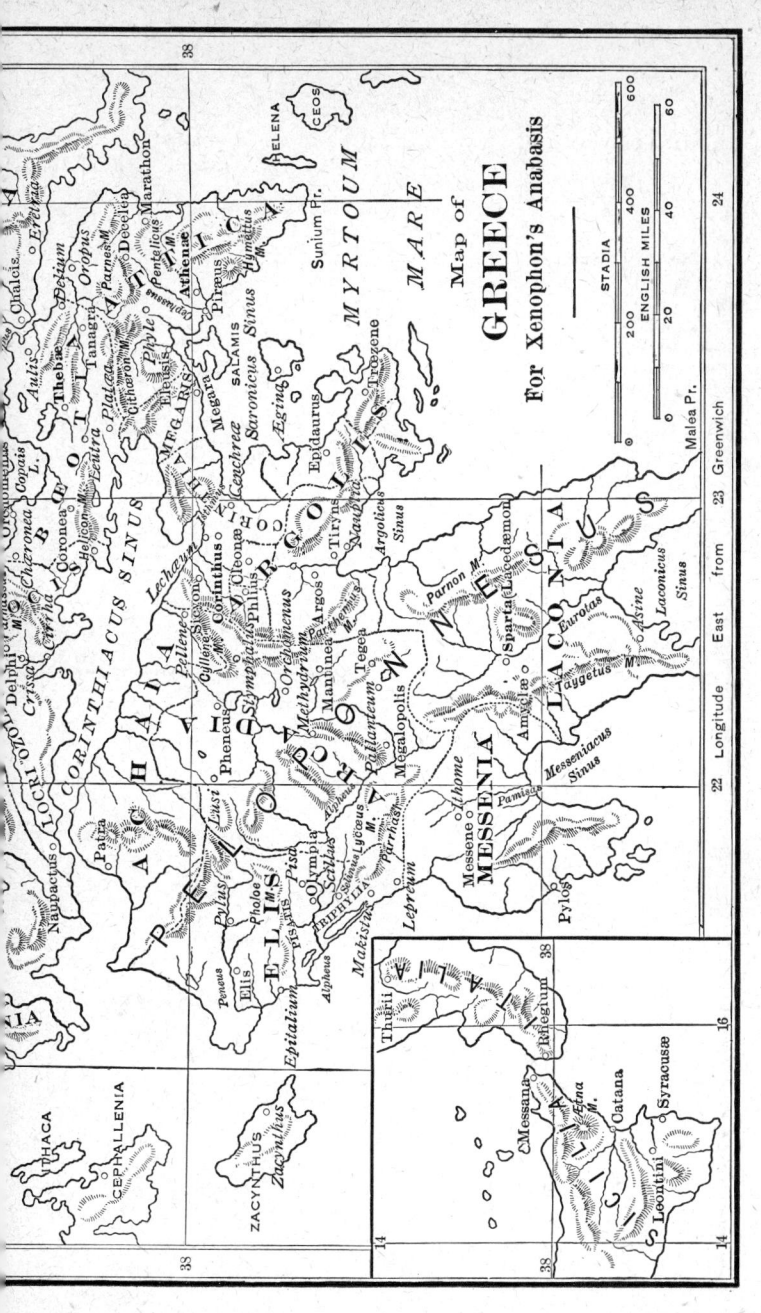

INTRODUCTION

I

XENOPHON, HIS LIFE, CHARACTER, AND WRITINGS

1. DATE OF XENOPHON'S BIRTH.—Xenophon, the author of the *Anabasis*, was an Athenian, the son of Gryllus and Diodōra. His birthplace was the deme Erchia, on the eastern slopes of the Hymettus range, some twelve miles from Athens. As to the date of his birth there has been much dispute, but it seems most probable that he was born about 431 B. C., the year in which the Peloponnesian war broke out. Certainly he makes it clear that at the time of Cyrus' expedition he was a young man, possibly, though hardly probably, under thirty (see *Anabasis* III, 1, §§ 14 and 25; III, 2, § 37.) The older view, accepting as authentic the story told in Diog. Lært. II, 22 (cf. Strabo p. 403), to the effect that Socrates bore the wounded Xenophon from the field of Delium (B. C. 424), places his birth about B. C. 444. This story is however all but certainly an echo of that told by Alcibiades in Plato's *Symposium* (220 de; Plut. *Alc.* 7) of his being saved by Socrates at Potidaea (B. C. 432), and lacks all credibility.

2. BOYHOOD AND TRAINING.—Of Xenophon's boyhood and youth no record has come down to us, but certain things may safely be assumed. His fondness for out-of-door sports is attested by the fact that among his writings are tracts on horsemanship and on hunting, and this fondness dates presumably from his boyhood. He must also be assumed to have had the training in music, letters, and gymnastics, which a well-to-do Athenian, such as Gryllus undoubtedly was, would naturally give his son; and it must be remembered not only that the Athens of Xenophon's boyhood days was the mistress of an empire, and a city of wealth and power, but that the

crowning manifestations of the Attic spirit in Art and Literature would be among the most potent formative influences surrounding his early years. Moreover it was a time when his country was at war, and by the time Xenophon had reached his eighteenth year the Spartans had occupied Decelēa, in Attic territory, and Xenophon must have been among those who served in arms against the invaders. To these facts we must add that Xenophon was a man of deeply religious nature, and we note further that service in arms and in the popular assembly must have done much to develop in him that versatility which enabled him later on to deal so ably with the most baffling and disheartening situations.

3. FRIENDSHIP WITH SOCRATES.—As a boy, or at least as a very young man, Xenophon became a pupil of Socrates, and was profoundly influenced by the unique personality of the great teacher. Diogenes Laertius tells a pretty story of the boy's first meeting with the philosopher. Socrates, he says, met Xenophon, a comely and modest boy, in a narrow way, and, holding his staff so as to block the boy's passage, asked him where provisions could be bought. On the boy's answering the question, he asked again: "And where are men made noble and good (καλοὶ κἀγαθοί)?" To this Xenophon could give no answer; and Socrates continued, "Follow me, then, and learn."

Whether this story be truth or fiction, it is certain that Xenophon was for years a follower of Socrates, and conceived for the homely and unpopular philosopher a deep and abiding affection, to which his *Memorabilia* bears abundant witness.

4. JOINS THE EXPEDITION OF CYRUS.—In the *Anabasis* III, 1, Xenophon tells us how he came to join the expedition of Cyrus, which the *Anabasis* has made famous. In the spring of 401, having seen the downfall of Athens after a protracted struggle, marked not only by disasters to her arms, but by greed and party-strife within her walls, Xenophon was invited by a friend, Proxenus of Boeotia, to join an expedition under the young Persian prince, Cyrus. Various motives

may have prompted him to accept the invitation, love of adventure, ambition (for the wealth and munificence of Cyrus were well known), and, it may be, a feeling of discontent with conditions at Athens. He tells us, however, that he asked the advice of Socrates, who bade him consult the oracle at Delphi. This Xenophon did, but, having already decided to go, merely asked the oracle to what gods he should sacrifice, in order to ensure success in his project. Having followed the oracle's instructions in this regard, he set sail, and joined Proxenus in Sardis. The latter introduced him to Cyrus, and Xenophon joined the expedition unofficially, as it were, and without rank in the army.

5. PROMINENCE DURING THE RETREAT.—We hear practically nothing of him during the upward march from Sardis to Babylonia, but after the treacherous seizure of the Greek generals, when the plight of the army seemed desperate, Xenophon comes to the front with remarkable courage, wisdom, and military skill, and becomes the real leader of the retreat. This remains true even if we accept the view that he has so shaped the narrative as to bring himself into undue prominence and to thrust others into the background (see below, § 13). With all allowances, we must still recognize his courage, his resourcefulness, and his devotion to the common good.

6. FRIENDSHIP WITH AGESILĀUS.—Xenophon's story of the Ten Thousand closes with his handing over the remnant of the army to the Spartan general Thibron in Asia Minor in the spring of 399, and we have no sure knowledge of his own movements during the years immediately following. He may have remained in Asia and taken part in Thibron's campaign against Tissaphernes, or he may have revisited Greece; but three years later we find him in the service of Agesilāus, king of Sparta, who was continuing the war against Persia. Between Agesilāus and Xenophon a strong friendship grew up, and a laudatory sketch of the king appears among Xenophon's writings.

When Agesilāus returned through Thrace and Macedonia,

Xenophon accompanied him, and must therefore have been present at the battle of Coronēa in 394. Whether or not he actually fought against his countrymen, who were arrayed on the side of the Thebans against the Spartans, cannot be positively stated; but in any case the bonds connecting him with Athens were by this time weak, if they had not already been severed. He had left Athens seven years before, seeking, possibly, to escape from a situation, which may well have seemed helpless and hopeless; he had lived for years with Asiatic and Peloponnesian Greeks; he had made an important campaign which had conclusively shown the weakness of Persia, the ancestral foe of Hellas, and he had doubtless been fired with a vision of a larger patriotism which cherished pan-Hellenic ideals, and looked forward to the conquest of Persia by Greek armies; in which case Sparta would be the natural leader.

7. BANISHMENT FROM ATHENS.—Be all this as it may, Xenophon at some time (between 400 and 394) and for some cause was banished from Athens, whether because of his participation in the expedition of Cyrus (we recall the warning given him by Socrates, *Anabasis* III, 1, § 5), or because of his close association with Sparta; or yet again because of his presence in the enemy's lines at Coronēa. Sparta gave the expatriated man a welcome, and at Sparta he dwelt for some time with his wife, Philesia, whom he had wedded while in Asia, and his two sons. These sons, therefore, grew up under Spartan, not Athenian, training.

8. RESIDENCE AT SCILLUS.—A few years later Xenophon was presented by the Spartans with an estate at Scillus, near Olympia, and there he lived for years, busied with his writing, and with the out-of-door exercises, the love of which never left him. Of his life at Scillus he gives us a glimpse in *Anabasis* V, 3, §§ 7-13.

9. REMOVAL FROM SCILLUS.—After some sixteen or seventeen years of this quiet life, the defeat of the Spartans at Leuctra (371) led to the recovery by the Elēans of the lands taken from them by the Spartans, and Xenophon was driven

out of Scillus. He appears then to have removed to Corinth, and to have made this city his home until his death, although the decree of banishment against him was revoked at Athens. Just when this action was taken we cannot say, but one of his sons was killed while fighting on the Athenian side at the battle of Mantinēa (362).

10. DEATH.—The date of Xenophon's death cannot be given with certainty, but he lived to a great age, if we may trust tradition, and in any case his death must be put later than 359 (357 ?), the date of the assassination of Alexander of Pheræ, to which event he refers in *Hellenica*, VI, 4, § 35ff.

11. PERSONAL TRAITS.—Xenophon's works, while not professedly autobiographical, are full of passages which throw a flood of light upon his own character. Certain points may be noted here in brief. He was at once something of a philosophical theorist and a man of action; or perhaps it is nearer the truth to say that he became through circumstances a man of action. Yet even so his native capacity and alertness reveal themselves. In the face of the most disheartening circumstances he never loses hope, and however baffling the problems before him his resourcefulness is boundless. He is careless of tradition and of theory in the varying situations of the retreat, but is quick to see what the situation calls for, and to act accordingly. Hence his military genius has been rated high, and the *Anabasis* abounds in illustrations of his tactical skill.*

Again he was ambitious and eager to win a name for himself. To this motive more than to any other we may perhaps ascribe his action in joining the expedition of Cyrus, and in the later books of the *Anabasis* many passages occur in which this side of his nature is, perhaps unconsciously, revealed; see the passages bearing upon his cherished idea of founding a colony (*e. g.* V, 6, §§ 15ff.), that expressing

---

* See the interesting remark of Cicero (*Ep. ad Q. Fratrem*, 1, 1, 8, 23), "Quos quidem libros (*i. e.* the *Cyropaedīa*) non sine causa noster ille Africanus de manibus ponere non solebat: nullum est enim praetermissum in his officium diligentis et moderati imperii."

his satisfaction when the supreme command was offered him (VI, 1, § 20), and others.

Furthermore, although he spent years in active campaigning and must have been brought into contact with all the barbarities of warfare, his own instincts are genuinely humane and philanthropic. His kindly treatment of the village chief (IV, 5, §§ 28ff.) was based rather on humanity than on policy merely, and this same trait of his nature is revealed by his comment on the scene following upon the capture of the Taochian stronghold, ἐνταῦθα δὴ δεινὸν ἦν θέαμα (IV, 7, § 12).

Perhaps the most striking character of Xenophon was, however, his simple, childlike trust in the gods. This is constantly brought out in his narrative. He consults the oracle before he sets out, when invited by Proxenus to join Cyrus (III, 1, §§ 5ff.); he recalls the omen of the eagle which appeared to him when he left Ephesus on his way to Sardis (VI, 1, § 23); it was through a dream, sent, as he devoutly believed, by the gods, that he was led to action on the memorable night following the seizure of the generals (III, 1, §§ 11ff.); it was a dream again that pointed the way to a successful solution of their problems when the Centrītes blocked their passage (IV, 3, § 8); and when the supreme command was offered to Xenophon, tempting as the offer was, he declined it because religious grounds deterred him from accepting (VI, 1, §§ 19ff.). It was doubtless from his reliance upon the gods and from his long experience in campaigning that he derived the stoic fortitude illustrated in a story told by Diogenes Laertius. According to this, Xenophon was engaged in offering sacrifice when the news of his son's death at Mantinēa (see § 9) was brought to him. On hearing the words, "Your son has fallen," he is said to have removed the chaplet from his brow, but when the messenger added, "Nobly," he replaced it, merely uttering the words, "I knew that my son was mortal."

In connection with these traits of character it is interesting to note the moral tone of the narrative. Reference need be made only to the stress laid upon the solemnity of the compact with Ariaeus, which so strikingly enhances our sense of moral indignation at the Persian's subsequent treachery (II, 2, §§ 8f.), and to Cleānor's vehement arraignment of both Ariaeus and Tissaphernes as godless breakers of faith (II, 5, § 39), a passage with which one inevitably contrasts the praise meted out to Cyrus in this regard (I, 9, § 7).

Lack of patriotism toward his native state is often made a reproach to Xenophon, who is sometimes spoken of as little better than an out-and-out traitor; but a larger view sees in this an evidence that what we may call pan-Hellenic patriotism, which in the case of Xenophon was a natural outgrowth from the circumstances of his life, became a larger thing than devotion to a single state, even though that state were Athens (cf. § 6). In this, as in his vision of a Hellenic conquest of Asia, he is the precursor of Alexander and his age.

Of Xenophon's honesty as an historian something is said in § 13.

12. XENOPHON AS A MAN OF LETTERS.—Xenophon was a productive writer, and the versatility of his genius is evidenced by the variety of subjects treated in his works. During the quiet of the years spent at Scillus (§ 8) we may well believe that his time was largely spent in writing, and a list of his works, compiled in antiquity, numbers forty books. With this our extant collection, if regard be had to its natural subdivisions, fairly well coincides, so that apparently all of the works ascribed to Xenophon have come down to us.

The list includes the following works :

1. Ἑλληνικά: a continuation of the history of Thucydides in seven books.
2. Κύρου ἀνάβασις: the present work; see the next section.
3. Κύρου παιδεία: a work in eight books, professedly an account of the training and career of Cyrus the Great, the founder of the Persian Empire, but really not so much a history as an historical romance, giving a sketch of an ideal ruler and of the writer's own political views.

4. Ἀγεσίλαος: a eulogistic sketch of the Spartan king, under whom Xenophon served in Asia Minor, and with whom he contracted a warm friendship.
5. Ἀπομνημονεύματα Σωκράτους: a collection in four books of the sayings of Socrates and of anecdotes regarding him, constituting a defence of the writer's beloved master and of his teachings regarded from their practical, rather than from their philosophical side.
6. Ἀπολογία Σωκράτους πρὸς τοὺς δικαστάς: a treatise, similar in scope to Plato's Apology, but of very dubious authenticity.
7. Συμπόσιον: a description of a symposium (drinking-party), with its accompaniment of music, dance, and philosophic discussion.
8. Οἰκονομικός: a Socratic dialogue, giving the author's views on the proper management of the household and farm.
9. Ἱέρων ἢ τυραννικός: a tract, contrasting the life of the tyrant with that of the private citizen.
10. Λακεδαιμονίων πολιτεία: an essay on the Spartan constitution, possibly spurious.
11. Ἀθηναίων πολιτεία: an essay on the Athenian constitution, certainly not by Xenophon.
12. Πόροι ἢ περὶ προσόδων: a tract on the Athenian revenues.
13. Κυνηγετικός: an interesting treatise on hunting and on the rearing of hunting dogs.
14. Περὶ ἱππικῆς: a tract on the choosing and the care of horses.
15. Ἱππαρχικός: a tract on the duties of a cavalry commander.

13. THE *Anabasis*, ITS PUBLICATION AND ITS CREDIBILITY. The *Anabasis* is full of a high interest, not only because of the stirring and important events which it describes, and of the author's skill as a narrator, but also because of the fact that the prominent part played by Xenophon in these events gives to the book the added charm of a personal narrative.

The title of the book, strictly speaking, fits only the first seven chapters of the first book, in which Cyrus' preparation for his upward march (ἀνάβασις) and the march itself are described. The bulk of the work is devoted to the narrative of the wonderful achievement of the Greek army in extricating itself from the perils menacing it after the death of Cyrus, and in particular after the seizure of its leaders. In this Xenophon played an important part, and the view has been held that the *Anabasis* was written by him for the purpose of glorifying himself, and that he distorts the true story of the events described in order to make himself more prominent. (See *e.g.* Gomperz, *Greek Thinkers*, II, 120ff., English Translation).

The fact that the *Anabasis* was published anonymously or under a pseudonym has been thought to lend support to this view, as though Xenophon felt that the portrait he draws of himself would be discredited if it were known to come from his own hand.

It is certainly true that in *Hellenica* III, 1, 2, Xenophon refers to the story of Cyrus' expedition as having been written by Themistogenes of Syracuse. Now of an historian of that name nothing whatever is known, and it is generally believed that Xenophon is here referring to his own work. Further, an *Anabasis* by Sophaenetus of Stymphālus, one of Cyrus' Greek generals, often mentioned in the *Anabasis*, is four times cited by the geographer Stephanus of Byzantium, and it has been thought that Xenophon may have written his own work in order to represent himself in a more flattering light than Sophænetus had done. Again, the historians Ephorus and Ctesias, from whom Diodōrus draws his account of the events narrated in the *Anabasis*, seem to have made little of Xenophon. Lastly, Xenophon besides using the third person throughout his work, speaks now and then as though his information had come to him at second hand (see *e. g.* I, 8, § 18; II, 1, § 14, with the note; and V, 4, § 34), which cannot have been the case if he were really as prominent in the retreat as he makes himself out to have been.

These are matters in which unity of opinion is hardly to be looked for. It should be said, however, that, if they predispose one to take an unfavorable view of Xenophon, it is none the less true that his work does not lack counter evidences of fairness of mind even when the matters reported do not tend to represent him in a particularly favorable light. For example, he attributes to himself the suggestion that the hollow square should be adopted as the formation in beginning the retreat (III, 2, § 36); yet he frankly states that they found the formation a bad one, which had to be altered (III, 4, § 19). It is noteworthy, too, that the ingenious plan for meeting the difficulties due to this formation is attributed to "the generals," not to Xenophon himself (III, 4, § 21). So, too, he tells us frankly that his inability properly to deal with the problems of guarding the rear called down upon him the censure of Chirisophus and the older generals (III, 3, § 11). The whole portrayal of the relations between Chirisophus and Xenophon seems marked by a spirit of fair-mindedness. The writer takes pains to mention their friendly coöperation (IV, 2, § 26), his own deference to Chirisophus, as a Lacedaemonian (III, 2, § 37), their playful banter (IV, 6, §§ 14ff.), their single misunderstanding (IV, 6, § 3). It is of interest, too, to note that the writer is at pains to account for Chirisophus' absence at the time of the seizure of the generals (II, 5, § 37), and that in III, 3, § 27, it is Chirisophus who takes Clearchus' place as virtual commander in chief, and speaks for the whole body in the colloquy with Mithradates. We may also refer to the words of praise meted out to subordinates, to the group of brave Arcadian captains whose rivalry in valor adds so much to the interest of the account of the assault on the Taochian fort (IV, 7, §§ 8ff.; see especially § 12); to Episthenes, who with his peltasts bore the brunt of Tissaphernes' charge (I, 10, § 7); and to the scout Democrates (IV, 4, § 15). Contrast, too, the comment upon Polycrates' faithfulness in the matter of procuring ships with the judgment passed upon the renegade Dexippus (V, 1, § 15f.). Again it is plain that Xenophon's sympathies were wholly with Clearchus in his rivalry with Menon; but at the same time he tells us that Clearchus, too, wished to win for himself the supreme command, and to brush aside all rivals

(II, 5, § 29), and despite appearances he abstains from accusing Menon of treachery (II, 6, § 28).

We may surely see frankness again in the writer's statements regarding his own ambitions, his desire to found a colony, and his gratification when the supreme command was offered to him; and his bearing in the vexatious situations brought about by the greed, jealousy, and bad faith of those with whom he was brought into contact must provoke our admiration. His defence, when with the other generals he was put on trial (V, 8, §§ 1ff.), and his speech before the Spartan ambassadors, when the disaffected were clamoring for his death (VII, 6, §§ 11ff.), deserve careful reading. Certain is it that there is nowhere the slightest evidence that he ever sought to use his position for private advantage at the expense of the interests of the whole army. After all the opportunities for gain-getting which fortune had put in his way, he tells us that he was compelled to sell his horse on reaching Lampsacus in order to secure funds for his journey. This of itself goes far to justify the estimate put upon Xenophon by Seuthes, τὰ μὲν ἄλλα οὐ κακός, φιλοστρατιώτης δέ.

For some remarks upon the style of the *Anabasis* see § 39.

II

PERSIA TO THE TIME OF CYRUS THE YOUNGER

14. THE PERSIAN EMPIRE; CYRUS THE GREAT.—The Persian Empire was founded in the sixth century B. C. by Cyrus the Great (died 529 B. C.). From earliest times the fertile region watered by the Tigris and the Euphrates has been the seat of great empires, Chaldaeans, Assyrians, Babylonians, Medes, and Persians succeeding one another. At the time of the accession of Cyrus to the throne the Persians were subject to the Medes, while in the west lay the great kingdom of Lydia, and to the south that of Babylon. Under Cyrus the Persians, a tribe of hardy mountaineers, were freed from

Median control, and began an irresistible series of conquests. The Lydian monarchy was overthrown and its capital, Sardis, taken in 546. By this the domain of Persia was extended to the coasts of Asia Minor, and the Greek cities dotting these coasts fell under its sway. In 538 Babylon was overthrown. Thus the empire founded by the great monarch extended over virtually all the region from the Ægæan to the Indus and from the Caspian Sea to the Persian Gulf. Within this vast area there were naturally many peoples whose subjugation was incomplete. Even in Xenophon's day the Cilicians were governed by their own rulers (*Anabasis*, I, 2, § 12), and the Pisidians (I, 1, § 11; I, 2, § 1; II, 5, § 13; III, 2, § 23), the Mysians (II, 5, § 13; III, 2, § 23), and the Lycaonians (III, 2, § 23) were at least rebellious, while the Cardūchi were practically independent.

Of Cyrus the Great, Xenophon has given a sketch, idealized and lacking in historic accuracy, in the *Cyropaedia*.

15. CAMBȳSES.—Cyrus was succeeded by his son, Cambȳses (529-522), who extended his father's conquests by campaigns against Phoenicia, Egypt, and Libya. By the conquest of Phoenicia Persia became a maritime, as well as an inland power. Cambȳses, on departing for Egypt, had murdered his younger brother, Bardiya (Bardes), or Smerdis, as the Greeks called him. Cambyses was of a jealous temperament, and was subject to fits of ungovernable passion. He was therefore both hated and feared by his subjects, while Bardiya was beloved. While Cambȳses was absent on his campaign against Egypt, a Magian proclaimed himself Bardiya, whom he happened to resemble in appearance, and seized the throne. On hearing of this Cambȳses, it appears, took his own life, although traditions differ. The false Bardiya, on his part, after a rule of only seven months, was assassinated by a band of conspirators led by Darīus, son of Hystaspes, a Persian noble of a younger branch of the royal house (Achaemenidae), who thereupon became king.

16. DARĪUS THE GREAT.—Darīus (521-485) during the first six years of his reign had to contend against opposition from

those who denied his right to rule, and to face rebellion in many parts of the empire, but by his energy, courage, and resourcefulness he finally triumphed over all his foes and established himself securely on the throne. He also extended the bounds of the empire by further conquests, and set himself to the colossal task of organizing and unifying his vast domain, which, it is estimated, included possibly as many as eighty millions of inhabitants, differing widely from one another in civilization, in government, in language, and in all the habits of life.

17. ORGANIZATION OF THE EMPIRE.—Darīus divided the empire into twenty-three satrapies, or provinces, each governed by a viceroy (satrap) appointed by the king and subject to removal at his will. Save for this fact the satraps were largely independent. They maintained their own courts, with palaces and game preserves ($\pi\alpha\rho\acute{\alpha}\delta\epsilon\iota\sigma o\iota$), and lived in regal state. They had supreme authority in all civil matters, levied and collected taxes, and controlled the local military forces, though the imperial troops and garrisons were under command of officers appointed by the king and responsible to him. Even these, however, were dependent upon the satrap for pay for their troops; but they formed a substantial check upon the satraps, and kept them from assuming real as well as virtual independence. So did likewise the royal secretary sent down to each province. This officer was the king's agent, and served as an independent channel through which the king could inform himself of what was going on. Moreover, inspectors (I, 1, § 5) were from time to time sent out by the king to the different provinces. Despite these checks upon their power, however, the satraps had by the time of Xenophon become practically independent sovereigns, and the king cared little about their doings, provided the tribute was regularly sent to him (I, 1, § 8). It was in this matter of collecting tribute that the system organized by Darīus proved most successful. The tribute was paid in kind (IV, 5, § 24), and was levied upon all the subjects of the empire except the Persians. The total revenue must have been enormous.

Another means of solidifying the empire was the maintenance of royal roads connecting the provinces with the capital, and the establishment along these of stations where couriers with relays of horses were posted. By this means it was possible to despatch messengers to or from the capital with surprising speed. These roads must not be assumed to have been anything like the great military roads of the Romans, yet by facilitating rapid communication they did much to unify the empire. The most famous of these roads, following probably an old trade route, ran from Nineveh to Susa and thence westward to Ephesus. On his upward march Cyrus availed himself of this royal road for a part of the distance.

Lastly it should be stated that Darīus sought to introduce a uniform system of gold and silver coinage, although from the nature of the case this attempt could not be wholly successful. The standard gold coin was, or came to be, called by the king's name, the daric (I, 1, § 9).

18. GREECE AND PERSIA.—A glance at the map shows how closely connected Greece and Asia Minor are, and how from the earliest times the intervening islands must have tended to promote intercourse. It was therefore but natural that, as successive migrations from the north into the Greek peninsula forced the already existing population to seek new homes, homes should be found first of all on the islands and on the neighboring coasts of Asia Minor. Thus the coasts of Asia Minor became studded with Greek cities, some of which, like Ephesus and Milētus, became rich and powerful. These cities during the seventh and sixth centuries before Christ were marked by a far more highly developed culture and civilization than were the cities of European Greece. These Ionian cities (for having been colonized by Ionians the district was called Ionia) fell under the sway of Lydia in the days of Lydian greatness, and when the empire of Croesus fell before the advance of Persia (§ 14) they, too, became subject to Persia.

19. THE IONIC REVOLT.—In 499 B. C. the Ionian cities

under the leadership of Aristagoras of Milētus expelled the
tyrants whom the power of Persia had imposed upon them,
and resolved to free themselves from Persian rule. Aristagoras went to Greece to seek help. He failed utterly at
Sparta, but Athens and the little town of Eretria on the
island of Euboea sent ships and men. Thanks to this assistance the Ionians were able to capture and burn Sardis, the
capital of Lydia; but their success was short-lived. The
Greeks were not united, nor was their leader a man of spirit.
Milētus fell after a siege, and the revolt was crushed.

20. THE PERSIAN EXPEDITIONS AGAINST GREECE.—After the
suppression of the revolt and the reorganization of Ionia,
Darīus in 492 sent forth an army and a fleet with the double
purpose of re-establishing Persian supremacy in Thrace and
Macedonia, and of proceeding against Greece in order to punish the states which had dared to take part in the war against
the Great King. The first project was successfully carried
out, though with heavy losses, but the fleet was wrecked in
attempting to round the promontory of Athos, and the
expedition against Greece was given up.

Darīus, however, was not minded to allow Athens and
Eretria to escape. In the picturesque story of Herodotus we
are told that he commanded one of his slaves to say daily
as dinner was served before him, "Master, remember the
Athenians." Hence, two years later the second expedition
was despatched. Eretria fell, but Athens was saved by the
genius of Miltiades and the valor of her citizens and those
of Plataea in the memorable battle of Marathon (490).
Nothing daunted, Darīus began preparations for a third
expedition, but died before they were completed.

He was succeeded by his son Xerxes (485-465), who after
a delay caused by the necessity of subjugating Egypt, which
had revolted, led a vast host by land and sea against Greece.
After he had triumphantly passed through Thrace, Macedonia, and Thessaly, and, aided by treachery, had forced the
pass at Thermopylae, his fleet was crushed in the battle of
Salamis (480), and the next year his army was defeated at

Plataea. Thus ended Persian attempts to subjugate European Greece, and Europe was not again to be menaced by an Oriental invasion for a full thousand years.

21. THE DECLINE OF PERSIA.—After this check put upon its career of conquest Persia rapidly declined. The very vastness of its power and wealth gave rise to luxury and decay. The court was maintained with great magnificence, but owing to the fact that it was made up of jealous and self-seeking men and women—slaves, eunuchs, and concubines, with hosts of greedy hangers-on—intrigue and strife abounded, and led only too often to the darkest crimes. Xerxes was murdered in 465 and was succeeded by his son, Artaxerxes I (Longimānus), who reigned until 425. He was followed by his son, Xerxes II., who after a reign of less than two months was murdered by his half-brother, Sogdianus, who in his turn suffered a like fate at the hands of his brother, Darīus, who seized the throne for himself.

22. DARĪUS II.—Darīus II, called Nothus (bastard), since he was the son of one of the royal concubines, was the father of Cyrus and Artaxerxes, with whose quarrel we have to do in the *Anabasis*. He married his half-sister (some authorities say his aunt), Parysatis, a woman of a strong and unscrupulous nature, whose influence at court became paramount. The reign of Darīus was marked by a series of insurrections and disorders in various parts of the empire, notably by the revolt of Egypt, which threw off Persian rule and maintained its independence, and by renewed activity on the part of the satraps of the western provinces in dealing with the Greek states (§ 26). These satraps were able and energetic men, Pharnabazus, who governed the northern provinces, and Tissaphernes, who was satrap of Caria on the south, though his dominion embraced Lydia as well. To these must be added Cyrus (§ 24), who was to become a dominant figure.

23. TISSAPHERNES.—Tissaphernes, as the story of the *Anabasis* makes all too clear, was a wily, unscrupulous Oriental. Instructed by the king to seek to regain control over the Greek cities, which had enjoyed virtual independence since

the failure of the Persian expeditions against Greece, he endeavored to carry out this purpose by aiding now Athens and now Sparta in their war against each other. By this means he hoped to weaken both, and thus secure for Persia a free hand. This policy was shrewdly planned, but was after a time interrupted by the energetic action of Cyrus, whose support of the cause of Sparta did much to secure her triumph, and to make the downfall of Athens inevitable.

III

CYRUS AND HIS EXPEDITION

24. CYRUS THE YOUNGER.—Cyrus, called the Younger to distinguish him from Cyrus the Great, was appointed by his father, Darīus, in 407, satrap of Lydia, Phrygia (the greater), and Cappadocia, and commander in chief ($κάρανος$) of one-fourth of the royal army,—of the troops, *i.e.*, whose mustering-place was the plain of Castōlus in western Asia (see Xenophon, *Hellenica*, I, 4, 3, and *Anabasis* I, 1, § 2). Cyrus was at this time a youth of seventeen, but he was ambitious and possessed of marked ability. The powers given to him were vast, and he was set over many older and more experienced men. Even Tissaphernes was reduced to a subordinate position, though he retained the satrapy of Caria and the control of the Greek cities on the coast, which were still under the power of Persia. Deeply incensed at being supplanted by a mere boy, Tissaphernes became the bitter enemy of Cyrus, and when the latter was summoned to Babylon on the occasion of his father's last illness (404) he found it wise to take Tissaphernes with him, ostensibly as his friend (I, 1, § 2), but we may well believe that the real ground was that he did not dare leave so dangerous a foe behind him.

Cyrus was the younger son (the family was large, but we are concerned merely with the two brothers, Cyrus and Artaxerxes), but was not without grounds for hoping that he would be designated his father's successor. Artaxerxes had been born before Darīus became king, and Cyrus was the eldest son "born in the purple." Moreover, he could count upon the support of the all-powerful queen mother, Parysatis. So strong was Cyrus' belief that he would succeed his father that he had already assumed the attitude of royalty, and had even, we are told, put to death two of his own first cousins, who had dared to come before him without assuming the posture which etiquette prescribed for those coming into the presence of the king.

25. ARTAXERXES II (MNEMON).—Cyrus came up to Babylon at his father's summons attended by a strong body-guard of Greek troops, but despite the support of Parysatis he failed in his ambitious purpose. Artaxerxes was named by Darīus as his successor. Enraged at this disappointment it may well be true, as was believed in antiquity, that Cyrus sought to murder his brother at the time of his coronation. Some declared that a priest charged Cyrus with intending to hide himself in the temple at Pasargadae and murder the king when he came thither, as custom demanded, to put on the robe of Cyrus the Great; and others went so far as to say that Cyrus was actually found lurking in the temple (so Plutarch, who gives both versions). Others, as Xenophon, regard these charges as malicious slanders uttered by Tissaphernes, who sought thus to avenge himself on his rival. In any case, Cyrus was seized and would have been put to death had it not been for the intercession of Parysatis. She secured his release, and sent him back in safety to his province (I, 1, § 3; the story is also picturesquely told by Plutarch).

Deeply angered at the baffling of his hopes and at the indignity put upon him, Cyrus resolved to wrest the throne from his brother by force, and straightway set about making preparations.

26. THE SITUATION AND THE RESOURCES OF CYRUS.—In planning to carry out his purpose Cyrus had certain advantages upon which he could rely. In the first instance he had

a strong ally in his mother, whose influence at court was immense, and whose strong imperious nature, at once vindictive and unscrupulous, would stop at nothing in seeking to further her ends. Again Cyrus had come to see the marked superiority of Greek over Persian troops, and was in a position to secure such troops for himself. He determined to gain control over the Greek cities of Ionia, and to this end made open war on Tissaphernes. As a result all these cities came over to his side save Milētus, in which Tissaphernes had a strong castle and a garrison. Moreover, the state of Greece at this time was a distinct advantage to Cyrus. It was in the period immediately following upon the overthrow of Athens by Sparta. The latter state owed her final success largely to the aid furnished by Cyrus, and he could rightly look to her for support in his undertaking. Finally, it should be noted that well equipped and well disciplined troops could now readily be had for hire, and that Cyrus was in a position to secure them, having already come into contact with them and having won for himself a name as a liberal paymaster.

27. CYRUS MUSTERS TROOPS.—His war with Tissaphernes made it easy for Cyrus to muster a considerable body of troops without arousing suspicion as to his ulterior purpose. He laid siege to Milētus and strengthened the garrisons in the various Ionian cities; and the king was pleased, rather than otherwise, at the thought that his rival was thus wasting his resources, the more so as Cyrus took pains to remit to him the proper tribute not from his own province alone, but also from the cities which he had taken from Tissaphernes (I, 1, § 8).

In this way the nucleus of a strong Greek force was mustered, but Cyrus was not blind to the magnitude of the task before him, and did not stop here. He furnished funds to Clearchus (§ 38), who collected and maintained a strong army in the Chersonēsus; to Aristippus, who was struggling to hold his ground against rivals in Thessaly; and sent word to other Greek officers to come and take service under him, alleging as his reason his war against Tissaphernes and, further, a desire to punish the Pisidians, a hardy tribe of mountaineers living to the south of his province, for their depredations committed on his territory. Furthermore, he entered into negotiations with Sparta, to which state he had rendered such signal service in the latter years of the Peloponnesian war; and although loath to enter openly upon war with the Great King the government acceded to his request, at least to the extent of sending a fleet with seven hundred hoplites under Chirisophus to the coast of Cilicia, where they joined the army of Cyrus on its upward march. Cyrus himself had, of course, in his official capacity control of the imperial troops in western Asia; but on these, as the sequel proved, little reliance could be placed.

28. THE ARMY OF CYRUS.—In the above-mentioned ways Cyrus gathered together a body of approximately thirteen thousand well-trained troops by the time he was ready to set out. These were drawn from all parts of the Greek world, but especially from central and northern Peloponnēsus (more than half of the whole army, Xenophon tells us, was made up of Arcadians or Achaeans, VI, 2, § 10). The Arcadians in particular were famous as fighting men, and are often singled out for special mention in Xenophon's narrative. The separate contingents with their commanders are given as follows:

Xenias, an Arcadian (I, 2, § 3), with 4000 hoplites.
Proxenus, a Boeotian (*ibid.*), with 1500 hoplites and 500 light-armed.
Sophaenetus, an Arcadian (*ibid.*), with 1000 hoplites.
Socrates, an Achaean (*ibid.*), with 500 hoplites.
Pasion, a Megarian (*ibid.*), with 300 hoplites and 300 peltasts.
Menon, a Thessalian (I. 2, § 6), with 1000 hoplites and 500 peltasts.
Clearchus, a Lacedaemonian (I, 2, § 9), with 1000 hoplites. 800 peltasts, 200 bowmen, and 40 horse.
Sosis, a Syracusan (*ibid.*), with 300 hoplites.
Agias (?), an Arcadian (*ibid.*), with 1000 hoplites.*

---

* See the note on I, 2, 56.

Chirisophus, a Lacedaemonian (I, 4, § 3), with 700 hoplites.

There is also mention of the troops which had been besieging Milētus (I, 2, § 2); these may, or may not, have been included in those brought by Pasion and Socrates, or by Xenias, since he was in general command of Cyrus' garrison troops; and lastly we are told of 400 deserters from the king's army (I, 4, § 3).

The number of troops is given in I, 2, § 9, after the review at Celaenae, as 11,000 hoplites and "about 2000" peltasts. Subsequent to this the 700 hoplites under Chirisophus joined the army; yet in I, 7, § 10, the number is given as 10,400 hoplites and 2500 peltasts. We have no means of explaining the discrepancy.

The heavy-armed soldier (ὁπλίτης; see the frontispiece) was equipped with helmet (κράνος), cuirass (θώραξ, or σπολάς), shield (ἀσπίς), and greaves (κνημῖδες), and carried a spear (δόρυ) and a short, straight, double-edged sword (ξίφος). The light-armed troops embraced (1) peltasts (πελτασταί), who carried a target (πέλτη) and spears; (2) javelin-throwers (ἀκοντισταί), who carried javelins alone;* (3) bowmen (τοξόται), whose equipment consisted of the bow (τόξον), quiver (φαρέτρα), and arrows (τοξεύματα, or οἰστοί); and slingers (σφενδονῆται), who carried merely their slings (σφενδόναι) and stones or slugs for hurling. No force of slingers was, however, organized until during the retreat (III, 3, §§ 16ff.).

The army was virtually without cavalry. Clearchus brought with him forty Thracian horsemen, but these deserted (II, 2, § 7) after the battle. During the retreat a small body of horse was organized (III, 3, §§ 19f.), which rendered good service.

Naturally, being composed of contingents under separate commands, the army was not strictly unified. Indeed on one occasion (I, 5, §§ 13ff.) the divisions of Clearchus and of Menon almost came to out-and-out fighting, and in general

---

* For information as to the ancient javelin and the method of hurling it with a thong (ἀγκύλη), see Gardiner, *Greek Athletic Sports and Festivals,* pp. 338ff., with the cuts on pp. 341 and 344.

each commander regarded himself as in large measure independent. All the more striking, however, is the unity and good discipline which were manifested during the retreat, at least up to the time when safety seemed assured. Then bickerings and mutual distrust showed themselves, and make the story told in the last two books of the *Anabasis,* in particular, one of petty jealousies, of strife, and disunion.

The men, with the exception of the Lacedaemonian contingent under Clearchus, were paid by Cyrus. The rate was at first a daric per month per man, but after the mutiny at Tarsus this was increased to a daric and a half (I, 3, § 21). This was liberal treatment, especially as he promised them pay in full until he should bring them back to Ionia. Ordinarily mercenaries were discharged whenever their employer had no further need of their services, and were left to find their way home as best they could. Moreover, Cyrus promised liberal bounties to the men in the event of his success (I, 4, § 13; I, 7, § 7). A captain received twice as much, a general four times as much, as a private.

There was no regular commissariat. The soldiers procured supplies from a market (ἀγορά) set up in the army. This was in the barbarian contingent (I, 3, § 14), and was maintained by orientals, chiefly by Lydians. These sutlers accompanied the army with wagons and pack-animals bearing supplies of flour and wine, and when we add to these the wagons laden with the camp equipment and the soldiers' baggage, and the hordes of hangers-on and camp-followers, both men and women, it will be seen that the train was of considerable size and a great hindrance to rapid progress. On the retreat, after the Persians had treacherously broken the truce, the Greeks burned their tents and superfluous baggage, and got supplies as best they could by pillage.

The army marched as a rule in column, and owing to the baggage train the line must have been of great length. During the retreat the hollow square was at first adopted as the wisest formation, but it was found to be impracticable. The battle line was ordinarily drawn up eight deep, but for a charge on rough or irregular ground the companies might be arranged in column, with open spaces between the columns (IV, 8, §§ 10ff.). The unit of organization was the enomoty (ἐνωμοτία), or company of twenty-four men with their commander (ἐνωμότάρχος); four of these made up the λόχος, under command of a captain (λοχαγός). Each unit was drilled so that the shift from column to line of battle and vice versa was attended with no confusion, and the rear men in each file were trained to act as leaders, when the order, "About face," was given (IV, 3, §§ 26 and 29).

Of the organization of the barbarian army of Cyrus little can be said, and it plays no part of importance in Xenophon's narrative. It numbered, according to Xenophon, 100,000 men (I, 7, § 10). The Greek and barbarian armies encamped separately (I, 3, § 14, and II, 4, § 10).

As to the size of the king's army, accurate information is lacking. Xenophon's estimate is based upon the reports of deserters (I, 7, §§ 12ff.) and is doubtless greatly exaggerated. Plutarch *Artox.* 13 (quoting Ctesias, see § 30) sets the number at 400,000.

29. THE ANABASIS, OR UPWARD MARCH.—At the head of the forces enumerated above, Cyrus set out from Sardis in March, 401 B. C. His course led him through Lydia and Phrygia, the general direction being somewhat south of east (as though he were indeed moving against the Pisidians), until he reached the city of Celaenae. Here he made a halt of thirty days, as some of his troops had not yet joined him. From this point he turned back and proceeded in a northwesterly direction to Ceramon Agora, whence the eastern march was again resumed. By this otherwise surprising detour, Cyrus avoided passing through a rugged country, in which it might have been difficult to obtain supplies and where he might have been delayed by opposition on the part of the very mountaineers against whom his expedition was ostensibly directed. At the same time the change in direction would not of necessity tend to arouse suspicion as to his ultimate goal.

It is impossible to determine accurately the distances covered in each day's march, although Xenophon gives them in "parasangs." The parasang was a Persian measure of length, but seems not to have been of uniform value. Following Herodotus, editors generally assume the parasang to have been equal to thirty stadia, or about three and a half English miles; but on this basis some of the day's marches recorded by Xenophon—marches made in the heat of a Babylonian summer or through deep snow—are of incredible length.

From Ceramon Agora the army proceeded by stages of unequal length, due doubtless to differences in the character of the country traversed, to the famous pass over the Taurus range in southeastern Asia Minor, called the Cilician gates. Here his course might easily have been checked by the Cilician king, Syennesis, who must have been forewarned by Tissaphernes (I, 2, § 4) of Cyrus' treasonable preparations. Syennesis was however not disposed to make an enemy of so formidable a prince as Cyrus, and seems to have acted in collusion with him. He had already sent his queen, Epyaxa, with a supply of money to visit Cyrus, and appears to have resolved to do no more than make a show of resistance. Moreover Cyrus had despatched Menon with a considerable force to escort the queen back to Cilicia, and these troops had availed themselves of a more direct route, and were in a position to attack Syennesis in the rear, had he really sought to defend the pass. He deserted his position, however, at the approach of Cyrus, and the latter passed through without encountering any opposition. The pass itself is a narrow defile 3600 feet in elevation and flanked on either side by high mountains. So strong is the position that it would have been impossible to force it, had any serious resistance been made.

Thus the army reached Tarsus. Here, as it was plain that Cyrus had some other design than an expedition against the Pisidians, whose territory they had long since left behind them, the soldiers mutinied and refused to go further. They suspected by this time that they were being led against the king, and such an expedition seemed to them a far more serious and dangerous undertaking than that for which they had been hired. The story of the clever stratagem by which Clearchus, who was in the confidence of Cyrus, won them back to their allegiance forms one of Xenophon's most interesting chapters. Finally, having become convinced that they were virtually in the power of Cyrus, and allured by the promise of a fifty per cent increase in pay, they were induced to accompany him at least as far as the Euphrates, where, he said, he wished to attack his foe Abrocomas. At that point he knew that they would find it impossible to desert.

Thus the march was resumed. Passing Issus they reached the so-called Gates of Syria and Cilicia, a narrow road between the cliffs and the coast, fortified by a wall at either end, where again opposition was to have been expected. To meet this contingency, Cyrus had ordered his fleet to meet him at this place in order that he might disembark troops within and without the walls and thus force a passage. Abrocomas, however, the commander of the king's forces, doubtless alarmed at the ease with which Cyrus had passed the Cilician Gates, made no resistance, but fled with the whole of his vast army (I, 4, §5).

From this point on no real opposition was met until the battle. At Thapsacus, where he purposed crossing the Euphrates, Cyrus was forced to reveal his purpose to the Greeks. They must have realized it before, but here, too, they made a show of indignation at the deceit practiced upon them. They were, however, helpless. Long marches through a desert country lay behind them, and they had no supplies. When Menon, therefore, urged his men to win the favor of Cyrus by prompt obedience they readily complied, and the whole army followed, crossing on foot, as Abrocomas had burned all the available boats.

From Thapsacus they proceeded along the left bank of the river until they reached the neighborhood of Babylonia (about September 1). The only events of importance, apart from the hardships attending a march through the desert, were the clash between Clearchus and Menon, which might so easily have led to disaster (I, 5, §§ 11ff.), and the attempted treason of the Persian noble, Orontas, whose trial and condemnation are vividly described (I, 6). Finally when they reached a huge trench that had been dug from the river to the ruins of the old Median wall (see the note on I, 7, 71), leaving but a narrow passage along the river some twenty feet wide, and found this, too, undefended, it seemed clear that the king had given up all intention of making any resistance. The battle array, which must have been maintained in daily expectation of a battle, was given up, and discipline was relaxed, as though their cause were already won.

30. THE BATTLE OF CUNAXA.—At length, on the third (?) of September, while the army was proceeding in this disorderly fashion, word was suddenly brought that the king was approaching with a large army. In the midst of great confusion the battle line was formed, the Greeks holding a position on the right wing next to the river. Of the battle itself Xenophon gives a graphic and picturesque account. After sacrifice and the singing of the pæan, the Greeks charged the enemy who at once turned and fled, while the Greeks followed in pursuit. Tissaphernes alone with a body of horse rode through the Greek peltasts and advanced against the camp of Cyrus. On the other hand the barbarian troops of Cyrus, under Ariaeus, seem to have offered no real resistance to the king's army, but fled at the first attack, or at least when the fall of Cyrus became known. Cyrus himself, with a body-guard of six hundred picked men, charged the king's center, where he knew his brother would be stationed. He had previously bidden Clearchus to lead the Greek hoplites against the Persian center, but the cautious Spartan had refused to expose his right flank to the enemy, and had advanced straight on with his flank guarded by the river. Cyrus and his men routed the body-guard of the king, six thousand strong, and their cause seemed to be won; but, carried away by passion as he caught sight of his brother, Cyrus rushed upon him to slay

him, and was himself struck down by a blow from a javelin. His faithful followers were slain one after another, fighting desperately over his dead body. After this the king marched upon Cyrus' camp, where he joined Tissaphernes and his detachment, and then turned back in order to attack the Greeks. These were still advancing in pursuit of the Persians who had given way at their first attack; but when they learned that their camp was being pillaged and presently saw the king's army approaching, they wheeled about to offer battle. The barbarians, however, did not venture to engage the Greeks, but fled; and the Greeks marched back to their devastated camp.

Such, in brief, is Xenophon's story of the battle. Another account, varying in important particulars, may be read in Plutarch's life of Artaxerxes. This is based in part upon the narrative of Ctesias, a Greek, who was for years court physician to Artaxerxes, and who is known to have written a history of Persia in twenty-three books. This work is known to us from abridgements preserved by the Byzantine scholar Photius, and from the fact that it was used by Plutarch and by the historian Diodōrus Siculus. Xenophon alludes to Ctesias (*Anabasis* I, 8, § 26) in a way which suggests that he was himself familiar with his narrative, and it may be that Xenophon's own story may be corrected here and there by information drawn from Ctesias. The latter's credibility as an historian is, however, far from being above question.

31. THE RETURN MARCH.—The victory of the Greeks demonstrated the superiority of Greek over Oriental troops, but all advantages which might have accrued to them from their triumph were nullified by the fact of Cyrus' death. They were now in the heart of the Persian empire, over a thousand miles from their starting point, and fully five hundred miles from the nearest Greek city. Moreover, their journey had brought them through a desert country, over which it was impossible for them to retrace their steps, without supplies, as they were. They had no resources and no guides; and all their hopes based upon Cyrus' promises had come to nothing.

Moreover, as they were soon to learn, they had to cope with the blackest treachery on the part of those claiming to be their friends.

All the greater must our admiration be for the courage and skill with which they met the difficulties surrounding them, and succeeded in fighting their way back to Greece. Whatever be our view as to the credibility of Xenophon's narrative, particularly as regards his own prominence (§ 13), we should not be blind to the really stupendous character of the achievement of this body of men, or withhold from Xenophon his due meed of praise. This little army proved conclusively that the Greek conquest of Persia was a possibility and only waited for an Alexander to become a fact. The reader of the *Anabasis* even feels ready to echo the words of a Greek writer of the fourth century of our era: ὁ γοῦν μέγας ᾿Αλέξανδρος οὐκ ἂν ἐγένετο μέγας, εἰ μὴ Ξενοφῶν.

32. NEGOTIATIONS.—On the day after the battle, when the news of Cyrus' death was brought to the Greeks by emissaries from Ariaeus, their reply was that they were victors, and that if Ariaeus would join them they would set him on the throne of Persia. Before his answer was received, however, heralds from the king came with the peremptory command that they should lay down their arms and throw themselves on the mercy of the king. In the face of this demand, and despite their really desperate situation, Clearchus put on a bold front, and the firm refusal to surrender led the envoys (one of whom was an expatriated Greek, and another, if we may trust his own statement, the court physician, Ctesias) to add the further message that the king promised a truce if they remained where they were, but that any change of position, whether in advance or retreat, would be construed as an act of war. To this Clearchus assented, though without stating what he would do.

The king's envoys then departed, and those sent to Ariaeus returned, bringing his answer declining their offer to set him on the throne, and declaring his intention to set out next morning for Ionia. At this the Greeks determined to throw in their lot with his. Reaching his camp about midnight they entered into a solemn compact and alliance with him, while he swore that he would guide them in all good faith.

At daybreak they set out, and their advance made such an impression on the king that next day envoys came from him to propose a truce. Emboldened by this change of attitude on the part of their foes, Clearchus demanded first of all to be led to supplies. This demand was granted, a truce was made, and the Greeks were led to villages where provisions were abundant. There Tissaphernes entered into negotiations with them, laying stress upon his influence with the king, and declaring that it was due to this influence that the king was willing to allow them to depart in safety. The Greek generals, apparently placing entire confidence in the treacherous Persian, made a compact with him and with the king's brother-in-law. Tissaphernes then left them, stating that he had business at court, and did not return for some weeks, during which time Ariaeus and his officers, having received assurances of immunity for themselves, showed less friendliness toward the Greeks. This gave rise to suspicions in the minds of the Greek officers, but Clearchus would listen to no arguments, declaring that their only hope was to remain loyal to the compact they had made.

32. TREACHERY.—At length Tissaphernes returned, after having received high honors at court, and the march began, during which Ariaeus and his men marched and encamped with the troops of Tissaphernes, and held aloof from the Greeks. Their course led them eastward to the Tigris, across which the Persians had resolved to lead them, presumably in the fear that the Greeks might conceivably seize a district in the fertile area between the rivers and establish themselves there. The Greeks, however, had no thought of violating their oaths, and no wish save to return to their own land with what speed they could. They crossed the river, therefore, trusting in the good faith of the Persians, and proceeded with Tissaphernes and his army to the point where the Greater Zab (Zapatas) joins the Tigris.

Here they halted for three days, and Clearchus, hoping that the feelings of mutual distrust which had become more and more apparent, might be dispelled by a frank discussion, sought an interview with Tissaphernes. The latter met his overtures with a great show of friendliness, and promised that, if Clearchus would bring his generals and captains to a conference, he would disclose the names of those who were acting treasonably toward the Greeks, and seeking to promote ill-feeling.

To this Clearchus assented, feeling certain in his own mind that Menon was the slanderer, and eager that the strife for supremacy between Menon and himself should be brought to an end by the death of his rival. He seems to have entertained no thought of treachery, and on returning to the camp, after having spent the night as the guest of Tissaphernes, urged that all the generals and captains should go to the proposed conference. Many protested against this, and pointed out the imprudence of putting all the commanding officers in the power of Tissaphernes, but Clearchus was insistent, and at last won his point, at least to the extent that four generals besides himself—Proxenus, Menon, Agias, and Socrates—with twenty captains should accept the invitation of Tissaphernes.

They went, therefore, and about two hundred of the men followed out of curiosity and to visit the Persian market. The generals were at once invited within, where at a given signal they were seized, while those without were cut down. The prisoners were taken in chains to Babylon, and after a short imprisonment were beheaded,—all, that is, save Menon, who is believed to have sought to win favor for himself by claiming that it was due to him that the plan of entrapping the Greek generals had succeeded. Xenophon is silent as to this, though he tells us that Menon was not beheaded as the others were, but was kept alive for a miserable year and then died in disgrace and torture. Apparently his attempt to win favor succeeded only in winning for him the fierce hatred of Parysatis.

34. REORGANIZATION.—The plight of the Greeks after the seizure of their generals was desperate indeed. All the difficulties that had menaced them after the death of Cyrus menaced them now, magnified and intensified a thousand fold. It was plain by this time that no further dependence could be placed either on Ariaeus or on Tissaphernes, who had broken their most solemn oaths; and left to themselves, as they were, the Greeks had now not even leaders to whom they could look for direction and guidance.

Of the utter despair that possessed the army during the night that followed the seizure of the generals, Xenophon gives a vivid picture in the opening chapter of the third book of the *Anabasis;* and even if we feel forced to assume that he has laid undue stress on the part played by him in the events of that night, it remains clear that through energetic action on the part of the few who had not lost heart the whole army was roused to action. Of these few, Xenophon was certainly one; and we must remember that the situation called not for energy alone and a clear vision of what was needed, but also for the ability to rouse the men from their despair by presenting a line of action to them in convincing and persuasive words. Hence it is in itself entirely credible that it was Xenophon rather than, for instance, Chirisophus, who came forward at this crisis; and we may follow Grote in his verdict that it was well for the army that the inspiration "fell upon one in whom a full measure of soldierly strength and courage was combined with the education of an Athenian, a democrat, and a philosopher."

In any case the army was roused to action; the stragglers were recalled; new generals were chosen to take the places of those who had been seized; and the men were led to realize that their only hope of safety lay in good discipline and in devotion to the common weal. It was voted to burn all the superfluous baggage, that their march might not be impeded by the size of the baggage-train, and to adopt the hollow square as their formation, the train and the light-armed being in the center and the hoplites on all sides of them. Chirisophus, as a Lacedaemonian, was to have the honor of leading the van, while Xenophon and Timasion, the two youngest of the generals, were to guard the rear.

35. FROM THE ZAB TO THE LAND OF THE CARDŪCHI.—Thus reorganized and inspired with fresh hope and courage, the army crossed the Zab, which was, according to Xenophon, four hundred feet wide, but at which Tissaphernes seems to have made no effort to check their progress. As they proceeded, however, a few hundred of the enemy's horse and light-armed assailed the Greeks in the rear and inflicted some damage. The Greek bowmen and javelin-throwers were unable to reach the foe, being a match for their adversaries neither in skill nor equipment, and being further compelled to shoot at longer range, since they were inside the hollow square. Xenophon attempted to charge the enemy with some of the hoplites who formed the rear of the square, but could accomplish nothing. He did no damage to the enemy and was himself compelled to bring his men back to the main body under fire. The first day was therefore a discouraging one; but that night a small body of fifty horse was equipped, and also a troop of slingers two hundred in number. Thereafter they met with better success in repelling the enemy, who continually hovered about their flanks, but even so they suffered considerably.

In particular the Greeks found that their formation (the hollow square) could not be maintained in passing over rough country or when rivers were to be crossed. Hence separate companies were formed, which were to fall behind when the way was narrow, and, on the other hand, were to fill up any gap that might be made in their line, adapting their formation to the space to be filled.

After fourteen days of marching, in the course of which they at times suffered severely and were compelled to halt frequently in order to procure supplies and to care for the wounded, the Greeks reached a point where farther progress seemed to be completely blocked. On the left was the Tigris, so deep that the soldiers could find no bottom with their spears, while high mountains shut them in on the right, and in front lay the rugged and mountainous country of the Cardūchi, a race of bold mountaineers who defied the Great King. Nevertheless the Greeks resolved to fight their way through this inhospitable region, knowing that thus they would reach Armenia, whence, they were told, it would be easy for them to make their way whithersoever they wished.

36. THROUGH THE LAND OF THE CARDŪCHI AND ARMENIA TO TRAPEZUS.—Making their start, therefore, under cover of the darkness the Greeks reached the first of the passes through the Cardūchian mountains before any resistance was undertaken, but as the rear-guard was descending from the pass into the villages beyond, the mountaineers assailed them with vigor. Xenophon even declares that had their foes had time to collect in larger numbers the whole Greek army might well have been destroyed. This was, however, but a foretaste of what was to follow; and the seven days which the Greeks spent in passing through this rugged region, beset by their fierce and determined foes and forced by lack of supplies to march even through heavy snow, were fraught with hardships and dangers beyond all that they had suffered at the hands of Tissaphernes and the Persians. Finally they reached a plain where they found comfortable quarters in villages along the Centrītes river, but here again their further progress seemed completely blocked. The river was two hundred feet in width and above their breasts in depth; and, as a new danger not heretofore experienced, Armenian cavalry were seen on the opposite bank ready to thwart any attempt on their part to cross. The Cardūchi, moreover, were seen to be gathering in their rear; so that their situation was critical.

Here again, however, Greek readiness in device, aided, as Xenophon devoutly believed, by the favor of heaven, found a means of coping with their difficulties, and the river was crossed by a clever stratagem. Thus they reached the high and undulating table-land of Armenia, a region of bitter cold —for it was now December. Over this they marched without any serious fighting, although the satrap Tiribazus, despite the fact that he had made an agreement with them that they would be allowed to pass through the country unmolested, if they did not burn the villages, followed closely after them, waiting for an opportunity for a treacherous attack. If, however, they had little fighting to do, they had to endure and many suffered from frozen extremities and from snow and the severity of the weather. Not only slaves and beasts of burden, but some also of the soldiers perished from cold, and many suffered from frozen extremities and from snow blindness; while at times the scarcity of provisions led to terrible sufferings and exhaustion. After all these hardships Xenophon records a week of feasting amid abundant supplies in Armenian villages, built half underground as at the present day.

Thence through various tribes, Taochi, Chalybes, Phasiāni, Scythēni, sometimes having to fight against stubborn opposition, they made their way by a route that can no longer be determined with certainty, until at length they reached a mountain which offered a view of the sea. In a striking word-picture, Xenophon brings vividly before us the scene as the soldiers pressed forward crying out θάλαττα θάλαττα, and embraced one another with tears. For they thought that the sight of the sea meant that their hardships and troubles were over and their safety assured. After six days more of marching through the land of the Macrōnes and Colchi, the latter of whom sought to oppose their progress, they reached the Greek city of Trapezus (Trebizond) on the shores of the Black Sea. Here with thanksgiving they offered to the gods the sacrifices they had vowed, and instituted games in truly Greek fashion.

37. FROM THE TRAPEZUS TO THE BOSPORUS.—At Trapezus the army remained thirty days for much-needed rest and in the hope that sufficient vessels might be collected to make it possible for them to proceed for the rest of the way by sea. Chirisophus was at his own suggestion despatched to Byzantium to seek to obtain transports from the Lacedaemonian admiral Anaxibius. Meanwhile passing merchantmen were

seized, and supplies were procured by pillaging expeditions into the territory of the Colchi and other neighboring tribes.

At length, in despair of obtaining more ships, they determined to set out, putting on board of the vessels they had the sick and wounded with the women and all the baggage, while the able-bodied proceeded by land. Thus a three-days' march brought them to Cerasus, where a halt of ten days was made, and after another journey of ten days they reached Cotyōra. Both of these were Greek cities, like Trapezus colonies of Sinōpe, a powerful city lying farther to the westward. At Cotyōra the governor would not admit them within the walls, and they had to resort to force to find shelter for their sick, although they abstained from further acts of violence. Their stay in this place was a long one (forty-five days), yet still Chirisophus did not appear. Envoys, however, came from Sinōpe, at which city they were promised a friendly welcome.

It was during their stay at Cotyōra that Xenophon seems to have conceived the idea of seizing some non-Greek city with the force now at his command, and of establishing a colony, which would have been certain to become rich and powerful. This plan was unfortunately divulged to the army by the soothsayer Silānus, and led to much bitterness against Xenophon, although he publicly renounced the project and successfully combatted the charges brought against him. It became more and more plain, however, that dissension was rife in the army and it required all of Xenophon's eloquence to restore good discipline. At this time the generals were individually brought to trial for their acts during their term of office.

Shortly after this, sufficient transports having been assembled from Sinōpe and from Heraclēa, a Greek city lying further to the west, the army set sail, and after a voyage of a day and a night reached Sinōpe. Here Chirisophus joined them, having failed utterly in his quest for ships; and here the army resolved to choose a single general in the place of those now in command. The supreme command was offered to Xenophon, but he declined out of deference to Chirisophus as a Lacedaemonian, and because the omens were unfavorable. Chirisophus was then chosen leader and the army sailed under his command to Heraclēa.

At this point it became clear that the good discipline which had done so much to save them in their day of peril was breaking down, and that many were now actuated by motives of greed and self-interest rather than by loyalty to the common weal. Dissensions broke out in the army which led to a revolt on the part of the Arcadians and Achaeans (who formed more than half of the whole army). These chose commanders of their own, while of the rest about half remained loyal to Chirisophus, while the other half attached themselves to Xenophon. The Arcadian division set out alone, but in attempting to pillage the country of Bithynia, it was surrounded, and would probably have been entirely destroyed had it not been rescued by Xenophon and his men. After this the whole army came together again at Calpē,—a point midway between Heraclēa and Byzantium—and chose Neon as its commander, Chirisophus' command having lasted only a week.

The location of Calpē was so favorable for the foundation of a colony that the soldiers hesitated to take even the ordinary measures for making it defensible, lest Xenophon should seek to make their stay permanent. Finally, however, Cleaander, the Lacedaemonian harmost (governor) of Byzantium, came to them, and although through the machinations of the renegade Dexippus serious trouble arose, and it looked for a time as though the Cyrēan troops would find themselves in open war with Sparta, the trouble was adjusted and Cleander was asked to assume the command of the army. Unfavorable omens, however, deterred him from acting as their leader, and he departed alone, promising that he would assist them when they reached Byzantium. The army then set out under its own commanders, and marched through Bithynia until it reached Chrysopolis, directly across the Bosporus from Byzantium.

37. CONCLUSION.—Here, when they seemed to have passed through all the dangers and hardships that were to befall

them, they were destined to meet again with treachery, this time at the hands of an unworthy Greek.

The Lacedaemonian admiral Anaxibius had been bribed by the satrap Pharnabazus to persuade the Greeks to cross over to the European side of the strait, and brought this about by a false promise that he would provide pay for them. When they had crossed, however, and were within the walls of Byzantium, Anaxibius, instead of providing them with pay, beguiled them outside the walls and bade them get supplies from Thracian villages in the neighborhood. At this the army attempted to re-enter the city but found the gates shut and barred. Incensed at this the soldiers burst down the gates, rushed once more within, and were about to sack the city, when Xenophon in earnest and persuasive words showed them the odium they would bring upon themselves by such a deed, and the inevitable retribution that would be exacted by the all-powerful Spartans. Brought to their senses by this plea, the soldiers withdrew again without the walls, and accepted the offer of an adventurer, Coeratadas, to take them under his command. But the proposal came to nothing, as the resources of Coeratadas proved wholly inadequate.

Meanwhile Anaxibius, having in his turn been deceived by Pharnabazus in the matter of the reward promised him for leading the Greeks from Asia to Europe, sought to avenge himself on the Persian satrap by leading the Greeks back into Asia to make war upon him. But he was thwarted in this plan by the newly-appointed harmost, Aristarchus, who having no thought of allowing Anaxibius to make a private war on Persia, threatened to sink them if they tried to cross.

Thwarted thus again, the army took service under the Thracian prince Seuthes, who promised them liberal pay and in addition special grants to the generals. For two months the army served under him, only to be defrauded of the promised pay, and left once more destitute. At this crisis, however, fortunately for them, Sparta determined upon war with Persia, and had need of troops. The army was led across into Asia and handed over to the Spartan general Thibron, and Xenophon's story ends with the account of a successful raid upon the estates of a wealthy Persian, whereby much booty was obtained.

IV

MISCELLANEOUS

38. PROMINENT PERSONAGES.—Space may be taken here for a few brief paragraphs regarding individuals prominent in the first four books of Xenophon's story, who, if mentioned, have received but a passing notice in the preceding sections.

(a) CLEARCHUS: Of Clearchus, the most prominent and the ablest (II, 2, § 5) of the Greek generals under Cyrus, Xenophon has himself given a sketch in II, 6, §§ 1-15, telling of his warlike character, his defiance of the Spartan ephors, and his banishment from Sparta. He was an experienced campaigner before he took service with Cyrus, and in Xenophon's story exhibits the traits of a typical Spartan. He was a severe disciplinarian (I, 5, § 11, n; II, 3, § 11; II, 6, §§ 9-10), and was feared rather than loved by his men.

During the battle of Cunaxa his undue caution led him to disregard Cyrus' command to charge the Persian center (I, 8, § 13, n.), and may be said to have been the indirect cause of Cyrus' death; while his credulity in trusting the promises of Tissaphernes led directly to the seizure of the Greek generals, himself included. At the same time he seems to have been an able commander, and his loss was a severe blow to the Greeks.

Of the strife between Clearchus and Menon, Xenophon says little (I, 5, §§ 11ff.; II, 5, § 28), and is apparently careful to be just, although his own sympathies are plainly on the side of Clearchus.

(b) MENON: Of Menon, too, Xenophon gives a sketch (II, 6, §§ 21-29), and one that is by no means flattering. He seems to have been an unprincipled adventurer, and we may well believe that after Cyrus' death he was ready to secure advantage for himself by betraying his comrades, although Xenophon is careful not to make direct charges. After the generals were seized there is ground for thinking that he sought to win favor for himself by claiming to have been instrumental in bringing about the success of Tissaphernes' plan, but the result was merely that he was kept alive for a year, and died under torture instead of being beheaded at once as the other generals were (II, 6, § 29). In this scholars generally see the work of Parysatis, whose wrath Menon incurred as being a traitor to Cyrus' cause.

(c) PROXENUS: To Proxenus Xenophon devotes what is not merely a biographical sketch, but a tribute of personal affection (II, 6, §§ 16-20). He is in every way an attractive figure—generous, high-minded, and cultivated; he had even studied under the famous Gorgias (II, 6, § 16). It was at his invitation that Xenophon joined the expedition of Cyrus, and allusions to their friendship abound (II, 4, § 15; II, 5, § 37; III, 1, §§ 4, 8, 9; V, 3, § 5).

(d) CHIRISOPHUS: Chirisophus, too, is an attractive figure. Sent by the Spartan ephors at the head of a body of seven hundred Lacedaemonian hoplites, he joined Cyrus at Issus (I, 4, § 3). After the seizure of the generals he becomes a central figure (he was himself absent at that time procuring supplies). As a Spartan he was a man of few words, and could not have played the part which Xenophon attributes to himself, and for which persuasive eloquence was indispensable, but he was given the post of honor, commanding the van, and conducted himself in a soldierly manner.

Between Chirisophus and Xenophon a cordial friendship grew up, and the latter defers to him, as to a more experienced commander, on more than one occasion.

From Trapezus, Chirisophus was at his own suggestion sent to Byzantium to endeavor to obtain ships from the Spartan admiral Anaxibius, but was unsuccessful.

When, at Sinōpe, the army determined to choose a single commander, and Xenophon positively declined the appointment, Chirisophus was chosen (VI, 1, § 32). His command lasted only a week and, worn and disgusted with the dissensions rife in the army, he fell sick and died at Calpē (VI, 4, § 11).

(e) XENIAS: Xenias seeems to have been a military adventurer. He was, as so many of the Cyrean Greeks, an Arcadian, and having taken service with Cyrus was made commander of the mercenary troops doing garrison duty in the Ionian cities (I, 2, § 1).

At Cyrus' summons he joined him at Sardis with a strong force of four thousand hoplites (I, 2, § 3)—the largest single contingent. At the same time Xenias is an insignificant figure. When the army mutinied at Tarsus and Clearchus declared his resolution to abide by the Greeks, rather than avail himself of the friendship of Cyrus, more than half of Xenias' troops went over to him, and Cyrus allowed Clearchus to retain them. This gave Clearchus a force larger than that of any other general, and when opportunity offered Xenias and another general, Pasion, deserted (I, 4, § 7).

(f) SOPHAENETUS: Sophaenetus, of Stymphālus in Arcadia, one of the Greek generals under Cyrus, plays a somewhat prominent part in Xenophon's narrative. He joined Cyrus at Sardis (or at Celaenae; see the note on I, 2, 56), and as a veteran commander (he is twice called πρεσβύτατος, V, 3, § 1, and VI, 5, § 13) is often mentioned. It was he, with Cleānor, who went to meet Ariaeus and those with him when they came to the Greek camp after the seizure of the generals (II, 5, § 37), and he was left in command of the camp when the army set out for a night attack upon Tiribazus (IV, 4, § 19). As one of the older men he was among those who sailed from Trapezus, while the main body marched by land (V, 3, § 1). He was fined for neglect of duty (V, 8, § 1).

A history of Cyrus' expedition is attributed to Sophaenetus (see § 13).

(g) CLEĀNOR: Cleānor of Orchomenus in Arcadia was chosen general in the place of Agias after the latter had been seized. He is mentioned as the "eldest" in II, 1, § 10 (see the note), and the speeches put into his mouth are marked by a distinct character. It is he who expostulates with Ariaeus and the other Persians after the seizure of the generals, and expresses the utmost moral indignation (II, 5, § 39), and he enlarges similarly upon the enormity of the Persian treachery in III, 2, §§ 4ff.

(h) AGASIAS: Agasias, also of Stymphālus in Arcadia, was one of the Greek captains and was a close friend of Xenophon's (VI, 6, § 11). He is often singled out for special mention as a brave soldier (IV, 1, § 27; IV, 7, § 11; V, 2, § 15; VII, 8, § 19). It was he who urged the choice of Xenophon as commander in chief, declaring that it was absurd always to defer to Lacedaemonians (VI, 1, § 30).

For protecting a soldier of his company who had been unjustly seized by Dexippus, he was involved in serious trouble with the Spartan harmost Cleander, but was set free on the representations of Xenophon (VI, 6, §§ 7ff.).

(i) CALLIMACHUS, ARISTONYMUS, AND ARISTEAS: These may be mentioned as like Agasias representative of a group of brave soldiers, each seeking to outdo the others in valor (see IV, 1, §§ 27f.; and IV, 7, §§ 8ff.).

39. STYLE OF THE ANABASIS.—"The Anabasis," says Dionysius of Halicarnassus, "what is it but a splendid hymn of praise in honor of the Hellenes who shared in the campaign."*

In this judgment sympathetic readers of the *Anabasis* will concur, and that the work deserves this enthusiastic praise is due not only to the character of the events narrated but also in no small measure to the art of the narrator. Many, to be sure, think only of the barren records of the early chapters of the first book—records which make upon one the impression that Xenophon was merely transcribing entries made in his diary,—as though the recurring ἐντεῦθεν ἐξελαύνει were a fair sample of the writer's literary ability,—forgetting that nowhere else in the whole work does this annalistic style reappear. It has indeed become fashionable of recent years not

---

* Quoted in Dakyns' *Xenophon*, p. xxvi.

only to decry Xenophon as a falsifier in his narrative and as one whose sins against the laws of pure "Attic," both as regards vocabulary and syntax, are manifold, but also as one who can lay claim to no merit as a stylist. Very different was the judgment of the Greeks who came after him—they are never weary of sounding his praises—and very different is the judgment of the Greeks of today. He was called, says Diogenes Laertius, "the Attic Muse"; Plutarch praises the vividness of his description of the battle of Cunaxa as making us almost see the scene with our own eyes; and a similar tribute is paid to Xenophon by Lucian with reference to the Panthea episode in the *Cyropoedia*.

This vividness is perhaps the most noteworthy trait in Xenophon's style. Worthy to be put side by side with the description of the battle in I, 8, are such passages as III, 4, §§ 38ff.; IV, 7, §§ 22ff.; V, 2, §§ 13ff.; and many others.

To produce this effect of vividness, besides the writer's own power of realizing vividly the scenes which he describes, many elements contribute—the frequent use of the historical present, the further treatment of the past as present in the use of the subjunctive instead of the optative in dependent clauses after secondary tenses, the frequent use of deictic pronouns and of graphic phrases such as ἔνθα δή, the use of dialogue, the insertion of speeches (see the next section), and very strikingly the preference, common to most Greek writers, for direct rather than indirect discourse. This last often leads to sudden shifts from the third person to the second or third, and is very frequent. See *e. g.* I, 3, §§ 14 and 16; IV, 1, § 19; IV, 8, § 4; V, 5, § 24; V, 6, § 19.

Again, while the style of the *Anabasis* is in the main flowing and easy, and while Xenophon is sparing in his use of rhetorical devices and in the employment of metaphors and similes, it would be a mistake to regard him as a careless writer. His style abounds in evidences of conscious art, a few of which may be noticed here.

Very striking is his fondness for what is called ποικιλία, or variation of phrase. This is scarcely to be noticed in early

Greek, but in Xenophon it is common. We have *e. g.* βούλει, ἐθέλω, and χρῄζεις in immediate succession in III, 4, § 41 (*cf.* II, 3, § 23, and V, 7, § 27); in II, 3, §§ 2-9, we have ἄχρι, μέχρι, and ἔστε; in I, 9, § 19, ἐκτῶντο is immediately followed by ἐπέπατο, and in II, 6, § 21, λαμβάνοι by κερδαίνοι. Sometimes the variation is simply one of form, as when ἕξει is immediately followed by σχήσει in III, 5, § 11, in II, 6, § 9, ἐνίοτε by ἔσθ' ὅτε, and in III, 1, § 20, ᾔδειν by ᾔδη; or of syntax, as when ἀγάλλομαι is used first with ἐπί and the dat., and then with the simple dat. (II, 6, § 26).

This desire to vary a phrase already used may perhaps be the reason for the choice of an occasional poetic word (as in οὐ τελέθει τὰ ἱερά, VI, 6, § 36).

Again, Xenophon is very fond of the figure, anaphora, and frequently begins successive clauses with an identical phrase. Instances abound; *e. g.* ἐπιδεικνὺς μὲν . . . ἐπιδεικνὺς δέ (I, 3, § 16); ὁρῶσι μὲν . . . ὁρῶσι δὲ, . . . ὁρῶσι δέ (IV, 3, § 7). Sometimes we have a combination of anaphora and varied phrase, as in ὀκνοίην μὲν . . . φοβοίμην δέ (I, 3, § 17), or in ἐπειδὰν δὲ . . . ἐπειδὰν δὲ . . . ἐπὶ δὲ τῷ τρίτῳ (II, 2, § 4).

Further, the chiastic arrangement of words is often sought. Sometimes this is a natural arrangement, when regard is had to emphatic expression, as in II, 4, § 16, πιστοὶ ὄντες Κύρῳ καὶ ὑμῖν εὖνοι, but even so it is a conscious, rather than an unconscious, device, and instances occur in rhetorical passages— in the speeches and in the biographical chapter II, 6, oftener than in the narrative itself. Sometimes, too, the chiastic arrangement is more elaborate; see the notes on II, 6, 5, and III, 1, 93. One especially effective form is called palindromic; see I, 7, § 13 (with the note); I, 10, § 3; II, 4, § 20; II, 5, § 3; IV, 7, § 3.

Other instances of conscious art in the matter of word arrangement, in cases where emphasis is sought, or where reference is had to euphony, alliteration, or to assonance, might easily be cited. Occasionally, too, it is plain that cacophony has been purposely avoided. In III, 1, § 23, *e. g.* μέν is omitted after ἔχομεν, because its use would have given an ill-sounding phrase; and the same grounds may have led to the omission of ἄν before ἀναστρέφοιο in II, 5, § 14; similarly we have the infrequent τὸ ποιούμενον in I, 10, § 12, because the normal τὸ γιγνόμενον would have given an unpleasant assonance with the following γιγνώσκειν. Possibly the choice of the infrequent infinitive construction after λέγει in III, 1, § 26, is similarly to be accounted for.

The un-Attic features and the frequent poeticisms in Xenophon's style have often been commented on. They are of interest, when considered in connection with the facts of his life, as showing that he was as pan-Hellenic in his style as in his politics. It should not be forgotten that he lived for years among Asiatic and Peloponnesian Greeks, and that during the formative years of his early life there was no Attic prose literature upon which his style could have been modeled, while there is abundant evidence that he was strongly influenced by the poets, not one of whom wrote pure "Attic."

40. THE SPEECHES IN THE ANABASIS.—The incorporation of speeches in historical narrative was to the Greek not only an effective and dramatic method of vivifying the narrative itself, but was so entirely in accord with the actual political life with which he was acquainted that a history without speeches would have seemed to him at once a tame and lifeless thing and an unnatural thing. It has been left for our modern age to question the right of the historian to avail himself of this device, and to find something of dishonesty in the incorporation of speeches unless he is in possession of an authentic record of the words actually used by the speaker on the particular occasion in question.

The ancients felt far otherwise; and it is impossible rightly to appreciate the art of historical composition in antiquity, or even rightly to weigh the content of the historical narrative, unless we can in a measure approach the problem from the antique point of view.

The first and most essential thing is to realize the value that to the Greeks of old the spoken word possessed, as contrasted with the written word. We must allow its due weight to the constant use of oratory in ancient political life, and must remember that there were no journals, no daily papers, indeed scarcely any prose literature, and no reading public until toward the end of the fifth century B. C. It was customary not for poets and orators alone, but for literary artists generally, to publish their works by public readings or recitations, rather than in written form.

Remembering these facts we shall realize that the historian's gift of historic imagination found in the dramatic scenes which form the background of the speeches, and in the speeches themselves, a splendid field for its exercise; and we who read the narrative after the lapse of centuries find our ability to comprehend events and their causes greatly helped by such a method of vivifying the past. Nor must we forget that history-writing is an art; and it may be questioned whether the modern theory of the science of history has not entailed losses which in part offset its gains in scientific accuracy.

Xenophon makes free use of speeches in the *Anabasis*. Some are represented as having been delivered on occasions when he was presumably present, others when he certainly was not present, and under such circumstances that it must have been impossible for him to learn precisely what was said. All must be regarded as free compositions by Xenophon himself rather than as authentic records of what was actually said by the various speakers. At the same time it would be going too far to deny them all historic value. There is also an artistic fitness in the way in which some of the speeches are made to accord with the character of the speaker. Those of Chirisophus, for example, and of Cleānor have a distinct character of their own.

In point of style, the speeches are quite different from the narrative portions of the work, and are at times highly rhetorical (see, *e. g.*, II, 5, §§ 3ff., especially § 9; and IV, 6, §§ 10ff.).

Of especial interest are the speeches put in the mouth of Xenophon himself, as they so admirably illustrate the influence of his Athenian training and his masterly power in dealing with men. We may refer not only to the speeches in III, 1 and 2, but in particular to that by which Xenophon restrained the angry soldiers in Byzantium (VII, 1, §§ 25-31), and to his striking address to Seuthes (VII, 7, §§ 21-47).

ΞΕΝΟΦΩΝΤΟΣ
ΚΤΡΟΥ ΑΝΑΒΑΣΙΣ

BOOK I

1 Ι. Δαρείου καὶ Παρυσάτιδος γίγνονται παῖδες δύο, πρεσβύτερος μὲν Ἀρταξέρξης, νεώτερος δὲ Κῦρος· ἐπεὶ δὲ ἠσθένει
Δαρεῖος καὶ ὑπώπτευε τελευτὴν τοῦ βίου, ἐβούλετο τὼ παῖδε
2 ἀμφοτέρω παρεῖναι. ὁ μὲν οὖν πρεσβύτερος παρὼν ἐτύγχανε·

CHAPTER I

1 **Δαρείου καὶ Παρυσάτιδος**: gen. of source (G. 1130, 2; H. 750; B. 365). This was Darius Nothus (*i.e.* the illegitimate), who came to the throne in 425 B. C. See the Introd., § 22.

γίγνονται: histor. pres. (G. 1252; H. 828; B. 525). This is particularly common with vbs. of relationship (genealogical present).

παῖδες δύο: δύο more commonly takes the plural than the dual (below τὼ παῖδε, with stress on the idea of *both*, ἀμφοτέρω). There were thirteen children in all, but only two appear in Xenophon's narrative. The following proper names are in apposition with παῖδες (G. 911; H. 623; B. 317). The clauses are, as often, balanced by μέν and δέ. The former may rarely be translated; the latter means *and* or *but*, as the context determines. Avoid cumbersome phrases such as *on the one hand—on the other*. Greek has a natural love of balance; English has not. For a sketch of the characters of the two brothers, see the Introd., §§ 24 and 25. Remember this was not Cyrus the Great.

2 **ἠσθένει**: *lay sick*. The tense is durative (G. 1250, 2; H. 829; B. 526).

3 **ὑπώπτευε**: G. 543; H. 362a; *cf.* B. 175. For the meaning, *cf.* Lat. *suspicor*.

τελευτὴν τοῦ βίου: the word θάνατος is ordinarily avoided; so, too, τελευτάω is the common vb. *to die* (ἀποθνήσκω denotes a violent death). In compound phrases like this the art. is regularly expressed only with the noun in the gen. Note the possessive force of the art., common in many languages.

4 **ἀμφοτέρω**: the predicate position is regular with pronouns. Here the postponement adds emphasis.

μὲν οὖν, *now*. μέν simply paves the way for the following δέ.

παρὼν ἐτύγχανε, *happened to be*

5 Κῦρον δὲ μεταπέμπεται ἀπὸ τῆς ἀρχῆς ἧς αὐτὸν σατράπην
ἐποίησε· καὶ στρατηγὸν δὲ αὐτὸν ἀπέδειξε πάντων ὅσοι εἰς Καστωλοῦ πεδίον ἀθροίζονται. ἀναβαίνει οὖν ὁ Κῦρος λαβὼν Τισσαφέρνην ὡς φίλον καὶ τῶν Ἑλλήνων ἔχων ὁπλίτας ἀνέβη

---

there. The supplementary partic. contains the main idea (G. 1586; H. 984; B. 660 n.).

5 **Κῦρον**: the obj. may be emphasized by being brought to the head of the sentence, the subj. by being postponed.

μεταπέμπεται: another histor. pres. For the voice, see G. 1242, 2; H. 813; B. 504.

ἀρχῆς, *province;* see the Introd., §§ 17 and 24.

σατράπην, *satrap*, a Persian word, familiar to the Greeks of Xenophon's day. Herodotus (about half a century earlier) uses ὕπαρχος as a Greek equivalent. In general, Greek was slow to borrow foreign words, and, as a rule, made borrowed words look like Greek formations. (*Cf.* παράδεισος and παρασάγγης, also Persian words.) For the pred. acc., see G. 1077; H. 726; B. 341.

6 **ἐποίησε ... ἀπέδειξε**: translate as if plpfs. (H. 837; B. 519, note 1; 528, 1; G. M. T. 58). Greek is less exact than Eng. in the use of past tenses; in expressing future relations far more exact.

καὶ ... δέ, *and ... also.* δέ is connective, καί intensive. Cyrus was not only satrap, but a military officer as well, commanding one of the four divisions of the imperial army; see the Introd., § 24. This fact calls for emphatic expression, and is brought into stronger prominence by the abandonment of the relative construction.

πάντων ὅσοι: ὅσος is the normal form of the relative when the antecedent is πᾶς.

7 **ἀθροίζονται**: habit. pres.; the review occurred each year. The plain of Castolus was the mustering place for the troops of lower Asia.

ἀναβαίνει ... ἀνέβη: histor. pres. and aor. side by side, as not infrequently. For the form ἀνέβη, see G. 798; 799; H. 489; B. 209; 211. Note the force of ἀνα-.

ὁ Κῦρος: the art. with proper names may serve (*a*) to mark the individual as famous; (*b*) to contrast him with someone else; or (*c*) it refers back to someone already mentioned.

λαβὼν ... ἔχων: circumstantial partics. (G. 1563; H. 968b; B. 652). It is a mistake to assume that *with* suffices as a translation. Cyrus *took with him* (λαβών) Tissaphernes, and went up *at the head of* (ἔχων) his troops. Note the chiastic order (ἀναβαίνει ... λαβὼν ... ἔχων ... ἀνέβη), often a mere rhetorical device, although at times the most natural arrangement. See the Introd., § 39.

Τισσαφέρνην: see the Introd., § 23. Proper names in -ης, of the third decl., often form the acc. in -ην, as if of the first decl.

8 **ὡς φίλον**: Cyrus' rapid advance-

Book I, Chap. I

3 τριακοσίους, ἄρχοντα δὲ αὐτῶν Ξενίαν Παρράσιον. ἐπεὶ δὲ
ἐτελεύτησε Δαρεῖος καὶ κατέστη εἰς τὴν βασιλείαν Ἀρταξέρξης, 10
Τισσαφέρνης διαβάλλει τὸν Κῦρον πρὸς τὸν ἀδελφὸν ὡς ἐπιβουλεύοι αὐτῷ. ὁ δὲ πείθεται καὶ λαμβάνει Κῦρον ὡς ἀποκτενῶν·
ἡ δὲ μήτηρ ἐξαιτησαμένη αὐτὸν ἀποπέμπει πάλιν ἐπὶ τὴν ἀρχήν.
4 Ὁ δ' ὡς ἀπῆλθε κινδυνεύσας καὶ ἀτιμασθείς, βουλεύεται

---

ment had aroused the jealousy of Tissaphernes. Perhaps Cyrus saw this, and took him with him, because he dared not leave him behind—or was he himself deceived?

τῶν Ἑλλήνων: emphatic by position; three hundred Greek hoplites afforded greater protection than many times that number of Orientals. For the equipment of the hoplite, see the Introd., § 28. The gen. τῶν Ἑλλήνων is partitive (G. 1088; H. 729e; B. 355).

9 **Ξενίαν**: see the Introd., § 38. Of the Greeks deemed worthy of special mention in the *Anabasis* many are Arcadians (*cf.* VI, 2, §10). Find Parrhasia on the map.

ἐπεὶ δὲ ἐτελεύτησε: *ἐπεί*, with the aor. may generally be rendered by the Eng. plpf.; in temporal clauses the Greek plpf. is exceptional.

10 **κατέστη**: with εἰς, because motion is implied.

11 **διαβάλλει**: *maligned, falsely accused;* yet it is possible that the charge was true; see the Introd., § 25.

ὡς ἐπιβουλεύοι, (*saying*) *that he was plotting against him.* The opt. is due to the indirect quotation; see G. 1487; H. 932, 2; B. 673. The histor. pres. is a secondary tense.

12 **ὁ δέ**: in this phrase, regularly referring to a new subj., the older use of the art. as a demonstrative survives (G. 981; 983; H. 654e; B. 443, 1). In such cases it is best written with the accent.

ὡς ἀποκτενῶν: G. 1563, 4; 1574; H. 969c; 978; B. 653, 5; 656, 3; ὡς shows that this was the avowed or assumed purpose of Artaxerxes; ἅτε, with the partic., on the other hand, makes a statement for which the writer is responsible (*e. g.* IV, 2, § 13).

13 **ἐξαιτησαμένη . . . ἀποπέμπει**, *begged him off* (*as a favor to herself,* mid.) *and sent him back.* Greek often uses a partic. and vb., instead of two vbs. coupled by καί. It is rich in partics., while Eng. is not. The use of the aor. indicates that the action of the partic. is prior to that of the vb. For the character of Parysatis, see the Introd., § 26.

14 **ὁ δέ**, *i. e., Cyrus,* another shift of subject.

ὡς: temporal; *cf.* Lat. *ut.*

βουλεύεται . . . ἀντ' ἐκείνου, *planned that he might never again be in the power of his brother, but, if possible, might be king in his place.* For the use of the fut. indic. in an obj. clause, see G. 1372; H. 885; B. 593. Such a clause must, of course, take as

15 ὅπως μήποτε ἔτι ἔσται ἐπὶ τῷ ἀδελφῷ, ἀλλά, ἢν δύνηται, βασιλεύσει ἀντ' ἐκείνου. Παρύσατις μὲν δὴ ἡ μήτηρ ὑπῆρχε τῷ Κύρῳ, φιλοῦσα αὐτὸν μᾶλλον ἢ τὸν βασιλεύοντα Ἀρταξέρξην. ὅστις δ' ἀφικνεῖτο τῶν παρὰ βασιλέως πρὸς αὐτὸν πάντας οὕτω 5 διατιθεὶς ἀπεπέμπετο ὥστε αὐτῷ μᾶλλον φίλους εἶναι ἢ βασιλεῖ.
20 καὶ τῶν παρ' ἑαυτῷ δὲ βαρβάρων ἐπεμελεῖτο ὡς πολεμεῖν τε

---

its negative μή, not οὐ; see G. 1610; H. 1021; B. 431, 1 and 4.

15 ἢν δύνηται, strictly, *if he should be able,* a fut. condition (G. 1403; H. 898; B. 604). The subjv. is retained, although following a secondary tense (histor. pres.) in virtual indir. disc. (G. 1502; H. 937; B. 677).

16 μέν: balanced by δέ, l. 18, serves to contrast the activity of Parysatis with that of Cyrus himself. Especially when coupled with δή, as here, μέν often marks the dismissal of one topic and the passing on to another.

ὑπῆρχε, *favored, supported.* Observe the force of the prep., *he had her to count upon.*

17 βασιλεύοντα: the partic. is a virtual adj.

18 ὅστις ἀφικνεῖτο: when a rel. has a general or an indefinite antecedent, it regularly takes the constructions of the general conditional sentence (G. 1429; 1431, 1 and 2; H. 913; 914b; B. 620; 625). The opt. would, therefore, be normal here, but the past indic. (as in the Eng. idiom) is also found; see G. 1432; H. 918; 894c; G. M. T. 535. This is especially common with ὅστις, which is itself indefinite.

τῶν παρὰ βασιλέως: the prepositional phrase, with the art., serves as a substantive (G. 952, 1 and 2; H. 666a, 621; B. 451, 1). The phrase is a condensed one; the full form would be, ὅστις δὲ τῶν παρὰ βασιλεῖ ἀφικνεῖτο παρὰ βασιλέως; cf. I, 2, §18, οἱ ἐκ τῆς ἀγορᾶς. This condensation is regular in Greek. βασιλεύς normally omits the art., G. 957; H. 660c; B. 446, note.

πάντας: legitimately follows ὅστις, which implies a plural. The relative, after πᾶς, is usually ὅσος. Observe the emphasis falling on the antecedent, when the relative precedes. These men were probably inspectors, sent out from Babylon.

19 ὥστε ... εἶναι: G. 1449, 1450; H. 953; B. 595. With the infin. (tendency) contrast the indic., ᾐσθάνετο, below, l. 39 (actual result). οὕτω often leads up to ὥστε.

αὐτῷ: for the case, see G. 1174; H. 765; B. 376.

μᾶλλον φίλους: commoner than the comp. form of this adj., although we have φιλαίτερον, I, 9, §29; cf. μάλιστα φίλος, VII, 6, §15.

20 καὶ ... δέ: see above, l. 6. δέ is not usually so far postponed; most frequently it is the second word in its clause. Here the postponement emphasizes the preceding words, and so marks

Book I, Chap. I

6 ἱκανοὶ εἴησαν καὶ εὐνοϊκῶς ἔχοιεν αὐτῷ. τὴν δὲ Ἑλληνικὴν δύναμιν ἤθροιζεν ὡς μάλιστα ἐδύνατο ἐπικρυπτόμενος, ὅπως ὅτι ἀπαρασκευότατον λάβοι βασιλέα. Ὧδε οὖν ἐποιεῖτο τὴν συλλογήν. ὁπόσας εἶχε φυλακὰς ἐν

the contrast, τῶν παρὰ βασιλέως ... τῶν παρ' ἑαυτῷ.

τῶν βαρβάρων: for the case, see G. 1102; H. 742; B. 356. The subj. of a depend. clause is often brought forward and made the obj. of the main vb. (prolepsis; see H. 878; B. 717, 18). This arrangement, very common in Greek, is infrequent in English, although it occurs in poetry, and in the authorized translation of the New Testament the Greek idiom is sometimes kept (*I knew thee that thou art an hard man*, Matt. XXV: 24).

ὡς . . . εἴησαν . . . ἔχοιεν: for the ordinary syntax of such an obj. clause, *cf.* ὅπως . . . ἔσται, l. 15, and the note. The subjv. (after secondary tenses the opt.) is also permitted, as in pure final clauses (G. 1374, 1; H. 885b; B. 593, 1). Xenophon allows the use of ὡς, instead of ὅπως (G. M. T. 351, 1 and App. IV); for this there are but few parallels in other Attic authors. He stands alone also (among prose writers) in making free use of ὡς, instead of ἵνα or ὅπως, in final clauses.

πολεμεῖν: dependent on ἱκανοί (G. 1526; H. 952; B. 641).

21 **εὐνοϊκῶς ἔχοιεν**: ἔχω, with advs., expresses a state or condition, and is best rendered by our vb. *to be*, with an adj.

τὴν δὲ Ἑλληνικὴν δύναμιν: note again the emphatic position.

22 **ἤθροιζεν**: *he set about collecting*. Note the tense.

ὡς μάλιστα ἐδύνατο ἐπικρυπτόμενος, *with all possible secrecy*. How lit.?

ὅπως λάβοι: G. 1365; H. 881; B. 590. ὅπως is Xenophon's favorite final particle, although ἵνα is freely used, and also ὡς (c. 3. 69). See G. M. T. 312, 3 and App. III.

ὅτι ἀπαρασκευότατον: ὅτι and ὡς are frequently used to intensify the meaning of a superlative (*cf.*, below, ὅτι πλείστους). With ὡς, not ὅτι, the vb. of ability is often expressed (above, l. 22).

24 **ὧδε**: as a rule, ὧδε looks forward, οὕτως back (G. 1005; H. 696; B. 482). The remainder of the chapter is taken up with the narrative of the various ways in which Cyrus sought to raise troops.

ἐποιεῖτο τὴν συλλογήν: a frequent periphrasis. ποιῶ (in the passive, γίγνομαι), with the verbal noun, may take the place of almost any vb. Here the use of the mid. emphasizes the activity of the subj.

ὁπόσας εἶχε . . . λαμβάνειν, *to the commanders of all the garrisons which he had in the cities he gave orders that they should severally enlist*. More regularly the Greek would be, φυλακῶν ὁπόσων εἶχε (by attraction for ὁπόσας εἶχε, G. 1031; H. 994; B.

25 ταῖς πόλεσι παρήγγειλε τοῖς φρουράρχοις ἑκάστοις λαμβάνειν
ἄνδρας Πελοποννησίους ὅτι πλείστους καὶ βελτίστους, ὡς ἐπιβουλεύοντος Τισσαφέρνους ταῖς πόλεσι. καὶ γὰρ ἦσαν αἱ Ἰωνικαὶ πόλεις Τισσαφέρνους τὸ ἀρχαῖον ἐκ βασιλέως δεδομέναι,
τότε δὲ ἀφειστήκεσαν πρὸς Κῦρον πᾶσαι πλὴν Μιλήτου· ἐν Μι- 7
30 λήτῳ δὲ Τισσαφέρνης προαισθόμενος τὰ αὐτὰ ταῦτα βουλευομένους, ἀποστῆναι πρὸς Κῦρον, τοὺς μὲν αὐτῶν ἀπέκτεινε τοὺς δ'

---

484). As it is, the antecedent is incorporated in the rel. clause (G. 1037; H. 995; B. 485). ὁπόσος implies the antecedent *all*; see the note on πάντας, l. 18. Distinguish between φυλακάς (from φυλακή) and φύλακας (from φύλαξ).

25 ἑκάστοις: pred. posit.; see on ἀμφοτέρω, l. 4. When it designates individuals, not groups, ἕκαστος is regularly in the sing. Here its close association with φρουράρχοις justifies the pl.

26 Πελοποννησίους: confessedly the best soldiers among the Greeks; *cf.* the note on Ξενίαν, l. 9.

ὡς ἐπιβουλεύοντος T., *alleging that T. was plotting against their cities.* See the note on ὡς ἀποκτενῶν, l. 12. For the gen. abs. see G. 1568; H. 970; B. 657.

27 καὶ γάρ, *and (with the more plausibility) for;* but the ellipsis is often hardly felt.

ἦσαν ... Τισσαφέρνους, *had belonged to T.* The impf. stands where English requires the plpf.; see the note on ἐποίησε, l. 6. When the impf. is thus used, the idea of duration is often prominent. For the pred. gen., see G. 1094, 1; H. 732a; B. 348, 1.

αἱ Ἰωνικαὶ πόλεις: see the Introd., § 26.

28 τὸ ἀρχαῖον: G. 1060; H. 719; B. 336.

ἐκ βασιλέως, *by the king*. ἐκ, common in Ionic Greek, may be used even in Attic of the agent, considered as the source; *cf.* ἀπό, l. 47.

29 ἀφειστήκεσαν: for the form, see G. 528; H. 359a; B. 172, 2.

πλὴν Μιλήτου: Tissaphernes kept the Milesians in check by a strong fortress which he had built.

30 προαισθόμενος ... βουλευομένους, *perceiving that some were forming this same plan* (προ-, *before their plan was ripe for execution*). Observe that the aor. partic. denotes an action prior to that of the principal vb.

τὰ αὐτά (often written ταὐτά): to be distinguished from ταῦτα (G. 399; H. 679; B. 475, 1). The case is acc. of the inner obj. (G. 1054; H. 716b; B. 334). In such phrases the pl. is normal in Greek, although Eng. often requires the sing.

βουλευομένους: partic. in indir. disc. (G. 1588; H. 982; B. 661). The indef. subj. of the partic. is omitted.

31 ἀποστῆναι: in appos. with τὰ αὐτὰ ταῦτα.

τοὺς μέν ... τοὺς δέ, *some* ...

ἐξέβαλεν. ὁ δὲ Κῦρος ὑπολαβὼν τοὺς φεύγοντας συλλέξας
στράτευμα ἐπολιόρκει Μίλητον καὶ κατὰ γῆν καὶ κατὰ θάλατταν
καὶ ἐπειρᾶτο κατάγειν τοὺς ἐκπεπτωκότας. καὶ αὕτη αὖ ἄλλη
πρόφασις ἦν αὐτῷ τοῦ ἀθροίζειν στράτευμα. πρὸς δὲ βασιλέα 35
8 πέμπων ἠξίου ἀδελφὸς ὢν αὐτοῦ δοθῆναι οἷ ταύτας τὰς πόλεις
μᾶλλον ἢ Τισσαφέρνην ἄρχειν αὐτῶν, καὶ ἡ μήτηρ συνέπραττεν
αὐτῷ ταῦτα· ὥστε βασιλεὺς τὴν μὲν πρὸς ἑαυτὸν ἐπιβουλὴν οὐκ
ᾐσθάνετο, Τισσαφέρνει δὲ ἐνόμιζε πολεμοῦντα αὐτὸν ἀμφὶ τὰ

others. For the art. as a demonstr. see on ὁ δέ, l. 12.

ἀπέκτεινε: aor. indic. (G. 672; H. 431; B. 204). This form might be impf., but ἐξέβαλεν shows that it is aor. For the latter form, see G. 675; H. 435; B. 207; 208.

32 ὑπολαβὼν ... συλλέξας ... ἐπολιόρκει, *having taken the exiles under his protection* (ὑπο-), *collected an army and laid siege to*. Observe that φεύγω supplies a passive to ἐκβάλλω; *cf.* ἐκπεπτωκότας, below.

34 κατάγειν, *restore*. Observe the force of the prep.; *cf.* κατέρχομαι, *come back from banishment*.

ἐκπεπτωκότας: ἐκπίπτω is the normal passive of ἐκβάλλω.

αὕτη: attracted to the gender of the pred. noun, a common construction (*cf.* Lat.). On the other hand the neut. is often kept. Since demonstr. pronouns regularly take the art., the absence of the art. shows that the noun is a part of the pred. and does not go directly with the pronoun.

35 αὐτῷ: dat. of possess. (G. 1173; H. 768; B. 379).

τοῦ ἀθροίζειν, *for collecting*. The infin. stands as a noun in the gen. (G. 1547; H. 959; B. 639).

Xen. is fond of the articular infin.

36 ἠξίου, *urged, asked as his right*, a durative tense.

ὤν, *inasmuch as he was*.

δοθῆναι οἷ: the infin. is the obj. of ἠξίου (G. 1518; H. 948; B. 638). οἷ is the indir. refl. (G. 987; H. 685; B. 471; 472); *i. e.*, while occurring in a subord. clause, it refers back to the main subj. Though enclitic, it is accented when emphatic (G. 144, 1; H. 263; B. 71, 2).

37 ἄρχειν, *continue to rule*.

αὐτῶν: for the case, see G. 1109; H. 741; B. 356.

συνέπραττεν αὐτῷ: the dat. is due to the comp. vb. (G. 1179; H. 775; B. 394).

38 ὥστε: see the note on ὥστε εἶναι, l. 19.

τὴν πρὸς ἑαυτὸν ἐπιβουλήν: the pr p. with its case has the value of an attrib. adj.; see the references cited in the note on τῶν παρὰ βασιλέως, l. 18. πρός is the most personal of the preps. governing the acc.; it may or may not denote hostility; ἐπί generally does.

39 Τισσαφέρνει: emphatic, *thought it was against T. that he was warring*, etc. For the dat., see

40 στρατεύματα δαπανᾶν· ὥστε οὐδὲν ἤχθετο αὐτῶν πολεμούντων.
καὶ γὰρ ὁ Κῦρος ἀπέπεμπε τοὺς γιγνομένους δασμοὺς βασιλεῖ
ἐκ τῶν πόλεων, ὧν Τισσαφέρνους ἐτύγχανεν ἔχων.

Ἄλλο δὲ στράτευμα αὐτῷ συνελέγετο ἐν Χερρονήσῳ τῇ 9
κατ' ἀντιπέρας Ἀβύδου τόνδε τὸν τρόπον. Κλέαρχος Λακεδαι-

G. 1177; H. 772; B. 392, 1, with the note. The partic. πολεμοῦντα is, of course, not due to indir. disc., but the emphasis is best brought out by some such rendering as that given above.

ἀμφί: more commonly εἰς is used in this phrase; *e. g.* c. 3. 15.

40 δαπανᾶν: infin. in indir. disc. (G. 1522, 1; H. 946; B. 646).

ὥστε... πολεμούντων, *so that he did not at all* (οὐδέν) *object to their being at war.* οὐδέν is the acc. of the inner obj., here, as often, scarcely differing in force from an adv. See the references cited in the note on τὰ αὐτὰ ταῦτα, l. 30.

αὐτῶν πολεμούντων: causal gen. abs.; see on ὡς ἐπιβουλεύοντος, ll. 26 f.

41 καὶ γάρ, *and (with more reason) for.* See l. 27 and the note.

ἀπέπεμπε, *continued to remit;* observe the tense. ἀπο- does not merely indicate separation; the revenues belonged to the king; so ἀποδίδωμι, *give back what is due,* ἀπαιτῶ, *ask what is due, etc.* Cf. Lat. re-.

δασμούς: the tribute was paid not in money only, but in the products of the different provinces, cattle, horses, *etc.*

42 ἐκ τῶν πόλεων . . . ἔχων, *from the cities belonging to T., which he* (*Cyrus*) *happened to hold.* The possess. gen. Τισσαφέρνους is incorporated in the rel. clause; see the notes on Τισσαφέρνους ἦσαν, ll. 27 f., and on ὁπόσας εἶχε φυλακάς, l. 24. ὧν is attracted to the case of its antecedent (see the references cited in the note just referred to). For the partic. with ἐτύγχανεν, see l. 4 and the note.

43 αὐτῷ: for such dats. consult G. 1157; H. 766; B. 377, note 2.

Χερρονήσῳ: since Χερρόνησος strictly means *peninsula,* a further designation may be added, although the presumption always is that the Thracian Chersonesus is meant; see the map.

τῇ κατ' ἀντιπέρας Ἀβύδου: it was at Abydus that Xerxes crossed the Hellespont. For the gen., see G. 1148; H. 757; B. 360. Note the third attrib. posit.; the epithet comes in as an afterthought. The student should observe that in all three positions the attrib. is immediately preceded by the art.; see G. 959, 1 and 2; H. 666; 667; 668; B. 452.

44 τόνδε τὸν τρόπον, *in the following manner.* See the note on ὧδε, l. 24. For the acc. as an adv., *cf.* τὸ ἀρχαῖον, l. 28, and the note. In the case of this word the dat. of manner and the adv. acc. are indistinguishable in meaning.

μόνιος φυγὰς ἦν· τούτῳ συγγενόμενος ὁ Κῦρος ἠγάσθη τε αὐτὸν 45
καὶ δίδωσιν αὐτῷ μυρίους δαρεικούς. ὁ δὲ λαβὼν τὸ χρυσίον
στράτευμα συνέλεξεν ἀπὸ τούτων τῶν χρημάτων καὶ ἐπολέμει ἐκ
Χερρονήσου ὁρμώμενος τοῖς Θρᾳξὶ τοῖς ὑπὲρ Ἑλλήσποντον οἰκοῦσι καὶ ὠφέλει τοὺς Ἕλληνας. ὥστε καὶ χρήματα συνεβάλλοντο αὐτῷ εἰς τὴν τροφὴν τῶν στρατιωτῶν αἱ Ἑλλησποντιακαὶ 50
πόλεις ἑκοῦσαι. τοῦτο δ' αὖ οὕτω τρεφόμενον ἐλάνθανεν αὐτῷ
τὸ στράτευμα.

10 Ἀρίστιππος δὲ ὁ Θετταλὸς ξένος ὢν ἐτύγχανεν αὐτῷ, καὶ
πιεζόμενος ὑπὸ τῶν οἴκοι ἀντιστασιωτῶν ἔρχεται πρὸς τὸν Κῦρον

Κλέαρχος: see the Introd., § 38, and II, 6, §§ 1–16. Asyndeton (omission of the connective) is not felt when the sentence but explains a preceding phrase, as here, or when the clause begins with a rel. pron. Often, too, although not always, a demonstr. serves as a connective (*cf.* the next clause in the text). Elsewhere asyndeton is rare in Greek, which abounds in connecting particles, and is generally a mark of haste or passion; see H. 1039; B. 717, 3.

45 τούτῳ: the pron. regularly refers back (see on ὧδε, l. 24).

ἠγάσθη, *took a liking to him*, ingressive aor. (G. 1260; H. 841; B. 529).

46 μυρίους δαρεικούς: a large sum, about $54,000.00; but Cyrus needed men and was willing to pay for them. The word δαρεικός suggests the French *Napoléon* and *Louis d'or* as names of coins; *cf.*, also, Eng. *sovereign*, so used.

47 συνέλεξεν . . . ἐπολέμει: note the change of tense.

ἀπό: of the means; *cf.* ἐκ of the agent, l. 28.

ἐκ Χερρονήσου: the natural base for operations against Thrace.

48 τοῖς Θρᾳξὶ τοῖς ὑπέρ: the formal attrib. posit.; see on τῇ κατ' ἀντιπέρας, ll. 43 f.

ὑπὲρ Ἑλλήσποντον: the acc. is freely used in phrases where motion is implied, not expressed.

49 ὥστε καί: καί is intensive, not connective.

50 εἰς: when not of motion, commonly, as here, of direction or purpose.

51 ἑκοῦσαι, *willingly* (G. 926; H. 619a; B. 425).

τοῦτο: with τὸ στράτευμα, despite the separation.

τρεφόμενον ἐλάνθανεν, *was secretly maintained* (*cf.* παρὼν ἐτύγχανε, l. 4, and the note).

53 Ἀρίστιππος: an aristocratic name.

Θετταλός: consult the map, whenever geographical names occur.

ξένος, *guest-friend;* but below, l. 55, ξένους, *mercenaries;* see the vocab.

54 οἴκοι: an attrib.; see on τὴν . . . ἐπιβουλήν, l. 38.

ἀντιστασιωτῶν: Thessaly was con-

55 καὶ αἰτεῖ αὐτὸν εἰς δισχιλίους ξένους καὶ τριῶν μηνῶν μισθόν, ὡς οὕτως περιγενόμενος ἂν τῶν ἀντιστασιωτῶν. ὁ δὲ Κῦρος δίδωσιν αὐτῷ εἰς τετρακισχιλίους καὶ ἓξ μηνῶν μισθόν, καὶ δεῖται αὐτοῦ μὴ πρόσθεν καταλῦσαι πρὸς τοὺς ἀντιστασιώτας πρὶν ἂν αὐτῷ συμβουλεύσηται. οὕτω δὲ αὖ τὸ ἐν Θετταλίᾳ ἐλάνθανεν
60 αὐτῷ τρεφόμενον στράτευμα.

Πρόξενον δὲ τὸν Βοιώτιον ξένον ὄντα ἐκέλευσε λαβόντα ἄν- 11
δρας ὅτι πλείστους παραγενέσθαι, ὡς ἐς Πισίδας βουλόμενος

stantly disturbed by strife among the nobles.

55 αἰτεῖ αὐτὸν . . . μισθόν, *asked him for pay* (G. 1069; H. 724; B. 340).

εἰς δισχιλίους . . . μισθόν, *pay for two thousand mercenaries and for three months.* Both phrases qualify μισθόν. For the gen. μηνῶν, see G. 1085; 5; H. 729d; B. 352.

ὡς οὕτως περιγενόμενος ἄν, *stating that (ὡς) he should thus get the better of.* See G. 1308, 1; H. 987a; B. 662 (direct, οὕτως περιγενοίμην ἄν).

56 ἀντιστασιωτῶν: for the case, see G. 1120; H. 749; B. 364.

57 δεῖται αὐτοῦ μή, *begged him not to.* δέομαι, taking the gen. (as a vb. expressing want, G. 1112; H. 743; B. 356), may take also an acc. of the inner obj. (here the infin. καταλῦσαι, G. 1114; H. 743a). Observe that the infin., unless in indir. disc., if negatived, takes μή, not οὐ (G. 1611; H. 1023; B. 633).

58 πρόσθεν: merely leads up to πρίν; it should not be translated. Cf. οὕτω . . . ὥστε, ll. 18 f.

καταλῦσαι πρός, *come to terms with.* The vb. means *bring to an end,* and may be used e. g.

both with πόλεμον and εἰρήνην; here the context makes clear which is to be supplied.

πρὶν ἄν . . . συμβουλεύσηται, *until he should have consulted with him (Cyrus).* πρίν (*until*) normally takes a finite mood; πρίν (*before*) the infin. (G. 1470). For the subjv. with ἄν, see G. 1471, 2; H. 924, 921; B. 627, 623. Cf. ἢν δύνηται, l. 15, and the note.

61 Πρόξενον: see the Introd., § 38, and II, 6, §§ 16–21. It was Proxenos who induced Xenophon to join the expedition (III, 1, § 4).

λαβόντα . . . παραγενέσθαι, *to enlist and come;* see on ἐξαιτησαμένη ἀποπέμπει, l. 13.

62 ὅτι πλείστους: see on ὅτι ἀπαρασκευότατον, ll. 22 f.

παραγενέσθαι: vbs. compounded with παρά very often imply motion; so even παρῆσαν, c. 2. 14.

ὡς . . . βουλόμενος . . . ὡς . . . παρεχόντων: in both cases ὡς gives the reason alleged by Cyrus; see on ὡς ἀποκτενῶν, l. 12.

ἐς Πισίδας, *into the country of the Pisidians,* a common use; the name of the people is more often expressed than the name of the country. Because of its

στρατεύεσθαι, ὡς πράγματα παρεχόντων τῶν Πισιδῶν τῇ ἑαυτοῦ χώρᾳ.

Σοφαίνετον δὲ τὸν Στυμφάλιον καὶ Σωκράτην τὸν Ἀχαιόν, 65
ξένους ὄντας καὶ τούτους, ἐκέλευσεν ἄνδρας λαβόντας ἐλθεῖν ὅτι
πλείστους, ὡς πολεμήσων Τισσαφέρνει σὺν τοῖς φυγάσι τοῖς
Μιλησίων. καὶ ἐποίουν οὕτως οὗτοι.

1 II. Ἐπεὶ δ' ἐδόκει ἤδη πορεύεσθαι αὐτῷ ἄνω, τὴν μὲν πρόφασιν ἐποιεῖτο ὡς Πισίδας βουλόμενος ἐκβαλεῖν παντάπασιν ἐκ
τῆς χώρας· καὶ ἀθροίζει ὡς ἐπὶ τούτους τό τε βαρβαρικὸν καὶ τὸ
Ἑλληνικόν. ἐνταῦθα καὶ παραγγέλλει τῷ τε Κλεάρχῳ λαβόντι

---

meaning, εἰς, expressing the limit of motion, is not used with the sing. of persons. The Pisidians were a hardy tribe, inhabiting the mountainous district south of Cyrus' satrapy (see the map), and enjoyed virtual independence.

65 **Στυμφάλιον . . . Ἀχαιόν**: find Stymphalus and Achaea on the map, and consult the note on Ξενίαν. l. 9.

66 **ξένους ὄντας καὶ τούτους**, *who were also guest-friends of his.*

CHAPTER II

1 **ἐπεὶ δ' . . . ἄνω**, *but when at length it seemed good to him to proceed inland*. Note the force of ἄνω, and cf. ἀναβαίνω, ἀνάβασις (the opposite is κατα-; see the vocab.). This was in the early part of 401 B.C.

τὴν μὲν πρόφασιν . . . ὡς . . . βουλόμενος, *he gave out that he wished*. Consult the notes on ὡς βουλόμενος, c. 1. 62, and on ἐποιεῖτο τὴν συλλογήν, c. 1. 24. Observe that the use of μέν, in this clause, leads one to expect a following clause with δέ, giving the real ground. This was, however, unnecessary. Well knowing that the Greeks would shrink from the undertaking, if they knew he intended to lead them on so long and so dangerous a journey, Cyrus hides his purpose; but even so starts inland. To the Greeks long journeys by land were always distasteful; they ordinarily traveled by water. Cyrus did not disclose his real purpose until they reached the Euphrates (I, 4, §11), when to turn back was a virtual impossibility. Even as it was they suspected that Cyrus was deceiving them, and mutinied (I, 3, §1), but were induced to proceed by promises of higher pay. The course of the march should be carefully followed on the map.

3 **τὸ βαρβαρικὸν . . . τὸ Ἑλληνικόν**: in such military phrases the neut. sing. is constantly used in a collective sense; no noun need be supplied.

4 **ἐνταῦθα**: *i.e.* to Sardis.

καί, *also*, not *and*.

παραγγέλλει: common in military writers; cf. pass the word.

5 ἥκειν ὅσον ἦν αὐτῷ στράτευμα, καὶ τῷ Ἀριστίππῳ συναλλαγέντι πρὸς τοὺς οἴκοι ἀποπέμψαι πρὸς ἑαυτὸν ὃ εἶχε στράτευμα· καὶ Ξενίᾳ τῷ Ἀρκάδι, ὃς αὐτῷ προεστήκει τοῦ ἐν ταῖς πόλεσι ξενικοῦ, ἥκειν παραγγέλλει λαβόντα πλὴν ὁπόσοι ἱκανοὶ ἦσαν τὰς ἀκροπόλεις φυλάττειν. ἐκάλεσε δὲ καὶ τοὺς Μίλητον πολι- 2
10 ορκοῦντας, καὶ τοὺς φυγάδας ἐκέλευσε σὺν αὐτῷ στρατεύεσθαι, ὑποσχόμενος αὐτοῖς, εἰ καλῶς καταπράξειεν ἐφ᾽ ἃ ἐστρατεύετο,

---

λαβόντι ἥκειν, *to come bringing.*
The partic. is in agreement with Κλεάρχῳ (*cf.* συναλλαγέντι) below. In such cases it should be noted that, while the vb. calls for a dat., the following infin. implies a subj. acc. The partic. varies in agreement. If it stands near the dat., as here, it may itself be dat.; but it is oftener acc., especially when it stands at a distance from the noun and in close proximity to the infin. See G. 928, 1; H. 941; B. 631, 1, and *cf.* λαβόντα, below, l. 8, after Ξενίᾳ.

5 ὅσον ... στράτευμα: the noun is incorporated in the rel. clause; see on ὁπόσας εἶχε, c. 1. 24.

Ἀριστίππῳ: Aristippus appears to have sent Menon in his place; see l. 34.

συναλλαγέντι: for the formation of the pres., see G. 580; H. 397; B. 195, 1.

6 τοὺς οἴκοι: no noun expressed; see on τῶν παρὰ βασιλέως, c. 1. 18.

7 Ξενίᾳ: he afterward proved a deserter (I, 4, § 7).

αὐτῷ, *under him* (*Cyrus*). This dat. is often best rendered by the Eng. possess., *was in command of his mercenaries.*

τοῦ ξενικοῦ: see on τὸ βαρβαρικόν, l. 3.

8 πλὴν ὁπόσοι ... φυλάττειν, *save as many as would suffice to defend the citadels.* The antecedent of the rel. is unexpressed, as often; if expressed, it would be τοσούτων. The ancient city regularly consisted of a fortified citadel and the lower town at its base; Mycenae, Corinth, and Athens are examples. Names of cities are often pl., *e. g.* Ἀθῆναι.

9 φυλάττειν: *cf.* πολεμεῖν, c. 1. 20, and the note.

δὲ καί, see on καὶ δέ, c. 1. 6.

ἐκάλεσε ... ἐκέλευσε: note the chiastic order; see on λαβὼν ... ἔχων, c. 1. 7.

τοὺς Μίλητον πολιορκοῦντας: the partic., with the art., is often best rendered by a rel. clause.

11 ὑποσχόμενος ... οἴκαδε: direct, ἐὰν καλῶς καταπράξω ἐφ᾽ ἃ στρατεύομαι, οὐ πρόσθεν παύσομαι πρὶν ἂν ὑμᾶς καταγάγω. For ἐὰν καταπράξω, see on ἢν δύνηται, c. 1. 15; for πρὶν ἂν καταγάγω, on πρὶν ἂν συμβουλεύσηται, c. 1. 58 f. The change to the opt. is due to the quotation after a secondary tense (G. 1487; H. 932, 2; B. 673). Similarly, στρατεύομαι might have been changed to στρατεύοιτο; but, in historical writers, a shift to the point of view of the narrator leads, not infrequently, to the

μὴ πρόσθεν παύσασθαι πρὶν αὐτοὺς καταγάγοι οἴκαδε. οἳ δὲ
ἡδέως ἐπείθοντο· ἐπίστευον γὰρ αὐτῷ· καὶ λαβόντες τὰ ὅπλα
παρῆσαν εἰς Σάρδεις. Ξενίας μὲν δὴ τοὺς ἐκ τῶν πόλεων λαβὼν παρεγένετο εἰς Σάρδεις ὁπλίτας εἰς τετρακισχιλίους, Πρόξενος δὲ παρῆν ἔχων ὁπλίτας μὲν εἰς πεντακοσίους καὶ χιλίους,
γυμνῆτας δὲ πεντακοσίους, Σοφαίνετος δὲ ὁ Στυμφάλιος ὁπλίτας ἔχων χιλίους, Σωκράτης δὲ ὁ Ἀχαιὸς ὁπλίτας ἔχων ὡς
πεντακοσίους, Πασίων δὲ ὁ Μεγαρεὺς τριακοσίους μὲν ὁπλίτας,
τριακοσίους δὲ πελταστὰς ἔχων παρεγένετο· ἦν δὲ καὶ οὗτος καὶ
ὁ Σωκράτης τῶν ἀμφὶ Μίλητον στρατευομένων. οὗτοι μὲν εἰς
Σάρδεις αὐτῷ ἀφίκοντο.

substitution of the past indic. (G. 1501, 1489; H. 936; B. 676). This corresponds to the Eng. idiom. παύσασθαι is governed by the vb. of promising, regarded as a vb. of will; hence the infin. is timeless and the neg. is μή, not οὐ (see G. 1496; H. 1024, end; B. 549, note). With vbs. of this class the fut. infin. is commoner; see G. 1286; H. 948a; B. 549, 2, with the note.

ἐφ' ἅ: the antecedent is omitted, as commonly when it is indef. (G. 1026; 1027; H. 996; B. 486); cf. πλὴν ὁπόσοι, c. 1. 8. Trans., *the objects of his expedition.*

12 πρόσθεν . . . πρίν: see c. 1. 58, and the note.

καταγάγοι: cf. κατάγειν, c. 1. 34, and the note.

14 παρῆσαν εἰς: see on παραγενέσθαι, c. 1. 62. Sardis was the capital of Lydia; see the map.

τοὺς ἐκ τῶν πόλεων: see on τῶν παρὰ βασιλέως, c. 1. 18.

15 ὁπλίτας: see the Introd., § 28.

εἰς, *about, to the number of.* It is still a prep., however, and governs the acc.; so does ἀμφί

(l. 59); ὡς (below, l. 18), and ὅσον (I, 8, § 6), on the other hand, are advs., and do not govern a case.

17 γυμνῆτας: see the Introd., § 28.

19 Μεγαρεύς: find Megara on the map.

20 πελταστάς: see the Introd., § 28.

ἦν: the vb. agrees with the nearer of two subjs.; see G. 901; H. 607; B. 496, 1.

21 τῶν . . . στρατευομένων: the partic. is impf., not pres.; see G. 1289; H. 856a; B. 542, 1. Render by the Eng. plpf. For the pred. gen., cf. Τισσαφέρνους, c. 1. 28 (there possess., here partit.).

οὗτοι μέν: no connective is needed; see on τούτῳ, c. 1. 45. μέν indicates that others came later (consult the note on μὲν δή, c. 1. 16). The total number of the troops thus far mentioned is 8,100, 7,300 of them hoplites.

22 αὐτῷ, *at his summons.* The translation of such dats. must vary in different connections; see the references given in the note on αὐτῷ, c. 1. 43.

Τισσαφέρνης δὲ κατανοήσας ταῦτα, καὶ μείζονα ἡγησάμενος 4
εἶναι ἢ ὡς ἐπὶ Πισίδας τὴν παρασκευήν, πορεύεται ὡς βασιλέα
ᾗ ἐδύνατο τάχιστα ἱππέας ἔχων ὡς πεντακοσίους. καὶ βασιλεὺς 5
μὲν δὴ ἐπεὶ ἤκουσε Τισσαφέρνους τὸν Κύρου στόλον, ἀντιπαρεσ-
κευάζετο.

Κῦρος δὲ ἔχων οὓς εἴρηκα ὡρμᾶτο ἀπὸ Σάρδεων· καὶ
ἐξελαύνει διὰ τῆς Λυδίας σταθμοὺς τρεῖς παρασάγγας εἴκοσι
καὶ δύο ἐπὶ τὸν Μαίανδρον ποταμόν. τούτου τὸ εὖρος δύο
πλέθρα· γέφυρα δὲ ἐπῆν ἑπτὰ ἐζευγμένη πλοίοις. τοῦτον 6

---

23 μείζονα: brought to the head of the clause for emphasis, although belonging to the pred.

24 εἶναι: see the note on δαπανᾶν, c. 1. 40.

ἢ ὡς ἐπί, freely, *than would be needed against.*

ὡς βασιλέα: ὡς, as a prep., denoting the limit, is used only with the acc. of words denoting persons; εἰς may not be used in such cases; see on ἐς Πισίδας, c. 1. 62.

25 ᾗ ἐδύνατο τάχιστα, *with all possible speed; cf.* ὡς μάλιστα ἐδύνατο, c. 1. 22, and Tissaphernes' own statement, II, 3, § 19.

26 μὲν δή: see on c. 1. 16.

ἤκουσεν: with gen., of the person (source), and acc., of the thing, as often; G. 1103; H. 742c; B. 365.

28 οὓς εἴρηκα, *the forces I have mentioned.*

ὡρμᾶτο: the date, according to accepted chronology, was Mar. 6th, 401 B.C.

29 σταθμούς: acc. of extent (G. 1062; H. 720; B. 338, with the note); so παρασάγγας, also.

παρασάγγας: a Persian word, made to look like Greek; see on σατράπην, c. 1. 5. For the length of the parasang, see the Introd., § 29.

εἴκοσι καὶ δύο: the καί might have been omitted; see G. 382, 1; H. 291b; B. 153.

30 Μαίανδρον: names of rivers stand regularly in the attrib. posit. The tortuous course of this stream has given us our word *meander.*

δύο πλέθρα: in expressions of measure we have either the pred. nom., as here; the gen. of measure (*e. g.* l. 47); or, less frequently, the adj. (*e. g.* πλεθριαῖον I, 5, § 4); again εὖρος may stand in the nom., as here, or in the acc. (acc. of specification, G. 1058; H. 718; B. 337). ἐστι, when a mere copula, is often omitted.

31 ἑπτὰ ἐζευγμένη πλοίοις, *made of* (lit. *joined by*) *seven boats.* For the dat., see G. 1181; H. 776; B. 387. ζευγνύναι γέφυραν and ζευγνύναι ποταμόν are both legitimate phrases. Pontoon bridges were very common in antiquity, and are still much used in many countries. Note the force of the perf., expressing a state. For the form, see G. 523; H. 365; B. 178, 1.

διαβὰς ἐξελαύνει διὰ Φρυγίας σταθμὸν ἕνα παρασάγγας ὀκτὼ
εἰς Κολοσσάς, πόλιν οἰκουμένην καὶ εὐδαίμονα καὶ μεγάλην.
ἐνταῦθα ἔμεινεν ἡμέρας ἑπτά· καὶ ἧκε Μένων Θετταλὸς ὁπλίτας
ἔχων χιλίους καὶ πελταστὰς πεντακοσίους, Δόλοπας καὶ Αἰνι- 35
7 ᾶνας καὶ Ὀλυνθίους. ἐντεῦθεν ἐξελαύνει σταθμοὺς τρεῖς παρασάγγας εἴκοσιν εἰς Κελαινάς, τῆς Φρυγίας πόλιν οἰκουμένην,
μεγάλην καὶ εὐδαίμονα. ἐνταῦθα Κύρῳ βασίλεια ἦν καὶ παράδεισος μέγας ἀγρίων θηρίων πλήρης, ἃ ἐκεῖνος ἐθήρευεν ἀπὸ

---

32 διαβάς: for the tense, see on ἐξαιτησαμένη, c. 1. 13; for the form, G. 798; 799; H. 489; B. 209; 211.

33 Κολοσσάς: see the map; in Xenophon's time a place of some importance, and even in Christian times the seat of one of the churches of Asia (cf. Paul's epistle). In common with almost all the ancient cities of Asia Minor and Mesopotamia it is now desolate; Smyrna, still an important commercial center, is an isolated exception.

πόλιν οἰκουμένην: the addition of this phrase shows that even in Xenophon's time many of these cities were deserted; he himself mentions instances (e.g. I, 5, § 4).

εὐδαίμονα καὶ μεγάλην: a favorite phrase of Xenophon's.

34 ἡμέρας: acc. of duration; cf. the note on σταθμούς, l. 29.

Μένων: apparently sent by Aristippus; see on l. 5. For a sketch of his character, see II, 6, §§ 21–30, and the Introd., § 38.

35 ἔχων: see on c. 1. 7. Cyrus' stay here was probably due to the fact that he was waiting for these troops.

36 ἐντεῦθεν: note the constant omission of the connective with these demonstr. advs., and consult the note on τούτῳ, c. 1. 45. Regarding the style of this passage, see the Introd., § 39.

38 Κύρῳ: see on αὐτῷ, c. 1. 35.

βασίλεια: distinct from βασιλεία (c. 1. 10). For the use of the pl, cf. Lat. *aedes*.

ἦν: sing. vb., with neut. pl. subj.; see G. 899, 2; H. 604; B. 498. To this rule Xenophon offers many exceptions, although most of them are easily explainable. For the agreement with the nearer of two subjs., see on ἦν, l. 20.

παράδεισος: another Persian word; see on σατράπην, c. 1. 5. Hunting has always been a favorite pastime with royalty (cf. I, 9, § 6, of Cyrus himself), and the Persian nobles often had game preserves, or parks; cf. I, 4, § 10.

39 ἀγρίων θηρίων: gen. with an adj. expressing fulness (G. 1139; 1140; cf. 1112; H. 753c; 743; B. 357).

ἀπὸ ἵππου, *on horseback*. The prep. is justified, because, in hunting, the action is exerted from the horse. ἐφ' ἵππου, also a common phrase, merely denotes the position of the rider on his horse.

40 ἵππου, ὁπότε γυμνάσαι βούλοιτο ἑαυτόν τε καὶ τοὺς ἵππους. διὰ μέσου δὲ τοῦ παραδείσου ῥεῖ ὁ Μαίανδρος ποταμός· αἱ δὲ πηγαὶ αὐτοῦ εἰσιν ἐκ τῶν βασιλείων· ῥεῖ δὲ καὶ διὰ τῆς Κελαινῶν πόλεως. ἔστι δὲ καὶ μεγάλου βασιλέως βασίλεια ἐν 8 Κελαιναῖς ἐρυμνὰ ἐπὶ ταῖς πηγαῖς τοῦ Μαρσύου ποταμοῦ ὑπὸ
45 τῇ ἀκροπόλει· ῥεῖ δὲ καὶ οὗτος διὰ τῆς πόλεως καὶ ἐμβάλλει εἰς τὸν Μαίανδρον· τοῦ δὲ Μαρσύου τὸ εὖρός ἐστιν εἴκοσι καὶ πέντε ποδῶν. ἐνταῦθα λέγεται Ἀπόλλων ἐκδεῖραι Μαρσύαν

40 ὁπότε... βούλοιτο, *whenever he wished*; a general temporal sentence. See the note on ἀφικνεῖτο, c. 1. 18. Observe that here and in the indir. disc. use, the Greek opt. is regularly to be translated by the Eng. past indic., not by a form with *could* or *would*.

γυμνάσαι... ἑαυτόν: the addition of the reflexive makes the act. vb. a virtual mid., and usually implies that the action in question is regarded as an unusual one; here, however, it is simply a means of including the two ideas, γυμνάσασθαι and γυμνάσαι τοὺς ἵππους, in one phrase.

41 διὰ μέσου... τοῦ παραδείσου, *through the middle of the park.* For the position of μέσου, see G. 978; H. 671; B. 454.

42 αὐτοῦ: for the position, see G. 977, 1; H. 673b; B. 457.

εἰσιν ἐκ, *are (in and flow) out from.* With this condensed phrase *cf.* ὅθεν (= ἐξ οὗ) αἱ πηγαί, below, l. 49. See also the note on τῶν παρὰ βασιλέως, c. 1. 18.

43 ἔστι: for the accent, see G. 144, 5; H. 480, 2; B. 262, 1.

μεγάλου βασιλέως: no art.; see on c. 1. 18.

45 καὶ οὗτος, *this too* (as well as the Meander).

ἐμβάλλει, *empties into.* The vb. is properly trans., but, in this sense, is regularly used without an obj.

47 ποδῶν: pred. gen. of measure; see the note on δύο πλέθρα, ll. 30 f.

λέγεται: the pers. construction in indir. disc. is decidedly preferred in Greek; see G. 1522, 1; H. 944; B. 634. In the pass. λέγω regularly takes the infin.; in the act. almost always ὡς or ὅτι, with a finite vb. (The infin. occurs, however, with the act., III, 1, § 26; V, 4, § 34; and VII, 5, § 13; and is regular when λέγω means *bid, move,* etc. The partic. also occurs, I, 3, § 15.)

Μαρσύαν: the story is as follows: Athene once, while playing the flute, chanced to catch sight of the reflection of her face in a pool of water, and, in disgust at her inflated cheeks and consequent disfigurement, flung the reed from her. The satyr Marsyas found it, and, puffed up with pride at the divine music he was able to produce upon it, dared to challenge Apollo to a contest. It was agreed by both that the victor might do what he would with the vanquished. Marsyas was defeated, the Muses

νικήσας ἐρίζοντά οἱ περὶ σοφίας, καὶ τὸ δέρμα κρεμάσαι ἐν τῷ ἄντρῳ ὅθεν αἱ πηγαί. διὰ δὲ τοῦτο ὁ ποταμὸς καλεῖται Μαρσύας. 9 ἐνταῦθα Ξέρξης, ὅτε ἐκ τῆς Ἑλλάδος ἡττηθεὶς τῇ μάχῃ ἀπ- 50 εχώρει, λέγεται οἰκοδομῆσαι ταῦτά τε τὰ βασίλεια καὶ τὴν Κελαινῶν ἀκρόπολιν. ἐνταῦθα ἔμεινε Κῦρος ἡμέρας τριάκοντα· καὶ ἧκε Κλέαρχος ὁ Λακεδαιμόνιος φυγὰς ἔχων ὁπλίτας χιλίους καὶ πελταστὰς Θρᾷκας ὀκτακοσίους καὶ τοξότας Κρῆτας διακοσίους. ἅμα δὲ καὶ Σῶσις παρῆν ὁ Συρακόσιος ἔχων ὁπλίτας 55 τριακοσίους, καὶ Σοφαίνετος Ἀρκάδας ἔχων ὁπλίτας χιλίους.

---

being judges, and, in punishment for his presumption, Apollo tied him to a tree and flayed him alive. Ovid, *Metamorphoses*, VI, 382-97, gives the story in brief. In Eng., see Matthew Arnold's *Empedocles on Etna* (the song of Charicles) and L. Morris's *Epic of Hades*. The legend furnished a favorite theme to ancient artists; the cut reproduces a statue in the Uffizi at Florence.

48 νικήσας ἐρίζοντά οἱ, *having conquered him in a contest;* lit. *contending with him (Apollo).* For the indir. reflexive, see on οἱ, c. 1. 36. The clause well illustrates the advantage Greek has over Eng. in the matter of pronouns.

σοφίας, *skill,* especially, as here, *musical skill.*

δέρμα for the suffix, see G. 837; H. 553, 1; B. 280.

49 ὅθεν: the use of an adv., instead of a prep., with the rel. is common also in Eng. For the omission of εἰσι, see l. 101. *Cf.*, also, the note on εἰσιν ἐκ τῶν βασιλείων, above, l. 42.

50 Ξέρξης: see the Introd., § 20.

τῆς Ἑλλάδος: Ἑλλάς, properly an adj., regularly has the art.

τῇ μάχῃ: *i. e.* the naval fight at Salamis. The use of the art. marks the battle as famous.

51 λέγεται οἰκοδομῆσαι: the pers. construction again; see on λέγεται ἐκδεῖραι, above, l. 47.

52 ἡμέρας τριάκοντα: this was the longest halt made on the upward march: Cyrus is waiting for reinforcements.

53 Κλέαρχος: re-read § 9 of the preceding chapter.

54 Θρᾷκας . . . Κρῆτας: both words are nouns, not adjs.; they are in appos. with πελταστάς and τοξότας respectively. The Cretans were famous bowmen.

55 Σῶσις: utterly unknown, and not again mentioned.

56 Σοφαίνετος: doubtless an error. A Sophaenetus had joined the army at Sardis with a thousand hoplites (above, l. 17). It has been suggested that we should read Ἀγίας, who is mentioned among the generals treacherously seized (II, 5, § 31), and who was also an Arcadian. Others would read Κλεάνωρ, who is prominent in Book II, and who

καὶ ἐνταῦθα Κῦρος ἐξέτασιν καὶ ἀριθμὸν τῶν Ἑλλήνων ἐποίησεν ἐν τῷ παραδείσῳ, καὶ ἐγένοντο οἱ σύμπαντες ὁπλῖται μὲν μύριοι 10 χίλιοι, πελτασταὶ δὲ ἀμφὶ τοὺς δισχιλίους.

60 Ἐντεῦθεν ἐξελαύνει σταθμοὺς δύο παρασάγγας δέκα εἰς Πέλτας, πόλιν οἰκουμένην. ἐνταῦθ' ἔμεινεν ἡμέρας τρεῖς· ἐν αἷς Ξενίας ὁ Ἀρκὰς τὰ Λύκαια ἔθυσε καὶ ἀγῶνα ἔθηκε· τὰ δὲ ἆθλα ἦσαν στλεγγίδες χρυσαῖ· ἐθεώρει δὲ τὸν ἀγῶνα καὶ Κῦρος. ἐντεῦθεν ἐξελαύνει σταθμοὺς δύο παρασάγγας δώδεκα ἐς Κερά-

took the place of Agias, after the latter was murdered (III, 1, §47). A third suggestion is that the name Σοφαίνετος is in its proper place here, and should be omitted from the text in the previous passage, where it might easily have been interpolated.

57 ἐξέτασιν: other reviews are mentioned in §14 of this chapter, in I, 7, §1, and in V, 3, §3. For the use of ποιῶ with a verbal noun, cf. ἐποιεῖτο τὴν συλλογήν, c. 1. 24.

58 ἐγένοντο οἱ σύμπαντες, *the whole number amounted to.*

μύριοι χίλιοι: note the Greek method of counting, not ἕνδεκα χίλιοι.

59 πελτασταί: the word here includes all light-armed troops.

ἀμφί, *about;* cf. εἰς, l. 15. Round numbers frequently have the art. (G. 948b; H. 664c), generally with a prep., as here. The actual totals, from the numbers given, are hoplites 10,600, light-armed 2,300.

60 ἐντεῦθεν: *i.e.* from Celaenae.

εἰς Πέλτας: Peltae was northwest of Celaenae; see the map. For a possible reason for this change in the direction of the march, see the Introd., §29.

62 τὰ Λύκαια ἔθυσε, *celebrated (with sacrifice) the Lycaea, i.e. the festival of* Ζεὺς Λύκαιος; see the vocab. Find Mt. Lycaeus on the map. Xenias, though absent, remembers the annual rite. Primitive worship often centers about mountain-tops; cf. the "high places" of the Bible. τὰ Λύκαια is the inner obj. of the vb. (cognate acc.); see on τὰ αὐτὰ ταῦτα, c. 1. 30.

ἀγῶνα: athletic contests formed an important part of Greek festivals.

ἔθηκε: for the form, see G. 670; H. 432; B. 205.

63 ἦσαν: the vb. is attracted to the number of the pred.; see G. 904; H. 610; B. 501; the neut. pl. subj. normally takes a sing. vb.; see on ἦν, l. 38.

στλεγγίδες, *strigils;* see the vocab. After exercising, naked, or nearly so, in the dust of the palaestra, the Greek athlete must have needed something of this sort, especially as the body was rubbed with oil before the contest.

64 Κεράμων ἀγοράν: cf. *Newmarket*, as the name of a town.

μων ἀγοράν, πόλιν οἰκουμένην, ἐσχάτην πρὸς τῇ Μυσίᾳ χώρᾳ. 65
11 ἐντεῦθεν ἐξελαύνει σταθμοὺς τρεῖς παρασάγγας τριάκοντα εἰς
Καΰστρου πεδίον, πόλιν οἰκουμένην. ἐνταῦθ' ἔμεινεν ἡμέρας
πέντε· καὶ τοῖς στρατιώταις ὠφείλετο μισθὸς πλέον ἢ τριῶν
μηνῶν, καὶ πολλάκις ἰόντες ἐπὶ τὰς θύρας ἀπῄτουν. ὁ δὲ
ἐλπίδας λέγων διῆγε καὶ δῆλος ἦν ἀνιώμενος· οὐ γὰρ ἦν πρὸς 70
τοῦ Κύρου τρόπου ἔχοντα μὴ ἀποδιδόναι. ἐνταῦθα ἀφικνεῖται
Ἐπύαξα ἡ Συεννέσιος γυνὴ τοῦ Κιλίκων βασιλέως παρὰ Κῦρον·

---

65 **ἐσχάτην πρός**, the last in the direction of.
67 **Καΰστρου πεδίον**: practically one word; cf. Eng. names of towns ending in -field.
68 **πλέον**: here indeclinable, as often.
τριῶν μηνῶν: for the case, see c. 1. 55 and the note. Three months' pay for 12,000 men (they were receiving a daric a month, I, 3, § 21) would amount to nearly $200,000, without allowing for the higher pay of the officers; see the Introd., § 28.
69 **ἐπὶ τὰς θύρας**: more than *to the door of his tent*. In oriental countries the gate of the palace is often the place where the king dispenses justice and where suppliants throng; the phrase, αἱ βασιλέως θύραι, therefore, often denotes *the king's court* (I, 9, § 3; II, 1, § 8); cf. II Sam. XV: 2–6; Esther II:19; and our modern phrase, *The Sublime Porte*, referring to the Turkish government.
ἀπῄτουν, *they kept demanding it.* For the force of the prep., see on ἀπέπεμπε, c. 1. 41.
70 **λέγων διῆγε**, *kept talking of.* For the suppl. partic., see on παρὼν ἐτύγχανε, c. 1. 4.

δῆλος ἦν ἀνιώμενος, *was evidently distressed;* a form of indir. disc., with the personal construction; see G. 1589; H. 981; B. 661. Cf. the personal construction with ἐλέγετο, below, l. 73.
πρὸς ... τρόπου, *in keeping with Cyrus' character.* τοῦ belongs to τρόπου, not to Κύρου.
71 **ἔχοντα**, *if able;* the acc., despite the preceding gen., Κύρου; see on λαβόντι, l. 4, adding to the references there given G. 928, 2; B. 631, 1.
μή: for the neg., see c. 1. 57, and the note.
72 **Συεννέσιος**: Ionic forms occur even in Attic in the case of proper names; see G. 255; H. 201d; B. 110, 2. The name, Syennesis, is Semitic, and was doubtless a title (cf. Pharaoh), but Xenophon uses it as an individual name. Cilicia was a dependency of Persia, but maintained its own court. Syennesis desired, apparently, to win favor both with Cyrus and with the king; he gives effectual aid to Cyrus, yet makes at least a show of obstructing his advance (cf. below, § 21).
τοῦ ... βασιλέως: in appos. with

καὶ ἐλέγετο Κύρῳ δοῦναι χρήματα πολλά. τῇ δ' οὖν στρατιᾷ 12
τότε ἀπέδωκε Κῦρος μισθὸν τεττάρων μηνῶν. εἶχε δὲ ἡ Κίλισσα
φυλακὴν περὶ αὐτὴν Κίλικας καὶ Ἀσπενδίους· ἐλέγετο δὲ καὶ
συγγενέσθαι Κῦρον τῇ Κιλίσσῃ.

Ἐντεῦθεν δὲ ἐξελαύνει σταθμοὺς δύο παρασάγγας δέκα εἰς 13
Θύμβριον, πόλιν οἰκουμένην. ἐνταῦθα ἦν παρὰ τὴν ὁδὸν κρήνη
ἡ Μίδου καλουμένη τοῦ Φρυγῶν βασιλέως, ἐφ' ᾗ λέγεται Μίδας
τὸν Σάτυρον θηρεῦσαι οἴνῳ κεράσας αὐτήν. ἐντεῦθεν ἐξελαύνει 14
σταθμοὺς δύο παρασάγγας δέκα εἰς Τυριάειον, πόλιν οἰκουμένην.
ἐνταῦθα ἔμεινεν ἡμέρας τρεῖς. καὶ λέγεται δεηθῆναι ἡ Κίλισσα
Κύρου ἐπιδεῖξαι τὸ στράτευμα αὐτῇ· βουλόμενος οὖν ἐπιδεῖξαι

Συεννέσιος. It is only when designating the king of Persia that βασιλεύς omits the art.

73 ἐλέγετο . . . δοῦναι, *it was rumored that she gave;* but in the Greek the construction is personal; see on λέγεται, 1. 47. Below, 1. 75, we have ἐλέγετο, with the acc. and infin., a much rarer use.

δ' οὖν, *be that as it may*, a regular formula in passing from rumor to fact; *cf.* below, § 22.

75 Ἀσπενδίους: consult the map.

78 Θύμβριον: Cyrus has resumed his eastern march; see the map.

ἦν . . . κρήνη . . . καλουμένη: retain the Greek order, and note the effect of the third attrib. position; see on τῇ κατ' ἀντιπέρας, c. 1. 43 f. When a form of εἰμί precedes its subj., it is often best rendered by our English phrase, *there is, there was*, etc.

παρὰ τὴν ὁδόν: motion is implied; hence the acc.; see the note on ὑπὲρ Ἑλλήσποντον, c. 1. 48, and *cf.* εἰσιν ἐκ, l. 42.

80 τὸν Σάτυρον: *i. e. Silenus.*

οἴνῳ κεράσας αὐτήν: οἴνῳ is dat. of association, rather than dat. of means; see G. 1175; H. 772; B. 392. For the formation of the present, κεράννυμι, see G. 608; 797, 1; H. 402e; B. 196, 5. Having thus caught Silenus, Midas did him no harm, but restored him to Dionysus, who, in return, allowed him to choose his own reward. Midas foolishly chose that whatever he touched might become gold. Of this plague he was finally healed by bathing in the river Pactolus, the sands of which were thereafter rich in gold. See Ovid, *Met.* XI, 90–145, and Saxe's poetical travesty, *The Choice of King Midas.*

81 Τυριάειον: of uncertain situation.

82 δεηθῆναι: with gen. and infin.; see on δεῖται, c. 1. 57 f.

83 ἐπιδεῖξαι: Cyrus' object was not only to please the queen, but also to impress her with the splendor and strength of his Greek troops.

ἐξέτασιν ποιεῖται ἐν τῷ πεδίῳ τῶν Ἑλλήνων καὶ τῶν βαρβάρων.
ἐκέλευσε δὲ τοὺς Ἕλληνας ὡς νόμος αὐτοῖς εἰς μάχην οὕτω
ταχθῆναι καὶ στῆναι, συντάξαι δ' ἕκαστον τοὺς ἑαυτοῦ. ἐτάχθησαν
οὖν ἐπὶ τεττάρων· εἶχε δὲ τὸ μὲν δεξιὸν Μένων καὶ
οἱ σὺν αὐτῷ, τὸ δὲ εὐώνυμον Κλέαρχος καὶ οἱ ἐκείνου, τὸ
δὲ μέσον οἱ ἄλλοι στρατηγοί· ἐθεώρει οὖν ὁ Κῦρος πρῶτον
μὲν τοὺς βαρβάρους· οἱ δὲ παρήλαυνον τεταγμένοι κατὰ
ἴλας καὶ κατὰ τάξεις· εἶτα δὲ τοὺς Ἕλληνας, παρελαύνων ἐφ'

84 τῶν Ἑλλήνων ... τῶν βαρβάρων: the repeated art. marks the two divisions as separate. How many barbarians Cyrus had at this time is not stated; in I, 7, § 10 they are said to number 100,000. Xenophon's interest, and ours, centers in the Greek troops.

85 οὕτω: resuming the ὡς-clause, may be omitted in translating; a demonstr. word is frequently so used after a rel.

86 στῆναι: the ingressive force, common in the first aor. (G. 1260; H. 841; B. 529), is marked also in the second aors., ἔστην and ἔσχον.

ἕκαστον: sc. στρατηγόν.

τοὺς ἑαυτοῦ, his own men. For the omitted noun, cf. τῶν παρὰ βασιλέως, c. 1. 18.

87 ἐπὶ τεττάρων, four deep. Cyrus wishes the army to present as impresssive an appearance as possible. Arranged in line of battle, four deep, 12,000 men (including the light-armed) would present a front nearly two miles long. Observe, also, that the barbarians march by Cyrus and the queen, but that the Greeks remain in battle array, while Cyrus and the queen drive past their front. On another occasion, when it was desirable that the Greeks should make an impression by their numbers, Clearchus has them march by, two abreast and with frequent halts, ὥστε τὸ στράτευμα καὶ (even) αὐτοῖς τοῖς Ἕλλησι δόξαι πάμπολυ εἶναι (seemed to be of vast extent), καὶ τὸν Πέρσην ἐκπεπλῆχθαι (was filled with amazement) θεωροῦντα.

εἶχε: for the agreement of the vb. with the nearer subj., see on ἦν, l. 20.

τὸ ... δεξιόν: no noun need be supplied; see the note on τό ... βαρβαρικόν, l. 3.

88 οἱ σὺν αὐτῷ, his men; scarcely different from οἱ ἐκείνου, below. Xen. makes wider use of the prep. σύν than is permitted in normal Attic prose.

τὸ ... εὐώνυμον, the left; see the vocab. Antique superstition avoided mentioning what was ill-omened, and often substituted a euphemistic term. In soothsaying the left was the side of ill omen; hence the word ἀριστερός was ordinarily avoided. Xen. has it, however, e.g. II, 3, § 11; II, 4, § 28.

89 πρῶτον μέν: balanced by εἶτα δέ, below, l. 91.

91 τοὺς Ἕλληνας: sc. ἐθεώρει.

ἅρματος καὶ ἡ Κίλισσα ἐφ' ἁρμαμάξης. εἶχον δὲ πάντες
κράνη χαλκᾶ καὶ χιτῶνας φοινικοῦς καὶ κνημῖδας καὶ τὰς
ἀσπίδας ἐκκεκαλυμμένας. ἐπειδὴ δὲ πάντας παρήλασε, στήσας 17
95 τὸ ἅρμα πρὸ τῆς φάλαγγος μέσης, πέμψας Πίγρητα τὸν ἑρμηνέα παρὰ τοὺς στρατηγοὺς τῶν Ἑλλήνων ἐκέλευσε προβαλέσθαι τὰ ὅπλα καὶ ἐπιχωρῆσαι ὅλην τὴν φάλαγγα. οἳ δὲ
ταῦτα προεῖπον τοῖς στρατιώταις· καὶ ἐπεὶ ἐσάλπιγξε, προ-
βαλόμενοι τὰ ὅπλα ἐπῇσαν. ἐκ δὲ τούτου θᾶττον προϊόντων
100 σὺν κραυγῇ ἀπὸ τοῦ αὐτομάτου δρόμος ἐγένετο τοῖς στρατιώταις
ἐπὶ τὰς σκηνάς, τῶν δὲ βαρβάρων φόβος πολύς, καὶ ἥ τε 18

---

93 χαλκᾶ: for the form see G. 310; H. 223; B. 118. Bronze was far more widely used in antiquity than it is now; steel and iron far less widely.

φοινικοῦς: the color of the Spartan uniform, according to Xen., *Rep. Lac.*, 11, 3.

94 ἐκκεκαλυμμένας: note the pred. posit. The shields were ordinarily kept in leathern cases; now they are uncovered and, doubtless, burnished — another touch of the λαμπρότης that impressed Ἐπύαξα.

παρήλασε: for the aor., where the English requires the plpf., see on ἐτελεύτησε, c. 1. 10.

στήσας: first aor., and so trans.; see the vocab.

95 μέσης: for the position, see on μέσου, l. 41.

96 προβαλέσθαι τὰ ὅπλα, *to advance arms* (in readiness for a charge).

97 ὅλην; for the posit., see G. 979; H. 672c; B. 455.

οἳ δέ, *and they*. See the note on ὃ δέ, c. 1. 12.

98 ἐσάλπιγξε: so-called impers. vbs. really contain their own subjects, here ὁ σαλπικτής, which is expressed with the vb. σημαίνω, IV, 3, §§ 29 and 32. See G. 897, 4; H. 602c; B. 305.

99 ἐκ ... τούτου, *upon this*. ἐκ often denotes immediate sequence.

θᾶττον, *faster and faster*. For the form see G. 357, 1; H. 253 with 74b; B. 134.

προϊόντων: sc. αὐτῶν, gen. abs., despite the following dat. For the omitted subj., see G. 1568, fine print; H. 972a; B. 657, 1, note 1.

100 ἀπὸ τοῦ αὐτομάτου, *of their own accord*. A prep. with the neut. of an adj. often stands for an adv.; *cf.* ἐκ τοῦ αὐτομάτου, c. 3. 62.

δρόμος ἐγένετο: see on ἐποιεῖτο τὴν συλλογήν, c. 1. 24.

101 τὰς σκηνάς, *the camp*, where were not only the quarters of the Greeks and the barbarians, (these were, however, separate), but the market, ἀγορά, of the sutlers as well. For the last, see the Introd., § 28.

τῶν δὲ βαρβάρων: subject. gen., G. 1094, 2; H. 729b; B. 349.

φόβος: forms of εἰμί, when it is a mere copula, may at any time be

Κίλισσα ἔφυγεν ἐπὶ τῆς ἁρμαμάξης καὶ οἱ ἐκ τῆς ἀγορᾶς καταλιπόντες τὰ ὤνια ἔφυγον. οἱ δὲ Ἕλληνες σὺν γέλωτι ἐπὶ τὰς σκηνὰς ἦλθον. ἡ δὲ Κίλισσα ἰδοῦσα τὴν λαμπρότητα καὶ τὴν τάξιν τοῦ στρατεύματος ἐθαύμασε. Κῦρος δὲ ἥσθη τόν ἐκ 105 τῶν Ἑλλήνων εἰς τοὺς βαρβάρους φόβον ἰδών.

19 Ἐντεῦθεν ἐξελαύνει σταθμοὺς τρεῖς παρασάγγας εἴκοσιν εἰς Ἰκόνιον, τῆς Φρυγίας πόλιν ἐσχάτην. ἐνταῦθα ἔμεινε τρεῖς ἡμέρας. ἐντεῦθεν ἐξελαύνει διὰ τῆς Λυκαονίας σταθμοὺς πέντε παρασάγγας τριάκοντα. ταύτην τὴν χώραν ἐπέτρεψε διαρπά- 110
20 σαι τοῖς Ἕλλησιν ὡς πολεμίαν οὖσαν. ἐντεῦθεν Κῦρος τὴν Κίλισσαν εἰς τὴν Κιλικίαν ἀποπέμπει τὴν ταχίστην ὁδόν· καὶ συνέπεμψεν αὐτῇ στρατιώτας οὓς Μένων εἶχε καὶ αὐτόν. Κῦρος δὲ μετὰ τῶν ἄλλων ἐξελαύνει διὰ Καππαδοκίας σταθμοὺς τέτ-

---

omitted, but such omissions are common only in the third person and are rare in other moods than the indic.

102 οἱ ἐκ τῆς ἀγορᾶς: see on τῶν παρὰ βασιλέως, c. 1. 18.

καταλιπόντες, *abandoning*, not simply *leaving*; the prep. is intensive.

103 ἔφυγον: the repetition of the vb. adds to the effect.

ἐπὶ τὰς σκηνάς, *to their tents;* not, as above, *to the camp.*

105 τάξιν: even in their charge the Greeks had not broken ranks.

ἐθαύμασε, *was seized with wonder.* Observe the tense, and see the note on ἠγάσθη, c. 1. 45. So, too, ἥσθη, below.

τὸν ... φόβον: all that intervenes between the art. and the noun serves as an attrib. of the noun: the terror literally proceeds *from* the Greeks *into* the hearts of the barbarians.

108 Ἰκόνιον: familiar from the Book of Acts, *e. g.* XIII:51.

ἐσχάτην: *cf.* 1. 65, and see the map.

110 διαρπάσαι: infin. of purpose, G. 1532; H. 951; B. 592. Cyrus has now left his own province, and, furthermore, the Lycaonians were rebellious (III, 2, § 23).

111 ὡς: with οὖσαν; see on ὡς ἀποκτενῶν, c. 1. 12.

112 τὴν ... ὁδόν, *by the shortest road;* a so-called adv. acc., here plainly a development from the inner obj. (cognate acc.).

113 καὶ αὐτόν, *and (Menon) himself.* This manoeuvre, by which a considerable force (Menon had 1,500 men, ll. 34 f.) was unexpectedly sent into Cilicia, made Syennesis' preparations for defense futile (assuming that they were seriously meant); see, below, § 21, end. Cyrus himself, with the main army, made a wide detour; see the map. This short road was, presumably, impassable for the baggage train.

115 ταρας παρασάγγας είκοσι καὶ πέντε πρὸς Δάνα, πόλιν οἰκουμένην μεγάλην καὶ εὐδαίμονα. ἐνταῦθα ἔμειναν ἡμέρας τρεῖς·
ἐν ᾧ Κῦρος ἀπέκτεινεν ἄνδρα Πέρσην Μεγαφέρνην, φοινικιστὴν
βασίλειον, καὶ ἕτερόν τινα τῶν ὑπάρχων δυνάστην, αἰτιασάμενος ἐπιβουλεύειν αὐτῷ.

120 Ἐντεῦθεν ἐπειρῶντο εἰσβάλλειν εἰς τὴν Κιλικίαν· ἡ δὲ εἰσ- 21
βολὴ ἦν ὁδὸς ἁμαξιτὸς ὀρθία ἰσχυρῶς καὶ ἀμήχανος εἰσελθεῖν
στρατεύματι, εἴ τις ἐκώλυεν. ἐλέγετο δὲ καὶ Συέννεσις εἶναι
ἐπὶ τῶν ἄκρων φυλάττων τὴν εἰσβολήν· διὸ ἔμειναν ἡμέραν ἐν
τῷ πεδίῳ. τῇ δὲ ὑστεραίᾳ ἧκεν ἄγγελος λέγων ὅτι λελοιπὼς

---

115 **Δάνα:** see the map.
117 **ἐν ᾧ:** we should have expected ἐν αἷς; cf. 61 f. In this phrase and in the similar ἀφ' οὗ, since (III, 2, § 14), the proper form of χρόνος is ordinarily supplied (ἐν τούτῳ τῷ χρόνῳ is a common phrase); but the rel. is certainly neut. in εἰς ὅ, until.
φοινικιστὴν βασίλειον, either, *wearer of the royal purple,* or, as a title, *dyer of the purple,* indicating one set in charge of the fisheries (the purple dye was obtained from a shell-fish) or the dye-houses of the king.
118 **ἕτερον . . . δυνάστην,** *another man of rank among his subordinates.*
119 **ἐπιβουλεύειν,** *of plotting;* infin. in indir. disc., as αἰτιασάμενος implies saying. αὐτούς readily supplies itself; and, in general, what supplies itself may be omitted.
120 **ἐπειρῶντο:** durative tense of effort.
εἰσβάλλειν: intrans., as ἐμβάλλει, above, l. 45.
ἡ δὲ εἰσβολή: a narrow pass between lofty mountains (7,000 to 8,000 feet in elevation) of the Taurus range, so completely commanding the approach to Asia Minor (Cilicia) from the S. E. that it was called Κιλικίας πύλαι.
121 **ἁμαξιτός:** the army was, of course, accompanied by an extensive baggage train; see the Introd., § 28.
ἰσχυρῶς: often used to intensify the meaning of an adj. Note that here its postponement gives an added force.
ἀμήχανος εἰσελθεῖν στρατεύματι, *difficult for an army to enter.* The adj. governs the dat. and the infin. as well, G. 1165; 1526; H. 767; 952; B. 378, 641.
122 **εἴ τις ἐκώλυεν,** *if anyone tried to prevent it.* For the tense, see G. 1255; H. 832; B. 527.
ἐλέγετο: again the personal construction; see on λέγεται . . . ἐκδεῖραι, l. 47.
εἶναι . . . φυλάττων: not a mere equivalent of φυλάττειν; εἶναι is a full vb.; progressive vb. forms are relatively rare in Greek. Syennesis makes at least a show of resistance.
124 **τῇ δ' ὑστεραίᾳ:** ἡμέρᾳ is regular-

εἴη Συέννεσις τὰ ἄκρα, ἐπεὶ ᾔσθετο ὅτι τὸ Μένωνος στράτευμα 125
ἤδη ἐν Κιλικίᾳ ἦν εἴσω τῶν ὀρέων, καὶ ὅτι τριήρεις ἤκουε
περιπλεούσας ἀπ' Ἰωνίας εἰς Κιλικίαν Ταμὼν ἔχοντα τὰς Λακεδαιμονίων καὶ αὐτοῦ Κύρου. Κῦρος δ' οὖν ἀνέβη ἐπὶ τὰ ὄρη
οὐδενὸς κωλύοντος, καὶ εἶδε τὰς σκηνὰς οὗ οἱ Κίλικες ἐφύλαττον.
ἐντεῦθεν δὲ κατέβαινεν εἰς πεδίον μέγα καὶ καλόν, ἐπίρρυτον, 130
καὶ δένδρων παντοδαπῶν σύμπλεων καὶ ἀμπέλων· πολὺ δὲ καὶ

ly omitted in this phrase. For the case, see G. 1192; H. 782; B. 385.

ἤκεν . . . λέγων: the remainder of the section is in indir. disc. after this secondary tense.

λελοιπὼς εἴη: direct λέλοιπε. For the opt., see on ἐπιβουλεύοι, c. 1. 11; for the form, see G. 733; H. 457; B. 221, 1.

125 ᾔσθετο: past indicatives, in subordinate clauses, remain, as a rule, unchanged; so, below, ἤκουε; see G. 1499; 1482; H. 925bc; B. 675, 1 and 3. Observe that the clause, ὅτι . . . τῶν ὀρέων, is quoted after ᾔσθετο, which is itself in indir. disc. This entails no difficulty.

126 καὶ ὅτι . . . ἤκουε: this clause is parallel with ἐπεὶ ᾔσθετο, and gives another reason for the action of Syennesis in abandoning the pass. What follows is quoted after ἤκουε, the principal vb. being ἔχοντα, despite the involved order (direct, Ταμὼς ἔχει). Trans.: *because he heard that Tamos was in charge of triremes belonging to the Lacedaemonians and to Cyrus himself which were sailing around from Ionia to Cilicia.* For the partic. in indir. disc., after ἤκουε, see G. 1588; H. 982; B. 661.

τριήρεις is brought to the head of the clause for emphasis: the possession of ships enabled Cyrus to disembark troops and attack the opposing force both in front and in the rear.

127 τὰς Λακ. . . καὶ αὐτοῦ Κύρου: for the order, see on τῇ κατ' ἀντιπέρας, c. 1. 44. For Cyrus' relations with the Lacedaemonians, see the Introd., § 26.

128 δ' οὖν: *cf.* l. 73, and the note.

129 οὐδενὸς κωλύοντος, *without opposition*. See the note on ἐπιβουλεύοντος Τισσαφέρνους, c. 1. 26 f.

τὰς σκηνάς: *cf.* l. 101, and the note.

οὗ, *where*.

ἐφύλαττον, *had been keeping guard*. In Greek the plpf. has no very wide range; here a durative tense was wanted; *cf.* ἦσαν, c. 1. 27.

130 κατέβαινεν: how different in force from the aor. ἀνέβη, above?

131 δένδρων . . . ἀμπέλων: gens. with an adj. of fulness; see on θηρίων, l. 39. σύμπλεων itself is not gen., but acc. sing., G. 305; 306; H. 227; B. 119; *cf.* 92.

πολύ: agreeing only with the nearest noun, but to be taken, also, with the others, G. 923; H. 620a; B. 421.

σήσαμον καὶ μελίνην καὶ κέγχρον καὶ πυροὺς καὶ κριθὰς φέρει. ὄρος δ' αὐτὸ περιεῖχεν ὀχυρὸν καὶ ὑψηλὸν πάντῃ ἐκ θαλάττης εἰς θάλατταν. καταβὰς δὲ διὰ τούτου τοῦ πεδίου ἤλασε σταθ- 23
135 μοὺς τέτταρας παρασάγγας πέντε καὶ εἴκοσιν εἰς Ταρσούς, τῆς Κιλικίας πόλιν μεγάλην καὶ εὐδαίμονα, οὗ ἦν τὰ Συεννέσιος βασίλεια τοῦ Κιλίκων βασιλέως· διὰ μέσου δὲ τῆς πόλεως ῥεῖ ποταμὸς Κύδνος ὄνομα, εὖρος δύο πλέθρων. ταύτην τὴν πόλιν 24 ἐξέλιπον οἱ ἐνοικοῦντες μετὰ Συεννέσιος εἰς χωρίον ὀχυρὸν ἐπὶ
140 τὰ ὄρη πλὴν οἱ τὰ καπηλεῖα ἔχοντες· ἔμειναν δὲ καὶ οἱ παρὰ τὴν θάλατταν οἰκοῦντες ἐν Σόλοις καὶ ἐν Ἰσσοῖς.

Ἐπύαξα δὲ ἡ Συεννέσιος γυνὴ προτέρα Κύρου πέντε ἡμέ- 25 ραις εἰς Ταρσοὺς ἀφίκετο· ἐν δὲ τῇ ὑπερβολῇ τῶν ὀρῶν τῇ εἰς τὸ

---

132 **φέρει**: pres. of lasting truth; cf. ἀθροίζονται, of habitual action, c. 1. 7.

πυροὺς καὶ κριθάς: both words are regularly used in the pl.

133 **αὐτό**: i.e. τὸ πεδίον.

ἐκ θαλάττης εἰς θάλατταν: see the map.

134 **ἤλασε**: Xen. prefers the compound, ἐξελαύνω, as a rule.

135 **Ταρσούς**: familiar as the birthplace of St. Paul. Ancient cities often had plural names (Ἀθῆναι, Σάρδεις, and, below, Σόλοι and Ἰσσοί), but, in this case, the sing., Ταρσός, is also found. Plural names may be due to the upper and lower city; cf. the note on ἀκροπόλεις, l. 9.

137 **μέσου**: used as a noun (G. 932, 1; H. 621 b; B. 424) with τῆς πόλεως depending on it, as a partit. gen. (gen. of the whole) (G. 1088; H. 729 e; B. 354, 355, last example).

138 **ὄνομα ... εὖρος**: accs. of specification (G. 1058; H. 718; B. 337).

εὖρος δύο πλέθρων: see the note on δύο πλέθρα, ll. 30 f. δύο is frequently treated as indeclinable.

139 **ἐξέλιπον εἰς**, had abandoned (and fled) to, a condensed phrase; cf. εἰσιν ἐκ, l. 42.

οἱ ἐνοικοῦντες, the inhabitants. A partic. with the art. is often equivalent to a noun, G. 1560; H. 966; B. 650, 1.

140 **πλήν**: here a conjunc. οὐκ ἐξέλιπον is, therefore, to be understood. As a prep. πλήν governs the gen. (see c. 1. 29) although there the gen. (antecedent to a rel.) is omitted.

οἱ τὰ καπηλεῖα ἔχοντες: these men were willing to take chances, hoping for business.

παρὰ τὴν θάλατταν: for the acc. cf. ὑπὲρ Ἑλλήσποντον, c. 1. 48. Find Soli and Issi on the map.

142 **προτέρα ... ἡμέραις**, five days before Cyrus. For the adj., where Eng. uses the adv., see G. 926; H. 619; B. 425; for the gen. Κύρου G. 1153; H. 755; B. 363; and for the dat., ἡμέραις, G. 1184; H. 781; B. 388.

143 **τῇ ὑπερβολῇ ... τῇ εἰς τὸ πεδίον**: the formal attrib. position; see on τῇ κατ' ἀντιπέρας, c. 1. 43 f. For

Book I, Chap. II

πεδίον δύο λόχοι τοῦ Μένωνος στρατεύματος ἀπώλοντο· οἱ μὲν
ἔφασαν ἁρπάζοντάς τι κατακοπῆναι ὑπὸ τῶν Κιλίκων, οἱ δὲ 145
ὑπολειφθέντας καὶ οὐ δυναμένους εὑρεῖν τὸ ἄλλο στράτευμα
οὐδὲ τὰς ὁδοὺς εἶτα πλανωμένους ἀπολέσθαι· ἦσαν δ' οὖν
οὗτοι ἑκατὸν ὁπλῖται. οἱ δ' ἄλλοι ἐπεὶ ἧκον, τήν τε πόλιν
τοὺς Ταρσοὺς διήρπασαν, διὰ τὸν ὄλεθρον τῶν συστρατιωτῶν
ὀργιζόμενοι, καὶ τὰ βασίλεια τὰ ἐν αὐτῇ. Κῦρος δ' ἐπεὶ 150
εἰσήλασεν εἰς τὴν πόλιν, μετεπέμπετο τὸν Συέννεσιν πρὸς
ἑαυτόν· ὁ δ' οὔτε πρότερον οὐδενί πω κρείττονι ἑαυτοῦ εἰς

---

the use of a prep. with its case as an attrib., see on πρὸς ἑαυτόν, c. 1. 38.

144 οἱ μὲν ... οἱ δέ: see on τοὺς μὲν ... τοὺς δέ, c. 1. 31. No connective is needed, as the clause explains the preceding one; see on Κλέαρχος, c. 1. 44.

145 ἁρπάζοντάς τι κατακοπῆναι, *that, while engaged in some act of plunder, they had been cut to pieces.* τι is the inner obj. of ἁρπάζοντας; see on τὰ αὐτὰ ταῦτα, c. 1. 30. αὐτούς, subj. of κατακοπῆναι, supplies itself; see on l. 119.

οἱ δέ: sc. ἔφασαν αὐτούς.

146 καὶ οὐ, *and not,* following a positive clause, but, below, οὐδέ, continuing the neg. οὐδέ, when there is no preceding neg., means *not even.*

τὸ ἄλλο στράτευμα, *the rest of the army:* see the vocab. So, below, οἱ ἄλλοι, *the rest,* i. e. of Menon's force.

147 εἶτα, *then,* resuming the partics.; *cf.* οὕτω, resuming ὡς, l. 85.

δ' οὖν: *cf.* l. 73, and the note.

148 ἑκατόν: ordinarily a single λόχος numbered 100 men (IV, 8, § 15).

οἱ δ' ἄλλοι: emphasized by being placed before ἐπεί; so Κῦρος, l. 150.

πόλιν ... Ταρσούς: apposition.

151 μετεπέμπετο: note the durative tense. For the voice, see on c. 1. 5. Here the force of the vb. is strengthened by the addition of πρὸς ἑαυτόν.

152 ὁ δ' ... ἤθελε, *but he declared that he had never before come into the power of anyone mightier than himself, and now he refused to come into Cyrus' power.* Syennesis said οὐκ ἦλθον, which is thrown into the infin. after ἔφη (*cf.* ἐπιβουλεύειν, l. 119, and the note). In such cases the neg., which belongs properly with the principal vb., is expressed with the vb. of saying (οὐκ ἔφη ἐλθεῖν, instead of ἔφη οὐκ ἐλθεῖν: *cf.* Lat. *nego*). The neg. here is οὔτε, not οὐκ, because ἔφη is made parallel with ἤθελε, although the parallelism (*neither ... nor*) should not be kept in translating. οὐδενί is used, not τινί, because it follows a neg.; see G. 1619; H. 1030; B. 433. For the dat., see G. 1175; 1177; H. 772a; B. 392; and *cf.* εἰς λόγους σοι ἐλθεῖν, II, 5, § 4. ἐθέλω with the neg., often means *refuse.* For the case of ἑαυτοῦ, see Κύρου, l. 142, and the note. With Κύρῳ, εἰς χεῖρας is to be supplied.

χεῖρας ἐλθεῖν ἔφη οὔτε τότε Κύρῳ ἰέναι ἤθελε, πρὶν ἡ γυνὴ αὐτὸν ἔπεισε καὶ πίστεις ἔλαβε. μετὰ δὲ ταῦτα ἐπεὶ συνε- 27 γένοντο ἀλλήλοις, Συέννεσις μὲν ἔδωκε Κύρῳ χρήματα πολλὰ εἰς τὴν στρατιάν, Κῦρος δὲ ἐκείνῳ δῶρα ἃ νομίζεται παρὰ βασιλεῖ τίμια, ἵππον χρυσοχάλινον καὶ στρεπτὸν χρυσοῦν καὶ ψέλια καὶ ἀκινάκην χρυσοῦν καὶ στολὴν Περσικήν, καὶ τὴν χώραν μηκέτι διαρπάζεσθαι· τὰ δὲ ἡρπασμένα ἀνδράποδα, ἤν που ἐντυγχάνωσιν ἀπολαμβάνειν.

III. Ἐνταῦθα ἔμεινεν ὁ Κῦρος καὶ ἡ στρατιὰ ἡμέρας εἴκοσιν· 1 οἱ γὰρ στρατιῶται οὐκ ἔφασαν ἰέναι τοῦ πρόσω· ὑπώπτευον γὰρ

153 πρίν: see c. 1.58, and the note. All temporal partics., when referring to definite past time, take, of course, the indic. For the subjv., with πρίν, see συμβουλεύσηται, c. 1.59, and the note; for the opt., καταγάγοι, l. 12. Observe that πρίν, *until*, regularly follows a neg.

154 ἔπεισε . . . ἔλαβε: a rapid shift of subj., common in Greek.

155 χρήματα πολλά: *cf.* l. 73.

156 εἰς: *cf.* c. 1.50.

Κῦρος δέ: *sc.* ἔδωκε.

παρὰ βασιλεῖ, *at court*. παρά, with the dat. of persons, regularly denotes, not nearness only, but characteristic locality—the place where the person in question properly is. Cyrus here usurps royal prerogatives; his gifts are such as the king alone could rightly bestow (Xen. *Cyropaedia*, VIII, 2, 8).

157 χρυσοῦν: for the decl., see on χαλκᾶ, l. 93.

158 στολήν: "*raiment*" formed no small item in the wealth of the Oriental; *cf.* III, 1, § 19 and Joshua, VII: 21.

159 τὴν χώραν . . . διαρπάζεσθαι, *that his country should no longer be pillaged* (διήρπασαν, above, l. 149). The clause supplies another obj. to ἔδωκε, as does also the following infin. clause, τὰ δὲ . . . ἀπολαμβάνειν. For the neg. μηκέτι, see on μὴ . . . καταλῦσαι, c. 1.58.

160 ἤν που ἐντυγχάνωσιν, *wherever they should find them*. For the subjv., *cf.* ἢν δύνηται, c. 1.15, and the note. The conditional with an indef. adv. is often tantamount to a rel.

ἀπολαμβάνειν: force of the prep.? See on ἀπέπεμπε, c. 1.41.

CHAPTER III

1 εἴκοσιν: a long stay, due to the mutiny.

2 οὐκ ἔφασαν ἰέναι, *declared they would not go*. They said, οὐκ ἴμεν (εἶμι is a fut., G. 1257; H. 477a; B. 524 note), but, in the infin. phrase, the neg. is expressed with the vb. of saying, see on οὔτε ἔφη, c. 2. 152. The pron. subj. of the infin., is regularly omitted when it is the same as the subj. of the vb. upon which the infin. depends (G. 895, 2; H. 940; B. 630); *cf.* μισθωθῆναι, below.

τοῦ πρόσω, *forward*, a local gen. (partit.); see G. 1138· H. 760a; B. 358.

ἤδη ἐπὶ βασιλέα ἰέναι· μισθωθῆναι δὲ οὐκ ἐπὶ τούτῳ ἔφασαν. πρῶτος δὲ Κλέαρχος τοὺς αὑτοῦ στρατιώτας ἐβιάζετο ἰέναι· οἱ δ' αὐτόν τε ἔβαλλον καὶ τὰ ὑποζύγια τὰ ἐκείνου, ἐπεὶ ἄρξαιν- 5
2 το προϊέναι. Κλέαρχος δὲ τότε μὲν μικρὸν ἐξέφυγε μὴ καταπετρωθῆναι, ὕστερον δ' ἐπεὶ ἔγνω ὅτι οὐ δυνήσεται βιάσασθαι, συνήγαγεν ἐκκλησίαν τῶν αὑτοῦ στρατιωτῶν. καὶ πρῶτον μὲν ἐδάκρυε πολὺν χρόνον ἑστώς· οἱ δὲ ὁρῶντες ἐθαύμαζον καὶ ἐσιώπων. εἶτα δὲ ἔλεξε τοιάδε. 10

ὑπώπτευον: see on ὑπώπτευε, c. 1. 3. ἰέναι is here a pres.
3 ἤδη, *by this time*. They were far past Pisidia (see the map), and had been three months on the march.
μισθωθῆναι: direct, οὐκ ἐμισθώθημεν. Note the order of the words.
ἐπὶ τούτῳ: *for this, on this basis*. ἐπί with the dat. is regular in contracts.
4 πρῶτος: adj., not adv.; *Clearchus was the first to*. πρῶτον, the adv., would merely contrast ἐβιάζετο with some subsequent act on his part; see G. 926; H. 619b; B. 425.
ἐβιάζετο: for the force of the tense, *cf.* ἐκώλυεν, c. 2. 122, and the note. This act was characteristic of Clearchus; see the Introd., § 38.
5 ἔβαλλον: βάλλω means *pelt*, rather than *throw;* the missile is oftener in the dat. (means) than in the acc. (direct obj.).
ἐπεὶ ἄρξαιντο: *cf.* ὁπότε βούλοιτο, c. 2. 40, and the note.
3 μικρόν, *barely*, an adv. acc.; see on τὸ ἀρχαῖον, c. 1. 28.
μή: to be omitted in translating. For its use with an infin., depending on a vb. which itself contains a neg. idea, see G. 1615; H. 1029; B. 434.

καταπετρωθῆναι: for the force of the prep., *cf.* κατακοπῆναι, c. 2. 145.
7 ἔγνω, *saw, came to know*. For the form, see G. 799; H. 489, 15; B. 209; *cf.* 256.
ὅτι οὐ δυνήσεται, *that he would not be able*. Eng. requires *would*, although in the Greek the direct form is retained (save for the necessary change of person; direct, οὐ δυνήσομαι). The change to the opt., after a secondary tense (see on ἐπιβουλεύοι, c. 1. 11), is never obligatory and is less common in the fut. than in other tenses.
8 συνήγαγεν: for the form, see G. 536; H. 436; B. 208, 1.
πρῶτον μὲν ... εἶτα δέ: *cf.* c. 2. 89-91.
9 ἐδάκρυε: the Greeks, like most southern peoples, were much more frank than we in emotional expression. These were, however, "crocodile tears."
πολὺν χρόνον: see the note on ἡμέρας, c. 2. 34.
ἑστώς: a perfect (G. 508; H. 336; B. 258). For its force, see on ἐξευγμένη, c. 2. 31. For the accent, see G. 117; H. 105; B. 65, 2. Trans., *stood and wept*. [tense.
ὁρῶντες, *as they looked*; note the
10 ἔλεξε: somewhat more formal than the commoner ἔλεγε.
τοιάδε, *about as follows; cf.* the

Ἄνδρες στρατιῶται, μὴ θαυμάζετε ὅτι χαλεπῶς φέρω τοῖς 3
παροῦσι πράγμασιν. ἐμοὶ γὰρ ξένος Κῦρος ἐγένετο καί με φεύγοντα ἐκ τῆς πατρίδος τά τε ἄλλα ἐτίμησε καὶ μυρίους ἔδωκε
δαρεικούς· οὓς ἐγὼ λαβὼν οὐκ εἰς τὸ ἴδιον κατεθέμην ἐμοὶ οὐδὲ
καθηδυπάθησα, ἀλλ' εἰς ὑμᾶς ἐδαπάνων. καὶ πρῶτον μὲν πρὸς 4
τοὺς Θρᾷκας ἐπολέμησα, καὶ ὑπὲρ τῆς Ἑλλάδος ἐτιμωρούμην
μεθ' ὑμῶν, ἐκ τῆς Χερρονήσου αὐτοὺς ἐξελαύνων βουλομένους
ἀφαιρεῖσθαι τοὺς ἐνοικοῦντας Ἕλληνας τὴν γῆν. ἐπειδὴ δὲ Κῦρος ἐκάλει, λαβὼν ὑμᾶς ἐπορευόμην, ἵνα εἴ τι δέοιτο ὠφελοίην

---

note on ὧδε, c. 1. 24. Xen. may not have heard the speech himself, but he could hardly have failed to learn what was said. This is not, then, one of the cases in which, for the sake of dramatic effect, the antique historian has permitted the insertion of an imaginary speech. See the Introd., § 40.

11 ἄνδρες στρατιῶται, *Fellow soldiers*. ἄνδρες is regularly added to such vocatives. In comedy we have even ἄνδρες ἰχθύες, and in Lucian, ἄνδρες θεοί. The familiar phrase in the Book of Acts, *Men and brethren*, is a mistranslation of ἄνδρες ἀδελφοί.

μὴ θαυμάζετε: for prohibitions, see G. 1346; H. 874; B. 584.

12 πράγμασιν: dat. of cause; see G. 1181; H. 776; 778; B. 391.

ξένος: *cf*. c. 1. 53, and the note.

ἐγένετο, *became*, not *was*.

φεύγοντα: see the Introd., § 38, and c. 1. 45. Note the emphasis given to this word by its position.

13 τά τε ἄλλα ... καί, *honored me in other things and* (*in particular*). Very commonly, after a form of ἄλλος with τε, καί introduces some fact singled out for special mention. τά ... ἄλλα is, of course, the inner obj.

ἔδωκε: *cf*. c. 1. 46.

14 οὐκ εἰς τὸ ἴδιον ... ἐμοί, did not store up for my own personal use.

οὐδέ, *nor*, when a neg. precedes; elsewhere *not even*.

15 καθηδυπάθησα: the prep. implies waste.

ἐδαπάνων: note the change to the durative tense in passing from the neg. to the positive statement. The neg. has a strong preference for the aor.

16 ἐτιμωρούμην: *sc*. αὐτούς.

17 ἐξελαύνων, here lit., *driving out*.

βουλομένους (with αὐτούς), *because they wished*.

18 ἀφαιρεῖσθαι ... γῆν, *to rob the Greeks dwelling there of their land*. For the two accs., see G. 1069; H. 724; B. 340. This vb. may also take an acc. and a gen. (separation), as in IV, 4, 12; see G. 1118; H. 748a; B. 362 note.

19 ἵνα ... ὑπ' ἐκείνου, *in order that, should he have any need of me, I might help him, in return for the good I had received at*

5 αὐτὸν ἀνθ' ὧν εὖ ἔπαθον ὑπ' ἐκείνου. ἐπεὶ δὲ ὑμεῖς οὐ βούλεσ- 20
θε συμπορεύεσθαι, ἀνάγκη δή μοι ἢ ὑμᾶς προδόντα τῇ Κύρου
φιλίᾳ χρῆσθαι ἢ πρὸς ἐκεῖνον ψευσάμενον μεθ' ὑμῶν εἶναι. εἰ
μὲν δὴ δίκαια ποιήσω οὐκ οἶδα, αἱρήσομαι δ' οὖν ὑμᾶς καὶ σὺν
ὑμῖν ὅ,τι ἂν δέῃ πείσομαι. καὶ οὔποτε ἐρεῖ οὐδεὶς ὡς ἐγὼ Ἕλληνας ἀγαγὼν εἰς τοὺς βαρβάρους, προδοὺς τοὺς Ἕλληνας 25
6 τὴν τῶν βαρβάρων φιλίαν εἱλόμην, ἀλλ' ἐπεὶ ὑμεῖς ἐμοὶ οὐ θέ-
λετε πείθεσθαι, ἐγὼ σὺν ὑμῖν ἕψομαι καὶ ὅ,τι ἂν δέῃ πείσομαι.
νομίζω γὰρ ὑμᾶς ἐμοὶ εἶναι καὶ πατρίδα καὶ φίλους καὶ συμμάχους, καὶ σὺν ὑμῖν μὲν ἂν οἶμαι εἶναι τίμιος ὅπου ἂν ὦ, ὑμῶν δὲ

his hands. For the final clause, see on ὅπως λάβοι, c. 1. 22 f.; for εἴ τι δέοιτο, representing ἐάν τι δέηται, after the opt. final clause, as though quoted after a secondary tense, see G. 1503; H. 937; B. 677; and, for the form ὠφελοίην, G. 737; H. 374a, end; B. 199, 1. ἀνθ' ὧν stands for ἀντὶ τούτων ἅ, the antecedent being omitted and the rel. attracted to the case it would have had, if expressed; see the notes on ἐφ' ἅ, c. 2. 11, and on ὁπόσας εἶχε φυλακάς, c. 1. 24. ὑπ' ἐκείνου is used because εὖ ἔπαθον is a virtual passive; see G. 1241; H. 820; B. 513. ἐκείνου is more emphatic than αὐτοῦ.

20 ὑμεῖς: emphatic, as personal pronouns always are when expressed in the nom.; see G. 985; H. 677; B. 467. Observe this in what follows.

21 ἀνάγκη ... μοι, I must. ἐστί is usually omitted in this phrase. For μοι, with the following acc., προδόντα, see the note on λαβόντι ἥκειν, c. 2. 4 f.

τῇ ... χρῆσθαι, to enjoy the friendship of Cyrus. The dat., with χρῶμαι, is dat. of means; see G. 1183; H. 777; B. 387 note.

22 εἰ, whether, introducing an indir. ques.; see G. 1605; H. 1016; B. 578.

23 δ' οὖν: cf. c. 2. 73.

σύν: cf. c. 2. 88, and the note.

24 ὅ,τι ἂν δέῃ, whatever may be necessary. The rel. is conditional; hence the subj. with ἄν; see G. 1434; H. 916; B. 620; 623; cf. the note on ὅστις ἀφικνεῖτο, c. 1. 18.

οὔποτε ... οὐδείς, never shall anyone say. For the repeated neg., see on οὐδενί, c. 2. 152. In a neg. sentence indef. words regularly become neg.

ὡς ... εἱλόμην: quoted, but, after the primary tense, there is no change of mood.

25 εἰς, into the country of; see the note on c. 1. 62.

26 ἐμοί: indir. obj. (G. 1159; 1160; H. 764, 2; B. 376).

27 σὺν ὑμῖν ἕψομαι: ἕπομαι usually takes the simple dat.

ὅ,τι ἂν δέῃ: see above, l. 24.

28 νομίζω: with acc. and infin., in indir. disc.

29 σὺν ὑμῖν ... τίμιος, with you, I think I should be held in honor. οἶμαι resumes νομίζω, and is expressed again in the next

30 ἔρημος ὢν οὐκ ἂν ἱκανὸς οἶμαι εἶναι οὔτ' ἂν φίλον ὠφελῆσαι οὔτ' ἂν ἐχθρὸν ἀλέξασθαι. ὡς ἐμοῦ οὖν ἰόντος ὅπῃ ἂν καὶ ὑμεῖς οὕτω τὴν γνώμην ἔχετε.

line. The direct form was σὺν ὑμῖν τίμιος ἂν εἴην (potential opt., for which see G. 1327 ff.; H. 872; B. 563). Here σὺν ὑμῖν supplies a virtual protasis; see G. 1413; H. 902; B. 614. For the change to the infin. with ἄν, see G. 1494; H. 964; B. 671. Observe that ἄν, like οὐ (see the note on οὔτε ἔφη, c. 2. 152), although belonging with the infin., is regularly expressed with the vb. of saying. This often causes ἄν to stand at the head of the sentence or clause, and so prepares the hearer or reader for the potential idea which is to follow. ἄν may then be repeated later on in the sentence (see below). By remembering that ἄν may not be used with the pres. indic. the student will be prevented from construing it with the vb. of saying.

ὅπου ἂν ὦ, *wherever I may be,* another condit. rel. clause; see on ὅ,τι ἂν δέῃ, l. 24. The subjv. is retained, although the opt. (by assimilation to ἂν ... εἴην, implied in ἂν εἶναι) would be more regular. See the note on ᾆ δοίη, below, § 17, and compare the retention of the subjv. after a secondary tense (see on ἢν δύνηται, c. 1. 15).

ὑμῶν δὲ ἔρημος, *but bereft of you* (G. 1140; H. 753c; B. 362, 2). This like σὺν ὑμῖν, above, supplies a protasis for the following potential clause.

30 οὐκ ἄν ... εἶναι: direct, οὐκ ἂν ... εἴην, as above.

οὔτ' ἂν ... ἀλέξασθαι, *either to ... or to.* We have οὔτε ... οὔτε, because a neg. precedes (see the note on οὐδενί, c. 2. 152). ἄν, repeated with both infins., belongs only with εἶναι. These infins. are governed by ἱκανός (see the note on c. 1. 20). ἀλέξασθαι is a poetic vb.; see the Introd., § 39.

31 ἐχθρόν, *a personal foe,* not merely a man with whom one happens to be at war (πολέμιος).

ὡς ἐμοῦ ... ὑμεῖς, *that, therefore, I shall go wherever you go* (ἴητε is to be supplied with ὑμεῖς, another condit. rel. clause). καί marks the parallelism between ἐμοῦ and ὑμεῖς. It should not be translated, but the pronouns should be strongly emphasized. The gen. abs., with ὡς (see the note on ὡς ἐπιβουλεύοντος, c. 1. 26 f.), is here a virtual form of indir. disc. See G. 1593, 2; B. 661, note 4; G. M. T. 918.

32 οὕτω ... ἔχετε, *be of this opinion.* οὕτω merely resumes the preceding ὡς-clause; see the note on οὕτω ταχθῆναι, c. 2. 85. In Eng. it is more natural to reverse the order of the clauses, and to translate, simply, *be of this opinion, then, that I,* etc. τὴν γνώμην ἔχετε is tantamount to γιγνώσκετε; see the note on ἐποιεῖτο τὴν συλλογήν, c. 1. 24.

Book I, Chap. III

7 Ταῦτα εἶπεν· οἱ δὲ στρατιῶται οἵ τε αὐτοῦ ἐκείνου καὶ οἱ ἄλλοι ταῦτα ἀκούσαντες ὅτι οὐ φαίη παρὰ βασιλέα πορεύεσθαι ἐπῄνεσαν· παρὰ δὲ Ξενίου καὶ Πασίωνος πλείους ἢ δισχίλιοι 8 λαβόντες τὰ ὅπλα καὶ τὰ σκευοφόρα ἐστρατοπεδεύσαντο παρὰ Κλεάρχῳ. Κῦρος δὲ τούτοις ἀπορῶν τε καὶ λυπούμενος μετεπέμπετο τὸν Κλέαρχον· ὁ δὲ ἰέναι μὲν οὐκ ἤθελε, λάθρᾳ δὲ τῶν στρατιωτῶν πέμπων αὐτῷ ἄγγελον ἔλεγε θαρρεῖν ὡς καταστησομένων τούτων εἰς τὸ δέον. μεταπέμπεσθαι δ' ἐκέλευεν αὐτόν· αὐτὸς δ' οὐκ ἔφη ἰέναι.

---

33 ταῦτα εἶπεν: normal asyn.; see on Κλέαρχος, c. 1. 44.

οἵ τε: the accent of οἵ is due to the following enclitic; see G. 143, 4; H. 115c; B. 70, 3.

οἵ ... ἐκείνου, *his own*. How lit.?

34 ταῦτα: despite the principle stated in the note on ὧδε, c. 1. 24, τοῦτο and ταῦτα often look forward to an explanatory clause. The words ὅτι ... πορεύεσθαι are omitted by some editors, as a needless gloss.

οὐ φαίη: for the position of the neg., see on οὔτε ἔφη, c. 2. 152.

πορεύεσθαι: direct; *οὐ πορεύομαι, I am not going*. The pres. is freely used for the fut., when the action depends solely on the will of the subj.; this is common also in Eng.

35 πλείους: not acc.; see G. 358; H. 236; B. 121. This episode gives a good idea of the lack of organization among Cyrus' troops, regarded as an army. Discipline, in a sense, there was, but it was coupled with a strong sense of democracy.

36 παρὰ Κλεάρχῳ: for the force of παρά, see c. 2. 156, and the note.

37 τούτοις ἀπορῶν: see l. 12, and the note.

μετεπέμπετο: force of the tense? *Cf.* c. 1. 2, and the note.

38 οὐκ ἤθελε: *cf.* c. 2. 152, and the note.

λάθρᾳ: with the gen.; see G. 1150; H. 757a end; B. 418.

39 ἔλεγε, *bade;* so generally, when (in the act.) it takes the infin. When used as a simple vb. of saying, λέγω (in the act.) almost invariably takes ὅτι or ὡς; see the note on λέγεται, c. 2. 47.

ὡς ... τὸ δέον, *assuring him that (ὡς) this would turn out all right*. See the note on ὡς ἐπιβουλεύοντος, c. 1. 26 f. τὸ δέον (partic. of δέω) is used as a noun; G. 932, 1; H. 621b; B. 650, 1.

40 μεταπέμπεσθαι: note the durative tense.

41 αὐτός: when the subj. of an infin. is the same as the subj. of the vb. governing it, modifiers of the subj. must be nom., not acc. Here the intensive pron. contrasts the activity of Clearchus with that of Cyrus; direct, αὐτὸς δ' οὐκ εἶμι, *for my part I will not come* (*cf.* οὔτε ἔφη, c. 2. 152, and the note).

Μετὰ δὲ ταῦτα συναγαγὼν τοὺς θ' ἑαυτοῦ στρατιώτας καὶ 9
τοὺς προσελθόντας αὐτῷ καὶ τῶν ἄλλων τὸν βουλόμενον ἔλεξε
τοιάδε. Ἄνδρες στρατιῶται, τὰ μὲν δὴ Κύρου δῆλον ὅτι οὕτως
45 ἔχει πρὸς ἡμᾶς ὥσπερ τὰ ἡμέτερα πρὸς ἐκεῖνον· οὔτε γὰρ ἡμεῖς
ἐκείνου ἔτι στρατιῶται, ἐπεί γε οὐ συνεπόμεθα αὐτῷ, οὔτε ἐκεῖνος
ἔτι ἡμῖν μισθοδότης. ὅτι μέντοι ἀδικεῖσθαι νομίζει ὑφ' ἡμῶν
οἶδα· ὥστε καὶ μεταπεμπομένου αὐτοῦ οὐκ ἐθέλω ἐλθεῖν, τὸ 10
μὲν μέγιστον αἰσχυνόμενος ὅτι σύνοιδα ἐμαυτῷ πάντα ἐψευσμέ-
50 νος αὐτόν, ἔπειτα καὶ δεδιὼς μὴ λαβών με δίκην ἐπιθῇ ὧν νομί-

---

42 θ': *i.e.* τε.

43 τοὺς προσελθόντας: *i.e.* the men of Xenias and Pasion; see l. 35.

τῶν ἄλλων: for the gen., see τῶν Ἑλλήνων, c. 1. 8, and the note.

τὸν βουλόμενον, *whoever wished (to come).*

44 ἄνδρες στρατιῶται: *cf.* l. 11, and the note.

τὰ μὲν ... πρὸς ἐκεῖνον, *Cyrus' affairs, you see* (δή) *evidently stand in the same relation to us, as ours to him.* τὰ Κύρου needs no noun; πράγματα comes easily to the mind.

δῆλον ὅτι: ἐστίν is regularly omitted, and the phrase (often written as one word, δηλονότι) becomes a virtual adv. For ἔχω with an adv., see on εὐνοϊκῶς ἔχοιεν, c. 1. 21; for ἐκεῖνον, instead of αὐτόν, *cf.* c. 2. 88, and the note.

45 οὔτε ... ἔτι: equivalent to οὐκέτι, but serving to mark the parallelism of the two neg. clauses. Note the omission of ἐσμέν and ἐστίν.

46 στρατιῶται: no art., *soldiers of his.*

ἐπεί γε: γε regularly emphasizes the preceding word.

47 ἡμῖν, *our;* see G. 1174; H. 765a; B. 376; and *cf.* the note on αὐτῷ, c. 2. 7.

ὅτι ... νομίζει ... οἶδα: retain the Greek order in translating. μέντοι is strongly adversative.

48 καὶ μεταπεμπομένου αὐτοῦ, *even though he keeps sending.* See G. 1573; H. 979; B. 656, 2.

τὸ μὲν μέγιστον, *chiefly* (continued by ἔπειτα καί, l. 50), an adv. acc.; see on τὸ ἀρχαῖον, c. 1. 28.

49 αἰσχυνόμενος, *from shame.* As Greek is far richer in partics. than Eng. (see the note on ἐξαιτησαμένη, c. 1. 13), the translation should vary with the context.

ἐμαυτῷ: with σύνοιδα (*cf. conscius,* with a dat., in Lat.). It may be omitted in translating, or rendered, *e. g., in my heart.*

πάντα, *utterly,* inner obj. of ἐψευσμένος.

ἐψευσμένος: for the form, see G. 523; H. 365; B. 178, 1. The partic. is quoted after σύνοιδα (see the note on ἔχοντα, c. 2. 127). For the case, see on αὐτός, l. 41; although here we might have had the dat., in agreement with ἐμαυτῷ (G. 1590; H. 982a; B. 661 note 2).

50 δεδιώς, *from fear,* parallel with αἰσχυνόμενος, above.

11 ζει ὑπ' ἐμοῦ ἠδικῆσθαι. ἐμοὶ οὖν δοκεῖ οὐχ ὥρα εἶναι ἡμῖν καθεύδειν οὐδ' ἀμελεῖν ἡμῶν αὐτῶν, ἀλλὰ βουλεύεσθαι ὅ,τι χρὴ ποιεῖν ἐκ τούτων. καὶ ἕως γε μένομεν αὐτοῦ σκεπτέον μοι δοκεῖ εἶναι ὅπως ὡς ἀσφαλέστατα μενοῦμεν, εἴ τε ἤδη δοκεῖ ἀπιέναι, ὅπως ὡς ἀσφαλέστατα ἄπιμεν, καὶ ὅπως τὰ ἐπιτήδεια ἕξομεν. 55 ἄνευ γὰρ τούτων οὔτε στρατηγοῦ οὔτε ἰδιώτου ὄφελος οὐδέν. ὁ
12 δ' ἀνὴρ πολλοῦ μὲν ἄξιος ᾧ ἂν φίλος ᾖ, χαλεπώτατος δ' ἐχθρὸς ᾧ ἂν πολέμιος ᾖ, ἔχει δὲ δύναμιν καὶ πεζὴν καὶ ἱππικὴν καὶ

μὴ ... ἐπιθῇ : see G. 1378; H. 887; B. 594.

ὧν ... ἠδικῆσθαι, lit., *for the things in which he thinks he has been wronged by me*. ὧν stands for τούτων ἅ (*cf*. l. 20, and the note), ἅ representing the inner obj. of ἠδικῆσθαι, retained in the pass. (G. 1239; H. 725c; B. 512).

51 ἐμοί: emphatic by position; retain the Greek order.

δοκεῖ, *it seems*, with depend. infin.; but in the Greek the construction is personal, with ὥρα as subj. This is regular in Greek (see the note on λέγεται, c. 2. 47), but is often unnatural in Eng. This infin. is the indir. disc. infin., and has its proper tense value. For the other use of δοκεῖ, see c. 2. 1.

καθεύδειν : with ὥρα; see G. 1521; H. 952; B. 641.

52 ἡμῶν αὐτῶν, *ourselves* (G. 401; H. 266; B. 141). For the case, see G. 1102; H. 742; B. 356.

ὅ,τι χρὴ ποιεῖν, sc. ἡμᾶς, *what we are to do*. ὅ,τι is the indir. interrog. (G. 1600; H. 1011; B. 580).

53 ἐκ τούτων, *in view of this*, not mere sequence.

ἕως, *while*. For γε, *cf*. ἐπεί γε, above, l. 46, and the note.

αὐτοῦ, *here*, the adv. of the intensive. *Cf*. the note on τοῦ πρόσω, l. 2.

σκεπτέον ... εἶναι : direct, σκεπτέον ἐστί. For the use of the verbal adj., see G. 1597; H. 990; B. 665.

54 ὅπως μενοῦμεν: for the obj. clause, after a vb. of striving, see the note on ὅπως ἔσται, c. 1. 15.

ὡς ἀσφαλέστατα : see c. 1. 22 f., and the note.

δοκεῖ, *seems best*, not *seems*.

55 ἄπιμεν : a fut.; see l. 2, and the note.

56 ἄνευ ... οὐδέν, *for without these neither general nor private is of any use whatever*. οὐδέν, for τι, in a neg. clause; see c. 2. 152, and the note. Neg. words, at the end of a clause, are regularly emphatic.

ὁ δ' ἀνήρ : *i. e. Cyrus*.

57 πολλοῦ ἄξιος, *valuable*. For the gen., see G. 1135; H. 753f; B. 353, 1.

ᾧ ἂν φίλος ᾖ : see the note on ὅ,τι ἂν δέῃ, l. 24.

ἐχθρός ... πολέμιος : *cf*. l. 31, and the note.

58 καὶ ... καὶ ... καί : the poly-

ναυτικὴν ἦν πάντες ὁμοίως ὁρῶμέν τε καὶ ἐπιστάμεθα· καὶ γὰρ
οὐδὲ πόρρω δοκοῦμέν μοι αὐτοῦ καθῆσθαι. ὥστε ὥρα λέγειν
ὅ,τι τις γιγνώσκει ἄριστον εἶναι.   ταῦτα εἰπὼν ἐπαύσατο.

Ἐκ δὲ τούτου ἀνίσταντο οἱ μὲν ἐκ τοῦ αὐτομάτου, λέξοντες ἃ ἐγίγνωσκον, οἱ δὲ καὶ ὑπ' ἐκείνου ἐγκέλευστοι, ἐπιδεικνύντες οἵα εἴη ἡ ἀπορία ἄνευ τῆς Κύρου γνώμης καὶ μένειν καὶ
ἀπιέναι.   εἷς δὲ δὴ εἶπε προσποιούμενος σπεύδειν ὡς τάχιστα
πορεύεσθαι εἰς τὴν Ἑλλάδα στρατηγοὺς μὲν ἑλέσθαι ἄλλους ὡς
τάχιστα, εἰ μὴ βούλεται Κλέαρχος ἀπάγειν· τὰ δ' ἐπιτήδει'
ἀγοράζεσθαι.—ἡ δ' ἀγορὰ ἦν ἐν τῷ βαρβαρικῷ στρατεύματι—

---

syndeton marks the gravity of the situation.

59 ὁμοίως: intensifies πάντες.

60 δοκοῦμεν: the construction with δοκῶ is nearly always personal.

αὐτοῦ: with πόρρω, *far from him*. See G. 1149; H. 757; B. 362, 3.

ὥρα: see above, l. 51. Note how cleverly Clearchus, who, at the outset, had won the good will of his listeners by his promise to stand by them, now leads them to realize the dangers that threaten them if they break with Cyrus.

62 ἐκ τοῦ αὐτομάτου: *cf.* c. 2. 100.

λέξοντες: fut. partic. of purpose; see on ὡς ἀποκτενῶν, c. 1.12. With ἐπιδεικνύντες, below, l. 63, the idea of purpose is less apparent, and the partic. is rather circumstantial.

63 οἱ δὲ καί, *and others too*.

ἐγκέλευστοι: the verbal adj. in -τος is often equivalent to a perf. pass. partic. (*cf.* the Lat. partic. in -tus); see G. 776, 2; H. 475, 1; B. 667; hence we have ὑπό, with the gen.

64 οἵα, *how utter*. οἷος is qualitative, ὅσος quantitative.

εἴη, the opt. is due to the indir. ques.; direct, ποία ἐστί.

καί . . . καί, *either . . . or*.

μένειν . . . ἀπιέναι: with ἀπορία; *cf.* ὥρα καθεύδειν, l. 51, and the note.

65 εἷς δὲ δή εἶπε, *and one man, in particular* (δή), *moved*.

προσποιούμενος: we are to think of him as really a tool of Clearchus'.

66 ἑλέσθαι: this, with all the following infins. as far as the end of the section (save ἀπάγειν, l. 67), is governed by εἶπε, *moved*. In this sense εἶπον always takes the infin.

67 εἰ μὴ βούλεται: the direct form is retained. The opt. would have been ambiguous, since it would suggest ἐὰν μὴ βούληται, as the direct form. The speaker means, *if he doesn't want to*, not, *if he shall prove unwilling*. Cf. the retention of past indics. in subordinate clauses (see the note on ᾔσθετο, c. 2. 125), and consult G. 1499; H. 933a; B. 673.

68 ἡ δ' ἀγορὰ . . . στρατεύματι: a parenthetical statement by the narrator (Xen.) to show how

καὶ συσκευάζεσθαι· ἐλθόντας δὲ Κῦρον αἰτεῖν πλοῖα, ὡς ἀπο-
πλέοιεν· ἐὰν δὲ μὴ διδῷ ταῦτα, ἡγεμόνα αἰτεῖν Κῦρον ὅστις διὰ 70
φιλίας τῆς χώρας ἀπάξει. ἐὰν δὲ μηδὲ ἡγεμόνα διδῷ, συντάτ-
τεσθαι τὴν ταχίστην, πέμψαι δὲ καὶ προκαταληψομένους τὰ
ἄκρα, ὅπως μὴ φθάσωσι μήτε Κῦρος μήτε οἱ Κίλικες καταλαβόντες, ὧν πολλοὺς καὶ πολλὰ χρήματα ἔχομεν ἀνηρπακότες.
οὗτος μὲν τοιαῦτα εἶπε. 75

15 Μετὰ δὲ τοῦτον Κλέαρχος εἶπε τοσοῦτον· Ὡς μὲν στρατη-

---

absurd the man's proposal was. The Greeks and the barbarians had separate camps. For the ἀγορά, cf. I, 5, § 6, and the Introd., § 28.

69 ἐλθόντας: in agreement with the unexpressed subj. of αἰτεῖν. One readily supplies τινάς.

αἰτεῖν: with two accs.; see c. 1. 55, and the note.

ὡς ἀποπλέοιεν: purpose; see c. 1. 22, and the note.

70 ἐὰν δὲ μὴ διδῷ: this offers a good illustration of the Greek love of directness. The direct form is retained in all of the conditional clauses, and, at the last, we have even a vb. in the first person (ἔχομεν). In all there is but a single opt. How many of the vbs. might have been in that mood?

ὅστις ... ἀπάξει: a rel. clause of purpose; see G. 1442; H. 911; B. 591. ὅστις is often used where Eng. more easily expresses the indef. idea with the antecedent, *some guide who.*

71 φιλίας: note the pred. posit., *through the country as friendly.*

72 τὴν ταχίστην, *with all speed,* an adv. acc.; see the note on τὸ ἀρχαῖον, c. 1. 28. Cf. τὴν ταχίστην ὁδόν, c. 2. 112.

προκαταληψομένους: cf. λέξοντες, above, l. 62, and the note, and, for the omission of the subj. of the partic., ἐλθόντας, above, l. 69.

τὰ ἄκρα: *i.e.* the pass through which they had come, or the heights commanding it.

73 ὅπως μὴ ... καταλαβόντες, *that neither Cyrus nor the Cilicians should seize them first.* For the partic. with φθάνω, see the note on παρὼν ἐτύγχανεν, c. 1. 4. Note the various ways in which purpose has been expressed in this section.

74 ὧν: the antecedent is οἱ Κίλικες. The gen. goes both with πολλούς and with πολλὰ χρήματα) *many men and much property*); with the former it is partitive, with the latter it is a gen. of possession.

ἔχομεν ἀνηρπακότες, *have seized and hold;* not a mere periphrastic vb. form; see G. 1262; H. 981a; B. 536, 2. With the use of the first person, the speaker falls into dir. disc.; cf. the note on ἐὰν δὲ μὴ διδῷ, above, l. 70.

75 τοιαῦτα, *to this effect.*

76 εἶπε τοσοῦτον, *said merely this* (*thus much and no more*).

ὡς μὲν ... λεγέτω, *let no one speak of me as intending to assume*

γήσοντα ἐμὲ ταύτην τὴν στρατηγίαν μηδεὶς ὑμῶν λεγέτω· πολλὰ γὰρ ἐνορῶ δι' ἃ ἐμοὶ τοῦτο οὐ ποιητέον· ὡς δὲ τῷ ἀνδρὶ ὃν
ἂν ἕλησθε πείσομαι ᾗ δυνατὸν μάλιστα, ἵνα εἰδῆτε ὅτι καὶ ἄρχεσθαι ἐπίσταμαι ὥς τις καὶ ἄλλος μάλιστα ἀνθρώπων. μετὰ
τοῦτον ἄλλος ἀνέστη, ἐπιδεικνὺς μὲν τὴν εὐήθειαν τοῦ τὰ πλοῖα
αἰτεῖν κελεύοντος, ὥσπερ πάλιν τὸν στόλον Κύρου ποιουμένου,
ἐπιδεικνὺς δὲ ὡς εὔηθες εἴη ἡγεμόνα αἰτεῖν παρὰ τούτου ᾧ λυ-

---

this command. This, like ὡς
ἐμοῦ ... ἰόντος, l. 31 (where see
the note), amounts to indir.
disc., although λέγω does not
take the partic. construction;
see G. 1593; B. 661, note 4; and
G. M. T. 919. On the analogy of
the preceding passage, this may
be construed as acc. abs. (G.
1569; 1570; H. 973; 974; B. 658,
with the note).

77 στρατηγίαν: cogn. acc. (inner
obj.); see the note on τὰ αὐτὰ
ταῦτα, c. 1. 30.

πολλὰ ... δι' ἅ, *many reasons
why.*

78 ποιητέον: sc. ἐστί; cf. σκεπτέον
l. 53, and the note. Here it
may be taken either as personal
or impersonal.

ὡς ... πείσομαι: the vb. of saying
must be supplied in positive
form.

ὃν ἂν ἕλησθε: cf. ὅ,τι ἂν δέῃ, l. 24,
and the note. Observe that
here the rel. is not attracted to
the case of the antecedent.

79 ᾗ δυνατὸν μάλιστα (sc. ἐστί), *to
the full extent of my power.*
Cf. ὅτι ἀπαρασκευότατον, c. 1. 22 f.,
and the note.

καὶ ἄρχεσθαι: *i. e. be ruled as well
as rule.*

80 ὥς τις καὶ ἄλλος ... ἀνθρώπων,
*as well as any other man in the
world.* ἀνθρώπων is partitive
gen., with the superlative adv.
μάλιστα (*most of all men*). This
addition intensifies the phrase.
ὥς τις καὶ ἄλλος, which is itself
inclusive; cf. εἴ τις καὶ ἄλλος,
I, 4, § 15.

81 ἐπιδεικνὺς μὲν ... ἐπιδεικνὺς δέ:
a good example of the figure
anaphora; see the Introd., § 39.
Similar is ὀκνοίην μὲν ἄν ...
φοβοίμην δ' ἄν, although there the
vb. first used gives place to a
stronger synonym.

82 ὥσπερ ... ποιουμένου, (lit.) *as
though it were backward that
Cyrus was making his march.*
The stress falls on πάλιν. The
text is, however, uncertain.
Some insert ἄν, and the corrector of the Paris MS. inserts μή
Note the shift of construction
with αἰτεῖν; above we had two
accs.

83 ὡς ... εἴη, *how foolish it was.*
ὡς is *how*, rather than *that*, and
should generally be translated
how in this use.

ᾧ ... πρᾶξιν, *whose undertaking
we are ruining*—another shift
to direct speech, always easy for
the Greek. For the dat. ᾧ, cf.
αὐτῷ, c. 2. 7, and the note.

μαινόμεθα τὴν πρᾶξιν. εἰ δὲ καὶ τῷ ἡγεμόνι πιστεύσομεν ὃν ἂν
Κῦρος διδῷ, τί κωλύει καὶ τὰ ἄκρα ἡμῖν κελεύειν Κῦρον προκαταλαβεῖν; ἐγὼ γὰρ ὀκνοίην μὲν ἂν εἰς τὰ πλοῖα ἐμβαίνειν ἃ
ἡμῖν δοίη, μὴ ἡμᾶς ταῖς τριήρεσι καταδύσῃ, φοβοίμην δ' ἂν
τῷ ἡγεμόνι ὃν δοίη ἕπεσθαι, μὴ ἡμᾶς ἀγάγῃ ὅθεν οὐκ ἔσται
ἐξελθεῖν· βουλοίμην δ' ἂν ἄκοντος ἀπιὼν Κύρου λαθεῖν
αὐτὸν ἀπελθών· ὃ οὐ δυνατόν ἐστιν. ἀλλ' ἐγώ φημι ταῦτα
μὲν φλυαρίας εἶναι· δοκεῖ δέ μοι ἄνδρας ἐλθόντας πρὸς Κῦρον

---

84 εἰ . . . πιστεύσομεν: for the tense, see G. 1391; H. 893c; B. 602 note 2. Note the difference between such a condition and the form with ἐάν.

85 τί κωλύει . . . προκαταλαβεῖν, *what hinders our bidding Cyrus to seize the heights for us as well?* For the constructions with vbs. of hindering, see G. 1549; H. 963; B. 643.

86 ἐγὼ γάρ, *for I, certainly.* The pron. is strongly emphasized.

ὀκνοίην ἄν: potential opt., for which the following condit. rel. clause supplies the protasis. *Cf.* σὺν ὑμῖν . . . ἂν εἶναι, l. 29, and the note. The vb., in such a rel. clause, generally agrees in mood with the subjv. or opt. upon which it depends; see G. 1270, 2; 1436; H. 919a; 917; B. 624; G. M. T. 177, I, a.

87 μὴ . . . καταδύσῃ, *lest he may sink us with his triremes* (dat. of means). The contrast between πλοῖον (*merchantman, transport*) and τριήρης or ναῦς (*ship of war*) is constantly emphasized. Observe that in the clause with μή the vb. is not assimilated to the opt. (G. 1270, 2; G. M. T. 180b; and the note on εἴη, II, 4, § 3).

88 ὃν δοίη: the mood exactly as in ἃ δοίη, above. Again the rel. is not attracted to the case of its antecedent.

ὅθεν, (*to a place*) *whence.*

οὐκ ἔσται, *it will be impossible*—stronger than οὐκ ἂν εἴη.

89 βουλοίμην . . . ἀπελθών, *and I should wish, were I to try to go away* (ἀπιών) *without Cyrus' consent, to get off without his knowledge*—another potent. opt., for which ἀπιών supplies a protasis. ἄκοντος Κύρου is gen. abs. In this construction the partic. ὄντος is almost never omitted, save with words which can, of themselves, be felt as partics. (ἑκών, ἄκων, *etc.*); see G. 1571; H. 972. For the phrase, λαθεῖν . . . ἀπελθών, *cf.* τρεφόμενον ἐλάνθανεν, c. 1. 51. Note the shift of tense, ἀπιών . . . ἀπελθών; and see G. 1586; 1290; H. 856b; B. 543.

90 ὅ: clauses beginning with a rel. are far commoner in Greek and Lat. than in Eng., and are often best rendered by a demonstr. with *and* or *but.*

ἐγώ: again strongly emphatic.

91 δοκεῖ δέ μοι, freely, *I recommend.* Five following infins. stand as subjs. to δοκεῖ.

ἄνδρας ἐλθόντας . . . ἐρωτᾶν, *that*

οἵτινες ἐπιτήδειοι σὺν Κλεάρχῳ ἐρωτᾶν ἐκεῖνον τί βούλεται
ἡμῖν χρῆσθαι· καὶ ἐὰν μὲν ἡ πρᾶξις ᾖ παραπλησία οἵαπερ
καὶ πρόσθεν ἐχρῆτο τοῖς ξένοις, ἕπεσθαι καὶ ἡμᾶς καὶ μὴ
95 κακίους εἶναι τῶν πρόσθεν τούτῳ συναναβάντων· ἐὰν δὲ μείζων 19
ἡ πρᾶξις τῆς πρόσθεν φαίνηται καὶ ἐπιπονωτέρα καὶ ἐπικιν-
δυνοτέρα, ἀξιοῦν ἢ πείσαντα ἡμᾶς ἄγειν ἢ πεισθέντα πρὸς
φιλίαν ἀφιέναι· οὕτω γὰρ καὶ ἑπόμενοι ἂν φίλοι αὐτῷ καὶ
πρόθυμοι ἐποίμεθα καὶ ἀπιόντες ἀσφαλῶς ἂν ἀπίοιμεν· ὅ,τι
100 δ' ἂν πρὸς ταῦτα λέγῃ ἀπαγγεῖλαι δεῦρο· ἡμᾶς δ' ἀκούσαντας
πρὸς ταῦτα βουλεύεσθαι.

Ἔδοξε ταῦτα, καὶ ἄνδρας ἑλόμενοι σὺν Κλεάρχῳ πέμπου- 20

suitable men go ... and ask.
The student should distinguish
between αἰτεῖν and ἐρωτᾶν.

92 οἵτινες ἐπιτήδειοι: sc. εἰσι. ὅστις
often serves to characterize.

τί ... χρῆσθαι, what use he wishes
to make of us. τί is the inner
obj., ἡμῖν, the dat. of means.

93 ᾖ: subjv. of εἰμί.

οἵαπερ: attracted from the acc.
(cf. τί, above) to the case of the
unexpressed antecedent. For
the dat., see G. 1175; H. 773; B.
392, 2.

94 πρόσθεν: the reference is to
the expedition mentioned in I,
1, § 2.

ἕπεσθαι καὶ ἡμᾶς, that we too follow
(as well as they).

μή: not οὐ, for the infin. is not in
indir. disc.

95 κακίους: for the form, cf. πλείους,
l. 35; there nom., here acc.

τούτῳ: i. e. Κύρῳ. The dat. is due
to the compound vb.; cf. αὐτῷ,
c. 1. 37.

τῶν συναναβάντων: for the gen., see
the note on Κύρου, c. 2. 142.

μείζων: for the form, see G. 361, 4;
84, 3; H. 253a, 68; B. 134; 39, 2.

96 τῆς πρόσθεν: πράξεως supplies
itself. For the case, cf. τῶν συναναβάντων, above.

ἐπιπονωτέρα: for the form, see G.
350, end; H. 249; B. 132, 1.

97 ἀξιοῦν: another subj. of δοκεῖ.
Upon it, in turn, ἄγειν and ἀφιέναι
depend. As its subj. we may
supply ἄνδρας (i. e. the envoys;
cf. l. 91), or ἡμᾶς (that we demand, acting through the envoys).

πείσαντα: in agreement with αὐτόν,
i. e. Κῦρον, to be supplied as
subj. of ἄγειν. The "persuasion"
meant is, of course, increase of
pay.

πρὸς φιλίαν, in friendship. The
prep., with its case, takes the
place of an adv.; cf. ἀπὸ τοῦ
αὐτομάτου, c. 2. 100.

98 ἑπόμενοι ... ἀπιόντες: equivalent to εἰ ἐποίμεθα ... εἰ ἀπίοιμεν.

φίλοι ... πρόθυμοι: pred. adjs.

100 ἀπαγγεῖλαι: sc. the envoys. This
infin. and, finally, βουλεύεσθαι, are
still subjs. of δοκεῖ.

101 πρὸς ταῦτα, in view of this.

102 ἔδοξε ταῦτα, this was determined on, a stock legal phrase.

σιν οἳ ἠρώτων Κῦρον τὰ δόξαντα τῇ στρατιᾷ. ὁ δ' ἀπεκρίνατο ὅτι ἀκούει Ἀβροκόμαν ἐχθρὸν ἄνδρα ἐπὶ τῷ Εὐφράτῃ ποταμῷ εἶναι, ἀπέχοντα δώδεκα σταθμούς· πρὸς τοῦτον οὖν ἔφη βού- 105
λεσθαι ἐλθεῖν· κἂν μὲν ᾖ ἐκεῖ, τὴν δίκην ἔφη χρῄζειν ἐπιθεῖναι αὐτῷ, ἢν δὲ φύγῃ, ἡμεῖς ἐκεῖ πρὸς ταῦτα βουλευσόμεθα· ἀκού-
21 σαντες δὲ ταῦτα οἱ αἱρετοὶ ἀγγέλλουσι τοῖς στρατιώταις· τοῖς δὲ ὑποψία μὲν ἦν ὅτι ἄγει πρὸς βασιλέα, ὅμως δὲ ἐδόκει ἕπεσθαι. προσαιτοῦσι δὲ μισθόν· ὁ δὲ Κῦρος ὑπισχνεῖται ἡμιόλιον 110
πᾶσι δώσειν οὗ πρότερον ἔφερον, ἀντὶ δαρεικοῦ τρία ἡμιδαρεικὰ

No connective is, of course, needed; *cf.* ταῦτα εἶπεν, l. 33, and the note.

103 οἳ ἠρώτων . . . τῇ στρατιᾷ, *who asked Cyrus the questions decided on by the army.* The vb. has both outer and inner obj.

104 ἀκούει: Greek, like Eng., often uses the pres. of vbs. of perception in cases where the perf. would be more logical. After the past tense we might, of course, have had ἀκούοι.

ἐχθρὸν ἄνδρα, *a foe of his.* For the difference between ἐχθρός and πολέμιος, see the note on l. 31.

105 εἶναι: indir. disc. after ἀκούει, which oftener takes the partic., as above, c. 2. 127, or ὅτι, as above, l. 34. With the infin. mere hearsay is indicated (G. 1592, 1 · H. 986).

ἀπέχοντα: with Ἀβροκόμαν.

δώδεκα: an understatement, not unnatural under the circumstances. As a matter of fact it took them nineteen days to reach Thapsacus, where they crossed the Euphrates.

ἔφη: resuming ἀπεκρίνατο, but with a shift to the infin. construc-tion. It is expressed again a line below.

106 κἂν (καὶ ἐὰν) . . . ᾖ, *if he should (prove to) be.* The direct form is retained, as so often, and in the next line we have the vb. in the first person, as above, ll. 83 f.

χρῄζειν: scarcely to be distinguished from the far commoner βούλεσθαι. Here its use avoids the repetition of the same word; see the Introd., § 39.

107 πρὸς ταῦτα: *cf.* above, l. 100.

108 αἱρετοί: for the force of the suffix -τος, see the note on ἐγκέλευστοι, l. 63.

τοῖς δέ: see the note on ὁ δέ, c. 1. 12.

109 ὅτι ἄγει: pres. indics., as well as opts., when quoted after a secondary tense, are necessarily rendered as past tenses in Eng.

ἐδόκει (*sc.* αὐτοῖς), *they concluded.* The tense implies deliberation.

110 προσαιτοῦσι: note the force of the prep.

111 δώσειν: indir. disc. after ὑπισχνεῖται; for the other construction, see c. 2. 11, and the note.

οὗ: attracted to the case of its omitted antecedent. The gen. is due to the fact that ἡμιόλιον

τοῦ μηνὸς τῷ στρατιώτῃ· ὅτι δὲ ἐπὶ βασιλέα ἄγοι οὐδὲ ἐνταῦθα ἤκουσεν οὐδεὶς ἐν τῷ γε φανερῷ.

IV. Ἐντεῦθεν ἐξελαύνει σταθμοὺς δύο παρασάγγας δέκα ἐπὶ τὸν Ψάρον ποταμόν, οὗ ἦν τὸ εὖρος τρία πλέθρα. ἐντεῦθεν ἐξελαύνει σταθμὸν ἕνα παρασάγγας πέντε ἐπὶ τὸν Πύραμον ποταμόν, οὗ ἦν τὸ εὖρος στάδιον. ἐντεῦθεν ἐξελαύνει σταθμοὺς δύο παρασάγγας πεντεκαίδεκα εἰς Ἰσσούς, τῆς Κιλικίας ἐσχάτην πόλιν ἐπὶ τῇ θαλάττῃ οἰκουμένην, μεγάλην καὶ εὐδαίμονα. ἐνταῦθα ἔμειναν ἡμέρας τρεῖς· καὶ Κύρῳ παρῆσαν αἱ ἐκ Πελοποννήσου νῆες τριάκοντα καὶ πέντε καὶ ἐπ' αὐταῖς ναύαρχος Πυθαγόρας Λακεδαιμόνιος. ἡγεῖτο δ' αὐταῖς Ταμὼς Αἰγύπτιος ἐξ Ἐφέσου, ἔχων ναῦς ἑτέρας Κύρου πέντε καὶ εἴκοσιν, αἷς ἐπολιόρκει Μίλητον ὅτε Τισσαφέρνει φίλη ἦν, καὶ συνεπολέμει

is felt as a comparative; *cf.* Κύρου, c. 2. 142, and the note, and G. 1154.

ἔφερον: *had been receiving. Cf.* ἐφύλαττον, c. 2. 129, and the note. With this use of φέρω, *cf.* μισθοφόροι, I, 4, § 3.

δαρεικοῦ: *cf.* c. 1. 46, and the note.

112 τοῦ μηνὸς τῷ στρατιώτῃ, *per month per man*. The art. is distributive, G. 951; H. 657c. For the gen. μηνός, see G. 1136; H. 759; B. 359.

οὐδέ: *cf.* c. 2. 146, and the note.

113 ἐν τῷ γε φανερῷ: *cf.* ἀπὸ τοῦ αὐτομάτου, c. 2. 100, and the note. γε implies that there was a secret understanding between Cyrus and some of the Greek leaders. This charge is made in I, 4, § 12.

CHAPTER IV

2 εὖρος . . . πλέθρα: see the note on δύο πλέθρα, c. 2. 30 f.

4 στάδιον: the commonest Greek measure of length (the length of the standard course for the foot race), roughly two hundred yards. The word makes its plural either regularly (στάδια, I, 8, § 17), or irregularly (στάδιοι, I, 4, § 4).

6 οἰκουμένην, *situated*.

7 Κύρῳ: *cf.* αὐτῷ, c. 2. 22, and the note. Many notions often blend in these dats. This is not mere advantage; Cyrus had summoned these ships (§ 5).

παρῆσαν: *cf.* c. 2. 14, and the note. For the mention of the fleet, *cf.* c. 2. 127.

Πελοποννήσου: on the connection of Sparta with the expedition, see the Introd., § 27.

8 ἐπ' αὐταῖς, *in command of them*. Contrast ἐπὶ τῶν νεῶν (below, l. 12), *on board of*.

9 ἡγεῖτο δ' αὐταῖς, *they were conducted by*. The dat. (as contrasted with the gen.) shows that he was not their regular commander.

11 ἐπολιόρκει . . . συνεπολέμει: *cf.* ἔφερον, above, c. 3. 111, and the

3 Κύρῳ πρὸς αὐτόν. παρῆν δὲ καὶ Χειρίσοφος Λακεδαιμόνιος ἐπὶ τῶν νεῶν, μετάπεμπτος ὑπὸ Κύρου, ἑπτακοσίους ἔχων ὁπλίτας, ὧν ἐστρατήγει παρὰ Κύρῳ. αἱ δὲ νῆες ὥρμουν παρὰ τὴν Κύρου σκηνήν. ἐνταῦθα καὶ οἱ παρὰ Ἀβροκόμα μισθοφόροι Ἕλληνες 15 ἀποστάντες ἦλθον παρὰ Κῦρον τετρακόσιοι ὁπλῖται καὶ συνεστρατεύοντο ἐπὶ βασιλέα.

4 Ἐντεῦθεν ἐξελαύνει σταθμὸν ἕνα παρασάγγας πέντε ἐπὶ πύλας τῆς Κιλικίας καὶ τῆς Συρίας. ἦσαν δὲ ταῦτα δύο τείχη, καὶ τὸ μὲν ἔσωθεν τὸ πρὸ τῆς Κιλικίας Συέννεσις εἶχε καὶ Κιλί- 20 κων φυλακή, τὸ δὲ ἔξω τὸ πρὸ τῆς Συρίας βασιλέως ἐλέγετο φυλακὴ φυλάττειν. διὰ μέσου δὲ ῥεῖ τούτων ποταμὸς Κάρσος

---

note. For the facts, see c. 32, and the Introd., § 26. The words ὅτε ... πρὸς αὐτόν are by many considered an interpolation.

12 Χειρίσοφος: see the Introd., §§ 27 and 38.

13 μετάπεμπτος: see the note on ἐγκέλευστοι, above, c. 3. 63. Here too we have ὑπό with the gen., a construction proper only with passives.

14 ὧν: the gen. is normal with vbs. meaning *command, be at the head of*, etc. (*cf.* c. 1. 37, and the note), but here the denominative force is so strong that the phrase is practically the same as ὧν στρατηγὸς ἦν; see G. 1109; 1110.

παρὰ Κύρῳ, *under Cyrus*.

ὥρμουν, *lay at anchor*.

15 σκηνήν: for the case, see Ἑλλήσποντον, c. 1. 48, and the note.

Ἀβροκόμα: a Doric form of the gen. (G. 188, 3; H. 146D). *Cf.* Συεννέσιος (Ionic), c. 2. 72, and the note.

19 πύλας: practically a proper name; hence no art. For a description of this pass, see the Introd., § 29.

ἦσαν: pl., although the subj. is neut. ταῦτα stands, however, for αὗται (attracted to the gender of the pred. noun; see on αὕτη, c. 1. 34), so this is hardly to be included among Xen.'s exceptions to the rule (see the note on ἦν, c. 2. 38).

20 τὸ μὲν ἔσωθεν: *sc.* τεῖχος. This is further explained by the addition of the phrase τὸ πρὸ τῆς Κιλικίας, as, below, τὸ δὲ ἔξω is explained by τὸ πρὸ τῆς Συρίας. The formal attrib. posit. lends itself to explicitness. With the use of the adv. in -θεν, *cf.* the use of ἐκ in, *e. g.*, ἐκ δεξιᾶς, *on the right*, where the Greek point of view differs from ours.

εἶχε: for the agreement, *cf.* ἦν, c. 2. 20, and the note. Syennesis was of course not there in person.

21 βασιλέως: emphatic position.

22 μέσου: a noun, as above, c. 2.137. Upon this word the gen τούτων depends; *cf.* below, τὸ μέσον τῶν τειχῶν.

ὄνομα, εὖρος πλέθρου. ἅπαν δὲ τὸ μέσον τῶν τειχῶν ἦσαν στάδιοι τρεῖς· καὶ παρελθεῖν οὐκ ἦν βίᾳ· ἦν γὰρ ἡ πάροδος
25 στενὴ καὶ τὰ τείχη εἰς τὴν θάλατταν καθήκοντα, ὕπερθεν δ' ἦσαν πέτραι ἠλίβατοι· ἐπὶ δὲ τοῖς τείχεσιν ἀμφοτέροις ἐφειστήκεσαν πύλαι. ταύτης ἕνεκα τῆς παρόδου Κῦρος τὰς ναῦς 5 μετεπέμψατο, ὅπως ὁπλίτας ἀποβιβάσειεν εἴσω καὶ ἔξω τῶν πυλῶν βιασομένους τοὺς πολεμίους εἰ φυλάττοιεν ἐπὶ ταῖς
30 Συρίαις πύλαις, ὅπερ ᾤετο ποιήσειν ὁ Κῦρος τὸν Ἀβροκόμαν, ἔχοντα πολὺ στράτευμα. Ἀβροκόμας δὲ οὐ τοῦτ' ἐποίησεν, ἀλλ' ἐπεὶ ἤκουσε Κῦρον ἐν Κιλικίᾳ ὄντα, ἀναστρέψας ἐκ Φοινίκης παρὰ βασιλέα ἀπήλαυνεν, ἔχων, ὡς ἐλέγετο, τριάκοντα μυριάδας στρατιᾶς.

23 εὖρος πλέθρου: see the note on δύο πλέθρα, c. 2. 30.

ἅπαν τὸ μέσον, *the whole space between.*

ἦσαν: attracted to the number of the pred. noun, although the subj. is sing. *Cf.* ἦσαν, c. 2. 63, and the note.

25 καθήκοντα: with ἦν, but not quite equivalent to καθῆκε. The partic. has the force of an adj. (like στενή); *cf.* φυλάττων, c. 2. 123, and the note.

26 ἠλίβατοι: a poetical word of uncertain etymology; see the Introd., § 39.

ἀμφοτέροις: for the posit., see c. 1. 4, and the note.

ἐφειστήκεσαν, *had been set* (and so *were*) *on.*

27 ταύτης: retain the Greek order, *it was because of this pass that.* Cyrus' preparations had been shrewdly planned.

28 εἴσω καὶ ἔξω: Cyrus himself is on the Cilician side; he means to land troops between the two walls (εἴσω), and also on the Syrian side (ἔξω), so as to be in a position to attack Abrocomas both in front and in the rear. For the gen. πυλῶν, see G. 1148; H. 757; B. 360.

29 βιασομένους: fut. partic. of purpose.

εἰ φυλάττοιεν: *cf.* εἴ τι δέοιτο, c. 3. 19, and the note.

30 ὅπερ: -περ makes the reference of the rel. more explicit.

31 ἔχοντα, *since he had.*

32 ἤκουσε ... ὄντα: *cf.* c. 2. 126, and the note.

ἀναστρέψας, *turning back.*

33 ὡς ἐλέγετο: it was doubtless impossible for Xen. to get at the truth in matters like this, but it was easy for the Greek to believe in the vast size of the Persian armies; *cf.* I, 7, §§ 11 and 12. Probably Abrocomas, like Syennesis, was waiting to see which side was to win before openly antagonizing either Cyrus or the king.

τριάκοντα ... στρατιᾶς: *cf.* I, 10, § 1, τέτταρες δ' ἐλέγοντο παρασάγγαι εἶναι τῆς ὁδοῦ. With this inversion of the usual case relation-

Book I, Chap. IV 45

6 Ἐντεῦθεν ἐξελαύνει διὰ Συρίας σταθμὸν ἕνα παρασάγγας 35
πέντε εἰς Μυρίανδον, πόλιν οἰκουμένην ὑπὸ Φοινίκων ἐπὶ τῇ
θαλάττῃ· ἐμπόριον δ' ἦν τὸ χωρίον καὶ ὥρμουν αὐτόθι ὁλκάδες
7 πολλαί. ἐνταῦθα ἔμεινεν ἡμέρας ἑπτά· καὶ Ξενίας ὁ Ἀρκὰς
καὶ Πασίων ὁ Μεγαρεὺς ἐμβάντες εἰς πλοῖον καὶ τὰ πλείστου
ἄξια ἐνθέμενοι ἀπέπλευσαν, ὡς μὲν τοῖς πλείστοις ἐδόκουν φιλο- 40
τιμηθέντες ὅτι τοὺς στρατιώτας αὐτῶν τοὺς παρὰ Κλεάρχου
ἀπελθόντας ὡς ἀπιόντας εἰς τὴν Ἑλλάδα πάλιν καὶ οὐ πρὸς
βασιλέα εἴα Κῦρος τὸν Κλέαρχον ἔχειν. ἐπεὶ δ' ἦσαν ἀφανεῖς,
διῆλθε λόγος ὅτι διώκοι αὐτοὺς Κῦρος τριήρεσι· καὶ οἱ μὲν
ηὔχοντο ὡς δειλοὺς ὄντας αὐτοὺς ληφθῆναι, οἱ δ' ᾤκτιρον εἰ 45
ἁλώσοιντο.

8 Κῦρος δὲ συγκαλέσας τοὺς στρατηγοὺς εἶπεν· Ἀπολελοί-
πασιν ἡμᾶς Ξενίας καὶ Πασίων. ἀλλ' εὖ γε μέντοι ἐπιστάσθων
ὅτι οὔτε ἀποδεδράκασιν· οἶδα γὰρ ὅπῃ οἴχονται· οὔτε ἀποπε-

---

ship, contrast the normal gen. of measure (*e. g.*, c. 2. 47).

36 οἰκουμένην: here the two meanings *inhabited* and *situated* are blended.

37 τὸ χωρίον: the subj., not the pred. noun, has the art.; see G. 956; H. 669; B. 449.

αὐτόθι: an older form of *αὐτοῦ*, *there*.

ὁλκάδες: *cf. πλοῖον*, as contrasted with *ναῦς* (c. 3. 87, and the note).

39 ἐμβάντες εἰς: note the preps., and *cf. ἐμβάλλει εἰς*, c. 2. 45.

τὰ πλείστου ἄξια, *their most valuable effects. Cf.* c. 3. 57, and the note.

40 ὡς μὲν τοῖς πλείστοις: note *μέν*; others thought differently.

ἐδόκουν: personal, in a case where Eng. requires the impersonal use; *cf.* c. 2. 47, and the note.

φιλοτιμηθέντες ὅτι ... ἔχειν, *jealous because Cyrus had permitted Clearchus to keep*, etc. For the form εἴα, see G. 537; H. 359; B. 172, 2.

41 τοὺς ... ἀπελθόντας, *who had gone over*. For the facts, see c. 3. 35.

42 ὡς ἀπιόντας: *cf. ὡς ἀποκτενῶν*, c. 1. 12, and the note. For *εἶμι*, as a fut., see c. 3. 2, and the note.

44 διώκοι, *was pursuing;* not *would pursue;* direct, *διώκει*.

45 ηὔχοντο ... ληφθῆναι, *prayed that they might be captured.*

εἰ ἁλώσοιντο, *if they were to be captured.* For the fut., *cf. πιστεύσομεν*, c. 3. 84, and the note, and, for the implied indir. disc., the note on εἴ τι δέοιτο, c. 3. 19. Cyrus' severity had already been shown (I, 2, §20); *cf.*, also, the Orontas episode in chap. vi, and Xenophon's own words in I, 9, §13.

47 γε μέντοι: *γε* emphasizes the preceding word and *μέντοι* is adversative, *however*.

48 ἀποδεδράκασιν: the word im-

50 φεύγασιν· ἔχω γὰρ τριήρεις ὥστε ἑλεῖν τὸ ἐκείνων πλοῖον·
ἀλλὰ μὰ τοὺς θεοὺς οὐκ ἔγωγε αὐτοὺς διώξω, οὐδ' ἐρεῖ οὐδεὶς ὡς
ἐγὼ ἕως μὲν ἂν παρῇ τις χρῶμαι, ἐπειδὰν δὲ ἀπιέναι βούληται,
συλλαβὼν καὶ αὐτοὺς κακῶς ποιῶ καὶ τὰ χρήματα ἀποσυλῶ.
ἀλλὰ ἰόντων εἰδότες ὅτι κακίους εἰσὶ περὶ ἡμᾶς ἢ ἡμεῖς περὶ
55 ἐκείνους. καίτοι ἔχω γε αὐτῶν καὶ τέκνα καὶ γυναῖκας ἐν
Τράλλεσι φρουρούμενα· ἀλλ' οὐδὲ τούτων στερήσονται, ἀλλ'
ἀπολήψονται τῆς πρόσθεν ἕνεκα περὶ ἐμὲ ἀρετῆς. καὶ ὁ μὲν 9
ταῦτα εἶπεν· οἱ δὲ Ἕλληνες, εἴ τις καὶ ἀθυμότερος ἦν πρὸς τὴν

plies stealth; it is regularly used of runaway slaves. ἀποφεύγω, on the other hand, implies speed. The two vbs. again occur side by side in II, 2, §13 and II, 5, §7.

οἴχονται: a pres., with the force of a perf. (G. 1256; H. 827, end; B. 521, note).

50 τριήρεις . . . πλοῖον: cf. above, c. 3. 87, and the note.

ὥστε: not of actual result; see the note on c. 1. 19.

51 μὰ τοὺς θεούς: a neg. oath; see G. 1066; 1067; H. 723; B. 344.

ἔγωγε: emphatic form, regularly used in oaths.

διώξω: more commonly the fut. of this vb. has the middle form.

οὐδ' ἐρεῖ οὐδείς: a postponed subj. is regularly to be emphasized. For the double neg., see c. 2. 152, and the note.

52 ἕως . . . ἂν παρῇ τις, *so long as one is with me*. See the note on ὅστις ἀφικνεῖτο, c. 1. 18, and cf. ἐπειδὰν βούληται, below.

χρῶμαι . . . ποιῶ . . . ἀποσυλῶ: quoted after ἐρεῖ ὡς. With χρῶμαι supply αὐτοῖς (for the pl. after τις, cf. ὅστις . . . πάντας, c. 1. 18, and the note).

53 καί . . . καί, *both . . . and.*

The order of the words brings αὐτούς and χρήματα into strong contrast.

54 ἰόντων: imperat., not partic.

κακίους: not acc.; cf. πλείους, c. 3. 35, and the note.

περί, *toward;* so again three lines below.

55 γε: cf. γε μέντοι, above, l. 47, and the note.

τέκνα καὶ γυναῖκας: in this phrase τέκνα commonly stands first (cf. III, 4, §46; V, 3, §1; yet see IV, 1, §8; VII, 4, §5, *etc.*). It is a word connoting affection. In the enumeration in III, 1, §3, παίδων comes last.

56 Τράλλεσι: in Caria; see the map.

φρουρούμενα: neut., since the women and children are regarded as chattels.

οὐδέ: see c. 2. 146, and the note.

στερήσονται: fut. mid. as pass. In the act., vbs. of depriving take either two accs. or acc. and gen.; see the note on ἀφαιρεῖσθαι, c. 3. 18.

58 εἴ τις καὶ . . . ἦν, freely, *even those who had been.*

ἀθυμότερος, *rather disheartened*— a frequent force of comp. adjs.

ἀνάβασιν, ἀκούοντες τὴν Κύρου ἀρετὴν ἥδιον καὶ προθυμότερον συνεπορεύοντο.

Μετὰ ταῦτα Κῦρος ἐξελαύνει σταθμοὺς τέτταρας παρασάγγας εἴκοσιν ἐπὶ τὸν Χάλον ποταμόν, ὄντα τὸ εὖρος πλέθρου, πλήρη δ' ἰχθύων μεγάλων καὶ πραέων, οὓς οἱ Σύροι θεοὺς ἐνόμιζον καὶ ἀδικεῖν οὐκ εἴων οὐδὲ τὰς περιστεράς. αἱ δὲ κῶμαι ἐν αἷς ἐσκήνουν Παρυσάτιδος ἦσαν εἰς ζώνην δεδομέναι. ἐντεῦθεν ἐξελαύνει σταθμοὺς πέντε παρασάγγας τριάκοντα ἐπὶ τὰς πηγὰς τοῦ Δάρδατος ποταμοῦ, οὗ τὸ εὖρος πλέθρου. ἐνταῦθα

---

59 ἀρετήν, *magnanimity;* but it may well have been policy.

ἥδιον ... προθυμότερον: for these advs., see G. 369; H. 259; B. 138.

61 μετὰ ταῦτα: no connective is needed; see the note on Κλέαρχος, c. 1. 44.

62 εὖρος πλέθρου: see the note on δύο πλέθρα, c. 2. 30 f. We have the opposite construction (of εὖρος), below, l. 67.

63 πλήρη: acc. masc. sing.; see G. 313; H. 230; B. 120.

ἰχθύων: for the case, see θηρίων, c. 2. 39, and the note.

πραέων: for the form, see G. 348; H. 247a; B. 128.

64 ἐνόμιζον: with two accs. (G. 1077; H. 726; B. 341). Both this vb. and the following εἴων might have been in the pres., as the statement is of lasting truth; but the past is equally natural in historical narrative.

οὐκ εἴων, *would not suffer.* The neg. with the imperf. is to be rendered *would not,* or *could not;* it rarely means merely *did not. Cf.* the note on ἐδαπάνων, c. 3. 15. For the augment of εἴων, see εἴα, above, c. 4. 43.

οὐδὲ τὰς περιστεράς, *or the doves either*, a second obj. to ἀδικεῖν. The words may be an interpolation. Fish were sacred to the Syrian goddess, Derceto, who, the legend said, had been changed into a fish, as her daughter Semiramis had been changed into a dove (Ovid, *Met.* IV, 44 ff.). Modern travelers speak of this superstition regarding fishes as still surviving in this region.

65 Παρυσάτιδος: *cf.* Τισσαφέρνους, c. 1. 28, and the note.

εἰς ζώνην, *for girdle money,* as we might say *for pin money.* The student will easily read the following passage from Plato, χώραν ... ἣν καλεῖν (ἔφη) τοὺς ἐπιχωρίους (*the natives*) ζώνην τῆς βασιλέως γυναικός· εἶναι δὲ καὶ ἄλλην ἣν αὖ καλεῖσθαι καλύπτραν (*veil*), καὶ ἄλλους πολλοὺς τόπους (*districts*) καλοὺς καὶ ἀγαθοὺς εἰς τὸν κόσμον (*adornment*) ἐξῃρημένους τὸν τῆς γυναικός (*Alc.* I, 123b). See also Cicero, *Verr.* II, 3, 33, 76: Solere aiunt reges barbaros Persarum ac Syrorum plures uxores habere, his autem uxoribus civitates attribuere hoc modo: Haec civitas mulieri in redimiculum

ἦσαν τὰ Βελέσυος βασίλεια τοῦ Συρίας ἄρξαντος, καὶ παράδεισος πάνυ μέγας καὶ καλός, ἔχων πάντα ὅσα ὧραι φύουσι.
70 Κῦρος δ' αὐτὸν ἐξέκοψεν καὶ τὰ βασίλεια κατέκαυσεν. ἐντεῦ- 11
θεν ἐξελαύνει σταθμοὺς τρεῖς παρασάγγας πεντεκαίδεκα ἐπὶ τὸν
Εὐφράτην ποταμόν, ὄντα τὸ εὖρος τεττάρων σταδίων· καὶ πόλις
αὐτόθι ᾠκεῖτο μεγάλη καὶ εὐδαίμων Θάψακος ὄνομα. ἐνταῦθα
ἔμεινεν ἡμέρας πέντε. καὶ Κῦρος μεταπεμψάμενος τοὺς στρα-
75 τηγοὺς τῶν Ἑλλήνων ἔλεγεν ὅτι ἡ ὁδὸς ἔσοιτο πρὸς βασιλέα
μέγαν εἰς Βαβυλῶνα· καὶ κελεύει αὐτοὺς λέγειν ταῦτα τοῖς
στρατιώταις καὶ ἀναπείθειν ἕπεσθαι. οἱ δὲ ποιήσαντες ἐκκλη- 12
σίαν ἀπήγγελλον ταῦτα· οἱ δὲ στρατιῶται ἐχαλέπαινον τοῖς
στρατηγοῖς, καὶ ἔφασαν αὐτοὺς πάλαι ταῦτ' εἰδότας κρύπτειν,

praebeat, haec in collum, haec in crinis. *Cf. Anab.* II, 4, § 27.

68 ἦσαν ... βασίλεια; see the note on ἦν, c. 2. 38.

ἄρξαντος : note the tense; a previous ruler must be meant, or, possibly, Belesys had relinquished his authority and fled as Cyrus approached.

Συρίας : for the case, *cf.* c. 1. 37, and the note.

παράδεισος: *cf.* c. 2. 38, and the note.

69 ἔχων ... φύουσι : the Greek loved the beauty of a rich vegetation; a barren, treeless land oppressed him. Herodotus (IV, 61) speaks of the steppes of Scythia as γῆ αἰνῶς ἄξυλος (*terribly treeless*). Xenophon's enthusiasm is, therefore, natural.

ὧραι: the art. is often omitted with words which denote time in a general sense.

70 αὐτόν : *i. e.* τὸν παράδεισον.

72 σταδίων : see the note on στάδιον, l. 4. The word may here be due to an error, as the width of the river at this place is now about 400 ft., *i. e.*, four *plethra*.

73 αὐτόθι : *cf.* l. 37, and the note.

Θάψακος : see the Introd., § 29.

ὄνομα : here acc., but in I, 5, § 4 it is nom. *Cf.* the two constructions of εὖρος (see c. 2. 30, and the note).

75 ἔσοιτο : direct, ἔσται. The use of the opt. in this tense is always due to the law of indir. disc.

βασιλέα : no art., even when used with an epithet; see the note on c. 2. 43. Observe the prep. used; πρός is more personal than εἰς.

77 ἀναπείθειν, *try to induce.*

ποιήσαντες ἐκκλησίαν: *cf. συνήγαγεν ἐκκλησίαν*, c. 3. 8.

78 ἐχαλέπαινον : perhaps no more than *made a show of anger*, for they must have seen the truth for some time past. Still by this attitude they hope to extort from Cyrus a promise of higher pay; and they are mercenaries, after all. For the dat., στρατηγοῖς, see G. 1159; H. 764, 2; B. 376.

79 πάλαι ... κρύπτειν, *had long been hiding.* For the pres., with πάλαι, see G. 1258; H. 826; B. 522. *Cf.* the similar use of *iam dudum*, in Latin.

καὶ οὐκ ἔφασαν ἰέναι, ἐὰν μή τις αὐτοῖς χρήματα διδῷ, ὥσπερ 80
τοῖς προτέροις μετὰ Κύρου ἀναβᾶσι, καὶ ταῦτα οὐκ ἐπὶ μάχην
ἰόντων, ἀλλὰ καλοῦντος τοῦ πατρὸς Κῦρον. ταῦτα οἱ στρατηγοὶ Κύρῳ ἀπήγγελλον. ὁ δ' ὑπέσχετο ἀνδρὶ ἑκάστῳ δώσειν
πέντε ἀργυρίου μνᾶς, ἐπὰν εἰς Βαβυλῶνα ἥκωσι, καὶ τὸν μισθὸν
ἐντελῆ μέχρι ἂν καταστήσῃ τοὺς Ἕλληνας εἰς Ἰωνίαν πάλιν. 85
τὸ μὲν δὴ πολὺ τοῦ Ἑλληνικοῦ οὕτως ἐπείσθη.

Μένων δὲ πρὶν δῆλον εἶναι τί ποιήσουσιν οἱ ἄλλοι στρατιῶται, πότερον ἕψονται Κύρῳ ἢ οὔ, συνέλεξε τὸ αὑτοῦ στρά-

εἰδότας: concessive, *although knowing*.
80 οὐκ ἔφασαν ἰέναι: *cf.* c. 3. 2, and the note.
ἐὰν μή τις διδῷ: *cf.* c. 1. 15, and the note. τις is, of course, Cyrus; but they are more concerned with the gift than with the giver.
χρήματα, *bounty, largess*, not *pay* (μισθός).
81 τοῖς προτέροις ... ἀναβᾶσι, lit., *the former ones who went up;* but see c. 3. 95, τῶν πρόσθεν ἀναβάντων, *those who went up before*. There is no real difference in meaning. Greek often prefers an adj. in cases where Eng. calls for an adv.; see the note on προτέρα, c. 2. 142. The reference is, of course, to the expedition mentioned in I, 1, § 2.
καὶ ταῦτα, *and that too*.
82 ἰόντων: sc. ἐκείνων. The gen. abs. frequently stands where we might have looked for a case in agreement (here ἰοῦσι). The partic. is again concessive; καλοῦντος, below, is causal.
83 ὑπέσχετο δώσειν: *cf.* c. 2. 11, and the note.
84 πέντε μνᾶς: not far from $100.

ἀργυρίου: gen. of material (G. 1085, 4; H. 729 f.; B. 352, with the note).
ἐπὰν ... ἥκωσι, *when they should reach Babylon*. The direct form is retained, as so often. *Cf.* μέχρι ἂν καταστήσῃ, below.
μισθὸν ἐντελῆ: *i. e.* the daric and a half, already promised (c. 3. 110), paid in full even after their service was properly over. From the Greek point of view this was munificence indeed, and doubts might easily arise on reflection (see I, 7, § 5); but, for the present, they are won.
86 τὸ ... πολύ, *the greater part* (G. 967; H. 665).
μὲν δή: *cf.* c. 1. 16, and the note.
87 πρὶν δῆλον εἶναι: for the constructions of πρίν, see the notes on πρὶν ἂν ... συμβουλεύσηται, c. 1. 58 f., and on πρὶν ἔπεισε, c. 2. 154. *Cf.* this same phrase 7 lines below, and also l. 102.
τί: the direct interrogative in an indir. quest. (G. 1012; H. 700; B. 490); below, in the same connection, we have the more regular ὅ,τι.
88 πότερον ... ἤ, *whether ... or*, a further explanation of τί ποιή-

τευμα χωρὶς τῶν ἄλλων καὶ ἔλεξε τάδε. "Ἄνδρες, ἐάν μοι 14
90 πεισθῆτε, οὔτε κινδυνεύσαντες οὔτε πονήσαντες τῶν ἄλλων
πλέον προτιμήσεσθε στρατιωτῶν ὑπὸ Κύρου. τί οὖν κελεύω
ποιῆσαι; νῦν δεῖται Κῦρος ἕπεσθαι τοὺς Ἕλληνας ἐπὶ βασιλέα·
ἐγὼ οὖν φημι ὑμᾶς χρῆναι διαβῆναι τὸν Εὐφράτην ποταμὸν
πρὶν δῆλον εἶναι ὅ,τι οἱ ἄλλοι Ἕλληνες ἀποκρινοῦνται Κύρῳ.
95 ἢν μὲν γὰρ ψηφίσωνται ἕπεσθαι, ὑμεῖς δόξετε αἴτιοι εἶναι 15
ἄρξαντες τοῦ διαβαίνειν, καὶ ὡς προθυμοτάτοις οὖσιν ὑμῖν χάριν
εἴσεται Κῦρος καὶ ἀποδώσει· ἐπίσταται δ' εἴ τις καὶ ἄλλος· ἢν
δὲ ἀποψηφίσωνται οἱ ἄλλοι, ἄπιμεν μὲν ἅπαντες τοὔμπαλιν,
ὑμῖν δὲ ὡς μόνοις πειθομένοις πιστοτάτοις χρήσεται καὶ εἰς
100 φρούρια καὶ εἰς λοχαγίας, καὶ ἄλλου οὗτινος ἂν δέησθε οἶδα ὅτι

σουσιν; see G. 1606; H. 1017;
B. 579.

οὔ: for the accent, see G. 138, 1;
H. 112a; B. 69, 1.

89 χωρὶς τῶν ἄλλων: *cf.* λάθρᾳ, c. 3.
38, and the note.

90 πεισθῆτε: deponent, not passive,
hearken to, obey.

οὔτε ... πονήσαντες, *without incurring either toil or danger.*

τῶν ἄλλων ... στρατιωτῶν: the
gen. is due to the comp. vb.
(G. 1132; H. 751; B. 370), and
the meaning is further emphasized by the redundant πλέον
(which would itself call for a
gen.; see on Κύρου, c. 2. 142). *Cf.*
I, 6, § 5, προτιμηθῆναι μάλιστα τῶν
Ἑλλήνων. For the fut. mid.,
used as a pass., *cf.* στερήσονται,
l. 56, and the note.

91 τί οὖν ... ποιῆσαι: a rhetorical
question.

92 δεῖται: with acc. and infin., asks
that the Greeks follow. The
construction with gen. and infin.
(*asks of the Greeks that they
follow*) is commoner. See, *e. g.,*
c. 2. 82 f., and the note.

93 ἐγώ: strongly emphatic.

χρῆναι: quoted after φημί, and
itself governing διαβῆναι.

96 ἄρξαντες, *because you began.*
For τοῦ διαβαίνειν, see G. 1547; H.
959; B. 639; for the case, G. 1099;
H. 738; B. 356.

καὶ ὡς ... ἀποδώσει, *and to you,
as being the most zealous, Cyrus will feel gratitude and will
show it.* Cf. the Lat. phrases,
gratias habere and *gratias
referre.* ὡς gives us Cyrus'
thought; so, below, l. 101.

97 ἐπίσταται: sc. χάριν ἀποδοῦναι.

εἴ τις καὶ ἄλλος: *cf.* c. 3. 80, and the
note.

98 ἀποψηφίσωνται: for the neg.
force of the prep., *cf.* ἀπεγνωκέναι
(I, 7, § 19) and ἀποδόξῃ (II, 3, § 9).

ἅπαντες, *all alike, i. e., we no less
than they.*

τοὔμπαλιν: by crasis (G. 42; H.
76; B. 43) for τὸ ἔμπαλιν.

99 ὑμῖν: emphatic.

πιστοτάτοις, *as most trustworthy.*

100 φρούρια ... λοχαγίας: desirable positions.

καὶ ἄλλου ... δέησθε, *and what-*

16 ὡς φίλοι τεύξεσθε Κύρου. ἀκούσαντες ταῦτα ἐπείθοντο καὶ διέβησαν πρὶν τοὺς ἄλλους ἀποκρίνασθαι. Κῦρος δ' ἐπεὶ ᾔσθετο διαβεβηκότας, ἥσθη τε καὶ τῷ στρατεύματι πέμψας Γλοῦν εἶπεν· Ἐγὼ μέν, ὦ ἄνδρες, ἤδη ὑμᾶς ἐπαινῶ· ὅπως δὲ καὶ ὑμεῖς ἐμὲ ἐπαινέσετε ἐμοὶ μελήσει, ἢ μηκέτι με Κῦρον 105
17 νομίζετε. οἱ μὲν δὴ στρατιῶται ἐν ἐλπίσι μεγάλαις ὄντες ηὔχοντο αὐτὸν εὐτυχῆσαι, Μένωνι δὲ καὶ δῶρα ἐλέγετο πέμψαι μεγαλοπρεπῶς. ταῦτα δὲ ποιήσας διέβαινε· συνείπετο δὲ καὶ τὸ ἄλλο στράτευμα αὐτῷ ἅπαν. καὶ τῶν διαβαινόντων τὸν ποταμὸν οὐδεὶς ἐβρέχθη ἀνωτέρω τῶν μαστῶν ὑπὸ τοῦ ποταμοῦ. 110
18 οἱ δὲ Θαψακηνοὶ ἔλεγον ὅτι οὐπώποθ' οὗτος ὁ ποταμὸς διαβατὸς γένοιτο πεζῇ εἰ μὴ τότε, ἀλλὰ πλοίοις, ἃ τότε Ἀβροκό-

---

ever else you may want. Cf. ὅ,τι ἂν δέῃ, c. 3. 24, and the note.
ἄλλου is generally explained as an instance of inverse attraction (G. 1035; H. 1003; B. 484, 2), but τεύξεσθε may itself properly take a gen. (e. g. I, 9, § 29). Similarly Κύρου may be taken as dependent on φίλοι, or as expressing the source (with τεύξεσθέ).
103 διαβεβηκότας (sc. αὐτούς), that they had crossed. For the partic. in indir. disc., cf. ἔχοντα, c. 2. 127, and the note. With the partic. αἰσθάνομαι denotes actual perception; contrast ᾔσθετο ὅτι, c. 2. 125.
ἥσθη: cf. ἠγάσθη, c. 1. 45, and the note.
104 Γλοῦν: he was the son of Tamos, Cyrus' admiral.
ἐγὼ ... ὑμᾶς ... ὑμεῖς ἐμέ: all strongly emphatic. For the chiastic order, see the Introd., § 39.
ὅπως ... ἐπαινέσετε: obj. clause after μελήσει; see the note on βουλεύεται ὅπως ... ἔσται, c. 1. 14. The obj. clause takes the place of the usual gen. with the

impers. μέλει (G. 1105; H. 742; B. 356). Cf. I, 8, § 13, end.
107 ηὔχοντο ... εὐτυχῆσαι: c,. ηὔχοντο ... ληφθῆναι, l. 45.
ἐλέγετο πέμψαι: for the pers. construction, see c. 2. 47, and the note.
108 μεγαλοπρεπῶς, in princely fashion.
109 ἅπαν: emphatic by postponement. They did not propose to sever connections with their paymaster.
110 τῶν μαστῶν: gen. with the comp. ἀνωτέρω. The pl. is used, because μαστός does not mean breast (i. e. chest), but one of the breasts.
ὑπό: a slight personification.
112 γένοιτο, had been, opt. in indir. disc.; the aor. instead of the plpf., as often.
εἰ μή, except.
ἀλλὰ πλοίοις: sc. διαβατὸς γένοιτο. A pontoon bridge had been built here by Xerxes.
ἃ ... διαβῇ: a statement added by Xen., not, of course, included in the quotation. The use of

μας προϊὼν κατέκαυσεν, ἵνα μὴ Κῦρος διαβῇ. ἐδόκει δὴ θεῖον εἶναι καὶ σαφῶς ὑποχωρῆσαι τὸν ποταμὸν Κύρῳ ὡς βασιλεύ- 115 σοντι.

Ἐντεῦθεν ἐξελαύνει διὰ τῆς Συρίας σταθμοὺς ἐννέα παρα- 19 σάγγας πεντήκοντα· καὶ ἀφικνοῦνται πρὸς τὸν Ἀράξην ποταμόν. ἐνταῦθα ἦσαν κῶμαι πολλαὶ μεσταὶ σίτου καὶ οἴνου. ἐνταῦθα ἔμειναν ἡμέρας τρεῖς καὶ ἐπεσιτίσαντο.

V. Ἐντεῦθεν ἐξελαύνει διὰ τῆς Ἀραβίας τὸν Εὐφράτην 1 ποταμὸν ἐν δεξιᾷ ἔχων σταθμοὺς ἐρήμους πέντε παρασάγγας τριάκοντα καὶ πέντε. ἐν τούτῳ δὲ τῷ τόπῳ ἦν μὲν ἡ γῆ πεδίον ἅπαν ὁμαλὲς ὥσπερ θάλαττα, ἀψινθίου δὲ πλῆρες· εἰ δέ τι καὶ 5 ἄλλο ἐνῆν ὕλης ἢ καλάμου, ἅπαντα ἦσαν εὐώδη ὥσπερ ἀρώματα· δένδρον δ' οὐδὲν ἐνῆν, θηρία δὲ παντοῖα, πλεῖστοι ὄνοι 2

the subj., rather than the opt., in final clauses, after secondary tenses, is a mark of vividness; the past is treated as present.

113 ἐδόκει . . . βασιλεύσοντι, *it seemed a miracle, and that the river had plainly given way before Cyrus, as before one who was to be king.* The river is said to be highest about the end of May and lowest in November. At its lowest there are but two feet of water or even less. It was now about the end of July, so the river might still be flowing somewhat full. This was doubtless the cause of the amazement of the natives, but allowance must be made for oriental exaggeration and flattery. Years later (69 B.C.) Lucullus and his army forded the river as Cyrus did, and Plutarch (*Lucull.* 24) tells a story similar to this. Alexander crossed by means of boats.

118 μεσταί: with the gen., as πλήρης, c. 2. 39.

119 ἐπεσιτίσαντο: for they now enter the desert of Arabia. Today the region through which they have been passing is also a desert.

CHAPTER V

2 ἔχων, *keeping. Cf.* the note on c. 1. 8.

3 τόπῳ, *region.*

πεδίον ἅπαν ὁμαλές, *wholly a level plain.* ἅπασα, in agreement with γῇ, would be more natural to us.

4 ὥσπερ θάλαττα: reference to the sea was always easy to the Greek.

εἰ δέ τι: equivalent to ὅ,τι δέ, *whatever.*

5 ὕλης, *brush,* as is plain from what follows.

ἅπαντα ἦσαν: see the note on c. 2. 38. For ἅπαντα, after τι, *cf.* πάντας, after ὅστις, c. 1. 18.

εὐώδη: commonly the case in waterless districts.

6 δένδρον: note the position, *trees there were none.* For the

ἄγριοι, πολλαὶ δὲ στρουθοὶ αἱ μεγάλαι· ἐνῆσαν δὲ καὶ ὠτίδες καὶ δορκάδες· ταῦτα δὲ τὰ θηρία οἱ ἱππεῖς ἐνίοτε ἐδίωκον. καὶ οἱ μὲν ὄνοι, ἐπεί τις διώκοι, προδραμόντες ἕστασαν· πολὺ γὰρ τῶν ἵππων ἔτρεχον θᾶττον· καὶ πάλιν, ἐπεὶ πλησιάζοιεν οἱ ἵπποι, ταὐτὸν ἐποίουν, καὶ οὐκ ἦν λαβεῖν, εἰ μὴ διαστάντες οἱ ἱππεῖς θηρῷεν διαδεχόμενοι. τὰ δὲ κρέα τῶν ἁλισκομένων ἦν παραπλήσια τοῖς ἐλαφείοις, ἁπαλώτερα δέ. στρουθὸν δὲ οὐδεὶς ἔλαβεν· οἱ δὲ διώξαντες τῶν ἱππέων ταχὺ ἐπαύοντο· πολὺ γὰρ ἀπέσπα φεύγουσα, τοῖς μὲν ποσὶ δρόμῳ, ταῖς δὲ πτέρυξιν αἴρουσα, ὥσπερ ἱστίῳ χρωμένη. τὰς δὲ ὠτίδας ἄν τις ταχὺ

Greek love of trees, see the note on c. 4 69.

ὄνοι ἄγριοι: still occasionally found in this region.

7 στρουθοὶ αἱ μεγάλαι, *ostriches*, later called στρουθοκάμηλοι. Note the order; αἱ μεγάλαι comes in as an afterthought, added for the sake of clearness. Without it στρουθοί might mean *sparrows*.

8 οἱ ἱππεῖς: the horsemen mentioned below (§ 13), as forming a part of Clearchus' force, are the only ones mentioned in the enumeration of the Greek troops. See the Introd , § 28.

9 ἐπεί τις διώκοι: *cf.* ὁπότε βούλοιτο, c. 2. 40, and the note, and ἐπεὶ πλησιάζοιεν, below.

προδραμόντες ἕστασαν, *would run forward and stop.* ἕστασαν, though plpf. (G. 508; H. 336; B. 258), has the force of an imperf., since the 2nd perf. of ἵστημι is practically a pres.

πολύ: emphatic by position and by its separation from θᾶττον.

11 ταὐτόν: *cf.* the note on τὰ αὐτά, c. 1. 30, and for the crasis, on τοὔμπαλιν, c. 4. 98. In this form the final ν often appears (G. 400; H. 265).

ἦν, *it was possible*; *cf.* c. 4. 24.

διαστάντες, *stationing themselves at intervals*. Note the prep., and *cf.* διαδεχόμενοι, below (*by relays*).

12 θηρῷεν: the opt., as διώκοι and πλησιάζοιεν, above; here conditional, there temporal.

13 τοῖς ἐλαφείοις, *venison* (sc. κρέασι). For the dat., see the note on c. 3. 93.

στρουθόν: note the position; *cf.* τὰς ὠτίδας, below, l. 16.

15 ἀπέσπα, *it drew off* (intrans.).

τοῖς μὲν . . . χρωμένη, lit. *using its feet in running and its wings (raising them) like a sail*. Both ποσί and πτέρυξιν are dats. of means with χρωμένη; δρόμῳ is dat. of manner, and αἴρουσα (sc. αὐτάς, *i. e.* τὰς πτέρυγας), also expressing manner, is added for graphic effect. ἱστίῳ naturally stands in the same case as πτέρυξιν. In reality the ostrich merely steadies itself with its wings.

16 ἄν τις . . . ἀνιστῇ, *if one start*

ἀνιστῇ ἔστι λαμβάνειν· πέτονται γὰρ βραχὺ ὥσπερ πέρδικες καὶ ταχὺ ἀπαγορεύουσι. τὰ δὲ κρέα αὐτῶν ἥδιστα ἦν.

Πορευόμενοι δὲ διὰ ταύτης τῆς χώρας ἀφικνοῦνται ἐπὶ τὸν Μάσκαν ποταμόν, τὸ εὖρος πλεθριαῖον. ἐνταῦθα ἦν πόλις ἐρήμη, μεγάλη, ὄνομα δ' αὐτῇ Κορσωτή· περιερρεῖτο δ' αὕτη ὑπὸ τοῦ Μάσκα κύκλῳ. ἐνταῦθ' ἔμειναν ἡμέρας τρεῖς καὶ ἐπεσιτίσαντο. ἐντεῦθεν ἐξελαύνει σταθμοὺς ἐρήμους τρεῖς καὶ δέκα παρασάγγας ἐνενήκοντα τὸν Εὐφράτην ποταμὸν ἐν δεξιᾷ ἔχων, καὶ ἀφικνεῖται ἐπὶ Πύλας. ἐν τούτοις τοῖς σταθμοῖς πολλὰ τῶν ὑποζυγίων ἀπώλετο ὑπὸ λιμοῦ· οὐ γὰρ ἦν χόρτος οὐδὲ ἄλλο οὐδὲν δένδρον, ἀλλὰ ψιλὴ ἦν ἅπασα ἡ χώρα· οἱ δὲ ἐνοικοῦντες ὄνους ἀλέτας παρὰ τὸν ποταμὸν ὀρύττοντες καὶ ποιοῦντες εἰς Βαβυλῶνα ἦγον καὶ ἐπώλουν καὶ ἀνταγοράζοντες

---

them up suddenly, a pres. general condit.

17 ἔστι: cf. ἦν, above, l. 11, and, for the accent, c. 2. 43, and the note.

18 ἀπαγορεύουσι, give out.

ἦν: the past tense resumes the narrative, after the general statements.

20 πλεθριαῖον: equivalent to πλέθρου; see the note on δύο πλέθρα, c. 2. 30 f. The adj. and the gen. are in many uses very nearly interchangeable.

21 ἐρήμη: of a city, this would naturally mean uninhabited (III, 4, § 10), yet they remain here three days and take in supplies. Perhaps the word means no more than in σταθμοὺς ἐρήμους, l. 2 (here, situated in the desert?), or had the inhabitants fled at Cyrus' approach? This, however, Xen. would surely have stated plainly (cf. c. 2. 139). πόλις ἐρήμη forms one idea, so there is no connective between it and the following adj.

ὄνομα δ' αὐτῇ: sc. ἦν. ὄνομα varies in construction, as εὖρος does.

περιερρεῖτο ὑπό: the act. of this vb. is treated as trans., so the passive construction is legitimate.

22 Μάσκα: see the note on Ἀβροκόμα, c. 4. 15.

23 ἐπεσιτίσαντο: this region is now a desert.

24 ἐνενήκοντα: very rapid marching; cf. below, § 7.

26 ὑπὸ λιμοῦ: preferred to λιμῷ, because of the slight personification.

27 οὐδ' ἄλλο οὐδὲν δένδρον, nor any tree either. For this idiomatic use of ἄλλος, see G. 966, 2; H. 705; B. 492 note 2.

28 ὄνους ἀλέτας, (upper) millstones. ἀλέτας is properly a noun, but it serves as an adj. The lower mill-stone was fixed; the upper one revolved upon it and was often turned by an ass; hence the name.

29 ποιοῦντες, shaping.

6 σῖτον ἔζων. τὸ δὲ στράτευμα ὁ σῖτος ἐπέλιπε, καὶ πρίασθαι οὐκ ἦν εἰ μὴ ἐν τῇ Λυδίᾳ ἀγορᾷ ἐν τῷ Κύρου βαρβαρικῷ, τὴν καπίθην ἀλεύρων ἢ ἀλφίτων τεττάρων σίγλων. ὁ δὲ σίγλος δύναται ἕπτ' ὀβολοὺς καὶ ἡμιωβόλιον Ἀττικούς· ἡ δὲ καπίθη δύο χοίνικας Ἀττικὰς ἐχώρει. κρέα οὖν ἐσθίοντες οἱ στρατιῶται 7 διεγίγνοντο. ἦν δὲ τούτων τῶν σταθμῶν οὓς πάνυ μακροὺς ἤλαυνεν, ὁπότε ἢ πρὸς ὕδωρ βούλοιτο διατελέσαι ἢ πρὸς χιλόν.

Καὶ δή ποτε στενοχωρίας καὶ πηλοῦ φανέντος ταῖς ἁμάξαις

30 **πρίασθαι**: sc. σῖτον.
31 **εἰ μή**, *save; cf.* c. 4. 112.
Λυδίᾳ: the Lydians were "a nation of shop-keepers." Tradition says that Cyrus the Great forbade them the use of arms and led them to devote themselves to such pursuits as would be least apt to keep alive the warlike spirit; see Herod. I, 155.
βαρβαρικῷ: no noun expressed; *cf.* c. 2. 3. For the market, *cf.* c. 3. 68, and the note.
32 **ἀλεύρων ἢ ἀλφίτων**: gens. of material, G. 1085, 4; H. 729f; B. 352 note. Barley meal, with wine, formed the staple food of the Greek soldier. It was ordinarily much cheaper than wheat flour, but, owing to the famine, now cost as much. The price mentioned ($0.45 a quart) was fully fifty times the usual price at Athens.
τεττάρων σίγλων: gen. of price, G. 1133; H. 746; B. 353. The σίγλος (*cf. shekel*) stood in the same relation to the Persian talent that the δραχμή did to the Greek; it was worth about $0.225.
33 **δύναται**, *amounts to*.
34 **κρέα οὖν ... διεγίγνοντο**, *it was by eating meat, therefore, that the soldiers got along*. The Greek ate but little meat (see above, on ἀλφίτων); to be forced to subsist on meat from lack of grain was accordingly a hardship. *Cf.* II, 1, § 6 end, and Caesar, *Gallic War*, VII, 17.
35 **ἦν ... ἤλαυνεν**, *some of these were the longest day's marches Cyrus made* (lit. *there were of these day's marches some which Cyrus marched very long*). For ἦν οὕς, see G. 1029; H. 998; B. 486 note. The rel., of course, takes the case called for by the syntax of the clause in which it stands (here cogn. acc. with ἤλαυνεν), and the vb. remains unchanged. This is common with ἔστιν, and εἰσὶν οἵ (οὕς) also occurs; but ἦν is very rare. μακρούς is, of course, pred.
36 **ὁπότε ... βούλοιτο**: *cf.* c. 2. 40, and the note. In dry countries one must push on until water is reached—a fact scarcely appreciated in regions where springs and streams abound.
38 **καὶ δή ποτε**: δή, as often, singles something out for special mention. *Cf.* c. 3. 65.

δυσπορεύτου ἐπέστη ὁ Κῦρος σὺν τοῖς περὶ αὐτὸν ἀρίστοις καὶ
40 εὐδαιμονεστάτοις καὶ ἔταξε Γλοῦν καὶ Πίγρητα λαβόντας τοῦ
βαρβαρικοῦ στρατοῦ συνεκβιβάζειν τὰς ἁμάξας. ἐπεὶ δ' ἐδόκουν 8
αὐτῷ σχολαίως ποιεῖν, ὥσπερ ὀργῇ ἐκέλευσε τοὺς περὶ αὐτὸν
Πέρσας τοὺς κρατίστους συνεπισπεῦσαι τὰς ἁμάξας. ἔνθα δὴ
μέρος τι τῆς εὐταξίας ἦν θεάσασθαι. ῥίψαντες γὰρ τοὺς πορ-
45 φυροῦς κάνδυς ὅπου ἔτυχεν ἕκαστος ἑστηκώς, ἵεντο ὥσπερ ἄν
δράμοι τις ἐπὶ νίκῃ καὶ μάλα κατὰ πρανοῦς γηλόφου, ἔχοντες
τούς τε πολυτελεῖς χιτῶνας καὶ τὰς ποικίλας ἀναξυρίδας, ἔνιοι
δὲ καὶ στρεπτοὺς περὶ τοῖς τραχήλοις καὶ ψέλια περὶ ταῖς
χερσίν· εὐθὺς δὲ σὺν τούτοις εἰσπηδήσαντες εἰς τὸν πηλὸν
50 θᾶττον ἢ ὥς τις ἂν ᾤετο μετεώρους ἐξεκόμισαν τὰς ἁμάξας. τὸ 9

φανέντος; in agreement with the nearer of the two subjs.

ταῖς ἁμάξαις: for the dat., *cf.* στρατεύματι, c. 2. 122.

39 σὺν τοῖς ... εὐδαιμονεστάτοις, *with the noblest and wealthiest of his retinue.*

40 τοῦ ... στρατοῦ: partitive gen., with λαβόντας, G. 1097, 1; H. 736; B. 356.

43 συνεπισπεῦσαι: in commands the aor. is more peremptory than the pres.

ἔνθα δὴ ... θεάσασθαι, *then it was that one might behold.* ... δή is very commonly used with temporal words. θεάσασθαι is stronger than ἰδεῖν.

44 τῆς εὐταξίας: *their (famous) discipline.* Cf. τῇ μάχῃ, c. 2. 50.

πορφοροῦς: *purple (scarlet)* has always been the color of royalty and nobility. For the form of the adj., *cf.* χαλκᾶ, c. 2. 93.

45 κάνδυς: these were long, flowing robes which impeded action.

ὅπου ἔτυχεν ... ἑστηκώς, *where each one happened to be standing.*

Cf. the note on παρὼν ἐτύγχανε, c. 1. 4. Observe the force of the perf. partic.

ὥσπερ ... νίκῃ, *as one would run in a race.* References to the great games are naturally very common in Greek literature. ἂν δράμοι is a potent. opt., for which ἐπὶ νίκῃ supplies a protasis; *cf.* σὺν ὑμῖν, c. 3. 29.

46 καὶ μάλα, *very*, modifying πρᾶνους. καί and μάλα are not to be separated (*cf.* IV, 1, § 23; IV, 6, § 16).

ἔχοντες, *having on.*

47 τούς τε ... καὶ τούς: the art. as with εὐταξίας, above, l. 44. ἀναξυρίδας is another Persian word; *cf.* the note on σατράπην, c. 1. 5.

48 στρεπτοὺς ... ψέλια: both mentioned by Herodotus (IX, 80) as stripped in quantities from the Persian dead at Plataea.

περὶ τοῖς τραχήλοις ... χερσίν: a purely local use of the prep. περί, with the dat., is uncommon in prose.

50 θᾶττον ... ᾤετο, *more quickly*

Book I, Chap. V

δὲ σύμπαν δῆλος ἦν Κῦρος ὡς σπεύδων πᾶσαν τὴν ὁδὸν καὶ οὐ
διατρίβων ὅπου μὴ ἐπισιτισμοῦ ἕνεκα ἤ τινος ἄλλου ἀναγκαίου
ἐκαθέζετο, νομίζων, ὅσῳ θᾶττον ἔλθοι, τοσούτῳ ἀπαρασκευ-
αστοτέρῳ βασιλεῖ μαχεῖσθαι, ὅσῳ δὲ σχολαίτερον, τοσούτῳ
πλέον συναγείρεσθαι βασιλεῖ στράτευμα. καὶ συνιδεῖν δ' ἦν 55
τῷ προσέχοντι τὸν νοῦν ἡ βασιλέως ἀρχὴ πλήθει μὲν χώρας καὶ
ἀνθρώπων ἰσχυρὰ οὖσα, τοῖς δὲ μήκεσι τῶν ὁδῶν καὶ τῷ διεσπάσθαι τὰς δυνάμεις ἀσθενής, εἴ τις διὰ ταχέων τὸν πόλεμον
ἐποιεῖτο.

---

than one would have thought. For the potential indic., see G. 1335-1337; B. 565. ὡς is redundant and should be omitted in translating.

μετεώρους ἐξεκόμισαν, they lifted up and bore out. For the use of the pred. adj., see G. 972; H. 618; B. 453, 1.

τὸ δὲ σύμπαν, and in general (adv. acc.).

51 δῆλος ... σπεύδων, Cyrus showed that he was hastening. δῆλος, used personally, takes a partic. (cf. c. 2. 70, and the note); used impersonally, it takes ὅτι with a finite vb. (cf. c. 3. 44). It is very unusual to have ὡς expressed with the partic., in the former construction, as here.

πᾶσαν τὴν ὁδόν: acc. of extent.

52 διατρίβων: construed as σπεύδων, above.

ὅπου μή, except where. The rel. is often equivalent to a conditional clause (e. g. ὅστις=εἴ τις); so this phrase is equivalent to εἰ μή που. Similarly, l. 4, we had the condit. equivalent to the rel.

53 νομίζων ... μαχεῖσθαι, thinking that the more quickly he should advance the more unprepared he should find (lit. fight against) the king. With ὅσῳ ... τοσούτῳ, cf. quanto ... tanto, and consult the note on ἡμέραις, c. 2. 142.

55 συναγείρεσθαι, was being collected. Note the change of tense.

βασιλεῖ: dat. of advantage, rather than of the agent.

καὶ συνιδεῖν ... τὸν νοῦν, and moreover (καί) one who gave close attention could see at a glance (συν-). For the dat., see G. 1172; H. 771; B. 382.

56 ἡ βασιλέως ἀρχὴ ... οὖσα, that the king's empire was. The nom. partic. follows, as though δήλη ἦν (cf. l. 51) had preceded, instead of συνιδεῖν ἦν.

πλήθει: G. 1182; H. 780; B. 390. The word goes both with χώρας (extent) and with ἀνθρώπων (multitude). μήκεσι and τῷ διεσπάσθαι stand in this same construction.

57 τῷ ... δυνάμεις, in the dispersion of its forces. For the infin. with the art., cf. c. 1. 35, and the note.

58 διὰ ταχέων: cf. ἀπὸ τοῦ αὐτομάτου, c. 2. 100, and the note.

59 ἐποιεῖτο: for the mood, cf. ἐκώλυεν, c. 2. 122; the condition is felt as logical rather than as general.

Πέραν δὲ τοῦ Εὐφράτου ποταμοῦ κατὰ τοὺς ἐρήμους σταθμοὺς ἦν πόλις εὐδαίμων καὶ μεγάλη, ὄνομα δὲ Χαρμάνδη· ἐκ
ταύτης οἱ στρατιῶται ἠγόραζον τὰ ἐπιτήδεια, σχεδίαις διαβαί-
νοντες ὧδε. διφθέρας ἃς εἶχον στεγάσματα ἐπίμπλασαν χόρτου
κούφου, εἶτα συνῆγον καὶ συνέσπων, ὡς μὴ ἅπτεσθαι τῆς κάρφης
τὸ ὕδωρ· ἐπὶ τούτων διέβαινον καὶ ἐλάμβανον τὰ ἐπιτήδεια,
οἶνόν τε ἐκ τῆς βαλάνου πεποιημένον τῆς ἀπὸ τοῦ φοίνικος καὶ
σῖτον μελίνης· τοῦτο γὰρ ἦν ἐν τῇ χώρᾳ πλεῖστον.

Ἀμφιλεξάντων δέ τι ἐνταῦθα τῶν τε τοῦ Μένωνος στρατιωτῶν καὶ τῶν τοῦ Κλεάρχου ὁ Κλέαρχος κρίνας ἀδικεῖν τὸν τοῦ
Μένωνος πληγὰς ἐνέβαλεν· ὁ δὲ ἐλθὼν πρὸς τὸ ἑαυτοῦ στρά-

---

60 τοῦ ποταμοῦ: gen. with πέραν, an improper prep., like λάθρᾳ, c. 3. 38.

61 ὄνομα: nom. or acc.?

62 ἠγόραζον: the supplies already laid in must have been nearly, or quite, exhausted.

63 ὧδε: *cf.* c. 1. 24, and the note. With what follows *cf.* II, 4, § 28, and III, 5, § 9, and the description, in Arrian (*An.* III, 29), of Alexander's crossing the Oxus. Inflated skins have long been used in Eastern countries (where wood is scarce), as a means of crossing rivers, whether singly, as a support for the individual swimmer, or collectively, as rafts or bridges. An account of methods, strikingly similar to those described in the text, in the German army of our own day, is given in the *Illustrierte Zeitung* for 1895, no. 2718 (Vollbrecht).

ἃς εἶχον στεγάσματα, *which they had as (tent-) coverings*.

χόρτου: for the case, *cf.* θηρίων, c. 2. 39.

64 συνέσπων, *sewed together*. Arrian uses ξυρράψαι, of the same act.

ὡς: for ὥστε, a usage rare in most prose writers, (G. 1456; H. 1054, 1 f.; B. 595; 645). See, further, the note on c. 1. 19, and, for the neg., on c. 1. 57.

κάρφης: for the case, see G. 1099; H. 738; B. 356.

66 τῆς βαλάνου ... τῆς ἀπὸ τοῦ φοίνικος, *the date*. For this the Greek has no word, hence the specifying phrase added to βάλανος (*nut*). Note the formal attrib. posit., and the exact use of the preps. ἐκ and ἀπό. Palm wine is said still to be much used in this region; *cf.* II, 3, § 14, where it is called simply οἶνος φοινίκων.

67 μελίνης: descript. gen. with σῖτον.

τοῦτο: neut., although referring to μελίνης, a construction always allowable in the case of words designating things.

68 ἀμφιλεξάντων τι, *having had some quarrel*. τι is, of course, the inner obj.

69 κρίνας ... ἐνέβαλεν, *deciding that Menon's man was in the*

τευμα ἔλεγεν· ἀκούσαντες δὲ οἱ στρατιῶται ἐχαλέπαινον καὶ
12 ὠργίζοντο ἰσχυρῶς τῷ Κλεάρχῳ. τῇ δὲ αὐτῇ ἡμέρᾳ Κλέαρχος
ἐλθὼν ἐπὶ τὴν διάβασιν τοῦ ποταμοῦ καὶ ἐκεῖ κατασκεψάμενος
τὴν ἀγορὰν ἀφιππεύει ἐπὶ τὴν ἑαυτοῦ σκηνὴν διὰ τοῦ Μένωνος
στρατεύματος σὺν ὀλίγοις τοῖς περὶ αὐτόν· Κῦρος δὲ οὔπω ἧκεν, 75
ἀλλ' ἔτι προσήλαυνε· τῶν δὲ Μένωνος στρατιωτῶν ξύλα σχίζων
τις ὡς εἶδε Κλέαρχον διελαύνοντα, ἵησι τῇ ἀξίνῃ· καὶ οὗτος μὲν
αὐτοῦ ἥμαρτεν· ἄλλος δὲ λίθῳ καὶ ἄλλος, εἶτα πολλοί, κραυγῆς
13 γενομένης. ὁ δὲ καταφεύγει εἰς τὸ ἑαυτοῦ στράτευμα, καὶ
εὐθὺς παραγγέλλει εἰς τὰ ὅπλα· καὶ τοὺς μὲν ὁπλίτας αὐτοῦ 80
ἐκέλευσε μεῖναι τὰς ἀσπίδας πρὸς τὰ γόνατα θέντας, αὐτὸς δὲ
λαβὼν τοὺς Θρᾷκας καὶ τοὺς ἱππέας οἳ ἦσαν αὐτῷ ἐν τῷ στρα-

---

wrong, flogged him. The sing., τόν, implies that the original dispute was between two men only. The flogging was doubtless done with the staff (βακτηρίᾳ), which the Spartan commander regularly carried; *cf.* II, 3, § 11—another instance of the severity of Clearchus, for which see also II, 6, § 9, and the Introd., § 38. Such occurrences were not rare: Xenophon was himself accused of having flogged soldiers; see his defense in V, 8, § 1.

72 **ἡμέρᾳ**: dat. of time; see the note on ὑστεραίᾳ, c. 2. 124.

73 **διάβασιν**: the word, properly designating the act of crossing, comes, by an easy extension, to include the means of crossing (II, 3, § 10), or as here, the place of crossing.

74 **ἀγοράν**: evidently the sutlers, bringing food across the river from Charmande, had arranged a market where they landed.

75 **ὀλίγοις**: pred., *being few, who were but few.*

77 **διελαύνοντα**, *as he rode through*

(*the camp*), a circumstantial partic.

ἵησι ... ἀξίνῃ: with vbs. of throwing or pelting the word denoting the missile is often omitted, or, if expressed, is, as a rule, not acc., but dat. (means). The person or thing pelted is regularly the dir. obj , *e. g.* c. 3. 5, which, in the case of ἵημι, would be a gen. See the note on κάρφης, l. 64.

78 **αὐτοῦ**: gen. with ἥμαρτεν, classed by some as partitive (see the references just given), by others, more correctly, as abl. (H. 748).

λίθῳ: sc. ἵησι.

79 **καταφεύγει**, *fled for refuge* (κατα-).

80 **αὐτοῦ**, *where they were.* The hoplites were to act as a reserve to be called upon, if needed. They form in readiness to advance, the spear grasped in the right hand and the shield on the left arm with its base resting on the left knee.

82 **τοὺς Θρᾷκας**: mere barbarian

τεύματι πλείους ἢ τετταράκοντα, τούτων δὲ οἱ πλεῖστοι Θρᾷκες, ἤλαυνεν ἐπὶ τοὺς Μένωνος, ὥστ' ἐκείνους ἐκπεπλῆχθαι καὶ
85 αὐτὸν Μένωνα, καὶ τρέχειν ἐπὶ τὰ ὅπλα· οἱ δὲ καὶ ἕστασαν ἀποροῦντες τῷ πράγματι. ὁ δὲ Πρόξενος—ἔτυχε γὰρ ὕστερος 14 προσιὼν καὶ τάξις αὐτῷ ἑπομένη τῶν ὁπλιτῶν—εὐθὺς οὖν εἰς τὸ μέσον ἀμφοτέρων ἄγων ἔθετο τὰ ὅπλα καὶ ἐδεῖτο τοῦ Κλεάρχου μὴ ποιεῖν ταῦτα. ὁ δ' ἐχαλέπαινεν ὅτι αὐτοῦ ὀλίγου δεή-
90 σαντος καταλευσθῆναι πράως λέγοι τὸ αὐτοῦ πάθος, ἐκέλευσέ τε αὐτὸν ἐκ τοῦ μέσου ἐξίστασθαι. ἐν τούτῳ δ' ἐπῄει καὶ Κῦρος 15 καὶ ἐπύθετο τὸ πρᾶγμα· εὐθὺς δ' ἔλαβε τὰ παλτὰ εἰς τὰς χεῖρας καὶ σὺν τοῖς παροῦσι τῶν πιστῶν ἦκεν ἐλαύνων εἰς τὸ μέσον, καὶ λέγει τάδε. Κλέαρχε καὶ Πρόξενε καὶ οἱ ἄλλοι οἱ 16

---

hirelings, not Greeks. There were 800 of them among Clearchus' troops. Some of them desert (II, 2, § 7).

ἱππέας: only here are mounted troops mentioned as forming a part of Cyrus' Greek forces. They, too, desert (II, 2, § 7).

83 πλείους: for the form, see the note on c. 3. 35.

84 ἐκπεπλῆχθαι, *were filled with terror*. The perf., especially of vbs. of emotion, may denote intense action. Observe that the infin. after ὥστε may denote the actual result (G. M. T. 583).

85 οἱ δέ: as if οἱ μέν had preceded.

ἕστασαν, *stood riveted to the spot* (Dakyns).

86 ὕστερος: *cf.* προτέρα, c. 2. 142, and the note.

87 τάξις . . . ἑπομένη: *sc.* ἔτυχε.

οὖν: resumptive, after the parenthetic words.

88 τὸ μέσον: *cf.* c. 4. 23.

ἔθετο τὰ ὅπλα, *halted under arms*. This is the commonest meaning of the phrase; for a different one, see below, § 17.

ἐδεῖτο, *implored*. For the construction, *cf.* c. 1. 57.

89 αὐτοῦ . . . πάθος, *when he* (Clearchus) *had barely escaped being stoned to death, he* (Proxenus) *spoke lightly of his experience*. ὀλίγου is gen. after δεήσαντος; for the phrase, see the vocab.

90 λέγοι: opt. in a causal sentence; see G. 1506; H. 925b; B. 598, note.

αὐτοῦ refers, with emphasis, to the main subj.

91 τε: thus used, without a balancing τε or καί, τε is rare in prose.

ἐν τούτῳ: *cf.* c. 2. 117, and the note.

92 τὰ παλτά; the Persian warrior regularly carried two spears.

93 τῶν πιστῶν: "*the Faithful*" was a title in Persia for the king's counsellors.

ἐλαύνων, *riding*.

94 οἱ ἄλλοι: in apposition with ὑμεῖς, implied in the vb. Such appositives must take the art., and are often found in connection with vocatives.

Κλέαρχε . . . Πρόξενε: Cyrus

παρόντες Ἕλληνες, οὐκ ἴστε ὅ,τι ποιεῖτε. εἰ γάρ τινα ἀλλήλοις 95
μάχην συνάψετε, νομίζετε ἐν τῇδε τῇ ἡμέρᾳ ἐμέ τε κατακεκόψεσθαι καὶ ὑμᾶς οὐ πολὺ ἐμοῦ ὕστερον· κακῶς γὰρ τῶν
ἡμετέρων ἐχόντων πάντες οὗτοι οὓς ὁρᾶτε βάρβαροι πολεμιώ-
τεροι ἡμῖν ἔσονται τῶν παρὰ βασιλεῖ ὄντων. ἀκούσας ταῦτα
ὁ Κλέαρχος ἐν ἑαυτῷ ἐγένετο· καὶ παυσάμενοι ἀμφότεροι κατὰ 100
χώραν ἔθεντο τὰ ὅπλα.

VI. Ἐντεῦθεν προϊόντων ἐφαίνετο ἴχνια ἵππων καὶ κόπρος.
ἠκάζετο δ᾽ εἶναι ὁ στίβος ὡς δισχιλίων ἵππων. οὗτοι προϊόντες ἔκαιον καὶ χιλὸν καὶ εἴ τι ἄλλο χρήσιμον ἦν. Ὀρόντας
δὲ Πέρσης ἀνὴρ γένει τε προσήκων βασιλεῖ καὶ τὰ πολέμια
λεγόμενος ἐν τοῖς ἀρίστοις Περσῶν ἐπιβουλεύει Κύρῳ καὶ 5

---

thinks that the quarrel is between these two. Menon does not appear as an aggressor.

95 εἰ συνάψετε: in conditional clauses implying a warning or a threat, εἰ, with the fut. indic., is regularly preferred to ἐάν, with the subjv.; see G. 1405.

96 ἐν ... ἡμέρᾳ, in the course of this day, slightly different from the simple dat. of time.

κατακεκόψεσθαι: the fut. perf. stands as a strong fut., with stress on the permanence of the result (and that will be the end of it), G. 1266; H. 855b; B. 538, note.

97 κακῶς ... ἐχόντων: the gen. abs. supplies a protasis to ἔσονται.

98 οὓς ὁρᾶτε; a direct appeal; there may well have been friction between the two armies.

99 τῶν ... ὄντων, than those with the king are; see G. 1155; H. 643b; B. 426, note 2.

ἀκούσας ταῦτα: no connective is needed.

100 ἐν ἑαυτῷ ἐγένετο, came to his senses.

κατὰ χώραν, in their quarters.
101 ἔθεντο τὰ ὅπλα, grounded their arms; cf. 1, 10, § 16.

CHAPTER VI

1 προϊόντων, as they advanced. The subj. of the partic., in this construction, may be omitted, whenever it is readily supplied by the context.

ἐφαίνετο, there kept appearing. For the sing. vb., cf. ἦν, c. 2. 38, and the note.

2 ὡς, about; cf. c. 2. 18.

ἵππων: pred. gen. of possession.

οὗτοι: ἵπποι, of course, implies ἱππεῖς.

προϊόντες, going on in advance of them; slightly different from προϊόντων, above.

3 εἴ τι ἄλλο, whatever else; cf. c. 5. 4, and the note.

4 γένει: dat. of respect; G. 1182; H. 780; B. 390.

τὰ πολέμια, in matters pertaining to war; acc. of respect.

5 λεγόμενος, reckoned.

καὶ πρόσθεν, formerly also (as well as now).

πρόσθεν πολεμήσας, καταλλαγεὶς δέ. οὗτος Κύρῳ εἶπεν, εἰ 2
αὐτῷ δοίη ἱππέας χιλίους, ὅτι τοὺς προκατακαίοντας ἱππέας
ἢ κατακαίνοι ἂν ἐνεδρεύσας ἢ ζῶντας πολλοὺς αὐτῶν ἂν ἕλοι
καὶ κωλύσειε τοῦ καίειν ἐπιόντας, καὶ ποιήσειεν ὥστε μήποτε
δύνασθαι αὐτοὺς ἰδόντας τὸ Κύρου στράτευμα βασιλεῖ διαγ-
γεῖλαι. τῷ δὲ Κύρῳ ἀκούσαντι ταῦτα ἐδόκει ὠφέλιμα εἶναι,
καὶ ἐκέλευεν αὐτὸν λαμβάνειν μέρος παρ' ἑκάστου τῶν ἡγεμόνων. ὁ δ' Ὀρόντας νομίσας ἑτοίμους εἶναι αὐτῷ τοὺς ἱππέας 3
γράφει ἐπιστολὴν παρὰ βασιλέα ὅτι ἥξοι ἔχων ἱππεῖς ὡς ἂν
δύνηται πλείστους· ἀλλὰ φράσαι τοῖς αὐτοῦ ἱππεῦσιν ἐκέλευεν
ὡς φίλιον αὐτὸν ὑποδέχεσθαι. ἐνῆν δὲ ἐν τῇ ἐπιστολῇ καὶ τῆς
πρόσθεν φιλίας ὑπομνήματα καὶ πίστεως. ταύτην τὴν ἐπιστολὴν δίδωσι πιστῷ ἀνδρί, ὡς ᾤετο· ὁ δὲ λαβὼν Κύρῳ δίδωσιν.
ἀναγνοὺς δὲ αὐτὴν ὁ Κῦρος συλλαμβάνει Ὀρόνταν, καὶ συγκαλεῖ 4
εἰς τὴν ἑαυτοῦ σκηνὴν Πέρσας τοὺς ἀρίστους τῶν περὶ αὐτὸν
ἑπτά, καὶ τοὺς τῶν Ἑλλήνων στρατηγοὺς ἐκέλευσενό πλίτας

6 καταλλαγείς: cf. συναλλαγέντι, c. 2. 5.

εἰ . . . δοίη: this clause forms part of the quotation, despite its position before ὅτι. It is unusual to have ὅτι so far postponed, although a single word is not infrequently placed before it for emphasis. Cf., however, II, 2, § 20.

8 κατακαίνοι: a poetical vb., used by Xen. alone among Attic prose writers. In his works, however, it is not infrequent. He has the simple καίνω (III, 2, § 39). ἄν, expressed with this vb. and with the following ἕλοι, is to be supplied also with κωλύσειε and with ποιήσειεν. In general, if expressed with one opt., ἄν may be omitted with others immediately following, in the same construction.

9 τοῦ καίειν ἐπιόντας, from burning as they advanced. The partic. agrees with the omitted subj. of καίειν. For the infin. with τοῦ, see the note on τοῦ διαβαίνειν, c. 4. 96, and add G. 1549; H. 963, 2; B. 643, 2.

ποιήσειεν . . . αὐτούς, would bring it about that they should never be able. The same construction occurs below, c. 6. 34; oftener ὥστε is omitted.

11 ἐδόκει: personal; ταῦτα is subj.

12 τῶν ἡγεμόνων: i. e., of course, from the Persian, not the Greek, commanders.

14 ἥξοι: direct ἥξω; but in δύνηται the mood of dir. disc. is retained.

ὡς ἂν . . . πλείστους: cf. c. 1. 22, and the note.

15 φράσαι: the subj. is αὐτόν, i. e., βασιλέα. This infin. governs ὑποδέχεσθαι.

21 ἑπτά: limiting τοὺς ἀρίστους.

ἀγαγεῖν, τούτους δὲ θέσθαι τὰ ὅπλα περὶ τὴν αὑτοῦ σκηνήν. οἳ δὲ ταῦτα ἐποίησαν, ἀγαγόντες ὡς τρισχιλίους ὁπλίτας.

5 Κλέαρχον δὲ καὶ εἴσω παρεκάλεσε σύμβουλον, ὅς γε καὶ αὐτῷ καὶ τοῖς ἄλλοις ἐδόκει προτιμηθῆναι μάλιστα τῶν Ἑλλή- νων. ἐπεὶ δ' ἐξῆλθεν, ἀπήγγειλε τοῖς φίλοις τὴν κρίσιν τοῦ 6 Ὀρόντα ὡς ἐγένετο· οὐ γὰρ ἀπόρρητον ἦν. ἔφη δὲ Κῦρον ἄρχειν τοῦ λόγου ὧδε. Παρεκάλεσα ὑμᾶς, ἄνδρες φίλοι, ὅπως σὺν ὑμῖν βουλευόμενος ὅ,τι δίκαιόν ἐστι καὶ πρὸς θεῶν καὶ πρὸς ἀνθρώπων, τοῦτο πράξω περὶ Ὀρόντα τουτουί. τοῦτον γὰρ πρῶτον μὲν ὁ ἐμὸς πατὴρ ἔδωκεν ὑπήκοον εἶναι ἐμοί· ἐπεὶ δὲ ταχθείς, ὡς ἔφη αὐτός, ὑπὸ τοῦ ἐμοῦ ἀδελφοῦ οὗτος ἐπολέμησεν ἐμοὶ ἔχων τὴν ἐν Σάρδεσιν ἀκρόπολιν καὶ ἐγὼ αὐτὸν προσπο-

---

Seven was a sacred number among the Persians.

22 θέσθαι τὰ ὅπλα: *cf.* c. 5. 88, and the note. Cyrus evidently fears trouble, and takes ample precautions. Three thousand Greek hoplites would form a strong guard, and would effectually prevent any attempt at rescue.

24 Κλέαρχον: note the emphatic position and the intensive καί; *Clearchus he even invited within*, as an adviser.

ὅς γε: causal. The rel. is often equivalent to ὅτι with the demonstr.

25 προτιμηθῆναι . . . τῶν Ἑλλήνων: *cf.* c. 4. 91, and the note.

26 τὴν κρίσιν: prolepsis; see the note on τῶν βαρβάρων, c. 1. 20.

27 ἔφη: sc. Κλέαρχος.

28 ἄρχειν τοῦ λόγου, *opened the debate.* ἄρχεσθαι would have meant, *began his speech* (III, 2, §7). The infin. is here imperf., G. 1494; H. 853a; B 671.

ὅπως, *in order that;* the vb. is πράξω, l. 30.

29 πρός, *in the sight of.*

30 τοῦτο: resuming the preceding rel.; *cf.* c. 2. 85, and the note.

τουτουί: equivalent to a gesture; see G. 412; H. 274; B. 147.

31 ὑπήκοον: Orontas was φρούραρχος in Sardis (see below, l. 33), and, therefore, under Cyrus, as commander-in-chief. On this question, see the Introd., § 24.

32 ταχθείς, ordered.

ὡς ἔφη αὐτός, *as he himself said.* αὐτός in the nom. is always intensive, = *ipse,* unless immediately preceded by the art. (ὁ αὐτός = *idem*).

33 αὐτόν: redundant with ὥστε δόξαι αὐτῷ. There is a shift in the construction: αὐτόν is expressed, as though παύσασθαι were to follow (*I made him cease*); but, instead of this, we have ὥστε δόξαι αὐτῷ (*so that he thought it better*), whereby αὐτόν is left without grammatical dependence (προσπολεμῶν would require a dat.). The result is that Orontas' act in concluding peace is represented as a voluntary one, not as one forced upon

λεμῶν ἐποίησα ὥστε δόξαι τούτῳ τοῦ πρὸς ἐμὲ πολέμου παύ-
35 σασθαι, καὶ δεξιὰν ἔλαβον καὶ ἔδωκα, μετὰ ταῦτα, ἔφη, ὦ 7
Ὀρόντα, ἔστιν ὅ,τι σε ἠδίκησα; ἀπεκρίνατο ὅτι οὔ. πάλιν δὴ
ὁ Κῦρος ἠρώτα· Οὐκοῦν ὕστερον, ὡς αὐτὸς σὺ ὁμολογεῖς, οὐδὲν
ὑπ' ἐμοῦ ἀδικούμενος ἀποστὰς εἰς Μυσοὺς κακῶς ἐποίεις τὴν
ἐμὴν χώραν ὅ,τι ἐδύνω; ἔφη Ὀρόντας. Οὐκοῦν, ἔφη ὁ Κῦρος,
40 ὁπότ' αὖ ἔγνως τὴν σαυτοῦ δύναμιν, ἐλθὼν ἐπὶ τὸν τῆς Ἀρτέμιδος βωμὸν μεταμέλειν τέ σοι ἔφησθα καὶ πείσας ἐμὲ πιστὰ

---

him; so that his present defection is the more worthy of punishment (Rehdantz). For the infin. with ὥστε, after ἐποίησα, cf. l. 9, and the note.

35 μετὰ ταῦτα: resumptive; the preceding vbs. have been introduced by ἐπεί. Now comes the apodosis, in the form of a direct address to Orontas. ἔφη is, therefore, parenthetic.

36 ἔστιν ... ἠδίκησα, *is there anything in which I have wronged you?* ὅ, τι is the inner obj.; cf. οὐδέν, below, l. 45.

ἀπεκρίνατο ὅτι οὔ, *he answered, No.* ὅτι, introducing a direct quotation, is a somewhat uncommon use; see G. 1477.

37 ἠρώτα: the imperf. has to do with the course of questioning; below, l. 47, we have the aor., of a single question.

οὐκοῦν: what answer is expected? See the vocab., and G. 1603; H. 1015; B. 572, 1. The vb. is, of course, ἐποίεις, two lines below.

αὐτὸς σύ: a good instance of the adj. force of the pron. In the first and second persons both prons. (personal and intensive) are often expressed; in the third the person is indicated by the vb.

οὐδέν: inner obj. of ἀδικούμενος, which is concessive. Cf. the act. construction, ὅ,τι σε ἠδίκησα, above, l. 36.

38 εἰς Μυσούς: see the note on εἰς Πισίδας, c. 1. 62. For the Mysians, cf. III, 2, §§ 23 and 24.

κακῶς ἐποίεις: with a direct obj.; see G. 1074; H. 712; B. 330.

39 ὅ, τι ἐδύνω, *as far as you were able.* The inner obj. has passed into an acc. of respect.

ἔφη, *said, Yes.*

40 δύναμιν, *weakness.* The word is relative, and the context determines its meaning.

τῆς Ἀρτέμιδος: probably the famous Ephesian Artemis; see Acts, chap. XIX. The altar has always been a place of refuge for the fugitive and the suppliant; but no more may be meant than that the oaths mentioned were sworn at Artemis' altar.

41 μεταμελεῖν σοι: he said, μεταμελεῖ μοι; cf. the biblical *It repenteth me* (Gen. IV:7), and the Lat. use of *paenitet*. μετα-, in composition, often implies change.

πάλιν ἔδωκάς μοι καὶ ἔλαβες παρ' ἐμοῦ; καὶ ταῦθ' ὡμολόγει
8 Ὀρόντας. Τί οὖν, ἔφη ὁ Κῦρος, ἀδικηθεὶς ὑπ' ἐμοῦ νῦν τὸ
τρίτον ἐπιβουλεύων μοι φανερὸς γέγονας; εἰπόντος δὲ τοῦ
Ὀρόντα ὅτι οὐδὲν ἀδικηθείς, ἠρώτησεν ὁ Κῦρος αὐτόν· Ὁμο- 45
λογεῖς οὖν περὶ ἐμὲ ἄδικος γεγενῆσθαι; Ἦ γὰρ ἀνάγκη, ἔφη
Ὀρόντας. ἐκ τούτου πάλιν ἠρώτησεν ὁ Κῦρος· Ἔτι οὖν ἂν
γένοιο τῷ ἐμῷ ἀδελφῷ πολέμιος, ἐμοὶ δὲ φίλος καὶ πιστός; ὁ δὲ
ἀπεκρίνατο ὅτι οὐδ' εἰ γενοίμην, ὦ Κῦρε, σοί γ' ἄν ποτε ἔτι
9 δόξαιμι. πρὸς ταῦτα Κῦρος εἶπε τοῖς παροῦσιν· Ὁ μὲν ἀνὴρ 50
τοιαῦτα μὲν πεποίηκε, τοιαῦτα δὲ λέγει· ὑμῶν δὲ σὺ πρῶτος,
ὦ Κλέαρχε, ἀπόφηναι γνώμην ὅ,τι σοι δοκεῖ. Κλέαρχος δὲ

---

42 **καὶ ταῦθ'**: καί is intensive, not connective.
43 **τὸ τρίτον**: adv. acc.
44 **ἐπιβουλεύων**: with φανερὸς γέγονας; *cf.* δῆλος ἦν ἀνιώμενος, c. 2. 70, and the note.
45 **Ὀρόντα**: for the form of the gen., *cf.* Ἀβροκόμα, c. 4. 15, and the note.
οὐδὲν ἀδικηθείς: Cyrus' question supplies the vb.
46 **περί**, *toward; cf.* c. 4. 54. περί regularly takes the acc. after vbs. of action, the gen. after vbs. of saying.
γεγενῆσθαι: quoted after ὁμολογεῖς; retain the tense. Note that, when the subj. of the infin. is the same as the subj. of the vb. of saying, it is unexpressed, and that a pred. noun or adj. is nom., not acc.
ἦ: one of the very few particles that may be rendered by *indeed*. Note that γάρ often implies assent, *yes, for.*
ἀνάγκη: sc. ἐστί.
47 **ἂν γένοιο**: potential opt. No protasis is to be supplied.

49 **ὅτι**: again introducing direct quotation; *cf.* l. 36, and the note.
οὐδ' εἰ: a good instance of the fondness of the neg. for the emphatic position at the head of the sentence. Grammatically it goes, of course, with δόξαιμι (*even if . . . I should never seem*).
σοί γε: for the force of γε, see c. 3. 46, and the note.
50 **πρὸς ταῦτα**, *in the light of these statements.*
51 **τοιαῦτα μὲν . . . τοιαῦτα δέ**: the figure anaphora; see the Introd., § 39.
πρῶτος: different from πρῶτον; see c. 3. 4, and the note.
52 **ἀπόφηναι**: aor. imv. mid., as is shown by the accent. Remember that the 1st aor. infin. act. always accents the penult, and that the infrequent opt. form, ἀποφῆναι (regularly ἀποφήνειε), has a long ultima (G. 113; H. 102b; B. 63).
ὅ,τι . . . δοκεῖ: an indir. quest., since ἀπόφηναι γνώμην implies statement.

εἶπε τάδε. Συμβουλεύω ἐγὼ τὸν ἄνδρα τοῦτον ἐκποδὼν ποιεῖσθαι ὡς τάχιστα, ὡς μηκέτι δέῃ τοῦτον φυλάττεσθαι, ἀλλὰ
σχολὴ ᾖ ἡμῖν τὸ κατὰ τοῦτον εἶναι τοὺς ἐθελοντὰς φίλους εὖ
ποιεῖν. ταύτῃ δὲ τῇ γνώμῃ ἔφη καὶ τοὺς ἄλλους προσθέσθαι.
 Μετὰ ταῦτα, ἔφη, κελεύοντος Κύρου ἔλαβον τῆς ζώνης τὸν
Ὀρόνταν ἐπὶ θανάτῳ ἅπαντες ἀναστάντες καὶ οἱ συγγενεῖς·
εἶτα δ' ἐξῆγον αὐτὸν οἷς προσετάχθη. ἐπεὶ δὲ εἶδον αὐτὸν
οἵπερ πρόσθεν προσεκύνουν, καὶ τότε προσεκύνησαν, καίπερ

---

53 **συμβουλεύω ἐγώ**: the act. is used of one who gives advice, the mid. of one who asks it. Note the emphasis on the pronoun.

ἐκποδὼν ποιεῖσθαι, *to put out of our way*. Note the voice; if the phrase were pass., γίγνεσθαι would be used.

54 **ὡς**: purpose.

τοῦτον: obj. of φυλάττεσθαι; see the vocab.

55 **ἡμῖν**: dat. of possessor. Does the use of the pl. suggest that Clearchus puts himself on the same plane with Cyrus?

τὸ ... εἶναι, *as far as this fellow is concerned*. τοῦτον is contemptuous, as often. For the idiomatic infin., see G. 1534, 1535; H. 956a; B. 642. The whole phrase stands as an acc. of specification.

ἐθελοντάς: a noun, in appos. with φίλους; the partic. is differently accented. Render, *those who are our friends of their own choosing*.

εὖ ποιεῖν: cf. κακῶς ἐποίεις, above, l. 38, and the note.

56 **ἔφη**: sc. Κλέαρχος. The indir. disc. is resumed, although only for a line. In the next line ἔφη is parenthetic, and refers the narrative to Clearchus, not to Xen.

57 **τῆς ζώνης**, *by the girdle*. For the case, see G. 1100; H. 738a; B. 356, with note 1. This act was symbolical among the Persians, and indicated condemnation. It sufficed for the king alone to touch the girdle of the man on trial before him. Xen., writing for Greek readers, adds ἐπὶ θανάτῳ (*as a sign of condemnation*).

58 **ἅπαντες ... συγγενεῖς**, *all, even those of his own kin*.

59 **οἷς προσετάχθη**, *who had been bidden, whose duty it was*, an impers. pass. This construction, so common in Lat., is regular in Greek with vbs. of commanding, and is frequent also with παρασκευάζω; elsewhere it is very rare.

60 **προσεκύνουν**: contrast the following aor., προσεκύνησαν. The vb. denotes the oriental manner of saluting a superior by prostrating oneself before him; cf. Dan. II, 46, and elsewhere in the Old Testament.

καὶ τότε ... καίπερ, *even then ... although*. καίπερ (*although*) takes a partic.; καίτοι (*and yet*) a vb. (*e.g.*, c. 4. 55).

11 εἰδότες ὅτι ἐπὶ θάνατον ἄγοιτο. ἐπεὶ δὲ εἰς τὴν Ἀρταπάτου σκηνὴν εἰσήχθη τοῦ πιστοτάτου τῶν Κύρου σκηπτούχων, μετὰ ταῦτα οὔτε ζῶντα Ὀρόνταν οὔτε τεθνηκότα οὐδεὶς εἶδε πώποτε οὐδὲ ὅπως ἀπέθανεν οὐδεὶς εἰδὼς ἔλεγεν· ἤκαζον δὲ ἄλλοι ἄλλως· τάφος δὲ οὐδεὶς πώποτε αὐτοῦ ἐφάνη. 65

1 VII. Ἐντεῦθεν ἐξελαύνει διὰ τῆς Βαβυλωνίας σταθμοὺς τρεῖς παρασάγγας δώδεκα. ἐν δὲ τῷ τρίτῳ σταθμῷ Κῦρος ἐξέτασιν ποιεῖται τῶν Ἑλλήνων καὶ τῶν βαρβάρων ἐν τῷ πεδίῳ περὶ μέσας νύκτας· ἐδόκει γὰρ εἰς τὴν ἐπιοῦσαν ἕω ἥξειν βασιλέα σὺν τῷ στρατεύματι μαχούμενον· καὶ ἐκέλευε Κλέαρ- 5 χον μὲν τοῦ δεξιοῦ κέρως ἡγεῖσθαι, Μένωνα δὲ τοῦ εὐωνύμου,
2 αὐτὸς δὲ τοὺς ἑαυτοῦ διέταξε. μετὰ δὲ τὴν ἐξέτασιν ἅμα τῇ

61 ἐπὶ θάνατον: limit of motion; not as ἐπὶ θανάτῳ, above.

63 οὔτε ... ἔλεγεν, *neither alive nor dead did anyone ever see Orontas, nor could anyone say with knowledge in what manner he was put to death*. For the accumulation of negatives, *cf*. οὐδενί, c. 2. 152, and the note. Observe, also, the force of the neg. with the impf. (*could not* or *would not*); see the note on c. 4. 64. Orontas may have been buried alive, Herodotus, VII, 114.

64 ἄλλοι ἄλλως: *cf. alii aliter* (H. 704a; B. 492, note 3).

CHAPTER VII

3 ἐξέτασιν ποιεῖται: *cf*. c. 1. 24, and the note.

4 νύκτας: pl., as we speak of *the watches of the night*.

ἐδόκει, *he thought*. This use of δοκῶ is not very common in Attic Greek.

εἰς ... ἕω, *next morning*. See G. 1207b; H. 796b; B. 405, and *cf*. II, 3, 25; III, 1, 3; and IV, 1, §15. These phrases seem often scarcely to differ from simple dats. of time. For the acc. ἕω, see G. 199; H. 161; B. 92, 3.

5 μαχούμενον, *to offer battle*; see the note on ἀποκτενῶν, c. 1. 12.

6 κέρως: for the form, see G. 228; H. 191; B. 115, 10; for the case, G. 1109; H. 741; B. 356. The dat. also occurs with ἡγεῖσθαι (*e. g.*, c. 4. 9; but the gen. prevails in cases where the individual is at the head of his own troops—*i. e.*, is leader *de iure*, as well as *de facto*. τὸ δεξιόν occurs, c. 2. 87, without any noun; see the note there. The right wing was the post of honor and of danger, for the side unprotected by the shield was exposed to a flank attack (see I, 8, § 13).

τοῦ εὐωνύμου: *i. e.*, of the Greek force. For the word, *cf*. c. 2. 88, and the note. The arrangement here given was followed in the battle (I, 8, § 4), the barbarians having their position on the Greek left.

7 ἅμα ... ἡμέρᾳ, *at dawn on the following day*. ἐπιούσῃ is not

ἐπιούσῃ ἡμέρᾳ ἧκον αὐτόμολοι παρὰ μεγάλου βασιλέως στρατιᾶς.

Κῦρος δὲ συγκαλέσας τοὺς στρατηγοὺς καὶ λοχαγοὺς τῶν Ἑλλήνων συνεβουλεύετό τε πῶς ἂν τὴν μάχην ποιοῖτο καὶ αὐτὸς παρῄνει θαρρύνων τοιάδε. Ὦ ἄνδρες Ἕλληνες, οὐκ 3 ἀνθρώπων ἀπορῶν βαρβάρων συμμάχους ὑμᾶς ἄγω, ἀλλὰ νομίζων ἀμείνονας καὶ κρείττους πολλῶν βαρβάρων ὑμᾶς εἶναι, διὰ τοῦτο προσέλαβον. ὅπως οὖν ἔσεσθε ἄνδρες ἄξιοι τῆς ἐλευθερίας ἧς κέκτησθε καὶ ἧς ὑμᾶς ἐγὼ εὐδαιμονίζω. εὖ γὰρ ἴστε ὅτι τὴν ἐλευθερίαν ἑλοίμην ἂν ἀντὶ ὧν ἔχω πάντων καὶ ἄλλων πολλαπλασίων. ὅπως δὲ καὶ εἰδῆτε εἰς οἷον ἔρχεσθε 4

---

usually added to this common phrase, but serves to make it more explicit. For the dat., see G. 1175, 1176; H. 772c; B. 392, 3.

10 τοὺς στρατηγοὺς καὶ λοχαγούς: the art., expressed but once, shows that both groups are regarded as forming a single class.

11 συνεβουλεύετο, *asked their advice;* contrast the act., above, c. 6. 53.

πῶς ἂν . . . ποιοῖτο, *how he should conduct the battle*, a potential opt., in an indir. quest. ὅπως would have been more normal than πῶς, but the dir. interrog. is often kept; see G. 1600; H. 1011; B. 580. Note the position of ἄν at the head of the clause.

12 τοιάδε, (*substantially*) *as follows.*

ὦ ἄνδρες Ἕλληνες: ὦ is commonly expressed with the voc. in Greek. For ἄνδρες, *cf.* c. 3. 11, and the note. With this word contrast ἀνθρώπων βαρβάρων (so again in § 4), and *cf.* the words of Herodotus (VII, 210), regarding the Persians at Thermopylae, ὅτι πολλοὶ μὲν ἄνθρωποι εἶεν, ὀλίγοι δὲ ἄνδρες.

13 ἀπορῶν: causal. Trans., *it is not because I lack barbarians that I . . . .* For the gen. ἀνθρώπων, see the note on c. 1. 29.

14 ἀμείνους . . . κρείττους, *braver . . . stronger.*

15 διὰ τοῦτο: resumes, with emphasis, the causal partic.

ὅπως . . . ἔσεσθε, *see that ye be.* See G. 1352, 1353; H. 885, 886; B. 583 note 3 (*cf.* 593).

16 ἧς κέκτησθε, *which you possess*, another case of attraction.

καὶ ἧς . . . εὐδαιμονίζω, *and for which I congratulate you.* The gen. is causal (G. 1126; H. 774; B. 366). Cyrus uses ἐγώ with emphasis; all the Persians were accounted the slaves (δοῦλοι) of the king. Cyrus knows to whom he is speaking.

17 ἴστε: imv., not indic.

ἀντὶ ὧν ἔχω πάντων, *in preference to all that I possess.* For the incorporation of the antecedent in the rel. clause, see the note on c. 1. 24.

18 εἰς οἷον . . . ἀγῶνα, *into what sort of a contest*, another indir. quest.

ἀγῶνα, ὑμᾶς εἰδὼς διδάξω. τὸ μὲν γὰρ πλῆθος πολὺ καὶ
κραυγῇ πολλῇ ἐπίασιν. ἂν δὲ ταῦτα ἀνάσχησθε, τὰ ἄλλα
καὶ αἰσχυνεῖσθαί μοι δοκῶ οἵους ἡμῖν γνώσεσθε τοὺς ἐν τῇ
χώρᾳ ὄντας ἀνθρώπους. ὑμῶν δὲ ἀνδρῶν ὄντων καὶ εὖ τῶν
ἐμῶν γενομένων, ἐγὼ ὑμῶν τὸν μὲν οἴκαδε βουλόμενον ἀπιέναι
τοῖς οἴκοι ζηλωτὸν ποιήσω ἀπελθεῖν, πολλοὺς δὲ οἶμαι ποιήσειν
τὰ παρ' ἐμοὶ ἑλέσθαι ἀντὶ τῶν οἴκοι.

Ἐνταῦθα Γαυλίτης παρὼν φυγὰς Σάμιος, πιστὸς δὲ Κύρῳ,
εἶπεν· Καὶ μήν, ὦ Κῦρε, λέγουσί τινες ὅτι πολλὰ ὑπισχνῇ νῦν
διὰ τὸ ἐν τοιούτῳ εἶναι τοῦ κινδύνου προσιόντος, ἂν δὲ εὖ
γένηταί τι, οὐ μεμνήσεσθαί σέ φασιν· ἔνιοι δὲ οὐδ' εἰ μεμνῇό τε

---

20 ἐπίασιν: fut., see the note on
ἰέναι, c. 3. 2.
ταῦτα: i. e. τὸ πλῆθος καὶ τὴν κραυγήν.
τὰ ἄλλα . . . ἀνθρώπους, *for the
rest, I think I shall even be
ashamed (to see) what sort of
men you will find those in our
country to be.* The indir. quest.,
οἵους . . . γνώσεσθε, is introduced
by αἰσχυνεῖσθαι; ἡμῖν is the ethical dat., and ὄντας is in indir.
disc. after γνώσεσθε.
22 ὄντων . . . γενομένων: the gen.
abs. in both instances expresses
condition. ἀνδρῶν is emphatic,
as above.
τῶν ἐμῶν is neut., *my affairs.*
ἐγὼ . . . ἀπελθεῖν, *I (on my part)
will cause those of you who
wish to return home, to return
as objects of envy to those at
home.* τὸν . . . βουλόμενον is lit.
him that wishes, but the pl. is
more in harmony with Eng.
usage. τοῖς οἴκοι is masc.; the dat.
depends upon the adj. ζηλωτόν.
25 τὰ παρ' ἐμοί, freely, *what I can
offer here.* τῶν οἴκοι is here neut.,
not masc.
26 φυγάς: an exile from a Greek

state often found an asylum at
one of the Persian courts.
πιστός: not here a title, one of
"the Faithful" (see c. 5. 93, and
the note), but simply *trusted by,*
in contrast with φυγάς. There
is no reason for the assumption
that Gaulites spoke at Cyrus'
instigation.
27 καὶ μήν, *and yet.*
28 διὰ τὸ . . . εἶναι, *because you are
in such a critical position.* For
the articular infin., see the note
on c. 1. 35. ἐν τοιούτῳ is further
explained by τοῦ κινδύνου προσιόντος, best taken as gen. abs. (*now
that the danger is approaching*).
29 τι, *your affairs;* but the vague
word is purposely chosen.
μεμνήσεσθαι; a mere fut., since
μέμνημαι is a present.
ἔνιοι δέ: sc. φασί.
οὐδ' εἰ . . . ὑπισχνῇ, *that, even if
you should remember and
should wish to, you would not
be able to repay all that you
promise.* For the form μεμνῇο,
see G. 734, 1; H. 465a; B. 227,
note. δύνασθαι ἄν represents an
original δύναιο ἄν.

καὶ βούλοιο δύνασθαι ἂν ἀποδοῦναι ὅσα ὑπισχνῇ. ἀκούσας 6
ταῦτα ἔλεξεν ὁ Κῦρος· Ἀλλ' ἔστι μὲν ἡμῖν, ὦ ἄνδρες, ἡ ἀρχὴ
ἡ πατρῴα πρὸς μὲν μεσημβρίαν μέχρι οὗ διὰ καῦμα οὐ δύνανται
οἰκεῖν ἄνθρωποι, πρὸς δὲ ἄρκτον μέχρι οὗ διὰ χειμῶνα· τὰ δ'
ἐν μέσῳ τούτων πάντα σατραπεύουσιν οἱ τοῦ ἐμοῦ ἀδελφοῦ
φίλοι. ἢν δ' ἡμεῖς νικήσωμεν, ἡμᾶς δεῖ τοὺς ἡμετέρους φίλους 7
τούτων ἐγκρατεῖς ποιῆσαι. ὥστε οὐ τοῦτο δέδοικα μὴ οὐκ ἔχω
ὅ,τι δῶ ἑκάστῳ τῶν φίλων, ἂν εὖ γένηται, ἀλλὰ μὴ οὐκ ἔχω
ἱκανοὺς οἷς δῶ. ὑμῶν δὲ τῶν Ἑλλήνων καὶ στέφανον ἑκάστῳ

---

31 ἔστι: not the copula, but a full vb.; hence the accent (*cf.* c. 2. 43, and the note). Trans. with πρός, *extends to*. Note the asseverative force of μέν.

ἡμῖν: dat. of advantage, not of possessor. Note the pl. of majesty.

32 μέχρι οὗ, *to a point where*.

33 τὰ δ' ... **πάντα**, *all that lies between*. For this use of μέσῳ, see c. 4. 23.

34 σατραπεύουσιν, *administer as satraps*. In III, 4, § 31 the vb. (in the meaning, *be satrap of*) governs the more regular gen.

35 ἡμεῖς ... ἡμετέρους: in emphatic contrast to what precedes.

36 ἐγκρατεῖς ποιῆσαι, *to put in control of*. The gen., τούτων, goes with this phrase, as with a vb. of ruling.

τοῦτο: when referring to a following clause, τοῦτο is more common than τόδε, despite the normal rule (see c. 1. 24, and the note).

μὴ οὐκ ἔχω, *that I shall not know (have)*. For the double neg., see G. 1362, 3; 1364; H. 887, 1033; B. 594; 432.

37 ὅ,τι δῶ, *what to give*. The deliberative subjv. appears in the indir. quest. (G. 1358; 1490; H. 866; 3; 932; B. 577; 581). οἷς δῶ, below, is to be explained in the same way. That sentence is rel., not interrog., but in such cases the subjv. seems to follow the analogy of the subjv. in deliberative questions; see G. M. T. 572. Others explain the words as a condit. rel. clause, with ἄν omitted. The rel. and the interrog. are not always strictly differentiated in Greek, Lat., or Eng.

ἂν εὖ γένηται, *if all goes well*.

38 ὑμῶν δέ: possibly the whole Greek force is meant, but, more probably, only the generals and captains present at the interview. The gen. depends on ἑκάστῳ, both words being emphasized by their separation from one another.

στέφανον ... χρυσοῦν: in this Cyrus is adopting a Greek custom. Among them crowns were regularly bestowed as rewards of extraordinary merit. The extravagance of Cyrus' promises is in keeping with his character as an oriental prince; yet he was doubtless sincere.

8 χρυσοῦν δώσω. οἱ δὲ ταῦτα ἀκούσαντες αὐτοί τε ἦσαν πολὺ προθυμότεροι καὶ τοῖς ἄλλοις ἐξήγγελλον.

Εἰσῆσαν δὲ παρ' αὐτὸν οἵ τε στρατηγοὶ καὶ τῶν ἄλλων Ἑλλήνων τινὲς ἀξιοῦντες εἰδέναι τί σφίσιν ἔσται, ἐὰν κρατήσωσιν. ὁ δὲ ἐμπιμπλὰς ἁπάντων τὴν γνώμην ἀπέπεμπε.
9 παρεκελεύοντο δὲ αὐτῷ πάντες ὅσοιπερ διελέγοντο μὴ μάχεσθαι, ἀλλ' ὄπισθεν ἑαυτῶν τάττεσθαι. ἐν δὲ τῷ καιρῷ τούτῳ Κλέαρχος ὡδέ πως ἤρετο τὸν Κῦρον· Οἴει γάρ σοι μαχεῖσθαι, ὦ Κῦρε, τὸν ἀδελφόν; Νὴ Δί', ἔφη ὁ Κῦρος, εἴπερ γε Δαρείου καὶ Παρυσάτιδός ἐστι παῖς, ἐμὸς δὲ ἀδελφός, οὐκ ἀμαχεὶ ταῦτ' ἐγὼ λήψομαι.

10 Ἐνταῦθα δὴ ἐν τῇ ἐξοπλισίᾳ ἀριθμὸς ἐγένετο τῶν μὲν Ἑλλήνων ἀσπὶς μυρία καὶ τετρακοσία, πελτασταὶ δὲ δισχίλιοι

---

39 **αὐτοί**: see c. 6. 37, and the note.
40 **ἐξήγγελλον**: *i. e.* to those who had not been called in for consultation.
41 **εἰσῆσαν**: note the tense. If the following words, οἵ τε στρατηγοί, are genuine, we must assume that the generals severally sought for confirmation of the promise.
42 **τί σφίσιν ἔσται**: for the indir. reflexive, *cf.* οἷ, c. 1. 36, and the note. Observe, also, that in the fut. the indic. is regularly retained in an indir. statement or quest. (also in an obj. clause after a secondary tense), although the fut. opt. exists only for the needs of indir. disc.
44 **μάχεσθαι**: *i. e.* in person.
45 **ἑαυτῶν**: with ὄπισθεν. The reflexive is indir.; yet ἑαυτῶν is preferred to σφῶν, which is rarely used. According to Plutarch, *Artox.* 8, Cyrus' answer was, τί λέγεις, ὦ Κλέαρχε; σὺ κελεύεις με τὸν βασιλείας ὀρεγόμενον (*reaching out for*) ἀνάξιον εἶναι βασιλείας.
46 **οἴει γάρ**, *why, do you suppose?* To the veteran Clearchus the mere fact that they have come so far without opposition is proof that the king will not dare to fight.
47 **νὴ Δί'**: for the acc. in an oath, *cf.* μὰ τοὺς θεούς, c. 4. 51.
48 **ἐμὸς δὲ ἀδελφός**, *and a brother of mine*.
ἀμαχεί: emphatic.
ταῦτα: *i. e.* the realm, described in § 6, perhaps said with a gesture.
50 **ἐξοπλισίᾳ**, *muster under arms*, almost = ἐξετάσει.
ἀριθμὸς ἐγένετο, *a numbering was made* (the pass. of ἀριθμὸν ποιεῖν, c. 2. 57).
51 **ἀσπίς**: *i. e.* ὁπλῖται. It was as easy for the Greek to use ἀσπίς in this collective sense, as, *e. g.*, ἵππος. So, in Eng., we speak of so many *horse*. The totals here

καὶ πεντακόσιοι, τῶν δὲ μετὰ Κύρου βαρβάρων δέκα μυριάδες καὶ ἅρματα δρεπανηφόρα ἀμφὶ τὰ εἴκοσι. τῶν δὲ πολεμίων ἐλέγοντο εἶναι ἑκατὸν καὶ εἴκοσι μυριάδες καὶ ἅρματα δρεπανηφόρα διακόσια. ἄλλοι δὲ ἦσαν ἑξακισχίλιοι ἱππεῖς, ὧν Ἀρταγέρσης ἦρχεν· οὗτοι δ' αὖ πρὸ αὐτοῦ βασιλέως τεταγμένοι ἦσαν. τοῦ δὲ βασιλέως στρατεύματος ἦσαν ἄρχοντες τέτταρες, τριάκοντα μυριάδων ἕκαστος, Ἀβροκόμας, Τισσαφέρνης, Γωβρύας, Ἀρβάκης. τούτων δὲ παρεγένοντο ἐν τῇ μάχῃ ἐνενήκοντα μυριάδες καὶ ἅρματα δρεπανηφόρα ἑκατὸν καὶ πεντήκοντα· Ἀβροκόμας δὲ ὑστέρησε τῆς μάχης ἡμέραις πέντε, ἐκ Φοινίκης ἐλαύνων. ταῦτα δὲ ἤγγελλον πρὸς Κῦρον οἱ αὐτομολήσαντες παρὰ μεγάλου βασιλέως πρὸ τῆς μάχης, καὶ μετὰ τὴν μάχην οἳ ὕστερον ἐλήφθησαν τῶν πολεμίων ταὐτὰ ἤγγελλον.

Ἐντεῦθεν δὲ Κῦρος ἐξελαύνει σταθμὸν ἕνα παρασάγγας τρεῖς συντεταγμένῳ τῷ στρατεύματι παντὶ καὶ τῷ Ἑλληνικῷ καὶ τῷ βαρβαρικῷ· ᾤετο γὰρ ταύτῃ τῇ ἡμέρᾳ μαχεῖσθαι

---

given cause difficulty; see the Introd., § 28.

52 δέκα μυριάδες: for the method of counting, regular in Greek, *cf.* c. 2. 58, and the note.

53 ἅρματα δρεπανηφόρα: described in § 10 of the next chapter.

54 ἑκατὸν . . . μυριάδες, probably the statement is grossly exaggerated (*cf.* c. 4. 33, and the note); Xen. gives it as a mere rumor. Ctesias (see the Introd., § 30) fixed the number as 400,000 (Plutarch, *Artox.* 13).

55 ἄλλοι, *besides*; *cf.* c. 5. 27, and the note.

Ἀρταγέρσης: slain by Cyrus himself, c. 8, § 24.

56 αὖ, *on their part*.

τοῦ: with στρατεύματος, not with βασιλέως.

58 Ἀβροκόμας: he seems to have been careful to keep out of Cyrus' way; *cf.* c. 4. 31.

61 τῆς μάχης: gen., since ὑστέρησε implies comparison.

ἡμέραις: *cf.* c. 2. 143, and the note.

62 ἤγγελλον . . . ἤγγελλον: the arrangement, causing the sentence to close with a word prominent at the opening (palindromic chiasm), throws great stress on ἤγγελλον (*cf.* I, 10, § 3). Xen. is careful to give the source of his information and to assure us that it was subsequently corroborated. Had he Ctesias' counter-statement in mind (Rehdantz)?

64 ταὐτά: not ταῦτα.

66 συντεταγμένῳ τῷ στρατεύματι: note that the posit. is pred. This dat. (of accompaniment) is especially common in military writers (G. 1189; 1190; H. 774; B. 392, 1.

βασιλέα· κατὰ γὰρ μέσον τὸν σταθμὸν τοῦτον τάφρος ἦν ὀρυκτὴ βαθεῖα, τὸ μὲν εὖρος ὀργυιαὶ πέντε, τὸ δὲ βάθος ὀργυιαὶ τρεῖς. παρετέτατο δὴ ἡ τάφρος ἄνω διὰ τοῦ πεδίου ἐπὶ δώδεκα παρασάγγας μέχρι τοῦ Μηδίας τείχους. [ἔνθα αἱ διώρυχες, ἀπὸ τοῦ Τίγρητος ποταμοῦ ῥέουσαι· εἰσὶ δὲ τέτταρες, τὸ μὲν εὖρος πλεθριαῖαι, βαθεῖαι δὲ ἰσχυρῶς, καὶ πλοῖα πλεῖ ἐν αὐταῖς σιταγωγά· εἰσβάλλουσι δὲ εἰς τὸν Εὐφράτην, διαλείπουσι δ' ἑκάστη παρασάγγην, γέφυραι δ' ἔπεισιν.] ἦν δὲ παρὰ τὸν Εὐφράτην πάροδος στενὴ μεταξὺ τοῦ ποταμοῦ καὶ τῆς τάφρου ὡς εἴκοσι ποδῶν τὸ εὖρος· ταύτην δὲ τὴν τάφρον βασιλεὺς

68 μέσον: for the position, cf. c. 2. 41, and the note.

τάφρος... ὀρυκτή: i. e. clearly artificial; cf., below, ll. 77 f., βασιλεὺς ποιεῖ.

69 εὖρος ὀργυιαὶ πέντε: Plutarch (Artox. 7) gives less credible measurements (depth and width ten fathoms each).

70 παρετέτατο: for the form, see G. 647; H. 448ab; B. 224 note.

ἄνω, inland.

δώδεκα παρασάγγας: this agrees closely with Plutarch's σταδίους τετρακοσίους.

71 τοῦ Μηδίας τεῖχος: the wall is described in II, 4, 12, where see the note. It seems originally to have been built from river to river to protect Babylonia from northern invaders. By Xen.'s time the southwestern end, at least, must have fallen in ruins, so that this trench was dug to bar Cyrus' advance.

[ἔνθα... ἔπεισιν]: this passage, which interrupts the narrative, is probably a note added by some editor or copyist.

διώρυχες: sc. εἰσί.

73 πλεθριαῖαι: adj, corresponding to the gen. of measure; cf. c. 2. 30, and the note.

74 εἰσβάλλουσι: cf. ἐμβάλλει, c. 2. 45.

διαλείπουσι: for the force of δια-, cf. διαστάντες, c. 5. 11. With ἑκάστη, in apposition with the subj. of a pl. vb., cf. the use of quisque, in Lat.

76 πάροδος: apparently Cyrus' rapid advance had prevented the completion of the trench; the opposite view—that the passage was left, in order that Cyrus might be enticed within—lacks all probability. Why this position, however, was not defended remains an unanswerable enigma. It would have been impossible for Cyrus to force it; and he had no supplies. Artaxerxes and his counselors seem to have been thoroughly afraid—and with good reason, as the sequel showed. Plutarch, Artox. 7, states that the king actually purposed abandoning the whole of the western part of his empire; but was dissuaded by Tiribazus.

77 ὡς, about, cf. c. 2. 18.

ποιεῖ: render by the Eng. plpf.,

ποιεῖ μέγας ἀντὶ ἐρύματος, ἐπειδὴ πυνθάνεται Κῦρον προσελαύνοντα. ταύτην δὴ τὴν πάροδον Κῦρός τε καὶ ἡ στρατιὰ 80 παρῆλθε καὶ ἐγένοντο εἴσω τῆς τάφρου. ταύτῃ μὲν οὖν τῇ 17 ἡμέρᾳ οὐκ ἐμαχέσατο βασιλεύς, ἀλλ' ὑποχωρούντων φανερὰ ἦσαν καὶ ἵππων καὶ ἀνθρώπων ἴχνη πολλά. ἐνταῦθα Κῦρος 18 Σιλανὸν καλέσας τὸν Ἀμπρακιώτην μάντιν ἔδωκεν αὐτῷ δαρεικοὺς τρισχιλίους, ὅτι τῇ ἑνδεκάτῃ ἀπ' ἐκείνης ἡμέρᾳ πρότερον 85 θυόμενος εἶπεν αὐτῷ ὅτι βασιλεὺς οὐ μαχεῖται δέκα ἡμερῶν, Κῦρος δ' εἶπεν· Οὐκ ἄρα ἔτι μαχεῖται, εἰ ἐν ταύταις οὐ μαχεῖται ταῖς ἡμέραις· ἐὰν δ' ἀληθεύσῃς, ὑπισχνοῦμαί σοι δέκα τάλαντα. τοῦτο τὸ χρυσίον τότε ἀπέδωκεν, ἐπεὶ παρῆλθον αἱ δέκα ἡμέραι. ἐπεὶ δ' ἐπὶ τῇ τάφρῳ οὐκ ἐκώλυε βασιλεὺς τὸ 19 90 Κύρου στράτευμα διαβαίνειν, ἔδοξε καὶ Κύρῳ καὶ τοῖς ἄλλοις ἀπεγνωκέναι τοῦ μάχεσθαι· ὥστε τῇ ὑστεραίᾳ Κῦρος ἐπορεύετο

---

and *cf.* the note on ἐφύλαττον, c. 2 129.

78 μέγας: the position is unusual; is contempt implied (Rehdantz)?

80 παρῆλθε: agreement with the nearer of two subjs. The next vb. is pl.

81 ἀλλ' ὑποχωρούντων, *nay, actually in retreat.* Note the order. It is not strange that Cyrus grew careless.

82 ἦσαν . . . ἴχνη: for the agreement *cf.* l. 95.

85 θυόμενος: for the difference in meaning between the act. and the mid. of this vb., see the vocab.

εἶπεν, *had said.*

ἡμερῶν: gen. of the time within which; see G. 1136; H. 759; B. 359.

86 ἔτι, *at all.*

εἰ . . . οὐ μαχεῖται: for the type of condition, see the note on εἰ πιστεύσομεν, c. 3. 84. οὐ is used, not μή, because Cyrus is but echoing Silanus' words, and οὐ μαχεῖται forms a single neg. idea (G. 1383; B. 600 note).

87 ἐὰν δ' ἀληθεύσῃς, *if you shall prove to have spoken the truth.*

88 δέκα τάλαντα: equivalent to the 3,000 darics mentioned above. A silver talent, therefore ($1,080), was worth 300 darics. On this basis the daric was worth only $3.60, while, by the weight of the gold, it should be $5.40. This shows that silver was worth half as much again, with reference to gold, as it is in our coinage, and practically three times as much as it is now in fact. The purchasing power of both metals was much greater than now.

ἀπέδωκεν: note the force of the prep. Cyrus is paying a debt.

89 οὐκ ἐκώλυε, *made no attempt to prevent.*

90 ἔδοξε: personal.

91 ἀπεγνωκέναι τοῦ μάχεσθαι, *to have*

20 ἠμελημένως μᾶλλον. τῇ δὲ τρίτῃ ἐπί τε τοῦ ἅρματος καθήμενος τὴν πορείαν ἐποιεῖτο καὶ ὀλίγους ἐν τάξει ἔχων πρὸ αὑτοῦ,
τὸ δὲ πολὺ αὐτῷ ἀνατεταραγμένον ἐπορεύετο καὶ τῶν ὅπλων
τοῖς στρατιώταις πολλὰ ἐπὶ ἁμαξῶν ἤγοντο καὶ ὑποζυγίων.   95

1 VIII. Καὶ ἤδη τε ἦν ἀμφὶ ἀγορὰν πλήθουσαν καὶ πλησίον ἦν ὁ σταθμὸς ἔνθα ἔμελλε καταλύειν, ἡνίκα Πατηγύας
ἀνὴρ Πέρσης τῶν ἀμφὶ Κῦρον χρηστὸς προφαίνεται ἐλαύνων
ἀνὰ κράτος ἱδροῦντι τῷ ἵππῳ, καὶ εὐθὺς πᾶσιν οἷς ἐνετύγχανεν
ἐβόα καὶ βαρβαρικῶς καὶ ἑλληνικῶς ὅτι βασιλεὺς σὺν στρατεύ- 5
ματι πολλῷ προσέρχεται ὡς εἰς μάχην παρεσκευασμένος. ἔνθα

given up the idea of fighting.
For this neg. force of ἀπο-, cf.
ἀποψηφίσωνται, c. 4. 98; for the
infin. with the art., see the note
on τοῦ διαβαίνειν, c. 4. 96. The
case is here due possibly to the
idea of separation; Xen., Hellenica VII, 5, 7, uses the acc.
with this vb.

92 ἠμελημένως: an adv. formed from
the partic. ἠμελημένος. This is
not overcommon; but the partic.,
felt as an adj., may even be compared (e. g. ἐρρωμενέστεροι, III, 1,
§ 42). The perf. partic. has an especially strong adjectival value.

94 τὸ δὲ πολύ: practically = οἱ δὲ
πολλοί. For such generalized
neuters, see the note on τὸ . . .
βαρβαρικόν, c. 2. 3.

ἀνατεταραγμένον, in a state of complete disorder.

τῶν ὅπλων: partitive gen. with
πολλά.

95 τοῖς στρατιώταις: dat. of advantage; contrast αὐτῷ, above.

ἤγοντο: a common custom. The
hoplite's shield, cuirass, and
helmet made up a heavy weight.
That Cyrus tolerated such laxity
at this time shows how completely confident he was that his
cause was already won. Cf.
Plutarch, Artox. 7. Note again
the pl. vb. with neut. pl. subj.
Cf. l. 82, and the note on c. 2. 38.

CHAPTER VIII

1 ἀμφὶ ἀγορὰν πλήθουσαν: i.e., about
the middle of the morning.

2 σταθμός, halting-place.

καταλύειν, to halt, i. e. for the morning meal (ἄριστον); cf. I, 10, § 19.

4 ἀνὰ κράτος, at full speed; cf. κατὰ
κράτος, below, § 19. Save in special uses ἀνά is scarcely used in
prose, although compounds are
very common.

ἱδροῦντι τῷ ἵππῳ, with his horse
bathed in sweat. The notions
of means, manner, and accompaniment are often blended in
the dat.

5 ἐβόα: note the tense. Xenophon's
description is very graphic.

βαρβαρικῶς: i. e. in Persian.

6 προσέρχεται: the retention of the
indic. adds greatly to the vividness of the passage.

ἔνθα δὴ . . . ἐγένετο, then indeed
ensued a scene of great confusion. The form, τάραχος, is

BATTLE OF CUNAXA

First Position of the Two Armies

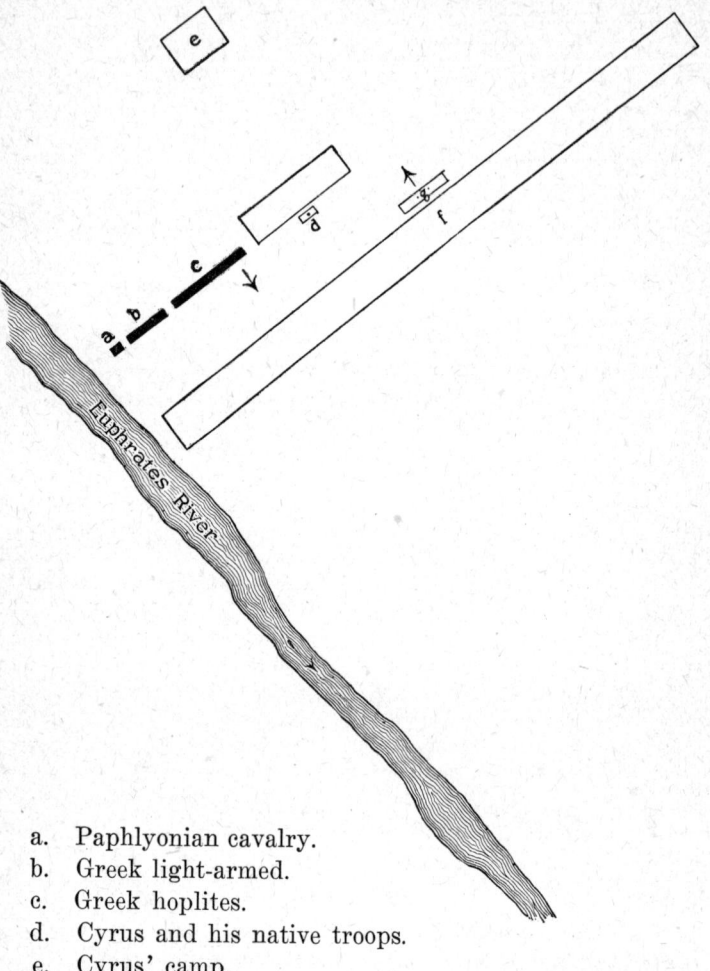

a. Paphlyonian cavalry.
b. Greek light-armed.
c. Greek hoplites.
d. Cyrus and his native troops.
e. Cyrus' camp.
f. Army of Artaxerxes.
g. Position of Artaxerxes.

BATTLE OF CUNAXA

Second Position of the Two Armies

The Greeks have advanced in pursuit of the Persians, who had fled before them. The king, whose army, save those facing the Greeks, had met with no opposition, proceeded against Cyrus' camp and pillaged it. There he was joined by Tissaphernes, who with his body of horse had ridden through the Greek peltasts. After this the king returned by the same way by which he had advanced,—*i. e.*, outside of what had originally been the left wing of Cyrus' army. The Greeks, seeing his advance, wheeled about in order to meet his attack. They therefore now face up-stream, the river being on their left, as it had before been on their right. Fearing that the king might attack them on the right flank, they were planning to fall back and bring the river in their rear (see the note on c. 10, 41); but the king meanwhile shifted his position, so as to face them.

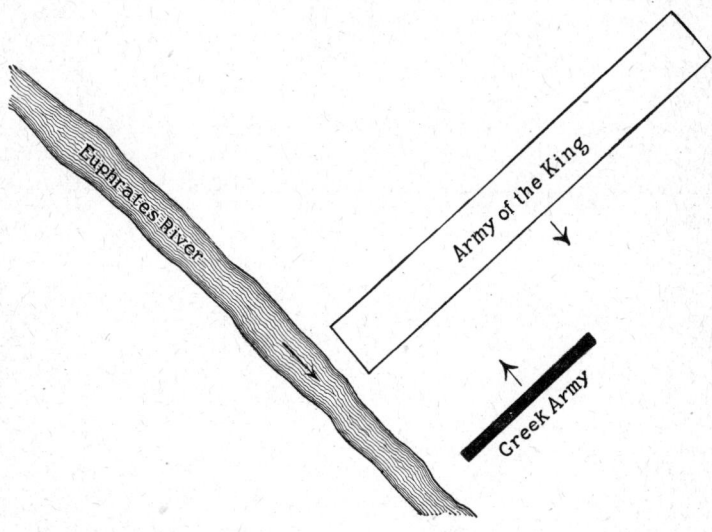

δὴ πολὺς τάραχος ἐγένετο· αὐτίκα γὰρ ἐδόκουν οἱ Ἕλληνες 2
καὶ πάντες δὲ ἀτάκτοις σφίσιν ἐπιπεσεῖσθαι· Κῦρός τε κατα- 3
πηδήσας ἀπὸ τοῦ ἅρματος τὸν θώρακα ἐνεδύετο καὶ ἀναβὰς
ἐπὶ τὸν ἵππον τὰ παλτὰ εἰς τὰς χεῖρας ἔλαβε, τοῖς τε ἄλλοις
πᾶσι παρήγγελλεν ἐξοπλίζεσθαι καὶ καθίστασθαι εἰς τὴν
ἑαυτοῦ τάξιν ἕκαστον. ἔνθα δὴ σὺν πολλῇ σπουδῇ καθί- 4
σταντο, Κλέαρχος μὲν τὰ δεξιὰ τοῦ κέρατος ἔχων πρὸς τῷ
Εὐφράτῃ ποταμῷ, Πρόξενος δὲ ἐχόμενος, οἱ δὲ ἄλλοι μετὰ
τοῦτον, Μένων δὲ [καὶ τὸ στράτευμα] τὸ εὐώνυμον κέρας ἔσχε
τοῦ Ἑλληνικοῦ. τοῦ δὲ βαρβαρικοῦ ἱππεῖς μὲν Παφλαγόνες 5
εἰς χιλίους παρὰ Κλέαρχον ἔστησαν ἐν τῷ δεξιῷ καὶ τὸ

---

found several times in Xen.; ταραχή is far commoner.

7 αὐτίκα: with ἐπιπεσεῖσθαι, but brought to the head of the clause for emphasis.

ἐδόκουν, *they thought; cf.* c. 7. 4.

8 σφίσιν: the reflexive is indirect.

ἐπιπεσεῖσθαι: the context makes clear what the subj. is. For the form, see G. 666; H. 426; B. 214.

9 τοῦ ἅρματος: the art. with this and with the following nouns is possessive.

10 τὸν ἵππον: Plutarch, *Artox.* 9 (from Ctesias; see the Introd., § 30), describes Cyrus' horse as γενναῖον (*high-bred*), ἄστομον (*hard-mouthed*), and ὑβριστήν (*fiery*); *cf.* Alexander's *Bucephalus.*

τὰ παλτά: *cf.* c. 5. 92.

τοῖς τε ἄλλοις . . . ἕκαστον: for ἕκαστον, after a pl., see the note on ἑκάστοις, c. 1. 25; and for the acc., after a dat., on λαβόντι, c. 2. 4.

11 ἐξοπλίζεσθαι: they were unarmed and had broken ranks.

13 τὰ δεξιὰ τοῦ κέρατος, *the extreme right;* see the plan and the Introd., § 30. The Greeks, as a body, formed the δεξιὸν κέρας of the whole force. With the form κέρατος contrast κέρως, c. 7. 6.

14 ἐχόμενος, *next to him* (*sc.* αὐτοῦ, partitive gen.).

15 [καὶ τὸ στράτευμα]: if these words are genuine, they must refer to Menon's own force. The text is, however, uncertain. For ἔσχε we should have expected εἶχε, although the context may perhaps justify the ingressive form.

16 τοῦ Ἑλληνικοῦ: added, because this was not the left of the whole force.

τοῦ δὲ βαρβαρικοῦ: brought by its position into strong contrast with the preceding Ἑλληνικοῦ. The gen. is partitive with ἱππεῖς.

17 εἰς, *to the number of; cf.* c. 2. 15.

παρὰ Κλέαρχον: acc., since ἔστησαν expresses motion.

ἐν τῷ δεξιῷ: these troops were, therefore, between Clearchus' hoplites and the river.

Ἑλληνικὸν πελταστικόν, ἐν δὲ τῷ εὐωνύμῳ Ἀριαῖός τε ὁ Κύρου
6 ὕπαρχος καὶ τὸ ἄλλο βαρβαρικόν, Κῦρος δὲ καὶ ἱππεῖς τούτου
ὅσον ἑξακόσιοι ⟨κατὰ τὸ μέσον⟩, ὡπλισμένοι θώραξι μὲν αὐτοὶ 20
καὶ παραμηριδίοις καὶ κράνεσι πάντες πλὴν Κύρου· Κῦρος δὲ
7 ψιλὴν ἔχων τὴν κεφαλὴν εἰς τὴν μάχην καθίστατο. οἱ δ'
ἵπποι πάντες εἶχον καὶ προμετωπίδια καὶ προστερνίδια· εἶχον
δὲ καὶ μαχαίρας οἱ ἱππεῖς Ἑλληνικάς.

8 Καὶ ἤδη τε ἦν μέσον ἡμέρας καὶ οὔπω καταφανεῖς ἦσαν 25
οἱ πολέμιοι· ἡνίκα δὲ δείλη ἐγίγνετο, ἐφάνη κονιορτὸς ὥσπερ
νεφέλη λευκή, χρόνῳ δὲ συχνῷ ὕστερον ὥσπερ μελανία τις ἐν
τῷ πεδίῳ ἐπὶ πολύ. ὅτε δὲ ἐγγύτερον ἐγίγνοντο, τάχα δὴ καὶ
χαλκός τις ἤστραπτε καὶ λόγχαι καὶ αἱ τάξεις καταφανεῖς
9 ἐγίγνοντο. καὶ ἦσαν ἱππεῖς μὲν λευκοθώρακες ἐπὶ τοῦ εὐω- 30

---

18 τῷ εὐωνύμῳ: *i. e.*, of the whole force.

Ἀριαῖος: see the Introd., § 32.

19 καὶ ἱππεῖς τούτου, *and horsemen of his, a body-guard of horsemen.*

20 ὅσον, *about;* see the note on c. 2. 15.

⟨κατὰ τὸ μέσον⟩: these words are conjecturally inserted as required by the sense. We must supply ἔστησαν.

αὐτοί: contrasted with οἱ δ' ἵπποι, below, l. 22.

21 πλὴν Κύρου: this has reference to the helmet alone, as the context shows. Cyrus was otherwise fully armed.

22 ψιλήν: pred. The word is emphasized by its position. Plutarch (*Artox.* 11) states that Cyrus wore the tiara—the badge of kingly authority.

οἱ δ' ἵπποι: δέ answers to μέν, above, l. 20. That cavalry horses should be protected by armor is recommended by Xen. in his treatise *De Re Equestri* XII, 8 (*cf.*, also, *Cyrop.* VI, 4, 1). It seems not to have been a Greek custom.

25 ἤδη τε ἦν . . . καί: *cf.* the opening words of the chapter.

26 δείλη, (*early*) *afternoon.* In III, 3, § 11, the word means *evening*. When doubt might exist in the mind of the hearer or reader, the adj. πρωΐα (*early*) might be added.

ἐγίγνετο, *was getting to be.*

ἐφάνη, *there appeared.* Retain the Greek order in this graphic description.

27 λευκή: a cloud of dust, seen in the distance, seems white in the sunshine.

χρόνῳ . . . πολύ, *and, some time afterward, a sort of* (τις) *blackness on the plain, extending over a great distance.*

28 καὶ χαλκός τις ἤστραπτε, *their bronze* (*armor*) *too* (καί) *began to flash here and there* (τις).

30 λευκοθώρακες: probably these

νύμου τῶν πολεμίων· Τισσαφέρνης ἐλέγετο τούτων ἄρχειν·
ἐχόμενοι δὲ γερροφόροι, ἐχόμενοι δὲ ὁπλῖται σὺν ποδήρεσι
ξυλίναις ἀσπίσιν. Αἰγύπτιοι δ' οὗτοι ἐλέγοντο εἶναι· ἄλλοι δ'
ἱππεῖς, ἄλλοι τοξόται. πάντες δ' οὗτοι κατὰ ἔθνη ἐν πλαισίῳ
35 πλήρει ἀνθρώπων ἕκαστον τὸ ἔθνος ἐπορεύοντο. πρὸ δὲ αὐτῶν 10
ἅρματα διαλείποντα συχνὸν ἀπ' ἀλλήλων τὰ δὴ δρεπανηφόρα
καλούμενα· εἶχον δὲ τὰ δρέπανα ἐκ τῶν ἀξόνων εἰς πλάγιον
ἀποτεταμένα καὶ ὑπὸ τοῖς δίφροις εἰς γῆν βλέποντα, ὡς διακόπτειν ὅτῳ ἐντυγχάνοιεν. ἡ δὲ γνώμη ἦν ὡς εἰς τὰς τάξεις
40 τῶν Ἑλλήνων ἐλῶντα καὶ διακόψοντα. ὃ μέντοι Κῦρος εἶπεν 11
ὅτε καλέσας παρεκελεύετο τοῖς Ἕλλησι τὴν κραυγὴν τῶν βαρ-

---

cuirasses were of linen (IV, 7, §15).

31 Τισσαφέρνης: normal asyndeton.

32 ἐχόμενοι: cf. ἐχόμενος, above, l. 14, and the note.
γερροφόροι: i.e., the Persian infantry. These wicker shields and the wooden Egyptian shields are mentioned (II, 1, § 6) as found in great quantities on the battlefield next day.

33 Αἰγύπτιοι: as Egypt was at this time in revolt, these may be assumed to be descendants of the Egyptians whom Cyrus the Great had settled in Persia (Xen., *Cyrop.* VII, 1, 45).

34 πάντες ... ἐπορεύοντο, *all of these were marching nation by nation* (a Persian custom), *each nation in a solid square.* ἕκαστον τὸ ἔθνος is in apposition with οὗτοι.

36 ἅρματα: retain the Greek order, and observe that ἅρματα has no article, while τὰ δὴ δρεπανηφόρα is purposely postponed. For the partic. καλούμενα, cf. c. 2. 79.
διαλείποντα ... ἀλλήλων, at considerable intervals from one another. See the note on διαστάντες, c. 5. 11.

37 εἶχον: for the pl., *cf.* c. 7. 95, and the note. With the description here given *cf.* Xen. *Cyrop.* VI, 1, 29 and 30.
εἰς πλάγιον ἀποτεταμένα, *extending out slantwise.*

38 ὡς διακόπτειν: ὡς for ὥστε; *cf.* c. 5. 64, and the note.

39 ὅτῳ ἐντυγχάνοιεν: for ὅτῳ ἂν ἐντυγχάνωσι, after the implied indir. disc. See the note on c. 3. 19.
ἡ δὲ γνώμη ... διακόψοντα, *the purpose was that they should drive through the ranks of the Greeks and cut them down.* The partics., ἐλῶντα and διακόψοντα, are in the acc. abs., a construction unusual, save with impers. vbs.

40 ὃ μέντοι ... εἶπεν: *cf.* c. 7. 20. The antecedent is τοῦτο, below.

41 τοῖς Ἕλλησι: dat. with παρεκελεύετο, the obj. of καλέσας being unexpressed. This is regular in Greek.

βάρων ἀνέχεσθαι, ἐψεύσθη τοῦτο· οὐ γὰρ κραυγῇ ἀλλὰ σιγῇ
ὡς ἀνυστὸν καὶ ἡσυχῇ ἐν ἴσῳ καὶ βραδέως προσῇσαν.

12 Καὶ ἐν τούτῳ Κῦρος παρελαύνων αὐτὸς σὺν Πίγρητι τῷ
ἑρμηνεῖ καὶ ἄλλοις τρισὶν ἢ τέτταρσι τῷ Κλεάρχῳ ἐβόα ἄγειν 45
τὸ στράτευμα κατὰ μέσον τὸ τῶν πολεμίων, ὅτι ἐκεῖ βασιλεὺς
13 εἴη· κἂν τοῦτ', ἔφη, νικῶμεν, πάνθ' ἡμῖν πεποίηται. ὁρῶν δὲ
ὁ Κλέαρχος τὸ μέσον στῖφος καὶ ἀκούων Κύρου ἔξω ὄντα τοῦ
εὐωνύμου βασιλέα—τοσοῦτον γὰρ πλήθει περιῆν βασιλεὺς ὥστε
μέσον τῶν ἑαυτοῦ ἔχων τοῦ Κύρου εὐωνύμου ἔξω ἦν—ἀλλ' ὅμως 50
ὁ Κλέαρχος οὐκ ἤθελεν ἀποσπάσαι ἀπὸ τοῦ ποταμοῦ τὸ δεξιὸν
κέρας, φοβούμενος μὴ κυκλωθείη ἑκατέρωθεν, τῷ δὲ Κύρῳ ἀπεκρίνατο ὅτι αὐτῷ μέλει ὅπως καλῶς ἔχοι.

---

42 τοῦτο, *in this*, acc. of specification.

οὐ γὰρ κραυγῇ: dat. of manner. Cyrus' expectation was, however, a reasonable one and is corroborated by what we are told of the advance of the Persians at Plataea (Herod. IX, 59) and again at Issus and at Arbela. Plutarch (*Artox.* 7) also speaks of the Greek surprise at the orderly advance of the Persians.

σιγῇ ὡς ἀνυστόν, *as quietly as possible*. ἀνυστόν is a poetical equivalent of δυνατόν.

43 ἐν ἴσῳ, *in even line; cf.* ὁμαλῶς, l. 55.

44 αὐτός, *by himself, i. e. unattended*. In such cases αὐτός practically = μόνος.

45 ἐβόα, *kept crying out to*. The vb. is construed as a vb. of commanding.

46 ὅτι ... εἴη: a causal sentence, with the construction of indir. disc.; *cf.* c. 5. 90, and the note. The more vivid form of direct speech is at once resumed.

47 πεποίηται: perf. for fut. perf., with a distinct gain in vividness; see G. 1264; H. 848; B. 537. ἡμῖν is dat. of the agent (G. 1186; H. 769; B. 380).

ὁρῶν, *although he saw;* so ἀκούων, below.

48 τὸ μέσον στῖφος, *the solid body at the centre (i. e.* the 6,000, mentioned, c. 7. 55.

Κύρου: *cf.* Τισσαφέρνους, c. 2. 26, and the note.

ὄντα: *cf.* c. 2. 126, and the note.

49 πλήθει: for the case, see G. 1182; H. 780; B. 390.

50 τοῦ: with εὐωνύμου, not with Κύρου. The former is governed by ἔξω; the latter is possessive.

ἀλλ' ὅμως, *despite all this*, resuming the concessive partics. above.

51 οὐκ ἤθελεν, *would not*. A Greek commander kept his right flank (the shieldless side) protected, if possible. Spartan generals were often overcautious.

53 ὅτι αὐτῷ μέλει, *that he was taking care*. Our idiom would more naturally have, *he would see;* but the Greek is pres., not fut.

ὅπως καλῶς ἔχοι, *that all should be*

Καὶ ἐν τούτῳ τῷ καιρῷ τὸ μὲν βαρβαρικὸν στράτευμα 14
ὁμαλῶς προῄει, τὸ δὲ Ἑλληνικὸν ἔτι ἐν τῷ αὐτῷ μένον συνετάττετο ἐκ τῶν ἔτι προσιόντων. καὶ ὁ Κῦρος παρελαύνων οὐ
πάνυ πρὸς αὐτῷ τῷ στρατεύματι κατεθεᾶτο ἑκατέρωσε ἀποβλέπων εἴς τε τοὺς πολεμίους καὶ τοὺς φίλους. ἰδὼν δὲ αὐτὸν 15
ἀπὸ τοῦ Ἑλληνικοῦ Ξενοφῶν Ἀθηναῖος, πελάσας ὡς συναντῆσαι ἤρετο εἴ τι παραγγέλλοι. ὁ δ' ἐπιστήσας εἶπε καὶ
λέγειν ἐκέλευε πᾶσιν ὅτι καὶ τὰ ἱερὰ καλὰ καὶ τὰ σφάγια καλά.
ταῦτα δὲ λέγων θορύβου ἤκουσε διὰ τῶν τάξεων ἰόντος, καὶ 16
ἤρετο τίς ὁ θόρυβος εἴη. ὁ δὲ εἶπεν ὅτι σύνθημα παρέρχεται

---

well. For the opt. in the obj. clause, see the note on ὡς εἴησαν, c. 1. 21. Plutarch (*Artox.* 8), after remarking that Clearchus, if inclined to be as cautious as this, ought to have remained at home, adds, ὁ δὲ (*i. e.* Κλέαρχος) αὐτῷ μέλειν εἰπὼν ὅπως ἕξει κάλλιστα, τὸ πᾶν διέφθειρεν. In this view modern scholars have generally concurred.

54 τὸ μὲν βαρβαρικὸν στράτευμα: *i. e.* the king's army.

55 ὁμαλῶς: *cf.* ἐν ἴσῳ, above, l. 43.

συνετάττετο, *was completing its formation.*

56 τῶν ἔτι προσιόντων: the army marched in column, so that the line was long.

οὐ πάνυ πρός, *at some little distance from.*

57 κατεθεᾶτο: attentive observation from a point of outlook (κατα-).

59 Ξενοφῶν Ἀθηναῖος: the first mention of Xen. in the *Anabasis*. For his position in the army, see III, 1, §§ 4 ff., and the Introd., § 4. Note the modest omission of the art. with Ἀθηναῖος.

πελάσας ὡς συναντῆσαι, *coming up to meet him.* πελάσας is one of Xen.'s poetic words. ὡς stands here for ὥστε, as above, l. 38.

60 εἴ τι παραγγέλλοι, *whether he had any commands to give.*

ἐπιστήσας, *reining in (his horse).*

61 τὰ ἱερά: omens (according to the old interpretation) drawn from the appearance of the vital organs, while σφάγια were omens drawn from the movements of the victims. It is now held that ἱερά was the general term for sacrifice and that σφάγια denoted special or propitiatory sacrifices. The Greek offered sacrifice before all important undertakings; if the omens at the first were unfavorable, he persisted in his sacrifice; see II, 2, § 3, and the note. Observe here the emphatic repetition of καλά.

62 ταῦτα ... λέγων, *while saying this;* note the tense.

θορύβου ... ἰόντος: for the case, see G. 1102; H. 742; B. 356. The partic. is not in indir. disc. (G. 1582; 1583; H. 968; B. 661 note 1, end).

63 τίς ... εἴη: dir. interrog., in an indir. ques. Just below we have

δεύτερον ἤδη. καὶ ὃς ἐθαύμασε τίς παραγγέλλει καὶ ἤρετο
ὅ,τι εἴη τὸ σύνθημα. ὁ δ' ἀπεκρίνατο Ζεὺς σωτὴρ καὶ νίκη. 65
17 ὁ δὲ Κῦρος ἀκούσας Ἀλλὰ δέχομαί τε, ἔφη, καὶ τοῦτο ἔστω.
ταῦτα δ' εἰπὼν εἰς τὴν αὑτοῦ χώραν ἀπήλαυνε.

Καὶ οὐκέτι τρία ἢ τέτταρα στάδια διειχέτην τὼ φάλαγγε
ἀπ' ἀλλήλων ἡνίκα ἐπαιάνιζόν τε οἱ Ἕλληνες καὶ ἤρχοντο
18 ἀντίοι ἰέναι τοῖς πολεμίοις. ὡς δὲ πορευομένων ἐξεκύμαινέ τι 70
τῆς φάλαγγος, τὸ ὑπολειπόμενον ἤρξατο δρόμῳ θεῖν· καὶ ἅμα
ἐφθέγξαντο πάντες οἷον τῷ Ἐνυαλίῳ ἐλελίζουσι, καὶ πάντες δὲ
ἔθεον. λέγουσι δέ τινες ὡς καὶ ταῖς ἀσπίσι πρὸς τὰ δόρατα

ὅ,τι εἴη. Both forms are common. Note, also, the free use of the indic., instead of the opt., in this section.

64 δεύτερον: the watchword was passed down the line and back again.

ἤδη: brought into prominence by its postponement.

καὶ ὅς, and he (Cyrus). The rel. with demonstrative force is found chiefly in this phrase (G. 1023, 2; H. 655a; B. 144a).

ἐθαύμασε: he himself should have been the one to give it.

66 ἀλλὰ δέχομαι, well, I accept it.

τοῦτο ἔστω, so be it. This probably means no more than be this the watchword; not as some have assumed, may victory be ours.

67 χώραν: cf. c. 5. 101. Where was Cyrus' position?

68 τὼ φάλαγγε: for the form τώ, as a fem.. see G. 388; H. 272a; B.144.

69 ἐπαιάνιζον: see the Introd., § 30.

ἤρχοντο: these augmented forms are always, in Attic prose, to be referred to ἄρχομαι, never to ἔρχομαι.

70 ἀντίοι: see the note on προτέρα, c. 2. 142.

πορευομένων: sc. αὐτῶν; cf. προϊόντων, c. 2. 99, and the note.

ἐξεκύμαινε . . . φάλαγγος, a part of the phalanx billowed out. The metaphor is graphic, but was natural to the Greek; cf. ὥσπερ θάλαττα, c. 5. 4, and the note.

71 τὸ ὑπολειπόμενον: the neut. is all the more natural, because of the preceding τι. In general, however, such phrases are common; see the note on τὸ βαρβαρικόν, c. 2. 3.

δρόμῳ θεῖν, to charge at double quick. The use of θεῖν is almost limited to this phrase in most prose writers. In Xen. it has a wider range (in IV, 8, § 28 there is no military connotation). The Greeks regularly charged the enemy on the run; see Herodotus' account of Marathon (VI, 112).

72 οἷον, such a shout as, inner obj.

Ἐνυαλίῳ: an epithet of Ares, the destroyer; cf. V, 2, § 14.

ἐλελίζουσι: the vb. is formed directly from the cry ἐλελεῦ (hurrah). This is the case with many vbs. in -ζω.

73 λέγουσι δέ τινες: probably an-

ἐδούπησαν φόβον ποιοῦντες τοῖς ἵπποις. πρὶν δὲ τόξευμα 19
ἐξικνεῖσθαι ἐκκλίνουσιν οἱ βάρβαροι καὶ φεύγουσι. καὶ ἐνταῦθα δὴ ἐδίωκον μὲν κατὰ κράτος οἱ Ἕλληνες, ἐβόων δὲ
ἀλλήλοις μὴ θεῖν δρόμῳ, ἀλλ' ἐν τάξει ἕπεσθαι. τὰ δ' 20
ἅρματα ἐφέροντο τὰ μὲν δι' αὐτῶν τῶν πολεμίων, τὰ δὲ καὶ
διὰ τῶν Ἑλλήνων κενὰ ἡνιόχων. οἳ δ' ἐπεὶ προΐδοιεν, διίσ-
ταντο· ἔστι δ' ὅστις καὶ κατελήφθη ὥσπερ ἐν ἱπποδρόμῳ
ἐκπλαγείς· καὶ οὐδὲν μέντοι οὐδὲ τοῦτον παθεῖν ἔφασαν, οὐδ'
ἄλλος δὲ τῶν Ἑλλήνων ἐν ταύτῃ τῇ μάχῃ ἔπαθεν οὐδεὶς
οὐδέν, πλὴν ἐπὶ τῷ εὐωνύμῳ τοξευθῆναί τις ἐλέγετο.

Κῦρος δ' ὁρῶν τοὺς Ἕλληνας νικῶντας τὸ καθ' αὑτοὺς καὶ 21
διώκοντας, ἡδόμενος καὶ προσκυνούμενος ἤδη ὡς βασιλεὺς ὑπὸ

other interpolated note, not by Xen. On this view τινες designates other historians; others consider that Xen. is quoting statements made by certain of the Greeks themselves after the battle, which seems very unlikely. With the whole passage *cf.* IV, 5, § 18.

74 ἐδούπησαν is a poetic word; Xen. has also the noun δοῦπος, II, 2, § 19.

πρὶν δὲ ... ἐξικνεῖσθαι, freely, *before the Greeks were within bowshot of them.* For the syntax of πρίν, see the note on c. 2. 153.

76 κατὰ κράτος: *cf.* ἀνὰ κράτος, above, 1. 4.

ἐβόων: *cf.* l. 5.

77 θεῖν δρόμῳ: here the phrase implies breaking ranks.

τὰ δ' ἅρματα ... τὰ μὲν ... τὰ δέ: partitive apposition (G. 914; H. 624d; B. 319).

78 ἐφέροντο: the vb. often denotes violent, uncontrollable motion; *cf.* IV, 2, § 3. The pl. vb. (see the note on c. 2. 38) is perhaps to be explained by the assumption that Xen. thinks of the chariots severally, rather than collectively.

79 κενὰ ἡνιόχων: the gen. as with ἔρημος, c. 3. 30.

ἐπεὶ προΐδοιεν: see the note on ὁπότε βούλοιτο, c. 2. 40.

διίσταντο, *opened ranks.* Note the prep., and *cf.* διαλείποντα, above, 1. 36.

80 ἔστι δ' ὅστις, *there was one man who.* The Greek expresses the indefinite idea by the rel.; Eng. by the antecedent. In these phrases the vb. is generally present, even in cases where the past would seem more logical. *Cf.* the note on ἦν οὕς, c. 5. 35. Xen. plainly refers to a single individual; *cf.* τοῦτον, below.

καί, *actually.*

81 ἐκπλαγείς, *scared out of his wits.*

οὐδὲ ... οὐδέ, *not even ... nor.*

82 οὐδεὶς οὐδέν: indef. words assume neg. form in a neg. sentence; see the note on οὐδενί, c. 2. 152.

84 τὸ καθ' αὑτούς, *those opposite them,* another collective neut.

85 ἡδόμενος ... προσκυνούμενος:

τῶν ἀμφ' αὑτόν, οὐδ' ὡς ἐξήχθη διώκειν, ἀλλὰ συνεσπειραμένην ἔχων τὴν τῶν σὺν ἑαυτῷ ἑξακοσίων ἱππέων τάξιν ἐπεμελεῖτο ὅ,τι ποιήσει βασιλεύς. καὶ γὰρ ᾔδει αὐτὸν ὅτι μέσον
22 ἔχοι τοῦ Περσικοῦ στρατεύματος. καὶ πάντες δ' οἱ τῶν βαρβάρων ἄρχοντες μέσον ἔχοντες τὸ αὑτῶν ἡγοῦνται, νομίζοντες 90
οὕτω καὶ ἐν ἀσφαλεστάτῳ εἶναι, ἢν ᾖ ἡ ἰσχὺς αὐτῶν ἑκατέρωθεν, καὶ εἴ τι παραγγεῖλαι χρῄζοιεν, ἡμίσει ἂν χρόνῳ αἰσθά-
23 νεσθαι τὸ στράτευμα. καὶ βασιλεὺς δὴ τότε μέσον ἔχων τῆς
αὑτοῦ στρατιᾶς ὅμως ἔξω ἐγένετο τοῦ Κύρου εὐωνύμου κέρατος.
ἐπεὶ δ' οὐδεὶς αὐτῷ ἐμάχετο ἐκ τοῦ ἀντίου οὐδὲ τοῖς αὑτοῦ 95
τεταγμένοις ἔμπροσθεν, ἐπέκαμπτεν ὡς εἰς κύκλωσιν.

24 Ἔνθα δὴ Κῦρος δείσας μὴ ὄπισθεν γενόμενος κατακόψῃ
τὸ Ἑλληνικὸν ἐλαύνει ἀντίος· καὶ ἐμβαλὼν σὺν τοῖς ἑξακοσίοις
νικᾷ τοὺς πρὸ βασιλέως τεταγμένους καὶ εἰς φυγὴν ἔτρεψε τοὺς
ἑξακισχιλίους, καὶ ἀποκτεῖναι λέγεται αὐτὸς τῇ ἑαυτοῦ χειρὶ 100

---

both concessive. For the latter
vb., *cf.* c. 6. 60.

86 οὐδ' ὥς, *not even thus*, resuming
the preceding partics. For the
use of ὥς (always accented) in
the sense of οὕτως, see G. 138, 3;
H. 120. It survives in prose only
after an intensive, καί or οὐδέ
(μηδέ).

συνεσπειραμένην ἔχων, *keeping in
close order*.

87 ἐπεμελεῖτο, *waited to see*, followed by an indir. ques.

88 ᾔδει αὐτὸν ὅτι, *knew that he*.
For the prolepsis, see c. 1. 20,
and the note.

90 μέσον . . . αὑτῶν, *holding the
centre of their own force*.

91 οὕτω: resumes the partic., and
is itself explained by the following condit. clause.

ἢν ᾖ: the condit. is general (G.
1393, 1; H. 894; B. 609).

92 καὶ εἰ . . . χρῄζοιεν, *and, should
they wish to give any orders*.

Note the change to the ideal
form (less vivid fut.).

ἡμίσει . . . χρόνῳ: the dat. of time
commonly has the prep.

ἂν . . . αἰσθάνεσθαι: direct, ἄν . . .
αἰσθάνοιτο; see the note on ἂν
εἶναι, c. 3. 29.

93 καὶ . . . δὴ τότε, *and so in this
case*. δή often introduces the
particular instance of a general
truth. *Cf.* c. 3. 65.

95 αὑτοῦ: with ἔμπροσθεν.

96 ὡς εἰς κύκλωσιν, *as if to surround* (the enemy). For this
movement, see the second position on the plan.

98 τοῖς ἑξακοσίοις: see l. 20.

99 τοὺς ἑξακισχιλίους: see c. 7. 55 f.
The words are postponed to emphasize the contrast—six hundred men routed six thousand.

100 αὐτὸς . . . χειρί, *himself with
his own hand*. αὐτός is redundant but forcible (G. 997; H. 688;
B. 473).

Ἀρταγέρσην τὸν ἄρχοντα αὐτῶν. ὡς δ' ἡ τροπὴ ἐγένετο, διασπείρονται καὶ οἱ Κύρου ἑξακόσιοι εἰς τὸ διώκειν ὁρμήσαντες, πλὴν πάνυ ὀλίγοι ἀμφ' αὐτὸν κατελείφθησαν, σχεδὸν οἱ ὁμοτράπεζοι καλούμενοι. σὺν τούτοις δὲ ὢν καθορᾷ βασιλέα καὶ τὸ ἀμφ' ἐκεῖνον στῖφος· καὶ εὐθὺς οὐκ ἠνέσχετο, ἀλλ' εἰπών, Τὸν ἄνδρα ὁρῶ, ἵετο ἐπ' αὐτὸν καὶ παίει κατὰ τὸ στέρνον καὶ τιτρώσκει διὰ τοῦ θώρακος, ὥς φησι Κτησίας ὁ ἰατρός, καὶ ἰᾶσθαι αὐτὸς τὸ τραῦμά φησι.

Παίοντα δ' αὐτὸν ἀκοντίζει τις παλτῷ ὑπὸ τὸν ὀφθαλμὸν βιαίως· καὶ ἐνταῦθα μαχόμενοι καὶ βασιλεὺς καὶ Κῦρος καὶ οἱ ἀμφ' αὐτοὺς ὑπὲρ ἑκατέρου, ὁπόσοι μὲν τῶν ἀμφὶ βασιλέα ἀπέθνησκον Κτησίας λέγει· παρ' ἐκείνῳ γὰρ ἦν· Κῦρος δὲ

101 **Ἀρταγέρσην**: see Plutarch, *Artox.* 9, for an account of the combat between the two.

102 **εἰς τὸ διώκειν**, *in pursuit.*

103 **πλήν**: the conjunc., not the prep.; see the note on c. 2. 140.

οἱ ὁμοτράπεζοι καλούμενοι, *his table companions, so called.* This was a title of honor among the Persians for the king's most trusted and most devoted followers. They were allowed to dine in the same room with the king, or in one immediately adjoining. No one might sit at the king's own table. In I, 9, 31 they are called συντράπεζοι.

104 **καθορᾷ**, *he caught sight of* (properly used of one looking down [κατα-] from a point of vantage).

105 **στῖφος**: doubtless the king's ὁμοτράπεζοι, loyally rallying to his defense, although the main body of the 6,000 had fled.

οὐκ ἠνέσχετο, *lost control of himself.* For the double augment, see G. 544; H. 361a; B. 175 note.

107 **Κτησίας**: see the Introd., § 30. He was for years the Persian court physician. Xen. mentions him only here and below, l. 112.

καὶ ἰᾶσθαι ... φησι, *and declares that he himself healed the wound.* It is not necessary to assume that the rel. ὅς has fallen out after ἰατρός. ἰᾶσθαι, if right, is the impf. infin. (G. 1285, 1; H. 853a; B. 671; G. M. T. 119). Some read, on conjecture, ἰάσασθαι.

109 **τις**: Mithradates, in Ctesias' account.

110 **μαχόμενοι**: translate as if gen. abs. The structure of the sentence shifts, so that, instead of the expected vb., we have the indir. ques., ὁπόσοι ἀπέθνησκον. Diodorus, perhaps drawing from Ephorus, a historian of the fourth century B.C., states that over 15,000 fell on the side of Artaxerxes, and 3,000 of Cyrus' barbarian troops.

112 **ἀπέθνησκον ... ἀπέθανε**: the

αὐτός τε ἀπέθανε καὶ ὀκτὼ οἱ ἄριστοι τῶν περὶ αὐτὸν ἔκειντο ἐπ' αὐτῷ. Ἀρταπάτης δ' ὁ πιστότατος αὐτῷ τῶν σκηπτούχων θεράπων λέγεται, ἐπειδὴ πεπτωκότα εἶδε Κῦρον, καταπηδήσας ἀπὸ τοῦ ἵππου περιπεσεῖν αὐτῷ. καὶ οἱ μέν φασι βασιλέα κελεῦσαί τινα ἐπισφάξαι αὐτὸν Κύρῳ, οἱ δ' ἑαυτὸν ἐπισφάξασθαι σπασάμενον τὸν ἀκινάκην· εἶχε γὰρ χρυσοῦν· καὶ στρεπτὸν δ' ἐφόρει καὶ ψέλια καὶ τἆλλα ὥσπερ οἱ ἄριστοι Περσῶν· ἐτετίμητο γὰρ ὑπὸ Κύρου δι' εὔνοιάν τε καὶ πιστότητα.

IX. Κῦρος μὲν οὖν οὕτως ἐτελεύτησεν, ἀνὴρ ὢν Περσῶν τῶν μετὰ Κῦρον τὸν ἀρχαῖον γενομένων βασιλικώτατός τε καὶ ἄρχειν ἀξιώτατος, ὡς παρὰ πάντων ὁμολογεῖται τῶν Κύρου δοκούντων

imperf. of the multitude, the aor. of the individual.

113 ἔκειντο: κεῖμαι is a passive of τίθημι: *were laid low*.

114 Ἀρταπάτης: see c. 6. 61.

116 περιπεσεῖν, *to have flung himself about him*.

αὐτῷ: the dat. is due to the compound vb. (G. 1179; H. 775; B. 304); *cf.* Κύρῳ, below.

117 ἑαυτὸν ἐπισφάξασθαι: the reflexive is redundant with the mid. vb., but serves to emphasize the reflexive idea (*cf.* αὐτὸς . . . ἑαυτοῦ χειρί, l. 100). As a rule, the simple mid. is used of actions that are normal or natural, the act. with the reflexive of actions that are abnormal.

119 ἐφόρει, *wore*. φορῶ is the frequentative of φέρω.

ὥσπερ . . . Περσῶν: for the dress and decorations of the Persian noble, see I, 2, § 27, and I, 5, § 8.

CHAPTER IX

This chapter is noteworthy as being, perhaps, the oldest biographical sketch in literature. It is, of course, idealized. Xen. portrays only the favorable sides of his hero's character; yet modern historians have generally followed him. It is striking that Xen. interrupts his account of the battle in order to introduce this sketch. *Cf.* the biographical sketches in II, 6.

1 ἀνὴρ ὤν, *a man who was*.

Περσῶν: partit. gen. with the following superlatives.

τῶν . . . γενομένων: note the effect of the third attrib. position; see the note on c. 5. 7, and *cf.* Κῦρον τὸν ἀρχαῖον, below.

2 Κῦρον τὸν ἀρχαῖον: Cyrus the Great, the founder of the Persian Empire (B.C. 560-529). Of his character and training Xen. gives an account in his *Cyropaedia*.

3 παρά: of the agent, like the normal ὑπό; *cf.* ἐκ, c. 1. 28, and II, 6, § 1, in an exactly parallel phrase.

τῶν . . . γενέσθαι, *who are reputed to have been intimately acquainted with Cyrus*.

ἐν πείρᾳ γενέσθαι. πρῶτον μὲν γὰρ ἔτι παῖς ὢν ὅτ' ἐπαιδεύετο 2
καὶ σὺν τῷ ἀδελφῷ καὶ σὺν τοῖς ἄλλοις παισί, πάντων πάντα
κράτιστος ἐνομίζετο. πάντες γὰρ οἱ τῶν ἀρίστων Περσῶν 3
παῖδες ἐπὶ ταῖς βασιλέως θύραις παιδεύονται· ἔνθα πολλὴν
μὲν σωφροσύνην καταμάθοι ἄν τις, αἰσχρὸν δ' οὐδὲν οὔτ' ἀκοῦσαι
οὔτ' ἰδεῖν ἔστι. θεῶνται δ' οἱ παῖδες καὶ τιμωμένους ὑπὸ βασι- 4
λέως καὶ ἀκούουσι, καὶ ἄλλους ἀτιμαζομένους· ὥστε εὐθὺς παῖδες
ὄντες μανθάνουσιν ἄρχειν τε καὶ ἄρχεσθαι· ἔνθα Κῦρος αἰδη- 5
μονέστατος μὲν πρῶτον τῶν ἡλικιωτῶν ἐδόκει εἶναι, τοῖς τε
πρεσβυτέροις καὶ τῶν ἑαυτοῦ ὑποδεεστέρων μᾶλλον πείθεσθαι,
ἔπειτα δὲ φιλιππότατος καὶ τοῖς ἵπποις ἄριστα χρῆσθαι· ἔκρινον
δ' αὐτὸν καὶ τῶν εἰς τὸν πόλεμον ἔργων, τοξικῆς τε καὶ ἀκοντί-
σεως, φιλομαθέστατον εἶναι καὶ μελετηρότατον. ἐπεὶ δὲ τῇ 6
ἡλικίᾳ ἔπρεπε, καὶ φιλοθηρότατος ἦν καὶ πρὸς τὰ θηρία μέντοι
φιλοκινδυνότατος. καὶ ἄρκτον ποτὲ ἐπιφερομένην οὐκ ἔτρεσεν,

---

4 πρῶτον μέν: continued by ἐπεὶ δέ, in § 6 and again in § 7.

ἔτι παῖς ὤν, *while still a boy.*

5 πάντα, *in everything.* The paronomasia (πάντων πάντα) seems to have been pleasing to the Greek ear; occurrences are common.

7 θύραις: *cf.* c. 2. 69, and the note.

8 σωφροσύνην: this was the prime virtue in the eyes of the Greek. We have no equivalent word. It may be rendered, in various connections, by *temperance, modesty, self-control,* or even *wisdom.* Note the stress that falls on the obj. because of its position; *cf.* αἰσχρὸν δ' οὐδέν, below.

9 ἔστι: for the meaning and the accent, see the notes on c. 2. 43 and c. 5. 11. We may question whether this statement is literally true.

τιμωμένους: sc. τινας.

11 αἰδημονέστατος: note the emphatic position. The word would naturally follow πρῶτον μέν.

12 τοῖς τε . . . πείθεσθαι, *and to be even* (καί) *more obedient to his elders than his inferiors* (were). τε, standing alone, without a balancing word (τε, καί, οὔτε, or μήτε), is unusual in prose.

14 φιλιππότατος: sc. ἐδόκει εἶναι.

χρῆσθαι, *to manage;* sc. ἐδόκει, simply.

ἔκρινον: the indef. third pers.; so, very commonly φασί, *they say.*

15 ἔργων: the gen. depends on the following adjs. (G. 1142; H. 754a; B. 351).

16 ἐπεὶ . . . ἔπρεπε, freely, *when he was of the proper age.*

18 ἄρκτον: the word is epicene (G. 158; H. 127).

ἐπιφερομένην: *cf.* ἐφέροντο, l. 78, and the note.

οὐκ ἔτρεσεν: a poetic vb. in a pregnant sense (*did not flee from*).

ἀλλὰ συμπεσὼν κατεσπάσθη ἀπὸ τοῦ ἵππου, καὶ τὰ μὲν ἔπαθεν, ὧν καὶ τὰς ὠτειλὰς εἶχεν, τέλος δὲ κατέκανε· καὶ τὸν πρῶτον 20 μέντοι βοηθήσαντα πολλοῖς μακαριστὸν ἐποίησεν.

7 Ἐπεὶ δὲ κατεπέμφθη ὑπὸ τοῦ πατρὸς σατράπης Λυδίας τε καὶ Φρυγίας τῆς μεγάλης καὶ Καππαδοκίας, στρατηγὸς δὲ καὶ πάντων ἀπεδείχθη οἷς καθήκει εἰς Καστωλοῦ πεδίον ἀθροίζεσθαι, πρῶτον μὲν ἐπέδειξεν αὐτὸν ὅτι περὶ πλείστου ποιοῖτο, 25 εἴ τῳ σπείσαιτο καὶ εἴ τῳ συνθοῖτο καὶ εἴ τῳ ὑπόσχοιτό τι, 8 μηδαμῶς ψεύδεσθαι. καὶ γὰρ οὖν ἐπίστευον μὲν αὐτῷ αἱ πόλεις ἐπιτρεπόμεναι, ἐπίστευον δ' οἱ ἄνδρες· καὶ εἴ τις πολέμιος ἐγένετο, σπεισαμένου Κύρου ἐπίστευε μηδὲν ἂν παρὰ τὰς σπονδὰς

---

19 συμπεσών, *grappling with it* (*the bear*). *Cf.* περιπεσεῖν, l. 116.

τὰ μὲν ... τέλος δέ: not infrequently some other word than τά stands with δέ, balancing τὰ μέν. τέλος is adv. acc.

20 κατέκανε: for this poetic vb., see the note on c. 6. 8.

καὶ ... μέντοι, *and yet;* i. e. despite the fact that help had been unnecessary.

21 πολλοῖς ... ἐποίησεν: see c. 7. 24, and the note.

22 κατεπέμφθη: *i. e.* down to the coast.

σατράπης, as satrap; see c. 1. 15, and the Introd., § 24.

23 Φρυγίας τῆς μεγάλης: *i. e.* the Persian province, as contrasted with the region in N. W. Asia Minor, also called Phrygia by the Greeks. Consult the map. Note again the third attributive position.

στρατηγὸς δὲ καί: emphatic; *cf.* c. 1. 6.

24 πάντων ... οἷς: in the parallel passage, just cited, we have more exactly πάντων ὅσοι.

οἷς καθήκει, *whose duty it is.*

25 πρῶτον μέν: balanced, loosely, by φανερὸς δέ in l. 36.

ἐπέδειξεν αὑτὸν ὅτι: for the prolepsis see the note on τῶν βαρβάρων, c. 1. 20.

περὶ πλείστου ποιοῖτο, *counted it of the utmost importance. Cf.* περὶ παντός, in l. 57. In these phrases the old sense of περί, *above*, survives. The following conditions are all general, and would have ἐάν with the subjv. in direct speech. Note the climax: a public contract, a private contract, a mere promise.

26 τῳ: *i. e.* τινι; see G. 416, 1; H. 277; B. 148.

συνθοῖτο: for the form, see G. 741; H. 445b; B. 170, 4; *cf.* προοῖτο (προΐημι) l. 34.

27 καὶ γάρ, *and (this policy had its effect) for.*

ἐπίστευον μὲν ... ἐπίστευον δ': an instance of anaphora (see the Introd., § 39), a figure much affected in rhetorical passages. The Greek order may be retained, if we render, *he won the confidence of.*

29 μηδὲν ἂν ... παθεῖν: direct,

30 παθεῖν. τοιγαροῦν ἐπεὶ Τισσαφέρνει ἐπολέμησε, πᾶσαι αἱ
πόλεις ἑκοῦσαι Κῦρον εἵλοντο ἀντὶ Τισσαφέρνους πλὴν Μιλησίων· οὗτοι δὲ ὅτι οὐκ ἤθελε τοὺς φεύγοντας προέσθαι ἐφοβοῦντο
αὐτόν. καὶ γὰρ ἔργῳ ἐπεδείκνυτο καὶ ἔλεγεν ὅτι οὐκ ἄν ποτε
προοῖτο, ἐπεὶ ἅπαξ φίλος αὐτοῖς ἐγένετο, οὐδ' εἰ ἔτι μὲν μείους
35 γένοιντο, ἔτι δὲ κάκιον πράξειαν.

Φανερὸς δ' ἦν καὶ εἴ τίς τι ἀγαθὸν ἢ κακὸν ποιήσειεν αὐτόν,
νικᾶν πειρώμενος· καὶ εὐχὴν δέ τινες αὐτοῦ ἐξέφερον ὡς εὔχοιτο
τοσοῦτον χρόνον ζῆν ἔστε νικῴη καὶ τοὺς εὖ καὶ τοὺς κακῶς ποι-

---

οὐδὲν ἂν . . . πάθοιμι. The change of the neg. from οὐδέν to μηδέν is due to the vb. of belief, ἐπίστευε; cf. μὴ παύσασθαι, c. 2. 12.

παρά, contrary to.

31 ἑκοῦσαι: cf. προτέρα, c. 2. 142, and the note.

Μιλησίων: by metonymy for the less personal Μιλήτου. For the facts, see c. 1. 32 ff., and the Introd., § 26.

33 καὶ γὰρ . . . ἔλεγεν, freely, he showed both by word and deed.

34 προοῖτο: see the note on συνθοῖτο, above, l. 26. The potential opt. with the neg. is often the strongest form of denial.

ἅπαξ: often used with temporal and conditional particles, like the Eng. once. It is to be distinguished from the indef. ποτέ, once upon a time.

οὐδ' εἰ . . . πράξειαν, no, not though they should become still fewer (in numbers) and should be in still greater straits. For this use of πράττω, see the vocab. The opts. are due to the condit., not to indir. disc. Note the anaphora, ἔτι μὲν . . . ἔτι δέ.

36 φανερὸς δ' ἦν . . . πειρώμενος, it was plain, also . . . that he endeavored. Cf. the use of δῆλος, c. 2. 70, and the note. Greek strongly prefers personal constructions.

εἴ τις . . . ποιήσειεν: a past general condition. This, with the corresponding relative and temporal constructions, is of frequent occurrence in this chapter, as was to be expected from the character of the subject-matter. The student will do well to review the matter in the grammar (G. 1393, 2; 1431, 2; H. 894, 2; 914B, 2; B. 610; 625). Note the ease with which ποιῶ takes two accs., the inner and the outer obj. (G. 1073; H. 725a; B. 340); cf. l. 38, where the advs. εὖ and κακῶς supply the place of one acc.

37 καὶ εὐχὴν δὲ . . . ὡς εὔχοιτο, and a prayer of his, too, men used to report, how he prayed. Exactly similar is Acts 20:35, Remember the words . . . how he said.

38 τοσοῦτον χρόνον . . . ἔστε, long enough to. ἔστε, until, is one of Xen.'s poetic words. It has no footing in any other prose author of the classic period. The same may be said of ἄχρι (II, 3, § 2).

οῦντας ἀλεξόμενος. καὶ γὰρ οὖν πλεῖστοι δὴ αὐτῷ ἑνί γε ἀνδρὶ
τῶν ἐφ' ἡμῶν ἐπεθύμησαν καὶ χρήματα καὶ πόλεις καὶ τὰ 40
ἑαυτῶν σώματα προέσθαι. οὐ μὲν δὴ οὐδὲ τοῦτ' ἄν τις εἴποι ὡς
τοὺς κακούργους καὶ ἀδίκους εἴα καταγελᾶν, ἀλλὰ ἀφειδέστατα
πάντων ἐτιμωρεῖτο· πολλάκις δ' ἦν ἰδεῖν παρὰ τὰς στειβομένας
ὁδοὺς καὶ ποδῶν καὶ χειρῶν καὶ ὀφθαλμῶν στερομένους ἀνθρώ-
πους· ὥστ' ἐν τῇ Κύρου ἀρχῇ ἐγένετο καὶ Ἕλληνι καὶ βαρ- 45
βάρῳ μηδὲν ἀδικοῦντι ἀδεῶς πορεύεσθαι ὅπῃ τις ἤθελεν, ἔχοντι
ὅ,τι προχωροίη.

ἕως is the normal word, although μέχρι also occurs, and πρίν is regular after real or implied negatives.

39 ἀλεξόμενος, *paying like for like,* another poetic word (see c. 3. 31, and the note).

πλεῖστοι δή, *by far the greatest number.*

αὐτῷ ... ἐφ' ἡμῶν, *to him above all other men of our time.* The dat. follows προέσθαι, below. ἑνί γε ἀνδρί stands in apposition with αὐτῷ. It adds a superlative force; hence the partit. gen. τῶν ἐφ' ἡμῶν.

40 χρήματα ... σώματα: note the climax.

41 προέσθαι, *entrust.* Contrast the meaning, *abandon,* above, l. 34; yet note that both usages come from the same original meaning.

οὐ μὲν δὴ ... ὡς, *not, however, that any one might say this, that.* In connection with δή, μέν often retains its original force as a particle of asseveration (= μήν). τοῦτο, in such phrases, regularly looks forward; *cf.* c. 7. 36.

42 κακούργους καὶ ἀδίκους: one class, hence the art. is expressed but once; *cf.* c. 7. 10, and the note.

καταγελᾶν: the word implies *with impunity; cf.* II, 4, § 4.

43 ἦν ἰδεῖν: see c. 4. 24; 5. 11, and *cf.* ἐγένετο, below, l. 45.

44 ὁδούς: the Persians maintained a system of roads connecting the different satrapies, although no other people in antiquity built roads as the Romans did. The Greeks themselves were not road-builders, using their ships as a means of communication; hence Greek writers often remark upon the Persian highways.

ποδῶν: this and the following gens. depend upon στερομένους. Barbarous mutilations have characterized oriental methods of punishment in all ages.

46 μηδὲν ἀδικοῦντι: the neg., μηδέν, shows that the partic. is conditional.

ὅπῃ τις ἤθελεν, *wherever he chose.* Note the indic. ἤθελεν. With words indefinite in themselves the indic. is often found, instead of the subjv. (with ἄν), or the opt.; see G. 1432; H. 918 (*cf.* 894c). *Cf.* ἀφικνεῖτο, c. 1. 18.

47 ὅ,τι προχωροίη, *whatsoever it was to his interest (to have).*

Τούς γε μέντοι ἀγαθοὺς εἰς πόλεμον ὡμολόγητο διαφερόντως τιμᾶν. καὶ πρῶτον μὲν ἦν αὐτῷ πόλεμος πρὸς Πισίδας
50 καὶ Μυσούς· στρατευόμενος οὖν καὶ αὐτὸς εἰς ταύτας τὰς χώρας
οὓς ἑώρα ἐθελόντας κινδυνεύειν, τούτους καὶ ἄρχοντας ἐποίει ἧς
κατεστρέφετο χώρας, ἔπειτα δὲ καὶ ἄλλοις δώροις ἐτίμα· ὥστε
φαίνεσθαι τοὺς μὲν ἀγαθοὺς εὐδαιμονεστάτους, τοὺς δὲ κακοὺς
δούλους τούτων ἀξίως εἶναι. τοιγαροῦν πολλὴ ἦν ἀφθονία
55 αὐτῷ τῶν ἐθελόντων κινδυνεύειν, ὅπου τις οἴοιτο Κῦρον αἰσθή-
σεσθαι. εἴς γε μὴν δικαιοσύνην εἴ τις φανερὸς γένοιτο ἐπιδείκνυσθαι βουλόμενος, περὶ παντὸς ἐποιεῖτο τούτους πλουσιωτέρως
ζῆν ποιεῖν τῶν ἐκ τοῦ ἀδίκου φιλοκερδούντων. καὶ γὰρ οὖν
ἄλλα τε πολλὰ δικαίως αὐτῷ διεχειρίζετο καὶ στρατεύματι ἀλη-

---

48 τούς γε μέντοι ... τιμᾶν: the emphasis due to the order is best retained by the Eng. periphrasis, *it was, however, the brave that he honored especially.* ὡμολόγητο is personal. It may be rendered by a subordinate clause, *as all men acknowledged.* Note that, when the pres. of a vb. denotes a state, the perf. (or plpf.) is merely intensive.

διαφερόντως: an adv. formed from the partic. See the note on ἠμελημένως, c. 7. 92.

49 πρῶτον μέν: these words go, in effect, with ἄρχοντας ἐποίει, below, l. 51, and are balanced by ἔπειτα δέ, l. 52. The clause, ἦν ... πόλεμος, may be made subordinate in translating.

50 καὶ αὐτός, *in his own person.* In this phrase καί is regular, but may rarely be translated.

51 ἑώρα: indic., as ἤθελεν, above.

ἧς ... χώρας: incorporation; *cf.* c. 1. 24, and the note.

55 ὅπου ... οἴοιτο: see the note on εἴ τις ... ποιήσειεν, l. 36.

Κῦρον: note the force of the proper name used instead of the pronoun.

56 εἴς γε μὴν δικαιοσύνην: with ἐπιδείκνυσθαι (*show himself conspicuous in*), but doubly emphasized by its position and by the parts. Note that the sentence closes with the words τῶν ... φιλοκερδούντων, thus contrasting the opposite ideas.

φανερός: *cf.* c. 2. 70, and the note.

57 περὶ παντὸς ἐποιεῖτο: *cf.* περὶ πλείστου ποιοῖτο, l. 25.

τούτους: after the general τις, as πάντας after ὅστις, c. 1. 18.

πλουσιωτέρως: a rare form of the comp. adv., G. 369; 370, 2; H. 259 with a; B. 138. The text is, however, conjectural.

58 ζῆν: governed by ποιεῖν.

ἐκ τοῦ ἀδίκου: *cf.* ἐκ τοῦ δικαίου, below, l. 66. ἐκ gives the source, and so, not infrequently, the means. *Cf.* its use of the agent, c. 1. 28.

59 δικαίως, *faithfully.*

αὐτῷ: dat. of advantage, not of the agent.

θινῷ ἐχρήσατο. καὶ γὰρ στρατηγοὶ καὶ λοχαγοί, οἳ χρημάτων 60
ἕνεκα πρὸς ἐκεῖνον ἔπλευσαν, ἔγνωσαν κερδαλεώτερον εἶναι
Κύρῳ καλῶς ὑπάρχειν ἢ τὸ κατὰ μῆνα κέρδος. ἀλλὰ μὴν εἴ
τίς γέ τι αὐτῷ προστάξαντι καλῶς ὑπηρετήσειεν, οὐδενὶ πώποτε
ἀχάριστον εἴασεν τὴν προθυμίαν. τοιγαροῦν κράτιστοι δὴ ὑπη-
ρέται παντὸς ἔργου Κύρῳ ἐλέχθησαν γενέσθαι. 65

Εἰ δέ τινα ὁρῴη δεινὸν ὄντα οἰκονόμον ἐκ τοῦ δικαίου καὶ
κατασκευάζοντά τε ἧς ἄρχοι χώρας καὶ προσόδους ποιοῦντα,
οὐδένα ἂν πώποτε ἀφείλετο, ἀλλ' ἀεὶ πλείω προσεδίδου· ὥστε
καὶ ἡδέως ἐπόνουν καὶ θαρραλέως ἐκτῶντο καὶ ὃ ἐπέπατο αὖ τις
ἥκιστα Κῦρον ἔκρυπτεν· οὐ γὰρ φθονῶν τοῖς φανερῶς πλου- 70

καί: singling out an important fact after ἄλλα; *cf.* c. 3. 13, and the note.

ἀληθινῷ, *worthy of the name.* The Greek army is meant, as is shown by what follows.

60 ἐχρήσατο, *acquired, secured.* The aor. is ingressive; *cf.* the note on ἠγάσθη, c. 1. 45. Contrast διεχείριζετο, above.

61 ἔπλευσαν: the means of motion is normally expressed in Greek; hence the frequent use of πλεῖν.

ἔγνωσαν: again ingressive, although second aor.; *cf.* ἔσχον and ἔστην.

62 ὑπάρχειν, *to serve.*
κατὰ μῆνα, *monthly.*

63 τι: inner obj. of ὑπηρετήσειεν.
οὐδενὶ ... προθυμίαν, *in the case of no one did he ever allow his zeal to go unrewarded.*

64 κράτιστοι δή: *cf.* πλεῖστοι δή, l. 39.

65 ἐλέχθησαν: personal in Greek, impersonal in Eng. Render, *it was said that Cyrus had.* Κύρῳ is dat. of possessor.

66 ὄντα: partic. in indir. disc.; so the two following partics.

ἐκ τοῦ δικαίου: *cf.* ἐκ τοῦ ἀδίκου, l. 58. Trans. as an adj. with οἰκονόμον.

67 ἧς ἄρχοι χώρας: incorporation, as above, l. 52, ἧς κατεστρέφετο χώρας, but here the antecedent is attracted to the case of the rel. ἄρχοι follows, of course, the construction of ὁρῴη.

68 οὐδένα ... ἀφείλετο, *he would never deprive him of it.* The ἄν is iterative (G. 1296; H. 835a; B. 568). Note that this gives the aor. the force of an impf.; with an impf. ἄν, in this sense, is sometimes found, but is never necessary. For οὐδένα, after τινα, *cf.* the note on οὐδενί, above, l. 63. Observe that pl. vbs. follow. For the two accs. (χώραν being understood), see G. 1069; H. 724; B. 340. *Cf.* ἔκρυπτεν, below, l. 70.

69 ἐπέπατο: a poetic vb. used several times by Xen. (again in III, 3, § 18). For the tense, see the note on κέκτησθε, c. 7. 16.

70 οὐ γὰρ φθονῶν ... πειρώμενος, *for he plainly did not envy ... but sought.* Distinguish between φαίνεσθαι with the infin. (*seem to*

τοῦσιν ἐφαίνετο, ἀλλὰ πειρώμενος χρῆσθαι τοῖς τῶν ἀποκρυπτομένων χρήμασι.

Φίλους γε μὴν ὅσους ποιήσαιτο καὶ εὔνους γνοίη ὄντας καὶ ἱκανοὺς κρίνειε συνεργοὺς εἶναι ὅ,τι τυγχάνοι βουλόμενος κατεργάζεσθαι, ὁμολογεῖται πρὸς πάντων κράτιστος δὴ γενέσθαι θεραπεύειν. καὶ γὰρ αὐτὸ τοῦτο οὗπερ αὐτὸς ἕνεκα φίλων ᾤετο δεῖσθαι, ὡς συνεργοὺς ἔχοι, καὶ αὐτὸς ἐπειρᾶτο συνεργὸς τοῖς φίλοις κράτιστος εἶναι τούτου ὅτου αἰσθάνοιτο ἕκαστον ἐπιθυμοῦντα. δῶρα δὲ πλεῖστα μὲν οἶμαι εἷς γε ἀνὴρ ἐλάμβανε διὰ πολλά· ταῦτα δὲ πάντων δὴ μάλιστα τοῖς φίλοις διεδίδου, πρὸς τοὺς τρόπους ἑκάστου σκοπῶν καὶ ὅτου μάλιστα ὁρῴη ἕκαστον δεόμενον. καὶ ὅσα τῷ σώματι αὐτοῦ κόσμον πέμποι τις ἢ ὡς εἰς πόλεμον ἢ ὡς εἰς καλλωπισμόν, καὶ περὶ

---

be) and φαίνεσθαι with the partic. (*manifestly to be*).

73 φίλους: doubly emphasized by its position and by the following parts. It is the obj. of θεραπεύειν, l. 76.

ὅσους: the rel. is conditional; hence the opts.

ὄντας: quoted after γνοίη.

74 ἱκανοὺς... κατεργάζεσθαι, *judged to be adequate co-workers in whatever he might wish to accomplish*.

75 πρὸς πάντων: πρός, of the agent, is rare.

76 αὐτὸ τοῦτο ... ἐπιθυμοῦντα, *the very thing, on account of which he thought he had need of friends, namely, that he might have co-workers, he on his own part* (καὶ αὐτός) *sought to bring about by being a most energetic co-worker with his friends in whatever he saw that each of them desired*. αὐτὸ τοῦτο is obj. acc., but, instead of expressing the governing vb. (*e.g.* πράττειν or παρέχειν), the writer substitutes the more explicit phrase, συνεργὸς ... εἶναι κ. τ. λ. Exactly similar is III, 5, §5. In Eng. the sentence may be rendered as above or αὐτὸ τοῦτο οὗπερ ... ἕνεκα may be rendered, *for the very reason for which*. In that case ἐπειρᾶτο ... εἶναι follows naturally. οὗπερ is used, not the simple οὗ, because of the preceding intensive, αὐτό. τούτου is governed by συνεργός, ὅτου by ἐπιθυμοῦντα.

79 εἷς γε ἀνήρ: *cf.* l. 39, ἑνί γε ἀνδρί.

80 πάντων δὴ μάλιστα, *above all men*.

διεδίδου: force of the prep.? *Cf.* c. 5. 11.

81 ὅτου: *i. e.* πρὸς τοῦτο ὅτου. The gen. depends on δεόμενον.

83 ὡς ... ὡς: giving the idea of the sender.

καὶ ... ἔφασαν, *also in the case of these they* (*i. e. people generally*) *said that he was wont to say*. λέγειν is impf. infin. *Cf.* ἰᾶσθαι, c. 8. 108, and the note.

τούτων λέγειν αὐτὸν ἔφασαν ὅτι τὸ μὲν ἑαυτοῦ σῶμα οὐκ ἂν
δύναιτο τούτοις πᾶσι κοσμηθῆναι, φίλους δὲ καλῶς κεκοσμη- 85
μένους μέγιστον κόσμον ἀνδρὶ νομίζοι. καὶ τὸ μὲν τὰ μεγάλα
νικᾶν τοὺς φίλους εὖ ποιοῦντα οὐδὲν θαυμαστόν, ἐπειδή γε καὶ
δυνατώτερος ἦν· τὸ δὲ τῇ ἐπιμελείᾳ περιεῖναι τῶν φίλων καὶ
τῷ προθυμεῖσθαι χαρίζεσθαι, ταῦτα ἔμοιγε μᾶλλον δοκεῖ ἀγαστὰ
εἶναι. Κῦρος γὰρ ἔπεμπε βίκους οἴνου ἡμιδεεῖς πολλάκις 90
ὁπότε πάνυ ἡδὺν λάβοι, λέγων ὅτι οὔπω δὴ πολλοῦ χρόνου
τούτου ἡδίονι οἴνῳ ἐπιτύχοι· τοῦτον οὖν σοὶ ἔπεμψε καὶ
δεῖταί σου τήμερον τοῦτον ἐκπιεῖν σὺν οἷς μάλιστα φιλεῖς.
πολλάκις δὲ χῆνας ἡμιβρώτους ἔπεμπε καὶ ἄρτων ἡμίσεα καὶ
ἄλλα τοιαῦτα, ἐπιλέγειν κελεύων τὸν φέροντα, Τούτους ἥσθη 95
Κῦρος· βούλεται οὖν καὶ σὲ τούτων γεύσασθαι. ὅπου δὲ χιλὸς
σπάνιος πάνυ εἴη, αὐτὸς δὲ δύναιτο παρασκευάσασθαι διὰ τὸ
πολλοὺς ἔχειν ὑπηρέτας καὶ διὰ τὴν ἐπιμέλειαν, διαπέμπων
ἐκέλευε τοὺς φίλους τοῖς τὰ ἑαυτῶν σώματα ἄγουσιν ἵπποις

---

84 οὐκ ἂν δύναιτο: potential opt.; νομίζοι, opt. in indir. disc.

86 καὶ τὸ μὲν ... θαυμαστόν, *now for him to outdo his friends in conferring great benefits was nothing strange.* τὰ μεγάλα is emphasized by its separation from εὖ ποιοῦντα, of which it is the inner obj.

89 τῷ προθυμεῖσθαι: dat. of respect, as the preceding ἐπιμελείᾳ.

ταῦτα: resuming τὸ ... περιεῖναι, which, owing to the two explanatory dats., has the effect of a pl. ἀγαστός, used several times by Xen., is rare in Attic Greek.

91 οὔπω ... χρόνου, *not for a long time.* For the gen., see G. 1136; H. 759; B. 359.

92 τούτου: the gen. follows the comp. ἡδίονι.

ἐπιτύχοι: direct, ἐπέτυχον, as said by Cyrus.

ἔπεμψε: the tense used by the messenger; *cf.* the epistolary impf. in Lat. With the shift from ἔπεμψε to δεῖται, *cf.* that from ἥσθη to βούλεται below, l. 96.

93 σὺν οἷς: *i.e.* σὺν τούτοις οὕς.

95 ἐπιλέγειν, *to say* (*in addition to the gift*).

96 τούτων: partit. gen. with γεύσασθαι. *Cf.* ζώνης, c. 6. 57. To receive gifts from the king's table was accounted a high honor.

97 σπάνιος πάνυ: the adv. gains force by its postponement. *Cf.* 2. 121.

διὰ τὸ ... ἔχειν: parallel with ἐπιμέλειαν. *Cf.* above, l. 89. The matter of supplies was carefully attended to by Persian military officials.

99 ἄγουσιν: partic., in agreement with ἵπποις. σώματα is its obj. Observe that ἑαυτῶν refers to

ἐμβάλλειν τοῦτον τὸν χιλόν, ὡς μὴ πεινῶντες τοὺς ἑαυτοῦ φίλους ἄγωσιν. εἰ δὲ δή ποτε πορεύοιτο καὶ πλεῖστοι μέλλοιεν ὄψεσθαι, προσκαλῶν τοὺς φίλους ἐσπουδαιολογεῖτο, ὡς δηλοίη οὓς τιμᾷ. ὥστε ἐγὼ μέν γε ἐξ ὧν ἀκούω οὐδένα κρίνω ὑπὸ πλειόνων πεφιλῆσθαι οὔτε Ἑλλήνων οὔτε βαρβάρων. τεκμήριον δὲ τούτου καὶ τόδε. παρὰ μὲν Κύρου δούλου ὄντος οὐδεὶς ἀπῄει πρὸς βασιλέα, πλὴν Ὀρόντας ἐπεχείρησε· καὶ οὗτος δὴ ὃν ᾤετο πιστόν οἱ εἶναι ταχὺ αὐτὸν ηὗρε Κύρῳ φιλαίτερον ἢ ἑαυτῷ· παρὰ δὲ βασιλέως πολλοὶ πρὸς Κῦρον ἀπῆλθον, ἐπειδὴ πολέμιοι ἀλλήλοις ἐγένοντο, καὶ οὗτοι μέντοι οἱ μάλιστα ὑπ' αὐτοῦ ἀγαπώμενοι, νομίζοντες παρὰ Κύρῳ ὄντες ἀγαθοὶ ἀξιωτέρας ἂν τιμῆς τυγχάνειν ἢ παρὰ βασιλεῖ. μέγα δὲ τεκμήριον καὶ τὸ ἐν τῇ τελευτῇ τοῦ βίου αὐτῷ γενόμενον ὅτι καὶ αὐτὸς ἦν ἀγαθὸς καὶ κρίνειν ὀρθῶς ἐδύνατο τοὺς πιστοὺς καὶ εὔνους καὶ βεβαίους.

φίλους, but ἑαυτοῦ, two lines below, to Cyrus. The context makes the reference of a reflexive clear.

101 ὄψεσθαι: the infin. after μέλλω is most commonly fut., although the pres. also occurs and, very rarely, the aor. Save for this use, the fut. infin. is found chiefly in indir. disc.

102 ἐσπουδαιολογεῖτο = σπουδῇ διελέγετο. The word is a rare one, occurring in Xen. alone of classic writers (Rehd.).

οὓς τιμᾷ: more definite than οὓς τιμῴη. In rel. clauses in which the direct form has the indic., not ἄν with the subjv., the change to the opt. is avoided.

104 Ἑλλήνων ... βαρβάρων: both gens. go with οὐδένα. The separation adds emphasis.

τεκμήριον ... τόδε: ἐστί is regularly omitted with this word. Note the exact use of the prons.

105 δούλου ὄντος, *slave though he was.* See the note on c. 7. 16.

106 οὗτος δή: contemptuous. For the facts, see c. 6. 18.

107 οἱ: indir. reflexive, see c. 1. 36, and the note. It is governed by πιστόν.

αὐτόν: here resuming the preceding rel. For this οὗτος is the usual word. It was perhaps avoided here, because it occurs just above, designating the main subj.

φιλαίτερον: G. 352; H. 250b; cf. B. 132, 2. The form is a rare one. We have μᾶλλον φίλους, c. 1. 19.

109 ὑπ' αὐτοῦ: *i.e.* the king.

110 ἀγαπώμενοι, *beloved,* and therefore *honored.*

ὄντες: equivalent to εἰ εἶεν.

ἂν ... τυγχάνειν: direct, ἂν τυγχάνοίμεθα.

111 τὸ ... γενόμενον, *that which happened.* With τεκμήριον, ἐστί is again omitted.

113 τούς: expressed but once with the three adjs., since they designate a single class. *Cf.* φίλοι καὶ συντράπεζοι, ll. 114 f.

31 ἀποθνήσκοντος γὰρ αὐτοῦ πάντες οἱ περὶ αὐτὸν φίλοι καὶ συντράπεζοι ἀπέθανον μαχόμενοι ὑπὲρ Κύρου πλὴν Ἀριαίου· οὗτος 115
δὲ τεταγμένος ἐτύγχανεν ἐπὶ τῷ εὐωνύμῳ τοῦ ἱππικοῦ ἄρχων·
ὡς δ' ᾔσθετο Κῦρον πεπτωκότα, ἔφυγεν ἔχων καὶ τὸ στράτευμα
πᾶν οὗ ἡγεῖτο.

1 X. Ἐνταῦθα δὴ Κύρου ἀποτέμνεται ἡ κεφαλὴ καὶ ἡ χεὶρ ἡ
δεξιά. βασιλεὺς δὲ [καὶ οἱ σὺν αὐτῷ] διώκων εἰσπίπτει εἰς τὸ
Κύρειον στρατόπεδον· καὶ οἱ μὲν μετὰ Ἀριαίου οὐκέτι ἵστανται
ἀλλὰ φεύγουσι διὰ τοῦ αὐτῶν στρατοπέδου εἰς τὸν σταθμὸν ἔνθεν
ὥρμηντο· τέτταρες δ' ἐλέγοντο παρασάγγαι εἶναι τῆς ὁδοῦ. 5
2 βασιλεὺς δὲ καὶ οἱ σὺν αυτῷ τά τε ἄλλα πολλὰ διαρπάζουσι

---

114 συντράπεζοι: cf. ὁμοτράπεζοι, c. 8. 103.
115 πλήν: how different from πλήν, above, l. 106.
116 τεταγμένος ... εὐωνύμῳ: see the plan, facing p. 76. For the use of the partic., cf. παρὼν ἐτύγχανε, c. 1. 4.
τοῦ ἱππικοῦ: gen. with ἄρχων. Ariaeus is elsewhere spoken of as commanding the whole of Cyrus' barbarian force. We can hardly assume that all were mounted.
118 οὗ ἡγεῖτο: for the force of the gen., as contrasted with the dat., after ἡγοῦμαι, see c. 4. 9 and the note.

CHAPTER X

1 ἐνταῦθα: the adv. resumes the narrative interrupted by c. 9.
ἀποτέμνεται: according to Persian custom; yet to the Greeks it seemed wanton barbarity. Cf. III, 1, § 17.
2 [καὶ οἱ σὺν αὐτῷ]: these words may be an interpolation. If genuine, they are to be regarded as parenthetic, since both vb. and partic. are in the sing., agreeing with βασιλεύς.
3 Κύρειον: equivalent to Κύρου. The use of the adj. instead of the gen. is common in poetry, but, in the case of proper names, is very rare in prose. It occurs also in English poets (Tennyson, A Niobean Daughter).
οἱ μὲν μετὰ Ἀριαίου: in the Greek of Xen.'s day such a phrase included the individual (Ariaeus and his men); later it became a somewhat pompous phrase for the individual alone. Above, l. 2, and below, l. 6, we have βασιλεὺς δὲ καὶ οἱ σὺν αὐτῷ, where the individual is brought into greater prominence.
4 ἔνθεν ὥρμηντο: i. e. on that morning. Some temporal adv. may have fallen out.
5 τῆς ὁδοῦ: for the case, see the note on στρατιᾶς, c. 4. 34. The clause affords a good instance of the Greek fondness for personal constructions.
6 διαρπάζουσι ... λαμβάνει: the former vb. expresses an act of the whole force, the latter an act

καὶ τὴν Φωκαΐδα τὴν Κύρου παλλακίδα τὴν σοφὴν καὶ καλὴν
λεγομένην εἶναι λαμβάνει. ἡ δὲ Μιλησία ληφθεῖσα ὑπὸ τῶν 3
ἀμφὶ βασιλέα ἐκφεύγει γυμνὴ πρὸς τῶν Ἑλλήνων, οἳ ἔτυχον
ἐν τοῖς σκευοφόροις ὅπλα ἔχοντες καὶ ἀντιταχθέντες πολλοὺς
μὲν τῶν ἁρπαζόντων ἀπέκτειναν, οἳ δὲ καὶ αὐτῶν ἀπέθανον·
οὐ μὴν ἔφυγόν γε, ἀλλὰ καὶ ταύτην ἔσωσαν καὶ τἆλλα ὁπόσα
ἐντὸς αὐτῶν καὶ χρήματα καὶ ἄνθρωποι ἐγένοντο πάντα ἔσωσαν.
ἐνταῦθα διέσχον ἀλλήλων βασιλεύς τε καὶ οἱ Ἕλληνες ὡς τριά- 4
κοντα στάδια, οἱ μὲν διώκοντες τοὺς καθ' αὑτούς, οἱ δ' ἁρπά-
ζοντες ὡς ἤδη πάντα νικῶντες.

Ἐπεὶ δ' ᾔσθοντο οἱ μὲν Ἕλληνες ὅτι βασιλεὺς σὺν τῷ 5
στρατεύματι ἐν τοῖς σκευοφόροις εἴη, βασιλεὺς δ' αὖ ἤκουσε
Τισσαφέρνους ὅτι οἱ Ἕλληνες νικῷεν τὸ καθ' αὑτοὺς καὶ εἰς τὸ

of the king's, *i.e.* one done at his bidding; hence the change of number.

τά τε ἄλλα . . . καί: a common phrase, throwing strong emphasis on the second member. Similarly ἄλλως τε καί means, *especially*. See c. 3. 12, and the note.

7 τὴν Φωκαΐδα: alluded to as one well known. She is said to have been called Milto, from her rosy cheeks (ἡ μίλτος = *red ochre*), but Cyrus called her Aspasia, after the famous consort of Pericles (Plut. *Artox.* 26; *Pericles* 24; Aelian, *Varia Historia* XII, 1).

σοφήν: not *witty;* Aelian speaks of her intelligence (σύνεσις) and states that Cyrus often turned to her for counsel.

9 γυμνή: *i. e.* without her outer garment, which was doubtless torn from her in her struggles to free herself.

πρὸς τῶν Ἑλλήνων, *towards the Greeks* (*cf.* II, 2, § 4). Others regard the gen. as partitive and supply τούτους or τινας; but such omission could scarcely be paralleled.

11 οἱ δὲ καὶ αὐτῶν: this balances πολλοὺς μέν, with a shift of construction.

12 οὐ μὴν ἔφυγόν γε: spoken with the pride of a Greek. μήν should always be felt as a particle of asseveration.

ταύτην: *i. e. τὴν Μιλησίαν*.

ὁπόσα: the antecedent is πάντα, postponed for emphasis.

13 ἐγένοντο: the pl. is here due to the vicinity of ἄνθρωποι.

ἔσωσαν: repeated to emphasize the achievement of this handful of Greeks. See also the note on ἤγγελλον, c. 7. 62.

14 διέσχον: *cf.* διειχέτην, c. 8. 68.

15 οἱ μὲν διώκοντες: *i. e. the Greeks.* The order is, therefore, chiastic.

18 αὖ, *on his part.*

19 Τισσαφέρνους: for the case, see c. 2. 26. Here the ὅτι-clause supplies the place of the acc.

νικῷεν . . . οἴχονται: the shift of

πρόσθεν οἴχονται διώκοντες, ἔνθα δὴ βασιλεὺς μὲν ἀθροίζει τε
τοὺς ἑαυτοῦ καὶ συντάττεται, ὁ δὲ Κλέαρχος ἐβουλεύετο Πρόξενον καλέσας, πλησιαίτατος γὰρ ἦν, εἰ πέμποιέν τινας ἢ
πάντες ἴοιεν ἐπὶ τὸ στρατόπεδον ἀρήξοντες. ἐν τούτῳ καὶ
βασιλεὺς δῆλος ἦν προσιὼν πάλιν ὡς ἐδόκει ὄπισθεν. καὶ οἱ
μὲν Ἕλληνες στραφέντες παρεσκευάζοντο ὡς ταύτῃ προσιόντος
καὶ δεξόμενοι, ὁ δὲ βασιλεὺς ταύτῃ μὲν οὐκ ἀπῆγεν, ᾗ δὲ
παρῆλθεν ἔξω τοῦ εὐωνύμου κέρατος ταύτῃ καὶ ἀπῆγεν, ἀναλαβὼν καὶ τοὺς ἐν τῇ μάχῃ πρὸς τοὺς Ἕλληνας αὐτομολήσαντας καὶ Τισσαφέρνην καὶ τοὺς σὺν αὐτῷ. ὁ γὰρ Τισσαφέρνης ἐν τῇ πρώτῃ συνόδῳ οὐκ ἔφυγεν, ἀλλὰ διήλασε παρὰ
τὸν ποταμὸν κατὰ τοὺς Ἕλληνας πελταστάς· διελαύνων δὲ
κατέκανε μὲν οὐδένα, διαστάντες δ' οἱ Ἕλληνες ἔπαιον καὶ

---

mood is virtually a change from indirect to the more vivid direct speech. This is very common. To begin with the indic. and later to change to the opt. is much less so.

21 ὁ δὲ Κλέαρχος: the order is again chiastic—Greeks, king, king, Clearchus.

22 πλησιαίτατος: for the form, *cf.* φιλαίτερον, c. 9. 107.

εἰ ... ἤ: an alternative indir. ques. (G. 1606; H. 1017; B. 579). The vbs. in direc. ques. would have been subjvs. (G. 1358; 1490; H. 866, 3; 932, 2; B. 577; 581).

23 ἀρήξοντες: a poetic vb.

ἐν τούτῳ: is the asyndeton felt?

24 δῆλος ἦν προσιών: *cf.* c. 2. 70, and the note. The king's force is meant. He himself had been wounded, and cannot have led them.

25 στραφέντες: *wheeling*; not simply "*about face*," but by a countermarch, so that the companies had the same men as before in their front ranks. The Greeks now face up-stream; see the plan facing p. 76.

ὡς: both with προσιόντος (gen. abs.; sc. αὐτοῦ) *in the expectation that*, and with δεξόμενοι, *with the intention of*.

27 παρῆλθεν: plpf. in Eng. For the fact, see c. 8. 96.

εὐωνύμου: referring to the original position of the Greeks. See the plan.

ταύτῃ: this postponement of the antecedent, very common in Greek, is rare in Eng.

καὶ ... καὶ ... καί: the first two only are co-ordinate.

28 αὐτομολήσαντας: many had doubtless deserted, thinking that Cyrus was victor. *Cf.* II, 1, § 6.

29 ὁ γὰρ Τ., *for, you remember, Tiss.*—resuming the narrative of c. 8.

30 δι-, παρά, κατά: note the prepositions. Where were the Greek peltasts stationed?

32 κατέκανε: see c. 6. 8, and the note.

διαστάντες, *opening their ranks*.

ἠκόντιζον αὐτούς· Ἐπισθένης δὲ Ἀμφιπολίτης ἦρχε τῶν πελταστῶν καὶ ἐλέγετο φρόνιμος γενέσθαι.

35 Ὁ δ' οὖν Τισσαφέρνης ὡς μεῖον ἔχων ἀπηλλάγη, πάλιν μὲν 8
οὐκ ἀναστρέφει, εἰς δὲ τὸ στρατόπεδον ἀφικόμενος τὸ τῶν Ἑλλήνων ἐκεῖ συντυγχάνει βασιλεῖ, καὶ ὁμοῦ δὴ πάλιν συνταξάμενοι
ἐπορεύοντο. ἐπεὶ δ' ἦσαν κατὰ τὸ εὐώνυμον τῶν Ἑλλήνων κέρας, 9
ἔδεισαν οἱ Ἕλληνες μὴ προσάγοιεν πρὸς τὸ κέρας καὶ περιπτύ-
40 ξαντες ἀμφοτέρωθεν αὐτοὺς κατακόψειαν· καὶ ἐδόκει αὐτοῖς
ἀναπτύσσειν τὸ κέρας καὶ ποιήσασθαι ὄπισθεν τὸν ποταμόν.
ἐν ᾧ δὲ ταῦτα ἐβουλεύοντο, καὶ δὴ βασιλεὺς παραμειψάμενος 10
εἰς τὸ αὐτὸ σχῆμα κατέστησεν ἀντίαν τὴν φάλαγγα ὥσπερ τὸ
πρῶτον μαχούμενος συνῄει. ὡς δὲ εἶδον οἱ Ἕλληνες ἐγγύς τε
45 ὄντας καὶ παρατεταγμένους, αὖθις παιανίσαντες ἐπῇσαν πολὺ
προθυμότερον ἢ πρόσθεν. οἱ δ' αὖ βάρβαροι οὐκ ἐδέχοντο, ἀλλὰ 11

33 **Ἀμφιπολίτης**: where was Amphipolis?
34 **γενέσθαι**, *to have shown himself*.
35 **ὡς ... ἀπηλλάγη**, *having come off with the worst of it*. For the phrase μεῖον ἔχων, cf. III, 2, § 17; III, 4, § 18. ἀπαλλάττομαι generally implies being well rid of a thing.
πάλιν ... ἀναστρέφει: he dared not charge the Greeks again. Note the emphatic position of οὐκ.
37 **ὁμοῦ δή**: sarcastic.
38 **τὸ εὐώνυμον**: see the note on c. 2. 88.
39 **ἔδεισαν**: ingressive aor.
προσάγοιεν ... κατακόψειαν: see the references cited in the note on μὴ ἐπιθῇ, c. 3. 50. περιπτύσσω is a poetic vb. So, too, ἀναπτύσσω, below.
41 **ἀναπτύσσειν**: what the proposed manoeuvre was cannot be determined with certainty. The most plausible view is that the Greeks, menaced with an attack upon their right flank, purposed to wheel so that their line should be parallel to the river instead of at right angles to it. The vb. ἀναπτύσσειν (*fold back*) admits of this view, and the phrase ποιήσασθαι ὄπισθεν τὸν ποταμόν distinctly favors it. Others, understanding the vb. to mean *fold out*, *unfold*, assume an extension of the wing; and still others imagine that the wing alone wheeled, not the whole line, so that the Greek front presented the appearance of two sides of a hollow square. The following phrase ἐν ᾧ ... ἐβουλεύοντο has led many to the belief that the projected manoeuvre was not carried out.
45 **ὄντας ... παρατεταγμένους**: partics. in indir. disc.
46 **ἐδέχοντο**: note the tense: *they could not bring themselves to*.

ἐκ πλέονος ἢ τὸ πρόσθεν ἔφευγον· οἱ δ᾽ ἐπεδίωκον μέχρι κώμης
12 τινός· ἐνταῦθα δ᾽ ἔστησαν οἱ Ἕλληνες· ὑπὲρ γὰρ τῆς κώμης
γήλοφος ἦν, ἐφ᾽ οὗ ἀνεστράφησαν οἱ ἀμφὶ βασιλέα, πεζοὶ μὲν
οὐκέτι, τῶν δὲ ἱππέων ὁ λόφος ἐνεπλήσθη, ὥστε τὸ ποιούμενον 50
μὴ γιγνώσκειν. καὶ τὸ βασίλειον σημεῖον ὁρᾶν ἔφασαν ἀετόν
13 τινα χρυσοῦν ἐπὶ πέλτῃ ἀνατεταμένον. ἐπεὶ δὲ καὶ ἐνταῦθ᾽
ἐχώρουν οἱ Ἕλληνες, λείπουσι δὴ καὶ τὸν λόφον οἱ ἱππεῖς· οὐ
μὴν ἔτι ἀθρόοι ἀλλ᾽ ἄλλοι ἄλλοθεν· ἐψιλοῦτο δ᾽ ὁ λόφος τῶν
14 ἱππέων· τέλος δὲ καὶ πάντες ἀπεχώρησαν. ὁ οὖν Κλέαρχος 55
οὐκ ἀνεβίβαζεν ἐπὶ τὸν λόφον, ἀλλ᾽ ὑπ᾽ αὐτὸν στήσας τὸ στρά-

---

47 **ἐκ πλέονος**, *when at a greater distance.*
κώμης τινός: perhaps Cunaxa; see Plut. *Artox.* 8.
49 **ἀνεστράφησαν**, *rallied;* note the prep.
οἱ ἀμφὶ βασιλέα: according to Diodorus (XIV, 23), Tissaphernes was their leader.
50 **τῶν δ᾽ ἱππέων**: a slight shift of construction, permissible also in Eng.
ὥστε . . . γιγνώσκειν: see the note on c. 1. 19. Tendency may include result, and when ὥστε takes the infin. there is no indication that the result does not follow. When used with the indic., however, there is positive indication that it does.
τὸ ποιούμενον, *what was going on.* As a rule, γίγνεσθαι supplies the pass. to ποιῶ, ποιεῖσθαι being used strictly of what is put into poetry.
51 **ἔφασαν**: does this indicate that Xen. was not with the main body? *Cf.* II, 1, § 14.
52 **τινα**, *a sort of. Cf.* μελανία τις, c. 8. 27. The Persian standard is again described by Xen. in *Cyrop.* VII, 1, 4, as ἀετὸς χρυσοῦς ἐπὶ δόρατος μακροῦ ἀνατεταμένος. From this it would appear that πέλτῃ here means, not a *target*, but a *lance;* and in the Greek lexicographers it is glossed by δόρυ, ἀκόντιον, and λόγχη. But these may be mere guesses from this passage. (Does ἐπὶ πέλτῃ mean *against a background in the shape of a shield?* [Smith].) A bas-relief, representing such a standard, has been found at Kuyunjik, the ancient Nineveh. See, further, Curtius, III, 3, 16.
ἀνατεταμένον: Curtius has *pinnas extendenti.*
ἐνταῦθ᾽: loosely used of the limit, as *there* in Eng.
53 **δή**: contemptuous again.
54 **ἄλλοι ἄλλοθεν**: the Greek, as often, expresses the "whence" idea. In Eng. we prefer to state the direction. For the phrase, see the note on ἄλλοι ἄλλως, c. 6. 64.
ἐψιλοῦτο: the tense paints the progress of the action; contrast ἀπεχώρησαν, below.
56 **ἀνεβίβαζεν**: apparently intrans., but the obj. supplies itself.
ὑπ᾽ αὐτόν, *at its foot.* στήσας and στάς must be distinguished.

τευμα πέμπει Λύκιον τὸν Συρακόσιον καὶ ἄλλον ἐπὶ τὸν λόφον
καὶ κελεύει κατιδόντας τὰ ὑπὲρ τοῦ λόφου τί ἐστιν ἀπαγγεῖλαι.
καὶ ὁ Λύκιος ἤλασέ τε καὶ ἰδὼν ἀπαγγέλλει ὅτι φεύγουσιν ἀνὰ 15
κράτος. σχεδὸν δ' ὅτε ταῦτα ἦν καὶ ἥλιος ἐδύετο.

Ἐνταῦθα δ' ἔστησαν οἱ Ἕλληνες καὶ θέμενοι τὰ ὅπλα ἀνε- 16
παύοντο· καὶ ἅμα μὲν ἐθαύμαζον ὅτι οὐδαμοῦ Κῦρος φαίνοιτο
οὐδ' ἄλλος ἀπ' αὐτοῦ οὐδεὶς παρῄει· οὐ γὰρ ᾔδεσαν αὐτὸν τεθνηκότα, ἀλλ' ᾔκαζον ἢ διώκοντα οἴχεσθαι ἢ καταληψόμενόν τι
προεληλακέναι· καὶ αὐτοὶ ἐβουλεύοντο εἰ αὐτοῦ μείναντες τὰ 17
σκευοφόρα ἐνταῦθα ἄγοιντο ἢ ἀπίοιεν ἐπὶ τὸ στρατόπεδον. ἔδοξεν αὐτοῖς ἀπιέναι· καὶ ἀφικνοῦνται ἀμφὶ δορπηστὸν ἐπὶ τὰς
σκηνάς. ταύτης μὲν τῆς ἡμέρας τοῦτο τὸ τέλος ἐγένετο. κατα- 18

---

58 **κατιδόντας**: καθορᾶν is regularly used of a scout or lookout. He looks down from some point of vantage. *Cf.* c. 8. 104.

ὑπέρ, *beyond*.

τί ἐστιν: τί sums up the preceding τά; it refers to the whole, as τά to the details. The clause is best construed with κατιδόντας (prolepsis).

59 **ἀνὰ κράτος**: see c. 8. 4, and the note.

60 **σχεδὸν . . . ἦν**, freely, *about this time*. καί marks the two events as parallel.

ἥλιος: with such words the art. is generally omitted.

61 **θέμενοι τὰ ὅπλα**: see c. 5. 88 and the note.

62 **φαίνοιτο**: opt. in a causal sentence; *cf.* c. 5. 90. With the whole *cf.* II, 1, § 2.

63 **τεθνηκότα**: indir. disc. In the perf. and plpf. the simple vb. is common.

64 **ᾔκαζον . . . προεληλακέναι**, *they fancied that they had either gone off in pursuit or had pushed forward to seize some position*. οἴχομαι has, as usual, the force of a perf.

65 **εἰ . . . ἤ**: *cf.* l. 22.

αὐτοῦ, *where they were*.

66 **ἔδοξεν**: the asyndeton is striking here. *Cf.* its normal use, *e. g.* c. 3. 102.

67 **ἀμφὶ δορπηστόν**, *about supper time*. The phrase is probably an old one. δεῖπνον was the Attic word for the evening meal— the chief meal of the day. (δόρπον is common in Homer, and δορπηστός occurs once in Aristophanes *Wasps* 103). In Greece, as in Europe to-day, there were but two regular meals daily— the ἄριστον (*déjeuner à la fourchette*), taken a little before noon, and the δεῖπνον. A barley cake, dipped in unmixed wine, was eaten on rising, and supplied the place of the modern *café*. On this subject, see Gulick, *Life of the Ancient Greeks* 141– 52.

68 **ταύτης μέν**: μέν concludes the

λαμβάνουσι δὲ τῶν τε ἄλλων χρημάτων τὰ πλεῖστα διηρπασ-
μένα καὶ εἴ τι σιτίον ἢ ποτὸν ἦν, καὶ τὰς ἁμάξας μεστὰς ἀλεύρων 70
καὶ οἴνου, ἃς παρεσκευάσατο Κῦρος, ἵνα εἴ ποτε σφόδρα τὸ στράτευμα λάβοι ἔνδεια, διαδιδοίη τοῖς Ἕλλησιν—ἦσαν δ' αὗται
τετρακόσιαι ὡς ἐλέγοντο ἅμαξαι—καὶ ταύτας τότε οἱ σὺν βασι-
19 λεῖ διήρπασαν. ὥστε ἄδειπνοι ἦσαν οἱ πλεῖστοι τῶν Ἑλλήνων·
ἦσαν δὲ καὶ ἀνάριστοι· πρὶν γὰρ δὴ καταλῦσαι τὸ στράτευμα 75
πρὸς ἄριστον βασιλεὺς ἐφάνη. ταύτην μὲν οὖν τὴν νύκτα οὕτω
διεγένοντο.

---

episode, as so often. *Cf.* μὲν δή, c. 1. 16, and μὲν οὖν, below, l. 76.

70 εἴ τι . . . ἦν, *whatever there was to eat or drink.* *Cf.* c. 5. 4 f., with the note. σιτίον is much rarer than σῖτος.

τὰς ἁμάξας: obj. of διήρπασαν, l. 74. After the parenthesis it is resumed by καὶ ταύτας.

μεστάς, *which had been full of;* but the ellipsis of οὔσας, the impf. partic. (G. 1289; H. 856a; B. 542, 1), is hardly felt.

73 ὡς ἐλέγοντο: a striking instance of the pers. construction.

74 ἦσαν . . . ἀνάριστοι: an emphatic clause. The chiasm heightens the effect.

75 καταλῦσαι: *cf.* c. 8. 2.

77 διεγένοντο: *cf.* c. 5. 34, and the note. μέν in this clause is balanced by δέ in II, 1, § 2. The originally connected narrative is interrupted by the later division into books and the introductory paragraph prefixed to Book II; see the next note. The part of the work properly called the *Anabasis* ends here.

BOOK II

I. ['Ως μὲν οὖν ἠθροίσθη Κύρῳ τὸ Ἑλληνικὸν ὅτε ἐπὶ 1
τὸν ἀδελφὸν Ἀρταξέρξην ἐστρατεύετο, καὶ ὅσα ἐν τῇ ἀνόδῳ
ἐπράχθη καὶ ὡς ἡ μάχη ἐγένετο καὶ ὡς Κῦρος ἐτελεύτησε καὶ
ὡς ἐπὶ τὸ στρατόπεδον ἐλθόντες οἱ Ἕλληνες ἐκοιμήθησαν
5 οἰόμενοι τὰ πάντα νικᾶν καὶ Κῦρον ζῆν, ἐν τῷ πρόσθεν λόγῳ
δεδήλωται.] ἅμα δὲ τῇ ἡμέρᾳ συνελθόντες οἱ στρατηγοὶ ἐθαύ- 2
μαζον ὅτι Κῦρος οὔτε ἄλλον πέμπει σημανοῦντα ὅ,τι χρὴ ποιεῖν
οὔτε αὐτὸς φαίνοιτο. ἔδοξεν οὖν αὐτοῖς συσκευασαμένοις ἃ
εἶχον καὶ ἐξοπλισαμένοις προϊέναι εἰς τὸ πρόσθεν ἕως Κύρῳ
10 συμμείξειαν. ἤδη δὲ ἐν ὁρμῇ ὄντων ἅμα ἡλίῳ ἀνέχοντι ἦλθε 3
Προκλῆς ὁ Τευθρανίας ἄρχων, γεγονὼς ἀπὸ Δαμαράτου τοῦ

CHAPTER I

The first section gives a recapitulation of Book I and is all but certainly not by Xen. The work was probably not divided into books until the time of the Alexandrian grammarians (third and second centuries B.C.), and the introductions, which are now found prefixed to all the books except the sixth, were probably added at that time or even later. The close connection between I, 10, § 19 and II, 1, § 2 (μέν—δέ) has been noted above.

3 ὡς, *how*. The five indirect questions in this section are subjs. of δεδήλωται.

5 νικᾶν, *be victorious*, has often the force of a perf., *to have conquered* (G. 1256; H. 827; B. 521).

6 δεδήλωται, *stands recorded*.

7 σημανοῦντα: purpose.

ὅ,τι χρὴ ποιεῖν: direct, τί χρή, a frequent substitute for the deliberative subjv.

8 συσκευασαμένοις: for the case of this and the following partics., see the note on λαβόντι, I, 2, 4 f.

9 εἰς τὸ πρόσθεν: *cf.* I, 10, 19 f. The direction was presumably toward Babylon.

ἕως . . . συμμείξειαν: direct, ἕως ἂν συμμείξωμεν.

10 ἤδη . . . ὄντων, *when they were now on the point of starting*, gen. abs. with omitted subj. *Cf.* προϊόντων, I, 2, 99.

ἡλίῳ, *cf.* I, 10, 60, and the note.

11 Τευθρανίας: see the map. This district had been given to Damaratus by Darius.

γεγονὼς ἀπό: he may well have been the grandson of Damaratus. For the latter, see the vocab.

Λάκωνος, καὶ Γλοῦς ὁ Ταμώ. οὗτοι ἔλεγον ὅτι Κῦρος μὲν τέθνηκεν, Ἀριαῖος δὲ πεφευγὼς ἐν τῷ σταθμῷ εἴη μετὰ τῶν ἄλλων βαρβάρων ὅθεν τῇ προτεραίᾳ ὥρμηντο, καὶ λέγει ὅτι ταύτην μὲν τὴν ἡμέραν περιμένοιεν αὐτούς, εἰ μέλλοιεν ἥκειν, τῇ δὲ ἄλλῃ ἀπιέναι φαίη ἐπὶ Ἰωνίας, ὅθενπερ ἦλθε. ταῦτα ἀκούσαντες οἱ στρατηγοὶ καὶ οἱ ἄλλοι Ἕλληνες πυνθανόμενοι βαρέως ἔφερον. Κλέαρχος δὲ τάδε εἶπεν· Ἀλλ' ὤφελε μὲν Κῦρος ζῆν· ἐπεὶ δὲ τετελεύτηκεν, ἀπαγγέλλετε Ἀριαίῳ ὅτι ἡμεῖς νικῶμέν τε βασιλέα καὶ ὡς ὁρᾶτε οὐδεὶς ἔτι ἡμῖν μάχεται, καὶ εἰ μὴ ὑμεῖς ἤλθετε, ἐπορευόμεθα ἂν ἐπὶ βασιλέα. ἐπαγγελλόμεθα δὲ Ἀριαίῳ, ἐὰν ἐνθάδε ἔλθῃ, εἰς τὸν θρόνον τὸν βασίλειον καθιεῖν αὐτόν· τῶν γὰρ μάχην νικώντων καὶ τὸ ἄρχειν ἐστί. ταῦτα εἰπὼν ἀποστέλλει τοὺς ἀγγέλους καὶ σὺν αὐτοῖς Χειρίσοφον τὸν Λάκωνα καὶ Μένωνα τὸν Θετταλόν· καὶ γὰρ αὐτὸς Μένων ἐβούλετο· ἦν γὰρ φίλος καὶ ξένος Ἀριαίου.

---

12 Γλοῦς: *cf.* I, 4, 104. He seems suddenly to have changed sides.

Ταμώ: *cf.* I, 4, 9. For the form of the gen., see G. 196; H. 159; B. 92.

ἔλεγον ὅτι: introducing indir. disc. which continues to the end of the section. τέθνηκεν (direct form retained), εἴη and λέγει (with φαίη which resumes it) are quoted after ἔλεγον ὅτι. λέγει ὅτι governs περιμένοιεν (direct, περιμένομεν) and ἀπιέναι depends upon φαίη. We have, therefore, double indir. disc.

13 πεφευγὼς: partic., not an opt. with εἴη. Render, *had fled and was.*

σταθμῷ: *cf.* I, 8, 2.

15 μέλλοιεν: direct, μέλλουσι.

16 τῇ δὲ ἄλλῃ, *on the next.*

ἀπιέναι: a fut. See on I, 3, 2.

ἐπί, *towards.*

17 ἀκούσαντες . . . πυνθανόμενοι: note the chiasm.

18 βαρέως ἔφερον: *cf.* I, 3, 11.

ἀλλ' ὤφελε . . . ζῆν, *Well, would that Cyrus were alive.* See G. 1512; H. 871a; B. 588.

20 ἡμεῖς: said with pride in contrast with the dead Cyrus.

21 εἰ μὴ . . . ἤλθετε, ἐπορευόμεθα ἄν: note the tenses, and see G. 1397; H. 895; B. 606.

22 ἐπαγγελλόμεθα: the mid. marks the act as voluntary.

23 βασίλειον: the adj. and the gen. stand close together; see, however, the note on Κύρειον, I, 10, 3.

καθιεῖν: for the formation of such futures, see G. 665, 3; H. 425; B. 215.

νικώντων: possess. gen. with ἐστί. *Cf.* Τισσαφέρνους, I, 1, 28.

25 Χειρίσοφον: see the Introd., §27. As a representative of the most powerful state in Greece he was wisely chosen.

26 φίλος καὶ ξένος: each word has

Οἱ μὲν ᾤχοντο, Κλέαρχος δὲ περιέμενε· τὸ δὲ στράτευμα 6
ἐπορίζετο σῖτον ὅπως ἐδύνατο ἐκ τῶν ὑποζυγίων κόπτοντες τοὺς
βοῦς καὶ ὄνους· ξύλοις δὲ ἐχρῶντο μικρὸν προϊόντες ἀπὸ τῆς
φάλαγγος οὗ ἡ μάχη ἐγένετο τοῖς τε οἰστοῖς πολλοῖς οὖσιν, οὓς
ἠνάγκαζον οἱ Ἕλληνες ἐκβάλλειν τοὺς αὐτομολοῦντας παρὰ
βασιλέως, καὶ τοῖς γέρροις καὶ ταῖς ἀσπίσι ταῖς ξυλίναις ταῖς
Αἰγυπτίαις· πολλαὶ δὲ καὶ πέλται καὶ ἅμαξαι ἦσαν φέρεσθαι
ἔρημοι· οἷς πᾶσι χρώμενοι κρέα ἕψοντες ἤσθιον ἐκείνην τὴν
ἡμέραν.

Καὶ ἤδη τε ἦν ἀμφὶ πλήθουσαν ἀγορὰν καὶ ἔρχονται παρὰ 7
βασιλέως καὶ Τισσαφέρνους κήρυκες οἱ μὲν ἄλλοι βάρβαροι, ἦν
δ' αὐτῶν Φαλῖνος εἷς Ἕλλην, ὃς ἐτύγχανε παρὰ Τισσαφέρνει
ὢν καὶ ἐντίμως ἔχων· καὶ γὰρ προσεποιεῖτο ἐπιστήμων εἶναι

its own force. For ξένος, see the vocab. and I, 1, 53.

27 οἱ μέν: a somewhat striking asyndeton.

περιέμενε: this compound is in place when the one waiting has nothing to do; *cf.* the colloquial Eng., *loaf around*.

28 σῖτον: here *food*, in the broadest sense.

ὅπως ἐδύνατο, *as best it could*. ὅπως is here the rel. adv. With this passage *cf.* the similar one, I, 5, § 6 end.

κόπτοντες: pl., because στράτευμα implies στρατιῶται.

τοὺς βοῦς καὶ ὄνους: the art. expressed but once; *cf.* I, 7, 10, and the note.

29 ξύλοις, *as fuel*, in appos. with οἰστοῖς, γέρροις, and ἀσπίσι, all of which are governed by ἐχρῶντο, the intervening clauses being parenthetic.

31 ἠνάγκαζον: trans. as if in plpf.

ἐκβάλλειν: *i.e.* out of their quivers.

αὐτομολοῦντας: *cf.* I, 7, 62.

33 ἦσαν φέρεσθαι: a somewhat rare use of the infin., in prose, at least; but one showing clearly its dat. force. See G. M. T. 772c. For the omitted οὖσαι with ἔρημοι, *cf.* I, 10, 70.

34 κρέα, *bits of meat*. The obj. is, as usual, expressed with but one of the two governing words (ἕψοντες ἤσθιον).

36 καὶ ἤδη τε ἦν: *cf.* I, 8, 1.

παρὰ βασιλέως: the others, Glus and Tamos, had come from Ariaeus, whom the Greeks considered their friend.

37 οἱ μὲν ἄλλοι: in appos. with κήρυκες. This would naturally be followed by εἷς δ' αὐτῶν Φαλῖνος Ἕλλην, but the order chosen is more pointed. This passage contradicts the statement of Ctesias (Plut. *Artox.* 13) that he himself was a member of the embassy.

39 ἐντίμως ἔχων: equivalent to ἔντιμος ὤν; *cf.* εὐνοϊκῶς ἔχοιεν, I, 1, 21.

προσεποιεῖτο: Xen. seems to believe him an impostor.

8 τῶν ἀμφὶ τάξεις τε καὶ ὁπλομαχίαν. οὗτοι δὲ προσελθόντες 40
καὶ καλέσαντες τοὺς τῶν Ἑλλήνων ἄρχοντας λέγουσιν ὅτι βασιλεὺς κελεύει τοὺς Ἕλληνας, ἐπεὶ νικῶν τυγχάνει καὶ Κῦρον ἀπέκτονε, παραδόντας τὰ ὅπλα ἰόντας ἐπὶ βασιλέως θύρας
9 εὑρίσκεσθαι ἄν τι δύνωνται ἀγαθόν. ταῦτα μὲν εἶπον οἱ βασιλέως κήρυκες· οἱ δὲ Ἕλληνες βαρέως μὲν ἤκουσαν, ὅμως δὲ 45
Κλέαρχος τοσοῦτον εἶπεν ὅτι οὐ τῶν νικώντων εἴη τὰ ὅπλα παραδιδόναι· ἀλλ', ἔφη, ὑμεῖς μέν, ὦ ἄνδρες στρατηγοί, τούτοις ἀποκρίνασθε ὅ,τι κάλλιστόν τε καὶ ἄριστον ἔχετε· ἐγὼ δὲ αὐτίκα ἥξω. ἐκάλεσε γάρ τις αὐτὸν τῶν ὑπηρετῶν, ὅπως ἴδοι τὰ ἱερὰ ἐξῃρημένα· ἔτυχε γὰρ θυόμενος. 50
10 Ἔνθα δὴ ἀπεκρίνατο Κλεάνωρ ὁ Ἀρκὰς πρεσβύτατος ὢν ὅτι πρόσθεν ἂν ἀποθάνοιεν ἢ τὰ ὅπλα παραδοίησαν· Πρόξενος

40 **τῶν ἀμφὶ τάξεις:** for the gen., see G. 1142; H. 754a; B. 351. ἐπιστήμων is used especially of scientific knowledge.

41 **λέγουσιν ὅτι:** the histor. pres. is a secondary tense, yet none of the following vbs. have been changed to the opt. The message is more peremptory in the direct form.

43 **βασιλέως θύρας:** cf. I, 2, 69, and the note.

44 **ἄν τι . . . ἀγαθόν,** whatever favor they could. See the note on εἰ δέ τι, I, 5, 4.

45 **βαρέως,** with anger, rather than with heavy hearts.

46 **τοσοῦτον,** (only) thus much, an example of Spartan brevity. Cf. I, 3, 76.

τῶν νικώντων: cf. I, 1, 28.

47 **ἀλλά:** with this Clearchus turns from the envoys to the Greeks. Xen. gives his words in direct form, ἔφη (said he) being parenthetic.

48 **κάλλιστόν τε καὶ ἄριστον,** most to your honor and to your advantage.

49 **αὐτίκα,** presently. The scant deference Clearchus shows to the envoys was politic. He was a wily Greek (cf. §§ 16,17, and 23; II, 3, § 9; and II, 4, § 26), yet in the end he was completely hoodwinked by Tiss.

50 **ἐξῃρημένα,** which had been taken out (from the victim). The inspection of the entrails, especially the nobler organs, was considered of great importance.

θυόμενος: cf. I, 7, 85, and the note.

51 **Κλεάνωρ:** see the Introd., § 38. πρεσβύτατος must have reference to honor and influence rather than to age, as in V, 3, § 1 Philesius and Sophaenetus are called the oldest. Cleanor is often brought into prominence. For precedence given to age, cf. III, 1, § 34, and Xenophon's words regarding himself, III, 1, § 25 end.

52 **ὅτι . . . παραδοίησαν,** that they

δὲ ὁ Θηβαῖος, Ἀλλ' ἐγώ, ἔφη, ὦ Φαλῖνε, θαυμάζω πότερα ὡς κρατῶν βασιλεὺς αἰτεῖ τὰ ὅπλα ἢ ὡς διὰ φιλίαν δῶρα. εἰ μὲν γὰρ ὡς κρατῶν, τί δεῖ αὐτὸν αἰτεῖν καὶ οὐ λαβεῖν ἐλθόντα; εἰ δὲ πείσας βούλεται λαβεῖν, λεγέτω τί ἔσται τοῖς στρατιώταις, ἐὰν αὐτῷ ταῦτα χαρίσωνται. πρὸς ταῦτα Φαλῖνος εἶπε· Βασιλεὺς νικᾶν ἡγεῖται, ἐπεὶ Κῦρον ἀπέκτεινε. τίς γὰρ αὐτῷ ἔτι τῆς ἀρχῆς ἀντιποιεῖται; νομίζει δὲ καὶ ὑμᾶς ἑαυτοῦ εἶναι, ἔχων ἐν μέσῃ τῇ ἑαυτοῦ χώρᾳ καὶ ποταμῶν ἐντὸς ἀδιαβάτων καὶ πλῆθος ἀνθρώπων ἐφ' ὑμᾶς δυνάμενος ἀγαγεῖν ὅσον οὐδ' εἰ παρέχοι ὑμῖν δύναισθε ἂν ἀποκτεῖναι. μετὰ τοῦτον Θεόπομπος Ἀθηναῖος εἶπεν· Ὦ Φαλῖνε, νῦν, ὡς σὺ ὁρᾷς, ἡμῖν οὐδὲν ἔστιν ἀγαθὸν ἄλλο εἰ μὴ ὅπλα καὶ ἀρετή. ὅπλα μὲν οὖν ἔχοντες οἰόμεθα ἂν καὶ τῇ ἀρετῇ χρῆσθαι, παραδόντες δ' ἂν ταῦτα καὶ τῶν σωμάτων στερηθῆναι. μὴ οὖν οἴου τὰ μόνα ἀγαθὰ ἡμῖν ὄντα ὑμῖν παραδώσειν, ἀλλὰ σὺν τούτοις καὶ περὶ τῶν ὑμετέρων ἀγαθῶν μαχούμεθα. ἀκούσας δὲ ταῦτα ὁ Φαλῖνος ἐγέλασε καὶ εἶπεν· Ἀλλὰ φιλοσόφῳ μὲν ἔοικας, ὦ νεανίσκε, καὶ λέγεις οὐκ

---

would die before they would give up their arms. ἄν goes with both vbs.

Πρόξενος: Xenophon's friend. See the Introd., § 38, and III, 1, §§ 4–10.

53 ὡς κρατῶν: gives the view of the king, not that of the Greeks; so, below, ὡς διὰ φιλίαν δῶρα, as gifts, alleging that he is our friend.

56 πείσας: contrasted with ὡς κρατῶν.

ἐὰν ... χαρίσωνται, if they grant him this favor. With the whole sentence cf. I, 7, 42.

58 αὐτῷ: dat. after the vb. of contending (G. 1177; H. 772; B. 376).

59 ἀρχῆς: G. 1128; H. 739a; B. 366.

ἑαυτοῦ: cf. νικώντων, l. 46.

ἔχων: causal, as δυνάμενος, below.

60 μέσῃ: for the position, see I, 2, 41, and the note.

61 ὅσον ... ἀποκτεῖναι, so great that, even if he should put them in your power, you would not be able to slay them.

62 Θεόπομπος: mentioned only here. The inferior MSS. give Ξενοφῶν; yet see the note on ἔφασαν, below, l. 72.

63 ὡς σὺ ὁρᾷς, as you can see for yourself.

64 εἰ μή, except. Cf. I, 4, 112.

ἔχοντες: equivalent to εἰ ἔχοιμεν; cf. παραδόντες, below.

65 ἄν: with χρῆσθαι; similarly the next ἄν goes with στερηθῆναι. Consult the note on I, 3, 29.

67 παραδώσειν: sc. ἡμᾶς, easily supplied from the preceding ἡμῖν.

68 ἐγέλασε, burst into a laugh, an ingressive aor.

ἀχάριστα· ἴσθι μέντοι ἀνόητος ὤν, εἰ οἴει τὴν ὑμετέραν ἀρετὴν 70
περιγενέσθαι ἂν τῆς βασιλέως δυνάμεως. ἄλλους δέ τινας
ἔφασαν λέγειν ὑπομαλακιζομένους ὡς καὶ Κύρῳ πιστοὶ ἐγένοντο
καὶ βασιλεῖ ἂν πολλοῦ ἄξιοι γένοιντο, εἰ βούλοιτο φίλος
γενέσθαι· καὶ εἴτε ἄλλο τι θέλοι χρῆσθαι εἴτ' ἔπ' Αἴγυπτον
στρατεύειν, συγκαταστρέψαιντ' ἂν αὐτῷ. 75
Ἐν τούτῳ Κλέαρχος ἧκε, καὶ ἠρώτησεν εἰ ἤδη ἀποκεκριμένοι εἶεν. Φαλῖνος δὲ ὑπολαβὼν εἶπεν· Οὗτοι μέν, ὦ Κλέαρχε,
ἄλλος ἄλλα λέγει· σὺ δ' ἡμῖν εἰπὲ τί λέγεις. ὁ δ' εἶπεν· Ἐγώ
σε, ὦ Φαλῖνε, ἄσμενος ἑώρακα, οἶμαι δὲ καὶ οἱ ἄλλοι πάντες·
σύ τε γὰρ Ἕλλην εἶ καὶ ἡμεῖς τοσοῦτοι ὄντες ὅσους σὺ ὁρᾷς· ἐν 80
τοιούτοις δὲ ὄντες πράγμασι συμβουλευόμεθά σοι τί χρὴ ποιεῖν

69 ἀλλά, well.
φιλοσόφῳ: i. e. one trained in argument, but unfitted for action.
70 ἀχάριστα: ironical, as we might say, *You argue very prettily.*
ἴσθι ... ὤν, *know that you are.* See G. 1588; H. 982 B. 661.
71 περιγενέσθαι ἄν, *could (possibly) get the better of.* Cf. I, 1, 56, and the notes.
72 ἔφασαν: Xen. again appears to give the narrative at second hand; cf. I, 8, 73.
λέγειν: imperf. infin., as I, 8, 107.
ὑπομαλακιζομένους: force of the prep.?
74 ἄλλο τι: inner obj. *for anything else.*
θέλοι: for this form, see the vocab·
75 συγκαταστρέψαιντο: instead of a conclusion that would follow equally well after either suggestion, we have a special phrase suiting the second one only. Cf. I, 9, 76 ff., and the note. Egypt, subdued by Cambyses, had revolted during the reign of Darius Nothus, and had not yet been permanently reconquered.

76 ἐν τούτῳ: asyndeton of rapid narrative; observe that Phalinus' answer is not given.
εἰ, *whether.*
77 ὑπολαβών: absolute, as often, *interrupting.*
οὗτοι ... ἄλλος ἄλλα λέγει: partit. appos. See the note on I, 8, 77. Here the vb. agrees with ἄλλος; the opposite agreement is found, e. g. I, 6, 64.
78 εἰπέ: for the accent, see G. 131, 2; H. 387b; B. 210 note.
λέγεις, *have to say, think.*
ἐγώ: emphatic, balancing σύ, above.
79 ἄσμενος: adj., where we use the adv. Cf. προτέρα, I, 2, 142, and the note.
οἶμαι: without influence on the construction. In this use the form οἶμαι is preferred; elsewhere οἴομαι.
80 τοσοῦτοι ὄντες ὅσους: stronger than πάντες ὅσους. Ἕλληνές ἐσμεν is easily supplied.
81 πράγμασι, *troubles, plight.*
συμβουλευόμεθα: note the meanings of the act. and the mid. of this vb.
τί, *as to what,* indir. ques.

περὶ ὧν λέγεις. σὺ οὖν πρὸς θεῶν συμβούλευσον ἡμῖν ὅ,τι σοι 17
δοκεῖ κάλλιστον καὶ ἄριστον εἶναι, καὶ ὅ σοι τιμὴν οἴσει εἰς τὸν
ἔπειτα χρόνον ἀεὶ λεγόμενον, ὅτι Φαλῖνός ποτε πεμφθεὶς παρὰ
85 βασιλέως κελεύσων τοὺς Ἕλληνας τὰ ὅπλα παραδοῦναι ξυμβου-
λευομένοις ξυνεβούλευσεν αὐτοῖς τάδε. οἶσθα δὲ ὅτι ἀνάγκη
λέγεσθαι ἐν τῇ Ἑλλάδι ἃ ἂν ξυμβουλεύσῃς. ὁ δὲ Κλέαρχος 18
ταῦτα ὑπήγετο βουλόμενος καὶ αὐτὸν τὸν παρὰ βασιλέως πρεσ-
βεύοντα ξυμβουλεῦσαι μὴ παραδοῦναι τὰ ὅπλα, ὅπως εὐέλπιδες
90 μᾶλλον εἶεν οἱ Ἕλληνες. Φαλῖνος δὲ ὑποστρέψας παρὰ τὴν
δόξαν αὐτοῦ εἶπεν· Ἐγώ, εἰ μὲν τῶν μυρίων ἐλπίδων μία τις 19
ὑμῖν ἐστι σωθῆναι πολεμοῦντας βασιλεῖ, συμβουλεύω μὴ παραδιδόναι τὰ ὅπλα· εἰ δέ τοι μηδεμία σωτηρίας ἐστὶν ἐλπὶς
ἄκοντος βασιλέως, ξυμβουλεύω σῴζεσθαι ὑμῖν ὅπῃ δυνατόν.
95 Κλέαρχος δὲ πρὸς ταῦτα εἶπεν· Ἀλλὰ ταῦτα μὲν δὴ σὺ λέγεις· 20
παρ' ἡμῶν δὲ ἀπάγγελλε τάδε ὅτι ἡμεῖς οἰόμεθα, εἰ μὲν δέοι
βασιλεῖ φίλους εἶναι, πλείονος ἂν ἄξιοι εἶναι φίλοι ἔχοντες τὰ

---

82 πρὸς θεῶν: he is put upon oath, as it were.

ὅ,τι ... καὶ ὅ, *whatever ... and a thing which*, a shift from the general to the particular.

83 εἰς ... χρόνον, *for all future time.*

84 ἀεὶ λεγόμενον, *when from time to time told.* The text is uncertain.

Φαλῖνος: far more effective than σύ. Xen. is giving the words of the supposed future narrator.

86 τάδε, *thus and so.* The actual advice is of course not given.

ἀνάγκη: for the omission of ἐστί, see I, 3, 21, and the note.

88 ταῦτα ὑπήγετο, *sought cunningly* (ὑπο-) *to draw him on in this.* ταῦτα is the inner obj.

καὶ αὐτὸν τὸν ... πρεσρεύοντα, *even the very one who was serving as ambassador.*

90 ὑποστρέψας, *cunningly evading him.* The metaphor is from wrestling.

παρά, *contrary to.*

91 τῶν μυρίων ἐλπίδων: the art. marks the numeral as the ordinary or proper one (a round number); it should not be translated.

μία τις, *a single one.*

92 σωθῆναι: the infin. depends upon ἐλπίς, understood with μία τις. Below we have σωτηρίας in a corresponding phrase.

94 ἄκοντος βασιλέως: cf. I, 3, 89, and the note.

95 μὲν δή: the matter is thus dismissed. Note the exact use of ταῦτα and τάδε with the emphatic pronouns σύ and ἡμεῖς. Cf. *iste* and *hic*.

97 πλείονος: cf. πολλοῦ, I, 3, 57.

ἂν ... εἶναι: direct, ἂν εἶμεν; so ἂν πολεμεῖν, below, representing ἂν

ὅπλα ἢ παραδόντες ἄλλῳ, εἰ δὲ δέοι πολεμεῖν, ἄμεινον ἂν πολεμεῖν ἔχοντες τὰ ὅπλα ἢ ἄλλῳ παραδόντες. ὁ δὲ Φαλῖνος εἶπε· Ταῦτα μὲν δὴ ἀπαγγελοῦμεν· ἀλλὰ καὶ τάδε ὑμῖν εἰπεῖν ἐκέλευσε βασιλεὺς ὅτι μένουσι μὲν ὑμῖν αὐτοῦ σπονδαὶ εἴησαν, προϊοῦσι δὲ καὶ ἀπιοῦσι πόλεμος. εἴπατε οὖν καὶ περὶ τούτου πότερα μενεῖτε καὶ σπονδαί εἰσιν ἢ ὡς πολέμου ὄντος παρ' ὑμῶν ἀπαγγείλω. Κλέαρχος δ' ἔλεξεν· Ἀπάγγελλε τοίνυν καὶ περὶ τούτου ὅτι καὶ ἡμῖν ταὐτὰ δοκεῖ ἅπερ καὶ βασιλεῖ. Τί οὖν ταῦτά ἐστιν; ἔφη ὁ Φαλῖνος. ἀπεκρίθη ὁ Κλέαρχος· Ἢν μὲν μένωμεν, σπονδαί, ἀπιοῦσι δὲ καὶ προϊοῦσι πόλεμος. ὁ δὲ πάλιν ἠρώτησε· Σπονδὰς ἢ πόλεμον ἀπαγγείλω; Κλέαρχος δὲ ταὐτὰ πάλιν ἀπεκρίνατο· Σπονδαὶ μένουσιν, ἀπιοῦσι δὲ ἢ προϊοῦσι πόλεμος. ὅ,τι δὲ ποιήσοι οὐ διεσήμηνε.

II. Φαλῖνος μὲν δὴ ᾤχετο καὶ οἱ σὺν αὐτῷ. οἱ δὲ παρὰ Ἀριαίου ἧκον Προκλῆς καὶ Χειρίσοφος· Μένων δὲ αὐτοῦ ἔμενε παρὰ Ἀριαίῳ· οὗτοι δὲ ἔλεγον ὅτι πολλοὺς φαίη ὁ Ἀριαῖος εἶναι Πέρσας ἑαυτοῦ βελτίους, οὓς οὐκ ἂν ἀνασχέσθαι αὐτοῦ βασιλεύ-

---

πολεμοῖμεν. The partics. ἔχοντες and παραδόντες supply in each case a new protasis.

101 μένουσι: conditional, as προϊοῦσι and ἀπιοῦσι, below.

εἴησαν: direct εἰσί. The pres. often covers the fut.; cf. εἰσιν, two lines below. Do not trans., would be.

102 εἴπατε: in the forms εἶπας and εἴπατε (indic. or imv.) this second aor. often has the first aor. vowel.

103 ὡς πολέμου ὄντος, that there is war. See I, 3, 31, and the note.

104 ἀπαγγείλω: observe that the subjv. question is followed by an imv. answer.

105 καὶ ἡμῖν ... καὶ βασιλεῖ: a rel. indicating sameness is regularly followed by καί. Often, as here, καί is expressed in both clauses emphasizing the parallelism.

106 ἀπεκρίθη: one of Xen.'s un-classic forms: ἀπεκρίνατο would be regular. Note the asyndeton; the answer comes quickly.

107 σπονδαί ... πόλεμος: note the chiasm.

110 ποιήσοι: fut. opts. are always due to indir. disc. (G. 1287; H. 855a; B. 548).

CHAPTER II

2 ἧκον, came back.

αὐτοῦ: the adv. (cf. I, 3, 11), further explained by παρὰ Ἀριαίῳ. For the relations of these two men to one another, see c. 1. 26.

3 ἔλεγον ... φαίη: the former of these vbs. has, in the act., almost invariably the construction with ὅτι; the latter virtually only the infin.

πολλούς: emphatic position.

4 βελτίους: i.e. in rank; cf. ἀρίστοις,

5 οντος· ἀλλ' εἰ βούλεσθε συναπιέναι, ἥκειν ἤδη κελεύει τῆς νυκτός. εἰ δὲ μή, αὔριον πρῲ ἀπιέναι φησίν. ὁ δὲ Κλέαρχος 2 εἶπεν· Ἀλλ' οὕτω χρὴ ποιεῖν· ἐὰν μὲν ἥκωμεν, ὥσπερ λέγετε· εἰ δὲ μή, πράττετε ὁποῖον ἄν τι ὑμῖν οἴησθε μάλιστα συμφέρειν. ὅ,τι δὲ ποιήσοι οὐδὲ τούτοις εἶπε.

10 Μετὰ ταῦτα ἤδη ἡλίου δύνοντος συγκαλέσας στρατηγοὺς καὶ 3 λοχαγοὺς ἔλεξε τοιάδε. Ἐμοί, ὦ ἄνδρες, θυομένῳ ἰέναι ἐπὶ βασιλέα οὐκ ἐγίγνετο τὰ ἱερά. καὶ εἰκότως ἄρα οὐκ ἐγίγνετο· ὡς γὰρ ἐγὼ νῦν πυνθάνομαι, ἐν μέσῳ ἡμῶν καὶ βασιλέως ὁ Τίγρης ποταμός ἐστι ναυσίπορος, ὃν οὐκ ἂν δυναίμεθα ἄνευ πλοίων δια-
15 βῆναι· πλοῖα δὲ ἡμεῖς οὐκ ἔχομεν. οὐ μὲν δὴ αὐτοῦ γε μένειν οἷόν τε· τὰ γὰρ ἐπιτήδεια οὐκ ἔστιν ἔχειν· ἰέναι δὲ παρὰ τοὺς

I, 5, 39. Xen. uses comparative forms both with and without the ν.

οὓς... βασιλεύοντος, *who would not endure his being king*. The influence of φαίη extends (exceptionally) even to the subordinate rel. clause. See G. 1524; H. 947; B. 671 note. The direct form was οἱ οὐκ ἂν ἀνάσχοιντο. αὐτοῦ βασιλεύοντος is gen. abs. *Cf* αὐτῶν πολεμούντων, I, 1, 40.

5 ἀλλ' εἰ βούλεσθε: a sudden shift to direct speech.

τῆς νυκτός: for the gen. of time, see the note on ἡμερῶν, I, 7, 85.

6 εἰ δὲ μή, *otherwise*. The phrase reverses a preceding assumption of whatever type, positive or negative. Here it is equivalent to ἐὰν δὲ μὴ ἥκητε, and below, l. 8, it follows ἐάν with the subj. See G. 1417; H. 906; B. 616, 3.

ἀπιέναι: fut., not pres. *Cf.* I, 3, 2, and the note.

7 ὥσπερ λέγετε: the ellipsis is easily supplied.

8 πράττετε: the imv. is more vivid than a clause with χρή.

ὁποῖον... τι: τι is often added to indefinite words.

9 ὅ,τι... εἶπε: retain the order in translating and remember οὐδέ is more than *not*.

10 δύνοντος: an Ionic form; *cf.* below, l. 62. The mid. is normal; *cf.* ἐδύετο, I, 10, 60.

11 ἰέναι: dat. infin. of purpose; *cf.* φέρεσθαι, c. 1. 33.

12 οὐκ ἐγίγνετο, *would not prove favorable*, i. e. after repeated trials. Contrast the aor. in IV, 5, § 8, ἐγένετο ἐπὶ τοῦ πρώτου καλὰ τὰ σφάγια.

ἄρα, *as I now see*, a constant use with the impf.

13 ἐν μέσῳ, *between. Cf.* I, 7, 34.

Τίγρης: Clearchus must have been misinformed, or he mistakes some canal for the river.

15 πλοῖα: note the emphatic position, and *cf.* τὰ γὰρ ἐπιτήδεια, below.

οὐ μὲν δή: *not that it is.*

16 οἷόν τε: see G. 1024b; H. 1000;

4 Κύρου φίλους πάνυ καλὰ ἡμῖν τὰ ἱερὰ ἦν. ὧδε οὖν χρὴ ποιεῖν·
ἀπιόντας δειπνεῖν ὅ,τι τις ἔχει· ἐπειδὰν δὲ σημήνῃ τῷ κέρατι ὡς
ἀναπαύεσθαι, συσκευάζεσθε· ἐπειδὰν δὲ τὸ δεύτερον, ἀνατίθεσθε
ἐπὶ τὰ ὑποζύγια· ἐπὶ δὲ τῷ τρίτῳ ἕπεσθε τῷ ἡγουμένῳ, τὰ μὲν 20
5 ὑποζύγια ἔχοντες πρὸς τοῦ ποταμοῦ, τὰ δὲ ὅπλα ἔξω. ταῦτ'
ἀκούσαντες οἱ στρατηγοὶ καὶ λοχαγοὶ ἀπῆλθον καὶ ἐποίουν οὕτω.
καὶ τὸ λοιπὸν ὃ μὲν ἦρχεν, οἱ δὲ ἐπείθοντο, οὐχ ἑλόμενοι, ἀλλὰ
ὁρῶντες ὅτι μόνος ἐφρόνει οἷα δεῖ τὸν ἄρχοντα, οἱ δ' ἄλλοι ἄπει-
6 ροι ἦσαν. [ἀριθμὸς τῆς ὁδοῦ ἣν ἦλθον ἐξ Ἐφέσου τῆς Ἰωνίας 25
μέχρι τῆς μάχης σταθμοὶ τρεῖς καὶ ἐνενήκοντα, παρασάγγαι
πέντε καὶ τριάκοντα καὶ πεντακόσιοι, στάδιοι πεντήκοντα καὶ
ἑξακισχίλιοι καὶ μύριοι· ἀπὸ δὲ τῆς μάχης ἐλέγοντο εἶναι εἰς
Βαβυλῶνα στάδιοι ἑξήκοντα καὶ τριακόσιοι.]

B. 641. The neut. has reference to circumstances; the personal masc. or fem., as a rule, to character.

ἰέναι: cf. l. 11.

18 σημήνῃ: the vb. contains its own subj. Cf. ἐσάλπιγξε, I, 2, 98.

τῷ κέρατι: an isolated use. Greek military signals were ordinarily given with the σάλπιγξ.

ὡς: Clearchus plans to deceive the enemy.

20 τῷ ἡγουμένῳ, *the van*, a collective neut.

21 πρός, *on the side of*.

τὰ δὲ ὅπλα = τοὺς ὁπλίτας, as often.

22 ἀπῆλθον . . . ἐποίουν: contrast the tenses.

23 τὸ λοιπόν, *in future*. In this general sense the gen., τοῦ λοιποῦ (e. g. V, 7, § 34), is somewhat commoner. The acc. often means *the rest of*, and may have a dependent gen. (e. g. III, 4, § 16).

ὃ μέν: *i. e.* Clearchus; see the Introd., § 38.

24 ἐφρόνει: the vb. is past indic., rather than opt., since the narrator looks back over the past.

25 ἀριθμός: this section is probably spurious. It reads like an interpolation and its figures do not agree in all particulars with those of Book I.

τῆς Ἰωνίας: a regular use of the gen. with local words.

26 μάχης, *battlefield;* so again below.

τρεῖς καὶ ἐνενήκοντα: eighty-four, according to Book I. Allowance must, of course, be made for the fact that Ephesus, not Sardis, is here taken as the starting-point. From Ephesus to Sardis was, however, only a three days' journey, so that a discrepancy of six σταθμοί remains. It will be noted that, if we allow eighteen parasangs for the additional three days' journey, we have, in this particular, complete agreement, as 517 is the total number according to Book I.

28 ἐλέγοντο: of this Xen. could

Anabasis

30 Ἐντεῦθεν ἐπεὶ σκότος ἐγένετο Μιλτοκύθης μὲν ὁ Θρᾷξ ἔχων 7
τούς τε ἱππέας τοὺς μεθ' ἑαυτοῦ εἰς τετταράκοντα καὶ τῶν πεζῶν
Θρᾳκῶν ὡς τριακοσίους ηὐτομόλησε πρὸς βασιλέα.

Κλέαρχος δὲ τοῖς ἄλλοις ἡγεῖτο κατὰ τὰ παρηγγελμένα, οἱ 8
δ' εἵποντο· καὶ ἀφικνοῦνται εἰς τὸν πρῶτον σταθμὸν παρ' Ἀρι-
35 αῖον καὶ τὴν ἐκείνου στρατιὰν ἀμφὶ μέσας νύκτας· καὶ ἐν τάξει
θέμενοι τὰ ὅπλα ξυνῆλθον οἱ στρατηγοὶ καὶ λοχαγοὶ τῶν Ἑλλήνων παρ' Ἀριαῖον· καὶ ὤμοσαν οἵ τε Ἕλληνες καὶ ὁ Ἀριαῖος
καὶ τῶν σὺν αὐτῷ οἱ κράτιστοι μήτε προδώσειν ἀλλήλους σύμ-
μαχοί τε ἔσεσθαι· οἱ δὲ βάρβαροι προσώμοσαν καὶ ἡγήσεσθαι
40 ἀδόλως. ταῦτα δὲ ὤμοσαν, σφάξαντες ταῦρον καὶ κάπρον καὶ 9
κριὸν εἰς ἀσπίδα, οἱ μὲν Ἕλληνες βάπτοντες ξίφος, οἱ δὲ βάρβαροι λόγχην. ἐπεὶ δὲ τὰ πιστὰ ἐγένετο, εἶπεν ὁ Κλέαρχος· 10

---

speak only from hearsay. Plut. *Artox.* 8, gives the distance as 500 stadia.

30 ἐντεῦθεν: *i. e.* from the plundered camp.

31 ἱππέας: see the note on I, 5, 82 f.

εἰς: *cf.* I, 2, 15, and the note.

35 μέσας νύκτας: for the pl., see I, 7, 4, and the note.

36 θέμενοι τὰ ὅπλα: see I, 5, 88, and the note. The partic. includes the troops, although agreeing with στρατηγοί and λοχαγοί.

38 μήτε ... τε, *not ... but.* The parallelism calls for τε ... τε, even when one clause is neg. In such cases Eng. generally uses the adversative, *but*. Note that vbs. of swearing, although usually taking the construction of indir. disc., have the neg. μή, never οὐ.

39 προσώμοσαν καί, *swore in addition that they would also.*

40 ἀδόλως, *without guile.* The word occurs often in treaties; *cf.* II, 3, § 26.

41 εἰς ἀσπίδα, *so that the blood ran into a shield. Cf.* εἰς ποταμόν, IV, 3, § 18. In solemn compacts three gods were often invoked and three victims slain (*cf.* the *suovetaurilia* of the Romans). The dipping of a weapon in the blood is doubtless symbolic: the one giving the oath invokes a like fate upon himself, if he prove faithless (Vollbrecht). The corrector of the Paris MS. adds a wolf to the list of victims, and, according to Plutarch, the wolf was the proper victim to sacrifice to Ahriman, the power of evil and darkness.

This is the most solemn compact recorded in the *Anabasis.* In most instances the oath and the giving of the hand suffice. (*e. g.* I, 6, 35, and II, 3, § 28). Perhaps Xen. wished to make the subsequent treachery of Ariaeus appear the more black.

42 ἐγένετο, *had been exchanged.* γίγνομαι must be translated as

Ἄγε δή, ὦ Ἀριαῖε, ἐπείπερ ὁ αὐτὸς ὑμῖν στόλος ἐστὶ καὶ ἡμῖν, εἰπὲ τίνα γνώμην ἔχεις περὶ τῆς πορείας, πότερον ἄπιμεν ἥνπερ ἤλθομεν ἢ ἄλλην τινὰ ἐννενοηκέναι δοκεῖς ὁδὸν κρείττω. ὁ δὲ εἶπεν· Ἢν μὲν ἤλθομεν ἀπιόντες παντελῶς ἂν ὑπὸ λιμοῦ ἀπολοίμεθα· ὑπάρχει γὰρ νῦν ἡμῖν οὐδὲν τῶν ἐπιτηδείων. ἑπτακαίδεκα γὰρ σταθμῶν τῶν ἐγγυτάτω οὐδὲ δεῦρο ἰόντες ἐκ τῆς χώρας οὐδὲν εἴχομεν λαμβάνειν· ἔνθα δέ τι ἦν, ἡμεῖς διαπορευόμενοι κατεδαπανήσαμεν. νῦν δ' ἐπινοοῦμεν πορεύεσθαι μακροτέραν μέν, τῶν δ' ἐπιτηδείων οὐκ ἀπορήσομεν. πορευτέον δ' ἡμῖν τοὺς πρώτους σταθμοὺς ὡς ἂν δυνώμεθα μακροτάτους, ἵνα ὡς πλεῖστον ἀποσπάσωμεν τοῦ βασιλικοῦ στρατεύματος· ἢν γὰρ ἅπαξ δύο ἢ τριῶν ἡμερῶν ὁδὸν ἀπόσχωμεν, οὐκέτι μὴ δύνηται βασιλεὺς ἡμᾶς καταλαβεῖν. ὀλίγῳ μὲν γὰρ στρατεύματι οὐ τολμήσει ἐφέπεσθαι· πολὺν δ' ἔχων στόλον οὐ δυνήσεται ταχέως πορεύεσθαι· ἴσως δὲ καὶ τῶν ἐπιτηδείων σπανιεῖ. ταύτην, ἔφη, τὴν γνώμην ἔχω ἔγωγε.

Ἦν δὲ αὕτη ἡ στρατηγία οὐδὲν ἄλλο δυναμένη ἢ ἀποδρᾶναι

---

the context demands. It may supply a passive to almost any vb.
43 ἄγε δή, come now.
44 ἥνπερ, the same as; sc. ὁδόν.
46 ὑπὸ λιμοῦ: a slight personification, common with this word. Cf. I, 5, 26.
47 ὑπάρχει, have to count upon, more than = ἔστι.
48 σταθμῶν: gen. of time.
ἐγγυτάτω: adv. as an attributive.
49 εἴχομεν, were we able.
50 κατεδαπανήσαμεν: for the force of the prep., cf. καθηδυπάθησα, I, 3, 15.
μακροτέραν: sc. ὁδόν.
51 ἐπιτηδείων: gen. with a word expressing want.
πορευτέον: verb. adj. in the impersonal construction, with acc. of the inner obj. (G. 1597; H. 990; B. 665). Trans., we must make. Cf. I, 5, 35.
52 ὡς ἄν . . . μακροτάτους, as long as possible.
53 ἅπαξ: cf. I, 9, 34.
54 ἡμερῶν: gen. of measure, with ὁδόν.
οὐκέτι μὴ δύνηται: emphatic neg. of the fut. (G. 1360; H. 1032; B. 569, 2).
57 σπανιεῖ: for the form, cf. καθιεῖν, c. 1. 23.
58 ἔγωγε, I, for my part. Note, also, the emphatic postponement of the word.
59 ἦν . . . δυναμένη, now this was a form of generalship which amounted to nothing else. The resolved vb. form (for ἐδύνατο) brings the partic. into stronger

60 ἢ ἀποφυγεῖν· ἡ δὲ τύχη ἐστρατήγησε κάλλιον. ἐπεὶ γὰρ ἡμέρα ἐγένετο, ἐπορεύοντο ἐν δεξιᾷ ἔχοντες τὸν ἥλιον, λογιζόμενοι ἥξειν ἅμα ἡλίῳ δύνοντι εἰς κώμας τῆς Βαβυλωνίας χώρας· καὶ τοῦτο μὲν οὐκ ἐψεύσθησαν. ἔτι δὲ ἀμφὶ δείλην ἔδοξαν πολεμίους ὁρᾶν ἱππέας· καὶ τῶν τε Ἑλλήνων οἳ μὴ ἔτυχον ἐν ταῖς τάξεσιν
65 ὄντες εἰς τὰς τάξεις ἔθεον, καὶ Ἀριαῖος, ἐτύγχανε γὰρ ἐφ' ἁμάξης πορευόμενος διότι ἐτέτρωτο, καταβὰς ἐθωρακίζετο καὶ οἱ σὺν αὐτῷ. ἐν ᾧ δὲ ὡπλίζοντο ἧκον λέγοντες οἱ προπεμφθέντες σκοποὶ ὅτι οὐχ ἱππεῖς εἶεν ἀλλ' ὑποζύγια νέμοιντο. καὶ εὐθὺς ἔγνωσαν πάντες ὅτι ἐγγύς που ἐστρατοπεδεύετο βασιλεύς· καὶ
70 γὰρ καπνὸς ἐφαίνετο ἐν κώμαις οὐ πρόσω.

Κλέαρχος δὲ ἐπὶ μὲν τοὺς πολεμίους οὐκ ἦγεν· ᾔδει γὰρ καὶ ἀπειρηκότας τοὺς στρατιώτας καὶ ἀσίτους ὄντας· ἤδη δὲ καὶ ὀψὲ ἦν· οὐ μέντοι οὐδὲ ἀπέκλινε, φυλαττόμενος μὴ δοκοίη φεύγειν, ἀλλ' εὐθύωρον ἄγων ἅμα τῷ ἡλίῳ δυομένῳ εἰς τὰς ἐγγυ-
75 τάτω κώμας τοὺς πρώτους ἔχων κατεσκήνωσεν, ἐξ ὧν διήρπαστο ὑπὸ τοῦ βασιλικοῦ στρατεύματος καὶ αὐτὰ τὰ ἀπὸ τῶν οἰκιῶν ξύλα. οἱ μὲν οὖν πρῶτοι ὅμως τρόπῳ τινὶ ἐστρατοπεδεύσαντο, οἱ δὲ ὕστεροι σκοταῖοι προσιόντες ὡς ἐτύγχανον ἕκαστοι ηὐλί-

---

relief. *Cf.* εἶναι φυλάττων, I, 2, 122 f. For this use of δύναμαι, *cf.* I, 5, 33.
ἀποδρᾶναι ... ἀποφυγεῖν: *cf.* I, 4, 49.
60 τύχη: almost personified.
62 δύνοντι: *cf.* l. 10, and the note.
τοῦτο ... ἐψεύσθησαν: *cf.* I, 8, 42.
63 δείλην: *cf.* I, 8, 26, and the note. It was not yet sunset, § 16.
ἔδοξαν, *they thought. Cf.* I, 7, 4, and the note.
64 οἳ μὴ ἔτυχον: the neg. shows that the rel. is indefinite.
65 ἐφ' ἁμάξης: *cf.* I, 7, 92.
67 ἐν ᾧ: *cf.* I, 2, 117, and the note.
68 εἶεν ... νέμοιντο: opt., since λέγοντες takes the time of ἧκον. For the pl. vb. with neut. pl. subj., *cf.* I, 2, 38, and the note.

71 ἦγεν: the obj., τὸ στράτευμα, is omitted.
72 ἀπειρηκότας, *were worn out. Cf.* ἀπαγορεύουσι, I, 5, 18.
73 οὐ μέντοι οὐδὲ ἀπέκλινε, *however he did not even turn aside either.*
74 εὐθύωρον, *straight on*, a poetic word. The adj. supplies the place of an inner obj.
75 ἐξ ὧν ... ξύλα: retain the order, *from which there had been taken ... even the very timbers.* For the pregnant use of the prep., *cf.* παρά, I, 1, 18, and the note.
77 τρόπῳ τινί, *after a fashion.*
78 σκοταῖοι: adj. for adv. again.
ηὐλίζοντο: the circumstances account for the choice of the

ζοντο, καὶ κραυγὴν πολλὴν ἐποίουν καλοῦντες ἀλλήλους, ὥστε
καὶ τοὺς πολεμίους ἀκούειν· ὥστε οἱ μὲν ἐγγύτατα τῶν πολε- 80
μίων καὶ ἔφυγον ἐκ τῶν σκηνωμάτων. δῆλον δὲ τοῦτο τῇ
18 ὑστεραίᾳ ἐγένετο· οὔτε γὰρ ὑποζύγιον ἔτ' οὐδὲν ἐφάνη οὔτε
στρατόπεδον οὔτε καπνὸς οὐδαμοῦ πλησίον. ἐξεπλάγη δέ, ὡς
ἔοικε, καὶ βασιλεὺς τῇ ἐφόδῳ τοῦ στρατεύματος. ἐδήλωσε δὲ
19 τοῦτο οἷς τῇ ὑστεραίᾳ ἔπραττε. προϊούσης μέντοι τῆς νυκτὸς 85
ταύτης καὶ τοῖς Ἕλλησι φόβος ἐμπίπτει, καὶ θόρυβος καὶ δοῦ-
20 πος ἦν οἷον εἰκὸς φόβου ἐμπεσόντος γίγνεσθαι. Κλέαρχος δὲ
Τολμίδην Ἠλεῖον, ὃν ἐτύγχανεν ἔχων παρ' ἑαυτῷ κήρυκα ἄριστον τῶν τότε, ἀνειπεῖν ἐκέλευσε σιγὴν κηρύξαντα ὅτι προαγο-
ρεύουσιν οἱ ἄρχοντες, ὃς ἂν τὸν ἀφέντα τὸν ὄνον εἰς τὰ ὅπλα 90
21 μηνύσῃ, ὅτι λήψεται μισθὸν τάλαντον. ἐπεὶ δὲ ταῦτα ἐκηρύχθη,
ἔγνωσαν οἱ στρατιῶται ὅτι κενὸς ὁ φόβος εἴη καὶ οἱ ἄρχοντες
σῶοι. ἅμα δὲ ὄρθρῳ παρήγγειλεν ὁ Κλέαρχος εἰς τάξιν τὰ
ὅπλα τίθεσθαι τοὺς Ἕλληνας ᾗπερ εἶχον ὅτε ἦν ἡ μάχη.

1 III. Ὁ δὲ δὴ ἔγραψα ὅτι βασιλεὺς ἐξεπλάγη τῇ ἐφόδῳ,
τῷδε δῆλον ἦν. τῇ μὲν γὰρ πρόσθεν ἡμέρᾳ πέμπων τὰ ὅπλα
παραδιδόναι ἐκέλευε, τότε δὲ ἅμα ἡλίῳ ἀνατέλλοντι κήρυκας
2 ἔπεμψε περὶ σπονδῶν. οἱ δ' ἐπεὶ ἦλθον πρὸς τοὺς προφύλακας,

---

durative tense. Contrast the aor. ἐστρατοπεδεύσαντο, l. 77.
81 καὶ ἔφυγον, *actually fled.*
83 ἐξεπλάγη: cf. ἐκπλαγείς, I, 8, 81. The word is a strong one, and is further emphasized by its position.
86 δοῦπος: a poetic word. Cf. ἐδούπησαν, I, 8, 74.
87 οἷον: masc., not neut. With εἰκός supply ἐστι.
89 τῶν τότε: sc. κηρύκων.
90 ὃς ἂν ... μηνύσῃ: a condit. rel. clause, forming a part of the indir. disc. despite its position before ὅτι. Cf. I, 6, 6 f., and the note.
τὸν ὄνον: i. e. the generals make nothing of the matter. A very similar story is told of the Athenian general Iphicrates in Polyaenus III, 9, 4.
91 τάλαντον: a large reward.
93 τὰ ὅπλα: the heavy arms were, as a rule, stacked in one place.
94 ᾗπερ εἶχον, *just as they stood.*

CHAPTER III

1 ὃ ... ἔγραψα: see c. 2. 83 f.
2 πέμπων: used without an obj., as *send* may be in Eng.
3 ἐκέλευε: with this vb. there is often a tendency to use the impf., rather than the aor.
4 περὶ σπονδῶν: a decided change

ἐζήτουν τοὺς ἄρχοντας. ἐπειδὴ δὲ ἀπήγγελλον οἱ προφύλακες, Κλέαρχος τυχὼν τότε τὰς τάξεις ἐπισκοπῶν εἶπεν τοῖς προφύλαξι κελεύειν τοὺς κήρυκας περιμένειν ἄχρι ἂν σχολάσῃ. ἐπεὶ δὲ κατέστησε τὸ στράτευμα ὥστε καλῶς ἔχειν ὁρᾶσθαι πάντῃ φάλαγγα πυκνήν, ἐκτὸς τῶν ὅπλων δὲ μηδένα καταφανῆ εἶναι, ἐκάλεσε τοὺς ἀγγέλους, καὶ αὐτός τε προῆλθε τούς τε εὐοπλοτάτους ἔχων καὶ εὐειδεστάτους τῶν αὑτοῦ στρατιωτῶν καὶ τοῖς ἄλλοις στρατηγοῖς ταὐτὰ ἔφρασεν. ἐπεὶ δὲ ἦν πρὸς τοῖς ἀγγέλοις, ἀνηρώτα τί βούλοιντο. οἱ δ' ἔλεγον ὅτι περὶ σπονδῶν ἥκοιεν ἄνδρες οἵτινες ἱκανοὶ ἔσονται τά τε παρὰ βασιλέως τοῖς Ἕλλησιν ἀπαγγεῖλαι καὶ τὰ παρὰ τῶν Ἑλλήνων βασιλεῖ. ὁ δὲ ἀπεκρίνατο· Ἀπαγγέλλετε τοίνυν αὐτῷ ὅτι μάχης δεῖ πρῶτον· ἄριστον γὰρ οὐκ ἔστιν οὐδ' ὁ τολμήσων περὶ σπονδῶν

---

in the king's attitude, commented on in III, 1, § 28.

6 ἐπισκοπῶν: supplementary partic. with τυχών.

7 ἄχρι, *until.* This word lacks prose warrant. It has been assumed that Xen. means to represent Clearchus as speaking in his own dialect; but, in view of our author's many poeticisms, this is, at best, highly uncertain. *Cf.* his use of ἔστε, below l. 30, a word used by no other prose author.

8 ὥστε ... ὁρᾶσθαι, *so that it presented a fine appearance.* This phrase is further explained by πάντῃ φάλαγγα πυκνήν. ὁρᾶσθαι limits and defines καλῶς (*for the looking*). See G. 1528; H. 952; B. 641. The act. infin. is regular in these phrases (*cf.* ὁρᾶν στυγνός [II, 6, § 9]), so that it may be regarded as doubtful whether we have here the pass., or the unAttic mid. in the sense of the act.

9 ἐκτὸς τῶν ὅπλων, *except the armed men.* The closed ranks of the hoplites in front would prevent the unarmed from being seen.

10 αὐτός τε: correlative with καὶ τοῖς ἄλλοις, below; the intervening τε and καί connect the adjs.

12 ταὐτά: *i.e.* they were to follow his example.

14 ἥκοιεν, *had come,* since ἥκω is in force a perf.

οἵτινες ... ἔσονται: a rel. clause of purpose. *Cf.* ὅστις ... ἀπάξει, I, 3, 70 f. Observe that in such a clause the indic. is usually retained, even after a secondary tense.

τά τε παρά: *i.e. proposals.* The context supplies the noun.

16 μάχης ... πρῶτον: both words are emphasized by their position.

17 ἄριστον ... ἄριστον: for the order, *cf.* ἤγγελλον ... ἤγγελλον, I, 7, 62 ff., and the note.

ἔστιν: for the accent, see G. 144, 5; H. 480; B. 262, 1.

ὁ τολμήσων (*sc.* ἔστι), *nor lives there a man who will dare.*

Book II, Chap. III

6 λέγειν τοῖς Ἕλλησι μὴ πορίσας ἄριστον. ταῦτα ἀκούσαντες
οἱ ἄγγελοι ἀπήλαυνον, καὶ ἦκον ταχύ· ᾧ καὶ δῆλον ἦν ὅτι
ἐγγύς που βασιλεὺς ἦν ἢ ἄλλος τις ᾧ ἐπετέτακτο ταῦτα πράττειν·
ἔλεγον δὲ ὅτι εἰκότα δοκοῖεν λέγειν βασιλεῖ, καὶ ἥκοιεν ἡγεμόνας
ἔχοντες οἳ αὐτούς, ἐὰν σπονδαὶ γένωνται, ἄξουσιν ἔνθεν ἕξουσι
7 τὰ ἐπιτήδεια. ὁ δὲ ἠρώτα εἰ αὐτοῖς τοῖς ἀνδράσι σπένδοιτο
τοῖς ἰοῦσι καὶ ἀπιοῦσιν, ἢ καὶ τοῖς ἄλλοις ἔσοιντο σπονδαί. οἱ
δέ, Ἅπασιν, ἔφασαν, μέχρι ἂν βασιλεῖ τὰ παρ' ὑμῶν διαγγελθῇ.
8 ἐπεὶ δὲ ταῦτα εἶπον, μεταστησάμενος αὐτοὺς ὁ Κλέαρχος ἐβου-
λεύετο· καὶ ἐδόκει τὰς σπονδὰς ποιεῖσθαι ταχὺ καὶ καθ' ἡσυ-
9 χίαν ἐλθεῖν τε ἐπὶ τὰ ἐπιτήδεια καὶ λαβεῖν. ὁ δὲ Κλέαρχος
εἶπε· Δοκεῖ μὲν κἀμοὶ ταῦτα· οὐ μέντοι ταχύ γε ἀπαγγελῶ,
ἀλλὰ διατρίψω ἔστ' ἂν ὀκνήσωσιν οἱ ἄγγελοι μὴ ἀποδόξῃ ἡμῖν
τὰς σπονδὰς ποιήσασθαι· οἶμαί γε μέντοι, ἔφη, καὶ τοῖς ἡμετέροις στρατιώταις τὸν αὐτὸν φόβον παρέσεσθαι. ἐπεὶ δὲ ἐδόκει
καιρὸς εἶναι, ἀπήγγελλεν ὅτι σπένδοιτο, καὶ εὐθὺς ἡγεῖσθαι
ἐκέλευε πρὸς τἀπιτήδεια.

---

18 μὴ πορίσας: conditional, as is shown by the neg. Clearchus keeps up his bold bearing, and with success; the envoys are ready enough to procure supplies.

19 ᾧ, *whereby*.

20 ᾧ ἐπετέτακτο, *to whom commands had been given*. See I, 6, 59, and the note.

21 δοκοῖεν ... ἥκοιεν ... ἕξουσι: direct, δοκεῖτε ... ἥκομεν ... ἕξετε. Note the rapid shift of subj, always easy in Greek.

23 αὐτοῖς: practically = μόνοις. *Cf.* I, 8, 44, and the note.

σπένδοιτο: *cf.* εἴησαν, c. 1. 101, and the note.

24 τοῖς ἰοῦσι: *i.e.* those going with the Persian envoys to obtain supplies. As a matter of fact, Clearchus leads the whole army (§ 6).

25 μέχρι ἂν ... διαγγελθῇ: in this chapter we have already had ἄχρι in the sense of *until* (l. 7, where see the note) and ἔστε occurs below, l. 30, μέχρι is not rare in prose, but is not nearly as common as ἕως. After negs. πρίν is regular; see I, 2, 12.

26 μεταστησάμενος αὐτούς, *having them retire*. *Cf.*, with change of voice, μεταστάντες, below (l. 86).

27 ἐδόκει: *i.e.* to the deliberating generals. Clearchus' own opinion follows.

30 ὀκνήσωσιν: ingressive.

ἀποδόξῃ: for the neg. force of the prep., *cf.* ἀποψηφίσωνται, I, 4, 98.

31 οἶμαι ... παρέσεσθαι: these words show that Clearchus, despite his bold front, was not unaware of the gravity of their situation.

33 σπένδοιτο: he said σπένδομαι.

Καὶ οἱ μὲν ἡγοῦντο, Κλέαρχος μέντοι ἐπορεύετο τὰς μὲν 10
σπονδὰς ποιησάμενος, τὸ δὲ στράτευμα ἔχων ἐν τάξει, καὶ αὐτὸς
ὠπισθοφυλάκει. καὶ ἐνετύγχανον τάφροις καὶ αὐλῶσιν ὕδατος
πλήρεσιν ὡς μὴ δύνασθαι διαβαίνειν ἄνευ γεφυρῶν· ἀλλ᾽
ἐποιοῦντο διαβάσεις ἐκ τῶν φοινίκων οἳ ἦσαν ἐκπεπτωκότες,
τοὺς δὲ καὶ ἐξέκοπτον. καὶ ἐνταῦθα ἦν Κλέαρχον καταμαθεῖν 11
ὡς ἐπεστάτει, ἐν μὲν τῇ ἀριστερᾷ χειρὶ τὸ δόρυ ἔχων, ἐν δὲ τῇ
δεξιᾷ βακτηρίαν· καὶ εἴ τις αὐτῷ δοκοίη τῶν πρὸς τοῦτο τεταγμένων βλακεύειν, ἐκλεγόμενος τὸν ἐπιτήδειον ἔπαισεν ἄν, καὶ
ἅμα αὐτὸς προσελάμβανεν εἰς τὸν πηλὸν ἐμβαίνων· ὥστε πᾶσιν
αἰσχύνην εἶναι μὴ οὐ συσπουδάζειν. καὶ ἐτάχθησαν πρὸς αὐτὸ 12
οἱ εἰς τριάκοντα ἔτη γεγονότες· ἐπεὶ δὲ Κλέαρχον ἑώρων σπου-

---

35 μέντοι balances μέν, but is more strongly adversative than δέ.

36 ποιησάμενος: concessive.

ἐν τάξει: ready, in case of an attack. He feared treachery.

37 ἐνετύγχανον: frequentative.

αὐλῶσιν: doubtless smaller ditches intersecting the τάφροι. The whole represents an elaborate system of irrigation, whereby the natural fertility of Babylonia was greatly enhanced. Cf. II, 4, § 13. From § 13 we infer that these had been flooded, in order to impede the progress of the Greeks.

38 ὡς μὴ δύνασθαι: cf. I, 5, 64, and the note.

39 διαβάσεις: cf. I, 5, 73, and the note. Many editors omit the word, as γεφύρας readily supplies itself as the obj.

οἳ ἦσαν ἐκπεπτωκότες, *which lay there, fallen*. The phrase is not a mere plpf. (= ἐξεπεπτώκεσαν); each element has its own force. Cf. the note on εἶναι ... φυλάττων, I, 2, 122 f.

40 Κλέαρχον: prolepsis; see on τῶν βαρβάρων, I, 1, 20.

41 τῇ ἀριστερᾷ χειρί: he is not cumbered with a shield, but carries his spear (τὸ δόρυ) in the left hand, leaving the right free to wield a stick (no art.). For the stick, see I, 5, 70, and for Clearchus as a disciplinarian, II, 6, § 8.

42 εἰ ... δοκοίη ... ἔπαισεν ἄν: the ἄν is frequentative (see I, 9, 68) and the condition is general.

44 εἰς τὸν πηλόν: cf. I, 5, 49.

45 μὴ οὐ συσπουδάζειν, *not to be equally zealous*. Such an infin. has regularly the neg. μή; it takes μὴ οὐ only when the leading vb. is neg.; see G. 1616; H. 1034; B. 434. Here the phrase ὥστε αἰσχύνην εἶναι implies negation. See G. M. T. 817, and cf. Anab. III, 1, § 13, where, however, the question, τί ἐμποδών;, is equivalent to οὐδὲν ἐμποδών. Such cases are exceptional.

πρὸς αὐτό: αὐτός is often used of the matter in hand.

13 δάζοντα, προσελάμβανον καὶ οἱ πρεσβύτεροι. πολὺ δὲ μᾶλλον
ὁ Κλέαρχος ἔσπευδεν, ὑποπτεύων μὴ αἰεὶ οὕτω πλήρεις εἶναι
τὰς τάφρους ὕδατος· οὐ γὰρ ἦν ὥρα οἵα τὸ πεδίον ἄρδειν· ἀλλ'
ἵνα ἤδη πολλὰ προφαίνοιτο τοῖς Ἕλλησι δεινὰ εἰς τὴν πορείαν, 50
τούτου ἕνεκα βασιλέα ὑπώπτευεν ἐπὶ τὸ πεδίον τὸ ὕδωρ
ἀφεικέναι.

14 Πορευόμενοι δὲ ἀφίκοντο εἰς κώμας ὅθεν ἀπέδειξαν οἱ ἡγεμόνες λαμβάνειν τὰ ἐπιτήδεια. ἐνῆν δὲ σῖτος πολὺς καὶ οἶνος
15 φοινίκων καὶ ὄξος ἑψητὸν ἀπὸ τῶν αὐτῶν. αὐταὶ δὲ αἱ βάλανοι 55
τῶν φοινίκων οἵας μὲν ἐν τοῖς Ἕλλησιν ἔστιν ἰδεῖν τοῖς οἰκέταις
ἀπέκειντο, αἱ δὲ τοῖς δεσπόταις ἀποκείμεναι ἦσαν ἀπόλεκτοι,
θαυμάσιαι τοῦ κάλλους καὶ μεγέθους, ἡ δὲ ὄψις ἠλέκτρου οὐδὲν

---

46 οἱ . . . γεγονότες, *those thirty years old and under.*

47 οἱ πρεσβύτεροι: observe how the chiastic order emphasizes this word.

48 ὑποπτεύων μὴ . . . εἶναι: for the neg., see the note on μηδὲν ἂν . . . παθεῖν, I, 9, 29. Some explain by assuming that the direct form was interrog., μὴ ἀεί εἰσιν;

49 οἵα . . . ἄρδειν: *cf.* the use of the infin. with ὥστε, οἷός τε, and οἷόν τε (G. 1526; H. 1000; B. 641; G. M. T. 759). The time for irrigation was summer; it was now October.

50 ἤδη, *at the start.*

51 τούτου ἕνεκα: resuming the final clause.

54 οἶνος φοινίκων, *palm-wine. Cf.* I, 5, 66, and the note.

55 ὄξος . . . αὐτῶν: presumably, after the juice had been pressed out for wine, the residue was boiled and an inferior drink made.

βάλανοι: *cf.* I, 5, 66, and the note. For the partitive appos., see the note on ἅρματα, I, 8, 78. Here the partitive gen. at the head of the sentence would have given an awkward succession of genitives.

56 ἐν τοῖς Ἕλλησιν: even when the name of a country is in common use (as ἡ Ἑλλάς) the Greek often prefers to use the name of the people in the pl. *Cf.* ἐς Πισίδας, I, 1, 62, and the note.

ἔστιν: *cf.* I, 5, 17, and the note.

57 ἀπέκειντο, *were laid aside.* κεῖμαι often supplies a pass. to τίθημι.

58 κάλλους . . . μεγέθους: causal gens. (G. 1126; H. 744; B. 366).

ἠλέκτρου: *i. e.* ἠλέκτρου ὄψεως. This shorter form of comparison is often preferred. *Cf.* III, 1, § 23, σώματα ἱκανώτερα τούτων, and see G. 1178; H. 773b. For ἤλεκτρον, see the vocab. Amber would seem a natural rendering here, but these dates were also called χρυσοβάλανοι; so that Xen. very probably had in mind the metal.

διέφερεν· τὰς δέ τινας ξηραίνοντες τραγήματα ἀπετίθεσαν. καὶ
ἦν καὶ παρὰ πότον ἡδὺ μέν, κεφαλαλγὲς δέ. ἐνταῦθα καὶ τὸν
ἐγκέφαλον τοῦ φοίνικος πρῶτον ἔφαγον οἱ στρατιῶται, καὶ οἱ
πολλοὶ ἐθαύμαζον τό τε εἶδος καὶ τὴν ἰδιότητα τῆς ἡδονῆς. ἦν
δὲ σφόδρα καὶ τοῦτο κεφαλαλγές. ὁ δὲ φοῖνιξ ὅθεν ἐξαιρεθείη
ὁ ἐγκέφαλος ὅλος ηὐαίνετο.

Ἐνταῦθα ἔμειναν ἡμέρας τρεῖς· καὶ παρὰ μεγάλου βασιλέως
ἧκε Τισσαφέρνης καὶ ὁ τῆς βασιλέως γυναικὸς ἀδελφὸς καὶ
ἄλλοι Πέρσαι τρεῖς· δοῦλοι δὲ πολλοὶ εἵποντο. ἐπεὶ δὲ
ἀπήντησαν αὐτοῖς οἱ τῶν Ἑλλήνων στρατηγοί, ἔλεγε πρῶτος
Τισσαφέρνης δι' ἑρμηνέως τοιάδε. Ἐγώ, ὦ ἄνδρες Ἕλληνες,
γείτων οἰκῶ τῇ Ἑλλάδι, καὶ ἐπεὶ ὑμᾶς εἶδον εἰς πολλὰ καὶ
ἀμήχανα πεπτωκότας, εὕρημα ἐποιησάμην εἴ πως δυναίμην
παρὰ βασιλέως αἰτήσασθαι δοῦναι ἐμοὶ ἀποσῶσαι ὑμᾶς εἰς τὴν
Ἑλλάδα. οἶμαι γὰρ ἂν οὐκ ἀχαρίστως μοι ἔχειν οὔτε πρὸς ὑμῶν
οὔτε πρὸς τῆς πάσης Ἑλλάδος. ταῦτα δὲ γνοὺς ᾐτούμην βασιλέα,

---

59 τὰς δέ τινας: τις is often added to ὁ μέν and ὁ δέ; cf. III, 3, § 19.
τραγήματα, for *sweetmeats*.
60 ἦν: the subj. is probably vague. It is unnecessary to evolve τὸ τράγημα from τραγήματα. ἡδύ is the substant. neut. in the pred. (*a pleasant thing*); see G. 925; H. 617; B. 423; and cf. II, 5, § 9.
61 ἐγκέφαλον τοῦ φοίνικος, *the cabbage of the palm.* Cf. Pliny, H. N., XIII, 4. Dulcis medulla earum (*i. e.* palmarum) in cacumine quod cerebrum apellant.
πρῶτον, *for the first time;* contrast πρῶτος, below, l. 68.
62 ἰδιότητα ... ἡδονῆς, *its peculiar flavor.*
63 ἐξαιρεθείη: frequentative.
66 γυναικός: her name was Statira.
70 γείτων: remember that ἡ Ἑλλάς includes the Greek cities of Asia Minor.

πολλὰ καὶ ἀμήχανα: after forms of πολύς, καί may often be left untranslated; cf. II, 4, § 21.
71 εὕρημα ἐποιησάμην, *I counted it a piece of good fortune.*
εἰ δυναίμην: oblique for ἐὰν δύνωμαι.
72 αἰτήσασθαι, *to win my request.* Note the tense and the voice.
δοῦναι, *that he should grant,* obj. of αἰτήσασθαι (cf. δοθῆναι, I, 1, 36), and itself governing ἀποσῶσαι.
73 οἶμαι ... ἔχειν, *for I think it would not be a thankless task.* For the position of ἄν, cf. I, 3, 29, and the note. Here ἄν precedes οὐκ because of the latter's close connection with ἀχαρίστως.
πρός: cf. I, 6, 29.
74 τῆς πάσης Ἑλλάδος: for πᾶς in the attrib. position, see G. 979; H. 672; B. 455.
ᾐτούμην: note the tense, and contrast αἰτήσασθαι, above.

λέγων αὐτῷ ὅτι δικαίως ἄν μοι χαρίζοιτο, ὅτι αὐτῷ Κῦρόν τε ἐπι- 75
στρατεύοντα πρῶτος ἤγγειλα καὶ βοήθειαν ἔχων ἅμα τῇ ἀγγελίᾳ
ἀφικόμην, καὶ μόνος τῶν κατὰ τοὺς Ἕλληνας τεταγμένων οὐκ
ἔφυγον, ἀλλὰ διήλασα καὶ συνέμειξα βασιλεῖ ἐν τῷ ὑμετέρῳ
στρατοπέδῳ ἔνθα βασιλεὺς ἀφίκετο, ἐπεὶ Κῦρον ἀπέκτεινε καὶ
τοὺς ξὺν Κύρῳ βαρβάρους ἐδίωξε σὺν τοῖσδε τοῖς παροῦσι νῦν 80
μετ' ἐμοῦ, οἵπερ αὐτῷ εἰσι πιστότατοι. καὶ περὶ μὲν τούτων
ὑπέσχετό μοι βουλεύσεσθαι· ἐρέσθαι δέ με ὑμᾶς ἐκέλευεν ἐλθόντα
τίνος ἕνεκεν ἐστρατεύσατε ἐπ' αὐτόν. καὶ συμβουλεύω ὑμῖν
μετρίως ἀποκρίνασθαι, ἵνα μοι εὐπρακτότερον ᾖ ἐάν τι δύνωμαι
ἀγαθὸν ὑμῖν παρ' αὐτοῦ διαπράξασθαι.
                                                                   85

Πρὸς ταῦτα μεταστάντες οἱ Ἕλληνες ἐβουλεύοντο· καὶ
ἀπεκρίναντο, Κλέαρχος δ' ἔλεγεν· Ἡμεῖς οὔτε συνήλθομεν ὡς
βασιλεῖ πολεμήσοντες οὔτε ἐπορευόμεθα ἐπὶ βασιλέα, ἀλλὰ
πολλὰς προφάσεις Κῦρος ηὕρισκεν, ὡς καὶ σὺ εὖ οἶσθα, ἵνα
ὑμᾶς τε ἀπαρασκεύους λάβοι καὶ ἡμᾶς ἐνθάδε ἀγάγοι. ἐπεὶ 90
μέντοι ἤδη αὐτὸν ἑωρῶμεν ἐν δεινῷ ὄντα, ᾐσχύνθημεν καὶ θεοὺς
καὶ ἀνθρώπους προδοῦναι αὐτόν, ἐν τῷ πρόσθεν χρόνῳ παρέ-

---

75 ἐπιστρατεύοντα: quoted after ἤγγειλα. ἀγγέλλω permits all three constructions, although the partic. is infrequent. For the fact, see I, 2, 23 ff.

78 διήλασα: cf. I, 10, 30

79 ἔνθα: cf. I, 10, 2 ff., and the note.

ἀπέκτεινε: Plut. *Artox.* 14 states that the king claimed to have slain Cyrus with his own hand.

80 τοῖσδε: said with a gesture.

81 αὐτῷ: i. e. the king.

82 ἐρέσθαι: in chiastic order with βουλεύσεσθαι.

84 μετρίως: i.e. less haughtily than before.

εὐπρακτότερον: verbal adjs. may of course be compared. For partics., see the note on ἠμελημένως, I, 7, 92.

85 διαπράξασθαι, win. Cf. διαπε-πραγμένος, below, l. 104. The prep. emphasizes the idea of accomplishment.

86 μεταστάντες: cf. μεταστησάμενος, above, l. 26, and note the difference in voice.

87 ἔλεγεν, was spokesman.

91 ἐν δεινῷ: at Thapsacus? See I, 5, 74 ff.

ᾐσχύνθημεν . . . αὐτόν, *we were ashamed both before gods and men to betray him*. αἰσχύνομαι takes an acc. of the thing of which one is ashamed, and also of the person before whom one feels shame. Here we have both, προδοῦναι supplying the place of one acc. See G. 1049, 1519; H. 712, 948; B. 329, 1; 638.

92 παρέχοντες: impf. partic., as is clear from the context.

χοντες ἡμᾶς αὐτοὺς εὖ ποιεῖν. ἐπεὶ δὲ Κῦρος τέθνηκεν, οὔτε
βασιλεῖ ἀντιποιούμεθα τῆς ἀρχῆς οὔτ' ἔστιν ὅτου ἕνεκα βουλοίμεθα ἂν τὴν βασιλέως χώραν κακῶς ποιεῖν, οὐδ' αὐτὸν ἀποκτεῖναι ἂν ἐθέλοιμεν, πορευοίμεθα δ' ἂν οἴκαδε, εἴ τις ἡμᾶς μὴ
λυποίη· ἀδικοῦντα μέντοι πειρασόμεθα σὺν τοῖς θεοῖς ἀμύ-
νασθαι· ἐὰν μέντοι τις ἡμᾶς καὶ εὖ ποιῶν ὑπάρχῃ, καὶ τούτου
εἴς γε δύναμιν οὐχ ἡττησόμεθα εὖ ποιοῦντες.   ὁ μὲν οὕτως εἶπεν·
ἀκούσας δὲ ὁ Τισσαφέρνης Ταῦτα, ἔφη, ἐγὼ ἀπαγγελῶ βασιλεῖ
καὶ ὑμῖν πάλιν τὰ παρ' ἐκείνου· μέχρι δ' ἂν ἐγὼ ἥκω αἱ σπονδαὶ
μενόντων· ἀγορὰν δὲ ἡμεῖς παρέξομεν.

Καὶ εἰς μὲν τὴν ὑστεραίαν οὐχ ἧκεν· ὥσθ' οἱ Ἕλληνες
ἐφρόντιζον· τῇ δὲ τρίτῃ ἥκων ἔλεγεν ὅτι διαπεπραγμένος ἥκοι
παρὰ βασιλέως δοθῆναι αὐτῷ σῴζειν τοὺς Ἕλληνας, καίπερ
πολλῶν ἀντιλεγόντων ὡς οὐκ ἄξιον εἴη βασιλεῖ ἀφεῖναι τοὺς ἐφ'
ἑαυτὸν στρατευσαμένους. τέλος δὲ εἶπε· Καὶ νῦν ἔξεστιν ὑμῖν
πιστὰ λαβεῖν παρ' ἡμῶν ἦ μὴν φιλίαν παρέξειν ὑμῖν τὴν χώραν

---

93 **εὖ ποιεῖν**: infin. of purpose.

94 **ἀντιποιούμεθα**: *cf.* c. 1. 59.

οὔτ' ἔστιν ὅτου ἕνεκα, *nor is there any reason why.*

βουλοίμεθα ... ἐθέλοιμεν: the difference in meaning is not to be pushed. Xen. often chooses to vary his language; see the Introd., §39. Note the potential opt., following an indic., and the chiastic order.

96 **τις**: often used when a definite person is meant (*cf.* II, 4, §22 end). Here the threatening tone is manifest.

97 **ἀδικοῦντα μέντοι**, *him that wrongs us, however*. The emphatic order should be retained.

σὺν τοῖς θεοῖς, *with heaven's help*. The phrase is a common one, but does not therefore lack force. For the tone, *cf.* II, 5, § 7; III, 2, § 10.

98 **καὶ εὖ ποιῶν**: **καί** marks this phrase as parallel with ἀδικοῦντα.

ὑπάρχῃ, *begin*, with supplementary partic.

καὶ τούτου: retain the order, *In his case also*. The gen. is due to the vb. of inferiority.

99 **εὖ ποιοῦντες**, *in doing good*, circumstantial partic. with ἡττησόμεθα.

ὁ μέν: is the asyndeton felt?

101 **ἥκω**: what mood?

102 **μενόντων**: not a partic.

103 **εἰς**: *cf*. I, 7, 4.

104 **διαπεπραγμένος**: *cf.* διαπράξασθαι, above, l. 85. Its obj. is the infin. clause.

105 **δοθῆναι ... Ἕλληνας**. *Cf.* δοῦναι, above, l. 72.

106 **ἄξιον**, *becoming*.

108 **πιστὰ λαβεῖν**: the phrase implies a promise, and so legitimately governs the infin.

καὶ ἀδόλως ἀπάξειν εἰς τὴν Ἑλλάδα ἀγορὰν παρέχοντας· ὅπου
δ' ἂν μὴ ᾖ πρίασθαι, λαμβάνειν ὑμᾶς ἐκ τῆς χώρας ἐάσομεν τὰ
ἐπιτήδεια. ὑμᾶς δὲ αὖ ἡμῖν δεήσει ὀμόσαι ἦ μὴν πορεύσεσθαι
ὡς διὰ φιλίας ἀσινῶς σῖτα καὶ ποτὰ λαμβάνοντας ὁπόταν μὴ
ἀγορὰν παρέχωμεν· ἢν δὲ παρέχωμεν ἀγοράν, ὠνουμένους ἕξειν
τὰ ἐπιτήδεια. ταῦτα ἔδοξε, καὶ ὤμοσαν καὶ δεξιὰς ἔδοσαν αὖ
Τισσαφέρνης καὶ ὁ τῆς βασιλέως γυναικὸς ἀδελφὸς τοῖς τῶν
Ἑλλήνων στρατηγοῖς καὶ λοχαγοῖς καὶ ἔλαβον παρὰ τῶν
Ἑλλήνων. μετὰ δὲ ταῦτα Τισσαφέρνης εἶπεν· Νῦν μὲν δὴ
ἄπειμι ὡς βασιλέα· ἐπειδὰν δὲ διαπράξωμαι ἃ δέομαι, ἥξω
συσκευασάμενος ὡς ἀπάξων ὑμᾶς εἰς τὴν Ἑλλάδα καὶ αὐτὸς
ἀπιὼν ἐπὶ τὴν ἐμαυτοῦ ἀρχήν.

IV. Μετὰ ταῦτα περιέμενον Τισσαφέρνην οἵ τε Ἕλληνες
καὶ ὁ Ἀριαῖος ἐγγὺς ἀλλήλων ἐστρατοπεδευμένοι ἡμέρας πλείους ἢ εἴκοσιν. ἐν δὲ ταύταις ἀφικνοῦνται πρὸς Ἀριαῖον καὶ οἱ
ἀδελφοὶ καὶ οἱ ἄλλοι ἀναγκαῖοι καὶ πρὸς τοὺς σὺν ἐκείνῳ Περσῶν

ἦ μήν, *verily*, a stereotyped formula in oaths.
109 ἀδόλως: *cf.* c. 2. 40.
ἀγοράν: see the Introd., §28.
ὅπου ... ἐάσομεν: a change to direct speech. ᾖ, of course, means, *be possible*.
112 διὰ φιλίας: sc. τῆς χώρας; *cf.* I, 3, 70 f., and the note.
ἀσινῶς: a poeticism. *Cf.* ἀσινέστατα, III, 3, §3, and ἐσίνοντο, III, 4, §16.
113 ὠνουμένους, *by purchase*.
ἕξειν: governed by the vb. of swearing.
114 ταῦτα ἔδοξε: the asyndeton is normal; *cf.* I, 3, 102.
δεξιάς: *cf.* I, 6, 35. The Persians make a great show of friendliness at the start, doubtless in order to induce the Greeks to leave their present position, in which they might well have maintained themselves indefinitely; *cf.* II, 4, §22, and III, 2, §24 ff.
118 ὡς βασιλέα: *cf.* I, 2, 24, and the note.
ἃ δέομαι: the antecedent is definite; contrast ὅ, τι ἂν δέῃ, I, 3, 24.

Chapter IV

1 περιέμενον: it was idle waiting; *cf.* c. 1. 27, and the note. During this time, according to Diodorus, XIV, 26, Tiss. went to Babylon, whither the king had gone to celebrate his victory. There he received high honors at the hands of the king, being invested with the command of the provinces that had belonged to Cyrus, and receiving, besides, the daughter of the king as his wife. On his part he promised to destroy the Greeks.
4 ἀναγκαῖοι: *cf. necessarii;* properly *blood-relations*.

5 τινες, ⟨οἳ⟩ παρεθάρρυνόν τε καὶ δεξιὰς ἐνίοις παρὰ βασιλέως
ἔφερον μὴ μνησικακήσειν βασιλέα αὐτοῖς τῆς σὺν Κύρῳ ἐπιστρατείας μηδὲ ἄλλου μηδενὸς τῶν παροιχομένων. τούτων δὲ 2
γιγνομένων ἔνδηλοι ἦσαν οἱ περὶ Ἀριαῖον ἧττον προσέχοντες
τοῖς Ἕλλησι τὸν νοῦν· ὥστε καὶ διὰ τοῦτο τοῖς μὲν πολλοῖς
10 τῶν Ἑλλήνων οὐκ ἤρεσκον, ἀλλὰ προσιόντες τῷ Κλεάρχῳ ἔλεγον καὶ τοῖς ἄλλοις στρατηγοῖς· Τί μένομεν; ἢ οὐκ ἐπιστάμεθα 3
ὅτι βασιλεὺς ἡμᾶς ἀπολέσαι ἂν περὶ παντὸς ποιήσαιτο, ἵνα καὶ
τοῖς ἄλλοις Ἕλλησι φόβος εἴη ἐπὶ βασιλέα μέγαν στρατεύειν;
καὶ νῦν μὲν ἡμᾶς ὑπάγεται μένειν διὰ τὸ διεσπάρθαι αὐτῷ τὸ
15 στράτευμα· ἐπὴν δὲ πάλιν ἁλισθῇ αὐτῷ ἡ στρατιά, οὐκ ἔστιν
ὅπως οὐκ ἐπιθήσεται ἡμῖν. ἴσως δέ που ἢ ἀποσκάπτει τι ἢ 4

---

5 παρεθάρρυνον: cf. the simple vb. I, 7, 12. For the force of the prep., cf. παρακελεύομαι (I, 7, 44), and παρακαλῶ (III, 1, §44).

6 μὴ μνησικακήσειν: the infin. after δεξιὰς ἔφερον, as after πιστὰ λαβεῖν, above, c. 3. 104. The neg. must, of course, be μή.

ἐπιστρατείας: causal gen.

8 ἔνδηλοι ἦσαν... προσέχοντες: cf. δῆλος ἦν ἀνιώμενος, I, 2, 70. Heretofore they had felt that their own safety depended on their alliance with the Greeks.

9 τοῖς ... πολλοῖς: see the note on τὸ ... πολύ, I, 4, 86.

10 ἤρεσκον ... ἔλεγον: again a rapid shift of subj.

11 ἢ οὐκ: ἤ properly introduces the second member of a double question, but here the first member is not expressed.

12 περὶ παντὸς ποιήσαιτο: cf. περὶ πλείστου ποιοῖτο, I, 9, 25, and the note

ἵνα ... εἴη: a potential opt. counts as a primary tense, but the vb. of a clause depending upon it may be assimilated to the opt. This regularly happens in the case of condit. rel. clauses (cf. ἅ δοίη, I, 3, 87, and the note); it is less frequent in the case of final clauses (cf. μὴ καταδύσῃ, I, 3, 87, and the note). Cf., however, III, 1, §18, and add to the references previously given H. 881b; B. 590, note 1.

13 στρατεύειν: after φόβος εἴη, as after φοβοῦμαι.

14 ὑπάγεται: cf. c. 1. 88, and the note.

διὰ τὸ διεσπάρθαι: cf. τῷ διεσπάσθαι, I, 5, 57.

15 ἐπὴν ... ἁλισθῇ: render by the fut. perf., as regularly after ἐπειδάν. ἁλίζω is one of Xen.'s poetic words; it recurs VI, 3, §3, and, in composition with σύν, VII, 3, §48.

οὐκ ἔστιν ὅπως οὐκ, *it is not possible that he will not;* i. e. he certainly will. Cf. οὐκ ἦν ὅπου οὐ, IV, 5, §31.

16 τι: the inner obj., *is digging some trench to cut us off* (ἀπο-). Cf. I, 10, 64.

ἀποτειχίζει, ὡς ἄπορος ᾖ ἡ ὁδός. οὐ γάρ ποτε ἑκών γε βουλήσεται ἡμᾶς ἐλθόντας εἰς τὴν Ἑλλάδα ἀπαγγεῖλαι ὡς ἡμεῖς τοσοίδε ὄντες ἐνικῶμεν τὸν βασιλέα ἐπὶ ταῖς θύραις αὐτοῦ καὶ
5 καταγελάσαντες ἀπήλθομεν. Κλέαρχος δὲ ἀπεκρίνατο τοῖς
ταῦτα λέγουσιν· Ἐγὼ ἐνθυμοῦμαι μὲν καὶ ταῦτα πάντα· ἐννοῶ δ' ὅτι εἰ νῦν ἄπιμεν, δόξομεν ἐπὶ πολέμῳ ἀπιέναι καὶ παρὰ τὰς σπονδὰς ποιεῖν. ἔπειτα πρῶτον μὲν ἀγορὰν οὐδεὶς παρέξει ἡμῖν οὐδὲ ὅθεν ἐπισιτιούμεθα· αὖθις δὲ ὁ ἡγησόμενος οὐδεὶς ἔσται· καὶ ἅμα ἂν ταῦτα ποιούντων ἡμῶν εὐθὺς Ἀριαῖος ἀποσταίη·
ὥστε φίλος ἡμῖν οὐδεὶς λελείψεται, ἀλλὰ καὶ οἱ πρόσθεν ὄντες
6 πολέμιοι ἡμῖν ἔσονται. ποταμὸς δ' εἰ μέν τις καὶ ἄλλος ἄρα ἡμῖν ἐστι διαβατέος οὐκ οἶδα· τὸν δ' οὖν Εὐφράτην οἴδαμεν ὅτι ἀδύνατον διαβῆναι κωλυόντων πολεμίων. οὐ μὲν δὴ ἂν μάχεσθαί γε δέῃ ἱππεῖς εἰσιν ἡμῖν ξύμμαχοι, τῶν δὲ πολεμίων ἱππεῖς

---

17 ἑκών γε: strongly emphatic, *not at least, if he can help it*.

19 τοσοίδε ὄντες, *although so few*. Cf. τοσοῦτον, c. 1. 46.

ἐπὶ ταῖς θύραις, *at his very doors*, a pardonable hyperbole. For θύραις, see I, 2, 69.

20 καταγελάσαντες: cf. I, 9, 42.

21 καὶ ταῦτα πάντα, *all this and more* (Pretor).

ἐννοῶ: varied from ἐνθυμοῦμαι.

22 εἰ . . . ἄπιμεν: observe the warning tone.

ἐπὶ πολέμῳ, *on a basis of war*, rather than indicating purpose, as ordinarily rendered. Cf. ἐπὶ γάμῳ, below, §8.

ἀπιέναι: a pres., not a fut.

24 ὅθεν, freely, *an opportunity to*. How lit.? For the fut. in such clauses, cf. ἀπάξει, I, 3, 71, and the note.

ὁ ἡγησόμενος: cf. ὁ τολμήσων, c. 3. 17, and ἡ ποιοῦσα, III, 1, §42.

26 λελείψεται: the tense denotes the state, *we shall find that*, etc.

With the whole passage cf. III, 1, §2.

ὄντες: sc. φίλοι.

27 ποταμός: note the emphatic position, which may be kept if the word be rendered as if it were an acc. of specification. Cf. Εὐφράτην, below, l. 28, and βασιλέα, l. 33. The word, although subj. of the interrogative clause, is put before the interrogative word; cf. 1, 9, 56, and the note.

τις καὶ ἄλλος: cf. I, 3, 80.

28 διαβατέος: the personal construction (G. 1595; H. 989; B. 664).

δ' οὖν: cf. I, 2, 73, and the note.

Εὐφράτην: felt as the obj. of οἴδαμεν, rather than of διαβῆναι (prolepsis; cf. βασιλέα, below, l. 33). For the Ionic form, οἴδαμεν, see G. 821, 1; H. 491a; B. 259a.

29 πολεμίων: no art., because wholly general.

οὐ μὲν δή: cf. I, 9, 41.

30 ἱππεῖς: on the absence of cavalry in the Greek army, see the

εἰσὶν οἱ πλεῖστοι καὶ πλείστου ἄξιοι· ὥστε νικῶντες μὲν τίνα ἂν ἀποκτείναιμεν; ἡττωμένων δὲ οὐδένα οἷόν τε σωθῆναι. ἐγὼ 7 μὲν οὖν βασιλέα, ᾧ οὕτω πολλά ἐστι τὰ σύμμαχα, εἴπερ προθυμεῖται ἡμᾶς ἀπολέσαι, οὐκ οἶδα ὅ,τι δεῖ αὐτὸν ὀμόσαι καὶ 35 δεξιὰν δοῦναι καὶ θεοὺς ἐπιορκῆσαι καὶ τὰ ἑαυτοῦ πιστὰ ἄπιστα ποιῆσαι Ἕλλησί τε καὶ βαρβάροις. τοιαῦτα πολλὰ ἔλεγεν.

Ἐν δὲ τούτῳ ἧκε Τισσαφέρνης ἔχων τὴν ἑαυτοῦ δύναμιν ὡς 8 εἰς οἶκον ἀπιὼν καὶ Ὀρόντας τὴν ἑαυτοῦ δύναμιν· ἦγε δὲ καὶ τὴν θυγατέρα τὴν βασιλέως ἐπὶ γάμῳ. ἐντεῦθεν δὲ ἤδη Τισσα- 9

note on I, 5, 82. The Greeks were conscious of their disadvantage in this respect (although in III, 2, § 18 Xen. tries to belittle it), and seek in a measure to make it good (III, 3, § 19). With the latter part of this section cf. III, 1, § 2 end.

τῶν δὲ ... ἄξιοι, *while of the enemy the most numerous and the most serviceable troops are cavalry*. The statement is, of course, exaggerated; but the cavalry under Tissaphernes were the only ones who had made any show of fighting against the Greeks at Cunaxa. Some editors omit οἱ (before πλεῖστοι), others render, *the most, with reference to other nations*, which is impossible.

31 τίνα ἂν ἀποκτείναιμεν: the rhetorical question is quite in keeping with the tone of the whole passage, which is due, of course, to Xen., not to Clearchus.

32 ἡττωμένων: sc. ἡμῶν.

οὐδένα ... σωθῆναι, *it is impossible that a single one should escape*. For οἷόν τε (sc. ἐστίν), cf. c. 2. 16, and the note. Observe the change from opt. to indic., marking the gravity of the situation.

33 βασιλέα: for the position, see the note on ποταμός, above, l. 27. Here the word is so far removed from the vb. that it is resumed by αὐτόν.

σύμμαχα: neut., because referring not to troops alone, but to situation, supplies, *etc.* Trans., *whom so many things conspire to help*.

εἴπερ, *assuming that*.

34 ὅ,τι δεῖ αὐτόν, *what need he has*, an indir. ques. For the acc. ὅ,τι, cf. I, 6, 36.

35 καὶ ... καὶ ... καὶ: the polysyndeton heightens the cumulative effect.

θεούς: for the case, see G. 1049; H. 712; B. 329, 1.

πιστὰ ἄπιστα: such instances of paronomasia are not rare in rhetorical passages.

36 τοιαῦτα: asyndeton with a demonstrative.

37 ὡς ... ἀπιών: this was Tissaphernes' avowed intention.

38 εἰς οἶκον, *homeward*. The art. is omitted in many old prepositional phrases.

Ὀρόντας: he was satrap of Armenia; cf. III, 5, § 17.

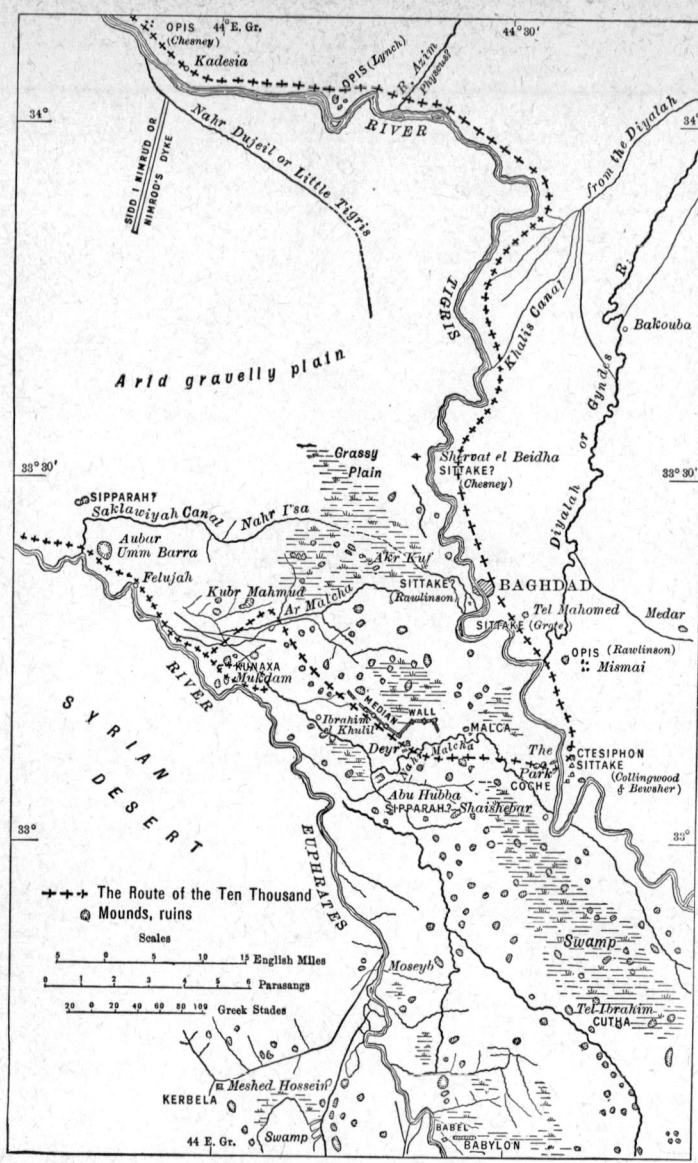

MAP OF A PART OF BABYLONIA
From actual survey
SHOWING MEDIAN WALL AND ROUTE OF THE TEN THOUSAND
(From Dakyns' Xenophon)

φέρνους ἡγουμένου καὶ ἀγορὰν παρέχοντος ἐπορεύοντο· ἐπορεύετο 40
δὲ καὶ Ἀριαῖος τὸ Κύρου βαρβαρικὸν ἔχων στράτευμα ἅμα
Τισσαφέρνει καὶ Ὀρόντᾳ καὶ ξυνεστρατοπεδεύετο σὺν ἐκείνοις.
οἱ δὲ Ἕλληνες ὑφορῶντες τούτους αὐτοὶ ἐφ' ἑαυτῶν ἐχώρουν
ἡγεμόνας ἔχοντες. ἐστρατοπεδεύοντο δὲ ἑκάστοτε ἀπέχοντες
ἀλλήλων παρασάγγην καὶ μεῖον· ἐφυλάττοντο δὲ ἀμφότεροι 45
ὥσπερ πολεμίους ἀλλήλους, καὶ εὐθὺς τοῦτο ὑποψίαν παρεῖχεν.
ἐνίοτε δὲ καὶ ξυλιζόμενοι ἐκ τοῦ αὐτοῦ καὶ χόρτον καὶ ἄλλα
τοιαῦτα ξυλλέγοντες πληγὰς ἐνέτεινον ἀλλήλοις· ὥστε καὶ τοῦτο
ἔχθραν παρεῖχε.

Διελθόντες δὲ τρεῖς σταθμοὺς ἀφίκοντο πρὸς τὸ Μηδίας κα- 50
λούμενον τεῖχος, καὶ παρῆλθον εἴσω αὐτοῦ. ἦν δὲ ᾠκοδομημένον

---

39 **τὴν θυγατέρα**: her name, according to Plutarch, was *Rhodogune*.

ἐπὶ γάμῳ, *as his wife.* Cf. ἐπὶ πολέμῳ, above, l. 22, and the note.

40 **ἐπορεύοντο**, *began their march.* Note that the next clause begins with the same vb. (epanastrophe).

41 **Ἀριαῖος**: for his changed bearing, *cf.* §1 of this chapter.

43 **ὑφορῶντες**, *regarding with suspicion.*

αὐτοὶ ἐφ' ἑαυτῶν, *alone by themselves.* The intensive is often combined with the reflexive; *cf.* I, 8, 100. For αὐτός virtually = μόνος, *cf.* I, 8, 44.

45 **ἀλλήλων**: *i. e.* the Greeks on the one hand and Tiss. and Ariaeus, with their armies, on the other.

μεῖον: so the MSS. πλέον has been conjectured, and seems to us more natural.

ἐφυλάττοντο... ἀλλήλους, *were ever on their guard against one another.*

48 **πληγὰς ἐνέτεινον**: of the simple vb. πλήττω only πέπληγμαι, ἐπλή-γην, and πληγήσομαι were in common use. Other tenses were supplied by other vbs. (παίω, πατάσσω, τύπτω), or by periphrases, as I, 5, 70, and in the present case.

50 **τὸ ... τεῖχος**: see I, 7, 71, and the note.

51 **παρῆλθον εἴσω αὐτοῦ**, either, passed within it, *i. e.* from the outside, or, passed along its inner side. The former rendering is the more natural one, but it is hard to see how the Greeks, after passing the trench described on I, 7, 68 ff., could have got outside the wall again. Possibly Xen. was in error in saying that the trench actually reached the wall, or, if the wall was largely broken down, they may have passed it without his mentioning the fact. At the same time, it seems impossible that the Greeks should by this time have got so far to the West. The accompanying map, reproduced, by permission from Dakyns' *Xenophon*, sug-

πλίνθοις ὀπταῖς ἐν ἀσφάλτῳ κειμέναις, εὖρος εἴκοσι ποδῶν, ὕψος δὲ ἑκατόν· μῆκος δ' ἐλέγετο εἶναι εἴκοσι παρασαγγῶν. ἀπεῖχε δὲ Βαβυλῶνος οὐ πολύ. ἐντεῦθεν δ' ἐπορεύθησαν σταθμοὺς δύο παρασάγγας ὀκτώ· καὶ διέβησαν διώρυχας δύο, τὴν μὲν ἐπὶ γεφύρας, τὴν δὲ ἐζευγμένην πλοίοις ἑπτά· αὗται δ' ἦσαν ἀπὸ τοῦ Τίγρητος ποταμοῦ· κατετέτμηντο δὲ ἐξ αὐτῶν καὶ τάφροι ἐπὶ τὴν χώραν, αἱ μὲν πρῶται μεγάλαι, ἔπειτα δὲ ἐλάττους· τέλος δὲ καὶ μικροὶ ὀχετοί, ὥσπερ ἐν τῇ Ἑλλάδι ἐπὶ τὰς μελίνας.

Καὶ ἀφικνοῦνται ἐπὶ τὸν Τίγρητα ποταμόν· πρὸς ᾧ πόλις ἦν μεγάλη καὶ πολυάνθρωπος ᾗ ὄνομα Σιττάκη, ἀπέχουσα τοῦ ποταμοῦ σταδίους πεντεκαίδεκα. οἱ μὲν οὖν Ἕλληνες παρ' αὐτὴν ἐσκήνησαν ἐγγὺς παραδείσου μεγάλου καὶ καλοῦ καὶ δασέος παντοίων δένδρων, οἱ δὲ βάρβαροι διαβεβηκότες τὸν Τίγρητα· οὐ μέντοι καταφανεῖς ἦσαν. μετὰ δὲ τὸ δεῖπνον ἔτυχον ἐν περιπάτῳ ὄντες πρὸ τῶν ὅπλων Πρόξενος καὶ Ξενοφῶν· καὶ προσ-

---

gests a widely different location for the wall (usually identified with the ruins known as *Sidd-i-Nimrud*) and also suits the second rendering. It shows, further, how uncertain the identifications are.

ἦν ... ᾠκοδομημένον = ᾠκοδόμητο, although the forms are not always identical in meaning. In the resolved form the partic. often has an independent (adjectival) meaning. Cf. εἶναι φυλάττων, I, 2, 122 f., and the note.

52 πλίνθοις ὀπταῖς: *i.e.* not merely sun-dried, as often.

εἴκοσι ποδῶν: see I, 2, 30 f., and the note. εὖρος, ὕψος, and μῆκος are all acc.

54 οὐ πολύ: this agrees with the identification given on the map, rather than with the common view.

55 διώρυχας ... τὴν μὲν ... τὴν δέ: partitive apposition.

56 ἐζευγμένην: cf. I, 2, 31, and the note.

58 ἐλάττους: for the form, see the note on I, 3, 35.

61 μεγάλη καὶ πολυάνθρωπος: yet the very site of Sittace is now uncertain; see the map. It was apparently on the west side of the river, as the Greeks encamp near it and do not cross until next morning (§ 24).

ὄνομα: nom., as I, 5, 21; more frequently it is acc.

63 δασέος: here construed with the gen., as an adj. of fulness; ordinarily it takes the dat. (means), as IV, 7, § 6, δασὺ πίτυσι. Others regard δασέος as abs., and the gen. as dependent on παράδεισος, which seems most unlikely.

64 οἱ δὲ βάρβαροι: sc. ἐσκήνησαν.

66 τῶν ὅπλων, *the camp*. Cf. III 1, § 3.

Πρόξενος καὶ Ξενοφῶν: for their

ἐλθὼν ἄνθρωπός τις ἠρώτησε τοὺς προφύλακας ποῦ ἂν ἴδοι
Πρόξενον ἢ Κλέαρχον. Μένωνα δὲ οὐκ ἐζήτει, καὶ ταῦτα παρ'
16 Ἀριαίου ὢν τοῦ Μένωνος ξένου. ἐπεὶ δὲ Πρόξενος εἶπεν ὅτι
αὐτός εἰμι ὃν ζητεῖς, εἶπεν ὁ ἄνθρωπος τάδε. Ἔπεμψέ με 70
Ἀριαῖος καὶ Ἀρτάοζος, πιστοὶ ὄντες Κύρῳ καὶ ὑμῖν εὖνοι, καὶ
κελεύουσι φυλάττεσθαι μὴ ὑμῖν ἐπιθῶνται τῆς νυκτὸς οἱ βάρ-
17 βαροι· ἔστι δὲ στράτευμα πολὺ ἐν τῷ πλησίον παραδείσῳ. καὶ
παρὰ τὴν γέφυραν τοῦ Τίγρητος ποταμοῦ πέμψαι κελεύουσι
φυλακήν, ὡς διανοεῖται αὐτὴν λῦσαι Τισσαφέρνης τῆς νυκτός, 75
ἐὰν δύνηται, ὡς μὴ διαβῆτε ἀλλ' ἐν μέσῳ ἀποληφθῆτε τοῦ
18 ποταμοῦ καὶ τῆς διώρυχος. ἀκούσαντες ταῦτα ἄγουσιν αὐτὸν
παρὰ τὸν Κλέαρχον καὶ φράζουσιν ἃ λέγει. ὁ δὲ Κλέαρχος
ἀκούσας ἐταράχθη σφόδρα καὶ ἐφοβεῖτο.
19 Νεανίσκος δέ τις τῶν παρόντων ἐννοήσας εἶπεν ὡς οὐκ ἀκό- 80
λουθα εἴη τό τε ἐπιθήσεσθαι καὶ τὸ λύσειν τὴν γέφυραν. δῆλον
γὰρ ὅτι ἐπιτιθεμένους ἢ νικᾶν δεήσει ἢ ἡττᾶσθαι. ἐὰν μὲν οὖν
νικῶσι, τί δεῖ λύειν αὐτοὺς τὴν γέφυραν; οὐδὲ γὰρ ἂν πολλαὶ

---

friendship see the Introd., § 38, and III, 1 § 4

67 ποῦ ἂν ἴδοι: potential opt. in an indir. ques. *Cf.* I, 6, 47 f.

68 καὶ ταῦτα ... ὤν: *and that too, although he came.* The circumstance was in itself suspicious; the warning would naturally have been given to Menon.

69 ὅτι: introducing dir. disc.; *cf.* I, 6, 36.

70 Ἔπεμψε: for the agreement, *cf.* I, 2, 20, and the note.

71 πιστοὶ ... εὖνοι: the chiastic order is often the natural one, when emphasis is desired (here on ὑμῖν).

73 ἔστι: accented at the head of the sentence (G. 144, 5; H. 480, 2; B. 262, 1).

74 παρὰ τὴν γέφυραν: an exception to the rule that παρά, expressing the limit, is, in prose, used only of persons.

75 ὡς διανοεῖται: causal; but, below, ὡς μὴ διαβῆτε, final.

78 φράζουσιν: φράζω regularly means, *tell in detail*; it is more than λέγω.

79 ἐταράχθη ... ἐφοβεῖτο: note the tenses.

80 νεανίσκος: it has been assumed that this was Xen. himself, or possibly the Theopompus of c. 1. 62.

ἐννοήσας, *on reflection.*

81 τό τε ... καὶ τὸ λύσειν, *the intention of attacking and of destroying.* For the fut. infin., thus used, see G. 1277; H. 855a; B. 548, 549; G. M. T. 113.

δῆλον γάρ: a shift to direct speech.

82 ἐπιτιθεμένους: *sc.* αὐτούς. It is equivalent to ἐὰν ἐπιτιθῶνται.

83 οὐδὲ ... σωθῶμεν, *for not even*

γέφυραι ὦσιν ἔχοιμεν ἂν ὅποι φυγόντες ἡμεῖς σωθῶμεν. ἐὰν δὲ 20
ἡμεῖς νικῶμεν, λελυμένης τῆς γεφύρας οὐχ ἕξουσιν ἐκεῖνοι ὅποι
φύγωσιν· οὐδὲ μὴν βοηθῆσαι πολλῶν ὄντων πέραν οὐδεὶς αὐτοῖς
δυνήσεται λελυμένης τῆς γεφύρας.

Ἀκούσας δὲ ὁ Κλέαρχος ταῦτα ἤρετο τὸν ἄγγελον πόση τις 21
εἴη χώρα ἡ ἐν μέσῳ τοῦ Τίγρητος καὶ τῆς διώρυχος. ὁ δὲ εἶπεν
ὅτι πολλὴ καὶ κῶμαι ἔνεισι καὶ πόλεις πολλαὶ καὶ μεγάλαι.
τότε δὴ καὶ ἐγνώσθη ὅτι οἱ βάρβαροι τὸν ἄνθρωπον ὑποπέμψαιεν, 22
ὀκνοῦντες μὴ οἱ Ἕλληνες διελόντες τὴν γέφυραν μείναιεν ἐν τῇ
νήσῳ ἐρύματα ἔχοντες ἔνθεν μὲν τὸν Τίγρητα, ἔνθεν δὲ τὴν διώ-
ρυχα· τὰ δ' ἐπιτήδεια ἔχοιεν ἐκ τῆς ἐν μέσῳ χώρας πολλῆς καὶ
ἀγαθῆς οὔσης καὶ τῶν ἐργασομένων ἐνόντων· εἶτα δὲ καὶ ἀπο-
στροφὴ γένοιτο εἴ τις βούλοιτο βασιλέα κακῶς ποιεῖν.

Μετὰ δὲ ταῦτα ἀνεπαύοντο· ἐπὶ μέντοι τὴν γέφυραν ὅμως 23
φυλακὴν ἔπεμψαν· καὶ οὔτε ἐπέθετο οὐδεὶς οὐδαμόθεν οὔτε πρὸς
τὴν γέφυραν οὐδεὶς ἦλθε τῶν πολεμίων, ὡς οἱ φυλάττοντες ἀπήγγελλον. ἐπειδὴ δὲ ἕως ἐγένετο, διέβαινον τὴν γέφυραν ἐζευγμένην 24
πλοίοις τριάκοντα καὶ ἑπτὰ ὡς οἷόν τε μάλιστα πεφυλαγμένως·
ἐξήγγελλον γάρ τινες τῶν παρὰ Τισσαφέρνους Ἑλλήνων ὡς δια-

---

though there be many bridges should we be able to save ourselves by flight. Note the blending of two forms (G. 1421, 2; H. 901a; B. 612, 1; G. M. T. 505). σωθῶμεν is the deliberative subjv. in an indir. ques.; so φύγωσιν, below. We might have had the opt. by assimilation; see the note on εἴη, above, l. 12.

85 λελυμένης τῆς γεφύρας: for the position and repetition of this phrase, cf. ἤγγελλον, I, 7, 62, and the note.

86 οὐδὲ μήν, no, nor.
βοηθῆσαι: emphatic position.
ὄντων: concessive.

90 πολλαὶ καὶ μεγάλαι: cf. c. 3. 70, and the note.

91 ὑποπέμψαιεν: cf. ὑπήγετο, c. 2. 88, and ὑπόπεμπτος, III, 3, § 4.

93 ἐρύματα, as defences. The word is uncommon in Attic prose.

95 οὔσης, which was.
καὶ . . ἐνόντων, and in which there were men to till it.
εἶτα δὲ καί, and furthermore (fearing) that.
ἀποστροφή, place of refuge, "base," a poetic word.

96 τις: cf. I, 4, 80, and the note.

97 μέντοι . . . ὅμως, however . . . none the less.

98 οὔτε . . . ἦλθε: for the accumulation of negatives, cf. I, 2, 152, and I, 8, 81 f.

101 πεφυλαγμένως: from the partic. See the note on ἠμελημένως, I, 7, 92.

βαινόντων μέλλοιεν ἐπιθήσεσθαι. ἀλλὰ ταῦτα μὲν ψευδῆ ἦν·
διαβαινόντων μέντοι ὁ Γλοῦς αὐτοῖς ἐπεφάνη μετ' ἄλλων σκοπῶν
εἰ διαβαίνοιεν τὸν ποταμόν· ἐπειδὴ δὲ εἶδεν, ᾤχετο ἀπελαύνων. 105
25 Ἀπὸ δὲ τοῦ Τίγρητος ἐπορεύθησαν σταθμοὺς τέτταρας παρασάγγας εἴκοσιν ἐπὶ τὸν Φύσκον ποταμόν, τὸ εὖρος πλέθρου·
ἐπῆν δὲ γέφυρα. καὶ ἐνταῦθα ᾠκεῖτο πόλις μεγάλη ὄνομα
Ὦπις· πρὸς ἣν ἀπήντησε τοῖς Ἕλλησιν ὁ Κύρου καὶ Ἀρτα-
ξέρξου νόθος ἀδελφὸς ἀπὸ Σούσων καὶ Ἐκβατάνων στρατιὰν 110
πολλὴν ἄγων ὡς βοηθήσων βασιλεῖ· καὶ ἐπιστήσας τὸ ἑαυτοῦ
26 στράτευμα παρερχομένους τοὺς Ἕλληνας ἐθεώρει. ὁ δὲ Κλέαρχος ἡγεῖτο μὲν εἰς δύο, ἐπορεύετο δὲ ἄλλοτε καὶ ἄλλοτε ἐφ-
ιστάμενος· ὅσον δ' οὖν χρόνον τὸ ἡγούμενον τοῦ στρατεύματος
ἐπιστήσειε, τοσοῦτον ἦν ἀνάγκη χρόνον δι' ὅλου τοῦ στρατεύ- 115
ματος γίγνεσθαι τὴν ἐπίστασιν· ὥστε τὸ στράτευμα καὶ αὐτοῖς
τοῖς Ἕλλησι δόξαι πάμπολυ εἶναι, καὶ τὸν Πέρσην ἐκπεπλῆχθαι
27 θεωροῦντα. ἐντεῦθεν δ' ἐπορεύθησαν διὰ τῆς Μηδίας σταθμοὺς
ἐρήμους ἓξ παρασάγγας τριάκοντα εἰς τὰς Παρυσάτιδος κώμας
τῆς Κύρου καὶ βασιλέως μητρός. ταύτας Τισσαφέρνης Κύρῳ 120
ἐπεγγελῶν διαρπάσαι τοῖς Ἕλλησιν ἐπέτρεψε πλὴν ἀνδραπό-

---

102 Ἑλλήνων: mercenaries, doubtless. Many Greeks took service
under Persian princes; cf. the
instances of Gaulites (I, 7, 26),
Ctesias (I, 8, 107), and Phalinus
(c. 1. 38).

διαβαινόντων: gen. abs., with subj.
omitted. We should have expected the dat. after ἐπιθήσεσθαι;
see, however, προϊόντων, I, 2, 99,
and a more striking instance,
below, l. 104, where αὐτοῖς follows.

104 σκοπῶν, to see whether. The
pres. partic. (conative) may express purpose.

105 ᾤχετο ἀπελαύνων, he rode off.
The circumstantial partic. with
οἴχομαι often expresses the means
of motion.

109 πρὸς ἥν: motion is implied.

111 βοηθήσων: he was too late, as
Abrocomas was (I, 7, 61).

112 παρερχομένους: ἔρχομαι is rarely
found, in prose, save in the pres.
indic.

113 εἰς δύο, two abreast. With the
whole passage, cf. the note on
ἐπὶ τεττάρων, I, 2, 87.

114 τὸ ἡγούμενον: cf. I, 2, 3, and
the note.

115 ἐπιστήσειε: frequentative.

116 καὶ αὐτοῖς τοῖς Ἕλλησι: the καί
is intensive, not parallel with καὶ
τὸν Πέρσην.

117 ἐκπεπλῆχθαι: see c. 3. 83, and
the note.

121 ἐπεγγελῶν: different from καταγελάσαντες, l. 20, in that ἐπι-, in

δων. ἐνῆν δὲ σῖτος πολὺς καὶ πρόβατα καὶ ἄλλα χρήματα. ἐντεῦθεν δ᾽ ἐπορεύθησαν σταθμοὺς ἐρήμους τέτταρας παρασάγγας εἴκοσι τὸν Τίγρητα ποταμὸν ἐν ἀριστερᾷ ἔχοντες. ἐν δὲ τῷ πρώτῳ σταθμῷ πέραν τοῦ ποταμοῦ πόλις ᾠκεῖτο μεγάλη καὶ εὐδαίμων ὄνομα Καιναί, ἐξ ἧς οἱ βάρβαροι διῆγον ἐπὶ σχεδίαις διφθερίναις ἄρτους, τυρούς, οἶνον.

V. Μετὰ ταῦτα ἀφικνοῦνται ἐπὶ τὸν Ζαπάταν ποταμόν, τὸ εὖρος τεττάρων πλέθρων. καὶ ἐνταῦθα ἔμειναν ἡμέρας τρεῖς· ἐν δὲ ταύταις ὑποψίαι μὲν ἦσαν, φανερὰ δὲ οὐδεμία ἐφαίνετο ἐπιβουλή. ἔδοξεν οὖν τῷ Κλεάρχῳ ξυγγενέσθαι τῷ Τισσαφέρνει καὶ εἴ πως δύναιτο παῦσαι τὰς ὑποψίας πρὶν ἐξ αὐτῶν πόλεμον γενέσθαι· καὶ ἔπεμψέν τινα ἐροῦντα ὅτι ξυγγενέσθαι αὐτῷ χρῄζει. ὁ δὲ ἑτοίμως ἐκέλευεν ἥκειν.

Ἐπειδὴ δὲ ξυνῆλθον, λέγει ὁ Κλέαρχος τάδε. Ἐγώ, ὦ Τισσαφέρνη, οἶδα μὲν ἡμῖν ὅρκους γεγενημένους καὶ δεξιὰς δεδομένας μὴ ἀδικήσειν ἀλλήλους· φυλαττόμενον δὲ σέ τε ὁρῶ ὡς πολεμίους ἡμᾶς καὶ ἡμεῖς ὁρῶντες ταῦτα ἀντιφυλαττόμεθα. ἐπεὶ δὲ σκοπῶν οὐ δύναμαι οὔτε σὲ αἰσθέσθαι πειρώμενον ἡμᾶς κακῶς

such compounds, denotes exultation over a fallen foe.
διαρπάσαι: cf. I, 2, 110.
πλὴν ἀνδραπόδων: i. e. they might not enslave the inhabitants.
124 ἐν δὲ . . . Καιναί: a very similar sentence occurs I, 5, 60 f.
127 σχεδίαις διφθερίναις: described in the passage just cited.
ἄρτους . . . οἶνον: asyndeton in an enumeration.

CHAPTER V

1 Ζαπάταν: at last a geographical point, the identification of which seems certain. See the map.
2 ἡμέρας τρεῖς: doubtless supplies were needed, so that the delay was not in itself a ground for suspicion.
3 ὑποψίαι: the pl. of abstract nouns is often concrete and has a cumulative force.
4 ξυγγενέσθαι, to have an interview with.
5 παῦσαι: also governed by ἔδοξεν.
πρίν, before. See I, 1, 58, and the note.
8 τάδε: on this speech see the Introd., § 40.
9 Τισσαφέρνη: a rare voc. form, as if of the first declension. Accusatives in -ην, on the other hand, are not uncommon; see e. g. Τισσαφέρνην, I, 1, 37.
γεγενημένους: cf. ἐγένετο, c. 2. 42.
10 ἀδικήσειν: cf. παρέξειν, c. 3. 108.
φυλαττόμενον . . . ἀντιφυλαττόμεθα: for the order, cf. the note on ἤγγελλον, I, 7, 62. For the fact, cf. c. 4. 43 ff.
12 οὔτε σὲ . . . ἐγώ τε: οὔθ᾽ ἡμᾶς

ποιεῖν ἐγώ τε σαφῶς οἶδα ὅτι ἡμεῖς γε οὐδὲ ἐπινοοῦμεν τοιοῦτον
οὐδέν, ἔδοξέ μοι εἰς λόγους σοι ἐλθεῖν, ὅπως εἰ δυναίμεθα ἐξέ-
5 λοιμεν ἀλλήλων τὴν ἀπιστίαν. καὶ γὰρ οἶδα ἀνθρώπους ἤδη
τοὺς μὲν ἐκ διαβολῆς τοὺς δὲ καὶ ἐξ ὑποψίας οἳ φοβηθέντες
ἀλλήλους φθάσαι βουλόμενοι πρὶν παθεῖν ἐποίησαν ἀνήκεστα
κακὰ τοὺς οὔτε μέλλοντας οὔτ' αὖ βουλομένους τοιοῦτον οὐδέν.
6 τὰς οὖν τοιαύτας ἀγνωμοσύνας νομίζων συνουσίαις μάλιστ' ἂν
παύεσθαι ἥκω καὶ διδάσκειν σε βούλομαι ὡς σὺ ἡμῖν οὐκ ὀρθῶς
7 ἀπιστεῖς. πρῶτον μὲν γὰρ καὶ μέγιστον οἱ θεῶν ἡμᾶς ὅρκοι
κωλύουσι πολεμίους εἶναι ἀλλήλοις· ὅστις δὲ τούτων σύνοιδεν
αὑτῷ παρημεληκώς, τοῦτον ἐγὼ οὔποτ' ἂν εὐδαιμονίσαιμι. τὸν

---

would follow logically, but there is a shift in the thought and the latter part of the sentence is the stronger for not being exactly parallel with the former. As to the attitude and intentions of the Greeks Clearchus had certain knowledge. For the correlation of οὔτε with τε, cf. μήτε . . . τε, c. 2. 38.

14 **εἰς λόγους σοι ἐλθεῖν:** cf. εἰς χεῖρας ἐλθεῖν, I, 2, 152 f., and the note.

15 **ἤδη,** *ere now.*

16 **οἳ . . . ἐποίησαν:** rel. clause, instead of the partic. in indir. disc., due, perhaps, to the desire to avoid a cumulation of partics. Cf. III, 2, § 23. Some, however, read ὅτι, for οἵ.

17 **φθάσαι . . . πρίν:** a frequent combination. Cf. πρόσθεν and πρότερον, leading up to πρίν (e. g. I, 1, 58).

18 **τοὺς . . . μέλλοντας . . . βουλομένους:** obj. of ἐποίησαν κακά: cf. I, 9, 36. μέλλοντας may perhaps be rendered *intending*, though it need not be regarded as trans.

19 **συνουσίαις:** emphatic position.

21 **πρῶτον μέν:** balanced by τῶν δ' ἀνθρωπίνων, below, l. 29.

οἱ θεῶν . . . ὅρκοι, *our oaths (sworn in the name) of the gods.* The gen. is objective (G. 1085, 3; H. 729c; B. 350).

22 **ὅστις . . . σύνοιδεν:** ὅστις, being itself indefinite, does not need the generalized construction; cf. ὅστις ἀφικνεῖτο, I, 1, 18, and the note.

τούτων: after παρημεληκώς; cf. ἡμῶν αὐτῶν, I, 3, 52. Note the emphasis the word receives from its position. For the partic., cf. ἐψευσμένος, I, 3, 49, and the note.

23 **τοῦτον:** resumptive, as often.

τὸν . . . πόλεμον, *a war against the gods.* The gen. is better taken as objective than as subjective (*the war the gods wage*), although the idea of the inevitability of retribution has led many to prefer the second rendering. The perjurer is, however, in a sense, the aggressor. The acc. is to be construed with οἶδα (prolepsis), rather than with ἀποφύγοι.

γὰρ θεῶν πόλεμον οὐκ οἶδα οὔτ' ἀπὸ ποίου ἂν τάχους φεύγων
25 τις ἀποφύγοι οὔτ' εἰς ποῖον ἂν σκότος ἀποδραίη οὔθ' ὅπως ἂν
εἰς ἐχυρὸν χωρίον ἀποσταίη. πάντῃ γὰρ πάντα τοῖς θεοῖς
ὕποχα καὶ πάντων ἴσον οἱ θεοὶ κρατοῦσι. περὶ μὲν δὴ τῶν
θεῶν τε καὶ τῶν ὅρκων οὕτω γιγνώσκω, παρ' οὓς ἡμεῖς τὴν
φιλίαν συνθέμενοι κατεθέμεθα· τῶν δ' ἀνθρωπίνων σὲ ἐγὼ ἐν
30 τῷ παρόντι νομίζω μέγιστον εἶναι ἡμῖν ἀγαθόν. σὺν μὲν γὰρ
σοὶ πᾶσα μὲν ὁδὸς εὔπορος, πᾶς δὲ ποταμὸς διαβατός, τῶν τε
ἐπιτηδείων οὐκ ἀπορία· ἄνευ δὲ σοῦ πᾶσα μὲν διὰ σκότους ἡ
ὁδός· οὐδὲν γὰρ αὐτῆς ἐπιστάμεθα· πᾶς δὲ ποταμὸς δύσπορος,
πᾶς δὲ ὄχλος φοβερός, φοβερώτατον δ' ἐρημία· μεστὴ γὰρ
35 πολλῆς ἀπορίας ἐστίν. εἰ δὲ δὴ καὶ μανέντες σε κατακτείναιμεν,
ἄλλο τι ἂν ἢ τὸν εὐεργέτην κατακτείναντες πρὸς βασιλέα τὸν
μέγιστον ἔφεδρον πολεμήσομεν; ὅσων δὲ δὴ καὶ οἵων ἂν ἐλπί-

---

24 ἀπό, with. Cf. I, 1, 47.
φεύγων ... ἀποφύγοι: observe the change of tense, and cf. the note on αἰτήσασθαι, c. 3. 70.
25 ἀποδραίη: see the note on ἀποδεδράκασιν, I, 4, 48. For the thought, cf. Ps. cxxxix : 7–12.
26 ἐχυρόν: the form ὀχυρόν is found I, 2, 133 and 139, and IV, 7, §17.
πάντῃ ... πάντα ... πάντων: a noteworthy instance of paronomasia.
27 πάντων: masc., not neut. It is the obj. of κρατοῦσι.
τῶν θεῶν ... ὅρκων: not a case of hendiadyoin (=τῶν θεῶν ὅρκων); each noun has independent value.
28 παρ' οὓς ... κατεθέμεθα, into whose keeping we consigned the friendship which we contracted.
29 τῶν δ' ἀνθρωπίνων, of things human; neut., not masc.
30 μέγιστον ... ἀγαθόν: ἀγαθόν has become a substantive and itself takes an adj.

σὺν ... σοί: cf. σὺν ὑμῖν, I, 3, 29.
31 πᾶσα ... ὁδός, every road; contrast πᾶσα ... ἡ ὁδός, below, l. 32, all our way.
πᾶσα μὲν ... πᾶς δέ: for the anaphora, cf. I, 3, 16.
τῶν τε: τε, rather than δέ, is often used to add a third clause.
34 φοβερώτατον: for the neut., cf. ἡδύ, c. 3. 60. Note the chiasm.
μεστὴ ... ἐστίν: a bold oxymoron. The literal rendering is perhaps the best.
35 εἰ δὲ δὴ καί: both δή and καί are intensive.
μανέντες, in a fit of madness; note the tense.
36 ἄλλο τι ... ἤ = nonne (G. 1604; H. 1015b; B. 573, note).
κατακτείναντες: purposely chosen, in a rhetorical passage, instead of the usual ἀποκτείναντες. Xen. has also κατακαίνω (e. g. I, 6, 8).
37 ἔφεδρον, a reserve combatant, i. e. one who draws a bye and fights the winner of the bout.

δων ἐμαυτὸν στερήσαιμι, εἰ σέ τι κακὸν ἐπιχειρήσαιμι ποιεῖν,
11 ταῦτα λέξω. ἐγὼ γὰρ Κῦρον ἐπεθύμησά μοι φίλον γενέσθαι,
νομίζων τῶν τότε ἱκανώτατον εἶναι εὖ ποιεῖν ὃν βούλοιτο· σὲ δὲ
νῦν ὁρῶ τήν τε Κύρου δύναμιν καὶ χώραν ἔχοντα καὶ τὴν σαυτοῦ
σῴζοντα, τὴν δὲ βασιλέως δύναμιν, ᾗ Κῦρος πολεμίᾳ ἐχρῆτο,
12 σοὶ ταύτην ξύμμαχον οὖσαν. τούτων δὲ τοιούτων ὄντων τίς
οὕτω μαίνεται ὅστις οὐ βούλεται σοὶ φίλος εἶναι; ἀλλὰ μὴν
ἐρῶ γὰρ καὶ ταῦτα ἐξ ὧν ἔχω ἐλπίδας καὶ σὲ βουλήσεσθαι
13 φίλον ἡμῖν εἶναι. οἶδα μὲν γὰρ ὑμῖν Μυσοὺς λυπηροὺς ὄντας,
οὓς νομίζω ἂν σὺν τῇ παρούσῃ δυνάμει ταπεινοὺς ὑμῖν παρασχεῖν·
οἶδα δὲ καὶ Πισίδας· ἀκούω δὲ καὶ ἄλλα ἔθνη πολλὰ
τοιαῦτα εἶναι, ἃ οἶμαι ἂν παῦσαι ἐνοχλοῦντα ἀεὶ τῇ ὑμετέρᾳ
εὐδαιμονίᾳ. Αἰγυπτίους δέ, οἷς μάλιστα ὑμᾶς γιγνώσκω τεθυμωμένους,
οὐχ ὁρῶ ποίᾳ δυνάμει συμμάχῳ χρησάμενοι μᾶλλον
14 ἂν κολάσαισθε τῆς νῦν σὺν ἐμοὶ οὔσης. ἀλλὰ μὴν ἔν γε τοῖς

Metaphors from the games are very common.

πολεμήσομεν: more effective than the opt. with ἄν.

39 ταῦτα: resuming the indir. ques., ὅσων . . . στερήσαιμι.

40 τῶν τότε: cf. c. 2. 89.

σέ: note the position. Cf. σοί, below, l. 43.

42 ἐχρῆτο: cf. II, 6, §13.

43 ξύμμαχον: fem.; see G. 304; H. 225; B. 119.

τούτων . . . ὄντων, quae cum ita sint.

44 ὅστις οὐ βούλεται: a rel. clause expressing result (G. 1445; H. 910; B. 597), where we might have looked for ὥστε μὴ βούλεσθαι. ὅστις often serves to characterize. Cf. the use of οἵτινες, below, l. 83, and ὅστις, II, 6, §6.

ἀλλὰ μὴν . . . γάρ: with ἀλλὰ γάρ there is regularly an ellipsis, as with καὶ γάρ; here, but (we can also be of service to you) for. The irregularity consists in the fact that what, to us, is the principal vb. is contained in the γάρ-clause. Cf. III, 2, §11. For ἀλλὰ μήν, cf. I, 9, 62, and below, l. 52.

46 οἶδα μὲν . . . οἶδα δέ: anaphora again.

Μυσούς: cf. III, 2, § 23.

47 νομίζω ἄν: for the position of ἄν, cf. I, 3, 29, and the note.

48 ἀκούω: with the infin. of hearsay.

49 ἐνοχλοῦντα, from disturbing.

50 Αἰγυπτίους, as for the Egyptians. By so rendering we keep the emphatic order. The word is, of course, obj. of κολάσαισθε.

μάλιστα . . . τεθυμωμένους: because of their revolt; see I, 8, 33. The perf. partic. is intensive.

52 τῆς . . . οὔσης = ἢ τῇ . . . οὔσῃ.

ἀλλὰ μήν: resuming the thought of § 11.

πέριξ οἰκοῦσι σὺ εἰ μὲν βούλοιο φίλος ὡς μέγιστος ἂν εἴης, εἰ
δέ τίς σε λυποίη, ὡς δεσπότης ἀναστρέφοιο ἔχων ἡμᾶς ὑπηρέτας, οἵ σοι οὐκ ἂν μισθοῦ ἕνεκα ὑπηρετοῖμεν ἀλλὰ καὶ τῆς
χάριτος ἣν σωθέντες ὑπὸ σοῦ σοὶ ἂν ἔχοιμεν δικαίως. ἐμοὶ μὲν
ταῦτα πάντα ἐνθυμουμένῳ οὕτω δοκεῖ θαυμαστὸν εἶναι τὸ σὲ
ἡμῖν ἀπιστεῖν ὥστε καὶ ἥδιστ᾽ ἂν ἀκούσαιμι τὸ ὄνομα τίς οὕτως
ἐστὶ δεινὸς λέγειν ὥστε σε πεῖσαι λέγων ὡς ἡμεῖς σοι ἐπιβου-
λεύομεν. Κλέαρχος μὲν οὖν τοσαῦτα εἶπε· Τισσαφέρνης δὲ
ὧδε ἀπημείφθη.

'Αλλ' ἥδομαι μέν, ὦ Κλέαρχε, ἀκούων σου φρονίμους λό-
γους· ταῦτα γὰρ γιγνώσκων εἴ τι ἐμοὶ κακὸν βουλεύοις, ἅμα ἂν
μοι δοκεῖς καὶ σαυτῷ κακόνους εἶναι. ὡς δ᾽ ἂν μάθῃς ὅτι οὐδ᾽
ἂν ὑμεῖς δικαίως οὔτε βασιλεῖ οὔτ᾽ ἐμοὶ ἀπιστοίητε, ἀντάκουσον.
εἰ γὰρ ὑμᾶς ἐβουλόμεθα ἀπολέσαι, πότερά σοι δοκοῦμεν ἱππέων

---

54 ἀναστρέφοιο, *would conduct yourself.* For the omission of ἄν, cf. I, 6, 9, and the note. The particle could, however, easily have been omitted by a copyist before ἀναστρέφοιο, and many insert it.

ὑπηρέτας: a strong word; they would do his bidding in all things.

55 οὐκ ἄν: for the position of ἄν, cf. I, 3, 29, and the note.

μισθοῦ: a frank admission of the fact that they are mercenaries.

56 ἥν: ἧς, with attraction, would be more regular.

σοῦ σοί: the collocation adds emphasis, as does also the postponement of δικαίως. Cf. ἡμεῖς σοί, below, l. 59.

57 τὸ ... ἀπιστεῖν, *your distrust of us.* The articular infin. is a favorite construction with Xen.

58 τὸ ὄνομα τίς: a blending of two constructions, ἀκούειν τίς, and ἀκούειν τὸ ὄνομα τούτου ὅστις.

59 λέγων, *by his mere words,* since proofs are lacking.

61 ἀπημείφθη: another of Xen.'s poeticisms. ἀμείβεσθαι, in this sense, has no footing in prose.

62 'Αλλ' ἥδομαι: for ἀλλά, beginning a speech, cf. I, 7, 31.

σου: cf. I, 2, 26, and the note.

63 ἄν ... δοκεῖς ... εἶναι: ἄν goes, of course, with εἶναι; cf. I, 3, 29, and the note. Observe that the personal construction cannot here be retained in Eng. Cf., below, ἀπορεῖν ... ἄν ... σοι δοκοῦμεν.

64 ὡς δ᾽ ἂν μάθῃς: Xen. stands alone among prose writers in using ὡς ἄν, in final clauses (G. 1367; H. 882; B. 590, note 2; G. M. T. 326, 2, and Appendix IV). Cf. his unusual fondness for ὡς, alone.

66 εἰ ἐβουλόμεθα: best taken as contrary to fact; see on εἰ μὴ ἤλθετε, c. 1. 21. Instead of the normal apodosis, Xen. has chosen

πλήθους ἀπορεῖν ἢ πεζῶν ἢ ὁπλίσεως ἐν ᾗ ὑμᾶς μὲν βλάπτειν
ἱκανοὶ εἴημεν ἄν, ἀντιπάσχειν δὲ οὐδεὶς κίνδυνος; ἀλλὰ χωρίων
ἐπιτηδείων ὑμῖν ἐπιτίθεσθαι ἀπορεῖν ἄν σοι δοκοῦμεν; οὐ τοσαῦτα
μὲν πεδία ἃ ὑμεῖς φίλια ὄντα σὺν πολλῷ πόνῳ διαπορεύεσθε,
τοσαῦτα δὲ ὄρη ὁρᾶτε ὑμῖν ὄντα πορευτέα, ἃ ἡμῖν ἔξεστι προκα-
ταλαβοῦσιν ἄπορα ὑμῖν παρέχειν, τοσοῦτοι δ' εἰσὶ ποταμοὶ ἐφ'
ὧν ἔξεστιν ἡμῖν ταμιεύεσθαι ὁπόσοις ἂν ὑμῶν βουλώμεθα μάχεσθαι; εἰσὶ δ' αὐτῶν οὓς οὐδ' ἂν παντάπασι διαβαίητε, εἰ μὴ
ἡμεῖς ὑμᾶς διαπορεύοιμεν. εἰ δ' ἐν πᾶσι τούτοις ἡττῴμεθα,
ἀλλὰ τό γέ τοι πῦρ κρεῖττον τοῦ καρποῦ ἐστιν· ὃν ἡμεῖς δυναί-
μεθ' ἂν κατακαύσαντες λιμὸν ὑμῖν ἀντιτάξαι, ᾧ ὑμεῖς οὐδ' εἰ
πάνυ ἀγαθοὶ εἴητε μάχεσθαι ἂν δύναισθε. πῶς ἂν οὖν ἔχοντες
τοσούτους πόρους πρὸς τὸ ὑμῖν πολεμεῖν, καὶ τούτων μηδένα
ἡμῖν ἐπικίνδυνον, ἔπειτα ἐκ τούτων πάντων τοῦτον ἂν τὸν τρόπον ἐξελοίμεθα ὃς μόνος μὲν πρὸς θεῶν ἀσεβής, μόνος δὲ πρὸς
ἀνθρώπων αἰσχρός; παντάπασι δὲ ἀπόρων ἐστὶ καὶ ἀμηχάνων

---

the more pointed rhetorical question, equally natural in Eng.

67 ἐν ᾗ, *by means of which*.

68 εἴημεν ἄν: ideal, not unreal; but the shift is an easy one. With the following οὐδεὶς κίνδυνος, ἂν εἴη is to be supplied.

ἀλλά: here best rendered by *or*. It anticipates objections.

69 οὐ=*nonne*. The vb. is ὁρᾶτε, below.

τοσαῦτα μὲν ... τοσαῦτα δὲ ... τοσοῦτοι: the anaphora is rhetorical, but vigorous.

70 φίλια ὄντα: concessive.

71 ὄντα πορευτέα: indir. disc., after ὁρᾶτε. For the construction of the verbal, see the note on διαβατέος, c. 4. 28. It goes also with πεδία, above, both phrases being an extension of ὁδὸν πορεύεσθαι.

72 εἰσί, *are there not?* The interrog. force of οὐ is still felt.

74 εἰσὶ δ' ... οὕς: cf. ἦν ... οὕς, I, 5, 35, and the note.

75 διαπορεύοιμεν: no other instance of the occurrence of this compound in the act. is known; διαβιβάζω supplies its place. The act. of the simple vb. occurs in a causative sense, but is rare in prose.

76 ἀλλὰ ... ἐστιν, *yet, at any rate, fire, as you know, is*.

77 κατακαύσαντες: Tiss. tries this, III, 5, §3. *Cf*., also, I, 6, 3.

λιμὸν ... ἀντιτάξαι: a fine metaphor.

78 πῶς ἄν: for the position of ἄν, cf. I, 3, 29. It is repeated below, l. 80.

79 μηδένα: not οὐδένα; ἔχοντες is felt as conditional.

81 πρός: cf. I, 6, 29.

82 ἐστί, *belongs to, is characteristic of*. The gens. are possessive.

καὶ ἐν ἀνάγκῃ ἐχομένων, καὶ τούτων πονηρῶν, οἵτινες ἐθέλουσι
δι' ἐπιορκίας τε πρὸς θεοὺς καὶ ἀπιστίας πρὸς ἀνθρώπους πράττειν τι. οὐχ οὕτως ἡμεῖς, ὦ Κλέαρχε, οὔτε ἀλόγιστοι οὔτε ἠλί-
θιοί ἐσμεν. ἀλλὰ τί δὴ ὑμᾶς ἐξὸν ἀπολέσαι οὐκ ἐπὶ τοῦτο
ἤλθομεν; εὖ ἴσθι ὅτι ὁ ἐμὸς ἔρως τούτου αἴτιος τὸ τοῖς Ἕλλησιν
ἐμὲ πιστὸν γενέσθαι, καὶ ᾧ Κῦρος ἀνέβη ξενικῷ διὰ μισθοδοσίας
πιστεύων τούτῳ ἐμὲ καταβῆναι δι' εὐεργεσίαν ἰσχυρόν. ὅσα δ'
ἐμοὶ χρήσιμοι ὑμεῖς ἐστε τὰ μὲν καὶ σὺ εἶπας, τὸ δὲ μέγιστον
ἐγὼ οἶδα· τὴν μὲν γὰρ ἐπὶ τῇ κεφαλῇ τιάραν βασιλεῖ μόνῳ ἔξεστιν ὀρθὴν ἔχειν, τὴν δ' ἐπὶ τῇ καρδίᾳ ἴσως ἂν ὑμῶν παρόντων
καὶ ἕτερος εὐπετῶς ἔχοι.

Ταῦτα εἰπὼν ἔδοξε τῷ Κλεάρχῳ ἀληθῆ λέγειν· καὶ εἶπεν·
Οὐκοῦν, ἔφη, οἵτινες τοιούτων ἡμῖν εἰς φιλίαν ὑπαρχόντων πει-

---

83 ἀνάγκῃ ἐχομένων, *the thralls of necessity.* Cf. ἀνάγκῃ κατεχομένων (II, 6, §13).

καὶ τούτων πονηρῶν: *cf.* καὶ ταῦτα, I, 4, 81. Observe the climax.

οἵτινες ἐθέλουσι: as if ἄποροί εἰσι had preceded. We should have looked for the simple infin.; *cf.* the use of ὅστις, II, 6, §6.

86 ἐξόν: acc. abs. (G. 1569; H. 973; B. 343). Note that the acc. abs. generally expresses an adversative relation, *although we had every chance to destroy you.*

87 ἔρως, *passion, burning desire,* a strong word.

τούτου: *i. e.* τοῦ ἡμᾶς μὴ ἐπὶ τοῦτο ἐλθεῖν. The gen. depends on αἴτιος.

τὸ ... γενέσθαι ... καταβῆναι: a clause, in the acc., defining the verbal noun ἔρως. Trans., *my burning desire to show myself ... and to go down.*

88 ᾧ ... ξενικῷ: military dat. of accompaniment; see on I, 7, 66. For the incorporation of the noun in the rel. clause, *cf.* I, 2, 5 and for the order (rel. first, resumed by demonstrative), *cf.* I, 9, 107.

μισθοδοσίας: acc., not gen.

89 ὅσα, in what respects. Cf. the acc. with χρῶμαι, *e. g.* I, 3, 93.

90 ἐστε: stronger than ἔσεσθε. Note the emphatic pronouns.

εἶπας: for the form, see c. 1. 102, and the note.

91 τιάραν ... ὀρθήν: a symbol of royalty. It is debatable whether by τὴν δ' ἐπὶ τῇ καρδίᾳ (sc. ὀρθήν) Tiss. means to indicate a desire on his part to set himself up as king with the help of the Greeks, or whether the phrase simply denotes the enjoyment of kingly power. The former view seems preferable.

93 ἕτερος: more modest than ἐγώ Cf. the use of τις to denote a definite individual (*e. g.* I, 4, 80).

94 εἶπεν: the subj. is easily supplied from the preceding dat.

95 οὐκοῦν: *cf.* I, 6, 37, and the note.

ρῶνται διαβάλλοντες ποιῆσαι πολεμίους ἡμᾶς ἄξιοί εἰσι τὰ
ἔσχατα παθεῖν; Καὶ ἐγὼ μέν γε, ἔφη ὁ Τισσαφέρνης, εἰ βού-
λεσθέ μοι οἵ τε στρατηγοὶ καὶ οἱ λοχαγοὶ ἐλθεῖν, ἐν τῷ ἐμφανεῖ
λέξω τοὺς πρὸς ἐμὲ λέγοντας ὡς σὺ ἐμοὶ ἐπιβουλεύεις καὶ τῇ
σὺν ἐμοὶ στρατιᾷ. Ἐγὼ δέ, ἔφη ὁ Κλέαρχος, ἄξω πάντας, καὶ
σοὶ αὖ δηλώσω ὅθεν ἐγὼ περὶ σοῦ ἀκούω. ἐκ τούτων δὴ τῶν
λόγων ὁ Τισσαφέρνης φιλοφρονούμενος τότε μὲν μένειν τε αὐτὸν
ἐκέλευε καὶ σύνδειπνον ἐποιήσατο.

Τῇ δὲ ὑστεραίᾳ ὁ Κλέαρχος ἀπελθὼν ἐπὶ τὸ στρατόπεδον
δῆλός τ' ἦν πάνυ φιλικῶς οἰόμενος διακεῖσθαι τῷ Τισσαφέρνει
καὶ ἃ ἔλεγεν ἐκεῖνος ἀπήγγελλεν, ἔφη τε χρῆναι ἰέναι παρὰ
Τισσαφέρνην οὓς ἐκέλευσεν, καὶ οἳ ἂν ἐλεγχθῶσι διαβάλλοντες
τῶν Ἑλλήνων, ὡς προδότας αὐτοὺς καὶ κακόνους τοῖς Ἕλλησιν

ἔφη: repeating εἶπεν; it is parenthetic.

τοιούτων ... ὑπαρχόντων, *when we have such grounds for*; see the note on ὑπῆρχε, I, 1, 16.

98 μοι: with ἐλθεῖν; less formal than πρός με.

οἱ ... στρατηγοὶ ... λοχαγοί: apposition with ὑμεῖς, contained in the vb.; *cf.* I, 5, 94, and the note. The art. is repeated, since the two groups do not form one class.

ἐν τῷ ἐμφανεῖ: *cf.* ἐν τῷ γε φανερῷ, I, 3, 113. Note the punctuation; this clause goes with λέξω, not with ἐλθεῖν.

101 ὅθεν = *those from whom*.

δή: the particle emphasizes the treachery of Tiss.

102 φιλοφρονούμενος, *with a great show of friendliness*.

103 σύνδειπνον ἐποιήσατο, *made him his guest at dinner* (note the mid.). This was a pledge of friendship among eastern peoples. *Cf.* ὁμοτράπεζοι, I, 8, 103 f., and συντράπεζοι, I, 9, 114 f., and the reference to the present passage in III, 2, §4.

105 δῆλός τ' ἦν ... διακεῖσθαι, *evidently thought that he stood on very friendly terms with*. For the use of δῆλος with a partic., see I, 2, 70, and for διακεῖσθαι, expressing a state, *cf.* II, 6, §12, and III, 1, §3. It serves as a pass. of διατιθέναι (*cf.* διατιθείς, I, 1, 19). Clearchus evidently felt flattered by the attention shown him.

107 οὓς ἐκέλευσεν: the subj. is Tiss., not Clearchus.

οἳ ἂν ... Ἑλλήνων, *whoever of the Greeks should be found guilty of making false charges*.

108 αὐτούς: less frequent in resuming a rel. than τούτους ... τούτους, however, would properly have stood at the head of the sentence, and would thus have deprived ὡς προδότας of its emphatic position.

ὄντας τιμωρηθῆναι. ὑπώπτευε δὲ εἶναι τὸν διαβάλλοντα Μένωνα,
εἰδὼς αὐτὸν καὶ συγγεγενημένον Τισσαφέρνει μετ' Ἀριαίου καὶ
στασιάζοντα αὐτῷ καὶ ἐπιβουλεύοντα, ὅπως τὸ στράτευμα ἅπαν
πρὸς αὐτὸν λαβὼν φίλος ᾖ Τισσαφέρνει. ἐβούλετο δὲ καὶ
Κλέαρχος ἅπαν τὸ στράτευμα πρὸς ἑαυτὸν ἔχειν τὴν γνώμην
καὶ τοὺς παραλυποῦντας ἐκποδὼν εἶναι. τῶν δὲ στρατιωτῶν
ἀντέλεγόν τινες αὐτῷ μὴ ἰέναι πάντας τοὺς λοχαγοὺς καὶ στρατηγοὺς μηδὲ πιστεύειν Τισσαφέρνει. ὁ δὲ Κλέαρχος ἰσχυρῶς
κατέτεινεν, ἔστε διεπράξατο πέντε μὲν στρατηγοὺς ἰέναι, εἴκοσι
δὲ λοχαγούς· συνηκολούθησαν δὲ ὡς εἰς ἀγορὰν καὶ τῶν ἄλλων
στρατιωτῶν ὡς διακόσιοι.

Ἐπεὶ δὲ ἦσαν ἐπὶ θύραις ταῖς Τισσαφέρνους, οἱ μὲν στρατηγοὶ
παρεκλήθησαν εἴσω, Πρόξενος Βοιώτιος, Μένων Θετταλός, Ἀγίας
Ἀρκάς, Κλέαρχος Λάκων, Σωκράτης Ἀχαιός· οἱ δὲ λοχαγοὶ
ἐπὶ θύραις ἔμενον. οὐ πολλῷ δὲ ὕστερον ἀπὸ τοῦ αὐτοῦ ση-

---

109 τιμωρηθῆναι: the infin. is governed by χρῆναι, above.

Μένωνα: for the strife between Clearchus and Menon, see I, 5, 68 ff. Clearchus' precedence dates from the events narrated in I, 3 (cf. I, 6, §5), and seems not to have been affected by Menon's action at Thapsacus (I, 4, §§13-17). Ctesias (see the Introd. 30) says: Κλεάρχῳ ἅπαντα ὁ Κῦρος συνεβούλευε, τοῦ δὲ Μένωνος λόγος οὐδεὶς ἦν.

110 μετ' Ἀριαίου: for his friendship with Menon, see c. 1. 26.

111 αὐτῷ: i. e. Κλεάρχῳ.

112 καὶ Κλέαρχος: a remark showing Xen.'s fairness; Menon was not the only schemer.

113 ἅπαν τὸ στράτευμα: a chiastic variation from τὸ στράτευμα ἅπαν, above.

115 ἀντέλεγον, *protested,* a durative tense, as κατέτεινεν, below.

The vb. takes μή, as implying a command.

116 ὁ δὲ Κλέαρχος: Ctesias' version is different. According to him, Menon was the prime mover and Clearchus was forced by the troops to go against his will. It was natural that Xen. should emphasize the activity of Clearchus, and Ctesias (in the Persian camp) that of Menon. We may well believe that each was scheming to get the other out of the way.

117 ἔστε: cf. I, 9, 38, and the note.

118 ὡς εἰς ἀγοράν: i. e. *unarmed.*

120 ἐπὶ θύραις ... Τισσ.: note the position; cf. I, 1, 43 f., and the note. For θύραις, cf. I, 2, 69, and the note.

123 πολλῷ: dat. of measure, but indistinguishable from the adv. πολύ.

ἀπό, *at.* The signal is said to have

μείου οἵ τ' ἔνδον ξυνελαμβάνοντο καὶ οἱ ἔξω κατεκόπησαν. μετὰ δὲ ταῦτα τῶν βαρβάρων τινὲς ἱππέων διὰ τοῦ πεδίου ἐλαύνοντες 125 ᾧτινι ἐντυγχάνοιεν Ἕλληνι ἢ δούλῳ ἢ ἐλευθέρῳ πάντας ἔκτεινον. οἱ δὲ Ἕλληνες τήν τε ἱππασίαν ἐθαύμαζον ἐκ τοῦ στρατοπέδου ὁρῶντες καὶ ὅ,τι ἐποίουν ἠμφεγνόουν, πρὶν Νίκαρχος Ἀρκὰς ἧκε φεύγων τετρωμένος εἰς τὴν γαστέρα καὶ τὰ ἔντερα ἐν ταῖς χερσὶν ἔχων, καὶ εἶπε πάντα τὰ γεγενημένα. ἐκ τούτου 130 δὴ οἱ Ἕλληνες ἔθεον ἐπὶ τὰ ὅπλα πάντες ἐκπεπληγμένοι καὶ νομίζοντες αὐτίκα ἥξειν αὐτοὺς ἐπὶ τὸ στρατόπεδον.

Οἱ δὲ πάντες μὲν οὐκ ἦλθον, Ἀριαῖος δὲ καὶ Ἀρτάοζος καὶ Μιθραδάτης, οἳ ἦσαν Κύρῳ πιστότατοι· ὁ δὲ τῶν Ἑλλήνων ἑρμηνεὺς ἔφη καὶ τὸν Τισσαφέρνους ἀδελφὸν σὺν αὐτοῖς ὁρᾶν 135 καὶ γιγνώσκειν· ξυνηκολούθουν δὲ καὶ ἄλλοι Περσῶν τεθωρακισμένοι εἰς τριακοσίους. οὗτοι ἐπεὶ ἐγγὺς ἦσαν, προσελθεῖν ἐκέλευον εἴ τις εἴη τῶν Ἑλλήνων στρατηγὸς ἢ λοχαγός, ἵνα ἀπαγγείλωσι τὰ παρὰ βασιλέως. μετὰ ταῦτα ἐξῆλθον φυλαττόμενοι τῶν Ἑλλήνων στρατηγοὶ μὲν Κλεάνωρ Ὀρχομένιος καὶ 140 Σοφαίνετος Στυμφάλιος, ξὺν αὐτοῖς δὲ Ξενοφῶν Ἀθηναῖος, ὅπως μάθοι τὰ περὶ Προξένου· Χειρίσοφος δὲ ἐτύγχανεν ἀπὼν ἐν

---

been the raising of a red flag over the tent of Tiss.

124 ξυνελαμβάνοντο . . . κατεκόπησαν: note the change in tense. With the whole cf. Caesar's action toward the Upsipites and Tencteri (B. G. IV, 13). It was thus, also, that the Parthians seized Crassus.

125 τινές: for the position, cf. III, 3, §4. It is permitted in Attic only when the subst. has an attrib. adj., but is common in Herodotus.

126 ᾧτινι ἐντυγχάνοιεν: see the note on ὅστις ἀφικνεῖτο, I, 1, 18, where again ὅστις is followed by a pl.

ἔκτεινον: the simple vb. only here in Xen.

128 ἐποίουν: instead of ποιοῖεν; see I, 2, 11, and the note.

ἠμφεγνόουν: for the double augment, cf. ἠνέσχετο, I, 8, 105, and the note.

πρίν: see the notes on I, 1, 53, and I, 9, 38. Here ἠμφεγνόουν implies a neg.

131 ἔθεον: see the note on θεῖν, I, 8, 71.

ἐκπεπληγμένοι: how different from ἐκπλαγέντες?

137 προσελθεῖν: they said, εἴ τίς ἐστι . . . προσελθέτω.

140 στρατηγοὶ μὲν . . . ξὺν αὐτοῖς δέ: Xen. held no rank, hence the two groups.

142 τὰ περί, the news about, a common phrase, oftener with the

κώμῃ τινὶ ξὺν ἄλλοις ἐπισιτιζομένοις. ἐπειδὴ δὲ ἔστησαν εἰς
ἐπήκοον, εἶπεν Ἀριαῖος τάδε. Κλέαρχος μέν, ὦ ἄνδρες Ἕλλη-
145 νες, ἐπεὶ ἐπιορκῶν τε ἐφάνη καὶ τὰς σπονδὰς λύων, ἔχει τὴν
δίκην καὶ τέθνηκε, Πρόξενος δὲ καὶ Μένων, ὅτι κατήγγειλαν
αὐτοῦ τὴν ἐπιβουλήν, ἐν μεγάλῃ τιμῇ εἰσιν. ὑμᾶς δὲ βασιλεὺς
τὰ ὅπλα ἀπαιτεῖ· αὐτοῦ γὰρ εἶναί φησιν, ἐπείπερ Κύρου ἦσαν
τοῦ ἐκείνου δούλου. πρὸς ταῦτα ἀπεκρίναντο οἱ Ἕλληνες, ἔλεγε
150 δὲ Κλεάνωρ ὁ Ὀρχομένιος· Ὦ κάκιστε ἀνθρώπων Ἀριαῖε καὶ
οἱ ἄλλοι ὅσοι ἦτε Κύρου φίλοι, οὐκ αἰσχύνεσθε οὔτε θεοὺς οὔτ'
ἀνθρώπους, οἵτινες ὀμόσαντες ἡμῖν τοὺς αὐτοὺς φίλους καὶ
ἐχθροὺς νομιεῖν, προδόντες ἡμᾶς σὺν Τισσαφέρνει τῷ ἀθεωτάτῳ
τε καὶ πανουργοτάτῳ τούς τε ἄνδρας αὐτοὺς οἷς ὤμνυτε ἀπολω-
155 λέκατε καὶ τοὺς ἄλλους ἡμᾶς προδεδωκότες ξὺν τοῖς πολεμίοις
ἐφ' ἡμᾶς ἔρχεσθε; ὁ δὲ Ἀριαῖος εἶπε· Κλέαρχος γὰρ πρόσθεν
ἐπιβουλεύων φανερὸς ἐγένετο Τισσαφέρνει τε καὶ Ὀρόντᾳ, καὶ
πᾶσιν ἡμῖν τοῖς ξὺν τούτοις. ἐπὶ τούτῳ Ξενοφῶν τάδε εἶπε.
Κλέαρχος μὲν τοίνυν εἰ παρὰ τοὺς ὅρκους ἔλυε τὰς σπονδάς,
160 τὴν δίκην ἔχει· δίκαιον γὰρ ἀπόλλυσθαι τοὺς ἐπιορκοῦντας·

---

acc. than the gen. For the friendship of Xen. and Proxenus, see the note on c. 4. 66.

Χειρίσοφος: his subsequent prominence justifies the special mention of him here.

143 ἔστησαν εἰς: motion, followed by rest.

145 ἐφάνη, *was proved*; *cf. φανερὸς ἐγένετο*, below, l. 157. See the note on ἐφαίνετο, I, 9, 70.

τὴν δίκην, *his deserts*.

148 ἀπαιτεῖ: for the two accs., see the note on I, 1, 55. Observe the emphatic position of ὑμᾶς and of αὐτοῦ, below.

ἦσαν: pl., despite the neut. pl. subj.; see the note on I, 2, 38.

149 ἐκείνου: *i. e. the king*, said from the standpoint of Ariaeus.

δούλου: cf. I, 9, 105, and the note.

ἀπεκρίναντο ... ἔλεγε: *cf.* c. 3. 87.

150 Κλεάνωρ: called πρεσβύτατος, c. 1. 51, and therefore entitled to take a prominent place. His words well express his outraged moral sense. Compare his words in III, 2, §§ 4 ff.

151 οἱ ἄλλοι: apposition; *cf.* I, 5, 94, and the note.

θεοὺς ... ἀνθρώπους: for the case, see the note on c. 3. 91.

152 οἵτινες, *seeing that you*. The rel. is often causal (G. 1461; H. 910; B. 598; 619, note).

ἡμῖν: the dat. goes with ὀμόσαντες, but is felt also with τοὺς αὐτούς (*the same as we*).

155 προδεδωκότες: varied from προδόντες, above. The repetition adds emphasis.

156 γάρ, (*we are not traitors*) *for.*

Πρόξενος δὲ καὶ Μένων ἐπείπερ εἰσὶν ὑμέτεροι μὲν εὐεργέται, ἡμέτεροι δὲ στρατηγοί, πέμψατε αὐτοὺς δεῦρο· δῆλον γὰρ ὅτι φίλοι γε ὄντες ἀμφοτέροις πειράσονται καὶ ὑμῖν καὶ ἡμῖν τὰ βέλτιστα ξυμβουλεῦσαι. πρὸς ταῦτα οἱ βάρβαροι πολὺν χρόνον διαλεχθέντες ἀλλήλοις ἀπῆλθον οὐδὲν ἀποκρινάμενοι.

VI. Οἱ μὲν δὴ στρατηγοὶ οὕτω ληφθέντες ἀνήχθησαν ὡς βασιλέα καὶ ἀποτμηθέντες τὰς κεφαλὰς ἐτελεύτησαν, εἷς μὲν αὐτῶν Κλέαρχος ὁμολογουμένως ἐκ πάντων τῶν ἐμπείρως αὐτοῦ ἐχόντων δόξας γενέσθαι ἀνὴρ καὶ πολεμικὸς καὶ φιλοπόλεμος ἐσχάτως. καὶ γὰρ δὴ ἕως μὲν πόλεμος ἦν τοῖς Λακεδαιμονίοις πρὸς τοὺς Ἀθηναίους παρέμενεν, ἐπειδὴ δὲ εἰρήνη ἐγένετο, πείσας τὴν αὑτοῦ πόλιν ὡς οἱ Θρᾷκες ἀδικοῦσι τοὺς Ἕλληνας καὶ διαπραξάμενος ὡς ἐδύνατο παρὰ τῶν ἐφόρων ἐξέπλει ὡς πολεμήσων τοῖς ὑπὲρ Χερρονήσου καὶ Περίνθου Θρᾳξίν. ἐπεὶ δὲ

γάρ is very common in answers, the context supplying *yes* or *no*. Here it may be rendered *but*.

161 Πρόξενος ... Μένων: best regarded as a real anacolouthon (nom. abs.). The emphasis may be retained by translating, *as regards Proxenus and Menon*. *Cf.* the note on ποταμός, c. 4. 27.

CHAPTER VI

2 τὰς κεφαλάς: acc. of the part affected (G. 1058; H. 718; B. 335; *cf.* III, 1, §31, τὰ ὦτα τετρυπημένον, *with his ears pierced*). Used with a pass. this suggests an act. construction ἀποτέμνειν τινὰ τὴν κεφαλήν (*cf.* βάλλειν with two accs.). Instead of this we have III, 1, §17, τοῦ ἀδελφοῦ ... ἀποτεμὼν τὴν κεφαλήν, and I, 10, 1 the regular pass., Κύρου ἀποτέμνεται ἡ κεφαλή.

εἷς μέν: balanced by Πρόξενος δέ, §16. It is a form of partitive appos. with οἱ στρατηγοί, εἷς μέν serving to bring the individual into stronger relief than ὁ μέν.

3 Κλέαρχος: see the Introd., §38.

ἐκ πάντων: with ὁμολογουμένως, *in the opinion of all*. For this use of ἐκ, *cf.* I, 1, 28, and the note.

τῶν ... ἐχόντων, *those acquainted with him*. *Cf.* I, 9, 3 f.

4 δόξας, *reputed*.

5 ἐσχάτως: a strong word in emphatic position.

δή: a specific instance of a general truth. The two characteristics (πολεμικός and φιλοπόλεμος) are taken up in reverse (chiastic) order. *Cf.* III, 1, §20.

πόλεμος: the Peloponnesian war, 431–404 B.C.

6 παρέμενεν, *could find service at home* (Dakyns).

7 τοὺς Ἕλληνας: *i. e.* those inhabiting the Chersonesus; see the map, and I, 1, 49.

8 διαπραξάμενος: *cf.* c. 3. 85.

ὡς ἐδύνατο, *no matter how*. Intrigue is implied.

10 μεταγνόντες πως οἱ ἔφοροι ἤδη ἔξω ὄντος ἀποστρέφειν αὐτὸν
ἐπειρῶντο ἐξ Ἰσθμοῦ, ἐνταῦθα οὐκέτι πείθεται, ἀλλ' ᾤχετο
πλέων εἰς Ἑλλήσποντον. ἐκ τούτου καὶ ἐθανατώθη ὑπὸ τῶν 4
ἐν Σπάρτῃ τελῶν ὡς ἀπειθῶν. ἤδη δὲ φυγὰς ὢν ἔρχεται πρὸς
Κῦρον, καὶ ὁποίοις μὲν λόγοις ἔπεισε Κῦρον ἄλλῃ γέγραπται,
15 δίδωσι δὲ αὐτῷ Κῦρος μυρίους δαρεικούς· ὁ δὲ λαβὼν οὐκ ἐπὶ 5
ῥᾳθυμίαν ἐτράπετο, ἀλλ' ἀπὸ τούτων τῶν χρημάτων συλλέξας
στράτευμα ἐπολέμει τοῖς Θρᾳξί, καὶ μάχῃ τε ἐνίκησε καὶ ἀπὸ
τούτου δὴ ἔφερε καὶ ἦγε τούτους καὶ πολεμῶν διεγένετο μέχρι
Κῦρος ἐδεήθη τοῦ στρατεύματος· τότε δὲ ἀπῆλθεν ὡς ξὺν ἐκείνῳ
20 αὖ πολεμήσων. ταῦτα οὖν φιλοπολέμου μοι δοκεῖ ἀνδρὸς ἔργα 6
εἶναι, ὅστις ἐξὸν μὲν εἰρήνην ἄγειν ἄνευ αἰσχύνης καὶ βλάβης
αἱρεῖται πολεμεῖν, ἐξὸν δὲ ῥᾳθυμεῖν βούλεται πονεῖν ὥστε πολεμεῖν, ἐξὸν δὲ χρήματα ἔχειν ἀκινδύνως αἱρεῖται πολεμῶν μείονα
ταῦτα ποιεῖν· ἐκεῖνος δὲ ὥσπερ εἰς παιδικὰ ἢ εἰς ἄλλην τινὰ
25 ἡδονὴν ἤθελε δαπανᾶν εἰς πόλεμον. οὕτω μὲν φιλοπόλεμος 7
ἦν· πολεμικὸς δὲ αὖ ταύτῃ ἐδόκει εἶναι ὅτι φιλοκίνδυνός τε ἦν

---

10 μεταγνόντες: cf. μεταμελεῖν, I, 6, 41, and the note.

ἤδη ... ὄντος: sc. αὐτοῦ. For the gen. abs., where we should have looked for a case in agreement, cf. I, 2, 99, and the note.

11 Ἰσθμοῦ: the isthmus of Corinth is meant.

ἐνταῦθα: resumptive.

ᾤχετο πλέων: cf. c. 4. 105, and the note.

12 καί, actually.

13 τελῶν: often used of high magistrates.

14 ἄλλῃ γέγραπται: note the tense. Xen. is perhaps referring to I, 1, §9 (which section should be compared throughout), but the arguments are not given.

15 ἐπὶ ῥᾳθυμίαν: cf. Clearchus' own words, I, 3, 15.

16 ἀπό: cf. I, 1, 47.

17 ἀπὸ τούτου, thenceforth.

18 ἔφερε καὶ ἦγε, plundered, a standing phrase. ἔφερε has reference to inanimate objects, ἦγε to live stock. Cf. ἔφερον, IV, 1, §8.

πολεμῶν διεγένετο: stronger than ἐπολέμει. Cf. λέγων διῆγε, I, 2, 70.

19 ἐδεήθη: for the fact, cf. 1, 2, 4.

21 ὅστις ... αἱρεῖται: instead of αἱρεῖσθαι. See the note on οἵτινες, c. 5. 83.

ἐξόν: cf. c. 5. 86. Note the anaphora and the parallel structure.

22 ὥστε πολεμεῖν, so it be for war. See G. 1453; H. 953b; B. 596.

26 πολεμικὸς δὲ αὖ: returning to the first characteristic, mentioned at the end of §1; see the note there.

φιλοκίνδυνός τε: parallel with καὶ ... φρόνιμος. The intervening

καὶ ἡμέρας καὶ νυκτὸς ἄγων ἐπὶ τοὺς πολεμίους καὶ ἐν τοῖς δεινοῖς φρόνιμος, ὡς οἱ παρόντες πανταχοῦ πάντες ὡμολόγουν. 8 καὶ ἀρχικὸς δ' ἐλέγετο εἶναι ὡς δυνατὸν ἐκ τοῦ τοιούτου τρόπου οἷον κἀκεῖνος εἶχεν. ἱκανὸς μὲν γὰρ ὥς τις καὶ ἄλλος φροντίζειν ἦν ὅπως ἔχοι ἡ στρατιὰ αὐτῷ τὰ ἐπιτήδεια καὶ παρασκευάζειν ταῦτα, ἱκανὸς δὲ καὶ ἐμποιῆσαι τοῖς παροῦσιν ὡς πειστέον 9 εἴη Κλεάρχῳ. τοῦτο δ' ἐποίει ἐκ τοῦ χαλεπὸς εἶναι· καὶ γὰρ ὁρᾶν στυγνὸς ἦν καὶ τῇ φωνῇ τραχύς, ἐκόλαζέ τε ἰσχυρῶς, καὶ ὀργῇ ἐνίοτε, ὡς καὶ αὐτῷ μεταμέλειν ἔσθ' ὅτε. καὶ γνώμῃ δ' 10 ἐκόλαζεν· ἀκολάστου γὰρ στρατεύματος οὐδὲν ἡγεῖτο ὄφελος εἶναι, ἀλλὰ καὶ λέγειν αὐτὸν ἔφασαν ὡς δέοι τὸν στρατιώτην φοβεῖσθαι μᾶλλον τὸν ἄρχοντα ἢ τοὺς πολεμίους, εἰ μέλλοι ἢ φυλακὰς φυλάξειν ἢ φίλων ἀφέξεσθαι ἢ ἀπροφασίστως ἰέναι 11 πρὸς τοὺς πολεμίους. ἐν μὲν οὖν τοῖς δεινοῖς ἤθελον αὐτοῦ

---

words καὶ ἡμέρας καὶ νυκτὸς ἄγων, κ.τ.λ., explain φιλοκίνδυνος. Do not connect ἄγων with ἦν. For the gens. ἡμέρας and νυκτός, cf. I, 7, 85, and the note.

28 φρόνιμος: cf. I, 10, 34.

πανταχοῦ πάντες: cf. c. 5. 26.

29 ὡς ... εἶχεν, as far as was possible for a man with such a temper as he had. καί with rel. words may often be left untranslated; cf. καὶ ἄλλος, just below, and see the notes on I, 3, 31, and I, 4, 97.

31 ὅπως ἔχοι: obj. clause after φροντίζειν.

αὐτῷ: cf. I, 1, 43, and the note.

32 ἐμποιῆσαι τοῖς παροῦσιν, to inspire in those about him (the feeling that). For the vb., cf. below, l. 69.

33 Κλεάρχῳ: the use of the proper name instead of the pron. has always a distinct force.

ἐκ τοῦ ... εἶναι, by being. Cf. I, 1, 35, and the note. Observe that χαλεπός must be nom., despite the fact that the clause is gen.

34 ὁρᾶν: dat. infin., parallel with the following τῇ φωνῇ; cf. ὁρᾶσθαι, c. 3. 8. In these cases dat. and acc. are indistinguishable.

ἐκόλαζέ τε: for the solitary τε, cf. I, 5, 91. Clearchus was a severe disciplinarian; cf. c. 3. 41, and the note, and III, 2, § 31.

35 ὡς = ὥστε.

ἔσθ' ὅτε: varied from ἐνίοτε, above. For the form, cf. the note on ἦν οὕς, I, 5, 35.

καὶ ... ἐκόλαζεν: repeated in chiastic order, a rhetorical feature common in this chapter.

36 ὄφελος: cf. I, 3, 56.

37 λέγειν ... ἔφασαν: cf. c. 1. 72, and the note.

38 εἰ μέλλοι, if he was to. After this vb. the fut. infin. is usual.

39 ἀφέξεσθαι, hold aloof from, abstain from injuring.

ἀκούειν σφόδρα καὶ οὐκ ἄλλον ᾑροῦντο οἱ στρατιῶται· καὶ γὰρ
τὸ στυγνὸν τότε φαιδρὸν αὐτοῦ ἐν τοῖς ἄλλοις προσώποις ἔφασαν
φαίνεσθαι καὶ τὸ χαλεπὸν ἐρρωμένον πρὸς τοὺς πολεμίους ἐδόκει εἶναι, ὥστε σωτήριον, οὐκέτι χαλεπὸν ἐφαίνετο· ὅτε δ' ἔξω 12
45 τοῦ δεινοῦ γένοιντο καὶ ἐξείη πρὸς ἄλλον ἀρξομένους ἀπιέναι,
πολλοὶ αὐτὸν ἀπέλειπον· τὸ γὰρ ἐπίχαρι οὐκ εἶχεν, ἀλλ' ἀεὶ
χαλεπὸς ἦν καὶ ὠμός· ὥστε διέκειντο πρὸς αὐτὸν οἱ στρατιῶται
ὥσπερ παῖδες πρὸς διδάσκαλον. καὶ γὰρ οὖν φιλίᾳ μὲν καὶ 13
εὐνοίᾳ ἑπομένους οὐδέποτε εἶχεν· οἵτινες δὲ ἢ ὑπὸ πόλεως τεταγ-
50 μένοι ἢ ὑπὸ τοῦ δεῖσθαι ἢ ἄλλῃ τινὶ ἀνάγκῃ κατεχόμενοι παρείη-
σαν αὐτῷ, σφόδρα πειθομένοις ἐχρῆτο. ἐπεὶ δὲ ἄρξαιντο νικᾶν 14
ξὺν αὐτῷ τοὺς πολεμίους, ἤδη μεγάλα ἦν τὰ χρησίμους ποιοῦντα
εἶναι τοὺς ξὺν αὐτῷ στρατιώτας· τό τε γὰρ πρὸς τοὺς πολεμίους
θαρραλέως ἔχειν παρῆν καὶ τὸ τὴν παρ' ἐκείνου τιμωρίαν φοβεῖ-
55 σθαι εὐτάκτους ἐποίει. τοιοῦτος μὲν δὴ ἄρχων ἦν· ἄρχεσθαι δὲ 15
ὑπὸ ἄλλων οὐ μάλα ἐθέλειν ἐλέγετο. ἦν δὲ ὅτε ἐτελεύτα ἀμφὶ
τὰ πεντήκοντα ἔτη.

41 σφόδρα: with ἀκούειν (*yield absolute obedience*), rather than with ἤθελον. Cf. σφόδρα πειθομένοις, l. 51.

42 τὸ στυγνὸν ... φαίνεσθαι: strongly rhetorical, *his gloominess then shone as a bright light*. φαιδρόν is pred. to φαίνεσθα (note the alliteration). αὐτοῦ, by its very unusual position, is strongly contrasted with τοῖς ἄλλοις. This phrase is one of very doubtful interpretation: either *among the faces of the rest* (in which fear was seen), or *reflected in the faces of the rest*. Some omit ἄλλοις, in which case αὐτοῦ ἐν τοῖς προσώποις means simply *in his face*, a poetical use of the pl. πρόσωπα referring to a single individual (Gildersleeve, *Syntax*, 48, 50).

44 σωτήριον οὐκέτι χαλεπόν: Plutarch (*Marius* 14) uses similar language of Marius.

45 ἀρξομένους, *to take service*, fut. mid. in pass. sense.

46 τὸ ... ἐπίχαρι, *charm of manner*. Retain the order.

47 διέκειντο: cf. c. 5. 105, and the note.

50 ὑπὸ ... δεῖσθαι: with κατεχόμενοι, and therefore parallel with the following dat., but the use of ὑπό gives a slight personification.

51 σφόδρα ... ἐχρῆτο, *he exacted absolute obedience*.

52 μεγάλα: the order must be retained, else this word loses its emphasis.

53 τό ... ἔχειν, *boldness in the face of the foe*.

56 οὐ μάλα, *not much*, but meaning, *not at all* (litotes).

Πρόξενος δὲ ὁ Βοιώτιος εὐθὺς μὲν μειράκιον ὢν ἐπεθύμει γενέσθαι ἀνὴρ τὰ μεγάλα πράττειν ἱκανός· καὶ διὰ ταύτην τὴν ἐπιθυμίαν ἔδωκε Γοργίᾳ ἀργύριον τῷ Λεοντίνῳ. ἐπεὶ δὲ συνεγένετο ἐκείνῳ, ἱκανὸς νομίσας ἤδη εἶναι καὶ ἄρχειν καὶ φίλος ὢν τοῖς πρώτοις μὴ ἡττᾶσθαι εὐεργετῶν, ἦλθεν εἰς ταύτας τὰς σὺν Κύρῳ πράξεις· καὶ ᾤετο κτήσεσθαι ἐκ τούτων ὄνομα μέγα καὶ δύναμιν μεγάλην καὶ χρήματα πολλά· τοσούτων δ᾽ ἐπιθυμῶν σφόδρα ἔνδηλον αὖ καὶ τοῦτο εἶχεν ὅτι τούτων οὐδὲν ἂν θέλοι κτᾶσθαι μετὰ ἀδικίας, ἀλλὰ σὺν τῷ δικαίῳ καὶ καλῷ ᾤετο δεῖν τούτων τυγχάνειν, ἄνευ δὲ τούτων μή. ἄρχειν δὲ καλῶν μὲν καὶ ἀγαθῶν δυνατὸς ἦν· οὐ μέντοι οὔτ᾽ αἰδῶ τοῖς στρατιώταις ἑαυτοῦ οὔτε φόβον ἱκανὸς ἐμποιῆσαι, ἀλλὰ καὶ ᾐσχύνετο μᾶλλον τοὺς στρατιώτας ἢ οἱ ἀρχόμενοι ἐκεῖνον· καὶ φοβούμενος μᾶλλον ἦν φανερὸς τὸ ἀπεχθάνεσθαι τοῖς στρατιώταις ἢ οἱ στρατιῶται τὸ ἀπιστεῖν ἐκείνῳ. ᾤετο δὲ ἀρκεῖν πρὸς τὸ ἀρχικὸν εἶναι καὶ δοκεῖν τὸν μὲν καλῶς ποιοῦντα ἐπαινεῖν, τὸν δὲ ἀδικοῦντα μὴ ἐπαινεῖν. τοιγαροῦν αὐτῷ οἱ μὲν καλοί τε καὶ

---

57 τὰ πεντήκοντα: for the art., cf. τοὺς δισχιλίους, I, 2, 59.

58 Πρόξενος δέ: see the Introd., § 38. δέ balances μέν in l. 2.
ἐπεθύμει, *cherished the desire*. How different from ἐπεθύμησε?

60 Γοργίᾳ: the most famous, perhaps, of the Greek "sophists." His fee is stated to have been 100 minae (nearly $2,000). Where was Leontini?

συνεγένετο ἐκείνῳ, *had completed his course with him*. συγγίγνεσθαι and συνεῖναι are regularly used to express the relations of teacher and pupil.

62 τοῖς πρώτοις, *the first men (of his day)*.

εὐεργετῶν: after ἡττᾶσθαι; cf. c. 3. 99.

63 καὶ ... καί: in enumerations both polysyndeton and asyndeton (l. 93) are common.

65 ἔνδηλον ... εἶχεν, *yet he made this too clear*.

67 μή: not οὐ, because going with τυγχάνειν, not with δεῖν; cf. μὴ ἐπαινεῖν, below, l. 74.

καλῶν ... ἀγαθῶν, *gentlemen*, i. e. men endowed with the ideal qualities, comeliness and manliness. The phrase is a common one; cf. § 20 and IV, 1, § 19.

68 αἰδῶ ... ἑαυτοῦ, *respect for himself*, obj. gen. For ἐμποιῆσαι, cf. l. 32.

70 οἱ ἀρχόμενοι: a synonym instead of the word just used.
φοβούμενος: after φανερὸς ἦν. Several instances of this use of the partic. occur in §§ 21 and 22. Cf. I, 2, 70, and the note.

72 ἀρκεῖν: the subj. is the clause τὸν μὲν ... τὸν δὲ ... ἐπαινεῖν.

73 ἀρχικόν: acc., not nom., since

ἀγαθοὶ τῶν συνόντων εὖνοι ἦσαν, οἱ δὲ ἄδικοι ἐπεβούλευον ὡς εὐμεταχειρίστῳ ὄντι. ὅτε δὲ ἀπέθνῃσκεν ἦν ἐτῶν ὡς τριάκοντα.

Μένων δὲ ὁ Θετταλὸς δῆλος ἦν ἐπιθυμῶν μὲν πλουτεῖν ἰσχυρῶς, ἐπιθυμῶν δὲ ἄρχειν, ὅπως πλείω λαμβάνοι, ἐπιθυμῶν δὲ τιμᾶσθαι, ἵνα πλείω κερδαίνοι· φίλος τε ἐβούλετο εἶναι τοῖς μέγιστα δυναμένοις, ἵνα ἀδικῶν μὴ διδοίη δίκην. ἐπὶ δὲ τὸ κατεργάζεσθαι ὧν ἐπιθυμοίη συντομωτάτην ᾤετο ὁδὸν εἶναι διὰ τοῦ ἐπιορκεῖν τε καὶ ψεύδεσθαι καὶ ἐξαπατᾶν, τὸ δ' ἁπλοῦν καὶ ἀληθὲς τὸ αὐτὸ τῷ ἠλιθίῳ εἶναι. στέργων δὲ φανερὸς μὲν ἦν οὐδένα, ὅτῳ δὲ φαίη φίλος εἶναι, τούτῳ ἔνδηλος ἐγίγνετο ἐπιβουλεύων. καὶ πολεμίου μὲν οὐδενὸς κατεγέλα, τῶν δὲ συνόντων πάντων ὡς καταγελῶν ἀεὶ διελέγετο. καὶ τοῖς μὲν τῶν πολεμίων κτήμασιν οὐκ ἐπεβούλευε· χαλεπὸν γὰρ ᾤετο εἶναι τὰ τῶν φυλαττομένων λαμβάνειν· τὰ δὲ τῶν φίλων μόνος ᾤετο εἰδέναι ῥᾷστον ὂν ἀφύλακτα λαμβάνειν. καὶ ὅσους μὲν αἰσθάνοιτο ἐπιόρκους καὶ ἀδίκους ὡς εὖ ὡπλισμένους ἐφοβεῖτο, τοῖς δὲ ὁσίοις καὶ ἀλήθειαν ἀσκοῦσιν ὡς ἀνάνδροις ἐπειρᾶτο χρῆσθαι.

---

the notion is an abstract one and there is no reference to the main subj.; contrast l. 33.

76 ὅτε δὲ ἀπέθνῃσκεν: Xen. varies the phrase in each case, both in stating the fact of death and in giving the age.

ἐτῶν: gen. of measure.

77 Μένων: see the Introd., § 38.

ἐπιθυμῶν: note the triple anaphora.

78 ὅπως ... ἵνα: note the varied phrases.

79 φίλος τε: for the solitary τε, cf. l. 34, and the note.

80 μέγιστα: adv. modifying δυναμένοις.

ἀδικῶν ... δίκην: note the alliteration.

ἐπὶ ... ὁδόν, *the shortest road leading to the accomplishment of his desires*. Why is ἐπιθυμοίη opt.?

83 τὸ αὐτό, *the same thing as, synonymous with.* For the dat., see G. 1175; H. 773; B. 392, 2.

στέργων: a strong word, properly denoting natural affection. Note the strong emphasis that falls both on στέργων and on οὐδένα, and also the chiastic order.

85 τῶν ... διελέγετο, *while, as for his associates, his whole conversation turned upon their ridicule.* The gen. is governed by καταγελῶν.

88 μόνος ... εἰδέναι, *thought that he knew better than any one else.* Cf. the use of εἷς in ἑνί γε ἀνδρί, I, 9, 39.

89 ὄν: partic. in indir. disc. after εἰδέναι.

ἀφύλακτα: trans. as causal.

92 ἀγάλλεται: with ἐπί, but below, ἠγάλλετο, with the simple dat.

26 ὥσπερ δέ τις ἀγάλλεται ἐπὶ θεοσεβείᾳ καὶ ἀληθείᾳ καὶ δικαιότητι, οὕτω Μένων ἠγάλλετο τῷ ἐξαπατᾶν δύνασθαι, τῷ πλάσασθαι ψευδῆ, τῷ φίλους διαγελᾶν· τὸν δὲ μὴ πανοῦργον τῶν ἀπαιδεύτων ἀεὶ ἐνόμιζεν εἶναι. καὶ παρ' οἷς μὲν ἐπεχείρει πρωτεύειν φιλίᾳ, διαβάλλων τοὺς πρώτους τοῦτο ᾤετο δεῖν κτήσασθαι. 27 τὸ δὲ πειθομένους τοὺς στρατιώτας παρέχεσθαι ἐκ τοῦ συναδικεῖν αὐτοῖς ἐμηχανᾶτο. τιμᾶσθαι δὲ καὶ θεραπεύεσθαι ἠξίου ἐπιδεικνύμενος ὅτι πλεῖστα δύναιτο καὶ ἐθέλοι ἂν ἀδικεῖν. εὐεργεσίαν δὲ κατέλεγεν, ὁπότε τις αὐτοῦ ἀφίστατο, ὅτι χρώμενος 28 αὐτῷ οὐκ ἀπώλεσεν αὐτόν. καὶ τὰ μὲν δὴ ἀφανῆ ἔξεστι περὶ αὐτοῦ ψεύδεσθαι, ἃ δὲ πάντες ἴσασι τάδ' ἐστί. παρὰ Ἀριστίππου μὲν ἔτι ὡραῖος ὢν στρατηγεῖν διεπράξατο τῶν ξένων, Ἀριαίῳ δὲ βαρβάρῳ ὄντι, ὅτι μειρακίοις καλοῖς ἥδετο, οἰκειότατος ἐγένετο, αὐτὸς δὲ παιδικὰ εἶχεν Θαρύπαν ἀγένειος ὢν γενειῶντα. 9 ἀποθνησκόντων δὲ τῶν συστρατήγων ὅτι ἐστράτευσαν ἐπὶ βασιλέα ξὺν Κύρῳ, ταὐτὰ πεποιηκὼς οὐκ ἀπέθανε, μετὰ δὲ τὸν τῶν ἄλλων θάνατον στρατηγῶν τιμωρηθεὶς ὑπὸ βασιλέως ἀπέθανεν, οὐχ ὥσπερ Κλέαρχος καὶ οἱ ἄλλοι στρατηγοὶ ἀποτμηθέντες τὰς

δικαιότητι: a Xenophontic word, for which δικαιοσύνη is usual.

93 τῷ ... τῷ ... τῷ: note the effect of the asyndeton.

94 διαγελᾶν: a rare compound.

τὸν ... μὴ πανοῦργον: μή shows that the phrase is general.

τῶν ἀπαιδεύτων: partitive gen. in the pred.

95 ἐπεχείρει: we should have expected the opt.; cf. ὅστις ἀφικνεῖτο, I, 1, 18, and ὁπότε τις ... ἀφίστατο, below.

96 διαβάλλων: in agreement with the main subj., although logically subordinated to δεῖν.

τοὺς πρώτους: i. e. those already first in their friendship.

τοῦτο: i. e. τὸ πρωτεύειν φιλίᾳ.

97 τὸ ... παρέχεσθαι: obj. of ἐμηχανᾶτο.

99 δύναιτο καὶ ἐθέλοι ἄν: direct, δύναμαι καὶ ἐθέλοιμ' ἄν. The shift of construction is appropriate to the meanings of the two vbs.

100 χρώμενος, *while associated with him*.

101 αὐτόν: emphatic repetition after αὐτῷ. Generally the pron. is expressed but once.

δή: emphasizing the contrast between ἀφανῆ and ἃ ... πάντες ἴσασι. By ἀφανῆ Menon's assumed treachery is doubtless meant.

102 Ἀριστίππου: cf. I, 1, 52 ff.

104 βαρβάρῳ ὄντι: said with indignation.

105 ἀγένειος ... γενειῶντα: contemptuous contrast.

107 πεποιηκώς: concessive.

109 ἀποτμηθέντες τὰς κεφαλάς: cf.

κεφαλάς, ὅσπερ τάχιστος θάνατος δοκεῖ εἶναι, ἀλλὰ ζῶν αἰκισθεὶς ἐνιαυτόν ὡς πονηρὸς λέγεται τῆς τελευτῆς τυχεῖν.

Ἀγίας δὲ ὁ Ἀρκὰς καὶ Σωκράτης ὁ Ἀχαιὸς καὶ τούτω ἀπε-
θανέτην. τούτων δὲ οὔθ᾽ ὡς ἐν πολέμῳ κακῶν οὐδεὶς κατεγέλα
οὔτ᾽ εἰς φιλίαν αὐτοὺς ἐμέμφετο. ἤστην δὲ ἄμφω ἀμφὶ τὰ
πέντε καὶ τριάκοντα ἔτη ἀπὸ γενεᾶς.

---

110 ὅσπερ: the rel. is attracted to the gender of the pred. noun.

ζῶν αἰκισθεὶς ἐνιαυτόν, *tortured alive for a year*. αἰκισθείς suggests mutilation, but we know nothing of the manner of his end.

112 Ἀγίας ... Σωκράτης: of these men nothing is known beyond what the *Anabasis* tells us.

καὶ τούτω: *they too*, but Eng. omits the pron. The dual groups the two together as contrasted with the others, but it is not consistently used.

114 εἰς, *with reference to*.

αὐτούς: μέμφομαι more often takes a dat.

115 ἀπὸ γενεᾶς: note the varied phrase.

BOOK III

1   I. [Ὅσα μὲν δὴ ἐν τῇ Κύρου ἀναβάσει οἱ Ἕλληνες ἔπραξαν μέχρι τῆς μάχης, καὶ ὅσα ἐπεὶ Κῦρος ἐτελεύτησεν ἐγένετο ἀπιόντων τῶν Ἑλλήνων σὺν Τισσαφέρνει ἐν ταῖς σπονδαῖς, ἐν
2 τῷ πρόσθεν λόγῳ δεδήλωται.] ἐπεὶ δὲ οἱ στρατηγοὶ συνειλημμένοι ἦσαν καὶ τῶν λοχαγῶν καὶ τῶν στρατιωτῶν οἱ συνεπισπό- 5
μενοι ἀπωλώλεσαν, ἐν πολλῇ δὴ ἀπορίᾳ ἦσαν οἱ Ἕλληνες, ἐννοούμενοι ὅτι ἐπὶ ταῖς βασιλέως θύραις ἦσαν, κύκλῳ δὲ αὐτοῖς πάντῃ πολλὰ καὶ ἔθνη καὶ πόλεις πολέμιαι ἦσαν, ἀγορὰν δὲ οὐδεὶς ἔτι παρέξειν ἔμελλεν, ἀπεῖχον δὲ τῆς Ἑλλάδος οὐ μεῖον ἢ μύρια στάδια, ἡγεμὼν δ' οὐδεὶς τῆς ὁδοῦ ἦν, ποταμοὶ δὲ διεῖρ- 10
γον ἀδιάβατοι ἐν μέσῳ τῆς οἴκαδε ὁδοῦ, προὐδεδώκεσαν δὲ αὐτοὺς καὶ οἱ σὺν Κύρῳ ἀναβάντες βάρβαροι, μόνοι δὲ καταλελειμμένοι ἦσαν οὐδὲ ἱππέα οὐδένα σύμμαχον ἔχοντες, ὥστε εὔδηλον ἦν

Chapter I

1 Ὅσα . . . δεδήλωται: with this introductory paragraph *cf.* II, 1, 1, and the note.

3 ἀπιόντων: temporal.

4 συνειλημμένοι ἦσαν . . . ἀπωλώλεσαν: plpf. in a temp. clause, instead of the normal aor.; see the note on ἐτελεύτησε, I, 1, 9.

7 ἐννοούμενοι: after eight depend. clauses, in which the despondency of the Greeks is effectively portrayed, this is resumed by ταῦτ' ἐννοούμενοι, l. 15.

ἐπὶ . . . θύραις: *cf.* I, 2, 69, and the note. The phrase is here an exaggerated one, but they are at least in the heart of the king's country.

ἦσαν: past indic., not opt., and so in the following clauses. This accords with Xen.'s point of view at the time of the composition of the *Anabasis*.

8 πολλά: to be taken with both nouns, although agreeing in gender with the nearer only; so, too, πολέμιαι, in the pred.

ἀγορὰν δέ: with this passage *cf.* the words of Clearchus in II, 4, § 5.

10 μύρια στάδια: a round number, like our *a thousand miles*. In reality the distance by the route over which they had come was far greater.

διεῖργον, *barred their progress.* ἐν μέσῳ is best taken in its literal sense, *in the midst of.*

13 ἱππέα οὐδένα: *cf.* with the whole passage II, 4, § 6, and the notes there.

151

ὅτι νικῶντες μὲν οὐδένα ἂν κατακάνοιεν, ἡττηθέντων δὲ αὐτῶν
οὐδεὶς ἂν λειφθείη· ταῦτ' ἐννοούμενοι καὶ ἀθύμως ἔχοντες ὀλίγοι
μὲν αὐτῶν εἰς τὴν ἑσπέραν σίτου ἐγεύσαντο, ὀλίγοι δὲ πῦρ ἀνέ-
καυσαν, ἐπὶ δὲ τὰ ὅπλα πολλοὶ οὐκ ἦλθον ταύτην τὴν νύκτα,
ἀνεπαύοντο δὲ ὅπου ἐτύγχανεν ἕκαστος, οὐ δυνάμενοι καθεύδειν
ὑπὸ λύπης καὶ πόθου πατρίδων, γονέων, γυναικῶν, παίδων, οὓς
οὔποτ' ἐνόμιζον ἔτι ὄψεσθαι. οὕτω μὲν δὴ διακείμενοι πάντες
ἀνεπαύοντο.

*Ἦν δέ τις ἐν τῇ στρατιᾷ Ξενοφῶν Ἀθηναῖος, ὃς οὔτε στρα-
τηγὸς οὔτε λοχαγὸς οὔτε στρατιώτης ὢν συνηκολούθει, ἀλλὰ
Πρόξενος αὐτὸν μετεπέμψατο οἴκοθεν ξένος ὢν ἀρχαῖος· ὑπισχνεῖτο δὲ αὐτῷ, εἰ ἔλθοι, φίλον αὐτὸν Κύρῳ ποιήσειν, ὃν αὐτὸς
ἔφη κρείττω ἑαυτῷ νομίζειν τῆς πατρίδος. ὁ μέντοι Ξενοφῶν
ἀναγνοὺς τὴν ἐπιστολὴν ἀνακοινοῦται Σωκράτει τῷ Ἀθηναίῳ
περὶ τῆς πορείας. καὶ ὁ Σωκράτης ὑποπτεύσας μή τι πρὸς τῆς

---

14 κατακάνοιεν: for the vb., *cf.* I, 6, 8, and the note.
15 ὀλίγοι μὲν ... ὀλίγοι δέ: partitive apposition with anaphora.
16 εἰς τὴν ἑσπέραν: *cf.* I, 7, 4.
17 ἐπὶ ... τὰ ὅπλα, *to their quarters*.
18 ὅπου ἐτύγχανεν: *cf.* II, 2, 78. There the pl. was used, denoting groups, here the sing. of individuals; *cf.* the note on ἑκάστοις, I, 1, 25.
19 ὑπό: again a slight personification.
πατρίδων: there were many states in Greece. Note the asyndeton and the order of the words. We begin with the most emphatic, and we have chiastic alliteration.
20 διακείμενοι: *cf.* διακεῖσθαι, II, 5, 105, and the note.
22 *Ἦν δέ τις: Xen. introduces himself modestly. He has been mentioned before, but only casually (I, 8, §§ 15 and 16, and II, 4, § 15); now he comes to the front.
Ἀθηναῖος: no art., but below, Σωκράτει τῷ Ἀθηναίῳ, since Socrates was famous.
24 αὐτόν: the rel. construction is given up, as regularly (G. 1040; H. 1005; B. 487).
25 εἰ ἔλθοι ... ποιήσειν: direct, ἐὰν ἔλθῃς ... ποιήσω.
αὐτός: for the combination of the intensive and the reflexive, *cf.* I, 8, 100, and the note.
26 τῆς πατρίδος: Boeotia.
27 ἀνακοινοῦται, *consulted with*, but, below, the act., ἀνακοινῶσαι, simply, *lay the matter before*.
28 ὑποπτεύσας ... γενέσθαι, *suspecting that his becoming a friend of Cyrus' might prejudice him with the state*. The infin. clause (φίλον ... γενέσθαι) is the subj. of εἴη. τι goes closely with ὑπαίτιον, *a matter for accusation*.

πόλεως ὑπαίτιον εἴη Κύρῳ φίλον γενέσθαι, ὅτι ἐδόκει ὁ Κῦρος προθύμως τοῖς Λακεδαιμονίοις ἐπὶ τὰς Ἀθήνας συμπολεμῆσαι, 30 συμβουλεύει τῷ Ξενοφῶντι ἐλθόντα εἰς Δελφοὺς ἀνακοινῶσαι 6 τῷ θεῷ περὶ τῆς πορείας. ἐλθὼν δ' ὁ Ξενοφῶν ἐπήρετο τὸν Ἀπόλλω τίνι ἂν θεῶν θύων καὶ εὐχόμενος κάλλιστα καὶ ἄριστα ἔλθοι τὴν ὁδὸν ἣν ἐπινοεῖ καὶ καλῶς πράξας σωθείη. καὶ ἀνεῖλεν 7 αὐτῷ ὁ Ἀπόλλων θεοῖς οἷς ἔδει θύειν. ἐπεὶ δὲ πάλιν ἦλθε, 35 λέγει τὴν μαντείαν τῷ Σωκράτει. ὁ δ' ἀκούσας ᾐτιᾶτο αὐτὸν ὅτι οὐ τοῦτο πρῶτον ἠρώτα πότερον λῷον εἴη αὐτῷ πορεύεσθαι ἢ μένειν, ἀλλ' αὐτὸς κρίνας ἰτέον εἶναι τοῦτ' ἐπυνθάνετο ὅπως ἂν κάλλιστα πορευθείη. ἐπεὶ μέντοι οὕτως ἤρου, ταῦτ', ἔφη, 8 χρὴ ποιεῖν ὅσα ὁ θεὸς ἐκέλευσεν. ὁ μὲν δὴ Ξενοφῶν οὕτω θυσά- 40 μενος οἷς ἀνεῖλεν ὁ θεὸς ἐξέπλει, καὶ καταλαμβάνει ἐν Σάρδεσι Πρόξενον καὶ Κῦρον μέλλοντας ἤδη ὁρμᾶν τὴν ἄνω ὁδόν, καὶ 9 συνεστάθη Κύρῳ. προθυμουμένου δὲ τοῦ Προξένου καὶ ὁ Κῦρος

---

29 ὅτι ... συμπολεμῆσαι: the allusion is to the latter part of the Peloponnesian war when Cyrus furnished the Lacedaemonians with funds; see the Introd., §26. Socrates' apprehensions were apparently well grounded. Xen. was subsequently banished, and an epigram quoted by Diogenes Laertius in his Greek life of Xen. contains the words, πολῖται φεύγειν κατέγνων τοῦ φίλου χάριν Κύρου.
31 ἐλθόντα: for the acc. after the dat., cf. I, 2, 4, and the note.
32 τῷ θεῷ: Apollo, of course; see below.
33 τίνι ... σωθείη, freely, *to whom of the gods he should sacrifice in order to*.
κάλλιστα καὶ ἄριστα: cf. II, 1, 83.
34 ἀνεῖλεν ... θύειν, *made answer (naming) the gods to whom he was to sacrifice*. θεοῖς is dat. by inverse attraction; see the note on ἄλλον, I, 4, 100. These gods were doubtless Zeus, Hermes, and Heracles. In any case Zeus was one of them; see VI, 1, §22. For the religious side of Xen.'s nature, see the Introd., §11.
37 τοῦτο: looking forward to the question; so again l. 38; cf. I, 3, 34, and the note.
λῷον = ἄμεινον; very rare in prose.
38 ἰτέον εἶναι: cf. I, 3, 53.
ὅπως ... πορευθείη: direct, πῶς ἂν ... πορευθείην; cf. I, 7, 2.
39 ἐπεὶ ... ἤρου: a shift to direct speech, as so often.
40 θυσάμενος: what is the force of θύεσθαι, as contrasted with θύειν?
42 ὁρμᾶν, *to set out on*, with cogn. acc., as ἔλθοι, above. The act. of this vb. is often intrans., like the mid.
τὴν ἄνω ὁδόν: for ἄνω, cf. I, 2, 1.
43 συνεστάθη, *was presented to*.

συμπρουθυμεῖτο μεῖναι αὐτόν, εἶπε δὲ ὅτι ἐπειδὰν τάχιστα ἡ
στρατεία λήξῃ, εὐθὺς ἀποπέμψει αὐτόν. ἐλέγετο δὲ ὁ στόλος
εἶναι εἰς Πισίδας. ἐστρατεύετο μὲν δὴ οὕτως ἐξαπατηθείς—
οὐχ ὑπὸ Προξένου· οὐ γὰρ ᾔδει τὴν ἐπὶ βασιλέα ὁρμὴν οὐδὲ
ἄλλος οὐδεὶς τῶν Ἑλλήνων πλὴν Κλεάρχου· ἐπεὶ μέντοι εἰς
Κιλικίαν ἦλθον, σαφὲς πᾶσιν ἤδη ἐδόκει εἶναι ὅτι ὁ στόλος εἴη
ἐπὶ βασιλέα. φοβούμενοι δὲ τὴν ὁδὸν καὶ ἄκοντες ὅμως οἱ
πολλοὶ δι' αἰσχύνην καὶ ἀλλήλων καὶ Κύρου συνηκολούθησαν·
ὧν εἷς καὶ Ξενοφῶν ἦν.

Ἐπεὶ δὲ ἀπορία ἦν, ἐλυπεῖτο μὲν σὺν τοῖς ἄλλοις καὶ οὐκ
ἐδύνατο καθεύδειν· μικρὸν δ' ὕπνου λαχὼν εἶδεν ὄναρ. ἔδοξεν
αὐτῷ βροντῆς γενομένης σκηπτὸς πεσεῖν εἰς τὴν πατρῴαν οἰκίαν,
καὶ ἐκ τούτου λάμπεσθαι πᾶσα. περίφοβος δ' εὐθὺς ἀνηγέρθη,
καὶ τὸ ὄναρ τῇ μὲν ἔκρινεν ἀγαθόν, ὅτι ἐν πόνοις ὢν καὶ κινδύ-
νοις φῶς μέγα ἐκ Διὸς ἰδεῖν ἔδοξε· τῇ δὲ καὶ ἐφοβεῖτο, ὅτι ἀπὸ
Διὸς μὲν βασιλέως τὸ ὄναρ ἐδόκει αὐτῷ εἶναι, κύκλῳ δὲ ἐδόκει

---

45 λήξῃ ... ἀποπέμψει: the direct form is retained in both vbs.
46 Πισίδας: cf. I, 2, 62.
ἐστρατεύετο ... ἐξαπατηθείς: retain the order.
51 ἀλλήλων ... Κύρου: obj. gens. after αἰσχύνην.
οἱ πολλοί: only Xenias and Pasion deserted (I, 4, § 7). The tone of the whole passage suggests that Xen. is defending his own course in the matter; cf. the notes on §5 of this chapter.
54 ὕπνου: partitive gen. with μικρόν. In such cases the word denoting the part stands, of course, in the acc., even if the vb. might properly take a gen.
εἶδεν ὄναρ: cf. IV, 3, § 8, for a similar occurrence. Dreams have in all ages been regarded as fraught with meaning; cf. Iliad I, 63, καὶ γάρ τ' ὄναρ ἐκ Διός ἐστιν.

ἔδοξεν αὐτῷ: explanatory asyndeton.
56 πᾶσα: note the emphatic position.
περίφοβος, in great fear. For the force of the prep., cf. περιγενέσθαι, περιεῖναι, and the phrase περὶ πολλοῦ (παντὸς) ποιεῖσθαι.
57 τῇ μὲν ... τῇ δέ, partly ... partly. The construction shifts slightly. ὅτι is causal in both clauses.
58 φῶς: not a mere variant for σκηπτός, but chosen because it commonly denotes a light of safety; so constantly in Homer.
ἀπὸ Διὸς ... βασιλέως, from Zeus as king: i. e. King Zeus suggested King Artaxerxes.
59 κύκλῳ: strongly emphatic.
60 μὴ οὐ: for the double neg., cf. I, 7, 36, and the note.
τῆς χώρας ... τῆς βασιλέως: the

λάμπεσθαι τὸ πῦρ, μὴ οὐ δύναιτο ἐκ τῆς χώρας ἐξελθεῖν τῆς βασιλέως, ἀλλ' εἴργοιτο πάντοθεν ὑπό τινων ἀποριῶν. ὁποῖόν τι μὲν δὴ ἐστὶ τὸ τοιοῦτον ὄναρ ἰδεῖν ἔξεστι σκοπεῖν ἐκ τῶν συμβάντων μετὰ τὸ ὄναρ. γίγνεται γὰρ τάδε. εὐθὺς ἐπειδὴ ἀνηγέρθη πρῶτον μὲν ἔννοια αὐτῷ ἐμπίπτει· τί κατάκειμαι; ἡ δὲ νὺξ προβαίνει· ἅμα δὲ τῇ ἡμέρᾳ εἰκὸς τοὺς πολεμίους ἥξειν. εἰ δὲ γενησόμεθα ἐπὶ βασιλεῖ, τί ἐμποδὼν μὴ οὐχὶ πάντα μὲν τὰ χαλεπώτατα ἐπιδόντας, πάντα δὲ τὰ δεινότατα παθόντας ὑβριζομένους ἀποθανεῖν; ὅπως δ' ἀμυνούμεθα οὐδεὶς παρασκευάζεται οὐδὲ ἐπιμελεῖται, ἀλλὰ κατακείμεθα ὥσπερ ἐξὸν ἡσυχίαν ἄγειν. ἐγὼ οὖν τὸν ἐκ ποίας πόλεως στρατηγὸν προσδοκῶ ταῦτα πράξειν; ποίαν δ' ἡλικίαν ἐμαυτῷ ἐλθεῖν ἀναμείνω; οὐ γὰρ ἔγωγ' ἔτι πρεσβύτερος ἔσομαι, ἐὰν τήμερον προδῶ ἐμαυτὸν τοῖς πολεμίοις.

---

formal order of the words (*cf.* I, 1, 43, and the note) suits well the gravity of the situation.

61 ὁποῖόν ... ἐστι, now what it betokens.

62 ἐκ τῶν συμβάντων: a sage reflection.

64 πρῶτον μέν: there is no ἔπειτα δέ, but ἐκ τούτου follows in l. 74.

τί κατάκειμαι: a vivid dramatic touch, quite in Homer's manner.

65 εἰκός: sc. ἐστι, which is often omitted.

66 εἰ δὲ γενησόμεθα: note the warning tone of the condition; *cf.* I, 5, 96, and the note.

ἐπὶ βασιλεῖ: *cf.* ἐπὶ τῷ ἀδελφῷ, I, 1, 15.

τί ἐμποδὼν ... ἀποθανεῖν, what is to prevent our beholding ... suffering ... and then being slain? μὴ οὐ is used, not μή alone, since the question, τί ἐμποδών, implies a neg.; see on μὴ οὐ συσπουδάζειν, II, 3, 45.

67 ἐπιδόντας: so Priam says of himself (*Iliad* XXII, 61) κακὰ πόλλ' ἐπιδόντα, having lived to see many ills.

68 ὅπως ... ἀμυνούμεθα: obj. clause after παρασκευάζεσθαι.

69 ἐξόν: *cf.* II, 5, 86, and the note.

70 ἐγὼ ... πράξειν, lit., now I, for my part, expect the general from what city to do this? ἐγώ is strongly emphasized by being placed before the interrogative word: although neither general nor captain he must act. Note that ποίας connotes quality; it is more than τίνος. What state, indeed, if not Athens?

71 ἀναμείνω: for the subjv. question, *cf.* I, 7, 37, and the note.

ἡλικίαν: Xen. was probably about thirty years old at this time; see the Introd., § 1. Note the modest tone of the whole; yet the Greeks owed their salvation to his energetic action.

Ἐκ τούτου ἀνίσταται καὶ συγκαλεῖ τοὺς Προξένου πρῶτον
λοχαγούς. ἐπεὶ δὲ συνῆλθον, ἔλεξεν. Ἐγώ, ὦ ἄνδρες λοχαγοί, οὔτε καθεύδειν δύναμαι, ὥσπερ οἶμαι οὐδ' ὑμεῖς, οὔτε κατα-
κεῖσθαι ἔτι, ὁρῶν ἐν οἵοις ἐσμέν. οἱ μὲν γὰρ πολέμιοι δῆλον
ὅτι οὐ πρότερον πρὸς ἡμᾶς τὸν πόλεμον ἐξέφηναν πρὶν ἐνόμισαν
καλῶς τὰ ἑαυτῶν παρασκευάσασθαι, ἡμῶν δ' οὐδεὶς οὐδὲν ἀντεπιμελεῖται ὅπως ὡς κάλλιστα ἀγωνιούμεθα. καὶ μὴν εἰ ὑφησόμεθα
καὶ ἐπὶ βασιλεῖ γενησόμεθα, τί οἰόμεθα πείσεσθαι; ὃς καὶ τοῦ
ὁμομητρίου ἀδελφοῦ καὶ τεθνηκότος ἤδη ἀποτεμὼν τὴν κεφαλὴν
καὶ τὴν χεῖρα ἀνεσταύρωσεν· ἡμᾶς δέ, οἷς κηδεμὼν μὲν οὐδεὶς
πάρεστιν, ἐστρατεύσαμεν δὲ ἐπ' αὐτὸν ὡς δοῦλον ἀντὶ βασιλέως
ποιήσοντες καὶ ἀποκτενοῦντες εἰ δυναίμεθα, τί ἂν οἰόμεθα παθεῖν; ἆρ' οὐκ ἂν ἐπὶ πᾶν ἔλθοι ὡς ἡμᾶς τὰ ἔσχατα αἰκισάμενος
πᾶσιν ἀνθρώποις φόβον παράσχοι τοῦ στρατεῦσαί ποτε ἐπ'

---

74 **Ἐκ τούτου**: is the asyndeton felt?

τοὺς Προξένου ... λοχαγούς: with these he was doubtless already acquainted.

76 **οἶμαι**: parenthetic; *cf.* I, 9, 79. δύνασθε is therefore to be supplied.

77 **ἐν οἵοις**, *in what straits; cf.* ἐν τοιούτοις ... πράγμασι, II, 1, 81.

δῆλον ὅτι: *cf.* I, 3, 44, and the note.

78 **πρότερον ... πρίν**: *cf.* πρόσθεν πρίν, I, 2, 12.

79 **οὐδέν**: inner obj. of ἀντεπιμελεῖται.

80 **καὶ μήν**, *and yet.* μήν is strongly adversative.

ὑφησόμεθα ... γενησόμεθα: again a warning condition.

81 **ὅς**, *a man who.* The rel. is causal; *cf.* ὅς γε, I, 6, 24.

82 **ὁμομητρίου**: this constituted the strongest tie of kinship.

καὶ ... ἤδη, *even though already dead*—*i. e.* it was wanton barbarity, although in harmony with Persian customs; *cf.* I, 10, 1.

83 **ἡμᾶς δέ**, *but as for us*, an independent acc., as the sentence stands, rather than the subj. of παθεῖν, which would properly be nom. Doubtless Xen. had in mind a trans. phrase (*e. g.* ποιεῖν αὐτόν) and shifted his thought as the sentence went on.

κηδεμὼν οὐδείς: there was no Parysatis to support their cause.

84 **δοῦλον**: *cf.* I, 7, 16.

85 **ἄν ... παθεῖν**: *cf.* I, 3, 29, and the note.

86 **ἐπὶ πᾶν ἔλθοι**, *make every effort.*

τὰ ἔσχατα: inner obj. of αἰκισάμενος.

87 **παράσχοι**: for the mood, *cf.* εἴη, II, 4, 12, and the note. That whole passage should be compared with this.

τοῦ στρατεῦσαι: obj. gen. with φόβον.

83 **ὅπως ... γενησόμεθα**: an obj. clause; despite the fact that

Book III, Chap. I 157

αὐτόν; ἀλλ' ὅπως τοι μὴ ἐπ' ἐκείνῳ γενησόμεθα πάντα ποιητέον.
19 ἐγὼ μὲν οὖν ἔστε μὲν αἱ σπονδαὶ ἦσαν οὔποτε ἐπαυόμην ἡμᾶς
μὲν οἰκτίρων, βασιλέα δὲ καὶ τοὺς σὺν αὐτῷ μακαρίζων, δια- 90
θεώμενος αὐτῶν ὅσην μὲν χώραν καὶ οἵαν ἔχοιεν, ὡς δὲ ἄφθονα
τὰ ἐπιτήδεια, ὅσους δὲ θεράποντας, ὅσα δὲ κτήνη, χρυσὸν δέ,
20 ἐσθῆτα δέ· τὰ δ' αὖ τῶν στρατιωτῶν ὁπότε ἐνθυμοίμην, ὅτι τῶν
μὲν ἀγαθῶν τούτων οὐδενὸς ἡμῖν μετείη, εἰ μὴ πριαίμεθα, ὅτου
δ' ὠνησόμεθα ᾔδειν ἔτι ὀλίγους ἔχοντας, ἄλλως δέ πως πορί- 95
ζεσθαι τὰ ἐπιτήδεια ἢ ὠνουμένους ὅρκους ἤδη κατέχοντας ἡμᾶς·
ταῦτ' οὖν λογιζόμενος ἐνίοτε τὰς σπονδὰς μᾶλλον ἐφοβούμην ἢ

ποιητέον has its own obj., πάντα.
The two together are equivalent
to a vb. of striving. *Cf.* the
similar sentence, below, § 35,
and the note.

89 ἔστε μέν: balanced by ἐπεὶ μέντοι
in l. 98. For the poetic word,
ἔστε, *cf.* I, 9, 38, and the note.

90 οἰκτίρων ... μακαρίζων: suppl.
partics. with ἐπαυόμην.

91 αὐτῶν, *in regard to them*. A
personal gen. is frequently found
with vbs. of *observing, wondering*, etc., often in connection
with the acc. of a demonstr. pron.
(*e. g.* σου ταῦτα θαυμάζω). This
acc. may be omitted and sometimes cannot easily be supplied,
so that some prefer to construe
the gen. directly with the vb.
Here the place of the acc. is
supplied by the following clauses.
Cf. III, 3, § 18.

92 χρυσὸν ... ἐσθῆτα: the omission of the exclamatory rel. is
natural at the end of the enumeration (*aye, and gold and raiment*). For ἐσθῆτα, *cf.* the note
on στολήν, I, 2, 158.

93 τὰ ... τῶν στρατιωτῶν, *the lot
of our men*, further explained by

the ὅτι-clause. This phrase precedes the temporal word for emphasis; *cf.* I, 9, 56. Observe that
the ideas expressed by οἰκτίρων
and μακαρίζων are taken up in
chiastic order; *cf.* II, 6, 5.

ὁπότε ἐνθυμοίμην: *cf.* ὁπότε βούλοιτο,
I, 2, 40, and the note. Owing to
the length of the clause, this
is resumed by ταῦτ' οὖν λογιζόμενος.

τῶν ... ἀγαθῶν τούτων: partitive
gen. with οὐδενός, which is itself
governed in the same way by
μετείη. μικρόν, l. 54, is different; see the note there.

94 εἰ μὴ πριαίμεθα: direct, ἐὰν μὴ
πριώμεθα.

ὅτου δ' ὠνησόμεθα, *wherewith to
buy*, a rel. final clause; *cf.* ὅστις
ἀπάξει, I, 3, 71, and the note.
For the gen. ὅτου, *cf.* σίγλων,
I, 5, 32, and the note.

95 ἔχοντας: indir. disc. after ᾔδειν;
κατέχοντας, after ἤδη.

ἄλλως ... πως ... ἢ ὠνουμένους,
otherwise than by purchase.

πορίζεσθαι, *from procuring*. The
infin. is governed by κατέχοντας,
a vb. of hindering.

97 ἐνίοτε: *cf.* ἔσθ' ὅτε, II, 6, 35.

νῦν τὸν πόλεμον. ἐπεὶ μέντοι ἐκεῖνοι ἔλυσαν τὰς σπονδάς, λε- 21
λύσθαι μοι δοκεῖ καὶ ἡ ἐκείνων ὕβρις καὶ ἡ ἡμετέρα ὑποψία. ἐν
100 μέσῳ γὰρ ἤδη κεῖται ταῦτα τὰ ἀγαθὰ ἆθλα ὁπότεροι ἂν ἡμῶν
ἄνδρες ἀμείνονες ὦσιν, ἀγωνοθέται δ' οἱ θεοί εἰσιν, οἳ σὺν ἡμῖν,
ὡς τὸ εἰκός, ἔσονται. οὗτοι μὲν γὰρ αὐτοὺς ἐπιωρκήκασιν· ἡμεῖς 22
δὲ πολλὰ ὁρῶντες ἀγαθὰ στερρῶς αὐτῶν ἀπειχόμεθα διὰ τοὺς
τῶν θεῶν ὅρκους· ὥστε ἐξεῖναί μοι δοκεῖ ἰέναι ἐπὶ τὸν ἀγῶνα
105 πολὺ σὺν φρονήματι μείζονι ἢ τούτοις. ἔτι δ' ἔχομεν σώματα 23
ἱκανώτερα τούτων καὶ ψύχη καὶ θάλπη καὶ πόνους φέρειν·
ἔχομεν δὲ καὶ ψυχὰς σὺν τοῖς θεοῖς ἀμείνονας· οἱ δὲ ἄνδρες καὶ
τρωτοὶ καὶ θνητοὶ μᾶλλον ἡμῶν, ἢν οἱ θεοὶ ὥσπερ τὸ πρόσθεν

---

98 ἔλυσαν ... λελύσθαι: the chiastic order gives to the second vb. an emphasis that well suits the meaning. Note, also, the force of the tense.

99 ἐν μέσῳ: in the great games of Greece the prizes were set forth in plain view. All such metaphors were easy for the Greek.

100 ἆθλα, *as prizes*, pred.

ὁπότεροι ... ὦσιν, *for whichever of us* (the two contending parties).

101 ἀγωνοθέται, *judges; cf.* the phrase ἀγῶνα ἔθηκε, I, 2, 62.

102 αὐτούς: for the acc., *cf.* θεούς, II, 4, 35, and the note.

103 τοὺς ... ὅρκους: *cf.* II, 5, 21, and the note.

104 ἐξεῖναι: *sc.* ἡμῖν, *it is permitted us.*

105 πολύ: strongly emphasized by its separation from μείζονι; *cf.* I, 5, 9.

ἢ τούτοις: agreeing in case with the omitted ἡμῖν.

ἔτι δ' ἔχομεν: μέν is omitted for euphony's sake, although ἔχομεν δέ follows.

106 τούτων, *than theirs.* For the "short comparison," *cf.* ἠλέκτρου, II, 3, 58, and the note.

ψύχη ... θάλπη: the pl. of abstract nouns is often concrete (*successive attacks of cold and heat*).

107 σὺν τοῖς θεοῖς, *with heaven's help.* The Greek shunned expressions which sounded like idle boasting.

ἀμείνονας, *braver,* not *better.*

οἱ δὲ ἄνδρες: *i. e. the enemy; cf.* c. 4. § 40, and ἀνθρώπους, IV, 2, § 7.

108 τρωτοί ... θνητοί: *i. e.* their armor is poorer and they are physically inferior. There are many flings at Persian effeminacy in Greek writers: the memory of Marathon and Salamis lived long, and Xen.'s hearers had had experience of their own to confirm it. *Cf.*, also, the words of Cyrus in I, 7, 14.

ἢν ... δίδωσιν: the apodosis implies the fut. (*we shall find them so, if*).

109 ἀλλ' ἴσως γάρ: there is no ellipsis: ἀλλ' introduces the appeal

24 νίκην ἡμῖν διδῶσιν. ἀλλ' ἴσως γὰρ καὶ ἄλλοι ταὐτὰ ἐνθυμοῦνται, πρὸς τῶν θεῶν μὴ ἀναμένωμεν ἄλλους ἐφ' ἡμᾶς ἐλθεῖν 110
παρακαλοῦντας ἐπὶ τὰ κάλλιστα ἔργα, ἀλλ' ἡμεῖς ἄρξωμεν τοῦ
ἐξορμῆσαι καὶ τοὺς ἄλλους ἐπὶ τὴν ἀρετήν· φάνητε τῶν λοχα-
25 γῶν ἄριστοι καὶ τῶν στρατηγῶν ἀξιοστρατηγότεροι. κἀγὼ δέ,
εἰ μὲν ὑμεῖς ἐθέλετε ἐξορμᾶν ἐπὶ ταῦτα, ἕπεσθαι ὑμῖν βούλομαι,
εἰ δ' ὑμεῖς τάττετ' ἐμὲ ἡγεῖσθαι, οὐδὲν προφασίζομαι τὴν ἡλικίαν, 115
ἀλλὰ καὶ ἀκμάζειν ἡγοῦμαι ἐρύκειν ἀπ' ἐμαυτοῦ τὰ κακά.

26 Ὁ μὲν ταῦτ' ἔλεξεν, οἱ δὲ ἀρχηγοὶ ἀκούσαντες ἡγεῖσθαι ἐκέλευον πάντες, πλὴν Ἀπολλωνίδης τις ἦν βοιωτιάζων τῇ φωνῇ·
οὗτος δ' εἶπεν ὅτι φλυαροίη ὅστις λέγει ἄλλως πως σωτηρίας ἂν

(μὴ ἀναμένωμεν), γάρ the subordinate clause.

110 πρὸς τῶν θεῶν: more formal, and hence more impressive than the commoner πρὸς θεῶν (II, 1, 82). For the subjv., see G. 1344; H. 866, 1; B. 585.

111 παρακαλοῦντας: fut., not pres. In pure vbs., if the final vowel of the theme is not lengthened in the fut. and aor. (contrast ἐκάλεσα with ἐποίησα), the σ of the fut. is regularly dropped, and contraction ensues (καλῶ as against ποιήσω). The same principle holds if the vowel ε is added to the theme (μαχοῦμαι, but γενήσομαι).

ἀλλ' . . . ἄρξωμεν, nay, let us be first to. With τοῦ ἐξορμῆσαι, cf. τοῦ διαβαίνειν, I, 4, 96.

112 φάνητε: note the abruptness of this effective climax.

113 τῶν στρατηγῶν: the gen. follows the comparative adj. Xen.'s audience was composed of λοχαγοί.

115 εἰ δ' ὑμεῖς: the expression of the pron. is a mark of modesty: he is ready to lead, but only if it is their wish.

οὐδὲν . . . τὴν ἡλικίαν: the inner and the outer obj. of προφασίζομαι. This passage is proof positive that Xen. was a young man at this time—probably not much over thirty; see the Introd., §1. The Greeks placed a man's prime (ἀκμή) at about forty.

116 ἐρύκειν: a poetic word. Xen. has ἀπήρυξα, V, 8, §25. The infin. is governed by ἀκμάζειν, as a vb. of ability.

117 ἀρχηγοί: another poeticism; many read λοχαγοί.

118 πλήν: cf. I, 2, 140, and the note. The new personage is introduced in an independent clause.

βοιωτιάζων τῇ φωνῇ, speaking the Boeotian dialect. He was, however, not a Boeotian, as the sequel shows.

119 φλυαροίη . . . λέγει: a rapid shift of mood in indir. disc.; the converse shift (indic. to opt.) is far less common.

ἄλλως πως . . . ἤ: cf. above, l. 95 f.

ἂν τυχεῖν: the infin. is unusual after λέγω (see the note on I, 2, 47), but, if the normal ὅτι . . . ἂν τύχοι had been used here, we

160   *Anabasis*

120 τυχεῖν ἢ βασιλέα πείσας, εἰ δύναιτο, καὶ ἅμα ἤρχετο λέγειν τὰς
ἀπορίας. ὁ μέντοι Ξενοφῶν μεταξὺ ὑπολαβὼν ἔλεξεν ὧδε. Ὦ 27
θαυμασιώτατε ἄνθρωπε, σύγε οὐδὲ ὁρῶν γιγνώσκεις οὐδὲ ἀκούων
μέμνησαι. ἐν ταὐτῷ γε μέντοι ἦσθα τούτοις ὅτε βασιλεύς, ἐπεὶ
Κῦρος ἀπέθανε, μέγα φρονήσας ἐπὶ τούτῳ πέμπων ἐκέλευε
125 παραδιδόναι τὰ ὅπλα. ἐπεὶ δὲ ἡμεῖς οὐ παραδόντες, ἀλλ' ἐξο- 28
πλισάμενοι ἐλθόντες παρεσκηνήσαμεν αὐτῷ, τί οὐκ ἐποίησε
πρέσβεις πέμπων καὶ σπονδὰς αἰτῶν καὶ παρέχων τὰ ἐπιτήδεια,
ἔστε σπονδῶν ἔτυχεν; ἐπεὶ δ' αὖ οἱ στρατηγοὶ καὶ λοχαγοί, 29
ὥσπερ δὴ σὺ κελεύεις, εἰς λόγους αὐτοῖς ἄνευ ὅπλων ἦλθον
130 πιστεύσαντες ταῖς σπονδαῖς, οὐ νῦν ἐκεῖνοι παιόμενοι, κεντού-
μενοι, ὑβριζόμενοι οὐδὲ ἀποθανεῖν οἱ τλήμονες δύνανται, καὶ
μάλ' οἶμαι ἐρῶντες τούτου; ἃ σὺ πάντα εἰδὼς τοὺς μὲν ἀμύνασθαι
κελεύοντας φλυαρεῖν φῄς, πείθειν δὲ πάλιν κελεύεις ἰόντας; ἐμοί, 30
ὦ ἄνδρες, δοκεῖ τὸν ἄνθρωπον τοῦτον μήτε προσίεσθαι εἰς ταὐτὸ

---

should have had an ill-sounding sentence. Observe the omission of the subj. of the infin. and the fact that πείσας is nom., not acc. The sentence is not general, but personal.

121 μεταξύ: sc. λέγοντα, *in the m'dst of his talk.* For ὑπολαβών, *cf.* II, 1, 77.

122 οὐδὲ ... οὐδέ, *not even ... nor.* Demosthenes (XXV, 89) cites the proverb, ὁρῶντας μὴ ὁρᾶν καὶ ἀκούοντας μὴ ἀκούειν. *Cf.*, also, Isa. vi:9 and Matt. xiii:13. Note the varied phrase in our text.

123 ἐν ταὐτῷ ... τούτοις, *present* (lit., *in the same place*) *with these men*. *Cf.* εἰς ταὐτὸ ἡμῖν, below, § 30.

ὅτε βασιλεύς: the allusion is to II, 1, §§ 7 ff.

126 τί οὐκ ἐποίησε: *cf.* ἆρ' οὐκ ἂν ἐπὶ πᾶν ἔλθοι, above, l. 86. For the events here alluded to, see II, 3, §§ 1 ff.

127 αἰτῶν ... παρέχων: the order is chiastic.

128 ἔστε: *cf.* I, 9, 38, and the note.

129 εἰς λόγους αὐτοῖς: *cf.* II, 1, §§ 25 f., and the note on I, 2, 152.

130 οὐ ... οὐδὲ ... δύνανται, *are they not ... unable even to die?* The first neg. is interrogative, the second intensive (*nonne ... ne quidem*).

παιόμενοι ... ὑβριζόμενοι: the asyndeton well marks the speaker's indignation. Observe that Xen. could not have known these facts at the time this speech is assumed to have been made. See the Introd., § 40.

132 ἐρῶντες τούτου: *i. e.* τοῦ ἀποθανεῖν, a strong phrase; *cf.* the note on ἔρως, II, 5, 87. The gen. is used as with ἐπιθυμῶ (*e. g.* IV, 1, § 14).

133 ἐμοί, ... δοκεῖ, *I move.*

134 μήτε ... τε: *cf.* II, 2, 38, and the note.

ἡμῖν αὐτοῖς ἀφελομένους τε τὴν λοχαγίαν σκεύη ἀναθέντας ὡς 135
τοιούτῳ χρῆσθαι. οὗτος γὰρ καὶ τὴν πατρίδα καταισχύνει καὶ
πᾶσαν τὴν Ἑλλάδα, ὅτι Ἕλλην ὢν τοιοῦτός ἐστιν. ἐντεῦθεν
ὑπολαβὼν Ἀγασίας Στυμφάλιος εἶπεν· Ἀλλὰ τούτῳ γε οὔτε
τῆς Βοιωτίας προσήκει οὐδὲν οὔτε τῆς Ἑλλάδος παντάπασιν,
ἐπεὶ ἐγὼ αὐτὸν εἶδον ὥσπερ Λυδὸν ἀμφότερα τὰ ὦτα τετρυ- 140
πημένον. καὶ εἶχεν οὕτως. τοῦτον μὲν οὖν ἀπήλασαν.

Οἱ δὲ ἄλλοι παρὰ τὰς τάξεις ἰόντες ὅπου μὲν στρατηγὸς
σῶος εἴη τὸν στρατηγὸν παρεκάλουν, ὁπόθεν δὲ οἴχοιτο τὸν
ὑποστράτηγον, ὅπου δ᾽ αὖ λοχαγὸς σῶος εἴη τὸν λοχαγόν.
ἐπεὶ δὲ πάντες συνῆλθον, εἰς τὸ πρόσθεν τῶν ὅπλων ἐκαθέ- 145
ζοντο· καὶ ἐγένοντο οἱ συνελθόντες στρατηγοὶ καὶ λοχαγοὶ
ἀμφὶ τοὺς ἑκατόν. ὅτε δὲ ταῦτα ἦν σχεδὸν μέσαι ἦσαν νύκτες.
ἐνταῦθα Ἱερώνυμος Ἠλεῖος πρεσβύτατος ὢν τῶν Προξένου
λοχαγῶν ἤρχετο λέγειν ὧδε. Ἡμῖν, ὦ ἄνδρες στρατηγοὶ καὶ
λοχαγοί, ὁρῶσι τὰ παρόντα ἔδοξε καὶ αὐτοῖς συνελθεῖν καὶ ὑμᾶς 150
παρακαλέσαι, ὅπως βουλευσαίμεθα εἴ τι δυναίμεθα ἀγαθόν.
λέξον δ᾽, ἔφη, καὶ σύ, ὦ Ξενοφῶν, ἅπερ καὶ πρὸς ἡμᾶς.

---

135 ἀφελομένους . . . χρῆσθαι, to
deprive him of his command
and packing our baggage on
him to use him in that capacity
(ὡς σκευοφόρῳ). The chiastic order emphasizes the contrast
between λοχαγίαν and σκεύη.

136 τὴν πατρίδα: assuming him to
be a Boeotian.

καταισχύνει: the prep. is intensive.

137 ἐντεῦθεν: cf. ἐκ τούτου, l. 74.

138 τούτῳ . . . προσήκει: cf. τῶν
μὲν . . . μετείη, l. 93.

140 ὥσπερ Λυδόν: gentile names
of barbarian races were often
used by the Greeks as synonymous with slave, but this word
has here an especial force. The
effeminacy of the Lydians was
proverbial; cf. the note on Λυδίᾳ

ἀγορᾷ, I, 5, 31. To wear earrings
marked a man as an Asiatic
(Juvenal I, 104).

τὰ ὦτα: for the case, cf. the note
on II, 6, 2.

143 εἴη . . . οἴχοιτο: for the mood,
see the note on ὅστις ἀφικνεῖτο,
I, 1, 18.

145 εἰς . . . ὅπλων, in front of. For
the acc. (rest following motion),
see the note on I, 2, 78.

146 ἐγένοντο: cf. I, 2, 58.

147 ἀμφὶ τοὺς ἑκατόν: cf. I, 2, 59,
and the note.

ὅτε . . . ἦσαν: cf. I, 10, 60.

μέσαι . . . νύκτες: cf. I, 7, 4, and
the note.

148 πρεσβύτατος: see the note on
Κλεάνωρ, II, 1, 51.

150 καὶ αὐτοῖς . . . καί, ourselves
to come together and . . . The

Ἐκ τούτου λέγει τάδε Ξενοφῶν. Ἀλλὰ ταῦτα μὲν δὴ πάντες ἐπιστάμεθα ὅτι βασιλεὺς καὶ Τισσαφέρνης οὓς μὲν ἐδυνήθησαν συνειλήφασιν ἡμῶν, τοῖς δ' ἄλλοις δῆλον ὅτι ἐπιβουλεύουσιν, ὡς ἢν δύνωνται ἀπολέσωσιν. ἡμῖν δέ γε οἶμαι πάντα ποιητέα ὡς μήποτε ἐπὶ τοῖς βαρβάροις γενώμεθα, ἀλλὰ μᾶλλον ἐκεῖνοι ἐφ' ἡμῖν. εὖ τοίνυν ἐπίστασθε ὅτι ὑμεῖς τοσοῦτοι ὄντες ὅσοι νῦν συνεληλύθατε μέγιστον ἔχετε καιρόν. οἱ γὰρ στρατιῶται οὗτοι πάντες πρὸς ὑμᾶς βλέπουσι, κἂν μὲν ὑμᾶς ὁρῶσιν ἀθύμους, πάντες κακοὶ ἔσονται, ἂν δὲ ὑμεῖς αὐτοί τε παρασκευαζόμενοι φανεροὶ ἦτε ἐπὶ τοὺς πολεμίους καὶ τοὺς ἄλλους παρακαλῆτε, εὖ ἴστε ὅτι ἕψονται ὑμῖν καὶ πειράσονται μιμεῖσθαι. ἴσως δέ τοι καὶ δίκαιόν ἐστιν ὑμᾶς διαφέρειν τι τούτων. ὑμεῖς γάρ ἐστε στρατηγοί, ὑμεῖς ταξίαρχοι καὶ λοχαγοί· καὶ ὅτε εἰρήνη ἦν ὑμεῖς καὶ χρήμασι καὶ τιμαῖς τούτων ἐπλεονεκτεῖτε· καὶ νῦν τοίνυν ἐπεὶ πόλεμός ἐστιν ἀξιοῦν δεῖ ὑμᾶς αὐτοὺς ἀμείνους τε τοῦ πλήθους εἶναι καὶ προβουλεύειν

---

intensive may be of any person; here it agrees with ἡμῖν.
152 ἅπερ καί: see the note on I, 3, 31.
153 Ἀλλά: cf. I, 7, 62.
155 ἡμῶν: partitive gen. with οὕς.
δῆλον ὅτι: cf. I, 3, 44, and the note.
156 ἡμῖν δέ γε: the contrast is, of course, with βασιλεὺς καὶ Τισσ., although formally δέ balances ταῦτα μέν.
157 πάντα ποιητέα: how different from πάντα ποιητέον, l. 88?
ὡς ... γενώμεθα: in view of the parallel sentence in § 18 (which cannot be final), this is best regarded as an obj. clause of an irregular type; cf. the note on ὡς εἴησαν, I, 1, 20 f.
158 ὑμεῖς: this pron. is expressed ten times in this and the following sections.
τοσοῦτοι ... ὅσοι: cf. II, 1, 80.

159 καιρόν, *opportunity*.
161 αὐτοί τε: cf. αὐτοῖς, above, l. 150, and the note.
162 παρασκευαζόμενοι: cf. the note on ἀνιώμενος, I, 2, 70.
163 εὖ ἴστε ὅτι: inserted for emphasis; not a mere adv., as δῆλον ὅτι.
164 διαφέρειν τι, *to excel in a measure*. τι is the inner obj.; cf. οὐδὲν διέφερεν, II, 3, 58 f.
165 τούτων: thrice in this section after a word implying comparison.
ὑμεῖς γάρ ... ὑμεῖς ... ὑμεῖς: for the emphatic repetition, cf. Arnold's *Rugby Chapel*,

We were weary, and we
Fearful, and we in our march
Fain to drop down and to die.

166 χρήμασι: *i. e.* higher pay.
167 ἀξιοῦν δεῖ, *it is right to demand that.*

Book III, Chap. I 163

38 τούτων καὶ προπονεῖν, ἤν που δέῃ. καὶ νῦν πρῶτον μὲν οἴομαι
ἂν ὑμᾶς μέγα ὠφελῆσαι τὸ στράτευμα, εἰ ἐπιμεληθείητε ὅπως 170
ἀντὶ τῶν ἀπολωλότων ὡς τάχιστα στρατηγοὶ καὶ λοχαγοὶ ἀντικατασταθῶσιν. ἄνευ γὰρ ἀρχόντων οὐδὲν ἂν οὔτε καλὸν οὔτε
ἀγαθὸν γένοιτο ὡς μὲν συνελόντι εἰπεῖν οὐδαμοῦ, ἐν δὲ δὴ τοῖς
πολεμικοῖς παντάπασιν. ἡ μὲν γὰρ εὐταξία σῴζειν δοκεῖ, ἡ
39 δὲ ἀταξία πολλοὺς ἤδη ἀπολώλεκεν. ἐπειδὰν δὲ καταστή- 175
σησθε τοὺς ἄρχοντας ὅσους δεῖ, ἢν καὶ τοὺς ἄλλους στρατιώτας
συλλέγητε καὶ παραθαρρύνητε, οἶμαι ἂν ὑμᾶς πάνυ ἐν καιρῷ
40 ποιῆσαι. νῦν γὰρ ἴσως καὶ ὑμεῖς αἰσθάνεσθε ὡς ἀθύμως μὲν
ἦλθον ἐπὶ τὰ ὅπλα, ἀθύμως δὲ πρὸς τὰς φυλακάς· ὥστε οὕτω
γ' ἐχόντων οὐκ οἶδα ὅ,τι ἄν τις χρήσαιτο αὐτοῖς εἴτε νυκτὸς δέοι 180
41 εἴτε καὶ ἡμέρας. ἢν δέ τις αὐτῶν τρέψῃ τὰς γνώμας, ὡς μὴ

---

168 αὐτούς: as αὐτοῖς, 1. 150.

προβουλεύειν ... προπονεῖν: force of the prep.? Plan and labor *for*, or *in a higher degree than?* Probably the former.

169 πρῶτον μέν: balanced by ἐπειδὰν δέ, at the beginning of § 39.

οἴομαι ἄν: for the order, *cf.* I, 3, 29. and the note. The type of condition chosen suits Xen.'s advisory tone. He has no authority.

170 ὅπως ... ἀντικατασταθῶσιν: again the subjv. in an obj. clause, but this time with the normal ὅπως, not ὡς.

172 οὐδὲν ἄν: ἄν is often expressed with the neg. (the emphatic word), even though far removed from its vb.

173 ὡς ... εἰπεῖν, *in a word*. For the dat., *cf.* G. 1172, 2; H. 771b; B. 382; for the infin., G. 1534; H. 956; B. 642, 1. The phrase modifies the strong word οὐδαμοῦ.

ἐν δὲ δή: the specific after the general; *cf.* I, 3, 65.

174 εὐταξία ... ἀταξία: note the rhetorical tone: anaphora with paronomasia.

175 ἀπολώλεκεν: the empiric (gnomic) perf., an appeal to experience; see G. 1295; H. 824b; Gildersleeve, *Syntax*, 257.

ἐπειδὰν ... καταστήσησθε, *when you shall have appointed* (see the note on II, 4, 15). After this subjv. the condit. clause has naturally the corresponding type, yet the apodosis is again in the ideal form.

177 πάνυ ἐν καιρῷ, *at a very opportune time*.

179 ἀθύμως δέ: with the omission of ὡς, *cf.* χρυσὸν ... ἐσθῆτα, c. 1. 92 f.

οὕτω γ' ἐχόντων (*sc.* αὐτῶν), *while they are thus minded*.

180 ὅ,τι ... αὐτοῖς, *what use any one could make of them. Cf.* I, 3, 92 f.

νυκτὸς ... ἡμέρας: *cf.* II, 6, 27.

181 αὐτῶν: with γνώμας, not with τις.

τοῦτο μόνον ἐννοῶνται τί πείσονται ἀλλὰ καὶ τί ποιήσουσι,
πολὺ εὐθυμότεροι ἔσονται. ἐπίστασθε γὰρ δὴ ὅτι οὔτε πλῆθός 42
ἐστιν οὔτε ἰσχὺς ἡ ἐν τῷ πολέμῳ τὰς νίκας ποιοῦσα, ἀλλ'
185 ὁπότεροι ἂν σὺν τοῖς θεοῖς ταῖς ψυχαῖς ἐρρωμενέστεροι ἴωσιν
ἐπὶ τοὺς πολεμίους, τούτους ὡς ἐπὶ τὸ πολὺ οἱ ἀντίοι οὐ
δέχονται. ἐντεθύμημαι δ' ἔγωγε, ὦ ἄνδρες, καὶ τοῦτο ὅτι 43
ὁπόσοι μὲν μαστεύουσι ζῆν ἐκ παντὸς τρόπου ἐν τοῖς πολεμικοῖς, οὗτοι μὲν κακῶς τε καὶ αἰσχρῶς ὡς ἐπὶ τὸ πολὺ ἀποθνή-
190 σκουσιν, ὁπόσοι δὲ τὸν μὲν θάνατον ἐγνώκασι πᾶσι κοινὸν εἶναι
καὶ ἀναγκαῖον ἀνθρώποις, περὶ δὲ τοῦ καλῶς ἀποθνήσκειν
ἀγωνίζονται, τούτους ὁρῶ μᾶλλόν πως εἰς τὸ γῆρας ἀφικνουμένους καὶ ἕως ἂν ζῶσιν εὐδαιμονέστερον διάγοντας. ἃ καὶ 44
ἡμᾶς δεῖ νῦν καταμαθόντας, ἐν τοιούτῳ γὰρ καιρῷ ἐσμεν,
195 αὐτούς τε ἄνδρας ἀγαθοὺς εἶναι καὶ τοὺς ἄλλους παρακαλεῖν.
ὃ μὲν ταῦτα εἰπὼν ἐπαύσατο. 45

Μετὰ δὲ τοῦτον εἶπε Χειρίσοφος· Ἀλλὰ πρόσθεν μέν, ὦ
Ξενοφῶν, τοσοῦτον μόνον σε ἐγίγνωσκον ὅσον ἤκουον Ἀθηναῖον
εἶναι, νῦν δὲ καὶ ἐπαινῶ σε ἐφ' οἷς λέγεις τε καὶ πράττεις καὶ
200 βουλοίμην ἂν ὅτι πλείστους εἶναι τοιούτους· κοινὸν γὰρ ἂν εἴη
τὸ ἀγαθόν. καὶ νῦν, ἔφη, μὴ μέλλωμεν, ὦ ἄνδρες, ἀλλ' ἀπελ- 46
θόντες ἤδη αἱρεῖσθε οἱ δεόμενοι ἄρχοντας, καὶ ἑλόμενοι ἥκετε

---

184 ἡ... ποιοῦσα, that which
brings about. Cf. c. 2. 96. Here
the partic. is attracted from the
abstract neut. to the gender of
ἰσχύς.

185 ὁπότεροι ἂν... ἴωσιν: cf. l. 100.
Note the position of the rel.
clause, resumed by τούτους, below.

σὺν τοῖς θεοῖς: cf. l. 107, and the
note.

186 ὡς ἐπὶ τὸ πολύ, for the most
part; cf. below, l. 189.

187 τοῦτο ὅτι: in this use τοῦτο
regularly looks forward; cf. I, 7,
36, and the note.

188 μαστεύουσι: a poetic word,
used several times by Xen.

ἐκ παντὸς τρόπου, at all hazards,
by hook or crook.

189 κακῶς... αἰσχρῶς: the words
go naturally together, as do καλός
and ἀγαθός.

192 τούτους ὁρῶ... ἀφικνουμένους:
a more effective form of statement than οὗτοι δὲ... ἀφικνοῦνται.

195 αὐτούς: cf. αὐτοῖς, l. 150.

198 τοσοῦτον... ὅσον, to this extent only, that.

ἤκουον... εἶναι: with the infin.
ἀκούω denotes mere hearsay.

201 μὴ μέλλωμεν: cf. μὴ ἀναμένωμεν,
l. 110.

202 αἱρεῖσθε... ἥκετε: imv., not
indic. The shift to the second

εἰς τὸ μέσον τοῦ στρατοπέδου καὶ τοὺς αἱρεθέντας ἄγετε· ἔπειτ᾽ ἐκεῖ συγκαλοῦμεν τοὺς ἄλλους στρατιώτας. παρέστω δ᾽ ἡμῖν, ἔφη, καὶ Τολμίδης ὁ κῆρυξ. καὶ ἅμα ταῦτ᾽ εἰπὼν ἀνέστη, ὡς μὴ μέλλοιτο ἀλλὰ περαίνοιτο τὰ δέοντα. ἐκ τούτου ᾑρέθησαν ἄρχοντες ἀντὶ μὲν Κλεάρχου Τιμασίων Δαρδανεύς, ἀντὶ δὲ Σωκράτους Ξανθικλῆς Ἀχαιός, ἀντὶ δὲ Ἀγίου Κλεάνωρ ὁ Ὀρχομένιος, ἀντὶ δὲ Μένωνος Φιλήσιος Ἀχαιός, ἀντὶ δὲ Προξένου Ξενοφῶν Ἀθηναῖος.

II. Ἐπεὶ δὲ ᾕρηντο, ἡμέρα τε σχεδὸν ὑπέφαινε καὶ εἰς τὸ μέσον ἧκον οἱ ἄρχοντες, καὶ ἔδοξεν αὐτοῖς προφυλακὰς καταστήσαντας συγκαλεῖν τοὺς στρατιώτας. ἐπεὶ δὲ καὶ οἱ ἄλλοι στρατιῶται συνῆλθον, ἀνέστη πρῶτος μὲν Χειρίσοφος ὁ Λακεδαιμόνιος καὶ ἔλεξεν ὧδε. Ἄνδρες στρατιῶται, χαλεπὰ μὲν τὰ παρόντα, ὁπότε ἀνδρῶν στρατηγῶν τοιούτων στερόμεθα καὶ

---

pers. is natural; Chirisophus is a general already.

οἱ δεόμενοι, *you who lack them.*

204 συγκαλοῦμεν: fut.; *cf.* the note on c. 1. 111.

205 Τολμίδης: *cf.* II, 2, 88.

ὡς μὴ μέλλοιτο, *that there might be no delay.* Strictly the vb. is pass. with τὰ δέοντα as its subj. —a rare use.

207 Δαρδανεύς: Dardanus, a city in the Troad; *cf.* map. Timasion had served under Clearchus, V, 6, § 24.

208 Κλεάνωρ: see the Introd., § 38. As he was already a general (although not mentioned in connection with the mustering of the army in book I; (see, however, the note on Σοφαίνετος, I, 2, 56), he seems to have had the troops of Agias added to his own. Observe the art. before Ὀρχομένιος; Cleanor was well known.

209 Φιλήσιος: mentioned in V, 3, § 1 as being, with Sophaenetus, πρεσβύτατος.

210 Ξενοφῶν: we are prepared for his election after the events of this night.

CHAPTER II.

1 ᾕρηντο: plpf. again; *cf.* c. 1. 4, and the note.

ὑπέφαινε, for the force of the prep., *cf.* ὑπομαλακιζομένους, II, 1, 72.

2 προφυλακάς: collective, but προφύλακας (II, 3, 4) individual.

καταστήσαντας: for acc. after the dat., *cf.* note on λαβόντι, I, 2, 4.

4 Χειρίσοφος: see the Introd., § 38. From now on he and Xen. eclipse all the others. Remember that Chirisophus held a commission from Sparta, then the leading state in Greece. πρῶτον μέν is balanced by ἐπὶ τούτῳ, in l. 13.

5 Ἄνδρες στρατιῶται: *cf.* I, 3, 11. The omission of ὦ makes the address less formal.

6 ὁπότε: *seeing that.*

ἀνδρῶν στρατηγῶν: apposition.

στερόμεθα: a perf. in sense, but with

λοχαγῶν καὶ στρατιωτῶν, πρὸς δ᾽ ἔτι καὶ οἱ ἀμφὶ Ἀριαῖον οἱ πρόσθεν σύμμαχοι ὄντες προδεδώκασιν ἡμᾶς· ὅμως δὲ δεῖ ἐκ τῶν παρόντων ἄνδρας ἀγαθοὺς τελέθειν καὶ μὴ ὑφίεσθαι, ἀλλὰ πειρᾶσθαι ὅπως ἢν μὲν δυνώμεθα καλῶς νικῶντες σῳζώμεθα· εἰ δὲ μή, ἀλλὰ καλῶς γε ἀποθνῄσκωμεν, ὑποχείριοι δὲ μηδέποτε γενώμεθα ζῶντες τοῖς πολεμίοις. οἴομαι γὰρ ἂν ἡμᾶς τοιαῦτα παθεῖν οἷα τοὺς ἐχθροὺς οἱ θεοὶ ποιήσειαν. ἐπὶ τούτῳ Κλεάνωρ ὁ Ὀρχομένιος ἀνέστη καὶ ἔλεξεν ὧδε. Ἀλλ᾽ ὁρᾶτε μέν, ὦ ἄνδρες, τὴν βασιλέως ἐπιορκίαν καὶ ἀσέβειαν, ὁρᾶτε δὲ τὴν Τισσαφέρνους ἀπιστίαν, ὅστις λέγων ὡς γείτων τε εἴη τῆς Ἑλλάδος καὶ περὶ πλείστου ἂν ποιήσαιτο σῶσαι ἡμᾶς, καὶ ἐπὶ τούτοις αὐτὸς ὀμόσας ἡμῖν, αὐτὸς δεξιὰς δούς, αὐτὸς ἐξαπατήσας συνέλαβε τοὺς στρατηγούς, καὶ οὐδὲ Δία ξένιον ᾐδέσθη, ἀλλὰ Κλεάρχῳ καὶ ὁμοτράπεζος γενόμενος αὐτοῖς τούτοις ἐξαπατήσας

---

vbs. of depriving the durative tenses prevail.

7 **πρὸς δ᾽ ἔτι**, *and furthermore*. The prep. is a mere adv.

9 **τελέθειν**: poetic for γίγνεσθαι. For subj. supply ἡμᾶς.

10 **ὅπως ... σῳζώμεθα**: obj. clause, instead of another infin.

11 **εἰ δὲ μή**: *cf*. II, 2, 6, and the note. The phrase generally, as here, introduces the unfavorable alternative.

ἀλλὰ ... γε, *yet at any rate*.

ἀποθνῄσκωμεν ... γενώμεθα: best regarded as governed by ὅπως, like σῳζώμεθα, above. The alternative is to regard them as hortative (*cf. ἀναμένωμεν*, above, c. 1. 110).

ὑποχείριοι ... ζῶντες: both strongly emphasized by their position.

13 **ποιήσειαν**: a wish; see G. 1507; H. 870; B. 587. Observe that in the imprecation the speaker uses ἐχθρούς, not πολεμίους; see the note on I, 3, 31.

Κλεάνωρ: with the speech, *cf*. Cleanor's words in II, 5, § 39.

16 **ὅστις**, *a man who*. ὅστις is frequently used to characterize.

λέγων: the reference is to the speech of Tiss. in II, 3, §§ 18 ff.

εἴη ... ἂν ποιήσαιτο: direct, εἰμι ... ἂν ποιησαίμην. The former vb. states a fact, the latter is hypothetical. [*this*.

17 **ἐπὶ τούτοις**, *in confirmation of*

18 **αὐτός**: note the indignant repetition of this word and the asyndeton.

19 **ᾐδέσθη**: *cf*. αἰδεσθείς, below, l. 24. The vb. is far stronger than αἰσχύνομαι (*cf.* II, 5, 151).

20 **ὁμοτράπεζος γενόμενος**: see II, 5, § 27.

αὐτοῖς τούτοις, *by these very means*. The pl. embraces the various details mentioned.

21 **Ἀριαῖος δὲ ... καὶ οὗτος**, *and Ariaeus ... he too*. For the facts alluded to, see II, 1, § 4, and II, 2, §§ 8 ff.

τοὺς ἄνδρας ἀπολώλεκεν. Ἀριαῖος δέ, ὃν ἡμεῖς ἠθέλομεν βασιλέα καθιστάναι, καὶ ἐδώκαμεν καὶ ἐλάβομεν πιστὰ μὴ προδώσειν ἀλλήλους, καὶ οὗτος οὔτε τοὺς θεοὺς δείσας οὔτε Κῦρον τεθνηκότα αἰδεσθείς, τιμώμενος μάλιστα ὑπὸ Κύρου ζῶντος νῦν πρὸς τοὺς ἐκείνου ἐχθίστους ἀποστὰς ἡμᾶς τοὺς Κύρου φίλους κακῶς ποιεῖν πειρᾶται. ἀλλὰ τούτους μὲν οἱ θεοὶ ἀποτείσαιντο· ἡμᾶς δὲ δεῖ ταῦτα ὁρῶντας μήποτε ἐξαπατηθῆναι ἔτι ὑπὸ τούτων, ἀλλὰ μαχομένους ὡς ἂν δυνώμεθα κράτιστα τοῦτο ὅ,τι ἂν δοκῇ τοῖς θεοῖς πάσχειν.

Ἐκ τούτου Ξενοφῶν ἀνίσταται ἐσταλμένος ἐπὶ πόλεμον ὡς ἐδύνατο κάλλιστα, νομίζων, εἴτε νίκην διδοῖεν οἱ θεοί, τὸν κάλλιστον κόσμον τῷ νικᾶν πρέπειν, εἴτε τελευτᾶν δέοι, ὀρθῶς ἔχειν τῶν καλλίστων ἑαυτὸν ἀξιώσαντα ἐν τούτοις τῆς τελευτῆς τυγχάνειν· τοῦ λόγου δὴ ἤρχετο ὧδε. Τὴν μὲν τῶν βαρβάρων ἐπιορκίαν τε καὶ ἀπιστίαν λέγει μὲν Κλεάνωρ, ἐπίστασθε δὲ καὶ ὑμεῖς οἶμαι. εἰ μὲν οὖν βουλόμεθα πάλιν αὐτοῖς διὰ φιλίας

---

22 ἐδώκαμεν: the rel. is not re-expressed in a different case; cf. c. 1. 24. Pl. forms, like ἐδώκαμεν, are rare; G. 670; H. 432; B. 205.

μὴ προδώσειν: after ἐλάβομεν πιστά; cf. II, 3, 108, and the note.

23 Κῦρον ... Κύρου ... Κύρου: note the pathetic repetition.

25 ἐχθίστους: the adj., although superlative, is felt as a noun; hence the gen. ἐκείνου. Somewhat similar is τῆς αὐτῶν πολεμίας χώρας, IV, 7, § 19.

26 ἀποτείσαιντο: another imprecation. Note the force of the prep. (*as is their due*).

28 τοῦτο ὅ,τι: ordinarily in such phrases τοῦτο is not expressed unless it follows the rel.

30 Ἐκ τούτου ... ἀνίσταται: note the asyndeton and the graphic force of the pres.

ἐσταλμένος, *arrayed*. Xen. wishes to make an impression, and he knows that his appearance will count for much.

32 ὀρθῶς ἔχειν, *that it was right*.

33 ἀξιώσαντα: the context supplies the pronominal subj.

34 τοῦ λόγου δή, *his speech*, contrasted with his action just mentioned. This speech is worthy of a close rhetorical study.

Τὴν μέν: μέν dismisses the topic and paves the way for another; there is no balancing δέ. Observe that the art. is expressed but once; the two nouns form one idea.

36 αὐτοῖς ... ἰέναι, *to be on terms of friendship with them*. Cf. below, διὰ παντὸς πολέμου ἰέναι, be on terms of absolute hostility. For the dat., cf. I, 2, 152, and the note.

ἰέναι, ἀνάγκη ἡμᾶς πολλὴν ἀθυμίαν ἔχειν, ὁρῶντας καὶ τοὺς στρατηγούς, οἳ διὰ πίστεως αὐτοῖς ἑαυτοὺς ἐνεχείρισαν, οἷα πεπόνθασιν· εἰ μέντοι διανοούμεθα σὺν τοῖς ὅπλοις ὧν τε 40 πεποιήκασι δίκην ἐπιθεῖναι αὐτοῖς καὶ τὸ λοιπὸν διὰ παντὸς πολέμου αὐτοῖς ἰέναι, σὺν τοῖς θεοῖς πολλαὶ ἡμῖν καὶ καλαὶ ἐλπίδες εἰσὶ σωτηρίας.

Τοῦτο δὲ λέγοντος αὐτοῦ πτάρνυταί τις· ἀκούσαντες δ' οἱ 9 στρατιῶται πάντες μιᾷ ὁρμῇ προσεκύνησαν τὸν θεόν, καὶ ὁ 45 Ξενοφῶν εἶπε· Δοκεῖ μοι, ὦ ἄνδρες, ἐπεὶ περὶ σωτηρίας ἡμῶν λεγόντων οἰωνὸς τοῦ Διὸς τοῦ σωτῆρος ἐφάνη, εὔξασθαι τῷ θεῷ τούτῳ θύσειν σωτήρια ὅπου ἂν πρῶτον εἰς φιλίαν χώραν ἀφικώμεθα, συνεπεύξασθαι δὲ καὶ τοῖς ἄλλοις θεοῖς θύσειν κατὰ δύναμιν. καὶ ὅτῳ δοκεῖ ταῦτ', ἔφη, ἀνατεινάτω τὴν χεῖρα. καὶ 50 ἀνέτειναν ἅπαντες. ἐκ τούτου ηὔξαντο καὶ ἐπαιάνισαν. ἐπεὶ δὲ τὰ τῶν θεῶν καλῶς εἶχεν, ἤρχετο πάλιν ὧδε.

Ἐτύγχανον λέγων ὅτι πολλαὶ καὶ καλαὶ ἐλπίδες ἡμῖν εἶεν 10 σωτηρίας. πρῶτον μὲν γὰρ ἡμεῖς μὲν ἐμπεδοῦμεν τοὺς τῶν θεῶν ὅρκους, οἱ δὲ πολέμιοι ἐπιωρκήκασί τε καὶ τὰς σπονδὰς 55 παρὰ τοὺς ὅρκους λελύκασιν. οὕτω δ' ἐχόντων εἰκὸς τοῖς μὲν

---

37 τοὺς στρατηγούς: prolepsis.
39 ὧν: *i. e.* τούτων ἅ; *cf.* I, 3, 20, and the note.
40 τὸ λοιπόν: *cf.* II, 2, 23, and the note.
41 πολλαί ... καὶ καλαί: *cf.* πολλὰ καὶ ἀμήχανα, II, 3, 70 f.
43 πτάρνυται: in antiquity (Hom. *Od.* 17. 545) the sneeze was commonly regarded as an omen (so still in many countries). Here the omen is favorable, since it accompanies mention of σωτηρία. So Xen. himself regards it as sent by Zeus Soter.
44 προσεκύνησαν: *cf.* I, 6, 60, although here it bears the religious sense, *worshipped*.
τὸν θεόν: *i. e.* the god who sent the omen.

46 οἰωνός, *omen*, a common use, see the vocab.
47 θύσειν σωτήρια, *to make thank-offerings for safety. Cf.* I, 2, 62, and the note. The fut. infin. follows εὔχεσθαι, as it follows vbs. of promising.
ὅπου ἄν ... ἀφικώμεθα: this vow was performed at Trapezus, IV, 8, § 25.
48 συνεπεύξασθαι: note the force of both preps., *to make at the same time an additional vow*.
49 ἀνατεινάτω: Greek popular assemblies regularly voted by a show of hands.
53 τοὺς ... ὅρκους: *cf.* II, 5, 21, and the note.
55 οὕτω δ' ἐχόντων, *since this is so. Cf.* c. 1. 141.

Book III, Chap. II

πολεμίοις ἐναντίους εἶναι τοὺς θεούς, ἡμῖν δὲ συμμάχους, οἵπερ ἱκανοί εἰσι καὶ τοὺς μεγάλους ταχὺ μικροὺς ποιεῖν καὶ τοὺς μικροὺς κἂν ἐν δεινοῖς ὦσι σῴζειν εὐπετῶς, ὅταν βούλωνται. 11 ἔπειτα δὲ ἀναμνήσω γὰρ ὑμᾶς καὶ τοὺς τῶν προγόνων τῶν ἡμετέρων κινδύνους, ἵνα εἰδῆτε ὡς ἀγαθοῖς τε ὑμῖν προσήκει εἶναι σῴζονταί τε σὺν τοῖς θεοῖς καὶ ἐκ πάνυ δεινῶν οἱ ἀγαθοί. ἐλθόντων μὲν γὰρ Περσῶν καὶ τῶν σὺν αὐτοῖς παμπληθεῖ στόλῳ ὡς ἀφανιούντων τὰς Ἀθήνας, ὑποστῆναι αὐτοὶ Ἀθη- 12 ναῖοι τολμήσαντες ἐνίκησαν αὐτούς. καὶ εὐξάμενοι τῇ Ἀρτέμιδι ὁπόσους κατακάνοιεν τῶν πολεμίων τοσαύτας χιμαίρας καταθύσειν τῇ θεῷ, ἐπεὶ οὐκ εἶχον ἱκανὰς εὑρεῖν, ἔδοξεν αὐτοῖς 13 κατ' ἐνιαυτὸν πεντακοσίας θύειν, καὶ ἔτι νῦν ἀποθύουσιν. ἔπειτα ὅτε Ξέρξης ὕστερον ἀγείρας τὴν ἀνάριθμητον στρατιὰν ἦλθεν ἐπὶ

---

57 τοὺς μεγάλους: for the thought, see Luke i:52, and, in general, the words of Clearchus, II, 5, § 7.
58 κἂν: *i. e.* καὶ ἐάν, *even if.*
59 ἔπειτα ... γάρ: with the whole *cf.* II, 5, 44 f., and the note. We may render by omitting γάρ, and treating ἀναμνήσω as the principal vb. By this long parenthesis the sequence is interrupted and the speaker goes on with ἐλθόντων μὲν γάρ.
60 ἀγαθοῖς: the pred. adj. takes the case of ὑμῖν. προσήκει may also take the acc. and infin. (below l. 80).
62 ἐλθόντων μέν: balanced by ἔπειτα ὅτε, below, l. 67.
παμπληθεῖ στόλῳ: for the dat., *cf.* στρατεύματι, I, 7, 66, and the note.
63 ὡς ἀφανιούντων, *to blot out of existence*. *Cf.* ὡς ἀποκτενῶν, I, 1, 12.
αὐτοί, *by themselves*; *cf.* I, 8, 44, and the note. As a matter of fact Athens had the support of a thousand Plataeans.

64 ἐνίκησαν: *i. e.* at Marathon, 490 B.C.
εὐξάμενοι ... ἔδοξεν αὐτοῖς, *having vowed ... they resolved*. The nom. abs. is not uncommon; ἔδοξεν αὐτοῖς is equivalent to a pers. vb.
65 τοσαύτας χιμαίρας: according to the scholiast on Aristophanes' *Knights*, 657, the vow was originally to sacrifice heifers, but because of the large number (Herodotus VI, 117 states that 6,400 of the barbarians were slain) an annual sacrifice of 500 she-goats was substituted.
67 ἀποθύουσιν: the prep. would naturally mean that the debt had not yet been paid in full (see on ἀπέπεμπε, I, 1, 41). The number 6,400, however, would have been reached in thirteen years, so that we must assume that an annual sacrifice was instituted. It appears to have been continued for centuries.
68 τὴν ... στρατιάν: for the art.; *cf.* τῇ μάχῃ, I, 2, 50. Herodotus

τὴν Ἑλλάδα, καὶ τότε ἐνίκων οἱ ἡμέτεροι πρόγονοι τοὺς τούτων
70 προγόνους καὶ κατὰ γῆν καὶ κατὰ θάλατταν. ὧν ἔστι μὲν
τεκμήρια ὁρᾶν τὰ τρόπαια, μέγιστον δὲ μαρτύριον ἡ ἐλευθερία
τῶν πόλεων ἐν αἷς ὑμεῖς ἐγένεσθε καὶ ἐτράφητε· οὐδένα γὰρ
ἄνθρωπον δεσπότην ἀλλὰ τοὺς θεοὺς προσκυνεῖτε. τοιούτων
μέν ἐστε προγόνων.

75 οὐ μὲν δὴ τοῦτό γε ἐρῶ ὡς ὑμεῖς καταισχύνετε αὐτούς· ἀλλ' 14
οὐ πολλαὶ ἡμέραι ἀφ' οὗ ἀντιταξάμενοι τούτοις τοῖς ἐκείνων
ἐκγόνοις πολλαπλασίους ὑμῶν αὐτῶν ἐνικᾶτε σὺν τοῖς θεοῖς.
καὶ τότε μὲν δὴ περὶ τῆς Κύρου βασιλείας ἄνδρες ἦτε ἀγαθοί· 15
νῦν δ' ὁπότε περὶ τῆς ὑμετέρας σωτηρίας ὁ ἀγών ἐστι πολὺ
80 δήπου ὑμᾶς προσήκει καὶ ἀμείνονας καὶ προθυμοτέρους εἶναι.
ἀλλὰ μὴν καὶ θαρραλεωτέρους νῦν πρέπει εἶναι πρὸς τοὺς 16
πολεμίους. τότε μὲν γὰρ ἄπειροι ὄντες αὐτῶν, τὸ δὲ πλῆθος
ἄμετρον ὁρῶντες, ὅμως ἐτολμήσατε σὺν τῷ πατρίῳ φρονήματι
ἰέναι εἰς αὐτούς· νῦν δὲ ὁπότε καὶ πεῖραν ἤδη ἔχετε αὐτῶν ὅτι
85 οὐ θέλουσι καὶ πολλαπλάσιοι ὄντες δέχεσθαι ὑμᾶς, τί ἔτι ὑμῖν
προσήκει τούτους φοβεῖσθαι;

μηδὲ μέντοι τοῦτο μεῖον δόξητε ἔχειν εἰ οἱ Κύρειοι πρόσθεν 17

---

makes the army of Xerxes to number more than two and a half millions of fighting men.

69 ἐνίκων: imperf., since there was a series of victories—Salamis, Plataea, and Mycale.

70 ἔστι ... ὁρᾶν: *cf.* II, 3, 56.

71 τεκμήρια: pred., *as proofs*.

ἡ ἐλευθερία: if ἔστιν ὁρᾶν is supplied, the construction must be personal (*cf.* ἀρχή, I, 7, 31). Observe, however, that ἐστι would suffice, and that the shift would be an easy one.

73 ἀλλά, *nay, on the contrary.*

75 οὐ μὲν δή: *cf.* I, 9, 41.

76 οὐ πολλαὶ ... ἀφ' οὗ, *not many days ago.*

77 πολλαπλασίους ὑμῶν, *although many times your number.* For the gen., *cf.* οὗ, I, 3, 111, and the note. Observe the acc., despite the nearness of the dat., ἐκγόνοις.

79 πολύ: for the position, *cf.* c. 1. 105.

80 ὑμᾶς: προσήκει far more frequently takes the dat. (above, l. 60).

83 ἄμετρον: pred.; *sc.* ὄν.

84 εἰς αὐτούς, *into their midst,* stronger than the normal ἐπ' αὐτούς.

ὁπότε ... ὅτι, *when from your experience with them you know that.*

87 μηδὲ ... δόξητε: G. 1346; H. 874; B. 584. For δοκῶ, meaning *think, cf.* I, 7, 4, and the note.

τοῦτο μεῖον ... ἔχειν, *that you are*

σὺν ἡμῖν ταττόμενοι νῦν ἀφεστήκασιν. ἔτι γὰρ οὗτοι κακίονές εἰσι τῶν ὑφ' ἡμῶν ἡττημένων· ἔφυγον γοῦν πρὸς ἐκείνους καταλιπόντες ἡμᾶς. τοὺς δ' ἐθέλοντας φυγῆς ἄρχειν πολὺ κρεῖττον 90 σὺν τοῖς πολεμίοις ταττομένους ἢ ἐν τῇ ἡμετέρᾳ τάξει ὁρᾶν.

18 εἰ δέ τις ὑμῶν ἀθυμεῖ ὅτι ἡμῖν μὲν οὐκ εἰσὶν ἱππεῖς, τοῖς δὲ πολεμίοις πολλοὶ πάρεισιν, ἐνθυμήθητε ὅτι οἱ μύριοι ἱππεῖς οὐδὲν ἄλλο ἢ μύριοί εἰσιν ἄνθρωποι· ὑπὸ μὲν γὰρ ἵππου ἐν μάχῃ οὐδεὶς πώποτε οὔτε δηχθεὶς οὔτε λακτισθεὶς ἀπέθανεν, οἱ 95 δὲ ἄνδρες εἰσὶν οἱ ποιοῦντες ὅ, τι ἂν ἐν ταῖς μάχαις γίγνηται.

19 οὐκοῦν τῶν ἱππέων πολὺ ἡμεῖς ἐπ' ἀσφαλεστέρου ὀχήματός ἐσμεν· οἱ μὲν γὰρ ἐφ' ἵππων κρέμανται φοβούμενοι οὐχ ἡμᾶς μόνον ἀλλὰ καὶ τὸ καταπεσεῖν· ἡμεῖς δ' ἐπὶ γῆς βεβηκότες πολὺ μὲν ἰσχυρότερον παίσομεν, ἤν τις προσίῃ, πολὺ δὲ μᾶλλον 100

---

at a disadvantage in this. Cf. I, 10, 35.

εἰ: see G. 1423; H. 926; B. 598, 1.

οἱ Κύρειοι: cf. I, 10, 3. The word must here denote Ariaeus and his men—Cyrus' barbarian troops. The text is perhaps corrupt.

88 ἔτι: strongly emphatic. For its position, cf. πολύ, l. 79.

89 ἐκείνους: i.e. τοὺς ὑφ' ὑμῶν ἡττημένους. With πρός, which the MSS. give, but which some editors omit, the meaning is: they sought safety by fleeing for refuge to cowards; therefore they are the greater cowards. It is literally true that Ariaeus' and Cyrus' barbarian troops had bought their safety by going over to the king's side. Xen. attempts in this and the next section to make the best of a bad situation by adopting a jocular tone, but he does not do this until he is sure of his ground. Contrast the words of Clearchus in II, 4, §5.

92 ἱππεῖς: cf. II, 4, §6, and the Introd., §28.

93 ἐνθυμήθητε: as though ὑμεῖς, not τις ὑμῶν, had preceded.

οἱ μύριοι: for the art. with round numbers, cf. I, 2, 59.

96 οἱ ποιοῦντες: cf. ἡ ... ποιοῦσα, c. 1. 184.

γίγνηται: plainly the pass. of ποιεῖν, cf. II, 2, 42, and the note. With this passage contrast III, 3, §16, where Xen. points out their need of cavalry. It is to be noted that his audience is composed largely of Peloponnesians, among whom, owing to the mountainous character of the country, cavalry was little used and little esteemed.

97 ἱππέων: gen. after the comparative. Note again the emphatic position of πολύ.

98 κρέμανται, *sit clinging*.

99 βεβηκότες, *with feet firmly planted*, note the tense.

ὅτου ἂν βουλώμεθα τευξόμεθα· ἑνὶ δὲ μόνῳ προέχουσιν οἱ
ἱππεῖς· φεύγειν αὐτοῖς ἀσφαλέστερόν ἐστιν ἢ ἡμῖν. εἰ δὲ δὴ 20
τὰς μὲν μάχας θαρρεῖτε, ὅτι δὲ οὐκέτι ὑμῖν Τισσαφέρνης ἡγήσε-
ται οὐδὲ βασιλεὺς ἀγορὰν παρέξει, τοῦτο ἄχθεσθε, σκέψασθε
105 πότερον κρεῖττον Τισσαφέρνην ἡγεμόνα ἔχειν, ὃς ἐπιβουλεύων
ἡμῖν φανερός ἐστιν, ἢ οὓς ἂν ἡμεῖς ἄνδρας λαβόντες ἡγεῖσθαι
κελεύωμεν, οἳ εἴσονται ὅτι ἤν τι περὶ ἡμᾶς ἁμαρτάνωσι, περὶ τὰς
ἑαυτῶν ψυχὰς καὶ σώματα ἁμαρτήσονται. τὰ δὲ ἐπιτήδεια 21
πότερον ὠνεῖσθαι κρεῖττον ἐκ τῆς ἀγορᾶς ἧς οὗτοι παρεῖχον
110 μικρὰ μέτρα πολλοῦ ἀργυρίου, μηδὲ τοῦτο ἔτι ἔχοντας, ἢ αὐτοὺς
λαμβάνειν, ἤνπερ κρατῶμεν, μέτρῳ χρωμένους ὁπόσῳ ἂν ἕκαστος
βούληται.

εἰ δὲ ταῦτα μὲν γιγνώσκετε ὅτι κρείττονα, τοὺς δὲ ποταμοὺς 22
ἄπορον νομίζετε εἶναι καὶ μεγάλως ἡγεῖσθε ἐξαπατηθῆναι δια-
115 βάντες, σκέψασθε εἰ ἄρα τοῦτο καὶ μωρότατον πεποιήκασιν οἱ
βάρβαροι. πάντες γὰρ ποταμοί, εἰ καὶ πρόσω τῶν πηγῶν

---

101 τεύξομεθα, *shall hit.*
103 τὰς ... μάχας θαρρεῖτε, *have courage for the fighting.* The acc. is used as after ἔτρεσεν, I, 9, 18.
104 τοῦτο: resuming the ὅτι-clause. It is the inner obj. of ἄχθεσθε; *cf.* οὐδὲν ἤχθετο, I, 1, 40.
105 κρεῖττον: *sc.* ἐστι.
106 ἄνδρας: incorporated in the rel. clause; *cf.* I, 1, 24.
107 περὶ ... σώματα: *i. e.* they will be scourged or even killed (*cf.* IV, 1, § 23). For the acc. after περί, *cf.* I, 4, 54. Observe that the art. is expressed but once; *cf.* I, 7, 10, and the note.
108 τὰ δὲ ἐπιτήδεια: see the note on ποταμός, II, 4, 27.
110 μηδὲ ... ἔχοντας: *cf.* c. 1. 95. The partic. agrees with ἡμᾶς, understood. We have μηδέ, not οὐδέ, because of the infin. construction.

αὐτούς: *cf.* αὐτοῖς, c. 1. 150, and the note.
113 ταῦτα: prolepsis. Observe how this serves to emphasize the word.
114 ἄπορον, *a hopeless difficulty.* *Cf.* ἡδύ, II, 3, 60, and the note.
διαβάντες: causal.
115 σκέψασθε ... βάρβαροι, *consider whether this is not the most foolish thing the barbarians have done.* We insert *not*, since an affirmative answer is expected. The thought is that the Persians would have done well to have got rid of the Greeks as soon as possible, instead of putting obstacles in their way— and besides the obstacles are not unsurmountable.
116 εἰ καί, *even if;* *i. e.* it makes no difference.
πρόσω: with the gen., *far from.*

ἄποροί εἰσι, προσιοῦσι πρὸς τὰς πηγὰς διαβατοὶ γίγνονται οὐδὲ
τὸ γόνυ βρέχοντες.

εἰ δὲ μήθ' οἱ ποταμοὶ διήσουσιν ἡγεμών τε μηδεὶς ἡμῖν φανεῖται, οὐδ' ὣς ἡμῖν γε ἀθυμητέον. ἐπιστάμεθα γὰρ Μυσούς, οὓς
οὐκ ἂν ἡμῶν φαίημεν βελτίους εἶναι, ὅτι ἐν βασιλέως χώρᾳ πολλάς τε καὶ εὐδαίμονας καὶ μεγάλας πόλεις οἰκοῦσιν, ἐπιστάμεθα
δὲ Πισίδας ὡσαύτως, Λυκάονας δὲ καὶ αὐτοὶ εἴδομεν ὅτι ἐν τοῖς
πεδίοις τὰ ἐρυμνὰ καταλαβόντες τὴν τούτων χώραν καρποῦνται·
καὶ ἡμᾶς δ' ἂν ἔφην ἔγωγε χρῆναι μήπω φανεροὺς εἶναι οἴκαδε
ὡρμημένους, ἀλλὰ κατασκευάζεσθαι ὡς αὐτοῦ οἰκήσοντας. οἶδα
γὰρ ὅτι καὶ Μυσοῖς βασιλεὺς πολλοὺς μὲν ἡγεμόνας ἂν δοίη,
πολλοὺς δ' ἂν ὁμήρους τοῦ ἀδόλως ἐκπέμψειν, καὶ ὁδοποιήσειέ
γ' ἂν αὐτοῖς καὶ εἰ σὺν τεθρίπποις βούλοιντο ἀπιέναι. καὶ ἡμῖν
γ' ἂν οἶδ' ὅτι τρισάσμενος ταῦτ' ἐποίει, εἰ ἑώρα ἡμᾶς μένειν

---

117 προσιοῦσι: for the dat., *cf.* συνελόντι, c. 1. 173, and the note.

119 διήσουσιν, *shall let us pass.*

120 οὐδ' ὣς: *cf.* I, 8, 86, and the note.

ἡμῖν γε: the particle adds emphasis.

Μυσούς: prolepsis. *Cf.* l. 37.

οὓς ... βελτίους: a clause marking the Greek contempt for Asiatics; see the note on Λυδόν, c. 1. 140.

123 Πισίδας: see I, 1, 62.

Λυκάονας ... εἴδομεν: *i. e.* on their upward march; see I, 2, 109.

124 τούτων: after βασιλέως, an easy shift, whereby the passage gains in force.

125 ἂν ἔφην, *I should say.* The protasis is not expressed, although ἀλλὰ γὰρ δέδοικα, below, l. 131, suggests that Xen. had in mind εἰ μὴ ἐδεδοίκη. ἔφην, of course, governs χρῆναι.

126 ὡρμημένους: after φανεροὺς εἶναι; *cf.* I, 2, 70, and the note.

ὡς ... οἰκήσοντας, *as if intending to make our homes here.*

128 τοῦ ... ἐκπέμψειν, *that he would send them forth without guile.* The gen. depends on ὁμήρους; *cf.* τοῦ στρατεῦσαι, c. 1. 87. For the fut. infin. with the art., *cf.* ἐπιθήσεσθαι and λύσειν, II, 4, 81, and the note.

129 καὶ εἰ: different from εἰ καί, above, l. 116, in that here the supposition is a most unlikely one.

σὺν τεθρίπποις: implying a triumphal progress, as though they were victors in the great games. For ancient roads, see I, 9, 44, and the note, and the Introd. § 17.

130 οἶδ' ὅτι: parenthetic; see the note on δῆλον ὅτι, I, 3, 44.

τρισάσμενος: adj. where we use the adv.; *cf.* προτέρα, I, 2, 142, and ἀργοί, below, which is parallel with ἐν ἀφθόνοις. The use of τρισ- (or its equivalents), with intensive force, is very common in

κατασκευαζομένους. ἀλλὰ γὰρ δέδοικα μή, ἂν ἅπαξ μάθωμεν
ἀργοὶ ζῆν καὶ ἐν ἀφθόνοις βιοτεύειν, καὶ Μήδων δὲ καὶ Περσῶν
καλαῖς καὶ μεγάλαις γυναιξὶ καὶ παρθένοις ὁμιλεῖν, μὴ ὥσπερ οἱ
λωτοφάγοι ἐπιλαθώμεθα τῆς οἴκαδε ὁδοῦ. δοκεῖ οὖν μοι εἰκὸς
καὶ δίκαιον εἶναι πρῶτον εἰς τὴν Ἑλλάδα καὶ πρὸς τοὺς οἰκείους
πειρᾶσθαι ἀφικνεῖσθαι καὶ ἐπιδεῖξαι τοῖς Ἕλλησιν ὅτι ἑκόντες
πένονται, ἐξὸν αὐτοῖς τοὺς νῦν σκληρῶς ἐκεῖ πολιτεύοντας ἐνθάδε
κομισαμένους πλουσίους ὁρᾶν.

ἀλλὰ γάρ, ὦ ἄνδρες, πάντα ταῦτα τἀγαθὰ δῆλον ὅτι τῶν
κρατούντων ἐστί· τοῦτο δὲ δεῖ λέγειν ὅπως ἂν πορευοίμεθά τε
ὡς ἀσφαλέστατα καὶ εἰ μάχεσθαι δέοι ὡς κράτιστα μαχοίμεθα.
πρῶτον μὲν τοίνυν, ἔφη, δοκεῖ μοι κατακαῦσαι τὰς ἁμάξας ἃς
ἔχομεν, ἵνα μὴ τὰ ζεύγη ἡμῶν στρατηγῇ, ἀλλὰ πορευώμεθα ὅπῃ
ἂν τῇ στρατιᾷ συμφέρῃ· ἔπειτα καὶ τὰς σκηνὰς συγκατακαῦσαι.
αὗται γὰρ αὖ ὄχλον μὲν παρέχουσιν ἄγειν, συνωφελοῦσι δ' οὐδὲν

Greek. Cf. Vergil's *ter quaterque beati* (*Aen.* I, 94) and the Eng. use of *thrice*—.

ἄν ... ἐποίει, εἰ ἑώρα: a shift from the ideal to the unreal; note the position of ἄν.

131 ἀλλὰ γάρ: for the ellipsis, *cf.* II, 5, 44, and the note. Here, as so often, we may render, *but the fact is.*

ἂν ἅπαξ: *cf.* II, 2, 53.

133 μὴ ὥσπερ: μή is repeated after the interposed condit. clause; so ἄν frequently, and in § 35, εἰ.

καλαῖς καὶ μεγάλαις: to the Greek, tallness was an important element of beauty.

134 λωτοφάγοι: see *Odyssey* IX, 83–104, and Herodotus IV, 177, and *cf.* Tennyson's "Lotus Eaters." The fruit of the lotus is actually used as a food in north Africa.

136 ἑκόντες, *of their own choosing.* *Cf.* τρισάσμενος, above, l. 130.

137 ἐξόν, *when they might.* Cf. II, 5, 86, and the note. The acc. abs. most frequently expresses an adversative relation.

τοὺς ... πολιτεύοντας: obj. of κομισαμένους. For the latter (acc. after dat.), see the note on λαβόντι, I, 2, 4. What Xen. here declares feasible Alexander subsequently accomplished.

140 τοῦτο: looking forward to the ὅπως-clause.

ὅπως ἄν: with μαχοίμεθα, as well as with πορευοίμεθα. For the opt. with ἄν in an indir. quest., *cf.* πῶς ἂν ... ποιοῖτο, I, 7, 11. Some of Xen.'s "irregular" object clauses with ὅπως ἄν are merely indir. quests. (*e. g.* IV, 3, § 14; V, 7, § 20). The two vbs., with their modifiers, are given in chiastic order.

143 ἡμῶν: with στρατηγῇ; see the note on I, 4, 14.

145 ὄχλον ... ἄγειν, *are a nuisance to carry.* ἄγειν defines ὄχλον (*in the matter of carrying*).

οὔτε εἰς τὸ μάχεσθαι οὔτ' εἰς τὸ τὰ ἐπιτήδεια ἔχειν. ἔτι δὲ καὶ τῶν ἄλλων σκευῶν τὰ περιττὰ ἀπαλλάξωμεν πλὴν ὅσα πολέμου ἕνεκεν ἢ σίτων ἢ ποτῶν ἔχομεν, ἵνα ὡς πλεῖστοι μὲν ἡμῶν ἐν τοῖς ὅπλοις ὦσιν, ὡς ἐλάχιστοι δὲ σκευοφορῶσι. κρατουμένων μὲν γὰρ ἐπίστασθε ὅτι πάντα ἀλλότρια· ἢν δὲ κρατῶμεν, καὶ 150 τοὺς πολεμίους δεῖ σκευοφόρους ἡμετέρους νομίζειν.

λοιπόν μοι εἰπεῖν ὅπερ καὶ μέγιστον νομίζω εἶναι. ὁρᾶτε γὰρ καὶ τοὺς πολεμίους ὅτι οὐ πρόσθεν ἐξενεγκεῖν ἐτόλμησαν πρὸς ἡμᾶς πόλεμον πρὶν τοὺς στρατηγοὺς ἡμῶν συνέλαβον, νομίζοντες ὄντων μὲν τῶν ἀρχόντων καὶ ἡμῶν πειθομένων ἱκανοὺς εἶναι 155 ἡμᾶς περιγενέσθαι τῷ πολέμῳ, λαβόντες δὲ τοὺς ἄρχοντας ἀναρχίᾳ ἂν καὶ ἀταξίᾳ ἐνόμιζον ἡμᾶς ἀπολέσθαι. δεῖ οὖν πολὺ μὲν τοὺς ἄρχοντας ἐπιμελεστέρους γενέσθαι τοὺς νῦν τῶν πρόσθεν, πολὺ δὲ τοὺς ἀρχομένους εὐτακτοτέρους καὶ πειθομένους μᾶλλον τοῖς ἄρχουσι νῦν ἢ πρόσθεν· ἢν δέ τις ἀπειθῇ, ψηφίσασθαι τὸν 160 ἀεὶ ὑμῶν ἐντυγχάνοντα σὺν τῷ ἄρχοντι κολάζειν· οὕτως οἱ πολέ-

---

It may be felt as acc. or as dat. Cf. ὁρᾶν, II, 6, 34, and the note.

147 ἀπαλλάξωμεν, *let us get rid of.* See the note on ἀπηλλάγη, I, 10, 35. For the subjv., *cf.* ἀναμένωμεν, c. 1. 110. The advice here given is carried out, c. 3. §1.

148 ἕνεκεν: with all three gens.

149 κρατουμένων: Xen. purposely avoids expressing ἡμῶν or using a vb. in the first person (ἢν … κρατώμεθα, parallel with ἢν δὲ κρατῶμεν, below). Render, *when men are conquered.*

150 πάντα ἀλλότρια, *all their goods become the property of others* (*i. e. of the foe*). γίγνεται or ἐστι is easily supplied.

καί: *i. e.* in addition to the bearers we have now.

152 λοιπόν (sc. ἐστιν), *it remains.*

ὁρᾶτε γάρ: the rest of the section is parenthetic. The important matter is told in § 30, with resumptive οὖν.

153 τοὺς πολεμίους: prolepsis.

οὐ πρόσθεν … πρίν, *not until.* Cf. I, 2, 58, and the note.

155 ἡμῶν πειθομένων … ἡμᾶς: *cf.* ἰόντων, I, 4, 82, with the note. Here the absolute construction was necessitated by the preceding gen. abs.

157 ἄν: with ἀπολέσθαι. For its position, see I, 3, 29, and the note.

πολὺ μέν … πολὺ δέ: anaphora of the strongly emphatic adv. (see the note on c. 1. 105) instead of the simple parallelism, τοὺς μὲν ἄρχοντας … τοὺς δὲ ἀρχομένους.

158 τοὺς νῦν τῶν πρόσθεν: for the emphatic collocation, *cf.* σὲ ἐγώ, II, 5, 29.

160 ψηφίσασθαι: sc. δεῖ.

161 κολάζειν: *cf.* the note on πληγὰς

μιοι πλεῖστον ἐψευσμένοι ἔσονται· τῇδε γὰρ τῇ ἡμέρᾳ μυρίους ὄψονται ἀνθ᾽ ἑνὸς Κλεάρχους τοὺς οὐδενὶ ἐπιτρέψοντας κακῷ εἶναι. ἀλλὰ γὰρ καὶ περαίνειν ἤδη ὥρα· ἴσως γὰρ οἱ πολέμιοι
165 αὐτίκα παρέσονται. ὅτῳ οὖν ταῦτα δοκεῖ καλῶς ἔχειν, ἐπικυρωσάτω ὡς τάχιστα, ἵνα ἔργῳ περαίνηται. εἰ δέ τι ἄλλο βέλτιον ἢ ταύτῃ, τολμάτω καὶ ὁ ἰδιώτης διδάσκειν· πάντες γὰρ κοινῆς σωτηρίας δεόμεθα.

Μετὰ ταῦτα Χειρίσοφος εἶπεν· Ἀλλ᾽ εἰ μέν τινος ἄλλου
170 δεῖ πρὸς τούτοις οἷς λέγει Ξενοφῶν, καὶ αὐτίκα ἐξέσται ποιεῖν· ἃ δὲ νῦν εἴρηκε δοκεῖ μοι ὡς τάχιστα ψηφίσασθαι ἄριστον εἶναι· καὶ ὅτῳ δοκεῖ ταῦτα, ἀνατεινάτω τὴν χεῖρα. ἀνέτειναν πάντες.

ἀναστὰς δὲ πάλιν εἶπε Ξενοφῶν· Ὦ ἄνδρες, ἀκούσατε ὧν
175 προσδοκεῖ μοι. δῆλον ὅτι πορεύεσθαι ἡμᾶς δεῖ ὅπου ἕξομεν τὰ ἐπιτήδεια· ἀκούω δὲ κώμας εἶναι καλὰς οὐ πλέον εἴκοσι σταδίων ἀπεχούσας· οὐκ ἂν οὖν θαυμάζοιμεν εἰ οἱ πολέμιοι, ὥσπερ οἱ δειλοὶ κύνες τοὺς μὲν παριόντας διώκοντες καὶ δάκνουσιν, ἢν δύνωνται, τοὺς δὲ διώκοντες φεύγουσιν, εἰ καὶ αὐτοὶ ἡμῖν ἀπιοῦσιν
180 ἐπακολουθοῖεν. ἴσως οὖν ἀσφαλέστερον ἡμῖν πορεύεσθαι πλαί-

---

ἐνέβαλεν, I, 5, 69. Xen. alludes to this compact, V, 8, § 21.

162 ἐψευσμένοι ἔσονται, *will find themselves deceived.* The compound form of the fut. perf., regular in the act., is not infrequent in the pass., and may be the only form in use.

163 Κλεάρχους: *i. e.* stern disciplinarians like him. See the note on I, 5, 69.

τοὺς . . . ἐπιτρέψοντας, *who will not permit.*

κακῷ: *cf.* ἀγαθοῖς, l. 60, and the note.

164 περαίνειν: with ὥρα; *cf.* καθεύδειν, I, 3, 51.

167 καὶ ὁ ἰδιώτης, *even though he be a private.*

170 καὶ αὐτίκα: *i. e.* presently (as well as now).

ποιεῖν, attend to, carry out; *cf.* below, l. 194.

172 ἀνέτειναν: vivid asyndeton.

174 ὧν προσδοκεῖ μοι, *what further measures recommend themselves to me.*

176 ἀκούω . . . εἶναι: *cf.* I, 3, 105, and the note.

177 εἰ οἱ πολέμιοι: resumed, after the simile, by εἰ καὶ αὐτοί.

178 διώκοντες καὶ δάκνουσιν: the καί is intensive, not connective — *go so far as to bite.*

179 εἰ καὶ αὐτοί, *if they too, I say.*

180 πλαίσιον: here a hollow square; see the Introd., § 34. Contrast I, 8, 35.

σιον ποιησαμένους τῶν ὅπλων, ἵνα τὰ σκευοφόρα καὶ ὁ πολὺς ὄχλος ἐν ἀσφαλεστέρῳ εἴη. εἰ οὖν νῦν ἀποδειχθείη τίνας χρὴ ἡγεῖσθαι τοῦ πλαισίου καὶ τὰ πρόσθεν κοσμεῖν καὶ τίνας ἐπὶ τῶν πλευρῶν ἑκατέρων εἶναι, τίνας δ' ὀπισθοφυλακεῖν, οὐκ ἂν ὁπότε οἱ πολέμιοι ἔλθοιεν βουλεύεσθαι ἡμᾶς δέοι, ἀλλὰ χρῴ- μεθα ἂν εὐθὺς τοῖς τεταγμένοις. εἰ μὲν οὖν ἄλλο τις βέλτιον ὁρᾷ, ἄλλως ἐχέτω· εἰ δέ, Χειρίσοφος μὲν ἡγοῖτο, ἐπειδὴ καὶ Λακεδαιμόνιός ἐστι· τῶν δὲ πλευρῶν ἑκατέρων δύο τὼ πρεσβυ- τάτω στρατηγὼ ἐπιμελοίσθην· ὀπισθοφυλακοῖμεν δ' ἡμεῖς οἱ νεώτατοι ἐγὼ καὶ Τιμασίων τὸ νῦν εἶναι. τὸ δὲ λοιπὸν πειρώ- μενοι ταύτης τῆς τάξεως βουλευσόμεθα ὅ,τι ἂν ἀεὶ κράτιστον δοκῇ εἶναι. εἰ δέ τις ἄλλο ὁρᾷ βέλτιον, λεξάτω. ἐπεὶ δ' οὐδεὶς ἀντέλεγεν, εἶπεν· Ὅτῳ δοκεῖ ταῦτα, ἀνατεινάτω τὴν χεῖρα. ἔδοξε ταῦτα. Νῦν τοίνυν, ἔφη, ἀπιόντας ποιεῖν δεῖ τὰ δεδογ- μένα. καὶ ὅστις τε ὑμῶν τοὺς οἰκείους ἐπιθυμεῖ ἰδεῖν, μεμνήσθω ἀνὴρ ἀγαθὸς εἶναι· οὐ γὰρ ἔστιν ἄλλως τούτου τυχεῖν· ὅστις τε ζῆν ἐπιθυμεῖ, πειράσθω νικᾶν· τῶν μὲν γὰρ νικώντων τὸ καίνειν, τῶν δὲ ἡττωμένων τὸ ἀποθνήσκειν ἐστί· καὶ εἴ τις δὲ χρημάτων ἐπιθυμεῖ, κρατεῖν πειράσθω· τῶν γὰρ νικώντων ἐστὶ καὶ τὰ ἑαυτῶν σῴζειν καὶ τὰ τῶν ἡττωμένων λαμβάνειν.

---

181 τῶν ὅπλων = τῶν ὁπλιτῶν, as often.

182 ἐν ἀσφαλεστέρῳ: *i. e.* in the center.

185 ὁπότε . . . ἔλθοιεν: for the mood, *cf.* δοίη, I, 3, 87, and the note.

187 εἰ δέ: exceptional for εἰ δὲ μή (G. M. T. 478. 2; H. 906b). We may understand καλῶς ἔχει, or something of that sort. Observe that if εἰ δὲ μή were used, it would not here, as usual, introduce the unfavorable alternative.

ἡγοῖτο: opt. for the more natural imv., an uncommon use in prose; so, again the two opts. that follow.

188 Λακεδαιμόνιος: this was the period of Spartan supremacy, and an Athenian is speaking.

190 τὸ νῦν εἶναι, *for the present;* *cf.* I, 6, 55.

194 ἔδοξε ταῦτα: *cf.* I, 3, 102, and the note.

τὰ δεδογμένα: *cf.* τὰ δόξαντα, I, 3, 103.

195 ὅστις τε: note the parallel clauses, ὅστις τε . . . ὅστις τε . . . εἴ τις.

μεμνήσθω εἶναι, *let him remember to be.*

197 τῶν . . . νικώντων . . . τῶν . . . ἡττομένων: both gens. are possessive.

καίνειν: Xen. has the simple form of this poetic vb. here and *Cyrop.* IV, 2, 24. For the compound, κατακαίνειν, *cf.* the note on I, 6, 8.

III. Τούτων λεχθέντων ἀνέστησαν καὶ ἀπελθόντες κατέκαιον τὰς ἁμάξας καὶ τὰς σκηνάς, τῶν δὲ περιττῶν ὅτου μὲν δέοιτό τις μετεδίδοσαν ἀλλήλοις, τὰ δὲ ἄλλα εἰς τὸ πῦρ ἐρρίπτουν. ταῦτα ποιήσαντες ἠριστοποιοῦντο. ἀριστοποιουμένων δὲ αὐτῶν ἔρχεται Μιθραδάτης σὺν ἱππεῦσιν ὡς τριάκοντα, καὶ καλεσάμενος τοὺς στρατηγοὺς εἰς ἐπήκοον λέγει ὧδε. Ἐγώ, ὦ ἄνδρες Ἕλληνες, καὶ Κύρῳ πιστὸς ἦν, ὡς ὑμεῖς ἐπίστασθε, καὶ νῦν ὑμῖν εὔνους· καὶ ἐνθάδε δ' εἰμὶ σὺν πολλῷ φόβῳ διάγων. εἰ οὖν ὁρῴην ὑμᾶς σωτήριόν τι βουλευομένους, ἔλθοιμι ἂν πρὸς ὑμᾶς καὶ τοὺς θεράποντας πάντας ἔχων. λέξατε οὖν πρός με τί ἐν νῷ ἔχετε ὡς φίλον τε καὶ εὔνουν καὶ βουλόμενον κοινῇ σὺν ὑμῖν τὸν στόλον ποιεῖσθαι. βουλευομένοις τοῖς στρατηγοῖς ἔδοξεν ἀποκρίνασθαι τάδε· καὶ ἔλεγε Χειρίσοφος· Ἡμῖν δοκεῖ, εἰ μέν τις ἐᾷ ἡμᾶς ἀπιέναι οἴκαδε, διαπορεύεσθαι τὴν χώραν ὡς ἂν δυνώμεθα ἀσινέστατα· ἢν δέ τις ἡμᾶς τῆς ὁδοῦ ἐπικωλύῃ, διαπολεμεῖν τούτῳ ὡς ἂν δυνώμεθα κράτιστα. ἐκ τούτου ἐπειρᾶτο Μιθραδάτης διδάσκειν ὡς ἄπορον εἴη βασιλέως ἄκοντος σωθῆναι. ἔνθα δὴ ἐγιγνώσκετο ὅτι ὑπόπεμπτος εἴη· καὶ γὰρ τῶν Τισσα-

CHAPTER III

1 **κατέκαιον**, set about burning; cf. the following impfs.
2 **τῶν . . . περιττῶν**: partitive; ὅτου, with δέοιτο.
3 **ἐρρίπτουν**: Xen. uses both ῥιπτῶ and ῥίπτω (ἔρριπτον, IV, 8, § 3). A difference in meaning is not to be insisted on.
5 **Μιθραδάτης**: cf. II, 5, 134.
6 **εἰς ἐπήκοον**: cf. II, 5, 143 f.
8 **εἰμὶ . . . διάγων**: for such forms, see the note on εἶναι . . . φυλάττων, I, 2, 122. Here we may render, And here I am—living in great fear.
11 **ὡς φίλον**: i. e. ὡς πρὸς φίλον. The prep. may be omitted before ὡς and ὥστε, as it often is before rel. prons.
13 **εἰ μέν τις ἐᾷ**, if we are permitted. For τις, cf. I, 4, 80.
15 **ἀσινέστατα**: cf. the note on ἀσινῶς, II, 3, 112.
τῆς ὁδοῦ: gen. with the vb. of hindering (separation).
διαπολεμεῖν, fight it out. Observe the parallelism in structure between the two clauses and the fact that both end with a superl. adv. In the second clause the threatening form of condition (εἴ τις . . . ἐπικωλύσει) is avoided.
17 **ὡς**, how, rather than that.
βασιλέως ἄκοντος: cf. ἄκοντος Κύρου, I, 3, 89, and the note.
18 **ὑπόπεμπτος**: cf. ὑποπέμψαιεν, II, 4, 91.
19 **τις**: for the position, cf. II, 5, 125.

5 φέρνους τις οἰκείων παρηκολουθήκει πίστεως ἕνεκα. καὶ ἐκ
τούτου ἐδόκει τοῖς στρατηγοῖς βέλτιον εἶναι δόγμα ποιήσασθαι 20
τὸν πόλεμον ἀκήρυκτον εἶναι ἔστ' ἐν τῇ πολεμίᾳ εἶεν· διέφθειρον
γὰρ προσιόντες τοὺς στρατιώτας, καὶ ἕνα γε λοχαγὸν διέφθειραν
Νίκαρχον Ἀρκάδα, καὶ ᾤχετο ἀπιὼν νυκτὸς σὺν ἀνθρώποις ὡς
εἴκοσι.

6 Μετὰ ταῦτα ἀριστήσαντες καὶ διαβάντες τὸν Ζαπάταν ποτα- 25
μὸν ἐπορεύοντο τεταγμένοι τὰ ὑποζύγια καὶ τὸν ὄχλον ἐν μέσῳ
ἔχοντες. οὐ πολὺ δὲ προεληλυθότων αὐτῶν ἐπιφαίνεται πάλιν
ὁ Μιθραδάτης, ἱππέας ἔχων ὡς διακοσίους καὶ τοξότας καὶ
7 σφενδονήτας εἰς τετρακοσίους μάλα ἐλαφροὺς καὶ εὐζώνους. καὶ
προσῄει μὲν ὡς φίλος ὢν πρὸς τοὺς Ἕλληνας· ἐπεὶ δ' ἐγγὺς 30
ἐγένοντο, ἐξαπίνης οἱ μὲν αὐτῶν ἐτόξευον καὶ ἱππεῖς καὶ πεζοί,
οἱ δ' ἐσφενδόνων καὶ ἐτίτρωσκον. οἱ δὲ ὀπισθοφύλακες τῶν
Ἑλλήνων ἔπασχον μὲν κακῶς, ἀντεποίουν δ' οὐδέν· οἵ τε γὰρ
Κρῆτες βραχύτερα τῶν Περσῶν ἐτόξευον καὶ ἅμα ψιλοὶ ὄντες
8 εἴσω τῶν ὅπλων κατεκέκλειντο, οἱ δὲ ἀκοντισταὶ βραχύτερα 35
ἠκόντιζον ἢ ὡς ἐξικνεῖσθαι τῶν σφενδονητῶν. ἐκ τούτου Ξενοφῶντι ἐδόκει διωκτέον εἶναι· καὶ ἐδίωκον τῶν ὁπλιτῶν καὶ τῶν

παρηκολουθήκει: the tense denotes the permanent relation.

πίστεως ἕνεκα, *to secure his good faith* (he had formerly been Κύρῳ πιστότατος, II, 5, 134).

20 δόγμα ποιήσασθαι: *cf.* ἐποιεῖτο τὴν συλλογήν, I, 1, 24, and the note.

21 ἔστ': see the note on I, 9, 38.

διέφθειρον ... διέφθειραν: the former vb. is conative, the latter records an actual occurrence.

23 Νίκαρχον: can this be the Nicarchus mentioned in II, 5, 128?

25 Ζαπάταν: *cf.* II, 5, 1.

26 τεταγμένοι: *i. e.* in the formation suggested by Xenophon, c. 2. 180 f.

31 ἐξαπίνης: an Ionicism, but more frequent in the *Anabasis* than the normal ἐξαίφνης.

καὶ ἱππεῖς καὶ πεζοί: apposition with οἱ μέν.

32 ἐτίτρωσκον: the subj. is the whole body (οἱ μέν as well as οἱ δέ).

33 ἀντεποίουν δ' οὐδέν, *could do nothing in retaliation*. Note the tense, and see the note on I, 4, 64.

34 Κρῆτες: see the note on I, 2, 54.

35 βραχύτερα ... ἢ ὡς, *not far enough to* (*a shorter distance than so as to*).

36 τῶν σφενδονητῶν: for the gen., see G. 1099; H. 739; B. 356.

37 ὁπλιτῶν ... πελταστῶν: partitive with οἵ.

πελταστῶν οἳ ἔτυχον σὺν αὐτῷ ὀπισθοφυλακοῦντες· διώκοντες
δὲ οὐδένα κατελάμβανον τῶν πολεμίων. οὔτε γὰρ ἱππεῖς ἦσαν
τοῖς Ἕλλησιν οὔτε οἱ πεζοὶ τοὺς πεζοὺς φεύγοντας ἐδύναντο
καταλαμβάνειν ἐν ὀλίγῳ χωρίῳ· πολὺ γὰρ οὐχ οἷόν τε ἦν ἀπὸ
τοῦ ἄλλου στρατεύματος διώκειν· οἱ δὲ βάρβαροι ἱππεῖς καὶ
φεύγοντες ἅμα ἐτίτρωσκον εἰς τοὔπισθεν τοξεύοντες ἀπὸ τῶν
ἵππων, ὁπόσον δὲ διώξειαν οἱ Ἕλληνες, τοσοῦτον πάλιν ἐπανα-
χωρεῖν μαχομένους ἔδει. ὥστε τῆς ἡμέρας διῆλθον οὐ πλέον
πέντε καὶ εἴκοσι σταδίων, ἀλλὰ δείλης ἀφίκοντο εἰς τὰς κώμας.

ἔνθα δὴ πάλιν ἀθυμία ἦν. καὶ Χειρίσοφος καὶ οἱ πρεσβύτατοι τῶν στρατηγῶν Ξενοφῶντα ᾐτιῶντο ὅτι ἐδίωκεν ἀπὸ τῆς
φάλαγγος καὶ αὐτός τε ἐκινδύνευε καὶ τοὺς πολεμίους οὐδὲν
μᾶλλον ἐδύνατο βλάπτειν. ἀκούσας δὲ Ξενοφῶν ἔλεγεν ὅτι
ὀρθῶς ᾐτιῶντο καὶ αὐτὸ τὸ ἔργον αὐτοῖς μαρτυροίη. ἀλλ' ἐγώ,
ἔφη, ἠναγκάσθην διώκειν, ἐπειδὴ ἑώρων ἡμᾶς ἐν τῷ μένειν κακῶς
μὲν πάσχοντας, ἀντιποιεῖν δὲ οὐ δυναμένους. ἐπειδὴ δὲ ἐδιώ-
κομεν, ἀληθῆ, ἔφη, ὑμεῖς λέγετε· κακῶς μὲν γὰρ ποιεῖν οὐδὲν
μᾶλλον ἐδυνάμεθα τοὺς πολεμίους, ἀνεχωροῦμεν δὲ παγχαλέπως.
τοῖς οὖν θεοῖς χάρις ὅτι οὐ σὺν πολλῇ ῥώμῃ ἀλλὰ σὺν ὀλίγοις
ἦλθον, ὥστε βλάψαι μὲν μὴ μεγάλα, δηλῶσαι δὲ ὧν δεόμεθα.

---

39 κατελάμβανον: the tense, as ἀντεποίουν, above. Cf. ἐδύνατο καταλαμβάνειν, below.

41 πολύ: in emphatic position because contrasted with ὀλίγῳ χωρίῳ.

οὐχ οἷόν τε ἦν: cf. II, 2, 16, and the note.

42 καὶ φεύγοντες ἅμα, even while fleeing. Cf. εὐθύς with partic., I, 9, 10.

43 εἰς τοὔπισθεν, backwards. This method of fighting, made famous by the Parthians, is said still to be characteristic of the Persians.

44 ὁπόσον, as far as.

45 μαχομένους: i. e. the Persians in turn pursued them.

τῆς ἡμέρας, in the course of the day. See the note on I, 7, 85. Cf. δείλης, below. They had, however, not started until after their ἄριστον.

46 τὰς κώμας: i. e. those mentioned, c. 2. 176.

49 οὐδὲν μᾶλλον, none the more; i. e. than if he had not incurred the risk. οὐδέν is, of course, inner obj.; so μεγάλα, below, l. 57.

51 τὸ ἔργον, the result.

52 ἐν τῷ μένειν, while staying (where we were).

54 ἀληθῆ . . . λέγετε: i. e. it was as you say.

56 τοῖς . . . χάρις, thank Heaven.

νῦν γὰρ οἱ πολέμιοι τοξεύουσι καὶ σφενδονῶσιν ὅσον οὔτε οἱ Κρῆτες ἀντιτοξεύειν δύνανται οὔτε οἱ ἐκ χειρὸς βάλλοντες ἐξικνεῖσθαι· ὅταν δὲ αὐτοὺς διώκωμεν, πολὺ μὲν οὐχ οἷόν τε χωρίον ἀπὸ τοῦ στρατεύματος διώκειν, ἐν ὀλίγῳ δὲ οὐδ' εἰ ταχὺς εἴη πεζὸς πεζὸν ἂν διώκων καταλαμβάνοι ἐκ τόξου ῥύματος. ἡμεῖς οὖν εἰ μέλλοιμεν τούτους εἴργειν ὥστε μὴ δύνασθαι βλάπτειν ἡμᾶς πορευομένους, σφενδονητῶν τὴν ταχίστην δεῖ καὶ ἱππέων. ἀκούω δ' εἶναι ἐν τῷ στρατεύματι ἡμῶν Ῥοδίους, ὧν τοὺς πολλούς φασιν ἐπίστασθαι σφενδονᾶν, καὶ τὸ βέλος αὐτῶν καὶ διπλάσιον φέρεσθαι τῶν Περσικῶν σφενδονῶν. ἐκεῖναι γὰρ διὰ τὸ χειροπληθέσι τοῖς λίθοις σφενδονᾶν ἐπὶ βραχὺ ἐξικνοῦνται, οἱ δὲ Ῥόδιοι καὶ ταῖς μολυβδίσιν ἐπίστανται χρῆσθαι. ἢν οὖν αὐτῶν ἐπισκεψώμεθα τίνες πέπανται σφενδόνας, καὶ τούτῳ μὲν δῶμεν αὐτῶν ἀργύριον, τῷ δὲ ἄλλας πλέκειν ἐθέλοντι ἄλλο ἀργύριον τελῶμεν, καὶ τῷ σφενδονᾶν ἐν τῷ τεταγμένῳ ἐθέλοντι ἄλλην τινὰ ἀτέλειαν εὑρίσκωμεν, ἴσως τινὲς φανοῦνται ἱκανοὶ ἡμᾶς ὠφελεῖν. ὁρῶ δὲ ἵππους ὄντας ἐν τῷ στρατεύματι, τοὺς μέν

---

58 ὅσον: of space, as ὁπόσον, above, l. 44.

59 οἱ ἐκ χειρὸς βάλλοντες: *i. e.* οἱ ἀκοντισταί.

62 ἐκ τόξου ῥύματος, *with a bowshot the start.* Cf. ἐκ πλέονος, I, 10, 47.

ἡμεῖς: assimilated to μέλλοιμεν, where we should have expected ἡμῖν (with δεῖ). Trans., as if the construction were personal, *we, if we are to . . . , have need of.* Cf. also the note on ποταμός, II, 4, 27. With μέλλω the potential form is less frequent; εἰ μέλλοιμεν would have been normal.

64 τὴν ταχίστην, *at once.* The ellipsis of a fem. noun (ὁδόν?) is hardly felt.

65 ἀκούω δ' εἶναι: see I, 3, 105, and the note.

ὧν . . . ἐπίστασθαι: acc. and infin. in a rel. clause, as c 2. 120 f. Note, however, that the rel. construction is given up in the next clause.

66 καὶ . . . φέρεσθαι, *carries even twice as far.* For the vb. *cf.* I, 8, 78.

67 διὰ τὸ . . . σφενδονᾶν, *because the stones they sling are as large as the fist.* Note that the adj. is pred.

69 αὐτῶν: see the note on c. 1. 91.

70 πέπανται: for the vb. *cf.* I, 9, 69, and the note. There was as yet no troop of slingers in the army.

τούτῳ: = τῷ πεπαμένῳ (κεκτημένῳ); sing. despite the preceding pl.

71 αὐτῶν, *for them, i. e. the slings.*

72 ἐν τῷ τεταγμένῳ, *wherever stationed.*

ἄλλην . . . ἀτέλειαν, *exemption from some other duty.*

75 τινας παρ' ἐμοί, τοὺς δὲ τῶν Κλεάρχου καταλελειμμένους, πολλοὺς δὲ καὶ ἄλλους αἰχμαλώτους σκευοφοροῦντας. ἂν οὖν τούτους
πάντας ἐκλέξαντες σκευοφόρα μὲν ἀντιδῶμεν, τοὺς δὲ ἵππους
εἰς ἱππέας κατασκευάσωμεν, ἴσως καὶ οὗτοί τι τοὺς φεύγοντας
ἀνιάσουσιν. ἔδοξε καὶ ταῦτα. καὶ ταύτης τῆς νυκτὸς σφενδο-
80 νῆται μὲν εἰς διακοσίους ἐγένοντο, ἵπποι δὲ καὶ ἱππεῖς ἐδοκιμάσθησαν τῇ ὑστεραίᾳ εἰς πεντήκοντα, καὶ σπολάδες καὶ θώρακες
αὐτοῖς ἐπορίσθησαν, καὶ ἵππαρχος ἐπεστάθη Λύκιος ὁ Πολυ-
στράτου Ἀθηναῖος.

IV. Μείναντες δὲ ταύτην τὴν ἡμέραν τῇ ἄλλῃ ἐπορεύοντο
πρῳαίτερον ἀναστάντες. χαράδραν γὰρ ἔδει αὐτοὺς διαβῆναι
ἐφ' ᾗ ἐφοβοῦντο μὴ ἐπιθοῖντο αὐτοῖς διαβαίνουσιν οἱ πολέμιοι.
διαβεβηκόσι δὲ αὐτοῖς πάλιν φαίνεται Μιθραδάτης, ἔχων ἱππέας
5 χιλίους, τοξότας δὲ καὶ σφενδονήτας εἰς τετρακισχιλίους· τοσούτους γὰρ ᾔτησε Τισσαφέρνην, καὶ ἔλαβεν ὑποσχόμενος, ἂν τούτους λάβῃ, παραδώσειν αὐτῷ τοὺς Ἕλληνας, καταφρονήσας,
ὅτι ἐν τῇ πρόσθεν προσβολῇ ὀλίγους ἔχων ἔπαθε μὲν οὐδέν,
πολλὰ δὲ κακὰ ἐνόμιζε ποιῆσαι. ἐπεὶ δὲ οἱ Ἕλληνες διαβεβη-

---

74 τοὺς μέν τινας, some few. Cf. II, 3, 59.

75 παρ' ἐμοί: Xen., as a man of means, had brought horses with him.

τῶν Κλεάρχου: for Clearchus' troop of horse see I, 5, 82; for their desertion, II, 2, 31. Evidently some horses had been left behind.

77 σκευοφόρα . . . ἀντιδῶμεν, put pack-animals in their places.

78 εἰς ἱππέας, for cavalry.

79 καὶ ταῦτα: καί is intensive, not connective. The asyndeton is regular.

80 ἐγένοντο, were equipped. γίγνομαι may supply a passive to almost any vb.

ἐδοκιμάσθησαν: the vb. is suggested by the Attic custom of having all candidates for cavalry service pass certain tests (a δοκιμασία) before the βουλή (Senate).

CHAPTER IV

1 μείναντες: i. e. this day was occupied with the equipment of the cavalry.

2 χαράδραν: i. e. a deep water course, presumably dry.

3 ἐπιθοῖντο: for the form see the note on I, 9, 26.

6 ᾔτησε: with two accs.; cf. I, 3, 69.

7 λάβῃ, παραδώσειν: he said, ἂν ... λάβω, παραδώσω.

καταφρονήσας: note the tense, having come to despise.

8 οὐδέν, πολλά: an effective chiasm.

κότες ἀπεῖχον τῆς χαράδρας ὅσον ὀκτὼ σταδίους, διέβαινε καὶ ὁ
Μιθραδάτης ἔχων τὴν δύναμιν. παρήγγελτο δὲ τῶν τε πελταστῶν οὓς ἔδει διώκειν καὶ τῶν ὁπλιτῶν, καὶ τοῖς ἱππεῦσιν εἴρητο
θαρροῦσι διώκειν ὡς ἐφεψομένης ἱκανῆς δυνάμεως. ἐπεὶ δὲ ὁ
Μιθραδάτης κατειλήφει, καὶ ἤδη σφενδόναι καὶ τοξεύματα ἐξικνοῦντο, ἐσήμηνε τοῖς Ἕλλησι τῇ σάλπιγγι, καὶ εὐθὺς ἔθεον
ὁμόσε οἷς εἴρητο καὶ οἱ ἱππεῖς ἤλαυνον· οἱ δὲ οὐκ ἐδέξαντο, ἀλλ᾽
ἔφευγον ἐπὶ τὴν χαράδραν. ἐν ταύτῃ τῇ διώξει τοῖς βαρβάροις
τῶν τε πεζῶν ἀπέθανον πολλοὶ καὶ τῶν ἱππέων ἐν τῇ χαράδρᾳ
ζωοὶ ἐλήφθησαν εἰς ὀκτωκαίδεκα. τοὺς δὲ ἀποθανόντας αὐτοκέλευστοι οἱ Ἕλληνες ᾐκίσαντο, ὡς ὅτι φοβερώτατον τοῖς πολεμίοις
εἴη ὁρᾶν.

καὶ οἱ μὲν πολέμιοι οὕτω πράξαντες ἀπῆλθον, οἱ δὲ Ἕλληνες
ἀσφαλῶς πορευόμενοι τὸ λοιπὸν τῆς ἡμέρας ἀφίκοντο ἐπὶ τὸν
Τίγρητα ποταμόν. ἐνταῦθα πόλις ἦν ἐρήμη μεγάλη, ὄνομα δ᾽
αὐτῇ ἦν Λάρισα· ᾤκουν δ᾽ αὐτὴν τὸ παλαιὸν Μῆδοι. τοῦ δὲ

---

10 ὅσον, *about;* cf. I, 2, 15.
11 παρήγγελτο... εἴρητο, *word had been passed ... commands had been given.* Only in the case of vbs. of saying and commanding, and of παρασκευάζω is the impers. pass. common in Greek — a marked contrast with Latin. *Cf.* οἷς εἴρητο, below.
πελταστῶν ... ὁπλιτῶν: partitive with οὕς.
13 θαρροῦσι, *boldly.*
15 ἐσήμηνε: *cf.* I, 2, 98, and the note.
16 οἷς εἴρητο: trans. as if pers., *those who had been ordered.*
17 τοῖς βαρβάροις, *on the part of the barbarians.*
19 αὐτοκέλευστοι: see the vocab. for similar compounds.
21 ὁρᾶν: *cf.* ὁρᾶσθαι, II, 3, 8, and the note.
23 τὸ λοιπὸν τῆς ἡμέρας: *cf.* II, 2, 23, and the note.

ἀφίκοντο ... ποταμόν: this proves that they had crossed the Zab at a point some distance above its junction with the Tigris.
25 Λάρισα: the ruins now called *Nimrud*, apparently identical with the Calah of Gen. x:11 and 12, but, in reality, a portion of the great complex of capitals making up the ancient Nineveh (see below). Included in these was also the Resen of Gen. x:12, and it has been assumed that this (in the form with the art. Al Resen) may have suggested to Xen. the name Larisa, which was, however, common in Greece, designating the citadels of various towns.
Μῆδοι: Xen. may refer to the relatively short period of Median occupation (before their empire was overthrown by Cyrus), but

τείχους αὐτῆς ἦν τὸ εὖρος πέντε καὶ εἴκοσι πόδες, ὕψος δ' ἑκατόν· τοῦ δὲ κύκλου ἡ περίοδος δύο παρασάγγαι· ᾠκοδόμητο δὲ πλίνθοις κεραμεαῖς· κρηπὶς δ' ὑπῆν λιθίνη τὸ ὕψος εἴκοσι ποδῶν. ταύτην βασιλεὺς Περσῶν ὅτε παρὰ Μήδων τὴν ἀρχὴν ἐλάμβα- 8
νον Πέρσαι πολιορκῶν οὐδενὶ τρόπῳ ἐδύνατο ἑλεῖν· ἥλιον δὲ νεφέλη προκαλύψασα ἠφάνισε μέχρι ἐξέλιπον οἱ ἄνθρωποι, καὶ οὕτως ἑάλω. παρὰ ταύτην τὴν πόλιν ἦν πυραμὶς λιθίνη, τὸ μὲν 9
εὖρος ἑνὸς πλέθρου, τὸ δὲ ὕψος δύο πλέθρων. ἐπὶ ταύτης πολλοὶ τῶν βαρβάρων ἦσαν ἐκ τῶν πλησίον κωμῶν ἀποπε-
φευγότες.

ἐντεῦθεν δ' ἐπορεύθησαν σταθμὸν ἕνα παρασάγγας ἓξ πρὸς 1
τεῖχος ἔρημον μέγα κείμενον· ὄνομα δὲ ἦν τῇ πόλει Μέσπιλα·

it is more likely that he is speaking loosely. Neither he nor his readers felt interested in the history of the despised barbarians, so he has nothing to say of the glory of Nineveh, "that great city."

26 **πόδες**: *cf.* πλέθρα, I, 2, 30, and the note. Contrast ὕψος, acc., and ποδῶν (below, l. 28).

27 **πλίνθοις**: *cf.* II, 4, 52.

28 **εἴκοσι ποδῶν**: a statement corroborated by excavations.

29 **βασιλεὺς Περσῶν**: Cyrus the Great.

30 **ἥλιον ... ἠφάνισε**: *cf.* "I will cover the sun with a cloud," Ezek. xxxii: 7. The passage is one of doubtful interpretation (the MSS. give ἥλιος ... νεφέλην προκαλύψας). Xen. may have meant that the city was shrouded in fog, or that there was an eclipse (there was one in 556 B.C.). Probably both here and in § 12 he is giving local traditions. To the popular mind there has always seemed a connection between darkness and disaster.

32 **πόλιν**: for the case, cf. I, 2, 78, and the note.

πυραμίς: not a pyramid, but, as the ruins still to be seen make clear, a structure of several stories, each smaller than the last. Its present height is said to be 141 feet and the base is 150 feet square. Presumably Xen. took no measurements himself, and it may well be that in his time the height was greater, in proportion to the base, than now.

λιθίνη: really of brick, with a stone facing. This was a natural and common mode of building: the base of durable stone and upon this a superstructure of material lighter and more easily worked.

34 **ἦσαν ... ἀποπεφευγότες**: each element has its own force; see on εἶναι ... φυλάττων, I, 2, 122.

36 **παρασάγγας ἕξ**: the actual distance between the ruins of Nimrud and those of Kuyunjik (Μέσπιλα) is eighteen miles.

37 **Μέσπιλα**: *cf.* the note on Λάρισα,

Μῆδοι δ' αὐτήν ποτε ᾤκουν. ἦν δὲ ἡ μὲν κρηπὶς λίθου ξεστοῦ κογχυλιάτου, τὸ εὖρος πεντήκοντα ποδῶν καὶ τὸ ὕψος πεντήκοντα. ἐπὶ δὲ ταύτῃ ἐπῳκοδόμητο πλίνθινον τεῖχος, τὸ μὲν εὖρος πεντήκοντα ποδῶν, τὸ δὲ ὕψος ἑκατόν· τοῦ δὲ τείχους ἡ περίοδος ἓξ παρασάγγαι. ἐνταῦθα λέγεται Μήδεια γυνὴ βασιλέως καταφυγεῖν ὅτε ἀπώλλυσαν τὴν ἀρχὴν ὑπὸ Περσῶν Μῆδοι. ταύτην δὲ τὴν πόλιν πολιορκῶν ὁ Περσῶν βασιλεὺς οὐκ ἐδύνατο οὔτε χρόνῳ ἑλεῖν οὔτε βίᾳ· Ζεὺς δὲ βροντῇ κατέπληξε τοὺς ἐνοικοῦντας, καὶ οὕτως ἑάλω.

Ἐντεῦθεν δ' ἐπορεύθησαν σταθμὸν ἕνα παρασάγγας τέτταρας. εἰς τοῦτον δὲ τὸν σταθμὸν Τισσαφέρνης ἐπεφάνη, οὕς τε αὐτὸς ἱππέας ἦλθεν ἔχων καὶ τὴν Ὀρόντα δύναμιν τοῦ τὴν

---

above. Nineveh was destroyed by Cyrus the Great in 549 B.C. It was the last and most noted of the capitals of the Assyrian empire, and is said (by Diodorus Siculus II, 3) to have been of such enormous extent that the circuit of its walls was 480 stadia, or nearly 60 miles. (This agrees with Jonah iii:3, "Now Nineveh was an exceeding great city of three days' journey.") The length given by Diodorus (150 stadia) corresponds roughly to the distance between Larisa and Mespila. These statements must be understood as including the capitals built at different periods, for the founder of each new dynasty established one of his own. Excavations at these sites have brought to light extensive remains of palaces and important works of art, many of which are in the British Museum.

38 Μῆδοι ... ᾤκουν: see the note on l. 25.

39 κογχυλιάτου: a hard fossiliferous stone, capable of receiving a high polish — still used as the common building material in this district.

42 ἓξ παρασάγγαι: apparently exaggerated; eight miles is the estimate of modern travelers.

Μήδεια: the name of one of the wives of Astyages, the last king of Media.

43 καταφυγεῖν: force of the prep.? Cf. I, 5, 79.

ὑπὸ: ἀπώλλυσαν is a virtual pass., *were being robbed of*.

45 βροντῇ κατέπληξε: a wholly obscure tradition, indicating apparently a connection between some phenomenon, believed to be supernatural, and the fall of the city.

48 εἰς: temporal; cf. I, 7, 4.

49 ἔχων: if the text is right this must be taken with ἦλθεν (cf. ἔχων ἀνέβη and ἔχων ἐβοήθει, below, and see the note on I, 1, 8, and also with ἐπεφάνη. Properly ἔχων should have been expressed

50 βασιλέως θυγατέρα ἔχοντος καὶ οὓς Κῦρος ἔχων ἀνέβη βαρβάρους καὶ οὓς ὁ βασιλέως ἀδελφὸς ἔχων βασιλεῖ ἐβοήθει, καὶ πρὸς τούτοις ὅσους βασιλεὺς ἔδωκεν αὐτῷ, ὥστε τὸ στράτευμα πάμπολυ ἐφάνη. ἐπεὶ δ᾽ ἐγγὺς ἐγένετο, τὰς μὲν τῶν τάξεων ὄπισθεν καταστήσας, τὰς δὲ εἰς τὰ πλάγια παραγαγὼν ἐμβαλεῖν
55 μὲν οὐκ ἐτόλμησεν οὐδ᾽ ἐβούλετο διακινδυνεύειν, σφενδονᾶν δὲ παρήγγειλε καὶ τοξεύειν. ἐπεὶ δὲ διαταχθέντες οἱ Ῥόδιοι ἐσφενδόνησαν καὶ οἱ τοξόται ἐτόξευσαν καὶ οὐδεὶς ἡμάρτανεν ἀνδρός, οὐδὲ γὰρ εἰ πάνυ προὐθυμεῖτο ῥᾴδιον ἦν, καὶ ὁ Τισσαφέρνης μάλα ταχέως ἔξω βελῶν ἀπεχώρει καὶ αἱ ἄλλαι τάξεις
60 ἀπεχώρησαν.

καὶ τὸ λοιπὸν τῆς ἡμέρας οἱ μὲν ἐπορεύοντο, οἱ δ᾽ εἵποντο· καὶ οὐκέτι ἐσίνοντο οἱ βάρβαροι τῇ τότε ἀκροβολίσει· μακρότερον γὰρ οἵ γε Ῥόδιοι τῶν Περσῶν ἐσφενδόνων καὶ τῶν τοξοτῶν. μεγάλα δὲ καὶ τόξα τὰ Περσικά ἐστιν· ὥστε χρήσιμα ἦν ὁπόσα
65 ἁλίσκοιτο τῶν τοξευμάτων τοῖς Κρησί, καὶ διετέλουν χρώμενοι τοῖς τῶν πολεμίων τοξεύμασι, καὶ ἐμελέτων τοξεύειν ἄνω ἱέντες μακράν. ηὑρίσκετο δὲ καὶ νεῦρα πολλὰ ἐν ταῖς κώμαις καὶ

---

again, but, as it is, we have ἔχων three times and ἔχοντος once in this sentence.

Ὀρόντα: for the form see I, 4, 15, and the note.

50 ἔχοντος: cf. II, 4, 39, and the note.

51 ὁ βασιλέως ἀδελφός: cf. II, 4, 110.

52 ὥστε ... ἐφάνη: cf. II, 4, 116 f.

53 τὰς μὲν ... τὰς δέ: i. e. the Greeks were threatened on three sides of the square.

54 ἐμβαλεῖν ... διακινδυνεύειν: note the chiasm.

56 διαταχθέντες, *stationed at intervals*.

58 ἀνδρός, *his man*.

οὐδὲ ... ῥᾴδιον ἦν: because of the dense ranks of the enemy.

62 ἐσίνοντο: cf. ἀσινῶς, II, 3, 112, and the note.

63 καὶ τῶν τοξοτῶν, *even than the bowmen*. That they could hurl their missiles farther than the Persian slingers has already been stated (above, c. 3. 65 f). The text of this passage is, however, very uncertain.

65 τῶν τοξευμάτων: these words are bracketed by Gemoll, in order that ὁπόσα may refer not to the arrows of the enemy, but to their bows. The Cretans could not make use of the long arrows of the Persians unless they used the captured bows as well.

διετέλουν χρώμενοι, *they made constant use of*. Cf. λέγων διῆγε, I, 2, 70.

66 ἄνω ἱέντες: i. e. so that they could recover the arrows.

νεῦρα, *cords*; not *bowstrings* (νευραί).

PLANS TO ILLUSTRATE III, 4, §§ 19-23

The Greeks found that the hollow square was a formation which could not always be maintained. Sometimes the wings would be forced to converge, and the men in the centre would then necessarily be thrown out of position; sometimes they would diverge, and a gap would then be formed in the line. To meet this difficulty the generals formed six companies of one hundred men each. These fell behind when the way was narrow, and thus allowed the wings to converge without confusion, and if there was a gap they filled it up, adapting their formation to the space to be filled.

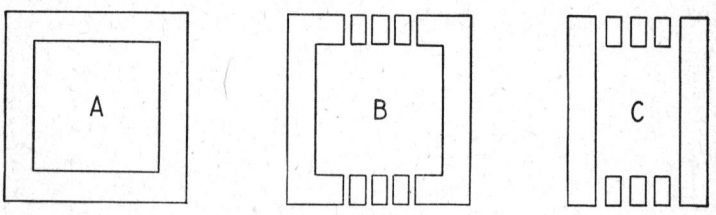

A. Original formation of the square.

BC. Possible arrangements with the six companies.

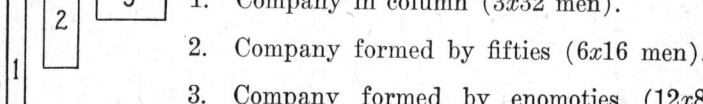

1. Company in column ($3x32$ men).
2. Company formed by fifties ($6x16$ men).
3. Company formed by enomoties ($12x8$ men).

μόλυβδος, ὥστε χρῆσθαι εἰς τὰς σφενδόνας. καὶ ταύτῃ μὲν τῇ ἡμέρᾳ, ἐπεὶ κατεστρατοπεδεύοντο οἱ Ἕλληνες κώμαις ἐπιτυχόντες, ἀπῆλθον οἱ βάρβαροι μεῖον ἔχοντες τῇ ἀκροβολίσει· τὴν δ' ἐπιοῦσαν ἡμέραν ἔμειναν οἱ Ἕλληνες καὶ ἐπεσιτίσαντο· ἦν γὰρ πολὺς σῖτος ἐν ταῖς κώμαις. τῇ δὲ ὑστεραίᾳ ἐπορεύοντο διὰ τοῦ πεδίου, καὶ Τισσαφέρνης εἵπετο ἀκροβολιζόμενος.

ἔνθα δὲ οἱ Ἕλληνες ἔγνωσαν πλαίσιον ἰσόπλευρον ὅτι πονηρὰ τάξις εἴη πολεμίων ἑπομένων. ἀνάγκη γάρ ἐστιν, ἢν συγκύπτῃ τὰ κέρατα τοῦ πλαισίου ἢ ὁδοῦ στενοτέρας οὔσης ἢ ὀρέων ἀναγκαζόντων ἢ γεφύρας, ἐκθλίβεσθαι τοὺς ὁπλίτας καὶ πορεύεσθαι πονήρως, ἅμα μὲν πιεζομένους, ἅμα δὲ ταραττομένους, ὥστε δυσχρήστους εἶναι ἀτάκτους ὄντας· ὅταν δ' αὖ διάσχῃ τὰ κέρατα, ἀνάγκη διασπᾶσθαι τοὺς τότε ἐκθλιβομένους καὶ κενὸν γίγνεσθαι τὸ μέσον τῶν κεράτων, καὶ ἀθυμεῖν τοὺς ταῦτα πάσχοντας πολεμίων ἑπομένων. καὶ ὁπότε δέοι γέφυραν διαβαίνειν ἢ ἄλλην τινὰ διάβασιν, ἔσπευδεν ἕκαστος βουλόμενος φθάσαι πρῶτος· καὶ εὐεπίθετον ἦν ἐνταῦθα τοῖς πολεμίοις. ἐπεὶ δὲ ταῦτ' ἔγνωσαν οἱ στρατηγοί, ἐποίησαν ἓξ λόχους ἀνὰ ἑκατὸν ἄνδρας, καὶ λοχαγοὺς ἐπέστησαν καὶ ἄλλους πεντηκοντῆρας

---

70 μεῖον ἔχοντες: cf. I, 10, 35.
72 πολὺς σῖτος: the plain is still noted for its fertility.
74 ἔγνωσαν, came to know, found (ingressive aor.).
πλαίσιον: prolepsis.
πονηρὰ τάξις: the normal depth of the Greek phalanx was eight ranks. If we assume this for each side of the square, and accept 9,600 as the probable number of the hoplites, we may conclude that each side of the square had a frontage of 300 men — i. e. would measure approximately 900 feet. It is apparent that this formation could not always be maintained.

75 ἢν συγκύπτῃ: the opposite of ὅταν ... διάσχῃ, below, l. 79. The following partics. are causal.
77 γεφύρας: sc. ἀναγκαζούσης.
80 τότε, in the former case.
81 τὸ μέσον, the space between; cf. I, 4, 23.
82 ὁπότε δέοι: a shift to the past, referring to their actual experience.
83 φθάσαι πρῶτος: redundant, but effective. Cf. πλέον προτιμήσεσθε, I, 4, 91.
84 εὐεπίθετον ἦν: probably impers. =ῥᾴδιον ἦν ἐπιτίθεσθαι.
85 ἀνὰ ... ἄνδρας, of a hundred men each.
86 ἄλλους, besides. Cf. ἄλλο, I, 5, 27, and the note.

καὶ ἄλλους ἐνωμοτάρχους. οὗτοι δὲ πορευόμενοι ὁπότε μὲν συγκύπτοι τὰ κέρατα ὑπέμενον, οἱ μὲν ὕστεροι, ὥστε μὴ ἐνοχλεῖν τοῖς κέρασι, τοὺς δὲ παρῆγον ἔξωθεν τῶν κεράτων. ὁπότε δὲ διάσχοιεν αἱ πλευραὶ τοῦ πλαισίου, τὸ μέσον ἂν ἐξεπίμπλασαν, εἰ μὲν στενότερον εἴη τὸ διέχον, κατὰ λόχους, εἰ δὲ πλατύτερον, κατὰ πεντηκοστῦς, εἰ δὲ πάνυ πλατύ, κατ' ἐνωμοτίας· ὥστε ἀεὶ ἔκπλεων εἶναι τὸ μέσον. εἰ δὲ καὶ διαβαίνειν τινὰ δέοι διάβασιν ἢ γέφυραν, οὐκ ἐταράττοντο, ἀλλ' ἐν τῷ μέρει οἱ λόχοι διέβαινον· καὶ εἴ που δέοι τι τῆς φάλαγγος, ἐπιπαρῆσαν οὗτοι. τούτῳ τῷ τρόπῳ ἐπορεύθησαν σταθμοὺς τέτταρας.

ἡνίκα δὲ τὸν πέμπτον ἐπορεύοντο, εἶδον βασίλειόν τι καὶ περὶ αὐτὸ κώμας πολλάς, τὴν δὲ ὁδὸν πρὸς τὸ χωρίον τοῦτο διὰ γηλόφων ὑψηλῶν γιγνομένην, οἳ καθῆκον ἀπὸ τοῦ ὄρους ὑφ' ᾧ ἦν ἡ κώμη. καὶ εἶδον μὲν τοὺς λόφους ἄσμενοι οἱ Ἕλληνες, ὡς εἰκὸς τῶν πολεμίων ὄντων ἱππέων· ἐπεὶ δὲ πορευόμενοι ἐκ τοῦ πεδίου ἀνέβησαν ἐπὶ τὸν πρῶτον γήλοφον καὶ κατέβαινον, ὡς ἐπὶ τὸν ἕτερον ἀναβαίνειν, ἐνταῦθα ἐπιγίγνονται οἱ βάρβαροι καὶ ἀπὸ τοῦ ὑψηλοῦ εἰς τὸ πρανὲς ἔβαλλον, ἐσφενδόνων, ἐτόξευον ὑπὸ μαστίγων, καὶ πολλοὺς ἐτίτρωσκον καὶ ἐκράτησαν τῶν Ἑλλήνων γυμνήτων καὶ κατέκλεισαν αὐτοὺς εἴσω τῶν

---

87 οὗτοι δέ: the nom. is continued by οἱ μὲν ... τοὺς δέ (part. appos.), but stands itself without pred. The text is again uncertain. οἱ μέν is a conjecture, adopted by recent editors. The MSS. give οἱ λοχαγοί, after ὕστεροι, but this appears to be but a gloss, explaining οὗτοι. For the manoeuvres here described, see the plan.

90 αἱ πλευραί: identical with τὰ κέρατα, above.

ἂν ἐξεπίμπλασαν: for the frequentative ἄν, cf. I, 9, 68, and the note.

91 τὸ διέχον, the gap.

93 ἔκπλεων: for the form, cf. σύμπλεων, I, 2, 131, and the note.

95 που: with τῆς φάλαγγος, at any part of.

97 βασίλειόν τι, a sort of palace. The pl. βασίλεια is more common.

98 τὴν δὲ ὁδὸν ... γιγνομένην: render by an independent clause. For the extended use of γίγνομαι, cf. II, 2, 42, and the note.

100 ἄσμενοι: cf. ἄσμενος, II, 1, 79.

104 εἰς τὸ πρανές, down hill.

ἔβαλλον ... ἐτόξευον: note the graphic asyndeton.

105 ὑπὸ μαστίγων: i. e. like slaves. Cf. Herodotus' account of the battle of Thermopylae (VII, 223).

ἐκράτησαν: the aor. gives the result, as often.

ὅπλων· ὥστε παντάπασι ταύτην τὴν ἡμέραν ἄχρηστοι ἦσαν ἐν
τῷ ὄχλῳ ὄντες καὶ οἱ σφενδονῆται καὶ οἱ τοξόται. ἐπεὶ δὲ
πιεζόμενοι οἱ Ἕλληνες ἐπεχείρησαν διώκειν, σχολῇ μὲν ἐπὶ τὸ
ἄκρον ἀφικνοῦνται ὁπλῖται ὄντες, οἱ δὲ πολέμιοι ταχὺ ἀπεπήδων.
πάλιν δὲ ὁπότε ἀπίοιεν πρὸς τὸ ἄλλο στράτευμα ταὐτὰ ἔπασχον,
καὶ ἐπὶ τοῦ δευτέρου γηλόφου ταὐτὰ ἐγίγνετο, ὥστε ἀπὸ τοῦ
τρίτου γηλόφου ἔδοξεν αὐτοῖς μὴ κινεῖν τοὺς στρατιώτας πρὶν
ἀπὸ τῆς δεξιᾶς πλευρᾶς τοῦ πλαισίου ἀνήγαγον πελταστὰς
πρὸς τὸ ὄρος. ἐπεὶ δ' οὗτοι ἐγένοντο ὑπὲρ τῶν ἑπομένων πολεμίων, οὐκέτι ἐπετίθεντο οἱ πολέμιοι τοῖς καταβαίνουσι, δεδοι-
κότες μὴ ἀποτμηθείησαν καὶ ἀμφοτέρωθεν αὐτῶν γένοιντο οἱ
πολέμιοι. οὕτω τὸ λοιπὸν τῆς ἡμέρας πορευόμενοι, οἱ μὲν τῇ
ὁδῷ κατὰ τοὺς γηλόφους, οἱ δὲ κατὰ τὸ ὄρος ἐπιπαριόντες, ἀφίκοντο εἰς τὰς κώμας· καὶ ἰατροὺς κατέστησαν ὀκτώ· πολλοὶ
γὰρ ἦσαν οἱ τετρωμένοι.

ἐνταῦθα ἔμειναν ἡμέρας τρεῖς καὶ τῶν τετρωμένων ἕνεκα καὶ
ἅμα ἐπιτήδεια πολλὰ εἶχον, ἄλευρα, οἶνον, κριθὰς ἵπποις συμβε-
βλημένας πολλάς. ταῦτα δὲ συνενηνεγμένα ἦν τῷ σατραπεύοντι
τῆς χώρας. τετάρτῃ δ' ἡμέρᾳ καταβαίνουσιν εἰς τὸ πεδίον. ἐπεὶ
δὲ κατέλαβεν αὐτοὺς Τισσαφέρνης σὺν τῇ δυνάμει, ἐδίδαξεν αὐτοὺς ἡ ἀνάγκη κατασκηνῆσαι οὗ πρῶτον εἶδον κώμην καὶ μὴ
πορεύεσθαι ἔτι μαχομένους· πολλοὶ γὰρ ἦσαν οἱ ἀπόμαχοι, οἵ
τε τετρωμένοι καὶ οἱ ἐκείνους φέροντες καὶ οἱ τῶν φερόντων τὰ

---

107 ἐν τῷ ὄχλῳ: i. e. the baggage train. These had from the first (c. 2. § 36) been within the hollow square.

113 πρὶν ... ἀνήγαγον, until they had brought; not, until they should have brought (πρὶν ... ἀναγάγοιεν). The indic. follows, as usual a neg. expression (ἔδοξεν ... μὴ κινεῖν being tantamount to οὐκ ἐκίνησαν).

116 ἐπετίθεντο: note the tense.

117 οἱ πολέμιοι: i. e. the Greeks, from the Persian standpoint.

118 οἱ μέν: the main body.

119 οἱ δέ: the peltasts.

120 ἰατρούς: hardly more than nurses.

123 εἶχον: an independent clause, where we might have looked for ἔχοντες.

ἄλευρα ... κριθάς: asyndeton in an enumeration.

124 τῷ σατραπεύοντι: dat. of the agent—or of advantage?

127 κατασκηνῆσαι: the word is general; they had burned their tents.

ὅπλα δεξάμενοι. ἐπεὶ δὲ κατεσκήνησαν καὶ ἐπεχείρησαν αὐτοῖς
ἀκροβολίζεσθαι οἱ βάρβαροι πρὸς τὴν κώμην προσιόντες, πολὺ
περιῆσαν οἱ Ἕλληνες· πολὺ γὰρ διέφερεν ἐκ χώρας ὁρμῶντας
ἀλέξασθαι ἢ πορευομένους ἐπιοῦσι τοῖς πολεμίοις μάχεσθαι.

ἡνίκα δ' ἦν ἤδη δείλη, ὥρα ἦν ἀπιέναι τοῖς πολεμίοις· οὔποτε
γὰρ μεῖον ἀπεστρατοπεδεύοντο οἱ βάρβαροι τοῦ Ἑλληνικοῦ
ἑξήκοντα σταδίων, φοβούμενοι μὴ τῆς νυκτὸς οἱ Ἕλληνες ἐπιθῶνται αὐτοῖς. πονηρὸν γὰρ νυκτός ἐστι στράτευμα Περσικόν.
οἵ τε γὰρ ἵπποι αὐτοῖς δέδενται καὶ ὡς ἐπὶ πολὺ πεποδισμένοι
εἰσὶ τοῦ μὴ φεύγειν ἕνεκα εἰ λυθείησαν, ἐάν τέ τις θόρυβος γίγνηται, δεῖ ἐπισάξαι τὸν ἵππον Πέρσῃ ἀνδρὶ καὶ χαλινῶσαι,
δεῖ καὶ θωρακισθέντα ἀναβῆναι ἐπὶ τὸν ἵππον. ταῦτα δὲ πάντα
χαλεπὰ νύκτωρ καὶ θορύβου ὄντος. τούτου ἕνεκα πόρρω ἀπε-
σκήνουν τῶν Ἑλλήνων.

ἐπεὶ δὲ ἐγίγνωσκον αὐτοὺς οἱ Ἕλληνες βουλομένους ἀπιέναι
καὶ διαγγελλομένους, ἐκήρυξε τοῖς Ἕλλησι συσκευάζεσθαι ἀκου-

130 **κατεσκήνησαν ... ἐπεχείρησαν**:
a sudden shift of subj.
132 **πολὺ γὰρ διέφερεν**, *it was a very
different thing*.
χώρας, *base, position*.
133 **ἀλέξασθαι**: *cf.* I, 3, 31, and the
note.
137 **πονηρόν**, *a wretched thing*.
The gender of the adj. is not
due to στράτευμα, but is to be
understood as φοβερώτατον, II, 5,
34. With this passage *cf.* the very
similar one, *Cyrop.* III, 3, 26 f.
138 **δέδενται**: the perf. marks the
state or condition.
αὐτοῖς: dat. of disadvantage, although we render by the possess.
gen. *Cf.* the note on I, 2, 7.
139 **τοῦ μὴ φεύγειν ἕνεκα**: equivalent to a final sentence — one of
the less common uses of the
artic. infin.
εἰ λυθείησαν, *(as they might do) if
they got loose*.

140 **Πέρσῃ ἀνδρί**: the dat. and
infin. with δεῖ is so unusual that
this is best rendered, *a Persian's horse must be saddled
and bridled for him*. Thus the
dat. is essentially the same as
αὐτοῖς, above (although not here
disadvantage), and we must understand θεράποντα (*squire*) or
possibly τινα as the subj. of the
infin., if a subj. be required (yet
it is not the squire, but the
horseman himself, that is subj.
of ἀναβῆναι). It should be remembered that χρή, too, takes
properly the acc. and infin. (not
the dat.). Exceptions to this
rule are few and, for the most
part, merely apparent.
ἐπισάξαι: the "saddle" was but a
cloth.
142 **θορύβου ὄντος**: the gen. abs. is
parallel with the adv.
145 **διαγγελλομένους**, *passing the*

ὄντων τῶν πολεμίων. καὶ χρόνον μέν τινα ἐπέσχον τῆς πορείας οἱ βάρβαροι, ἐπειδὴ δὲ ὀψὲ ἐγίγνετο, ἀπῇσαν· οὐ γὰρ ἐδόκει λύειν αὐτοὺς νυκτὸς πορεύεσθαι καὶ κατάγεσθαι ἐπὶ τὸ στρατό-
37 πεδον. ἐπειδὴ δὲ σαφῶς ἀπιόντας ἤδη ἑώρων οἱ Ἕλληνες, ἐπορεύοντο καὶ αὐτοὶ ἀναζεύξαντες καὶ διῆλθον ὅσον ἑξήκοντα 150 σταδίους. καὶ γίγνεται τοσοῦτον μεταξὺ τῶν στρατευμάτων ὥστε τῇ ὑστεραίᾳ οὐκ ἐφάνησαν οἱ πολέμιοι οὐδὲ τῇ τρίτῃ, τῇ δὲ τετάρτῃ νυκτὸς προελθόντες καταλαμβάνουσι χωρίον ὑπερδέξιον οἱ βάρβαροι, ᾗ ἔμελλον οἱ Ἕλληνες παριέναι, ἀκρωνυχίαν ὄρους, ὑφ' ἣν ἡ κατάβασις ἦν εἰς τὸ πεδίον. 155

38 ἐπειδὴ δὲ ἑώρα Χειρίσοφος προκατειλημμένην τὴν ἀκρωνυχίαν, καλεῖ Ξενοφῶντα ἀπὸ τῆς οὐρᾶς καὶ κελεύει λαβόντα
39 τοὺς πελταστὰς παραγενέσθαι εἰς τὸ πρόσθεν· ὁ δὲ Ξενοφῶν τοὺς μὲν πελταστὰς οὐκ ἦγεν. ἐπιφαινόμενον γὰρ ἑώρα Τισσαφέρνην καὶ τὸ στράτευμα πᾶν· αὐτὸς δὲ προσελάσας ἠρώτα Τί 160 καλεῖς; ὁ δὲ λέγει αὐτῷ· Ἔξεστιν ὁρᾶν· κατείληπται γὰρ ἡμῖν ὁ ὑπὲρ τῆς καταβάσεως λόφος, καὶ οὐκ ἔστι παρελθεῖν, εἰ μὴ

word (from rank to rank); παρα- is commoner.

ἐκήρυξε: for the omission of the subj., cf. ἐσάλπιγξε, I, 2, 98, and the note.

147 οὐ γὰρ . . . λύειν, it did not seem to be worth while. λύειν is here used, as not rarely by the poets, in the sense of λυσιτελεῖν.

νυκτός: with both the following infins.

150 καὶ αὐτοί, they too (as well as the Persians). αὐτός is frequently thus used with καί. Often it is best to leave the pron. untranslated and to render the whole simply, also. English is much more restricted in its use of pronouns than Greek is.

ἀναζεύξαντες: freely used; they had burned their wagons. Cf. κατασκηνῆσαι, l. 127, and the note.

153 χωρίον ὑπερδέξιον, a commanding position on their right.

154 ἀκρωνυχίαν: appos. with χωρίον.

155 ὑφ' ἥν: why not ὑφ' ᾗ? See the note on παρὰ τὴν ὁδόν, I, 2, 78. The Tigris was on their left, so that they could not make a détour.

156 ἐπειδὴ δὲ ἑώρα: the following vivid narrative is in Xen.'s best style.

158 παραγενέσθαι: a vb. of motion; cf. I, 1, 62, and the note.

159 οὐκ ἦγεν: he could not, as the next sentence shows.

160 αὐτός: almost=μόνος.

161 ἔξεστιν . . . ἔστι: the former is the stronger word.

ἡμῖν: dat. of disadvantage.

162 εἰ μὴ . . . ἀποκόψομεν: a "warning" condition, marking the

τούτους ἀποκόψομεν. ἀλλὰ τί οὐκ ἦγες τοὺς πελταστάς; ὃ δὲ 40
λέγει ὅτι οὐκ ἐδόκει αὐτῷ ἔρημα καταλιπεῖν τὰ ὄπισθεν πολεμίων ἐπιφαινομένων. Ἀλλὰ μὴν ὥρα γ', ἔφη, βουλεύεσθαι
πῶς τις τοὺς ἄνδρας ἀπελᾷ ἀπὸ τοῦ λόφου. ἐνταῦθα Ξενοφῶν 41
ὁρᾷ τοῦ ὄρους τὴν κορυφὴν ὑπὲρ αὐτοῦ τοῦ ἑαυτῶν στρατεύματος οὖσαν, καὶ ἀπὸ ταύτης ἔφοδον ἐπὶ τὸν λόφον ἔνθα ἦσαν
οἱ πολέμιοι, καὶ λέγει· Κράτιστον, ὦ Χειρίσοφε, ἡμῖν ἵεσθαι
ὡς τάχιστα ἐπὶ τὸ ἄκρον. ἢν γὰρ τοῦτο λάβωμεν, οὐ δυνήσονται
μένειν οἱ ὑπὲρ τῆς ὁδοῦ. ἀλλά, εἰ βούλει, μένε ἐπὶ τῷ στρατεύματι, ἐγὼ δ' ἐθέλω πορεύεσθαι· εἰ δὲ χρῄζεις, πορεύου ἐπὶ τὸ
ὄρος, ἐγὼ δὲ μενῶ αὐτοῦ. Ἀλλὰ δίδωμί σοι, ἔφη ὁ Χειρίσοφος, 42
ὁπότερον βούλει ἑλέσθαι. εἰπὼν ὁ Ξενοφῶν ὅτι νεώτερός ἐστιν
αἱρεῖται πορεύεσθαι, κελεύει δέ οἱ συμπέμψαι ἀπὸ τοῦ στόματος
ἄνδρας· μακρὸν γὰρ ἦν ἀπὸ τῆς οὐρᾶς λαβεῖν. καὶ ὁ Χειρίσο- 43
φος συμπέμπει τοὺς ἀπὸ τοῦ στόματος πελταστάς, ἔλαβε δὲ
τοὺς κατὰ μέσον πλαισίου. συνέπεσθαι δ' ἐκέλευσεν καὶ τοὺς
τριακοσίους οὓς αὐτὸς εἶχε τῶν ἐπιλέκτων ἐπὶ τῷ στόματι τοῦ
πλαισίου.

ἐντεῦθεν ἐπορεύοντο ὡς ἐδύναντο τάχιστα. οἱ δ' ἐπὶ τοῦ λό- 44
φου πολέμιοι ὡς ἐνόησαν αὐτῶν τὴν πορείαν ἐπὶ τὸ ἄκρον, εὐθὺς

---

gravity of the situation. τούτους is said with a gesture.

166 πῶς ... ἀπελᾷ, *how we shall dislodge*—an indir. ques. with dir. interrog. (*cf.* I, 8, 63, and the note). The indefinite third pers. is far commoner in Greek than in Eng.

167 κορυφήν: called below τὸ ἄκρον and τὸ ὄρος. This was, of course, higher than the spur (ἀκρωνυχίαν) held by the enemy.

ὑπὲρ αὐτοῦ ... στρατεύματος: the pron. is intensive; the whole may be rendered, *right above their own army*.

172 ἐγὼ δ' ἐθέλω, *I am ready, volunteer.* Note the emphatic expression of the subj.; the one who proposes the plan is also ready to carry it out. Observe that the balancing σὺ μέν is omitted. The language is varied (βούλει, ἐθέλω, χρῄζεις), as often.

174 εἰπών: asyndeton in rapid narrative.

175 οἱ: indir. reflexive. *Cf.* I, 1, 36, and the note. In prose κελεύω does not govern a dat.

177 τοὺς ἀπὸ τοῦ στόματος: *cf.* the note on τῶν παρὰ βασιλέως, I, 1, 18.

ἔλαβε: *i. e.* to replace those taken by Xen.

178 τοὺς τριακοσίους: since these are called "picked men" they may well have been three of the

45 καὶ αὐτοὶ ὥρμησαν ἀμιλλᾶσθαι ἐπὶ τὸ ἄκρον. καὶ ἐνταῦθα
πολλὴ μὲν κραυγὴ ἦν τοῦ Ἑλληνικοῦ στρατεύματος διακελευομένων τοῖς ἑαυτῶν, πολλὴ δὲ κραυγὴ τῶν ἀμφὶ Τισσαφέρνην
46 τοῖς ἑαυτῶν διακελευομένων. Ξενοφῶν δὲ παρελαύνων ἐπὶ τοῦ
ἵππου παρεκελεύετο· Ἄνδρες, νῦν ἐπὶ τὴν Ἑλλάδα νομίζετε
ἁμιλλᾶσθαι, νῦν πρὸς τοὺς παῖδας καὶ τὰς γυναῖκας, νῦν ὀλίγον
47 πονήσαντες ἀμαχεὶ τὴν λοιπὴν πορευσόμεθα. Σωτηρίδας δὲ ὁ
Σικυώνιος εἶπεν· Οὐκ ἐξ ἴσου, ὦ Ξενοφῶν, ἐσμέν· σὺ μὲν γὰρ
48 ἐφ᾽ ἵππου ὀχῇ, ἐγὼ δὲ χαλεπῶς κάμνω τὴν ἀσπίδα φέρων. καὶ
ὃς ἀκούσας ταῦτα καταπηδήσας ἀπὸ τοῦ ἵππου ὠθεῖται αὐτὸν
ἐκ τῆς τάξεως καὶ τὴν ἀσπίδα ἀφελόμενος ὡς ἐδύνατο τάχιστα
ἔχων ἐπορεύετο· ἐτύγχανε δὲ καὶ θώρακα ἔχων τὸν ἱππικόν·
ὥστ᾽ ἐπιέζετο. καὶ τοῖς μὲν ἔμπροσθεν ὑπάγειν παρεκελεύετο,
49 τοῖς δὲ ὄπισθεν παριέναι μόλις ἑπόμενος. οἱ δ᾽ ἄλλοι στρατιῶται παίουσι καὶ βάλλουσι καὶ λοιδοροῦσι τὸν Σωτηρίδαν, ἔστε
ἠνάγκασαν ἀναλαβόντα τὴν ἀσπίδα πορεύεσθαι. ὁ δ᾽ ἀναβάς,
ἕως μὲν βάσιμα ἦν, ἐπὶ τοῦ ἵππου ἦγεν, ἐπεὶ δὲ ἄβατα ἦν,

λόχοι mentioned in §21. Others assume that they formed Chirisophus' body-guard.

183 καὶ αὐτοί: as above, l. 150.

ἀμιλλᾶσθαι, *to race.*

184 πολλὴ μέν ... πολλὴ δέ: anaphora. The rhetorical effect is heightened by the chiastic arrangement, διακελευομένων τοῖς ἑαυτῶν ... τοῖς ἑαυτῶν διακελευομένων. For the pl. partic. after στρατεύματος, *cf.* κόπτοντες, II, 1, 28, and the note.

185 τῶν ἀμφὶ Τισσαφέρνην: Tiss. is included; *cf.* I, 10, 3, and the note.

187 Ἄνδρες: the formal ὦ would plainly be out of place here.

νῦν ... νῦν ... νῦν: the anaphora is forcible.

188 παῖδας ... γυναῖκας: *cf.* I, 4, 55, and the note.

190 οὐκ ἐξ ἴσου, *not on an equal footing.*

191 καὶ ὅς: *cf.* I, 8, 64, and the note.

194 ἔχων, *with it* (the shield).

θώρακα ... ἱππικόν: this was of metal and so heavier than the leathern cuirass of the hoplite. The horseman, of course, carried no shield.

195 ὑπάγειν, *to lead on (whether he kept up or not).* The rendering ordinarily given (*lead on slowly*) does not well suit the race for the summit.

196 παριέναι, *to pass him by.*

μόλις ἑπόμενος: causal; *since he could hardly keep up.*

197 ἔστε, *until.* Cf. I, 9, 38, and the note.

198 ὁ δ᾽: *i. e.* Xen.

199 βάσιμα ... ἄβατα: *i. e.* for the

200 καταλιπὼν τὸν ἵππον ἔσπευδε πεζῇ. καὶ φθάνουσιν ἐπὶ τῷ ἄκρῳ γενόμενοι τοὺς πολεμίους.

V. ἔνθα δὴ οἱ μὲν βάρβαροι στραφέντες ἔφευγον ᾗ ἕκαστος 1 ἐδύνατο, οἱ δὲ Ἕλληνες εἶχον τὸ ἄκρον. οἱ δὲ ἀμφὶ Τισσαφέρνην καὶ Ἀριαῖον ἀποτραπόμενοι ἄλλην ὁδὸν ᾤχοντο. οἱ δὲ ἀμφὶ Χειρίσοφον καταβάντες ἐστρατοπεδεύοντο ἐν κώμῃ μεστῇ πολ-
5 λῶν ἀγαθῶν. ἦσαν δὲ καὶ ἄλλαι κῶμαι πολλαὶ πλήρεις πολλῶν ἀγαθῶν ἐν τούτῳ τῷ πεδίῳ παρὰ τὸν Τίγρητα ποταμόν. ἡνίκα 2 δ' ἦν δείλη ἐξαπίνης οἱ πολέμιοι ἐπιφαίνονται ἐν τῷ πεδίῳ, καὶ τῶν Ἑλλήνων κατέκοψάν τινας τῶν ἐσκεδασμένων ἐν τῷ πεδίῳ καθ' ἁρπαγήν. καὶ γὰρ νομαὶ πολλαὶ βοσκημάτων διαβιβα-
10 ζόμεναι εἰς τὸ πέραν τοῦ ποταμοῦ κατελήφθησαν. ἐνταῦθα 3 Τισσαφέρνης καὶ οἱ σὺν αὐτῷ καίειν ἐπεχείρησαν τὰς κώμας. καὶ τῶν Ἑλλήνων μάλα ἠθύμησάν τινες, ἐννοούμενοι μὴ τὰ ἐπιτήδεια, εἰ καίοιεν, οὐκ ἔχοιεν ὁπόθεν λαμβάνοιεν. καὶ οἱ 4 μὲν ἀμφὶ Χειρίσοφον ἀπῇσαν ἐκ τῆς βοηθείας· ὁ δὲ Ξενοφῶν
15 ἐπεὶ κατέβη, παρελαύνων τὰς τάξεις ἡνίκα ἀπὸ τῆς βοηθείας ἀπήντησαν [οἱ Ἕλληνες] ἔλεγεν· Ὁρᾶτε, ὦ ἄνδρες Ἕλληνες, 5

---

horse. With these adjs. no noun need be supplied; *cf.* βατά, IV, 6, § 17.

200 φθάνουσιν: with dir. obj. and supplementary partic. as well. The experience here narrated seems to have taught Xen. a lesson; see VII, 3, § 45.

CHAPTER V

3 ἄλλην ὁδόν: an extension of the inner obj.: trans., *by another road*. Such accs. are often virtual advs.

5 ἀγαθῶν = ἐπιτηδείων.

7 ἐξαπίνης: *cf.* c. 3. 31, and the note.

9 νομαὶ . . . βοσκημάτων, *grazing herds*.

διαβιβαζόμεναι, *while being transported*; note the tense.

11 καίειν ἐπεχείρησαν: *cf.* the words of Tiss., II, 5, 76.

12 μὴ . . . οὐκ ἔχοιεν: ἐννοούμενοι implies fear. For μὴ οὐκ, *cf.* II, 3, 45, and the note.

13 ὁπόθεν λαμβάνοιεν: direct, πόθεν λαμβάνωμεν; with the whole *cf.* the note on ὅ, τι δῶ, I, 7, 37.

14 βοηθείας: they had evidently gone to the aid of the Greeks scattered in search of booty (§ 2).

15 ἐπεὶ κατέβη: he had a longer and a harder descent to make — from the κορυφή.

16 [οἱ Ἕλληνες]: *i. e.* οἱ ἀμφὶ Χειρίσοφον; but the words have all the appearance of a gloss, indicating that ἀπήντησαν has not here a hostile sense.

ὑφιέντας τὴν χώραν ἤδη ὑμετέραν εἶναι· ἃ γὰρ ὅτε ἐσπένδοντο διεπράττοντο, μὴ καίειν τὴν βασιλέως χώραν, νῦν αὐτοὶ καίουσιν ὡς ἀλλοτρίαν. ἀλλ' ἐάν που καταλείπωσί γε αὐτοῖς ἐπιτήδεια, 6 ὄψονται καὶ ἡμᾶς ἐνταῦθα πορευομένους. ἀλλ', ὦ Χειρίσοφε, ἔφη, δοκεῖ μοι βοηθεῖν ἐπὶ τοὺς καίοντας ὡς ὑπὲρ τῆς ἡμετέρας. ὁ δὲ Χειρίσοφος εἶπεν· Οὔκουν ἔμοιγε δοκεῖ· ἀλλὰ καὶ ἡμεῖς, ἔφη, καίωμεν, καὶ οὕτω θᾶττον παύσονται.

7 Ἐπεὶ δὲ ἐπὶ τὰς σκηνὰς ἦλθον, οἱ μὲν ἄλλοι περὶ τὰ ἐπιτήδεια ἦσαν, στρατηγοὶ δὲ καὶ λοχαγοὶ συνῆσαν. καὶ ἐνταῦθα πολλὴ ἀπορία ἦν. ἔνθεν μὲν γὰρ ὄρη ἦν ὑπερύψηλα, ἔνθεν δὲ ὁ ποταμὸς τοσοῦτος βάθος ὡς μηδὲ τὰ δόρατα ὑπερέχειν πειρω- 8 μένοις τοῦ βάθους. ἀπορουμένοις δ' αὐτοῖς προσελθών τις ἀνὴρ Ῥόδιος εἶπεν· Ἐγὼ θέλω, ὦ ἄνδρες, διαβιβάσαι ὑμᾶς κατὰ τετρακισχιλίους ὁπλίτας, ἂν ἐμοὶ ὧν δέομαι ὑπηρετήσητε 9 καὶ τάλαντον μισθὸν πορίσητε. ἐρωτώμενος δὲ ὅτου δέοιτο, Ἀσκῶν, ἔφη, δισχιλίων δεήσομαι· πολλὰ δ' ὁρῶ πρόβατα καὶ αἶγας καὶ βοῦς καὶ ὄνους, ἃ ἀποδαρέντα καὶ φυσηθέντα ῥᾳδίως 10 ἂν παρέχοι τὴν διάβασιν. δεήσομαι δὲ καὶ τῶν δεσμῶν οἷς

---

17 **ὑφιέντας**: sc. αὑτούς, *i. e.* τοὺς Πέρσας.

ἃ γάρ ... χώραν, lit. *the thing which they stipulated, when they made the treaty, that we should not do*. ἅ for ὅ, as frequently ταῦτα for τοῦτο—a course of action, rather than a concrete act.

18 **νῦν αὐτοὶ καίουσιν**: we should have expected ποιοῦσιν, but a more explicit word is substituted; *cf*. I, 9, 76.

21 **βοηθεῖν ἐπί**, *bear aid against*, as always.

22 **καίωμεν**: *cf*. the note on ἀναμένωμεν, c. 1. 110.

24 **ἐπὶ τὰς σκηνάς,** *to their quarters. Cf*. the note on κατασκηνῆσαι, c. 4. 127.

περὶ ... ἦσαν, *were busied with*.

26 **ἔνθεν μὲν ... ἔνθεν δέ**, *on the one side ... on the other*.

27 **ὡς**=ὥστε; *cf*. I, 5, 64, and the note.

πειρωμένοις τοῦ βάθους, *when they tried the depth*. For the dat., see the note on προσέχοντι, I, 5, 56. *Cf*. διαβάντι, below, l. 54.

29 **θέλω**, *volunteer; cf*. c. 4. 172.

30 **κατά**: distributive; *cf*. I, 8, 34.

ὑπηρετήσητε, freely, *supply*.

33 **ἅ**, *beasts which*, although with φυσηθέντα we think, of course, of the skins (δέρματα)—a shift made easy by the preceding ἀποδαρέντα.

34 **διάβασιν**, *means of crossing; cf*. the note on I, 5, 73. The Rhodian had seen skins used in this or similar ways; *cf*. I, 5, 63, and the note.

δεσμῶν, *thongs*.

35 χρῆσθε περὶ τὰ ὑποζύγια· τούτοις ζεύξας τοὺς ἀσκοὺς πρὸς
ἀλλήλους, ὁρμίσας ἕκαστον ἀσκὸν λίθους ἀρτήσας καὶ ἀφεὶς
ὥσπερ ἀγκύρας εἰς τὸ ὕδωρ, διαγαγὼν καὶ ἀμφοτέρωθεν δήσας
ἐπιβαλῶ ὕλην καὶ γῆν ἐπιφορήσω· ὅτι μὲν οὖν οὐ καταδύσεσθε 11
αὐτίκα μάλα εἴσεσθε· πᾶς γὰρ ἀσκὸς δύ' ἄνδρας ἕξει τοῦ μὴ
40 καταδῦναι. ὥστε δὲ μὴ ὀλισθάνειν ἡ ὕλη καὶ ἡ γῆ σχήσει.
ἀκούσασι ταῦτα τοῖς στρατηγοῖς τὸ μὲν ἐνθύμημα χαρίεν ἐδόκει 12
εἶναι, τὸ δ' ἔργον ἀδύνατον. ἦσαν γὰρ οἱ κωλύσοντες πέραν
πολλοὶ ἱππεῖς, οἳ εὐθὺς τοῖς πρώτοις οὐδὲν ἂν ἐπέτρεπον τούτων
ποιεῖν.

45 ἐνταῦθα τὴν μὲν ὑστεραίαν ἐπανεχώρουν εἰς τοὔμπαλιν εἰς 13
τὰς ἀκαύστους κώμας, κατακαύσαντες ἔνθεν ἐξῇσαν· ὥστε οἱ
πολέμιοι οὐ προσήλαυνον, ἀλλὰ ἐθεῶντο καὶ ὅμοιοι ἦσαν θαυμάζουσιν ὅποι ποτὲ τρέψονται οἱ Ἕλληνες καὶ τί ἐν νῷ ἔχοιεν.

---

35 **περί**, *in connection with*, not merely *around* (of girths).

ζεύξας ... δήσας, note the array of partics. ζεύξας, ὁρμίσας, διαγαγών, and δήσας are co-ordinate, and give the successive stages of construction. ἀρτήσας and ἀφείς are subordinate to ὁρμίσας (*anchoring them by attaching and letting down*).

37 **διαγαγὼν ... δήσας**: the line of inflated skins was to be carried across the stream and made fast on both banks.

38 **ἐπιβαλῶ ... ἐπιφορήσω**: chiasm.

39 **ἕξει τοῦ μὴ καταδῦναι**, *will keep from sinking*. For the gen. of the infin. (after a vb. of hindering), *cf.* τοῦ καίειν, I, 6, 9, and the note. For μή, cf. I, 3, 6, and the note. Below we have the varied phrase, ὥστε μὴ ὀλισθάνειν.

40 **σχήσει**: sing., since ὕλη and γῆ form one idea (the covering of earth and brush).

41 **χαρίεν**: *cf.* οὐκ ἀχάριστα, II, 1, 70.

42 **οἱ κωλύσοντες**, *men to prevent it*. With this πολλοὶ ἱππεῖς stands in appos.

43 **ἂν ἐπέτρεπον**: past potential (unreal); the condition is suppressed, as often.

45 **τὴν ὑστεραίαν**: acc. of duration. **εἰς τοὔμπαλιν**: the opposite of εἰς τὸ πρόσθεν (I, 10, 19 f). The reason for this march was plainly the hope of finding some means of egress from their present position. Its exact direction, however, cannot be determined. The Greeks can hardly have retraced their steps over the hills where they had been so harassed. It has been assumed that they followed some valley leading eastward.

46 **ἔνθεν**=τὰς κώμας ἐξ ὧν. *Cf.* II, 5, 101.

47 **ὅμοιοι ... θαυμάζουσιν**, *seemed lost in wonder*. The best MS. has θαυμάζειν.

48 **τρέψονται ... ἔχοιεν**: the fut. is of all tenses the one least apt

ἐνταῦθα οἱ μὲν ἄλλοι στρατιῶται ἐπὶ τὰ ἐπιτήδεια ἦσαν· οἱ δὲ στρατηγοὶ πάλιν συνῆλθον, καὶ συναγαγόντες τοὺς ἑαλωκότας ἤλεγχον τὴν κύκλῳ πᾶσαν χώραν τίς ἑκάστη εἴη. οἱ δὲ ἔλεγον ὅτι τὰ πρὸς μεσημβρίαν τῆς ἐπὶ Βαβυλῶνα εἴη καὶ Μηδίαν, δι' ἧσπερ ἥκοιεν, ἡ δὲ πρὸς ἕω ἐπὶ Σοῦσά τε καὶ Ἐκβάτανα φέροι, ἔνθα θερίζειν λέγεται βασιλεύς, ἡ δὲ διαβάντι τὸν ποταμὸν πρὸς ἑσπέραν ἐπὶ Λυδίαν καὶ Ἰωνίαν φέροι, ἡ δὲ διὰ τῶν ὀρέων καὶ πρὸς ἄρκτον τετραμμένη ὅτι εἰς Καρδούχους ἄγοι. τούτους δὲ ἔφασαν οἰκεῖν ἀνὰ τὰ ὄρη καὶ πολεμικοὺς εἶναι, καὶ βασιλέως οὐκ ἀκούειν, ἀλλὰ καὶ ἐμβαλεῖν ποτε εἰς αὐτοὺς βασιλικὴν στρατιὰν δώδεκα μυριάδας· τούτων δ' οὐδέν' ἀπονοστῆσαι διὰ τὴν δυσχωρίαν. ὁπότε μέντοι πρὸς τὸν σατράπην ἐν τῷ πεδίῳ σπείσαιντο, καὶ ἐπιμειγνύναι σφῶν τε πρὸς ἐκείνους καὶ ἐκείνων πρὸς ἑαυτούς. ἀκούσαντες ταῦτα οἱ στρατηγοὶ ἐκάθισαν χωρὶς τοὺς ἑκασταχόσε φάσκοντας εἰδέναι, οὐδὲν δῆλον ποιήσαντες ὅποι πορεύεσθαι ἔμελλον. ἐδόκει δὲ τοῖς στρατηγοῖς

---

to change to the opt. in indir. quests. or quotations.

51 ἤλεγχον ... εἴη, *asked about the whole surrounding country, what it was in each direction* (ἑκάστη). The prolepsis is admissible in Eng.

52 τὰ πρός, *the region toward.*

τῆς ἐπὶ ... εἴη: sc. ὁδοῦ, *formed part of, was on.*

53 δι' ἧσπερ ἥκοιεν, *the very road over which they had come.*

54 θερίζειν: in *Cyrop.* VIII, 6, 22 it is stated that the king spent the winter season (seven months) in Babylon, the spring (three months) in Susa, and the hot season (two months) in Ecbatana.

διαβάντι: see the note on πειρωμένοις, above, l. 27 f.

56 ὅτι: note the repetition—possibly intended to emphasize the route finally decided on.

εἰς Καρδούχους: see the note on ἐς Πισίδας, I, 1, 62.

57 ἀνά: distributive, *throughout, among.*

πολεμικούς: the Kurds of today defy the Turks, and mock at their attempts to collect tribute.

58 ἀκούειν, *obey; cf.* II, 6, 41.

59 δώδεκα μυριάδας: appos. with στρατιάν; we might have looked for the gen.

ἀπονοστῆσαι: another poeticism.

60 ὁπότε ... σπείσαιντο: still governed by ἔφασαν; direct, ὁπόταν σπείσωνται. In the following, σφῶν and ἑαυτούς denote the Persians (properly indir. reflexives, but ἑαυτούς is substituted for the infrequent σφᾶς); ἐκείνους and ἐκείνων the Carduchi. With σφῶν and ἐκείνων supply τινας. καί, before ἐπιμειγνύναι, is intensive (*actually, even*).

63 τοὺς ... εἰδέναι, *those who*

65 ἀναγκαῖον εἶναι διὰ τῶν ὀρέων εἰς Καρδούχους ἐμβάλλειν· τούτους γὰρ διελθόντας ἔφασαν εἰς Ἀρμενίαν ἥξειν, ἧς Ὀρόντας ἦρχε πολλῆς καὶ εὐδαίμονος. ἐντεῦθεν δ' εὔπορον ἔφασαν εἶναι ὅποι τις ἐθέλοι πορεύεσθαι. ἐπὶ τούτοις ἐθύσαντο, ὅπως ἡνίκα καὶ δοκοίη τῆς ὥρας τὴν πορείαν ποιοῖντο· τὴν γὰρ ὑπερβολὴν
70 τῶν ὀρέων ἐδεδοίκεσαν μὴ προκαταληφθείη· καὶ παρήγγειλαν, ἐπειδὴ δειπνήσαιεν, συσκευασαμένους πάντας ἀναπαύεσθαι, καὶ ἕπεσθαι ἡνίκ' ἄν τις παραγγέλλῃ.

---

claimed to know the country in each direction.

66 ἔφασαν: *i. e.* the captives; direct, τούτους διελθόντες ἥξετε.

68 ἐθύσαντο: *cf.* I, 7, 85, and the note.

ἡνίκα ... ὥρας, at whatsoever (καὶ) time it might seem best. ἡνίκα takes the gen., as local advs. do.

69 ὑπερβολήν: prolepsis.

72 ἡνίκ' ... παραγγέλλῃ, when the word should be passed (*i. e.* from mouth to mouth; no signal was to be given).

BOOK IV

1 I. [Ὅσα μὲν δὴ ἐν τῇ ἀναβάσει ἐγένετο μέχρι τῆς μάχης, καὶ ὅσα μετὰ τὴν μάχην ἐν ταῖς σπονδαῖς ἃς βασιλεὺς καὶ οἱ σὺν Κύρῳ ἀναβάντες Ἕλληνες ἐποιήσαντο, καὶ ὅσα παραβάντος τὰς σπονδὰς βασιλέως καὶ Τισσαφέρνους ἐπολεμήθη πρὸς τοὺς Ἕλληνας ἐπακολουθοῦντος τοῦ Περσικοῦ στρατεύματος, ἐν τῷ 5
2 πρόσθεν λόγῳ δεδήλωται. ἐπεὶ δὲ ἀφίκοντο ἔνθα ὁ μὲν Τίγρης ποταμὸς παντάπασιν ἄπορος ἦν διὰ τὸ βάθος καὶ μέγεθος, πάροδος δὲ οὐκ ἦν, ἀλλὰ τὰ Καρδούχεια ὄρη ἀπότομα ὑπὲρ αὐτοῦ τοῦ ποταμοῦ ἐκρέματο, ἐδόκει δὴ τοῖς στρατηγοῖς διὰ τῶν ὀρέων
3 πορευτέον εἶναι. ἤκουον γὰρ τῶν ἁλισκομένων ὅτι εἰ διέλθοιεν 10 τὰ Καρδούχεια ὄρη, ἐν τῇ Ἀρμενίᾳ τὰς πηγὰς τοῦ Τίγρητος ποταμοῦ, ἢν μὲν βούλωνται, διαβήσονται, ἢν δὲ μὴ βούλωνται, περιίασι. καὶ τοῦ Εὐφράτου δὲ τὰς πηγὰς ἐλέγετο οὐ πρόσω τοῦ
4 Τίγρητος εἶναι, καὶ ἔστιν οὕτως ἔχον. τὴν δ' εἰς τοὺς Καρδούχους ἐμβολὴν ὧδε ποιοῦνται, ἅμα μὲν λαθεῖν πειρώμενοι, ἅμα 15 δὲ φθάσαι πρὶν τοὺς πολεμίους καταλαβεῖν τὰ ἄκρα.]

CHAPTER I

For the opening sections consult the note on II, 1, 1. Sec. 1 gives a recapitulation of the narrative up to the point now reached, while secs. 2–4 (omitted in the best MS.) give a restatement of the matter contained in the concluding sections of the preceding book. In all probability the first four sections are a later addition and are not by Xen. Note that sec. 5 takes up the narrative again and follows closely on the end of Book III.

3 ὅσα ... ἐπολεμήθη: ὅσα would have been the inner obj. in the act. phrase.

8 ἀπότομα ... ἐκρέματο, *hung sheer over the very stream.*

10 τῶν ἁλισκομένων: for the case, *cf.* Τισσαφέρνους, I, 2, 26.

13 ἐλέγετο: the personal use is far commoner.

τοῦ Τίγρητος=τῶν τοῦ Τίγρητος πηγῶν. *Cf.* the note on ἠλέκτρου, II, 3, 58.

14 ἔστιν οὕτως ἔχον=οὕτως ἔχει. *Cf.* the note on εἶναι ... φυλάττων, I, 2, 122 f. The text is, however, conjectural.

15 ἅμα μὲν ... ἅμα δέ: *cf.* III, 4, 78.

16 φθάσαι πρίν: *cf.* II, 5, 17, and the note.

ἡνίκα δ' ἦν ἀμφὶ τὴν τελευταίαν φυλακὴν καὶ ἐλείπετο τῆς 5
νυκτὸς ὅσον σκοταίους διελθεῖν τὸ πεδίον, τηνικαῦτα ἀναστάντες
ἀπὸ παραγγέλσεως πορευόμενοι ἀφικνοῦνται ἅμα τῇ ἡμέρᾳ πρὸς
τὸ ὄρος. ἔνθα δὴ Χειρίσοφος μὲν ἡγεῖτο τοῦ στρατεύματος λα- 6
βὼν τὸ ἀμφ' αὑτὸν καὶ τοὺς γυμνῆτας πάντας, Ξενοφῶν δὲ σὺν
τοῖς ὀπισθοφύλαξιν ὁπλίταις εἵπετο οὐδένα ἔχων γυμνῆτα· οὐδεὶς
γὰρ κίνδυνος ἐδόκει εἶναι μή τις ἄνω πορευομένων ἐκ τοῦ ὄπισθεν
ἐπίσποιτο. καὶ ἐπὶ μὲν τὸ ἄκρον ἀναβαίνει Χειρίσοφος πρίν 7
τινας αἰσθέσθαι τῶν πολεμίων· ἔπειτα δ' ὑφηγεῖτο· ἐφείπετο
δὲ ἀεὶ τὸ ὑπερβάλλον τοῦ στρατεύματος εἰς τὰς κώμας τὰς ἐν
τοῖς ἄγκεσί τε καὶ μυχοῖς τῶν ὀρέων. ἔνθα δὴ οἱ μὲν Καρδοῦχοι 8
ἐκλιπόντες τὰς οἰκίας ἔχοντες καὶ γυναῖκας καὶ παῖδας ἔφευγον
ἐπὶ τὰ ὄρη. τὰ δὲ ἐπιτήδεια πολλὰ ἦν λαμβάνειν, ἦσαν δὲ καὶ
χαλκώμασι παμπόλλοις κατεσκευασμέναι αἱ οἰκίαι, ὧν οὐδὲν
ἔφερον οἱ Ἕλληνες, οὐδὲ τοὺς ἀνθρώπους ἐδίωκον, ὑποφειδόμενοι,
εἴ πως ἐθελήσειαν οἱ Καρδοῦχοι διιέναι αὐτοὺς ὡς διὰ φιλίας
τῆς χώρας, ἐπείπερ βασιλεῖ πολέμιοι ἦσαν· τὰ μέντοι ἐπιτή- 9
δεια ὅτῳ τις ἐπιτυγχάνοι ἐλάμβανεν· ἀνάγκη γὰρ ἦν. οἱ δὲ

18 ὅσον ... πεδίον, *enough for crossing the plain in the dark.* For the infin., *cf.* οἷα ... ἄρδειν, II, 3, 49, and the note. *Cf.* c. 8. §12.

σκοταίους: adj. for adv.; *cf.* προτέρα, I, 2, 142, and the note.

19 ἀπὸ παραγγέλσεως: *cf.* the last note on the preceding book.

21 τὸ ἀμφ' αὐτόν: no noun need be supplied; *cf.* τὸ ὑπερβάλλον, below, l. 26, and the note on I, 2, 3.

22 ὁπλίταις: in appos. with the preceding noun.

23 πορευομένων: sc. αὐτῶν. We might have looked for the dat., but *cf.* the note on I, 2, 99. As a matter of fact the Persians pursued them no farther.

26 ἀεί: primarily with ἐφείπετο, although it is felt also with τὸ ὑπερβάλλον=*each division as it crossed.*

27 μυχοῖς: a poetic word, used also by Thucyd. VII, 5, 2.

28 γυναῖκας ... παῖδας: *cf.* I, 4, 55, and the note.

31 ἔφερον: *cf.* the note on II, 6, 18. Observe the force of the tense of this vb. and of the following ἐδίωκον.

ὑποφειδόμενοι: note the force of the prep.; they had an object in view. *Cf.* ὑπήγετο, II, 1, 88, and the note.

32 εἴ πως, *in the hope that.* See G. 1420; H. 907.

διιέναι: *cf.* διήσουσιν, III, 2, 119.

φιλίας: pred., *cf.* I, 3, 71, and the note.

34 ὅτῳ: collective sing. after a pl.; *cf.* ὅστις ... πάντας, I, 1, 18. The

Καρδοῦχοι οὔτε καλούντων ὑπήκουον οὔτε ἄλλο φιλικὸν οὐδὲν ἐποίουν. ἐπεὶ δὲ οἱ τελευταῖοι τῶν Ἑλλήνων κατέβαινον εἰς τὰς κώμας ἀπὸ τοῦ ἄκρου ἤδη σκοταῖοι—διὰ γὰρ τὸ στενὴν εἶναι τὴν ὁδὸν ὅλην τὴν ἡμέραν ἡ ἀνάβασις αὐτοῖς ἐγένετο καὶ κατάβασις—τότε δὴ συλλεγέντες τινὲς τῶν Καρδούχων τοῖς τελευταίοις ἐπετίθεντο, καὶ ἀπέκτεινάν τινας καὶ λίθοις καὶ τοξεύμασι κατέτρωσαν, ὀλίγοι ὄντες· ἐξ ἀπροσδοκήτου γὰρ αὐτοῖς ἐπέπεσε τὸ Ἑλληνικόν. εἰ μέντοι τότε πλείους συνελέγησαν, ἐκινδύνευσεν ἂν διαφθαρῆναι πολὺ τοῦ στρατεύματος. καὶ ταύτην μὲν τὴν νύκτα οὕτως ἐν ταῖς κώμαις ηὐλίσθησαν· οἱ δὲ Καρδοῦχοι πυρὰ πολλὰ ἔκαιον κύκλῳ ἐπὶ τῶν ὀρέων καὶ συνεώρων ἀλλήλους.

ἅμα δὲ τῇ ἡμέρᾳ συνελθοῦσι τοῖς στρατηγοῖς καὶ λοχαγοῖς τῶν Ἑλλήνων ἔδοξε τῶν τε ὑποζυγίων τὰ ἀναγκαῖα καὶ δυνατώτατα ἔχοντας πορεύεσθαι, καταλιπόντας τἆλλα, καὶ ὅσα ἦν νεωστὶ αἰχμάλωτα ἀνδράποδα ἐν τῇ στρατιᾷ πάντα ἀφεῖναι. σχολαίαν γὰρ ἐποίουν τὴν πορείαν πολλὰ ὄντα τὰ ὑποζύγια καὶ τὰ αἰχμάλωτα, πολλοὶ δὲ οἱ ἐπὶ τούτοις ὄντες ἀπόμαχοι ἦσαν,

---

best attested reading is ὅτι, emended by some to ὅπου.

35 καλούντων: sc. αὐτῶν, *when they called.* Again note the force of the impf. with the neg. (ὑπήκουον).

37 διὰ γὰρ τὸ ... εἶναι, *on account of the narrowness of the road.* Cf. the note on I, 1, 35.

38 ἐγένετο, *lasted.* The aor. may be used with words expressing duration and the impf. with words implying speed. It depends on the point of view; with ἐπετίθεντο we shift to the impf.

41 ἐξ ἀπροσδοκήτου: cf. ἀπὸ τοῦ αὐτομάτου, I, 2, 100, and the note. With this phrase, cf. the Lat. *ex improviso.*

42 πλείους, *in larger numbers.*

43 ἐκινδύνευσεν ἂν διαφθαρῆναι, would have been in danger of destruction.

πολύ, *much of;* but τὸ πολύ, I, 4, 86, *the greater part of.*

45 συνεώρων, *kept each other in view* (Pretor)—presumably by means of fire signals; but συνεβόων is a plausible emendation (cf. VI, 3, § 6); see, however, VI, 2, § 13.

48 ἀναγκαῖα, *indispensable.*

49 ἔχοντας ... καταλιπόντας: acc. after dat. See the note on I, 2, 4.

51 σχολαίαν: note the emphasis given to this word by its position.

ἐποίουν, *rendered.* The mid., I, 1, 21, is different. The subj. is neut., but the idea of plurality is marked.

διπλάσιά τε ἐπιτήδεια ἔδει πορίζεσθαι καὶ φέρεσθαι πολλῶν
τῶν ἀνθρώπων ὄντων. δόξαν δὲ ταῦτα ἐκήρυξαν οὕτω ποιεῖν.

55 Ἐπεὶ δὲ ἀριστήσαντες ἐπορεύοντο, ὑποστήσαντες ἕν τῷ στενῷ 14
οἱ στρατηγοί, εἴ τι εὑρίσκοιεν τῶν εἰρημένων μὴ ἀφειμένον, ἀφῃ-
ροῦντο, οἱ δ' ἐπείθοντο, πλὴν εἴ τις ἔκλεψεν, οἷον ἢ παιδὸς ἐπιθυμήσας ἢ γυναικὸς τῶν εὐπρεπῶν. καὶ ταύτην μὲν τὴν ἡμέραν
οὕτως ἐπορεύθησαν, τὰ μέν τι μαχόμενοι τὰ δέ τι ἀναπαυόμενοι.
60 εἰς δὲ τὴν ὑστεραίαν γίγνεται χειμὼν πολύς, ἀναγκαῖον δ' ἦν 15
πορεύεσθαι· οὐ γὰρ ἦν ἱκανὰ τἀπιτήδεια. καὶ ἡγεῖτο μὲν Χειρίσοφος, ὠπισθοφυλάκει δὲ Ξενοφῶν. καὶ οἱ πολέμιοι ἰσχυρῶς 16
ἐπετίθεντο, καὶ στενῶν ὄντων τῶν χωρίων ἐγγὺς προσιόντες ἐτόξευον καὶ ἐσφενδόνων· ὥστε ἠναγκάζοντο οἱ Ἕλληνες ἐπιδιώκοντες
65 καὶ πάλιν ἀναχάζοντες σχολῇ πορεύεσθαι· καὶ θαμινὰ παρήγγελλεν ὁ Ξενοφῶν ὑπομένειν, ὅτε οἱ πολέμιοι ἰσχυρῶς ἐπικέοιντο.
ἐνταῦθα ὁ Χειρίσοφος ἄλλοτε μὲν ὅτε παρεγγυῷτο ὑπέμενε, τότε 17
δὲ οὐχ ὑπέμενεν, ἀλλ' ἦγε ταχέως καὶ παρηγγύα ἕπεσθαι, ὥστε
δῆλον ἦν ὅτι πρᾶγμά τι εἴη· σχολὴ δ' οὐκ ἦν ἰδεῖν παρελθόντι

---

52 ἀπόμαχοι: cf. III, 4, 128.
53 διπλάσια: not to be taken literally; yet the train was large.
54 δόξαν ... ταῦτα: acc. abs.; see
the note on ἐξόν, II, 5, 86. ταῦτα
is best taken as subj. (cf. ταῦτα
ἔδοξε). Xen. has also δόξαντα ταῦτα
(Hell. III, 2, 19), δοξάντων τούτων (Hell. I, 7, 30), and δόξαντος
τούτου (Hell. I, 1, 36).
55 ὑποστήσαντες, posting men (with
a covert purpose, ὑπο-; cf. II, 1, 88).
56 εἴ τι, whatever; cf. I, 5, 4.
τῶν εἰρημένων, of the objects above
mentioned. This is simpler than
to take the phrase, as is usually
done, as = τούτων ἃ εἴρητο ἀφεῖναι,
of the things they had been ordered to abandon.
57 οἱ δ': i. e. the men, οἱ στρατιῶται.
ἔκλεψεν, smuggled through (Vollbrecht).

οἷον, for example.
58 εὐπρεπῶν: part. gen. The other
gens. are governed by ἐπιθυμήσας.
They would more naturally have
been expressed in the acc. (objs.
of ἔκλεψεν).
59 τὰ μέν ... τὰ δέ, now ... now.
For the added τι, cf. II, 3, 59.
60 εἰς: cf. I, 7, 4.
χειμών: it was now about the middle of November.
65 ἀναχάζοντες: a poetic word, as
is also the θαμινά, below.
παρήγγελλεν: i. e. to Chirisophus.
66 ἐπικέοιντο: frequentative.
67 ἄλλοτε μὲν ... τότε δέ: co-
ordination (parataxis), where to
us subordination (although ...
yet) is more natural.
ὅτε παρεγγυῷτο, whenever word was
passed. Impers. pass.; see on
παρήγγελτο, III, 4, 11.

τὸ αἴτιον τῆς σπουδῆς· ὥστε ἡ πορεία ὁμοία φυγῇ ἐγίγνετο τοῖς ὀπισθοφύλαξι. καὶ ἐνταῦθα ἀποθνήσκει ἀνὴρ ἀγαθὸς Λακωνικὸς Λεώνυμος τοξευθεὶς διὰ τῆς ἀσπίδος καὶ τῆς σπολάδος εἰς τὰς πλευράς, καὶ Βασίας Ἀρκὰς διαμπερὲς τὴν κεφαλήν.

ἐπεὶ δὲ ἀφίκοντο ἐπὶ σταθμόν, εὐθὺς ὥσπερ εἶχεν ὁ Ξενοφῶν ἐλθὼν πρὸς τὸν Χειρίσοφον ᾐτιᾶτο αὐτὸν ὅτι οὐχ ὑπέμενεν, ἀλλ' ἠναγκάζοντο φεύγοντες ἅμα μάχεσθαι. καὶ νῦν δύο καλώ τε καὶ ἀγαθὼ ἄνδρε τέθνατον καὶ οὔτε ἀνελέσθαι οὔτε θάψαι ἐδυνάμεθα. ἀποκρίνεται ὁ Χειρίσοφος· Βλέψον, ἔφη, πρὸς τὰ ὄρη καὶ ἰδὲ ὡς ἄβατα πάντα ἐστί· μία δ' αὕτη ὁδὸς ἣν ὁρᾷς ὀρθία, καὶ ἐπὶ ταύτῃ ἀνθρώπων ὁρᾶν ἔξεστί σοι ὄχλον τοσοῦτον, οἳ κατειληφότες φυλάττουσι τὴν ἔκβασιν. ταῦτ' ἐγὼ ἔσπευδον καὶ διὰ τοῦτό σε οὐχ ὑπέμενον, εἴ πως δυναίμην φθάσαι πρὶν κατειλῆφθαι τὴν ὑπερβολήν· οἱ δ' ἡγεμόνες οὓς ἔχομεν οὔ φασιν εἶναι ἄλλην

---

69 πρᾶγμά τι, *some trouble*.

παρελθόντι: the omission of τινι or Ξενοφῶντι is natural; so in Eng., *there was no time to go forward and see*.

73 διαμπερές, *straight through*, a poetic word.

τὴν κεφαλήν: (*sc.* τοξευθείς). For the acc., see the note on τὰς κεφαλάς, II, 6, 67 f.

74 ὥσπερ εἶχεν, *just as he was*; emphasizing εὐθύς.

75 ὑπέμενεν... ἠναγκάζοντο: rapid shift of subj.

76 καὶ νῦν: transition to dir. speech.

καλώ τε καὶ ἀγαθώ: *cf.* II, 6, 67, and the note.

77 τέθνατον, *are lying dead*. Note the tense.

ἀνελέσθαι: the recovery and interment of the bodies of those slain in battle was to the Greeks a sacred duty. (The events following upon the battle of Arginusae, 406 B.C., are the best illustration of this.)

78 ἀποκρίνεται: asyndeton in dialogue. After this vb. the following ἔφη is redundant; it is none the less often inserted in colloquial narrative.

79 μία δ' αὕτη ... ὀρθία, *there is this one road which you see, a steep one.* With numerals οὗτος omits the art. It is here said with a gesture (so τοσοῦτον, below). *Cf.* c. 7. § 4.

81 ἔκβασιν: it is not necessary to understand the word of a pass in the strict sense. It means a way out of the narrow valleys in which they now were. Below it is called ὑπερβολή.

ταῦτ': best taken as the inner obj. of ἔσπευδον, although it is sometimes used for διὰ ταῦτα.

82 εἴ πως: *cf.* l. 32, and the note.

φθάσαι πρίν: *cf.* II, 5, 17, and the note.

83 οὔ φασιν: *cf.* I, 3, 2, and the note.

ὁδόν. ὁ δὲ Ξενοφῶν λέγει· Ἀλλ' ἐγὼ ἔχω δύο ἄνδρας. ἐπεὶ 22
γὰρ ἡμῖν πράγματα παρεῖχον, ἐνηδρεύσαμεν, ὅπερ ἡμᾶς καὶ
ἀναπνεῦσαι ἐποίησε, καὶ ἀπεκτείναμέν τινας αὐτῶν, καὶ ζῶντας
προὐθυμήθημεν λαβεῖν αὐτοῦ τούτου ἕνεκα ὅπως ἡγεμόσιν εἰδόσι
τὴν χώραν χρησαίμεθα.

Καὶ εὐθὺς ἀγαγόντες τοὺς ἀνθρώπους ἤλεγχον διαλαβόντες 23
εἴ τινα εἰδεῖεν ἄλλην ὁδὸν ἢ τὴν φανεράν. ὁ μὲν οὖν ἕτερος οὐκ
ἔφη μάλα πολλῶν φόβων προσαγομένων· ἐπεὶ δὲ οὐδὲν ὠφέλι-
μον ἔλεγεν, ὁρῶντος τοῦ ἑτέρου κατεσφάγη. ὁ δὲ λοιπὸς ἔλεξεν 24
ὅτι οὗτος μὲν οὐ φαίη διὰ ταῦτα εἰδέναι ὅτι αὐτῷ ἐτύγχανε θυγάτηρ ἐκεῖ παρ' ἀνδρὶ ἐκδεδομένη· αὐτὸς δ' ἔφη ἡγήσεσθαι δυνατὴν
καὶ ὑποζυγίοις πορεύεσθαι ὁδόν· ἐρωτώμενος δ' εἰ εἴη τι ἐν αὐτῇ 25
δυσπάριτον χωρίον, ἔφη εἶναι ἄκρον ὃ εἰ μή τις προκαταλήψοιτο,
ἀδύνατον ἔσεσθαι παρελθεῖν.

ἐνταῦθα δ' ἐδόκει συγκαλέσαντας λοχαγοὺς καὶ πελταστὰς 2
καὶ τῶν ὁπλιτῶν λέγειν τε τὰ παρόντα καὶ ἐρωτᾶν εἴ τις αὐτῶν

85 πράγματα παρεῖχον, *were bothering us; cf.* I, 1, 63.
ὅπερ: neut., because referring to the preceding clause.
86 ἀναπνεῦσαι: the word recalls Homeric usage and was, therefore, probably felt as a poeticism, although Demosth. also has it (18, 195).
87 ἡγεμόσιν, *as guides; sc.* αὐτοῖς.
89 διαλαβόντες: note the force of the prep.
90 εἰδεῖεν: indir. ques.; dir., ἴστε.
οὐκ ἔφη, *said, No.* It is not necessary to supply εἰδέναι.
91 φόβων: here concrete; *threats,* or possibly *forms of torture. Cf.* ὑποψίαι, II, 5, 3, and the note.
92 ἔλεγεν: note the tense; he persistently refused to speak.
ὁρῶντος τοῦ ἑτέρου, *before the eyes of the other.*
93 ὅτι ... ἐκδεδομένη, *because he happened to have a married daughter living there with her husband.* Note that παρά (like the German *bei* and the French *chez*) implies characteristic locality (*at her husband's house*).
ἐτύγχανε: in causal clauses the indic. is often retained; *cf.* I, 2, 126.
94 δυνατὴν ... ὁδόν, *a road over which even the beasts of burden could travel.* The personal construction should be noted.
96 ὃ εἰ μή τις προκαταλήψοιτο: the rel. and condit. clauses are combined, as rarely in Eng.; render, *and if they should not first occupy this.* Note that the condit. is of the warning type.
98 συγκαλέσαντας: acc., despite its nearness to ἐδόκει.
λοχαγοὺς ... τῶν ὁπλιτῶν, *the captains, both those who were peltasts and those the hoplites.*
99 εἴ τις ... γενέσθαι, *if there was*

PLAN TO ILLUSTRATE IV

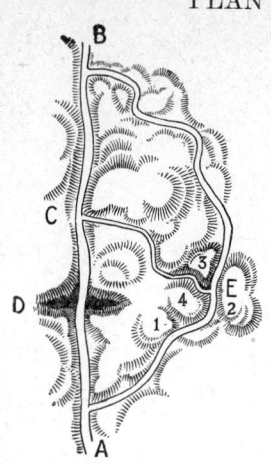

A B   Steep road.
C   Position of Carduchi.
D   Ravine
E   Position seized by the volunteers.
1   First hill seized by Xenophon.
2   Second hill seized by Xenophon.
3   Height which the volunteers were to have seized, and third hill seized by Xenophon.
4   Hill opposite the height (c. 2, 75).

The Greeks are passing along a road ACB which leads up a steep ascent to a plateau beyond (c. 1, 79). A point C on this road is occupied by the Carduchi. The guide agreed to lead them by a circuitous route AEB (c. 1, 94) over which even the baggage train could pass; the sequel showed that the train could not have proceeded by the road ACB. This circuitous road was commanded by a height (c. 1, 96) which must be seized. For this purpose a call for volunteers was issued (c. 1, 99). These set out, two thousand strong, along the road AE, with instructions to seize and occupy the hill and at daybreak to advance against the enemy at C. The main body was to make a simultaneous attack along the direct road (c. 2, 5). As the volunteers started, Xenophon, to divert the attention of the enemy (c. 2, 9) led the rear-guard along the road toward C. Crossing this was a ravine D (c. 2, 11) which it was impossible to cross, as the enemy rolled down huge stones from their position at C. Meanwhile the volunteers reached the point E (c. 2, 22) and there found a guard of the enemy sitting about a fire. These they dispersed, and themselves occupied the position (c. 2, 24), thinking that it was the height. It was not, however; and the guide seems not to have undeceived them. At daybreak they proceeded against the position C (c. 2, 29), which the Carduchi abandoned at their approach (c. 2, 32). Here at

C the volunteers were joined by Chirisophus and the main body of the Greeks, who had crossed the ravine D as best they could, some even drawing one another up by their spears (c. 2, 36). They then advanced to the plateau beyond.

Xenophon, on his part, dividing the rear-guard and placing the baggage train between the two halves (c. 2, 39), proceeded by the road AEB. As they advanced they came upon a hill (1 in the plan) which the enemy had occupied (c. 2, 42). This they took by a spirited charge in company columns (c. 2, 47), and, leaving a guard here, proceeded on their way. A second hill (2 in the plan) was met (c. 2, 51) and taken in the same way (c. 2, 59). Still another height remained (3 in the plan), higher and steeper than the others (c. 2, 60), and apparently commanding them. This was the one which the volunteers were to have occupied, and it was on one of the lower spurs of this that they had surprised the guard of the Carduchi (c. 2, 61). As Xenophon proceeded to attack this the enemy suddenly left it (c. 2, 63), and by making a détour re-occupied the first hill, overpowering the guard that had been left there and threatening the train. Xenophon with the youngest of the men occupied the hill 3 and bade the rest advance along the road EB, and halt under arms on the plateau beyond (c. 2, 69). While they were doing this the enemy occupied a hill (4 on the plan) over against the height (c. 2, 75). A truce was now made according to which the Carduchi agreed to restore the dead, and Xenophon not to burn the villages (c. 2, 78). Trusting in this, Xenophon and his men left the commanding height, although the numbers of the enemy had now greatly increased (c. 2, 80). As they did this the Carduchi rushed and seized the height (c. 2, 82), and rolled stones down upon the retreating Greeks (c. 2, 84). Finally, however, Xenophon and his men joined the main body under Chirisophus (c. 2, 89) and encamped in villages on the plateau, where there were abundant supplies (c. 2, 80). By negotiating with the enemy an arrangement was made whereby the bodies of the dead were restored to the Greeks, while they on their part released the guide (c. 2, 92).

ἔστιν ὅστις ἀνὴρ ἀγαθὸς ἐθέλοι ἂν γενέσθαι καὶ ὑποστὰς ἐθε- 100
λοντὴς πορεύεσθαι. ὑφίσταται τῶν μὲν ὁπλιτῶν Ἀριστώνυμος
Μεθυδριεὺς καὶ Ἀγασίας Στυμφάλιος ἀντιστασιάζων δὲ αὐτοῖς
Καλλίμαχος Παρράσιος ἔφη ἐθέλειν πορεύεσθαι προσλαβὼν
ἐθελοντὰς ἐκ παντὸς τοῦ στρατεύματος· ἐγὼ γάρ, ἔφη, οἶδα ὅτι
ἕψονται πολλοὶ τῶν νέων ἐμοῦ ἡγουμένου. ἐκ τούτου ἐρωτῶσιν 105
εἴ τις καὶ τῶν γυμνήτων ταξιάρχων ἐθέλοι συμπορεύεσθαι.
ὑφίσταται Ἀριστέας Χῖος, ὃς πολλαχοῦ πολλοῦ ἄξιος τῇ στρατιᾷ
εἰς τὰ τοιαῦτα ἐγένετο.

II. Καὶ ἦν μὲν δείλη, οἱ δ' ἐκέλευον αὐτοὺς ἐμφαγόντας
πορεύεσθαι. καὶ τὸν ἡγεμόνα δήσαντες παραδιδόασιν αὐτοῖς,
καὶ συντίθενται τὴν μὲν νύκτα, ἢν λάβωσι τὸ ἄκρον, τὸ χωρίον
φυλάττειν, ἅμα δὲ τῇ ἡμέρᾳ τῇ σάλπιγγι σημαίνειν· καὶ τοὺς
μὲν ἄνω ὄντας ἰέναι ἐπὶ τοὺς κατέχοντας τὴν φανερὰν ἔκβασιν, 5
αὐτοὶ δὲ συμβοηθήσειν ἐκβαίνοντες ὡς ἂν δύνωνται τάχιστα.
ταῦτα συνθέμενοι οἱ μὲν ἐπορεύοντο πλῆθος ὡς δισχίλιοι· καὶ
ὕδωρ πολὺ ἦν ἐξ οὐρανοῦ· Ξενοφῶν δὲ ἔχων τοὺς ὀπισθοφύλακας ἡγεῖτο πρὸς τὴν φανερὰν ἔκβασιν, ὅπως ταύτῃ τῇ ὁδῷ οἱ

---

any one among them who would be glad to show his valor. For γενέσθαι=show oneself, cf. I, 10, 34.

100 καὶ ... πορεύεσθαι, freely, by offering to go as a volunteer. Grammatically πορεύεσθαι depends upon ἐθέλοι ἄν.

101 ὑφίσταται: asyndeton, as below, l. 107. Note that all the volunteers from the hoplites are Arcadians, and cf. the note on I, 1, 9.

104 ἐγώ ... ἐμοῦ: said with pride.

106 γυμνήτων ταξιάρχων: appos., as πελταστάς, above, l. 98.

ἐθέλοι, was ready. Not potential, as above.

CHAPTER II

1 δείλη: cf. I, 8, 26, and the note.
οἱ δ': i.e. Xen. and Chirisophus.

ἐμφαγόντας, to eat something and. This cpd. is used of hasty eating.

3 συντίθενται, made an agreement with them (i. e. Xen. and Chirisophus with the volunteers).

ἄκρον: the height mentioned above, c. 1. 20. For this whole episode, study the plan and the accompanying comments.

4 τοὺς ... ἄνω ὄντας: the volunteers.

5 τὴν φανερὰν ἔκβασιν: cf. c. 1. 21.

6 αὐτοὶ δὲ συμβοηθήσειν: construed after συντίθενται, as after a vb. of promising (that they themselves would).

7 συνθέμενοι οἱ μὲν ... Ξεν ... δέ: part. appos.; cf. I, 8, 77, and the note.

8 ὕδωρ ... ἐξ οὐρανοῦ, rain.

10 πολέμιοι προσέχοιεν τὸν νοῦν καὶ ὡς μάλιστα λάθοιεν οἱ περι-
ιόντες. ἐπεὶ δὲ ἦσαν ἐπὶ χαράδρᾳ οἱ ὀπισθοφύλακες ἣν ἔδει
διαβάντας πρὸς τὸ ὄρθιον ἐκβαίνειν, τηνικαῦτα ἐκυλίνδουν οἱ
βάρβαροι ὁλοιτρόχους ἁμαξιαίους καὶ μείζους καὶ ἐλάττους, οἳ
φερόμενοι πρὸς τὰς πέτρας παίοντες διεσφενδονῶντο· καὶ παντά-
15 πασιν οὐδὲ πελάσαι οἷόν τ' ἦν τῇ εἰσόδῳ. ἔνιοι δὲ τῶν λοχαγῶν,
εἰ μὴ ταύτῃ δύναιντο, ἄλλῃ ἐπειρῶντο· καὶ ταῦτα ἐποίουν μέχρι
σκότος ἐγένετο· ἐπεὶ δὲ ᾤοντο ἀφανεῖς εἶναι ἀπιόντες, τότε
ἀπῆλθον ἐπὶ τὸ δεῖπνον· ἐτύγχανον δὲ καὶ ἀνάριστοι ὄντες
αὐτῶν οἱ ὀπισθοφυλακήσαντες. οἱ μέντοι πολέμιοι οὐδὲν ἐπαύ-
20 σαντο δι' ὅλης τῆς νυκτὸς κυλινδοῦντες τοὺς λίθους· τεκμαίρεσθαι
δ' ἦν τῷ ψόφῳ.

οἱ δ' ἔχοντες τὸν ἡγεμόνα κύκλῳ περιόντες καταλαμβάνουσι
τοὺς φύλακας ἀμφὶ πῦρ καθημένους· καὶ τοὺς μὲν κατακαίνοντες
τοὺς δὲ καταδιώξαντες αὐτοὶ ἐνταῦθ' ἔμενον ὡς τὸ ἄκρον κατέ-
25 χοντες. οἱ δ' οὐ κατεῖχον, ἀλλὰ μαστὸς ἦν ὑπὲρ αὐτῶν παρ'

10 προσέχοιεν τὸν νοῦν: cf. I, 5, 56.
11 ἣν ἔδει ... ἐκβαίνειν, which they must cross in order to make their way out up the ascent.
13 ὁλοιτρόχους: an Homeric word.
ἁμαξιαίους: Xen. has the word again, *Hell.* II, 4, 7. It is not a mere gloss on the preceding.
14 φερόμενοι: cf. ἐφέροντο, I, 8, 78, and the note.
διεσφενδονῶντο, were flung as from slings in all directions.
καὶ ... ἦν, and it was absolutely impossible even to approach. For the poetic πελάσαι, cf. I, 8, 59.
15 εἰσόδῳ, the entrance, i. e. to the ἔκβασις, which must have been a pass through the mountains.
16 εἰ μὴ ... δύναιντο: general condit. with frequentative impf. in the apodosis.
18 τὸ δεῖπνον: for the Greek meals, see I, 10, 67, and the note.

19 οἱ ὀπισθοφυλακήσαντες: these had been fighting steadily (c. 1. § 16).
οὐδὲν ἐπαύσαντο: οὐδέν in such cases is stronger than οὐκ.
23 τοὺς φύλακας: i. e. of the Carduchi.
κατακαίνοντες: cf. I, 6, 8, and the note.
24 ὡς ... κατέχοντες, in the belief that they held.
25 οἱ δ': note that here (exceptionally) the subj. does not change.
μαστός, a hill; see the vocab., and cf. below, §§ 14, 18, and 20. The word thus used savors of poetry, although such metaphors were easy to the Greek (cf. ἀκρωνυχία). This was apparently the ἄκρον which they were to have occupied.

ὃν ἦν ἡ στενὴ αὕτη ὁδὸς ἐφ' ᾗ ἐκάθηντο οἱ φύλακες. ἔφοδος μέντοι αὐτόθεν ἐπὶ τοὺς πολεμίους ἦν οἳ ἐπὶ τῇ φανερᾷ ὁδῷ ἐκάθηντο. καὶ τὴν μὲν νύκτα ἐνταῦθα διήγαγον· ἐπεὶ δ' ἡμέρα ὑπέφαινεν, ἐπορεύοντο σιγῇ συντεταγμένοι ἐπὶ τοὺς πολεμίους· καὶ γὰρ ὁμίχλη ἐγένετο, ὥστ' ἔλαθον ἐγγὺς προσελθόντες· ἐπεὶ δὲ εἶδον ἀλλήλους, ἥ τε σάλπιγξ ἐφθέγξατο καὶ ἀλαλάξαντες ἵεντο ἐπὶ τοὺς ἀνθρώπους. οἱ δὲ οὐκ ἐδέξαντο, ἀλλὰ λιπόντες τὴν ὁδὸν φεύγοντες ὀλίγοι ἀπέθνῃσκον· εὔζωνοι γὰρ ἦσαν. οἱ δὲ ἀμφὶ Χειρίσοφον ἀκούσαντες τῆς σάλπιγγος εὐθὺς ἵεντο ἄνω κατὰ τὴν φανερὰν ὁδόν· ἄλλοι δὲ τῶν στρατηγῶν κατὰ ἀτριβεῖς ὁδοὺς ἐπορεύοντο ᾗ ἔτυχον ἕκαστοι ὄντες, καὶ ἀναβάντες ὡς ἐδύναντο ἀνίμων ἀλλήλους τοῖς δόρασι. καὶ οὗτοι πρῶτοι συνέμειξαν τοῖς προκαταλαβοῦσι τὸ χωρίον.

Ξενοφῶν δὲ ἔχων τῶν ὀπισθοφυλάκων τοὺς ἡμίσεις ἐπορεύετο ᾗπερ οἱ τὸν ἡγεμόνα ἔχοντες· εὐοδωτάτη γὰρ ἦν τοῖς ὑποζυγίοις·

---

26 ἡ στενὴ αὕτη ὁδός: for the position of αὕτη, see G. 975; H. 673c; B. 458. This path led to the main position of the Carduchi; hence the guard.

27 αὐτόθεν: *i. e. from where they were*, although they had not taken the height. They are thus able to carry out their original plan of attacking the main body of the enemy, as outlined in § 1.

28 διήγαγον: here with dir. obj.; it is abs. in III, 1, 193; III, 3, 8.

29 ὑπέφαινεν: *cf.* III, 2, 1, and the note.

31 ἐφθέγξατο: we, also, speak of the trumpet's *voice*.

ἀλαλάξαντες: ἀλαλάζω is a poetical equivalent of ἐλελίζω (I, 8, 72). It occurs again in VI, 5, §§ 26, and 27.

32 τοὺς ἀνθρώπους: *i. e. the enemy*, as often; *cf.* ἄνδρες, III, 1, 107. Note the rapidity with which the subj. shifts in this section.

33 ὀλίγοι: limiting appos.

εὔζωνοι: *cf.* III, 3, 29. This clause gives the reason why but few were killed.

34 ἵεντο ... ἐπορεύοντο: chiasm.

36 ὡς ἐδύναντο, *as best they could*.

37 ἀνίμων: the word is a graphic one; it is used of drawing buckets from a well.

συνέμειξαν: *cf.* II, 1, 10.

38 τὸ χωρίον: *i. e.* the position which the enemy had been occupying.

39 Ξενοφῶν δέ: we now learn of the experiences of the rear-guard and the train, while they endeavored to follow the circuitous road over which the volunteers had gone.

τοὺς ἡμίσεις: assimilation in gender; we also have τὸ ἥμισυ, as a noun.

40 εὐοδωτάτη: it was, in fact, the only road; see below.

τοὺς δὲ ἡμίσεις ὄπισθεν τῶν ὑποζυγίων ἔταξε. πορευόμενοι δ'
ἐντυγχάνουσι λόφῳ ὑπὲρ τῆς ὁδοῦ κατειλημμένῳ ὑπὸ τῶν πολεμίων, οὓς ἢ ἀποκόψαι ἦν ἀνάγκη ἢ διεζεῦχθαι ἀπὸ τῶν ἄλλων
Ἑλλήνων. καὶ αὐτοὶ μὲν ἂν ἐπορεύθησαν ᾗπερ οἱ ἄλλοι, τὰ
δὲ ὑποζύγια οὐκ ἦν ἄλλῃ ἢ ταύτῃ ἐκβῆναι. ἔνθα δὴ παρακελευσάμενοι ἀλλήλοις προσβάλλουσι πρὸς τὸν λόφον ὀρθίοις τοῖς
λόχοις, οὐ κύκλῳ ἀλλὰ καταλιπόντες ἄφοδον τοῖς πολεμίοις, εἰ
βούλοιντο φεύγειν. καὶ τέως μὲν αὐτοὺς ἀναβαίνοντας ὅπῃ ἐδύνατο ἕκαστος οἱ βάρβαροι ἐτόξευον καὶ ἔβαλλον, ἐγγὺς δ' οὐ
προσίεντο, ἀλλὰ φυγῇ λείπουσι τὸ χωρίον. καὶ τοῦτόν τε
παρεληλύθεσαν οἱ Ἕλληνες καὶ ἕτερον ὁρῶσιν ἔμπροσθεν λόφον
κατεχόμενον ἐπὶ τοῦτον αὖθις ἐδόκει πορεύεσθαι. ἐννοήσας δ'
ὁ Ξενοφῶν μή, εἰ ἔρημον καταλίποι τὸν ἑαλωκότα λόφον, πάλιν
λαβόντες οἱ πολέμιοι ἐπιθοῖντο τοῖς ὑποζυγίοις παριοῦσιν—ἐπὶ
πολὺ δ' ἦν τὰ ὑποζύγια ἅτε διὰ στενῆς τῆς ὁδοῦ πορευόμενα—
καταλείπει ἐπὶ τοῦ λόφου λοχαγοὺς Κηφισόδωρον Κηφισοφῶντος
Ἀθηναῖον καὶ Ἀμφικράτην Ἀμφιδήμου Ἀθηναῖον καὶ Ἀρχα-

---

42 λόφῳ: this was not the ἄκρον (μαστός); see the plan.

43 διεζεῦχθαι, to be cut off once for all; note the tense.

44 τὰ δὲ ὑποζύγια: subj. of διαβῆναι.

46 ὀρθίοις τοῖς λόχοις, with companies in column. See the Introd., §28. Such a formation was well adapted to rough ground, where the phalanx could hardly have been used.

47 ἄφοδον: they did not wish to force an engagement.

εἰ βούλοιντο: see G. 1420; H. 907; B. 613.

50 προσίεντο: for the vb., cf. III, 1, 134.

τε ... καί: co-ordination; freely, when the Greeks had passed this, they saw another. (ὁρῶσιν is dat. of the partic., with ἐδόκει.)

This second hill is also distinct from the ἄκρον; see the plan.

52 ἐννοήσας: cf. III, 5, 12. The aor. is ingressive.

54 ἐπιθοῖντο: for the form, see G. 741; H. 445b; B. 170, 4.

ἐπὶ πολὺ δ' ἦν, stretched over a long distance. Cf. I, 8, 28.

55 ἅτε: with causal partic.; see G. 1575; H. 977; B. 656, 1. For the difference between ἅτε and ὡς, see the note on I, 1, 12. Cf. c. 5. §18; c. 8. §27.

στενῆς: pred. (because the road over which they were passing was narrow).

56 Κηφισοφῶντος ... Ἀμφιδήμου: in such cases the omitted word is regularly υἱός. These men are both Athenians, and at Athens it was the custom to

γόραν Ἀργεῖον φυγάδα, αὐτὸς δὲ σὺν τοῖς λοιποῖς ἐπορεύετο ἐπὶ τὸν δεύτερον λόφον, καὶ τῷ αὐτῷ τρόπῳ καὶ τοῦτον αἱροῦσιν.

14 ἔτι δὲ αὐτοῖς τρίτος μαστὸς λοιπὸς ἦν πολὺ ὀρθιώτατος ὁ ὑπὲρ τῆς ἐπὶ τῷ πυρὶ καταληφθείσης φυλακῆς τῆς νυκτὸς ὑπὸ
15 τῶν ἐθελοντῶν. ἐπεὶ δ' ἐγγὺς ἐγένοντο οἱ Ἕλληνες, λείπουσιν οἱ βάρβαροι ἀμαχητὶ τὸν μαστόν, ὥστε θαυμαστὸν πᾶσι γενέσθαι καὶ ὑπώπτευον δείσαντας αὐτοὺς μὴ κυκλωθέντες πολιορκοῖντο ἀπολιπεῖν. οἱ δ' ἄρα ἀπὸ τοῦ ἄκρου καθορῶντες τὰ ὄπισθεν
16 γιγνόμενα πάντες ἐπὶ τοὺς ὀπισθοφύλακας ἐχώρουν. καὶ Ξενοφῶν μὲν σὺν τοῖς νεωτάτοις ἀνέβαινεν ἐπὶ τὸ ἄκρον, τοὺς δὲ ἄλλους ἐκέλευσεν ὑπάγειν, ὅπως οἱ τελευταῖοι λόχοι προσμείξειαν, καὶ προελθόντας κατὰ τὴν ὁδὸν ἐν τῷ ὁμαλῷ θέσθαι τὰ ὅπλα.

17 καὶ ἐν τούτῳ τῷ χρόνῳ ἦλθεν Ἀρχαγόρας ὁ Ἀργεῖος πεφευγὼς καὶ λέγει ὡς ἀπεκόπησαν ἀπὸ τοῦ λόφου καὶ ὅτι τεθνᾶσι

---

give the father's name as well as that of the man in question.

60 τρίτος μαστός: this was the ἄκρον of c. 1. 25, which the volunteers should have occupied.

ὁ . . . ἐθελοντῶν, *the one above the outpost which had been surprised at the fire during the night by the volunteers.* In such cases it is not necessary that *all* the defining words should stand between art. and noun (G. 969; H. 667a). Had they done so in this case the sentence would have been less clear.

63 ἀμαχητί: but I, 7, 48, and elsewhere, ἀμαχεί.

64 αὐτοὺς . . . ἀπολιπεῖν: quoted after ὑπώπτευον (subj., the Greeks); δείσαντας is causal. Note the shift from the infin. after ὥστε to an independ. vb.

65 ἄρα, *as it proved.*

66 τοὺς ὀπισθοφύλακας: *i. e.* those left to guard the first hill, as § 17 shows. The Carduchi had seen from their position on the height what was happening in their rear, and now make a détour, intending to overpower these men and attack the Greeks from behind.

67 νεωτάτοις: the younger men were often chosen for arduous or hazardous duty; *cf.* II, 3, 45 f. By occupying this height Xen. secures the road for the passage of the train.

68 ὑπάγειν, *lead on slowly;* not quite as III, 4, 195.

69 θέσθαι τὰ ὅπλα: *cf.* I, 5, 88, and the note.

71 πεφευγώς: not equivalent to φυγάς, but = *having made his escape; cf.* II, 1, 13. Note the vivid indics. in indir. disc.

Κηφισόδωρος καὶ Ἀμφικράτης καὶ ἄλλοι ὅσοι μὴ ἁλάμενοι κατὰ τῆς πέτρας πρὸς τοὺς ὀπισθοφύλακας ἀφίκοντο. ταῦτα δὲ διαπραξάμενοι οἱ βάρβαροι ἧκον ἐπ' ἀντίπορον λόφον τῷ μαστῷ· καὶ ὁ Ξενοφῶν διελέγετο αὐτοῖς δι' ἑρμηνέως περὶ σπονδῶν καὶ τοὺς νεκροὺς ἀπῄτει. οἱ δὲ ἔφασαν ἀποδώσειν ἐφ' ᾧ μὴ καίειν τὰς οἰκίας. συνωμολόγει ταῦτα ὁ Ξενοφῶν. ἐν ᾧ δὲ τὸ μὲν ἄλλο στράτευμα παρῄει, οἱ δὲ ταῦτα διελέγοντο, πάντες οἱ ἐκ τούτου τοῦ τόπου συνερρύησαν ἐνταῦθα πολέμιοι. καὶ ἐπεὶ ἤρξαντο καταβαίνειν ἀπὸ τοῦ μαστοῦ πρὸς τοὺς ἄλλους ἔνθα τὰ ὅπλα ἔκειντο, ἵεντο δὴ οἱ πολέμιοι πολλῷ πλήθει καὶ θορύβῳ· καὶ ἐπεὶ ἐγένοντο ἐπὶ τῆς κορυφῆς τοῦ μαστοῦ ἀφ' οὗ Ξενοφῶν κατέβαινεν, ἐκυλίνδουν πέτρους· καὶ ἑνὸς μὲν κατέαξαν τὸ σκέλος, Ξενοφῶντα δὲ ὁ ὑπασπιστὴς ἔχων τὴν ἀσπίδα ἀπέλιπεν· Εὐρύλοχος δὲ Λουσιεὺς προσέδραμεν αὐτῷ ὁπλίτης, καὶ πρὸ ἀμφοῖν προβεβλημένος ἀπεχώρει, καὶ οἱ ἄλλοι πρὸς τοὺς συντεταγμένους ἀπῆλθον.

ἐκ δὲ τούτου πᾶν ὁμοῦ ἐγένετο τὸ Ἑλληνικόν, καὶ ἐσκήνησαν αὐτοῦ ἐν πολλαῖς καὶ καλαῖς οἰκίαις καὶ ἐπιτηδείοις δαψιλέσι· καὶ γὰρ οἶνος πολὺς ἦν, ὥστε ἐν λάκκοις κονιατοῖς εἶχον. Ξενο-

---

73 ὅσοι μή, *all who had not.* μή is generic; *cf.* II, 2, 64, and the note.

75 ἀντίπορον, *opposite,* another poetic word. This may, or may not, have been the height seized by the volunteers in the night. Note the free position of τῷ μαστῷ.

77 τοὺς νεκρούς: *cf.* the note on c. 1. 77.

ἐφ' ᾧ μὴ καίειν, *on condition that they should not burn.* See G. 1460; H. 999a; B. 596.

78 ἐν ᾧ, *while.* For such phrases, *cf.* the note on I, 2, 117.

80 οἱ ἐκ: *cf.* τῶν παρὰ βασιλέως, I, 1, 18, and the note.

συνερρύησαν: a vivid metaphor; *cf.* V, 2, § 3.

81 ἤρξαντο: *i. e.* Xen. and the νεώτατοι.

82 ἔνθα τὰ ὅπλα ἔκειντο, *where the hoplites stood under arms.* The phrase is the pass. of τίθεσθαι τὰ ὅπλα.

84 ἐκυλίνδουν . . . κατέαξαν: note the tenses.

85 ἀπέλιπεν, *had left in the lurch,* doubtless through fear.

87 προβεβλημένος, *with his shield thrown before them both.* With this use of the mid. *cf.* διηγκυλομένους and ἐπιβεβλημένους, c. 3. § 28. τοὺς συντεταγμένους: *cf.* above, § 16.

90 δαψιλέσι: a poetic word, used occasionally by Xen.; *cf.* c. 4. § 2.

91 ἐν λάκκοις: such cisterns are still to be seen in Kurdistan and

φῶν δὲ καὶ Χειρίσοφος διεπράξαντο ὥστε λαβόντες τοὺς νεκροὺς
ἀπέδοσαν τὸν ἡγεμόνα· καὶ πάντα ἐποίησαν τοῖς ἀποθανοῦσιν
ἐκ τῶν δυνατῶν ὥσπερ νομίζεται ἀνδράσιν ἀγαθοῖς.

τῇ δὲ ὑστεραίᾳ ἄνευ ἡγεμόνος ἐπορεύοντο· μαχόμενοι δ᾽ οἱ 95
πολέμιοι καὶ ὅπῃ εἴη στενὸν χωρίον προκαταλαμβάνοντες ἐκώλυον τὰς παρόδους. ὁπότε μὲν οὖν τοὺς πρώτους κωλύοιεν,
Ξενοφῶν ὄπισθεν ἐκβαίνων πρὸς τὰ ὄρη ἔλυε τὴν ἀπόφραξιν
τῆς ὁδοῦ τοῖς πρώτοις ἀνωτέρω πειρώμενος γίγνεσθαι τῶν κωλυόντων, ὁπότε δὲ τοῖς ὄπισθεν ἐπιθοῖντο, Χειρίσοφος ἐκβαίνων 100
καὶ πειρώμενος ἀνωτέρω γίγνεσθαι τῶν κωλυόντων ἔλυε τὴν
ἀπόφραξιν τῆς παρόδου τοῖς ὄπισθεν· καὶ ἀεὶ οὕτως ἐβοήθουν
ἀλλήλοις καὶ ἰσχυρῶς ἀλλήλων ἐπεμέλοντο.

ἦν δὲ καὶ ὁπότε αὐτοῖς τοῖς ἀναβᾶσι πολλὰ πράγματα
παρεῖχον οἱ βάρβαροι πάλιν καταβαίνουσιν· ἐλαφροὶ γὰρ ἦσαν 105
ὥστε καὶ ἐγγύθεν φεύγοντες ἀποφεύγειν· οὐδὲν γὰρ εἶχον ἄλλο
ἢ τόξα καὶ σφενδόνας. ἄριστοι δὲ καὶ τοξόται ἦσαν· εἶχον δὲ
τόξα ἐγγὺς τριπήχη, τὰ δὲ τοξεύματα πλέον ἢ διπήχη· εἷλκον
δὲ τὰς νευρὰς ὁπότε τοξεύοιεν πρὸς τὸ κάτω τοῦ τόξου τῷ ἀρι-

Armenia. The custom was familiar to the Greeks, as well.

92 διεπράξαντο ὥστε: *cf. ποιήσειεν ὥστε*, I, 6, 9, and the note. Here the use of the indic. emphasizes the fact that the terms of the contract were actually fulfilled.

93 τὸν ἡγεμόνα: *cf.* c. 1. § 24.

τοῖς ἀποθανοῦσιν, *in honor of the dead.* *Cf.* the note on c. 1. 77.

94 ἐκ τῶν δυνατῶν: limiting *πάντα*. **νομίζεται**, *is held right.*

96 ὅπῃ εἴη, *wherever there was.* *Cf.* the general temporal sentences below.

ἐκώλυον: conative, as *κωλύοιεν*, below.

97 τὰς παρόδους, *their passage.* The pl. refers to the several occasions.

98 ἀπόφραξιν, *blockade*, a rare word.

104 ἦν δὲ καὶ ὁπότε, *and sometimes, too.* *Cf.* ἔσθ᾽ ὅτε, II, 6, 35, and the note on ἦν οὕς, I, 5, 35.

αὐτοῖς, freely, *even.*

πράγματα παρεῖχον: *cf.* I, 1, 63.

105 ἐλαφροί: tantamount to *εὔζωνοι* (l. 33), with which it is joined, III, 3, 29.

106 ὥστε ... ἀποφεύγειν, *so as to make good their escape even when fleeing from near at hand.* For *ἀποφεύγειν*, *cf.* the note on I, 4, 48; with *ἐγγύθεν*, *cf.* ἐκ πλέονος, I, 10, 47, and ἐκ τόξου ῥύματος, III, 3, 62.

108 ἐγγύς, *nearly.*

109 πρὸς τὸ κάτω ... προσβαίνοντες, *planting the left foot against the base of the bow.* Some assume that Xen. means to indicate a sort of cross-bow, but

110 στερῷ ποδὶ προσβαίνοντες. τὰ δὲ τοξεύματα ἐχώρει διὰ τῶν ἀσπίδων καὶ διὰ τῶν θωράκων. ἐχρῶντο δὲ αὐτοῖς οἱ Ἕλληνες, ἐπεὶ λάβοιεν, ἀκοντίοις ἐναγκυλῶντες. ἐν τούτοις τοῖς χωρίοις οἱ Κρῆτες χρησιμώτατοι ἐγένοντο. ἦρχε δὲ αὐτῶν Στρατοκλῆς Κρής.

III. Ταύτην δ' αὖ τὴν ἡμέραν ηὐλίσθησαν ἐν ταῖς κώμαις 1 ταῖς ὑπὲρ τοῦ πεδίου παρὰ τὸν Κεντρίτην ποταμόν, εὖρος ὡς δίπλεθρον, ὃς ὁρίζει τὴν Ἀρμενίαν καὶ τὴν τῶν Καρδούχων χώραν. καὶ οἱ Ἕλληνες ἐνταῦθα ἀνέπνευσαν ἄσμενοι ἰδόντες 5 πεδίον· ἀπεῖχε δὲ τῶν ὀρέων ὁ ποταμὸς ἓξ ἢ ἑπτὰ στάδια τῶν Καρδούχων. τότε μὲν οὖν ηὐλίσθησαν μάλα ἡδέως καὶ τἀπι- 2 τήδεια ἔχοντες καὶ πολλὰ τῶν παρεληλυθότων πόνων μνημονεύοντες. ἑπτὰ γὰρ ἡμέρας ὅσασπερ ἐπορεύθησαν διὰ τῶν Καρδούχων πάσας μαχόμενοι διετέλεσαν, καὶ ἔπαθον κακὰ ὅσα 10 οὐδὲ τὰ σύμπαντα ὑπὸ βασιλέως καὶ Τισσαφέρνους. ὡς οὖν ἀπηλλαγμένοι τούτων ἡδέως ἐκοιμήθησαν.

---

this seems very unlikely. *Cf.* Arrian, *Ind.* 16, τὸ τόξον κάτω ἐπὶ τὴν γῆν θέντες καὶ τῷ ἀριστερῷ ἀντιβάντες, and Diod. Sic. III, 8, (ξύλινα τόξα) οἷς τοξεύουσι μὲν τῷ ποδὶ προσβαίνοντες.

112 ἀκοντίοις: appos. with αὐτοῖς.

ἐναγκυλῶντες: the javelin was fitted with a thong (ἀγκύλη) attached to the middle of the shaft. By means of this greater force and greater certainty of aim were attained. See the Introd., § 28, and *cf.* διηγκυλωμένους, c. 4. 28.

113 Κρῆτες: *cf.* I, 2, 54, and the note.

CHAPTER III

2 Κεντρίτην ποταμόν: the present Butan Tchai, an eastern tributary of the Tigris; see the map.

3 δίπλεθρον: *cf.* πλεθριαῖον, I, 5, 20, and the note. Consult, also, the note on δύο πλέθρα, I, 2, 30 f.

4 ἀνέπνευσαν: *cf.* c. 1. 86.

ἄσμενοι: *cf.* προτέρα, I, 2, 142, and the note.

5 τῶν Καρδούχων: with ὀρέων.

7 πολλά: inner obj. of μνημονεύοντες. Render freely, *often.* The thought is a common one. Most familiar is, perhaps, Vergil's Forsan et haec olim meminisse iuvabit.

8 ἑπτά: only five days have been enumerated. The difficulty is usually met by assuming that Xen. includes the next two days, in which they were beset by the same enemies.

9 μαχόμενοι διετέλεσαν: *cf.* διετέλουν χρώμενοι, III, 4, 65.

κακά: yet had not the mountainous country saved them from the pursuit by Tiss. and the Persians, they might well have succumbed in the end.

Ἅμα δὲ τῇ ἡμέρᾳ ὁρῶσιν ἱππέας που πέραν τοῦ ποταμοῦ ἐξωπλισμένους ὡς κωλύσοντας διαβαίνειν, πεζοὺς δ' ἐπὶ ταῖς ὄχθαις παρατεταγμένους ἄνω τῶν ἱππέων ὡς κωλύσοντας εἰς τὴν Ἀρμενίαν ἐκβαίνειν. ἦσαν δ' οὗτοι Ὀρόντα καὶ Ἀρτούχα Ἀρμένιοι καὶ Μάρδοι καὶ Χαλδαῖοι μισθοφόροι. ἐλέγοντο δὲ οἱ Χαλδαῖοι ἐλεύθεροί τε καὶ ἄλκιμοι εἶναι· ὅπλα δ' εἶχον γέρρα μακρὰ καὶ λόγχας. αἱ δὲ ὄχθαι αὗται ἐφ' ὧν παρατεταγμένοι οὗτοι ἦσαν τρία ἢ τέτταρα πλέθρα ἀπὸ τοῦ ποταμοῦ ἀπεῖχον· ὁδὸς δὲ μία ὁρωμένη ἦν ἄγουσα ἄνω ὥσπερ χειροποίητος· ταύτῃ ἐπειρῶντο διαβαίνειν οἱ Ἕλληνες. ἐπεὶ δὲ πειρωμένοις τό τε ὕδωρ ὑπὲρ τῶν μαστῶν ἐφαίνετο, καὶ τραχὺς ἦν ὁ ποταμὸς μεγάλοις λίθοις καὶ ὀλισθηροῖς, καὶ οὔτ' ἐν τῷ ὕδατι τὰ ὅπλα ἦν ἔχειν,—εἰ δὲ μή, ἥρπαζεν ὁ ποταμός·—ἐπί τε τῆς κεφαλῆς τὰ ὅπλα εἴ τις φέροι, γυμνοὶ ἐγίγνοντο πρὸς τὰ τοξεύματα καὶ τἆλλα βέλη, ἀνεχώρησαν καὶ αὐτοῦ ἐστρατοπεδεύσαντο παρὰ τὸν ποταμόν. ἔνθα δὲ αὐτοὶ τὴν πρόσθεν νύκτα ἦσαν ἐπὶ τοῦ ὄρους ἑώρων τοὺς Καρδούχους πολλοὺς συνειλεγμένους

---

11 ἀπηλλαγμένοι: cf. ἀπηλλάγη, I, 10, 35, and the note. Their troubles were, however, not yet over.

15 ἐκβαίνειν: used as ἔκβασιν, c. 2. 5, and below, l. 88.

Ὀρόντα ... Ἀρτούχα: for these gen. forms, cf. Ἀβροκόμα, I, 4, 15, and the note.

17 ἐλεύθεροι: yet they were nominally under Persian rule.

ἄλκιμοι: a poetic word, occurring again, c. 7. § 15.

ὅπλα: appos, as ἀκοντίοις, above, c. 2. 112.

20 ὁδὸς ... ἄγουσα, freely, *there was a single road in sight, which led*. For the form ἦν ἄγουσα, cf. the note on εἶναι ... φυλάττων, I, 2, 122 f. Here, too, each element has its own force.

χειροποίητος: "made" roads were not common until Roman days; see the note on I, 9, 44. Remains of an ancient causeway are reported by travelers as still to be seen in this region, but the exact locality is uncertain.

21 πειρωμένοις: cf. III, 5, 27, and the note.

22 ὁ ποταμός, *the river bed*.

23 οὔτ': balanced by τε, below.

24 εἰ δὲ μή: cf. II, 2, 6, and the note. This clause is parenthetic.

25 γυμνοὶ ... πρός, *exposed to*. Note the pl. after the collective τις, and the postponement of the condit. part. (cf. the note on II, 4, 27).

27 παρὰ τὸν ποταμόν: further defining αὐτοῦ (*where they were*).

ἦσαν, *had been*. See the note on I, 2, 129.

ἐν τοῖς ὅπλοις. ἐνταῦθα δὴ πολλὴ ἀθυμία ἦν τοῖς Ἕλλησιν,
30 ὁρῶσι μὲν τοῦ ποταμοῦ τὴν δυσπορίαν, ὁρῶσι δὲ τοὺς διαβαίνειν
κωλύσοντας, ὁρῶσι δὲ τοῖς διαβαίνουσιν ἐπικεισομένους τοὺς
Καρδούχους ὄπισθεν.

ταύτην μὲν οὖν τὴν ἡμέραν καὶ νύκτα ἔμειναν ἐν πολλῇ 8
ἀπορίᾳ ὄντες. Ξενοφῶν δὲ ὄναρ εἶδεν· ἔδοξεν ἐν πέδαις δεδέσθαι,
35 αὗται δὲ αὐτῷ αὐτόμαται περιρρυῆναι, ὥστε λυθῆναι καὶ διαβαίνειν ὁπόσον ἐβούλετο. ἐπεὶ δὲ ὄρθρος ἦν, ἔρχεται πρὸς τὸν
Χειρίσοφον καὶ λέγει ὅτι ἐλπίδας ἔχει καλῶς ἔσεσθαι, καὶ διηγεῖται αὐτῷ τὸ ὄναρ. ὁ δὲ ἥδετό τε καὶ ὡς τάχιστα ἕως ὑπέ- 9
φαινεν ἐθύοντο πάντες παρόντες οἱ στρατηγοί· καὶ τὰ ἱερὰ καλὰ
40 ἦν εὐθὺς ἐπὶ τοῦ πρώτου. καὶ ἀπιόντες ἀπὸ τῶν ἱερῶν οἱ στρατηγοὶ καὶ λοχαγοὶ παρήγγελλον τῇ στρατιᾷ ἀριστοποιεῖσθαι.

καὶ ἀριστῶντι τῷ Ξενοφῶντι προσέτρεχον δύο νεανίσκω· ᾔδε- 1
σαν γὰρ πάντες ὅτι ἐξείη αὐτῷ καὶ ἀριστῶντι καὶ δειπνοῦντι
προσελθεῖν καὶ εἰ καθεύδοι ἐπεγείραντα εἰπεῖν, εἴ τίς τι ἔχοι
45 τῶν πρὸς τὸν πόλεμον. καὶ τότε ἔλεγον ὅτι τυγχάνοιεν φρύ- 1
γανα συλλέγοντες ὡς ἐπὶ πῦρ, κἄπειτα κατίδοιεν ἐν τῷ πέραν
ἐν πέτραις καθηκούσαις ἐπ' αὐτὸν τὸν ποταμὸν γέροντά τε καὶ

---

30 ὁρῶσι μὲν ... ὁρῶσι δὲ ... ὁρῶσι δέ: triple anaphora.
31 ἐπικεισομένους: cf. c. 1. 65. We have ἐπιθήσεσθαι, II, 4, 81.
34 ὄναρ: cf. III, 1, 54.
ἔδοξεν: normal asyn.
35 περιρρυῆναι, to slip off his feet.
διαβαίνειν, could move his legs, take a step. This is a proper meaning of the word (for the simple vb., cf. βεβηκότες, III, 2, 99, and the note). This cpd. is, however, generally trans., to pass through, cross, and is doubtless chosen with reference to their crossing the river.
37 ἐλπίδας ἔχει = ἐλπίζει, and so followed by the fut. infin. Cf. the note on πιστὰ λαβεῖν, II, 3, 108.

38 ὡς τάχιστα: ὡς is the temp. conjunc., not, as so often, an intensifying adv.
40 ἐπὶ τοῦ πρώτου: cf. VI, 5, § 2, where the word ἱερείου (victim) is added.
43 αὐτῷ: i. e. Ξενοφῶντι; dat. after προσελθεῖν.
44 ἔχοι: sc. λέγειν.
45 καὶ τότε, and so in this case— an illustration of what has just been said.
τυγχάνοιεν: imperf. opt.; see G. 1488; H. 935b; B. 675, 1, note. The vbs. were in dir. disc. ἐτυγχάνομεν and κατείδομεν.
46 ἐν τῷ πέραν: cf. εἰς τὸ πέραν, III, 5, 10.
47 καθηκούσαις: cf. καθήκοντα, I, 4, 25.

γυναῖκα καὶ παιδίσκας ὥσπερ μαρσίπους ἱματίων κατατιθεμέ-
12 νους ἐν πέτρᾳ ἀντρώδει. ἰδοῦσι δὲ σφίσι δόξαι ἀσφαλὲς εἶναι
διαβῆναι· οὐδὲ γὰρ τοῖς πολεμίοις ἱππεῦσι προσβατὸν εἶναι
κατὰ τοῦτο. ἐκδύντες δ' ἔφασαν ἔχοντες τὰ ἐγχειρίδια γυμνοὶ
ὡς νευσόμενοι διαβαίνειν· πορευόμενοι δὲ πρόσθεν διαβῆναι
πρὶν βρέξαι τὰ αἰδοῖα· καὶ διαβάντες, λαβόντες τὰ ἱμάτια
πάλιν ἥκειν.

13 εὐθὺς οὖν Ξενοφῶν αὐτός τε ἔσπενδε καὶ τοῖς νεανίσκοις ἐγχεῖν
ἐκέλευε καὶ εὔχεσθαι τοῖς φήνασι θεοῖς τά τε ὀνείρατα καὶ τὸν
πόρον καὶ τὰ λοιπὰ ἀγαθὰ ἐπιτελέσαι. σπείσας δ' εὐθὺς ἦγε
τοὺς νεανίσκους παρὰ τὸν Χειρίσοφον, καὶ διηγοῦνται ταυτά.
14 ἀκούσας δὲ καὶ ὁ Χειρίσοφος σπονδὰς ἐποίει. σπείσαντες δὲ
τοῖς μὲν ἄλλοις παρήγγελλον συσκευάζεσθαι, αὐτοὶ δὲ συγκα-
λέσαντες τοὺς στρατηγοὺς ἐβουλεύοντο ὅπως ἂν κάλλιστα διαβαῖεν καὶ τούς τε ἔμπροσθεν νικῷεν καὶ ὑπὸ τῶν ὄπισθεν μηδὲν
15 πάσχοιεν κακόν. καὶ ἔδοξεν αὐτοῖς Χειρίσοφον μὲν ἡγεῖσθαι
καὶ διαβαίνειν ἔχοντα τὸ ἥμισυ τοῦ στρατεύματος, τὸ δ' ἥμισυ
ἔτι ὑπομένειν σὺν Ξενοφῶντι, τὰ δὲ ὑποζύγια καὶ τὸν ὄχλον ἐν
μέσῳ τούτων διαβαίνειν.

---

48 **ὥσπερ**, freely, *what appeared to be*.
49 **δόξαι**: infin., as though ἔφασαν, not ἔλεγον ὅτι, had preceded. This is of common occurrence.
52 **ὡς νευσόμενοι**, *thinking that they would have to swim*.
πρόσθεν ... πρίν: cf. I, 1, 58, and the note. Observe the neg. force of πρίν. We might render πρὶν βρέξαι, *without wetting*.
53 **λαβόντες**: this explains their motive in crossing—to steal the clothing.
55 **τοῖς νεανίσκοις**: dat. after ἐγχεῖν, not after ἐκέλευε, which does not take a dat. in Attic prose. We need not supply any word; in Eng., too, we can say *bade pour*.
56 **φήνασι**, *who had shown*. This has both ὀνείρατα and πόρον as objs. The former is perhaps pl. because the dream had two distinct phases.
καὶ ... ἐπιτελέσαι, lit., *that they would bring to accomplishment also the remaining blessings* (i. e. whatever was wanting to success). The infin. is governed by εὔχεσθαι.
59 **σπονδὰς ἐποίει** = ἔσπενδε.
61 **ὅπως ἄν ... διαβαῖεν ... νικῷεν ... πάσχοιεν**: poten. opt. in an indir. quest., rather than an obj. clause of irregular type. *Cf.* III, 2, 140, and the note.
64 **τὸ ἥμισυ**: probably felt as a noun, although στρατεύματος is

PLAN TO ILLUSTRATE IV, 3, §§ 3-34

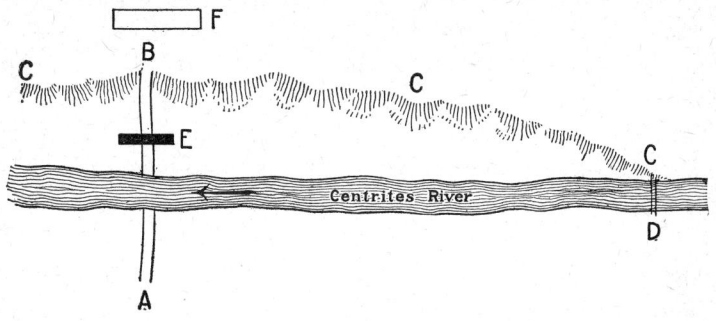

The road AB crossing the river is guarded by Armenian cavalry at E and by a force of footmen (F) on the bluffs above (CCC). The young men have discovered a ford D where the bluffs come so close to the river as to leave no room for the enemy's cavalry. Chirisophus, with half the army and the train, crosses the river at the ford D, Xenophon and the other half remaining behind. As Chirisophus crosses, Xenophon marches back quickly to the crossing AB, and the Armenian cavalry, fearing an attack on both sides, flee. Xenophon then returns to the ford D and, as the Carduchi threaten to attack him in the rear, forms his men facing them. The Greeks charge and the Carduchi turn and flee. Then at the sound of the trumpet the Greeks wheel about quickly and cross the river before the enemy discover the trick.

ἐπεὶ δὲ ταῦτα καλῶς εἶχεν ἐπορεύοντο· ἡγοῦντο δ' οἱ νεα-
νίσκοι ἐν ἀριστερᾷ ἔχοντες τὸν ποταμόν· ὁδὸς δὲ ἦν ἐπὶ τὴν
διάβασιν ὡς τέτταρες στάδιοι. πορευομένων δ' αὐτῶν ἀντιπαρῇσαν αἱ τάξεις τῶν ἱππέων. ἐπειδὴ δὲ ἦσαν κατὰ τὴν διάβασιν
καὶ τὰς ὄχθας τοῦ ποταμοῦ, ἔθεντο τὰ ὅπλα, καὶ αὐτὸς πρῶτος
Χειρίσοφος στεφανωσάμενος καὶ ἀποδὺς ἐλάμβανε τὰ ὅπλα καὶ
τοῖς ἄλλοις πᾶσι παρήγγελλε, καὶ τοὺς λοχαγοὺς ἐκέλευεν
ἄγειν τοὺς λόχους ὀρθίους, τοὺς μὲν ἐν ἀριστερᾷ τοὺς δ' ἐν δεξιᾷ
ἑαυτοῦ. καὶ οἱ μὲν μάντεις ἐσφαγιάζοντο εἰς τὸν ποταμόν· οἱ
δὲ πολέμιοι ἐτόξευον καὶ ἐσφενδόνων· ἀλλ' οὔπω ἐξικνοῦντο· ἐπεὶ
δὲ καλὰ ἦν τὰ σφάγια, ἐπαιάνιζον πάντες οἱ στρατιῶται καὶ
ἀνηλάλαζον, συνωλόλυζον δὲ καὶ αἱ γυναῖκες ἅπασαι. πολλαὶ
γὰρ ἦσαν ἑταῖραι ἐν τῷ στρατεύματι.

καὶ Χειρίσοφος μὲν ἐνέβαινε καὶ οἱ σὺν ἐκείνῳ· ὁ δὲ Ξενοφῶν
τῶν ὀπισθοφυλάκων λαβὼν τοὺς εὐζωνοτάτους ἔθει ἀνὰ κράτος
πάλιν ἐπὶ τὸν πόρον τὸν κατὰ τὴν ἔκβασιν τὴν εἰς τὰ τῶν
Ἀρμενίων ὄρη, προσποιούμενος ταύτῃ διαβὰς ἀποκλείσειν τοὺς

---

itself neut. *Cf.* the note on τοὺς ἡμίσεις, c. 2. 39.

69 ἀντιπαρῇσαν, *kept abreast of them* (on the opposite bank).

70 διάβασιν: *i. e.* the ford discovered by the youths.

κατὰ ... τὰς ὄχθας, *at the ford and opposite the bluffs* (§ 3).

72 στεφανωσάμενος: a Spartan custom. Xen. *Repub. Lac.* 13, 8, gives as a law of Lycurgus, μηδένα Λακεδαιμονίων ἀστεφάνωτον εἶναι (*i. e.* when facing the foe). *Cf.* Plut. *Lycurg.* 22).

73 παρήγγελλε: *i. e.* to follow his example.

74 τοὺς λόχους ὀρθίους: *cf.* c. 2. 46, and the note.

75 ἐσφαγιάζοντο εἰς: *cf.* σφάξαντες εἰς, II, 2, 40 f., and the note.

78 ἀνηλάλαζον, συνωλόλυζον: for the former vb., *cf.* c. 2. 31, and the note. The latter is almost invariably used of a cry raised by women, whether of fear or (oftener) of joy. Note the chiastic order.

79 ἑταῖραι: *cf.* Motley's description of the army of Alva (*Dutch Republic*, Part III, chap. i).

81 εὐζωνοτάτους: *cf.* c. 2. 33.

ἀνὰ κράτος: *cf.* I, 8, 4, and below, l. 87.

82 τὸν πόρον τὸν κατά: the formal position is due to a desire for clearness. This was the regular ford which the enemy had been guarding. For ἔκβασιν, *cf.* c. 2. 5.

83 προσποιούμενος ... ἀποκλείσειν, *pretending that he was going to cross there and cut off.*

21 παρὰ τὸν ποταμὸν ἱππεῖς. οἱ δὲ πολέμιοι ὁρῶντες μὲν τοὺς
ἀμφὶ Χειρίσοφον εὐπετῶς τὸ ὕδωρ περῶντας, ὁρῶντες δὲ τοὺς 85
ἀμφὶ Ξενοφῶντα θέοντας εἰς τοὔμπαλιν, δείσαντες μὴ ἀπο-
ληφθείησαν φεύγουσιν ἀνὰ κράτος ὡς πρὸς τὴν τοῦ ποταμοῦ
ἄνω ἔκβασιν. ἐπεὶ δὲ κατὰ τὴν ὁδὸν ἐγένοντο, ἔτεινον ἄνω πρὸς
22 τὸ ὄρος. Λύκιος δ' ὁ τὴν τάξιν ἔχων τῶν ἱππέων καὶ Αἰσχίνης
ὁ τὴν τάξιν τῶν πελταστῶν ἀμφὶ Χειρίσοφον ἐπεὶ ἑώρων ἀνὰ 90
κράτος φεύγοντας, εἵποντο· οἱ δὲ στρατιῶται ἐβόων μὴ ἀπολεί-
23 πεσθαι, ἀλλὰ συνεκβαίνειν ἐπὶ τὸ ὄρος. Χειρίσοφος δ' αὖ ἐπεὶ
διέβη, τοὺς ἱππέας οὐκ ἐδίωκεν, εὐθὺς δὲ κατὰ τὰς προσηκούσας
ὄχθας ἐπὶ τὸν ποταμὸν ἐξέβαινεν ἐπὶ τοὺς ἄνω πολεμίους. οἱ
δὲ ἄνω, ὁρῶντες μὲν τοὺς ἑαυτῶν ἱππέας φεύγοντας, ὁρῶντες 95
δ' ὁπλίτας σφίσιν ἐπιόντας, ἐκλείπουσι τὰ ὑπὲρ τοῦ ποταμοῦ
ἄκρα.

4 Ξενοφῶν δ' ἐπεὶ τὰ πέραν ἑώρα καλῶς γιγνόμενα, ἀπεχώρει
τὴν ταχίστην πρὸς τὸ διαβαῖνον στράτευμα· καὶ γὰρ οἱ Καρδοῦχοι φανεροὶ ἤδη ἦσαν εἰς τὸ πεδίον καταβαίνοντες ὡς ἐπιθη- 100
5 σόμενοι τοῖς τελευταίοις. καὶ Χειρίσοφος μὲν τὰ ἄνω κατεῖχε,

---

84 ὁρῶντες μὲν . . . ὁρῶντες δέ: anaphora, as so often; *cf.* l. 30.

87 ὡς πρὸς . . . ἔκβασιν, *apparently to the road which led up from the river*. τοῦ ποταμοῦ is governed by the prep. in the verbal noun ἔκβασιν. Others construe with ἄνω, but the order is against this.

88 ἔτεινον, *they hastened on*, not a common prose use. They made no attempt to defend the road after all.

89 Λύκιος: *cf.* III, 3, 82. Aeschines is mentioned again, c. 4. § 18.

91 στρατιῶται: *i. e.* the hoplites with Chirisophus.

ἐβόων . . . ὄρος, *kept shouting to them not to fall behind, but to pursue them right up to the mountain*. The vbs. were imv. in dir. disc. The alternative rendering, *protested that they (the hoplites) should not be left behind, but should join in the pursuit*, is unlikely. The heavy armed men would be no help, but rather a hindrance.

92 δ' αὖ, *on his part*, contrasted with Lycius and Aeschines.

94 ὄχθας: the πέτραι of § 11. For the order, *cf.* c. 2. 75.

τοὺς ἄνω πολεμίους: *cf.* § 3.

98 ἀπεχώρει: *i. e.* from the main ford to that discovered by the youths.

99 τὴν ταχίστην: *cf.* I, 3, 72.

100 φανεροὶ . . . ἦσαν: with partic.; *cf.* δῆλος ἦν ἀνιώμενος, I, 2, 70.

Λύκιος δὲ σὺν ὀλίγοις ἐπιχειρήσας ἐπιδιῶξαι ἔλαβε τῶν σκευοφόρων τὰ ὑπολειπόμενα καὶ μετὰ τούτων ἐσθῆτά τε καλὴν καὶ ἐκπώματα. καὶ τὰ μὲν σκευοφόρα τῶν Ἑλλήνων καὶ ὁ ὄχλος
105 ἀκμὴν διέβαινε, Ξενοφῶν δὲ στρέψας πρὸς τοὺς Καρδούχους ἀντία τὰ ὅπλα ἔθετο, καὶ παρήγγειλε τοῖς λοχαγοῖς κατ' ἐνωμοτίας ποιήσασθαι ἕκαστον τὸν ἑαυτοῦ λόχον, παρ' ἀσπίδα παραγαγόντας τὴν ἐνωμοτίαν ἐπὶ φάλαγγος· καὶ τοὺς μὲν λοχαγοὺς καὶ τοὺς ἐνωμοτάρχους πρὸς τῶν Καρδούχων ἰέναι,
110 οὐραγοὺς δὲ καταστήσασθαι πρὸς τοῦ ποταμοῦ. οἱ δὲ Καρδοῦχοι ὡς ἑώρων τοὺς ὀπισθοφύλακας τοῦ ὄχλου ψιλουμένους καὶ ὀλίγους ἤδη φαινομένους, θᾶττον δὴ ἐπῇσαν ᾠδάς τινας ᾄδοντες. ὁ δὲ Χειρίσοφος, ἐπεὶ τὰ παρ' αὐτῷ ἀσφαλῶς εἶχε, πέμπει παρὰ Ξενοφῶντα τοὺς πελταστὰς καὶ σφενδονήτας καὶ
115 τοξότας καὶ κελεύει ποιεῖν ὅ,τι ἂν παραγγέλλῃ.

ἰδὼν δ' αὐτοὺς διαβαίνοντας Ξενοφῶν πέμψας ἄγγελον κελεύει αὐτοῦ μεῖναι ἐπὶ τοῦ ποταμοῦ μὴ διαβάντας· ὅταν δ'

---

102 **τῶν σκευοφόρων**: *i. e.* of the enemy.
103 **τὰ ὑπολειπόμενα**, *those that kept falling behind;* note the tense.
ἐσθῆτα: *cf.* I, 2, 158, and the note.
105 **ἀκμὴν διέβαινε**, *were in the midst of crossing. Cf. ἀρχήν* and *τέλος* used as advs.
106 **κατ' ἐνωμοτίας**: the troops were presumably formed in company columns (§ 17). Xen. now orders his captains to form by enomoties and by deploying the companies to the left (παρ' ἀσπίδα) to form the phalanx.
107 **ἕκαστον**: sing. after a pl.; *cf.* I, 7, 74.
109 **πρός**, *on the side of, facing. Cf.* II, 2, 21.
110 **οὐραγούς**, *rear men.* These were picked men, trained in tactics, for whenever the order "about face!" was given, they became the leaders; so in this case. The omission of the art. is striking.
111 **τοῦ ὄχλου**: here *the main body;* not *the train*, which would be absurd.
112 **θᾶττον δή**: marks their confidence.
ᾠδάς τινας: the war chant of the barbarians seems hardly music to the Greek.
114 **πέμπει**: *i. e.* back across the stream. Note that one art. suffices for the three following nouns.
117 **αὐτοῦ μεῖναι**, *to stay where they were.*
ἐπί, *on the bank of.*
μὴ διαβάντας, *without crossing. μή*, not *οὐ*, because of the command.

ἄρξωνται αὐτοὶ διαβαίνειν, ἐναντίους ἔνθεν καὶ ἔνθεν σφῶν ἐμβαίνειν ὡς διαβησομένους, διηγκυλωμένους τοὺς ἀκοντιστὰς καὶ
ἐπιβεβλημένους τοὺς τοξότας· μὴ πρόσω δὲ τοῦ ποταμοῦ προ- 120
29 βαίνειν. τοῖς δὲ παρ' ἑαυτῷ παρήγγειλεν, ἐπειδὰν σφενδόνη
ἐξικνῆται καὶ ἀσπὶς ψοφῇ, παιανίσαντας θεῖν εἰς τοὺς πολεμίους, ἐπειδὰν δ' ἀναστρέψωσιν οἱ πολέμιοι καὶ ἐκ τοῦ ποταμοῦ
ὁ σαλπικτὴς σημήνῃ τὸ πολεμικόν, ἀναστρέψαντας ἐπὶ δόρυ
ἡγεῖσθαι μὲν τοὺς οὐραγούς, θεῖν δὲ πάντας καὶ διαβαίνειν ὅτι 125
τάχιστα ᾗ ἕκαστος τὴν τάξιν εἶχεν, ὡς μὴ ἐμποδίζειν ἀλλήλους·
ὅτι οὗτος ἄριστος ἔσοιτο ὃς ἂν πρῶτος ἐν τῷ πέραν γένηται.
30 οἱ δὲ Καρδοῦχοι ὁρῶντες ὀλίγους ἤδη τοὺς λοιπούς—πολλοὶ
γὰρ καὶ τῶν μένειν τεταγμένων ᾤχοντο ἐπιμελόμενοι οἱ μὲν
ὑποζυγίων, οἱ δὲ σκευῶν, οἱ δ' ἑταιρῶν—ἐνταῦθα δὴ ἐπέκειντο 130
31 θρασέως καὶ ἤρχοντο σφενδονᾶν καὶ τοξεύειν. οἱ δὲ Ἕλληνες
παιανίσαντες ὥρμησαν δρόμῳ ἐπ' αὐτούς· οἱ δὲ οὐκ ἐδέξαντο·
καὶ γὰρ ἦσαν ὡπλισμένοι ὡς μὲν ἐν τοῖς ὄρεσιν ἱκανῶς πρὸς τὸ

---

118 **αὐτοί**: Xen. and his men.
ἐναντίους, *to meet them*.
ἔνθεν καὶ ἔνθεν σφῶν, *above and below them*.
119 **διηγκυλωμένους**, *with their fingers on the thong (of the javelin)*.
120 **ἐπιβεβλημένους**, *with their arrows on the string*. Both partics. are mid., not pass. With the latter phrase, *cf.* V, 2, § 12.
πρόσω ... τοῦ ποταμοῦ, *far into the river*. The gen. is local (partitive); *cf.* I, 3, 2, and the note. Contrast πρόσω τῶν πηγῶν, III, 2, 116 (*far from their sources*).
122 **ψοφῇ**, *ring*, when struck by a missile.
εἰς: stronger than ἐπί, as indicating a hand-to-hand conflict.
124 **ὁ σαλπικτής**: rarely expressed (*cf.* l. 135); see the note on ἐσάλπιγξε, I, 2, 98.

τὸ πολεμικόν: of course to deceive the enemy.
ἐπὶ δόρυ: contrast παρ' ἀσπίδα, above, l. 107.
126 **εἶχεν**: instead of ἔχοι; see the note on III, 1, 7.
ὡς: for ὥστε; *cf.* I, 5, 64, and the note.
127 **ὅτι**, *adding that*. A vb. of saying is, as often, implied in the preceding vb. of commanding.
129 **τῶν μένειν τεταγμένων**: really half of the army; *cf.* § 15.
133 **ὡς ... ἱκανῶς**, *well enough for mountaineers*. In such phrases ὡς has a limiting force; *cf.* Lat. *ut*.
ἱκανῶς ... ἱκανῶς: note that the chiastic order best brings out the emphasis. The Carduchi were doubtless without defensive armor, save the shield; and so were no match for hoplites.

ἐπιδραμεῖν καὶ φεύγειν, πρὸς δὲ τὸ εἰς χεῖρας δέχεσθαι οὐχ
135 ἱκανῶς. ἐν τούτῳ σημαίνει ὁ σαλπικτής· καὶ οἱ μὲν πολέμιοι 32
ἔφευγον πολὺ ἔτι θᾶττον, οἱ δὲ Ἕλληνες τἀναντία στρέψαντες
ἔφευγον διὰ τοῦ ποταμοῦ ὅτι τάχιστα. τῶν δὲ πολεμίων οἱ 33
μέν τινες αἰσθόμενοι πάλιν ἔδραμον ἐπὶ τὸν ποταμὸν καὶ
τοξεύοντες ὀλίγους ἔτρωσαν, οἱ δὲ πολλοὶ καὶ πέραν ὄντων τῶν
140 Ἑλλήνων ἔτι φανεροὶ ἦσαν φεύγοντες. οἱ δὲ ὑπαντήσαντες 34
ἀνδριζόμενοι καὶ προσωτέρω τοῦ καιροῦ προϊόντες ὕστερον τῶν
μετὰ Ξενοφῶντος διέβησαν πάλιν· καὶ ἐτρώθησάν τινες καὶ
τούτων.

IV. Ἐπεὶ δὲ διέβησαν, συνταξάμενοι ἀμφὶ μέσον ἡμέρας 1
ἐπορεύθησαν διὰ τῆς Ἀρμενίας πεδίον ἅπαν καὶ λείους γηλόφους
οὐ μεῖον ἢ πέντε παρασάγγας· οὐ γὰρ ἦσαν ἐγγὺς τοῦ ποταμοῦ
κῶμαι διὰ τοὺς πολέμους τοὺς πρὸς τοὺς Καρδούχους. εἰς δὲ 2
5 ἣν ἀφίκοντο κώμην μεγάλη τε ἦν καὶ βασίλειον εἶχε τῷ σατράπῃ καὶ ἐπὶ ταῖς πλείσταις οἰκίαις τύρσεις ἐπῆσαν· ἐπιτήδεια
δ' ἦν δαψιλῆ. ἐντεῦθεν δ' ἐπορεύθησαν σταθμοὺς δύο παρα- 3
σάγγας δέκα μέχρι ὑπερῆλθον τὰς πηγὰς τοῦ Τίγρητος ποταμοῦ.

136 τἀναντία στρέψαντες, wheeling about so as to face the opposite direction (stronger than ἀναστρέψαντες, above, l. 124). The acc. is the inner obj., felt almost as an adv.
137 οἱ μέν τινες: cf. II, 3, 59, and the note.
139 καὶ... Ἑλλήνων, even when the Greeks were on the other side.
140 οἱ δὲ ὑπαντήσαντες: i. e. those sent by Chirisophus.
141 προσωτέρω τοῦ καιροῦ, farther than they should have.

CHAPTER IV

2 πεδίον ... γηλόφους: acc. of the country traversed, an extension of the inner obj. Cf. the note on II, 5, 71. This statement is usually said not to agree with the actual character of the country; but their route is wholly uncertain. If they turned westward it accords well (Karbe, Marsch der Zehntausend, p. 27).
5 κώμην: incorporation (see I, 1, 24, and the note) is rare when the antecedent is the subj. of the sentence. Cf. Vergil's Urbem quam statuo vestra est (Aen. I, 673).
τῷ σατράπῃ: Orontas.
6 τύρσεις: a statement true of the architecture in these regions today.
7 δαψιλῆ: cf. c. 2. 90, and the note.
8 ὑπερῆλθον: this must not be taken too literally. They now cross a ridge which forms the watershed between the two great rivers. The Teleboas (l. 10),

ἐντεῦθεν δ' ἐπορεύθησαν σταθμοὺς τρεῖς παρασάγγας πεντεκαίδεκα ἐπὶ τὸν Τηλεβόαν ποταμόν· οὗτος δ' ἦν καλὸς μέν, 10
4 μέγας δ' οὔ· κῶμαι δὲ πολλαὶ περὶ τὸν ποταμὸν ἦσαν. ὁ δὲ
τόπος οὗτος Ἀρμενία ἐκαλεῖτο ἡ πρὸς ἑσπέραν. ὕπαρχος δ' ἦν
αὐτῆς Τιρίβαζος, ὁ καὶ βασιλεῖ φίλος γενόμενος, καὶ ὁπότε
5 παρείη, οὐδεὶς ἄλλος βασιλέα ἐπὶ τὸν ἵππον ἀνέβαλλεν. οὗτος
προσήλασεν ἱππέας ἔχων, καὶ προπέμψας ἑρμηνέα εἶπεν ὅτι 15
βούλοιτο διαλεχθῆναι τοῖς ἄρχουσι. τοῖς δὲ στρατηγοῖς ἔδοξεν
6 ἀκοῦσαι· καὶ προσελθόντες εἰς ἐπήκοον ἠρώτων τί θέλει. ὁ δὲ
εἶπεν ὅτι σπείσασθαι βούλοιτο ἐφ' ᾧ μήτε αὐτὸς τοὺς Ἕλληνας
ἀδικεῖν μήτε ἐκείνους καίειν τὰς οἰκίας, λαμβάνειν τε τἀπιτήδεια ὅσων δέοιντο. ἔδοξε ταῦτα τοῖς στρατηγοῖς καὶ ἐσπείσαντο 20
ἐπὶ τούτοις.

7 Ἐντεῦθεν δ' ἐπορεύθησαν σταθμοὺς τρεῖς διὰ πεδίου παρασάγγας πεντεκαίδεκα· καὶ Τιρίβαζος παρηκολούθει ἔχων τὴν
ἑαυτοῦ δύναμιν ἀπέχων ὡς δέκα σταδίους· καὶ ἀφίκοντο εἰς
βασίλεια καὶ κώμας πέριξ πολλὰς πολλῶν τῶν ἐπιτηδείων 25
8 μεστάς. στρατοπεδευομένων δ' αὐτῶν γίγνεται τῆς νυκτὸς χιὼν
πολλή· καὶ ἕωθεν ἔδοξε διασκηνῆσαι τὰς τάξεις καὶ τοὺς στρατηγοὺς κατὰ τὰς κώμας· οὐ γὰρ ἑώρων πολέμιον οὐδένα καὶ

---

whatever its identification, plainly flows into the Euphrates.

Τίγρητος: certainly not the Tigris proper, but some tributary. Just what stream it was cannot be determined.

12 ἡ πρὸς ἑσπέραν, *western*.

ὕπαρχος, *lieutenant* (cf. I, 1, 5), apparently subordinate to Orontas, although some assume that Tiribazus, too, was satrap (of western, as Orontas of eastern, Armenia).

14 ἀνέβαλλεν, *assisted to mount*. The ancients had no stirrups.

17 εἰς ἐπήκοον: cf. II, 5, 143 f. They are on their guard.

18 ἐφ' ᾧ: cf. c. 2. 77, and the note.

μήτε ... μήτε ... τε, *neither ... nor ... but*. Cf. II, 2, 38, and the note.

20 ἔδοξε: normal asyndeton.

21 ἐπὶ τούτοις: cf. III, 5, 68, and the note on II, 4, 22.

23 παρηκολούθει: doubtless waiting for an opportunity to attack.

25 πολλῶν: pred., *in great abundance*. The paronomasia is intentional.

26 χιὼν πολλή: it was late November, and they were at an elevation of nearly four thousand feet in the latitude of Philadelphia.

27 διασκηνῆσαι: for the force of the prep., cf. I, 5, 11, and the note.

ἀσφαλὲς ἐδόκει εἶναι διὰ τὸ πλῆθος τῆς χιόνος. ἐνταῦθα εἶχον 9
30 ὅσα ἐστὶν ἀγαθά, ἱερεῖα, σῖτον, οἴνους παλαιοὺς εὐώδεις, ἀσταφίδας, ὄσπρια παντοδαπά. τῶν δὲ ἀποσκεδαννυμένων τινὲς ἀπὸ τοῦ στρατοπέδου ἔλεγον ὅτι κατίδοιεν νύκτωρ πολλὰ πυρὰ φαίνοντα. ἐδόκει δὴ τοῖς στρατηγοῖς οὐκ ἀσφαλὲς εἶναι δια- 10
σκηνοῦν, ἀλλὰ συναγαγεῖν τὸ στράτευμα πάλιν. ἐντεῦθεν
35 συνῆλθον· καὶ γὰρ ἐδόκει διαιθριάζειν. νυκτερευόντων δ' αὐτῶν 11
ἐνταῦθα ἐπιπίπτει χιὼν ἄπλετος, ὥστε ἀπέκρυψε καὶ τὰ ὅπλα καὶ τοὺς ἀνθρώπους κατακειμένους· καὶ τὰ ὑποζύγια συνεπόδισεν ἡ χιών· καὶ πολὺς ὄκνος ἦν ἀνίστασθαι· κατακειμένων γὰρ ἀλεεινὸν ἦν ἡ χιὼν ἐπιπεπτωκυῖα ὅτῳ μὴ παραρρυείη.
40 ἐπεὶ δὲ Ξενοφῶν ἐτόλμησε γυμνὸς ἀναστὰς σχίζειν ξύλα, τάχ' 12
ἀναστάς τις καὶ ἄλλος ἐκείνου ἀφελόμενος ἔσχιζεν. ἐκ δὲ τούτου καὶ ἄλλοι ἀναστάντες πῦρ ἔκαιον καὶ ἐχρίοντο· πολὺ 13
γὰρ ἐνταῦθα ηὑρίσκετο χρῖμα, ᾧ ἐχρῶντο ἀντ' ἐλαίου, σύειον

---

30 **ἱερεῖα**: properly *sacrificial beasts*, but freely used of animals slaughtered for food. For the asyndeton in an enumeration, *cf.* II, 4, 127.
31 **τινές**: another instance of freedom of position.
33 **φαίνοντα**, *blazing*.
ἐδόκει: with different meanings with the two following infins.— first *seemed*, then *seemed best*. So not infrequently.
34 **ἐντεῦθεν**: *cf. ἐκ τούτου.*
35 **διαιθριάζειν**, *to be clearing up*. With such vbs. the subj. ὁ Ζεύς, ὁ θεός, is sometimes expressed (Aristoph. *Birds* 1501 f.; Xen. *Cyn.* 8, 1). For the omitted subj., see the note on ἐσάλπιγξε, I, 2, 98.
δια-, of course, denotes the breaking up of the clouds.
36 **ἄπλετος**: another poetic word.
37 **συνεπόδισεν**: *cf. πεποδισμένοι εἰσί*, III, 4, 138.

38 **κατακειμένων**: gen. abs. with omitted subj. (*cf. προϊόντων*, I, 2, 99, and the note); for the abs. construction, where we might have looked for the dat., *cf.* I, 4, 82, and the note.
39 **ἀλεεινόν**, *a source of warmth*. For the neut. adj. thus used, *cf. ἡδύ*, II, 3, 60, and the note.
ὅτῳ μή, freely, *if it didn't slip off one*. The rel. is equivalent to the gen. condit.
40 **ἐτόλμησε**, *summed up courage*.
γυμνός, *without his cloak*; *cf.* I, 10, 41 **τις καὶ ἄλλος**: *cf.* I, 3, 80. [9.
ἀφελόμενος: sc. τὴν ἀξίνην or τὰ ξύλα. This vb. is often construed with two accs. (*e. g.* I, 3, 18).
42 **ἐχρίοντο**: the use of oil to keep the skin in good condition and the limbs supple was universal among the Greeks.
43 **ἐλαίου**: this was the normal unguent in Greece.

καὶ σησάμινον καὶ ἀμυγδάλινον ἐκ τῶν πικρῶν καὶ τερμίνθινον. ἐκ δὲ τῶν αὐτῶν τούτων καὶ μύρον ηὑρίσκετο.

Μετὰ ταῦτα ἐδόκει πάλιν διασκηνητέον εἶναι εἰς τὰς κώμας εἰς στέγας. ἔνθα δὴ οἱ στρατιῶται σὺν πολλῇ κραυγῇ καὶ ἡδονῇ ἦσαν ἐπὶ τὰς στέγας καὶ τὰ ἐπιτήδεια· ὅσοι δὲ ὅτε τὸ πρότερον ἀπῆσαν τὰς οἰκίας ἐνέπρησαν ὑπὸ ἀτασθαλίας, δίκην ἐδίδοσαν κακῶς σκηνοῦντες. ἐντεῦθεν ἔπεμψαν νυκτὸς Δημοκράτην Τημνίτην ἄνδρας δόντες ἐπὶ τὰ ὄρη ἔνθα ἔφασαν οἱ ἀποσκεδαννύμενοι καθορᾶν τὰ πυρά· οὗτος γὰρ ἐδόκει καὶ πρότερον πολλὰ ἤδη ἀληθεῦσαι τοιαῦτα, τὰ ὄντα τε ὡς ὄντα καὶ τὰ μὴ ὄντα ὡς οὐκ ὄντα. πορευθεὶς δὲ τὰ μὲν πυρὰ οὐκ ἔφη ἰδεῖν, ἄνδρα δὲ συλλαβὼν ἧκεν ἄγων ἔχοντα τόξον Περσικὸν καὶ φαρέτραν καὶ σάγαριν οἵανπερ καὶ αἱ Ἀμαζόνες ἔχουσιν. ἐρωτώμενος δὲ ποδαπὸς εἴη Πέρσης μὲν ἔφη εἶναι, πορεύεσθαι δ' ἀπὸ τοῦ Τιριβάζου στρατοπέδου, ὅπως ἐπιτήδεια λάβοι. οἱ δὲ ἠρώτων αὐτὸν τὸ στράτευμα ὁπόσον τ' εἴη καὶ ἐπὶ τίνι συνειλεγμένον. ὁ δὲ εἶπεν ὅτι Τιρίβαζος εἴη ἔχων τήν τε αὐτοῦ δύναμιν καὶ μισθοφόρους Χάλυβας καὶ Ταόχους· παρεσκευάσθαι δὲ αὐτὸν ἔφη ὡς ἐπὶ τῇ ὑπερβολῇ τοῦ ὄρους ἐν

---

44 ἐκ τῶν πικρῶν: added for clearness' sake. The preceding adj. supplies the noun. The whole phrase=ἐκ τῶν πικρῶν ἀμυγδαλῶν; but the adj. form is preferred in order to conform to what precedes.

45 ἐκ δὲ τῶν αὐτῶν τούτων, made from these same ingredients. Cf. II, 3, 55.

47 εἰς στέγας, under cover; it is, therefore, not redundant after εἰς τὰς κώμας.

σὺν πολλῇ . . . ἡδονῇ, with loud shouts of joy—a good instance of hendiadyoin (one idea expressed by two words).

49 ὑπὸ ἀτασθαλίας, in wanton folly. The word is Homeric.

51 Τημνίτην: Temnus was a city in Aeolis; but the text is uncertain.

54 τὰ μὴ ὄντα: the generic μή (giving the class); see G. 1613; H. B. 431, 1. Below we have οὐκ ὄντα, because in each case he reported οὐκ ἔστι.

πορευθείς, on his return.

55 ἧκεν ἄγων, brought with him.

56 Ἀμαζόνες: familiar to Xen.'s readers from many works of art.

59 τὸ στράτευμα: prolepsis. This was the army which had been reported in § 9.

60 εἴη ἔχων, it was T., with.

62 παρεσκευάσθαι . . . ἔφη: if in indir. disc. a vb. of saying is reexpressed, it is almost invariably

τοῖς στενοῖς ἧπερ μοναχῇ εἴη πορεία, ἐνταῦθα ἐπιθησόμενον τοῖς Ἕλλησιν.

ἀκούσασι τοῖς στρατηγοῖς ταῦτα ἔδοξε τὸ στράτευμα συναγαγεῖν· καὶ εὐθὺς φύλακας καταλιπόντες καὶ στρατηγὸν ἐπὶ τοῖς μένουσι Σοφαίνετον Στυμφάλιον ἐπορεύοντο ἔχοντες ἡγεμόνα τὸν ἁλόντα ἄνθρωπον. ἐπειδὴ δὲ ὑπερέβαλλον τὰ ὄρη, οἱ πελτασταὶ προϊόντες καὶ κατιδόντες τὸ στρατόπεδον οὐκ ἔμειναν τοὺς ὁπλίτας, ἀλλ' ἀνακραγόντες ἔθεον ἐπὶ τὸ στρατόπεδον. οἱ δὲ βάρβαροι ἀκούσαντες τὸν θόρυβον οὐχ ὑπέμειναν, ἀλλ' ἔφευγον· ὅμως δὲ καὶ ἀπέθανόν τινες τῶν βαρβάρων καὶ ἵπποι ἑάλωσαν εἰς εἴκοσι καὶ ἡ σκηνὴ ἡ Τιριβάζου ἑάλω καὶ ἐν αὐτῇ κλῖναι ἀργυρόποδες καὶ ἐκπώματα καὶ οἱ ἀρτοκόποι καὶ οἱ οἰνοχόοι φάσκοντες εἶναι. ἐπειδὴ δὲ ἐπύθοντο ταῦτα οἱ τῶν ὁπλιτῶν στρατηγοί, ἐδόκει αὐτοῖς ἀπιέναι τὴν ταχίστην ἐπὶ τὸ στρατόπεδον, μή τις ἐπίθεσις γένοιτο τοῖς καταλελειμμένοις. καὶ εὐθὺς ἀνακαλεσάμενοι τῇ σάλπιγγι ἀπῇσαν, καὶ ἀφίκοντο αὐθημερὸν ἐπὶ τὸ στρατόπεδον.

V. Τῇ δ' ὑστεραίᾳ ἐδόκει πορευτέον εἶναι ὅπῃ δύναιντο τάχιστα πρὶν ἢ συλλεγῆναι τὸ στράτευμα πάλιν καὶ καταλα-

---

a form of φημί, no matter what the original vb. was. So, too, a second clause often has the infin., even when φημί is not inserted. Note the tense of παρεσκευάσθαι, *all was in readiness*.

ὡς: with ἐπιθησόμενον.

63 ἐνταῦθα: resumptive, as demonstr. words so often are.

66 ἐπί, *in command of*.

67 Σοφαίνετον: see the Introd., §38.

ἡγεμόνα: *cf.* ἀκοντίοις, c. 2. 112, and the note.

69 τὸ στρατόπεδον: *i. e.* that of Tiribazus.

70 ἀνακραγόντες, *raising a shout* (ingressive aor.)

74 κλῖναι: similarly Herodotus (IX, 80 and 82) mentions among the spoils captured in the camp of Mardonius at Plataea, κλίνας τε χρυσέας καὶ ἀργυρέας εὖ ἐστρωμένας καὶ τραπέζας τε χρυσέας καὶ ἀργυρέας καὶ παρασκευὴν (dishes) μεγαλοπρεπέα. There is mention there, too, of ἀρτοκόποι and ὀψοποιοί (*cooks*).

75 φάσκοντες εἶναι, *claiming to be;* cf. καλούμενοι; I, 8, 104.

76 τὸ στρατόπεδον: *i. e.* their own camp, guarded by Sophaenetus.

77 ἐπίθεσις γένοιτο: *i. e.* on the part of Tiribazus.

78 ἀνακαλεσάμενοι, *sounding a recall*.

CHAPTER V

2 πρὶν ἤ: this poetical equivalent of the simple πρίν is found twice

βεῖν τὰ στενά. συσκευασάμενοι δ' εὐθὺς ἐπορεύοντο διὰ χιόνος
πολλῆς ἡγεμόνας ἔχοντες πολλούς· καὶ αὐθημερὸν ὑπερβαλόντες
τὸ ἄκρον ἐφ' ᾧ ἔμελλεν ἐπιτίθεσθαι Τιρίβαζος κατεστρατοπε- 5
2 δεύσαντο. ἐντεῦθεν δ' ἐπορεύθησαν σταθμοὺς ἐρήμους τρεῖς παρασάγγας πεντεκαίδεκα ἐπὶ τὸν Εὐφράτην ποταμόν, καὶ διέβαινον
αὐτὸν βρεχόμενοι πρὸς τὸν ὀμφαλόν. ἐλέγοντο δ' οὐδ' αἱ πηγαὶ
πρόσω εἶναι.

3 ἐντεῦθεν ἐπορεύοντο διὰ χιόνος πολλῆς καὶ πεδίου σταθμοὺς 10
τρεῖς παρασάγγας δέκα. ὁ δὲ τρίτος ἐγένετο χαλεπὸς καὶ
ἄνεμος βορρᾶς ἐναντίος ἔπνει παντάπασιν ἀποκαίων πάντα καὶ
4 πηγνὺς τοὺς ἀνθρώπους. ἔνθα δὴ τῶν μάντεών τις εἶπε σφαγιάσασθαι τῷ ἀνέμῳ, καὶ σφαγιάζεται· καὶ πᾶσι δὴ περιφανῶς
ἔδοξεν λῆξαι τὸ χαλεπὸν τοῦ πνεύματος. ἦν δὲ τῆς χιόνος τὸ 15
βάθος ὀργυιά· ὥστε καὶ τῶν ὑποζυγίων καὶ τῶν ἀνδραπόδων
5 πολλὰ ἀπώλετο καὶ τῶν στρατιωτῶν ὡς τριάκοντα. διεγένοντο

---

again in Xen. and once in Thucydides, but is otherwise foreign to Attic prose. See G. M. T. 652.

3 τὰ στενά: cf. c. 4. 63.

4 ἡγεμόνας: apparently prisoners taken in the attack on the camp.

5 ἔμελλεν, was to have.

7 τὸν Εὐφράτην: i. e. the eastern branch, now known as the Murad Su.

10 διὰ ... πεδίου, over a plain covered with deep snow.

11 παρασάγγας δέκα: the text is uncertain, but so little can be said with definiteness about the route of the Greeks after they crossed the Centrites, that sure emendation is impossible.

τρίτος: sc. σταθμός.

12 ἐναντίος, in their faces.

ἀποκαίων, parching, blasting—a strong word to denote the effect of cold. In a fragment of one of the comic poets we have, ἀπέκαυσεν ἡ πάχνη (frost) τὰς ἀμπέλους (vines), and Xen. even has (Anab. VII, 4, § 3), καὶ τῶν Ἑλλήνων πολλῶν καὶ ῥῖνες (noses) ἀπεκαίοντο καὶ ὦτα. So, in Lat., adurere (Verg. Georg. I, 93) and torrere (Varr. ap. Non. 452, 11) are used of cold. Cf. Milton, Paradise Lost II, 594. The parching air | Burns frore, and cold performs the work of fire.

13 εἶπε σφαγιάσασθαι, bade sacrifice. No subj. of the infin. need be supplied; so, too, σφαγιάζεται may be rendered, sacrifice was made. To the Greeks the winds were divinities, and the Athenians, in particular, worshiped Boreas, who had wedded, the legend said, Oreithyia, the daughter of Erectheus.

17 διεγένοντο ... καίοντες, they got through the night, however, by keeping up fires. Cf. I, 5, 34.

δὲ τὴν νύκτα πῦρ καίοντες· ξύλα δ' ἦν ἐν τῷ σταθμῷ πολλά· οἱ δὲ ὀψὲ προσιόντες ξύλα οὐκ εἶχον. οἱ οὖν πάλαι ἥκοντες καὶ πῦρ καίοντες οὐ προσίεσαν πρὸς τὸ πῦρ τοὺς ὀψίζοντας, εἰ μὴ μεταδοῖεν αὐτοῖς πυροὺς ἢ ἄλλο εἴ τι ἔχοιεν βρωτόν. ἔνθα δὴ 6 μετεδίδοσαν ἀλλήλοις ὧν εἶχον ἕκαστοι. ἔνθα δὲ τὸ πῦρ ἐκαίετο, διατηκομένης τῆς χιόνος βόθροι ἐγένοντο μεγάλοι ἔστε ἐπὶ τὸ δάπεδον· οὗ δὴ παρῆν μετρεῖν τὸ βάθος τῆς χιόνος.

ἐντεῦθεν δὲ τὴν ἐπιοῦσαν ἡμέραν ὅλην ἐπορεύοντο διὰ χιόνος, 7 καὶ πολλοὶ τῶν ἀνθρώπων ἐβουλιμίασαν. Ξενοφῶν δ' ὀπισθοφυλακῶν καὶ καταλαμβάνων τοὺς πίπτοντας τῶν ἀνθρώπων ἠγνόει ὅ,τι τὸ πάθος εἴη. ἐπειδὴ δὲ εἶπέ τις αὐτῷ τῶν ἐμπείρων 8 ὅτι σαφῶς βουλιμιῶσι κἄν τι φάγωσιν ἀναστήσονται, περιὼν περὶ τὰ ὑποζύγια, εἴ πού τι ὁρῴη βρωτόν, διεδίδου καὶ διέπεμπε διδόντας τοὺς δυναμένους παρατρέχειν τοῖς βουλιμιῶσιν. ἐπειδὴ 9 δέ τι ἐμφάγοιεν, ἀνίσταντο καὶ ἐπορεύοντο.

πορευομένων δὲ Χειρίσοφος μὲν ἀμφὶ κνέφας πρὸς κώμην ἀφικνεῖται, καὶ ὑδροφορούσας ἐκ τῆς κώμης πρὸς τῇ κρήνῃ

---

20 οὐ προσίεσαν, *would not admit to.* Cf. III, I, 134.

21 πυρούς: with μεταδιδόναι the obj. shared is commonly in the partitive gen. (*cf.* below, ὧν εἶχον). The acc. is rare (save in the case of the word μέρος, *part*) and denotes, of course, the part given.

ἄλλο εἴ τι, *whatever else,* εἴ τι ἄλλο, or ὅ,τι ἄλλο, would have been more usual.

ἔνθα . . . ἔνθα: the former is demonstr., the latter rel.

23 ἔστε ἐπί, *clear to.* For ἔστε, see the note on I, 9, 38. μέχρι before preps. is not uncommon (*Anab.* VI, 4, § 26), and in V, 5, § 4 (a spurious passage) we have ἄχρι εἰς.

24 δάπεδον: a poetic word.
παρῆν, *it was possible.*
26 ἐβουλιμίασαν, *were attacked by* boulimy (*ravenous hunger*). βου- in composition often denotes something huge (βούπαις, *a great overgrown boy*); so, too ἱππο- and *horse-* in Eng. (*horse-radish, horse-laugh*).

27 τοὺς πίπτοντας τῶν ἀνθρώπων, *those of the men who sank exhausted.* Note the tense.

30 διεδίδου: *cf.* I, 9, 80.

31 διδόντας, *to give;* sc. τινάς. The pres. partic. often stands where the fut. (of purpose) might have been looked for (*cf.* ἐπεφάνη σκοπῶν, II, 4, 104). It is more graphic.

παρατρέχειν, *to run along the ranks.*
τοῖς βουλιμιῶσιν: the dat. is governed by διδόντας.

33 κνέφας: a poeticism. [κόρας.
34 ἐκ τῆς κώμης: with γυναῖκας καὶ **πρὸς τῇ κρήνῃ:** the art., since the

γυναῖκας καὶ κόρας καταλαμβάνει ἔμπροσθεν τοῦ ἐρύματος. αὗται ἠρώτων αὐτοὺς τίνες εἶεν. ὁ δ' ἑρμηνεὺς εἶπε περσιστὶ ὅτι παρὰ βασιλέως πορεύονται πρὸς τὸν σατράπην. αἱ δὲ ἀπεκρίναντο ὅτι οὐκ ἐνταῦθα εἴη, ἀλλ' ἀπέχει ὅσον παρασάγγην. οἱ δ', ἐπεὶ ὀψὲ ἦν, πρὸς τὸν κωμάρχην συνεισέρχονται εἰς τὸ ἔρυμα σὺν ταῖς ὑδροφόροις. Χειρίσοφος μὲν οὖν καὶ ὅσοι ἐδυνήθησαν τοῦ στρατεύματος ἐνταῦθα ἐστρατοπεδεύσαντο, τῶν δ' ἄλλων στρατιωτῶν οἱ μὴ δυνάμενοι διατελέσαι τὴν ὁδὸν ἐνυκτέρευσαν ἄσιτοι καὶ ἄνευ πυρός· καὶ ἐνταῦθά τινες ἀπώλοντο τῶν στρατιωτῶν.

ἐφείποντο δὲ τῶν πολεμίων συνειλεγμένοι τινὲς καὶ τὰ μὴ δυνάμενα τῶν ὑποζυγίων ἥρπαζον καὶ ἀλλήλοις ἐμάχοντο περὶ αὐτῶν. ἐλείποντο δὲ τῶν στρατιωτῶν οἵ τε διεφθαρμένοι ὑπὸ τῆς χιόνος τοὺς ὀφθαλμοὺς οἵ τε ὑπὸ τοῦ ψύχους τοὺς δακτύλους τῶν ποδῶν ἀποσεσηπότες. ἦν δὲ τοῖς μὲν ὀφθαλμοῖς ἐπικούρημα τῆς χιόνος εἴ τις μέλαν τι ἔχων πρὸ τῶν ὀφθαλμῶν ἐπορεύετο, τῶν δὲ ποδῶν εἴ τις κινοῖτο καὶ μηδέποτε ἡσυχίαν ἔχοι καὶ εἰς τὴν νύκτα ὑπολύοιτο· ὅσοι δὲ ὑποδεδεμένοι ἐκοιμῶντο εἰσεδύοντο εἰς τοὺς πόδας οἱ ἱμάντες καὶ τὰ ὑποδήματα περιεπήγνυντο· καὶ γὰρ ἦσαν, ἐπειδὴ ἐπέλιπε τὰ ἀρχαῖα ὑποδήματα, καρβάτιναι πεποιημέναι ἐκ τῶν νεοδάρτων βοῶν.

---

villagers had a common spring, as usual.

38 ὅσον, *about; cf.* I, 2, 15. [bodied.
40 ὅσοι ἐδυνήθησαν, *all the able-*
42 οἱ μὴ δυνάμενοι: the generic μή again; *cf.* τὰ μὴ δυνάμενα, below.
47 οἵ τε ... τοὺς ὀφθαλμούς, *those whose eyes had been blinded.*
48 οἵ τε ... ἀποσεσηπότες, *those who had lost their toes through mortification* (as a result of their having been frozen). For the accs. ὀφθαλμούς and δακτύλους, *cf.* the note on τὰς κεφαλάς, II, 6, 2. ὑπό, as so often, gives a slight personification. Note that the order is chiastic.

49 τοῖς ... ὀφθαλμοῖς: dat. of advantage.
ἐπικούρημα τῆς χιόνος, *a protection against the snow.* The gen. is objective.
50 ἐπορεύετο: the logical indic., instead of the generalized opt. Contrast κινοῖτο and the following opts., below.
51 τῶν δὲ ποδῶν, *and (a protection) for the feet.* Another objective gen., but in a different sense.
52 ὑπολύοιτο, *took off his shoes.* Contrast ὑποδεδεμένοι, below, *(with their shoes on).*
54 ἦσαν: sc. αὐτοῖς, *they had.*
55 καρβάτιναι: not the normal

διὰ τὰς τοιαύτας οὖν ἀνάγκας ὑπελείποντό τινες τῶν στρατιωτῶν· καὶ ἰδόντες μέλαν τι χωρίον διὰ τὸ ἐκλελοιπέναι αὐτόθι τὴν χιόνα εἴκαζον τετηκέναι· καὶ ἐτετήκει διὰ κρήνην τινὰ ἣ πλησίον ἦν ἀτμίζουσα ἐν νάπῃ. ἐνταῦθ' ἐκτραπόμενοι ἐκάθηντο καὶ οὐκ ἔφασαν πορεύεσθαι. ὁ δὲ Ξενοφῶν ἔχων ὀπισθοφύλακας ὡς ᾔσθετο, ἐδεῖτο αὐτῶν πάσῃ τέχνῃ καὶ μηχανῇ μὴ ἀπολείπεσθαι, λέγων ὅτι ἕπονται πολλοὶ πολέμιοι συνειλεγμένοι, καὶ τελευτῶν ἐχαλέπαινεν. οἱ δὲ σφάττειν ἐκέλευον· οὐ γὰρ ἂν δύνασθαι πορευθῆναι. ἐνταῦθα ἔδοξε κράτιστον εἶναι τοὺς ἑπομένους πολεμίους φοβῆσαι, εἴ τις δύναιτο, μὴ ἐπίοιεν τοῖς κάμνουσι. καὶ ἦν μὲν σκότος ἤδη, οἱ δὲ προσῇσαν πολλῷ θορύβῳ ἀμφὶ ὧν εἶχον διαφερόμενοι. ἔνθα δὴ οἱ ὀπισθοφύλακες

---

sandals, but a sort of brogue made of a single piece of untanned hide, drawn up around the foot by thongs. Such brogues were easily made, and were common among the country people of Greece.

βοῶν, *oxen*, and so (by metonomy) *ox-hides*.

56 ἀνάγκας, *straits*.

57 διὰ τὸ ἐκλελοιπέναι: the clause explains μέλαν. For the infin. with the art., see the note on I, 6, 9.

59 ἦν ἀτμίζουσα: not a progressive vb. form; each element has its full value. This warm spring does not suffice to identify the place. Several such springs are known.

νάπῃ: the form νάπος occurs three times in VI, 5.

60 πορεύεσθαι: what they said was οὐ πορευόμεθα, *we are going no farther*. The pres. is often used for the fut. in cases where the action depends upon the will of the subj. For the position of the neg., *cf*. the note on I, 2, 152.

ὀπισθοφύλακας, *a detachment of the rear-guard*.

61 πάσῃ τέχνῃ καὶ μηχανῇ, *by all manner of means*. The phrase (a stereotyped one; *cf*. VII, 2, § 8) strengthens ἐδεῖτο, itself a strong word.

63 τελευτῶν, *finally*.

ἐχαλέπαινεν: *cf*. the narrative in V, 8, where Xen., accused by one of the men, a mule-driver, of having acted with undue severity toward him at this time, clears himself by showing that the fellow was attempting to bury alive an exhausted soldier whom he had been bidden to carry. The time of the flogging is there given as ὅπου καὶ ῥίγει ἀπωλλύμεθα καὶ χιὼν πλείστη ἦν.

σφάττειν: neither subj. nor obj. need be expressed. The men said simply σφάττε.

64 ἂν δύνασθαι: supply ἔφασαν, from ἐκέλευον; *cf*. c. 4. 62. and the note. In neg. clauses the potential opt. is one of the strongest forms of denial.

67 ἀμφὶ ὧν ... διαφερόμενοι, *quar-*

ἅτε ὑγιαίνοντες ἐξαναστάντες ἔδραμον εἰς τοὺς πολεμίους· οἱ δὲ κάμνοντες ἀνακραγόντες ὅσον ἐδύναντο μέγιστον τὰς ἀσπίδας πρὸς τὰ δόρατα ἔκρουσαν. οἱ δὲ πολέμιοι δείσαντες ἧκαν 70 αὑτοὺς κατὰ τῆς χιόνος εἰς τὴν νάπην, καὶ οὐδεὶς ἔτι οὐδαμοῦ ἐφθέγξατο.

καὶ Ξενοφῶν μὲν καὶ οἱ σὺν αὐτῷ εἰπόντες τοῖς ἀσθενοῦσιν ὅτι τῇ ὑστεραίᾳ ἥξουσί τινες ἐπ᾽ αὐτούς, πορευόμενοι πρὶν τέτταρα στάδια διελθεῖν ἐντυγχάνουσιν ἐν τῇ ὁδῷ ἀναπαυομένοις 75 ἐπὶ τῆς χιόνος τοῖς στρατιώταις ἐγκεκαλυμμένοις, καὶ οὐδὲ φυλακὴ οὐδεμία καθειστήκει· καὶ ἀνίστασαν αὐτούς. οἱ δ᾽ ἔλεγον ὅτι οἱ ἔμπροσθεν οὐχ ὑποχωροῖεν. ὁ δὲ παριὼν καὶ παραπέμπων τῶν πελταστῶν τοὺς ἰσχυροτάτους ἐκέλευε σκέψασθαι τί εἴη τὸ κωλῦον. οἱ δὲ ἀπήγγελλον ὅτι ὅλον οὕτως ἀναπαύοιτο 80 τὸ στράτευμα. ἐνταῦθα καὶ οἱ περὶ Ξενοφῶντα ηὐλίσθησαν αὐτοῦ ἄνευ πυρὸς καὶ ἄδειπνοι, φυλακὰς οἵας ἐδύναντο καταστησάμενοι. ἐπεὶ δὲ πρὸς ἡμέραν ἦν, ὁ μὲν Ξενοφῶν πέμψας πρὸς τοὺς ἀσθενοῦντας τοὺς νεωτάτους ἀναστήσαντας ἐκέλευεν ἀναγκάζειν προϊέναι. 85

ἐν δὲ τούτῳ Χειρίσοφος πέμπει τῶν ἐκ τῆς κώμης σκεψομένους πῶς ἔχοιεν οἱ τελευταῖοι. οἱ δὲ ἄσμενοι ἰδόντες τοὺς μὲν ἀσθενοῦντας τούτοις παρέδοσαν κομίζειν ἐπὶ τὸ στρατόπεδον,

---

reling about their booty. ἀμφί with the gen. (instead of περί) is used by Xen. alone among Attic prose writers.

68 ἅτε ὑγιαίνοντες: cf. the note on I, 1, 12.
εἰς: *into the midst of*, cf. I, 1, 62, and the note.
69 ὅσον ἐδύναντο μέγιστον, *as loud as they could* (inner obj.). μέγας is regularly used of the voice.
τὰς ἀσπίδας... ἔκρουσαν: cf. I, 8, 73 f.
70 δείσαντες, *seized with fear*. Note the tense.
ἧκαν αὑτούς, *flung themselves*. The act. with the reflexive is always stronger than the mid. It is often used of unusual or unnatural actions.
74 ἐπ᾽ αὐτούς, *to get them*.
77 ἀνίστασαν, *tried to make them get up*. They supposed that the men had succumbed to the drowsiness preceding death from cold.
80 ὅλον: an easy exaggeration. As a matter of fact the van had reached a village (§§ 9 and 22).
86 τῶν ἐκ: see on I, 1, 18. The gen. is partitive (sc. τινάς).
87 οἱ δέ: apparently the men sent by Xen. to bring up the sick.
ἄσμενοι: cf. II, 1, 79, and the note.

αὐτοὶ δὲ ἐπορεύοντο, καὶ πρὶν εἴκοσι στάδια διεληλυθέναι ἦσαν
90 πρὸς τῇ κώμῃ ἔνθα Χειρίσοφος ηὐλίζετο. ἐπεὶ δὲ συνεγένοντο
ἀλλήλοις, ἔδοξε κατὰ τὰς κώμας ἀσφαλὲς εἶναι τὰς τάξεις σκηνοῦν. καὶ Χειρίσοφος μὲν αὐτοῦ ἔμενεν, οἱ δὲ ἄλλοι διαλαχόντες
ἃς ἑώρων κώμας ἐπορεύοντο ἕκαστοι τοὺς ἑαυτῶν ἔχοντες. ἔνθα
δὴ Πολυκράτης Ἀθηναῖος λοχαγὸς ἐκέλευσεν ἀφιέναι ἑαυτόν·
95 καὶ λαβὼν τοὺς εὐζώνους, θέων ἐπὶ τὴν κώμην ἣν εἰλήχει Ξενοφῶν καταλαμβάνει πάντας ἔνδον τοὺς κωμήτας καὶ τὸν κωμάρχην καὶ πώλους εἰς δασμὸν βασιλεῖ τρεφομένους ἑπτακαίδεκα,
καὶ τὴν θυγατέρα τοῦ κωμάρχου ἐνάτην ἡμέραν γεγαμημένην· ὁ
δ' ἀνὴρ αὐτῆς λαγῶς ᾤχετο θηράσων καὶ οὐχ ἑάλω ἐν τῇ κώμῃ.
100 αἱ δ' οἰκίαι ἦσαν κατάγειοι, τὸ μὲν στόμα ὥσπερ φρέατος,
κάτω δ' εὐρεῖαι· αἱ δὲ εἴσοδοι τοῖς μὲν ὑποζυγίοις ὀρυκταί, οἱ δὲ
ἄνθρωποι κατέβαινον ἐπὶ κλίμακος. ἐν δὲ ταῖς οἰκίαις ἦσαν
αἶγες, ὄϊες, βόες, ὄρνιθες, καὶ τὰ ἔκγονα τούτων· τὰ δὲ κτήνη
πάντα χιλῷ ἔνδον ἐτρέφοντο. ἦσαν δὲ καὶ πυροὶ καὶ κριθαὶ

---

92 **αὐτοῦ**: *i. e.* in the village where he was.

διαλαχόντας ... κώμας, *distributing among themselves by lot the villages which they saw.* κώμας is incorporated in the rel. clause; *cf.* I, 1, 24.

94 **ἐκέλευσεν**, *urged;* as a subordinate he could hardly order.

ἀφιέναι, *that he be given leave to set out.*

95 **θέων**: this vb. is rarely used without military connotations; *cf.* the note on I, 8, 71.

96 **καὶ ... καὶ ... καί**: in enumerations we have either polysyndeton, as here, or asyndeton, as below, l. 103.

97 **δασμόν**: *cf.* I, 1, 41, and the note.

ἑπτακαίδεκα: the number seems incorrect; see below, § 35.

98 **ἐνάτην ἡμέραν**, *eight days before.*

99 **ἀνήρ**, *husband,* as often.

100 **κατάγειοι**: Xenophon's description of these underground, or semi-underground, houses agrees, in the main, with the accounts of modern travelers. They are not, to be sure, entirely underground nor are they entered by a hole in the roof, but they are none the less largely covered with earth for the sake of warmth, often being excavated in hill-sides; and the inhabitants share them with the domestic animals.

τὸ μὲν στόμα: probably in partitive appos. with οἰκίαι, which is immediately resumed as subj. It may also be taken as acc. of specification.

103 **ὄρνιθες**, *poultry,* as often.

104 **ἐτρέφοντο**: for the pl. vb. with neut. pl. subj., see the note on I, 2, 38. Observe that here

καὶ ὄσπρια καὶ οἶνος κρίθινος ἐν κρατῆρσιν. ἐνῆσαν δὲ καὶ
αὐταὶ αἱ κριθαὶ ἰσοχειλεῖς, καὶ κάλαμοι ἐνέκειντο, οἱ μὲν
μείζους οἱ δὲ ἐλάττους, γόνατα οὐκ ἔχοντες· τούτους ἔδει ὁπότε
τις διψῴη λαβόντα εἰς τὸ στόμα μύζειν. καὶ πάνυ ἄκρατος ἦν,
εἰ μή τις ὕδωρ ἐπιχέοι· καὶ πάνυ ἡδὺ συμμαθόντι τὸ πῶμα ἦν.

ὁ δὲ Ξενοφῶν τὸν ἄρχοντα τῆς κώμης ταύτης σύνδειπνον
ἐποιήσατο καὶ θαρρεῖν αὐτὸν ἐκέλευε λέγων ὅτι οὔτε τῶν τέκνων
στερήσοιτο τήν τε οἰκίαν αὐτοῦ ἀντεμπλήσαντες τῶν ἐπιτηδείων
ἀπίασιν, ἢν ἀγαθόν τι τῷ στρατεύματι ἐξηγησάμενος φαίνηται
ἔστ' ἂν ἐν ἄλλῳ ἔθνει γένωνται. ὁ δὲ ταῦτα ὑπισχνεῖτο, καὶ
φιλοφρονούμενος οἶνον ἔφρασεν ἔνθα ἦν κατορωρυγμένος. ταύτην μὲν τὴν νύκτα διασκηνήσαντες οὕτως ἐκοιμήθησαν ἐν πᾶσιν
ἀφθόνοις πάντες οἱ στρατιῶται, ἐν φυλακῇ ἔχοντες τὸν κωμάρχην
καὶ τὰ τέκνα αὐτοῦ ὁμοῦ ἐν ὀφθαλμοῖς.

τῇ δ' ἐπιούσῃ ἡμέρᾳ Ξενοφῶν λαβὼν τὸν κωμάρχην πρὸς
Χειρίσοφον ἐπορεύετο· ὅπου δὲ παρίοι κώμην, ἐτρέπετο πρὸς
τοὺς ἐν ταῖς κώμαις καὶ κατελάμβανε πανταχοῦ εὐωχουμένους
καὶ εὐθυμουμένους, καὶ οὐδαμόθεν ἀφίεσαν πρὶν παραθεῖναι

---

the idea of plurality is emphasized.

105 **οἶνος κρίθινος**, *barley-wine* (i.e. beer).

106 **ἰσοχειλεῖς**, *floating level with the brim*.

107 **γόνατα**, *joints*. For such metaphors, cf. ἀκρωνυχία, III, 4, 154, and μαστός, c. 2. 25.

108 **ἄκρατος**, *strong*. The Greeks were a temperate people, regularly diluting their wine with more than its bulk of water.

109 **συμμαθόντι**, when one became accustomed to it. For the dat., cf. I, 5, 55.

110 **σύνδειπνον ἐποιήσατο**: cf. II, 5, 103.

111 **οὔτε . . . τε**: cf. II, 2, 38, and the note. The parallelism is sought even where the subj. changes.

112 **στερήσοιτο**: fut. mid. as pass.
ἀντεμπλήσαντες . . . ἀπίασιν, they would fill (in recompense) before they left.

113 **ἐξηγησάμενος φαίνηται**, should prove to have suggested. Cf. the note on I, 9, 70.

114 **ἔστ' ἄν**. see the note on I, 9, 38.

115 **οἶνον**: prolepsis. This was doubtless grape wine.

116 **ἐν πᾶσιν ἀφθόνοις**: cf. III, 2, 132. Here the strong phrase, followed by πάντες οἱ στρατιῶται, emphasizes the contrast with their recent hardships.

122 **οὐδαμόθεν ἀφίεσαν**, *in no case would they let them go*.
παραθεῖναι: this, with διακονῶ (cf.

αὐτοῖς ἄριστον· οὐκ ἦν δ' ὅπου οὐ παρετίθεσαν ἐπὶ τὴν αὐτὴν
τράπεζαν κρέα ἄρνεια, ἐρίφεια, χοίρεια, μόσχεια, ὀρνίθεια, σὺν
125 πολλοῖς ἄρτοις τοῖς μὲν πυρίνοις τοῖς δὲ κριθίνοις. ὁπότε δέ
τις φιλοφρονούμενός τῳ βούλοιτο προπιεῖν, εἷλκεν ἐπὶ τὸν κρα-
τῆρα, ἔνθεν ἐπικύψαντα ἔδει ῥοφοῦντα πίνειν ὥσπερ βοῦν. καὶ
τῷ κωμάρχῃ ἐδίδοσαν λαμβάνειν ὅ,τι βούλοιτο. ὁ δὲ ἄλλο μὲν
οὐδὲν ἐδέχετο, ὅπου δέ τινα τῶν συγγενῶν ἴδοι, πρὸς ἑαυτὸν ἀεὶ
130 ἐλάμβανεν. ἐπεὶ δ' ἦλθον πρὸς Χειρίσοφον, κατελάμβανον
κἀκείνους σκηνοῦντας ἐστεφανωμένους τοῦ ξηροῦ χιλοῦ στεφά-
νοις, καὶ διακονοῦντας Ἀρμενίους παῖδας σὺν ταῖς βαρβαρικαῖς
στολαῖς· τοῖς δὲ παισὶν ἐδείκνυσαν ὥσπερ ἐνεοῖς ὅ,τι δέοι
ποιεῖν.

135 ἐπεὶ δ' ἀλλήλους ἐφιλοφρονήσαντο Χειρίσοφος καὶ Ξενοφῶν, κοινῇ δὴ ἀνηρώτων τὸν κωμάρχην διὰ τοῦ περσίζοντος
ἑρμηνέως τίς εἴη ἡ χώρα. ὁ δ' ἔλεγεν ὅτι Ἀρμενία. καὶ πάλιν
ἠρώτων τίνι οἱ ἵπποι τρέφονται. ὁ δ' ἔλεγεν ὅτι βασιλεῖ
δασμός· τὴν δὲ πλησίον χώραν ἔφη εἶναι Χάλυβας, καὶ τὴν
140 ὁδὸν ἔφραζεν ᾗ εἴη. καὶ αὐτὸν τότε μὲν ᾤχετο ἄγων ὁ Ξενοφῶν
πρὸς τοὺς ἑαυτοῦ οἰκέτας, καὶ ἵππον ὃν εἰλήφει παλαίτερον

διακονοῦντας, below, l. 132), is the regular word for serving at table.

123 **οὐκ ἦν δ' ὅπου οὐ**: for the strong phrase, *cf.* οὐκ ἔστιν ὅπως οὐκ, II, 4, 15, and the common οὐδεὶς ὅστις οὐ (*everybody*).

126 **προπιεῖν**, *to drink his health*.

127 **βοῦν**: attracted to the case of αὐτόν. We should have looked for βοῦς (sc. πίνει).

129 **ἐδέχετο**: note the tense; *he would accept nothing else*.

131 **σκηνοῦντας**: here=εὐωχουμένους.

ἐστεφανωμένους: the garland was an indispensable accompaniment of a Greek banquet, even when there was nothing but hay to make it of.

133 **ὥσπερ ἐνεοῖς**: the boys, of course, understood no Greek.

139 **Χάλυβας**: the name of the people for the name of the country; *cf.* Πισίδας, I, I, 62, and the note.

140 **αὐτόν**: the comarch. The word is strongly emphasized by its position.

τότε μέν: contrast ἐπεὶ δ', below, c. 6. 1.

141 **πρὸς ... οἰκέτας**, *to his family* (*i. e. the comarch's*). The reflexive refers back to the emphatic word, here the obj., not the subj. of the sentence; see G. 994; H. 683, b; B. 470. The comarch's relatives were in the village where Xen. and his men were quartered (§ 24).

δίδωσι τῷ κωμάρχῃ ἀναθρέψαντι καταθῦσαι, ὅτι ἤκουεν αὐτὸν
ἱερὸν εἶναι τοῦ Ἡλίου, δεδιὼς μὴ ἀποθάνῃ· ἐκεκάκωτο γὰρ
ὑπὸ τῆς πορείας· αὐτὸς δὲ τῶν πώλων λαμβάνει, καὶ τῶν ἄλλων
36 στρατηγῶν καὶ λοχαγῶν ἔδωκεν ἑκάστῳ πῶλον. ἦσαν δ' οἱ 145
ταύτῃ ἵπποι μείονες μὲν τῶν Περσικῶν, θυμοειδέστεροι δὲ πολύ.
ἐνταῦθα δὴ καὶ διδάσκει ὁ κωμάρχης περὶ τοὺς πόδας τῶν ἵππων
καὶ τῶν ὑποζυγίων σακία περιειλεῖν, ὅταν διὰ τῆς χιόνος
ἄγωσιν· ἄνευ γὰρ τῶν σακίων κατεδύοντο μέχρι τῆς γαστρός.

1   VI. Ἐπεὶ δ' ἡμέρα ἦν ὀγδόη, τὸν μὲν ἡγεμόνα παραδίδωσι
Χειρισόφῳ, τοὺς δὲ οἰκέτας καταλείπει τῷ κωμάρχῃ, πλὴν τοῦ
υἱοῦ τοῦ ἄρτι ἡβάσκοντος· τοῦτον δὲ Πλεισθένει Ἀμφιπολίτῃ
δίδωσι φυλάττειν, ὅπως εἰ καλῶς ἡγήσοιτο, ἔχων καὶ τοῦτον
ἀπίοι. καὶ εἰς τὴν οἰκίαν αὐτοῦ εἰσεφόρησαν ὡς ἐδύναντο 5
2 πλεῖστα, καὶ ἀναζεύξαντες ἐπορεύοντο. ἡγεῖτο δ' αὐτοῖς ὁ κωμάρχης λελυμένος διὰ χιόνος· καὶ ἤδη τε ἦν ἐν τῷ τρίτῳ

εἰλήφει: see III, 3, § 19 or IV, 4, § 21.

παλαίτερον, *oldish,* a common force of the comp.

142 **ἀναθρέψαντι καταθῦσαι,** *to fatten up and sacrifice.*

143 **ἱερόν,** *sacred to;* with possess. gen. The Persians sacrificed horses at the feast of Mithras, the sun god.

εἶναι: how different from ὄντα? Cf. I, 3, 105, and the note.

144 **ὑπό**: again a slight touch of personification.

τῶν πώλων: partitive gen.

145 **ἑκάστῳ**: this suggests a far larger number than the seventeen mentioned in § 24. Possibly the number is incorrect, or Xen. may have meant the generals and captains of his own division.

146 **μείονες**: this description of the Armenian horses is corroborated by modern travelers. We think of the mustang of our western plains.

πολύ: emphatic position.

148 **σακία**: a sort of snow-shoe. The custom still prevails in the Caucasus.

CHAPTER VI

1 **τὸν μὲν ἡγεμόνα,** *him (i. e. the comarch), as guide.* τῷ κωμάρχῃ just below (dat. of advantage, instead of possess. gen.) seems to have been added, if genuine, for the sake of parallelism.

4 **ὅπως ... ἀπίοι,** *intending, if he should prove an honest guide, to let him go home, taking his son with him.*

7 **λελυμένος,** *free from bonds.* Contrast c. 2. 2.

καὶ ἤδη τε ἦν ... καί: cf. I, 8, 1. The vb. is probably impers., as there.

σταθμῷ, καὶ Χειρίσοφος αὐτῷ ἐχαλεπάνθη ὅτι οὐκ εἰς κώμας ἤγαγεν. ὁ δ' ἔλεγεν ὅτι οὐκ εἶεν ἐν τῷ τόπῳ τούτῳ. ὁ δὲ Χειρίσοφος αὐτὸν ἔπαισεν, ἔδησε δ' οὔ. ἐκ δὲ τούτου ἐκεῖνος τῆς νυκτὸς ἀποδρὰς ᾤχετο καταλιπὼν τὸν υἱόν. τοῦτό γε δὴ Χειρισόφῳ καὶ Ξενοφῶντι μόνον διάφορον ἐν τῇ πορείᾳ ἐγένετο, ἡ τοῦ ἡγεμόνος κάκωσις καὶ ἀμέλεια. Πλεισθένης δὲ ἠράσθη τοῦ παιδὸς καὶ οἴκαδε κομίσας πιστοτάτῳ ἐχρῆτο.

μετὰ τοῦτο ἐπορεύθησαν ἑπτὰ σταθμοὺς ἀνὰ πέντε παρασάγγας τῆς ἡμέρας παρὰ τὸν Φᾶσιν ποταμόν, εὖρος πλεθριαῖον. ἐντεῦθεν ἐπορεύθησαν σταθμοὺς δύο παρασάγγας δέκα· ἐπὶ δὲ τῇ εἰς τὸ πεδίον ὑπερβολῇ ἀπήντησαν αὐτοῖς Χάλυβες καὶ Τάοχοι καὶ Φασιανοί. Χειρίσοφος δ' ἐπεὶ κατεῖδε τοὺς πολεμίους ἐπὶ τῇ ὑπερβολῇ, ἐπαύσατο πορευόμενος, ἀπέχων εἰς τριάκοντα σταδίους, ἵνα μὴ κατὰ κέρας ἄγων πλησιάσῃ τοῖς πολεμίοις· παρήγγειλε δὲ καὶ τοῖς ἄλλοις παράγειν τοὺς λόχους, ὅπως ἐπὶ φάλαγγος γένοιτο τὸ στράτευμα. ἐπεὶ δὲ ἦλθον οἱ ὀπισθοφύλακες, συνεκάλεσε στρατηγοὺς καὶ λοχαγούς, καὶ ἔλεξεν ὧδε. Οἱ μὲν πολέμιοι, ὡς ὁρᾶτε, κατέχουσι τὰς ὑπερβολὰς τοῦ ὄρους· ὥρα δὲ βουλεύεσθαι ὅπως ὡς κάλλιστα ἀγωνι-

---

8 **ἐχαλεπάνθη**: the deponent form is rare. A real pass. is found in Plato.

οὐκ εἰς κώμας: from the description in §25 it will be clear that villages could easily have escaped notice, unless the guide chose to reveal them; Chirisophus' anger may, therefore, have been justified. At the same time, if the villages were widely scattered, the guide may have been honest.

10 **ἔδησε δ' οὔ**: said not to mark Chirisophus' clemency, but his lack of caution.

11 **ἀποδρὰς ᾤχετο**: cf. II, 4, 105, and the note.

12 **διάφορον**, disagreement.

13 **ἠράσθη**: ingressive aor.; cf. I, 1, 45.

14 **ἐχρῆτο**, found. Cf. the Lat. utor.

15 **ἀνά**: cf. III, 4, 85.

16 **Φᾶσιν**: certainly not the familiar Phasis, which flows into the Euxine from the east, although the Greeks doubtless thought it was. It must have been a branch of the Araxes; see the map.

πλεθριαῖον: cf. I, 2, 30 f., and the note.

18 **ὑπερβολῇ**: cf. I, 2, 143.

21 **κατὰ κέρας**, in column—the order of march.

22 **παράγειν**: i. e. παρ' ἀσπίδα.

26 **ὅπως . . . ἀγωνιούμεθα**: cf. I, 1, 14, and the note.

8 οὔμεθα. ἐμοὶ μὲν οὖν δοκεῖ παραγγεῖλαι μὲν ἀριστοποιεῖσθαι τοῖς στρατιώταις, ἡμᾶς δὲ βουλεύεσθαι εἴτε τήμερον εἴτε αὔριον
9 δοκεῖ ὑπερβάλλειν τὸ ὄρος. Ἐμοὶ δέ γε, ἔφη ὁ Κλεάνωρ, δοκεῖ, ἐπὰν τάχιστα ἀριστήσωμεν, ἐξοπλισαμένους ὡς κράτιστα ἰέναι ἐπὶ τοὺς ἄνδρας. εἰ γὰρ διατρίψομεν τὴν τήμερον ἡμέραν, οἵ τε νῦν ἡμᾶς ὁρῶντες πολέμιοι θαρραλεώτεροι ἔσονται καὶ ἄλλους εἰκὸς τούτων θαρρούντων πλείους προσγενέσθαι.

10 μετὰ τοῦτον Ξενοφῶν εἶπεν· Ἐγὼ δ' οὕτω γιγνώσκω. εἰ μὲν ἀνάγκη ἐστὶ μάχεσθαι, τοῦτο δεῖ παρασκευάσασθαι ὅπως ὡς κράτιστα μαχούμεθα· εἰ δὲ βουλόμεθα ὡς ῥᾷστα ὑπερβάλλειν, τοῦτό μοι δοκεῖ σκεπτέον εἶναι ὅπως ὡς ἐλάχιστα μὲν τραύματα λάβω-
11 μεν, ὡς ἐλάχιστα δὲ σώματα ἀνδρῶν ἀποβάλωμεν. τὸ μὲν οὖν ὄρος ἐστὶ τὸ ὁρώμενον πλέον ἢ ἐφ' ἑξήκοντα στάδια, ἄνδρες δ' οὐδαμοῦ φυλάττοντες ἡμᾶς φανεροί εἰσιν ἀλλ' ἢ κατ' αὐτὴν τὴν ὁδόν· πολὺ οὖν κρεῖττον τοῦ ἐρήμου ὄρους καὶ κλέψαι τι πειρᾶσθαι λαθόντας καὶ ἁρπάσαι φθάσαντας, εἰ δυναίμεθα, μᾶλλον ἢ πρὸς ἰσχυρὰ χωρία καὶ ἀνθρώπους παρεσκευασμένους μάχεσθαι.

---

28 ἡμᾶς δέ: expressed for the sake of emphasis, although there is no change of subj.

29 ὑπερβάλλειν: note the tense.

Κλεάνωρ: see the Introd., § 38.

31 εἰ γὰρ διατρίψομεν: a warning condition; *cf.* I, 5, 95, and the note.

33 πλείους: pred. (*in larger numbers*).

προσγενέσθαι: after εἰκός the pres. or aor. infin. is common, not the fut. alone.

34 Ξενοφῶν: the following rhetorical speech is in marked contrast with the author's narrative style; see the Introd., § 40.

37 ὅπως ... λάβωμεν .... ἀποβάλωμεν: obj. clause with subj.; *cf.* I, 1, 20, and the note.

38 σώματα ἀνδρῶν: a strong phrase for *men*.

39 τὸ ὁρώμενον: with ὄρος. Its position suggests that it was an after-thought.

ἐπί: *cf. ἐπὶ πολύ*, I, 8, 28.

40 ἀλλ' ἤ, *save only*.

41 τοῦ ἐρήμου ὄρους: partitive gen. with τι. The position is emphatic.

κλέψαι ... καὶ ἁρπάσαι: both infins. depend on πειρᾶσθαι. The former has reference to stealth, the latter to a sudden dash, such as that described in III, 4, §§ 44 ff. The distinction is made clearer by the accompanying partics. Note that the usual construction of λανθάνω and φθάνω is here reversed; see G. M. T. 893.

42 εἰ δυναίμεθα: ideal opt., where ἢν δυνώμεθα might have been expected.

μᾶλλον ἤ: after κρεῖττον; the second comp. is, of course, redundant.

πολὺ γὰρ ῥᾷον ὄρθιον ἀμαχεὶ ἰέναι ἢ ὁμαλὲς ἔνθεν καὶ ἔνθεν 12
45 πολεμίων ὄντων, καὶ νύκτωρ ἀμαχεὶ μᾶλλον ἂν τὰ πρὸ ποδῶν
ὁρῴη τις ἢ μεθ' ἡμέραν μαχόμενος, καὶ ἡ τραχεία τοῖς ποσὶν
ἀμαχεὶ ἰοῦσιν εὐμενεστέρα ἢ ἡ ὁμαλὴ τὰς κεφαλὰς βαλλομένοις.
καὶ κλέψαι δ' οὐκ ἀδύνατόν μοι δοκεῖ εἶναι, ἐξὸν μὲν νυκτὸς 13
ἰέναι, ὡς μὴ ὁρᾶσθαι, ἐξὸν δ' ἀπελθεῖν τοσοῦτον ὡς μὴ αἴσθησιν
50 παρέχειν. δοκοῦμεν δ' ἄν μοι ταύτῃ προσποιούμενοι προσβαλεῖν
ἐρημοτέρῳ ἂν τῷ ὄρει χρῆσθαι· μένοιεν γὰρ αὐτοῦ μᾶλλον
ἀθρόοι οἱ πολέμιοι. ἀτὰρ τί ἐγὼ περὶ κλοπῆς συμβάλλομαι; 14
ὑμᾶς γὰρ ἔγωγε, ὦ Χειρίσοφε, ἀκούω τοὺς Λακεδαιμονίους ὅσοι
ἐστὲ τῶν ὁμοίων εὐθὺς ἐκ παίδων κλέπτειν μελετᾶν, καὶ οὐκ
55 αἰσχρὸν εἶναι ἀλλὰ καλὸν κλέπτειν ὅσα μὴ κωλύει νόμος.
ὅπως δὲ ὡς τάχιστα κλέπτητε καὶ πειρᾶσθε λανθάνειν, νόμι- 15

---

44 πολὺ γὰρ ῥᾷον. the two projects, κλέψαι and ἁρπάσαι, are taken up in chiastic order (cf. the note on II, 6, 5). Xen. wishes to close with κλέψαι.

ὄρθιον ... ὁμαλές: the adjs. supply the place of a subst. inner obj.; cf. εὐθύωρον, II, 2, 74, and the note. Cf., also, the note on πεδίον, c. 4. 2.

45 τὰ πρὸ ποδῶν, freely, *one's path.*

46 τοῖς ποσίν: with τραχεῖα; but the words may be spurious.

47 ἰοῦσιν ... βαλλομένοις: for the dat., cf. I, 5, 55, and the note. (ἰοῦσιν is not in agreement with τοῖς ποσίν).

τὰς κεφαλάς: cf. II, 6, 2, and the note.

48 κλέψαι, emphatic position,

ἐξὸν ... ἐξόν: acc. abs.; cf. II, 5, 86, and the note.

49 αἴσθησιν παρέχειν: *i. e. to be heard.*

50 δοκοῦμεν δ' ἄν ... χρῆσθαι: the personal construction cannot be literally rendered. For the repeated ἄν, cf. I, 3, 29, and the note.

51 μένοιεν: ἄν is to be supplied from the preceding sentence. Only in such cases may the potential opt. omit ἄν; see the note on I, 6, 8, and G. M. T. 226.

52 ἀτάρ: save in Plato, not common in Attic prose. Note that the style here is conversational.

ἐγώ: note the emphasis and the contrast with ὑμᾶς.

συμβάλλομαι: sc. λόγους or γνώμην, *express an opinion.*

53 ὑμᾶς ... τοὺς Λακεδαιμονίους, appos. Cf. I, 5, 94, and the note.

54 τῶν ὁμοίων, *the peers*, a technical name for those of Dorian stock at Sparta. The other inhabitants were restricted in civic rights (Helots, Perioeci).

ἐκ παίδων, *from boyhood.* Cf. *inde a pueris.*

55 ὅσα μὴ κωλύει νόμος: the rations served to Spartan boys were but scanty and they were allowed to

μον παρ' ὑμῖν ἐστιν, ἐὰν ληφθῆτε κλέπτοντες, μαστιγοῦσθαι.
νῦν οὖν μάλα σοι καιρός ἐστιν ἐπιδείξασθαι τὴν παιδείαν, καὶ
φυλάξασθαι μὴ ληφθῶμεν κλέπτοντες τοῦ ὄρους, ὡς μὴ πληγὰς
λάβωμεν.

Ἀλλὰ μέντοι, ἔφη ὁ Χειρίσοφος, κἀγὼ ὑμᾶς τοὺς Ἀθηναίους
ἀκούω δεινοὺς εἶναι κλέπτειν τὰ δημόσια, καὶ μάλα ὄντος δεινοῦ
κινδύνου τῷ κλέπτοντι, καὶ τοὺς κρατίστους μέντοι μάλιστα,
εἴπερ ὑμῖν οἱ κράτιστοι ἄρχειν ἀξιοῦνται· ὥστε ὥρα καὶ σοὶ
ἐπιδείκνυσθαι τὴν παιδείαν. Ἐγὼ μὲν τοίνυν, ἔφη ὁ Ξενοφῶν,
ἕτοιμός εἰμι τοὺς ὀπισθοφύλακας ἔχων, ἐπειδὰν δειπνήσωμεν,
ἰέναι καταληψόμενος τὸ ὄρος. ἔχω δὲ καὶ ἡγεμόνας· οἱ γὰρ
γυμνῆτες τῶν ἑπομένων ἡμῖν κλωπῶν ἔλαβόν τινας ἐνεδρεύ-
σαντες· τούτων καὶ πυνθάνομαι ὅτι οὐκ ἄβατόν ἐστι τὸ ὄρος,
ἀλλὰ νέμεται αἰξὶ καὶ βουσίν· ὥστε ἐάνπερ ἅπαξ λάβωμέν τι
τοῦ ὄρους, βατὰ καὶ τοῖς ὑποζυγίοις ἔσται. ἐλπίζω δὲ οὐδὲ τοὺς

---

steal food. If caught, however, they were severely punished.

58 μάλα ... καιρός ἐστιν: cf. πάνυ ἐν καιρῷ, III, 1, 177.

ἐπιδείξασθαι: the aor. of the single act. Contrast κλέπτειν (above), of the habit.

59 πληγὰς λάβωμεν: this periphrasis often supplies the pass. of the defective vb., πλήττω. Its perf. act. is regularly supplied by the phrase, πληγὰς δέδωκα. Cf. the note on II, 4, 48.

62 δεινοὺς ... κλέπτειν, *terrible fellows at stealing*. From such a use it is easy to see how δεινός comes to mean *clever*. Charges of bribery and peculation were common at Athens. Were we to believe Aristophanes and the orators, we should conclude that few men in public life were honest.

ὄντος: concessive, with intensive καί.

δεινοῦ: chosen to refer back to δεινούς. The penalty was a fine of double the amount appropriated, loss of civic rights, banishment, or even death.

63 κρατίστους, *your best men*.

64 εἴπερ, *that is, if*.

ὑμῖν: ethical dat. (*to be your rulers*). The asperity of Chirisophus' answer has led some to see in this episode a reminiscence of the quarrel mentioned in § 3.

65 ἐπιδείκνυσθαι, perhaps, *to set about showing;* not exactly as ἐπιδείξασθαι, above.

68 κλωπῶν: chosen doubtless with reference to κλέπτειν; see, however, c. 5. § 12.

69 τούτων καὶ πυνθάνομαι, *I learn from them, besides other things*.

70 νέμεται αἰξὶ καὶ βουσίν, *is grazed over by goats and cattle*. In the act. construction the subj. is the herdsmen, not the animals.

71 βατά: cf. III, 4, 199.

πολεμίους μενεῖν ἔτι, ἐπειδὰν ἴδωσιν ἡμᾶς ἐν τῷ ὁμοίῳ ἐπὶ τῶν ἄκρων· οὐδὲ γὰρ νῦν ἐθέλουσι καταβαίνειν εἰς τὸ ἴσον ἡμῖν. ὁ δὲ Χειρίσοφος εἶπε· Καὶ τί δεῖ σὲ ἰέναι καὶ λιπεῖν τὴν ὀπισθοφυλακίαν; ἀλλὰ ἄλλους πέμψον, ἂν μή τινες ἐθέλοντες ἀγαθοὶ φαίνωνται.

ἐκ τούτου Ἀριστώνυμος Μεθυδριεὺς ἔρχεται ὁπλίτας ἔχων καὶ Ἀριστέας ὁ Χῖος γυμνῆτας καὶ Νικόμαχος Οἰταῖος γυμνῆτας· καὶ σύνθημα ἐποιήσαντο, ὁπότε ἔχοιεν τὰ ἄκρα, πυρὰ καίειν πολλά. ταῦτα συνθέμενοι ἠρίστων· ἐκ δὲ τοῦ ἀρίστου προήγαγεν ὁ Χειρίσοφος τὸ στράτευμα πᾶν ὡς δέκα σταδίους πρὸς τοὺς πολεμίους, ὅπως ὡς μάλιστα δοκοίη ταύτῃ προσάξειν.

Ἐπειδὴ δὲ ἐδείπνησαν καὶ νὺξ ἐγένετο, οἱ μὲν ταχθέντες ᾤχοντο, καὶ καταλαμβάνουσι τὸ ὄρος, οἱ δὲ ἄλλοι αὐτοῦ ἀνεπαύοντο. οἱ δὲ πολέμιοι ἐπεὶ ᾔσθοντο τὸ ὄρος ἐχόμενον, ἐγρηγόρεσαν καὶ ἔκαιον πυρὰ πολλὰ διὰ νυκτός. ἐπειδὴ δὲ ἡμέρα ἐγένετο Χειρίσοφος μὲν θυσάμενος ἦγε κατὰ τὴν ὁδόν, οἱ δὲ τὸ ὄρος καταλαβόντες κατὰ τὰ ἄκρα ἐπῇσαν. τῶν δὲ πολεμίων τὸ μὲν πολὺ ἔμενεν ἐπὶ τῇ ὑπερβολῇ τοῦ ὄρους, μέρος δ' αὐτῶν ἀπήντα τοῖς κατὰ τὰ ἄκρα. πρὶν δὲ ὁμοῦ εἶναι τοὺς

---

72 ἐν τῷ ὁμοίῳ, *on a level with them.*

73 εἰς τὸ ἴσον ἡμῖν, *to the same level with us.*

75 ἀλλά, *no*, or *rather*. It implies a preceding negation (*Do not go yourself*).

77 Ἀριστώνυμος ... Ἀριστέας: *cf.* c. 1. §§ 27 and 28. The use of the art. with Χῖος is perhaps intended to signalize Aristeas' well-known bravery. *Cf.* Σωκράτει τῷ Ἀθηναίῳ, III, 1, 27.

78 Οἰταῖος: find Mount Oeta on the map.

79 σύνθημα ἐποιήσαντο = συνέθεντο; *cf.* ταῦτα συνθέμενοι, below, and the note on I, 1, 24. The mid. is reciprocal. *Cf.* c. 2. 7.

80 ἐκ ... τοῦ ἀρίστου, *immediately after breakfast* (lunch).

83 οἱ μὲν ταχθέντες: *i. e.* the volunteers, § 20.

86 ἐγρηγόρεσαν, *kept watch*. When the perf. of a vb. has the force of a pres. (*e. g.* ἐγρήγορα, *am awake*), the plpf. has, of course, the force of an impf.

διὰ νυκτός: *cf.* the stronger phrase δι' ὅλης τῆς νυκτός, c. 2. 20.

87 θυσάμενος: *cf.* I, 7, 85; contrast θύσαντες, below, l. 98.

88 κατὰ τὰ ἄκρα ἐπῇσαν, *advanced against them along the heights.*

89 τὸ μὲν πολύ: *cf.* I, 4, 86.

90 τοὺς πολλούς: *i. e.* the two main bodies. The following gen., ἀλλήλων, depends upon ὁμοῦ, which

πολλοὺς ἀλλήλων, συμμειγνύασιν οἱ κατὰ τὰ ἄκρα, καὶ νικῶσιν οἱ Ἕλληνες καὶ διώκουσιν. ἐν τούτῳ δὲ καὶ οἱ ἐκ τοῦ πεδίου οἱ μὲν πελτασταὶ τῶν Ἑλλήνων δρόμῳ ἔθεον πρὸς τοὺς παρατεταγμένους, Χειρίσοφος δὲ βάδην ταχὺ ἐφείπετο σὺν τοῖς ὁπλίταις. οἱ δὲ πολέμιοι οἱ ἐπὶ τῇ ὁδῷ ἐπειδὴ τὸ ἄνω ἑώρων ἡττώμενον, φεύγουσι· καὶ ἀπέθανον μὲν οὐ πολλοὶ αὐτῶν, γέρρα δὲ πάμπολλα ἐλήφθη· ἃ οἱ Ἕλληνες ταῖς μαχαίραις κόπτοντες ἀχρεῖα ἐποίουν. ὡς δ' ἀνέβησαν, θύσαντες καὶ τρόπαιον στησάμενοι κατέβησαν εἰς τὸ πεδίον, καὶ εἰς κώμας πολλῶν καὶ ἀγαθῶν γεμούσας ἦλθον.

VII. Ἐκ δὲ τούτων ἐπορεύθησαν εἰς Ταόχους σταθμοὺς πέντε παρασάγγας τριάκοντα· καὶ τὰ ἐπιτήδεια ἐπέλειπε· χωρία γὰρ ᾤκουν ἰσχυρὰ οἱ Τάοχοι, ἐν οἷς καὶ τὰ ἐπιτήδεια ἅπαντα εἶχον ἀνακεκομισμένοι. ἐπεὶ δ' ἀφίκοντο πρὸς χωρίον ὃ πόλιν μὲν οὐκ εἶχεν οὐδ' οἰκίας—συνεληλυθότες δ' ἦσαν

---

here follows the analogy of ἐγγύς and πλησίον. Ordinarily, as a word denoting sameness, it takes a dat.

92 οἱ ἐκ τοῦ πεδίου: *i. e.* the main body of the Greeks. Note the partitive appos. in the following.

93 δρόμῳ ἔθεον: *cf.* I, 8, 71, and the note.

94 βάδην ταχύ, *at a quick pace.*

95 τὸ ἄνω = τοὺς ἄνω, *their men above.* For the neut., *cf.* the note on I, 2, 3.

98 τρόπαιον στησάμενοι: This was the regular sequel to a Greek victory. The trophy, whether elaborate, as often, or simple, as it must have been in this case, was at once a thank-offering to the gods and a monument to their own valor (note that the vb. is regularly mid.)

100 γεμούσας: after so many privations Xen. uses strong words to express abundance, when they meet it. *Cf.* c. 2. § 22.

CHAPTER VII

1 Ἐκ δὲ τούτων: probably neut., *after these events*, rather than fem., *out of these villages.*

εἰς Ταόχους: note again the name of the people, instead of the name of the country. This name still survives.

2 ἐπέλειπε: *cf.* I, 5, 30, but note the difference in tense.

3 ἐν οἷς: not εἰς ἅ, because of εἶχον. They kept the provisions in the strongholds, whither they had brought them. For the phrase εἶχον ἀνακεκομισμένοι, *cf.* ἔχομεν ἀνηρπακότες, I, 3, 74, and the note.

5 συνεληλυθότες ... ἦσαν, *had gathered.* The plpf. is not rarely resolved into perf. partic. and copula; see, however, the note

αὐτόσε καὶ ἄνδρες καὶ γυναῖκες καὶ κτήνη πολλά—Χειρίσοφος μὲν οὖν πρὸς τοῦτο προσέβαλλεν εὐθὺς ἥκων· ἐπειδὴ δὲ ἡ πρώτη τάξις ἀπέκαμνεν, ἄλλη προσῄει καὶ αὖθις ἄλλη· οὐ γὰρ ἦν ἀθρόοις περιστῆναι, ἀλλ' ἀπότομον ἦν κύκλῳ.

10 ἐπειδὴ δέ Ξενοφῶν ἦλθε σὺν τοῖς ὀπισθοφύλαξι καὶ πελτα- 3 σταῖς καὶ ὁπλίταις, ἐνταῦθα δὴ λέγει Χειρίσοφος· Εἰς καλὸν ἥκετε· τὸ γὰρ χωρίον αἱρετέον· τῇ γὰρ στρατιᾷ οὐκ ἔστι τὰ ἐπιτήδεια, εἰ μὴ ληψόμεθα τὸ χωρίον. ἐνταῦθα δὴ κοινῇ ἐβου- 4 λεύοντο· καὶ τοῦ Ξενοφῶντος ἐρωτῶντος τί τὸ κωλῦον εἴη 15 εἰσελθεῖν εἶπεν ὁ Χειρίσοφος· Μία αὕτη πάροδός ἐστιν ἣν ὁρᾷς· ὅταν δέ τις ταύτῃ πειρᾶται παριέναι, κυλινδοῦσι λίθους ὑπὲρ ταύτης τῆς ὑπερεχούσης πέτρας· ὃς δ' ἂν καταληφθῇ, οὕτω διατίθεται. ἅμα δ' ἔδειξε συντετριμμένους ἀνθρώπους καὶ σκέλη καὶ πλευράς. Ἢν δὲ τοὺς λίθους ἀναλώσωσιν, ἔφη ὁ Ξενοφῶν, 5 20 ἄλλο τι ἢ οὐδὲν κωλύει παριέναι; οὐ γὰρ δὴ ἐκ τοῦ ἐναντίου ὁρῶμεν εἰ μὴ ὀλίγους τούτους ἀνθρώπους, καὶ τούτων δύο ἢ τρεῖς ὡπλισμένους. τὸ δὲ χωρίον, ὡς καὶ σὺ ὁρᾷς, σχεδὸν τρία ἡμί- 6 πλεθρά ἐστιν ὃ δεῖ βαλλομένους διελθεῖν· τούτου δὲ ὅσον πλέθρον δασὺ πίτυσι διαλειπούσαις μεγάλαις, ἀνθ' ὧν ἑστηκότες

---

on ἦσαν ἐκπεπτωκότες, II, 3, 39, and on εἶναι ... φυλάττων, I, 2, 122 f.

6 αὐτόσε: the rel. construction is given up as often.

Χειρίσοφος μὲν οὖν: the sentence makes a new start (anacolouthon).

7 εὐθὺς ἥκων, *immediately on his arrival.*

11 εἰς καλόν, *opportunely.*

12 τὸ χωρίον ... τὸ χωρίον: note the effect of the chiastic order. Cf. I, 7, 62, and the note.

13 εἰ μὴ ληψόμεθα: a warning condition; cf. I, 5, 96, and the note.

15 Μία ... ὁρᾷς: cf. c. 1. 79, and the note.

6 κυλινδοῦσι: for the form, cf. ἐρρίπτουν, III, 3, 3, and the note.

17 οὕτω διατίθεται, *fares thus.* For the vb. cf. διατιθείς, I, 1, 19.

18 σκέλη καὶ πλευράς: cf. the note on τὰς κεφαλάς, II, 6, 2.

20 ἄλλο τι ἤ: cf. II, 5, 36, and the note.

ἐκ τοῦ ἐναντίου, *on the other side.*

21 εἰ μή, *except.*

τούτους, *yonder.* No art.

22 χωρίον, *space.*

τρία ἡμίπλεθρα: *i. e.* 150 ft. For the form of expression, cf. τρία ἡμιδαρεικά, I, 3, 110.

23 βαλλομένους, *under fire.*

ὅσον: cf. I, 2, 15, and the note.

24 δασὺ πίτυσι: the adj. has here its normal construction (with a dat. of means). In II, 4, 63, it was construed with a gen., after

ἄνδρες τί ἂν πάσχοιεν ἢ ὑπὸ τῶν φερομένων λίθων ἢ ὑπὸ τῶν κυλινδομένων; τὸ λοιπὸν οὖν γίγνεται ὡς ἡμίπλεθρον, ὃ δεῖ ὅταν λωφήσωσιν οἱ λίθοι παραδραμεῖν. Ἀλλὰ εὐθύς, ἔφη ὁ Χειρίσοφος, ἐπειδὰν ἀρξώμεθα εἰς τὸ δασὺ προσιέναι, φέρονται οἱ λίθοι πολλοί. Αὐτὸ ἄν, ἔφη, τὸ δέον εἴη· θᾶττον γὰρ ἀναλώσουσι τοὺς λίθους. ἀλλὰ πορευώμεθα ἔνθεν ἡμῖν μικρόν τι παραδραμεῖν ἔσται, ἢν δυνώμεθα, καὶ ἀπελθεῖν ῥᾴδιον, ἢν βουλώμεθα.

Ἐντεῦθεν ἐπορεύοντο Χειρίσοφος καὶ Ξενοφῶν καὶ Καλλίμαχος Παρράσιος λοχαγός· τούτου γὰρ ἡγεμονία ἦν τῶν ὀπισθοφυλάκων λοχαγῶν ἐκείνῃ τῇ ἡμέρᾳ· οἱ δὲ ἄλλοι λοχαγοὶ ἔμενον ἐν τῷ ἀσφαλεῖ. μετὰ τοῦτο οὖν ἀπῆλθον ὑπὸ τὰ δένδρα ἄνθρωποι ὡς ἑβδομήκοντα, οὐχ ἁθρόοι ἀλλὰ καθ' ἕνα, ἕκαστος φυλαττόμενος ὡς ἐδύνατο. Ἀγασίας δὲ ὁ Στυμφάλιος καὶ Ἀριστώνυμος Μεθυδριεὺς καὶ οὗτοι τῶν ὀπισθοφυλάκων λοχαγοὶ ὄντες, καὶ ἄλλοι δέ, ἐφέστασαν ἔξω τῶν δένδρων· οὐ γὰρ ἦν ἀσφαλῶς ἐν τοῖς δένδροις ἑστάναι πλέον ἢ τὸν ἕνα λόχον. ἔνθα δὴ Καλλίμαχος μηχανᾶταί τι· προὔτρεχεν ἀπὸ τοῦ δένδρου ὑφ' ᾧ ἦν αὐτὸς δύο ἢ τρία βήματα· ἐπειδὴ δὲ οἱ λίθοι φέροιντο, ἀνέχαζεν

---

the analogy of words expressing fulness. See the note there.

διαλειπούσαις, *standing at intervals. Cf.* I, 5, 11.

ἀνθ' ὧν, *behind which.*

25 τί ἂν πάσχοιεν: the incorporation of the question in the rel. clause adds vividness.

φερομένων: *cf.* I, 8, 78, and the note, and φέρονται, below, l. 28.

29 πολλοί, pred., *in large numbers.*

αὐτὸ ... εἴη: *that is the very thing we want.*

30 ἔνθεν, (*to a point*) *whence.*

μικρόν τι: *i. e.* the space estimated as 50 ft. (§ 6).

31 ἀπελθεῖν, *to get back; i. e.* if an advance should prove impossible.

33 Καλλίμαχος: *cf.* c. 1. 103.

34 ὀπισθοφυλάκων λοχαγῶν: appos.

35 ἐκείνῃ τῇ ἡμέρᾳ: from this it appears that the several λόχοι held the front position (the post of danger) on successive days.

36 ἀπῆλθον, *departed, set out;* not as ἀπελθεῖν, above.

37 ὡς ἑβδομήκοντα: *i. e.* his λόχος.

καθ' ἕνα, *one at a time. Cf.* κατὰ ἔθνη, I, 8, 34, and the corresponding distributive use of ἄνα (*e. g.* c. 6. 15).

38 Ἀγασίας: *cf.* the Introd., § 38.

39 Ἀριστώνυμος: *cf.* c. 1. 101.

40 καὶ ἄλλοι δέ, *and others, too.*

42 προὔτρεχεν: explanatory asyndeton. Note the tenses.

43 βήματα: acc. of extent.

ἀνέχαζεν: for the vb., *cf.* c. 1. 65, and the note.

εὐπετῶς· ἐφ' ἑκάστης δὲ τῆς προδρομῆς πλέον ἢ δέκα ἅμαξαι
πετρῶν ἀνηλίσκοντο. ὁ δὲ Ἀγασίας ὡς ὁρᾷ τὸν Καλλίμαχον 11
ἃ ἐποίει, καὶ τὸ στράτευμα πᾶν θεώμενον, δείσας μὴ οὐ πρῶτος
παραδράμῃ εἰς τὸ χωρίον, οὐ [δὲ] τὸν Ἀριστώνυμον πλησίον
ὄντα παρακαλέσας οὐδὲ Εὐρύλοχον τὸν Λουσιέα ἑταίρους ὄντας
οὐδὲ ἄλλον οὐδένα χωρεῖ αὐτός, καὶ παρέρχεται πάντας. ὁ δὲ 12
Καλλίμαχος ὡς ὁρᾷ αὐτὸν παριόντα, ἐπιλαμβάνεται αὐτοῦ τῆς
ἴτυος· ἐν δὲ τούτῳ παραθεῖ αὐτοὺς Ἀριστώνυμος Μεθυδριεύς,
καὶ μετὰ τοῦτον Εὐρύλοχος Λουσιεύς· πάντες γὰρ οὗτοι ἀντεποιοῦντο ἀρετῆς καὶ διηγωνίζοντο πρὸς ἀλλήλους· καὶ οὕτως
ἐρίζοντες αἱροῦσι τὸ χωρίον. ὡς γὰρ ἅπαξ εἰσέδραμον, οὐδεὶς
πέτρος ἄνωθεν ἠνέχθη. ἐνταῦθα δὴ δεινὸν ἦν θέαμα. αἱ γὰρ 13
γυναῖκες ῥίπτουσαι τὰ παιδία εἶτα ἑαυτὰς ἐπικατερρίπτουν, καὶ
οἱ ἄνδρες ὡσαύτως. ἐνταῦθα δὴ καὶ Αἰνείας Στυμφάλιος
λοχαγὸς ἰδών τινα θέοντα ὡς ῥίψοντα ἑαυτὸν στολὴν ἔχοντα
καλὴν ἐπιλαμβάνεται ὡς κωλύσων· ὁ δὲ αὐτὸν ἐπισπᾶται, καὶ 14
ἀμφότεροι ᾤχοντο κατὰ τῶν πετρῶν φερόμενοι καὶ ἀπέθανον.
ἐντεῦθεν ἄνθρωποι μὲν πάνυ ὀλίγοι ἐλήφθησαν, βόες δὲ καὶ ὄνοι
πολλοὶ καὶ πρόβατα.

Ἐντεῦθεν ἐπορεύθησαν διὰ Χαλύβων σταθμοὺς ἑπτὰ παρα- 1
σάγγας πεντήκοντα. οὗτοι ἦσαν ὧν διῆλθον ἀλκιμώτατοι, καὶ
εἰς χεῖρας ᾖσαν. εἶχον δὲ θώρακας λινοῦς μέχρι τοῦ ἤτρου, ἀντὶ

---

44 ἅμαξαι, *wagon-loads*.
45 Καλλίμαχον ἃ ἐποίει: prolepsis.
46 δείσας μὴ οὐ πρῶτος παραδράμῃ, *afraid that he* (*himself*) *would not be the first to get in.*
49 αὐτός, *alone*, a frequent use; *cf.* I, 8, 44.
50 αὐτοῦ τῆς ἴτυος, *the rim of his shield.* αὐτοῦ may be taken with τῆς ἴτυος, or directly with ἐπιλαμβάνεται (*catches hold of him by his shield*). ἴτυς is a poetic word.
52 ἀντεποιοῦντο ἀρετῆς: *cf.* II, 1, 59. ἀρετή is here *reputation* for valor.
54 ἅπαξ: *cf.* I, 9, 34.

55 δεινόν: Xen. was not lacking in humanity.
56 ῥίπτουσαι . . . ἐπικατερρίπτουν: note the durative tenses and the exact use of the preps.
58 στολὴν . . . καλήν: *cf.* the note on I, 2, 158.
60 ᾤχοντο . . . φερόμενοι: *cf.* II, 4, 105, and the note.
64 ὧν: gen. by attraction; the antecedent would have been partitive.
ἀλκιμώτατοι: for the adj., *cf.* c. 3. 17, and the note.
65 εἰς χεῖρας ᾖσαν: *cf.* I, 2, 152, although the sense differs.

16 δὲ τῶν πτερύγων σπάρτα πυκνὰ ἐστραμμένα. εἶχον δὲ καὶ κνημῖδας καὶ κράνη καὶ παρὰ τὴν ζώνην μαχαίριον ὅσον ξυήλην Λακωνικήν, ᾧ ἔσφαττον ὧν κρατεῖν δύναιντο, καὶ ἀποτέμνοντες ἂν τὰς κεφαλὰς ἔχοντες ἐπορεύοντο, καὶ ᾖδον καὶ ἐχόρευον ὁπότε οἱ πολέμιοι αὐτοὺς ὄψεσθαι ἔμελλον. εἶχον δὲ καὶ δόρυ ὡς 70
17 πεντεκαίδεκα πήχεων μίαν λόγχην ἔχον. οὗτοι ἐνέμενον ἐν τοῖς πολίσμασιν· ἐπεὶ δὲ παρέλθοιεν οἱ Ἕλληνες, εἵποντο ἀεὶ μαχούμενοι. ᾤκουν δὲ ἐν τοῖς ὀχυροῖς, καὶ τὰ ἐπιτήδεια ἐν τούτοις ἀνακεκομισμένοι ἦσαν· ὥστε μηδὲν λαμβάνειν αὐτόθεν τοὺς Ἕλληνας, ἀλλὰ διετράφησαν τοῖς κτήνεσιν ἃ ἐκ τῶν Ταόχων 75
18 ἔλαβον. ἐκ τούτων οἱ Ἕλληνες ἀφίκοντο ἐπὶ Ἅρπασον ποταμόν, εὖρος τεττάρων πλέθρων. ἐντεῦθεν ἐπορεύθησαν διὰ Σκυθηνῶν σταθμοὺς τέτταρας παρασάγγας εἴκοσι διὰ πεδίου εἰς κώμας· ἐν αἷς ἔμειναν ἡμέρας τρεῖς καὶ ἐπεσιτίσαντο.

9 ἐντεῦθεν διῆλθον σταθμοὺς τέτταρας παρασάγγας εἴκοσι πρὸς 80 πόλιν μεγάλην καὶ εὐδαίμονα καὶ οἰκουμένην ἣ ἐκαλεῖτο Γυμνιάς. ἐκ ταύτης ὁ τῆς χώρας ἄρχων τοῖς Ἕλλησιν ἡγεμόνα πέμπει, ὅπως
10 διὰ τῆς ἑαυτῶν πολεμίας χώρας ἄγοι αὐτούς. ἐλθὼν δ᾽ ἐκεῖνος

---

66 **πτερύγων**: the lower part of the cuirass (θώραξ) was necessarily of pliant material, so as not to interfere with the movement of the body. It was called πτέρυξ (*flap*), and was usually of leather or felt, at times covered with metal plates.

σπάρτα πυκνὰ ἐστραμμένα, *thickly plaited cords*.

67 **ξυήλην**: acc. by attraction; *cf.* ὥσπερ βοῦν, c. 5. 127.

69 **ἂν ... ἐπορεύοντο**: frequentative; *cf.* I, 9, 68, and the note. Translate, *would carry them with them as they marched*.

70 **ἔμελλον**: we should have expected μέλλοιεν, but see the note on I, 5, 59.

71 **μίαν λόγχην**: the Greek spear had a spike (στύραξ, σαυρωτήρ) at the butt end also, by which it could be stuck into the ground.

73 **μαχούμενοι**, *ready to fight*.

ἐν τούτοις: *cf.* ἐν οἷς, l. 3, and the note.

75 **διετράφησαν**: the dependent construction (with ὥστε) is given up. For the force of δια- *cf.* διεγένοντο, I, 5, 34. Whenever the Greeks had to subsist on meat Xen. lays stress on the fact.

ἅ: no assimilation, such as usually takes place.

76 **Ἅρπασον**: of wholly uncertain identification.

83 **ἑαυτῶν**: gen. after πολεμίας, a somewhat rare use. It is permissible, because πολέμιος may easily be felt as a substantive. *Cf.* τοὺς ἐκείνου ἐχθίστους, III, 2, 25, and ἑαυτοῦ, below l. 86. ἑαυτῶν

λέγει ὅτι ἄξει αὐτοὺς πέντε ἡμερῶν εἰς χωρίον ὅθεν ὄψονται
θάλατταν· εἰ δὲ μή, τεθνάναι ἐπηγγείλατο. καὶ ἡγούμενος
ἐπειδὴ ἐνέβαλλεν εἰς τὴν ἑαυτοῦ πολεμίαν, παρεκελεύετο αἴθειν
καὶ φθείρειν τὴν χώραν· ᾧ καὶ δῆλον ἐγένετο ὅτι τούτου ἕνεκα
ἔλθοι, οὐ τῆς τῶν Ἑλλήνων εὐνοίας. καὶ ἀφικνοῦνται ἐπὶ τὸ
ὄρος τῇ πέμπτῃ ἡμέρᾳ· ὄνομα δὲ τῷ ὄρει ἦν Θήχης. ἐπεὶ δὲ οἱ
πρῶτοι ἐγένοντο ἐπὶ τοῦ ὄρους, κραυγὴ πολλὴ ἐγένετο. ἀκούσας
δὲ ὁ Ξενοφῶν καὶ οἱ ὀπισθοφύλακες ᾠήθησαν ἔμπροσθεν ἄλλους
ἐπιτίθεσθαι πολεμίους· εἵποντο γὰρ ὄπισθεν ἐκ τῆς καιομένης
χώρας, καὶ αὐτῶν οἱ ὀπισθοφύλακες ἀπέκτεινάν τέ τινας καὶ
ἐζώγρησαν ἐνέδραν ποιησάμενοι, καὶ γέρρα ἔλαβον δασειῶν
βοῶν ὠμοβόεια ἀμφὶ τὰ εἴκοσιν. ἐπειδὴ δὲ βοὴ πλείων τε
ἐγίγνετο καὶ ἐγγύτερον καὶ οἱ ἀεὶ ἐπιόντες ἔθεον δρόμῳ ἐπὶ τοὺς
ἀεὶ βοῶντας καὶ πολλῷ μείζων ἐγίγνετο ἡ βοὴ ὅσῳ δὴ πλείους
ἐγίγνοντο, ἐδόκει δὴ μεῖζόν τι εἶναι τῷ Ξενοφῶντι, καὶ ἀναβὰς ἐφ᾽
ἵππον καὶ Λύκιον καὶ τοὺς ἱππέας ἀναλαβὼν παρεβοήθει· καὶ
τάχα δὴ ἀκούουσι βοώντων τῶν στρατιωτῶν Θάλαττα θάλαττα
καὶ παρεγγυώντων. ἔνθα δὴ ἔθεον πάντες καὶ οἱ ὀπισθοφύλακες,

---

refers, of course, to the people of the ἄρχων.

84 πέντε ἡμερῶν, *within five days;* see the note on I, 7, 85.

85 τεθνάναι: force of the tense?

86 αἴθειν: poetic for καίειν.

88 τῶν Ἑλλήνων: object. gen.

89 Θήχης: again of uncertain identification.

91 ἄλλους: explained by the following.

94 δασειῶν βοῶν ὠμοβόεια, *made of raw ox-hides with the shaggy hair left on.* βοῶν (gen. of material) here means *ox-hides*, as c. 5. 55. *Cf.*, also, V, 4, § 12. Greek loves to bring into close connection words from the same stem, even when one is redundant.

95 ἀμφὶ τὰ εἴκοσιν: for the art., *cf.* I, 2, 59, and the note.

96 ἐγίγνετο, *kept growing.* Note the succession of graphic impfs.

98 μεῖζόν τι, *something more serious.*

100 Θάλαττα θάλαττα: the sight of the sea was to the Greeks as the sight of land to storm-tossed mariners. Their perils seemed now to be over, for, since the shores of the Euxine were studded with Greek cities, they were sure to meet kindred people, and might expect easy transportation by sea (*cf.* V, I, § 2) after the terrible hardships they had been enduring. The Greek love of the sea is highly characteristic.

101 ἔθεον, *broke into a run.*

25 καὶ τὰ ὑποζύγια ἠλαύνετο καὶ οἱ ἵπποι. ἐπεὶ δὲ ἀφίκοντο
πάντες ἐπὶ τὸ ἄκρον, ἐνταῦθα δὴ περιέβαλλον ἀλλήλους καὶ
στρατηγοὺς καὶ λοχαγοὺς δακρύοντες. καὶ ἐξαπίνης ὅτου δὴ
παρεγγυήσαντος οἱ στρατιῶται φέρουσι λίθους καὶ ποιοῦσι 105
26 κολωνὸν μέγαν. ἐνταῦθα ἀνετίθεσαν δερμάτων πλῆθος ὠμο-
βοείων καὶ βακτηρίας καὶ τὰ αἰχμάλωτα γέρρα, καὶ ὁ ἡγεμὼν
27 αὐτός τε κατέτεμνε τὰ γέρρα καὶ τοῖς ἄλλοις διεκελεύετο. μετὰ
ταῦτα τὸν ἡγεμόνα οἱ Ἕλληνες ἀποπέμπουσι δῶρα δόντες ἀπὸ
κοινοῦ ἵππον καὶ φιάλην ἀργυρᾶν καὶ σκευὴν Περσικὴν καὶ 110
δαρεικοὺς δέκα· ᾔτει δὲ μάλιστα τοὺς δακτυλίους, καὶ ἔλαβε
πολλοὺς παρὰ τῶν στρατιωτῶν. κώμην δὲ δείξας αὐτοῖς οὗ
σκηνήσουσι καὶ τὴν ὁδὸν ἣν πορεύσονται εἰς Μάκρωνας, ἐπεὶ
ἑσπέρα ἐγένετο, ᾤχετο τῆς νυκτὸς ἀπιών.

1   VIII. Ἐντεῦθεν δ' ἐπορεύθησαν οἱ Ἕλληνες διὰ Μακρώνων
σταθμοὺς τρεῖς παρασάγγας δέκα. τῇ πρώτῃ δὲ ἡμέρᾳ ἀφίκοντο
ἐπὶ τὸν ποταμὸν ὃς ὥριζε τὴν τῶν Μακρώνων καὶ τὴν τῶν Σκυθη-
2 νῶν. εἶχον δ' ὑπὲρ δεξιῶν χωρίον οἷον χαλεπώτατον καὶ ἐξ

---

102 ἠλαύνετο, *were hurried on.*
104 δακρύοντες: how different from δακρύσαντες? This emotional outburst needs no apology; *cf.* the note on I, 3, 9.
ἐξαπίνης: *cf.* III, 3, 31, and the note.
ὅτου δὴ παρεγγυήσαντος, *some one or other giving the word*; *cf.* V, 2, § 24, ὅτου δὴ ἐνάψαντος. In these cases ὅτου is felt as the subj. of the partic., but it is really attracted from the nom. (παρεγγυήσαντός τινος ὅστις δὴ ἦν).
106 ἀνετίθεσαν: a technical word; note the durative tense.
δερμάτων: above, we had βοῶν in this sense (l. 94).
108 κατέτεμνε: *cf.* c. 6. 97.
109 ἀπὸ κοινοῦ, *from the common stock.*
111 τοὺς δακτυλίους: the Greek, unless a slave, regularly wore a ring.
113 σκηνήσουσι . . . πορεύσονται: for the rel. clause of purpose, *cf.* I, 3, 70, and the note.
114 ᾤχετο . . . ἀπιών: *cf.* II, 5, 105, and the note.

CHAPTER VIII

3 τὴν τῶν . . . τὴν τῶν: χώραν easily supplies itself.
4 ὑπὲρ δεξιῶν, *above them on the right; cf.* ὑπερδέξιον, III, 4, 153. Both are more descriptive than the simple ἐκ δεξιᾶς (*cf.* ἐξ ἀριστερᾶς) or ἐν δεξιᾷ (I, 5, 2). The tense of εἶχον suggests that χωρίον means, not *position*, but *continuous country*.
οἷον χαλεπώτατον: οἷον is used with the superlative, as are ὅτι and

5 ἀριστερᾶς ἄλλον ποταμόν, εἰς ὃν ἐνέβαλλεν ὁ ὁρίζων, δι' οὗ ἔδει διαβῆναι. ἦν δὲ οὗτος δασὺς δένδρεσι παχέσι μὲν οὔ, πυκνοῖς δέ. ταῦτ' ἐπεὶ προσῆλθον οἱ Ἕλληνες ἔκοπτον, σπεύδοντες ἐκ τοῦ χωρίου ὡς τάχιστα ἐξελθεῖν. οἱ δὲ Μάκρωνες ἔχοντες γέρρα 3 καὶ λόγχας καὶ τριχίνους χιτῶνας κατ' ἀντιπέραν τῆς διαβάσεως
10 παρατεταγμένοι ἦσαν καὶ ἀλλήλοις διεκελεύοντο καὶ λίθους εἰς τὸν ποταμὸν ἔρριπτον· ἐξικνοῦντο γὰρ οὒ οὐδ' ἔβλαπτον οὐδέν.

Ἔνθα δὴ προσέρχεται Ξενοφῶντι τῶν πελταστῶν ἀνὴρ 4 Ἀθήνησι φάσκων δεδουλευκέναι, λέγων ὅτι γιγνώσκοι τὴν φωνὴν τῶν ἀνθρώπων. καὶ οἶμαι, ἔφη, ἐμὴν ταύτην πατρίδα εἶναι·
15 καὶ εἰ μή τι κωλύει ἐθέλω αὐτοῖς διαλεχθῆναι. Ἀλλ' οὐδὲν 5 κωλύει, ἔφη, ἀλλὰ διαλέγου καὶ μάθε πρῶτον τίνες εἰσίν. οἱ δ' εἶπον ἐρωτήσαντος ὅτι Μάκρωνες. Ἐρώτα τοίνυν, ἔφη, αὐτοὺς τί ἀντιτετάχαται καὶ χρῄζουσιν ἡμῖν πολέμιοι εἶναι. οἱ 6 δ' ἀπεκρίναντο Ὅτι ὑμεῖς ἐπὶ τὴν ἡμετέραν χώραν ἔρχεσθε.
20 λέγειν ἐκέλευον οἱ στρατηγοὶ ὅτι οὐ κακῶς γε ποιήσοντες, ἀλλὰ βασιλεῖ πολεμήσαντες ἀπερχόμεθα εἰς τὴν Ἑλλάδα, καὶ ἐπὶ θάλατταν βουλόμεθα ἀφικέσθαι. ἠρώτων ἐκεῖνοι εἰ δοῖεν ἂν 7

ὡς (cf. I, 1, 22, and the note), but it is much less common.

5 ἐνέβαλλεν: cf. I, 2, 45.

ὁ ὁρίζων, *the boundary stream.*

6 δασύς, *thickly bordered with;* cf. the note on c. 7. 24.

δένδρεσι: we have the form δένδροις in c. 7. 41.

7 ἔκοπτον: the reason is given by σπεύδοντες; cf. συνεξέκοπτον, below l. 26.

9 τριχίνους: *i. e. woven of (goat's?) hair.*

κατ' ἀντιπέραν: cf. κατ' ἀντιπέρας, I, 1, 44.

13 Ἀθήνησι: locative; see G. 296; H. 220; B. 76 note.

φάσκων, *declaring*, not *alleging*. The forms of φημί, save in the indic., are indeterminate, and may be either pres. or aor. When a pres. is desired, forms of φάσκω are freely used without appreciable difference of meaning.

14 ταύτην: sc. χώραν. This is subj., πατρίδα pred. Note the transition to direct speech.

17 ἐρωτήσαντος: sc. αὐτοῦ.

ὅτι: introducing direct speech; cf. I, 6, 36.

18 ἀντιτετάχαται: for the form, cf. G. 701; H. 464a; B. 226a. Contrast παρατεταγμένοι ἦσαν, above, l. 10.

20 λέγειν ἐκέλευον: asyndeton is common in dialogue.

21 ἐπὶ θάλατταν: the chiastic order strongly emphasizes these words.

22 δοῖεν ἄν: potential opt. in an indir. ques. cf. I, 7, 11.

τούτων τὰ πιστά. οἳ δ' ἔφασαν καὶ δοῦναι καὶ λαβεῖν ἐθέλειν. ἐντεῦθεν διδόασιν οἱ Μάκρωνες βαρβαρικὴν λόγχην τοῖς Ἕλλησιν, οἱ δὲ Ἕλληνες ἐκείνοις Ἑλληνικήν· ταῦτα γὰρ ἔφασαν πιστὰ εἶναι· θεοὺς δ' ἐπεμαρτύραντο.

8 Μετὰ δὲ τὰ πιστὰ εὐθὺς οἱ Μάκρωνες τὰ δένδρα συνεξέκοπτον τήν τε ὁδὸν ὡδοποίουν ὡς διαβιβάσοντες ἐν μέσοις ἀναμεμειγμένοι τοῖς Ἕλλησι, καὶ ἀγορὰν οἵαν ἐδύναντο παρεῖχον, καὶ παρήγαγον ἐν τρισὶν ἡμέραις ἕως ἐπὶ τὰ Κόλχων ὅρια
9 κατέστησαν τοὺς Ἕλληνας. ἐνταῦθα ἦν ὄρος μέγα· καὶ ἐπὶ τούτου οἱ Κόλχοι παρατεταγμένοι ἦσαν. καὶ τὸ μὲν πρῶτον οἱ Ἕλληνες ἀντιπαρετάξαντο φάλαγγα, ὡς οὕτως ἄξοντες πρὸς τὸ ὄρος· ἔπειτα δὲ ἔδοξε τοῖς στρατηγοῖς βουλεύσασθαι συλλεγεῖσιν ὅπως ὡς κάλλιστα ἀγωνιοῦνται.

10 ἔλεξεν οὖν Ξενοφῶν ὅτι δοκοίη παύσαντας τὴν φάλαγγα λόχους ὀρθίους ποιῆσαι· ἡ μὲν γὰρ φάλαγξ διασπασθήσεται εὐθύς· τῇ μὲν γὰρ ἄνοδον τῇ δὲ εὔοδον εὑρήσομεν τὸ ὄρος· καὶ εὐθὺς τοῦτο ἀθυμίαν ποιήσει ὅταν τεταγμένοι εἰς φάλαγγα ταύ-
11 την διεσπασμένην ὁρῶσιν. ἔπειτα ἂν μὲν ἐπὶ πολλῶν τεταγμένοι προσάγωμεν, περιττεύσουσιν ἡμῶν οἱ πολέμιοι καὶ τοῖς περιττοῖς χρήσονται ὅ,τι ἂν βούλωνται· ἐὰν δὲ ἐπ' ὀλίγων τεταγμένοι ὦμεν, οὐδὲν ἂν εἴη θαυμαστὸν εἰ διακοπείη ἡμῶν ἡ φάλαγξ ὑπὸ ἀθρόων καὶ βελῶν καὶ ἀνθρώπων πολλῶν ἐμπεσόντων· εἰ δέ πῃ
12 τοῦτο ἔσται, τῇ φάλαγγι κακὸν ἔσται. ἀλλά μοι δοκεῖ ὀρθίους

---

23 τὰ πιστά, *the* (*proper*) *pledges.*
28 διαβιβάσοντες: with this vb. the contracted fut. is commoner.
33 ἀντιπαρετάξαντο φάλαγγα: the acc. is an extension of the inner obj.; below, l. 39, we have εἰς φάλαγγα.
34 βουλεύσασθαι συλλεγεῖσιν, *to come together and consult.* Note the dat., συλλεγεῖσιν; the acc. would be normal, since it follows the infin. See the note on I, 2, 4.
35 ὅπως ... ἀγωνιοῦνται: obj. clause, although the interrog. tone is clear.
37 λόχους ὀρθίους: *cf.* c. 2. 46, and the note.
διασπασθήσεται: *cf.* III, 4, 80. Note again the shift to direct speech.
40 ἐπὶ πολλῶν, *many deep. Cf.* below, ἐπ' ὀλίγων, *few deep.*
41 περιττεύσουσιν ἡμῶν: *i. e.* their line will be longer than ours.
42 ὅ,τι ἂν βούλωνται: *e. g.* for a flank attack. For the inner obj. with χρήσονται, *cf.* I, 3, 93.
44 ἀθρόων: the text is uncertain.

τοὺς λόχους ποιησαμένους τοσοῦτον χωρίον κατασχεῖν διαλιπόντας τοῖς λόχοις ὅσον ἔξω τοὺς ἐσχάτους λόχους γενέσθαι τῶν πολεμίων κεράτων· καὶ οὕτως ἐσόμεθα τῆς τε τῶν πολεμίων φάλαγγος ἔξω οἱ ἔσχατοι λόχοι, καὶ ὀρθίους ἄγοντες οἱ κράτιστοι
50 ἡμῶν πρῶτοι προσίασιν, ᾗ τε ἂν εὔοδον ᾖ ταύτῃ ἕκαστος ἄξει ὁ λόχος. καὶ εἴς τε τὸ διαλεῖπον οὐ ῥᾴδιον ἔσται τοῖς πολεμίοις 13 εἰσελθεῖν ἔνθεν καὶ ἔνθεν λόχων ὄντων, διακόψαι τε οὐ ῥᾴδιον ἔσται λόχον ὄρθιον προσιόντα. ἄν τέ τις πιέζηται τῶν λόχων, ὁ πλησίον βοηθήσει. ἤν τε εἰς πῃ δυνηθῇ τῶν λόχων ἐπὶ τὸ
55 ἄκρον ἀναβῆναι, οὐδεὶς μηκέτι μείνῃ τῶν πολεμίων.

ταῦτα ἔδοξε, καὶ ἐποίουν ὀρθίους τοὺς λόχους. Ξενοφῶν δὲ 14 ἀπιὼν ἐπὶ τὸ εὐώνυμον ἀπὸ τοῦ δεξιοῦ ἔλεγε τοῖς στρατιώταις· Ἄνδρες, οὗτοί εἰσιν οὓς ὁρᾶτε μόνοι ἔτι ἡμῖν ἐμποδὼν τὸ μὴ ἤδη εἶναι ἔνθα πάλαι σπεύδομεν· τούτους ἤν πως δυνώμεθα, καὶ
60 ὠμοὺς δεῖ καταφαγεῖν.

As it stands ἀθρόων (pred. after ἐμπεσόντων) is to be taken both with βελῶν and ἀνθρώπων.

εἰ ... ἔσται: a warning condition again.

46 κατασχεῖν, *to cover*. With this τοῖς λόχοις is to be construed (as dat. of means).

διαλιπόντας, *stationing them at intervals*.

47 ὅσον ... γενέσθαι: for the infin. after ὅσον, as after ὥστε, *cf.* c. 1. 18, and the note on οἷα ... ἄρδειν, II, 3, 49.

ἔξω: with τῶν πολεμίων κεράτων, but emphasized by its position.

49 οἱ ἔσχατοι λόχοι: limiting apposition with the subj. of ἐσόμεθα.

οἱ κράτιστοι ἡμῶν, *our bravest captains*. In this formation each captain led his own company. For the bravery of individual captains, see *e. g.* c. 1. § 27 and c. 7. §§ 9 ff.

50 ταύτῃ: resuming the rel., as often.

ἄξει: intrans.

51 τὸ διαλεῖπον: *cf.* III, 4, 91, τὸ διέχον.

55 οὐδεὶς μηκέτι μείνῃ: for the double neg., see the note on II, 2, 54.

58 ἐμποδὼν τὸ μὴ ... εἶναι: for the infin. with τὸ μή after a word of hindering, see G. 1551; H. 961a; B. 642, 1; 643.

59 πάλαι σπεύδομεν, *have long been striving*—a regular force of the pres. with πάλαι.

60 ὠμοὺς ... καταφαγεῖν: a proverbial phrase which occurs again in *Hell.* III, 3, 6. It may be a reminiscence from Homer; see *Iliad* IV, 35; XXII, 347; XXIV, 212. Compare also *Much Ado about Nothing* Act IV, sc. 1, I would eat his heart in the market-place.

Ἐπεὶ δ' ἐν ταῖς χώραις ἕκαστοι ἐγένοντο καὶ τοὺς λόχους ὀρθίους ἐποιήσαντο, ἐγένοντο μὲν λόχοι τῶν ὁπλιτῶν ἀμφὶ τοὺς ὀγδοήκοντα, ὁ δὲ λόχος ἕκαστος σχεδὸν εἰς τοὺς ἑκατόν· τοὺς δὲ πελταστὰς καὶ τοὺς τοξότας τριχῇ ἐποιήσαντο, τοὺς μὲν τοῦ εὐωνύμου ἔξω, τοὺς δὲ τοῦ δεξιοῦ, τοὺς δὲ κατὰ μέσον, σχεδὸν ἑξακοσίους ἑκάστους. ἐκ τούτου παρηγγύησαν οἱ στρατηγοὶ εὔχεσθαι· εὐξάμενοι δὲ καὶ παιανίσαντες ἐπορεύοντο. καὶ Χειρίσοφος μὲν καὶ Ξενοφῶν καὶ οἱ σὺν αὐτοῖς πελτασταὶ τῆς τῶν πολεμίων φάλαγγος ἔξω γενόμενοι ἐπορεύοντο· οἱ δὲ πολέμιοι ὡς εἶδον αὐτούς, ἀντιπαραθέοντες οἱ μὲν ἐπὶ τὸ δεξιὸν οἱ δὲ ἐπὶ τὸ εὐώνυμον διεσπάσθησαν, καὶ πολὺ τῆς αὑτῶν φάλαγγος ἐν τῷ μέσῳ κενὸν ἐποίησαν. οἱ δὲ κατὰ τὸ Ἀρκαδικὸν πελτασταί, ὧν ἦρχεν Αἰσχίνης ὁ Ἀκαρνάν, νομίσαντες φεύγειν ἀνακραγόντες ἔθεον· καὶ οὗτοι πρῶτοι ἐπὶ τὸ ὄρος ἀναβαίνουσι· συνεφείπετο δὲ αὐτοῖς καὶ τὸ Ἀρκαδικὸν ὁπλιτικόν, ὧν ἦρχε Κλεάνωρ ὁ Ὀρχομένιος. οἱ δὲ πολέμιοι, ὡς ἤρξαντο θεῖν, οὐκέτι ἔστησαν, ἀλλὰ φυγῇ ἄλλος ἄλλῃ ἐτράπετο.

οἱ δὲ Ἕλληνες ἀναβάντες ἐστρατοπεδεύοντο ἐν πολλαῖς κώμαις καὶ τἀπιτήδεια πολλὰ ἐχούσαις. καὶ τὰ μὲν ἄλλα οὐδὲν ὅ,τι

---

61 χώραις, *places; cf.* κατὰ χώραν, I, 5, 100.

63 ὀγδοήκοντα . . . ἑκατόν: this gives roughly 8,000, as against the original total of 11,700 (see I, 2, 58 f., and I, 4, 13). Similarly only 1,800 peltasts are here accounted for, while the original number was 2,300. Most of these losses occurred after the Greeks entered the Carduchian mountains.

εἰς τοὺς ἑκατόν: for the art., *cf.* I, 2, 59, and the note. The company properly numbered 100 men (*cf.* I, 2, 148, and the note), but this number can hardly have been always maintained.

66 παρεγγύησαν: less common than the equivalent παραγγέλλω, but occurring four times in this book.

67 Χειρίσοφος . . . Ξενοφῶν: they led the columns at the extreme right and left.

70 ἀντιπαραθέοντες: for the preps., *cf.* above, l. 33. The Colchians sought to avoid being outflanked. Note the partitive appos.

72 κατὰ τὸ Ἀρκαδικόν, *in the Arcadian division.* This, it appears, was in the centre.

73 φεύγειν: *i. e.* τοὺς πολεμίους.

75 ὁπλιτικόν, ὧν: the pl. is justified, since ὁπλιτικόν=ὁπλῖται.

76 ὡς ἤρξαντο: *i. e.* οἱ πελτασταί.

79 τὰ μὲν ἄλλα, *for the rest* (adv. acc.). **οὐδέν:** *sc.* ἦν.

ὅ,τι καί: καί may be rendered, *at*

καὶ ἐθαύμασαν· τὰ δὲ σμήνη πολλὰ ἦν αὐτόθι, καὶ τῶν κηρίων ὅσοι ἔφαγον τῶν στρατιωτῶν πάντες ἄφρονές τε ἐγίγνοντο καὶ ἤμουν καὶ κάτω διεχώρει αὐτοῖς καὶ ὀρθὸς οὐδεὶς ἐδύνατο ἵστασθαι, ἀλλ' οἱ μὲν ὀλίγον ἐδηδοκότες σφόδρα μεθύουσιν ἐῴκεσαν, οἱ δὲ πολὺ μαινομένοις, οἱ δὲ καὶ ἀποθνῄσκουσιν. ἔκειντο δὲ οὕτω πολλοὶ ὥσπερ τροπῆς γεγενημένης, καὶ πολλὴ ἦν ἀθυμία. τῇ δ' ὑστεραίᾳ ἀπέθανε μὲν οὐδείς, ἀμφὶ δὲ τὴν αὐτήν πως ὥραν ἀνεφρόνουν· τρίτῃ δὲ καὶ τετάρτῃ ἀνίσταντο ὥσπερ ἐκ φαρμακοποσίας.

Ἐντεῦθεν δ' ἐπορεύθησαν δύο σταθμοὺς παρασάγγας ἑπτά, καὶ ἦλθον ἐπὶ θάλατταν εἰς Τραπεζοῦντα πόλιν Ἑλληνίδα οἰκουμένην ἐν τῷ Εὐξείνῳ Πόντῳ Σινωπέων ἀποικίαν ἐν τῇ Κόλχων χώρᾳ. ἐνταῦθα ἔμειναν ἡμέρας ἀμφὶ τὰς τριάκοντα ἐν ταῖς τῶν Κόλχων κώμαις· κἀντεῦθεν ὁρμώμενοι ἐλῄζοντο τὴν Κολχίδα. ἀγορὰν δὲ παρεῖχον τῷ στρατοπέδῳ Τραπεζούντιοι, καὶ ἐδέξαντό τε τοὺς Ἕλληνας καὶ ξένια ἔδοσαν βοῦς καὶ ἄλφιτα καὶ οἶνον. συνδιεπράττοντο δὲ καὶ ὑπὲρ τῶν πλησίον Κόλχων τῶν ἐν τῷ πεδίῳ μάλιστα οἰκούντων, καὶ ξένια καὶ παρ' ἐκείνων ἦλθον βόες.

all. Here it lessens the force of the vb.; oftener it accentuates it.

82 κάτω διεχώρει αὐτοῖς, *suffered from diarrhoea.*

83 μεθύουσιν . . . ἀποθνῄσκουσιν: partics., of course, like μαινομένοις.

87 ἀνεφρόνουν, *began to recover their senses.* Note the force of the prep., and *cf.* ἀναπνεῦσαι, c. 1. 86.

τρίτῃ δὲ καὶ τετάρτῃ: in such phrases in Greek, καί is commoner than the disjunct. ἤ.

ἐκ φαρμακοποσίας: the accounts of modern travelers with reference to the existence of poisonous honey in this region tend, for the most part, to corroborate Xenophon's account. They differ widely from one another regarding the flower from which the honey is extracted, and some hold that it is unwholesome only if eaten raw. Professor Koch denies the existence of poisonous honey, and thinks the Greeks must have eaten honey that was spoiled.

90 Τραπεζοῦντα: here at last we are on certain ground; this was the modern Trebizond.

95 ἐδέξαντο: *i. e. into the city.*

96 συνδιεπράττοντο: *i. e. in conjunction with the Colchians.*

ὑπέρ: *i. e. that they should not be pillaged.*

97 ξένια: in appos. with βόες.

25 μετὰ δὲ τοῦτο τὴν θυσίαν ἣν ηὔξαντο παρεσκευάζοντο·
ἦλθον δ' αὐτοῖς ἱκανοὶ βόες ἀποθῦσαι τῷ Διὶ σωτήρια καὶ τῷ
Ἡρακλεῖ ἡγεμόσυνα καὶ τοῖς ἄλλοις θεοῖς ἃ ηὔξαντο. ἐποίησαν
δὲ καὶ ἀγῶνα γυμνικὸν ἐν τῷ ὄρει ἔνθαπερ ἐσκήνουν. εἵλοντο
δὲ Δρακόντιον Σπαρτιάτην, ὃς ἔφυγε παῖς ὢν οἴκοθεν, παῖδα
ἄκων κατακανὼν ξυήλῃ πατάξας, δρόμου τ' ἐπιμεληθῆναι καὶ
τοῦ ἀγῶνος προστατῆσαι.

26 ἐπειδὴ δὲ ἡ θυσία ἐγένετο, τὰ δέρματα παρέδοσαν τῷ Δρα-
κοντίῳ, καὶ ἡγεῖσθαι ἐκέλευον ὅπου τὸν δρόμον πεποιηκὼς εἴη.
ὁ δὲ δείξας οὗπερ ἑστηκότες ἐτύγχανον Οὗτος ὁ λόφος, ἔφη,
κάλλιστος τρέχειν ὅπου ἄν τις βούληται. Πῶς οὖν, ἔφασαν,
δυνήσονται παλαίειν ἐν σκληρῷ καὶ δασεῖ οὕτως; ὃ δ' εἶπε·
27 Μᾶλλόν τι ἀνιάσεται ὁ καταπεσών. ἠγωνίζοντο δὲ παῖδες μὲν
στάδιον τῶν αἰχμαλώτων οἱ πλεῖστοι, δόλιχον δὲ Κρῆτες πλείους

99 **ηὔξαντο**, *had vowed.* See III, 2, § 9.
100 **ἀποθῦσαι**: for the cpd., *cf.* I, 3, 67, and the note on ἀπέπεμπε, I, 1, 41. They are fulfilling an obligation.
101 **ἡγεμόσυνα**, *thank-offerings for guidance.* The word occurs here only. ἡγεμών was a standing title of Heracles (*e. g.* VI, 2, § 15). His own wide wanderings made him the fitting patron of all wanderers.
102 **ἔνθαπερ**, *right where.* The force of the enclitic περ should always be noted.
104 **ἄκων**: *i. e.* he was not a murderer. The Greeks, however, regarded one who had slain another even involuntarily as polluted, and he was obliged to go for a time, at least, into banishment, *i. e.* according to the primitive view, to go beyond the range of the ghost of the slain man.

106 **δέρματα**: the skins of the victims were to serve as prizes (*cf. Iliad* XXII, 159 f.).
111 **Μᾶλλόν . . . καταπεσών**, *so much the worse for him who is thrown*—a reply worthy of the Spartan.
ἠγωνίζοντο . . . στάδιον: the acc. is cognate (inner obj.). So, too, with πάλην, πυγμήν, and παγκράτιον the vb. ἠγωνίζοντο is to be supplied. With δόλιχον (sc. δρόμον) ἔθεον is expressed, but it is very probable that ἠγωνίζοντο should be understood there, too, ἔθεον being regarded as a gloss. The στάδιον was the oldest of the Olympic contests, and the victor in this was the Olympic victor for the year. It was a straightaway dash of approximately 200 yards.
παῖδες: races for boys formed a regular part of Greek athletic contests.
112 **αἰχμαλώτων οἱ πλεῖστοι**: excused by the fact that there

ἢ ἑξήκοντα, [ἔθεον] πάλην δὲ καὶ πυγμὴν καὶ παγκράτιον ἕτεροι, καὶ καλὴ θέα ἐγένετο· πολλοὶ γὰρ κατέβησαν καὶ ἅτε θεωμένων τῶν ἑταίρων πολλὴ φιλονικία ἐγίγνετο. ἔθεον δὲ καὶ ἵπποι καὶ ἔδει αὐτοὺς κατὰ τοῦ πρανοῦς ἐλάσαντας ἐν τῇ θαλάττῃ ἀπο στρέψαντας πάλιν πρὸς τὸν βωμὸν ἄγειν. καὶ κάτω μὲν οἱ πολλοὶ ἐκυλινδοῦντο· ἄνω δὲ πρὸς τὸ ἰσχυρῶς ὄρθιον μόγις βάδην ἐπορεύοντο οἱ ἵπποι· ἔνθα πολλὴ κραυγὴ καὶ γέλως καὶ παρακέλευσις ἐγίγνετο.

---

were no Greek boys in the army. In the great games of Greece only those of genuine Hellenic stock might compete.

δόλιχον: this was a long race, a test of endurance. At Olympia it was 24 stadia, but the length seems to have varied.

113 παγκράτιον: a composite contest in which the arts both of the wrestler and the boxer were allowed.

114 κατέβησαν: the technical term for entering the lists (in arenam *de*scendere).

ἅτε: *cf.* I, 1, 12, and the note.

116 αὐτούς: *i. e.* the horses, obj. of ἄγειν and the accompanying partics. We must understand ἱππέας as subj.

117 βωμόν, *mound,* of earth or turf. Doubtless it was the "altar" on which the victims had been sacrificed.

BOOK V

1 I. [Ὅσα μὲν δὴ ἐν τῇ ἀναβάσει τῇ μετὰ Κύρου ἔπραξαν οἱ Ἕλληνες, καὶ ὅσα ἐν τῇ πορείᾳ τῇ μέχρι ἐπὶ θάλατταν τὴν ἐν τῷ Εὐξείνῳ Πόντῳ, καὶ ὡς εἰς Τραπεζοῦντα πόλιν Ἑλληνίδα ἀφίκοντο, καὶ ὡς ἀπέθυσαν ἃ ηὔξαντο σωτήρια θύσειν ἔνθα πρῶτον εἰς φιλίαν γῆν ἀφίκοιντο, ἐν τῷ πρόσθεν λόγῳ δεδήλωται.]

2 Ἐκ δὲ τούτου ξυνελθόντες ἐβουλεύοντο περὶ τῆς λοιπῆς πορείας· ἀνέστη δὲ πρῶτος Λέων Θούριος καὶ ἔλεξεν ὧδε. Ἐγὼ μὲν τοίνυν, ἔφη, ὦ ἄνδρες, ἀπείρηκα ἤδη ξυσκευαζόμενος καὶ βαδίζων καὶ τρέχων καὶ τὰ ὅπλα φέρων καὶ ἐν τάξει ὢν καὶ φυλακὰς φυλάττων καὶ μαχόμενος, ἐπιθυμῶ δὲ ἤδη παυσάμενος τούτων τῶν πόνων, ἐπεὶ θάλατταν ἔχομεν, πλεῖν τὸ λοιπὸν καὶ 3 ἐκταθεὶς ὥσπερ Ὀδυσσεὺς ἀφικέσθαι εἰς τὴν Ἑλλάδα. ταῦτα ἀκούσαντες οἱ στρατιῶται ἀνεθορύβησαν ὡς εὖ λέγει· καὶ ἄλλος ταὐτὰ ἔλεγε, καὶ πάντες οἱ παριόντες. ἔπειτα δὲ Χειρίσοφος 4 ἀνέστη καὶ εἶπεν ὧδε. Φίλος μοί ἐστιν, ὦ ἄνδρες, Ἀναξίβιος, ναυαρχῶν δὲ καὶ τυγχάνει. ἢν οὖν πέμψητέ με, οἴομαι ἂν ἐλθεῖν καὶ τριήρεις ἔχων καὶ πλοῖα τὰ ἡμᾶς ἄξοντα· ὑμεῖς δὲ εἴπερ πλεῖν βούλεσθε, περιμένετε ἔστ' ἂν ἐγὼ ἔλθω· ἥξω δὲ ταχέως. ἀκούσαντες ταῦτα οἱ στρατιῶται ἥσθησάν τε καὶ ἐψηφίσαντο πλεῖν αὐτὸν ὡς τάχιστα.

5 Μετὰ τοῦτον Ξενοφῶν ἀνέστη καὶ ἔλεξεν ὧδε. Χειρίσοφος μὲν δὴ ἐπὶ πλοῖα στέλλεται, ἡμεῖς δὲ ἀναμενοῦμεν. ὅσα μοι οὖν 6 δοκεῖ καιρὸς εἶναι ποιεῖν ἐν τῇ μονῇ, ταῦτα ἐρῶ. πρῶτον μὲν τὰ ἐπιτήδεια δεῖ πορίζεσθαι ἐκ τῆς πολεμίας· οὔτε γὰρ ἀγορὰ ἔστιν ἱκανὴ οὔτε ὅτου ὠνησόμεθα εὐπορία εἰ μὴ ὀλίγοις τισίν· ἡ δὲ χώρα πολεμία· κίνδυνος οὖν πολλοὺς ἀπόλλυσθαι, ἢν ἀμελῶς 7 τε καὶ ἀφυλάκτως πορεύησθε ἐπὶ τὰ ἐπιτήδεια. ἀλλά μοι δοκεῖ σὺν προνομαῖς λαμβάνειν τὰ ἐπιτήδεια, ἄλλως δὲ μὴ πλανᾶσθαι, ὡς σῴζησθε, ἡμᾶς δὲ τούτων ἐπιμελεῖσθαι. ἔδοξε ταῦτα.

8 Ἔτι τοίνυν ἀκούσατε καὶ τάδε. ἐπὶ λείαν γὰρ ὑμῶν ἐκπορεύσονταί τινες. οἴομαι οὖν βέλτιστον εἶναι ἡμῖν εἰπεῖν τὸν

μέλλοντα εξιέναι, φράζειν δε και όποι, ίνα και το πλήθος ειδώμεν των εξιόντων και των μενόντων και ξυμπαρασκευάζωμεν, εάν τι δέη, κἂν βοηθήσαί τισι καιρός ᾖ, ειδώμεν όποι δεήσει
35 βοηθείν, και εάν τις των απειροτέρων εγχειρῇ ποι, ξυμβουλεύωμεν πειρώμενοι ειδέναι την δύναμιν εφ' ους αν ίωσιν. έδοξε και ταύτα.

Εννοείτε δε και τόδε, έφη. σχολή τοις πολεμίοις λήζεσθαι, και δικαίως ημίν επιβουλεύουσιν· έχομεν γαρ τα εκείνων· υπερ-
40 κάθηνται δε ημών. φυλακάς δή μοι δοκεί δείν περί το στρατόπεδον είναι· εάν ουν κατά μέρος φυλάττωμεν και σκοπώμεν, ήττον αν δύναιντο ημάς θηράν οι πολέμιοι.

Έτι τοίνυν τάδε οράτε. ει μεν ηπιστάμεθα σαφώς ότι ήξει πλοία Χειρίσοφος άγων ικανά, ουδέν αν έδει ων μέλλω λέγειν·
45 νυν δ' επεί τούτο άδηλον, δοκεί μοι πειράσθαι πλοία συμπαρασκευάζειν και αυτόθεν. ην μεν γαρ έλθῃ, υπαρχόντων ενθάδε εν αφθονωτέροις πλευσόμεθα· αν δε μη άγῃ, τοις ενθάδε χρησόμεθα. ορώ δε εγώ πλοία πολλάκις παραπλέοντα· ει ουν αιτησάμενοι παρά Τραπεζουντίων μακρά πλοία κατάγοιμεν και
50 φυλάττοιμεν, τα πηδάλια παραλυόμενοι, έως αν ικανά τα άξοντα γένηται, ίσως αν ουκ απορήσαιμεν κομιδής οίας δεόμεθα. έδοξε και ταύτα.

Εννοήσατε δ', έφη, ει εικός και τρέφειν από κοινού ους αν κατάγωμεν όσον αν χρόνον ημών ένεκεν μένωσι, και ναύλον
55 ξυνθέσθαι, όπως ωφελούντες και ωφελώνται. έδοξε και ταύτα.

Δοκεί τοίνυν μοι, έφη, ην άρα και ταύτα ημίν μη εκπεραίνηται ώστε αρκείν πλοία, τας οδούς ας δυσπόρους ακούομεν είναι ταις παρά θάλατταν οικούσαις πόλεσιν εντείλασθαι οδοποιείν· πείσονται γαρ και δια το φοβείσθαι και δια το βούλεσθαι ημών
60 απαλλαγήναι.

Ενταύθα δε ανέκραγον ως ου δέοι οδοιπορείν. ο δε ως έγνω την αφροσύνην αυτών, επεψήφισε μεν ουδέν, τας δε πόλεις εκούσας έπεισεν οδοποιείν, λέγων ότι θάττον απαλλάξονται, ην εύποροι γένωνται αι οδοί. έλαβον δε και πεντηκόντορον παρά
65 των Τραπεζουντίων, ᾗ επέστησαν Δέξιππον Λάκωνα περίοικον. ούτος αμελήσας του ξυλλέγειν πλοία αποδράς ᾤχετο έξω του

Πόντου, ἔχων τὴν ναῦν. οὗτος μὲν οὖν δίκαια ἔπαθεν ὕστερον·
ἐν Θράκῃ γὰρ παρὰ Σεύθῃ πολυπραγμονῶν τι ἀπέθανεν ὑπὸ
Νικάνδρου τοῦ Λάκωνος. ἔλαβον δὲ καὶ τριακόντορον, ᾗ ἐπεστάθη Πολυκράτης Ἀθηναῖος, ὃς ὁπόσα λαμβάνοι πλοῖα κατῆγεν
ἐπὶ στρατόπεδον. καὶ τὰ μὲν ἀγώγιμα εἴ τι ἦγον ἐξαιρούμενοι
φύλακας καθίστασαν, ὅπως σῶα εἴη, τοῖς δὲ πλοίοις ἐχρήσαντο
εἰς παραγωγήν. ἐν ᾧ δὲ ταῦτα ἦν ἐπὶ λείαν ἐξῇσαν οἱ Ἕλληνες,
καὶ οἱ μὲν ἐλάμβανον, οἱ δὲ καὶ οὔ. Κλεαίνετος δὲ ἐξαγαγὼν
καὶ τὸν ἑαυτοῦ καὶ ἄλλον λόχον πρὸς χωρίον χαλεπὸν αὐτός τε
ἀπέθανε καὶ ἄλλοι πολλοὶ τῶν σὺν αὐτῷ.

II. Ἐπεὶ δὲ τὰ ἐπιτήδεια οὐκέτι ἦν λαμβάνειν ὥστε ἀπαυ-
θημερίζειν ἐπὶ τὸ στρατόπεδον, ἐκ τούτου λαβὼν Ξενοφῶν
ἡγεμόνας τῶν Τραπεζουντίων ἐξάγει εἰς Δρίλας τὸ ἥμισυ τοῦ
στρατεύματος, τὸ δὲ ἥμισυ κατέλιπε φυλάττειν τὸ στρατόπεδον·
οἱ γὰρ Κόλχοι, ἅτε ἐκπεπτωκότες ἐκ τῶν οἰκιῶν, πολλοὶ ἦσαν
ἀθρόοι καὶ ὑπερεκάθηντο ἐπὶ τῶν ἄκρων. οἱ δὲ Τραπεζούντιοι
ὁπόθεν μὲν τὰ ἐπιτήδεια ῥᾴδιον ἦν λαβεῖν οὐκ ἦγον· φίλοι γὰρ
αὐτοῖς ἦσαν· εἰς δὲ τοὺς Δρίλας προθύμως ἦγον, ὑφ᾽ ὧν κακῶς
ἔπασχον, εἰς χωρία τε ὀρεινὰ καὶ δύσβατα καὶ ἀνθρώπους πολε-
μικωτάτους τῶν ἐν τῷ Πόντῳ.

Ἐπεὶ δὲ ἦσαν ἐν τῇ ἄνω χώρᾳ οἱ Ἕλληνες, ὁποῖα τῶν
χωρίων τοῖς Δρίλαις ἁλώσιμα εἶναι ἐδόκει ἐμπιμπράντες ἀπῇ-
σαν· καὶ οὐδὲν ἦν λαμβάνειν εἰ μὴ ὗς ἢ βοῦς ἢ ἄλλο τι κτῆνος
τὸ πῦρ διαπεφευγός. ἓν δὲ ἦν χωρίον μητρόπολις αὐτῶν· εἰς
τοῦτο πάντες ξυνερρυήκεσαν. περὶ δὲ τοῦτο ἦν χαράδρα ἰσχυρῶς
βαθεῖα, καὶ πρόσοδοι χαλεπαὶ πρὸς τὸ χωρίον. οἱ δὲ πελτασταὶ
προδραμόντες στάδια πέντε ἢ ἓξ τῶν ὁπλιτῶν, διαβάντες τὴν
χαράδραν, ὁρῶντες πρόβατα πολλὰ καὶ ἄλλα χρήματα προσέβαλλον πρὸς τὸ χωρίον· ξυνείποντο δὲ καὶ δορυφόροι πολλοὶ
οἱ ἐπὶ τὰ ἐπιτήδεια ἐξωρμημένοι· ὥστε ἐγένοντο οἱ διαβάντες
πλείους ἢ εἰς χιλίους ἀνθρώπους. ἐπεὶ δὲ μαχόμενοι οὐκ ἐδύναντο λαβεῖν τὸ χωρίον, καὶ γὰρ τάφρος ἦν περὶ αὐτὸ εὐρεῖα
ἀναβεβλημένη καὶ σκόλοπες ἐπὶ τῆς ἀναβολῆς καὶ τύρσεις
πυκναὶ ξύλιναι πεποιημέναι, ἀπιέναι δὴ ἐπεχείρουν· οἱ δὲ
ἐπέκειντο αὐτοῖς. ὡς δὲ οὐκ ἐδύναντο ἀποτρέχειν, ἦν γὰρ ἐφ᾽

ἑνὸς ἡ κατάβασις ἐκ τοῦ χωρίου εἰς τὴν χαράδραν, πέμπουσι
πρὸς Ξενοφῶντα. ὁ δὲ ἡγεῖτο τοῖς ὁπλίταις. ὁ δὲ ἐλθὼν λέγει 7
ὅτι ἔστι χωρίον χρημάτων πολλῶν μεστόν· τοῦτο οὔτε λαβεῖν
δυνάμεθα· ἰσχυρὸν γάρ ἐστιν· οὔτε ἀπελθεῖν ῥᾴδιον· μάχονται
γὰρ ἐπεξεληλυθότες καὶ ἡ ἄφοδος χαλεπή.

Ἀκούσας ταῦτα ὁ Ξενοφῶν προσαγαγὼν πρὸς τὴν χαράδραν 8
τοὺς μὲν ὁπλίτας θέσθαι ἐκέλευσε τὰ ὅπλα, αὐτὸς δὲ διαβὰς
σὺν τοῖς λοχαγοῖς ἐσκοπεῖτο πότερον εἴη κρεῖττον ἀπαγαγεῖν
καὶ τοὺς διαβεβηκότας ἢ καὶ τοὺς ὁπλίτας διαβιβάζειν, ὡς
ἁλόντος ἂν τοῦ χωρίου. ἐδόκει γὰρ τὸ μὲν ἀπαγαγεῖν οὐκ 9
εἶναι ἄνευ πολλῶν νεκρῶν, ἑλεῖν δ' ἂν ᾤοντο καὶ οἱ λοχαγοὶ τὸ
χωρίον, καὶ ὁ Ξενοφῶν ξυνεχώρησε τοῖς ἱεροῖς πιστεύσας· οἱ
γὰρ μάντεις ἀποδεδειγμένοι ἦσαν ὅτι μάχη μὲν ἔσται, τὸ δὲ
τέλος καλὸν τῆς ἐξόδου. καὶ τοὺς μὲν λοχαγοὺς ἔπεμπε δια- 10
βιβάσοντας τοὺς ὁπλίτας, αὐτὸς δ' ἔμενεν ἀναχωρίσας ἅπαντας
τοὺς πελταστάς, καὶ οὐδένα εἴα ἀκροβολίζεσθαι. ἐπεὶ δ' ἧκον 11
οἱ ὁπλῖται, ἐκέλευσε τὸν λόχον ἕκαστον ποιῆσαι τῶν λοχαγῶν
ὡς ἂν κράτιστα οἴηται ἀγωνιεῖσθαι· ἦσαν γὰρ οἱ λοχαγοὶ πλησίον ἀλλήλων οἳ πάντα τὸν χρόνον ἀλλήλοις περὶ ἀνδραγαθίας
ἀντεποιοῦντο. καὶ οἱ μὲν ταῦτ' ἐποίουν· ὁ δὲ τοῖς πελτασταῖς 12
πᾶσι παρήγγειλε διηγκυλωμένους ἰέναι, ὡς ὁπόταν σημήνῃ
ἀκοντίζειν, καὶ τοὺς τοξότας ἐπιβεβλῆσθαι ἐπὶ ταῖς νευραῖς, ὡς
ὁπόταν σημήνῃ τοξεύειν, καὶ τοὺς γυμνῆτας λίθων ἔχειν μεστὰς
τὰς διφθέρας· καὶ τοὺς ἐπιτηδείους ἔπεμψε τούτων ἐπιμεληθῆναι.

Ἐπεὶ δὲ πάντα παρεσκεύαστο καὶ οἱ λοχαγοὶ καὶ οἱ ὑπολό- 13
χαγοι καὶ οἱ ἀξιοῦντες τούτων μὴ χείρους εἶναι πάντες παρατεταγμένοι ἦσαν, καὶ ἀλλήλους μὲν δὴ ξυνεώρων· μηνοειδὴς γὰρ
διὰ τὸ χωρίον ἡ τάξις ἦν· ἐπεὶ δ' ἐπαιάνισαν καὶ ἡ σάλπιγξ 14
ἐφθέγξατο, ἅμα τε τῷ Ἐνυαλίῳ ἠλέλιξαν καὶ ἔθεον δρόμῳ οἱ
ὁπλῖται, καὶ τὰ βέλη ὁμοῦ ἐφέρετο, λόγχαι, τοξεύματα, σφενδόναι, πλεῖστοι δ' ἐκ τῶν χειρῶν λίθοι, ἦσαν δὲ οἳ καὶ πῦρ προσέ-
φερον. ὑπὸ δὲ τοῦ πλήθους τῶν βελῶν ἔλιπον οἱ πολέμιοι 15
τά τε σταυρώματα καὶ τὰς τύρσεις· ὥστε Ἀγασίας Στυμφάλιος
καταθέμενος τὰ ὅπλα ἐν χιτῶνι μόνον ἀνέβη, καὶ ἄλλον εἷλκε,
καὶ ἄλλος ἀνεβεβήκει, καὶ ἑαλώκει τὸ χωρίον, ὡς ἐδόκει.

16 Καὶ οἱ μὲν πελτασταὶ καὶ οἱ ψιλοὶ ἐσδραμόντες ἥρπαζον ὅ,τι ἕκαστος ἐδύνατο· ὁ δὲ Ξενοφῶν στὰς κατὰ τὰς πύλας ὁπόσους ἐδύνατο κατεκώλυσε τῶν ὁπλιτῶν ἔξω· πολέμιοι γὰρ
17 ἄλλοι ἐφαίνοντο ἐπ' ἄκροις τισὶν ἰσχυροῖς. οὐ πολλοῦ δὲ χρόνου μεταξὺ γενομένου κραυγή τε ἐγένετο ἔνδον καὶ ἔφευγον οἱ μὲν καὶ ἔχοντες ἃ ἔλαβον, τάχα δέ τις καὶ τετρωμένος· καὶ πολὺς ἦν ὠθισμὸς ἀμφὶ τὰ θύρετρα. καὶ ἐρωτώμενοι οἱ ἐκπίπτοντες ἔλεγον ὅτι ἄκρα τέ ἐστιν ἔνδον καὶ οἱ πολέμιοι πολλοί,
18 οἳ παίουσιν ἐκδεδραμηκότες τοὺς ἔνδον ἀνθρώπους. ἐνταῦθα ἀνειπεῖν ἐκέλευσε Τολμίδην τὸν κήρυκα ἰέναι εἴσω τὸν βουλόμενόν τι λαμβάνειν. καὶ ἵενται πολλοὶ εἴσω, καὶ νικῶσι τοὺς ἐκπίπτοντας οἱ εἰσωθούμενοι καὶ κατακλείουσι τοὺς πολεμίους
19 πάλιν εἰς τὴν ἄκραν. καὶ τὰ μὲν ἔξω τῆς ἄκρας πάντα διηρπάσθη, καὶ ἐξεκομίσαντο οἱ Ἕλληνες· οἱ δὲ ὁπλῖται ἔθεντο τὰ ὅπλα, οἱ μὲν περὶ τὰ σταυρώματα, οἱ δὲ κατὰ τὴν ὁδὸν τὴν ἐπὶ
20 τὴν ἄκραν φέρουσαν. ὁ δὲ Ξενοφῶν καὶ οἱ λοχαγοὶ ἐσκόπουν εἰ οἷόν τε εἴη τὴν ἄκραν λαβεῖν· ἦν γὰρ οὕτω σωτηρία ἀσφαλής, ἄλλως δὲ πάνυ χαλεπὸν ἐδόκει εἶναι ἀπελθεῖν· σκοπουμένοις δὲ αὐτοῖς ἔδοξε παντάπασιν ἀνάλωτον εἶναι τὸ χωρίον.

21 Ἐνταῦθα παρεσκευάζοντο τὴν ἄφοδον, καὶ τοὺς μὲν σταυροὺς ἕκαστοι τοὺς καθ' αὑτοὺς διῄρουν, καὶ τοὺς ἀχρείους καὶ φορτία ἔχοντας ἐξεπέμποντο καὶ τῶν ὁπλιτῶν τὸ πλῆθος καταλιπόντες
22 οἱ λοχαγοὶ οἷς ἕκαστος ἐπίστευεν. ἐπεὶ δὲ ἤρξαντο ἀποχωρεῖν, ἐπεξέθεον ἔνδοθεν πολλοὶ γέρρα καὶ λόγχας ἔχοντες καὶ κνημῖδας καὶ κράνη Παφλαγονικά, καὶ ἄλλοι ἐπὶ τὰς οἰκίας ἀνέβαινον τὰς
23 ἔνθεν καὶ ἔνθεν τῆς εἰς τὴν ἄκραν φερούσης ὁδοῦ· ὥστε οὐδὲ διώκειν ἀσφαλὲς ἦν κατὰ τὰς πύλας τὰς εἰς τὴν ἄκραν φερούσας. καὶ γὰρ ξύλα μεγάλα ἐπερρίπτουν ἄνωθεν, ὥστε χαλεπὸν ἦν καὶ μένειν καὶ ἀπιέναι· καὶ ἡ νὺξ φοβερὰ ἦν ἐπιοῦσα.

24 Μαχομένων δὲ αὐτῶν καὶ ἀπορουμένων θεῶν τις αὐτοῖς μηχανὴν σωτηρίας δίδωσιν. ἐξαπίνης γὰρ ἀνέλαμψεν οἰκία τῶν ἐν δεξιᾷ ὅτου δὴ ἐνάψαντος. ὡς δ' αὕτη ξυνέπιπτεν, ἔφευ-
25 γον οἱ ἀπὸ τῶν ἐν δεξιᾷ οἰκιῶν. ὡς δὲ ἔμαθεν ὁ Ξενοφῶν τοῦτο παρὰ τῆς τύχης, ἐνάπτειν ἐκέλευε καὶ τὰς ἐν ἀριστερᾷ οἰκίας, αἳ ξύλιναι ἦσαν, ὥστε καὶ ταχὺ ἐκαίοντο. ἔφευγον οὖν καὶ οἱ

ἀπὸ τούτων τῶν οἰκιῶν. οἱ δὲ κατὰ στόμα δὴ ἔτι μόνοι ἐλύπουν 26
καὶ δῆλοι ἦσαν ὅτι ἐπικείσονται ἐν τῇ ἐξόδῳ τε καὶ καταβάσει.
ἐνταῦθα παραγγέλλει φορεῖν ξύλα ὅσοι ἐτύγχανον ἔξω ὄντες τῶν
βελῶν εἰς τὸ μέσον ἑαυτῶν καὶ τῶν πολεμίων. ἐπεὶ δὲ ἱκανὰ ἤδη
100 ἦν, ἐνῆψαν· ἐνῆπτον δὲ καὶ τὰς παρ' αὐτὸ τὸ χαράκωμα οἰκίας,
ὅπως οἱ πολέμιοι ἀμφὶ ταῦτα ἔχοιεν. οὕτω μόλις ἀπῆλθον ἀπὸ 27
τοῦ χωρίου, πῦρ ἐν μέσῳ ἑαυτῶν καὶ τῶν πολεμίων ποιησάμενοι. καὶ κατεκαύθη πᾶσα ἡ πόλις καὶ αἱ οἰκίαι καὶ αἱ
τύρσεις καὶ τὰ σταυρώματα καὶ τἆλλα πάντα πλὴν τῆς ἄκρας.
105 Τῇ δὲ ὑστεραίᾳ ἀπῇσαν οἱ Ἕλληνες ἔχοντες τὰ ἐπιτήδεια. 28
ἐπεὶ δὲ τὴν κατάβασιν ἐφοβοῦντο τὴν εἰς Τραπεζοῦντα, πρανὴς
γὰρ ἦν καὶ στενή, ψευδενέδραν ἐποιήσαντο· καὶ ἀνὴρ Μυσὸς 29
καὶ τοὔνομα τοῦτο ἔχων τῶν Κρητῶν λαβὼν δέκα ἔμενεν ἐν
λασίῳ χωρίῳ καὶ προσεποιεῖτο τοὺς πολεμίους πειρᾶσθαι λανθά-
110 νειν. αἱ δὲ πέλται αὐτῶν ἄλλοτε καὶ ἄλλοτε διεφαίνοντο χαλ-
καῖ οὖσαι. οἱ μὲν οὖν πολέμιοι ταῦτα διορῶντες ἐφοβοῦντο ὡς 30
ἐνέδραν οὖσαν· ἡ δὲ στρατιὰ ἐν τούτῳ κατέβαινεν. ἐπεὶ δὲ
ἐδόκει ἤδη ἱκανὸν ὑπεληλυθέναι, τῷ Μυσῷ ἐσήμηνε φεύγειν ἀνὰ
κράτος· καὶ ὃς ἐξαναστὰς φεύγει καὶ οἱ σὺν αὐτῷ. καὶ οἱ μὲν 31
115 ἄλλοι Κρῆτες, ἁλίσκεσθαι γὰρ ἔφασαν τῷ δρόμῳ, ἐκπεσόντες
ἐκ τῆς ὁδοῦ εἰς ὕλην κατὰ τὰς νάπας καλινδούμενοι ἐσώθησαν, ὁ
Μυσὸς δὲ κατὰ τὴν ὁδὸν φεύγων ἐβόα βοηθεῖν· καὶ ἐβοήθησαν 32
αὐτῷ, καὶ ἀνέλαβον τετρωμένον. καὶ αὐτοὶ ἐπὶ πόδα ἀνεχώρουν
βαλλόμενοι οἱ βοηθήσαντες καὶ ἀντιτοξεύοντές τινες τῶν Κρη-
120 τῶν. οὕτως ἀφίκοντο ἐπὶ τὸ στρατόπεδον πάντες σῶοι ὄντες.

III. Ἐπεὶ δὲ οὔτε Χειρίσοφος ἧκεν οὔτε πλοῖα ἱκανὰ ἦν 1
οὔτε τὰ ἐπιτήδεια ἦν λαμβάνειν ἔτι, ἐδόκει ἀπιτέον εἶναι. καὶ
εἰς μὲν τὰ πλοῖα τούς τε ἀσθενοῦντας ἐνεβίβασαν καὶ τοὺς ὑπὲρ
τετταράκοντα ἔτη καὶ παῖδας καὶ γυναῖκας καὶ τῶν σκευῶν ὅσα
5 μὴ ἀνάγκη ἦν ἔχειν. καὶ Φιλήσιον καὶ Σοφαίνετον τοὺς πρεσ-
βυτάτους τῶν στρατηγῶν εἰσβιβάσαντες τούτων ἐκέλευον ἐπι-
μελεῖσθαι· οἱ δὲ ἄλλοι ἐπορεύοντο· ἡ δὲ ὁδὸς ὡδοποιημένη ἦν. 2
καὶ ἀφικνοῦνται πορευόμενοι εἰς Κερασοῦντα τριταῖοι πόλιν
Ἑλληνίδα ἐπὶ θαλάττῃ Σινωπέων ἄποικον ἐν τῇ Κολχίδι χώρᾳ.
10 ἐνταῦθα ἔμειναν ἡμέρας δέκα· καὶ ἐξέτασις σὺν τοῖς ὅπλοις 3

ἐγίγνετο καὶ ἀριθμός, καὶ ἐγένοντο ὀκτακισχίλιοι καὶ ἑξακόσιοι.
οὗτοι ἐσώθησαν. οἱ δὲ ἄλλοι ἀπώλοντο ὑπό τε τῶν πολεμίων
καὶ χιόνος καὶ εἴ τις νόσῳ.

4 Ἐνταῦθα καὶ διαλαμβάνουσι τὸ ἀπὸ τῶν αἰχμαλώτων ἀργύριον γενόμενον. καὶ τὴν δεκάτην ἣν τῷ Ἀπόλλωνι ἐξεῖλον καὶ
τῇ Ἐφεσίᾳ Ἀρτέμιδι διέλαβον οἱ στρατηγοὶ τὸ μέρος ἕκαστος
φυλάττειν τοῖς θεοῖς· ἀντὶ δὲ Χειρισόφου Νέων ὁ Ἀσιναῖος
5 ἔλαβε. Ξενοφῶν οὖν τὸ μὲν τοῦ Ἀπόλλωνος ἀνάθημα ποιησάμενος ἀνατίθησιν εἰς τὸν ἐν Δελφοῖς τῶν Ἀθηναίων θησαυρὸν
καὶ ἐπέγραψε τό τε αὐτοῦ ὄνομα καὶ τὸ Προξένου, ὃς σὺν Κλεάρ-
6 χῳ ἀπέθανεν· ξένος γὰρ ἦν αὐτοῦ. τὸ δὲ τῆς Ἀρτέμιδος τῆς
Ἐφεσίας, ὅτ᾽ ἀπῄει σὺν Ἀγησιλάῳ ἐκ τῆς Ἀσίας τὴν εἰς Βοιω-
τοὺς ὁδόν, καταλείπει παρὰ Μεγαβύζῳ τῷ τῆς Ἀρτέμιδος νεω-
κόρῳ, ὅτι αὐτὸς κινδυνεύσων ἐδόκει ἰέναι, καὶ ἐπέστειλεν, ἢν μὲν
αὐτὸς σωθῇ, αὐτῷ ἀποδοῦναι· ἢν δέ τι πάθῃ, ἀναθεῖναι ποιησά-
μενον τῇ Ἀρτέμιδι ὅ,τι οἴοιτο χαριεῖσθαι τῇ θεῷ.

7 Ἐπειδὴ δ᾽ ἔφευγεν ὁ Ξενοφῶν, κατοικοῦντος ἤδη αὐτοῦ ἐν
Σκιλλοῦντι ὑπὸ τῶν Λακεδαιμονίων οἰκισθέντος παρὰ τὴν Ὀλυμπίαν ἀφικνεῖται Μεγάβυζος εἰς Ὀλυμπίαν θεωρήσων καὶ ἀποδίδωσι τὴν παρακαταθήκην αὐτῷ. Ξενοφῶν δὲ λαβὼν χωρίον
8 ὠνεῖται τῇ θεῷ ὅπου ἀνεῖλεν ὁ θεός. ἔτυχε δὲ διαρρέων διὰ τοῦ
χωρίου ποταμὸς Σελινοῦς. καὶ ἐν Ἐφέσῳ δὲ παρὰ τὸν τῆς
Ἀρτέμιδος νεὼν Σελινοῦς ποταμὸς παρρεῖ. καὶ ἰχθύες τε ἐν
ἀμφοτέροις ἔνεισι καὶ κόγχαι· ἐν δὲ τῷ ἐν Σκιλλοῦντι χωρίῳ
9 καὶ θῆραι πάντων ὁπόσα ἐστὶν ἀγρευόμενα θηρία. ἐποίησε δὲ
καὶ βωμὸν καὶ ναὸν ἀπὸ τοῦ ἱεροῦ ἀργυρίου, καὶ τὸ λοιπὸν δὲ ἀεὶ
δεκατεύων τὰ ἐκ τοῦ ἀγροῦ ὡραῖα θυσίαν ἐποίει τῇ θεῷ, καὶ
πάντες οἱ πολῖται καὶ οἱ πρόσχωροι ἄνδρες καὶ γυναῖκες μετεῖχον
τῆς ἑορτῆς. παρεῖχε δὲ ἡ θεὸς τοῖς σκηνοῦσιν ἄλφιτα, ἄρτους,
οἶνον, τραγήματα, καὶ τῶν θυομένων ἀπὸ τῆς ἱερᾶς νομῆς λάχος,
10 καὶ τῶν θηρευομένων δέ. καὶ γὰρ θήραν ἐποιοῦντο εἰς τὴν
ἑορτὴν οἵ τε Ξενοφῶντος παῖδες καὶ οἱ τῶν ἄλλων πολιτῶν, οἱ
δὲ βουλόμενοι καὶ ἄνδρες ξυνεθήρων· καὶ ἡλίσκετο τὰ μὲν ἐξ
αὐτοῦ τοῦ ἱεροῦ χώρου, τὰ δὲ καὶ ἐκ τῆς Φολόης, σύες καὶ δορ-
κάδες καὶ ἔλαφοι.

Ἔστι δὲ ἡ χώρα ᾗ ἐκ Λακεδαίμονος εἰς Ὀλυμπίαν πορεύονται ὡς εἴκοσι στάδιοι ἀπὸ τοῦ ἐν Ὀλυμπίᾳ Διὸς ἱεροῦ. ἔνι δ' ἐν τῷ ἱερῷ χώρῳ καὶ λειμὼν καὶ ὄρη δένδρων μεστά, ἱκανὰ σῦς καὶ αἶγας καὶ βοῦς τρέφειν καὶ ἵππους, ὥστε καὶ τὰ τῶν εἰς τὴν ἑορτὴν ἰόντων ὑποζύγια εὐωχεῖσθαι. περὶ δὲ αὐτὸν τὸν ναὸν ἄλσος ἡμέρων δένδρων ἐφυτεύθη ὅσα ἐστὶ τρωκτὰ ὡραῖα. ὁ δὲ ναὸς ὡς μικρὸς μεγάλῳ τῷ ἐν Ἐφέσῳ ᾔκασται, καὶ τὸ ξόανον ἔοικεν ὡς κυπαρίττινον χρυσῷ ὄντι τῷ ἐν Ἐφέσῳ. καὶ στήλη ἕστηκε παρὰ τὸν ναὸν γράμματα ἔχουσα· ΙΕΡΟΣ Ο ΧΩΡΟΣ ΤΗΣ ΑΡΤΕΜΙΔΟΣ. ΤΟΝ ΕΧΟΝΤΑ ΚΑΙ ΚΑΡΠΟΥΜΕΝΟΝ ΤΗΝ ΜΕΝ ΔΕΚΑΤΗΝ ΚΑΤΑΘΥΕΙΝ ΕΚΑΣΤΟΥ ΕΤΟΥΣ. ΕΚ ΔΕ ΤΟΥ ΠΕΡΙΤΤΟΥ ΤΟΝ ΝΑΟΝ ΕΠΙΣΚΕΥΑΖΕΙΝ. ΑΝ ΔΕ ΤΙΣ ΜΗ ΠΟΙΗΙ ΤΑΥΤΑ ΤΗΙ ΘΕΩΙ ΜΕΛΗΣΕΙ.

IV. Ἐκ Κερασοῦντος δὲ κατὰ θάλατταν μὲν ἐκομίζοντο οἵπερ καὶ πρόσθεν, οἱ δὲ ἄλλοι κατὰ γῆν ἐπορεύοντο. ἐπεὶ δὲ ἦσαν ἐπὶ τοῖς Μοσσυνοίκων ὁρίοις, πέμπουσιν εἰς αὐτοὺς Τιμησίθεον τὸν Τραπεζούντιον πρόξενον ὄντα τῶν Μοσσυνοίκων, ἐρωτῶντες πότερον ὡς διὰ φιλίας ἢ διὰ πολεμίας πορεύσονται τῆς χώρας. οἱ δὲ εἶπον ὅτι οὐ διήσοιεν· ἐπίστευον γὰρ τοῖς χωρίοις. ἐντεῦθεν λέγει ὁ Τιμησίθεος ὅτι πολέμιοι τούτοις εἰσὶν οἱ ἐκ τοῦ ἐπέκεινα. καὶ ἐδόκει καλέσαι ἐκείνους, εἰ βούλοιντο ξυμμαχίαν ποιήσασθαι· καὶ πεμφθεὶς ὁ Τιμησίθεος ἧκεν ἄγων τοὺς ἄρχοντας. ἐπεὶ δὲ ἀφίκοντο, συνῆλθον οἵ τε τῶν Μοσσυνοίκων ἄρχοντες καὶ οἱ στρατηγοὶ τῶν Ἑλλήνων· καὶ ἔλεξε Ξενοφῶν, ἡρμήνευε δὲ Τιμησίθεος· Ὦ ἄνδρες Μοσσύνοικοι, ἡμεῖς βουλόμεθα διασωθῆναι πρὸς τὴν Ἑλλάδα πεζῇ· πλοῖα γὰρ οὐκ ἔχομεν· κωλύουσι δὲ οὗτοι ἡμᾶς οὓς ἀκούομεν ὑμῖν πολεμίους εἶναι. εἰ οὖν βούλεσθε, ἔξεστιν ὑμῖν ἡμᾶς λαβεῖν ξυμμάχους καὶ τιμωρήσασθαι εἴ τί ποτε ὑμᾶς οὗτοι ἠδίκησαν, καὶ τὸ λοιπὸν ὑμῶν ὑπηκόους εἶναι τούτους. εἰ δὲ ἡμᾶς ἀφήσετε, σκέψασθε πόθεν αὖθις ἂν τοσαύτην δύναμιν λάβοιτε ξύμμαχον. πρὸς ταῦτα ἀπεκρίνατο ὁ ἄρχων τῶν Μοσσυνοίκων ὅτι καὶ βούλοιντο ταῦτα καὶ δέχοιντο τὴν ξυμμαχίαν. Ἄγετε δή, ἔφη ὁ Ξενοφῶν, τί ἡμῶν δεήσεσθε χρήσασθαι, ἂν ξύμμαχοι ὑμῶν γενώμεθα, καὶ

10 ὑμεῖς τί οἷοί τε ἔσεσθε ἡμῖν ξυμπρᾶξαι περὶ τῆς διόδου; οἱ δὲ εἶπον ὅτι ἱκανοί ἐσμεν εἰς τὴν χώραν εἰσβάλλειν ἐκ τοῦ ἐπὶ θάτερα τὴν τῶν ὑμῖν τε καὶ ἡμῖν πολεμίων, καὶ δεῦρο ὑμῖν πέμψαι ναῦς τε καὶ ἄνδρας οἵτινες ὑμῖν ξυμμαχοῦνταί τε καὶ τὴν ὁδὸν ἡγήσονται.

11 Ἐπὶ τούτοις πιστὰ δόντες καὶ λαβόντες ᾤχοντο. καὶ ἧκον τῇ ὑστεραίᾳ ἄγοντες τριακόσια πλοῖα μονόξυλα καὶ ἐν ἑκάστῳ τρεῖς ἄνδρας, ὧν οἱ μὲν δύο ἐκβάντες εἰς τάξιν ἔθεντο τὰ ὅπλα,
12 ὁ δὲ εἷς ἔμενε. καὶ οἱ μὲν λαβόντες τὰ πλοῖα ἀπέπλευσαν, οἱ δὲ μένοντες ἐξετάξαντο ὧδε. ἔστησαν ἀνὰ ἑκατὸν μάλιστα οἷον χοροὶ ἀντιστοιχοῦντες ἀλλήλοις, ἔχοντες γέρρα πάντες λευκῶν βοῶν δασέα, ἠκασμένα κιττοῦ πετάλῳ, ἐν δὲ τῇ δεξιᾷ παλτὸν ὡς ἔξπηχυ, ἔμπροσθεν μὲν λόγχην ἔχον, ὄπισθεν δὲ τοῦ ξύλου
13 σφαιροειδές. χιτωνίσκους δὲ ἐνεδεδύκεσαν ὑπὲρ γονάτων, πάχος ὡς λινοῦ στρωματοδέσμου, ἐπὶ τῇ κεφαλῇ δὲ κράνη σκύτινα οἷάπερ τὰ Παφλαγονικά, κρωβύλον ἔχοντα κατὰ μέσον, ἐγγύ-
14 τατα τιαροειδῆ· εἶχον δὲ καὶ σαγάρεις σιδηρᾶς. ἐντεῦθεν ἐξῆρχε μὲν αὐτῶν εἷς, οἱ δὲ ἄλλοι ἅπαντες ἐπορεύοντο ᾄδοντες ἐν ῥυθμῷ, καὶ διελθόντες διὰ τῶν τάξεων καὶ διὰ τῶν ὅπλων τῶν Ἑλλήνων ἐπορεύοντο εὐθὺς πρὸς τοὺς πολεμίους ἐπὶ χωρίον ὃ ἐδόκει ἐπιμαχώτατον εἶναι.

15 Ὠικεῖτο δὲ τοῦτο πρὸ τῆς πόλεως τῆς Μητροπόλεως καλουμένης αὐτοῖς καὶ ἐχούσης τὸ ἀκρότατον τῶν Μοσσυνοίκων. καὶ περὶ τούτου ὁ πόλεμος ἦν· οἱ γὰρ ἀεὶ τοῦτ' ἔχοντες ἐδόκουν ἐγκρατεῖς εἶναι καὶ πάντων Μοσσυνοίκων, καὶ ἔφασαν τούτους οὐ δικαίως ἔχειν τοῦτο, ἀλλὰ κοινὸν ὂν καταλαβόντας πλεονεκτεῖν.

16 Εἵποντο δ' αὐτοῖς καὶ τῶν Ἑλλήνων τινές, οὐ ταχθέντες ὑπὸ τῶν στρατηγῶν, ἀλλὰ ἁρπαγῆς ἕνεκεν. οἱ δὲ πολέμιοι προσιόντων τέως μὲν ἡσύχαζον· ἐπεὶ δ' ἐγγὺς ἐγένοντο τοῦ χωρίου, ἐκδραμόντες τρέπονται αὐτούς, καὶ ἀπέκτειναν συχνοὺς τῶν βαρβάρων καὶ τῶν ξυναναβάντων Ἑλλήνων τινάς, καὶ ἐδίωκον μέχρι οὗ εἶδον
17 τοὺς Ἕλληνας βοηθοῦντας· εἶτα δὲ ἀποτραπόμενοι ᾤχοντο, καὶ ἀποτεμόντες τὰς κεφαλὰς τῶν νεκρῶν ἐπεδείκνυσαν τοῖς Ἕλλησι
18 καὶ τοῖς ἑαυτῶν πολεμίοις, καὶ ἅμα ἐχόρευον νόμῳ τινὶ ᾄδοντες. οἱ δὲ Ἕλληνες μάλα ἤχθοντο ὅτι τούς τε πολεμίους ἐπεποιή-

κεσαν θρασυτέρους καὶ ὅτι οἱ ἐξελθόντες Ἕλληνες σὺν αὐτοῖς ἐπεφεύγεσαν μάλα ὄντες συχνοί· ὃ οὔπω πρόσθεν ἐπεποιήκεσαν ἐν τῇ στρατείᾳ.

60 Ξενοφῶν δὲ ξυγκαλέσας τοὺς Ἕλληνας εἶπεν· Ἄνδρες 19 στρατιῶται, μηδὲν ἀθυμήσητε ἕνεκα τῶν γεγενημένων· ἴστε γὰρ ὅτι καὶ ἀγαθὸν οὐ μεῖον τοῦ κακοῦ γεγένηται. πρῶτον μὲν 20 γὰρ ἐπίστασθε ὅτι οἱ μέλλοντες ἡμῖν ἡγεῖσθαι τῷ ὄντι πολέμιοί εἰσιν οἷσπερ καὶ ἡμᾶς ἀνάγκη· ἔπειτα δὲ καὶ τῶν Ἑλλήνων οἱ
65 ἀμελήσαντες τῆς ξὺν ἡμῖν τάξεως καὶ ἱκανοὶ ἡγησάμενοι εἶναι ξὺν τοῖς βαρβάροις ταὐτὰ πράττειν ἅπερ σὺν ἡμῖν δίκην δεδώκασιν· ὥστε αὖθις ἧττον τῆς ἡμετέρας τάξεως ἀπολείψονται. ἀλλ' ὑμᾶς δεῖ παρασκευάζεσθαι ὅπως καὶ τοῖς φίλοις οὖσι τῶν 21 βαρβάρων δόξητε κρείττους αὐτῶν εἶναι καὶ τοῖς πολεμίοις
70 δηλώσητε ὅτι οὐχ ὁμοίοις ἀνδράσι μαχοῦνται νῦν τε καὶ ὅτε τοῖς ἀτάκτοις ἐμάχοντο.

Ταύτην μὲν οὖν τὴν ἡμέραν οὕτως ἔμειναν· τῇ δὲ ὑστεραίᾳ 22 θύσαντες ἐπεὶ ἐκαλλιερήσαντο, ἀριστήσαντες, ὀρθίους τοὺς λόχους ποιησάμενοι, καὶ τοὺς βαρβάρους ἐπὶ τὸ εὐώνυμον κατὰ
75 ταὐτὰ ταξάμενοι ἐπορεύοντο τοὺς τοξότας μεταξὺ τῶν λόχων ἔχοντες, ὑπολειπομένου δὲ μικρὸν τοῦ στόματος τῶν ὁπλιτῶν. ἦσαν γὰρ τῶν πολεμίων οἱ εὔζωνοι κατατρέχοντες τοῖς λίθοις 23 ἔβαλλον. τούτους ἀνέστελλον οἱ τοξόται καὶ πελτασταί. οἱ δ' ἄλλοι βάδην ἐπορεύοντο πρῶτον μὲν ἐπὶ τὸ χωρίον ἀφ' οὗ τῇ
80 προτεραίᾳ οἱ βάρβαροι ἐτρέφθησαν καὶ οἱ ξὺν αὐτοῖς· ἐνταῦθα γὰρ οἱ πολέμιοι ἦσαν ἀντιτεταγμένοι. τοὺς μὲν οὖν πελταστὰς 24 ἐδέξαντο οἱ βάρβαροι καὶ ἐμάχοντο, ἐπειδὴ δὲ ἐγγὺς ἦσαν οἱ ὁπλῖται, ἐτρέποντο. καὶ οἱ μὲν πελτασταὶ εὐθὺς εἵποντο διώκοντες ἄνω πρὸς τὴν πόλιν, οἱ δὲ ὁπλῖται ἐν τάξει εἵποντο.
85 ἐπεὶ δὲ ἄνω ἦσαν πρὸς ταῖς Μητροπόλεως οἰκίαις, ἐνταῦθα οἱ 25 πολέμιοι ὁμοῦ δὴ πάντες γενόμενοι ἐμάχοντο καὶ ἐξηκόντιζον τοῖς παλτοῖς, καὶ ἄλλα δόρατα ἔχοντες παχέα μακρά, ὅσα ἀνὴρ ἂν φέροι μόλις, τούτοις ἐπειρῶντο ἀμύνασθαι ἐκ χειρός. ἐπεὶ 26 δὲ οὐχ ὑφίεντο οἱ Ἕλληνες, ἀλλὰ ὁμόσε ἐχώρουν, ἔφευγον οἱ
90 βάρβαροι καὶ ἐντεῦθεν λείποντες ἅπαντες τὸ χωρίον. ὁ δὲ βασιλεὺς αὐτῶν ὁ ἐν τῷ μόσσυνι τῷ ἐπ' ἄκρου ᾠκοδομημένῳ, ὃν τρέ-

φουσι πάντες κοινῇ αὐτοῦ μένοντα καὶ φυλάττουσιν, οὐκ ἤθελεν ἐξελθεῖν, οὐδὲ ὁ ἐν τῷ πρότερον αἱρεθέντι χωρίῳ, ἀλλ' αὐτοῦ σὺν τοῖς μοσσύνοις κατεκαύθησαν.

27 Οἱ δὲ Ἕλληνες διαρπάζοντες τὰ χωρία ηὕρισκον θησαυροὺς ἐν ταῖς οἰκίαις ἄρτων, νενημένων πατρίους, ὡς ἔφασαν οἱ Μοσσύνοικοι, τὸν δὲ νέον σῖτον ξὺν τῇ καλάμῃ ἀποκείμενον· ἦσαν δὲ 28 ζειαὶ αἱ πλεῖσται. καὶ δελφίνων τεμάχη ἐν ἀμφορεῦσιν ηὑρίσκετο τεταριχευμένα καὶ στέαρ ἐν τεύχεσι τῶν δελφίνων, ᾧ 29 ἐχρῶντο οἱ Μοσσύνοικοι καθάπερ οἱ Ἕλληνες τῷ ἐλαίῳ· κάρυα δὲ ἐπὶ τῶν ἀνώγεων ἦν πολλὰ τὰ πλατέα οὐκ ἔχοντα διαφυὴν οὐδεμίαν. τούτῳ καὶ πλείστῳ σίτῳ ἐχρῶντο ἕψοντες καὶ ἄρτους ὀπτῶντες. οἶνος δὲ ηὑρίσκετο ὃς ἄκρατος μὲν ὀξὺς ἐφαίνετο εἶναι ὑπὸ τῆς αὐστηρότητος, κερασθεὶς δὲ εὐώδης τε καὶ ἡδύς.

30 Οἱ μὲν δὴ Ἕλληνες ἀριστήσαντες ἐνταῦθα ἐπορεύοντο εἰς τὸ πρόσω, παραδόντες τὸ χωρίον τοῖς ξυμμαχήσασι τῶν Μοσσυνοίκων. ὁπόσα δὲ καὶ ἄλλα παρῆσαν χωρία τῶν ξὺν τοῖς πολεμίοις ὄντων, τὰ εὐπροσοδώτατα οἱ μὲν ἔλειπον, οἱ δὲ 31 ἑκόντες προσεχώρουν. τὰ δὲ πλεῖστα τοιάδε ἦν τῶν χωρίων. ἀπεῖχον αἱ πόλεις ἀπ' ἀλλήλων στάδια ὀγδοήκοντα, αἱ δὲ πλέον αἱ δὲ μεῖον· ἀναβοώντων δὲ ἀλλήλων ξυνήκουον εἰς τὴν ἑτέραν ἐκ τῆς ἑτέρας πόλεως· οὕτως ὑψηλή τε καὶ κοίλη ἡ χώρα ἦν. 32 ἐπεὶ δὲ πορευόμενοι ἐν τοῖς φίλοις ἦσαν, ἐπεδείκνυσαν αὐτοῖς παῖδας τῶν εὐδαιμόνων σιτευτούς, τεθραμμένους καρύοις ἑφθοῖς, ἁπαλοὺς καὶ λευκοὺς σφόδρα καὶ οὐ πολλοῦ δέοντας ἴσους τὸ μῆκος καὶ τὸ πλάτος εἶναι, ποικίλους δὲ τὰ νῶτα καὶ τὰ ἔμ- 33 προσθεν πάντα ἐστιγμένους ἀνθέμια. ἐζήτουν δὲ καὶ ταῖς ἑταίραις ἃς ἦγον οἱ Ἕλληνες, ἐμφανῶς ξυγγίγνεσθαι· νόμος γὰρ ἦν οὗτός σφισι. λευκοὶ δὲ πάντες οἱ ἄνδρες καὶ αἱ 34 γυναῖκες. τούτους ἔλεγον οἱ στρατευσάμενοι βαρβαρωτάτους διελθεῖν καὶ πλεῖστον τῶν Ἑλληνικῶν νόμων κεχωρισμένους. ἔν τε γὰρ ὄχλῳ ὄντες ἐποίουν ἅπερ ἂν ἄνθρωποι ἐν ἐρημίᾳ ποιήσειαν, μόνοι τε ὄντες ὅμοια ἔπραττον ἅπερ ἂν μετ' ἄλλων ὄντες, διελέγοντό τε αὐτοῖς καὶ ἐγέλων ἐφ' ἑαυτοῖς καὶ ὠρχοῦντο ἐφιστάμενοι ὅπου τύχοιεν ὥσπερ ἄλλοις ἐπιδεικνύμενοι.

V. Διὰ ταύτης τῆς χώρας οἱ Ἕλληνες, διά τε τῆς πολεμίας καὶ τῆς φιλίας, ἐπορεύθησαν ὀκτὼ σταθμούς, καὶ ἀφικνοῦνται εἰς Χάλυβας. οὗτοι ὀλίγοι τε ἦσαν καὶ ὑπήκοοι τῶν Μοσσυνοίκων, καὶ ὁ βίος ἦν τοῖς πλείστοις αὐτῶν ἀπὸ σιδηρείας. ἐντεῦθεν ἀφικνοῦνται εἰς Τιβαρηνούς. ἡ δὲ τῶν Τιβαρηνῶν χώρα πολὺ ἦν πεδινωτέρα καὶ χωρία εἶχεν ἐπὶ θαλάττῃ ἧττον ἐρυμνά. καὶ οἱ στρατηγοὶ ἔχρῃζον πρὸς τὰ χωρία προσβάλλειν καὶ τὴν στρατιὰν ὀνηθῆναί τι, καὶ τὰ ξένια ἃ ἧκε παρὰ Τιβαρηνῶν οὐκ ἐδέχοντο, ἀλλ' ἐπιμεῖναι κελεύσαντες ἔστε βουλεύσαιντο ἐθύοντο. καὶ πολλὰ καταθυσάντων τέλος ἀπεδείξαντο οἱ μάντεις πάντες γνώμην ὅτι οὐδαμῇ προσίοιντο οἱ θεοὶ τὸν πόλεμον. ἐντεῦθεν δὴ τὰ ξένια ἐδέξαντο, καὶ ὡς διὰ φιλίας πορευόμενοι δύο ἡμέρας ἀφίκοντο εἰς Κοτύωρα πόλιν Ἑλληνίδα, Σινωπέων ἄποικον, οὖσαν δ' ἐν τῇ Τιβαρηνῶν χώρᾳ.

[Μέχρι ἐνταῦθα ἐπέζευσεν ἡ στρατιά. πλῆθος τῆς καταβάσεως τῆς ὁδοῦ ἀπὸ τῆς ἐν Βαβυλῶνι μάχης ἄχρι εἰς Κοτύωρα σταθμοὶ ἑκατὸν εἴκοσι δύο, παρασάγγαι ἑξακόσιοι καὶ εἴκοσι, στάδιοι μύριοι καὶ ὀκτακισχίλιοι καὶ ἑξακόσιοι, χρόνου πλῆθος ὀκτὼ μῆνες.]

Ἐνταῦθα ἔμειναν ἡμέρας τετταράκοντα πέντε. ἐν δὲ ταύταις πρῶτον μὲν τοῖς θεοῖς ἔθυσαν, καὶ πομπὰς ἐποίησαν κατὰ ἔθνος ἕκαστοι τῶν Ἑλλήνων καὶ ἀγῶνας γυμνικούς. τὰ δ' ἐπιτήδει' ἐλάμβανον τὰ μὲν ἐκ τῆς Παφλαγονίας, τὰ δ' ἐκ τῶν χωρίων τῶν Κοτυωριτῶν· οὐ γὰρ παρεῖχον ἀγοράν, οὐδὲ εἰς τὸ τεῖχος τοὺς ἀσθενοῦντας ἐδέχοντο.

Ἐν τούτῳ ἔρχονται ἐκ Σινώπης πρέσβεις, φοβούμενοι περὶ τῶν Κοτυωριτῶν τῆς τε πόλεως, ἣν γὰρ ἐκείνων καὶ φόρον ἐκείνοις ἔφερον, καὶ περὶ τῆς χώρας, ὅτι ἤκουον δῃουμένην. καὶ ἐλθόντες εἰς τὸ στρατόπεδον ἔλεγον· προηγόρει δὲ Ἑκατώνυμος δεινὸς νομιζόμενος εἶναι λέγειν· Ἔπεμψεν ἡμᾶς, ὦ ἄνδρες στρατιῶται, ἡ τῶν Σινωπέων πόλις ἐπαινέσοντάς τε ὑμᾶς ὅτι νικᾶτε Ἕλληνες ὄντες βαρβάρους, ἔπειτα δὲ καὶ ξυνησθησομένους ὅτι διὰ πολλῶν τε καὶ δεινῶν, ὡς ἡμεῖς ἠκούσαμεν, πραγμάτων σεσωμένοι πάρεστε. ἀξιοῦμεν δὲ Ἕλληνες ὄντες καὶ αὐτοὶ ὑφ' ὑμῶν ὄντων Ἑλλήνων ἀγαθὸν μέν τι πάσχειν, κακὸν δὲ μηδέν·

οὐδὲ γὰρ ἡμεῖς ὑμᾶς οὐδὲν πώποτε ὑπήρξαμεν κακῶς ποιοῦντες.
Κοτυωρῖται δὲ οὗτοι εἰσὶ μὲν ἡμέτεροι ἄποικοι, καὶ τὴν χώραν ἡμεῖς αὐτοῖς ταύτην παραδεδώκαμεν βαρβάρους ἀφελόμενοι· διὸ καὶ δασμὸν ἡμῖν φέρουσιν οὗτοι τεταγμένον καὶ Κερασούντιοι καὶ Τραπεζούντιοι· ὥστε ὅ,τι ἂν τούτους κακὸν ποιήσητε ἡ Σινωπέων πόλις νομίζει πάσχειν. νῦν δὲ ἀκούομεν ὑμᾶς εἴς τε τὴν πόλιν βίᾳ παρεληλυθότας ἐνίους σκηνοῦν ἐν ταῖς οἰκίαις καὶ ἐκ τῶν χωρίων βίᾳ λαμβάνειν ὧν ἂν δέησθε οὐ πείθοντας. ταῦτ᾽ οὖν οὐκ ἀξιοῦμεν· εἰ δὲ ταῦτα ποιήσετε, ἀνάγκη ἡμῖν καὶ Κορύλαν καὶ Παφλαγόνας καὶ ἄλλον ὅντινα ἂν δυνώμεθα φίλον ποιεῖσθαι.

Πρὸς ταῦτα ἀναστὰς Ξενοφῶν ὑπὲρ τῶν στρατιωτῶν εἶπεν· Ἡμεῖς δέ, ὦ ἄνδρες Σινωπεῖς, ἥκομεν ἀγαπῶντες ὅτι τὰ σώματα διεσωσάμεθα καὶ τὰ ὅπλα· οὐ γὰρ ἦν δυνατὸν ἅμα τε χρήματα ἄγειν καὶ φέρειν καὶ τοῖς πολεμίοις μάχεσθαι. καὶ νῦν ἐπεὶ εἰς τὰς Ἑλληνίδας πόλεις ἤλθομεν, ἐν Τραπεζοῦντι μέν, παρεῖχον γὰρ ἡμῖν ἀγοράν, ὠνούμενοι εἴχομεν τὰ ἐπιτήδεια, καὶ ἀνθ᾽ ὧν ἐτίμησαν ἡμᾶς καὶ ξένια ἔδωκαν τῇ στρατιᾷ, ἀντετιμῶμεν αὐτούς, καὶ εἴ τις αὐτοῖς φίλος ἦν τῶν βαρβάρων, τούτων ἀπειχόμεθα· τοὺς δὲ πολεμίους αὐτῶν ἐφ᾽ οὓς αὐτοὶ ἡγοῖντο κακῶς ἐποιοῦμεν ὅσον ἐδυνάμεθα. ἐρωτᾶτε δὲ αὐτοὺς ὁποίων τινῶν ἡμῶν ἔτυχον· πάρεισι γὰρ ἐνθάδε οὓς ἡμῖν ἡγεμόνας διὰ φιλίαν ἡ πόλις ξυνέπεμψεν. ὅποι δ᾽ ἂν ἐλθόντες ἀγορὰν μὴ ἔχωμεν, ἄν τε εἰς βάρβαρον γῆν ἄν τε εἰς Ἑλληνίδα, οὐχ ὕβρει ἀλλὰ ἀνάγκῃ λαμβάνομεν τὰ ἐπιτήδεια. καὶ Καρδούχους καὶ Τάοχους καὶ Χαλδαίους καίπερ βασιλέως οὐχ ὑπηκόους ὄντας ὅμως καὶ μάλα φοβεροὺς ὄντας πολεμίους ἐκτησάμεθα διὰ τὸ ἀνάγκην εἶναι λαμβάνειν τὰ ἐπιτήδεια, ἐπεὶ ἀγορὰν οὐ παρεῖχον. Μάκρωνας δὲ καίπερ βαρβάρους ὄντας, ἐπεὶ ἀγορὰν οἵαν ἐδύναντο παρεῖχον, φίλους τε ἐνομίζομεν εἶναι καὶ βίᾳ οὐδὲν ἐλαμβάνομεν τῶν ἐκείνων.

Κοτυωρίτας δέ, οὓς ὑμετέρους φατὲ εἶναι, εἴ τι αὐτῶν εἰλήφαμεν, αὐτοὶ αἴτιοί εἰσιν· οὐ γὰρ ὡς φίλοι προσεφέροντο ἡμῖν, ἀλλὰ κλείσαντες τὰς πύλας οὔτε εἴσω ἐδέχοντο οὔτε ἔξω ἀγορὰν ἔπεμπον· ᾐτιῶντο δὲ τὸν παρ᾽ ὑμῶν ἁρμοστὴν τούτων αἴτιον εἶναι. ὃ δὲ λέγεις βίᾳ παρελθόντας σκηνοῦν, ἡμεῖς ἠξιοῦμεν τοὺς κάμνοντας εἰς τὰς στέγας δέξασθαι· ἐπεὶ δὲ οὐκ ἀνέῳγον τὰς πύλας, ᾗ ἡμᾶς ἐδέχετο αὐτὸ τὸ χωρίον ταύτῃ εἰσελθόντες ἄλλο μὲν οὐδὲν βίαιον ἐποιήσαμεν, σκηνοῦσι δ' ἐν ταῖς στέγαις οἱ κάμνοντες τὰ αὐτῶν δαπανῶντες, καὶ τὰς πύλας φρουροῦμεν, ὅπως μὴ ἐπὶ τῷ ὑμετέρῳ ἁρμοστῇ ὦσιν οἱ κάμνοντες ἡμῶν, ἀλλ' ἐφ' ἡμῖν ᾖ κομίσασθαι ὅταν βουλώμεθα. οἱ δὲ ἄλλοι, ὡς ὁρᾶτε, σκηνοῦμεν ὑπαίθριοι ἐν τῇ τάξει, παρεσκευασμένοι, ἂν μέν τις εὖ ποιῇ, ἀντευποιεῖν, ἂν δὲ κακῶς, ἀλέξασθαι.

Ἃ δὲ ἠπείλησας ὡς ἢν ὑμῖν δοκῇ Κορύλαν καὶ Παφλαγόνας ξυμμάχους ποιήσεσθε ἐφ' ἡμᾶς, ἡμεῖς δὲ ἢν μὲν ἀνάγκῃ ᾖ πολεμήσομεν καὶ ἀμφοτέροις· ἤδη γὰρ καὶ ἄλλοις πολλαπλασίοις ὑμῶν ἐπολεμήσαμεν. ἂν δὲ δοκῇ ἡμῖν καὶ φίλον ποιεῖσθαι τὸν Παφλαγόνα — ἀκούομεν δὲ αὐτὸν καὶ ἐπιθυμεῖν τῆς ὑμετέρας πόλεως καὶ χωρίων τῶν ἐπιθαλαττίων — πειρασόμεθα ξυμπράττοντες αὐτῷ ὧν ἐπιθυμεῖ φίλοι γίγνεσθαι.

Ἐκ τούτου μάλα μὲν δῆλοι ἦσαν οἱ ξυμπρέσβεις τῷ Ἑκατωνύμῳ χαλεπαίνοντες τοῖς εἰρημένοις, παρελθὼν δ' αὐτῶν ἄλλος εἶπεν ὅτι οὐ πόλεμον ποιησόμενοι ἥκοιεν ἀλλὰ ἐπιδείξοντες ὅτι φίλοι εἰσί. καὶ ξενίοις, ἢν μὲν ἔλθητε πρὸς τὴν Σινωπέων πόλιν, ἐκεῖ δεξόμεθα, νῦν δὲ τοὺς ἐνθάδε κελεύσομεν διδόναι ἃ δύνανται· ὁρῶμεν γὰρ πάντα ἀληθῆ ὄντα ἃ λέγετε. ἐκ τούτου ξένιά τε ἔπεμπον οἱ Κοτυωρῖται καὶ οἱ στρατηγοὶ τῶν Ἑλλήνων ἐξένιζον τοὺς τῶν Σινωπέων πρέσβεις, καὶ πρὸς ἀλλήλους πολλά τε καὶ φιλικὰ διελέγοντο τά τε ἄλλα καὶ περὶ τῆς λοιπῆς πορείας ἀνεπυνθάνοντο ὧν ἑκάτεροι ἐδέοντο.

VI. Ταύτῃ μὲν τῇ ἡμέρᾳ τοῦτο τὸ τέλος ἐγένετο. τῇ δὲ ὑστεραίᾳ ξυνέλεξαν οἱ στρατηγοὶ τοὺς στρατιώτας. καὶ ἐδόκει αὐτοῖς περὶ τῆς λοιπῆς πορείας παρακαλέσαντας τοὺς Σινωπέας βουλεύεσθαι. εἴτε γὰρ πεζῇ δέοι πορεύεσθαι, χρήσιμοι ἂν ἐδόκουν εἶναι οἱ Σινωπεῖς· ἔμπειροι γὰρ ἦσαν τῆς Παφλαγονίας· εἴτε κατὰ θάλατταν, προσδεῖν ἐδόκει Σινωπέων· μόνοι γὰρ ἂν ἐδόκουν ἱκανοὶ εἶναι πλοῖα παρασχεῖν ἀρκοῦντα τῇ στρατιᾷ. καλέσαντες οὖν τοὺς πρέσβεις ξυνεβουλεύοντο, καὶ ἠξίουν Ἕλληνας ὄντας Ἕλλησι τούτῳ πρῶτον καλῶς δέχεσθαι τῷ εὔνους τε εἶναι καὶ τὰ κάλλιστα ξυμβουλεύειν.

3 Ἀναστὰς δὲ Ἑκατώνυμος πρῶτον μὲν ἀπελογήσατο περὶ οὗ
εἶπεν ὡς τὸν Παφλαγόνα φίλον ποιήσοιντο, ὅτι οὐχ ὡς τοῖς
Ἕλλησι πολεμησόντων σφῶν εἴποι, ἀλλ' ὅτι ἐξὸν τοῖς βαρβάροις φίλους εἶναι τοὺς Ἕλληνας αἱρήσονται. ἐπεὶ δὲ ξυμβου-
4 λεύειν ἐκέλευον, ἐπευξάμενος εἶπεν ὧδε. Εἰ μὲν ξυμβουλεύοιμι
ἃ βέλτιστά μοι δοκεῖ, πολλά μοι καὶ ἀγαθὰ γένοιτο· εἰ δὲ μή,
τἀναντία. αὕτη γὰρ ἡ ἱερὰ ξυμβουλὴ λεγομένη εἶναι δοκεῖ
μοι παρεῖναι· νῦν γὰρ δὴ ἂν μὲν εὖ ξυμβουλεύσας φανῶ, πολλοὶ
ἔσονται οἱ ἐπαινοῦντές με, ἂν δὲ κακῶς, πολλοὶ ἔσεσθε οἱ καταρώ-
5 μενοι. πράγματα μὲν οὖν οἶδ' ὅτι πολὺ πλείω ἕξομεν, ἐὰν κατὰ
θάλατταν κομίζησθε· ἡμᾶς γὰρ δεήσει τὰ πλοῖα πορίζειν· ἢν δὲ
6 κατὰ γῆν στέλλησθε, ὑμᾶς δεήσει τοὺς μαχομένους εἶναι. ὅμως
δὲ λεκτέα ἃ γιγνώσκω· ἔμπειρος γάρ εἰμι καὶ τῆς χώρας τῆς
Παφλαγόνων καὶ τῆς δυνάμεως. ἔχει γὰρ ἀμφότερα, καὶ πεδία
κάλλιστα καὶ ὄρη ὑψηλότατα.

7 Καὶ πρῶτον μὲν οἶδα εὐθὺς ᾗ τὴν εἰσβολὴν ἀνάγκη ποιεῖσθαι·
οὐ γὰρ ἔστιν ἄλλη ἢ ᾗ τὰ κέρατα τοῦ ὄρους τῆς ὁδοῦ καθ' ἑκά-
τερά ἐστιν ὑψηλά, ἃ κρατεῖν κατέχοντες καὶ πάνυ ὀλίγοι δύναιντ'
ἄν· τούτων δὲ κατεχομένων οὐδ' ἂν οἱ πάντες ἄνθρωποι δύναιντ'
ἂν διελθεῖν. ταῦτα δὲ καὶ δείξαιμι ἄν, εἴ μοί τινα βούλεσθε
ξυμπέμψαι.

8 Ἔπειτα δὲ οἶδα καὶ πεδία ὄντα καὶ ἱππείαν ἣν αὐτοὶ οἱ βάρβαροι νομίζουσι κρείττω εἶναι ἁπάσης τῆς βασιλέως ἱππείας.
καὶ νῦν οὗτοι οὐ παρεγένοντο βασιλεῖ καλοῦντι, ἀλλὰ μεῖζον
φρονεῖ ὁ ἄρχων αὐτῶν.

9 Ἢν δὲ καὶ δυνηθῆτε τά τε ὄρη κλέψαι ἢ φθάσαι λαβόντες
καὶ ἐν τῷ πεδίῳ κρατῆσαι μαχόμενοι τούς τε ἱππεῖς τούτων καὶ
πεζῶν μυριάδας πλέον ἢ δώδεκα, ἥξετε ἐπὶ τοὺς ποταμούς,
πρῶτον μὲν τὸν Θερμώδοντα, εὖρος τριῶν πλέθρων, ὃν χαλεπὸν
οἶμαι διαβαίνειν ἄλλως τε καὶ πολεμίων πολλῶν ἔμπροσθεν
ὄντων, πολλῶν δὲ ὄπισθεν ἑπομένων· δεύτερον δὲ Ἶριν, τρί-
πλεθρον ὡσαύτως· τρίτον δὲ Ἅλυν, οὐ μεῖον δυοῖν σταδίοιν, ὃν
οὐκ ἂν δύναισθε ἄνευ πλοίων διαβῆναι· πλοῖα δὲ τίς ἔσται ὁ
παρέχων; ὡς δ' αὔτως καὶ ὁ Παρθένιος ἄβατος· ἐφ' ὃν ἔλθοιτε
ἄν, εἰ τὸν Ἅλυν διαβαίητε.

Ἐγὼ μὲν οὖν οὐ χαλεπὴν ὑμῖν εἶναι νομίζω τὴν πορείαν ἀλλὰ παντάπασιν ἀδύνατον. ἂν δὲ πλέητε, ἔστιν ἐνθένδε μὲν εἰς Σινώπην παραπλεῦσαι, ἐκ Σινώπης δὲ εἰς Ἡράκλειαν· ἐξ Ἡρακλείας δὲ οὔτε πεζῇ οὔτε κατὰ θάλατταν ἀπορία· πολλὰ γὰρ καὶ πλοῖά ἐστιν ἐν Ἡρακλείᾳ.

Ἐπεὶ δὲ ταῦτ᾽ ἔλεξεν, οἱ μὲν ὑπώπτευον φιλίας ἕνεκα τῆς Κορύλα λέγειν· καὶ γὰρ ἦν πρόξενος αὐτῷ· οἱ δὲ καὶ ὡς δῶρα ληψόμενον διὰ τὴν ξυμβουλὴν ταύτην· οἱ δὲ ὑπώπτευον καὶ τούτου ἕνεκα λέγειν ὡς μὴ πεζῇ ἰόντες τὴν Σινωπέων τι χώραν κακὸν ἐργάζοιντο. οἱ δ᾽ οὖν Ἕλληνες ἐψηφίσαντο κατὰ θάλατταν τὴν πορείαν ποιεῖσθαι. μετὰ ταῦτα Ξενοφῶν εἶπεν· Ὦ Σινωπεῖς, οἱ μὲν ἄνδρες ᾕρηνται πορείαν ἣν ὑμεῖς ξυμβουλεύετε· οὕτω δὲ ἔχει· εἰ μὲν πλοῖα ἔσεσθαι μέλλει ἱκανὰ ὡς ἀριθμῷ ἕνα μὴ καταλείπεσθαι ἐνθάδε, ἡμεῖς ἂν πλέοιμεν· εἰ δὲ μέλλοιμεν οἱ μὲν καταλείψεσθαι οἱ δὲ πλεύσεσθαι, οὐκ ἂν ἐμβαίημεν εἰς τὰ πλοῖα. γιγνώσκομεν γὰρ ὅτι ὅπου μὲν ἂν κρατῶμεν, δυναίμεθα ἂν καὶ σῴζεσθαι καὶ τὰ ἐπιτήδεια ἔχειν· εἰ δέ που ἥττους τῶν πολεμίων ληφθησόμεθα, εὔδηλον δὴ ὅτι ἐν ἀνδραπόδων χώρᾳ ἐσόμεθα. ἀκούσαντες ταῦτα οἱ Σινωπεῖς ἐκέλευον πέμπειν πρέσβεις. καὶ πέμπουσι Καλλίμαχον Ἀρκάδα καὶ Ἀρίστωνα Ἀθηναῖον καὶ Σαμόλαν Ἀχαιόν. καὶ οἱ μὲν ᾤχοντο.

Ἐν δὲ τούτῳ τῷ χρόνῳ Ξενοφῶντι, ὁρῶντι μὲν ὁπλίτας πολλοὺς τῶν Ἑλλήνων, ὁρῶντι δὲ πελταστὰς πολλοὺς καὶ τοξότας καὶ σφενδονήτας καὶ ἱππεῖς δὲ καὶ μάλα ἤδη διὰ τὴν τριβὴν ἱκανούς, ὄντας δ᾽ ἐν τῷ Πόντῳ, ἔνθα οὐκ ἂν ἀπ᾽ ὀλίγων χρημάτων τοσαύτη δύναμις παρεσκευάσθη, καλὸν αὐτῷ ἐδόκει εἶναι χώραν καὶ δύναμιν τῇ Ἑλλάδι προσκτήσασθαι πόλιν κατοικίσαντας. καὶ γενέσθαι ἂν αὐτῷ ἐδόκει μεγάλη, καταλογιζομένῳ τό τε αὐτῶν πλῆθος καὶ τοὺς περιοικοῦντας τὸν Πόντον. καὶ ἐπὶ τούτοις ἐθύετο πρίν τινι εἰπεῖν τῶν στρατιωτῶν Σιλανὸν παρακαλέσας τὸν Κύρου μάντιν γενόμενον τὸν Ἀμπρακιώτην. ὁ δὲ Σιλανὸς δεδιὼς μὴ γένηται ταῦτα καὶ καταμείνῃ που ἡ στρατιά, ἐκφέρει εἰς τὸ στράτευμα λόγον ὅτι Ξενοφῶν βούλεται καταμεῖναι τὴν στρατιὰν καὶ πόλιν οἰκίσαι καὶ ἑαυτῷ ὄνομα καὶ δύναμιν περιποιήσασθαι. αὐτὸς δ᾽ ὁ Σιλανὸς ἐβούλετο ὅτι τάχιστα εἰς τὴν Ἑλλάδα ἀφικέσθαι· οὓς γὰρ παρὰ Κύρου ἔλαβε τρισχιλίους δαρεικοὺς ὅτε τὰς δέκα ἡμέρας ἠλήθευσε θυόμενος Κύρῳ, καὶ διεσεσώκει.

19 Τῶν δὲ στρατιωτῶν, ἐπεὶ ἤκουσαν, τοῖς μὲν ἐδόκει βέλτιστον εἶναι καταμεῖναι, τοῖς δὲ πολλοῖς οὔ. Τιμασίων δὲ ὁ Δαρδανεὺς καὶ Θώραξ ὁ Βοιώτιος πρὸς ἐμπόρους τινὰς παρόντας τῶν Ἡρακλεωτῶν καὶ Σινωπέων λέγουσιν ὅτι εἰ μὴ ἐκποριοῦσι τῇ στρατιᾷ μισθὸν ὥστε ἔχειν τὰ ἐπιτήδεια ἐκπλέοντας, ὅτι κινδυνεύσει μεῖναι τοσαύτη δύναμις ἐν τῷ Πόντῳ· βούλεται γὰρ Ξενοφῶν καὶ ἡμᾶς παρακαλεῖ, ἐπειδὰν ἔλθῃ τὰ πλοῖα, τότε εἰπεῖν ἐξαίφνης
20 τῇ στρατιᾷ, Ἄνδρες, νῦν μὲν ὁρῶμεν ἡμᾶς ἀπόρους ὄντας καὶ ἐν τῷ ἀπόπλῳ ἔχειν τὰ ἐπιτήδεια καὶ ὡς οἴκαδε ἀπελθόντας ὀνῆσαί τι τοὺς οἴκοι· εἰ δὲ βούλεσθε τῆς κύκλῳ χώρας περὶ τὸν Πόντον οἰκουμένης ἐκλεξάμενοι ὅποι ἂν βούλησθε κατασχεῖν, καὶ τὸν μὲν ἐθέλοντα ἀπιέναι οἴκαδε, τὸν δ' ἐθέλοντα μένειν αὐτοῦ, πλοῖα δ' ὑμῖν πάρεστιν, ὥστε ὅπῃ ἂν βούλησθε ἐξαίφνης ἂν ἐπιπέσοιτε.

21 Ἀκούσαντες ταῦτα οἱ ἔμποροι ἀπήγγελλον ταῖς πόλεσι· ξυνέπεμψε δ' αὐτοῖς Τιμασίων Δαρδανεὺς Εὐρύμαχόν τε τὸν Δαρδανέα καὶ Θώρακα τὸν Βοιώτιον ταὐτὰ ἐροῦντας. Σινωπεῖς δὲ καὶ Ἡρακλεῶται ταῦτα ἀκούσαντες πέμπουσι πρὸς τὸν Τιμασίωνα καὶ κελεύουσι προστατεῦσαι λαβόντα χρήματα ὅπως
22 ἐκπλεύσῃ ἡ στρατιά. ὁ δὲ ἄσμενος ἀκούσας ἐν ξυλλόγῳ τῶν στρατιωτῶν ὄντων λέγει τάδε. Οὐ δεῖ προσέχειν μονῇ, ὦ ἄνδρες, οὐδὲ τῆς Ἑλλάδος οὐδὲν περὶ πλείονος ποιεῖσθαι. ἀκούω δέ τινας θύεσθαι ἐπὶ τούτῳ οὐδ' ὑμῖν λέγοντας. ὑπισχνοῦμαι δὲ ὑμῖν, ἂν ἐκπλέητε, ἀπὸ νουμηνίας μισθοφορὰν παρέξειν κυζικηνὸν ἑκάστῳ τοῦ μηνός· καὶ ἄξω ὑμᾶς εἰς τὴν Τρῳάδα, ἔνθεν καί εἰμι φυγάς, καὶ ὑπάρξει ὑμῖν ἡ ἐμὴ πόλις· ἑκόντες γάρ
24 με δέξονται. ἡγήσομαι δὲ αὐτὸς ἐγὼ ἔνθεν πολλὰ χρήματα λήψεσθε. ἔμπειρος δέ εἰμι τῆς Αἰολίδος καὶ τῆς Φρυγίας καὶ τῆς Τρῳάδος καὶ τῆς Φαρναβάζου ἀρχῆς πάσης, τὰ μὲν διὰ τὸ ἐκεῖθεν εἶναι, τὰ δὲ διὰ τὸ ξυνεστρατεῦσθαι ἐν αὐτῇ σὺν Κλεάρχῳ τε καὶ Δερκυλίδᾳ.

25. Ἀναστὰς αὖθις Θώραξ ὁ Βοιώτιος, ὃς περὶ στρατηγίας Ξενοφῶντι ἐμάχετο, ἔφη, εἰ ἐξέλθοιεν ἐκ τοῦ Πόντου, ἔσεσθαι αὐτοῖς

Χερρόνησον χώραν καλὴν καὶ εὐδαίμονα ὥστε ἐξεῖναι τῷ βουλομένῳ ἐνοικεῖν, τῷ δὲ μὴ βουλομένῳ ἀπιέναι οἴκαδε. γελοῖον δὲ εἶναι ἐν τῇ Ἑλλάδι οὔσης χώρας πολλῆς καὶ ἀφθόνου ἐν τῇ βαρβάρων μαστεύειν. ἔστε δ' ἄν, ἔφη, ἐκεῖ γένησθε, κἀγὼ καθάπερ Τιμασίων ὑπισχνοῦμαι ὑμῖν τὴν μισθοφοράν. ταῦτα δὲ ἔλεγεν εἰδὼς ἃ Τιμασίωνι οἱ Ἡρακλεῶται καὶ οἱ Σινωπεῖς ὑπισχνοῦντο ὥστε ἐκπλεῖν. ὁ δὲ Ξενοφῶν ἐν τούτῳ ἐσίγα.

Ἀναστὰς δὲ Φιλήσιος καὶ Λύκων οἱ Ἀχαιοὶ ἔλεγον ὡς δεινὸν εἴη ἰδίᾳ μὲν Ξενοφῶντα πείθειν τε καταμένειν καὶ θύεσθαι ὑπὲρ τῆς μονῆς, εἰς δὲ τὸ κοινὸν μηδὲν ἀγορεύειν περὶ τούτων.

Ὥστε ἠναγκάσθη ὁ Ξενοφῶν ἀναστῆναι καὶ εἰπεῖν τάδε. Ἐγώ, ὦ ἄνδρες, θύομαι μὲν ὡς ὁρᾶτε ὁπόσα δύναμαι καὶ ὑπὲρ ὑμῶν καὶ ὑπὲρ ἐμαυτοῦ ὅπως ταῦτα τυγχάνω καὶ λέγων καὶ νοῶν καὶ πράττων ὁποῖα μέλλει ὑμῖν τε κάλλιστα καὶ ἄριστα ἔσεσθαι καὶ ἐμοί. καὶ νῦν ἐθυόμην περὶ αὐτοῦ τούτου εἰ ἄμεινον εἴη ἄρχεσθαι λέγειν εἰς ὑμᾶς καὶ πράττειν περὶ τούτων ἢ παντάπασι μηδὲ ἅπτεσθαι τοῦ πράγματος. Σιλανὸς δέ μοι ὁ μάντις ἀπεκρίνατο τὸ μὲν μέγιστον, τὰ ἱερὰ καλὰ εἶναι· ᾔδει γὰρ καὶ ἐμὲ οὐκ ἄπειρον ὄντα διὰ τὸ ἀεὶ παρεῖναι τοῖς ἱεροῖς· ἔλεξε δὲ ὅτι ἐν τοῖς ἱεροῖς φαίνοιτό τις δόλος καὶ ἐπιβουλὴ ἐμοί, ὡς ἄρα γιγνώσκων ὅτι αὐτὸς ἐπεβούλευε διαβάλλειν με πρὸς ὑμᾶς. ἐξήνεγκε γὰρ τὸν λόγον ὡς ἐγὼ πράττειν ταῦτα διανοοίμην ἤδη οὐ πείσας ὑμᾶς. ἐγὼ δὲ εἰ μὲν ἑώρων ἀποροῦντας ὑμᾶς, τοῦτ' ἂν ἐσκόπουν ἀφ' οὗ ἂν γένοιτο ὥστε λαβόντας ὑμᾶς πόλιν τὸν μὲν βουλόμενον ἀποπλεῖν ἤδη, τὸν δὲ μὴ βουλόμενον, ἐπεὶ κτήσαιτο ἱκανὰ ὥστε καὶ τοὺς ἑαυτοῦ οἰκείους ὠφελῆσαί τι. ἐπεὶ δὲ ὁρῶ ὑμῖν καὶ τὰ πλοῖα πέμποντας Ἡρακλεώτας καὶ Σινωπεῖς ὥστε ἐκπλεῖν, καὶ μισθὸν ὑπισχνουμένους ὑμῖν ἄνδρας ἀπὸ νουμηνίας, καλόν μοι δοκεῖ εἶναι σῳζομένους ἔνθα βουλόμεθα μισθὸν τῆς σωτηρίας λαμβάνειν, καὶ αὐτός τε παύομαι ἐκείνης τῆς διανοίας, καὶ ὁπόσοι πρὸς ἐμὲ προσῇσαν λέγοντες ὡς χρὴ ταῦτα πράττειν, ἀναπαύεσθαί φημι χρῆναι.

Οὕτω γὰρ γιγνώσκω· ὁμοῦ μὲν ὄντες πολλοὶ ὥσπερ νυνὶ δοκεῖτε ἄν μοι καὶ ἔντιμοι εἶναι καὶ ἔχειν τὰ ἐπιτήδεια· ἐν γὰρ τῷ κρατεῖν ἐστι καὶ τὸ λαμβάνειν τὰ τῶν ἡττόνων· διασπασθέντες δ' ἂν καὶ κατὰ μικρὰ γενομένης τῆς δυνάμεως οὔτ' ἂν τροφὴν δύναισθε λαμβάνειν οὔτε χαίροντες ἂν ἀπαλλάξαιτε. δοκεῖ οὖν μοι ἅπερ ὑμῖν, ἐκπορεύεσθαι εἰς τὴν Ἑλλάδα, καὶ ἐάν τις μέντοι ἀπολιπὼν ληφθῇ πρὶν ἐν ἀσφαλεῖ εἶναι πᾶν τὸ στράτευμα, κρίνεσθαι αὐτὸν ὡς ἀδικοῦντα. καὶ ὅτῳ δοκεῖ, ἔφη, ταῦτα, ἀράτω τὴν χεῖρα. ἀνέτειναν ἅπαντες.

Ὁ δὲ Σιλανὸς ἐβόα, καὶ ἐπεχείρει λέγειν ὡς δίκαιον εἴη ἀπιέναι τὸν βουλόμενον. οἱ δὲ στρατιῶται οὐκ ἠνείχοντο, ἀλλ' ἠπείλουν αὐτῷ ὅτι εἰ λήψονται ἀποδιδράσκοντα, τὴν δίκην ἐπιθήσοιεν. ἐντεῦθεν ἐπεὶ ἔγνωσαν οἱ Ἡρακλεῶται ὅτι ἐκπλεῖν δεδογμένον εἴη καὶ Ξενοφῶν αὐτὸς ἐπεψηφικὼς εἴη, τὰ μὲν πλοῖα πέμπουσι, τὰ δὲ χρήματα ἃ ὑπέσχοντο Τιμασίωνι καὶ Θώρακι ἐψευσμένοι ἦσαν. ἐνταῦθα δὲ ἐκπεπληγμένοι ἦσαν καὶ ἐδεδίεσαν τὴν στρατιὰν οἱ τὴν μισθοφορὰν ὑπεσχημένοι. παραλαβόντες οὖν οὗτοι καὶ τοὺς ἄλλους στρατηγοὺς οἷς ἀνεκεκοίνωντο ἃ πρόσθεν ἔπραττον, πάντες δ' ἦσαν πλὴν Νέωνος τοῦ Ἀσιναίου, ὃς Χειρισόφῳ ὑπεστρατήγει, Χειρίσοφος δὲ οὔπω παρῆν, ἔρχονται πρὸς Ξενοφῶντα, καὶ λέγουσιν ὅτι μεταμέλοι αὐτοῖς, καὶ δοκοίη κράτιστον εἶναι πλεῖν εἰς Φᾶσιν, ἐπεὶ πλοῖα ἔστι, καὶ κατασχεῖν τὴν Φασιανῶν χώραν. Αἰήτου δὲ υἱδοῦς ἐτύγχανε βασιλεύων αὐτῶν. Ξενοφῶν δὲ ἀπεκρίνατο ὅτι οὐδὲν ἂν τούτων εἴποι εἰς τὴν στρατιάν· ὑμεῖς δὲ ξυλλέξαντες, ἔφη, εἰ βούλεσθε, λέγετε. ἐνταῦθα ἀποδείκνυται Τιμασίων ὁ Δαρδανεὺς γνώμην οὐκ ἐκκλησιάζειν ἀλλὰ τοὺς αὐτοῦ ἕκαστον λοχαγοὺς πρῶτον πειρᾶσθαι πείθειν. καὶ ἀπελθόντες ταῦτ' ἐποίουν.

VII. Ταῦτα οὖν οἱ στρατιῶται ἀνεπύθοντο ταραττόμενα. καὶ ὁ Νέων λέγει ὡς Ξενοφῶν ἀναπεπεικὼς τοὺς ἄλλους στρατηγοὺς διανοεῖται ἄγειν τοὺς στρατιώτας ἐξαπατήσας πάλιν εἰς Φᾶσιν. ἀκούσαντες δ' οἱ στρατιῶται χαλεπῶς ἔφερον, καὶ ξύλλογοι ἐγίγνοντο καὶ κύκλοι ξυνίσταντο [καὶ μάλα φοβεροὶ ἦσαν μὴ ποιήσειαν οἷα καὶ τοὺς τῶν Κόλχων κήρυκας ἐποίησαν καὶ τοὺς ἀγορανόμους· ὅσοι μὴ εἰς τὴν θάλατταν κατέφυγον κατελεύσθησαν]. ἐπεὶ δὲ ᾐσθάνετο Ξενοφῶν, ἔδοξεν αὐτῷ ὡς τάχιστα ξυναγαγεῖν αὐτῶν ἀγοράν, καὶ μὴ ἐᾶσαι ξυλλεγῆναι αὐτομάτους· καὶ ἐκέλευσε τὸν κήρυκα ξυλλέξαι ἀγοράν. οἱ δ' ἐπεὶ τοῦ κήρυκος ἤκουσαν, ξυνέδραμον καὶ μάλα ἑτοίμως. ἐνταῦθα Ξενοφῶν τῶν μὲν στρατηγῶν οὐ κατηγόρει, ὅτι ἦλθον πρὸς αὐτόν, λέγει δὲ ὧδε.

Ἀκούω τινὰ διαβάλλειν, ὦ ἄνδρες, ἐμὲ ὡς ἐγὼ ἄρα ἐξαπατήσας ὑμᾶς μέλλω ἄγειν εἰς Φᾶσιν. ἀκούσατε οὖν μου πρὸς θεῶν, καὶ ἐὰν μὲν ἐγὼ φαίνωμαι ἀδικεῖν, οὐ χρή με ἐνθένδε ἀπελθεῖν πρὶν ἂν δῶ δίκην· ἂν δ᾽ ὑμῖν φαίνωνται ἀδικεῖν οἱ ἐμὲ διαβάλλοντες, οὕτως αὐτοῖς χρῆσθαι ὥσπερ ἄξιον. ὑμεῖς δέ, ἔφη, ἴστε δήπου ὅθεν ἥλιος ἀνίσχει καὶ ὅπου δύεται, καὶ ὅτι ἐὰν μέν τις εἰς τὴν Ἑλλάδα μέλλῃ ἰέναι, πρὸς ἑσπέραν δεῖ πορεύεσθαι· ἢν δέ τις βούληται εἰς τοὺς βαρβάρους, τοὔμπαλιν πρὸς ἕω. ἔστιν οὖν ὅστις τοῦτο ἂν δύναιτο ὑμᾶς ἐξαπατῆσαι ὡς ἥλιος ἔνθεν μὲν ἀνίσχει, δύεται ἐνταῦθα, ἔνθα δὲ δύεται, ἀνίσχει ἐντεῦθεν; ἀλλὰ μὴν καὶ τοῦτό γε ἐπίστασθε ὅτι βορέας μὲν ἔξω τοῦ Πόντου εἰς τὴν Ἑλλάδα φέρει, νότος δὲ εἴσω εἰς Φᾶσιν, καὶ λέγεται, ὅταν βορρᾶς πνέῃ, ὡς καλοὶ πλοῖ εἰσιν εἰς τὴν Ἑλλάδα. τοῦτ᾽ οὖν ἔστιν ὅπως τις ἂν ὑμᾶς ἐξαπατήσαι ὥστε ἐμβαίνειν ὁπόταν νότος πνέῃ; ἀλλὰ γὰρ ὁπόταν γαλήνη ᾖ ἐμβιβῶ. οὐκοῦν ἐγὼ μὲν ἐν ἑνὶ πλοίῳ πλεύσομαι, ὑμεῖς δὲ τοὐλάχιστον ἐν ἑκατόν. πῶς ἂν οὖν ἐγὼ ἢ βιασαίμην ὑμᾶς ξὺν ἐμοὶ πλεῖν μὴ βουλομένους ἢ ἐξαπατήσας ἄγοιμι; ποιῶ δ᾽ ὑμᾶς ἐξαπατηθέντας καὶ γοητευθέντας ὑπ᾽ ἐμοῦ ἥκειν εἰς Φᾶσιν· καὶ δὴ ἀποβαίνομεν εἰς τὴν χώραν· γνώσεσθε δήπου ὅτι οὐκ ἐν τῇ Ἑλλάδι ἐστέ· καὶ ἐγὼ μὲν ἔσομαι ὁ ἐξηπατηκὼς εἷς, ὑμεῖς δὲ οἱ ἐξηπατημένοι ἐγγὺς μυρίων ἔχοντες ὅπλα. πῶς ἂν οὖν ἀνὴρ μᾶλλον δοίη δίκην ἢ οὕτω περὶ αὑτοῦ τε καὶ ὑμῶν βουλευόμενος;

Ἀλλ᾽ οὗτοί εἰσιν οἱ λόγοι ἀνδρῶν καὶ ἠλιθίων κἀμοὶ φθονούντων, ὅτι ἐγὼ ὑφ᾽ ὑμῶν τιμῶμαι. καίτοι οὐ δικαίως γ᾽ ἄν μοι φθονοῖεν· τίνα γὰρ αὐτῶν ἐγὼ κωλύω ἢ λέγειν εἴ τις τι ἀγαθὸν δύναται ἐν ὑμῖν, ἢ μάχεσθαι εἴ τις ἐθέλει ὑπὲρ ὑμῶν τε καὶ ἑαυτοῦ, ἢ ἐγρηγορέναι περὶ τῆς ὑμετέρας ἀσφαλείας ἐπιμελούμενον; τί γάρ, ἄρχοντας αἱρουμένων ὑμῶν ἐγώ τινι ἐμποδών εἰμι; παρίημι, ἀρχέτω· μόνον ἀγαθόν τι ποιῶν ὑμᾶς φαινέσθω. ἀλλὰ γὰρ ἐμοὶ μὲν ἀρκεῖ περὶ τούτων τὰ εἰρημένα· εἰ δέ τις ὑμῶν ἢ αὐτὸς ἐξαπατηθῆναι ἂν οἴεται ταῦτα ἢ ἄλλον ἐξαπατῆσαι

12 ταῦτα, λέγων διδασκέτω. ὅταν δὲ τούτων ἅλις ἔχητε, μὴ ἀπέλθητε πρὶν ἂν ἀκούσητε οἷον ὁρῶ ἐν τῇ στρατιᾷ ἀρχόμενον πρᾶγμα· ὃ εἰ ἔπεισι καὶ ἔσται οἷον ὑποδείκνυσιν, ὥρα ἡμῖν βουλεύεσθαι ὑπὲρ ἡμῶν αὐτῶν μὴ κάκιστοί τε καὶ αἴσχιστοι ἄνδρες ἀποφαινώμεθα καὶ πρὸς θεῶν καὶ πρὸς ἀνθρώπων καὶ φίλων καὶ πολεμίων.

13 Ἀκούσαντες δὲ ταῦτα οἱ στρατιῶται ἐθαύμασάν τε ὅ,τι εἴη καὶ λέγειν ἐκέλευον. ἐκ τούτου ἄρχεται πάλιν· Ἐπίστασθέ που ὅτι χωρία ἦν ἐν τοῖς ὄρεσι βαρβαρικά, φίλια τοῖς Κερασουντίοις, ὅθεν κατιόντες τινὲς καὶ ἱερεῖα ἐπώλουν ἡμῖν καὶ ἄλλα ὧν εἶχον, δοκοῦσι δέ μοι καὶ ὑμῶν τινες εἰς τὸ ἐγγυτάτω χωρίον
14 τούτων ἐλθόντες ἀγοράσαντές τι πάλιν ἀπελθεῖν. τοῦτο καταμαθὼν Κλεάρετος ὁ λοχαγὸς ὅτι καὶ μικρὸν εἴη καὶ ἀφύλακτον διὰ τὸ φίλιον νομίζειν εἶναι, ἔρχεται ἐπ᾽ αὐτοὺς τῆς νυκτὸς ὡς
15 πορθήσων, οὐδενὶ ἡμῶν εἰπών. διενενόητο δέ, εἰ λάβοι τόδε τὸ χωρίον, εἰς μὲν τὸ στράτευμα μηκέτι ἐλθεῖν, εἰσβὰς δὲ εἰς πλοῖον ἐν ᾧ ἐτύγχανον οἱ ξύσκηνοι αὐτοῦ παραπλέοντες, καὶ ἐνθέμενος εἴ τι λάβοι, ἀποπλέων οἴχεσθαι ἔξω τοῦ Πόντου. καὶ ταῦτα ξυνωμολόγησαν αὐτῷ οἱ ἐκ τοῦ πλοίου σύσκηνοι, ὡς ἐγὼ νῦν
16 αἰσθάνομαι. παρακαλέσας οὖν ὁπόσους ἔπειθεν ἦγεν ἐπὶ τὸ χωρίον. πορευόμενον δ᾽ αὐτὸν φθάνει ἡμέρα γενομένη, καὶ ξυστάντες οἱ ἄνθρωποι ἀπὸ ἰσχυρῶν τόπων βάλλοντες καὶ παίοντες τόν τε Κλεάρετον ἀποκτείνουσι καὶ τῶν ἄλλων συχνούς,
17 οἱ δέ τινες καὶ εἰς Κερασοῦντα αὐτῶν ἀποχωροῦσι. ταῦτα δ᾽ ἦν ἐν τῇ ἡμέρᾳ ᾗ ἡμεῖς δεῦρο ἐξωρμῶμεν πεζῇ· τῶν δὲ πλεόντων ἔτι τινὲς ἦσαν ἐν Κερασοῦντι, οὔπω ἀνηγμένοι.

Μετὰ τοῦτο, ὡς οἱ Κερασούντιοι λέγουσιν, ἀφικνοῦνται τῶν ἐκ τοῦ χωρίου τρεῖς ἄνδρες τῶν γεραιτέρων πρὸς τὸ κοινὸν τὸ ἡμέτερον χρῄζοντες ἐλθεῖν. ἐπεὶ δ᾽ ἡμᾶς οὐ κατέλαβον, πρὸς τοὺς Κερασουντίους ἔλεγον ὅτι θαυμάζοιεν τί ἡμῖν δόξειεν ἐλθεῖν
18 ἐπ᾽ αὐτούς. ἐπεὶ μέντοι σφεῖς λέγειν, ἔφασαν, ὅτι οὐκ ἀπὸ κοινοῦ γένοιτο τὸ πρᾶγμα, ἥδεσθαί τε αὐτοὺς καὶ μέλλειν ἐνθάδε πλεῖν, ὡς ἡμῖν λέξαι τὰ γενόμενα καὶ τοὺς νεκροὺς κελεύειν
19 αὐτοὺς θάπτειν λαβόντας. τῶν δ᾽ ἀποφυγόντων τινὰς Ἑλλήνων τυχεῖν ἔτι ὄντας ἐν Κερασοῦντι· αἰσθόμενοι δὲ τοὺς βαρβάρους

ὅποι ἴοιεν αὐτοί τε ἐτόλμησαν βαλεῖν τοῖς λίθοις καὶ τοῖς ἄλλοις
παρεκελεύοντο. καὶ οἱ ἄνδρες ἀποθνῄσκουσι τρεῖς ὄντες οἱ
πρέσβεις καταλευσθέντες.

Ἐπεὶ δὲ τοῦτο ἐγένετο, ἔρχονται πρὸς ἡμᾶς οἱ Κερασούντιοι
85 καὶ λέγουσι τὸ πρᾶγμα· καὶ ἡμεῖς οἱ στρατηγοὶ ἀκούσαντες
ἠχθόμεθά τε τοῖς γεγενημένοις καὶ ἐβουλευόμεθα ξὺν τοῖς Κερασουντίοις ὅπως ἂν ταφείησαν οἱ τῶν Ἑλλήνων ιεκροί. συγκα-
θήμενοι δ' ἔξωθεν τῶν ὅπλων ἐξαίφνης ἀκούομεν θορύβου πολλοῦ
Παῖε παῖε, βάλλε βάλλε, καὶ τάχα δὴ ὁρῶμεν πολλοὺς προσ-
90 θέοντας λίθους ἔχοντας ἐν ταῖς χερσί, τοὺς δὲ καὶ ἀναιρουμένους.
καὶ οἱ μὲν Κερασούντιοι, ὡς δὴ καὶ ἑωρακότες τὸ παρ' ἑαυτοῖς
πρᾶγμα, δείσαντες ἀποχωροῦσι πρὸς τὰ πλοῖα. ἦσαν δὲ νὴ
Δία καὶ ἡμῶν οἳ ἔδεισαν. ἐγώ γε μὴν ἦλθον πρὸς αὐτοὺς καὶ
ἠρώτων ὅ,τι ἐστὶ τὸ πρᾶγμα. τῶν δὲ ἦσαν μὲν οἳ οὐδὲν ᾔδεσαν,
95 ὅμως δὲ λίθους εἶχον ἐν ταῖς χερσίν. ἐπεὶ δὲ εἰδότι τινὶ ἐπέτυχον, λέγει μοι ὅτι οἱ ἀγορανόμοι δεινότατα ποιοῦσι τὸ στράτευμα. ἐν τούτῳ τις ὁρᾷ τὸν ἀγορανόμον Ζήλαρχον πρὸς τὴν
θάλατταν ἀποχωροῦντα, καὶ ἀνέκραγεν· οἱ δὲ ὡς ἤκουσαν,
ὥσπερ ἢ συὸς ἀγρίου ἢ ἐλάφου φανέντος ἵενται ἐπ' αὐτόν. οἱ
100 δ' αὖ Κερασούντιοι ὡς εἶδον ὁρμῶντας καθ' αὑτούς, σαφῶς νομίζοντες ἐπὶ σφᾶς ἵεσθαι, φεύγουσι δρόμῳ καὶ ἐμπίπτουσιν εἰς
τὴν θάλατταν. ξυνεισέπεσον δὲ καὶ ἡμῶν αὐτῶν τινες, καὶ ἐπνί-
γετο ὅστις νεῖν μὴ ἐτύγχανεν ἐπιστάμενος. καὶ τούτους τί
δοκεῖτε; ἠδίκουν μὲν οὐδέν, ἔδεισαν δὲ μὴ λύττα τις ὥσπερ
105 κυσὶν ἡμῖν ἐμπεπτώκοι.

Εἰ οὖν ταῦτα τοιαῦτα ἔσται, θεάσασθε οἵα ἡ κατάστασις
ἡμῖν ἔσται τῆς στρατιᾶς. ὑμεῖς μὲν οἱ πάντες οὐκ ἔσεσθε
κύριοι οὔτε ἀνελέσθαι πόλεμον ᾧ ἂν βούλησθε οὔτε καταλῦσαι,
ἰδίᾳ δὲ ὁ βουλόμενος ἄξει στράτευμα ἐφ' ὅ,τι ἂν θέλῃ. κἄν
110 τινες πρὸς ὑμᾶς ἴωσι πρέσβεις εἰρήνης δεόμενοι ἢ ἄλλου τινός,
κατακτείναντες τούτους οἱ βουλόμενοι ποιήσουσιν ὑμᾶς τῶν
λόγων μὴ ἀκοῦσαι τῶν πρὸς ὑμᾶς ἰόντων. ἔπειτα δὲ οὓς μὲν ἂν
ὑμεῖς πάντες ἕλησθε ἄρχοντας, ἐν οὐδεμιᾷ χώρᾳ ἔσονται, ὅστις
δὲ ἂν ἑαυτὸν ἕληται στρατηγὸν καὶ ἐθέλῃ λέγειν Βάλλε βάλλε,
115 οὗτος ἔσται ἱκανὸς καὶ ἄρχοντα κατακανεῖν καὶ ἰδιώτην ὃν ἂν

ὑμῶν ἐθέλῃ ἄκριτον, ἢν ὦσιν οἱ πεισόμενοι αὐτῷ, ὥσπερ καὶ νῦν ἐγένετο. οἷα δὲ ὑμῖν καὶ διαπεπράχασιν οἱ αὐθαίρετοι οὗτοι στρατηγοὶ σκέψασθε. Ζήλαρχος μὲν ὁ ἀγορανόμος εἰ μὲν ἀδικεῖ ὑμᾶς, οἴχεται ἀποπλέων οὐ δοὺς ὑμῖν δίκην· εἰ δὲ μὴ ἀδικεῖ, φεύγει ἐκ τοῦ στρατεύματος δείσας μὴ ἀδίκως ἄκριτος ἀποθάνῃ. οἱ δὲ καταλεύσαντες τοὺς πρέσβεις διεπράξαντο ὑμῖν μόνοις μὲν τῶν Ἑλλήνων εἰς Κερασοῦντα μὴ ἀσφαλὲς εἶναι ἂν μὴ σὺν ἰσχύι ἀφικνῆσθε· τοὺς δὲ νεκροὺς οὓς πρόσθεν αὐτοὶ οἱ κατακανόντες ἐκέλευον θάπτειν, τούτους διεπράξαντο μηδὲ ξὺν κηρυκείῳ ἔτι ἀσφαλὲς εἶναι ἀνελέσθαι. τίς γὰρ ἐθελήσει κῆρυξ ἰέναι κήρυκας ἀπεκτονώς; ἀλλ᾽ ἡμεῖς Κερασουντίων θάψαι αὐτοὺς ἐδεήθημεν. εἰ μὲν οὖν ταῦτα καλῶς ἔχει, δοξάτω ὑμῖν, ἵνα ὡς τοιούτων ἐσομένων καὶ φυλακὴν ἰδίᾳ ποιήσῃ τις καὶ τὰ ἐρυμνὰ ὑπερδέξια πειρᾶται ἔχων σκηνοῦν. εἰ μέντοι ὑμῖν δοκεῖ θηρίων ἀλλὰ μὴ ἀνθρώπων εἶναι τὰ τοιαῦτα ἔργα, σκοπεῖτε παῦλάν τινα αὐτῶν· εἰ δέ μή, πρὸς Διὸς πῶς ἢ θεοῖς θύσομεν ἡδέως ποιοῦντες ἔργα ἀσεβῆ, ἢ πολεμίοις πῶς μαχούμεθα, ἢν ἀλλήλους κατακαίνωμεν; πόλις δὲ φιλία τίς ἡμᾶς δέξεται, ἥτις ἂν ὁρᾷ τοσαύτην ἀνομίαν ἐν ἡμῖν; ἀγορὰν δὲ τίς ἄξει θαρρῶν, ἢν περὶ τὰ μέγιστα τοιαῦτα ἐξαμαρτάνοντες φαινώμεθα; οὗ δὲ δὴ πάντων οἰόμεθα τεύξεσθαι ἐπαίνου, τίς ἡμᾶς τοιούτους ὄντας ἐπαινέσει; ἡμεῖς μὲν γὰρ οἶδ᾽ ὅτι πονηροὺς ἂν φαίημεν εἶναι τοὺς τὰ τοιαῦτα ποιοῦντας.

Ἐκ τούτου ἀνιστάμενοι πάντες ἔλεγον τοὺς μὲν τούτων ἄρξαντας δοῦναι δίκην, τοῦ δὲ λοιποῦ μηκέτι ἐξεῖναι ἀνομίας ἄρξαι· ἐὰν δέ τις ἄρξῃ, ἄγεσθαι αὐτοὺς ἐπὶ θανάτῳ· τοὺς δὲ στρατηγοὺς εἰς δίκας πάντας καταστῆσαι· εἶναι δὲ δίκας καὶ εἴ τι ἄλλο τις ἠδίκητο ἐξ οὗ Κῦρος ἀπέθανε· δικαστὰς δὲ τοὺς λοχαγοὺς ἐποιήσαντο. παραινοῦντος δὲ Ξενοφῶντος καὶ τῶν μάντεων συμβουλευόντων ἔδοξε καθῆραι τὸ στράτευμα. καὶ ἐγένετο καθαρμός.

VIII. Ἔδοξε δὲ καὶ τοὺς στρατηγοὺς δίκην ὑποσχεῖν τοῦ παρεληλυθότος χρόνου. καὶ διδόντων Φιλήσιος μὲν ὦφλε καὶ Ξανθικλῆς τῆς φυλακῆς τῶν γαυλικῶν χρημάτων τὸ μείωμα εἴκοσι μνᾶς, Σοφαίνετος δέ, ὅτι αἱρεθεὶς * * κατημέλει, δέκα μνᾶς.

Ξενοφῶντος δὲ κατηγόρησάν τινες φάσκοντες παίεσθαι ὑπ' αὐτοῦ καὶ ὡς ὑβρίζοντος τὴν κατηγορίαν ἐποιοῦντο. καὶ ὁ Ξενοφῶν ἐκέλευσεν εἰπεῖν τὸν πρῶτον λέξαντα ποῦ καὶ ἐπλήγη. ὁ δὲ ἀπεκρίνατο· Ὅπου καὶ ῥίγει ἀπωλλύμεθα καὶ χιὼν πλείστη ἦν. ὁ δὲ εἶπεν· Ἀλλὰ μὴν χειμῶνός γε ὄντος οἵου λέγεις, σίτου δὲ ἐπιλελοιπότος, οἴνου δὲ μηδ' ὀσφραίνεσθαι παρόν, ὑπὸ δὲ πόνων πολλῶν ἀπαγορευόντων, πολεμίων δὲ ἑπομένων, εἰ ἐν τοιούτῳ καιρῷ ὕβριζον, ὁμολογῶ καὶ τῶν ὄνων ὑβριστότερος εἶναι, οἷς φασιν ὑπὸ τῆς ὕβρεως κόπον οὐκ ἐγγίγνεσθαι. ὅμως δὲ καὶ λέξον, ἔφη, ἐκ τίνος ἐπλήγης. πότερον ᾔτουν τί σε καὶ ἐπεί μοι οὐκ ἐδίδους ἔπαιον; ἀλλ' ἀπῄτουν; ἀλλὰ περὶ παιδικῶν μαχόμενος; ἀλλὰ μεθύων ἐπαρῴνησα; ἐπεὶ δὲ τούτων οὐδὲν ἔφησεν, ἐπήρετο αὐτὸν εἰ ὁπλιτεύει. οὐκ ἔφη· πάλιν εἰ πελτάζοι. οὐδὲ τοῦτ' ἔφη, ἀλλ' ἡμίονον ἐλαύνειν ταχθεὶς ὑπὸ τῶν συσκήνων ἐλεύθερος ὤν. ἐνταῦθα δὴ ἀναγιγνώσκει αὐτὸν καὶ ἤρετο· Ἦ σὺ εἶ ὁ τὸν κάμνοντα ἀγαγών; Ναὶ μὰ Δί', ἔφη· σὺ γὰρ ἠνάγκαζες· τὰ δὲ τῶν ἐμῶν συσκήνων σκεύη διέρριψας. Ἀλλ' ἡ μὲν διάρριψις, ἔφη ὁ Ξενοφῶν, τοιαύτη τις ἐγένετο. διέδωκα ἄλλοις ἄγειν καὶ ἐκέλευσα πρὸς ἐμὲ ἀπαγαγεῖν, καὶ ἀπολαβὼν ἅπαντα σῶα ἀπέδωκά σοι, ἐπειδὴ καὶ σὺ ἐμοὶ ἀπέδειξας τὸν ἄνδρα. οἷον δὲ τὸ πρᾶγμα ἐγένετο ἀκούσατε, ἔφη· καὶ γὰρ ἄξιον.

Ἀνὴρ κατελείπετο διὰ τὸ μηκέτι δύνασθαι πορεύεσθαι. καὶ ἐγὼ τὸν μὲν ἄνδρα τοσοῦτον ἐγίγνωσκον ὅτι εἷς ἡμῶν εἴη· ἠνάγκασα δὲ σὲ τοῦτον ἄγειν, ὡς μὴ ἀπόλοιτο· καὶ γάρ, ὡς ἐγὼ οἶμαι, πολέμιοι ἡμῖν ἐφείποντο. συνέφη τοῦτο ὁ ἄνθρωπος. Οὐκοῦν, ἔφη ὁ Ξενοφῶν, ἐπεὶ προὔπεμψά σε, καταλαμβάνω αὖθις σὺν τοῖς ὀπισθοφύλαξι προσιὼν βόθρον ὀρύττοντα ὡς κατορύξοντα τὸν ἄνθρωπον, καὶ ἐπιστὰς ἐπῄνουν σε. ἐπεὶ δὲ παρεστηκότων ἡμῶν συνέκαμψε τὸ σκέλος ἀνήρ, ἀνέκραγον οἱ παρόντες ὅτι ζῇ ὁ ἀνήρ, σὺ δ' εἶπας Ὁπόσα γε βούλεται· ὡς ἔγωγε αὐτὸν οὐκ ἄξω. ἐνταῦθα ἔπαισά σε· ἀληθῆ λέγεις· ἔδοξας γάρ μοι εἰδότι ἐοικέναι ὅτι ἔζη. Τί οὖν; ἔφη, ἧττόν τι ἀπέθανεν, ἐπεὶ ἐγώ σοι ἀπέδειξα αὐτόν; Καὶ γὰρ ἡμεῖς, ἔφη ὁ Ξενοφῶν, πάντες ἀποθανούμεθα· τούτου οὖν ἕνεκα ζῶντας ἡμᾶς δεῖ κατορυχθῆναι;

Τοῦτον μὲν ἀνέκραγον ὡς ὀλίγας παίσειεν· ἄλλους δ' ἐκέλευε λέγειν διὰ τί ἕκαστος ἐπλήγη. ἐπεὶ δὲ οὐκ ἀνίσταντο, αὐτὸς ἔλεγεν· Ἐγώ, ὦ ἄνδρες, ὁμολογῶ παῖσαι δὴ ἄνδρας ἕνεκεν ἀταξίας ὅσοις σῴζεσθαι μὲν ἤρκει δι' ὑμῶν ἐν τάξει τε ἰόντων καὶ μαχομένων ὅπου δέοι, αὐτοὶ δὲ λιπόντες τὰς τάξεις προθέοντες ἁρπάζειν ἤθελον καὶ ἡμῶν πλεονεκτεῖν. εἰ δὲ τοῦτο πάντες ἐποιοῦμεν, ἅπαντες ἂν ἀπωλόμεθα. ἤδη δὲ καὶ μαλακιζόμενόν τινα καὶ οὐκ ἐθέλοντα ἀνίστασθαι ἀλλὰ προϊέμενον αὐτὸν τοῖς πολεμίοις καὶ ἔπαισα καὶ ἐβιασάμην πορεύεσθαι. ἐν γὰρ τῷ ἰσχυρῷ χειμῶνι καὶ αὐτός ποτε ἀναμένων τινὰς συσκευαζομένους καθεζόμενος συχνὸν χρόνον κατέμαθον ἀναστὰς μόλις καὶ τὰ σκέλη ἐκτείνας. ἐν ἐμαυτῷ οὖν πεῖραν λαβὼν ἐκ τούτου καὶ ἄλλον, ὁπότε ἴδοιμι καθήμενον καὶ βλακεύοντα, ἤλαυνον· τὸ γὰρ κινεῖσθαι καὶ ἀνδρίζεσθαι παρεῖχε θερμασίαν τινὰ καὶ ὑγρότητα, τὸ δὲ καθῆσθαι καὶ ἡσυχίαν ἔχειν ἑώρων ὑπουργὸν ὂν τῷ τε ἀποπήγνυσθαι τὸ αἷμα καὶ τῷ ἀποσήπεσθαι τοὺς τῶν ποδῶν δακτύλους, ἅπερ πολλοὺς καὶ ὑμεῖς ἴστε παθόντας. ἄλλον δέ γε ἴσως ἀπολειπόμενόν που διὰ ῥᾳστώνην καὶ κωλύοντα καὶ ὑμᾶς τοὺς πρόσθεν καὶ ἡμᾶς τοὺς ὄπισθεν πορεύεσθαι ἔπαισα πύξ, ὅπως μὴ λόγχῃ ὑπὸ τῶν πολεμίων παίοιτο. καὶ γὰρ οὖν νῦν ἔξεστιν αὐτοῖς σωθεῖσιν, εἴ τι ὑπ' ἐμοῦ ἔπαθον παρὰ τὸ δίκαιον, δίκην λαβεῖν. εἰ δ' ἐπὶ τοῖς πολεμίοις ἐγένοντο, τί μέγα ἂν οὕτως ἔπαθον ὅτου δίκην ἂν ἠξίουν λαμβάνειν;

Ἁπλοῦς μοι, ἔφη, ὁ λόγος· εἰ μὲν ἐπ' ἀγαθῷ ἐκόλασά τινα, ἀξιῶ ὑπέχειν δίκην οἵαν καὶ γονεῖς υἱοῖς καὶ διδάσκαλοι παισί· καὶ γὰρ οἱ ἰατροὶ καίουσι καὶ τέμνουσιν ἐπ' ἀγαθῷ. εἰ δὲ ὕβρει νομίζετέ με ταῦτα πράττειν, ἐνθυμήθητε ὅτι νῦν ἐγὼ θαρρῶ σὺν τοῖς θεοῖς μᾶλλον ἢ τότε καὶ θρασύτερός εἰμι νῦν ἢ τότε καὶ οἶνον πλείω πίνω, ἀλλ' ὅμως οὐδένα παίω· ἐν εὐδίᾳ γὰρ ὁρῶ ὑμᾶς. ὅταν δὲ χειμὼν ᾖ καὶ θάλαττα μεγάλη ἐπιφέρηται, οὐχ ὁρᾶτε ὅτι καὶ νεύματος μόνου ἕνεκα χαλεπαίνει μὲν πρῳρεὺς τοῖς ἐν πρῴρᾳ, χαλεπαίνει δὲ κυβερνήτης τοῖς ἐν πρύμνῃ; ἱκανὰ γὰρ ἐν τῷ τοιούτῳ καὶ μικρὰ ἁμαρτηθέντα πάντα συνεπιτρῖψαι. ὅτι δὲ δικαίως ἔπαιον αὐτοὺς καὶ ὑμεῖς κατεδικάσατε· ἔχοντες ξίφη, οὐ ψήφους, παρέστατε, καὶ ἐξῆν ὑμῖν ἐπικουρεῖν αὐτοῖς, εἰ ἐβούλεσθε· ἀλλὰ μὰ Δία οὔτε τούτοις ἐπεκουρεῖτε οὔτε σὺν ἐμοὶ τὸν ἀτακτοῦντα ἐπαίετε. τοιγαροῦν ἐξουσίαν ἐποιήσατε τοῖς κακοῖς αὐτῶν ὑβρίζειν ἐῶντες αὐτούς.

Οἶμαι γάρ, εἰ ἐθέλετε σκοπεῖν, τοὺς αὐτοὺς εὑρήσετε καὶ τότε κακίστους καὶ νῦν ὑβριστοτάτους. Βοΐσκος γοῦν ὁ πύκτης ὁ Θετταλὸς τότε μὲν διεμάχετο ὡς κάμνων ἀσπίδα μὴ φέρειν, νῦν δέ, ὡς ἀκούω, Κοτυωριτῶν πολλοὺς ἤδη ἀποδέδυκεν. ἢν οὖν σωφρονῆτε, τοῦτον τἀναντία ποιήσετε ἢ τοὺς κύνας ποιοῦσι· τοὺς μὲν γὰρ κύνας τοὺς χαλεποὺς τὰς μὲν ἡμέρας διδέασι, τὰς δὲ νύκτας ἀφιᾶσι, τοῦτον δέ, ἢν σωφρονῆτε, τὴν νύκτα μὲν δήσετε, τὴν δὲ ἡμέραν ἀφήσετε.

Ἀλλὰ γάρ, ἔφη, θαυμάζω ὅτι εἰ μέν τινι ὑμῶν ἀπηχθόμην, μέμνησθε καὶ οὐ σιωπᾶτε, εἰ δέ τῳ ἢ χειμῶνα ἐπεκούρησα ἢ πολέμιον ἀπήρυξα ἢ ἀσθενοῦντι ἢ ἀποροῦντι συνεξεπόρισά τι, τούτων δὲ οὐδεὶς μέμνηται, οὐδ' εἴ τινα καλῶς τι ποιοῦντα ἐπῄνεσα οὐδ' εἴ τινα ἄνδρα ὄντα ἀγαθὸν ἐτίμησα ὡς ἐδυνάμην, οὐδὲν τούτων μέμνησθε. ἀλλὰ μὴν καλόν τε καὶ δίκαιον καὶ ὅσιον καὶ ἥδιον τῶν ἀγαθῶν μᾶλλον ἢ τῶν κακῶν μεμνῆσθαι.

Ἐκ τούτου μὲν δὴ ἀνίσταντο καὶ ἀνεμίμνησκον. καὶ περιεγένετο ὥστε καλῶς ἔχειν.

BOOK VI

1 I. Ἐκ τούτου δὲ ἐν τῇ διατριβῇ οἱ μὲν ἀπὸ τῆς ἀγορᾶς ἔζων, οἱ δὲ καὶ ληζόμενοι ἐκ τῆς Παφλαγονίας. ἐκλώπευον δὲ καὶ οἱ Παφλαγόνες εὖ μάλα τοὺς ἀποσκεδαννυμένους, καὶ τῆς νυκτὸς τοὺς πρόσω σκηνοῦντας ἐπειρῶντο κακουργεῖν· καὶ πολε-
2 μικώτατα πρὸς ἀλλήλους εἶχον ἐκ τούτων. ὁ δὲ Κορύλας, ὃς ἐτύγχανε τότε Παφλαγονίας ἄρχων, πέμπει παρὰ τοὺς Ἕλληνας πρέσβεις ἔχοντας ἵππους καὶ στολὰς καλάς, λέγοντας ὅτι Κορύ-
3 λας ἕτοιμος εἴη τοὺς Ἕλληνας μήτε ἀδικεῖν μήτε ἀδικεῖσθαι. οἱ δὲ στρατηγοὶ ἀπεκρίναντο ὅτι περὶ μὲν τούτων σὺν τῇ στρατιᾷ βουλεύσοιντο, ἐπὶ ξένια δὲ ἐδέχοντο αὐτούς· παρεκάλεσαν δὲ καὶ τῶν ἄλλων ἀνδρῶν οὓς ἐδόκουν δικαιοτάτους εἶναι.

4 Θύσαντες δὲ βοῦς τῶν αἰχμαλώτων καὶ ἄλλα ἱερεῖα εὐωχίαν μὲν ἀρκοῦσαν παρεῖχον, κατακείμενοι δὲ ἐν σκίμποσιν ἐδείπνουν, καὶ ἔπινον ἐκ κερατίνων ποτηρίων, οἷς ἐνετύγχανον ἐν τῇ χώρᾳ.
5 ἐπεὶ δὲ σπονδαί τε ἐγένοντο καὶ ἐπαιάνισαν, ἀνέστησαν πρῶτον μὲν Θρᾷκες καὶ πρὸς αὐλὸν ὠρχήσαντο σὺν τοῖς ὅπλοις καὶ ἥλλοντο ὑψηλά τε καὶ κούφως καὶ ταῖς μαχαίραις ἐχρῶντο·
6 τέλος δὲ ὁ ἕτερος τὸν ἕτερον παίει, ὡς πᾶσιν ἐδόκει· ὁ δ' ἔπεσε τεχνικῶς πως. καὶ ἀνέκραγον οἱ Παφλαγόνες. καὶ ὃ μὲν σκυλεύσας τὰ ὅπλα τοῦ ἑτέρου ἐξῄει ᾄδων τὸν Σιτάλκαν· ἄλλοι δὲ
7 τῶν Θρᾳκῶν τὸν ἕτερον ἐξέφερον ὡς τεθνηκότα· ἦν δὲ οὐδὲν πεπονθώς. μετὰ τοῦτο Αἰνιᾶνες καὶ Μάγνητες ἀνέστησαν, οἳ
8 ὠρχοῦντο τὴν καρπαίαν καλουμένην ἐν τοῖς ὅπλοις. ὁ δὲ τρόπος τῆς ὀρχήσεως ἦν, ὃ μὲν παραθέμενος τὰ ὅπλα σπείρει καὶ ζευγηλατεῖ, πυκνὰ δὲ στρεφόμενος ὡς φοβούμενος, λῃστὴς δὲ προσέρχεται. ὃ δ' ἐπειδὰν προΐδηται, ἀπαντᾷ ἁρπάσας τὰ ὅπλα καὶ μάχεται πρὸ τοῦ ζεύγους· καὶ οὗτοι ταῦτ' ἐποίουν ἐν ῥυθμῷ πρὸς τὸν αὐλόν· καὶ τέλος ὁ λῃστὴς δήσας τὸν ἄνδρα καὶ τὸ ζεῦγος ἀπάγει· ἐνίοτε δὲ καὶ ὁ ζευγηλάτης τὸν λῃστήν· εἶτα παρὰ τοὺς βοῦς ζεύξας ὀπίσω τὼ χεῖρε δεδεμένον ἐλαύνει. μετὰ τοῦτο Μυσὸς εἰσῆλθεν ἐν ἑκατέρᾳ τῇ χειρὶ ἔχων πέλτην, καὶ

τοτὲ μὲν ὡς δύο ἀντιτα ττομένων μιμούμενος ὠρχεῖτο, τοτὲ δὲ ὡς
πρὸς ἕνα ἐχρῆτο ταῖς πέλταις, τοτὲ δ' ἐδινεῖτο καὶ ἐξεκυβίστα
ἔχων τὰς πέλτας, ὥστε ὄψιν καλὴν φαίνεσθαι. τέλος δὲ τὸ
περσικὸν ὠρχεῖτο κρούων τὰς πέλτας καὶ ὤκλαζε καὶ ἐξανί-
στατο· καὶ ταῦτα πάντα ἐν ῥυθμῷ ἐποίει πρὸς τὸν αὐλόν. ἐπὶ
δὲ τούτῳ οἱ Μαντινεῖς καὶ ἄλλοι τινὲς τῶν Ἀρκάδων ἀναστάντες
ἐξοπλισάμενοι ὡς ἐδύναντο κάλλιστα ᾖσάν τε ἐν ῥυθμῷ πρὸς
τὸν ἐνόπλιον ῥυθμὸν αὐλούμενοι καὶ ἐπαιάνισαν καὶ ὠρχήσαντο
ὥσπερ ἐν ταῖς πρὸς τοὺς θεοὺς προσόδοις. ὁρῶντες δὲ οἱ Παφλαγόνες δεινὰ ἐποιοῦντο πάσας τὰς ὀρχήσεις ἐν ὅπλοις εἶναι.
ἐπὶ τούτοις ὁρῶν ὁ Μυσὸς ἐκπεπληγμένους αὐτούς, πείσας τῶν
Ἀρκάδων τινὰ πεπαμένον ὀρχηστρίδα εἰσάγει σκευάσας ὡς ἐδύνατο κάλλιστα καὶ ἀσπίδα δοὺς κούφην αὐτῇ. ἡ δὲ ὠρχήσατο
πυρρίχην ἐλαφρῶς. ἐνταῦθα κρότος ἦν πολύς, καὶ οἱ Παφλαγόνες ἤροντο εἰ καὶ γυναῖκες συνεμάχοντο αὐτοῖς. οἱ δ' ἔλεγον
ὅτι αὗται καὶ αἱ τρεψάμεναι εἶεν βασιλέα ἐκ τοῦ στρατοπέδου.
τῇ μὲν νυκτὶ ταύτῃ τοῦτο τὸ τέλος ἐγένετο.

Τῇ δὲ ὑστεραίᾳ προσῆγον αὐτοὺς εἰς τὸ στράτευμα· καὶ
ἔδοξε τοῖς στρατιώταις μήτε ἀδικεῖν Παφλαγόνας μήτε ἀδικεῖσθαι. μετὰ τοῦτο οἱ μὲν πρέσβεις ᾤχοντο· οἱ δὲ Ἕλληνες,
ἐπειδὴ πλοῖα ἱκανὰ ἐδόκει παρεῖναι, ἀναβάντες ἔπλεον ἡμέραν
καὶ νύκτα πνεύματι καλῷ ἐν ἀριστερᾷ ἔχοντες τὴν Παφλαγονίαν.
τῇ δ' ἄλλῃ ἀφικνοῦνται εἰς Σινώπην καὶ ὡρμίσαντο εἰς Ἁρμή-
νην τῆς Σινώπης. Σινωπεῖς δὲ οἰκοῦσι μὲν ἐν τῇ Παφλαγονικῇ,
Μιλησίων δὲ ἄποικοί εἰσιν. οὗτοι δὲ ξένια πέμπουσι τοῖς
Ἕλλησιν ἀλφίτων μεδίμνους τρισχιλίους, οἴνου δὲ κεράμια
χίλια καὶ πεντακόσια.

Καὶ Χειρίσοφος ἐνταῦθα ἦλθε τριήρη ἔχων. καὶ οἱ μὲν
στρατιῶται προσεδόκων ἄγοντά τι σφίσιν ἥκειν· ὁ δ' ἦγε μὲν
οὐδέν, ἀπήγγελλε δὲ ὅτι ἐπαινοίη αὐτοὺς καὶ Ἀναξίβιος ὁ ναύαρχος καὶ οἱ ἄλλοι, καὶ ὅτι ὑπισχνεῖτο Ἀναξίβιος, εἰ ἀφίκοιντο
ἔξω τοῦ Πόντου, μισθοφορὰν αὐτοῖς ἔσεσθαι. καὶ ἐν ταύτῃ τῇ
Ἁρμήνῃ ἔμειναν οἱ στρατιῶται ἡμέρας πέντε.

Ὡς δὲ τῆς Ἑλλάδος ἐδόκουν ἐγγὺς γίγνεσθαι, ἤδη μᾶλλον ἢ
πρόσθεν εἰσῄει αὐτοὺς ὅπως ἂν καὶ ἔχοντές τι οἴκαδε ἀφίκωνται.

18 ἡγήσαντο οὖν, εἰ ἕνα ἕλοιντο ἄρχοντα, μᾶλλον ἂν ἢ πολυαρχίας
οὔσης δύνασθαι τὸν ἕνα χρῆσθαι τῷ στρατεύματι καὶ νυκτὸς καὶ
ἡμέρας, καὶ εἴ τι δέοι λανθάνειν, μᾶλλον ἂν κρύπτεσθαι, καὶ εἴ
τι αὖ δέοι φθάνειν, ἧττον ἂν ὑστερίζειν· οὐ γὰρ ἂν λόγων δεῖν
πρὸς ἀλλήλους, ἀλλὰ τὸ δόξαν τῷ ἑνὶ περαίνεσθαι ἄν· τὸν δ'
ἔμπροσθεν χρόνον ἐκ τῆς νικώσης ἔπραττον πάντα οἱ στρατηγοί.

19 Ὡς δὲ ταῦτα διενοοῦντο, ἐτράποντο ἐπὶ τὸν Ξενοφῶντα· καὶ
οἱ λοχαγοὶ ἔλεγον προσιόντες αὐτῷ ὅτι ἡ στρατιὰ οὕτω γιγνώσκει, καὶ εὔνοιαν ἐνδεικνύμενος ἕκαστος ἔπειθεν αὐτὸν ὑποστῆναι
20 τὴν ἀρχήν. ὁ δὲ Ξενοφῶν τῇ μὲν ἐβούλετο ταῦτα, νομίζων καὶ
τὴν τιμὴν μείζω οὕτως ἑαυτῷ γίγνεσθαι πρὸς τοὺς φίλους καὶ εἰς
τὴν πόλιν τοὔνομα μεῖζον ἀφίξεσθαι αὐτοῦ, τυχὸν δὲ καὶ ἀγαθοῦ
21 τινος ἂν αἴτιος τῇ στρατιᾷ γενέσθαι. τὰ μὲν δὴ τοιαῦτα ἐνθυμή-
ματα ἐπῆρεν αὐτὸν ἐπιθυμεῖν αὐτοκράτορα γενέσθαι ἄρχοντα.
ὁπότε δ' αὖ ἐνθυμοῖτο ὅτι ἄδηλον μὲν παντὶ ἀνθρώπῳ ὅπῃ τὸ
μέλλον ἕξει, διὰ τοῦτο δὲ καὶ κίνδυνος εἴη καὶ τὴν προειργασ-
μένην δόξαν ἀποβαλεῖν, ἠπορεῖτο.

22 Διαπορουμένῳ δὲ αὐτῷ διακρῖναι ἔδοξε κράτιστον εἶναι τοῖς
θεοῖς ἀνακοινῶσαι· καὶ παραστησάμενος δύο ἱερεῖα ἐθύετο τῷ
Διὶ τῷ βασιλεῖ, ὅσπερ αὐτῷ μαντευτὸς ἦν ἐκ Δελφῶν· καὶ τὸ
ὄναρ δὴ ἀπὸ τούτου τοῦ θεοῦ ἐνόμιζεν ἑωρακέναι ὃ εἶδεν ὅτε
23 ἤρχετο ἐπὶ τὸ συνεπιμελεῖσθαι τῆς στρατιᾶς καθίστασθαι. καὶ
ὅτε ἐξ Ἐφέσου ὡρμᾶτο Κύρῳ συσταθησόμενος, αἰετὸν ἀνεμιμνή-
σκετο ἑαυτῷ δεξιὸν φθεγγόμενον, καθήμενον μέντοι, ὅνπερ ὁ μάντις προπέμπων αὐτὸν ἔλεγεν ὅτι μέγας μὲν οἰωνὸς εἴη καὶ οὐκ
ἰδιωτικός, καὶ ἔνδοξος, ἐπίπονος μέντοι· τὰ γὰρ ὄρνεα μάλιστα
ἐπιτίθεσθαι τῷ αἰετῷ καθημένῳ· οὐ μέντοι χρηματιστικὸν εἶναι
τὸν οἰωνόν· τὸν γὰρ αἰετὸν πετόμενον μᾶλλον λαμβάνειν τὰ
24 ἐπιτήδεια. οὕτω δὴ θυομένῳ αὐτῷ διαφανῶς ὁ θεὸς σημαίνει
μήτε προσδεῖσθαι τῆς ἀρχῆς μήτε εἰ αἱροῖντο ἀποδέχεσθαι.
τοῦτο μὲν δὴ οὕτως ἐγένετο.

25 Ἡ δὲ στρατιὰ συνῆλθε, καὶ πάντες ἔλεγον ἕνα αἱρεῖσθαι·
καὶ ἐπεὶ τοῦτο ἔδοξε, προὐβάλλοντο αὐτόν. ἐπεὶ δὲ ἐδόκει
δῆλον εἶναι ὅτι αἱρήσονται αὐτόν, εἴ τις ἐπιψηφίζοι, ἀνέστη καὶ
ἔλεξε τάδε.

Ἐγώ, ὦ ἄνδρες, ἥδομαι μὲν ὑπὸ ὑμῶν τιμώμενος, εἴπερ ἄν- 26
θρωπός εἰμι, καὶ χάριν ἔχω καὶ εὔχομαι δοῦναί μοι τοὺς θεοὺς
αἴτιόν τινος ὑμῖν ἀγαθοῦ γενέσθαι· τὸ μέντοι ἐμὲ προκριθῆναι
ὑπὸ ὑμῶν ἄρχοντα Λακεδαιμονίου ἀνδρὸς παρόντος οὔτε ὑμῖν
μοι δοκεῖ συμφέρον εἶναι, ἀλλ' ἧττον ἂν διὰ τοῦτο τυγχάνειν,
εἴ τι δέοισθε παρ' αὐτῶν· ἐμοί τε αὖ οὐ πάνυ τι νομίζω ἀσφαλὲς
εἶναι τοῦτο. ὁρῶ γὰρ ὅτι καὶ τῇ πατρίδι μου οὐ πρόσθεν ἐπαύ- 27
σαντο πολεμοῦντες πρὶν ἐποίησαν πᾶσαν τὴν πόλιν ὁμολογεῖν
Λακεδαιμονίους καὶ αὐτῶν ἡγεμόνας εἶναι. ἐπεὶ δὲ τοῦτο 28
ὡμολόγησαν, εὐθὺς ἐπαύσαντο πολεμοῦντες καὶ οὐκέτι πέρα
ἐπολιόρκησαν τὴν πόλιν. εἰ οὖν ταῦτα ὁρῶν ἐγὼ δοκοίην ὅπου
δυναίμην ἐνταῦθ' ἄκυρον ποιεῖν τὸ ἐκείνων ἀξίωμα, ἐκεῖνο ἐννοῶ
μὴ λίαν ἂν ταχὺ σωφρονισθείην. ὃ δὲ ὑμεῖς ἐννοεῖτε ὅτι ἧττον 29
ἂν στάσις εἴη ἑνὸς ἄρχοντος ἢ πολλῶν, εὖ ἴστε ὅτι ἄλλον μὲν
ἑλόμενοι οὐχ εὑρήσετε ἐμὲ στασιάζοντα· νομίζω γὰρ ὅστις ἐν
πολέμῳ ὢν στασιάζει πρὸς ἄρχοντα, τοῦτον πρὸς τὴν ἑαυτοῦ
σωτηρίαν στασιάζειν· ἐὰν δὲ ἐμὲ ἕλησθε, οὐκ ἂν θαυμάσαιμι εἴ
τινα εὕροιτε καὶ ὑμῖν καὶ ἐμοὶ ἀχθόμενον.

Ἐπεὶ ταῦτα εἶπε, πολὺ πλείονες ἀνίσταντο λέγοντες ὡς δέοι 30
αὐτὸν ἄρχειν. Ἀγασίας δὲ Στυμφάλιος εἶπεν ὅτι γελοῖον εἴη,
εἰ οὕτως ἔχοι· ἢ ὀργιοῦνται Λακεδαιμόνιοι καὶ ἐὰν σύνδειπνοι
συνελθόντες μὴ Λακεδαιμόνιον συμποσίαρχον αἱρῶνται; ἐπεὶ εἰ
οὕτω γε τοῦτο ἔχει, ἔφη, οὐδὲ λοχαγεῖν ἡμῖν ἔξεστιν, ὡς ἔοικεν,
ὅτι Ἀρκάδες ἐσμέν. ἐνταῦθα δὴ ὡς εὖ εἰπόντος τοῦ Ἀγασίου
ἀνεθορύβησαν.

Καὶ ὁ Ξενοφῶν ἐπεὶ ἑώρα πλείονος ἐνδέον, παρελθὼν εἶπεν· 31
Ἀλλ', ὦ ἄνδρες, ἔφη, ὡς πάνυ εἰδῆτε, ὀμνύω ὑμῖν θεοὺς πάντας
καὶ πάσας, ἦ μὴν ἐγώ, ἐπεὶ τὴν ὑμετέραν γνώμην ᾐσθανόμην,
ἐθυόμην εἰ βέλτιον εἴη ὑμῖν τε ἐμοὶ ἐπιτρέψαι ταύτην τὴν ἀρχὴν
καὶ ἐμοὶ ὑποστῆναι· καί μοι οἱ θεοὶ οὕτως ἐν τοῖς ἱεροῖς ἐσή-
μηναν ὥστε καὶ ἰδιώτην ἂν γνῶναι ὅτι τῆς μοναρχίας ἀπέχεσθαί
με δεῖ.

Οὕτω δὴ Χειρίσοφον αἱροῦνται. Χειρίσοφος δ' ἐπεὶ ᾑρέθη, 32
παρελθὼν εἶπεν· Ἀλλ', ὦ ἄνδρες, τοῦτο μὲν ἴστε ὅτι οὐδ' ἂν
ἔγωγε ἐστασίαζον, εἰ ἄλλον εἵλεσθε· Ξενοφῶντα μέντοι, ἔφη,

ὠνήσατε οὐχ ἑλόμενοι. ὡς καὶ νῦν Δέξιππος ἤδη διέβαλλεν αὐτὸν πρὸς Ἀναξίβιον ὅ,τι ἐδύνατο καὶ μάλα ἐμοῦ αὐτὸν σιγάζοντος. ὁ δ᾽ ἔφη νομίζειν αὐτὸν Τιμασίωνι μᾶλλον ἂν συνάρχειν ἐθελῆσαι Δαρδανεῖ ὄντι τοῦ Κλεάρχου στρατεύματος ἢ ἑαυτῷ Λάκωνι ὄντι. ἐπεὶ μέντοι ἐμὲ εἵλεσθε, ἔφη, καὶ ἐγὼ πειράσομαι ὅ,τι ἂν δύνωμαι ὑμᾶς ἀγαθὸν ποιεῖν. καὶ ὑμεῖς οὕτω παρασκευάζεσθε ὡς αὔριον, ἐὰν πλοῦς ᾖ, ἀναξόμενοι· ὁ δὲ πλοῦς ἔσται εἰς Ἡράκλειαν· ἅπαντας οὖν δεῖ ἐκεῖσε πειρᾶσθαι κατασχεῖν· τὰ δ᾽ ἄλλα, ἐπειδὰν ἐκεῖσε ἔλθωμεν, βουλευσόμεθα.

II. Ἐντεῦθεν τῇ ὑστεραίᾳ ἀναγόμενοι πνεύματι ἔπλεον καλῷ ἡμέρας δύο παρὰ γῆν. καὶ παραπλέοντες [ἐθεώρουν τήν τε Ἰασονίαν ἀκτήν, ἔνθα ἡ Ἀργὼ λέγεται ὁρμίσασθαι, καὶ τῶν ποταμῶν τὰ στόματα, πρῶτον μὲν τοῦ Θερμώδοντος, ἔπειτα δὲ τοῦ Ἴριος, ἔπειτα δὲ τοῦ Ἅλυος, μετὰ τοῦτον τοῦ Παρθενίου· τοῦτον δὲ παραπλεύσαντες] ἀφίκοντο εἰς Ἡράκλειαν πόλιν Ἑλληνίδα Μεγαρέων ἄποικον, οὖσαν δ᾽ ἐν τῇ Μαριανδυνῶν χώρᾳ. καὶ ὡρμίσαντο παρὰ τῇ Ἀχερουσιάδι Χερρονήσῳ, ἔνθα λέγεται ὁ Ἡρακλῆς ἐπὶ τὸν Κέρβερον κύνα καταβῆναι ᾗ νῦν τὰ σημεῖα δεικνύασι τῆς καταβάσεως τὸ βάθος πλέον ἢ ἐπὶ δύο στάδια. ἐνταῦθα τοῖς Ἕλλησιν οἱ Ἡρακλεῶται ξένια πέμπουσιν ἀλφίτων μεδίμνους τρισχιλίους καὶ οἴνου κεράμια δισχίλια καὶ βοῦς εἴκοσι καὶ οἷς ἑκατόν. ἐνταῦθα διὰ τοῦ πεδίου ῥεῖ ποταμὸς Λύκος ὄνομα, εὖρος ὡς δύο πλέθρων.

Οἱ δὲ στρατιῶται συλλεγέντες ἐβουλεύοντο τὴν λοιπὴν πορείαν πότερον κατὰ γῆν ἢ κατὰ θάλατταν χρὴ πορευθῆναι ἐκ τοῦ Πόντου. ἀναστὰς δὲ Λύκων Ἀχαιὸς εἶπε· Θαυμάζω μέν, ὦ ἄνδρες, τῶν στρατηγῶν ὅτι οὐ πειρῶνται ἡμῖν ἐκπορίζειν σιτηρέσιον· τὰ μὲν γὰρ ξένια οὐ μὴ γένηται τῇ στρατιᾷ τριῶν ἡμερῶν σιτία· ὁπόθεν δ᾽ ἐπισιτισάμενοι πορευσόμεθα οὐκ ἔστιν, ἔφη. ἐμοὶ οὖν δοκεῖ αἰτεῖν τοὺς Ἡρακλεώτας μὴ ἔλαττον ἢ τρισχιλίους κυζικηνούς· ἄλλος δ᾽ εἶπε μὴ ἔλαττον ἢ μυρίους· καὶ ἑλομένους πρέσβεις αὐτίκα μάλα ἡμῶν καθημένων πέμπειν πρὸς τὴν πόλιν, καὶ εἰδέναι ὅ,τι ἂν ἀπαγγέλλωσι, καὶ πρὸς ταῦτα βουλεύεσθαι. ἐντεῦθεν προὐβάλλοντο πρέσβεις πρῶτον μὲν Χειρίσοφον, ὅτι ἄρχων ᾕρητο· ἔστι δ᾽ οἳ καὶ Ξενοφῶντα.

οἳ δὲ ἰσχυρῶς ἀπεμάχοντο· ἀμφοῖν γὰρ ταὐτὰ ἐδόκει μὴ ἀναγκάζειν πόλιν Ἑλληνίδα καὶ φιλίαν ὅ,τι μὴ αὐτοὶ ἐθέλοντες διδοῖεν. ἐπεὶ δ' οὗτοι ἐδόκουν ἀπρόθυμοι εἶναι, πέμπουσι Λύκωνα Ἀχαιὸν καὶ Καλλίμαχον Παρράσιον καὶ Ἀγασίαν Στυμφάλιον. οὗτοι ἐλθόντες ἔλεγον τὰ δεδογμένα· τὸν δὲ Λύκωνα ἔφασαν καὶ ἐπαπειλεῖν, εἰ μὴ ποιήσοιεν ταῦτα. ἀκούσαντες δ' οἱ Ἡρακλεῶται βουλεύσεσθαι ἔφασαν· καὶ εὐθὺς τά τε χρήματα ἐκ τῶν ἀγρῶν συνῆγον καὶ τὴν ἀγορὰν εἴσω ἀνεσκεύασαν, καὶ αἱ πύλαι ἐκέκλειντο καὶ ἐπὶ τῶν τειχῶν ὅπλα ἐφαίνετο.

Ἐκ τούτου οἱ ταράξαντες ταῦτα τοὺς στρατηγοὺς ᾐτιῶντο διαφθείρειν τὴν πρᾶξιν· καὶ συνίσταντο οἱ Ἀρκάδες καὶ οἱ Ἀχαιοί· προειστήκει δὲ μάλιστα αὐτῶν Καλλίμαχός τε ὁ Παρράσιος καὶ Λύκων ὁ Ἀχαιός. οἱ δὲ λόγοι ἦσαν αὐτοῖς ὡς αἰσχρὸν εἴη ἄρχειν Ἀθηναῖον Πελοποννησίων καὶ Λακεδαιμόνιον μηδεμίαν δύναμιν παρεχομένους εἰς τὴν στρατιάν καὶ τοὺς μὲν πόνους σφᾶς ἔχειν, τὰ δὲ κέρδη ἄλλους, καὶ ταῦτα τὴν σωτηρίαν σφῶν κατειργασμένων· εἶναι γὰρ τοὺς κατειργασμένους Ἀρκάδας καὶ Ἀχαιούς, τὸ δ' ἄλλο στράτευμα οὐδὲν εἶναι — καὶ ἦν δὲ τῇ ἀληθείᾳ ὑπὲρ ἥμισυ τοῦ στρατεύματος Ἀρκάδες καὶ Ἀχαιοί — εἰ οὖν σωφρονοῖεν, αὐτοὶ συστάντες καὶ στρατηγοὺς ἑλόμενοι ἑαυτῶν καθ' ἑαυτοὺς ἂν τὴν πορείαν ποιοῖντο καὶ πειρῶντο ἀγαθόν τι λαμβάνειν. ταῦτ' ἔδοξε· καὶ ἀπολιπόντες Χειρίσοφον εἴ τινες ἦσαν παρ' αὐτῷ Ἀρκάδες ἢ Ἀχαιοὶ καὶ Ξενοφῶντα συνέστησαν καὶ στρατηγοὺς αἱροῦνται ἑαυτῶν δέκα· τούτους δὲ ἐψηφίσαντο ἐκ τῆς νικώσης ὅ,τι δοκοίη τοῦτο ποιεῖν. ἡ μὲν οὖν τοῦ παντὸς ἀρχὴ Χειρισόφῳ ἐνταῦθα κατελύθη ἡμέρᾳ ἕκτῃ ἢ ἑβδόμῃ ἀφ' ἧς ᾑρέθη.

Ξενοφῶν μέντοι ἐβούλετο κοινῇ μετὰ τῶν μεινάντων τὴν πορείαν ποιεῖσθαι, νομίζων οὕτως ἀσφαλεστέραν εἶναι ἢ ἰδίᾳ ἕκαστον στέλλεσθαι· ἀλλὰ Νέων ἔπειθεν αὐτὸν καθ' αὑτὸν πορεύεσθαι, ἀκούσας τοῦ Χειρισόφου ὅτι Κλέανδρος ὁ ἐν Βυζαντίῳ ἁρμοστὴς φαίη τριήρεις ἔχων ἥξειν εἰς Κάλπης λιμένα· ὅπως οὖν μηδεὶς μετάσχοι, ἀλλ' αὐτοὶ καὶ οἱ αὐτῶν στρατιῶται ἐκπλεύσειαν ἐπὶ τῶν τριήρων, διὰ ταῦτα συνεβούλευε. καὶ Χειρίσοφος, ἅμα μὲν ἀθυμῶν τοῖς γεγενημένοις, ἅμα δὲ μισῶν

ἐκ τούτου τὸ στράτευμα, ἐπιτρέπει αὐτῷ ποιεῖν ὅ,τι βούλεται.
15 Ξενοφῶν δὲ ἔτι μὲν ἐπεχείρησεν ἀπαλλαγεὶς τῆς στρατιᾶς ἐκπλεῦσαι· θυομένῳ δὲ αὐτῷ τῷ ἡγεμόνι Ἡρακλεῖ καὶ κοινουμένῳ, πότερα λῷον καὶ ἄμεινον εἴη στρατεύεσθαι ἔχοντι τοὺς παραμείναντας τῶν στρατιωτῶν ἢ ἀπαλλάττεσθαι, ἐσήμηνεν ὁ θεὸς
16 τοῖς ἱεροῖς συστρατεύεσθαι. οὕτω γίγνεται τὸ στράτευμα τρίχα, Ἀρκάδες μὲν καὶ Ἀχαιοὶ πλείους ἢ τετρακισχίλιοι, ὁπλῖται πάντες, Χειρισόφῳ δ' ὁπλῖται μὲν εἰς τετρακοσίους καὶ χιλίους, πελτασταὶ δὲ εἰς ἑπτακοσίους, οἱ Κλεάρχου Θρᾷκες, Ξενοφῶντι δὲ ὁπλῖται μὲν εἰς ἑπτακοσίους καὶ χιλίους, πελτασταὶ δὲ εἰς τριακοσίους. ἱππικὸν δὲ μόνος οὗτος εἶχεν, ἀμφὶ τετταράκοντα ἱππέας.

17 Καὶ οἱ μὲν Ἀρκάδες διαπραξάμενοι πλοῖα παρὰ τῶν Ἡρακλεωτῶν πρῶτοι πλέουσιν, ὅπως ἐξαίφνης ἐπιπεσόντες τοῖς Βιθυνοῖς λάβοιεν ὅτι πλεῖστα· καὶ ἀποβαίνουσιν εἰς Κάλπης
18 λιμένα κατὰ μέσον πως τῆς Θρᾴκης. Χειρίσοφος δ' εὐθὺς ἀπὸ τῆς πόλεως τῶν Ἡρακλεωτῶν ἀρξάμενος πεζῇ ἐπορεύετο διὰ τῆς χώρας· ἐπεὶ δὲ εἰς τὴν Θρᾴκην ἐνέβαλε, παρὰ τὴν θάλατταν
19 ᾔει· καὶ γὰρ ἠσθένει. Ξενοφῶν δὲ πλοῖα λαβὼν ἀποβαίνει ἐπὶ τὰ ὅρια τῆς Θρᾴκης καὶ τῆς Ἡρακλεώτιδος καὶ διὰ μεσογείας ἐπορεύετο.

1 III. [Ὃν μὲν οὖν τρόπον ἥ τε Χειρισόφου ἀρχὴ τοῦ παντὸς κατελύθη καὶ τῶν Ἑλλήνων τὸ στράτευμα ἐσχίσθη ἐν τοῖς ἐπάνω εἴρηται.]

2 Ἔπραξαν δ' αὐτῶν ἕκαστοι τάδε. οἱ μὲν Ἀρκάδες ὡς ἀπέβησαν νυκτὸς εἰς Κάλπης λιμένα, πορεύονται εἰς τὰς πρώτας κώμας, στάδια ἀπὸ θαλάττης ὡς τριάκοντα. ἐπεὶ δὲ φῶς ἐγένετο, ἦγεν ἕκαστος ὁ στρατηγὸς τὸν αὑτοῦ λόχον ἐπὶ κώμην· ὁποία δὲ μείζων ἐδόκει εἶναι, σύνδυο λόχους ἦγον οἱ στρατηγοί.
3 συνεβάλλοντο δὲ καὶ λόφον εἰς ὃν δέοι πάντας ἀλίζεσθαι· καὶ ἅτε ἐξαίφνης ἐπιπεσόντες ἀνδράποδά τε πολλὰ ἔλαβον καὶ
4 πρόβατα πολλὰ περιεβάλλοντο. οἱ δὲ Θρᾷκες ἠθροίζοντο οἱ διαφεύγοντες· πολλοὶ δὲ διέφευγον πελτασταὶ ὄντες ὁπλίτας ἐξ αὐτῶν τῶν χειρῶν. ἐπεὶ δὲ συνελέγησαν, πρῶτον, μὲν τῳ Σμίκρητος λόχῳ ἑνὸς τῶν Ἀρκάδων στρατηγῶν ἀπιόντι ἤδη εἰς

τὸ συγκείμενον καὶ πολλὰ χρήματα ἄγοντι ἐπιτίθενται. καὶ τέως μὲν ἐμάχοντο ἅμα πορευόμενοι οἱ Ἕλληνες, ἐπὶ δὲ διαβάσει χαράδρας τρέπονται αὐτούς, καὶ αὐτόν τε τὸν Σμίκρητα ἀποκτιννύασι καὶ τοὺς ἄλλους πάντας· ἄλλου δὲ λόχου τῶν δέκα στρατηγῶν τοῦ Ἡγησάνδρου ὀκτὼ μόνους ἔλιπον· καὶ αὐτὸς Ἡγήσανδρος ἐσώθη.

Καὶ οἱ ἄλλοι δὲ λόχοι συνῆλθον οἱ μὲν σὺν πράγμασιν οἱ δὲ ἄνευ πραγμάτων· οἱ δὲ Θρᾷκες ἐπεὶ ηὐτύχησαν τοῦτο τὸ εὐτύχημα, συνεβόων τε ἀλλήλους καὶ συνελέγοντο ἐρρωμένως τῆς νυκτός. καὶ ἅμα ἡμέρᾳ κύκλῳ περὶ τὸν λόφον ἔνθα οἱ Ἕλληνες ἐστρατοπεδεύοντο ἐτάττοντο καὶ ἱππεῖς πολλοὶ καὶ πελτασταί, καὶ ἀεὶ πλέονες συνέρρεον· καὶ προσέβαλλον πρὸς τοὺς ὁπλίτας ἀσφαλῶς· οἱ μὲν γὰρ Ἕλληνες οὔτε τοξότην εἶχον οὔτε ἀκοντιστὴν οὔτε ἱππέα· οἱ δὲ προσθέοντες καὶ προσελαύνοντες ἠκόντιζον· ὁπότε δὲ αὐτοῖς ἐπίοιεν, ῥᾳδίως ἀπέφευγον· ἄλλοι δὲ ἄλλῃ ἐπετίθεντο. καὶ τῶν μὲν πολλοὶ ἐτιτρώσκοντο, τῶν δὲ οὐδείς· ὥστε κινηθῆναι οὐκ ἐδύναντο ἐκ τοῦ χωρίου, ἀλλὰ τελευτῶντες καὶ ἀπὸ τοῦ ὕδατος εἶργον αὐτοὺς οἱ Θρᾷκες. ἐπεὶ δὲ ἀπορία πολλὴ ἦν, διελέγοντο περὶ σπονδῶν· καὶ τὰ μὲν ἄλλα ὡμολόγητο αὐτοῖς, ὁμήρους δὲ οὐκ ἐδίδοσαν οἱ Θρᾷκες αἰτούντων τῶν Ἑλλήνων, ἀλλ' ἐν τούτῳ ἴσχετο. τὰ μὲν δὴ τῶν Ἀρκάδων οὕτως εἶχε.

Χειρίσοφος δὲ ἀσφαλῶς πορευόμενος παρὰ θάλατταν ἀφικνεῖται εἰς Κάλπης λιμένα.

Ξενοφῶντι δὲ διὰ τῆς μεσογείας πορευομένῳ οἱ ἱππεῖς προκαταθέοντες ἐντυγχάνουσι πρεσβύταις πορευομένοις ποι. καὶ ἐπεὶ ἤχθησαν παρὰ Ξενοφῶντα, ἐρωτᾷ αὐτοὺς εἴ που ᾔσθηνται ἄλλου στρατεύματος ὄντος Ἑλληνικοῦ. οἱ δὲ ἔλεγον πάντα τὰ γεγενημένα, καὶ νῦν ὅτι πολιορκοῦνται ἐπὶ λόφου, οἱ δὲ Θρᾷκες πάντες περικεκυκλωμένοι εἶεν αὐτούς. ἐνταῦθα τοὺς μὲν ἀνθρώπους τούτους ἐφύλαττεν ἰσχυρῶς, ὅπως ἡγεμόνες εἶεν ὅποι δέοι· σκοποὺς δὲ καταστήσας συνέλεξε τοὺς στρατιώτας καὶ ἔλεξεν·

Ἄνδρες στρατιῶται, τῶν Ἀρκάδων οἱ μὲν τεθνᾶσιν, οἱ δὲ λοιποὶ ἐπὶ λόφου τινὸς πολιορκοῦνται. νομίζω δ' ἔγωγε, εἰ ἐκεῖνοι ἀπολοῦνται, οὐδ' ἡμῖν εἶναι οὐδεμίαν σωτηρίαν, οὕτω μὲν πολλῶν

13 ὄντων τῶν πολεμίων, οὕτω δὲ τεθαρρηκότων. κράτιστον οὖν ἡμῖν ὡς τάχιστα βοηθεῖν τοῖς ἀνδράσιν, ὅπως εἰ ἔτι εἰσὶ σῶοι, σὺν ἐκείνοις μαχώμεθα καὶ μὴ μόνοι λειφθέντες μόνοι καὶ κινδυ-
16 νεύωμεν. ἡμεῖς γὰρ ἀποδραίημεν ἂν οὐδαμοῖ ἐνθένδε· πολλὴ
(14) μὲν γάρ, ἔφη, εἰς Ἡράκλειαν πάλιν ἀπιέναι, πολλὴ δὲ εἰς Χρυσόπολιν διελθεῖν· οἱ δὲ πολέμιοι πλησίον· εἰς Κάλπης δὲ λιμένα, ἔνθα Χειρίσοφον εἰκάζομεν εἶναι, εἰ σέσωται, ἐλαχίστη ὁδός. ἀλλὰ δὴ ἐκεῖ μὲν οὔτε πλοῖά ἐστιν οἷς ἀποπλευσούμεθα,
17 μένουσι δὲ αὐτοῦ οὐδὲ μιᾶς ἡμέρας ἔστι τὰ ἐπιτήδεια. τῶν δὲ
(15) πολιορκουμένων ἀπολομένων σὺν τοῖς Χειρισόφου μόνοις κάκιόν ἐστι διακινδυνεύειν ἢ τῶνδε σωθέντων πάντας εἰς ταὐτὸν ἐλθόντας κοινῇ τῆς σωτηρίας ἔχεσθαι. ἀλλὰ χρὴ παρασκευασαμένους τὴν γνώμην πορεύεσθαι ὡς νῦν ἢ εὐκλεῶς τελευτῆσαι ἔστιν ἢ κάλλιστον ἔργον ἐργάσασθαι Ἕλληνας τοσούτους σώ-
18 σαντας. καὶ ὁ θεὸς ἴσως ἄγει οὕτως, ὃς τοὺς μεγαληγορήσαντας
(16) ὡς πλέον φρονοῦντας ταπεινῶσαι βούλεται, ἡμᾶς δὲ τοὺς ἀπὸ τῶν θεῶν ἀρχομένους ἐντιμοτέρους ἐκείνων καταστῆσαι. ἀλλ' ἕπεσθαι χρὴ καὶ προσέχειν τὸν νοῦν, ὡς ἂν τὸ παραγγελλόμενον
14 δύνησθε ποιεῖν. νῦν μὲν οὖν στρατοπεδευσώμεθα προελθόντες
(17) ὅσον ἂν δοκῇ καιρὸς εἶναι εἰς τὸ δειπνοποιεῖσθαι· ἕως δ' ἂν πορευώμεθα, Τιμασίων ἔχων τοὺς ἱππεῖς προελαυνέτω ἐφορῶν ἡμᾶς καὶ σκοπείτω τὰ ἔμπροσθεν, ὡς μηδὲν ἡμᾶς λάθῃ.

15 Ταῦτ' εἰπὼν ἡγεῖτο. παρέπεμψε δὲ καὶ τῶν γυμνήτων
(18) ἀνθρώπους εὐζώνους εἰς τὰ πλάγια καὶ εἰς τὰ ἄκρα, ὅπως εἴ πού τί ποθεν καθορῷεν, σημαίνοιεν· ἐκέλευε δὲ καίειν ἅπαντα
19 ὅτῳ ἐντυγχάνοιεν καυσίμῳ. οἱ δὲ ἱππεῖς σπειρόμενοι ἐφ' ὅσον καλῶς εἶχεν ἔκαιον, καὶ οἱ πελτασταὶ ἐπιπαριόντες κατὰ τὰ ἄκρα ἔκαιον πάντα ὅσα καύσιμα ἑώρων, καὶ ἡ στρατιὰ δέ, εἴ τινι παραλειπομένῳ ἐντυγχάνοιεν· ὥστε πᾶσα ἡ χώρα αἴθεσθαι
20 ἐδόκει καὶ τὸ στράτευμα πολὺ εἶναι. ἐπεὶ δὲ ὥρα ἦν, κατεστρατοπεδεύσαντο ἐπὶ λόφον ἐκβάντες, καὶ τά τε τῶν πολεμίων πυρὰ ἑώρων, ἀπεῖχον δὲ ὡς τετταράκοντα σταδίους, καὶ αὐτοὶ ὡς
21 ἐδύναντο πλεῖστα πυρὰ ἔκαιον. ἐπεὶ δὲ ἐδείπνησαν τάχιστα, παρηγγέλθη τὰ πυρὰ κατασβεννύναι πάντα. καὶ τὴν μὲν νύκτα φυλακὰς ποιησάμενοι ἐκάθευδον· ἅμα δὲ τῇ ἡμέρᾳ προσευξάμενοι

τοῖς θεοῖς, συνταξάμενοι ὡς εἰς μάχην ἐπορεύοντο ᾗ ἐδύναντο τάχιστα. Τιμασίων δὲ καὶ οἱ ἱππεῖς ἔχοντες τοὺς ἡγεμόνας καὶ προελαύνοντες ἐλάνθανον αὑτοὺς ἐπὶ τῷ λόφῳ γενόμενοι ἔνθα ἐπολιορκοῦντο οἱ Ἕλληνες. καὶ οὐχ ὁρῶσιν οὔτε φίλιον στράτευμα οὔτε πολέμιον—καὶ ταῦτα ἀπαγγέλλουσι πρὸς τὸν Ξενοφῶντα καὶ τὸ στράτευμα—γρᾴδια δὲ καὶ γερόντια καὶ πρόβατα ὀλίγα καὶ βοῦς καταλελειμμένους. καὶ τὸ μὲν πρῶτον θαῦμα ἦν τί εἴη τὸ γεγενημένον, ἔπειτα δὲ καὶ τῶν καταλελειμμένων ἐπυνθάνοντο ὅτι οἱ μὲν Θρᾷκες ἀφ' ἑσπέρας ᾤχοντο ἀπιόντες, καὶ τοὺς Ἕλληνας δ' ἔφασαν οἴχεσθαι· ὅποι δέ, οὐκ εἰδέναι.

Ταῦτα ἀκούσαντες οἱ ἀμφὶ Ξενοφῶντα, ἐπεὶ ἠρίστησαν, συσκευασάμενοι ἐπορεύοντο, βουλόμενοι ὡς τάχιστα συμμεῖξαι τοῖς ἄλλοις εἰς Κάλπης λιμένα. καὶ πορευόμενοι ἑώρων τὸν στίβον τῶν Ἀρκάδων καὶ Ἀχαιῶν κατὰ τὴν ἐπὶ Κάλπης ὁδόν. ἐπεὶ δὲ ἀφίκοντο εἰς τὸ αὐτό, ἅσμενοί τε εἶδον ἀλλήλους καὶ ἠσπάζοντο ὥσπερ ἀδελφούς. καὶ ἐπυνθάνοντο οἱ Ἀρκάδες τῶν περὶ Ξενοφῶντα τί τὰ πυρὰ κατασβέσειαν· ἡμεῖς μὲν γάρ, ἔφασαν, ᾠόμεθα ὑμᾶς τὸ μὲν πρῶτον, ἐπειδὴ τὰ πυρὰ οὐκέθ' ἑωρῶμεν, τῆς νυκτὸς ἥξειν ἐπὶ τοὺς πολεμίους· καὶ οἱ πολέμιοι δέ, ὥς γ' ἡμῖν ἐδόκουν, τοῦτο δείσαντες ἀπῆλθον· σχεδὸν γὰρ ἀμφὶ τοῦτον τὸν χρόνον ἀπῇσαν. ἐπεὶ δὲ οὐκ ἀφίκεσθε, ὁ δὲ χρόνος ἐξῆκεν, ᾠόμεθα ὑμᾶς πυθομένους τὰ παρ' ἡμῖν φοβηθέντας οἴχεσθαι ἀποδράντας ἐπὶ θάλατταν· καὶ ἐδόκει ἡμῖν μὴ ἀπολείπεσθαι ὑμῶν. οὕτως οὖν καὶ ἡμεῖς δεῦρο ἐπορεύθημεν.

IV. Ταύτην μὲν οὖν τὴν ἡμέραν αὐτοῦ ηὐλίζοντο ἐπὶ τοῦ αἰγιαλοῦ πρὸς τῷ λιμένι. τὸ δὲ χωρίον τοῦτο ὃ καλεῖται Κάλπης λιμὴν ἔστι μὲν ἐν τῇ Θρᾴκῃ τῇ ἐν τῇ Ἀσίᾳ· ἀρξαμένη δὲ ἡ Θρᾴκη αὕτη ἐστὶν ἀπὸ τοῦ στόματος τοῦ Πόντου μέχρι Ἡρακλείας ἐπὶ δεξιὰ εἰς τὸν Πόντον εἰσπλέοντι. καὶ τριήρει μέν ἐστιν εἰς Ἡράκλειαν ἐκ Βυζαντίου κώπαις ἡμέρας μακρᾶς πλοῦς· ἐν δὲ τῷ μέσῳ ἄλλη μὲν πόλις οὐδεμία οὔτε φιλία οὔτε Ἑλληνίς, ἀλλὰ Θρᾷκες Βιθυνοί· καὶ οὓς ἂν λάβωσι τῶν Ἑλλήνων ἐκπίπτοντας ἢ ἄλλως πως δεινὰ ὑβρίζειν λέγονται τοὺς Ἕλληνας. ὁ δὲ Κάλπης λιμὴν ἐν μέσῳ μὲν κεῖται ἑκατέ-

ρωθεν πλεόντων ἐξ Ἡρακλείας καὶ Βυζαντίου, ἔστι δ᾽ ἐν τῇ
θαλάττῃ προκείμενον χωρίον, τὸ μὲν εἰς τὴν θάλατταν καθῆκον
αὐτοῦ πέτρα ἀπορρώξ, ὕψος ὅπῃ ἐλάχιστον οὐ μεῖον εἴκοσιν
ὀργυιῶν, ὁ δὲ αὐχὴν ὁ εἰς τὴν γῆν ἀνήκων τοῦ χωρίου μάλιστα
τεττάρων πλέθρων τὸ εὖρος· τὸ δ᾽ ἐντὸς τοῦ αὐχένος χωρίον 15
4 ἱκανὸν μυρίοις ἀνθρώποις οἰκῆσαι. λιμὴν δ᾽ ὑπ᾽ αὐτῇ τῇ πέτρᾳ
τὸ πρὸς ἑσπέραν αἰγιαλὸν ἔχων. κρήνη δὲ ἡδέος ὕδατος καὶ
ἄφθονος ῥέουσα ἐπ᾽ αὐτῇ τῇ θαλάττῃ ὑπὸ τῇ ἐπικρατείᾳ τοῦ
χωρίου. ξύλα δὲ πολλὰ μὲν καὶ ἄλλα, πάνυ δὲ πολλὰ καὶ
5 καλὰ ναυπηγήσιμα ἐπ᾽ αὐτῇ τῇ θαλάττῃ. τὸ δὲ ὄρος εἰς μεσό- 20
γειαν μὲν ἀνήκει ὅσον ἐπὶ εἴκοσι σταδίους, καὶ τοῦτο γεῶδες καὶ
ἄλιθον· τὸ δὲ παρὰ θάλατταν πλέον ἢ ἐπὶ εἴκοσι σταδίους δασὺ
6 πολλοῖς καὶ παντοδαποῖς καὶ μεγάλοις ξύλοις. ἡ δὲ ἄλλη
χώρα καλὴ καὶ πολλή, καὶ κῶμαι ἐν αὐτῇ εἰσι πολλαὶ καὶ
οἰκούμεναι· φέρει γὰρ ἡ γῆ καὶ κριθὰς καὶ πυροὺς καὶ ὄσπρια 25
πάντα καὶ μελίνας καὶ σήσαμα καὶ σῦκα ἀρκοῦντα καὶ ἀμπέλους
πολλὰς καὶ ἡδυοίνους καὶ τἆλλα πάντα πλὴν ἐλαῶν.

7 Ἡ μὲν χώρα ἦν τοιαύτη. ἐσκήνουν δ᾽ ἐν τῷ αἰγιαλῷ πρὸς
τῇ θαλάττῃ· εἰς δὲ τόπον πόλισμα ἂν γενόμενον οὐκ ἐβούλοντο
στρατοπεδεύεσθαι, ἀλλὰ ἐδόκει καὶ τὸ ἐλθεῖν ἐνταῦθα ἐξ ἐπι- 30
8 βουλῆς εἶναι, βουλομένων τινῶν κατοικίσαι πόλιν. τῶν γὰρ
στρατιωτῶν οἱ πλεῖστοι ἦσαν οὐ σπάνει βίου ἐκπεπλευκότες ἐπὶ
ταύτην τὴν μισθοφοράν, ἀλλὰ τὴν Κύρου ἀρετὴν ἀκούοντες, οἱ
μὲν καὶ ἄνδρας ἄγοντες, οἱ δὲ καὶ προσανηλωκότες χρήματα,
καὶ τούτων ἕτεροι ἀποδεδρακότες πατέρας καὶ μητέρας, οἱ δὲ καὶ 35
τέκνα καταλιπόντες ὡς χρήματ᾽ αὐτοῖς κτησάμενοι ἥξοντες
πάλιν, ἀκούοντες καὶ τοὺς ἄλλους τοὺς παρὰ Κύρῳ πολλὰ καὶ
ἀγαθὰ πράττειν. τοιοῦτοι ὄντες ἐπόθουν εἰς τὴν Ἑλλάδα
σῴζεσθαι.

9 Ἐπειδὴ δὲ ὑστέρα ἡμέρα ἐγένετο τῆς εἰς ταὐτὸν συνόδου, ἐπ᾽ 40
ἐξόδῳ ἐθύετο Ξενοφῶν· ἀνάγκη γὰρ ἦν ἐπὶ τὰ ἐπιτήδεια ἐξάγειν·
ἐπενόει δὲ καὶ τοὺς νεκροὺς θάπτειν. ἐπεὶ δὲ τὰ ἱερὰ καλὰ
ἐγένετο, εἵποντο καὶ οἱ Ἀρκάδες, καὶ τοὺς μὲν νεκροὺς τοὺς
πλείστους ἔνθαπερ ἔπεσον ἑκάστους ἔθαψαν· ἤδη γὰρ ἦσαν
πεμπταῖοι καὶ οὐχ οἷόν τε ἀναιρεῖν ἔτι ἦν· ἐνίους δὲ τοὺς ἐκ τῶν 45

ὁδῶν συνενεγκόντες ἔθαψαν ἐκ τῶν ὑπαρχόντων ὡς ἐδύναντο
κάλλιστα· οὓς δὲ μὴ ηὕρισκον, κενοτάφιον αὐτοῖς ἐποίησαν
μέγα, καὶ στεφάνους ἐπέθεσαν. ταῦτα δὲ ποιήσαντες ἀνεχώρησαν ἐπὶ τὸ στρατόπεδον. καὶ τότε μὲν δειπνήσαντες ἐκοιμή-
50 θησαν. τῇ δὲ ὑστεραίᾳ συνῆλθον οἱ στρατιῶται πάντες· συνῆγε
δὲ μάλιστα ὁ Ἀγασίας τε ὁ Στυμφάλιος λοχαγὸς καὶ Ἱερώνυμος
Ἠλεῖος λοχαγὸς καὶ ἄλλοι οἱ πρεσβύτατοι τῶν Ἀρκάδων. καὶ
δόγμα ἐποιήσαντο, ἐάν τις τοῦ λοιποῦ μνησθῇ δίχα τὸ στράτευμα
ποιεῖν, θανάτῳ αὐτὸν ζημιοῦσθαι, καὶ κατὰ χώραν ἀπιέναι ᾗπερ
55 πρόσθεν εἶχε τὸ στράτευμα καὶ ἄρχειν τοὺς πρόσθεν στρατηγούς. καὶ Χειρίσοφος μὲν ἤδη ἐτετελευτήκει φάρμακον πιὼν
πυρέττων· τὰ δ᾽ ἐκείνου Νέων Ἀσιναῖος παρέλαβε.

Μετὰ δὲ ταῦτα ἀναστὰς εἶπε Ξενοφῶν· Ὦ ἄνδρες στρατιῶται, τὴν μὲν πορείαν, ὡς ἔοικε πεζῇ ποιητέον· οὐ γὰρ ἔστι
60 πλοῖα· ἀνάγκη δὲ πορεύεσθαι ἤδη· οὐ γὰρ ἔστι μένουσι τὰ
ἐπιτήδεια. ἡμεῖς οὖν, ἔφη, θυσόμεθα· ὑμᾶς δὲ δεῖ παρασκευάζεσθαι ὡς μαχουμένους εἴ ποτε καὶ ἄλλοτε· οἱ γὰρ πολέμιοι
ἀνατεθαρρήκασιν. ἐκ τούτου ἐθύοντο οἱ στρατηγοί, μάντις δὲ
παρῆν Ἀρηξίων Ἀρκάς· ὁ δὲ Σιλανὸς ὁ Ἀμπρακιώτης ἤδη
65 ἀπεδεδράκει πλοῖον μισθωσάμενος ἐξ Ἡρακλείας. θυομένοις δὲ
ἐπὶ τῇ ἀφόδῳ οὐκ ἐγίγνετο τὰ ἱερά. ταύτην μὲν οὖν τὴν ἡμέραν
ἐπαύσαντο. καί τινες ἐτόλμων λέγειν ὡς ὁ Ξενοφῶν βουλόμενος
τὸ χωρίον οἰκίσαι πέπεικε τὸν μάντιν λέγειν ὡς τά ἱερὰ οὐ
γίγνεται ἐπὶ ἀφόδῳ. ἐντεῦθεν κηρύξας τῇ αὔριον παρεῖναι ἐπὶ
70 τὴν θυσίαν τὸν βουλόμενον, καὶ μάντις εἴ τις εἴη, παραγγείλας
παρεῖναι ὡς συνθεασόμενον τὰ ἱερά, ἔθυε· καὶ ἐνταῦθα παρῆσαν
πολλοί. θυομένῳ δὲ πάλιν εἰς τρὶς ἐπὶ τῇ ἀφόδῳ οὐκ ἐγίγνετο
τὰ ἱερά. ἐκ τούτου χαλεπῶς εἶχον οἱ στρατιῶται· καὶ γὰρ τὰ
ἐπιτήδεια ἐπέλιπεν ἃ ἔχοντες ἦλθον, καὶ ἀγορὰ οὐδεμία πω
75 παρῆν.

Ἐκ τούτου ξυνελθόντων εἶπε πάλιν Ξενοφῶν· Ὦ ἄνδρες,
ἐπὶ μὲν τῇ πορείᾳ, ὡς ὁρᾶτε, τὰ ἱερὰ οὔπω γίγνεται· τῶν δ᾽
ἐπιτηδείων ὁρῶ ὑμᾶς δεομένους· ἀνάγκη οὖν μοι δοκεῖ εἶναι
θύεσθαι περὶ αὐτοῦ τούτου. ἀναστάς τις εἶπεν· Καὶ εἰκότως
80 ἄρα ἡμῖν οὐ γίγνεται τὰ ἱερά· ὡς γὰρ ἐγὼ ἀπὸ τοῦ αὐτομάτου

χθὲς ἥκοντος πλοίῳ ἤκουσά τινος Κλέανδρος ὁ ἐκ Βυζαντίου
19 ἁρμοστὴς μέλλει ἥξειν πλοῖα καὶ τριήρεις ἔχων. ἐκ τούτου δὲ
ἀναμένειν μὲν πᾶσιν ἐδόκει· ἐπὶ δὲ τὰ ἐπιτήδεια ἀνάγκη ἦν ἐξιέναι. καὶ ἐπὶ τούτῳ πάλιν ἐθύετο εἰς τρίς, καὶ οὐκ ἐγίγνετο τὰ
ἱερά. καὶ ἤδη καὶ ἐπὶ σκηνὴν ἰόντες τὴν Ξενοφῶντος ἔλεγον ὅτι 85
οὐκ ἔχοιεν τὰ ἐπιτήδεια. ὁ δ' οὐκ ἂν ἔφη ἐξαγαγεῖν μὴ γιγνομένων τῶν ἱερῶν.

20   Καὶ πάλιν τῇ ὑστεραίᾳ ἐθύετο, καὶ σχεδόν τι πᾶσα ἡ στρατιὰ διὰ τὸ μέλειν ἅπασιν ἐκυκλοῦντο περὶ τὰ ἱερά· τὰ δὲ θύματα
ἐπελελοίπει. οἱ δὲ στρατηγοὶ ἐξῆγον μὲν οὔ, συνεκάλεσαν δέ. 90
21 εἶπεν οὖν Ξενοφῶν· Ἴσως οἱ πολέμιοι συνειλεγμένοι εἰσὶ καὶ
ἀνάγκη μάχεσθαι· εἰ οὖν καταλιπόντες τὰ σκεύη ἐν τῷ ἐρυμνῷ
χωρίῳ ὡς εἰς μάχην παρεσκευασμένοι ἴοιμεν, ἴσως ἂν τὰ ἱερὰ
22 προχωροίη ἡμῖν. ἀκούσαντες δ' οἱ στρατιῶται ἀνέκραγον ὡς
οὐδὲν δέοι εἰς τὸ χωρίον ἄγειν, ἀλλὰ θύεσθαι ὡς τάχιστα. καὶ 95
πρόβατα μὲν οὐκέτι ἦν, βοῦν δὲ ὑπὸ ἁμάξης πριάμενοι ἐθύοντο·
καὶ Ξενοφῶν Κλεάνορος ἐδεήθη τοῦ Ἀρκάδος προθυμεῖσθαι εἴ
τι ἐν τούτῳ εἴη. ἀλλ' οὐδ' ὣς ἐγένοντο.

23   Νέων δὲ ἦν μὲν στρατηγὸς κατὰ τὸ Χειρισόφου μέρος, ἐπεὶ
δὲ ἑώρα τοὺς ἀνθρώπους ὡς εἶχον δεινῶς τῇ ἐνδείᾳ, βουλόμενος 100
αὐτοῖς χαρίζεσθαι, εὑρών τινα ἄνθρωπον Ἡρακλεώτην, ὃς ἔφη
κώμας ἐγγὺς εἰδέναι ὅθεν εἴη λαβεῖν τὰ ἐπιτήδεια, ἐκήρυξε τὸν
βουλόμενον ἰέναι ἐπὶ τὰ ἐπιτήδεια, ὡς ἡγεμόνος ἐσομένου. ἐξ-
έρχονται δὴ σὺν δορατίοις καὶ ἀσκοῖς καὶ θυλάκοις καὶ ἄλλοις
ἀγγείοις εἰς δισχιλίους ἀνθρώπους. ἐπειδὴ δὲ ἦσαν ἐν ταῖς 105
24 κώμαις καὶ διεσπείροντο ὡς ἐπὶ τὸ λαμβάνειν, ἐπιπίπτουσιν
αὐτοῖς οἱ Φαρναβάζου ἱππεῖς πρῶτοι· βεβοηθηκότες γὰρ ἦσαν
τοῖς Βιθυνοῖς, βουλόμενοι σὺν τοῖς Βιθυνοῖς, εἰ δύναιντο, ἀποκω-
λῦσαι τοὺς Ἕλληνας μὴ ἐλθεῖν εἰς τὴν Φρυγίαν· οὗτοι οἱ ἱππεῖς
ἀποκτείνουσι τῶν ἀνδρῶν οὐ μεῖον πεντακοσίους· οἱ δὲ λοιποὶ 110
25 ἐπὶ τὸ ὄρος ἀνέφυγον. ἐκ τούτου ἀπαγγέλλει τις ταῦτα τῶν
ἀποφευγόντων εἰς τὸ στρατόπεδον. καὶ ὁ Ξενοφῶν, ἐπεὶ οὐκ
ἐγεγένητο τὰ ἱερὰ ταύτῃ τῇ ἡμέρᾳ, λαβὼν βοῦν ὑπὸ ἁμάξης, οὐ
γὰρ ἦν ἄλλα ἱερεῖα, σφαγιασάμενος ἐβοήθει καὶ οἱ ἄλλοι οἱ
26 μέχρι τριάκοντα ἐτῶν ἅπαντες. καὶ ἀναλαβόντες τοὺς λοιποὺς 115

ἄνδρας εἰς τὸ στρατόπεδον ἀφικνοῦνται. καὶ ἤδη μὲν ἀμφὶ ἡλίου δυσμὰς ἦν καὶ οἱ Ἕλληνες μάλ' ἀθύμως ἔχοντες ἐδειπνοποιοῦντο, καὶ ἐξαπίνης διὰ τῶν λασίων τῶν Βιθυνῶν τινες ἐπιγενόμενοι τοῖς προφύλαξι τοὺς μὲν κατέκαινον τοὺς δὲ ἐδίωξαν 120 μέχρι εἰς τὸ στρατόπεδον. καὶ κραυγῆς γενυμένης εἰς τὰ ὅπλα 27 πάντες ἔδραμον οἱ Ἕλληνες· καὶ διώκειν μὲν καὶ κινεῖν τὸ στρατόπεδον νυκτὸς οὐκ ἀσφαλὲς ἐδόκει εἶναι· δασέα γὰρ ἦν τὰ χωρία· ἐν δὲ τοῖς ὅπλοις ἐνυκτέρευον φυλαττόμενοι ἱκανοῖς φύλαξι.

V. Τὴν μὲν νύκτα οὕτω διήγαγον· ἅμα δὲ τῇ ἡμέρᾳ οἱ 1 στρατηγοὶ εἰς τὸ ἐρυμνὸν χωρίον ἡγοῦντο· οἳ δὲ εἵποντο ἀναλαβόντες τὰ ὅπλα καὶ τὰ σκεύη. πρὶν δὲ ἀρίστου ὥραν εἶναι ἀπετάφρευον ᾗ ἡ εἴσοδος ἦν εἰς τὸ χωρίον, καὶ ἀπεσταύρωσαν 5 ἅπαν, καταλιπόντες τρεῖς πύλας. καὶ πλοῖον ἐξ Ἡρακλείας ἧκεν ἄλφιτα ἄγον καὶ ἱερεῖα καὶ οἶνον· πρῲ δ' ἀναστὰς Ξενοφῶν 2 ἐθύετο ἐπ' ἐξόδῳ, καὶ γίγνεται τὰ ἱερὰ ἐπὶ τοῦ πρώτου ἱερείου. καὶ ἤδη τέλος ἐχόντων τῶν ἱερῶν ὁρᾷ αἰετὸν αἴσιον ὁ μάντις Ἀρηξίων Παρράσιος, καὶ ἡγεῖσθαι κελεύει τὸν Ξενοφῶντα. καὶ 3 10 διαβάντες τὴν τάφρον τὰ ὅπλα τίθενται, καὶ ἐκήρυξαν ἀριστήσαντας ἐξιέναι τοὺς στρατιώτας σὺν τοῖς ὅπλοις, τὸν δὲ ὄχλον καὶ τὰ ἀνδράποδα αὐτοῦ καταλιπεῖν. οἱ μὲν δὴ ἄλλοι πάντες 4 ἐξῇσαν, Νέων δὲ οὔ· ἐδόκει γὰρ κάλλιστον εἶναι τοῦτον φύλακα καταλιπεῖν τῶν ἐπὶ στρατοπέδου. ἐπεὶ δ' οἱ λοχαγοὶ καὶ οἱ 15 στρατιῶται ἀπέλειπον αὐτόν, αἰσχυνόμενοι μὴ ἐφέπεσθαι τῶν ἄλλων ἐξιόντων, κατέλιπον αὐτοῦ τοὺς ὑπὲρ πέντε καὶ τετταράκοντα ἔτη. καὶ οὗτοι μὲν ἔμενον, οἱ δ' ἄλλοι ἐπορεύοντο. πρὶν 5 δὲ πεντεκαίδεκα στάδια διεληλυθέναι ἐνέτυχον ἤδη νεκροῖς· καὶ τὴν οὐρὰν τοῦ κέρατος ποιησάμενοι κατὰ τοὺς πρώτους φανέντας 20 νεκροὺς ἔθαπτον πάντας ὁπόσους ἐπελάμβανε τὸ κέρας. ἐπεὶ 6 δὲ τοὺς πρώτους ἔθαψαν, προαγαγόντες καὶ τὴν οὐρὰν αὖθις ποιησάμενοι κατὰ τοὺς πρώτους τῶν ἀτάφων ἔθαπτον τὸν αὐτὸν τρόπον ὁπόσους ἐπελάμβανεν ἡ στρατιά. ἐπεὶ δὲ εἰς τὴν ὁδὸν ἧκον τὴν ἐκ τῶν κωμῶν, ἔνθα ἔκειντο ἀθρόοι, συνενεγκόντες 25 αὐτοὺς ἔθαψαν.

Ἤδη δὲ πέρα μεσούσης τῆς ἡμέρας προάγοντες τὸ στρά- 7 τευμα ἔξω τῶν κωμῶν ἐλάμβανον τὰ ἐπιτήδεια ὅ,τι τις ὁρῴη

ἐντὸς τῆς φάλαγγος, καὶ ἐξαίφνης ὁρῶσι τοὺς πολεμίους ὑπερ-
βάλλοντας κατὰ λόφους τινὰς ἐκ τοῦ ἐναντίου, τεταγμένους ἐπὶ
φάλαγγος ἱππέας τε πολλοὺς καὶ πεζούς· καὶ γὰρ Σπιθριδάτης
καὶ Ῥαθίνης ἦκον παρὰ Φαρναβάζου ἔχοντες τὴν δύναμιν.
8 ἐπεὶ δὲ κατεῖδον τοὺς Ἕλληνας οἱ πολέμιοι, ἔστησαν ἀπέχοντες
αὐτῶν ὅσον πεντεκαίδεκα σταδίους. ἐκ τούτου εὐθὺς ὁ Ἀρηξίων
ὁ μάντις τῶν Ἑλλήνων σφαγιάζεται, καὶ ἐγένετο ἐπὶ τοῦ πρώτου
9 καλὰ τὰ σφάγια. ἔνθα δὴ Ξενοφῶν λέγει· Δοκεῖ μοι, ὦ ἄνδρες
στρατηγοί, ἐπιτάξασθαι τῇ φάλαγγι λόχους φύλακας ἵν' ἄν που
δέῃ ὦσιν οἱ ἐπιβοηθήσοντες τῇ φάλαγγι καὶ οἱ πολέμιοι τεταραγ-
μένοι ἐμπίπτωσιν εἰς τεταγμένους καὶ ἀκεραίους. συνεδόκει
10 ταῦτα πᾶσιν. Ὑμεῖς μὲν τοίνυν, ἔφη, προηγεῖσθε τὴν πρὸς τοὺς
ἐναντίους, ὡς μὴ ἑστήκωμεν, ἐπεὶ ὤφθημεν καὶ εἴδομεν τοὺς
πολεμίους· ἐγὼ δὲ ἥξω τοὺς τελευταίους λόχους καταχωρίσας
11 ᾗπερ ὑμῖν δοκεῖ. ἐκ τούτου οἱ μὲν ἥσυχοι προῆγον, ὁ δὲ τρεῖς
ἀφελὼν τὰς τελευταίας τάξεις ἀνὰ διακοσίους ἄνδρας τὴν μὲν
ἐπὶ τὸ δεξιὸν ἐπέτρεψεν ἐφέπεσθαι ἀπολιπόντας ὡς πλέθρον·
Σαμόλας Ἀχαιὸς ταύτης ἦρχε τῆς τάξεως· τὴν δ' ἐπὶ τῷ μέσῳ
ἐχώρισεν ἕπεσθαι· Πυρρίας Ἀρκὰς ταύτης ἦρχε τῆς τάξεως· τὴν
δὲ μίαν ἐπὶ τῷ εὐωνύμῳ· Φρασίας Ἀθηναῖος ταύτῃ ἐφειστήκει.
12 Προϊόντες δέ, ἐπεὶ ἐγένοντο οἱ ἡγούμενοι ἐπὶ νάπει μεγάλῳ
καὶ δυσπόρῳ, ἔστησαν ἀγνοοῦντες εἰ διαβατέον εἴη τὸ νάπος.
καὶ παρεγγυῶσι στρατηγοὺς καὶ λοχαγοὺς παριέναι ἐπὶ τὸ
13 ἡγούμενον. καὶ ὁ Ξενοφῶν θαυμάσας ὅ,τι τὸ ἴσχον εἴη τὴν
πορείαν καὶ ταχὺ ἀκούων τὴν παρεγγύην, ἐλαύνει ᾗ τάχιστα.
ἐπεὶ δὲ συνῆλθον, λέγει Σοφαίνετος πρεσβύτατος ὢν τῶν στρατηγῶν ὅτι βουλῆς οὐκ ἄξιον εἴη εἰ διαβατέον ἐστὶ τοιοῦτον
νάπος.

14 Καὶ ὁ Ξενοφῶν σπουδῇ ὑπολαβὼν ἔλεξεν· Ἀλλ' ἴστε μέν
με, ὦ ἄνδρες, οὐδένα πω κίνδυνον προξενήσαντα ὑμῖν ἐθελού-
σιον· οὐ γὰρ δόξης ὁρῶ δεομένους ὑμᾶς εἰς ἀνδρειότητα, ἀλλὰ
15 σωτηρίας. νῦν δὲ οὕτως ἔχει· ἀμαχεὶ μὲν ἐνθένδε οὐκ ἔστιν
ἀπελθεῖν· ἢν γὰρ μὴ ἡμεῖς ἴωμεν ἐπὶ τοὺς πολεμίους, οὗτοι
16 ἡμῖν ὁπόταν ἀπίωμεν ἕψονται καὶ ἐπιπεσοῦνται. ὁρᾶτε δὴ
πότερον κρεῖττον ἰέναι ἐπὶ τοὺς ἄνδρας προβαλλομένους τὰ

ὅπλα ἢ μεταβαλλομένους ὄπισθεν ἡμῶν ἐπιόντας τοὺς πολεμίους
θεᾶσθαι. ἴστε μέντοι ὅτι τὸ μὲν ἀπιέναι ἀπὸ πολεμίων οὐδενὶ
καλῷ ἔοικε, τὸ δὲ ἐφέπεσθαι καὶ τοῖς κακίοσι θάρρος ἐμποιεῖ.
ἐγὼ γοῦν ἥδιον ἂν σὺν ἡμίσεσιν ἐπιοίην ἢ σὺν διπλασίοις ἀποχωροίην. καὶ τούτους οἶδ' ὅτι ἐπιόντων μὲν ἡμῶν οὐδ' ὑμεῖς
ἐλπίζετε δέξασθαι ἡμᾶς, ἀπιόντων δὲ πάντες ἐπιστάμεθα ὅτι
τολμήσουσιν ἐφέπεσθαι. τὸ δὲ διαβάντας ὄπισθεν νάπος χαλεπὸν ποιήσασθαι μέλλοντας μάχεσθαι ἆρ' οὐχὶ καὶ ἁρπάσαι
ἄξιον; τοῖς μὲν γὰρ πολεμίοις ἐγὼ βουλοίμην ἂν εὔπορα πάντα
φαίνεσθαι ὥστε ἀποχωρεῖν· ἡμᾶς δὲ καὶ ἀπὸ τοῦ χωρίου δεῖ
διδάσκεσθαι ὅτι οὐκ ἔστι μὴ νικῶσι σωτηρία. θαυμάζω δ' ἔγωγε
καὶ τὸ νάπος τοῦτο εἴ τις μᾶλλον φοβερὸν νομίζει εἶναι τῶν
ἄλλων ὧν διαπεπορεύμεθα χωρίων. πῶς γὰρ δὴ διαβατὸν τὸ
πεδίον, εἰ μὴ νικήσομεν τοὺς ἱππέας; πῶς δὲ ἃ διεληλύθαμεν
ὄρη, ἢν πελτασταὶ τοσοίδε ἐφέπωνται; ἢν δὲ δὴ καὶ σωθῶμεν
ἐπὶ θάλατταν, πόσον τι νάπος ὁ Πόντος; ἔνθα οὔτε πλοῖα ἔστι
τὰ ἀπάξοντα οὔτε σῖτος ᾧ θρεψόμεθα μένοντες, δεήσει δέ, ἢν
θᾶττον ἐκεῖ γενώμεθα, θᾶττον πάλιν ἐξιέναι ἐπὶ τὰ ἐπιτήδεια.
οὐκοῦν νῦν κρεῖττον ἠριστηκότας μάχεσθαι ἢ αὔριον ἀναρίστους.
ἄνδρες, τά τε ἱερὰ ἡμῖν καλὰ οἵ τε οἰωνοὶ αἴσιοι τά τε σφάγια
κάλλιστα· ἴωμεν ἐπὶ τοὺς ἄνδρας. οὐ δεῖ ἔτι τούτους, ἐπεὶ ἡμᾶς
πάντως εἶδον, ἡδέως δειπνῆσαι οὐδ' ὅπου ἂν θέλωσι σκηνῆσαι.

Ἐντεῦθεν οἱ λοχαγοὶ ἡγεῖσθαι ἐκέλευον, καὶ οὐδεὶς ἀντέλεγε.
καὶ ὃς ἡγεῖτο, παραγγείλας διαβαίνειν ᾗ ἕκαστος ἐτύγχανε τοῦ
νάπους ὤν· θᾶττον γὰρ ἁθρόον ἐδόκει ἂν οὕτω πέραν γενέσθαι
τὸ στράτευμα ἢ εἰ κατὰ τὴν γέφυραν ἢ ἐπὶ τῷ νάπει ἦν ἐξεμηρύοντο. ἐπεὶ δὲ διέβησαν, παριὼν παρὰ τὴν φάλαγγα ἔλεγεν·
Ἄνδρες, ἀναμιμνήσκεσθε ὅσας δὴ μάχας σὺν τοῖς θεοῖς ὁμόσε
ἰόντες νενικήκατε καὶ οἷα πάσχουσιν οἱ πολεμίους φεύγοντες, καὶ
τοῦτο ἐννοήσατε ὅτι ἐπὶ ταῖς θύραις τῆς Ἑλλάδος ἐσμέν. ἀλλ'
ἕπεσθε ἡγεμόνι τῷ Ἡρακλεῖ καὶ ἀλλήλους παρακαλεῖτε ὀνομαστί. ἡδύ τοι ἀνδρεῖόν τι καὶ καλὸν νῦν εἰπόντα καὶ ποιήσαντα
μνήμην ἐν οἷς ἐθέλει παρέχειν ἑαυτοῦ.

Ταῦτα παρελαύνων ἔλεγε καὶ ἅμα ὑφηγεῖτο ἐπὶ φάλαγγος,
καὶ τοὺς πελταστὰς ἑκατέρωθεν ποιησάμενοι ἐπορεύοντο ἐπὶ τοὺς

πολεμίους. παρήγγελτο δὲ τὰ μὲν δόρατα ἐπὶ τὸν δεξιὸν ὦμον
ἔχειν, ἕως σημαίνοι τῇ σάλπιγγι· ἔπειτα δὲ εἰς προσβολὴν
καθέντας ἕπεσθαι βάδην καὶ μηδένα δρόμῳ διώκειν. ἐκ τούτου
σύνθημα παρῄει Ζεὺς σωτήρ, Ἡρακλῆς ἡγεμών. οἱ δὲ πολέμιοι
ὑπέμενον, νομίζοντες καλὸν ἔχειν τὸ χωρίον. ἐπεὶ δ᾿ ἐπλησίαζον,
ἀλαλάξαντες οἱ Ἕλληνες πελτασταὶ ἔθεον ἐπὶ τοὺς πολεμίους
πρίν τινα κελεύειν· οἱ δὲ πολέμιοι ἀντίοι ὥρμησαν, οἱ θ᾿ ἱππεῖς
καὶ τὸ στῖφος τῶν Βιθυνῶν· καὶ τρέπονται τοὺς πελταστάς.
ἀλλ᾿ ἐπεὶ ὑπηντίαζεν ἡ φάλαγξ τῶν ὁπλιτῶν ταχὺ πορευομένη
καὶ ἅμα ἡ σάλπιγξ ἐφθέγξατο καὶ ἐπαιάνιζον καὶ μετὰ ταῦτα
ἠλάλαζον καὶ ἅμα τὰ δόρατα καθίεσαν, ἐνταῦθα οὐκέτι ἐδέξαντο
οἱ πολέμιοι, ἀλλὰ ἔφευγον. καὶ Τιμασίων μὲν ἔχων τοὺς ἱππεῖς
ἐφείπετο, καὶ ἀπεκτίννυσαν ὅσουσπερ ἐδύναντο ὡς ὀλίγοι ὄντες.
τῶν δὲ πολεμίων τὸ μὲν εὐώνυμον εὐθὺς διεσπάρη, καθ᾿ ὃ οἱ
Ἕλληνες ἱππεῖς ἦσαν, τὸ δὲ δεξιὸν ἅτε οὐ σφόδρα διωκόμενον
ἐπὶ λόφου συνέστη. ἐπεὶ δὲ εἶδον οἱ Ἕλληνες ὑπομένοντας
αὐτούς, ἐδόκει ῥᾷστόν τε καὶ ἀκινδυνότατον εἶναι ἰέναι ἤδη ἐπ᾿
αὐτούς. παιανίσαντες οὖν εὐθὺς ἐπέκειντο· οἳ δ᾿ οὐχ ὑπέμειναν.
καὶ ἐνταῦθα οἱ πελτασταὶ ἐδίωκον μέχρι τὸ δεξιὸν διεσπάρη·
ἀπέθανον δὲ ὀλίγοι· τὸ γὰρ ἱππικὸν φόβον παρεῖχε τὸ τῶν
πολεμίων πολὺ ὄν. ἐπεὶ δὲ εἶδον οἱ Ἕλληνες τό τε Φαρναβάζου ἱππικὸν ἔτι συνεστηκὸς καὶ τοὺς Βιθυνοὺς ἱππέας πρὸς τοῦτο
συναθροιζομένους καὶ ἀπὸ λόφου τινὸς καταθεωμένους τὰ γιγνόμενα ἀπειρήκεσαν μέν, ὅμως δὲ ἐδόκει καὶ ἐπὶ τούτους ἰτέον
εἶναι οὕτως ὅπως δύναιντο, ὡς μὴ τεθαρρηκότες ἀναπαύσαιντο.
συνταξάμενοι δὴ πορεύονται. ἐντεῦθεν οἱ πολέμιοι ἱππεῖς φεύγουσι κατὰ τοῦ πρανοῦς ὁμοίως ὥσπερ ὑπὸ ἱππέων διωκόμενοι·
νάπος γὰρ αὐτοὺς ὑπεδέχετο, ὃ οὐκ ᾔδεσαν οἱ Ἕλληνες, ἀλλὰ
προαπετράποντο διώκοντες· ὀψὲ γὰρ ἦν. ἐπανελθόντες δὲ ἔνθα
ἡ πρώτη συμβολὴ ἐγένετο, στησάμενοι τρόπαιον ἀπῇσαν ἐπὶ
θάλατταν περὶ ἡλίου δυσμάς· στάδιοι δ᾿ ἦσαν ὡς ἑξήκοντα ἐπὶ
τὸ στρατόπεδον.

VI. Ἐντεῦθεν οἱ μὲν πολέμιοι εἶχον ἀμφὶ τὰ ἑαυτῶν καὶ
ἀπήγοντο καὶ τοὺς οἰκέτας καὶ τὰ χρήματα ὅποι ἐδύναντο προ-
σωτάτω· οἱ δὲ Ἕλληνες προσέμενον μὲν Κλέανδρον καὶ τὰς

τριήρεις καὶ τὰ πλοῖα ὡς ἥξοντα, ἐξιόντες δ' ἑκάστης ἡμέρας σὺν
τοῖς ὑποζυγίοις καὶ τοῖς ἀνδραπόδοις ἐφέροντο ἀδεῶς πυροὺς καὶ
κριθάς, οἶνον, ὄσπρια, μελίνας, σῦκα· ἅπαντα γὰρ ἀγαθὰ εἶχεν
ἡ χώρα πλὴν ἐλαίου. καὶ ὁπότε μὲν καταμένοι τὸ στράτευμα 2
ἀναπαυόμενον, ἐξῆν ἐπὶ λείαν ἰέναι, καὶ ἐλάμβανον οἱ ἐξιόντες·
ὁπότε δὲ ἐξίοι πᾶν τὸ στράτευμα, εἴ τις χωρὶς ἀπελθὼν λάβοι
τι, δημόσιον ἔδοξεν εἶναι. ἤδη δὲ ἦν πάντων ἀφθονία· καὶ γὰρ 3
ἀγοραὶ πάντοθεν ἀφικνοῦντο ἐκ τῶν Ἑλληνίδων πόλεων καὶ οἱ
παραπλέοντες ἄσμενοι κατῆγον, ἀκούοντες ὡς οἰκίζοιτο πόλις
καὶ λιμὴν εἴη. ἔπεμπον δὲ καὶ οἱ πολέμιοι ἤδη οἳ πλησίον 4
ᾤκουν πρὸς Ξενοφῶντα, ἀκούοντες ὅτι οὗτος πολίζει τὸ χωρίον,
ἐρωτῶντες ὅ,τι δέοι ποιοῦντας φίλους εἶναι. ὁ δ' ἐπεδείκνυεν
αὐτοὺς τοῖς στρατιώταις.

Καὶ ἐν τούτῳ Κλέανδρος ἀφικνεῖται δύο τριήρεις ἔχων, 5
πλοῖον δ' οὐδέν. ἐτύγχανε δὲ τὸ στράτευμα ἔξω ὂν ὅτε ἀφίκετο
καὶ ἐπὶ λείαν τινὲς οἰχόμενοι ἄλλοσε εἰς τὸ ὄρος εἰλήφεσαν πρόβατα πολλά· ὀκνοῦντες δὲ μὴ ἀφαιρεθεῖεν τῷ Δεξίππῳ λέγουσιν, ὃς ἀπέδρα τὴν πεντηκόντορον ἔχων ἐκ Τραπεζοῦντος, καὶ
κελεύουσι διασώσαντα αὐτοῖς τὰ πρόβατα τὰ μὲν αὐτὸν λαβεῖν,
τὰ δὲ σφίσιν ἀποδοῦναι. εὐθὺς δ' ἐκεῖνος ἀπελαύνει τοὺς περιε- 6
στῶτας τῶν στρατιωτῶν καὶ λέγοντας ὅτι δημόσια εἴη, καὶ τῷ
Κλεάνδρῳ λέγει ἐλθὼν ὅτι ἁρπάζειν ἐπιχειροῦσιν. ὁ δὲ κελεύει
τὸν ἁρπάζοντα ἄγειν πρὸς αὐτόν. καὶ ὁ μὲν λαβὼν ἦγέ τινα· 7
περιτυχὼν δ' Ἀγασίας ἀφαιρεῖται· καὶ γὰρ ἦν αὐτῷ ὁ ἀγόμενος
λοχίτης. οἱ δ' ἄλλοι οἱ παρόντες τῶν στρατιωτῶν ἐπιχειροῦσι
βάλλειν τὸν Δέξιππον, ἀνακαλοῦντες τὸν προδότην. ἔδεισαν δὲ
καὶ τῶν τριηριτῶν πολλοὶ καὶ ἔφευγον εἰς τὴν θάλατταν, καὶ
Κλέανδρος δ' ἔφευγε. Ξενοφῶν δὲ καὶ οἱ ἄλλοι στρατηγοὶ 8
κατεκώλυόν τε καὶ τῷ Κλεάνδρῳ ἔλεγον ὅτι οὐδὲν εἴη πρᾶγμα,
ἀλλὰ τὸ δόγμα αἴτιον εἴη τοῦ στρατεύματος ταῦτα γενέσθαι.
ὁ δὲ Κλέανδρος ὑπὸ τοῦ Δεξίππου τε ἀνερεθιζόμενος καὶ αὐτὸς
ἀχθεσθεὶς ὅτι ἐφοβήθη, ἀποπλευσεῖσθαι ἔφη καὶ κηρύξειν μηδεμίαν πόλιν δέχεσθαι αὐτούς, ὡς πολεμίους. ἦρχον δὲ τότε
πάντων τῶν Ἑλλήνων οἱ Λακεδαιμόνιοι. ἐνταῦθα πονηρὸν
τὸ πρᾶγμα ἐδόκει εἶναι τοῖς Ἕλλησι, καὶ ἐδέοντο μὴ ποιεῖν

ταῦτα. ὃ δ' οὐκ ἂν ἄλλως ἔφη γενέσθαι, εἰ μή τις ἐκδώσει τὸν
ἄρξαντα βάλλειν καὶ τὸν ἀφελόμενον. ἦν δὲ ὃν ἐξῄτει Ἀγασίας
διὰ τέλους φίλος τῷ Ξενοφῶντι· ἐξ οὗ καὶ διέβαλλεν αὐτὸν ὁ
Δέξιππος.

Καὶ ἐντεῦθεν ἐπειδὴ ἀπορία ἦν, συνήγαγον τὸ στράτευμα οἱ
ἄρχοντες· καὶ ἔνιοι μὲν αὐτῶν παρ' ὀλίγον ἐποιοῦντο τὸν Κλέανδρον, τῷ δὲ Ξενοφῶντι οὐκ ἐδόκει φαῦλον εἶναι, ἀλλ' ἀναστὰς
ἔλεξεν· Ὦ ἄνδρες στρατιῶται, ἐμοὶ δὲ οὐδὲν φαῦλον δοκεῖ εἶναι
τὸ πρᾶγμα, εἰ ἡμῖν οὕτως ἔχων τὴν γνώμην Κλέανδρος ἄπεισιν
ὥσπερ λέγει. εἰσὶ μὲν γὰρ ἐγγὺς αἱ Ἑλληνίδες πόλεις· τῆς δὲ
Ἑλλάδος Λακεδαιμόνιοι προεστήκασιν· ἱκανοὶ δέ εἰσι καὶ εἷς
ἕκαστος Λακεδαιμονίων ἐν ταῖς πόλεσιν ὅ,τι βούλονται διαπράτ-
τεσθαι. εἰ οὖν οὗτος πρῶτον μὲν ἡμᾶς Βυζαντίου ἀποκλείσει,
ἔπειτα δὲ τοῖς ἄλλοις ἁρμοσταῖς παραγγελεῖ εἰς τὰς πόλεις μὴ
δέχεσθαι ὡς ἀπιστοῦντας Λακεδαιμονίοις καὶ ἀνόμους ὄντας, ἔτι
δὲ πρὸς Ἀναξίβιον τὸν ναύαρχον οὗτος ὁ λόγος περὶ ἡμῶν ἥξει,
χαλεπὸν ἔσται καὶ μένειν καὶ ἀποπλεῖν· καὶ γὰρ ἐν τῇ γῇ
ἄρχουσι Λακεδαιμόνιοι καὶ ἐν τῇ θαλάττῃ τὸν νῦν χρόνον.
οὔκουν δεῖ οὔτε ἑνὸς ἀνδρὸς ἕνεκα οὔτε δυοῖν ἡμᾶς τοὺς ἄλλους
τῆς Ἑλλάδος ἀπέχεσθαι, ἀλλὰ πειστέον ὅ,τι ἂν κελεύωσι· καὶ
γὰρ αἱ πόλεις ἡμῶν ὅθεν ἐσμὲν πείθονται αὐτοῖς. ἐγὼ μὲν οὖν,
καὶ γὰρ ἀκούω Δέξιππον λέγειν πρὸς Κλέανδρον ὡς οὐκ ἂν
ἐποίησεν Ἀγασίας ταῦτα, εἰ μὴ ἐγὼ αὐτὸν ἐκέλευσα, ἐγὼ μὲν
οὖν ἀπολύω καὶ ὑμᾶς τῆς αἰτίας καὶ Ἀγασίαν, ἂν αὐτὸς
Ἀγασίας φήσῃ ἐμέ τι τούτων αἴτιον εἶναι, καὶ καταδικάζω
ἐμαυτοῦ, εἰ ἐγὼ πετροβολίας ἢ ἄλλου τινὸς βιαίου ἐξάρχω, τῆς
ἐσχάτης δίκης ἄξιος εἶναι, καὶ ὑφέξω τὴν δίκην. φημὶ δὲ καὶ
εἴ τινα ἄλλον αἰτιᾶται, χρῆναι ἑαυτὸν παρασχεῖν Κλεάνδρῳ
κρῖναι· οὕτω γὰρ ἂν ὑμεῖς ἀπολελυμένοι τῆς αἰτίας εἴητε. ὡς
δὲ νῦν ἔχει, χαλεπὸν εἰ οἰόμενοι ἐν τῇ Ἑλλάδι καὶ ἐπαίνου καὶ
τιμῆς τεύξεσθαι ἀντὶ δὲ τούτων οὐδ' ὅμοιοι τοῖς ἄλλοις ἐσόμεθα,
ἀλλ' εἰρξόμεθα ἐκ τῶν Ἑλληνίδων πόλεων.

Μετὰ ταῦτα ἀναστὰς εἶπεν Ἀγασίας· Ἐγώ, ὦ ἄνδρες,
ὄμνυμι θεοὺς καὶ θεὰς ἦ μὴν μήτε με Ξενοφῶντα κελεῦσαι
ἀφελέσθαι τὸν ἄνδρα μήτε ἄλλον ὑμῶν μηδένα· ἰδόντι δέ μοι

ἄνδρα ἀγαθὸν ἀγόμενον τῶν ἐμῶν λοχιτῶν ὑπὸ Δεξίππου, ὃν
ὑμεῖς ἐπίστασθε ὑμᾶς προδόντα, δεινὸν ἔδοξεν εἶναι· καὶ ἀφειλόμην, ὁμολογῶ. καὶ ὑμεῖς μὲν μὴ ἐκδῶτέ με· ἐγὼ δὲ ἐμαυτόν,
ὥσπερ Ξενοφῶν λέγει, παρασχήσω κρίναντι Κλεάνδρῳ ὅ,τι ἂν
βούληται ποιῆσαι· τούτου ἕνεκα μήτε πολεμεῖτε Λακεδαιμονίοις
σῴζοισθέ τε ἀσφαλῶς ὅποι θέλει ἕκαστος. συμπέμψατε μέντοι
μοι ὑμῶν αὐτῶν ἑλόμενοι πρὸς Κλέανδρον οἵτινες, ἄν τι ἐγὼ
παραλίπω, καὶ λέξουσιν ὑπὲρ ἐμοῦ καὶ πράξουσιν.

Ἐκ τούτου ἔδωκεν ἡ στρατιὰ οὕστινας βούλοιτο προελό-
μενον ἰέναι. ὁ δὲ προείλετο τοὺς στρατηγούς. μετὰ ταῦτα
ἐπορεύοντο πρὸς Κλέανδρον Ἀγασίας καὶ οἱ στρατηγοὶ καὶ ὁ
ἀφαιρεθεὶς ἀνὴρ ὑπὸ Ἀγασίου. καὶ ἔλεγον οἱ στρατηγοί·
Ἔπεμψεν ἡμᾶς ἡ στρατιὰ πρὸς σέ, ὦ Κλέανδρε, καὶ ἐκέλευσέ
σε, εἴτε πάντας αἰτιᾷ, κρίναντα σὲ αὐτὸν χρῆσθαι ὅ,τι ἂν βούλῃ,
εἴτε ἕνα τινὰ ἢ δύο ἢ καὶ πλείους αἰτιᾷ τούτους ἀξιοῦσι παρασχεῖν σοι ἑαυτοὺς εἰς κρίσιν. εἴ τι οὖν ἡμῶν τινα αἰτιᾷ,
πάρεσμέν σοι ἡμεῖς· εἴ τι δὲ ἄλλον τινά, φράσον· οὐδεὶς γὰρ
ἀπέσται ὅστις ἂν ἡμῖν ἐθέλῃ πείθεσθαι. μετὰ ταῦτα παρελθὼν
ὁ Ἀγασίας εἶπεν· Ἐγώ εἰμι, ὦ Κλέανδρε, ὁ ἀφελόμενος Δεξίππου ἄγοντος τοῦτον τὸν ἄνδρα καὶ παίειν κελεύσας Δέξιππον.
τοῦτον μὲν γὰρ οἶδα ἄνδρα ἀγαθὸν ὄντα, Δέξιππον δὲ οἶδα
αἱρεθέντα ὑπὸ τῆς στρατιᾶς ἄρχειν τῆς πεντηκοντόρου ἧς ᾐτησάμεθα παρὰ Τραπεζουντίων ἐφ' ᾧτε πλοῖα συλλέγειν ὡς σῳ-
ζοίμεθα, καὶ ἀποδράντα Δέξιππον καὶ προδόντα τοὺς στρατιώτας
μεθ' ὧν ἐσώθη. καὶ τούς τε Τραπεζουντίους ἀπεστερήκαμεν
τὴν πεντηκόντορον καὶ κακοὶ δοκοῦμεν εἶναι διὰ τοῦτον, αὐτοί
τε τὸ ἐπὶ τούτῳ ἀπολώλαμεν. ἤκουε γάρ, ὥσπερ ἡμεῖς, ὡς
ἄπορον εἴη πεζῇ ἀπιόντας τοὺς ποταμούς τε διαβῆναι καὶ
σωθῆναι εἰς τὴν Ἑλλάδα. τοῦτον οὖν τοιοῦτον ὄντα ἀφειλόμην.
εἰ δὲ σὺ ἦγες ἢ ἄλλος τις τῶν παρὰ σοῦ, καὶ μὴ τῶν παρ' ἡμῶν
ἀποδράντων, εὖ ἴσθι ὅτι οὐδὲν ἂν τούτων ἐποίησα. νόμιζε δέ,
ἂν ἐμὲ νῦν ἀποκτείνῃς, δι' ἄνδρα δειλόν τε καὶ πονηρὸν ἄνδρα
ἀγαθὸν ἀποκτείνων.

Ἀκούσας ταῦτα ὁ Κλέανδρος εἶπεν ὅτι Δέξιππον μὲν οὐκ
ἐπαινοίη, εἰ ταῦτα πεποιηκὼς εἴη· οὐ μέντοι ἔφη νομίζειν οὐδ'

εἰ παμπόνηρος ἦν Δέξιππος βίᾳ χρῆναι πάσχειν αὐτόν, ἀλλὰ κριθέντα, ὥσπερ καὶ ὑμεῖς νῦν ἀξιοῦτε, τῆς δίκης τυχεῖν. νῦν οὖν ἄπιτε καταλιπόντες τόνδε τὸν ἄνδρα· ὅταν δ' ἐγὼ κελεύσω, πάρεστε πρὸς τὴν κρίσιν. αἰτιῶμαι δὲ οὔτε τὴν στρατιὰν οὔτε ἄλλον οὐδένα ἔτι, ἐπεὶ οὗτος αὐτὸς ὁμολογεῖ ἀφελέσθαι τὸν ἄνδρα. ὁ δὲ ἀφαιρεθεὶς εἶπεν· Ἐγώ, ὦ Κλέανδρε, εἰ καὶ οἴει με ἀδικοῦντά τι ἄγεσθαι, οὔτε ἔπαιον οὐδένα οὔτε ἔβαλλον, ἀλλ' εἶπον ὅτι δημόσια εἴη τὰ πρόβατα· ἦν γὰρ τῶν στρατιωτῶν δόγμα, εἴ τις ὁπότε ἡ στρατιὰ ἐξίοι ἰδίᾳ λῄζοιτο, δημόσια εἶναι τὰ ληφθέντα. ταῦτα εἶπον· ἐκ τούτου με λαβὼν οὗτος ἦγεν, ἵνα μὴ φθέγγοιτο μηδείς, ἀλλ' αὐτὸς λαβὼν τὸ μέρος διασώσειε τοῖς λῃσταῖς παρὰ τὴν ῥήτραν τὰ χρήματα. πρὸς ταῦτα ὁ Κλέανδρος εἶπεν· Ἐπεὶ τοίνυν συναίτιος εἶ, κατάμενε, ἵνα καὶ περὶ σοῦ βουλευσώμεθα.

Ἐκ τούτου οἱ μὲν ἀμφὶ Κλέανδρον ἠρίστων· τὴν δὲ στρατιὰν συνήγαγε Ξενοφῶν καὶ συνεβούλευε πέμψαι ἄνδρας πρὸς Κλέανδρον παραιτησομένους περὶ τῶν ἀνδρῶν. ἐκ τούτου ἔδοξεν αὐτοῖς πέμψαντας στρατηγοὺς καὶ λοχαγοὺς καὶ Δρακόντιον τὸν Σπαρτιάτην καὶ τῶν ἄλλων οἳ ἐδόκουν ἐπιτήδειοι εἶναι δεῖσθαι Κλεάνδρου κατὰ πάντα τρόπον ἀφεῖναι τὼ ἄνδρε. ἐλθὼν οὖν ὁ Ξενοφῶν λέγει· Ἔχεις μέν, ὦ Κλέανδρε, τοὺς ἄνδρας, καὶ ἡ στρατιά σοι ὑφεῖτο ὅ,τι ἐβούλου ποιῆσαι καὶ περὶ τούτων καὶ περὶ αὐτῶν ἁπάντων. νῦν δέ σε αἰτοῦνται καὶ δέονται δοῦναι σφίσι τὼ ἄνδρε καὶ μὴ κατακαίνειν· πολλὰ γὰρ ἐν τῷ ἔμπροσθεν χρόνῳ περὶ τὴν στρατιὰν ἐμοχθησάτην. ταῦτα δέ σου τυχόντες ὑπισχνοῦνταί σοι ἀντὶ τούτων, ἢν βούλῃ ἡγεῖσθαι αὐτῶν καὶ ἢν οἱ θεοὶ ἵλεῳ ὦσιν, ἐπιδείξειν σοι καὶ ὡς κόσμιοί εἰσι καὶ ὡς ἱκανοὶ τῷ ἄρχοντι πειθόμενοι τοὺς πολεμίους σὺν τοῖς θεοῖς μὴ φοβεῖσθαι. δέονται δέ σου καὶ τοῦτο, παραγενόμενον καὶ ἄρξαντα ἑαυτῶν πεῖραν λαβεῖν καὶ Δεξίππου καὶ σφῶν τῶν ἄλλων οἷος ἕκαστός ἐστι, καὶ τὴν ἀξίαν ἑκάστοις νεῖμαι. ἀκούσας ταῦτα ὁ Κλέανδρος, Ἀλλὰ ναὶ τὼ σιώ, ἔφη, ταχύ τοι ὑμῖν ἀποκρινοῦμαι. καὶ τώ τε ἄνδρε ὑμῖν δίδωμι καὶ αὐτὸς παρέσομαι· καὶ ἢν οἱ θεοὶ παραδιδῶσιν, ἐξηγήσομαι εἰς τὴν Ἑλλάδα. καὶ πολὺ οἱ λόγοι οὗτοι ἀντίοι εἰσὶν ἢ οὓς ἐγὼ

περὶ ὑμῶν ἐνίων ἤκουον ὡς τὸ στράτευμα ἀφίστατε ἀπὸ
Λακεδαιμονίων.

Ἐκ τούτου οἱ μὲν ἐπαινοῦντες ἀπῆλθον, ἔχοντες τὼ ἄνδρε·
Κλέανδρος δὲ ἐθύετο ἐπὶ τῇ πορείᾳ καὶ ξυνῆν Ξενοφῶντι φιλικῶς
καὶ ξενίαν ξυνεβάλλοντο. ἐπεὶ δὲ καὶ ἑώρα αὐτοὺς τὸ παραγγελλόμενον εὐτάκτως ποιοῦντας, καὶ μᾶλλον ἔτι ἐπεθύμει ἡγεμὼν
γενέσθαι αὐτῶν. ἐπεὶ μέντοι θυομένῳ αὐτῷ ἐπὶ τρεῖς ἡμέρας
οὐκ ἐγίγνετο τὰ ἱερά, συγκαλέσας τοὺς στρατηγοὺς εἶπεν· Ἐμοὶ
μὲν οὐ τελέθει τὰ ἱερὰ ἐξάγειν· ὑμεῖς μέντοι μὴ ἀθυμεῖτε τούτου
ἕνεκα· ὑμῖν γάρ, ὡς ἔοικε, δέδοται ἐκκομίσαι τοὺς ἄνδρας· ἀλλὰ
πορεύεσθε. ἡμεῖς δὲ ὑμᾶς, ἐπειδὰν ἐκεῖσε ἥκητε, δεξόμεθα ὡς
ἂν δυνώμεθα κάλλιστα.

Ἐκ τούτου ἔδοξε τοῖς στρατιώταις δοῦναι αὐτῷ τὰ δημόσια
πρόβατα· ὁ δὲ δεξάμενος πάλιν αὐτοῖς ἀπέδωκε. καὶ οὗτος μὲν
ἀπέπλει. οἱ δὲ στρατιῶται διαθέμενοι τὸν σῖτον ὃν ἦσαν συγκεκομισμένοι καὶ τἆλλα ἃ εἰλήφεσαν ἐξεπορεύοντο διὰ τῶν
Βιβυνῶν. ἐπεὶ δὲ οὐδενὶ ἐνέτυχον πορευόμενοι τὴν ὀρθὴν ὁδόν,
ὥστε ἔχοντές τι εἰς τὴν φιλίαν ἐλθεῖν, ἔδοξεν αὐτοῖς τοὔμπαλιν
ὑποστρέψαντας ἐλθεῖν μίαν ἡμέραν καὶ νύκτα. τοῦτο δὲ ποιήσαντες ἔλαβον πολλὰ καὶ ἀνδράποδα καὶ πρόβατα· καὶ ἀφίκοντο ἑκταῖοι εἰς Χρυσόπολιν τῆς Καλχηδονίας, καὶ ἐκεῖ ἔμειναν
ἡμέρας ἑπτὰ λαφυροπωλοῦντες.

BOOK VII

1 I. [Ὅσα μὲν δὴ ἐν τῇ ἀναβάσει τῇ μετὰ Κύρου ἔπραξαν οἱ Ἕλληνες μέχρι τῆς μάχης, καὶ ὅσα ἐπεὶ Κῦρος ἐτελεύτησεν ἐν τῇ πορείᾳ μέχρι εἰς τὸν Πόντον ἀφίκοντο, καὶ ὅσα ἐκ τοῦ Πόντου πεζῇ ἐξιόντες καὶ ἐκπλέοντες ἐποίουν μέχρι ἔξω τοῦ στόματος ἐγένοντο ἐν Χρυσοπόλει τῆς Ἀσίας, ἐν τῷ πρόσθεν λόγῳ δεδήλωται.]

2 Ἐκ τούτου δὲ Φαρνάβαζος φοβούμενος τὸ στράτευμα μὴ ἐπὶ τὴν αὑτοῦ χώραν στρατεύηται, πέμψας πρὸς Ἀναξίβιον τὸν ναύαρχον — ὃ δ' ἔτυχεν ἐν Βυζαντίῳ ὤν — ἐδεῖτο διαβιβάσαι τὸ στράτευμα ἐκ τῆς Ἀσίας, καὶ ὑπισχνεῖτο πάντα ποιήσειν 3 αὐτῷ ὅσα δέοι. καὶ ὁ Ἀναξίβιος μετεπέμψατο τοὺς στρατηγοὺς καὶ λοχαγοὺς εἰς Βυζάντιον, καὶ ὑπισχνεῖτο, εἰ διαβαῖεν, μισθο- 4 φορὰν ἔσεσθαι τοῖς στρατιώταις. οἱ μὲν δὴ ἄλλοι ἔφασαν βουλευσάμενοι ἀπαγγελεῖν, Ξενοφῶν δὲ εἶπεν αὐτῷ ὅτι ἀπαλλάξοιτο ἤδη ἀπὸ τῆς στρατιᾶς καὶ βούλοιτο ἀποπλεῖν. ὁ δὲ Ἀναξίβιος ἐκέλευσεν αὐτὸν συνδιαβάντα ἔπειτα οὕτως ἀπαλλάττεσθαι. ἔφη οὖν ταῦτα ποιήσειν.

5 Σεύθης δὲ ὁ Θρᾷξ πέμπει Μηδοσάδην καὶ κελεύει Ξενοφῶντα συμπροθυμεῖσθαι ὅπως διαβῇ τὸ στράτευμα, καὶ ἔφη 6 αὐτῷ ταῦτα συμπροθυμηθέντι ὅτι οὐ μεταμελήσει. ὃ δ' εἶπεν· Ἀλλὰ τὸ μὲν στράτευμα διαβήσεται· τούτου ἕνεκα μηδὲν τελείτω μήτε ἐμοὶ μήτε ἄλλῳ μηδενί· ἐπειδὰν δὲ διαβῇ, ἐγὼ μὲν ἀπαλλάξομαι, πρὸς δὲ τοὺς διαμένοντας καὶ ἐπικαιρίους ὄντας προσφερέσθω ὡς ἂν αὐτῷ δοκῇ ἀσφαλές.

7 Ἐκ τούτου διαβαίνουσι πάντες εἰς τὸ Βυζάντιον οἱ στρατιῶται. καὶ μισθὸν μὲν οὐκ ἐδίδου ὁ Ἀναξίβιος, ἐκήρυξε δὲ λαβόντας τὰ ὅπλα καὶ τὰ σκεύη τοὺς στρατιώτας ἐξιέναι, ὡς ἀποπέμψων τε ἅμα καὶ ἀριθμὸν ποιήσων. ἐνταῦθα οἱ στρατιῶται ἤχθοντο, ὅτι οὐκ εἶχον ἀργύριον ἐπισιτίζεσθαι εἰς τὴν 8 πορείαν, καὶ ὀκνηρῶς συνεσκευάζοντο. καὶ ὁ Ξενοφῶν Κλεάνδρῳ τῷ ἁρμοστῇ ξένος γεγενημένος προσελθὼν ἠσπάζετο αὐτὸν

ὡς ἀποπλευσούμενος ἤδη. ὁ δὲ αὐτῷ λέγει· Μὴ ποιήσῃς ταῦτα· εἰ δὲ μή, ἔφη, αἰτίαν ἕξεις, ἐπεὶ καὶ νῦν τινὲς ἤδη σὲ αἰτιῶνται ὅτι οὐ ταχὺ ἐξέρπει τὸ στράτευμα. ὁ δ' εἶπεν· Ἀλλ' αἴτιος μὲν ἔγωγε οὐκ εἰμὶ τούτου, οἱ δὲ στρατιῶται αὐτοὶ ἐπισιτισμοῦ δεόμενοι διὰ τοῦτο ἀθυμοῦσι πρὸς τὴν ἔξοδον. Ἀλλ' ὅμως, ἔφη, ἐγώ σοι συμβουλεύω ἐξελθεῖν μὲν ὡς πορευσόμενον, ἐπειδὰν δ' ἔξω γένηται τὸ στράτευμα, τότε ἀπαλλάττεσθαι. Ταῦτα τοίνυν, ἔφη ὁ Ξενοφῶν, ἐλθόντες πρὸς Ἀναξίβιον διαπραξόμεθα. οὕτως ἐλθόντες ἔλεγον ταῦτα.

Ὁ δὲ ἐκέλευεν οὕτω ποιεῖν καὶ ἐξιέναι τὴν ταχίστην συσκευασαμένους, καὶ προσανεῖπεν, ὃς ἂν μὴ παρῇ εἰς τὴν ἐξέτασιν καὶ εἰς τὸν ἀριθμόν, ὅτι αὐτὸς αὑτὸν αἰτιάσεται. ἐντεῦθεν ἐξῇσαν οἵ τε στρατηγοὶ πρῶτοι καὶ οἱ ἄλλοι. καὶ ἄρδην πάντες πλὴν ὀλίγων ἔξω ἦσαν, καὶ Ἐτεόνικος εἱστήκει παρὰ τὰς πύλας ὡς ὁπότε ἔξω γένοιντο πάντες συγκλείσων τὰς πύλας καὶ τὸν μοχλὸν ἐμβαλῶν. ὁ δὲ Ἀναξίβιος συγκαλέσας τοὺς στρατηγοὺς καὶ τοὺς λοχαγοὺς ἔλεγεν· Τὰ μὲν ἐπιτήδεια, ἔφη, λαμβάνετε ἐκ τῶν Θρᾳκίων κωμῶν· εἰσὶ δὲ αὐτόθι πολλαὶ κριθαὶ καὶ πυροὶ καὶ τἆλλα ἐπιτήδεια· λαβόντες δὲ πορεύεσθε εἰς Χερρόνησον, ἐκεῖ δὲ Κυνίσκος ὑμῖν μισθοδοτήσει. ἐπακούσαντες δέ τινες τῶν στρατιωτῶν ταῦτα, ἢ καὶ τῶν λοχαγῶν τις διαγγέλλει εἰς τὸ στράτευμα. καὶ οἱ μὲν στρατηγοὶ ἐπυνθάνοντο περὶ τοῦ Σεύθου πότερα πολέμιος εἴη ἢ φίλος, καὶ πότερα διὰ τοῦ ἱεροῦ ὄρους δέοι πορεύεσθαι ἢ κύκλῳ διὰ μέσης τῆς Θρᾴκης. ἐν ᾧ δὲ ταῦτα διελέγοντο οἱ στρατιῶται ἀναρπάσαντες τὰ ὅπλα θέουσι δρόμῳ πρὸς τὰς πύλας, ὡς πάλιν εἰς τὸ τεῖχος εἰσιόντες. ὁ δὲ Ἐτεόνικος καὶ οἱ σὺν αὐτῷ ὡς εἶδον προσθέοντας τοὺς ὁπλίτας, συγκλείουσι τὰς πύλας καὶ τὸν μοχλὸν ἐμβάλλουσιν. οἱ δὲ στρατιῶται ἔκοπτον τὰς πύλας καὶ ἔλεγον ὅτι ἀδικώτατα πάσχοιεν ἐκβαλλόμενοι εἰς τοὺς πολεμίους· κατασχίσειν τε τὰς πύλας ἔφασαν, εἰ μὴ ἑκόντες ἀνοίξουσιν. ἄλλοι δὲ ἔθεον ἐπὶ θάλατταν καὶ παρὰ τὴν χηλὴν τὸ τεῖχος ὑπερβαίνουσιν εἰς τὴν πόλιν, ἄλλοι δὲ οἳ ἐτύγχανον ἔνδον ὄντες τῶν στρατιωτῶν, ὡς ὁρῶσι τὰ ἐπὶ ταῖς πύλαις πράγματα, διακόπτοντες ταῖς ἀξίναις τὰ κλεῖθρα ἀναπετανύασι τὰς πύλας, οἱ δ' εἰσπίπτουσιν.

Ὁ δὲ Ξενοφῶν ὡς εἶδε τὰ γιγνόμενα, δείσας μὴ ἐφ' ἁρπαγὴν τράποιτο τὸ στράτευμα καὶ ἀνήκεστα κακὰ γένοιτο τῇ πόλει καὶ ἑαυτῷ καὶ τοῖς στρατιώταις, ἔθει καὶ συνεισπίπτει εἴσω τῶν πυλῶν σὺν τῷ ὄχλῳ. οἱ δὲ Βυζάντιοι ὡς εἶδον τὸ στράτευμα βίᾳ εἰσπῖπτον, φεύγουσιν ἐκ τῆς ἀγορᾶς, οἱ μὲν εἰς τὰ πλοῖα, οἱ δὲ οἴκαδε, ὅσοι δὲ ἔνδον ἐτύγχανον ὄντες, ἔξω, οἱ δὲ καθεῖλκον τὰς τριήρεις, ὡς ἐν ταῖς τριήρεσι σῴζοιντο, πάντες δὲ ᾤοντο ἀπολωλέναι, ὡς ἑαλωκυίας τῆς πόλεως. ὁ δὲ Ἐτεόνικος εἰς τὴν ἄκραν ἀποφεύγει. ὁ δὲ Ἀναξίβιος καταδραμὼν ἐπὶ θάλατταν ἐν ἁλιευτικῷ πλοίῳ περιέπλει εἰς τὴν ἀκρόπολιν, καὶ εὐθὺς μεταπέμπεται ἐκ Καλχηδόνος φρουρούς· οὐ γὰρ ἱκανοὶ ἐδόκουν εἶναι οἱ ἐν τῇ ἀκροπόλει σχεῖν τοὺς ἄνδρας.

Οἱ δὲ στρατιῶται ὡς εἶδον Ξενοφῶντα, προσπίπτουσι πολλοὶ αὐτῷ καὶ λέγουσι· Νῦν σοι ἔξεστιν, ὦ Ξενοφῶν, ἀνδρὶ γενέσθαι. ἔχεις πόλιν, ἔχεις τριήρεις, ἔχεις χρήματα, ἔχεις ἄνδρας τοσούτους. νῦν ἄν, εἰ βούλοιο, σύ τε ἡμᾶς ὀνήσαις καὶ ἡμεῖς σὲ μέγαν ποιήσαιμεν. ὁ δ' ἀπεκρίνατο· Ἀλλ' εὖ γε λέγετε καὶ ποιήσω ταῦτα· εἰ δὲ τούτων ἐπιθυμεῖτε, θέσθε τὰ ὅπλα ἐν τάξει ὡς τάχιστα· βουλόμενος αὐτοὺς κατηρεμίσαι· καὶ αὐτός τε παρηγγύα ταῦτα καὶ τοὺς ἄλλους ἐκέλευε παρεγγυᾶν τίθεσθαι τὰ ὅπλα. οἱ δὲ αὐτοὶ ὑφ' ἑαυτῶν ταττόμενοι οἵ τε ὁπλῖται ἐν ὀλίγῳ χρόνῳ εἰς ὀκτὼ ἐγένοντο καὶ οἱ πελτασταὶ ἐπὶ τὸ κέρας ἑκάτερον παρεδεδραμήκεσαν. τὸ δὲ χωρίον οἷον κάλλιστον ἐκτάξασθαί ἐστι τὸ Θρᾴκιον καλούμενον, ἔρημον οἰκιῶν καὶ πεδινόν. ἐπεὶ δὲ ἔκειτο τὰ ὅπλα καὶ κατηρεμίσθησαν, συγκαλεῖ ὁ Ξενοφῶν τὴν στρατιὰν καὶ λέγει τάδε. Ὅτι μὲν ὀργίζεσθε, ὦ ἄνδρες στρατιῶται, καὶ νομίζετε δεινὰ πάσχειν ἐξαπατώμενοι οὐ θαυμάζω. ἢν δὲ τῷ θυμῷ χαριζώμεθα καὶ Λακεδαιμονίους τε τοὺς παρόντας τῆς ἐξαπάτης τιμωρησώμεθα καὶ τὴν πόλιν τὴν οὐδὲν αἰτίαν διαρπάσωμεν, ἐνθυμεῖσθε ἃ ἔσται ἐντεῦθεν. πολέμιοι μὲν ἐσόμεθα ἀποδεδειγμένοι Λακεδαιμονίοις καὶ τοῖς συμμάχοις. οἷος δὲ πόλεμος ἂν γένοιτο εἰκάζειν δὴ πάρεστιν, ἑωρακότας καὶ ἀναμνησθέντας τὰ νῦν δὴ γεγενημένα. ἡμεῖς γὰρ οἱ Ἀθηναῖοι ἤλθομεν εἰς τὸν πόλεμον τὸν πρὸς Λακεδαιμονίους καὶ τοὺς συμμάχους ἔχοντες τριήρεις τὰς μὲν ἐν θαλάττῃ τὰς δ' ἐν τοῖς

νεωρίοις οὐκ ἐλάττους τριακοσίων, ὑπαρχόντων δὲ πολλῶν χρημάτων ἐν τῇ πόλει καὶ προσόδου οὔσης κατ' ἐνιαυτὸν ἀπό τε τῶν ἐνδήμων καὶ τῆς ὑπερορίας οὐ μεῖον χιλίων ταλάντων· ἄρχοντες
105 δὲ τῶν νήσων ἁπασῶν καὶ ἔν τε τῇ Ἀσίᾳ πολλὰς ἔχοντες πόλεις καὶ ἐν τῇ Εὐρώπῃ ἄλλας τε πολλὰς καὶ αὐτὸ τοῦτο τὸ Βυζάντιον, ὅπου νῦν ἐσμεν, ἔχοντες κατεπολεμήθημεν οὕτως ὡς πάντες ὑμεῖς ἐπίστασθε. νῦν δὲ δὴ τί ἂν οἰόμεθα παθεῖν, Λακεδαιμονίοις μὲν καὶ τῶν ἀρχαίων συμμάχων ὑπαρχόντων, Ἀθηναίων
110 δὲ καὶ οἳ ἐκείνοις τότε ἦσαν σύμμαχοι πάντων προσγεγενημένων, Τισσαφέρνους δὲ καὶ τῶν ἐπὶ θαλάττῃ ἄλλων βαρβάρων πάντων πολεμίων ἡμῖν ὄντων, πολεμιωτάτου δὲ αὐτοῦ τοῦ ἄνω βασιλέως, ὃν ἤλθομεν ἀφαιρησόμενοι τὴν ἀρχὴν καὶ ἀποκτενοῦντες, εἰ δυναίμεθα; τούτων δὴ πάντων ὁμοῦ ὄντων ἔστι τις οὕτως ἄφρων
115 ὅστις οἴεται ἂν ἡμᾶς περιγενέσθαι; μὴ πρὸς θεῶν μαινώμεθα μηδ' αἰσχρῶς ἀπολώμεθα πολέμιοι ὄντες καὶ ταῖς πατρίσι καὶ τοῖς ἡμετέροις αὐτῶν φίλοις τε καὶ οἰκείοις. ἐν γὰρ ταῖς πόλεσίν εἰσι πάντες ταῖς ἐφ' ἡμᾶς στρατευσομέναις, καὶ δικαίως, εἰ βάρβαρον μὲν πόλιν οὐδεμίαν ἠθελήσαμεν κατασχεῖν, καὶ ταῦτα
120 κρατοῦντες, Ἑλληνίδα δὲ εἰς ἣν πρώτην ἤλθομεν πόλιν, ταύτην ἐξαλαπάξομεν. ἐγὼ μὲν τοίνυν εὔχομαι πρὶν ταῦτα ἐπιδεῖν ὑφ' ὑμῶν γενόμενα μυρίας ἐμέ γε κατὰ τῆς γῆς ὀργυιὰς γενέσθαι. καὶ ὑμῖν δὲ συμβουλεύω Ἕλληνας ὄντας τοῖς τῶν Ἑλλήνων προεστηκόσι πειθομένους πειρᾶσθαι τῶν δικαίων τυγχάνειν.
125 ἐὰν δὲ μὴ δύνησθε ταῦτα, ἡμᾶς δεῖ ἀδικουμένους τῆς γοῦν Ἑλλάδος μὴ στέρεσθαι. καὶ νῦν μοι δοκεῖ πέμψαντας Ἀναξιβίῳ εἰπεῖν ὅτι ἡμεῖς οὐδὲν βίαιον ποιήσοντες παρεληλύθαμεν εἰς τὴν πόλιν, ἀλλ' ἢν μὲν δυνώμεθα παρ' ὑμῶν ἀγαθόν τι εὑρίσκεσθαι, εἰ δὲ μή, ἀλλὰ δηλώσοντες ὅτι οὐκ ἐξαπατώμενοι ἀλλὰ
130 πειθόμενοι ἐξερχόμεθα.

Ταῦτα ἔδοξε, καὶ πέμπουσιν Ἱερώνυμόν τε τὸν Ἠλεῖον ἐροῦντα ταῦτα καὶ Εὐρύλοχον Ἀρκάδα καὶ Φιλήσιον Ἀχαιόν. οἱ μὲν ταῦτα ᾤχοντο ἐροῦντες.

Ἔτι δὲ καθημένων τῶν στρατιωτῶν προσέρχεται Κοιρατάδας
135 Θηβαῖος, ὃς οὐ φεύγων τὴν Ἑλλάδα περιῄει ἀλλὰ στρατηγιῶν καὶ ἐπαγγελλόμενος, εἴ τις ἢ πόλις ἢ ἔθνος στρατηγοῦ δέοιτο·

καὶ τότε προσελθὼν ἔλεγεν ὅτι ἕτοιμος εἴη ἡγεῖσθαι αὐτοῖς εἰς τὸ Δέλτα καλούμενον τῆς Θρᾴκης, ἔνθα πολλὰ καὶ ἀγαθὰ λήψοιντο· ἔστε δ' ἂν μόλωσιν, εἰς ἀφθονίαν παρέξειν ἔφη καὶ σιτία καὶ ποτά. ἀκούουσι ταῦτα τοῖς στρατιώταις καὶ τὰ παρὰ 140 Ἀναξιβίου ἅμα ἀπαγγελλόμενα—ἀπεκρίνατο γὰρ ὅτι πειθομένοις αὐτοῖς οὐ μεταμελήσει, ἀλλὰ τοῖς τε οἴκοι τέλεσι ταῦτα ἀπαγγελεῖ καὶ αὐτὸς βουλεύσοιτο περὶ αὐτῶν ὅ,τι δύναιτο ἀγαθόν—ἐκ τούτου οἱ στρατιῶται τόν τε Κοιρατάδαν δέχονται στρατηγὸν καὶ ἔξω τοῦ τείχους ἀπῆλθον. ὁ δὲ Κοιρατάδας 145 συντίθεται αὐτοῖς εἰς τὴν ὑστεραίαν παρέσεσθαι ἐπὶ τὸ στράτευμα ἔχων καὶ ἱερεῖα καὶ μάντιν καὶ σιτία καὶ ποτὰ τῇ στρατιᾷ. ἐπεὶ δὲ ἐξῆλθον, ὁ Ἀναξίβιος ἔκλεισε τὰς πύλας καὶ ἐκήρυξεν ὅς ἂν ἁλῷ ἔνδον ὢν τῶν στρατιωτῶν ὅτι πεπράσεται. τῇ δ' ὑστεραίᾳ Κοιρατάδας μὲν ἔχων τὰ ἱερεῖα καὶ τὸν μάντιν ἧκε καὶ ἄλφιτα 150 φέροντες εἵποντο αὐτῷ εἴκοσιν ἄνδρες καὶ οἶνον ἄλλοι εἴκοσι καὶ ἐλαῶν τρεῖς καὶ σκορόδων ἀνὴρ ὅσον ἐδύνατο μέγιστον φορτίον καὶ ἄλλος κρομμύων. ταῦτα δὲ καταθέμενος ὡς ἐπὶ δάσμευσιν ἐθύετο. Ξενοφῶν δὲ μεταπεμψάμενος Κλέανδρον ἐκέλευε διαπρᾶξαι ὅπως εἰς τὸ τεῖχος εἰσέλθοι καὶ ἀποπλεῦσαι ἐκ Βυζαν- 155 τίου. ἐλθὼν δ' ὁ Κλέανδρος μάλα μόλις ἔφη διαπραξάμενος ἥκειν· λέγειν γὰρ Ἀναξίβιον ὅτι οὐκ ἐπιτήδειον εἴη τοὺς μὲν στρατιώτας πλησίον εἶναι τοῦ τείχους, Ξενοφῶντα δὲ ἔνδον· τοὺς Βυζαντίους δὲ στασιάζειν καὶ πονηροὺς εἶναι πρὸς ἀλλήλους· ὅμως δὲ εἰσιέναι, ἔφη, ἐκέλευεν, εἰ μέλλεις σὺν αὐτῷ 160 ἐκπλεῖν. ὁ μὲν δὴ Ξενοφῶν ἀσπασάμενος τοὺς στρατιώτας εἴσω τοῦ τείχους ἀπῄει σὺν Κλεάνδρῳ. ὁ δὲ Κοιρατάδας τῇ μὲν πρώτῃ ἡμέρᾳ οὐκ ἐκαλλιέρει οὐδὲ διεμέτρησεν οὐδὲν τοῖς στρατιώταις· τῇ δ' ὑστεραίᾳ τὰ μὲν ἱερεῖα εἱστήκει παρὰ τὸν βωμὸν καὶ Κοιρατάδας ἐστεφανωμένος ὡς θύσων· προσελθὼν δὲ Τιμα- 165 σίων ὁ Δαρδανεὺς καὶ Νέων ὁ Ἀσιναῖος καὶ Κλεάνωρ ὁ Ὀρχομένιος ἔλεγον Κοιρατάδᾳ μὴ θύειν, ὡς οὐχ ἡγησόμενον τῇ στρατιᾷ, εἰ μὴ δώσει τὰ ἐπιτήδεια. ὁ δὲ κελεύει διαμετρεῖσθαι. ἐπεὶ δὲ πολλῶν ἐνέδει αὐτῷ ὥστε ἡμέρας σῖτον ἑκάστῳ γενέσθαι τῶν στρατιωτῶν, ἀναλαβὼν τὰ ἱερεῖα ἀπῄει καὶ τὴν στρατηγίαν 170 ἀπειπών.

II. Νέων δὲ ὁ Ἀσιναῖος καὶ Φρυνίσκος ὁ Ἀχαιὸς καὶ Φιλήσιος ὁ Ἀχαιὸς καὶ Ξανθικλῆς ὁ Ἀχαιὸς καὶ Τιμασίων ὁ Δαρδανεὺς ἐπέμενον ἐπὶ τῇ στρατιᾷ, καὶ εἰς κώμας τῶν Θρᾳκῶν προελθόντες τὰς κατὰ Βυζάντιον ἐστρατοπεδεύοντο. καὶ οἱ στρατηγοὶ ἐστασίαζον, Κλεάνωρ μὲν καὶ Φρυνίσκος πρὸς Σεύθην βουλόμενοι ἄγειν· ἔπειθε γὰρ αὐτούς, καὶ ἔδωκε τῷ μὲν ἵππον, τῷ δὲ γυναῖκα· Νέων δὲ εἰς Χερρόνησον, οἰόμενος, εἰ ὑπὸ Λακεδαιμονίοις γένοιντο, παντὸς ἂν προεστάναι τοῦ στρατεύματος· Τιμασίων δὲ προὐθυμεῖτο πέραν εἰς τὴν Ἀσίαν πάλιν διαβῆναι, οἰόμενος ⟨οὕτως⟩ ἂν οἴκαδε κατελθεῖν. καὶ οἱ στρατιῶται ταὐτὰ ἐβούλοντο. διατριβομένου δὲ τοῦ χρόνου πολλοὶ τῶν στρατιωτῶν, οἱ μὲν τὰ ὅπλα ἀποδιδόμενοι κατὰ τοὺς χώρους ἀπέπλεον ὡς ἐδύναντο, οἱ δὲ καὶ εἰς τὰς πόλεις κατεμείγνυντο. Ἀναξίβιος δ' ἔχαιρε ταῦτα ἀκούων, διαφθειρόμενον τὸ στράτευμα· τούτων γὰρ γιγνομένων ᾤετο μάλιστα χαρίζεσθαι Φαρναβάζῳ.

Ἀποπλέοντι δὲ Ἀναξιβίῳ ἐκ Βυζαντίου συναντᾷ Ἀρίσταρχος ἐν Κυζίκῳ διάδοχος Κλεάνδρῳ Βυζαντίου ἁρμοστής· ἐλέγετο δὲ ὅτι καὶ ναύαρχος διάδοχος Πῶλος ὅσον οὐ παρείη ἤδη εἰς Ἑλλήσποντον. καὶ Ἀναξίβιος τῷ μὲν Ἀριστάρχῳ ἐπιστέλλει ὁπόσους ἂν εὕρῃ ἐν Βυζαντίῳ τῶν Κύρου στρατιωτῶν ὑπολελειμμένους ἀποδόσθαι· ὁ δὲ Κλέανδρος οὐδένα ἐπεπράκει, ἀλλὰ καὶ τοὺς κάμνοντας ἐθεράπευεν οἰκτίρων καὶ ἀναγκάζων οἰκίᾳ δέχεσθαι· Ἀρίσταρχος δ' ἐπεὶ ἦλθε τάχιστα, οὐκ ἐλάττους τετρακοσίων ἀπέδοτο. Ἀναξίβιος δὲ παραπλεύσας εἰς Πάριον πέμπει παρὰ Φαρναβάζοι κατὰ τὰ συγκείμενα. ὃ δ' ἐπεὶ ᾔσθετο Ἀρίσταρχόν τε ἥκοντα εἰς Βυζάντιον ἁρμοστὴν καὶ Ἀναξίβιον οὐκέτι ναυαρχοῦντα, Ἀναξιβίου μὲν ἠμέλησε, πρὸς Ἀρίσταρχον δὲ διεπράττετο τὰ αὐτὰ περὶ τοῦ Κύρου στρατεύματος ἅπερ πρὸς Ἀναξίβιον.

Ἐκ τούτου ὁ Ἀναξίβιος καλέσας Ξενοφῶντα κελεύει πάσῃ τέχνῃ καὶ μηχανῇ πλεῦσαι ἐπὶ τὸ στράτευμα ὡς τάχιστα, καὶ συνέχειν τε αὐτὸ καὶ συναθροίζειν τῶν διεσπαρμένων ὡς ἂν πλείστους δύνηται, καὶ παραγαγόντα εἰς τὴν Πέρινθον διαβιβάζειν εἰς τὴν Ἀσίαν ὅτι τάχιστα· καὶ δίδωσιν αὐτῷ τριακόντορον καὶ ἐπιστολὴν καὶ ἄνδρα συμπέμπει κελεύσοντα τοὺς Περινθίους ὡς τάχιστα Ξενοφῶντα προπέμψαι τοῖς ἵπποις ἐπὶ τὸ στράτευμα. καὶ ὁ μὲν Ξενοφῶν διαπλεύσας ἀφικνεῖται ἐπὶ τὸ στράτευμα· οἱ δὲ στρατιῶται ἐδέξαντο ἡδέως καὶ εὐθὺς εἵποντο ἄσμενοι ὡς διαβησόμενοι ἐκ τῆς Θρᾴκης εἰς τὴν Ἀσίαν.

Ὁ δὲ Σεύθης ἀκούσας ἥκοντα πάλιν πέμψας πρὸς αὐτὸν κατὰ θάλατταν Μηδοσάδην ἐδεῖτο τὴν στρατιὰν ἄγειν πρὸς ἑαυτόν, ὑπισχνούμενος αὐτῷ ὅ,τι ᾤετο λέγων πείσειν. ὁ δ᾽ ἀπεκρίνατο ὅτι οὐδὲν οἷόν τε εἴη τούτων γενέσθαι. καὶ ὁ μὲν ταῦτα ἀκούσας ᾤχετο. οἱ δὲ Ἕλληνες ἐπεὶ ἀφίκοντο εἰς Πέρινθον, Νέων μὲν ἀποσπάσας ἐστρατοπεδεύσατο χωρὶς ἔχων ὡς ὀκτακοσίους ἀνθρώπους· τὸ δ᾽ ἄλλο στράτευμα πᾶν ἐν τῷ αὐτῷ παρὰ τὸ τεῖχος τὸ Περινθίων ἦν.

Μετὰ ταῦτα Ξενοφῶν μὲν ἔπραττε περὶ πλοίων, ὅπως ὅτι τάχιστα διαβαῖεν. ἐν δὲ τούτῳ ἀφικόμενος Ἀρίσταρχος ⟨ὁ⟩ ἐκ Βυζαντίου ἁρμοστής, ἔχων δύο τριήρεις, πεπεισμένος ὑπὸ Φαρναβάζου τοῖς τε ναυκλήροις ἀπεῖπε μὴ διάγειν ἐλθών τε ἐπὶ τὸ στράτευμα τοῖς στρατιώταις εἶπε μὴ περαιοῦσθαι εἰς τὴν Ἀσίαν. ὁ δὲ Ξενοφῶν ἔλεγεν ὅτι Ἀναξίβιος ἐκέλευσε καὶ ἐμὲ πρὸς τοῦτο ἔπεμψεν ἐνθάδε. πάλιν δ᾽ Ἀρίσταρχος ἔλεξεν· Ἀναξίβιος μὲν τοίνυν οὐκέτι ναύαρχος, ἐγὼ δὲ τῇδε ἁρμοστής· εἰ δέ τινα ὑμῶν λήψομαι ἐν τῇ θαλάττῃ, καταδύσω. ταῦτ᾽ εἰπὼν ᾤχετο εἰς τὸ τεῖχος. τῇ δ᾽ ὑστεραίᾳ μεταπέμπεται τοὺς στρατηγοὺς καὶ λοχαγοὺς τοῦ στρατεύματος. ἤδη δὲ ὄντων πρὸς τῷ τείχει ἐξαγγέλλει τις τῷ Ξενοφῶντι ὅτι εἰ εἴσεισι, συλληφθήσεται καὶ ἢ αὐτοῦ τι πείσεται ἢ καὶ Φαρναβάζῳ παραδοθήσεται. ὁ δὲ ἀκούσας ταῦτα τοὺς μὲν προπέμπεται, αὐτὸς δὲ εἶπεν ὅτι θῦσαί τι βούλοιτο. καὶ ἀπελθὼν ἐθύετο εἰ παρεῖεν αὐτῷ οἱ θεοὶ πειρᾶσθαι πρὸς Σεύθην ἄγειν τὸ στράτευμα. ἑώρα γὰρ οὔτε διαβαίνειν ἀσφαλὲς ὂν τριήρεις ἔχοντος τοῦ κωλύσοντος, οὔτ᾽ ἐπὶ Χερρόνησον ἐλθὼν κατακλεισθῆναι ἐβούλετο καὶ τὸ στράτευμα ἐν πολλῇ σπάνει πάντων γενέσθαι ἔνθα πείθεσθαι μὲν ἀνάγκη τῷ ἐκεῖ ἁρμοστῇ, τῶν δ᾽ ἐπιτηδείων οὐδὲν ἔμελλεν ἕξειν τὸ στράτευμα.

Καὶ ὁ μὲν ἀμφὶ ταῦτ᾽ εἶχεν· οἱ δὲ στρατηγοὶ καὶ οἱ λοχαγοὶ ἥκοντες παρὰ τοῦ Ἀριστάρχου ἀπήγγελλον ὅτι νῦν μὲν ἀπιέναι σφᾶς κελεύει, τῆς δείλης δὲ ἥκειν· ἔνθα καὶ δήλη μᾶλλον ἐδόκει ἡ ἐπιβουλή. ὁ οὖν Ξενοφῶν, ἐπεὶ ἐδόκει τὰ ἱερὰ καλὰ εἶναι αὐτῷ καὶ τῷ στρατεύματι ἀσφαλῶς πρὸς Σεύθην ἰέναι, παραλαβὼν Πολυκράτην τὸν Ἀθηναῖον λοχαγὸν καὶ παρὰ τῶν στρατηγῶν ἑκάστου ἄνδρα—πλὴν παρὰ Νέωνος—ᾧ ἕκαστος ἐπίστευεν ᾤχετο τῆς νυκτὸς ἐπὶ τὸ Σεύθου στράτευμα ἑξήκοντα στάδια. ἐπεὶ δ' ἐγγὺς ἦν αὐτοῦ, ἐπιτυγχάνει πυροῖς ἐρήμοις. καὶ τὸ μὲν πρῶτον ᾤετο μετακεχωρηκέναι ποι τὸν Σεύθην· ἐπεὶ δὲ θορύβου τε ᾔσθετο καὶ σημαινόντων ἀλλήλοις τῶν περὶ Σεύθην, κατέμαθεν ὅτι τούτου ἕνεκα τὰ πυρὰ κεκαυμένα εἴη τῷ Σεύθῃ πρὸ τῶν νυκτοφυλάκων ὅπως οἱ μὲν φύλακες μὴ ὁρῷντο ἐν τῷ σκότει ὄντες μήτε ὁπόσοι μήτε ὅπου εἶεν, οἱ δὲ προσιόντες μὴ λανθάνοιεν, ἀλλὰ διὰ τὸ φῶς καταφανεῖς εἶεν.

Ἐπεὶ δὲ ᾔσθετο, προπέμπει τὸν ἑρμηνέα ὃν ἐτύγχανεν ἔχων, καὶ εἰπεῖν κελεύει Σεύθῃ ὅτι Ξενοφῶν πάρεστι βουλόμενος συγγενέσθαι αὐτῷ. οἱ δὲ ἤροντο εἰ Ἀθηναῖος ἀπὸ τοῦ στρατεύματος. ἐπειδὴ δὲ ἔφη οὗτος εἶναι, ἀναπηδήσαντες ἐδίωκον· καὶ ὀλίγον ὕστερον παρῆσαν πελτασταὶ ὅσον διακόσιοι, καὶ παραλαβόντες Ξενοφῶντα καὶ τοὺς σὺν αὐτῷ ἦγον πρὸς Σεύθην. ὁ δ' ἦν ἐν τύρσει μάλα φυλαττόμενος, καὶ ἵπποι περὶ αὐτὴν κύκλῳ ἐγκεχαλινωμένοι· διὰ γὰρ τὸν φόβον τὰς μὲν ἡμέρας ἐχίλου τοὺς ἵππους, τὰς δὲ νύκτας ἐγκεχαλινωμένοις ἐφυλάττετο. ἐλέγετο γὰρ καὶ πρόσθεν Τήρης ὁ τούτου πρόγονος ἐν ταύτῃ τῇ χώρᾳ πολὺ ἔχων στράτευμα ὑπὸ τούτων τῶν ἀνδρῶν πολλοὺς ἀπολέσαι καὶ τὰ σκευοφόρα ἀφαιρεθῆναι· ἦσαν δ' οὗτοι Θυνοί, πάντων λεγόμενοι εἶναι μάλιστα νυκτὸς πολεμικώτατοι.

Ἐπεὶ δ' ἐγγὺς ἦσαν, ἐκέλευσεν εἰσελθεῖν Ξενοφῶντα ἔχοντα δύο οὓς βούλοιτο. ἐπειδὴ δὲ ἔνδον ἦσαν, ἠσπάζοντο μὲν πρῶτον ἀλλήλους καὶ κατὰ τὸν Θρᾴκιον νόμον κέρατα οἴνου προὔπινον· παρῆν δὲ καὶ Μηδοσάδης τῷ Σεύθῃ, ὅσπερ ἐπρέσβευεν αὐτῷ πάντοσε. ἔπειτα δὲ Ξενοφῶν ἤρχετο λέγειν· Ἔπεμψας πρὸς ἐμέ, ὦ Σεύθη, εἰς Καλχηδόνα πρῶτον Μηδοσάδην τουτονί, δεόμενός μου συμπροθυμηθῆναι διαβῆναι τὸ στράτευμα ἐκ τῆς Ἀσίας, καὶ ὑπισχνούμενός μοι, εἰ ταῦτα πράξαιμι, εὖ ποιήσειν, ὡς ἔφη Μηδοσάδης οὗτος. ταῦτα εἰπὼν ἐπήρετο τὸν Μηδοσάδην εἰ ἀληθῆ ταῦτα εἴη. ὁ δ' ἔφη. Αὖθις ἦλθε Μηδοσάδης οὗτος ἐπεὶ ἐγὼ διέβην πάλιν ἐπὶ τὸ στράτευμα ἐκ Παρίου, ὑπισχνούμενος, εἰ ἄγοιμι τὸ στράτευμα πρὸς σέ, τἆλλα τέ σε φίλῳ μοι χρήσεσθαι καὶ ἀδελφῷ καὶ τὰ παρὰ θαλάττῃ μοι χωρία ὧν σὺ κρατεῖς ἔσεσθαι παρὰ σοῦ. ἐπὶ τούτοις πάλιν ἤρετο τὸν Μηδοσάδην εἰ ἔλεγε ταῦτα. ὁ δὲ συνέφη καὶ ταῦτα. Ἴθι νυν, ἔφη, ἀφήγησαι τούτῳ τί σοι ἀπεκρινάμην ἐν Καλχηδόνι πρῶτον. Ἀπεκρίνω ὅτι τὸ στράτευμα διαβήσοιτο εἰς Βυζάντιον καὶ οὐδὲν τούτου ἕνεκα δέοι τελεῖν οὔτε σοὶ οὔτε ἄλλῳ· αὐτὸς δὲ ἐπεὶ διαβαίης, ἀπιέναι ἔφησθα· καὶ ἐγένετο οὕτως ὥσπερ σὺ ἔλεγες. Τί γὰρ ἔλεγον, ἔφη, ὅτε κατὰ Σηλυμβρίαν ἀφίκου; Οὐκ ἔφησθα οἷόν τε εἶναι, ἀλλ' εἰς Πέρινθον ἐλθόντας διαβαίνειν εἰς τὴν Ἀσίαν. Νῦν τοίνυν, ἔφη ὁ Ξενοφῶν, πάρειμι καὶ ἐγὼ καὶ οὗτος Φρυνίσκος εἷς τῶν στρατηγῶν καὶ Πολυκράτης οὗτος εἷς τῶν λοχαγῶν, καὶ ἔξω εἰσὶν ἀπὸ τῶν στρατηγῶν ὁ πιστότατος ἑκάστῳ πλὴν ⟨ἀπὸ⟩ Νέωνος τοῦ Λακωνικοῦ. εἰ οὖν βούλει πιστοτέραν εἶναι τὴν πρᾶξιν, καὶ ἐκείνους κάλεσαι. τὰ δὲ ὅπλα σὺ ἐλθὼν εἰπέ, ὦ Πολύκρατες, ὅτι ἐγὼ κελεύω καταλιπεῖν, καὶ αὐτὸς ἐκεῖ καταλιπὼν τὴν μάχαιραν εἴσιθι.

Ἀκούσας ταῦτα ὁ Σεύθης εἶπεν ὅτι οὐδενὶ ἂν ἀπιστήσειεν Ἀθηναίων· καὶ γὰρ ὅτι συγγενεῖς εἶεν εἰδέναι καὶ φίλους εὔνους ἔφη νομίζειν. μετὰ ταῦτα δ' ἐπεὶ εἰσῆλθον οὓς ἔδει, πρῶτον Ξενοφῶν ἐπήρετο Σεύθην ὅ,τι δέοιτο χρῆσθαι τῇ στρατιᾷ. ὁ δὲ εἶπεν ὧδε· Μαισάδης ἦν πατήρ μοι, ἐκείνου δὲ ἦν ἀρχὴ Μελανδῖται καὶ Θυνοὶ καὶ Τρανίψαι. ἐκ ταύτης οὖν τῆς χώρας, ἐπεὶ τὰ Ὀδρυσῶν πράγματα ἐνόσησεν, ἐκπεσὼν ὁ πατὴρ αὐτὸς μὲν ἀποθνήσκει νόσῳ, ἐγὼ δ' ἐξετράφην ὀρφανὸς παρὰ Μηδόκῳ τῷ νῦν βασιλεῖ. ἐπεὶ δὲ νεανίσκος ἐγενόμην, οὐκ ἐδυνάμην ζῆν εἰς ἀλλοτρίαν τράπεζαν ἀποβλέπων· καὶ ἐκαθεζόμην ἐνδίφριος αὐτῷ ἱκέτης δοῦναί μοι ὁπόσους δυνατὸς εἴη ἄνδρας, ὅπως καὶ τοὺς ἐκβαλόντας ἡμᾶς εἴ τι δυναίμην κακὸν ποιοίην καὶ ζῴην μὴ εἰς τὴν ἐκείνου τράπεζαν ἀποβλέπων. ἐκ τούτου μοι δίδωσι τοὺς ἄνδρας καὶ τοὺς ἵππους οὓς ὑμεῖς ὄψεσθε ἐπειδὰν ἡμέρα γένηται. καὶ νῦν ἐγὼ ζῶ τούτους ἔχων, ληζόμενος τὴν ἐμαυτοῦ πατρῴαν χώραν. εἰ δέ μοι ὑμεῖς παραγένοισθε, οἶμαι ἂν σὺν τοῖς θεοῖς ῥᾳδίως ἀπολαβεῖν τὴν ἀρχήν. ταῦτ' ἐστὶν ἃ ἐγὼ δέομαι.

Τί ἂν οὖν, ἔφη ὁ Ξενοφῶν, σὺ δύναιο, εἰ ἔλθοιμεν, τῇ τε στρατιᾷ διδόναι καὶ τοῖς λοχαγοῖς καὶ τοῖς στρατηγοῖς; λέξον, ἵνα οὗτοι ἀπαγγέλλωσιν. ὁ δ' ὑπέσχετο τῷ μὲν στρατιώτῃ κυζικηνόν, τῷ δὲ λοχαγῷ διμοιρίαν, τῷ δὲ στρατηγῷ τετραμοιρίαν, καὶ γῆν ὁπόσην ἂν βούλωνται καὶ ζεύγη καὶ χωρίον ἐπὶ θαλάττῃ τετειχισμένον. Ἐὰν δέ, ἔφη ὁ Ξενοφῶν, ταῦτα πειρώμενοι μὴ διαπράξωμεν, ἀλλά τις φόβος ὑπὸ Λακεδαιμονίων ᾖ, δέξῃ εἰς τὴν σεαυτοῦ, ἐάν τις ἀπιέναι βούληται παρὰ σέ; ὁ δ' εἶπε· Καὶ ἀδελφούς γε ποιήσομαι καὶ ἐνδιφρίους καὶ κοινωνοὺς ἁπάντων ὧν ἂν δυνώμεθα κτᾶσθαι. σοὶ δέ, ὦ Ξενοφῶν, καὶ θυγατέρα δώσω καὶ εἴ τις σοὶ ἔστι θυγάτηρ, ὠνήσομαι Θρᾳκίῳ νόμῳ, καὶ Βισάνθην οἴκησιν δώσω, ὅπερ ἐμοὶ κάλλιστον χωρίον ἐστὶ τῶν ἐπὶ θαλάττῃ.

III. Ἀκούσαντες ταῦτα καὶ δεξιὰς δόντες καὶ λαβόντες ἀπήλαυνον· καὶ πρὸ ἡμέρας ἐγένοντο ἐπὶ στρατοπέδῳ καὶ ἀπήγγειλαν ἕκαστοι τοῖς πέμψασιν. ἐπεὶ δὲ ἡμέρα ἐγένετο, ὁ μὲν Ἀρίσταρχος πάλιν ἐκάλει τοὺς στρατηγούς· τοῖς δ' ἔδοξε τὴν μὲν πρὸς Ἀρίσταρχον ὁδὸν ἐᾶσαι, τὸ δὲ στράτευμα συγκαλέσαι. καὶ συνῆλθον πάντες πλὴν οἱ Νέωνος· οὗτοι δὲ ἀπεῖχον ὡς δέκα στάδια. ἐπεὶ δὲ συνῆλθον, ἀναστὰς Ξενοφῶν εἶπε τάδε. Ἄνδρες, διαπλεῖν μὲν ἔνθα βουλόμεθα Ἀρίσταρχος τριήρεις ἔχων κωλύει· ὥστε εἰς πλοῖα οὐκ ἀσφαλὲς ἐμβαίνειν· οὗτος δὲ αὐτὸς κελεύει εἰς Χερρόνησον βίᾳ διὰ τοῦ ἱεροῦ ὄρους πορεύεσθαι· ἢν δὲ κρατήσαντες τούτου ἐκεῖσε ἔλθωμεν, οὔτε πωλήσειν ἔτι ὑμᾶς φησιν ὥσπερ ἐν Βυζαντίῳ, οὔτε ἐξαπατήσεσθαι ἔτι ὑμᾶς, ἀλλὰ λήψεσθαι μισθόν, οὔτε περιόψεσθαι ἔτι ὥσπερ νυνὶ δεομένους τῶν ἐπιτηδείων. οὗτος μὲν ταῦτα λέγει· Σεύθης δέ φησιν, ἂν πρὸς ἐκεῖνον ἴητε, εὖ ποιήσειν ὑμᾶς· νῦν οὖν σκέψασθε πότερον ἐνθάδε μένοντες τοῦτο βουλεύσεσθε ἢ εἰς τὰ ἐπιτήδεια ἐπανελθόντες. ἐμοὶ μὲν οὖν δοκεῖ, ἐπεὶ ἐνθάδε οὔτε ἀργύριον ἔχομεν ὥστε ἀγοράζειν οὔτε ἄνευ ἀργυρίου ἐῶσι λαμβάνειν, ἐπανελθόντας εἰς τὰς κώμας ὅθεν οἱ ἥττους ἐῶσι λαμβάνειν, ἐκεῖ ἔχοντας τὰ ἐπιτήδεια ἀκούοντας ὅ,τι τις ἡμῶν

6 δεῖται, αἱρεῖσθαι ὅ,τι ἂν ἡμῖν δοκῇ κράτιστον εἶναι. καὶ ὅτῳ, ἔφη, ταῦτα δοκεῖ, ἀράτω τὴν χεῖρα. ἀνέτειναν ἅπαντες. Ἀπιόντες τοίνυν, ἔφη, συσκευάζεσθε, καὶ ἐπειδὰν παραγγέλλῃ τις, ἕπεσθε τῷ ἡγουμένῳ.

7 Μετὰ ταῦτα Ξενοφῶν μὲν ἡγεῖτο, οἳ δ' εἵποντο. Νέων δὲ καὶ παρ' Ἀριστάρχου ἄγγελοι ἔπειθον ἀποτρέπεσθαι· οἳ δ' οὐχ ὑπήκουον. ἐπεὶ δ' ὅσον τριάκοντα στάδια προεληλύθεσαν, ἀπαντᾷ Σεύθης. καὶ ὁ Ξενοφῶν ἰδὼν αὐτὸν προσελάσαι ἐκέλευσεν, ὅπως ὅτι πλείστων ἀκουόντων εἴποι αὐτῷ ἃ ἐδόκει 8 συμφέρειν. ἐπεὶ δὲ προσῆλθεν, εἶπε Ξενοφῶν· Ἡμεῖς πορευόμεθα ὅπου μέλλει ἕξειν τὸ στράτευμα τροφήν· ἐκεῖ δ' ἀκούοντες καὶ σοῦ καὶ τῶν τοῦ Λακωνικοῦ αἱρησόμεθα ἃ ἂν κράτιστα δοκῇ εἶναι. ἢν οὖν ἡμῖν ἡγήσῃ ὅπου πλεῖστά ἐστιν ἐπιτήδεια, ὑπὸ 9 σοῦ νομιοῦμεν ξενίζεσθαι. καὶ ὁ Σεύθης ἔφη· Ἀλλὰ οἶδα κώμας πολλὰς ἀθρόας καὶ πάντα ἐχούσας τὰ ἐπιτήδεια ἀπεχούσας ἡμῶν ὅσον διελθόντες ἂν ἡδέως ἀριστῷτε. Ἡγοῦ τοίνυν, 10 ἔφη ὁ Ξενοφῶν. ἐπεὶ δ' ἀφίκοντο εἰς αὐτὰς τῆς δείλης, συνῆλθον οἱ στρατιῶται, καὶ εἶπεν ὁ Σεύθης τοιάδε. Ἐγώ, ὦ ἄνδρες, δέομαι ὑμῶν στρατεύεσθαι σὺν ἐμοί, καὶ ὑπισχνοῦμαι ὑμῖν δώσειν τοῖς στρατιώταις κυζικηνόν, λοχαγοῖς δὲ καὶ στρατηγοῖς τὰ νομιζόμενα· ἔξω δὲ τούτων τὸν ἄξιον τιμήσω. σῖτα δὲ καὶ ποτὰ ὥσπερ καὶ νῦν ἐκ τῆς χώρας λαμβάνοντες ἕξετε· ὁπόσα δ' ἂν ἁλίσκηται ἀξιώσω αὐτὸς ἔχειν, ἵνα ταῦτα διατιθέμενος ὑμῖν 11 τὸν μισθὸν πορίζω. καὶ τὰ μὲν φεύγοντα καὶ ἀποδιδράσκοντα ἡμεῖς ἱκανοὶ ἐσόμεθα διώκειν καὶ μαστεύειν· ἂν δέ τις ἀνθιστῆται, 12 σὺν ὑμῖν πειρασόμεθα χειροῦσθαι. ἐπήρετο ὁ Ξενοφῶν· Πόσον δὲ ἀπὸ θαλάττης ἀξιώσεις συνέπεσθαί σοι τὸ στράτευμα; ὁ δ' ἀπεκρίνατο· Οὐδαμῇ πλέον ἑπτὰ ἡμερῶν, μεῖον δὲ πολλαχῇ.

13 Μετὰ ταῦτα ἐδίδοτο λέγειν τῷ βουλομένῳ· καὶ ἔλεγον **πολλοὶ** κατὰ ταὐτὰ ὅτι παντὸς ἄξια λέγει Σεύθης· χειμὼν γὰρ εἴη **καὶ** οὔτε οἴκαδε ἀποπλεῖν τῷ τοῦτο βουλομένῳ δυνατὸν εἴη, διαγενέσθαι τε ἐν φιλίᾳ οὐχ οἷόν τε, εἰ δέοι ὠνουμένους ζῆν, ἐν δὲ τῇ πολεμίᾳ διατρίβειν καὶ τρέφεσθαι ἀσφαλέστερον μετὰ Σεύθου ἢ μόνους, ὄντων ἀγαθῶν τοσούτων. εἰ δὲ μισθὸν προσλήψοιντο, εὕρημα ἐδόκει εἶναι. ἐπὶ τούτοις εἶπεν ὁ Ξενοφῶν·

Εἴ τις ἀντιλέγει, λεγέτω· εἰ δὲ μή, ἐπιψηφιῶ ἐγὼ ταῦτα. 14
ἐπεὶ δὲ οὐδεὶς ἀντέλεγεν, ἐπεψήφισε, καὶ ἔδοξε ταῦτα. εὐθὺς
δὲ Σεύθῃ εἶπε ταῦτα, ὅτι συστρατεύσοιντο αὐτῷ.

Μετὰ τοῦτο οἱ μὲν ἄλλοι κατὰ τάξεις ἐσκήνησαν, στρατη- 15
γοὺς δὲ καὶ λοχαγοὺς ἐπὶ δεῖπνον Σεύθης ἐκάλεσε, πλησίον
κώμην ἔχων. ἐπεὶ δ' ἐπὶ θύραις ἦσαν ὡς ἐπὶ δεῖπνον παριόντες, 16
ἦν τις Ἡρακλείδης Μαρωνείτης· οὗτος προσιὼν ἑνὶ ἑκάστῳ
οὕστινας ᾤετο ἔχειν τι δοῦναι Σεύθῃ, πρῶτον μὲν πρὸς Παρια-
νούς τινας, οἳ παρῆσαν φιλίαν διαπραξόμενοι πρὸς Μήδοκον τὸν
Ὀδρυσῶν βασιλέα καὶ δῶρα ἄγοντες αὐτῷ τε καὶ τῇ γυναικί,
ἔλεγεν ὅτι Μήδοκος μὲν ἄνω εἴη δώδεκα ἡμερῶν ἀπὸ θαλάττης
ὁδόν, Σεύθης δ' ἐπεὶ τὸ στράτευμα τοῦτο εἴληφεν, ἄρχων ἔσοιτο
ἐπὶ θαλάττῃ. γείτων οὖν ὢν ἱκανώτατος ἔσται ὑμᾶς καὶ εὖ καὶ 17
κακῶς ποιεῖν. ἢν οὖν σωφρονῆτε, τούτῳ δώσετε ὅ,τι ἂν ἄγητε·
καὶ ἄμεινον ὑμῖν διακείσεται ἢ ἐὰν Μηδόκῳ τῷ πρόσω οἰκοῦντι
διδῶτε. τούτους μὲν οὖν οὕτως ἔπειθεν.

Αὖθις δὲ Τιμασίωνι τῷ Δαρδανεῖ προσελθών, ἐπεὶ ἤκουσεν 18
αὐτῷ εἶναι καὶ ἐκπώματα καὶ τάπιδας βαρβαρικάς, ἔλεγεν ὅτι
νομίζοιτο ὁπότε ἐπὶ δεῖπνον καλέσαι ὁ Σεύθης δωρεῖσθαι αὐτῷ
τοὺς κληθέντας. οὗτος δ' ἢν μέγας ἐνθάδε γένηται, ἱκανὸς ἔσται
σε καὶ οἴκαδε καταγαγεῖν καὶ ἐνθάδε πλούσιον ποιῆσαι. τοιαῦτα 19
προὐμνᾶτο ἑκάστῳ προσιών. προσελθὼν δὲ καὶ Ξενοφῶντι
ἔλεγε· Σὺ καὶ πόλεως μεγίστης εἶ καὶ παρὰ Σεύθῃ τὸ σὸν ὄνομα
μέγιστόν ἐστι, καὶ ἐν τῇδε τῇ χώρᾳ ἴσως ἀξιώσεις καὶ τείχη
λαμβάνειν, ὥσπερ καὶ ἄλλοι τῶν ὑμετέρων ἔλαβον, καὶ χώραν·
ἄξιον οὖν σοι καὶ μεγαλοπρεπέστατα τιμῆσαι Σεύθην. εὔνους 20
δέ σοι ὢν παραινῶ. εὖ οἶδα γὰρ ὅτι ὅσῳ ἂν μείζω τούτῳ
δωρήσῃ, τοσούτῳ μείζω ὑπὸ τούτου ἀγαθὰ πείσῃ. ἀκούων
ταῦτα Ξενοφῶν ἠπόρει· οὐ γὰρ διεβεβήκει ἔχων ἐκ Παρίου εἰ
μὴ παῖδα καὶ ὅσον ἐφόδιον.

Ἐπεὶ δὲ εἰσῆλθον ἐπὶ τὸ δεῖπνον τῶν τε Θρᾳκῶν οἱ κρά- 21
τιστοι τῶν παρόντων καὶ οἱ στρατηγοὶ καὶ οἱ λοχαγοὶ τῶν
Ἑλλήνων καὶ εἴ τις πρεσβεία παρῆν ἀπὸ πόλεως, τὸ δεῖπνον
μὲν ἦν καθημένοις κύκλῳ· ἔπειτα δὲ τρίποδες εἰσηνέχθησαν
πᾶσιν· οὗτοι δ' ἦσαν κρεῶν μεστοὶ νενεμημένων, καὶ ἄρτοι

ζυμῖται μεγάλοι προσπεπερονημένοι ἦσαν πρὸς τοῖς κρέασι.
22 μάλιστα δ' αἱ τράπεζαι κατὰ τοὺς ξένους αἰεὶ ἐτίθεντο· νόμος
γὰρ ἦν—καὶ πρῶτος τοῦτο ἐποίει Σεύθης, καὶ ἀνελόμενος τοὺς
ἑαυτῷ παρακειμένους ἄρτους διέκλα κατὰ μικρὸν καὶ ἐρρίπτει
οἷς αὐτῷ ἐδόκει, καὶ τὰ κρέα ὡσαύτως, ὅσον μόνον γεύσασθαι
23 ἑαυτῷ καταλιπώ . καὶ οἱ ἄλλοι δὲ κατὰ ταὐτὰ ἐποίουν καθ'
οὓς αἱ τράπεζαι ἔκειντο. Ἀρκὰς δέ τις Ἀρύστας ὄνομα, φαγεῖν
δεινός, τὸ μὲν διαρριπτεῖν εἴα χαίρειν, λαβὼν δὲ εἰς τὴν χεῖρα
ὅσον τριχοίνικον ἄρτον καὶ κρέα θέμενος ἐπὶ τὰ γόνατα ἐδείπνει.
24 κέρατα δὲ οἴνου περιέφερον, καὶ πάντες ἐδέχοντο· ὁ δ' Ἀρύστας,
ἐπεὶ παρ' αὐτὸν φέρων τὸ κέρας ὁ οἰνοχόος ἧκεν, εἶπεν ἰδὼν τὸν
Ξενοφῶντα οὐκέτι δειπνοῦντα, Ἐκείνῳ, ἔφη, δός· σχολάζει γὰρ
25 ἤδη, ἐγὼ δὲ οὐδέπω. ἀκούσας Σεύθης τὴν φωνὴν ἠρώτα τὸν
οἰνοχόον τί λέγει. ὁ δὲ οἰνοχόος εἶπεν· ἑλληνίζειν γὰρ ἠπίστατο. ἐνταῦθα μὲν δὴ γέλως ἐγένετο.

26 Ἐπειδὴ δὲ προὐχώρει ὁ πότος, εἰσῆλθεν ἀνὴρ Θρᾷξ ἵππον
ἔχων λευκόν, καὶ λαβὼν κέρας μεστὸν εἶπε, Προπίνω σοι, ὦ
Σεύθη, καὶ τὸν ἵππον τοῦτον δωροῦμαι, ἐφ' οὗ καὶ διώκων ὃν ἂν
27 θέλῃς αἱρήσεις καὶ ἀποχωρῶν οὐ μὴ δείσῃς τὸν πολέμιον. ἄλλος
παῖδα εἰσάγων οὕτως ἐδωρήσατο προπίνων, καὶ ἄλλος ἱμάτια
τῇ γυναικί. καὶ Τιμασίων προπίνων ἐδωρήσατο φιάλην τε
28 ἀργυρᾶν καὶ τάπιδα ἀξίαν δέκα μνῶν. Γνήσιππος δέ τις Ἀθηναῖος ἀναστὰς εἶπεν ὅτι ἀρχαῖος εἴη νόμος κάλλιστος τοὺς μὲν
ἔχοντας διδόναι τῷ βασιλεῖ τιμῆς ἕνεκα, τοῖς δὲ μὴ ἔχουσι διδόναι τὸν βασιλέα, ἵνα καὶ ἐγώ, ἔφη, ἔχω σοι δωρεῖσθαι καὶ τιμᾶν.
29 ὁ δὲ Ξενοφῶν ἠπορεῖτο τί ποιήσει· καὶ γὰρ ἐτύγχανεν ὡς τιμώμενος ἐν τῷ πλησιαιτάτῳ δίφρῳ Σεύθῃ καθήμενος. ὁ δὲ Ἡρακλείδης ἐκέλευεν αὐτῷ τὸ κέρας ὀρέξαι τὸν οἰνοχόον. ὁ δὲ
Ξενοφῶν, ἤδη γὰρ ὑποπεπωκὼς ἐτύγχανεν, ἀνέστη θαρραλέως
30 δεξάμενος τὸ κέρας καὶ εἶπεν· Ἐγὼ δέ σοι, ὦ Σεύθη, δίδωμι
ἐμαυτὸν καὶ τοὺς ἐμοὺς τούτους ἑταίρους φίλους εἶναι πιστούς,
καὶ οὐδένα ἄκοντα, ἀλλὰ πάντας μᾶλλον ἔτι ἐμοῦ σοι βουλο-
31 μένους φίλους εἶναι. καὶ νῦν πάρεισιν οὐδέν σε προσαιτοῦντες,
ἀλλὰ καὶ προϊέμενοι καὶ πονεῖν ὑπὲρ σοῦ καὶ προκινδυνεύειν
ἐθέλοντες· μεθ' ὧν, ἂν οἱ θεοὶ θέλωσι, πολλὴν χώραν τὴν μὲν

ἀπολήψῃ πατρῴαν οὖσαν, τὴν δὲ κτήσῃ, πολλοὺς δὲ ἵππους,
πολλοὺς δὲ ἄνδρας καὶ γυναῖκας καλὰς κτήσῃ, οὓς οὐ λήζεσθαί
σε δεήσει, ἀλλ' αὐτοὶ φέροντες παρέσονται πρὸς σὲ δῶρα.
ἀναστὰς ὁ Σεύθης συνεξέπιε καὶ συγκατεσκεδάσατο μετ' αὐτοῦ 32
τὸ κέρας. μετὰ ταῦτα εἰσῆλθον κέρασί τε οἵοις σημαίνουσιν
αὐλοῦντες καὶ σάλπιγξιν ὠμοβοείαις ῥυθμούς τε καὶ οἷον μαγά-
διδι σαλπίζοντες. καὶ αὐτὸς Σεύθης ἀναστὰς ἀνέκραγέ τε 33
πολεμικὸν καὶ ἐξήλατο ὥσπερ βέλος φυλαττόμενος μάλα
ἐλαφρῶς. εἰσῇσαν δὲ καὶ γελωτοποιοί.

Ὡς δ' ἦν ἥλιος ἐπὶ δυσμαῖς, ἀνέστησαν οἱ Ἕλληνες καὶ 34
εἶπον ὅτι ὥρα νυκτοφύλακας καθιστάναι καὶ σύνθημα παραδιδόναι. καὶ Σεύθην ἐκέλευον παραγγεῖλαι ὅπως εἰς τὰ Ἑλληνικὰ
στρατόπεδα μηδεὶς τῶν Θρᾳκῶν εἴσεισι νυκτός· οἵ τε γὰρ πολέμιοι Θρᾷκες καὶ ὑμεῖς οἱ φίλοι. ὡς δ' ἐξῇσαν, συνανέστη ὁ 35
Σεύθης οὐδέν τι μεθύοντι ἐοικώς. ἐξελθὼν δ' εἶπεν αὐτοὺς
τοὺς στρατηγοὺς ἀποκαλέσας· Ὦ ἄνδρες, οἱ πολέμιοι ἡμῶν οὐκ
ἴσασί πω τὴν ἡμετέραν συμμαχίαν· ἢν οὖν ἔλθωμεν ἐπ' αὐτοὺς
πρὶν φυλάξασθαι ὥστε μὴ ληφθῆναι ἢ παρασκευάσασθαι ὥστε
ἀμύνασθαι, μάλιστ' ἂν λάβοιμεν καὶ ἀνθρώπους καὶ χρήματα.
συνεπῄνουν ταῦτα οἱ στρατηγοὶ καὶ ἡγεῖσθαι ἐκέλευον. ὁ δ' 36
εἶπε· Παρασκευασάμενοι ἀναμένετε· ἐγὼ δὲ ὁπόταν καιρὸς ᾖ
ἥξω πρὸς ὑμᾶς, καὶ τοὺς πελταστὰς καὶ ὑμᾶς ἀναλαβὼν ἡγήσομαι σὺν τοῖς ἵπποις. καὶ ὁ Ξενοφῶν εἶπε· Σκέψαι τοίνυν, 37
εἴπερ νυκτὸς πορευσόμεθα, εἰ ὁ Ἑλληνικὸς νόμος κάλλιον ἔχει·
μεθ' ἡμέραν μὲν γὰρ ἐν ταῖς πορείαις ἡγεῖται τοῦ στρατεύματος
ὁποῖον ἂν ἀεὶ πρὸς τὴν χώραν συμφέρῃ, ἐάν τε ὁπλιτικὸν ἐάν
τε πελταστικὸν ἐάν τε ἱππικόν· νύκτωρ δὲ νόμος τοῖς Ἕλλησιν
ἡγεῖσθαί ἐστιν τὸ βραδύτατον· οὕτω γὰρ ἥκιστα διασπᾶται τὰ 38
στρατεύματα καὶ ἥκιστα λανθάνουσιν ἀποδιδράσκοντες ἀλλή-
λους· οἱ δὲ διασπασθέντες πολλάκις καὶ περιπίπτουσιν ἀλλήλοις καὶ ἀγνοοῦντες κακῶς ποιοῦσι καὶ πάσχουσιν. εἶπεν 39
οὖν Σεύθης· Ὀρθῶς λέγετε καὶ ἐγὼ τῷ νόμῳ τῷ ὑμετέρῳ
πείσομαι. καὶ ὑμῖν μὲν ἡγεμόνας δώσω τῶν πρεσβυτάτων τοὺς
ἐμπειροτάτους τῆς χώρας, αὐτὸς δ' ἐφέψομαι τελευταῖος τοὺς
ἵππους ἔχων· ταχὺ γὰρ πρῶτος, ἂν δέῃ, παρέσομαι. σύνθημα

δ' εἶπον Ἀθηναίαν κατὰ τὴν συγγένειαν. ταῦτα εἰπόντες ἀνεπαύοντο.

40 Ἡνίκα δ' ἦν ἀμφὶ μέσας νύκτας παρῆν Σεύθης ἔχων τοὺς ἱππέας τεθωρακισμένους καὶ τοὺς πελταστὰς σὺν τοῖς ὅπλοις. καὶ ἐπεὶ παρέδωκε τοὺς ἡγεμόνας, οἱ μὲν ὁπλῖται ἡγοῦντο, οἱ δὲ 41 πελτασταὶ εἵποντο, οἱ δ' ἱππεῖς ὠπισθοφυλάκουν· ἐπεὶ δ' ἡμέρα ἦν, ὁ Σεύθης παρήλαυνεν εἰς τὸ πρόσθεν καὶ ἐπῄνεσε τὸν Ἑλληνικὸν νόμον. πολλάκις γὰρ ἔφη νύκτωρ αὐτὸς καὶ σὺν ὀλίγοις πορευόμενος ἀποσπασθῆναι σὺν τοῖς ἵπποις ἀπὸ τῶν πεζῶν· νῦν δ' ὥσπερ δεῖ ἀθρόοι πάντες ἅμα τῇ ἡμέρᾳ φαινόμεθα. ἀλλὰ ὑμεῖς μὲν περιμένετε αὐτοῦ καὶ ἀναπαύσασθε, ἐγὼ δὲ σκεψά- 42 μενός τι ἥξω. ταῦτ' εἰπὼν ἤλαυνε δι' ὄρους ὁδόν τινα λαβών. ἐπεὶ δ' ἀφίκετο εἰς χιόνα πολλήν, ἐσκέψατο εἰ εἴη ἴχνη ἀνθρώπων ἢ πρόσω ἡγούμενα ἢ ἐναντία. ἐπεὶ δὲ ἀτριβῆ ἑώρα τὴν 43 ὁδόν, ἧκε ταχὺ πάλιν καὶ ἔλεγεν· Ἄνδρες, καλῶς ἔσται, ἢν θεὸς θέλῃ· τοὺς γὰρ ἀνθρώπους λήσομεν ἐπιπεσόντες. ἀλλ' ἐγὼ μὲν ἡγήσομαι τοῖς ἵπποις, ὅπως ἄν τινα ἴδωμεν, μὴ διαφυγὼν σημήνῃ τοῖς πολεμίοις· ὑμεῖς δ' ἕπεσθε· κἂν λειφθῆτε, τῷ στίβῳ τῶν ἵππων ἕπεσθε. ὑπερβάντες δὲ τὰ ὄρη ἥξομεν εἰς κώμας πολλάς τε καὶ εὐδαίμονας.

44 Ἡνίκα δ' ἦν μέσον ἡμέρας, ἤδη τε ἦν ἐπὶ τοῖς ἄκροις καὶ κατιδὼν τὰς κώμας ἧκεν ἐλαύνων πρὸς τοὺς ὁπλίτας καὶ ἔλεγεν· Ἀφήσω ἤδη καταθεῖν τοὺς μὲν ἱππέας εἰς τὸ πεδίον, τοὺς δὲ πελταστὰς ἐπὶ τὰς κώμας. ἀλλ' ἕπεσθε ὡς ἂν δύνησθε τάχιστα, 45 ὅπως ἐάν τις ὑφιστῆται, ἀλέξησθε. ἀκούσας ταῦτα ὁ Ξενοφῶν κατέβη ἀπὸ τοῦ ἵππου. καὶ ὃς ἤρετο· Τί καταβαίνεις ἐπεὶ σπεύδειν δεῖ; Οἶδα, ἔφη, ὅτι οὐκ ἐμοῦ μόνου δέῃ· οἱ δὲ ὁπλῖται 46 θᾶττον δραμοῦνται καὶ ἥδιον, ἐὰν καὶ ἐγὼ πεζὸς ἡγῶμαι. μετὰ ταῦτα ᾤχετο, καὶ Τιμασίων μετ' αὐτοῦ ἔχων ἱππεῖς ὡς τετταράκοντα τῶν Ἑλλήνων. Ξενοφῶν δὲ παρηγγύησε τοὺς εἰς τριάκοντα ἔτη παριέναι ἀπὸ τῶν λόχων εὐζώνους. καὶ αὐτὸς μὲν 47 ἐτρόχαζε τούτους ἔχων, Κλεάνωρ δ' ἡγεῖτο τῶν ἄλλων. ἐπεὶ δ' ἐν ταῖς κώμαις ἦσαν, Σεύθης ἔχων ὅσον τριάκοντα ἱππέας προσελάσας εἶπε· Τάδε δή, ὦ Ξενοφῶν, ἃ σὺ ἔλεγες· ἔχονται οἱ ἄνθρωποι· ἀλλὰ γὰρ ἔρημοι οἱ ἱππεῖς οἴχονταί μοι ἄλλος ἄλλῃ

διώκων, καὶ δέδοικα μὴ συστάντες ἀθρόοι που κακόν τι ἐργά-
σωνται οἱ πολέμιοι. δεῖ δὲ καὶ ἐν ταῖς κώμαις καταμένειν τινὰς
ἡμῶν· μεσταὶ γάρ εἰσιν ἀνθρώπων. Ἀλλ' ἐγὼ μέν, ἔφη ὁ 48
Ξενοφῶν, σὺν οἷς ἔχω τὰ ἄκρα καταλήψομαι· σὺ δὲ Κλεάνορα
κέλευε διὰ τοῦ πεδίου παρατεῖναι τὴν φάλαγγα παρὰ τὰς κώμας.
ἐπεὶ ταῦτα ἐποίησαν, συνηλίσθησαν ἀνδράποδα μὲν εἰς χίλια,
βόες δὲ δισχίλιοι, πρόβατα ἄλλα μύρια. τότε μὲν δὴ αὐτοῦ
ηὐλίσθησαν.

IV. Τῇ δ' ὑστεραίᾳ κατακαύσας ὁ Σεύθης τὰς κώμας παντε- 1
λῶς καὶ οἰκίαν οὐδεμίαν λιπών, ὅπως φόβον ἐνθείη καὶ τοῖς
ἄλλοις οἷα πείσονται, ἂν μὴ πείθωνται, ἀπῄει πάλιν. καὶ τὴν 2
μὲν λείαν ἀπέπεμψε διατίθεσθαι Ἡρακλείδην εἰς Πέρινθον,
ὅπως ἂν μισθὸς γένοιτο τοῖς στρατιώταις· αὐτὸς δὲ καὶ οἱ
Ἕλληνες ἐστρατοπεδεύοντο ἀνὰ τὸ Θυνῶν πεδίον. οἱ δ' ἐκλιπόντες ἔφευγον εἰς τὰ ὄρη. ἦν δὲ χιὼν πολλὴ καὶ ψῦχος 3
οὕτως ὥστε τὸ ὕδωρ ὃ ἐφέροντο ἐπὶ δεῖπνον ἐπήγνυτο καὶ ὁ οἶνος
ὁ ἐν τοῖς ἀγγείοις, καὶ τῶν Ἑλλήνων πολλῶν καὶ ῥῖνες ἀπε-
καίοντο καὶ ὦτα. καὶ τότε δῆλον ἐγένετο οὗ ἕνεκα οἱ Θρᾷκες 4
τὰς ἀλωπεκᾶς ἐπὶ ταῖς κεφαλαῖς φοροῦσι καὶ τοῖς ὠσί, καὶ
χιτῶνας οὐ μόνον περὶ τοῖς στέρνοις ἀλλὰ καὶ περὶ τοῖς μηροῖς,
καὶ ζειρὰς μέχρι τῶν ποδῶν ἐπὶ τῶν ἵππων ἔχουσιν, ἀλλ' οὐ
χλαμύδας. ἀφιεὶς δὲ τῶν αἰχμαλώτων ὁ Σεύθης εἰς τὰ ὄρη 5
ἔλεγεν ὅτι εἰ μὴ καταβήσονται οἰκήσοντες καὶ πείσονται, ὅτι
κατακαύσει καὶ τούτων τὰς κώμας καὶ τὸν σῖτον, καὶ ἀπολοῦνται
τῷ λιμῷ. ἐκ τούτου κατέβαινον καὶ γυναῖκες καὶ παῖδες καὶ
πρεσβύτεροι· οἱ δὲ νεώτεροι ἐν ταῖς ὑπὸ τὸ ὄρος κώμαις ηὐλίζοντο. καὶ ὁ Σεύθης καταμαθὼν ἐκέλευσε τὸν Ξενοφῶντα τῶν 6
ὁπλιτῶν τοὺς νεωτάτους λαβόντα συνεπισπέσθαι. καὶ ἀναστάντες τῆς νυκτὸς ἅμα τῇ ἡμέρᾳ παρῆσαν εἰς τὰς κώμας. καὶ
οἱ μὲν πλεῖστοι ἐξέφυγον· πλησίον γὰρ ἦν τὸ ὄρος· ὅσους δὲ
ἔλαβε κατηκόντισεν ἀφειδῶς Σεύθης.

Ἐπισθένης δ' ἦν τις Ὀλύνθιος παιδεραστής, ὃς ἰδὼν παῖδα 7
καλὸν ἡβάσκοντα ἄρτι πέλτην ἔχοντα μέλλοντα ἀποθνῄσκειν,
προσδραμὼν Ξενοφῶντα ἱκέτευε βοηθῆσαι παιδὶ καλῷ. καὶ ὃς 8
προσελθὼν τῷ Σεύθῃ δεῖται μὴ ἀποκτεῖναι τὸν παῖδα, καὶ τοῦ

Ἐπισθένους διηγεῖται τὸν τρόπον, καὶ ὅτι λόχον ποτὲ συνελέξατο σκοπῶν οὐδὲν ἄλλο ἢ εἴ τινες εἶεν καλοί, καὶ μετὰ τούτων ἦν ἀνὴρ ἀγαθός. ὁ δὲ Σεύθης ἤρετο· Ἦ καὶ θέλοις ἄν, ὦ Ἐπίσθενες, ὑπὲρ τούτου ἀποθανεῖν; ὁ δ᾽ ὑπερανατείνας τὸν τράχηλον, Παῖε, ἔφη, εἰ κελεύει ὁ παῖς καὶ μέλλει χάριν εἰδέναι. ἐπήρετο ὁ Σεύθης τὸν παῖδα εἰ παίσειεν αὐτὸν ἀντ᾽ ἐκείνου. οὐκ εἴα ὁ παῖς, ἀλλ᾽ ἱκέτευε μηδέτερον κατακαίνειν. ἐνταῦθα ὁ Ἐπισθένης περιβαλὼν τὸν παῖδα εἶπεν· Ὥρα σοι, ὦ Σεύθη, περὶ τοῦδέ μοι διαμάχεσθαι· οὐ γὰρ μεθήσω τὸν παῖδα. ὁ δὲ Σεύθης γελῶν ταῦτα μὲν εἴα· ἔδοξε δὲ αὐτῷ αὐτοῦ αὐλισθῆναι, ἵνα μηδ᾽ ἐκ τούτων τῶν κωμῶν οἱ ἐπὶ τοῦ ὄρους τρέφοιντο. καὶ αὐτὸς μὲν ἐν τῷ πεδίῳ ὑποκαταβὰς ἐσκήνου, ὁ δὲ Ξενοφῶν ἔχων τοὺς ἐπιλέκτους ἐν τῇ ὑπὸ τὸ ὄρος ἀνωτάτω κώμῃ, καὶ οἱ ἄλλοι Ἕλληνες ἐν τοῖς ὀρεινοῖς καλουμένοις Θρᾳξὶ πλησίον κατεσκήνησαν.

Ἐκ τούτου ἡμέραι τ᾽ οὐ πολλαὶ διετρίβοντο καὶ οἱ ἐκ τοῦ ὄρους Θρᾷκες καταβαίνοντες πρὸς τὸν Σεύθην περὶ σπονδῶν καὶ ὁμήρων διεπράττοντο. καὶ ὁ Ξενοφῶν ἐλθὼν ἔλεγε τῷ Σεύθῃ ὅτι ἐν πονηροῖς σκηνοῖεν καὶ πλησίον εἶεν οἱ πολέμιοι· ἥδιόν τ᾽ ἂν ἔξω αὐλίζεσθαι ἔφη ἐν ἐχυροῖς χωρίοις μᾶλλον ἢ ἐν τοῖς στεγνοῖς, ὥστε ἀπολέσθαι. ὁ δὲ θαρρεῖν ἐκέλευε καὶ ἔδειξεν ὁμήρους παρόντας αὐτῶν. ἐδέοντο δὲ καὶ αὐτοῦ Ξενοφῶντος καταβαίνοντές τινες τῶν ἐκ τοῦ ὄρους συμπρᾶξαι σφίσι τὰς σπονδάς. ὁ δ᾽ ὡμολόγει καὶ θαρρεῖν ἐκέλευε καὶ ἠγγυᾶτο μηδὲν αὐτοὺς κακὸν πείσεσθαι πειθομένους Σεύθῃ. οἱ δ᾽ ἄρα ταῦτ᾽ ἔλεγον κατασκοπῆς ἕνεκα.

Ταῦτα μὲν τῆς ἡμέρας ἐγένετο· εἰς δὲ τὴν ἐπιοῦσαν νύκτα ἐπιτίθενται ἐλθόντες ἐκ τοῦ ὄρους οἱ Θυνοί. καὶ ἡγεμὼν μὲν ἦν ὁ δεσπότης ἑκάστης τῆς οἰκίας· χαλεπὸν γὰρ ἦν ἄλλως τὰς οἰκίας σκότους ὄντος ἀνευρίσκειν ἐν ταῖς κώμαις· καὶ γὰρ αἱ οἰκίαι κύκλῳ περιεσταύρωντο μεγάλοις σταυροῖς τῶν προβάτων ἕνεκα. ἐπεὶ δ᾽ ἐγένοντο κατὰ τὰς θύρας ἑκάστου τοῦ οἰκήματος, οἱ μὲν εἰσηκόντιζον, οἱ δὲ τοῖς σκυτάλοις ἔβαλλον, ἃ ἔχειν ἔφασαν ὡς ἀποκόψοντες τῶν δοράτων τὰς λόγχας, οἱ δ᾽ ἐνεπίμπρασαν, καὶ Ξενοφῶντα ὀνομαστὶ καλοῦντες ἐξιόντα ἐκέλευον ἀποθνή-

σκειν, ἢ αὐτοῦ ἔφασαν κατακαυθήσεσθαι αὐτόν. καὶ ἤδη τε διὰ 16
τοῦ ὀρόφου ἐφαίνετο πῦρ, καὶ ἐντεθωρακισμένοι οἱ περὶ τὸν Ξενοφῶντα ἔνδον ἦσαν ἀσπίδας καὶ μαχαίρας καὶ κράνη ἔχοντες, καὶ
Σιλανὸς Μακίστιος ἐτῶν ὡς ὀκτωκαίδεκα σημαίνει τῇ σάλπιγγι·
καὶ εὐθὺς ἐκπηδῶσιν ἐσπασμένοι τὰ ξίφη καὶ οἱ ἐκ τῶν ἄλλων
σκηνωμάτων. οἱ δὲ Θρᾷκες φεύγουσιν, ὥσπερ δὴ τρόπος ἦν 17
αὐτοῖς, ὄπισθεν περιβαλλόμενοι τὰς πέλτας· καὶ αὐτῶν ὑπεραλ-
λομένων τοὺς σταυροὺς ἐλήφθησάν τινες κρεμασθέντες ἐνεχο-
μένων τῶν πελτῶν τοῖς σταυροῖς· οἱ δὲ καὶ ἀπέθανον διαμαρτόντες
τῶν ἐξόδων· οἱ δὲ Ἕλληνες ἐδίωκον ἔξω τῆς κώμης. τῶν δὲ 18
Θυνῶν ὑποστραφέντες τινὲς ἐν τῷ σκότει τοὺς παρατρέχοντας
παρ' οἰκίαν καιομένην ἠκόντιζον εἰς τὸ φῶς ἐκ τοῦ σκότους· καὶ
ἔτρωσαν Ἱερώνυμόν τε Ἐπιταλιέα λοχαγὸν καὶ Θεογένην
Λοκρὸν λοχαγόν· ἀπέθανε δὲ οὐδείς· κατεκαύθη μέντοι καὶ
ἐσθής τινων καὶ σκεύη. Σεύθης δὲ ἧκε βοηθῶν σὺν ἑπτὰ 19
ἱππεῦσι τοῖς πρώτοις καὶ τὸν σαλπικτὴν ἔχων τὸν Θρᾴκιον.
καὶ ἐπείπερ ᾔσθετο, ὅσονπερ χρόνον ἐβοήθει, τοσοῦτον καὶ τὸ
κέρας ἐφθέγγετο αὐτῷ· ὥστε καὶ τοῦτο φόβον συμπαρέσχε τοῖς
πολεμίοις. ἐπεὶ δ' ἦλθεν, ἐδεξιοῦτό τε καὶ ἔλεγεν ὅτι οἴοιτο
τεθνεῶτας πολλοὺς εὑρήσειν.

Ἐκ τούτου ὁ Ξενοφῶν δεῖται τοὺς ὁμήρους τε αὐτῷ παρα- 20
δοῦναι καὶ ἐπὶ τὸ ὄρος, εἰ βούλεται, συστρατεύεσθαι· εἰ δὲ μή,
αὐτὸν ἐᾶσαι. τῇ οὖν ὑστεραίᾳ παραδίδωσιν ὁ Σεύθης τοὺς ὁμή- 21
ρους, πρεσβυτέρους ἄνδρας ἤδη, τοὺς κρατίστους, ὡς ἔφασαν,
τῶν ὀρεινῶν, καὶ αὐτὸς ἔρχεται σὺν τῇ δυνάμει. ἤδη δὲ εἶχε καὶ
τριπλασίαν δύναμιν ὁ Σεύθης· ἐκ γὰρ τῶν Ὀδρυσῶν ἀκούοντες
ἃ πράττει ὁ Σεύθης πολλοὶ κατέβαινον συστρατευσόμενοι. οἱ 22
δὲ Θυνοὶ ἐπεὶ εἶδον ἀπὸ τοῦ ὄρους πολλοὺς μὲν ὁπλίτας, πολλοὺς
δὲ πελταστάς, πολλοὺς δὲ ἱππεῖς, καταβάντες ἱκέτευον σπείσασθαι, καὶ πάντα ὡμολόγουν ποιήσειν καὶ πιστὰ λαμβάνειν
ἐκέλευον. ὁ δὲ Σεύθης καλέσας τὸν Ξενοφῶντα ἐπεδείκνυεν ἃ 23
λέγοιεν, καὶ οὐκ ἂν ἔφη σπείσασθαι, εἰ Ξενοφῶν βούλοιτο τιμωρήσασθαι αὐτοὺς τῆς ἐπιθέσεως. ὁ δ' εἶπεν· Ἀλλ' ἔγωγε 24
ἱκανὴν νομίζω καὶ νῦν δίκην ἔχειν, εἰ οὗτοι δοῦλοι ἔσονται ἀντ'
ἐλευθέρων. συμβουλεύειν μέντοι ἔφη αὐτῷ τὸ λοιπὸν ὁμήρους

λαμβάνειν τοὺς δυνατωτάτους κακόν τι ποιεῖν, τοὺς δὲ γέροντας
οἴκοι ἐᾶν. οἱ μὲν οὖν ταύτῃ πάντες δὴ προσωμολόγουν.

V. Ὑπερβάλλουσι δὲ πρὸς τοὺς ὑπὲρ Βυζαντίου Θρᾷκας
εἰς τὸ Δέλτα καλούμενον· αὕτη δ' ἦν οὐκέτι ἀρχὴ Μαισάδου,
ἀλλὰ Τήρους τοῦ Ὀδρύσου [ἀρχαίου τινός]. καὶ ὁ Ἡρακλείδης
ἐνταῦθα ἔχων τὴν τιμὴν τῆς λείας παρῆν. καὶ Σεύθης ἐξαγαγὼν ζεύγη ἡμιονικὰ τρία, οὐ γὰρ ἦν πλείω, τὰ δ' ἄλλα βοεικά,
καλέσας Ξενοφῶντα ἐκέλευε λαβεῖν, τὰ δὲ ἄλλα διανεῖμαι τοῖς
στρατηγοῖς καὶ λοχαγοῖς. Ξενοφῶν δὲ εἶπεν· Ἐμοὶ τοίνυν
ἀρκεῖ καὶ αὖθις λαβεῖν· τούτοις δὲ τοῖς στρατηγοῖς δωροῦ οἳ
σὺν ἐμοὶ ἠκολούθησαν καὶ λοχαγοῖς. καὶ τῶν ζευγῶν λαμβάνει
ἓν μὲν Τιμασίων ὁ Δαρδανεύς, ἓν δὲ Κλεάνωρ ὁ Ὀρχομένιος, ἓν
δὲ Φρυνίσκος ὁ Ἀχαιός· τὰ δὲ βοεικὰ ζεύγη τοῖς λοχαγοῖς
κατεμερίσθη. τὸν δὲ μισθὸν ἀποδίδωσιν ἐξεληλυθότος ἤδη τοῦ
μηνὸς εἴκοσι μόνον ἡμερῶν· ὁ γὰρ Ἡρακλείδης ἔλεγεν ὅτι οὐ
πλέον ἐμπολῆσαι. ὁ οὖν Ξενοφῶν ἀχθεσθεὶς εἶπεν ἐπομόσας·
Δοκεῖς μοι, ὦ Ἡρακλείδη, οὐχ ὡς δεῖ κήδεσθαι Σεύθου· εἰ γὰρ
ἐκήδου, ἧκες ἂν φέρων πλήρη τὸν μισθὸν καὶ προσδανεισάμενος,
εἰ μὴ ἄλλως ἐδύνω, καὶ ἀποδόμενος τὰ σαυτοῦ ἱμάτια.

Ἐντεῦθεν ὁ Ἡρακλείδης ἠχθέσθη τε καὶ ἔδεισε μὴ ἐκ τῆς
Σεύθου φιλίας ἐκβληθείη, καὶ ὅ,τι ἐδύνατο ἀπὸ ταύτης τῆς
ἡμέρας Ξενοφῶντα διέβαλλε πρὸς Σεύθην. οἱ μὲν δὴ στρατιῶται Ξενοφῶντι ἐνεκάλουν ὅτι οὐκ εἶχον τὸν μισθόν· Σεύθης
δὲ ἤχθετο αὐτῷ ὅτι ἐντόνως τοῖς στρατιώταις ἀπῄτει τὸν μισθόν.
καὶ τέως μὲν ἀεὶ ἐμέμνητο ὡς, ἐπειδὰν ἐπὶ θάλατταν ἀπέλθῃ,
παραδώσει αὐτῷ Βισάνθην καὶ Γάνον καὶ Νέον τεῖχος· ἀπὸ δὲ
τούτου τοῦ χρόνου οὐδενὸς ἔτι τούτων ἐμέμνητο. ὁ γὰρ Ἡρακλείδης καὶ τοῦτο διεβεβλήκει ὡς οὐκ ἀσφαλὲς εἴη τείχη παραδιδόναι ἀνδρὶ δύναμιν ἔχοντι.

Ἐκ τούτου ὁ μὲν Ξενοφῶν ἐβουλεύετο τί χρὴ ποιεῖν περὶ
τοῦ ἔτι ἄνω στρατεύεσθαι· ὁ δ' Ἡρακλείδης εἰσαγαγὼν τοὺς
ἄλλους στρατηγοὺς πρὸς Σεύθην λέγειν τε ἐκέλευεν αὐτοὺς ὅτι
οὐδὲν ἂν ἧττον σφεῖς ἀγάγοιεν τὴν στρατιὰν ἢ Ξενοφῶν, τόν τε
μισθὸν ὑπισχνεῖτο αὐτοῖς ἐντὸς ὀλίγων ἡμερῶν ἔκπλεων παρέσεσθαι δυοῖν μηνοῖν, καὶ συστρατεύεσθαι ἐκέλευε. καὶ ὁ Τιμασίων

εἶπεν· Ἐγὼ μὲν τοίνυν οὐδ' ἂν πέντε μηνῶν μισθὸς μέλλῃ εἶναι στρατευσαίμην ἂν ἄνευ Ξενοφῶντος. καὶ ὁ Φρυνίσκος καὶ ὁ Κλεάνωρ συνωμολόγουν τῷ Τιμασίωνι. ἐντεῦθεν ὁ Σεύθης ἐλοι- 11 δόρει τὸν Ἡρακλείδην ὅτι οὐ παρεκάλει καὶ Ξενοφῶντα. ἐκ δὲ τούτου παρακαλοῦσιν αὐτὸν μόνον. ὁ δὲ γνοὺς τοῦ Ἡρακλείδου τὴν πανουργίαν ὅτι βούλοιτο αὐτὸν διαβάλλειν πρὸς τοὺς ἄλλους στρατηγούς, παρέρχεται λαβὼν τούς τε στρατηγοὺς πάντας καὶ τοὺς λοχαγούς.

Καὶ ἐπεὶ πάντες ἐπείσθησαν, συνεστρατεύοντο καὶ ἀφικνοῦνται 12 ἐν δεξιᾷ ἔχοντες τὸν Πόντον διὰ τῶν Μελινοφάγων καλουμένων Θρᾳκῶν εἰς τὸν Σαλμυδησσόν. ἔνθα τῶν εἰς τὸν Πόντον πλεου- σῶν νεῶν πολλαὶ ὀκέλλουσι καὶ ἐκπίπτουσι· τέναγος γάρ ἐστιν ἐπὶ πάμπολυ τῆς θαλάττης. καὶ Θρᾷκες οἱ κατὰ ταῦτα οἰκοῦντες 13 στήλας ὁρισάμενοι τὰ καθ' αὑτοὺς ἐκπίπτοντα ἕκαστοι λήζονται· τέως δὲ ἔλεγον πρὶν ὁρίσασθαι ἁρπάζοντας πολλοὺς ὑπ' ἀλλή- λων ἀποθνῄσκειν. ἐνταῦθα ηὑρίσκοντο πολλαὶ μὲν κλῖναι, 14 πολλὰ δὲ κιβώτια, πολλαὶ δὲ βίβλοι γεγραμμέναι, καὶ τἆλλα πολλὰ ὅσα ἐν ξυλίνοις τεύχεσι ναύκληροι ἄγουσιν. ἐντεῦθεν ταῦτα καταστρεψάμενοι ἀπῇσαν πάλιν. ἔνθα δὴ Σεύθης εἶχε 15 στράτευμα ἤδη πλέον τοῦ Ἑλληνικοῦ· ἔκ τε γὰρ Ὀδρυσῶν πολὺ ἔτι πλείους κατεβεβήκεσαν καὶ οἱ αἰεὶ πειθόμενοι συνεστρα- τεύοντο. κατηυλίσθησαν δ' ἐν τῷ πεδίῳ ὑπὲρ Σηλυμβρίας ὅσον τριάκοντα σταδίους ἀπέχοντες τῆς θαλάττης. καὶ μισθὸς μὲν 16 οὐδείς πω ἐφαίνετο· πρὸς δὲ τὸν Ξενοφῶντα οἵ τε στρατιῶται παγχαλέπως εἶχον ὅ τε Σεύθης οὐκέτι οἰκείως διέκειτο, ἀλλ' ὁπότε συγγενέσθαι αὐτῷ βουλόμενος ἔλθοι, πολλαὶ ἤδη ἀσχολίαι ἐφαίνοντο.

VI. Ἐν τούτῳ τῷ χρόνῳ σχεδὸν ἤδη δύο μηνῶν ὄντων 1 ἀφικνεῖται Χαρμῖνός τε ὁ Λάκων καὶ Πολύνικος παρὰ Θίβρωνος, καὶ λέγουσιν ὅτι Λακεδαιμονίοις δοκεῖ στρατεύεσθαι ἐπὶ Τισσα- φέρνην, καὶ Θίβρων ἐκπέπλευκεν ὡς πολεμήσων, καὶ δεῖται ταύτης τῆς στρατιᾶς καὶ λέγει ὅτι δαρεικὸς ἑκάστῳ ἔσται μισθὸς τοῦ μηνός, καὶ τοῖς λοχαγοῖς διμοιρία, τοῖς δὲ στρατηγοῖς τετρα- μοιρία.

Ἐπεὶ δ' ἦλθον οἱ Λακεδαιμόνιοι, εὐθὺς ὁ Ἡρακλείδης 2

πυθόμενος ὅτι ἐπὶ τὸ στράτευμα ἥκουσι λέγει τῷ Σεύθῃ ὅτι κάλλιστόν τι γεγένηται· οἱ μὲν γὰρ Λακεδαιμόνιοι δέονται τοῦ στρατεύματος, σὺ δὲ οὐκέτι δέῃ· ἀποδιδοὺς δὲ τὸ στράτευμα χαριῇ αὐτοῖς, σὲ δὲ οὐκέτι ἀπαιτήσουσι τὸν μισθόν, ἀλλ' 3 ἀπαλλάξονται ἐκ τῆς χώρας. ἀκούσας ταῦτα ὁ Σεύθης κελεύει παράγειν· καὶ ἐπεὶ εἶπον ὅτι ἐπὶ τὸ στράτευμα ἥκουσιν, ἔλεγεν ὅτι τὸ στράτευμα ἀποδίδωσι, φίλος τε καὶ σύμμαχος εἶναι βούλεται, καλεῖ τε αὐτοὺς ἐπὶ ξένια· καὶ ἐξένιζε μεγαλοπρεπῶς. Ξενοφῶντα δὲ οὐκ ἐκάλει, οὐδὲ τῶν ἄλλων στρατηγῶν οὐδένα. 4 ἐρωτώντων δὲ τῶν Λακεδαιμονίων τίς ἀνὴρ εἴη Ξενοφῶν ἀπεκρίνατο ὅτι τὰ μὲν ἄλλα εἴη οὐ κακός, φιλοστρατιώτης δέ· καὶ διὰ τοῦτο χεῖρόν ἐστιν αὐτῷ. καὶ οἳ εἶπον, Ἀλλ' ἦ δημαγωγεῖ ὁ 5 ἀνὴρ τοὺς ἄνδρας; καὶ ὁ Ἡρακλείδης, Πάνυ μὲν οὖν, ἔφη. Ἆρ' οὖν, ἔφασαν, μὴ καὶ ἡμῖν ἐναντιώσεται τῆς ἀπαγωγῆς; Ἀλλ' ἢν ὑμεῖς, ἔφη ὁ Ἡρακλείδης, συλλέξαντες αὐτοὺς ὑπόσχησθε τὸν μισθόν, ὀλίγον ἐκείνῳ προσχόντες ἀποδραμοῦνται σὺν ὑμῖν. 6 Πῶς οὖν ἄν, ἔφασαν, ἡμῖν συλλεγεῖεν; Αὔριον ὑμᾶς, ἔφη ὁ Ἡρακλείδης, πρῲ ἄξομεν πρὸς αὐτούς· καὶ οἶδα, ἔφη, ὅτι ἐπειδὰν ὑμᾶς ἴδωσιν, ἄσμενοι συνδραμοῦνται. αὕτη μὲν ἡ ἡμέρα οὕτως ἔληξεν.

7 Τῇ δ' ὑστεραίᾳ ἄγουσιν ἐπὶ τὸ στράτευμα τοὺς Λάκωνας Σεύθης τε καὶ Ἡρακλείδης, καὶ συλλέγεται ἡ στρατιά. τὼ δὲ Λάκωνε ἐλεγέτην ὅτι Λακεδαιμονίοις δοκεῖ πολεμεῖν Τισσαφέρνει τῷ ὑμᾶς ἀδικήσαντι· ἢν οὖν ἴητε σὺν ἡμῖν, τόν τε ἐχθρὸν τιμωρήσεσθε καὶ δαρεικὸν ἕκαστος οἴσει τοῦ μηνὸς ὑμῶν, λοχαγὸς δὲ 8 τὸ διπλοῦν, στρατηγὸς δὲ τὸ τετραπλοῦν. καὶ οἱ στρατιῶται ἄσμενοί τε ἤκουσαν καὶ εὐθὺς ἀνίσταταί τις τῶν Ἀρκάδων τοῦ Ξενοφῶντος κατηγορήσων. παρῆν δὲ καὶ Σεύθης βουλόμενος 9 εἰδέναι τί πραχθήσεται, καὶ ἐν ἐπηκόῳ εἱστήκει ἔχων ἑρμηνέα· ξυνίει δὲ καὶ αὐτὸς ἑλληνιστὶ τὰ πλεῖστα. ἔνθα δὴ λέγει ὁ Ἀρκάς· Ἀλλ' ἡμεῖς μέν, ὦ Λακεδαιμόνιοι, καὶ πάλαι ἂν ἦμεν παρ' ὑμῖν, εἰ μὴ Ξενοφῶν ἡμᾶς δεῦρο πείσας ἀπήγαγεν, ἔνθα δὴ ἡμεῖς μὲν τὸν δεινὸν χειμῶνα στρατευόμενοι καὶ νύκτα καὶ ἡμέραν οὐδὲν πεπαύμεθα· ὁ δὲ τοὺς ἡμετέρους πόνους ἔχει· καὶ Σεύθης 10 ἐκεῖνον μὲν ἰδίᾳ πεπλούτικεν, ἡμᾶς δὲ ἀποστερεῖ τὸν μισθόν·

ὥστε [ὅ γε πρῶτος λέγων] ἐγὼ μὲν εἰ τοῦτον ἴδοιμι καταλευσθέντα καὶ δόντα δίκην ὧν ἡμᾶς περιεῖλκε, καὶ τὸν μισθὸν ἄν μοι δοκῶ ἔχειν καὶ οὐδὲν ἐπὶ τοῖς πεπονημένοις ἄχθεσθαι. μετὰ τοῦτον ἄλλος ἀνέστη ὁμοίως καὶ ἄλλος. ἐκ δὲ τούτου Ξενοφῶν ἔλεξεν ὧδε.

Ἀλλὰ πάντα μὲν ἄρα ἄνθρωπον ὄντα προσδοκᾶν δεῖ, ὁπότε γε καὶ ἐγὼ νῦν ὑφ᾽ ὑμῶν αἰτίας ἔχω ἐν ᾧ πλείστην προθυμίαν ἐμαυτῷ γε δοκῶ συνειδέναι περὶ ὑμᾶς παρεσχημένος. ἀπετραπόμην μέν γε ἤδη οἴκαδε ὡρμημένος, οὐ μὰ τὸν Δία οὔτοι πυνθανόμενος ὑμᾶς εὖ πράττειν, ἀλλὰ μᾶλλον ἀκούων ἐν ἀπόροις εἶναι ὡς ὠφελήσων εἴ τι δυναίμην. ἐπεὶ δὲ ἦλθον, Σεύθου τουτουὶ πολλοὺς ἀγγέλους πρὸς ἐμὲ πέμποντος καὶ πολλὰ ὑπισχνουμένου μοι, εἰ πείσαιμι ὑμᾶς πρὸς αὐτὸν ἐλθεῖν, τοῦτο μὲν οὐκ ἐπεχείρησα ποιεῖν, ὡς αὐτοὶ ὑμεῖς ἐπίστασθε. ἦγον δὲ ὅθεν ᾠόμην τάχιστ᾽ ἂν ὑμᾶς εἰς τὴν Ἀσίαν διαβῆναι. ταῦτα γὰρ καὶ βέλτιστα ἐνόμιζον ὑμῖν εἶναι καὶ ὑμᾶς ᾔδειν βουλομένους. ἐπεὶ δ᾽ Ἀρίσταρχος ἐλθὼν σὺν τριήρεσιν ἐκώλυε διαπλεῖν ἡμᾶς, ἐκ τούτου, ὅπερ εἰκὸς δήπου ἦν, συνέλεξα ὑμᾶς, ὅπως βουλευσαίμεθα ὅ,τι χρὴ ποιεῖν. οὐκοῦν ὑμεῖς ἀκούοντες μὲν Ἀριστάρχου ἐπιτάττοντος ὑμῖν εἰς Χερρόνησον πορεύεσθαι, ἀκούοντες δὲ Σεύθου πείθοντος ἑαυτῷ συστρατεύεσθαι, πάντες μὲν ἐλέγετε σὺν Σεύθῃ ἰέναι, πάντες δ᾽ ἐψηφίσασθε ταῦτα; τί οὖν ἐγὼ ἐνταῦθα ἠδίκησα ἀγαγὼν ὑμᾶς ἔνθα πᾶσιν ὑμῖν ἐδόκει; ἐπεί γε μὴν ψεύδεσθαι ἤρξατο Σεύθης περὶ τοῦ μισθοῦ, εἰ μὲν ἐπαινῶ αὐτόν, δικαίως ἄν με καὶ αἰτιῷσθε καὶ μισοῖτε· εἰ δὲ πρόσθεν αὐτῷ πάντων μάλιστα φίλος ὢν νῦν πάντων διαφορώτατός εἰμι, πῶς ἂν ἔτι δικαίως ὑμᾶς αἱρούμενος ἀντὶ Σεύθου ὑφ᾽ ὑμῶν αἰτίαν ἔχοιμι περὶ ὧν πρὸς τοῦτον διαφέρομαι;

Ἀλλ᾽ εἴποιτ᾽ ἂν ὅτι ἔξεστι καὶ τὰ ὑμέτερα ἔχοντα παρὰ Σεύθου τεχνάζειν. οὐκοῦν δῆλον τοῦτό γέ ἐστιν, εἴπερ ἐμοὶ ἐτέλει τι Σεύθης, οὐχ οὕτως ἐτέλει δήπου ὡς ὧν τε ἐμοὶ δοίη στέροιτο καὶ ἄλλα ὑμῖν ἀποτείσειεν, ἀλλ᾽ οἶμαι, εἰ ἐδίδου, ἐπὶ τούτῳ δὴ ἐδίδου ὅπως ἐμοὶ δοὺς μεῖον μὴ ἀποδοίη ὑμῖν τὸ πλέον. εἰ τοίνυν οὕτως ἔχειν οἴεσθε, ἔξεστιν ὑμῖν αὐτίκα μάλα ματαίαν ταύτην τὴν πρᾶξιν ἀμφοτέροις ἡμῖν ποιῆσαι, ἐὰν πράττητε αὐτὸν τὰ χρήματα. δῆλον γὰρ ὅτι Σεύθης, εἰ ἔχω τι παρ' αὐτοῦ, ἀπαιτήσει με, καὶ ἀπαιτήσει μέντοι δικαίως, ἐὰν μὴ βεβαιῶ τὴν πρᾶξιν αὐτῷ ἐφ' ᾗ ἐδωροδόκουν. ἀλλὰ πολλοῦ μοι δοκῶ δεῖν τὰ ὑμέτερα ἔχειν· ὀμνύω γὰρ ὑμῖν θεοὺς ἅπαντας καὶ πάσας μηδ' ἃ ἐμοὶ ἰδίᾳ ὑπέσχετο Σεύθης ἔχειν· πάρεστι δὲ καὶ αὐτὸς καὶ ἀκούων σύνοιδέ μοι εἰ ἐπιορκῶ· ἵνα δὲ μᾶλλον θαυμάσητε, συνεπόμνυμι μηδὲ ἅ οἱ ἄλλοι στρατηγοὶ ἔλαβον εἰληφέναι, μὴ τοίνυν μηδὲ ὅσα τῶν λοχαγῶν ἔνιοι.

Καὶ τί δὴ ταῦτ' ἐποίουν; ᾤμην, ἄνδρες, ὅσῳ μᾶλλον συμφέροιμι τούτῳ τὴν τότε πενίαν, τοσούτῳ μᾶλλον αὐτὸν φίλον ποιήσεσθαι, ὁπότε δυνασθείη. ἐγὼ δὲ ἅμα τε αὐτὸν ὁρῶ εὖ πράττοντα καὶ γιγνώσκω δὴ αὐτοῦ τὴν γνώμην. εἴποι δή τις ἄν, οὔκουν αἰσχύνῃ οὕτω μώρως ἐξαπατώμενος; ναὶ μὰ Δία ᾐσχυνόμην μεντἂν, εἰ ὑπὸ πολεμίου γε ὄντος ἐξηπατήθην· φίλῳ δὲ ὄντι ἐξαπατᾶν αἴσχιόν μοι δοκεῖ εἶναι ἢ ἐξαπατᾶσθαι. ἐπεὶ εἴ γε πρὸς φίλους ἐστὶ φυλακή, πᾶσαν οἶδα ἡμᾶς φυλαξαμένους ὡς μὴ παρασχεῖν τούτῳ πρόφασιν δικαίαν μὴ ἀποδιδόναι ἡμῖν ἃ ὑπέσχετο· οὔτε γὰρ ἠδικήσαμεν τοῦτον οὐδὲν οὔτε κατεβλακεύσαμεν τὰ τούτου οὐδὲ μὴν κατεδειλιάσαμεν οὐδὲν ἐφ' ὅ,τι ἡμᾶς οὗτος παρεκάλεσεν.

Ἀλλά, φαίητε ἄν, ἔδει τὰ ἐνέχυρα τότε λαβεῖν, ὡς μηδ' εἰ ἐβούλετο ἐδύνατο ἐξαπατᾶν. πρὸς ταῦτα δὴ ἀκούσατε ἃ ἐγὼ οὐκ ἄν ποτε εἶπον τούτου ἐναντίον, εἰ μή μοι παντάπασιν ἀγνώμονες ἐδοκεῖτε εἶναι ἢ λίαν εἰς ἐμὲ ἀχάριστοι. ἀναμνήσθητε γὰρ ἐν ποίοις τισὶ πράγμασιν ὄντες ἐτυγχάνετε, ἐξ ὧν ὑμᾶς ἐγὼ ἀνήγαγον πρὸς Σεύθην. οὐκ εἰς μὲν Πέρινθον προσῇτε πόλιν, Ἀρίσταρχος δ' ὑμᾶς ὁ Λακεδαιμόνιος οὐκ εἴα εἰσιέναι ἀποκλείσας τὰς πύλας; ὑπαίθριοι δ' ἔξω ἐστρατοπεδεύετε, μέσος δὲ χειμὼν ἦν, ἀγορᾷ δὲ ἐχρῆσθε σπάνια μὲν ὁρῶντες τὰ ὤνια, σπάνια δ' ἔχοντες ὅτων ὠνήσεσθε, ἀνάγκη δὲ ἦν μένειν ἐπὶ Θρᾴκης· τριήρεις γὰρ ἐφορμοῦσαι ἐκώλυον διαπλεῖν· εἰ δὲ μένοι τις, ἐν πολεμίᾳ εἶναι, ἔνθα πολλοὶ μὲν ἱππεῖς ἦσαν ἐναντίοι, πολλοὶ δὲ πελτασταί, ἡμῖν δὲ ὁπλιτικὸν μὲν ἦν ᾧ ἁθρόοι μὲν ἰόντες ἐπὶ τὰς κώμας ἴσως ἂν ἐδυνάμεθα σῖτον λαμβάνειν οὐδέν τι ἄφθονον, ὅτῳ δὲ διώκοντες ἂν ἢ ἀνδράποδα ἢ πρόβατα κατελαμβάνομεν οὐκ ἦν ἡμῖν· οὔτε γὰρ ἱππικὸν οὔτε πελταστικὸν ἔτι ἐγὼ συνεστηκὸς κατέλαβον παρ' ὑμῖν.

Εἰ οὖν ἐν τοιαύτῃ ἀνάγκῃ ὄντων ὑμῶν μηδ' ὁντιναοῦν μισθὸν 27 προσαιτήσας Σεύθην σύμμαχον ὑμῖν προσέλαβον, ἔχοντα καὶ ἱππέας καὶ πελταστὰς ὧν ὑμεῖς προσεδεῖσθε, ἦ κακῶς ἂν ἐδόκουν ὑμῖν βεβουλεῦσθαι πρὸ ὑμῶν; τούτων γὰρ δήπου κοινωνήσαντες 28 καὶ σῖτον ἀφθονώτερον ἐν ταῖς κώμαις ηὑρίσκετε διὰ τὸ ἀναγκάζεσθαι τοὺς Θρᾷκας κατὰ σπουδὴν μᾶλλον φεύγειν, καὶ προβάτων καὶ ἀνδραπόδων μᾶλλον μετέσχετε. καὶ πολέμιον οὐκέτι 29 οὐδένα ἑωρῶμεν ἐπειδὴ τὸ ἱππικὸν ἡμῖν προσεγένετο· τέως δὲ θαρραλέως ἡμῖν ἐφείποντο οἱ πολέμιοι καὶ ἱππικῷ καὶ πελταστικῷ κωλύοντες μηδαμῇ κατ' ὀλίγους ἀποσκεδαννυμένους τὰ ἐπιτήδεια ἀφθονώτερα ἡμᾶς πορίζεσθαι. εἰ δὲ δὴ ὁ συμπαρέχων 30 ὑμῖν ταύτην τὴν ἀσφάλειαν μὴ πάνυ πολὺν μισθὸν προσετέλει τῆς ἀσφαλείας, τοῦτο δή τι σχέτλιον πάθημα καὶ διὰ τοῦτο οὐδαμῇ οἴεσθε χρῆναι ζῶντα ἐμὲ ἀνεῖναι;

Νῦν δὲ δὴ πῶς ἀπέρχεσθε; οὐ διαχειμάσαντες μὲν ἐν ἀφθό- 31 νοις τοῖς ἐπιτηδείοις, περιττὸν δ' ἔχοντες τοῦτο εἴ τι ἐλάβετε παρὰ Σεύθου; τὰ γὰρ τῶν πολεμίων ἐδαπανᾶτε. καὶ ταῦτα πράττοντες οὔτε ἄνδρας ἐπείδετε ὑμῶν αὐτῶν ἀποθανόντας οὔτε ζῶντας ἀπεβάλετε. εἰ δέ τι καλὸν πρὸς τοὺς ἐν τῇ Ἀσίᾳ βαρ- 32 βάρους ἐπέπρακτο ὑμῖν, οὐ καὶ ἐκεῖνο σῶον ἔχετε καὶ πρὸς ἐκείνοις νῦν ἄλλην εὔκλειαν προσειλήφατε καὶ τοὺς ἐν τῇ Εὐρώπῃ Θρᾷκας ἐφ' οὓς ἐστρατεύσασθε κρατήσαντες; ἐγὼ μὲν ὑμᾶς φημι δικαίως ἂν ὧν ἐμοὶ χαλεπαίνετε τούτων τοῖς θεοῖς χάριν εἰδέναι ὡς ἀγαθῶν.

Καὶ τὰ μὲν δὴ ὑμέτερα τοιαῦτα. ἄγετε δὴ πρὸς θεῶν καὶ 33 τὰ ἐμὰ σκέψασθε ὡς ἔχει. ἐγὼ γὰρ ὅτε μὲν πρότερον ἀπῇα οἴκαδε, ἔχων μὲν ἔπαινον πολὺν πρὸς ὑμῶν ἀπεπορευόμην, ἔχων δὲ δι' ὑμᾶς καὶ ὑπὸ τῶν ἄλλων Ἑλλήνων εὔκλειαν. ἐπιστευόμην δὲ ὑπὸ Λακεδαιμονίων· οὐ γὰρ ἄν με ἔπεμπον πάλιν πρὸς ὑμᾶς. νῦν δὲ ἀπέρχομαι πρὸς μὲν Λακεδαιμονίους ὑφ' ὑμῶν διαβεβλη- 34 μένος, Σεύθῃ δὲ ἀπηχθημένος ὑπὲρ ὑμῶν, ὃν ἤλπιζον εὖ ποιήσας μεθ' ὑμῶν ἀποστροφὴν καὶ ἐμοὶ καλὴν καὶ παισίν, εἰ γένοιντο, καταθήσεσθαι. ὑμεῖς δ', ὑπὲρ ὧν ἐγὼ ἀπήχθημαί τε πλεῖστα 35

καὶ ταῦτα πολὺ κρείττοσιν ἐμαυτοῦ, πραγματευόμενός τε οὐδὲ
νῦν πω πέπαυμαι ὅ,τι δύναμαι ἀγαθὸν ὑμῖν, τοιαύτην ἔχετε
γνώμην περὶ ἐμοῦ.

Ἀλλ' ἔχετε μέν με οὔτε φεύγοντα λαβόντες οὔτε ἀποδιδράσκοντα· ἢν δὲ ποιήσητε ἃ λέγετε, ἴστε ὅτι ἄνδρα κατακεκονότες
ἔσεσθε πολλὰ μὲν δὴ πρὸ ὑμῶν ἀγρυπνήσαντα, πολλὰ δὲ σὺν
ὑμῖν πονήσαντα καὶ κινδυνεύσαντα καὶ ἐν τῷ μέρει καὶ παρὰ τὸ
μέρος, θεῶν δ' ἵλεων ὄντων καὶ τρόπαια βαρβάρων πολλὰ δὴ
σὺν ὑμῖν στησάμενον, ὅπως δέ γε μηδενὶ τῶν Ἑλλήνων πολέμιοι γένοισθε, πᾶν ὅσον ἐγὼ ἐδυνάμην πρὸς ὑμᾶς διατεινάμενον.
καὶ γὰρ νῦν ὑμῖν ἔξεστιν ἀνεπιλήπτως πορεύεσθαι ὅπῃ ἂν ἔλησθε
καὶ κατὰ γῆν καὶ κατὰ θάλατταν. ὑμεῖς δέ, ὅτι πολλὴ ὑμῖν
εὐπορία φαίνεται, καὶ πλεῖτε ἔνθα δὴ ἐπεθυμεῖτε πάλαι, δέονταί
τε ὑμῶν οἱ μέγιστον δυνάμενοι, μισθὸς δὲ φαίνεται, ἡγεμόνες δὲ
ἥκουσι Λακεδαιμόνιοι οἱ κράτιστοι νομιζόμενοι εἶναι, νῦν δὴ
καιρὸς ὑμῖν δοκεῖ εἶναι ὡς τάχιστα ἐμὲ κατακαίνεν; οὐ μὴν ὅτε
γε ἐν τοῖς ἀπόροις ἦμεν, ὦ πάντων μνημονικώτατοι, ἀλλὰ καὶ
πατέρα ἐμὲ ἐκαλεῖτε καὶ αἰεὶ ὡς εὐεργέτου μεμνῆσθαι ὑπισχνεῖσθε.
οὐ μέντοι ἀγνώμονες οὐδὲ οὗτοί εἰσιν οἱ νῦν ἥκον ἐφ' ὑμᾶς·
ὥστε, ὡς ἐγὼ οἶμαι, οὐδὲ τούτοις δοκεῖτε βελτίονες εἶναι τοιοῦτοι
ὄντες περὶ ἐμέ. ταῦτ' εἰπὼν ἐπαύσατο.

Χαρμῖνος δὲ ὁ Λακεδαιμόνιος ἀναστὰς εἶπεν· Οὐ τὼ σιώ,
ἀλλ' ἐμοὶ μέντοι οὐ δικαίως δοκεῖτε τῷ ἀνδρὶ τούτῳ χαλεπαίνειν·
ἔχω γὰρ καὶ αὐτὸς αὐτῷ μαρτυρῆσαι. Σεύθης γὰρ ἐρωτῶντος
ἐμοῦ καὶ Πολυνίκου περὶ Ξενοφῶντος τίς ἀνὴρ εἴη ἄλλο μὲν
οὐδὲν εἶχε μέμψασθαι, ἄγαν δὲ φιλοστρατιώτην ἔφη αὐτὸν εἶναι·
διὸ καὶ χεῖρον αὐτῷ εἶναι πρὸς ἡμῶν τε τῶν Λακεδαιμονίων καὶ
πρὸς αὐτοῦ. ἀναστὰς ἐπὶ τούτῳ Εὐρύλοχος Λουσιάτης εἶπεν·
Καὶ δοκεῖ γέ μοι, ἄνδρες Λακεδαιμόνιοι, τοῦτο ὑμᾶς πρῶτον
ἡμῶν στρατηγῆσαι, παρὰ Σεύθου ἡμῖν τὸν μισθὸν ἀναπρᾶξαι ἢ
ἑκόντος ἢ ἄκοντος, καὶ μὴ πρότερον ἡμᾶς ἀπαγαγεῖν. Πολυκράτης δὲ Ἀθηναῖος εἶπεν ἐνετὸς ὑπὸ Ξενοφῶντος· Ὁρῶ γε
μήν, ἔφη, ὦ ἄνδρες, καὶ Ἡρακλείδην ἐνταῦθα παρόντα, ὃς παραλαβὼν τὰ χρήματα ἃ ἡμεῖς ἐπονήσαμεν, ταῦτα ἀποδόμενος οὔτε
Σεύθῃ ἀπέδωκεν οὔτε ἡμῖν τὰ γιγνόμενα, ἀλλ' αὐτὸς κλέψας

πέπαται. ἢν οὖν σωφρονῶμεν, ἑξόμεθα αὐτοῦ· οὐ γὰρ δὴ οὗτός γε, ἔφη, Θρᾷξ ἐστιν, ἀλλ' Ἕλλην ὢν Ἕλληνας ἀδικεῖ.

Ταῦτα ἀκούσας ὁ Ἡρακλείδης μάλα ἐξεπλάγη· καὶ προσελθὼν τῷ Σεύθῃ λέγει· Ἡμεῖς ἢν σωφρονῶμεν, ἄπιμεν ἐντεῦθεν ἐκ τῆς τούτων ἐπικρατείας. καὶ ἀναβάντες ἐπὶ τοὺς ἵππους ᾤχοντο ἀπελαύνοντες εἰς τὸ ἑαυτῶν στρατόπεδον. καὶ ἐντεῦθεν Σεύθης πέμπει Ἀβροζέλμην τὸν ἑαυτοῦ ἑρμηνέα πρὸς Ξενοφῶντα καὶ κελεύει αὐτὸν καταμεῖναι παρ' ἑαυτῷ ἔχοντα χιλίους ὁπλίτας, καὶ ὑπισχνεῖται αὐτῷ ἀποδώσειν τά τε χωρία τὰ ἐπὶ θαλάττῃ καὶ τὰ ἄλλα ἃ ὑπέσχετο, καὶ ἐν ἀπορρήτῳ ποιησάμενος λέγει ὅτι ἀκήκοε Πολυνίκου ὡς εἰ ὑποχείριος ἔσται Λακεδαιμονίοις, σαφῶς ἀποθανοῖτο ὑπὸ Θίβρωνος. ἐπέστελλον δὲ ταῦτα καὶ ἄλλοι πολλοὶ τῷ Ξενοφῶντι ὡς διαβεβλημένος εἴη καὶ φυλάττεσθαι δέοι. ὁ δὲ ἀκούων ταῦτα δύο ἱερεῖα λαβὼν ἐθύετο τῷ Διὶ τῷ βασιλεῖ πότερά οἱ λῷον καὶ ἄμεινον εἴη μένειν παρὰ Σεύθῃ ἐφ' οἷς Σεύθης λέγει ἢ ἀπιέναι σὺν τῷ στρατεύματι. ἀναιρεῖ αὐτῷ ἀπιέναι.

VII. Ἐντεῦθεν Σεύθης μὲν ἀπεστρατοπεδεύσατο προσωτέρω· οἱ δὲ Ἕλληνες ἐσκήνησαν εἰς κώμας ὅθεν ἔμελλον πλεῖστα ἐπισιτισάμενοι ἐπὶ θάλατταν ἥξειν. αἱ δὲ κῶμαι αὗται ἦσαν δεδομέναι ὑπὸ Σεύθου Μηδοσάδῃ. ὁρῶν οὖν ὁ Μηδοσάδης δαπανώμενα τὰ ἐν ταῖς κώμαις ὑπὸ τῶν Ἑλλήνων χαλεπῶς ἔφερε· καὶ λαβὼν ἄνδρα Ὀδρύσην δυνατώτατον τῶν ἄνωθεν καταβεβηκότων καὶ ἱππέας ὅσον τριάκοντα ἔρχεται καὶ προκαλεῖται Ξενοφῶντα ἐκ τοῦ Ἑλληνικοῦ στρατεύματος. καὶ ὃς λαβών τινας τῶν λοχαγῶν καὶ ἄλλους τῶν ἐπιτηδείων προσέρχεται. ἔνθα δὴ λέγει Μηδοσάδης· Ἀδικεῖτε, ὦ Ξενοφῶν, τὰς ἡμετέρας κώμας πορθοῦντες. προλέγομεν οὖν ὑμῖν, ἐγώ τε ὑπὲρ Σεύθου καὶ ὅδε ἀνὴρ παρὰ Μηδόκου ἥκων τοῦ ἄνω βασιλέως, ἀπιέναι ἐκ τῆς χώρας· εἰ δὲ μή, οὐκ ἐπιτρέψομεν ὑμῖν, ἀλλ' ἐὰν ποιῆτε κακῶς τὴν ἡμετέραν χώραν, ὡς πολεμίους ἀλεξόμεθα.

Ὁ δὲ Ξενοφῶν ἀκούσας ταῦτα εἶπεν· Ἀλλὰ σοὶ μὲν τοιαῦτα λέγοντι καὶ ἀποκρίνασθαι χαλεπόν· τούτου δ' ἕνεκα τοῦ νεανίσκου λέξω, ἵν' εἰδῇ οἷοί τε ὑμεῖς. ἡμεῖς μὲν γάρ, ἔφη, πρὶν ὑμῖν φίλοι γενέσθαι ἐπορευόμεθα διὰ ταύτης τῆς χώρας ὅποι

ἐβουλόμεθα, ἣν μὲν ἐθέλοιμεν πορθοῦντες, ἣν δὲ θέλοιμεν καίοντες,
6 καὶ σὺ ὁπότε πρὸς ἡμᾶς ἔλθοις πρεσβεύων, ηὐλίζου τότε παρ'
ἡμῖν οὐδένα φοβούμενος τῶν πολεμίων· ὑμεῖς δὲ οὐκ ἦτε εἰς
τήνδε τὴν χώραν, ἢ εἴ ποτε ἔλθοιτε, ὡς ἐν κρειττόνων χώρᾳ
7 ηὐλίζεσθε ἐγκεχαλινωμένοις τοῖς ἵπποις. ἐπεὶ δὲ ἡμῖν φίλοι
ἐγένεσθε καὶ δι' ἡμᾶς σὺν θεοῖς ἔχετε τήνδε τὴν χώραν, νῦν δὴ
ἐξελαύνετε ἡμᾶς ἐκ τῆσδε τῆς χώρας ἣν παρ' ἡμῶν ἐχόντων
κατὰ κράτος παρελάβετε· ὡς γὰρ αὐτὸς οἶσθα, οἱ πολέμιοι οὐχ
8 ἱκανοὶ ἦσαν ἡμᾶς ἐξελαύνειν. καὶ οὐχ ὅπως δῶρα δοὺς καὶ εὖ
ποιήσας ἀνθ' ὧν εὖ ἔπαθες ἀξιοῖς ἡμᾶς ἀποπέμψασθαι, ἀλλ'
ἀποπορευομένους ἡμᾶς οὐδ' ἐναυλισθῆναι ὅσον δύνασαι ἐπιτρέ-
9 πεις. καὶ ταῦτα λέγων οὔτε θεοὺς αἰσχύνῃ οὔτε τόνδε τὸν
ἄνδρα, ὃς νῦν μέν σε ὁρᾷ πλουτοῦντα, πρὶν δὲ ἡμῖν φίλον
γενέσθαι ἀπὸ λῃστείας τὸν βίον ἔχοντα, ὡς αὐτὸς ἔφησθα.
10 ἀτὰρ τί καὶ πρὸς ἐμὲ λέγεις ταῦτα; ἔφη· οὐ γὰρ ἔγωγ' ἔτι ἄρχω,
ἀλλὰ Λακεδαιμόνιοι, οἷς ὑμεῖς παρεδώκατε τὸ στράτευμα ἀπαγαγεῖν οὐδὲν ἐμὲ παρακαλέσαντες, ὦ θαυμαστότατοι, ὅπως ὥσπερ
ἀπηχθανόμην αὐτοῖς ὅτε πρὸς ὑμᾶς ἦγον, οὕτω καὶ χαρισαίμην
νῦν ἀποδιδούς.

11 Ἐπεὶ ταῦτα ἤκουσεν ὁ Ὀδρύσης, εἶπεν· Ἐγὼ μέν, ὦ Μηδόσαδες, κατὰ τῆς γῆς καταδύομαι ὑπὸ τῆς αἰσχύνης ἀκούων
ταῦτα. καὶ εἰ μὲν πρόσθεν ἠπιστάμην, οὐδ' ἂν συνηκολούθησά
σοι· καὶ νῦν ἄπειμι. οὐδὲ γὰρ ἂν Μήδοκός με ὁ βασιλεὺς ἐπαι-
12 νοίη, εἰ ἐξελαύνοιμι τοὺς εὐεργέτας. ταῦτ' εἰπὼν ἀναβὰς ἐπὶ
τὸν ἵππον ἀπήλαυνε καὶ σὺν αὐτῷ οἱ ἄλλοι ἱππεῖς πλὴν τεττάρων ἢ πέντε. ὁ δὲ Μηδοσάδης, ἐλύπει γὰρ αὐτὸν ἡ χώρα
πορθουμένη, ἐκέλευε τὸν Ξενοφῶντα καλέσαι τὼ Λακεδαιμονίω.
13 καὶ ὃς λαβὼν τοὺς ἐπιτηδειοτάτους προσῆλθε τῷ Χαρμίνῳ καὶ
Πολυνίκῳ καὶ ἔλεγεν ὅτι καλεῖ αὐτοὺς Μηδοσάδης προερῶν
14 ἅπερ αὐτῷ, ἀπιέναι ἐκ τῆς χώρας. οἴομαι ἂν οὖν, ἔφη, ὑμᾶς
ἀπολαβεῖν τῇ στρατιᾷ τὸν ὀφειλόμενον μισθόν, εἰ εἴποιτε ὅτι
δεδέηται ὑμῶν ἡ στρατιὰ συναναπρᾶξαι τὸν μισθὸν ἢ παρ' ἑκόντος
ἢ παρ' ἄκοντος Σεύθου, καὶ ὅτι τούτων τυχόντες προθύμως ἂν συνέπεσθαι ὑμῖν φασι· καὶ ὅτι δίκαια ὑμῖν δοκοῦσι λέγειν· καὶ ὅτι ὑπέ-
σχεσθε αὐτοῖς τότε ἀπιέναι ὅταν τὰ δίκαια ἔχωσιν οἱ στρατιῶται.

Ἀκούσαντες οἱ Λάκωνες ταῦτα ἔφασαν ἐρεῖν καὶ ἄλλα ὁποῖα
ἂν δύνωνται κράτιστα· καὶ εὐθὺς ἐπορεύοντο ἔχοντες πάντας
τοὺς ἐπικαιρίους. ἐλθὼν δὲ ἔλεξε Χαρμῖνος· Εἰ μὲν σύ τι
ἔχεις, ὦ Μηδόσαδες, πρὸς ἡμᾶς λέγειν, εἰ δὲ μή, ἡμεῖς πρὸς σὲ
ἔχομεν. ὁ δὲ Μηδοσάδης μάλα δὴ ὑφειμένως· Ἀλλ' ἐγὼ μὲν
λέγω, ἔφη, καὶ Σεύθης τὰ αὐτά, ὅτι ἀξιοῦμεν τοὺς φίλους ἡμῖν
γεγενημένους μὴ κακῶς πάσχειν ὑφ' ὑμῶν. ὅ,τι γὰρ ἂν τούτους
κακῶς ποιῆτε ἡμᾶς ἤδη ποιεῖτε· ἡμέτεροι γάρ εἰσιν. Ἡμεῖς
τοίνυν, ἔφασαν οἱ Λάκωνες, ἀπίοιμεν ἂν ὁπότε τὸν μισθὸν ἔχοιεν
οἱ ταῦτα ὑμῖν καταπράξαντες· εἰ δὲ μή, ἐρχόμεθα μὲν καὶ νῦν
βοηθήσοντες τούτοις καὶ τιμωρησόμενοι ἄνδρας οἳ τούτους παρὰ
τοὺς ὅρκους ἠδίκησαν. ἢν δὲ δὴ καὶ ὑμεῖς τοιοῦτοι ἦτε, ἐνθένδε
ἀρξόμεθα τὰ δίκαια λαμβάνειν. ὁ δὲ Ξενοφῶν εἶπεν· Ἐθέλοιτε
ἂν τούτοις, ὦ Μηδόσαδες, ἐπιτρέψαι, ἐπειδὴ φίλους ἔφατε εἶναι
ὑμῖν, ἐν ὦν τῇ χώρᾳ ἐσμέν, ὁπότερ' ἂν ψηφίσωνται, εἴθ' ὑμᾶς
προσήκει ἐκ τῆς χώρας ἀπιέναι εἴτε ἡμᾶς; ὃ δὲ ταῦτα μὲν οὐκ
ἔφη· ἐκέλευε δὲ μάλιστα μὲν αὐτὼ τὼ Λάκωνε ἐλθεῖν παρὰ
Σεύθην περὶ τοῦ μισθοῦ, καὶ οἴεσθαι ἂν Σεύθην πεῖσαι· εἰ δὲ
μή, Ξενοφῶντα σὺν αὐτῷ πέμπειν, καὶ συμπράξειν ὑπισχνεῖτο.
ἐδεῖτο δὲ τὰς κώμας μὴ καίειν.

Ἐντεῦθεν πέμπουσι Ξενοφῶντα καὶ σὺν αὐτῷ οἳ ἐδόκουν
ἐπιτηδειότατοι εἶναι. ὃ δὲ ἐλθὼν λέγει πρὸς τὸν Σεύθην· Οὐδὲν
ἀπαιτήσων, ὦ Σεύθη, πάρειμι, ἀλλὰ διδάξων, ἢν δύνωμαι, ὡς οὐ
δικαίως μοι ἠχθέσθης ὅτι ὑπὲρ τῶν στρατιωτῶν ἀπήτουν σε
προθύμως ἃ ὑπέσχου αὐτοῖς· σοὶ γὰρ ἔγωγε οὐχ ἧττον ἐνόμιζον
σύμφορον εἶναι ἀποδοῦναι ἢ ἐκείνοις ἀπολαβεῖν. πρῶτον μὲν
γὰρ οἶδα μετὰ τοὺς θεοὺς εἰς τὸ φανερόν σε τούτους καταστήσαντας, ἐπεί γε βασιλέα σε ἐποίησαν πολλῆς χώρας καὶ πολλῶν
ἀνθρώπων· ὥστε οὐχ οἷόν τέ σοι λανθάνειν οὔτε ἤν τι καλὸν
οὔτε ἤν τι αἰσχρὸν ποιήσῃς.

Τοιούτῳ δὲ ὄντι ἀνδρὶ μέγα μέν μοι ἐδόκει εἶναι μὴ δοκεῖν
ἀχαρίστως ἀποπέμψασθαι ἄνδρας εὐεργέτας, μέγα δὲ εὖ ἀκούειν
ὑπὸ ἑξακισχιλίων ἀνθρώπων, τὸ δὲ μέγιστον μηδαμῶς ἄπιστον
σαυτὸν καταστῆσαι ὅ,τι λέγοις. ὁρῶ γὰρ τῶν μὲν ἀπίστων
ματαίους καὶ ἀδυνάτους καὶ ἀτίμους τοὺς λόγους πλανωμένους·

οἵ δ' ἂν φανεροὶ ὦσιν ἀλήθειαν ἀσκοῦντες, τούτων οἱ λόγοι, ἤν τι δέωνται, οὐδὲν μεῖον δύνανται ἀνύσασθαι ἢ ἄλλων ἡ βία· ἤν τέ τινας σωφρονίζειν βούλωνται, γιγνώσκω τὰς τούτων ἀπειλὰς οὐχ ἧττον σωφρονιζούσας ἢ ἄλλων τὸ ἤδη κολάζειν· ἤν τέ τῳ τι ὑπισχνῶνται οἱ τοιοῦτοι ἄνδρες, οὐδὲν μεῖον διαπράττονται ἢ ἄλλοι παραχρῆμα διδόντες.

25 Ἀναμνήσθητι δὲ καὶ σὺ τί προτελέσας ἡμῖν συμμάχους ἡμᾶς ἔλαβες. οἶσθ' ὅτι οὐδέν· ἀλλὰ πιστευθεὶς ἀληθεύσειν ἃ ἔλεγες ἐπῆρας τοσούτους ἀνθρώπους συστρατεύεσθαί τε καὶ κατεργάσασθαί σοι ἀρχὴν οὐ τριάκοντα μόνον ἀξίαν ταλάντων, ὅσα οἴονται δεῖν οὗτοι νῦν ἀπολαβεῖν, ἀλλὰ πολλαπλασίων. 26 οὐκοῦν τοῦτο μὲν πρῶτον τὸ πιστεύεσθαι, τὸ καὶ τὴν βασιλείαν σοι κατεργασάμενον, τούτων τῶν χρημάτων πιπράσκεται;

27 Ἴθι δὴ ἀναμνήσθητι πῶς μέγα ἡγοῦ τότε καταπρᾶξαι ἃ νῦν καταστρεψάμενος ἔχεις. ἐγὼ μὲν εὖ οἶδ' ὅτι ηὔξω ἂν τὰ νῦν πεπραγμένα μᾶλλόν σοι καταπραχθῆναι ἢ πολλαπλάσια τού- 28 των τῶν χρημάτων γενέσθαι. ἐμοὶ τοίνυν μεῖζον βλάβος καὶ αἴσχιον δοκεῖ εἶναι τὸ ταῦτα νῦν μὴ κατασχεῖν ἢ τότε μὴ λαβεῖν, ὅσῳπερ χαλεπώτερον ἐκ πλουσίου πένητα γενέσθαι ἢ ἀρχὴν μὴ πλουτῆσαι, καὶ ὅσῳ λυπηρότερον ἐκ βασιλέως ἰδιώ- 29 την φανῆναι ἢ ἀρχὴν μὴ βασιλεῦσαι. οὐκοῦν ἐπίστασαι μὲν ὅτι οἱ νῦν σοι ὑπήκοοι γενόμενοι οὐ φιλίᾳ τῇ σῇ ἐπείσθησαν ὑπὸ σοῦ ἄρχεσθαι ἀλλ' ἀνάγκῃ, καὶ ὅτι ἐπιχειροῖεν ἂν πάλιν 30 ἐλεύθεροι γίγνεσθαι, εἰ μή τις αὐτοὺς φόβος κατέχοι. ποτέρως οὖν οἴει μᾶλλον ἂν φοβεῖσθαί τε αὐτοὺς καὶ σωφρονεῖν τὰ πρὸς σέ, εἰ ὁρῷέν σοι τοὺς στρατιώτας οὕτω διακειμένους ὡς νῦν τε μένοντας ἄν, εἰ σὺ κελεύοις, αὖθίς τ' ἂν ταχὺ ἐλθόντας, εἰ δέοι, ἄλλους τε τούτων περὶ σοῦ ἀκούοντας πολλὰ ἀγαθὰ ταχὺ ἄν σοι ὁπότε βούλοιο παραγενέσθαι, ἢ εἰ καταδοξάσειαν μήτ' ἂν ἄλλους σοι ἐλθεῖν δι' ἀπιστίαν ἐκ τῶν νῦν γεγενημένων τούτους 31 τε αὐτοῖς εὐνουστέρους εἶναι ἢ σοί; ἀλλὰ μὴν οὐδὲ πλήθει γε ἡμῶν λειφθέντες ὑπεῖξάν σοι, ἀλλὰ προστατῶν ἀπορίᾳ. οὐκοῦν νῦν καὶ τοῦτο κίνδυνος μὴ λάβωσι προστάτας αὐτῶν τινας τούτων οἳ νομίζουσιν ὑπὸ σοῦ ἀδικεῖσθαι, ἢ καὶ τούτων κρείττονας τοὺς Λακεδαιμονίους, ἐὰν μὲν οἱ στρατιῶται ὑπισχνῶνται

προθυμότερον αὐτοῖς συστρατεύσεσθαι, ἂν τὰ παρὰ σοῦ νῦν ἀναπράξωσιν, οἱ δὲ Λακεδαιμόνιοι διὰ τὸ δεῖσθαι τῆς στρατιᾶς συναινέσωσιν αὐτοῖς ταῦτα. ὅτι γε μὴν οἱ νῦν ὑπὸ σοὶ Θρᾷκες γενόμενοι πολὺ ἂν προθυμότερον ἴοιεν ἐπί σε ἢ σύν σοι οὐκ ἄδηλον· σοῦ μὲν γὰρ κρατοῦντος δουλεία ὑπάρχει αὐτοῖς, κρατουμένου δέ σου ἐλευθερία.

Εἰ δὲ καὶ τῆς χώρας προνοεῖσθαι ἤδη τι δεῖ ὡς σῆς οὔσης, ποτέρως ἂν οἴει ἀπαθῆ κακῶν μᾶλλον αὐτὴν εἶναι, εἰ οὗτοι οἱ στρατιῶται ἀπολαβόντες ἃ ἐγκαλοῦσιν εἰρήνην καταλιπόντες οἴχοιντο, ἢ εἰ οὗτοί τε μένοιεν ὡς ἐν πολεμίᾳ σύ τε ἄλλους πειρῷο πλέονας τούτων ἔχων ἀντιστρατοπεδεύεσθαι δεομένους τῶν ἐπιτηδείων; ἀργύριον δὲ ποτέρως ἂν πλέον ἀναλωθείη, εἰ τούτοις τὸ ὀφειλόμενον ἀποδοθείη, ἢ εἰ ταῦτά τε ὀφείλοιντο ἄλλους τε κρείττονας δέοι σε μισθοῦσθαι; ἀλλὰ γὰρ Ἡρακλείδῃ, ὡς πρὸς ἐμὲ ἐδήλου, πάμπολυ δοκεῖ τοῦτο τὸ ἀργύριον εἶναι. ἦ μὴν πολύ γέ ἐστιν ἔλαττον νῦν σοι καὶ λαβεῖν τοῦτο καὶ ἀποδοῦναι ἢ πρὶν ἡμᾶς ἐλθεῖν πρὸς σὲ δέκατον τούτου μέρος. οὐ γὰρ ἀριθμός ἐστιν ὁ ὁρίζων τὸ πολὺ καὶ τὸ ὀλίγον, ἀλλ' ἡ δύναμις τοῦ τε ἀποδιδόντος καὶ τοῦ λαμβάνοντος. σοὶ δὲ νῦν ἡ κατ' ἐνιαυτὸν πρόσοδος πλείων ἔσται ἢ ἔμπροσθεν τὰ παρόντα πάντα ἃ ἐκέκτησο.

Ἐγὼ μέν, ὦ Σεύθη, ταῦτα ὡς φίλου ὄντος σου προὐνοούμην, ὅπως σύ τε ἄξιος δοκοίης εἶναι ὧν οἱ θεοί σοι ἔδωκαν ἀγαθῶν ἐγώ τε μὴ διαφθαρείην ἐν τῇ στρατιᾷ. εὖ γὰρ ἴσθι ὅτι νῦν ἐγὼ οὔτ' ἂν ἐχθρὸν βουλόμενος κακῶς ποιῆσαι δυνηθείην σὺν ταύτῃ τῇ στρατιᾷ οὔτ' ἂν εἴ σοι πάλιν βουλοίμην βοηθῆσαι, ἱκανὸς ἂν γενοίμην. οὕτω γὰρ πρός με ἡ στρατιὰ διάκειται. καίτοι αὐτόν σε μάρτυρα σὺν θεοῖς εἰδόσι ποιοῦμαι ὅτι οὔτε ἔχω παρὰ σοῦ ἐπὶ τοῖς στρατιώταις οὐδὲν οὔτε ᾔτησα πώποτε εἰς τὸ ἴδιον τὰ ἐκείνων οὔτε ἃ ὑπέσχου μοι ἀπῄτησα· ὄμνυμι δέ σοι μηδὲ ἀποδιδόντος δέξασθαι ἄν, εἰ μὴ καὶ οἱ στρατιῶται ἔμελλον τὰ ἑαυτῶν συναπολαμβάνειν. αἰσχρὸν γὰρ ⟨ἂν⟩ ἦν τὰ μὲν ἐμὰ διαπεπρᾶχθαι, τὰ δ' ἐκείνων περιιδεῖν κακῶς ἔχοντα ἄλλως τε καὶ τιμώμενον ὑπ' ἐκείνων. καίτοι Ἡρακλείδῃ γε λῆρος πάντα δοκεῖ εἶναι πρὸς τὸ ἀργύριον ἔχειν ἐκ παντὸς τρόπου· ἐγὼ δέ, ὦ

Σεύθη, οὐδὲν νομίζω ἀνδρὶ ἄλλως τε καὶ ἄρχοντι κάλλιον εἶναι κτῆμα οὐδὲ λαμπρότερον ἀρετῆς καὶ δικαιοσύνης καὶ γενναιότητος. ὁ γὰρ ταῦτα ἔχων πλουτεῖ μὲν ὄντων φίλων πολλῶν, πλουτεῖ δὲ καὶ ἄλλων βουλομένων γενέσθαι, καὶ εὖ μὲν πράττων ἔχει τοὺς συνησθησομένους, ἐὰν δέ τι σφαλῇ, οὐ σπανίζει τῶν βοηθησόντων.

Ἀλλὰ γὰρ εἰ μήτε ἐκ τῶν ἔργων κατέμαθες ὅτι σοι ἐκ τῆς ψυχῆς φίλος ἦν, μήτε ἐκ τῶν ἐμῶν λόγων δύνασαι τοῦτο γνῶναι, ἀλλὰ τοὺς τῶν στρατιωτῶν λόγους πάντας κατανόησον· παρῆσθα γὰρ καὶ ἤκουες ἃ ἔλεγον οἱ ψέγειν ἐμὲ βουλόμενοι. κατηγόρουν γάρ μου πρὸς Λακεδαιμονίους ὡς σὲ περὶ πλείονος ποιοίμην ἢ Λακεδαιμονίους, αὐτοὶ δ᾽ ἐνεκάλουν ἐμοὶ ὡς μᾶλλον μέλει μοι ὅπως τὰ σὰ καλῶς ἔχοι ἢ ὅπως τὰ ἑαυτῶν· ἔφασαν δέ με καὶ δῶρα ἔχειν παρὰ σοῦ. καίτοι τὰ δῶρα ταῦτα πότερον οἴει αὐτοὺς κακόνοιάν τινα ἐνιδόντας μοι πρὸς σὲ αἰτιᾶσθαί με ἔχειν παρὰ σοῦ ἢ προθυμίαν πολλὴν περὶ σὲ κατανοήσαντας; ἐγὼ μὲν οἶμαι πάντας ἀνθρώπους νομίζειν εὔνοιαν δεῖν ἀποδείκνυσθαι τούτῳ παρ᾽ οὗ ἂν δῶρά τις λαμβάνῃ. σὺ δὲ πρὶν μὲν ὑπηρετῆσαί τί σοι ἐμὲ ἐδέξω ἡδέως καὶ ὄμμασι καὶ φωνῇ καὶ ξενίοις καὶ ὅσα ἔσοιτο ὑπισχνούμενος οὐκ ἐνεπίμπλασο· ἐπεὶ δὲ κατέπραξας ἃ ἐβούλου καὶ γεγένησαι ὅσον ἐγὼ ἐδυνάμην μέγιστος, νῦν οὕτω με ἄτιμον ὄντα ἐν τοῖς στρατιώταις τολμᾷς περιορᾶν; ἀλλὰ μὴν ὅτι σοι δόξει ἀποδοῦναι πιστεύω καὶ τὸν χρόνον διδάξειν σε καὶ αὐτόν γέ σε οὐχὶ ἀνέξεσθαι τοὺς σοὶ προεμένους εὐεργεσίαν ὁρῶντά σοι ἐγκαλοῦντας. δέομαι οὖν σου, ὅταν ἀποδιδῷς, προθυμεῖσθαι ἐμὲ παρὰ τοῖς στρατιώταις τοιοῦτον ποιῆσαι οἷόνπερ καὶ παρέλαβες.

Ἀκούσας ταῦτα ὁ Σεύθης κατηράσατο τῷ αἰτίῳ τοῦ μὴ πάλαι ἀποδεδόσθαι τὸν μισθόν· καὶ πάντες Ἡρακλείδην τοῦτον ὑπώπτευσαν εἶναι· ἐγὼ γάρ, ἔφη, οὔτε διενοήθην πώποτε ἀποστερῆσαι ἀποδώσω τε. ἐντεῦθεν πάλιν εἶπεν ὁ Ξενοφῶν· Ἐπεὶ τοίνυν διανοῇ ἀποδιδόναι, νῦν ἐγώ σου δέομαι δι᾽ ἐμοῦ ἀποδοῦναι, καὶ μὴ περιιδεῖν με διὰ σὲ ἀνομοίως ἔχοντα ἐν τῇ στρατιᾷ νῦν τε καὶ ὅτε πρὸς σὲ ἀφικόμεθα. ὁ δ᾽ εἶπεν· Ἀλλ᾽ οὔτ᾽ ἐν τοῖς στρατιώταις ἔσῃ δι᾽ ἐμὲ ἀτιμότερος ἄν τε μένῃς παρ᾽

ἐμοὶ χιλίους μόνους ὁπλίτας ἔχων, ἐγώ σοι τά τε χωρία ἀποδώσω καὶ τἆλλα ἃ ὑπεσχόμην. ὃ δὲ πάλιν εἶπεν· Ταῦτα μὲν ἔχειν οὕτως οὐχ οἷόν τε· ἀπόπεμπε δὲ ἡμᾶς. Καὶ μήν, ἔφη ὁ Σεύθης, καὶ ἀσφαλέστερόν γέ σοι οἶδα ὂν παρ' ἐμοὶ μένειν ἢ ἀπιέναι. ὃ δὲ πάλιν εἶπεν· Ἀλλὰ τὴν μὲν σὴν πρόνοιαν ἐπαινῶ· ἐμοὶ δὲ μένειν οὐχ οἷόν τε· ὅπου δ' ἂν ἐγὼ ἐντιμότερος ὦ, νόμιζε καὶ σοὶ τοῦτο ἀγαθὸν ἔσεσθαι. ἐντεῦθεν λέγει Σεύθης· Ἀργύριον μὲν οὐκ ἔχω ἀλλ' ἢ μικρόν τι, καὶ τοῦτό σοι δίδωμι, τάλαντον· βοῦς δὲ ἑξακοσίους καὶ πρόβατα εἰς τετρακισχίλια καὶ ἀνδράποδα εἰς εἴκοσι καὶ ἑκατόν. ταῦτα λαβὼν καὶ τοὺς τῶν ἀδικησάντων σε ὁμήρους προσλαβὼν ἄπιθι. γελάσας ὁ Ξενοφῶν εἶπεν· Ἢν οὖν μὴ ἐξικνῆται ταῦτ' εἰς τὸν μισθόν, τίνος τάλαντον φήσω ἔχειν; ἆρ' οὐκ, ἐπειδὴ καὶ ἐπικίνδυνόν μοί ἐστιν, ἀπιόντα γε ἄμεινον φυλάττεσθαι πέτρους; ἤκουες δὲ τὰς ἀπειλάς. τότε μὲν δὴ αὐτοῦ ἔμεινε.

Τῇ δ' ὑστεραίᾳ ἀπέδωκέ τε αὐτοῖς ἃ ὑπέσχετο καὶ τοὺς ἐλῶντας συνέπεμψεν. οἱ δὲ στρατιῶται τέως μὲν ἔλεγον ὡς ὁ Ξενοφῶν οἴχοιτο ὡς Σεύθην οἰκήσων καὶ ἃ ὑπέσχετο αὐτῷ ληψόμενος· ἐπεὶ δὲ εἶδον, ἥσθησαν καὶ προσέθεον. Ξενοφῶν δ' ἐπεὶ εἶδε Χαρμῖνόν τε καὶ Πολύνικον, Ταῦτα, ἔφη, σέσωται δι' ὑμᾶς τῇ στρατιᾷ καὶ παραδίδωμι αὐτὰ ἐγὼ ὑμῖν· ὑμεῖς δὲ διαθέμενοι διάδοτε τῇ στρατιᾷ. οἱ μὲν οὖν παραλαβόντες καὶ λαφυροπώλας καταστήσαντες ἐπώλουν, καὶ πολλὴν εἶχον αἰτίαν. Ξενοφῶν δὲ οὐ προσῄει, ἀλλὰ φανερὸς ἦν οἴκαδε παρασκευαζόμενος· οὐ γάρ πω ψῆφος αὐτῷ ἐπῆκτο Ἀθήνησι περὶ φυγῆς. προσελθόντες δὲ αὐτῷ οἱ ἐπιτήδειοι ἐν τῷ στρατοπέδῳ ἐδέοντο μὴ ἀπελθεῖν πρὶν ἀπαγάγοι τὸ στράτευμα καὶ Θίβρωνι παραδοίη.

VIII. Ἐντεῦθεν διέπλευσαν εἰς Λάμψακον, καὶ ἀπαντᾷ τῷ Ξενοφῶντι Εὐκλείδης μάντις Φλειάσιος ὁ Κλεαγόρου υἱὸς τοῦ τὰ ἐντοίχια ἐν Λυκείῳ γεγραφότος. οὗτος συνήδετο τῷ Ξενοφῶντι ὅτι ἐσέσωτο, καὶ ἠρώτα αὐτὸν πόσον χρυσίον ἔχει. ὃ δ' αὐτῷ ἐπομόσας εἶπεν ἦ μὴν ἔσεσθαι μηδὲ ἐφόδιον ἱκανὸν οἴκαδε ἀπιόντι, εἰ μὴ ἀπόδοιτο τὸν ἵππον καὶ ἃ ἀμφ' αὑτὸν εἶχεν. ὃ δ' αὐτῷ οὐκ ἐπίστευεν. ἐπεὶ δ' ἔπεμψαν Λαμψακηνοὶ ξένια τῷ Ξενοφῶντι καὶ ἔθυε τῷ Ἀπόλλωνι, παρεστήσατο

τὸν Εὐκλείδην· ἰδὼν δὲ τὰ ἱερὰ Εὐκλείδης εἶπεν ὅτι πείθοιτο
αὐτῷ μὴ εἶναι χρήματα. Ἀλλ' οἶδα, ἔφη, ὅτι κἂν μέλλῃ ποτὲ
ἔσεσθαι, φαίνεταί τι ἐμπόδιον, ἂν μηδὲν ἄλλο, σὺ σαυτῷ. συνω-
4 μολόγει ταῦτα ὁ Ξενοφῶν. ὃ δὲ εἶπεν· Ἐμπόδιος γάρ σοι ὁ
Ζεὺς ὁ μειλίχιός ἐστι, καὶ ἐπήρετο εἰ ἤδη θύσειεν, ὥσπερ οἴκοι,
ἔφη, εἰώθειν ἐγὼ ὑμῖν θύεσθαι καὶ ὁλοκαυτεῖν. ὃ δ' οὐκ ἔφη ἐξ
ὅτου ἀπεδήμησε τεθυκέναι τούτῳ τῷ θεῷ. συνεβούλευσεν οὖν
αὐτῷ θύεσθαι καθὰ εἰώθει, καὶ ἔφη συνοίσειν ἐπὶ τὸ βέλτιον.
5 τῇ δὲ ὑστεραίᾳ Ξενοφῶν προσελθὼν εἰς Ὀφρύνιον ἐθύετο καὶ
6 ὡλοκαύτει χοίρους τῷ πατρίῳ νόμῳ, καὶ ἐκαλλιέρει. καὶ ταύτῃ
τῇ ἡμέρᾳ ἀφικνεῖται Βίων καὶ Ναυσικλείδης χρήματα δώσοντες
τῷ στρατεύματι, καὶ ξενοῦνται τῷ Ξενοφῶντι καὶ ἵππον ὃν ἐν
Λαμψάκῳ ἀπέδοτο πεντήκοντα δαρεικῶν, ὑποπτεύοντες αὐτὸν
δι' ἔνδειαν πεπρακέναι, ὅτι ἤκουον αὐτὸν ἥδεσθαι τῷ ἵππῳ,
λυσάμενοι ἀπέδοσαν καὶ τὴν τιμὴν οὐκ ἤθελον ἀπολαβεῖν.

7 Ἐντεῦθεν ἐπορεύοντο διὰ τῆς Τρῳάδος, καὶ ὑπερβάντες τὴν
Ἴδην εἰς Ἄντανδρον ἀφικνοῦνται πρῶτον, εἶτα παρὰ θάλατταν
8 πορευόμενοι [τῆς Ἀσίας] εἰς Θήβης πεδίον. ἐντεῦθεν δι'
Ἀδραμυτίου καὶ Κυτωνίου ὁδεύσαντες εἰς Καΐκου πεδίον ἐλθόντες
Πέργαμον καταλαμβάνουσι τῆς Μυσίας.

Ἐνταῦθα δὴ ξενοῦται Ξενοφῶν Ἑλλάδι τῇ Γογγύλου τοῦ
9 Ἐρετριέως γυναικὶ καὶ Γοργίωνος καὶ Γογγύλου μητρί. αὕτη
δ' αὐτῷ φράζει ὅτι Ἀσιδάτης ἐστὶν ἐν τῷ πεδίῳ ἀνὴρ Πέρσης·
τοῦτον ἔφη αὐτόν, εἰ ἔλθοι τῆς νυκτὸς σὺν τριακοσίοις ἀνδράσι,
λαβεῖν ἂν καὶ αὐτὸν καὶ γυναῖκα καὶ παῖδας καὶ τὰ χρήματα·
εἶναι δὲ πολλά. ταῦτα δὲ καθηγησομένους ἔπεμψε τόν τε
αὐτῆς ἀνεψιὸν καὶ Δαφναγόραν, ὃν περὶ πλείστου ἐποιεῖτο.
10 ἔχων οὖν ὁ Ξενοφῶν τούτους παρ' ἑαυτῷ ἐθύετο. καὶ Βασίας ὁ
Ἠλεῖος μάντις παρὼν εἶπεν ὅτι κάλλιστα εἴη τὰ ἱερὰ αὐτῷ καὶ
11 ὁ ἀνὴρ ἁλώσιμος εἴη. δειπνήσας οὖν ἐπορεύετο τούς τε λοχαγοὺς τούς μάλιστα φίλους λαβὼν καὶ . . . πιστοὺς γεγενημένους διὰ παντός, ὅπως εὖ ποιῆσαι αὐτούς. συνεξέρχονται δὲ
αὐτῷ καὶ ἄλλοι βιασάμενοι εἰς ἑξακοσίους· οἱ δὲ λοχαγοὶ ἀπήλαυνον, ἵνα μὴ μεταδοῖεν τὸ μέρος, ὡς ἑτοίμων δὴ χρημάτων.
12 Ἐπεὶ δὲ ἀφίκοντο περὶ μέσας νύκτας, τὰ μὲν πέριξ ὄντα

ἀνδράποδα τῆς τύρσιος καὶ χρήματα τὰ πλεῖστα ἀπέδρα αὐτοὺς παραμελοῦντας, ὡς τὸν Ἀσιδάτην αὐτὸν λάβοιεν καὶ τὰ ἐκείνου. πυργομαχοῦντες δὲ ἐπεὶ οὐκ ἐδύναντο λαβεῖν τὴν τύρσιν— ὑψηλὴ γὰρ ἦν καὶ μεγάλη καὶ προμαχεῶνας καὶ ἄνδρας πολλοὺς καὶ μαχίμους ἔχουσα—διορύττειν ἐπεχείρησαν τὸν πύργον. ὁ δὲ τοῖχος ἦν ἐπ' ὀκτὼ πλίνθων γηΐνων τὸ εὖρος. ἅμα δὲ τῇ ἡμέρᾳ διωρώρυκτο· καὶ ὡς τὸ πρῶτον διεφάνη, ἐπάταξεν ἔνδοθεν βουπόρῳ τις ὀβελίσκῳ διαμπερὲς τὸν μηρὸν τοῦ ἐγγυτάτω· τὸ δὲ λοιπὸν ἐκτοξεύοντες ἐποίουν μηδὲ παριέναι ἔτι ἀσφαλὲς εἶναι. κεκραγότων δὲ αὐτῶν καὶ πυρσευόντων ἐκβοηθοῦσιν Ἰταμένης μὲν ἔχων τὴν ἑαυτοῦ δύναμιν, ἐκ Κομανίας δὲ ὁπλῖται Ἀσσύριοι καὶ Ὑρκάνιοι ἱππεῖς καὶ οὗτοι βασιλέως μισθοφόροι ὡς ὀγδοήκοντα, καὶ ἄλλοι πελτασταὶ εἰς ὀκτακοσίους, ἄλλοι δ' ἐκ Παρθενίου, ἄλλοι δ' ἐξ Ἀπολλωνίας καὶ ἐκ τῶν πλησίον χωρίων καὶ ἱππεῖς.

Ἐνταῦθα δὴ ὥρα ἦν σκοπεῖν πῶς ἔσται ἡ ἄφοδος· καὶ λαβόντες ὅσοι ἦσαν βόες καὶ πρόβατα ἤλαυνον καὶ ἀνδράποδα ἐντὸς πλαισίου ποιησάμενοι, οὐ τοῖς χρήμασιν ἔτι προσέχοντες τὸν νοῦν, ἀλλὰ μὴ φυγῇ εἴη ἡ ἄφοδος, εἰ καταλιπόντες τὰ χρήματα ἀπίοιεν, καὶ οἵ τε πολέμιοι θρασύτεροι εἶεν καὶ οἱ στρατιῶται ἀθυμότεροι· νῦν δὲ ἀπῇσαν ὡς περὶ τῶν χρημάτων μαχούμενοι. ἐπεὶ δὲ ἑώρα Γογγύλος ὀλίγους μὲν τοὺς Ἕλληνας, πολλοὺς δὲ τοὺς ἐπικειμένους, ἐξέρχεται καὶ αὐτὸς βίᾳ τῆς μητρὸς ἔχων τὴν ἑαυτοῦ δύναμιν, βουλόμενος μετασχεῖν τοῦ ἔργου· συνεβοήθει δὲ καὶ Προκλῆς ἐξ Ἁλισάρνης καὶ Τευθρανίας ὁ ἀπὸ Δαμαράτου. οἱ δὲ περὶ Ξενοφῶντα ἐπεὶ πάνυ ἤδη ἐπιέζοντο ὑπὸ τῶν τοξευμάτων καὶ σφενδονῶν, πορευόμενοι κύκλῳ, ὅπως τὰ ὅπλα ἔχοιεν πρὸ τῶν τοξευμάτων, μόλις διαβαίνουσι τὸν Κάρκασον ποταμόν, τετρωμένοι ἐγγὺς οἱ ἡμίσεις. ἐνταῦθα δὲ Ἀγασίας ὁ Στυμφάλιος λοχαγὸς τιτρώσκεται, τὸν πάντα χρόνον μαχόμενος πρὸς τοὺς πολεμίους. καὶ διασῴζονται ἀνδράποδα ὡς διακόσια ἔχοντες καὶ πρόβατα ὅσον θύματα.

Τῇ δὲ ὑστεραίᾳ θυσάμενος ὁ Ξενοφῶν ἐξάγει νύκτωρ πᾶν τὸ στράτευμα, ὅπως ὅτι μακροτάτην ἔλθοι τῆς Λυδίας, εἰς τὸ μὴ διὰ τὸ ἐγγὺς εἶναι φοβεῖσθαι, ἀλλ' ἀφυλακτεῖν. ὁ δὲ Ἀσιδάτης

ἀκούσας ὅτι πάλιν ἐπ' αὐτὸν τεθυμένος εἴη ὁ Ξενοφῶν καὶ παντὶ
τῷ στρατεύματι ἥξοι, ἐξαυλίζεται εἰς κώμας ὑπὸ τὸ Παρθένιον
22 πόλισμα ἐχούσας. ἐνταῦθα οἱ περὶ Ξενοφῶντα συντυγχάνουσιν
αὐτῷ καὶ λαμβάνουσιν αὐτὸν καὶ γυναῖκα καὶ παῖδας καὶ τοὺς
ἵππους καὶ πάντα τὰ ὄντα· καὶ οὕτω τὰ πρότερα ἱερὰ ἀπέβη.
23 Ἔπειτα πάλιν ἀφικνοῦνται εἰς Πέργαμον. ἐνταῦθα τὸν θεὸν
ἠσπάσατο Ξενοφῶν· συνέπραττον γὰρ καὶ οἱ Λάκωνες καὶ οἱ
λοχαγοὶ καὶ οἱ ἄλλοι στρατηγοὶ καὶ οἱ στρατιῶται ὥστ' ἐξαίρετα
λαβεῖν καὶ ἵππους καὶ ζεύγη καὶ τἆλλα· ὥστε ἱκανὸν εἶναι καὶ
ἄλλον ἤδη εὖ ποιεῖν.
24 Ἐν τούτῳ Θίβρων παραγενόμενος παρέλαβε τὸ στράτευμα καὶ
συμμείξας τῷ ἄλλῳ Ἑλληνικῷ ἐπολέμει πρὸς Τισσαφέρνην καὶ
Φαρνάβαζον.
25 [Ἄρχοντες δὲ οἵδε τῆς βασιλέως χώρας ὅσην ἐπήλθομεν.
Λυδίας Ἀρτίμας, Φρυγίας Ἀρτακάμας, Λυκαονίας καὶ Καππαδοκίας Μιθραδάτης, Κιλικίας Συέννεσις, Φοινίκης καὶ Ἀραβίας
Δέρνης, Συρίας καὶ Ἀσσυρίας Βέλεσυς, Βαβυλῶνος Ῥωπάρας,
Μηδίας Ἀρβάκας, Φασιανῶν καὶ Ἑσπεριτῶν Τιρίβαζος· Καρδοῦχοι δὲ καὶ Χάλυβες καὶ Χαλδαῖοι καὶ Μάκρωνες καὶ Κόλχοι
καὶ Μοσσύνοικοι καὶ Κοῖτοι καὶ Τιβαρηνοὶ αὐτόνομοι· Παφλαγονίας Κορύλας, Βιθυνῶν Φαρνάβαζος, τῶν ἐν Εὐρώπῃ Θρᾳκῶν
26 Σεύθης. ἀριθμὸς συμπάσης τῆς ὁδοῦ τῆς ἀναβάσεως καὶ καταβάσεως σταθμοὶ διακόσιοι δεκαπέντε, παρασάγγαι χίλιοι ἑκατὸν
πεντήκοντα, στάδια τρισμύρια τετρακισχίλια διακόσια πεντήκοντα πέντε. χρόνου πλῆθος τῆς ἀναβάσεως καὶ καταβάσεως
ἐνιαυτὸς καὶ τρεῖς μῆνες.]

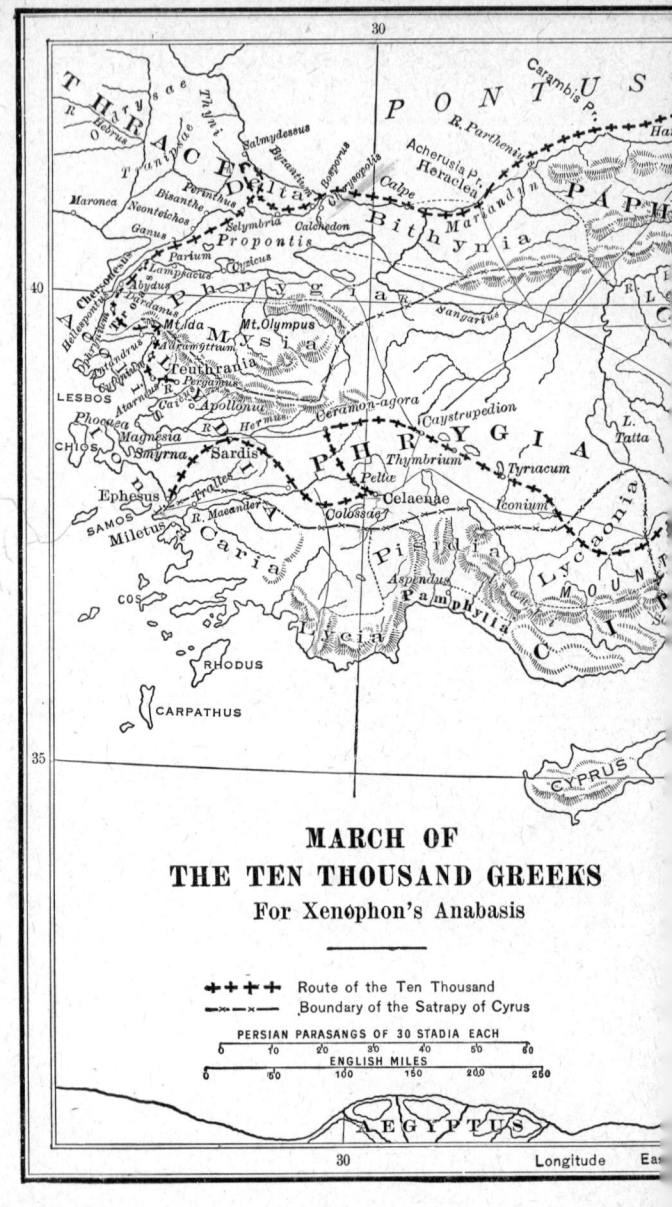

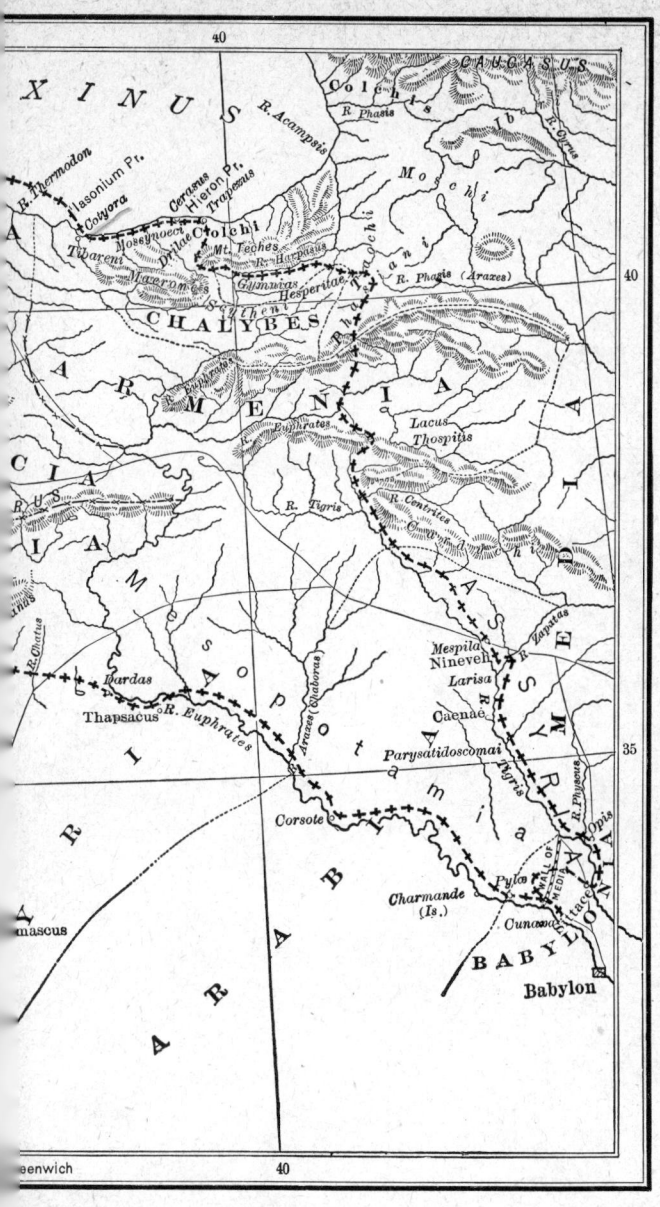

VOCABULARY

[References given in the Vocabulary are to chapter and section, not to chapter and line. The use of a hyphen, prefixed to verb forms, indicates that the form in question occurs only in compounds.]

A

ἀ-, inseparable prefix, 1) privative, giving the word a negative meaning; before vowels ἀν-; *cf.* Lat. *in-*, Eng. *un-*.
2) copulative, signifying union, as in ἀκόλουθος; in the older period ἁ-; *cf.* ἅπας, ἁθρόος.
3) euphonic, chiefly before liquids or double consonants; *cf.* ἀμύνω.

ἅ, ἅπερ, see ὅς, ὅσπερ.

ἄβατος, -ον (ἀ-priv.+βαίνω), *not to be trodden or traversed, impassable;* of rivers, *unfordable.*

Ἀβροζέλμης, -ου, ὁ, *Abrozelmes,* a Thracian, interpreter to Seuthes.

Ἀβροκόμας, -ου, Doric gen. -α, *Abrocomas,* satrap of Phoenicia and Syria, and commander of one of the four divisions of the army of Artaxerxes.

Ἄβυδος, -ου, ὁ, *Abydus,* a city on the Hellespont.

ἀγαγεῖν, ἀγάγῃ, ἀγαγών, see ἄγω.

ἀγαθός, -ή, -όν, *good* in the widest sense, of persons or things, and hence to be variously rendered, *brave, excellent, upright, useful, favorable;* of land, *fertile,* II, 4, 22; of a dream, *auspicious,* III, 1, 12. As subst. (τὸ) ἀγαθόν, *good, benefit, advantage, etc.;* in pl. *provisions, blessings,* III, 1, 20; ἀγαθόν τί ποιεῖν τινα, *do one some service,* 1, 9, 11; ἀγαθὰ πάσχειν, *receive benefits,* VII, 3, 20; ἐπ' ἀγαθῷ, *for one's good,* V, 8, 18; καλὸς καὶ ἀγαθός, or καλὸς κἀγαθός, *"gentleman,"* II, 6, 19n. Comp. ἀμείνων, βελτίων, κρείττων, sup. ἄριστος, βέλτιστος, κράτιστος.

ἀγάλλω, *glorify,* a poetic vb.; in mid., *glory* or *delight in,* with dat., or ἐπί with dat.

ἄγαμαι, ἠγάσθην, *admire;* aor., *took a liking to.*

ἄγαν, adv., *very, exceedingly.*

ἀγαπάω, ἀγαπήσω, etc., *love, esteem,* I, 9, 29; *be well content, be glad,* V, 5, 13.

Ἀγασίας, -ου, ὁ, *Agasias,* of Stymphālus in Arcadia, one of the Greek captains and a close friend of Xenophon.

ἀγαστός, -ή, -όν (verbal of ἄγαμαι), *admirable.*

ἀγγεῖον, -ου, τό (dim. of ἄγγος, *vessel*) *vessel, jar.*

ἀγγελία, -ας, ἡ (ἀγγέλλω), *message.*

ἀγγέλλω, ἀγγελῶ, ἤγγειλα, ἤγγελκα, ἤγγελμαι, ἠγγέλθην, *announce, report, bring news.*

ἄγγελος, -ου, ὁ (ἀγγέλλω, Eng., *angel*), *messenger, scout, herald.*

ἀγείρω, ἤγειρα, *collect.*

ἀγένειος, -ον (ἀ-priv. + γένειον, *chin, beard*), *beardless.*

Ἀγησίλαος, -ου, ὁ, *Agesilāus,* king of Sparta from 398 to 360 B.C.; commanded an expedition against Persia in 396, in which Xenophon took part.

Ἀγίας, -ου, ὁ, *Agias*, an Arcadian general under Cyrus, treacherously slain after the battle of Cunaxa.

ἄγκος, -ους, τό (*cf.* Lat. *angulus*, Eng. *angle, ankle*), *bend;* hence *glen, valley*.

ἄγκυρα, -ας, ἡ (*cf.* ἄγκος), *anchor*.

ἀγνοέω, ἀγνοήσω (ἀ-priv. + νοέω), *not know* or *recognize, be in doubt*.

ἀγνωμωσύνη, -ης, ἡ (*cf.* the following word), *want of knowledge, folly;* in pl., *misunderstandings*, II, 5, 6.

ἀγνώμων (ἀ-priv. + γνώμη), *senseless, lacking judgment*.

ἀγορά, -ᾶς, ἡ (ἀγείρω), *assembly*, V, 7, 3; *place of assembly*, esp. *market-place, market;* then in general, *market, provisions*, V, 5, 19. ἀμφὶ ἀγορὰν πλήθουσαν, *about full market time, i.e. in the middle of the morning*, I, 8, 1, II, 1, 7; ἀπὸ τῆς ἀγορᾶς ζῆν, *live by purchasing provisions*, (not by plunder), VI, 1, 1.

ἀγοράζω, ἀγοράσω, etc. (ἀγορά), *frequent the market, buy*.

ἀγορανόμος, -ου, ὁ (ἀγορά + νέμω), *master* or *inspector of the market*.

ἀγορεύω (ἀγορά), *speak in the assembly, speak, say*.

ἀγρεύω, ἀγρεύσω (ἄγρα, *chase*, akin to ἄγω), *hunt, chase, catch*.

ἄγριος, -α, -ον (ἀγρός), *living in the fields, wild*.

ἀγρός, -οῦ (*cf.* Lat. *ager*, Eng. *acre*), *field, land, country*.

ἀγρυπνέω (ἀγρέω = ἀγρεύω + ὕπνος), *lie awake*.

ἄγω, ἄξω, ἤγαγον, ἦχα, ἦγμαι, ἤχθην, *lead, drive, bring, carry;* without obj., of a general, I, 3, 21; of the troops, IV, 8, 9; of a road, III, 5, 15; *carry off*, VI, 6, 21; hence φέρειν καὶ ἄγειν (*ferre et agere*), *plunder, i.e. carry off* the goods and *drive off* the stock, II, 6, 5; ἄγε (ἄγετε) δή, *come now*, II, 2, 10; ἡσυχίαν ἄγειν, *keep quiet*, III, 1, 14; partic. ἄγων, like ἔχων, loosely translated, *with*, II, 4, 25.

ἀγώγιμος, -ον (ἄγω), *that may be carried;* τὰ ἀγώγιμα, *freight, cargo*.

ἀγών, -ῶνος, ὁ (ἄγω), orig. *assembly*, used esp. of the great games of Greece; hence, *contest, struggle, game;* ἀγῶνα τιθέναι (I, 2, 10) or ποιεῖν (IV, 8, 25), *institute* or *hold games*.

ἀγωνίζομαι, ἀγωνιοῦμαι, etc. (ἀγών), *contend in games;* hence, generally, *strive, contend, fight*.

ἀγωνοθέτης, -ου, ὁ (ἀγών + τίθημι), *judge* or *director of a contest*.

ἄδειπνος, -ον (ἀ-priv. + δεῖπνον), *without dinner, dinnerless*.

ἀδελφός, -οῦ, ὁ (ἀ-copulative + δελφύς, *womb*), *brother*.

ἀδεῶς, adv. (ἀ-priv. + δέος, *fear*), *without fear, fearlessly*.

ἄδηλος, -ον (ἀ-priv. + δῆλος), *unclear, uncertain, doubtful*.

ἀδιάβατος, -ον (ἀ-priv. + διαβατός), *not to be crossed* or *forded*.

ἀδικέω, -ήσω, etc. (ἄδικος), *be unjust, be in the wrong, do wrong;* with acc., *do wrong to, injure;* often with inner obj., I, 9, 13; so in pass., I, 6, 8. The pres. has often the force of a perf., *be in the wrong, i.e. have done wrong;* in the pass., *have suffered wrong*.

ἀδικία, -ας, ἡ (ἄδικος), *injustice, wrong*.

ἄδικος, -ον (ἀ-priv. + δίκη), *unjust, wrong;* τὸ ἄδικον, *injustice*, 1, 9, 16.

ἀδίκως, adv. (ἄδικος), *unfairly, unjustly;* sup. ἀδικώτατα πάσχειν, *be treated most unjustly,* VII, 1, 16.

ἀδόλως, adv. (ἀ-priv.+δόλος), *without treachery or guile.*

Ἀδραμύτιον or **Ἀδραμύττιον**, -ου, τό, Adramyttium, a city on the coast of Mysia.

ἀδύνατος, -ον (ἀ-priv.+δυνατός), *unable;* of things, *impossible, impracticable;* ἀδύνατον, with or without ἐστι, *it is impossible.*

ᾄδω, ᾖδον, ᾄσομαι (*cf.* ᾠδή), *sing, chant.*

ἀεί, adv. (older form αἰεί, *cf.* Lat. aevum, Eng. *aye, ever*), *always, ever, from time to time.*

ἀετός, -οῦ (older form αἰετός; *cf.* Lat. avis), *eagle.*

ἄθεος, -ον (ἀ-priv.+θεός, Eng. *atheist*), *godless, impious.*

Ἀθῆναι, -ῶν, αἱ, Athens.

Ἀθηναία, -ας, ἡ (*cf.* Ἀθῆναι), Athēna, goddess of war and wisdom, and patron goddess of Athens; in VII, 3, 39, the watchword of Seuthes and the Greeks.

Ἀθηναῖος, -α, -ον (Ἀθῆναι), *Athenian;* masc. as subst. *an Athenian.*

Ἀθήνησι, locative adv. (Ἀθῆναι), *at Athens.*

ἆθλον, -ου, τό (*cf.* ἀθλητής, athlete), *prize,* in a contest.

ἀθροίζω, ἀθροίσω, etc. (ἀθρόος), *collect, assemble;* mid. intrans., *muster.*

ἀθρόος, -α, -ον (ἀ-copulative+θρόος, *noise*), lit. *in a noisy crowd,* then *together, in a body.*

ἀθυμέω, ἀθυμήσω, etc. (ἄθυμος), *be despondent, disheartened.*

ἀθυμητέον (verbal of ἀθυμέω), *one must be discouraged.*

ἀθυμία, -ας, ἡ (ἄθυμος), *discouragement, despondency.*

ἄθυμος, -ον (ἀ-priv.+θυμός), *without courage, despondent, dejected.*

ἀθύμως, adv. (ἄθυμος), *despondently, dejectedly;* ἀθύμως ἔχειν, *be dejected.*

αἱ, αἵ, see ὁ, ὅς.

αἰγιαλός, -οῦ, ὁ, *seashore, beach.*

Αἰγύπτιος, -α, -ον (Αἴγυπτος), *Egyptian;* masc. as subst., *an Egyptian.*

Αἴγυπτος, -ου, ἡ, *Egypt,* conquered by Cambyses and made a part of the Persian empire, but at the time of the *Anabasis* in revolt and independent.

αἰδέομαι, αἰδέσομαι, ᾐδεσάμην, ᾔδεσμαι, ᾐδέσθην (αἰδώς), *respect, reverence.*

αἰδήμων, -ον, gen. -ονος, sup. αἰδημονέστατος (αἰδέομαι), *respectful, modest.*

αἰδοῖον, -ου, τό, generally pl. (αἰδέομαι), *the pudenda, private parts.*

αἰδώς, -οῦς, ἡ (αἰδέομαι), *respect, reverence.*

αἰεί, see ἀεί.

αἰετός, see ἀετός.

Αἰήτης, -ου, ὁ, Aeētes, king of Colchis.

αἴθω, *burn;* mid. intrans., *be on fire.*

αἰκίζω, oftener dep. αἰκίζομαι, αἰκιοῦμαι, etc. (ἀεικής, *unseemly,* ἀ-priv.+εἰκός), *outrage, maltreat, torture.*

αἷμα, -ατος, τό, *blood.*

Αἰνείας, -ου, Aenēas, of Stymphālus in Arcadia, a captain in the Greek army.

Αἰνιᾶνες, -ων, οἱ, *the Aenianians,* a Thessalian people.

αἴξ, αἰγός, ἡ, *goat.*

Αἰολίς, -ίδος, ἡ, Aeolis, a district on the northwestern coast of Asia Minor.

αἱρετέος, -α, -ον (verbal of αἱρέω), *must be taken.*

αἱρετός, -ή, -όν (αἱρέω), taken, chosen; οἱ αἱρετοί, the delegates, envoys.

αἱρέω, αἱρήσω, εἷλον, ᾕρηκα, ᾕρημαι, ᾑρέθην, take, capture, seize; mid. choose, prefer, elect; pass., be chosen, be elected.

αἴρω, ἀρῶ, ἦρα, etc., raise.

αἷς, see ὅς.

αἰσθάνομαι, αἰσθήσομαι, ᾐσθόμην, ᾔσθημαι, perceive, observe, learn, with acc., ὅτι, ὡς, or with a partic. clause; with gen., hear, hear of.

αἴσθησις, -εως, ἡ (αἰσθάνομαι), perception; αἴσθησιν παρέχειν, be perceived, IV, 6, 13.

αἴσιος, -ον (αἶσα, portion, fate), auspicious, favorable.

Αἰσχίνης, -ου, ὁ, Aeschines, an Arcadian, in command of the Greek peltasts.

αἰσχρός, -ά, -όν (αἰδέομαι), shameful, base, disgraceful. Comp. αἰσχίων, sup. αἴσχιστος.

αἰσχρῶς, adv. (αἰσχρός), shamefully, disgracefully.

αἰσχύνη, -ης, ἡ (αἰδέομαι), shame, disgrace.

αἰσχύνω, αἰσχυνῶ, ᾔσχυνα, ᾐσχύνθην, dishonor, put to shame; mid. and pass., be ashamed; with acc., feel shame before, II, 3, 22.

αἰτέω, αἰτήσω, etc., ask for, demand; mid., beseech, ask for as a favor. The vb. may take two accs. (I, 3, 14 n.), or the source may be expressed by παρά.

αἰτία, -ας, ἡ (αἰτέω), charge, blame; αἰτίαν ἔχειν, be blamed.

αἰτιάομαι, αἰτιάσομαι, etc. (αἰτία), blame, censure, accuse, charge.

αἴτιος, -α, -ον (αἰτέω), chargeable, responsible, to blame for, the cause of, abs. or with gen. τὸ αἴτιον, the cause, IV, 1, 17.

αἰχμάλωτος, -ον (αἰχμή, spear+ ἁλίσκομαι), taken by the spear, captured; οἱ αἰχμάλωτοι, prisoners; τὰ αἰχμάλωτα, booty.

Ἀκαρνάν, -ᾶνος, ὁ, an Acarnanian, inhabitant of Acarnania in the southwestern part of north Greece.

ἄκαυστος, -ον (ἀ-priv.+καίω), unburnt.

ἀκέραιος, -ον, sound, fresh, of troops.

ἀκήρυκτος, -ον (ἀ-priv. + κηρύττω), without heralds, without a truce.

ἀκινάκης, -ου, ὁ, (a Persian word), a short, straight sword, dagger.

ἀκίνδυνος, -ον (ἀ-priv.+κίνδυνος), without danger, safe.

ἀκινδύνως, adv. (ἀκίνδυνος), without danger.

ἀκμάζω, ἀκμάσω (ἀκμή), be at one's prime, at one's best.

ἀκμή, -ῆς, ἡ (√ ἀκ, cf. ἀκόντιον, ἄκρος, Eng., acme), point, edge; ἀκμήν, as adv., at the point of, just.

ἀκόλαστος, -ον (ἀ-priv.+κολάζω), unpunished, undisciplined.

ἀκολουθέω, ἀκολουθήσω, etc. (ἀ-copulative + κέλευθος, way), accompany, follow.

ἀκόλουθος, -ον (ἀ-copulative+κέλευθος, way), going the same way, consistent.

ἀκοντίζω, ἀκοντιῶ (ἀκόντιον), hurl the javelin, hit with the javelin.

ἀκόντιον, -ου, τό (√ ἀκ; cf. ἀκμή), javelin, hurled with the aid of a thong; see IV, 2, 28 n.

ἀκόντισις, -εως, ἡ (ἀκοντίζω), javelin-throwing.

ἀκοντιστής, -οῦ, ὁ (ἀκοντίζω), javelin-thrower.

ἀκούω, ἀκούσομαι, ἤκουσα, ἀκήκοα, ἠκούσθην, hear, hear of, abs. or with acc.; with gen., of the sound heard, IV, 2, 8; often with gen. of source, hear from; foll. by ὅτι, by acc. and infin. (of hearsay), or by acc. and partic. (if what is heard be marked as a fact); with gen., *hearken to, obey.* εὖ ἀκούειν (*bene audire*), as pass. of εὖ λέγειν, *be well spoken of,* VII, 7, 23. The pres., as in Eng., is often used where the perf. would be more logical, *e. g.* I, 9, 28.

ἄκρα, -ας, ἡ (ἄκρος), *summit, height, citadel.*

ἄκρατος, -ον (ἀ-priv.+κεράννυμι), *unmixed, strong,* of wine.

ἄκριτος, -ον (ἀ-priv.+κρίνω), *without a trial.*

ἀκροβολίζομαι, aor. ἠκροβολισάμην (ἄκρος+βάλλω), *throw from a distance;* hence, *skirmish,*

ἀκροβόλισις, -εως, ἡ (ἀκροβολίζομαι), *skirmish.*

ἀκρόπολις, -εως, ἡ (ἄκρος+πόλις), *upper city, citadel, acropolis.*

ἄκρος, -α, -ον (cf. ἀκμή), *highest, topmost, the top of;* τὸ ἄκρον, *height, summit;* so τὰ ἄκρα, *the heights.*

ἀκρωνυχία, -ας, ἡ (ἄκρος+ὄνυξ, *nail*), *tip of the nail;* then *spur of a mountain.*

ἀκτή, -ῆς, ἡ (ἄγνυμι, *break*), *shore, coast, promontory.*

ἄκυρος, -ον (κῦρος, *power, authority*), *of no force, invalid, null and void.*

ἄκων, -ουσα, -ον (ἀ-priv.+ἑκών), *unwilling,* used as a partic., ἄκοντος Κύρου, *against the will of Cyrus, without the consent of Cyrus,* I, 3, 17; with the force of an adv., *unwillingly, unintentionally,* IV, 8, 25.

ἀλαλάζω, ἀλαλάξομαι, ἠλάλαξα (ἀλαλή, an imitative word, *battle-cry*), *raise the battle-cry, shout.*

ἀλεεινός, -ή, -όν (ἀλέα, *warmth*), *warm;* in neut., *a source of warmth.*

ἀλέξω, ἀλέξομαι, ἠλεξάμην, *ward off;* in the *Anabasis* always mid., *ward off from oneself, repel, requite.*

ἀλέτης, -ου, ὁ (ἀλέω, *grind*), *a grinder;* ὄνος ἀλέτης, *the upper millstone,* I, 5, 5.

ἄλευρον, -ου, τό (ἀλέω), *wheat-flour,* always in pl.

ἀλήθεια, -ας, ἡ (ἀληθής), *truth, candor;* τῇ ἀληθείᾳ, *in fact, in truth.*

ἀληθεύω, ἀληθεύσω, etc. (ἀληθής), *speak the truth, tell the truth about, report truly.*

ἀληθής, -ές (ἀ-priv.+λήθω=λανθάνω), *unconcealed, manifest;* hence *true;* τὸ ἀληθές, *the truth.*

ἀληθινός, -ή, -όν (ἀληθής), *real, genuine, worthy of the name.*

ἁλιευτικός, -ή, -όν (ἁλιεύω, *fish,* from ἅλς, *the sea;* cf. Lat. *sal,* Eng. *salt*), *belonging to fishing or a fisherman;* with πλοῖον, *a fishing-boat.*

ἁλίζω, ἥλισα, ἡλίσθην (ἅλις), *gather, collect;* mid. intrans., *assemble,* VI, 3, 3.

ἄλιθος, -ον (ἀ-priv.+λίθος), *stoneless, free from stones.*

ἅλις, adv., *in crowds, in abundance, enough,* with gen.

Ἁλισάρνη, -ης, *Halisarne,* a city in Mysia.

ἁλίσκομαι, ἁλώσομαι, ἑάλων, ἑάλωκα, a pass. of αἱρέω, *be taken, be captured, be seized.*

ἄλκιμος, -ον (ἀλκή, *strength, valor*), *warlike, brave,* a poetic word.

ἀλλά (ἄλλος), conj., more strongly adversative than δέ, *otherwise, on the other hand, but;* at the beginning of a speech often, *well, well but;* in replies sometimes, *nay, on the contrary,* often coupled with other particles, but always with adversative force; ἀλλὰ γάρ, often implying an ellipsis, *but . . . for,* III, 2, 25; ἀλλ' ἤ, *except.*

ἄλλῃ, adv. (ἄλλος), *in another way, place,* or *manner, elsewhere.*

ἀλλήλων, -οις, reciprocal pron. (ἄλλος), *one another, each other.*

ἄλλοθεν, adv. (ἄλλος) *from another place;* ἄλλοι ἄλλοθεν, *some in one way others in another,* I, 10, 13 n.

ἅλλομαι, ἁλοῦμαι, ἡλάμην, 2 aor. ἡλόμην (Lat. *salio*), *leap, jump.*

ἄλλος, -η, -ο (Lat. *alius*), *other, another;* with art., *the rest of,* I, 2, 15; τῇ ἄλλῃ (ἡμέρᾳ), *the next (day),* II, 1, 3; with alternative or distributive force, ἄλλος καὶ ἄλλος, I, 5, 12; ἄλλοι . . . ἄλλοι, *some . . . others,* I, 8, 9; ἄλλοι ἄλλως (*alii aliter*), *some in one way others in another,* I, 6, 11; so ἄλλος ἄλλα λέγει, II, 1, 5; ἄλλος ἄλλῃ, IV, 8, 19; sometimes pleonastic, *besides;* I, 5, 5; so especially with numerals, I, 7, 11; εἴ τις καὶ ἄλλος and ὥς τις καὶ ἄλλος, see καί; in questions expecting an affirmative answer, ἄλλο τι ἤ; = *nonne?*

ἄλλοσε (ἄλλος), *to another place, elsewhere.*

ἄλλοτε, adv. (ἄλλος), *at another time, at other times;* ἄλλοτε καὶ ἄλλοτε, *every now and then,* II, 4, 26; εἴ ποτε καὶ ἄλλοτε; see καί.

ἀλλότριος, -α, -ον (ἄλλος), *belonging to another, foreign.*

ἄλλως, adv. (ἄλλος), *otherwise, in another way, differently;* aimlessly, rashly, V, 1, 7; ἄλλως ἔχειν or γίγνεσθαι, *be different,* III, 2, 37, VI, 6, 10; ἄλλως πως, *in any other way,* III, 1, 20; ἄλλως τε καί, *for other reasons and particularly, i.e. especially,* V, 6, 9; VII, 7, 40; ἄλλοι ἄλλως; see ἄλλος.

ἀλόγιστος, -ον (ἀ-priv.+λογίζομαι), *unreasoning, senseless, foolish.*

ἄλσος, -ους, τό, *sacred enclosure,* esp. *grove.*

Ἅλυς, -υος, ὁ, *the Halys,* the principal river of Asia Minor, flowing into the Euxine.

ἄλφιτον, -ου, τό, *barley meal,* always pl.

ἀλωπεκῆ, -ῆς (ἀλώπηξ, *fox*), *fox-skin cap,* worn by Thracians, VII, 4, 4.

ἁλώσιμος, -ον (ἁλίσκομαι), *that may be captured, easy to capture.*

ἁλώσοιντο, see ἁλίσκομαι.

ἅμα, (cf. ὁμοῦ, Lat., *simul*, Eng. *same*), *at the same time, at the same time with* (dat.), *together with;* ἅμα τῇ ἡμέρᾳ, *at day-break,* II, 1, 2; cf. ἅμα τῇ ἐπιούσῃ ἡμέρᾳ, *on the following day at dawn,* I, 7, 2; ἅμα ἡλίῳ ἀνέχοντι, ἀνατέλλοντι, *at sunrise,* II, 1, 3; 3, 1; ἅμα ἡλίῳ δύνοντι, *at sunset,* II, 2, 13; ἅμα μέν . . . ἅμα δέ, *both . . . and,* III, 4, 19; with partics. (strictly with the accompanying vb.), *as soon as.*

Ἀμαζών, -όνος, ἡ, *an Amazon,* one of the mythical tribe of female warriors.

ἅμαξα, -ης, ἡ (ἅμα + ἄγω), *a wagon, cart;* ἅμαξα πετρῶν, *a wagon-load of stones,* IV, 7, 10; βοῦς ὑπὸ ἁμάξης, *a draught-ox,* VI, 4, 22, 25.

ἁμαξαῖος, -α, -ον (ἅμαξα), *of* stones, *large enough to load a wagon.*

ἁμαξιτός, -ον (ἅμαξα), *passable for wagons,* ὁδὸς ἁμαξιτός *wagon-road,* I, 2, 21.

ἁμαρτάνω, ἁμαρτήσομαι, ἥμαρτον, ἡμάρτηκα, ἡμάρτημαι, ἡμαρτήθην, *miss the mark*, *miss* (with gen.), I. 5, 12; *do wrong*, *sin against*, III, 2, 20; μικρὰ ἁμαρτηθέντα, *small errors*, V, 8, 20.

ἀμαχεί, adv. (ἀ-priv.+μάχομαι), *without fighting*, *without a struggle*.

ἀμαχητί, adv. =the foregoing.

ἀμείνων, -ον, comp. of ἀγαθός, *better*, *braver*; neut. as adv., II, 1, 20.

ἀμέλεια, -ας, ἡ (cf. ἀμελέω), *carelessness*, *neglect*.

ἀμελέω, -ήσω, etc. (ἀ-priv.+μέλει), *be careless*, *be negligent of*, *neglect*, with gen.

ἀμελῶς, adv. (ἀμελής, *careless*; cf. ἀμελέω), *carelessly*, *negligently*.

ἄμετρος, -ον (ἀ-priv.+μέτρον), *without measure*, *countless*.

ἀμήχανος, -ον (ἀ-priv.+μηχανή), *without resource* or *means*; *impossible*, I, 2, 21; πολλὰ καὶ ἀμήχανα, *many difficulties*, II, 3, 18.

ἁμιλλάομαι, ἁμιλλήσομαι, etc., dep. pass. (ἅμιλλα, *contest*), *contend*, *vie with*, *race for* (with ἐπί or πρός).

ἄμπελος, -ου, ἡ, *vine*.

Ἀμπρακιώτης, -ου, ὁ, *an Ambraciot*, citizen of Ambracia in Epirus.

ἀμυγδάλινος, -η, -ον (ἀμυγδάλη, *almond*), *of almonds*, IV, 4, 13 n.

ἀμύνω, ἀμυνῶ, ἤμυνα (ἀ-euphonic+√μυ, cf. μύνη, *excuse* and Lat. *moenia*, *walls*), *ward off*; mid. *ward off from oneself*, *defend oneself against*, *requite*, *punish*.

ἀμφί, prep. (cf. ἄμφω, Lat. *ambi-*), lit., *on both sides of;* hence (1) with gen. (a poetic use), *about*, *concerning*, IV, 5, 17 n.; (2) with acc., *about*, *round about*, of place, ἀμφὶ Μίλητον, I, 2, 3; of persons, τῶν ἀμφὶ Κῦρον, I, 8, 1; in such phrases the individual is oftener included, οἱ ἀμφὶ Ἀριαῖον, *Ariaeus and his men*, III, 2, 2; of time, ἀμφὶ ἀγορὰν πλήθουσαν, *about full market time*, I, 8, 1; ἀμφὶ δορπηστόν, I, 10, 17; with various objects, ἀμφὶ τὰ στρατεύματα δαπανᾶν, *spend money on his armies*, I, 1, 8; τὰ ἀμφὶ τάξεις, *tactics*, II, 1, 7; ἀμφὶ ταῦτα ἔχειν, *to be busied about this*, V, 2, 26; with numerals, I, 2, 9, and frequently.

ἀμφιγνοέω, impf. ἠμφιγνόουν, ἠμφεγνόησα, ἠμφεγνοήθην (ἀμφί+νοέω, for γνοέω), *think on both sides*, *be in doubt*.

Ἀμφίδημος, -ου, ὁ, *Amphidēmus*, father of Amphicrates.

Ἀμφικράτης, -ους, ὁ, *Amphicrates*, an Athenian, a captain in the Greek army.

ἀμφιλέγω (λέγω), *speak on both sides*, *quarrel*.

Ἀμφιπολίτης, -ου, ὁ, *an Amphipolitan*, citizen of Amphipolis, a colony of Athens on the Strymon in Macedonia.

ἀμφορεύς, -έως, ὁ (Homeric ἀμφιφορεύς, ἀμφί+φέρω), *a large jar with two handles*.

ἀμφότερος, -α, -ον (ἄμφω), *both*. In the *Anabasis* only dual or pl.

ἀμφοτέρωθεν, adv. (ἀμφότερος), *from both sides*, *on both sides*.

ἄμφω (cf. ἀμφί, Lat. *ambo*, Eng. *both*), gen. and dat. ἀμφοῖν, *both*.

ἄν, post-pos. modal part. for which there is no English equivalent (cf. Lat. *an*), used as follows: (1) with the condit. part. εἰ (see ἐάν), with relatives (ὅς, ὅστις, ὁπόσος, etc.), and with temporal words ὅτε, ὁπότε, ἐπεί, ἐπειδή (see ὅταν, ὁπόταν, ἐπάν, ἐπειδάν); ἕως.

πρίν, μέχρι, ἔστε, with the vb. in the subj., either referring to the fut. or made general in the pres.; with ὡς and the subj. in a final clause; (2) with vbs. (a) with opt. in an apodosis, the protasis being often only implied or entirely suppressed (potential opt.); (b) with secondary tenses of the indic. in apodoses of conditions contrary to fact (past potential), (c) with infin. or partic., representing either of these constructions, (d) with impf. or aor. indic. in an iterative sense I, 9, 19 n.

ἄν stands regularly near the head of its clause and may be repeated with the vb., if that is postponed; sometimes it is repeated several times, I, 3, 6 n.; on the other hand, it may be omitted with the vb., if it has been expressed with a preceding vb. in the same construction, I, 6, 2 n.

ἄν, see ἐάν.

ἀν-, see ἀ-.

ἀνά, prep. with acc. (cf. Eng. on), up, up along, over, throughout; often distributive, ἀνὰ ἑκατὸν ἄνδρας, a hundred men each, III, 4, 21; of manner, ἀνὰ κράτος, up to or with all one's might, at full speed, I, 8, 1 (cf. κατὰ κράτος). In composition ἀνά frequently means back or again.

ἀναβαίνω, (βαίνω), go up, ascend; especially go up from the coast; go inland; of a horse, mount; of a ship, embark on, both with ἐπί.

ἀναβάλλω (βάλλω), throw up, of a mound; help to mount, IV, 4, 4.

ἀνάβασις, -εως, ἡ (ἀναβαίνω), a going up, ascent, a march inland, esp. of the march of Cyrus against his brother, and hence the proper title of Xenophon's history.

ἀναβιβάζω (βιβάζω, -βιβάσω or -βιβῶ, -ἐβίβασα, make to go), make go up, lead up.

ἀναβοάω (βοάω), shout aloud, call.

ἀναβολή, -ῆς, ἡ (ἀναβάλλω), earth thrown up, mound.

ἀναγιγνώσκω (γιγνώσκω), know again (something seen before), recognize, V, 8, 6; read I, 6, 4.

ἀναγκάζω, ἀναγκάσω, etc. (ἀνάγκη), force, compel.

ἀναγκαῖος, -α, -ον (ἀνάγκη), necessary; οἱ ἀναγκαῖοι, one's relatives, Lat. necessarii, II, 4, 1.

ἀνάγκη, -ης, ἡ, necessity, force; with or without ἐστι, it is necessary, one must, with dat. or acc. and infin.; ἀνάγκῃ ἔχεσθαι or κατέχεσθαι, be constrained by necessity, II, 5, 21; II, 6, 13; ἐν ἀνάγκῃ εἶναι, be in straits, VII, 6, 27.

ἀναγνούς, see ἀναγιγνώσκω.

ἀνάγω (ἄγω), lead or take up, lead inland; mid. put to sea, set sail.

ἀναζεύγνυμι (ζεύγνυμι), yoke up, hence break camp, III, 4, 37; IV, 6, 1.

ἀναθαρρέω (cf. θρασύς), take courage, recover courage.

ἀναθεῖναι, ἀναθείς, see ἀνατίθημι.

ἀνάθημα, -ατος, τό (ἀνατίθημι), a thing set up, votive offering, V, 3, 5.

ἀναθορυβέω (θορυβέω, -ήσω, raise an uproar; cf. θόρυβος), cry out aloud, applaud.

ἀναθρέψαντι, see ἀνατρέφω.

ἀναιρέω (αἱρέω), take up, pick up, carry off for burial (in this

sense chiefly mid.); of an oracle, *take up a subject;* hence *answer,* III, 1, 6; of war, *undertake, begin.*
ἀνακαίω (καίω), *kindle.*
ἀνακαλέω (καλέω) *call again, call aloud, call back, sound the recall.*
ἀνακοινόω (κοινόω), *consult, confer with,* act. or mid.
ἀνακομίζω (κομίζω), *carry up;* mid., *store up for oneself.*
ἀνακράζω (κράζω, *scream*) only in aor. ἀνέκραγον, *shout aloud, cry out.*
ἀναλαλάζω (ἀλαλάζω), **raise the** *war-cry.*
ἀναλαμβάνω (λαμβάνω), *take up, pick up, take along with.*
ἀναλάμπω (λάμπω), *blaze up,* aor. *burst into a blaze.*
ἀναλίσκω, ἀναλώσω, ἀνήλωσα, ἀνήλωκα, ἀνήλωμαι, ἀνηλώθην, *use up, spend, exhaust.*
ἀνάλωτος, -ον (ἀ-priv.+ἀλωτός, verbal of ἀλίσκομαι), *not be taken, impregnable.*
ἀναμείγνυμι (μείγνυμι, μείξω, ἔμειξα, μέμειγμαι, ἐμείχθην, 2 aor. pass. ἐμίγην, *mix*), *mingle with.*
ἀναμένω (μένω), *remain, wait, wait for.*
ἀναμιμνῄσκω (μιμνῄσκω), *remind one of* (with two accs.), III, 2, 11; *make mention of,* V, 8, 26; mid. and pass., *call to mind, remember,* VI, 1, 23.
ἄνανδρος, -ον (ἀ-priv.+ἀνήρ) *unmanly, cowardly.*
'Ἀναξίβιος, -ον, ὁ, *Anaxibius,* a Spartan admiral in command at Byzantium.
ἀναξυρίδες, -ίδων, αἱ (Persian word), *trousers.*
ἀναπαύω (παύω), *cause to cease;* mid., *rest, refresh oneself, pass the night.*
ἀναπείθω (πείθω), *persuade, induce.*
ἀναπετάννυμι (πετάννυμι, *spread out;* cf. Lat. *pandeo, pateo*), *throw open.*
ἀναπηδάω (πηδάω, πηδήσω, etc., *leap*), *leap up, spring upon one's horse.*
ἀναπνέω (πνέω), *breathe again, recover breath.*
ἀναπράττω (πράττω), *exact, collect,* of money due.
ἀναπτύσσω (πτύσσω, πτύξω, etc., *fold*), *unfold, fold back,* I, 10, 9 n.
ἀναπυνθάνομαι (πυνθάνομαι), *inquire carefully, learn by questioning.*
ἀναρίθμητος, -ον (ἀ-priv.+ἀριθμέω, *count*), *innumerable.*
ἀνάριστος, -ον (ἀ-priv.+ἄριστον), *without breakfast, breakfastless.*
ἀναρπάζω (ἁρπάζω), *snatch up, seize, carry off.*
ἀναρχία, -ας, ἡ (ἀ-priv.+ἄρχω), *lack of government, anarchy.*
ἀνασκευάζω (σκευάζω), *pack up, remove.*
ἀναστάς, see ἀνίστημι.
ἀνασταυρόω (σταυρόω, σταυρώσω, *fence with stakes;* cf. σταυρός), *set up on a stake, impale.*
ἀναστέλλω (στέλλω), *send back;* hence *repulse.*
ἀναστῆναι, ἀναστήσας, see ἀνίστημι.
ἀναστρέφω (στρέφω), *turn back* or *about, face about, retreat;* mid., *conduct oneself, behave,* II, 5, 14; pass., *face about, rally,* I, 10, 12.
ἀνασχέσθαι, ἀνάσχωμαι, see ἀνέχω.
ἀναταράττω (ταράττω), *stir up;* perf. pass. partic. ἀνατεταραγμένον, *in disorder,* I, 7, 20.
ἀνατείνω (τείνω) *stretch up, hold up,* esp. of the hands in voting;

αἰετὸς ἀνατεταμένος, *an eagle with wings outspread*, I, 10, 12.
ἀνατέλλω (τέλλω, ἔτειλα, *make to rise*), intr., *rise*, of the sun.
ἀνατίθημι (τίθημι), *put upon, pack upon*, II, 2, 4; *set up, dedicate*, V, 3, 5 and 6.
ἀνατρέφω (τρέφω), *fatten up*.
ἀναφεύγω (φεύγω), *flee up*.
ἀναφρονέω (φρονέω), *come to one's senses, recover one's senses*.
ἀναχάζω, only in pres. (Homeric χάζω, *withdraw*), *withdraw, retreat*.
ἀναχωρέω (χωρέω), *withdraw, retire, retreat*; ἀναχωρεῖν ἐπὶ πόδα, *give ground step by step*, V, 2, 32.
ἀναχωρίζω (χωρίζω), *make to withdraw or retire*.
ἄνδρα, see ἀνήρ.
ἀνδραγαθία, -ας, ἡ (ἀνήρ + ἀγαθός), *bravery, valor*.
ἀνδράποδον, -ου, τό (ἀνήρ + πούς?), *slave*, esp. *captive* taken in war.
ἀνδρεῖος, -α, -ον (ἀνήρ), *manly, courageous*.
ἀνδρειότης, -ητος, ἡ (ἀνήρ), *manliness, valor, courage*.
ἀνδρίζομαι (ἀνήρ), *play the man, act bravely*.
ἀνέβην, see ἀναβαίνω.
ἀνεγείρω (ἐγείρω), trans., *wake up, awaken*; pass., *be aroused, wake up*.
ἀνεῖλον, see ἀναιρέω.
ἀνεῖναι, see ἀνίημι.
ἀνεῖπον (εἶπον), *proclaim*.
ἀνελέσθαι, see ἀναιρέω.
ἄνεμος, -ου, ὁ (cf. Lat. *anima, animus*), *wind*.
ἀνεπιλήπτως, adv. (ἀ-priv. + verbal of ἐπιλαμβάνω), *not to be laid hold of, in security, blamelessly*.
ἀνερεθίζω (ἐρεθίζω, *excite*), *excite, provoke*; pass., *be instigated*.

ἀνερωτάω (ἐρωτάω), *ask, demand*.
ἀνέστην, see ἀνίστημι.
ἀνεστράφην, see ἀναστρέφω.
ἄνευ, improper prep., *without*, foll. by gen.
ἀνευρίσκω (εὑρίσκω), *find out, discover*.
ἀνέχω, impf. mid. ἠνειχόμην, 2 aor. ἠνεσχόμην, with double augment (ἔχω), *hold up*; mid., *bear up under, endure, control oneself*.
ἀνεψιός, -οῦ, ὁ (cf. Lat. *nepos*), *first cousin*.
ἀνέῳγον, ἀνέῳξα, see ἀνοίγω.
ἀνήγαγον, see ἀνάγω.
ἀνηγέρθη, see ἀνεγείρω.
ἀνηγμένος, see ἀνάγω.
ἀνήκεστος, -ον (ἀ-priv. + ἀκέομαι, *heal*), *that cannot be healed or made good, irreparable*.
ἀνήκω (ἥκω), *extend to, reach*.
ἀνήρ, ἀνδρός, ὁ, *man* (Lat. *vir*) as contrasted with woman or child or with ἄνθρωπος *human being* (I, 7, 3 n); hence in varying senses, *husband*, IV, 5, 24; *soldier*, I, 1, 11; often joined with words denoting nationality, in which case it is not to be translated, ἄνδρα Πέρσην, *a Persian*, I, 2, 20; very common in addresses, ἄνδρες στρατιῶται, *men, fellow soldiers*, I, 3, 3. Cf. ἄνθρωπος.
ἀνηρώτα, see ἀνερωτάω.
ἀνήχθησαν, see ἀνάγω.
ἀνθ', see ἀντί.
ἀνθέμιον, -ου, τό (ἄνθος, *flower*), *flower, flower-pattern*, V, 4, 32.
ἀνθίστημι (ἵστημι), *set up against*; mid., *rise up against, oppose*.
ἀνθρώπινος, -η, -ον (ἄνθρωπος), *human*; neut., pl., *things human*, as contrasted with the gods.
ἄνθρωπος, -ου, ὁ, ἡ, *man, human*

being, pl. *men, people;* with words denoting nationality, like ἀνήρ, VI, 4, 23; often contemptuous, III, 1, 27.

ἀνιάω, ἀνιάσω, etc. (ἀνία, *grief*), *grieve, trouble, harass;* mid., *be distressed,* I, 2, 11; *be hurt,* IV, 8, 26.

ἀνίημι (ἵημι), *send back;* hence, *let go,* VII, 6, 30.

ἀνιμάω (ἱμάω, *draw;* cf. ἱμάς), *draw up.*

ἀνίστημι (ἵστημι), *cause to stand, rouse up,* I, 5, 3; mid., with perf. and 2 aor. act., *stand up, get up, rise.*

ἄνοδος, -ον (ἀ-priv.+ὁδός), *impassable.*

ἄνοδος, -ου, ἡ (ἀνά+ὁδός), *way up, upward march;* cf. ἀνάβασις.

ἀνόητος, -ον (ἀ-priv.+νοέω), *senseless, foolish.*

ἀνοίγω, ἀνοίξω, with double augment throughout, impf. ἀνέῳγον (οἴγω or οἴγνυμι, *open*), *open, throw open.*

ἀνομία, -ας, ἡ (ἀ-priv.+νόμος), *lawlessness.*

ἀνομοίως, adv. (ἀ-priv.+ὅμοιος), *differently.*

ἄνομος, -ον (ἀ-priv.+νόμος), *lawless.*

ἀντ', see ἀντί.

ἀνταγοράζω, (ἀγοράζω), *buy in exchange.*

ἀντακούω (ἀκούω), *hear in turn, hear in reply.*

Ἄντανδρος, -ου, ἡ, *Antandrus,* a city in the Troad.

ἀντεμπίμπλημι (πίμπλημι), *fill in return* or *in requital.*

ἀντεπιμελέομαι (ἐπιμελέομαι), *take care in turn, take counter measures.*

ἀντευποιέω (ποιέω), *do good in return.*

ἀντί, by elision ἀντ' or ἀνθ', prep. with gen., *over against, opposite, against;* hence, *instead of,* I, 1, 4; *in return for,* I, 3, 4; ἀνθ' ὧν ἑστηκότες, *standing behind which,* IV, 7, 6.

ἀντιδίδωμι (δίδωμι), *give in return* or *in place of.*

ἀντικαθίστημι (ἵστημι), *appoint instead* or *in place of.*

ἀντιλέγω (λέγω), *say against* or *in opposition* (ὅτι or infin.); *speak against, object,* abs.

ἀντίος, -α, -ον (ἀντί), *opposite, against, facing;* ἀντίοι ἰέναι, *go to meet, go against,* I, 8, 17; οἱ ἀντίοι, *the enemy,* III, 1, 42; ἐκ τοῦ ἀντίου, *from the opposite side, from the side of the enemy,* I, 8, 23; λόγοι ἀντίοι ἢ οὓς ἤκουον, *words the very opposite of those I heard* (a rare use), VI, 6, 34.

ἀντιπαραθέω (θέω), *run along opposite.*

ἀντιπαρασκευάζομαι (σκευάζω), *make counter preparations.*

ἀντιπαρατάττομαι (τάττω), *array oneself against.*

ἀντιπάρειμι (εἶμι), *march along opposite* or *on the other side.*

ἀντιπάσχω (πάσχω), *suffer in return.*

ἀντιπέραν or ἀντιπέρας, adv. (ἀντί+πέραν), *over against, opposite,* with gen. and preceded by κατά.

ἀντιποιέω (ποιέω), *do in return, retaliate;* mid., *contend with someone* (dat.) *for something* (gen.), II, 1, 11; *vie with one another in* (gen.), IV, 7, 12.

ἀντίπορος, -ον (ἀντί+√περ; cf. περάω), *over against, opposite,* a poetic word, IV, 2, 18.

ἀντιστασιάζω (στασιάζω), *contend against, vie with.*

ἀντιστασιώτης, -ου, ὁ (ἀντί+στάσις, faction), an opponent, rival.
ἀντιστοιχέω (στοιχέω, be in a row, στοῖχος, row), stand in rows over against.
ἀντιστρατοπεδεύομαι (στρατοπεδεύω), encamp against.
ἀντιτάττω (τάττω), draw up or array against.
ἀντιτιμάω (τιμάω), honor in return.
ἀντιτοξεύω (τοξεύω), shoot in return, shoot back.
ἀντιφυλάττομαι (φυλάττω), be on one's guard in turn, take counter precautions.
ἄντρον, -ου, τό (hence Lat. antrum), cave.
ἀντρώδης, -ες (ἄντρον+εἶδος), cave-like; πέτρα ἀντρώδης, a rocky cavern.
ἀνυστός, -ή, -όν (verbal of ἀνύω), that may be accomplished; possible; σιγῇ ὡς ἀνυστόν, as silently as possible, I, 8, 11.
ἀνύω, ἀνύσω, etc. (pres. regularly ἀνύτω), accomplish.
ἄνω, adv. (ἀνά), comp. ἀνωτέρω, sup. ἀνωτάτω, up, upwards, above, inland, with gen., IV, 3, 3; τὰ ἄνω, the heights, IV, 3, 25; ἡ ἄνω ὁδός, the journey inland, III, 1, 8.
ἀνώγεων, -ω, τό (ἄνω+γῆ), upper floor, loft, a dubious word, V, 4, 29.
ἄνωθεν, adv. (ἄνω), from above, from the interior.
ἀξία, -ας, ἡ (ἄξιος), worth, value, price, deserts.
ἀξίνη, -ης, ἡ (Lat. ascia, Eng. axe), axe.
ἄξιος, -α, -ον (ἄγω), weighing as much as, worth, worthy of (gen.); ἄξιον (ἐστι), be worth while, be fitting; πολλοῦ (πλείονος, πλείστου) ἄξιος, of great (more, the

most) value; so παντὸς ἄξιος, VII, 3, 13.
ἀξιοστράτηγος, -ον (ἄξιος+στρατηγός), worthy to be general.
ἀξιόω, ἀξιώσω, etc. (ἄξιος), deem fit or proper, ask, claim.
ἀξίωμα, -ατος, τό (ἀξιόω), worth, authority.
ἀξίως, adv. (ἄξιος), worthily, deservedly, I, 9, 15.
ἄξων, -ονος, ὁ (ἄνω), axle.
ἀπ', see ἀπό.
ἀπαγγέλλω (ἀγγέλλω), bring back word, announce, report.
ἀπαγορεύω, ἀπερῶ, ἀπεῖπον, ἀπείρηκα (ἀγορεύω), renounce, give up, grow weary.
ἀπάγω (ἄγω), lead or carry back or off; march back.
ἀπαγωγή, -ῆς, ἡ (ἄγω), removal, departure.
ἀπαθής, -ές (ἀ-priv.+πάθος), without experience in, free from (gen.).
ἀπαίδευτος, -ον (ἀ-priv.+παιδεύω), uneducated, ignorant.
ἀπαίρω (αἴρω), raise from; intr. of ships, set sail, depart.
ἀπαιτέω (αἰτέω), claim as one's right or due, demand; with two accs., II, 5, 38.
ἀπαλλάττω (ἀλλάττω, ἀλλάξω, ἤλλαξα, -ήλλαχα, ἤλλαγμαι, -ηλλάχθην or ἠλλάγην), change from, set free, remove; intr., depart, be freed from, be well rid of, I, 10, 8.
ἀπαλός, -ή, -όν, tender, delicate, soft.
ἀπαμείβομαι, in aor. pass. ἀπημείφθη (ἀμείβω, change), exchange words, answer, reply, II, 5, 15 n.
ἀπαντάω, ἀπαντήσομαι, ἀπήντησα, ἀπήντηκα, meet or, in a hostile sense, encounter.
ἅπαξ, adv., once.
ἀπαράσκευος, -ον (ἀ-priv. + παρασκευή), unprepared.

ἅπας, ἅπασα, ἅπαν (πᾶς), *all together, the whole of, entire;* with art. gen. in pred. posit.

ἀπαυθημερίζω (*cf.* αὐθημερόν), *return on the same day.*

ἀπεγνωκέναι, see ἀπογιγνώσκω.

ἀπεδόμην, see ἀποδίδωμι.

ἀπέδρα, etc., see ἀποδιδράσκω.

ἀπέδωκα, see ἀποδίδωμι.

ἀπέθανον, see ἀποθνήσκω.

ἀπειθέω, -ήσω, etc. (ἀ-priv.+πείθομαι), *disobey.*

ἀπειλέω, ἀπειλήσω, etc. (ἀπειλή), *threaten.*

ἀπειλή, -ῆς, ἡ, *threat.*

ἄπειμι (εἶμι), *go away, go back, retreat* (the pres. often with fut. force; *cf.* εἶμι).

ἄπειμι (εἰμί), *be away,* or *absent.*

ἀπεῖπον (εἶπον), *renounce,* VII, 1, 41; *forbid,* with dat. and infin., VII, 2, 12.

ἀπειρηκότας, see ἀπαγορεύω.

ἄπειρος, -ον (ἀ-priv. + πεῖρα), *unskilled, unacquainted with,* abs. or with gen.

ἀπεῖχον, see ἀπέχω.

ἀπέκτονε, see ἀποκτείνω.

ἀπελαύνω (ἐλαύνω), *drive away* or *out, expel;* intr. *march* or *ride away.*

ἀπελθεῖν, ἀπελθών, etc., see ἀπέρχομαι.

ἅπερ, see ὅσπερ.

ἀπερύκω (ἐρύκω), *ward off.*

ἀπέρχομαι (ἔρχομαι), *come* (or *go*) *back* or *away, depart, return, retreat; go forth,* IV, 7, 8.

ἀπεχθάνομαι, ἀπεχθήσομαι, ἀπηχθόμην, ἀπήχθημαι (ἀπό+ἔχθος, *hatred*), *incur one's enmity* or *hatred.*

ἀπέχω (ἔχω), *keep off* or *from;* mid., *hold oneself aloof from, abstain from,* II, 6, 10, etc.; act. intr., *be away from, distant from,* I, 3, 20.

ἀπήγαγεν, see ἀπάγω.

ἀπῄει, see ἄπειμι (εἶμι).

ἀπήλασα, ἀπήλαυνον, see ἀπελαύνω.

ἀπῆλθον, see ἀπέρχομαι.

ἀπηλλάγη, see ἀπαλλάττω.

ἀπημείφθη, see ἀπαμείβομαι.

ἀπῆρα, see ἀπαίρω.

ἀπιστέω, ἀπιστήσω, etc. (ἄπιστος), *distrust, disbelieve, disobey* (dat.).

ἀπιστία, -ας, ἡ (ἄπιστος), *distrust, suspicion,* II, 5, 4; *faithlessness, treachery,* II, 5, 21; III, 2, 8.

ἄπιστος, -ον (ἀ-priv.+πείθω), *not to be trusted, faithless.*

ἀπιτέον (verbal of ἄπειμι), *one must go* or *depart.*

ἄπλετος, -ον, *boundless, immeasurable.*

ἁπλοῦς, -ῆ, -οῦν (ἀ-copulative+√πλα, *cf.* πίμπλημι), *simple, frank;* τὸ ἁπλοῦν, *frankness, candor,* II, 6, 22.

ἀπό, by elision ἀπ' or ἀφ', prep. with gen. (Lat. *a, ab,* Eng. *off*), (1) of place, *from, away from;* often with pregnant construction, τὰ ἀπὸ τῶν οἰκιῶν ξύλα, II, 2, 16 n.; (2) of time, *from, since, after,* ἀπὸ τούτου, *from this time on,* II, 6, 5; ἀφ' οὗ, *since,* III, 2, 14; (3) of source, I, 5, 10; so of descent, II, 1, 3; (4) of means, ἀπὸ τούτων τῶν χρημάτων, I, 1, 9; (5) of cause, ἀπὸ τοῦ αὐτομάτου, *at their own bidding,* I, 2, 17; ἀπὸ τοῦ αὐτοῦ σημείου, *at the same signal,* II, 5, 32.

So the phrase ἀπό (ἀφ') ἵππου means *on horseback,* but denotes that the rider's attention is directed away from the horse; contrast ἐφ' ἵππου. In composition ἀπο- denotes *from, away, back, in return,* or it may have a neg. force (see ἀποψηφίζομαι, ἀποδοκέω).

ἀποβαίνω (βαίνω), *step off,* esp. *disembark;* of events, *turn out, come true,* VII, 8, 22.

ἀποβάλλω (βάλλω), *cast away, lose.*

ἀποβιβάζω (βιβάζω, βιβάσω or βιβῶ, -εβίβασα, *make to go,* causative of βαίνω), trans., *disembark.*

ἀποβλέπω (βλέπω), *look away* (from other things) *to,* 1, 8, 14; *look* (for support), *to,* VII, 2, 33.

ἀπαγιγνώσκω (γιγνώσκω), *decide against, give up the intention of,* I, 7, 19.

ἀποδαρέντα, see ἀποδέρω.

ἀποδεδράκασιν, see ἀποδιδράσκω.

ἀποδείκνυμι (δείκνυμι), *point out, direct,* with infin., *appoint;* mid., *declare* (with or without γνώμην) foll. by ὅτι or by infin.; pass., *be declared, pointed out.*

ἀποδέρω (δέρω, δερῶ, ἔδειρα, δέδαρμαι, ἐδάρην, *flay*), *strip the hide off, flay, skin.*

ἀποδέχομαι (δέχομαι), *receive from, accept.*

ἀποδημέω, -ήσω, etc. (δῆμος), *be or go away from home.*

ἀποδιδράσκω (-διδράσκω, -δράσομαι, -έδραν, -δέδρακα, *run*), *run away, escape* (by stealth), I, 4, 8, *etc.; run away from, abandon* (acc.), VI, 4, 8.

ἀποδίδωμι (δίδωμι), *give back, render,* esp. what is due, *restore, return, pay; fulfil a promise,* I, 7, 5; mid., *sell,* VII, 2, 3.

ἀποδοκεῖ, impers. (δοκέω), *it seems best not to,* II, 3, 9.

ἀποδοῦναι, see ἀποδίδωμι.

ἀποδραίη, ἀποδρᾶναι, see ἀποδιδράσκω.

ἀποδραμοῦμαι, see ἀποτρέχω.

ἀποδύω (δύω), *strip off, spoil* (a fallen foe); mid., with 2 aor. act., *strip oneself.*

ἀποδώσει, see ἀποδίδωμι.

ἀποθανεῖν, see ἀποθνήσκω.

ἀποθνήσκω (θνήσκω), *die, be killed, be put to death.* οἱ ἀποθανόντες, *the dead.*

ἀποθύω (θύω), *sacrifice* or *offer* (in payment of a vow).

ἀποικία, -ας, ἡ (ἀπό+οἰκέω), *colony* IV, 8, 22.

ἄποικος, -ον (ἀπό+οἶκος), *away from home,* οἱ ἄποικοι, *colonists;* πόλις ἄποικος, *colony.*

ἀποκαίω or ἀποκάω (καίω), *burn off,* also of cold, IV, 5, 3, hence, *freeze off,* VII, 4, 3.

ἀποκαλέω (καλέω), *call aside.*

ἀποκάμνω (κάμνω), *grow weary, flag.*

ἀπόκειμαι (κεῖμαι), *be laid or stored away.*

ἀποκλείω (κλείω), *shut off, cut off, exclude from,* VI, 6, 13; *shut, bolt,* VII, 6, 24.

ἀποκλίνω (κλίνω, κλινῶ, etc.; cf. κλῖμαξ, *ladder,* Lat. *inclino, bend,* Eng. *lean*), intr. *turn aside,* II, 2, 16.

ἀποκόπτω (κόπτω), *cut* or *strike off, beat off, dislodge* an enemy.

ἀποκρίνομαι (κρίνω), *answer, reply.*

ἀποκρύπτω (κρύπτω), *hide from,* acc.; I, 9, 19; *conceal,* IV, 4, 11.

ἀποκτείνω (κτείνω); the pass. is supplied by ἀποθνήσκω, *kill, slay, put to death.*

ἀποκτίννυμι, a parallel form to ἀποκτείνω, only used in pres. and impf., VI, 3, 5; 5, 28.

ἀποκωλύω (κωλύω), *hinder from, prevent,* with μή and infin.

ἀπολαμβάνω (λαμβάνω), *take back, take from, receive, recover;* pass. as a military phrase, *be cut off.*

ἀπολείπω (λείπω), *leave behind, desert, abandon; leave a space,* VI, 5, 11; mid. and pass., *be left behind, fall behind.*

ἀπόλεκτος, -ον (ἀπό+λέγω), *selected, choice.*

ἀποληφθῆτε, ἀπολήψονται, see ἀπολαμβάνω.

ἀπόλλυμι (ὄλλυμι, ὀλῶ, ὤλεσα, -ολώλεκα, ὠλόμην, ὄλωλα), *destroy, kill, lose;* mid. and 2 pf. and plpf. act., *be destroyed, perish, die,* as a virtual pass., often foll. by ὑπό with the gen. of the agent.

Ἀπόλλων, -ωνος, acc. -ωνα or -ω, *Apollo,* son of Zeus and Leto, the god of prophecy, music, poetry, etc.; his most noted oracle was at Delphi (see III, 1, 6).

Ἀπολλωνία, -ας, ἡ, *Apollonia,* a town in Mysia.

Ἀπολλωνίδης, -ου, ὁ, *Apollonides,* a Lydian pretending to be a Boeotian, III, 1, 26.

ἀπολογέομαι, ἀπολογήσομαι, etc. (ἀπό+λέγω; cf. Eng. *apology), say in defense.*

ἀπολύω (λύω), *loose from, acquit.*

ἀπολωλέκατε, see ἀπόλλυμι.

ἀπομάχομαι (μάχομαι), *fight off, fight against, resist.*

ἀπόμαχος, -ον (ἀπό+μάχη), *not fighting, disabled;* οἱ ἀπόμαχοι, *the non-combatants.*

ἀπονοστέω (νοστέω, *go home,* from νόστος, *return), return home.*

ἀποπέμπω (πέμπω), *send off, send back;* esp. *send what is due, remit,* I, 1, 8; mid., *dismiss,* I, 1, 5.

ἀποπήγνυμι (πήγνυμι), *freeze, curdle.*

ἀποπηδάω (πηδάω, πηδήσω, *leap), leap down.*

ἀποπλέω (πλέω), *sail off or back, sail home.*

ἀπόπλους, -ου, ὁ (πλοῦς), *voyage back or home.*

ἀποπορεύομαι (πορεύομαι), *go away, depart.*

ἀπορέω, -ήσω (ἄπορος), *be without resource, be in doubt, at a loss,* act. and mid.; *be in want of,* with gen., I, 7, 3.

ἀπορία, -ας, ἡ (ἄπορος), *lack of resource, difficulty, perplexity; lack, want,* with gen., II, 5, 9.

ἄπορος, -ον (ἀ-priv.+πόρος), *without means or resource, at a loss, perplexed;* of roads, etc., *impassable;* of actions, *difficult;* τὸ ἄπορον, *difficulty, obstacle,* III, 2, 22; ἄπορόν ἐστι, *it is impracticable,* III, 3, 4.

ἀπόρρητος, -ον (ἀπό+verbal of εἴρω), *not to be told, secret;* ἐν ἀπορρήτῳ ποιησάμενος, *putting him under pledge of secrecy,* VII, 6, 43.

ἀπορρώξ, -ῶγος, ὁ, ἡ (cf. ῥήγνυμι, *break,* Lat. *frangere,* Eng. *break), broken off, abrupt, sheer.*

ἀποσήπομαι, with 2 perf. act. ἀποσέσηπα (σήπω, *make to rot,* cf. Eng. *antiseptic), rot off, lose by mortification.*

ἀποσκάπτω (σκάπτω, σκάψω, etc., *dig), dig off;* ἀποσκάπτει τι, *is digging some trench to cut us off,* II, 4, 4.

ἀποσκεδάννυμι (σκεδάννυμι), *scatter abroad;* mid. and pass., *be dispersed, straggle.*

ἀποσκηνόω (σκηνόω), *encamp at a distance from,* III, 4, 35.

ἀποσπάω (σπάω), *draw off or away from, withdraw;* pass., *be separated from.*

ἀποσταυρόω (σταυρόω, *fence off, from,* σταυρός), *stake off, shut off by a palisade.*

ἀποστέλλω (στέλλω), *send back.*

ἀποστερέω (στερέω), *rob, defraud,* abs. or with 2 accs.

ἀποστῆναι, see ἀφίστημι.

ἀποστρατοπεδεύομαι (στρατοπεδεύω), encamp away from, gen.
ἀποστρέφω (στρέφω), turn back, induce to return.
ἀποστροφή, -ῆς, ἡ (ἀποστρέφω), a turning back, hence, place of refuge, base for operations, II, 4, 22; VII, 6, 34.
ἀποσυλάω (συλάω, συλήσω, etc., strip, rob), strip off, rob of.
ἀποσχεῖν, ἀπόσχωμεν, see ἀπέχω.
ἀποσῴζω (σῴζω), lead back in safety.
ἀποταφρεύω (ταφρεύω, dig a trench, from τάφρος), shut off by a trench, trench off, VI, 5, 1.
ἀποτείνω (τείνω), stretch, extend.
ἀποτειχίζω (τειχίζω), wall off, shut off by a wall, II, 4, 4.
ἀποτέμνω (τέμνω), cut off; lit. or as a military phrase, cut off, intercept.
ἀποτίθημι (τίθημι), put or store away.
ἀποτίνω (τίνω, τείσω, ἔτεισα, etc., pay), pay back; mid., exact payment, requite, punish.
ἀποτμηθέντες, see ἀποτέμνω.
ἀπότομος, -ον (ἀπό+τέμνω), cut-off, sheer, steep.
ἀποτρέπω (τρέπω), turn back or away; mid., intr. turn back, turn aside.
ἀποτρέχω (τρέχω), run back, run away.
ἀποφαίνω (φαίνω), show forth; mid. and pass., appear, declare (one's own opinion), I, 6, 9.
ἀποφεύγω (φεύγω), flee away, escape (by speed, contrast ἀποδιδράσκω).
ἀπόφηναι, see ἀποφαίνω.
ἀπόφραξις, -εως, ἡ (ἀπό+φράττω, fence in, cf. Lat. farcio, stuff full), a fencing off, hence blockade.
ἀποχωρέω (χωρέω), depart, withdraw, retreat.
ἀποψηφίζομαι (ψηφίζομαι), vote against, vote in the negative, I, 4, 15.
ἀπρόθυμος, -ον (ἀ-priv.+πρόθυμος), unwilling.
ἀπροσδόκητος, -ον (ἀ-priv.+προσδοκάω), unexpected; ἐξ ἀποσδοκήτου, unexpectedly, IV, 1, 10.
ἀπροφασίστως, adv. (ἀ-priv.+προφασίζομαι, make excuses), without making excuses, without hesitation, II, 6, 10.
ἅπτω, ἅψω, etc. (Lat. aptus, fit) fasten; mid., lay hold of, touch (with gen.).
ἀπώλετο, see ἀπόλλυμι.
ἄρα, post-positive inferential part., therefore, accordingly, then, so.
ἆρα, interrog. part., ἆρα οὐ (Lat. nonne), III, 1, 18; ἆρα μή (Lat. num), VII, 6, 5.
Ἀραβία, -ας, ἡ, Arabia, the great peninsula between the Red Sea and the Persian Gulf. In the Anabasis, I, 5, 1, the name is applied to the district east of the Euphrates.
Ἀράξης, -ου, ὁ, the Araxes, a name given by Xen. to a tributary of the Euphrates, the modern Khabur.
ἀράτω, see αἴρω.
Ἀρβάκας, -ου, ὁ, Arbacas, satrap of Media.
Ἀρβάκης, -ου, ὁ, Arbaces, one of the four generals of Artaxerxes' army.
Ἀργεῖος, -α, -ον ("Αργος, τό, Argos) Argive; masc. as subst., an Argive, a native of Argos, the capital of Argolis.
ἀργός, -ον (ἀ-priv.+ἔργον), lazy, idle.
ἀργύριον, -ου, τό (dim. of ἄργυρος, silver, Lat. argentum), piece of silver, silver coin, money.
ἀργυρόπους, -οδος, ὁ, ἡ (ἄργυρος, silver+πούς), silver-footed.

ἀργυροῦς, -ᾶ, -οῦν (ἄργυρος, silver), of silver, silver.

Ἀργώ, -οῦς, ἡ, the Argo, the ship of the Argonauts.

ἄρδην, adv. (αἴρω), lit. raised up, then wholly, quite.

ἄρδω, water, irrigate.

ἀρέσκω, ἀρέσω, ἠρέσθην (√ἀρ, fit), suit, please, dat.

ἀρετή, -ῆς, ἡ (cf. ἄριστος), fitness, excellence, esp. in war, valor, II, 1, 12; magnanimity, I, 4, 9; faithfulness, service, I, 4, 8.

ἀρήγω, ἀρήξω, help, succor.

Ἀρηξίων, -ωνος, ὁ, Arexion, of Parrhasia, a soothsayer in the Greek army.

Ἀριαῖος, -ου, ὁ, Ariaeus, commander of the barbarian force under Cyrus. See the Introd., § 32.

ἀριθμός, -οῦ, ὁ, number, numbering, enumeration; extent, τῆς ὁδοῦ, II, 2, 6.

Ἀρίσταρχος, -ου, ὁ, Aristarchus, a Spartan, successor to Cleander as harmost of Byzantium.

ἀριστάω, ἀριστήσω, etc. (ἄριστον) take breakfast.

Ἀριστέας, -ου, ὁ, Aristeas, of Chios, commander of a company of light-armed troops in the Greek army.

ἀριστερός, -ά, -όν, left; ἐν ἀριστερᾷ (sc. χειρί) or ἐξ ἀριστερᾶς (sc. χειρός), on the left.

Ἀρίστιππος, -ου, ὁ, Aristippus, a Thessalian noble who raised an army for Cyrus.

ἄριστον, -ου, τό, breakfast or lunch; see the note on I, 10, 17.

ἀριστοποιέομαι (ἄριστον+ποιέω), get or prepare breakfast.

ἄριστος, -η, -ον (√ἀρ, suit, fit), sup. of ἀγαθός, best, bravest, noblest, most honorable; ἄριστα, as adv., in the best way, best.

Ἀρίστων, -ωνος, ὁ, Ariston, an Athenian in the Greek army.

Ἀριστώνυμος, -ου, ὁ, Aristonymus, a captain in the Greek army, distinguished for his bravery.

Ἀρκαδικός, -ή, -όν (Ἀρκάς), of Arcadia, Arcadian; τὸ Ἀρκαδικόν, the Arcadian force, IV, 8, 18.

Ἀρκάς, -άδος, ὁ, an Arcadian, native of Arcadia, the central state of Peloponnesus. As to the Arcadians in Cyrus' army, see VI, 2, 10.

ἀρκέω, ἀρκέσω, ἤρκεσα (Lat. arceo, cf. ἀρήγω, ἀλκή), be enough, suffice; ἀρκῶν, as adj., enough, V, 6, 1.

ἄρκτος, -ου, ἡ (akin to Lat. ursus), bear (the fem. used for both sexes); the constellation Ursa Maior, the Bear, the North.

ἅρμα, -ατος, τό, chariot, war chariot.

ἁρμάμαξα, -ης, ἡ (ἅρμα+ἅμαξα), covered carriage.

Ἀρμενία, -ας, ἡ, Armenia, the high table-land of western Asia, southeast of the Euxine.

Ἀρμένιος, -α, -ον (Ἀρμενία), belonging to Armenia, Armenian.

Ἁρμήνη, -ης, ἡ, Harmēne, a town on the Euxine near Sinōpe.

ἁρμοστής, -οῦ, ὁ (ἁρμόζω, fit, join), one who sets in order; esp. administrator, harmost, a title given to officers sent out by Sparta to govern subject states.

ἄρνειος, -α, -ον (ἀρνός, of a lamb, no nom.), of a lamb, lamb's, with κρέα, IV, 5, 31.

ἁρπαγή, -ῆς, ἡ (ἁρπάζω), plundering, plunder, pillage; καθ' ἁρπαγήν, after booty, III, 5, 2.

ἁρπάζω, ἁρπάσω, etc. (cf. Lat. rapio), snatch, seize, carry off, plunder, rob.

"Άρπασος, -ου, ὁ, the *Harpasus*, a river bounding the land of the Chalybes and the Scythīni.

'Αρταγέρσης, -ου, ὁ, *Artagerses*, a Persian noble in command of the king's mounted body-guard at Cunaxa, I, 7, 11; said to have been slain by Cyrus, I, 8, 24.

'Αρτακάμας, -α, ὁ, *Artacamas*, satrap of Phrygia.

'Αρταξέρξης, the name of several kings of Persia; in the Anabasis Artaxerxes II (called Mnemon, because of his good memory), son of Darius II and Parysatis and elder brother of Cyrus. He reigned from 405 B. C. to 362 B. C.

'Αρτάοζος, -ου, ὁ, *Artaozus*, a friend of Cyrus, who with Ariaeus proved faithless to the Greeks after Cunaxa.

'Αρταπάτης, -ου, ὁ, *Artapates*, a Persian noble, in the confidence of Cyrus, and slain over his dead body.

ἀρτάω, ἀρτήσω, etc. (cf. αἴρω?), *fasten, suspend*.

"Άρτεμις, -ιδος, ἡ, *Artemis*, daughter of Zeus and Leto, goddess of the chase, III, 2, 12; identified with the Asiatic goddess, whose temple at Ephesus was worldrenowned, V, 3, 4.

ἄρτι, adv. *just now, just*.

'Αρτίμας, -α, ὁ *Artimas*, satrap of Lydia.

ἀρτοκόπος, -ου, ὁ (ἄρτος + √ κοπ, *cook, cf*. Lat. *coquo*), *baker*.

ἄρτος, -ου, ὁ, *a loaf of bread* (wheaten or barley).

'Αρτούχας, -α, ὁ, *Artūchas*, a general in the Persian army.

'Αρύστας, -α (or -ου?), *Arystas*, an Arcadian.

'Αρχαγόρας, -α, or -ου, ὁ, *Archagoras*, an exile from Argos, a captain in the Greek army.

ἀρχαῖος, -α, -ον (ἄρχω), *old, ancient*; Κῦρον τὸν ἀρχαῖον, *Cyrus the Elder*, I, 9, 1; τὸ ἀρχαῖον, as adv., *formerly*, I, 1, 6.

ἀρχή, -ῆς, ἡ (ἄρχω), *beginning*; ἀρχήν, as adv., *in the first place*; with neg., *at all*, VII, 7, 28; *the first place*, hence, *sovereignty*, II, 1, 11; II, 3, 23, etc.; *empire*, I, 5, 9; *province*, I, 1, 2.

ἀρχηγός, -οῦ, ὁ (ἄρχω + ἄγω), *leader, commander*, rare in prose, III 1, 26.

ἀρχικός, -ή, -όν (ἄρχω), *fit to command*.

ἄρχω, ἄρξω, ἦρξα, ἦργμαι, ἤρχθην, *begin, be first*, with gen. or with infin.; *lead, command, rule, rule over*, abs., or with gen.; mid., *begin*, abs., or with gen.; *start from;* pass., *be begun, be governed, obey*; τὸ ἄρχειν, *government, sovereignty*; ὁ ἄρχων. see the word; οἱ ἀρχόμενοι, *subjects, soldiers*.

ἄρχων, -οντος, ὁ (properly partic. of ἄρχω), *ruler, commander*.

ἄρωμα, -ατος, τό, (Eng. *aroma*), in pl. *spices, fragrant herbs*.

ἀσέβεια, -ας, ἡ (see the following word), *impiety*.

ἀσεβής, -ές (ἀ-priv.+σέβομαι, *worship*), *impious, sacrilegious*.

ἀσθενέω, -ήσω, etc. (ἀσθενής), *be weak, be sick*; οἱ ἀσθενοῦντες, *the sick*, IV, 5, 19.

ἀσθενής, -ές (ἀ-priv. + σθένος *strength*), *without strength, weak*.

'Ασία, -ας, ἡ, *Asia*.

'Ασιδάτης, -ου, ὁ, *Asidates*, a wealthy Persian, captured by Xenophon.

'Ασιναῖος, -ου, ὁ ('Ασίνη, *Asine*), *an Asinaean, a man of Asine,* a town of Laconia.

ἀσινῶς, adv. (σίνομαι), *harmlessly;* in sup. ἀσινέστατα, III, 3, 3.

ἄσιτος, -ον (ἀ-priv.+σῖτος), *without food.*

ἀσκέω, ἀσκήσω (cf. Eng. *ascetic*), *practise, cultivate.*

ἀσκός, -οῦ, ὁ, *skin, leathern bag, wine-skin.*

ἄσμενος, -ον (cf. ἥδομαι), *glad,* used where in Eng. an adv. is required, *gladly, with pleasure.*

ἀσπάζομαι, ἀσπάσομαι, *greet, salute, welcome, take leave of.*

'Ασπένδιος, -ον, ὁ ("Ασπενδος, *Aspendus*), *an Aspendian,* inhabitant of Aspendus, a city in Pamphylia.

ἀσπίς, -ίδος, ἡ, *shield,* esp. the large oval shield of the Greek hoplite; by metonomy = ὁπλίτης; παρ' ἀσπίδα, *to the left,* IV, 3, 26.

'Ασσυρία, -ας, ἡ, *Assyria,* in the *Anabasis* the region about the Tigris, a province of the Persian empire. The word also designates the Assyrian empire, which flourished in the seventh century B. C.

'Ασσύριος, -α, -ον ('Ασσυρία), *Assyrian.*

ἀσταφίς, -ίδος, ἡ, pl. in collective sense, *dried grapes, raisins.*

ἀστράπτω, aor. ἤστραψα, *flash.*

ἀσφάλεια, -ας, ἡ (ἀ-priv.+σφάλλω), *security, safety.*

ἀσφαλέστατα, see ἀσφαλῶς.

ἀσφαλέστερος, see ἀσφαλής.

ἀσφαλής, -ές (ἀ-priv.+σφάλλω), *not to be tripped up, sure, secure, safe;* comp. ἀσφαλέστερος; sup., ἀσφαλέστατος; ἐν (τῷ) ἀσφαλεῖ, *in a safe place,* IV, 7, 8; so in comp., III, 2, 36; in sup., I, 8, 22.

ἄσφαλτος, -ου, ἡ (Eng. *asphalt*), *asphalt, bitumen.*

ἀσφαλῶς, adv. (ἀσφαλής), *firmly, securely, safely;* sup. ἀσφαλέστατα.

ἀσχολία, -ας, ἡ (ἀ-priv.+σχολή), *lack of leisure, occupation, engagement.*

ἀτακτέω (ἀ-priv.+τάττω), *be disorderly.*

ἄτακτος, -η, -ον (ἀ-priv.+τάττω), *in disorder.*

ἀταξία, -ας (ἀ-priv.+τάττω), *disorder, lack of discipline, insubordination.*

ἀτάρ, conj., *but, yet, however,* always standing first in its sentence.

ἀτασθαλία, -ας, ἡ, *wantonness, folly,* a poetic word, IV, 4, 14.

ἄταφος, -ον (θάπτω), *unburied.*

ἅτε, adv. (acc. neut. pl. of ὅστε), *as, inasmuch as, because,* with causal partic., IV, 2, 13 n.

ἀτέλεια, -ας, ἡ (ἀ-priv.+τέλος), *exemption from a tax or duty.*

ἀτιμάζω, ἀτιμάσω, etc. (ἄτιμος), *dishonor, disgrace.*

ἄτιμος, -ον (ἀ-priv.+τιμή), *in dishonor, without honor.*

ἀτμίζω (ἀτμός, *vapor*), *steam.*

ἀτριβής, -ές (ἀ-priv.+τριβή), *untrodden.*

'Αττικός, -ή, -όν, *of* or *belonging to Attica, Attic, Athenian.*

αὖ, post-positive adv. (cf. αὖθις and Lat., *autem*), to be variously rendered, *again, moreover, on the contrary, on his part.*

αὐαίνω, αὐανῶ, ηὔηνα, αὐάνθην (αὔω, *dry*), *dry;* mid., intrans., *dry up, wither.*

αὐθαίρετος, -ον (αὐτός+αἱρέω), *self-appointed.*

αὐθημερόν, adv. (αὐτός+ἡμέρα), *on the same day.*

αὖθις, adv. (αὖ), *again, in turn, afterwards.*

αὐλέω, αὐλήσω (αὐλός), *play the flute or pipe;* pass., of dancers, *be accompanied on the flute,* VI, 1, 11.

αὐλίζομαι, αὐλίσομαι, ηὐλισάμην or ηὐλίσθην (αὐλή, *court-yard*), *bivouac, camp in the open air, pass the night.*

αὐλός, -οῦ, ὁ, *flute, pipe.*

αὐλών, -ῶνος, ὁ, *channel, canal.*

αὔριον, adv., *tomorrow;* ἡ αὔριον (sc. ἡμέρα), *the morrow.*

αὐστηρότης, -ητος, ἡ (αὐστηρός, *dry rough,* Eng. *austere,* cf. ἀναίνω), *harshness of taste, sharpness,* V, 4, 29.

αὐτίκα, adv. (αὐτός; cf. ἡνίκα), *at the very moment, immediately,* followed by strengthening μάλα, III, 5, 11; VII, 6, 17.

αὐτόθεν, adv. (αὐτός), *from the very spot, hence, thence.*

αὐτόθι, adv. (αὐτός), *right here* or *there, on the very spot;* cf. αὐτοῦ.

αὐτοκέλευστος, -ον (αὐτός + κελεύω), *self-bidden, of one's own accord.*

αὐτοκράτωρ, -ορος, ὁ, ἡ (αὐτός + κρατέω), *one's own master, with full powers.*

αὐτόματος (αὐτός +√/μα, *think*), *of one's own accord, unbidden;* ἀπὸ (or ἐκ) τοῦ αὐτομάτου, as adv., *unbidden, voluntarily.*

αὐτομολέω, -ήσω, etc. (αὐτόμολος), *desert;* οἱ αὐτομολήσαντες, *the deserters.*

αὐτόμολος, -ον, ὁ (αὐτός +√/μολ; cf. βλώσκω), *a deserter.*

αὐτόνομος, -ον (αὐτός + νέμω), *self-governed, independent.*

αὐτός, -ή, -ό (neut. with art. ταὐτόν, I, 5, 2), intensive pron., *self;* to be variously rendered, sometimes, *by oneself, of one's own accord;* standing alone in the nom. or with nouns or prons. in any case, αὐτὸς σύ, I, 6, 7; αὐτὸς Μένων, II, 1, 5; αὐτοῦ Κύρου, I, 2, 21; αὐτοῖς τούτοις, III, 2, 4; frequently=μόνος, *alone,* III, 2, 11; IV, 7, 11; often for emphasis coupled with the reflexive, αὐτὸς τῇ ἑαυτοῦ χειρί, I, 8, 24; αὐτοὶ ἐφ' ἑαυτῶν, II, 4, 10. With possessives, τοῖς ἡμετέροις αὐτῶν φίλοις, where the intensive agrees with the gen. of the pers. pron. implied in the possessive; sometimes best rendered by *just, exactly, right;* ὑπὲρ αὐτοῦ τοῦ ἑαυτῶν στρατεύματος, *right above their own army,* III, 4, 41; in the oblique cases=the 3d pers. pron., *him, her, it, them,* used sometimes where a reflexive might have been expected, I, 1, 5; the gen. αὐτοῦ, αὐτῆς, αὐτῶν regularly takes the place of a possessive pron., *his, her, its, their.* With the art.: in the pred. posit. always intensive, αὐτῷ τῷ στρατεύματι, I, 8, 14; in the attrib. posit.=*the same,* τὰ αὐτὰ ταῦτα, *these same things,* I, 1, 7; ἐπὶ τὴν αὐτὴν τράπεζαν, IV, 5, 31. The neut. is often used of place, εἰς ταὐτό, III, 1, 30; ἐκ τοῦ αὐτοῦ, II, 4, 11; ἐν τῷ αὐτῷ, I, 8, 14; in this use, often followed by a dat., III, 1, 30.

αὐτόσε, adv. (αὐτός), *to the very place, thither.*

αὐτοῦ, adv. (αὐτός), *in the very place, there, here;* αὐτοῦ που, *somewhere here, hereabouts.*

αὐτοῦ, see ἑαυτοῦ.

αὔτως, adv. (αὐτός), only in the phrase ὡς δ' αὔτως, *in the very manner, just so*, V, 6, 9; cf. ὡσαύτως.

αὐχήν, -ένος, ὁ, *neck, isthmus*.

ἀφ', see ἀπό.

ἀφαιρέω (αἱρέω), *take away, deprive of, rob*, the person robbed standing either in acc., I, 3, 4, or the gen., IV, 4, 12; *rescue*, VI, 6, 10.

ἀφανής, -ές (φαίνω), *invisible, out of sight, hidden, unknown*.

ἀφανίζω, ἀφανιῶ, ἠφάνισα, etc. (ἀ-priv.+φαίνω), *hide, blot out, annihilate*.

ἀφειδῶς, adv. (ἀφειδής, *lavish, unsparing*), *without sparing, mercilessly*, VII, 4, 6; sup., I, 9, 13.

ἀφειστήκεσαν, see ἀφίστημι.

ἀφέξεσθαι, see ἀπέχω.

ἀφεστήξει, see ἀφίστημι.

ἀφηγέομαι (ἡγέομαι), *set forth, tell*.

ἀφήσετε, see ἀφίημι.

ἀφθονία, -ας, ἡ (ἄφθονος), *plenty, abundance*; εἰς ἀφθονίαν, *in abundance*, VII, 1, 33.

ἄφθονος, -ον (cf. φθονέω), *ungrudging, liberal*; of things, *plenteous, abundant*; ἐν ἀφθόνοις, *in abundance*, III, 2, 25; stronger, ἐν πᾶσιν ἀφθόνοις, IV, 5, 29; cf. V, 1, 10.

ἀφίημι (ἵημι), *send off* or *away, let go, set free*; of water, *let flow*; of animals, *loose*; *reject*, V, 4, 7.

ἀφικνέομαι, -ίξομαι, -ικόμην, -ῖγμαι (ἱκνέομαι), *come, arrive at, reach*.

ἀφιππεύω (ἵππευω, ἱππεύσω, etc., *ride*), *ride back* or *away*.

ἀφίστημι (ἵστημι), *cause to stand away from, lead to revolt*, VI, 6, 34; oftener (in mid., with 2 aor. and 2 perf. systems act.), *revolt, withdraw, go over to*.

ἄφοδος, -ου, ἡ (ἀπό+ὁδός), *a going away* or *back, retreat, way of escape*.

ἀφροσύνη, -ης, ἡ (ἀ-priv.+φρήν), *folly*.

ἄφρων, -ον (ἀ-priv.+φρήν), *without sense, foolish, out of one's head*, IV, 8, 20.

ἀφυλακτέω (ἀ-priv.+φυλάττω), *be off one's guard*.

ἀφύλακτος, -ον (ἀ-priv.+φυλάττω), *unguarded*.

ἀφυλάκτως, adv. (ἀφύλακτος), *unguardedly*.

'Αχαιός, -οῦ, ὁ, *a native of Achaea*, a country on the northern coast of Peloponnesus, *an Achaean*.

ἀχάριστος, -ον (ἀ-priv.+χαρίζομαι), *graceless, unpleasant, unthankful, unrewarded*, I, 9, 18; οὐκ ἀχάριστα λέγειν, *speak prettily enough*, II, 1, 13.

ἀχαρίστως, adv. (ἀχάριστος), *without thanks*, ἀχαρίστως ἔχειν, *be a thankless task*, II, 3, 18.

'Αχερουσιάς, -άδος, ἡ ('Αχέρων, Acheron), *Acherusian*; 'Αχερουσιὰς Χερρόννησος, *peninsula of Acheron*, near Heraclea on the Euxine.

ἄχθομαι, ἀχθέσομαι, ἠχθέσθην (ἄχθος, *burden, distress*), *be burdened, distressed, vexed*.

ἀχρεῖος, -ον (ἀ-priv.+χράομαι), *useless, unserviceable*.

ἄχρηστος, -ον (ἀ-priv.+χράομαι), *useless*.

ἄχρι, adv., *utterly*; ἄχρι εἰς, *all the way to*, V, 5, 4; as conj., *till, until*, II, 3, 2 n.

ἀψίνθιον, -ου, τό, *wormwood*.

B

Βαβυλών -ῶνος, ἡ (Gate of God), Babylon, the famous capital of Babylonia, built on both sides of the Euphrates.

Βαβυλωνία, -ας, ἡ (Βαβυλώνιος), Babylonia, the district in which Babylon was situated, I, 7, 1.

Βαβυλώνιος, -α, -ον (Βαβυλών), of Babylon, with χώρα.

βάδην, adv. (βαίνω), at a walk, step by step; βάδην ταχύ, in quick step, IV, 6, 25.

βαδίζω, βαδιοῦμαι, ἐβάδισα (βαίνω), walk, go.

βάθος, -ους, τό (βαθύς), depth.

βαθύς, -εῖα, -ύ, deep.

βαίνω, βήσομαι, -έβην, βέβηκα, go, walk; properly, take a step, hence in perf., stand firm, i. e., with legs apart, III, 2, 19.

βακτηρία, -ας (βαίνω), walking stick, staff.

βάλανος, -ου, ἡ (Lat. glans), acorn; ἡ βάλανος ἡ ἀπὸ τοῦ φοίνικος, date, I, 5, 10 n.

βάλλω, βαλῶ, ἔβαλον, βέβληκα, βέβλημαι, ἐβλήθην, throw, hit, pelt, the missile, if expressed, being, usually, in the dat. (means); pass., βαλλόμενοι, under fire; οἱ ἐκ χειρὸς βάλλοντες=οἱ ἀκοντισταί, III, 3, 15.

βάπτω, βάψω, ἔβαψα, βέβαμμαι, ἐβάφην (cf. Eng. baptize), dip, dip in.

βαρβαρικός, -ή, -όν (βάρβαρος), un-Greek, barbarian, barbaric; τὸ βαρβαρικόν, the Persian force (of Cyrus), I, 2, 1.

βαρβαρικῶς, adv. (βαρβαρικός), in a foreign tongue, in Persian.

βάρβαρος, -ον, adj. (imitative of the sound of an unknown tongue; Eng. barbarous; cf. Lat. balbus), foreign, barbarian, uncivilized, in sup. V, 4, 34; as a noun, barbarian, foreigner, used of all non-Greeks, but in the Anabasis, especially of the Persians.

βαρέως, adv. (βαρύς, heavy), heavily; βαρέως φέρειν, bear ill, take to heart (cf. Lat. graviter ferre), II, 1, 4; βαρέως ἀκούειν, hear with anger, II, 1, 9.

Βασίας, -ου, ὁ, Basias: (1) an Arcadian in the Greek army, killed by the Carduchi, IV, 1, 18; (2) a soothsayer from Elis, VII, 8, 10.

βασιλεία, -ας, ἡ (βασιλεύς), sovereignty, royal power, kingdom.

βασίλειος, -ον (βασιλεύς), royal, pertaining to a king; neut., βασίλεια τά, royal residence, palace.

βασιλεύς, -έως, ὁ, king, especially the king of Persia. Thus used it is a virtual title, and has no art.

βασιλεύω, βασιλεύσω, etc. (βασιλεύς), be king, rule over, abs., or with gen.

βασιλικός, -ή, -όν (βασιλεύς), royal, kingly, fit to be king.

βάσιμος, -ον (βαίνω), passable; ἕως βάσιμα ἦν, as long as he could ride, III, 4, 49.

βατός, -ή, -όν (βαίνω), passable; traversable.

βέβαιος, -α, -ον (βαίνω), steadfast, trusty.

βεβαιόω, -ώσω, etc. (βέβαιος) make firm, confirm, fulfil.

βεβηκότες, see βαίνω.

Βέλεσυς, -υος, ὁ, Belesys, a satrap of Syria and Assyria.

βέλος, -ους, τό (βάλλω), thing thrown, missile; ἔξω τῶν βελῶν, out of range.

βελτίων, -ον and **βέλτιστος**, -η, -ον (cf. βούλομαι), used as comp. and sup. of ἀγαθός, better, best in whatever respect, whether of quality, character, or rank; cf. ἀγαθός.

βῆμα, -ατος, τό (βαίνω), step, stride.
βία, -ας, ἡ, strength, force, violence; βίᾳ, by force; with gen., in spite of.
βιάζομαι, βιάσομαι, etc. (βία), force, compel, overpower; abs., thrust or obtrude oneself, VII, 8, 11.
βίαιος, -α, -ον (βία), violent, τὸ βίαιον, act of violence.
βιαίως, adv. (βίαιος), with violence; ἀκοντίζει βιαίως, dealt a heavy blow with a javelin, I, 8, 27.
βίβλος, -ου, ἡ (cf. Eng. Bible), properly the pith of the papyrus plant which, when pressed, was used as paper; hence, manuscript, book.
Βιθυνός, -ή, -όν, Bithynian; οἱ Βιθυνοί, the Bithynians. Bithynia was a district in northwestern Asia Minor, on the Euxine.
βῖκος, -ου, ὁ, a large earthen jar or vessel.
βίος, -ου, ὁ (Lat. vivus), life; means of living, V, 5, 1; VI, 4, 8.
βιοτεύω, βιοτεύσω, etc. (βίος), live.
Βισάνθη, -ης, ἡ, Bisanthe, a Thracian city on the Propontis.
Βίων, -ωνος, ὁ, Bion, a Spartan, messenger from Thibron to the Greeks.
βλάβη, -ης, ἡ (βλάπτω), hurt, harm, damage.
βλάβος, -ους, τό (βλάβη) = the foregoing, VII, 7, 28.
βλακεύω (βλάξ, slack, lazy), be slack, shirk.
βλάπτω, βλάψω, ἔβλαψα, βέβλαφα, βέβλαμμαι, ἐβλάφθην or ἐβλάβην (βλάβη), harm, hurt, injure.
βλέπω, βλέψω, etc., look, esp. look to one for help (πρός), III, 1, 36; of things, look towards, face, I, 8, 10.
βλώσκω, μολοῦμαι, ἔμολον (for μλώσκω; cf. αὐτόμολος), go, come, VII,

1, 33, an isolated occurrence of a purely poetic vb.
βοάω, βοήσομαι, ἐβόησα (βοή), shout, call out.
βοεικός, -ή, -όν (βοῦς), belonging to oxen; ζευγὸς βοεικόν, an ox-team, VII, 5, 2, 4.
βοή, -ῆς, ἡ, shout, call, cry.
βοήθεια, -ας, ἡ (βοή+θέω), help, assistance.
βοηθέω, -ήσω, etc. (βοή+θέω), run in answer to a cry for help, aid, rescue, with ἐπί and the acc., bear aid against, III, 5, 6.
βόθρος, -ου, ὁ, pit, hollow.
Βοΐσκος, -ου, ὁ, Boiscus, a Thessalian boxer.
Βοιωτία, -ας, ἡ (Βοιώτιος), Boeotia, the country in northern Greece adjoining Attica.
βοιωτιάζω (Βοιώτιος), play the Boeotian, with φωνῇ, speak the Boeotian dialect, III, 1, 26.
Βοιώτιος, -ου, and Βοιωτός, -οῦ, ὁ, a native of Boeotia, a Boeotian.
Βορέας, -ου, or Βορρᾶς, -ᾶ, ὁ, Boreas, the Northwind.
βόσκημα, -ατος, τό (βόσκω, feed), beast, in pl., cattle.
βουλεύω, βουλεύσω, etc. (βουλή), plan, devise, rarely act., II, 5, 16; commonly mid., take counsel, plan, deliberate, determine, often with obj. clause.
βουλή, -ῆς, ἡ (βουλεύω), consultation, deliberation.
βουλιμιάω, ἐβουλιμίασα (βοῦς+λιμός), suffer from boulimy or ravenous hunger, IV, 5, 7, 8 n.
βούλομαι, βουλήσομαι, βεβούλημαι, ἐβουλήθην (cf. Lat. volo, Eng. will), will, wish; cf. ἐθέλω; prefer, choose, II, 6, 6; τὸν βουλόμενον, him that wishes, whoever wishes, I, 3, 9.

βουπόρος, -ον (βοῦς+√περ), lit. *piercing an ox*; with ὀβελίσκος, *a spit large enough for a whole ox*, VII, 8, 14.

βοῦς, βοός, ὁ, ἡ (Lat. *bos*), *ox, cow; ox-hide*, IV, 5, 14.

βραδέως, adv. (βραδύς), *slowly*.

βραδύς, -εῖα, -ύ, *slow*; sup. βραδύτατος, VII, 3, 37.

βραχύς, -εῖα, -ύ (*cf.* Lat. *brevis*), *short*, whether of space or time; πέτονται βραχύ, *they fly but a little way*, I, 5, 3; βραχύτερα ἐτόξευον, *did not shoot as far as*, III, 3, 7; ἐπὶ βραχὺ ἐξικνοῦνται, *they have a short range*, III, 3, 17.

βρέχω, βρέξω, ἐβρεξα, etc., *wet*, in pass., *be* or *get wet*.

βροντή, -ῆς, ἡ (for βρομτή; *cf.* βρέμω, *roar*), *thunder, thunder-clap*.

βρωτός, -ή, -όν (βιβρώσκω, *eat*), *eatable*.

Βυζάντιον, -ου, τό, *Byzantium*, an important city on the Bosporus, the modern Constantinople.

Βυζάντιος, -α, -ον, *belonging to Byzantium*; οἱ Βυζάντιοι, *the Byzantines*.

βωμός, -οῦ, ὁ (βαίνω), *a raised place*, esp. *altar*.

Γ

γαλήνη, -ης, ἡ, *calm*.

γαμέω, γαμῶ, ἔγημα, γεγάμηκα, γεγάμημαι, *marry*, act., of the man, mid. and pass., of the woman.

γάμος, -ου, ὁ (*cf.* Eng. *bigamy*), *wedding, marriage*; ἄγειν ἐπὶ γαμῷ, *take home as one's wife*, II, 4, 8.

Γάνος, -ου, ἡ, *Ganus*, a Thracian city on the Propontis.

γάρ, post-pos. causal conj. (γέ+ἄρα), giving, as a rule, the reason or explanation of a statement made or implied in the context, or confirming it; to be variously rendered, *for, because, namely, now*; in questions, *then*, I, 7, 9, etc.; often with ellipsis, καὶ γάρ, *and . . . . for*, I, 1, 6 n.; ἀλλὰ γάρ *but* (*no more of this*) *for but the fact is*, III, 2, 25 n; καὶ γὰρ οὖν, *and therefore*, 1, 9, 8.

γαστήρ, -ρός, ἡ (Eng. *gastric*), *belly*

γαυλικός, -ή, -όν (γαῦλος, *merchantman*), *of* or *for a merchant vessel*; γαυλικὰ χρήματα, *cargoes*, V, 8, 1.

Γαυλίτης, -ου, ὁ, *Gaulītes*, a Samian exile.

γέ, intensive particle, enclitic and post-pos. emphasizing the preceding word or the clause in which it stands, *yes, certainly, surely, at least*; often best rendered by emphasis. γε is often added to other particles, γε μήν, γε μέντοι, γε δή, etc. For these Eng. has no equivalents.

γεγενῆσθαι, **γέγονα**, see γίγνομαι.

γείτων, -ονος, ὁ (γῆ), *neighbor*.

γελάω, γελάσομαι, ἐγέλασα, ἐγελάσθην, *laugh*, abs. or with ἐπί and dat.

γελοῖος, -α, -ον (γελάω), *laughable, absurd*.

γέλως, -ωτος, ὁ (γελάω), *laughter*.

γελωτοποιός, -οῦ, ὁ (γέλως+ποιέω), *jester, clown*.

γέμω, only in pres. and imperf., *be full of*, gen.

γενεά, -ᾶς, ἡ (√γεν), *birth*.

γενειάω (γένειον, *chin, beard*), *grow* or *wear a beard*.

γενναιότης, -ητος, ἡ (γενναῖος, *of good birth*), *nobility, generosity*.

γένος, -ους, τό (γίγνομαι, *cf.* Lat. *genus*), *family, race*.

γεραιός, -ά, -όν (γέρων), *old*; comp., οἱ γεραίτεροι, *elders*, V, 7, 17.

γερόντιον, -ου, τό, (dim. of γέρων), *feeble old man*.

γέρρον, -ου, τό, *wicker shield*.

γερροφόρος, -ον (γέρρον+φέρω), *bearing* or *armed with a wicker shield*.

γέρων, -οντος, ὁ (akin to Eng. *gray*), *old man*.

γεύω, γεύσω, ἔγευσα, γέγευμαι (Lat. *gusto*, *taste*, Eng. *choose*), *give a taste of*; mid., *taste*, abs. or with gen.

γέφυρα, -ας, ἡ, *bridge, embankment*, VI, 5, 22; γέφυρα ἐζευγμένη πλοίοις, *pontoon bridge*, I, 2, 5.

γεώδης, -ες (γῆ+εἶδος) *earthy, loamy*.

γῆ, γῆς, ἡ, *earth, land, country*; καὶ κατὰ γῆν καὶ κατὰ θάλατταν, *by land and sea*, I, 1, 7; παρὰ γῆν, *along the coast*.

γήϊνος, -η, -ον (γῆ), *of earth, earthen*.

γήλοφος, -ου, ὁ (γῆ+λόφος), *hill, hillock*.

γῆρας, γήρως, τό (γέρων), *old age*.

γίγνομαι, γενήσομαι, ἐγενόμην, γέγονα, γεγένημαι (√γεν), *become, be*; of men, *be born*, with gen. or with ἀπό and the gen., *become, get*; of things, *become, be made*; of events, *take place, happen*, the translation varying with the context; of day, *dawn*, II, 2, 13; of afternoon, *draw on*, I, 8, 8; of rain or snow, *fall*, IV, 1, 15; of numbers, *amount to*, I, 2, 9; of sounds, *arise*, I, 8, 2; of sacrifices, *be favorable*, II, 2, 3; often =the pass. of ποιέω or other vbs.; thus of oaths, *be exchanged, be given*, II, 2, 10; of taxes, *be paid in*, I, 1, 8; rarely, with infin., *be possible*, I, 9, 13; with predicate adj., *show oneself*, I, 6, 8. ἐν ἑαυτῷ ἐγένετο, *came to his senses*, I, 5, 17; οἱ εἰς τριάκοντα ἔτη γεγονότες, *those thirty years old and under*, II, 3, 12.

γιγνώσκω, γνώσομαι, ἔγνων, ἔγνωκα, ἔγνωσμαι, ἐγνώσθην (cf. Lat. *nosco*, Eng., *know*), *know, learn, recognize*.

Γλοῦς, -οῦ, ὁ, *Glus*, son of Tamos, an Egyptian who deserted Cyrus' cause after the battle of Cunaxa.

Γνήσιππος, -ου, ὁ, *Gnesippus*, an Athenian captain.

γνοίη, see γιγνώσκω.

γνώμη, -ης, ἡ (γιγνώσκω), *opinion, judgment, purpose*; ἄνευ τῆς Κύρου γνώμης, *without Cyrus' consent*, I, 3, 13; ἐμπιμπλάναι τὴν γνώμην τινός, *satisfy one's desires*, I, 7, 8; πρός τινα τὴν γνώμην ἔχειν, *be devoted to one*, II, 5, 29.

γνῶναι, γνώσεσθε, see γιγνώσκω.

Γογγύλος, -ου, ὁ, (1) *Gongylus*, a Greek living at Pergamus; (2) his son of the same name.

γοητεύω, ἐγοητεύθην (γόης, *sorcerer*), *bewitch*.

γονεύς, -έως, ὁ (γίγνομαι), *begetter, father*; in pl. *parents*, III, 1, 3.

γόνυ, γόνατος, τό (cf. Lat. *genu*, Eng. *knee*), *knee*; of reeds, etc., *knot, joint*, IV, 5, 26.

Γοργίας, -ου, ὁ, *Gorgias*, of Leontīni in Sicily, a famous rhetorician and "sophist," teacher of Proxenus.

Γοργίων, -ωνος, ὁ, *Gorgion*, a son of the elder Gongylus.

γοῦν, post-positive particle (γε+οὖν), *at least, at any rate, certainly*.

γρᾴδιον, -ου, τό (dim. of γραῦς, *old woman*; cf. γέρων), *feeble old woman*.

γράμμα, -ατος, τό (γράφω), *what is written, letter of the alphabet*; pl., *inscription*, V, 3, 13.

γράφω, γράψω, ἔγραψα, γέγραφα, γέγραμμαι, ἐγράφην (Lat. *scribo*, Eng.

grave, graphic, etc.) mark, draw, paint; most commonly, *write.*

γυμνάζω, γυμνάσω, etc. (γυμνός), *exercise.*

γυμνής, -ῆτος, ὁ (γυμνός) *light-armed foot-soldier.*

Γυμνιάς, -άδος, ἡ, *Gymnias,* a city in the territory of the Scythīni.

γυμνικός, -ή, -όν (γυμνός), *gymnastic.*

γυμνός, -ή, -όν (Eng. *gymnast*), *naked, lightly clad, without one's cloak;* of soldiers, *without armour, defenseless.*

γυνή, γυναικός, ἡ, (√γεν, γίγνομαι, Eng. *queen*), *woman, wife.*

Γωβρύας, -ου, ὁ, *Gobryas,* one of the four generals of Artaxerxes army.

Δ

δ', by elision for δέ.

δάκνω, δήξομαι, ἔδακον, δέδηγμαι, ἐδήχθην, *bite.*

δακρύω, δακρύσω, etc. (δάκρυ, *tear; cf.* Lat. *lacrima,* Eng. *tear*), *shed tears, weep.*

δακτύλιος, -ου, ὁ (*cf.* δάκτυλος), *ring.*

δάκτυλος, -ου, ὁ (δείκνυμι), *finger;* of the foot, *toe.*

Δαμάρατος, -ου, ὁ, *Demarātus,* king of Sparta, who, when deposed, fled to Persia. He accompanied Xerxes on his expedition against Greece.

Δάνα, τά, *Dana,* a city in southern Cappadocia.

δαπανάω, δαπανήσω, etc., *spend, expend,* of money, I, 1, 8; of goods, *consume,* VII, 6, 31.

δάπεδον, -ου, τό, *earth, ground,* IV, 5, 6, a poetic word.

Δαρδανεύς, -έως, ὁ (Δάρδανος, *Dardanus*), a *Dardanian,* native of Dardanus in the Troad.

Δάρδας, -ατος, ὁ, *Dardas,* a river in Syria.

δαρεικός, -οῦ, ὁ (Δαρεῖος?), *daric,* a Persian gold coin, worth about $5.40, but exchanged for 20 Attic drachmae, I, 7, 18 n.

Δαρεῖος, -ου, ὁ, *Darīus,* a common name of Persian kings; in the *Anabasis Darīus II* (named Ὦχος, but called ὁ νόθος, as he was a natural son of Artaxerxes I), who reigned from 425 to 405 B.C.

δάσμευσις, -εως, ὁ (δατέομαι, *divide*), *distribution.*

δασμός, -οῦ, ὁ (δατέομαι, *divide*), lit., *division, share;* hence, *tribute, tax,* paid in money or in kind.

δασύς, -εῖα, -ύ (*cf.* Lat. *densus, thick*), *thick, thickly grown with* (gen. or dat.), II, 4, 14; of hides, *shaggy,* IV, 7, 22; τὸ δασύ, *thicket, copse,* IV, 7, 7.

Δαφναγόρας, -ου, ὁ, *Daphnagoras,* a Mysian.

δαψιλής, -ές, *plentiful, abundant.*

δέ, post-pos. conj., *but, and;* generally adversative, but less strongly so than ἀλλά. δέ is generally the second word in its clause, although it may be further postponed; it is commonly balanced by μέν in a preceding clause, but not necessarily (I, 7, 5); sometimes it occurs in an apodosis, V, 6, 20, *e. g.,* a survival of older co-ordination. When it is combined with καί, each word has its own force, δέ connective, καί intensive, καί . . . δέ, I, 1, 2; δὲ καί, I, 2, 3.

-δε, a suffix added: (1) to names of places, generally in the acc., to denote motion toward, *-ward, to;* οἴκαδε, *homeward;* (2) to demonstrative prons. for emphasis, ὅδε, τοσόσδε, etc.

δεδιώς, see δείδω.

δεδογμένα, see δοκέω.

δέδοικα, see δείδω.

δεδομέναι, see δίδωμι.

δέῃ, δεηθῆναι, δεῖ, see δέω, lack.

δείδω, a pres. unused in Attic, from which we have perf. δέδια, or δέδοικα (with pres. force), and aor. ἔδεισα, etc., be afraid, fear; the aor. is regularly ingressive, be seized with fear, I, 8, 24.

δείκνυμι, δείξω, ἔδειξα, δέδειχα, δέδειγμαι, ἐδείχθην (cf. old Lat. deico = dico), point out, show; make signs to, IV, 5, 33.

δείλη, -ης, ἡ, afternoon (early or late), evening, I, 8, 8 n; ἀμφὶ δείλην, toward evening, II, 2, 14.

δειλός, -ή, -όν (δείδω), cowardly, timid.

δεινός, -ή, -όν (δείδω), terrible, horrible, awful, severe; τὸ δεινόν, peril, danger; clever, skilful, I, 9, 19, etc.; δεινότατα ποιεῖν τινα, treat with outrageous indignity, V, 7, 23; cf. κακῶς ποιεῖν τινα.

δεινῶς, adv. (δεινός) terribly, dreadfully; ἔχειν δεινῶς, be in a terrible plight.

δειπνέω, δειπνήσω, etc., dine.

δεῖπνον, -ου, τό, the principal meal of the day, evening meal, dinner.

δειπνοποιέω (δεῖπνον+ποιέω), get dinner, mid., dine.

δείσας, δείσῃς, see δείδω.

δεῖσθαι, see δέω, lack.

δέκα, indecl. (Lat., decem), ten.

δεκαπέντε, indecl. (δέκα+πέντε), fifteen.

δεκατεύω (δέκατος), exact the tenth or tithe.

δέκατος, -η, -ον (δέκα), tenth; ἡ δεκάτη, tithe.

Δέλτα, τό, indecl. (Eng. delta), the Delta, a peninsula in Thrace, so called from its triangular shape.

δελφίς, -ῖνος, ὁ, dolphin.

Δελφοί, -ῶν, οἱ, Delphi, a town of Phocis, famed for its oracle of Apollo.

δένδρον, -ου, τό, dat. pl. δένδροις or δένδρεσσι, tree.

δέξασθαι, see δέχομαι.

δεξιόομαι, δεξιώσομαι, ἐδεξιωσάμην (δεξιά), give the right hand, greet, welcome.

δεξιός, -ά, -όν (cf. Lat. dexter), right, on the right; the noun is often omitted, ἐν τῇ δεξιᾷ, in the right hand, II, 3, 11; ἐν δεξιᾷ, on the right, I, 5, 1; δεξιὰν (δεξιὰς) δοῦναι, give the right hand (as a pledge), promise, II, 3, 28; cf. I, 6, 6; τὸ δεξιόν (with or without κέρας), the right wing, the right, I, 2, 15; cf. I, 7, 1. In divination the right was the propitious side; αἰετὸς δεξιός, VI, 1, 23.

Δέξιππος, -ου, ὁ, Dexippus, a faithless Laconian.

δέοι, δέομαι, δέον, see δέω, lack.

Δερκυλίδας, -α, ὁ, Dercylidas, a Spartan admiral.

δέρμα, -ατος, τό (δέρω, flay), skin, hide.

Δέρνης, -ου, ὁ, Dernes, satrap of Phoenicia and Arabia.

δεσμός, -οῦ, ὁ, but pl. often δεσμά (δέω), band, halter, strap.

δεσπότης, -ου, ὁ (whence Eng. despot), master, lord.

δεῦρο, adv., hither, here.

δεύτερος, -α, -ον (δύο), second; as adv., (τὸ) δεύτερον, for the second time.

δέχομαι, δέξομαι, etc., receive, accept; of friends, receive hospitably, welcome; of foes, receive or *await the attack of;* εἰς χεῖρας δέχεσθαί τινα, *come to close quarters with one,* IV, 3, 31.

δέω, δήσω, ἔδησα, δέδεκα, δέδεμαι, ἐδέθην, *bind, tie, fetter.*

δέω, δεήσω, ἐδέησα, δεδέηκα, δεδέημαι, ἐδεήθην, *lack, want, need:* (1) pers., rare in act., ὀλίγου δεῖν, with infin., *lack little of being,* I, 5, 14; so οὐ πολλοῦ δεῖν, V, 4, 32; common in mid., abs., or with gen.; also, *wish, desire,* with gen., with acc. of inner obj. (τι etc.), or with acc. and infin. *beg, ask,* with gen. of pers. and infin.; (2) impers. (δεῖ, ἔδει, δέῃ, δέοι, δεῖν, δέον), *there is need, one must,* with infin. expressed or understood; so with acc. and infin.; in III, 4, 35 (see the note) we have apparently dat. and infin.; with gen. of the thing needed, II, 3, 5. εἰς τὸ δέον, *satisfactorily,* I, 3, 8; αὐτὸ τὸ δέον, *the very thing we want,* IV, 7, 7; τί δεῖ, *what need is there?* II, 1, 10.

δή, post-positive particle with intensive force, emphasizing as a rule the immediately preceding word, and often best rendered by emphasis; *aye, now, indeed, truly, exactly,* sometimes with contemptuous tone; often with imvs., II, 2, 10, or with superlatives, I, 9, 18.

δῆλος, -η, -ον, *plain, clear, evident, manifest;* δῆλον ἦν ὅτι, *it was clear that,* II, 3, 6; δῆλον ὅτι as adv. *clearly, evidently,* I, 3, 9; often in pers. construction with partic., δῆλος ἦν ἀνιώμενος, *was manifestly troubled or distressed,* I, 2, 11.

δηλόω, δηλώσω, etc. (δῆλος), *make clear, make known, show.*

δημαγωγέω, δημαγωγήσω, etc. (δῆμος, *people*+ἄγω), *play the demagogue, curry favor with* (acc.), VII, 6, 4.

Δημοκράτης, -ους, ὁ, *Democrates* of Temnus, a scout.

δημόσιος, -α, -ον (δῆμος, *the people,* cf. Eng. *democracy*), *belonging to the people, public,* τὰ δημόσια, *public money,* IV, 6, 16.

δηόω, δηώσω, ἐδῄωσα (epic δήϊος, *hostile*), *lay waste, ravage.*

δήπου, adv. (δή+που), *surely, of course.*

δῆσαι, see δέω, *bind.*

δηχθείς, see δάκνω.

διά (by elision δι'), prep. with gen. or acc., *through:* (1) with gen., *through, throughout, during, by means of,* of place, of means, or of time; often forming adv. phrases, διὰ ταχέων, *quickly,* I, 5, 9; διὰ σκότους, *in darkness,* II, 5, 9; διὰ φιλίας ἰέναι with dat., *enter upon friendship with,* III, 2, 8; cf. διὰ παντὸς πολέμου ἰέναι, *ibid.;* (2) with acc., *through, on account of, for the sake of, thanks to,* often with art. and infin., *on account of the fact that, because,* I, 7, 5; διὰ τοῦτο, *for this reason,* I, 7, 3; πολλὰ δι' ἅ, *many reasons why,* I, 3, 15. In composition, besides the literal meaning δια- may denote thoroughness (*through and through*), and it often means *apart.*

Δία, Διί, Διός, see Ζεύς.

διαβαίνω (βαίνω), *take a step,* or *stride,* IV, 3, 8; generally trans., *go over, go through, cross.*

διαβάλλω (βάλλω), properly, *throw across,* but in the *Anabasis* always, *slander, calumniate, accuse falsely.*

διαβάς, see διαβαίνω.
διάβασις, -εως, ἡ (διαβαίνω), a crossing, then, means of crossing (ford, bridge, etc.), or place of crossing.
διαβατέος, -α, -ον (verbal of διαβαίνω), that must be crossed.
διαβατός, -ή, -όν (verbal from διαβαίνω), crossable, fordable.
διαβεβηκότας, see διαβαίνω.
διαβιβάζω (βιβάζω, βιβάσω, or βιβῶ, etc., make go), make go across, transport across.
διαβολή, -ῆς, ἡ (διαβάλλω), slander, calumny, false charges.
διαγγέλλω (ἀγγέλλω), bear word through, report, pass the word.
διαγελάω (γελάω), laugh to scorn.
διαγίγνομαι (γίγνομαι), get through, pass (of time), continue, live, exist.
διαγκυλόομαι, perf. διηγκύλωμαι (cf. ἐναγκυλάω), hold the javelin by the thong, ready for casting.
διάγω (ἄγω), carry through, or across, transport; of time, spend, live; with partic., ἐλπίδας λέγων διῆγε, kept constantly talking of his hopes, I, 2, 11.
διαγωνίζομαι (ἀγωνίζομαι), strive earnestly, vie with (πρὸς).
διαδέχομαι (δέχομαι), receive at intervals or in succession; εἰ μὴ θηρῷεν διαδεχόμενοι, if they did not relieve one another in the chase, I, 5, 2.
διαδίδωμι (δίδωμι), distribute.
διάδοχος, -ον, ὁ (διαδέχομαι), successor.
διαζεύγνυμι (ζεύγνυμι), separate.
διαθεάομαι (θεάομαι), look through, observe, consider.
διαιθριάζω (αἰθρία, clear sky), be clearing up (of weather).
διαιρέω (αἱρέω), tear apart, destroy.

διάκειμαι (κεῖμαι), be disposed, feel; ἄμεινον ὑμῖν διακείσεται, it will be better for you, VII, 3, 17.
διακελεύομαι (κελεύω), urge on, encourage.
διακινδυνεύω (κινδυνεύω), venture all, risk a battle.
διακλάω (κλάω, break; cf. Eng. iconoclast), break in two, or in pieces.
διακονέω (διάκονος, servant, Eng. deacon), serve at table.
διακόπτω (κόπτω), cut through, cut in pieces.
διακόσιοι -αι, -α (δύο+ἑκατόν), two hundred.
διακρίνω (κρίνω), discern between, decide.
διαλαγχάνω (λαγχάνω), distribute by lot.
διαλαμβάνω (λαμβάνω), take separately, IV, 1, 23; divide, V, 3, 4.
διαλέγομαι, διαλέξομαι, διείλεγμαι, διελέχθην (λέγω), talk with, converse with, dat.; discuss.
διαλείπω (λείπω), leave a space between, be stationed at intervals, stand apart; τὸ διαλεῖπον, space between, gap, interval, IV, 8, 13.
διαμάχομαι (μάχομαι), fight it out.
διαμένω (μένω), stay through to the end, remain.
διαμετρέω (μετρέω), measure out; mid., serve out rations.
διαμπερές, adv. (διά+ √περ), straight through.
διανέμω (νέμω), divide or distribute among.
διανοέομαι (διά+νοῦς), intend, purpose, mean.
διάνοια, -ας, ἡ (διά+νοῦς), purpose, intention.
διαπέμπω (πέμπω), send in different directions, distribute.
διαπλέω (πλέω), sail across.

διαπολεμέω (πολεμέω), *war or fight to the end, fight it out.*
διαπορεύω (πορεύω), *carry across;* mid., *march through.*
διαπορέω (ἀπορέω), *be utterly at a loss.*
διαπράττω (πράττω), *work out, accomplish, settle, arrange, negotiate,* act. or mid.
διαρπάζω (ἁρπάζω), *lay waste, sack, plunder,* stronger than the simple vb.
διαρρέω (ῥέω), *flow through.*
διαρρίπτω and **διαρριπτέω** (ῥίπτω), *throw about, scatter.*
διάρριψις, -εως, ἡ (διαρρίπτω), *a scattering around.*
διασημαίνω (σημαίνω), *indicate clearly, announce.*
διασκηνέω (σκηνέω), *encamp apart, go into separate quarters.*
διασκηνητέον (verbal of διασκηνέω), *one must encamp apart.*
διασκηνόω (σκηνόω), *encamp or be encamped apart.*
διασπάω (σπάω), *draw apart,* in the *Anabasis* only pass., *be scattered, dispersed.*
διασπείρω (σπείρω), *scatter about* (as seed); in the *Anabasis* only of soldiers, *be scattered, dispersed.*
διασφενδονάω (σφενδονάω), *hurl in all directions* (as from a sling).
διάσχῃ, see διέχω.
διασῴζω (σῴζω), *bring through safely, save, preserve;* pass., *come through safely, arrive safely at* (πρός).
διατάττω (τάττω), *draw up in array;* pass., *be stationed at intervals.*
διατείνω (τείνω), *stretch out;* mid., *do one's utmost.*
διατελέω (τελέω), *bring to an end, complete;* with or without ὁδόν, *reach, arrive at;* with partic. *continue to do.*
διατήκω (τήκω), *melt;* pass., intrans., *melt away.*
διατίθημι (τίθημι), *arrange, manage, dispose, treat;* mid., *dispose of one's own, sell.*
διατρέφω (τρέφω), *nourish, support.*
διατριβή, -ῆς, ἡ (διατρίβω), *delay.*
διατρίβω (τρίβω, τρίψω, ἔτριψα, etc., *rub*), *rub through, waste, spend,* of time; abs. *waste time, delay.*
διαφαίνω (φαίνω), *show through,* pass., *shine* or *be seen through;* impers. διεφάνη, *light shone through,* VII, 8, 14.
διαφανῶς, adv. (φαίνω), *clearly, plainly.*
διαφερόντως, adv. (from partic. διαφέρων), *pre-eminently,*
διαφέρω (φέρω), *bear through or apart;* intrans., *differ, be different from, surpass* (gen.); mid., *be at variance, quarrel;* πολὺ διέφερεν, *it was a very different thing,* III, 4, 33.
διαφεύγω (φεύγω), *slip through, escape.*
διαφθείρω (φθείρω), *destroy or corrupt utterly, bribe, spoil.*
διάφορος, -ον (διαφέρω), *different,* esp. *at variance with;* τὸ διάφορον, *disagreement.*
διαφυή, -ῆς, ἡ (διά+φύω), *a growth between, division.*
διαχειμάζω, -άσω, etc. (χεῖμα, *winter;* cf. χιών), *spend the winter.*
διαχειρίζω (χειρίζω, *handle*), *manage, administer.*
διαχωρέω (χωρέω), *go through;* κάτω διεχώρει αὐτοῖς, *they suffered from diarrhoea,* IV, 8, 20.
διδάσκαλος, -ον, ὁ (διδάσκω), *teacher, schoolmaster.*

διδάσκω, διδάξω, ἐδίδαξα, etc., *teach, show, inform;* pass., *learn.*

δίδημι, 3 pers. pl. διδέασι (epic for δέω), *bind, tie up.*

δίδωμι, δώσω, ἔδωκα, δέδωκα, δέδομαι, ἐδόθην (cf. Lat. *do*), *give* (in pres. and imperf. sometimes, *offer*), *grant, permit, bestow, pay; give to wife;* of the gods, *ordain;* so the pass. δέδοται, *it is ordained, is permitted,* VI, 6, 36; δίκην διδόναι, etc., *pay the penalty,* II, 6, 21. The partic. δούς may sometimes be rendered *with* (cf. ἔχων and λαβών), IV, 4, 15.

διείργω (εἴργω), *keep apart, cut off.*

διελαύνω (ἐλαύνω), *drive, ride* or *march through.*

διελόντες, see διαιρέω.

διέρχομαι (ἔρχομαι), *go* or *march through, traverse;* of a rumor, *spread abroad.*

διεσπάρθαι, see διασπείρω.

διέχω (ἔχω), *hold apart, separate;* τὸ διέχον, *the space between, interval,* III, 4, 22; intr., *be apart* or *separate,* I, 8, 17.

διηγέομαι (ἡγέομαι), *set out in detail, tell.*

διηγκυλωμένους, see διαγκυλόομαι.

διήλασε, see διελαύνω.

δίιημι (ἵημι), *send through, let go through, grant a passage.*

διίστημι (ἵστημι), *set apart;* mid. and 2 aor. act. intr., *stand apart, stand at intervals, open ranks.*

δίκαιος, -α, -ον (δίκη), *fair, right, just, lawful;* δίκαιον (ἐστι), with acc. and infin., *it is right that,* II, 5, 41; so in pers. constr., δικαιοτάτους, *most deserving* (to be invited), VI, 1, 3; τὸ δίκαιον, *justice,* in pl., *one's rights, one's deserts,* V, 1, 15; ἐκ τοῦ δικαίου, *justly,* I, 9, 19; so σὺν τῷ δικαίῳ, II, 6, 18; παρὰ τὸ δίκαιον, *unjustly,* V, 8, 17.

δικαιοσύνη, -ης, ἡ (δίκαιος), *justice.*

δικαιότης, -ητος, ἡ (δίκαιος), *justice.*

δικαίως, adv. (δίκαιος), *justly, rightly, fitly.*

δικαστής, -οῦ, ὁ (δικάζω, *judge,* from δίκη), *judge, juryman.*

δίκη, -ης, ἡ (δείκνυμι), *justice, right, one's deserts, satisfaction* (to one wronged), *penalty* (for the wrongdoer), *reckoning, trial;* ἔχει τὴν δίκην, *has his deserts,* II, 5, 38, but ἱκανὴν νομίζω δίκην ἔχειν, *I consider that I am abundantly satisfied,* VII, 4, 24; δίκην ἐπιθεῖναι or λαβεῖν, *inflict punishment;* δίκην δοῦναι, *pay the penalty;* so δίκην ὑπέχειν, VI, 6, 15; but in V, 8, 1, *render account.*

διμοιρία, -ας, ἡ (δύο+μοῖρα, *portion*), *double share* or *portion.*

δινέω (δίνη, *whirlpool*), *whirl around;* mid. intrans., VI, 1, 9.

διό (i.e. δι' ὅ), *on account of which, wherefore.*

δίοδος, -ου, ἡ (διὰ + ὁδός), *way through, passage.*

διοράω (ὁράω), *see through.*

διορύττω (ὀρύττω), *dig through.*

διότι (δι' ὅτι), *on account of which, because.*

δίπηχυς, -υ (δύο+πῆχυς), *two cubits long.*

διπλάσιος, -α, -ον (διπλάζω, *double,* from δύο+ √πλα), *twofold, twice as great, as much, as many* etc.; διπλάσιον, as adv., *twice as far.*

δίπλεθρος, -ον (δύο+πλέθρον), *of two plethra;* with εὖρος, *two plethra wide,* IV, 3, 1.

διπλοῦς, -ῆ, -οῦν (δύο+ √πλα), *twofold, double.*

δίς, numeral adv. (δύο), *twice;* in the *Anabasis* only in composition.

δισχίλιοι, -αι, -α (δύο+χίλιοι), *two thousand.*

διφθέρα, -ας, ἡ (*cf.* Eng. *diphtheria*), *a tanned skin* or *hide;* hence, *a leathern bag,* V, 2, 12.

διφθέρινος, -η, -ον (διφθέρα), *made of hide,* or *leather.*

δίφρος, -ου, ὁ (δύο+φέρω), lit., *holding two; the body* (of a chariot) on which the driver and the warrior stood.

δίχα, adv. (δύο), *in two parts.*

διψάω (δίψα, *thirst*), *be thirsty.*

διωκτέον (verbal of διώκω), *one must pursue.*

διώκω, διώξω (or -ομαι), ἐδίωξα, δεδίωχα, *pursue, chase;* intr., *speed, make haste.*

δίωξις, -εως, ἡ (διώκω), *pursuit.*

διῶρυξ, -υχος, ἡ (διορύττω), *ditch, canal.*

δόγμα, -ατος, τό (δοκέω), *what seems good, opinion, decree, ordinance.*

δοθῆναι, see δίδωμι.

δοκέω, δόξω, ἔδοξα, δέδογμαι, ἐδόχθην (*cf.* Lat. *decet*), *think, consider, suppose,* an uncommon use in Attic, though not rare in the *Anabasis,* I, 7, 1; far more commonly intrans., *seem, appear;* also, *seem good,* hence *be determined, resolved;* in this use it is either pers. or impers.; μοι δοκῶ, *methinks,* I, 7, 4; ἔδοξε ταῦτα, *this was decided on,* I, 3, 20; *cf.* τὰ δόξαντα τῇ στρατιᾷ, *ibid.,* τὸ δόξαν, *the resolution,* VI, 1, 18; so τὰ δεδογμένα, III, 2, 39; δόξαν δὲ ταῦτα, *when this was resolved on* (acc. abs.), IV, 1, 13 n.

δοκιμάζω, δοκιμάσω (δοκέω), *test, approve.*

δόλιχος, -ου, ὁ (δολιχός, *long*), *long race* or *course,* as contrasted with the στάδιον. Its length varied, IV, 8, 27 n.

Δόλοπες, -ων, οἱ, *Dolopians,* a Thessalian people.

δόλος, -ου, ὁ (*cf.* Lat., *dolus, deceit*), *deceit, guile.*

δόξα, -ης, ἡ (δοκέω), *opinion, expectation, reputation, glory;* παρὰ τὴν δόξαν, *contrary to his expectations,* II, 1, 18.

δοράτιον, -ου, τό (δόρυ), *small spear;* in VI, 4, 23, *pole* (for carrying booty).

δορκάς, -άδος, ἡ (δέρκομαι, *see*), *gazelle* (so named from its large bright eyes).

δορπηστός, -οῦ, ὁ (δόρπον, *evening meal*), *supper time.*

δόρυ, -ατος, τό (akin to δρῦς, *oak,* Eng. *tree*), *stem* (of a sapling), then *spear-shaft, spear;* ἐπὶ δόρυ; *to the right,* IV, 3, 29; (τὰ δόρατα) εἰς προβολὴν καθέντας, *lowering their spears for the charge,* VI, 5, 25; *cf.* 27.

δορυφόρος, -ου, ὁ (δόρυ+φέρω), *spear bearer;* in the *Anabasis, pole-bearer* (*i. e.* for carrying booty), V, 2, 4; *cf.* δοράτιον.

δουλεία, -ας, ἡ (δοῦλος), *slavery, servitude.*

δουλεύω, δουλεύσω, etc. (δοῦλος), *be a slave.*

δοῦλος, -ου, ὁ, *slave,* lit., and as a term applied to all subjects of the Persian king.

δοῦναι, see δίδωμι.

δουπέω, aor., ἐδούπησα (δοῦπος), *make a dull sound* or *din, strike heavily.*

δοῦπος, -ου, ὁ, *dull noise, din, uproar,* a poetic word, II, 2, 19.

Δρακόντιος, -ου, ὁ, *Dracontius,* a Spartan exile in the Greek army.

δράμοι, δραμοῦνται, see τρέχω.

δρεπανηφόρος, -ον (δρέπανον+φέρω), scythe-bearing, epithet of chariots.

δρέπανον, -ου, τό (δρέπω, pluck), reaping hook, sickle, scythe.

Δρίλαι, -ῶν, οἱ, the Drilae, a warlike tribe in Pontus.

δρόμος, -ου, ὁ (cf. ἔδραμον), a running, run; δρόμῳ θεῖν (ὁρμᾶν, φεύγειν), to run at double-quick, I, 8, 18; a race-course, IV, 8, 26.

δύναμαι, δυνήσομαι, δεδύνημαι, ἐδυνήθην, be able, abs., or with infin., can; very often with relative words and superlatives, e. g. ὡς μάλιστα ἐδύνατο ἐπικρυπτόμενος, with all possible secrecy, I, 1, 6; of things, be worth, amount to, I, 5, 6; οἱ μέγιστα δυνάμενοι, the most powerful, II, 6, 21.

δύναμις, -εως, ἡ (δύναμαι), ability, means, power, influence; most frequently, force or forces, troops; εἴς γε δύναμιν, as far as our power goes, II, 3, 23.

δυνάστης, -ου, ὁ (δύναμαι), a man of influence, nobleman, prince.

δυνατός, -ή, -όν (δύναμαι), able, powerful; possible, practicable; ὡς δυνατόν, as far as possible, II, 6, 8; ἐκ τῶν δυνατῶν, as far as their power went, IV, 2, 23.

δύνω, only in pres. system, of the sun, enter the sea, set, cf. δύω.

δύο, -οῖν (Lat. duo, Eng. two), two, generally indecl. although the gen. δυοῖν occurs; εἰς δύο, two abreast, II, 4, 26.

δυσ- (Eng. dys-peptic, etc.), an inseparable prefix signifying hard, with difficulty.

δύσβατος, -ον (δυσ-+βαίνω), hard to travel or traverse.

δυσμαί, -ῶν, αἱ (δύω), going down, setting (of the sun), only pl.

δυσπάριτος, -ον (δυσ-+πάρειμι), hard to pass.

δυσπόρευτος, -ον (δυσ-+πορεύω), hard to pass through, I, 5, 7.

δυσπορία, -ας, ἡ (δυσ-+ √ περ), difficulty of passing or crossing.

δύσπορος, -ον (δυσ-+ √ περ), hard to travel, hard to cross (of roads, rivers, etc.).

δύσχρηστος, -ον (δυσ-+χρηστός), verbal of χράομαι), hard to use, useless.

δυσχωρία, -ας, ἡ (δυσ-+χώρα), ruggedness of country, rough country.

δύω, δύσω, etc., 2 aor., ἔδυν, in the Anabasis only in pres. and impf. mid. and always of the sun, enter the sea, set; cf. δύνω.

δῶ, see δίδωμι.

δώδεκα, indecl. (δύο+δέκα), twelve.

δωρέομαι, δωρήσομαι (δῶρον), give as a present, present someone (dat.) with (acc.).

δωροδοκέω, δωροδοκήσω, etc. (δῶρον+δέχομαι), receive presents or bribes.

δῶρον, -ου, τό (δίδωμι), present, gift.

δώσω, see δίδωμι.

E

ἐᾷ, see ἐάω.

ἑάλω, see ἁλίσκομαι.

ἐάν, also ἤν or ἄν, (in crasis κἄν=καὶ ἐάν), conj. (εἰ+ἄν), if, if perchance, only with subj.; ἐὰν μή, unless, I, 4, 12; ἄν τε ... ἄν τε, be it ... or be it, whether ... or, V. 5. 16.

ἐάνπερ or ἤνπερ, conj., strengthened form of ἐάν, if.

ἑαυτοῦ, -ῆς, -οῦ, or, contracted, αὑτοῦ, etc., reflexive pron. (stem ἑ+

αὐτός), *himself, herself, itself* only in oblique cases. The gen. often takes the place of a possess. pron., *his own, their own.*

ἐάω, εἴων, ἐάσω, εἴασα, εἴακα, etc., *allow, permit, let go, let alone, give up;* with neg., *forbid;* ἐὰν χαίρειν; see χαίρω.

ἑβδομήκοντα (ἑπτά), *seventy.*

ἕβδομος, -η, -ον (ἑπτά), *seventh.*

ἐγ-, by euphony for ἐν before palatals.

ἐγγίγνομαι (γίγνομαι), *be born in, arise in.*

ἐγγυάω, ἠγγύησα, etc. (ἐγγύη, *pledge*), *pledge;* mid. *promise.*

ἐγγύθεν, adv. (ἐγγύς), *from close at hand.*

ἐγγύς, adv., comp. ἐγγύτερον, sup. ἐγγυτάτω or ἐγγύτατα, *near,* abs. or with gen.

ἐγείρω, ἐγερῶ, ἤγειρα, ἐγρήγορα, *rouse;* in 2 perf. intrans., *lie awake, keep watch.*

ἐγκαλέω (καλέω), *call in, claim, demand; call up against, blame, accuse* (dat.).

ἐγκαλύπτω (καλύπτω, καλύψω, ἐκάλυψα, κεκάλυμμαι, *cover*), *cover;* mid., *wrap oneself up.*

ἔγκειμαι (κεῖμαι), *lie in, be in.*

ἐγκέλευστος, -ον (ἐν+κελεύω), *bidden* or *instigated by* (ὑπό).

ἐγκέφαλος, -ον, ὁ (properly an adj., sc. μυελός, *marrow,* from ἐν+κεφαλή), *the brain;* of the palm, *the crown* (a cabbage-like growth at the top), or possibly *the pith,* II, 3, 16.

ἐγκρατής, -ες (ἐν+κράτος), *possessed of, master of.*

ἐγρηγόρεσαν, see ἐγείρω.

ἐγχαλινόω (χαλινόω), *put on a bridle;* perf. pass. partic. ἐγκεχαλινωμένοι, *bridled* (of horses).

ἐγχειρέω, ἐγχειρήσω, ἐνεχείρησα (ἐν+χείρ), *put one's hand to, make an attempt.*

ἐγχειρίδιον, -ου, τό (ἐν+χείρ), *dagger.*

ἐγχειρίζω, ἐγχειριοῦμαι, etc. (ἐν+χείρ), *put into one's hand, entrust.*

ἐγχέω (χέω, χεῶ, ἔχεα, *pour;* cf. Eng. *gush*), *pour in, fill a cup* especially for libations.

ἐγώ, ἐμοῦ or μοῦ, pl. ἡμεῖς, pers. pron. (Lat. *ego, me,* Eng. *I, me*), *I,* pl. *we,* the nom. used only when emphatic.

ἔγωγε (ἐγώ+γε), *I for my part, I certainly.*

ἐδεδοίκεσαν, see δείδω.

ἔδει, see δέω, *lack.*

ἔδεισαν, see δείδω.

ἐδηδοκότες, see ἐσθίω.

ἔδραμον, etc., see τρέχω.

ἔδωκα, see δίδωμι.

ἔζη, ἔζων, see ζάω.

ἐθελοντής, -οῦ, ὁ (ἐθέλω), *volunteer;* οἱ ἐθελονταὶ φίλοι, *those who are friends of their own choosing,* I, 6, 9.

ἐθελούσιος, -α, -ον (ἐθέλω), *willing, voluntary, of one's own accord.*

ἐθέλω (rarely θέλω), ἐθελήσω, ἠθέλησα, ἠθέληκα, *wish, be willing, volunteer.* As contrasted with βούλομαι, ἐθέλω often means *be willing,* rather than *wish;* it is a more poetic word, and belongs to a higher sphere (ἂν οἱ θεοὶ θέλωσι, VII, 3, 31; *cf.* 43). Forms of θέλω (after consonants as well as vowels) are commoner in the *Anabasis* than in most prose writings.

ἔθετο, ἔθηκε, see τίθημι.

ἔθνος, -ους, τό, *tribe, people, nation;* κατὰ ἔθνη (ἔθνος), see κατά.

εἰ, conj., *if,* introducing conditional clauses with indic. or opt.; also used to introduce indir. ques., *whether;* εἰ ... ἤ, *whether ... or,* II, 3, 7; εἰ καί, or καὶ εἰ, *although, even if;* εἰ μή, *if not,* after a neg., *unless,* I, 4, 18; εἰ δὲ μή, *otherwise,* II, 2, 1 n.; so εἰ δέ, III, 2, 37 n.; εἰ τις, εἴ τι are often equivalent to ὅστις and ὅτι.

εἴα, εἴασε, see ἐάω.

εἰδέναι, εἰδῆτε, see οἶδα.

εἶδον (*cf.* Lat. *video,* Eng. *wit, wot*), used as 2 aor. of ὁράω, *see, look, perceive.*

εἶδος, -ους, τό (εἶδον), *shape, appearance.*

εἰδότες, see οἶδα.

εἰκάζω, εἰκάσω, ᾔκασα, ᾔκασμαι, εἰκάσθην (ἔοικα, εἰκός), *liken, compare, infer, suppose;* perf. pass., *resemble.*

εἰκός, -ότος, neut. partic. of ἔοικα, *natural, probable, reasonable,* with or without ἐστί and followed by acc. and infin.; εἰκότα λέγειν, *say what is reasonable,* II, 3, 6; ὡς εἰκός or ὡς τὸ εἰκός, *as is likely, in all probability,* III, 1, 21; III, 4, 24.

εἴκοσι, indecl., *twenty.*

εἰκότως, adv. (εἰκός), *naturally, with good reason.*

εἴληφε, εἰλήφει, see λαμβάνω.

εἰλήχει, see λαγχάνω.

εἷλκον, see ἕλκω.

εἱλόμην, εἷλον, etc., see αἱρέω.

εἰμί, ἦν, ἔσομαι (for ἐσμί, old Lat. *esum,* Eng. *am*), *be,* either as the substantive vb., *be, exist,* or as a mere copula; with pred. gen. in various senses, *be sprung from, belong to, consist of,* etc.; often with dat. of possessor; with rel. words, ἔστι δ' ὅστις, *there is one who,* i.e., *somebody,* I, 8, 20; ἔστιν (ἦσαν) οἵ, *some,* V, 2, 14; similarly ἦν οὕς, I, 5, 7 n.: ἔσθ' ὅτε, *sometimes,* II, 6, 9; οὐκ ἦν ὅπου οὐ, *everywhere,* IV, 5, 31; τὰ ὄντα, *facts,* IV, 4, 15 (but *possessions,* VII, 8, 22); τῷ ὄντι, *in fact,* V, 4, 20; impers. ἔστιν (ἦν), *it is (was) possible,* I, 4, 4; sometimes with partic., as a periphrastic vb. form, ἦν δυναμένη= ἐδύνατο, II, 2, 13 n.; in infin. phrases, τὸ νῦν εἶναι, *for the present,* III, 2, 37; τὸ κατὰ τούτοι εἶναι, *as far as this fellow is concerned,* I, 6, 9.

εἶμι, impf. ᾖα (*cf.* Lat. *eo, ire*), *go, come, proceed.* The pres. indic. has always a fut. sense and so the infin. and partic. when in indir. disc., I, 3, 1; imv. ἴθι, in exhortations, *come now,* like ἄγε, VII, 2, 26; VII, 7, 27; εἰς χεῖρας ἰέναι, *come to close quarters,* IV, 7, 15; but εἰς χεῖρας ἐλθεῖν τινι, *come into one's power,* I, 2, 26.

εἶπας, εἴπατε, see εἶπον.

εἴπερ (εἰ+πέρ), *if in fact, if really; inasmuch as,* VI, 1, 26.

εἵπετο, see ἕπομαι.

εἶπον, only 2 aor.; the pres. in use is λέγω, fut. ἐρῶ, perf. εἴρηκα, etc. (*cf.* ἔπος, *word, verse;* Lat. *voco;* Eng. *epic*), *say, speak, tell;* with infin., *bid, command, move, propose.* In 2 pers. forms with 1 aor. vowel occur, εἶπας, II, 5, 23; εἴπατε, imv., II, 1, 21.

εἴργω, εἴρξω, εἶρξα, εἴργμαι, εἴρχθην, *shut out, keep away* (ἐκ or ἀπό with gen.), VI, 3, 8; fut. mid. as pass., VI, 6, 16; *prevent, hinder,* ὥστε μή, III, 3, 16; *shut in hem in,* III, 1, 12.

εἴρηκα, εἴρημαι, see εἴρω.

εἰρήνη, -ης, ἡ, *peace.*

εἴρητο, see εἴρω.

εἴρω, epic vb. of which fut. ἐρῶ, perf. εἴρηκα and εἴρημαι, and aor. pass. ἐρρήθην, are used in Attic, supplementing the forms of λέγω and φημί, *say, mention;* also, *tell, order,* in impers. pass., III, 4, 3.

εἰς (also ἐς, orig. ἐν-ς), prep. with the acc. only, *into, to, up to;* of place, after vbs. of motion; sometimes the motion is only implied, II, 5, 33; of persons (in the pl.), especially common with the names of peoples, ἐς Πισίδας, *into the country of the Pisidians,* I, 1, 11, etc.; εἰς τοὺς πολεμίους, *against the enemy,* stronger than ἐπί, IV, 5, 18; after a vb. of speaking, εἰς τὴν στρατιάν, V, 6, 37; of direction or purpose, εἰς τὴν τροφήν, I, 1, 9; after a vb. of expending, I, 3, 3; of measure, εἰς δύναμιν, *to the extent of our power,* II, 3, 23; with numerals, *up to, about,* I, 2, 3; of time, *up to, at,* I, 7, 1; II, 3, 25; εἰς τὴν νύκτα, *for the night,* IV, 5, 13; εἰς δύο, *two abreast,* II, 4, 26; εἰς ὀκτώ, *eight deep,* VII, 1, 23. In composition εἰσ- signifies *into, in.*

εἷς, μία, ἕν, gen. ἑνός, μιᾶς, ἑνός, numeral adj., *one;* sometimes as indef. pron. like τις, I, 3, 14; combined with τις, II, 1, 19; so εἷς ἕκαστος, VI, 6, 12; ἕνα μή, stronger than μηδένα, *no one,* V, 6, 12; often in intensive phrases, I, 9, 12 n.; I, 9, 22.

εἰσάγω (ἄγω), *lead* or *bring in* or *into.*

εἰσακοντίζω (ἀκοντίζω), *hurl in javelins.*

εἰσβαίνω (βαίνω), *enter, go on board, embark.*

εἰσβάλλω (βάλλω), *throw into;* intr., *invade;* of rivers, *empty into.*

εἰσβιβάζω (βιβάζω, βιβάσω or βιβῶ, -εβίβασα, *make go*), *cause to embark, put on board.*

εἰσβολή, -ῆς, ἡ (εἰσβάλλω), *invasion,* V, 6, 7; *entrance, pass,* I, 2, 21.

εἰσδύομαι (δύω), *enter into, sink* or *cut into.*

εἰσέδραμον, see εἰστρέχω.

εἴσειμι (εἶμι), *go in, enter, come into the presence of;* of thoughts, *occur to,* VI, 1, 17.

εἰσελαύνω (ἐλαύνω), *march into.*

εἰσελθεῖν, see εἰσέρχομαι.

εἰσέρχομαι (ἔρχομαι), *come in, enter.*

εἴσεται, see οἶδα.

εἴσοδος, -ου, ἡ (εἰς+ὁδός), *way in, entrance.*

εἰσπηδάω (πηδάω, πηδήσομαι, ἐπήδησα, *leap*), *leap* or *spring into.*

εἰσπίπτω (πίπτω), *fall into, rush into, fall upon.*

εἰσπλέω (πλέω), *sail into.*

εἱστήκει, see ἵστημι.

εἰστρέχω (τρέχω), *run* or *rush in.*

εἰσφέρω (φέρω), *bear* or *carry in.*

εἰσφορέω (φορέω), *bear* or *carry into.*

εἴσω (εἰς), *within, inside of.*

εἰσωθέω (ὠθέω), *thrust in;* mid., *force one's way in.*

εἶτα, adv., *then, thereupon, afterwards.*

εἴτε, conj. (εἰ+τέ), doubled in disjunctive clauses, *whether . . . or.*

εἶχε, see ἔχω.

εἴωθα, 2 perf. as pres., and εἰώθη, 2 plpf. as impf., of epic vb. ἔθω, *be accustomed* (cf. ἔθος, τό, *custom,* ἦθος, τό, *character,* Eng. *ethic*), *be accustomed, be wont,* with infin., VII, 8, 4.

εἴων, see ἐάω.

ἐκ (before vowels ἐξ), prep. with the gen. (cf. Lat. *e, ex*); (1) of place, *out of, from, away from;* according to Greek idiom often used where Eng. requires *in* or *on*, ἐξ ἀριστερᾶς, *on the left,* IV, 8, 2; (2) of time, *since, after,* denoting immediate sequence, ἐκ τούτου, *upon this, thereupon,* I, 2, 17; ἐκ τοῦ ἀρίστου, *after breakfast,* IV, 6, 21; ἐκ παίδων, *from boyhood,* IV, 6, 14; (3) of source, ἐκ τούτου, *therefore, in consequence of this,* II, 6, 4; τὸν ἐκ τῶν Ἑλλήνων φόβον, *the fear inspired by the Greeks,* I, 2, 18; of the agent with pass. vbs., much rarer than ὑπό, ἐκ βασιλέως δεδομέναι, I, 1, 6; ἐκ τῶν παρόντων, *in view of our present circumstances,* III, 2, 3; ἐκ τῆς νικώσης (sc. γνώμης), *in accordance with a majority vote,* VI, 1, 18; often forming adv. phrases, ἐκ τοῦ αὐτομάτου, *of their own accord,* I, 3, 13; ἐκ τοῦ δικαίου, *justly,* I, 9, 19; ἐκ παντὸς τρόπου, *in every way, by hook or crook,* III, 1, 43; ἐξ ἀπροσδοκήτου, *unexpectedly,* IV, 1, 10; ἐκ τῶν δυνατῶν, *as well as they could,* IV, 2, 23, etc.

ἑκασταχόσε, adv. (ἕκαστος), *in every direction,* III, 5, 17.

ἕκαστος, -η, -ον (sup. form; cf. ἑκάτερος), *each, every,* used of more than two; the sing. often stands in appos. to a pl., I, 7, 15.

ἑκάστοτε, adv. (ἕκαστος), *on each occasion, always.*

ἑκάτερος, -α, -ον (comp. form; cf. ἕκαστος), *each of two* in the pl., *both;* καθ' ἑκάτερα, *on both sides,* V, 6, 7.

ἑκατέρωθεν, adv. (ἑκάτερος), *on both sides.*

ἑκατέρωσε, adv. (ἑκάτερος), *in both directions.*

ἑκατόν, indecl. (cf. Lat. *centum*), *one hundred.*

Ἑκατώνυμος, -ου, ὁ, *Hecatonymus,* an envoy from Sinōpe.

ἐκβαίνω (βαίνω), *step out,* esp., *disembark; go forth, march out,* IV, 2, 1.

ἐκβάλλω (βάλλω), *throw away, drive out, expel, banish.*

ἔκβασις, -εως, ἡ (ἐκ+βαίνω), *a going out, way out, pass.*

Ἐκβάτανα, τά, *Ecbatana,* capital of Media, and summer residence of the Persian king.

ἐκβοηθέω (βοηθέω), *come forth to the rescue.*

ἔκγονος, -ον (ἐκ+ √γεν), *born of;* οἱ ἔκγονοι, *descendants,* III, 2, 14; of animals, τὰ ἔκγονα, *young,* IV, 5, 25.

ἐκδεδράμηκα, see ἐκτρέχω.

ἐκδέρω (δέρω, δερῶ, ἔδειρα, δέδαρμαι, ἐδάρην, *flay,* cf. Eng. *tear*), *strip off the skin, flay.*

ἐκδίδωμι (δίδωμι), *give up, surrender; give away in marriage,* IV, 1, 24.

ἐκδραμεῖν, see ἐκτρέχω.

ἐκδύω (δύω), *strip off;* mid. and 2 aor. act., *strip oneself,* IV, 3, 12.

ἐκεῖ, adv., *there, in that place, thither.*

ἐκεῖθεν, adv. (ἐκεῖ), *thence.*

ἐκεῖνος, -η, -ο, dem. pron. (ἐκεῖ), *that, that one, he,* of a person or thing remote from the speaker, cf. Lat. *ille;* sometimes merely an emphatic third pers. pron.

ἐκεῖσε, adv. (ἐκεῖ), *to that place, thither.*

ἐκέκτησο, see κτάομαι.

ἐκήρυξε, ἐκηρύχθη, see κηρύττω.

ἐκθλίβω (θλίβω, θλίψω, etc., *squeeze*), *squeeze out, crowd out.*

ἐκκαλύπτω (καλύπτω, καλύψω, ἐκάλυψα, κεκάλυμμαι, ἐκαλύφθην), *uncover*.

ἐκκλησία, -ας, ἡ (ἐκ+καλέω; cf. Eng. *ecclesiastic*), *assembly, meeting*.

ἐκκλησιάζω, ἐκκλησιάσω, *hold an assembly*.

ἐκκλίνω (κλίνω, *bend*), *bend out of line, give way*, of troops.

ἐκκομίζω (κομίζω), *carry off* or *out*; of troops, *bring off*, VI, 6, 36; mid., *carry off for one's own use*, V, 2, 19.

ἐκκόπτω (κόπτω), *cut off* or *away, cut down*.

ἐκκυβιστάω (κυβιστάω, *tumble, cf.* κύπτω, *stoop*), *turn a somersault*.

ἐκκυμαίνω (κυμαίνω, *swell, surge*; κῦμα, *wave*), *billow out*, of the curving front of a charging line of troops.

ἐκλέγω (ἐκ+λέγω, *gather, pick, cf.* συλλέγω), *pick out, select*, mid., *choose*.

ἐκλείπω (λείπω), *leave, abandon*; with εἰς, *leave one place for another, leave and flee to*, I, 2, 24; intrans., *give out*; of snow, *melt away*, IV, 5, 15.

ἐκμηρύομαι (μηρύω, *wind*), *wind out*; of an army, *defile*, VI, 5, 22.

ἐκπέμπω (πέμπω), *send out, send away*; mid., *send away from oneself, dismiss*, V, 2, 21.

ἐκπεπληγμένος, ἐκπεπλῆχθαι, see ἐκπλήττω.

ἐκπεραίνω (περαίνω), *bring to completion, accomplish*; with ὥστε, *bring it about that*, V, 1, 13.

ἐκπηδάω (πηδάω, *leap*), *leap forth*.

ἐκπίμπλημι (πίμπλημι), *fill up*.

ἐκπίνω (ἐκ+πίνω), *drink up, drain, quaff*.

ἐκπίπτω (πίπτω), *fall out*; commonly as pass. of ἐκβάλλω, *be banished, exiled*; οἱ ἐκπεπτωκότες, *the exiles*, I, 1, 7; of violent motion, *rush* or *hurry out*, V, 2, 17; cf. V, 2, 31; *be cast away, shipwrecked*, VI, 4, 2.

ἐκπλαγείς, see ἐκπλήττω.

ἐκπλέω (πλέω), *sail forth* or *away*.

ἔκπλεως, -ων, gen. -ω (πίμπλημι), *filled up, quite full*.

ἐκπλήττω, 2 aor. pass. ἐξεπλάγην (πλήττω), *strike out* (of one's senses); pass., *be amazed, startled, scared out of one's wits*.

ἐκποδών, adv. (ἐκ+πούς), *out of the way*; ἐκποδὼν ποιεῖσθαι, *put out of the way*, I, 6, 9.

ἐκπορεύομαι (πορεύομαι), *go forth, go out*.

ἐκπορίζω (πορίζω), *provide, procure*.

ἔκπωμα, -ατος, τό (ἐκπίνω), *drinking-cup*.

ἐκταθείς, see ἐκτείνω.

ἑκταῖος, -α, -ον (ἕξ), *on the sixth day*.

ἐκτάττω (τάττω), *draw out in battle array*.

ἐκτείνω (τείνω), *stretch out*; ἐκταθείς, *stretched out at full length* (of a sleeper), V, 1, 2.

ἐκτοξεύω (τοξεύω), *shoot arrows from*.

ἐκτός, adv. (ἕξ), *outside of, apart from*.

ἕκτος, -η, -ον (ἕξ), *sixth*.

ἐκτρέπω (τρέπω), *turn out*; pass. and 2 aor. mid. ἐτραπόμην, intrans., *turn aside*, IV, 5, 15.

ἐκτρέφω (τρέφω), *bring up, rear*.

ἐκτρέχω (τρέχω), *run* or *rush forth, make a sally*.

ἐκτῶντο, see κτάομαι.

ἐκφαίνω (φαίνω), *show forth, bring to light*; of war, *declare*, III, 1, 16.

ἐκφέρω (φέρω), *bear out, carry out*; with πόλεμον, *begin*, III, 2, 29; of news, etc., *report, announce*, I, 9, 11.

ἐκφεύγω (φεύγω), *flee out of, flee away, escape;* with μή and infin., I, 3, 2.

ἑκών, -οῦσα, -όν, *willing, of one's own choice;* often best rendered as adv., *willingly.*

ἐλάα, or ἐλαία, -ας, ἡ, *olive tree, olive.*

ἔλαβον, see λαμβάνω.

ἔλαιον, -ου, τό (ἐλάα), *olive oil, oil.*

ἐλάττων, -ον, gen. -ονος (ἐλαχύς, *small;* cf. Lat. *levis*, Eng. *light*), used as comp. of μικρός, *smaller, less,* in pl., *fewer;* ἔλαττόν ἐστι, with infin., *it is a lesser thing to,* i.e., *it is easier to,* VII, 7, 35.

ἐλαύνω (ἐλῶ, ἤλασα, ἐλήλακα, ἐλήλαμαι, ἠλάθην), *drive, ride, march,* abs. or with acc.

ἐλάφειος, -ον (ἔλαφος), *of or belonging to deer;* τὰ ἐλάφεια (sc. κρέα) *venison,* I, 5, 2.

ἔλαφος, -ου, ὁ, ἡ, *deer,* whether stag or hind.

ἐλαφρός, -ά, -όν, *light, light-armed, nimble, active.*

ἐλαφρῶς, adv. (ἐλαφρός), *lightly, nimbly.*

ἐλάχιστος, -η, -ον (cf. ἐλάττων), used as sup. of μικρός, *least, smallest,* in pl., *fewest;* τοὐλάχιστον, as adv., *at least,* V, 7, 8.

ἐλέγχω (ἐλέγξω, ἤλεγξα, ἐλήλεγμαι, ἠλέγχθην), *examine, question, refute, convict.*

ἐλεῖν, see αἱρέω.

ἐλελίζω, ἠλέλιξα (ἐλελεῦ, imitative, *a war cry*), *cry;* ἐλελεῦ, *raise the war cry;* cf. ἀλαλάζω.

ἐλέσθαι, see αἱρέω.

ἐλευθερία, -ας, ἡ (ἐλεύθερος), *liberty, freedom.*

ἐλεύθερος, -α, -ον, *free, independent.*

ἐλέχθησαν, see λέγω.

ἐλήφθην, see λαμβάνω.

ἐλθεῖν, see ἔρχομαι.

ἕλκω, impf. εἷλκον, *drag, draw.*

Ἑλλάς, -άδος, ἡ (cf. Ἕλλην): (1) *Hellas, Greece,* in the widest sense, the Greek world; (2) *Hellas,* a woman of Mysia, wife of Gongylus and hostess of Xenophon, VII, 8, 8.

Ἕλλην, -ηνος (cf. Eng. *Hellenic*), *a Greek.* In the *Anabasis* generally designating the Greek mercenaries of Cyrus; as adj., *Greek,* I, 10, 7.

ἑλληνίζω (Ἕλλην), *speak Greek.*

Ἑλληνικός, -ή, -όν (Ἕλλην), *Hellenic, Greek;* τὸ Ἑλληνικόν, *the Greek army.*

ἑλληνικῶς, adv. (Ἑλληνικός), *in Greek.*

Ἑλληνίς, -ίδος, ἡ (Ἕλλην), fem. adj., *Greek.*

ἑλληνιστί, adv. (ἑλληνίζω), *in Greek.*

Ἑλλησποντιακός, -ή, -όν (Ἑλλήσποντος), of cities, *lying on the Hellespont.*

Ἑλλήσποντος, -ου, ὁ (Ἕλλης+πόντος), *the Hellespont* (sea of Helle), *the Dardanelles.*

ἐλπίζω, ἤλπισα (ἐλπίς), *hope, expect.*

ἐλπίς, -ίδος, ἡ (cf. Lat. *voluptas*), *hope, expectation.*

ἐμ-, by euphony for ἐν- before labials.

ἔμαθεν, see μανθάνω.

ἐμαυτοῦ, -ῆς, reflex. pron., pl. ἡμῶν αὐτῶν, etc. (stem of ἐμέ+αὐτός), *of myself, myself.*

ἐμβαίνω (βαίνω), *go in, enter, embark,* abs. or with εἰς and acc.

ἐμβάλλω (βάλλω), *cast* or *throw in, put in, throw before* (χιλὸν ἵπποις), I, 9, 27; intrans., of rivers, *empty into* (εἰς), I, 2, 8; in military lang., *make an invasion* or *attack;* πληγὰς ἐμβάλλειν, *inflict blows,* I, 5, 1.

ἐμβιβάζω (βιβάζω, βιβάσω or βιβῶ, ἐβίβασα, make go), cause to embark, put on board.

ἐμβολή, -ῆς, ἡ (ἐμβάλλω), invasion.

ἔμεινε, see μένω.

ἐμέω, ἤμουν (Lat. vomo, vomit; cf. Eng. emetic), vomit.

ἐμέμνητο, see μιμνήσκω.

ἐμμένω (μένω), stay in.

ἐμός, -ή, όν (cf. ἐμέ, Lat. meus, Eng. my), my, mine.

ἔμπαλιν, adv. back; in the Anabasis always with the art. τοὔμπαλιν, I, 4, 15; εἰς τοὔμπαλιν, III, 5, 13.

ἐμπεδόω, impf. ἠμπέδουν, ἐμπεδώσω, etc. (ἔμπεδος, fixed in the ground, firm), hold fast, abide by, III, 2, 10.

ἔμπειρος, -ον (ἐν+πεῖρα), acquainted with, experienced.

ἐμπείρως, adv. (ἔμπειρος), with experience; ἐμπείρως ἔχειν, gen., be personally acquainted with, II, 6, 1.

ἐμπίμπλημι (πίμπλημι), fill full, satisfy; pass., be filled with, I, 10, 12; ὑπισχνούμενος οὐκ ἐνεπίμπλασο, you couldn't sate yourself with promising, VII, 7, 46.

ἐμπίμπρημι (πίμπρημι, πρήσω, ἔπρησα, burn), set on fire, burn. The simple vb. is poetic.

ἐμπίπτω (πίπτω), fall upon, seize, attack; of thoughts, occur to, II, 2, 19, etc.

ἔμπλεως, -ων, gen. -ω (πίμπλημι), full of (gen.).

ἐμποδίζω (ποδίζω), hinder, impede.

ἐμπόδιος, -ον (ἐν+πούς), in the way, hindering; τὸ ἐμπόδιον, the hindrance, VII, 8, 3.

ἐμποδών, adv. (ἐν+πούς), before one's feet, in the way; ἐμποδὼν εἶναι, be in the way, hinder.

ἐμποιέω (ποιέω), create in, inspire in.

ἐμπολάω, ἐμπολήσω, etc., gain or realize by sale, VII, 5, 4.

ἐμπόριον, -ου, τό (ἔμπορος), trading-place, emporium.

ἔμπορος, -ου, ὁ (cf. πορεύομαι), merchant.

ἐμπρήσαντες, see ἐμπίμπρημι.

ἔμπροσθεν, adv. (ἐν+πρόσθεν), before, in front of, with gen., I, 8, 23; IV, 5, 9; ὁ ἔμπροσθεν λόγος, the foregoing narrative, II, 1, 1; οἱ ἔμπροσθεν, those in front, III, 4, 48, etc.; τὸν ἔμπροσθεν χρόνον, hitherto, VI, 1, 18; τὰ ἔμπροσθεν, the front parts of the body, contrasted with the back, V, 4, 32, but VI, 3, 14, the country in front.

ἐμφάγοιεν, ἐμφαγόντας, see ἐνέφαγον.

ἐμφανής, -ές (ἐν+φαίνω), evident, manifest; ἐν τῷ ἐμφανεῖ, openly, II, 5, 25.

ἐμφανῶς, adv. (ἐμφανής), openly, V, 4, 33.

ἐν, prep. with the dat. only (Lat. and Eng. in), in; (1) of place, in, at, in the midst of, among, before; ἐν ὅπλοις, under arms, III, 2, 28; ἐν τῷ γε φανερῷ, openly at least, I, 3, 21; ἐν ὀφθαλμοῖς, in sight, IV, 5, 29; (2) of time, in, during, within, at, often ἐν τούτῳ, meanwhile, I, 5, 15; ἐν ᾧ, during which time, while, I, 2, 20; so ἐν αἷς (sc. ἡμέραις), I, 2, 10; (3) of means or manner, in, with, by, II, 5, 17. In composition ἐν- becomes ἐγ- before a palatal, and ἐμ- before a labial or before μ.

ἔν, see εἷς.

ἐναγκυλάω (ἐν+ἀγκύλη, thong), fit with a thong, of javelins, IV, 2, 28 n.

ἐναντιόομαι, -ώσομαι, etc. (ἐναντίος), oppose, withstand.

ἐναντίος, -α, -ον (ἐν+ἀντίος), opposite, over against, facing, opposed to, hostile; οἱ ἐναντίοι, the enemy, VI, 5, 10; τἀναντία, the reverse, V, 6, 4; τἀναντία στρέψαντες, turning in the opposite direction, facing about, IV, 3, 32; ἐκ τοῦ ἐναντίου, on the opposite side, IV, 7, 5.

ἐνάπτω (ἅπτω), kindle, set on fire.

ἔνατος, -η, -ον (ἐννέα), ninth.

ἐναυλίζομαι (αὐλίζομαι), bivouac or encamp in.

ἔνδεια, -ας, ἡ (ἐν+δέω), need, want, scarcity, poverty.

ἐνδείκνυμι (δείκνυμι), show, show forth, declare, mid., VI, 1, 19.

ἐνδέκατος, -η, -ον (εἷς+δέκα), eleventh.

ἐνδέω (δέω), lack; impers., there is need of (gen.); ἑώρα πλείονος ἐνδέον, he saw that there was need of more (argument), VI, 1, 31.

ἔνδηλος, -ον (ἐν+δῆλος), evident, plain, manifest.

ἔνδημος, -ον (ἐν+δῆμος, land, people), native, at home; τὰ ἔνδημα, home revenues, VII, 1, 27.

ἐνδίφριος, -ον (δίφρος), on the same seat with one, at one's table.

ἔνδοθεν, adv. (ἔνδον), from within.

ἔνδον, adv. (ἐν), inside, within.

ἔνδοξος, -ον (δόξα), glorious, famous; of omens, portending glory, VI, 1, 23.

ἐνδύω (δύω), put on; in perf. tenses, wear, V, 4, 13.

ἐνέδρα, -ας, ἡ (ἐν+ἕδρα, seat), ambuscade.

ἐνεδρεύω, aor. ἐνήδρευσα (ἐνέδρα), set an ambush, lie in ambush.

ἐνεῖδον (εἶδον), see, observe in.

ἔνειμι (εἰμί), be in, be on, be there.

ἕνεκα or **ἕνεκεν**, improper prep., generally post-pos., on account of, for the sake of.

ἐνενήκοντα (ἐννέα), ninety.

ἐνεός, -ά, -όν, dumb, deaf and dumb.

ἐνετός, -ή, -όν (ἑτός, verbal of ἵημι), set on, instigated by (ὑπό), VII, 6, 41.

ἐνέφαγον (ἔφαγον), only aor., eat hastily, eat something.

ἐνεχείρησαν, see ἐγχειρίζω.

ἐνέχυρον, -ου, τό (ἔχω), pledge, security.

ἐνέχω (ἔχω), hold in, entangle.

ἔνθα, adv. of place or time (ἐν), rel., where or whither; dem., here; of time, then, often with emphatic δή.

ἐνθάδε, adv. of place (ἔνθα), hither, here.

ἔνθαπερ, adv. (ἔνθα), just where.

ἔνθεν, local adv. (ἐν), dem., from there, thence; rel., whence; ἔνθεν ... ἔνθεν, on this side ... on that; ἔνθεν καὶ ἔνθεν, on both sides.

ἐνθένδε, local adv. (ἐν), from this place, hence; of persons, VII, 7, 17 (=ἀφ' ὑμῶν).

ἐνθυμέομαι, ἐνθυμήσομαι, ἐντεθύμημαι, ἐνεθυμήθην (ἐν+θυμός), bear in mind, reflect, consider; perf., I have noted, observed, III, 1, 43.

ἐνθύμημα, -ατος, τό (ἐνθυμέομαι), thought, idea, plan.

ἐνθωρακίζω (θωρακίζω), put on one's breastplate; perf. pass. partic. ἐντεθωρακισμένοι, clad in armor, VII, 4, 16.

ἔνι, for ἔνεστι, see ἔνειμι.

ἐνί, see εἷς.

ἐνιαυτός, -οῦ, ὁ, year; κατ' ἐνιαυτόν, yearly, annually.

ἔνιοι, -αι, -α, some.

ἐνίοτε, adv. (ἔνιοι [?]+ὅτε), sometimes.

ἐννέα, indecl., nine.

ἐννοέω (νοέω), *have in mind, think, devise, ponder;* with μή, *fear that,* IV, 2, 13; mid., *consider, reflect.*

ἔννοια, -ας, ἡ (ἐν + νοῦς), *thought, reflection.*

ἐνοικέω (οἰκέω), *live in, inhabit;* οἱ ἐνοικοῦντες, *the inhabitants.*

ἐνόπλιος, -ον (ἐν + ὅπλον), *in arms;* with ῥυθμός, *martial,* VI, 1, 11.

ἐνοράω (ὁράω), *see in* (something or somebody); πολλὰ ἐνορῶ δι' ἅ, *I see many reasons* (in the project) *why,* I, 3, 15.

ἑνός, see εἷς.

ἐνοχλέω, -ήσω, aor. and perf. with double augment in all voices (*cf.* ὄχλος), *crowd upon, trouble.*

ἐνταῦθα, adv. of place, *here, there;* loosely, *thither;* of time, *then, thereupon;* μέχρι ἐνταῦθα, *hitherto,* V, 5, 4.

ἐντείνω (τείνω), *stretch tight;* πληγὰς ἐντείνειν, *inflicted blows upon,* II, 4, 11.

ἐντελής, -ές (ἐν + τέλος), *complete, in full.*

ἐντέλλομαι, ἐντελοῦμαι, ἐνετειλάμεν (*cf.* τέλος), *enjoin upon, command.*

ἔντερον, -ου, τό (ἐν), *intestine.*

ἐντεῦθεν, adv. of place, *thence, from there;* of time, *then, thereafter;* of cause, *as a result of this,* VII, 1, 25.

ἐντίθημι (τίθημι), *put or place in, put on board ship; inspire* or *instil in* (φόβον), VII, 4, 1.

ἔντιμος, -ον (ἐν + τιμή), *in honor, esteemed.*

ἐντίμως, adv. (ἔντιμος), in the phrase ἐντίμως ἔχειν, *be held in honor,* II, 1, 7.

ἐντοίχιος, -ον (τοῖχος), *on the wall;* τὰ ἐντοίχια, *wall paintings,* VII, 8, 1.

ἐντόνως, adv. (ἔντονος, *eager,* fr. τείνω), *earnestly, strenuously.*

ἐντός, adv. with gen. (ἐν), *within,* of place or time.

ἐντυγχάνω (τυγχάνω), *light upon, fall in with, find.*

Ἐνυάλιος, -ου, ὁ (Ἐνυώ, *goddess of war*), *Enyalius,* a name of Ares, the god of war.

ἐνωμοτάρχος, -ου, ὁ (*cf.* ἐνωμοτία), *commander of an enomoty.*

ἐνωμοτία, -ας, ἡ (ἐνώμοτος, *sworn in; cf.* ὄμνυμι), *a sworn band;* esp. of soldiers, *enomoty,* forming one quarter of the λόχος and numbering therefore ordinarily twenty-five men.

ἐξ, see ἐκ.

ἕξ, indecl. (Lat. *sex,* Eng. *six*), *six.*

ἐξαγγέλλω (ἀγγέλλω), *tell out, report.*

ἐξάγω (ἄγω), *lead* or *bring out, march out;* pass. οὐδ' ὡς ἐξήχθη διώκειν, *not even thus was he induced to pursue,* I, 8, 21.

ἐξαίρετος, -ον (αἱρέω), *selected, picked.*

ἐξαιρέω (αἱρέω), *take out, remove; unload,* V, 1, 16; of tithes, *dedicate,* V, 3, 4; mid., *pick out, select* (for oneself), II, 5, 20.

ἐξαιτέω (αἰτέω), *ask, demand* (esp. the surrender of a person), VI, 6, 11; mid., *beg off,* I, 1, 3.

ἐξαίφνης, adv. (ἄφνω), *suddenly, unexpectedly; cf.* ἐξαπίνης.

ἑξακισχίλιοι, -αι, -α (ἕξ + χίλιοι), *six thousand.*

ἐξακοντίζω (ἀκοντίζω), *throw the javelin, hurl* (from within a fortress), V, 4, 25.

ἑξακόσιοι, -αι, -α (ἕξ + ἑκατόν), *six hundred.*

ἐξαλαπάζω, -άξω, *plunder, sack,* epic vb. used only here in Attic, VII, 1, 29.

ἐξάλλομαι (ἅλλομαι), *leap out* or *aside*.
ἐξαμαρτάνω (ἁμαρτάνω), *err, do wrong*.
ἐξανίστημι (ἵστημι), *make stand up*; mid. with 2 aor. and 2 perf. act., intrans., *stand up, rise* or *start up*.
ἐξαπατάω (ἀπατάω, ἀπατήσω, etc., *deceive*; ἀπάτη, *deceit*), *deceive utterly*.
ἐξαπάτη, -ης, ἡ (ἀπάτη, *deceit*), *gross deceit*, VII, 1, 25.
ἐξαπίνης, adv., an Ionic word for which Attic usually has ἐξαίφνης, *suddenly, unexpectedly*.
ἐξάρχω (ἄρχω), *begin, lead off*.
ἐξαυλίζομαι (αὐλίζομαι), *break camp*.
ἔξειμι (εἰμί), only impers. ἔξεστι, *it is permitted, allowed, possible*; so the partic. ἐξόν often in acc. abs., generally in adversative or concessive sense, II, 5, 22.
ἔξειμι (εἶμι), *go out* or *forth*.
ἐξελαύνω (ἐλαύνω), *drive out, expel*; commonly intrans., *march*, generally with σταθμόν (σταθμούς).
ἐξενεγκεῖν, see ἐκφέρω.
ἐξεπλάγη, see ἐκπλήττω.
ἐξέρπω (ἕρπω, *creep*, Lat. *serpo*), *creep out*; of an army, *march forth*, VII, 1, 8.
ἐξέρχομαι (ἔρχομαι), *go* or *come out, march out, escape*; of time, *run out, elapse*, VII, 5, 4.
ἐξέτασις, -εως, ἡ (ἐξετάζω, *examine*), *review, inspection*.
ἐξηγέομαι (ἡγέομαι), *lead forth*, VI, 6, 34; *narrate, disclose, suggest*, IV, 5, 28.
ἐξήκοντα, indecl. (ἕξ), *sixty*.
ἐξήκω (ἥκω), *run out, expire* (of time), pres. in sense of perf., VI, 3, 26.
ἐξήνεγκε, see ἐκφέρω.

ἐξικνέομαι (ἱκνέομαι, ἵξομαι, ἱκόμην, ἷγμαι), *reach*; of missiles, *reach the mark*; βραχὺ ἐξικνεῖσθαι, *have a short range*, III, 3, 17; of value, *amount to, suffice for*, VII, 5, 4.
ἐξίστημι (ἵστημι), *cause to stand out of*; mid., *stand aside*; ἐκ τοῦ μέσου ἐξίστασθαι, *get out of the way*, I, 5, 14.
ἔξοδος, -ου, ἡ (ἐξ+ὁδός, Eng. *exodus*), *way out, expedition, sally*.
ἔξομεν, see ἔχω.
ἐξοπλίζω (ὁπλίζω), *arm fully*; mid., *arm oneself*.
ἐξοπλισία, -ας, ἡ (ἐξοπλίζω), *complete armament*; ἐν τῇ ἐξοπλισίᾳ, *under arms*, I, 7, 10.
ἐξορμάω (ὁρμάω), *urge on, incite*; intrans., *set out, rush forth*.
ἐξουσία, -ας, ἡ (ἔξεστι), *possibility, power*.
ἑξπῆχυς, -υ (ἕξ+πῆχυς), *six cubits long*.
ἔξω (ἐξ), *outside of, without, beyond*, often with gen.; τὸ ἔξω, *the outer*, I, 4, 4; ἔξω βελῶν, *out of range*, III, 4, 15; ἔξω τούτων, *besides this*, VII, 3, 10.
ἔξωθεν, adv. (ἔξω), *from without, without, outside of*, gen.
ἔοικα, perf. as pres., ἐῴκη, plpf. as impf. (no pres. in use; fut., εἴξω, rare; cf. εἰκάζω), *be like, look like* (dat., occasionally with acc. of respect); ὡς ἔοικε, parenthetical, *as it seems*, II, 2, 18; οὐδενὶ καλῷ ἔοικε, *it doesn't look at all honorable*, VI, 5, 17. Neut. partic. εἰκός, see the word.
ἑορακότες, see ὁράω.
ἑορτή, -ῆς, ἡ, *festival*.
ἐπ', by elision for ἐπί.
ἐπαγγέλλω (ἀγγέλλω), *proclaim*; mid., *offer oneself, promise*.

ἐπάγω (ἄγω), *bring forward, propose* (of a vote), VII, 7, 57.

ἔπαθον, see πάσχω.

ἐπαινέω, -έσομαι, -ῄνεσα (ἔπαινος), *praise, commend;* often in declining an offer, *thank one for*, VII, 7, 52.

ἔπαινος, -ου, ὁ (αἶνος, *tale, praise*), *commendation*.

ἐπαίρω (αἴρω), *raise up, excite, induce.*

ἐπακολουθέω (ἀκολουθέω), *follow after, pursue*.

ἐπακούω (ἀκούω), *listen to, hearken, overhear*.

ἐπάν or ἐπήν, temporal conj. (ἐπεί+ἄν), *when, whenever*, only with subj.

ἐπαναχωρέω (χωρέω), *retreat, withdraw.*

ἐπανέρχομαι (ἔρχομαι), *go back, return.*

ἐπάνω, adv. (ἄνω), *above;* in the phrase ἐν τοῖς ἐπάνω εἴρηται, *has been told above, in what precedes*, VI, 3, 1.

ἐπαπειλέω (ἀπειλέω), *add threats*.

ἐπεγγελάω (γελάω), *laugh at, insult, mock at*.

ἐπεγείρω (ἐγείρω), *wake up, arouse*.

ἐπεί, conj.: (1) temporal, *when, after, whenever;* with indic., of definite past time; with opt. in indir. disc., after a secondary tense, or when expressing repeated action in the past; with infin. by assimilation in indir. disc., V, 7, 18; ἐπεὶ τάχιστα, *as soon as* (*cum primum*), VI, 3, 21; (2) causal, *since, because,* with indic.

ἐπειδάν, temporal conj. with subj. (ἐπειδή+ἄν), *when, after that, as soon as, whenever.* After ἐπειδάν the aor. subj. is often best rendered by the Eng. fut. pf.

ἐπειδή, temporal and causal conj. (ἐπεί+δή), *when, after, since, because*.

ἐπεῖδον (εἶδον), *behold, see, experience*.

ἔπειμι (εἰμί), *be over, be upon*.

ἔπειμι (εἶμι), *go on* or *against, advance, attack, come forward;* ἡ ἐπιοῦσα ἡμέρα (ἕως, νύξ), *the following day,* etc.

ἐπείπερ, causal conj. (ἐπεί+περ), *since, seeing that*.

ἔπεισα, ἐπείσθησαν, see πείθω.

ἔπειτα, adv. (εἶτα), *thereupon, then;* in enumerations, *then, in the next place;* εἰς τὸν ἔπειτα χρόνον, *in after times*, II, 1, 17.

ἐπέκεινα, adv. (ἐπί+ἐκεῖνα), *on the farther side, beyond,* V, 4, 3.

ἐπεκθέω (θέω), *sally out against*.

ἐπεξέρχομαι (ἔρχομαι), *sally out against*.

ἐπέπατο, see πάομαι.

ἐπεπράκει, see πιπράσκω.

ἐπέπρακτο, see πράττω.

ἐπέρομαι (ἔρομαι), only in 2 aor. ἐπηρόμην, etc., *ask again* or *farther, inquire, ask*.

ἐπέρχομαι (ἔρχομαι), *come upon;* of countries, *visit, traverse.*

ἔπεσον, see πίπτω.

ἐπεύχομαι (εὔχομαι), *pray to, invoke, call to witness*.

ἐπεφεύγεσαν, see φεύγω.

ἐπέχω (ἔχω), *hold back, restrain;* intrans., *refrain from;* ἐπέσχον τῆς πορείας, *they delayed their march*, III, 4, 36.

ἐπήκοος, -ον (ἐπί+ἀκούω), *hearing;* εἰς ἐπήκοον (ἐν ἐπηκόῳ, after vbs. of rest), *within hearing distance.*

ἐπῆκτο, see ἐπάγω.

ἐπήν, see ἐπάν.

ἐπῇρεν, see ἐπαίρω.

ἐπήρετο, see ἐπέρομαι.
ἐπί, before vowels ἐπ' or ἐφ', prep. with gen., dat., and acc., *upon*. With gen., of place, *upon, on*, ἐφ' ἵππων, *on horseback*, III, 2, 19 (*cf.* ἀπό); ἐπὶ Θρᾴκης, *on the coast of Thrace*, VII, 6, 25; of direction, *toward*, II, 1, 3; of time, *in the time of*, I, 9, 12; *at*, IV, 7, 10, *cf.* IV, 3, 9; of manner, ἐπὶ τεττάρων, *four deep*, I, 2, 15; ἐπὶ φάλαγγος, *in line of battle*, IV, 3, 26; ἐφ' ἑνός, *in single file;* ἐφ' ἑαυτῶν, *by themselves*, II, 4, 10.

With dat., of place, *on, upon, by, at, near;* of time, *at*, ἐπὶ τῷ τρίτῳ, *at the third* (signal), II, 2, 4; frequently ἐπὶ τούτῳ (τούτοις), *thereupon;* of dependence, *in the power of*, I, 1, 4; of command, *over, in command of*, I, 4, 2; of aim or purpose, *for*, ἐπὶ τούτῳ, *for this*, I, 3, 1; *cf.* ἐπὶ θανάτῳ, I, 6, 10; τὸ ἐπὶ τούτῳ, *as far as he is concerned*, VI, 6, 23; so ἐφ' ᾧ or ἐφ' ᾧτε with infin. *on condition that;* sometimes merely giving circumstances, ἐπὶ γάμῳ, *as his wife,* II, 4, 8; ἐπὶ πολέμῳ, *on a basis of war*, II, 4, 5; ἐπί is thus common in contracts and treaties.

With acc., *on, upon, to;* often in a hostile sense, *against;* of extent, *over, along;* ἐπὶ πολύ, I, 8, 8; ἐπὶ βραχύ, III, 3, 17; of time, *for, during*, VI, 6, 36; ὡς ἐπὶ τὸ πολύ, *for the most part*, III, 1, 42; of aim or purpose, *for;* ἐφ' ἃ ἐστρατεύετο, *the objects of his expedition*, I, 2, 2.

In composition ἐπι- signifies *upon, over, to, toward, against, besides,* but is sometimes merely intensive.

ἐπιβάλλω (βάλλω), *throw on;* ἐπιβεβλημένοι τοξόται, *bowmen with their arrows on the string*, IV, 3, 28 n.; V, 2, 12.
ἐπιβοηθέω (βοηθέω), *come to the aid of* (dat.).
ἐπιβουλεύω (βουλεύω), *plot against*, with dat.; with infin. *plot, scheme.*
ἐπιβουλή, -ῆς, ἡ (βουλή), *scheme, design, plot.*
ἐπιγίγνομαι (γίγνομαι), *come upon, attack.*
ἐπιγράφω (γράφω), *inscribe upon.*
ἐπιδείκνυμι (δείκνυμι), *show, display, make clear, point out;* mid., *show oneself, distinguish oneself, show.*
ἐπιδιώκω (διώκω), *pursue after, chase.*
ἐπιδόντας, see ἐπεῖδον.
ἐπιδραμεῖν, see ἐπιτρέχω.
ἐπιέζετο, see πιέζω.
ἐπιθαλάττιος, -α, -ον (ἐπί+θάλαττα), *on the sea.*
ἐπίθεσις, -εως, ἡ (ἐπιτίθημι), *attack.*
ἐπιθυμέω, ἐπιθυμήσω, etc. (ἐπί+θυμός), *set one's heart on, desire, long for, be enamored of,* with infin. or with gen.
ἐπιθυμία, -ας, ἡ (*cf.* ἐπιθυμέω), *desire.*
ἐπικαίριος, -ον (καιρός), *in season, suitable, available*, VII, 1, 6; τοὺς ἐπικαιρίους, *the proper representatives* (according to others, *the chief men*), VII, 7, 15.
ἐπικάμπτω (κάμπτω, κάμψω, etc., *bend*), *bend toward;* of an army, *wheel.*
ἐπικαταριπτέω (ῥιπτέω), *throw down after.*
ἐπίκειμαι (κεῖμαι), *lie or be set upon;* of an enemy, *attack; cf.* ἐπιτίθημι.

ἐπικίνδυνος, -ον (κίνδυνος), *dangerous.*

ἐπικουρέω, ἐπικουρήσω, *etc.* (ἐπίκουρος, *ally*), *help, aid* (dat.); with acc. of thing, *aid one* (dat.) *against, ward off from one,* V, 8, 25.

ἐπικούρημα, -ατος, τό (ἐπικουρέω), *help, protection.*

ἐπικράτεια, -ας, ἡ (κράτος), *power over, mastery.*

ἐπικρύπτω (κρύπτω), *hide, conceal;* mid., *conceal oneself, act secretly.*

ἐπικύπτω (κύπτω, *stoop*), *stoop or bend over.*

ἐπικυρόω (κυρόω, κυρώσω, *etc.,* *make valid,* from κῦρος, τό, *power, authority*), *confirm, ratify.*

ἐπικωλύω (κωλύω), *hinder, debar from,* gen.

ἐπιλαμβάνω (λαμβάνω), *take in, include,* VI, 5, 5 and 6; *lay hold of, catch,* IV, 7, 12, 13.

ἐπιλανθάνομαι (λανθάνω), *forget,* with gen.

ἐπιλέγω (λέγω), *say besides, add.*

ἐπιλείπω (λείπω), *leave behind;* in pass. τὸ ἐπιλειπόμενον, *those* (*the part*) *left behind,* I, 8, 18; of things, *give out, fail.*

ἐπίλεκτος, -ον (λέγω), *picked out, selected;* οἱ ἐπίλεκτοι, *picked men,* III, 4, 43; VII, 4, 11.

ἐπιμαρτύρομαι (μαρτύρομαι, aor. ἐμαρτυράμην, *call to witness,* from μάρτυς), *call to witness, invoke.*

ἐπίμαχος, -ον (ἐπί+μάχομαι), *that may be attacked, open to attack.*

ἐπιμείγνυμι (μείγνυμι, μείξω, *etc., mix*), *mix with;* mid. intrans., *mingle with, have dealings with,* III, 5, 16.

ἐπιμέλεια, -ας, ἡ (ἐπιμελέομαι), *care, pains, attention.*

ἐπιμελέομαι and ἐπιμέλομαι, ἐπιμελήσομαι, ἐπιμεμέλημαι, ἐπεμελήθην (μέλει), *care for, look out for, attend to.*

ἐπιμελής, -ές, comp. ἐπιμελέστερος (*cf.* ἐπιμελέομαι), *careful, watchful.*

ἐπιμέλομαι, see ἐπιμελέομαι.

ἐπιμένω (μένω), *remain at or with,* VII, 2, 1; *wait for, wait,* V, 5, 2.

ἐπινοέω (νοέω), *purpose, intend.*

ἐπιορκέω, ἐπιορκήσω, *etc.* (ἐπίορκος), *swear falsely, perjure oneself* (θεούς, *by the gods*).

ἐπιορκία, -ας, ἡ (ἐπίορκος), *perjury.*

ἐπίορκος, -ον (ἐπί+ὅρκος), *foresworn.*

ἐπιπάρειμι (εἶμι), *march on beside,* or *parallel with; advance to bear aid,* or *for service,* III, 4, 23.

ἐπιπίπτω (πίπτω), *fall upon, attack* (dat.); of snow, *fall* (on one).

ἐπίπονος, -ον (πόνος), *toilsome, laborious;* of a bird of omen, *portending toil or suffering,* VI. 1, 23.

ἐπιρριπτέω (ῥιπτέω), *throw at,* or *upon.*

ἐπίρρυτος, -ον (ῥέω), *watered, well watered.*

ἐπισάττω (σάττω, ἔσαξα, *load*), *load on, saddle,* III, 4, 35 n.

Ἐπισθένης, -ους, ὁ, *Episthenes,* (1) of Amphipolis, captain of the Greek peltasts at Cunaxa; (2) an Olynthian of the same name.

ἐπισιτίζομαι (σιτίζομαι, σιτιοῦμαι, *etc.*), *collect* or *lay in supplies, forage.*

ἐπισιτισμός, -οῦ, ὁ (ἐπισιτίζομαι), *a laying in of supplies, provisioning; supplies,* VII, 1, 9.

ἐπισκέπτομαι (σκέπτομαι), *look into, examine, inquire.*

ἐπισκευάζω (σκευάζω), *fit out, repair.*

ἐπισκοπέω (σκοπέω), *inspect, review.*

ἐπισπάω (σπάω), *draw after;* mid., *draw after oneself.*

ἐπίσποιτο, see ἐφέπομαι.

ἐπίσταμαι, impf. ἠπιστάμην (ἵστημι; *cf.* Germ. *verstehen*), *know, understand,* with ὅτι or partic.; *know how,* with infin.

ἐπίστασις, -εως, ἡ (ἐπί+ἵστημι), *a stopping, halt.*

ἐπιστατέω (ἐπί+ἵστημι), *be a commander* or *overseer, rule.*

ἐπιστέλλω (στέλλω), *send to, send word* (cf. ἐπιστολή); *direct, command.*

ἐπιστήμων, -ον (ἐπίσταμαι), *acquainted with, versed* or *skilled in* (gen.).

ἐπιστολή, -ῆς, ἡ (ἐπιστέλλω; *cf.* Eng. *epistle*), *letter.*

ἐπιστρατεία, -ας, ἡ (ἐπιστρατεύω), *march* or *make an expedition against.*

ἐπιστρατεύω (στρατεύω), *take the field against, march against.*

ἐπισφάττω (σφάττω), *slay upon* (as a victim).

Ἐπιταλιεύς, -έως, ὁ (Ἐπιτάλιον), *inhabitant of Epitalium* in Elis, VII, 4, 18 (where the MSS. have the corrupt form εὐοδέα or ἐνοδίαν).

ἐπιτάττω (τάττω), *draw up in addition* or *behind* (as a reserve force), VI, 5, 9; *command, give orders;* ᾧ ἐπετέτακτο, *to whom orders had been given,* II, 3, 6.

ἐπιτελέω (τελέω), *bring to an end, fulfil, accomplish.*

ἐπιτήδειος, -α, -ον (ἐπιτηδές, *on purpose, enough*), *adapted to, suitable, fit, necessary;* οἱ ἐπιτήδειοι, *close friends* (Lat. *necessarii*), VII, 7, 57; τὰ ἐπιτήδεια, *provisions, supplies,* I, 3, 11, and often; τὸν ἐπιτήδειον ἔπαισεν ἄν, *he would strike the proper one* (*i.e.,* the one deserving it), II, 3, 11.

ἐπιτίθημι (τίθημι), *put upon, lay upon;* of penalties, *inflict;* mid., *attack.*

ἐπιτρέπω (τρέπω), *turn over to, entrust, grant, permit; refer a thing to another,* VII, 7, 18; mid., *give oneself up to for protection,* I, 9, 8.

ἐπιτρέχω, aor. ἐπέδραμον (τρέχω), *run upon, charge.*

ἐπιτυγχάνω (τυγχάνω), *chance upon, fall in with, find,* dat.

ἐπιφαίνομαι (φαίνω), *come in sight, appear.*

ἐπιφέρω (φέρω), *bring upon* or *against;* mid., *rush upon, attack;* of a heavy sea, V, 8, 20.

ἐπιφορέω (φορέω), *carry upon, place upon* (by making frequent trips), III, 5, 10.

ἐπίχαρις, -ι, gen. -ιτος (ἐπί+χάρις), *gracious, pleasing;* τὸ ἐπίχαρι, *grace of manner,* II, 6, 12.

ἐπιχειρέω, ἐπιχειρήσω, etc. (ἐπί+χείρ), *put one's hand to, attempt, try.*

ἐπιχέω (χέω, *pour*), *pour on* or *in.*

ἐπιχωρέω (χωρέω), *move against, advance.*

ἐπιψηφίζω (ψηφίζω), *put to vote.*

ἔπλευσαν, see πλέω.

ἐπλήγην, see πλήττω.

ἐποικοδομέω (οἰκοδομέω), *build upon.*

ἕπομαι, εἱπόμην, ἕψομαι, ἑσπόμην (√σεπ; *cf.* Lat. *sequor*), *follow, attend, accompany, pursue,* abs., with dat. or with σύν and dat.

ἐπόμνυμι (ὄμνυμι), *swear to a thing.*

ἐπριάμην, opt. πριαίμην, inf. πρίασθαι, partic. πριάμενος; defective vb., used as the aor. of ὠνέομαι, *buy.*

ἑπτά, indecl. (Lat. *septem*, Eng. *seven*), *seven.*

ἑπτακαίδεκα, indecl. (ἑπτά+δέκα), seventeen.

ἑπτακόσιοι, -αι, -α (ἑπτά+ἑκατόν), seven hundred.

Ἐπύαξα, -ης, ἡ, Epyaxa, wife of Syennesis, king of Cilicia.

ἐπύθετο, see πυνθάνομαι.

ἔραμαι (cf. ἔρως), love; aor. ἠράσθην, fall in love with, take a liking to.

ἐράω (cf. ἔρως), love, long for, with gen.

ἐργάζομαι, ἐργάσομαι, εἰργασάμην, εἴργασμαι, -ειργάσθην (ἔργον), work, labor, till (sc. γῆν), do, accomplish; with two accs., do to, inflict upon.

ἔργον, -ου, τό (originally ϝέργον, cf. Eng. work), work, deed, action; execution (of a work), III, 5, 12; ἔργῳ, in fact, in deed, contrasted with words, I, 9, 10; cf. III, 2, 32; τὰ εἰς τὸν πόλεμον ἔργα, deeds of war, I, 9, 5.

ἐρεῖ, see εἴρω.

ἐρέσθαι, see ἔρομαι.

Ἐρετριεύς, -έως, ὁ (Ἐρετρία), an Eretrian, native of Eretria, a city on the western coast of Euboea.

ἐρημία, -ας, ἡ (ἔρημος), solitude, privacy, V, 4, 34; desert, II, 5, 9.

ἔρημος, -η, -ον, or -ος, -ον (Eng. eremite, hermit), deserted, empty, unprotected, abandoned by, bereft of, without (gen.); σταθμοὶ ἔρημοι, marches through the desert, I, 5, 1; ἔρημοι οἱ ἱππεῖς, the cavalry unsupported (by infantry), VII, 3, 47.

ἐρίζω, in the Anabasis only in pres. (ἔρις, strife), strive, contend with (dat.).

ἐρίφειος, -α, -ον (ἔριφος, kid), of a kid, kids', with κρέα, IV, 5, 31.

ἑρμηνεύς, -έως, ὁ (Ἑρμῆς, Hermes, the messenger of Zeus), interpreter.

ἑρμηνεύω (ἑρμηνεύς ; cf. Eng. hermeneutic), act as interpreter, interpret.

ἔρομαι, in Attic only in fut. ἐρήσομαι and 2 aor. ἠρόμην, cf. ἐρωτάω, ask, inquire.

ἐροῦντα, see εἴρω.

ἐρρήθην, see εἴρω.

ἐρρωμένος, -η, -ον (perf. pass. partic. of ῥώννυμι, make strong), as adj., strong, resolute, comp. ἐρρωμενέστερος; (τὸ) ἐρρωμένον, strength, II, 6, 11.

ἐρρωμένως, adv. (ἐρρωμένος), strongly, vigorously.

ἐρύκω, keep back, ward off.

ἔρυμα, -ατος, τό, defense, wall.

ἐρυμνός, -ή, -όν, fortified, strong; neut. pl., strongholds, III, 2, 23.

ἔρχομαι, ἦλθον, ἐλήλυθα, come, go. Of the pres. the indic. alone is in common use, the other moods being supplied by εἶμι, which also supplies the fut. and impf.; εἰς χεῖρας ἐλθεῖν, come into the power of (dat.), I, 2, 26, or come to close quarters with, IV, 3, 31; εἰς λόγους σοι ἐλθεῖν, have an interview with you, II, 5, 4; ἐπὶ πᾶν ἐλθεῖν, have recourse to everything, leave nothing undone, III, 1, 18.

ἐρῶ, see εἴρω.

ἐρῶντες, see ἐράω.

ἔρως, -ωτος, ὁ (ἔραμαι; cf. Eng. erotic), love, desire.

ἐρωτάω, ἐρωτήσω, etc. (cf. ἔρομαι), ask, inquire.

ἐς, see εἰς.

ἐσέσωτο, see σῴζω.

ἔσθ' by elision and euphony for ἐστί.

ἐσθής, -ῆτος, ἡ (ἕννυμι, *put on*, for ϝέσνυμι; *cf.* Lat. *vestis*, Eng. *wear*), *clothing, raiment*.
ἐσθίω, ἔδομαι, ἐδήδοκα, ἠδέσθην, 2 aor. ἔφαγον *q.v.* (for ἐδθίω, Lat. *edo*, Eng. *eat*), *eat*.
ἐσκεδασμένων, see σκεδάννυμι.
ἐσκέψατο, see σκέπτομαι.
ἔσοιτο, see εἰμί.
ἐσπείσαντο, see σπένδω
ἐσπέρα, -ας, ἡ (Lat. *vesper*), *evening*, πρὸς ἑσπέραν, *toward the west*.
Ἑσπερῖται, -ῶν, οἱ, *the Hesperītae*, a people living in western Armenia.
ἐσταλμένος, see στέλλω.
ἑστάναι, see ἵστημι.
ἔστε adv. (ἐς [εἰς]+τε), *all the way to;* as temporal conj. (poetic), *up to, until*.
ἔστηκε, ἑστηκώς, ἔστησαν, see ἵστημι.
ἐστιγμένος, see στίζω.
ἐστραμμένα, see στρέφω.
ἑστώς, see ἵστημι.
ἔσχατος, -η, -ον (ἐξ), *last, farthest, extreme, severest, uttermost, worst* (δίκη) VI, 6, 15; τὰ ἔσχατα παθεῖν, *suffer the extreme penalty* (*i. e.* death), II, 5, 24; τὰ ἔσχατα αἰκισάμενος, *inflicting the extremest tortures*, III, 1, 18.
ἐσχάτως, adv. (ἔσχατος), *in the extremest degree, exceedingly*.
ἔσχε, see ἔχω.
ἔσωθεν, adv., *from within, inside;* τὸ ἔσωθεν, *the inner* (τεῖχος), I, 4, 4.
ἑταίρα, -ας, ἡ (*cf.* ἑταῖρος), *courtesan*.
ἑταῖρος, -ου, ὁ (*cf.* ἑταίρα), *companion, comrade, friend*.
ἐτάχθησαν, see τάττω.
Ἐτεόνικος, -ου, ὁ, *Eteonīcus*, a Spartan officer at Byzantium.
ἕτερος, -α, -ον (by crasis θάτερον for τὸ ἕτερον), *the other of two, the one, the other;* loosely like ἄλλος, *other;* τούτων ἕτεροι, *others than these, others besides*, VI, 4, 8; ἐκ τοῦ ἐπὶ θάτερα, *on the other side*, V, 4, 10.
ἐτετίμητο, see τιμάω.
ἐτέτρωτο, see τιτρώσκω.
ἔτι, adv., of time, *yet, still, longer, again;* of degree, with comp., *still, even;* ἔτι δέ, πρὸς δ' ἔτι, *furthermore, besides*.
ἕτοιμος, -η, -ον, *ready, prepared, at hand, certain*.
ἑτοίμως, adv. (ἕτοιμος), *readily, willingly*.
ἔτος, -ους, τό (*cf.* Lat. *vetus*, old, Eng. *wether*), *year*.
ἐτράπετο, see τρέπω.
ἐτράφητε, see τρέφω.
ἔτυχον, see τυγχάνω.
εὖ, adv., *well, easily, fortunately;* esp. εὖ ποιεῖν, *treat well* (*cf.* κακῶς ποιεῖν, I, 4, 8); εὖ πάσχειν, *be well treated;* εὖ πράττειν, *fare well;* εὖ μάλα, *thoroughly, roundly*, VI, 1, 1.
εὐδαιμονία, -ας (εὐδαίμων), *happiness, prosperity*.
εὐδαιμονίζω, εὐδαιμονιῶ, etc. (εὐδαίμων), *deem happy, congratulate* (for, gen.).
εὐδαιμόνως, adv. (εὐδαίμων), comp. εὐδαιμονέστερον, *prosperously, happily*.
εὐδαίμων, -ον, comp. εὐδαιμονέστερος, sup. εὐδαιμονέστατος (εὖ+δαίμων, *divinity, fate*), *happy, prosperous, wealthy;* with μέγας, a favorite epithet of cities in Xenophon.
εὔδηλος, -ον (εὖ+δῆλος), *entirely clear, manifest*.
εὐδία, -ας, ἡ, *fair weather*.
εὐειδής, -ές, sup. εὐειδέστατος (εὖ+εἶδος), *good looking, of good presence*.

εὔελπις, gen. -ιδος (εὖ+ἐλπίς), *of good hope, hopeful.*

εὐεπίθετος, -ον (εὖ+ἐπιτίθημι), *easily attacked;* εὐεπίθετον ἦν, *it was easy to attack,* III, 4, 20.

εὐεργεσία, -ας, ἡ (εὖ+ἔργον), *well-doing, conferring of benefits, kindness.*

εὐεργετέω, εὐεργετήσω, etc. (εὖ+ἔργον), *do well, confer favors.*

εὐεργέτης, -ου, ὁ (εὖ+ἔργον), *benefactor.*

εὔζωνος, -ον (ζώνη), *well girt,* hence, *active, agile.*

εὐήθεια, -ας, ἡ (εὐήθης), *simplicity, silliness.*

εὐήθης, -ες (εὖ+ἦθος, *disposition*), *simple-minded, silly.*

εὐθυμέομαι (εὖ+θυμός), *be in good spirits, enjoy oneself.*

εὔθυμος, -ον (εὖ+θυμός), *cheerful, of good courage.*

εὐθύς, adv., *straightway, at once, immediately;* εὐθύς παῖδες ὄντες, *even from boyhood,* I, 9, 4; so εὐθύς καὶ ἐκ παίδων, IV, 6, 14; εὐθὺς ἐπειδή, *as soon as,* III, 1, 13; *cf.* IV, 7, 7.

εὐθύωρος, -ον (εὐθύς), neut. as adv., *straight on.*

εὔκλεια, -ας, ἡ (κλέος, τό, *fame*), *fair fame, glory.*

Εὐκλείδης, -ου, ὁ, *Euclīdes,* a soothsayer from Phlius, a friend of Xenophon.

εὐκλεῶς, adv. (εὐκλεής, *glorious; cf.* εὔκλεια), *gloriously.*

εὐμενής, -ες (εὖ+μένος, *might, then, temper*), *well disposed, kindly,* hence, of a road, *easy, comfortable,* IV, 6, 12, in comp.

εὐμεταχείριστος, -ον (εὖ+μεταχειρίζομαι, *manage*), *easy to deal with* or *manage.*

εὔνοια, -ας, ἡ (εὖ+νοῦς), *good will, kindness.*

εὐνοϊκῶς, adv. (εὔνους), *kindly;* with ἔχειν, *be well-disposed.*

εὔνους, -ουν, comp. εὐνούστερος (εὖ+νοῦς), *well-disposed, friendly, devoted.*

εὔξασθαι, see εὔχομαι.

εὔξεινος, -ον (εὖ+ξένος), *hospitable;* Πόντος Εὔξεινος, the *Euxine* or *Black Sea,* a euphemism for the older name Ἄξενος, *inhospitable; cf. Cape of Good Hope,* for the older *Stormy Cape* or *Cape of Storms.*

εὔοδος, -ον (εὖ+ὁδός), *easy to travel.*

εὔοπλος, -ον (εὖ+ὅπλον), *well armed.*

εὐπετῶς, adv. (εὐπετής, *easy*), *easily.*

εὐπορία, -ας, ἡ (εὔπορος), *means of providing, means, abundance.*

εὔπορος, -ον (εὖ+πόρος), *easy to traverse, easy to pass through* or *over;* εὐπορόν ἐστι *it is easy* (lit. *traveling is easy*), III, 5, 17.

εὔπρακτος, -ον (εὖ+verbal of πράττω), *easy to be done, easy.*

εὐπρεπής, -ες (εὖ+πρέπω), *good looking, comely, handsome.*

εὐπρόσοδος, -ον (εὖ+πρός+ὁδός), *easy of access, easy to approach.*

εὕρημα, -ατος, τό (εὑρίσκω), *what is found, a "find," a piece of good luck.*

εὑρίσκω (εὑρήσω, ηὗρον, ηὕρηκα, ηὕρημαι, ηὑρέθην), *find, discover, devise.*

εὖρος, -ους, τό (εὐρύς), *breadth, width.*

Εὐρύλοχος, -ου, ὁ, *Eurylochus,* an Arcadian hoplite.

Εὐρύμαχος, -ου, ὁ, *Eurymachus,* of Dardanus, an opponent of Xenophon.

εὐρύς, -εῖα, -ύ, *broad, wide.*

Εὐρώπη, -ης, ἡ, *Europe.*

εὔτακτος, -ον (εὖ+τάττω), of troops, well-disciplined.

εὐτάκτως, adv. (εὔτακτος), in an orderly or well-disciplined manner.

εὐταξία, -ας, ἡ (εὖ+τάττω), good order, discipline.

εὐτυχέω, εὐτυχήσω, etc. (εὖ+τύχη), be fortunate, be successful.

εὐτύχημα, -ατος, τό (εὐτυχέω), piece of good fortune, advantage, success.

Εὐφράτης, -ου, ὁ, the Euphrātes, the chief river of western Asia.

εὐχή, -ῆς, ἡ (εὔχομαι), prayer.

εὔχομαι (εὔξομαι, ηὐξάμην), pray, pray that (acc. infin.), pray for, wish, vow.

εὐώδης, -ες (εὖ+ὄζω, smell, Lat. odor), sweet-smelling, fragrant.

εὐώνυμος, -ον (εὖ+ὄνομα), properly of good name, of good omen, so by a euphemism, the left, ἀριστερός being avoided as unlucky, since omens on the left were bad; in military language, τὸ εὐώνυμον (with or without κέρας), the left wing, the left, I, 2, 15 n.; cf. δεξιός.

εὐωχέω, entertain; in mid., feast, have abundance.

εὐωχία, -ας, ἡ (εὐωχέω), feast, banquet.

ἐφ', see ἐπί.

ἔφαγον, 2 aor., eat. The pres. in use is ἐσθίω, q. v.

ἐφάνη, see φαίνω.

ἔφασαν, ἔφατε, see φημί.

ἔφεδρος, -ον (ἐπί+ἕδρα, seat), sitting by, as subst., ὁ ἔφεδρος, antagonist—properly a third contestant who sits by and fights with the victor of the first bout, II, 5, 10.

ἐφέπομαι (ἕπομαι), follow after pursue.

Ἐφέσιος, -α, -ον (Ἔφεσος), of Ephesus, Ephesian.

Ἔφεσος, -ου, ἡ, Ephesus, an ancient city on the coast of Lydia, famed for its temple of Artemis.

ἔφη, see φημί.

ἐφθός, -ή, -όν (cf. ἕψω), boiled.

ἐφίστημι (ἵστημι), set beside or on, cause to stop, of a horse, rein in, I, 8, 15; set over or in command of; intrans. in mid. and in 2 aor., perf., and plpf. act., be set in or on, of gates, I, 4, 4; be put in command of, perf. command, VI, 5, 11; halt, I, 5, 7.

ἐφόδιον, -ου, τό (ὁδός), money for a journey, traveling expenses.

ἔφοδος, -ου, ἡ (ἐπί+ὁδός), way to, approach; advance, attack.

ἐφοράω (ὁράω), oversee, keep in sight.

ἐφορμέω (ὁρμέω), lie at anchor over against, blockade.

ἔφορος, -ου, ὁ (ἐπί+ὁράω), overseer, ephor. The five ephors, elected annually, were the highest magistrates of the Spartan state, having authority even over the kings.

ἔφυγε, see φεύγω.

ἔχθρα, -ας, ἡ (ἔχθος, hatred), hatred, ill-will.

ἐχθρός, -ά, -όν (τὸ ἔχθος, hatred), hating, hated, hostile, often as subst., enemy, I, 3, 6 n.; sup. οἱ ἐκείνου ἔχθιστοι, his bitterest foes, III, 2, 5.

ἐχυρός, -ά, -όν (ἔχω), that may be held; of a fortress, strong, defensible; cf. ὀχυρός.

ἔχω, ἕξω and σχήσω, ἔσχον, ἔσχηκα, -έσχημαι, have, in the widest sense and therefore to be variously rendered; lit. have, possess, οἱ ἔχοντες, the rich, VII, 3, 28; hold, II, 3, 11; have on, wear, I, 5, 8; have to wife, III, 4, 13; obtain, get, I, 3, 11; keep from, prevent, III, 5, 11; have power, be able, II, 2, 11; be busied with, ἀμφί, V, 2, 26; ἔχων, having, often rendered with, has generally a fuller meaning, e. g., keeping, II, 3, 10; at the head of, I, 2, 5, etc.; cf. λαβών; often ἔχω is intrans., especially when used with advs., and may be rendered be; εὐνοϊκῶς ἔχειν, be well disposed, I, 1, 5; εἶχεν οὕτως, it was so, III, 1, 31; cf. ἔχουσαι, intrans., VII, 8, 21; μεῖον ἔχειν, have the worst of it, I, 10, 8; χάριν ἔχειν feel grateful, II, 5, 14; αἰτίαν ἔχειν, (as pass. of αἰτιάομαι) be accused, VII, 1, 8; ἡσυχίαν ἔχειν, keep still, IV, 5, 13; ἔνδηλον καὶ τοῦτο εἶχεν, he made this too clear, II, 6, 18. Sometimes ἔχω is used with a past partic., but is not a mere composite vb. form; see I, 3, 14 and IV, 7, 1; mid. have hold of, come next to, be next, abs. or with gen., I, 8, 4; pass. ἐν ἀνάγκῃ ἔχεσθαι, be the thrall of necessity, II, 5, 21.

ἑψητός, -ή, -όν (verbal of ἕψω), boiled, made by boiling.

ἕψομαι, see ἕπομαι.

ἕψω, ἑψήσω, ἥψησα, boil.

ἕωθεν, adv. (ἕως), from dawn, at dawn, in the early morning.

ἑῴκεσαν, see ἔοικα.

ἑῶντες, see ἐάω.

ἑώρα, ἑώρακα, ἑώρων, see ὁράω.

ἕως, ἕω, ἡ (akin to Eng. east), dawn, daybreak; πρὸς ἕω, eastward, III, 5, 15; V, 7, 6.

ἕως, temporal conj., as long as, while, until.

Z

Ζαπάτας, -ου, ὁ, the Zab, a tributary of the Tigris.

ζάω, ζήσω, live, be alive.

ζειαί, -ῶν, αἱ, a coarse grain, spelt, only in pl.; cf. πυροί and κριθαί.

ζειρά, -ᾶς, ἡ, cloak or mantle reaching to the feet, worn by Thracian horsemen in winter.

ζευγηλατέω (ζυγόν+ἐλαύνω), drive a yoke of oxen.

ζευγηλάτης, -ου, ὁ (ζυγόν+ἐλαύνω), one who drives a yoke of oxen, a teamster.

ζεύγνυμι, ζεύξω, ἔζευξα, etc. (Lat. iungo, Eng. yoke), yoke, join, fasten; esp. of bridges, ζευγνύναι γέφυραν or ζευγνύναι ποταμόν, so in pass., I, 2, 5; II, 4, 13.

ζεῦγος, -ους, τό (ζυγόν, yoke), yoke or pair of animals; in pl. cattle.

Ζεύς, Διός, ὁ (cf. Sanskrit Dyaus, old Lat. Diespiter), Zeus, son of Rhea and Cronus, and king of the gods.

Ζήλαρχος, -ου, ὁ, Zelarchus, a commissary in the Greek army.

ζηλωτός, -ή, -όν (verbal adj. of ζηλόω, envy, from ζῆλος, envy; cf. Eng. zeal, jealous), enviable, an object of envy.

ζημιόω (ζημία, loss, fine), fine, punζῆν, see ζάω. [ish.

ζητέω, ζητήσω, etc., seek for, ask for; with infin., desire.

ζυμίτης, -ου, adj. (ζύμη, leaven; cf. Eng. zymotic), leavened.

ζωγρέω, ζωγρήσω, ἐζώγρησα (ζωός+ἀγρέω, catch), take alive.

ζῶν, see ζάω.

ζώνη, -ης, ἡ (ζώννυμι, gird, Eng. zone), girdle, belt. Women's girdles were often richly decorated, hence of the Persian queen, κῶμαι εἰς ζώνην δεδομέναι, villages given for girdle-money ("*pin money*"), *i.e.*, she enjoyed the revenues for personal use, I, 4, 9; a soldier's belt was of metal or leather.

ζωός, -ή, -όν (ζάω), *living, alive*.

H

ἤ, conj.: (1) disjunctive, *or*; ἤ ... ἤ, *either ... or*, I, 3, 5; in indir. double ques., πότερον (πότερα, εἰ) ... ἤ, *whether ... or*; in a direct question, with the former member unexpressed, II, 4, 3; (2) comparative, *than* (after comparative or words implying comp. rison ἄλλος, ἐναντίος, etc.).

ἦ, adv. (Eng. *yea*), *in truth, truly*; in oaths ἦ μήν; see μήν.

ἦ, interrogative part., implying nothing as to the answer expected, but often implying feeling.

ἡ, see ὁ.

ᾗ, dat. sing. fem. of rel. ὅς, used as adv. (sc. ὁδῷ?), *in what place, where, in what way, how;* ᾗ ἐδύνατο τάχιστα, *as quickly as he could,* I, 2, 4, etc.,; ᾗ δυνατὸν μάλιστα, *with all my power, with all my heart,* I, 3, 15.

ᾖ, see εἰμί.

ἡβάσκω (ἥβη, *youth*), *grow from boyhood to youth*.

ἤγαγον, see ἄγω.

ἠγάσθη, see ἄγαμαι.

ἤγγειλα, see ἀγγέλλω.

ἠγγυᾶτο, see ἐγγυάω.

ἡγεμονία, -ας, ἡ (ἡγεμών), *leadership, command*.

ἡγεμόσυνα, -ων, τά (sc. ἱερά), *thank-offerings* (for safe conduct).

ἡγεμών, -όνος, ὁ (ἡγέομαι, ἄγω), *leader, guide, commander*; as a title of Heracles, VI, 2, 15.

ἡγέομαι, ἡγήσομαι, etc. (*cf.* ἄγω), *lead, conduct, guide*, abs. or with dat.; τὸ ἡγούμενον, *the van,* II, 2, 4; *command, be leader of,* abs. or with gen. or dat., I, 4, 2 n; *think, believe* (*cf.* Lat. *duco*), I, 2, 4.

Ἡγήσανδρος, -ου, ὁ, *Hegesander,* one of the generals of the Arcadian army.

ᾔδει, ᾔδεσαν, see οἶδα.

ἡδέως, adv., comp. ἥδιον, sup. ἥδιστα (ἡδύς), *gladly, with pleasure*.

ἤδη, adv. (ἦ+δή?), *now, ere now, by this time, already, at once*.

ἥδομαι, ἡσθήσομαι, ἥσθην (ἡδύς, *suavis*, *sweet*), *be glad, delight in, enjoy*, abs., with dat., or with partic.

ἡδονή, -ῆς, ἡ (ἡδύς), *pleasure, delight*; of fruit, *flavor, taste,* II, 3, 16.

ἡδύοινος, -ον (ἡδύς+οἶνος), *producing sweet wine*.

ἡδύς, -εῖα, -ύ, comp. ἡδίων, sup. ἥδιστος (*cf.* ἥδομαι, Lat. *suavis*), *sweet, delicious, pleasant*.

ἤθελε, see ἐθέλω.

ἧκαν, see ἵημι.

ἥκιστα, see ἥττων.

ἥκω, ἥξω, pres. with perf. force, *be come, have come, arrive, come back*.

ἤλασε, see ἐλαύνω.

ἤλεγχον, see ἐλέγχω.

Ἠλεῖος, -α, -ον (Ἦλις, *Elis*), *an Elēan*, a native of Elis, a state in the western part of the Peloponnesus.

ἤλεκτρον, -ου, τό (*cf.* Eng. *electric*), a name given by the Greeks to *amber*, and to the metal *electrum*, a compound of four parts of gold to one of silver.

ἦλθον, see ἔρχομαι.

ἠλίβατος, -ον, poetic adj., *steep, sheer, precipitous.*

ἠλίθιος, -α, -ον, *foolish, stupid;* τὸ ἠλίθιον, *folly, stupidity,* II, 6, 22.

ἡλικία, -ας, ἡ (ἡλίκος, *as old as*), *age,* esp. *prime of life, manhood.*

ἡλικιώτης, -ου, ὁ (ἡλικία), *a person of one's own age, comrade,*

ἥλιος, -ου, ὁ (cf. Eng. *heliotrope,* etc.), *the sun,* generally without art.; as a god, *Helios,* the sun-god, IV, 5, 35.

ἡμεῖς, see ἐγώ.

ἠμελημένως, adv. from perf. pass. partic. of ἀμελέω, *carelessly.*

ἦμεν, see εἰμί.

ἡμέρα, -ας, ἡ, *day,* whether contrasted with night or as designating the whole period of 24 hrs.; μέσον ἡμέρας, *noon,* I, 8, 8; ἅμα τῇ ἡμέρᾳ, *at daybreak,* II, 1, 2; τὰς μὲν ἡμέρας ... τὰς δὲ νύκτας, *by day ... by night,* V, 8, 24; so ἡμέρας καὶ νυκτός, II, 6, 7; distributive, τῆς ἡμέρας, *a day, per diem,* IV, 6, 4; but in III, 3, 11, *in the course of the day;* cf. δέκα ἡμερῶν, *within ten days,* I, 7, 18; ὅλην τὴν ἡμέραν, *all day long,* IV, 1, 10; πρὸς ἡμέραν, *near dawn,* IV, 5, 21; μεθ' ἡμέραν, *by day,* IV, 6, 12.

ἥμερος, -α, -ον, *tame,* of trees, *cultivated.*

ἡμέτερος, -α, -ον (ἡμεῖς), *our;* τὰ ἡμέτερα, *our affairs* or *circumstances,* I, 3, 9.

ἡμι-, a prefix (Lat. *semi-,* Eng. *hemi-*), *half.*

ἡμίβρωτος, -ον (ἡμι-+verbal of βιβρώσκω, *eat*), *half-eaten.*

ἡμιδαρεικόν, -ου, τό (ἡμι-+δαρεικός), *half a daric.*

ἡμιδεής, -ές (ἡμι-+δέω, *need, lack*), *half-full.*

ἡμιόλιος, -α, -ον (ἡμι-+ὅλος), *half as much again,* with gen. of comparison, I, 3, 21.

ἡμιονικός, -ή, -όν (ἡμίονος), *belonging to mules;* ζεῦγος ἡμιονικόν, *mule team,* VII, 5, 2.

ἡμίονος, -ου, ὁ (ὄνος), *mule.*

ἡμίπλεθρον, -ου, τό (πλέθρον), *half a plethrum.*

ἥμισυς, -εια, -υ (cf. ἡμι-), *half;* as subst., *half, the half,* with gen. I, 9, 26.

ἡμιωβόλιον, -ου, τό (ὀβολός), *half an obol.*

ἤμουν, see ἐμέω.

ἠμφεγνόουν, see ἀμφιγνοέω.

ἡμῶν αὐτῶν, see ἐμαυτοῦ.

ἤν, contr. for ἐάν.

ἦν, imperf. of εἰμί.

ἠνέχθη, see φέρω.

ἡνίκα, temporal conj., *when,*

ἡνίοχος, -ου, ὁ (ἡνία, τά, *reins*+ἔχω), *driver, charioteer.*

ἤνπερ, contr. for ἐάνπερ.

ἥνπερ, see ὅσπερ.

ἥξειν, see ἥκω.

ᾗπερ, dat. fem. sing. of ὅσπερ, as adv., *in the very manner* or *place in which, just as, just where.*

ἠπιστάμεθα, see ἐπίσταμαι.

Ἡράκλεια, -ας, ἡ, *Heraclēa,* a Greek city in Bithynia.

Ἡρακλείδης, -ου, ὁ (Ἡρακλῆς), *Heraclīdes,* a Thracian from Maronea, in the service of Seuthes.

Ἡρακλεώτης, -ου, ὁ (Ἡράκλεια), *an inhabitant of Heraclēa, a Heracleot.*

Ἡρακλῆς, -έους, ὁ, *Heracles,* Lat. *Hercules,* son of Zeus and Alcmena, the greatest of the Greek heroes. For twelve years he was forced by Hera to serve Eurystheus, king of Argos, and thus performed his twelve labors, the last of which was the bringing of Cerberus to the upper world, VI, 2, 2. He was the patron and guide of wanderers, IV, 8, 25 n.

ἠράσθη, see ἔραμαι.

ᾑρέθησαν, ᾕρηντο, see αἱρέω.

ᾐρόμην, ἔρομαι.

ἥσθη, see ἥδομαι.

ἡσυχάζω (ἥσυχος), *keep quiet.*

ἡσυχῇ, adv. (ἥσυχος), *quietly, in silence.*

ἡσυχία, -ας, ἡ (ἥσυχος), *quiet, rest;* καθ' ἡσυχίαν, *at one's ease,* II, 3, 8; ἡσυχίαν ἄγειν, *take one's ease,* III, 1, 14; ἡσυχίαν ἔχειν, *keep still,* IV, 5, 13; V, 8, 15; *cf.* εἰρήνην ἄγειν, *enjoy peace,* II, 6, 6.

ἥσυχος, -ον, *still, quiet, in silence.*

ᾐτησάμεθα, see αἰτέω.

ἦτρον, -ου, τό, *belly, abdomen.*

ἡττάομαι, ἡττήσομαι or ἡττηθήσομαι, etc. (ἥττων), *be less* or *weaker than* (gen.), *be surpassed, outdone, defeated.*

ἥττων, -ον, gen. -ονος, *inferior, weaker,* used as comp. of κακός; neut. as adv., ἧττον, *less,* II, 4, 2; οὐδὲν ἧττον, *none the less,* VII, 5, 9; sup. ἥκιστα, *least of all, not at all, by no means,* I, 9, 19; VII, 3, 38.

ηὔχοντο, see εὔχομαι.

ηὗρε, see εὑρίσκω.

ηὐτύχησαν, see εὐτυχέω.

ἤχθησαν, see ἄγω.

Θ

θ', by elision and euphony for τέ.

θάλαττα, -ης, ἡ, *sea.*

θάλπος, -ους, τό (θάλπω, *warm*), *heat,* in pl. III, 1, 23 n.

θαμινά, adv. (θάμα, *often*), *often.*

θάνατος, -ου, ὁ (θνῄσκω), *death;* ἐπὶ θανάτῳ, *as a sign of condemnation to death,* I, 6, 10; ἐπὶ θανάτῳ ἄγεσθαι, *be prosecuted on a capital charge,* V, 7, 34.

θανατόω, θανατώσω, etc. (θάνατος), *condemn to death.*

θάπτω (θάψω, ἔθαψα, τέθαμμαι, ἐτάφην), *bury.*

θαρραλέος, -α, -ον (θρασύς), *bold, confident.*

θαρραλέως, adv. (θαρραλέος), *boldly, confidently.*

θαρρέω, -ήσω, etc. (θρασύς), *be confident, be of good courage;* with acc., *have no fear of,* III, 2, 20; partic. as adv., *confidently,* III, 4, 3.

θάρρος, -ους, τό (θρασύς), *confidence, courage.*

θαρρύνω (θρασύς), *make confident, encourage, hearten.*

Θαρύπας, -ου, ὁ, *Tharypas,* a favorite of Menon's.

θάτερον, see ἕτερος.

θᾶττον, see ταχύς.

θαῦμα, -ατος, τό (*cf.* θεάομαι), *a wonder, marvel.*

θαυμάζω (θαυμάσομαι, ἐθαύμασα, τεθαύμακα, ἐθαυμάσθην), *wonder at, be surprised, admire.*

θαυμάσιος, -α, -ον (θαυμάζω), *marvelous, remarkable.*

θαυμαστός, -ή, -όν (θαυμάζω), *wonderful, strange; cf.* θαυμάσιος.

Θαψακηνός, -οῦ, ὁ (Θάψακος), *inhabitant of Thapsacus,* in pl., I, 4, 18.

Θάψακος, ου, ἡ (Heb. *Tiphsah, ford,* I Kings, 4:24), *Thapsacus,* an important city on the west bank of the Euphrates.

θέα, -ας, ἡ (*cf.* θεάομαι, Eng. *theatre*), *sight, spectacle.*

θεά, -ᾶς, ἡ (θεός), *goddess.*

θέαμα, -ατος, τό (θεάομαι), *sight, spectacle.*

θεάομαι, θεάσομαι, *etc.* (θέα), *gaze at, watch, see.*

θεῖος, -α, -ον (θεός), *divine, miraculous.*

θέλω, see ἐθέλω.

-θεν, suffix denoting the place whence.

Θεογένης, -ους, ὁ, *Theogenes,* a Locrian, captain in the Greek army.

Θεόπομπος, -ου, ὁ, *Theopompus,* an Athenian.

θεός, -οῦ, ὁ, ἡ, *divinity, god, goddess,* the sing. having the art. only when a definite god is meant; σὺν (τοῖς) θεοῖς, *with the aid of heaven;* πρὸς θεῶν, *before* or *in the sight of the gods.*

θεοσέβεια, -ας, ἡ (θεός+σέβομαι, *worship*), *reverence for the gods, piety.*

θεραπεύω, θεραπεύσω, *etc.* (θεράπων, *cf.* Eng. *therapeutic*), *attend, serve, wait upon.*

θεράπων, -οντος, ὁ, *servant, attendant* (not a born slave, δοῦλος).

θερίζω, (θέρος, *summer*), *spend the summer.*

θερμασία, -ας, ἡ (θερμός, *hot; cf.* Eng. *thermometer*), *warmth.*

Θερμώδων, -οντος, ὁ, *the Thermōdon,* a river in Cappadocia.

θέσθαι, see τίθημι.

Θετταλία, -ας, ἡ (Θετταλός), *Thessaly,* the largest state in northern Greece, bordering upon Macedonia.

Θετταλός, -οῦ, ὁ, *a Thessalian.*

θέω (θεύσομαι), *run, charge;* chiefly, but not solely, in the military phrase, θεῖν δρόμῳ, *charge at double quick, on the run.*

θεωρέω, θεωρήσω, *etc.* (θέα), *look at, view, be spectator; of troops, review.*

Θηβαῖος, -ου, ὁ (Θῆβαι, *Thebes*), *a Theban,* inhabitant of Thebes in Boeotia.

Θήβη, -ης, ἡ, *Thebe,* a small city in the Troad; Θήβης πεδίον, the neighboring district, VII, 8, 7.

θήρα, -ας, ἡ (θήρ, *wild beast, cf.* Lat. *ferus,* Eng. *deer*), *hunt, chase.*

θηράω, θηράσω, *etc.* (θήρα), *hunt, chase.*

θηρεύω, θηρεύσω, *etc.* (θήρα), *hunt, chase, catch.*

θηρίον, -ου, τό (θήρα), *beast, animal.*

θησαυρός, -οῦ, ὁ, (τίθημι), *treasure, store,* V, 4, 27; *treasury,* V, 3, 5.

Θήχης, ου, ὁ, *Theches,* a mountain in Pontus.

-θι, a suffix denoting the place where.

Θίβρων, -ωνος, ὁ, *Thibron,* a Spartan general, warring against Tissaphernes.

θνῄσκω (θανοῦμαι, ἔθανον, τέθνηκα), regularly used in compounds (chiefly ἀπο-), save in the perf. and plpf., *die, be killed;* in perf. *be dead, fallen in battle,* I, 6, 11. In the pf., save in the sing. indic. 2 pf. forms are found, τέθνατον, IV, 1, 19; τεθνᾶσι, IV, 2, 17; τεθνάναι, IV, 7, 20; τεθνεῶτας, VII, 4, 19.

θνητός, -ή, -όν (verbal of θνῄσκω), *mortal.*

θόρυβος, -ου, ὁ, *noise, confusion, disturbance.*

Θούριος, -ου, ὁ, *a Thurian,* inhabitant of Thurii, an Athenian colony in southern Italy.

Θρᾴκη, -ης, ἡ (Θρᾷξ), *Thrace:* (1) the region in Europe lying north of the Aegean and west of the

Euxine; (2) in Asia, the region south of the Euxine extending from the Bosphorus to Heraclēa.

Θράκιος, -α, -ον (Θρᾷξ), Thracian; τὸ Θράκιον, the Thracian quarter (in Byzantium).

Θρᾷξ, -κός, ὁ, a native of Thrace, Thracian.

θρασέως, adv. (θρασύς), boldly.

θρασύς, -εῖα, -υ (cf. Eng. dare), bold, daring.

θρεψόμεθα, see τρέφω.

θρόνος, -ου, ὁ (Eng. throne), seat, chair, throne.

θυγάτηρ, -τρός, ἡ (cf. Eng. daughter), daughter.

θύλακος, -ου, ὁ, bag, sack.

θῦμα, -ατος, τό (θύω), sacrifice, victim.

Θύμβριον, -ου, τό, Thymbrium, a city of Phrygia.

θυμοειδής, -ές (θυμός+εἶδος), high-spirited, of horses.

θυμόομαι, θυμώσομαι, etc. (θυμός), be angry or wroth.

θυμός, -οῦ, ὁ, heart, feelings, wrath.

Θυνοί, -ῶν, οἱ, the Thyni, a Thracian tribe.

θύρα, -ας, ἡ (Lat. foris, Eng. door), door, commonly in pl. of folding doors; ἐπὶ ταῖς βασιλέως θύραις, at the king's court, I, 9, 3, but in II, 4, 4, at his very gates; cf. VI, 5, 23 and see I, 2, 11 n.

θύρετρα, τά (θύρα), doors, gates.

θυσία, -ας, ἡ, sacrifice.

θύω (θύσω, ἔθυσα, τέθυκα, τέθυμαι, ἐτύθην), sacrifice, abs., or with acc. of victim, and dat. of the god; mid., have a sacrifice offered, offer sacrifice, esp. with a view to learning about the future; τὰ Λύκαια ἔθυσε, celebrated the Lycaea (see the word) with sacrifice, I, 2, 10; θύειν σωτήρια, sacrifice thank-offerings for safety, III, 2, 9; τὰ θυόμενα, the victims, V, 3, 9.

θωρακίζω, ἐθωράκισα, etc. (θώραξ), arm with a breastplate or cuirass; mid., put on one's breastplate, II, 2, 14; pass. aor. and pf. partic., clad in armor.

θώραξ, -ακος, ὁ, breastplate, cuirass.

Θώραξ, -ακος, ὁ, Thorax, a Boeotian in the Greek army.

I

ἰάομαι, ἰάσομαι, heal, cure.

Ἰασονία ἀκτή, ἡ, Jason's cape, a promontory in Pontus near Sinōpe. Here according to legend, the Argonauts under Jason landed.

ἰατρός, -οῦ, ὁ (ἰάομαι), physician, surgeon.

ἰδέ (ἰδεῖν), see εἶδον.

Ἴδη, -ης, ἡ, Ida, a mountain in the Troad, famed as the scene of the judgment of Paris.

ἴδιος, -α, -ον (cf. Eng. idiom), one's own, personal, private; εἰς τὸ ἴδιον, for one's own use, I, 3, 3; adv. ἰδίᾳ, privately, V, 6, 27.

ἰδιότης, -ητος, ἡ (ἴδιος), peculiarity.

ἰδιώτης, -ου, ὁ (ἴδιος; cf. Eng. idiot), private person, subject, private soldier; amateur, one without special knowledge, VI, 1, 31.

ἰδιωτικός, -ή, -όν (ἰδιώτης), of a private person, private, common.

ἴδοι, ἰδοῦσα, see εἶδον.

ἱδρόω, ἱδρώσω (ἱδρώς, sweat, Lat. sudor, Eng. sweat), sweat.

ἰδών, see εἶδον.

ἵεντο, see ἵημι.

ἱερεῖον, -ου, τό (ἱερός), *animal for sacrifice;* in pl., *cattle, for food,* since a portion of the slain beast was always offered to the gods.

ἱερός, -ά, -όν (cf. Eng. *hierarchy*), *holy, sacred* (to a god, gen., V, 3, 13); as subst. τὸ ἱερόν. *temple,* V, 3, 11; in pl. τὰ ἱερά, *sacrifice, vitals,* of the victims, or *omens,* drawn from their inspection, I, 8, 15. and often; ἡ ἱερὰ συμβουλὴ λεγομένη εἶναι, "*sacred counsel" as the proverb goes* (alluding to the proverb ἱερὸν ἡ συμβουλή), V, 6, 4; Ἱερὸν ὄρος, *sacred mountain,* in Thrace, VII, 1, 14.

Ἱερώνυμος, -ου, ὁ, *Hieronymus,* of Elis, a Greek captain.

ἵημι (ἥσω, ἧκα, -εῖκα, -εῖμαι, -είθην), *send, throw, hurl,* with dat. of the missile; ἧκαν ἑαυτούς, *they flung themselves, rushed,* IV, 5, 18; so mid., *run, rush, charge.*

ἴθι, see εἶμι.

ἱκανός, -ή, -όν (ἱκνέομαι, ἱκάνω), *sufficient, enough, adequate, able, fit,* abs., or with infin.

ἱκανῶς, adv. (ἱκανός), *sufficiently, adequately, well enough.*

ἱκετεύω, -εύσω, etc. (ἱκνέομαι), *implore, beseech.*

ἱκέτης, -ου, ὁ (ἱκνέομαι), *suppliant.*

Ἰκόνιον, -ου, τό, *Iconium,* a city of Phrygia.

ἵλεως, -ων, gen. -ω, *propitious, favorable,* of gods.

ἴλη, -ης, ἡ (εἴλω, *hem in*), *band, troop,* esp. of cavalry.

ἱμάς, -άντος, ὁ, *thong, strap.*

ἱμάτιον, -ου, τό, *outer garment, cloak, himation;* in pl., *clothes,* IV, 3, 11.

ἵνα, final particle, *that, in order that,* with subj. or opt.

ἵππαρχος, -ου, ὁ (ἵππος+ἄρχω), *cavalry, commander.*

ἱππασία, -ας, ἡ (ἵππος), *a riding to and fro.*

ἱππεία, -ας, ἡ (ἵππος), *cavalry.*

ἱππεύς, -έως, ὁ, *horseman, cavalryman.*

ἱππικός, -ή, -όν (ἵππος), *of or belonging to a horse* or *to cavalry;* ἱππικὴ δύναμις, *cavalry force,* I, 3, 12; τὸ ἱππικόν, *cavalry,* I, 9, 31.

ἱππόδρομος, -ου, ὁ (ἵππος+δρόμος), *a race-course, hippodrome.*

ἵππος, -ου, ὁ (for ἴκκος, Lat. *equus*), *horse,* pl. οἱ ἵπποι, *cavalry,* VII, 3, 39; ἀπὸ or ἐφ' ἵππου, *on horseback,* I. 2, 7; III, 4, 47.

Ἶρις, acc. Ἶριν, ὁ, *the Iris,* a river in Pontus.

ἴσθι, see οἶδα.

ἰσθμός, -οῦ, ὁ (Eng. *isthmus*), *isthmus;* as a proper name, *the Isthmus of Corinth,* II, 6, 3.

ἴσμεν, see οἶδα.

ἰσόπλευρος, -ον (ἴσος+πλευρά), *with equal sides, equilateral.*

ἴσος, -η, -ον (cf. Eng. *isosceles*), *equal;* ἐν ἴσῳ, *in equal step, evenly,* I, 8, 11; οὐκ ἐξ ἴσου ἐσμέν, *we are not on an equal footing,* III, 4, 47; εἰς τὸ ἴσον ἡμῖν, *to the same level with us,* IV, 6, 18; ἴσους τὸ μῆκος καὶ τὸ πλάτος, *as broad as they were long,* V, 4, 32; adv. ἴσον, *equally, alike,* II, 5, 7.

ἰσοχειλής, -ές (ἴσος+χεῖλος, *lip*), *up to the brim.*

Ἰσσοί, -ῶν, οἱ, *Issi* or *Issus,* a city of Cilicia.

ἴστε, see οἶδα.

ἵστημι (στήσω, ἔστησα, ἔστηκα, ἐστάθην), 2 aor. ἔστην, 2 perf. infin. ἑστάναι (Lat. *stare,* Eng. *stand*), *make stand* or *stop, station,* *place, set up;* intr. in mid. (except 1 aor.) and 2 aor., 1 and 2 perf., and 1 and 2 plpf. act., *stand, halt, be stationed, hold one's ground,* I, 10, 1.

ἱστίον, -ου, τό (dimin. of ἱστός, *mast, cf.* ἵστημι), *sail.*

ἰσχυρός, -ά, -όν (ἰσχύς), *strong, mighty,* of persons and places.

ἰσχυρῶς, (ἰσχυρός), *strongly, violently, exceedingly.*

ἰσχύς, -ύος, ἡ, *strength, might, force;* of an army, I, 8, 22; V. 7, 30.

ἴσχω (parallel form to ἔχω, only in pres. and impf.), *hold, hinder;* pass., ἐν τούτῳ ἴσχετο, *in this there was a hitch,* VI, 3, 9.

ἴσως, adv. (ἴσος), *equally, probably, perhaps, I suppose.*

Ἰταμένης, -ου, ὁ, *Itamenes,* a Persian.

ἰτέον (verbal of εἶμι), *one must go.*

ἴτυς, -υος, ἡ, *rim,* of a shield.

ἰχθύς, -ύος, ὁ (cf. Eng. *ichthyology*), *fish.*

ἰχνίον, -ου, τό (dim. of ἴχνος), *footstep, track.* The word is mainly confined to poetry.

ἴχνος, -ους, τό, *footstep, track.*

Ἰωνία, -ας, ἡ (Ἴων, *Ion,* the mythical founder of the Ionian tribe), *Ionia,* a name given to the coast of Asia Minor and the adjacent islands, between Aeolis and Caria.

Ἰωνικός, -ή, -όν (Ἰωνία), *belonging to Ionia, Ionian, Ionic.*

K

κἀγαθά, for καὶ ἀγαθά.

κἀγώ, for καὶ ἐγώ.

καθ', by elision and euphony for κατά.

καθά, adv. for καθ' ἅ, *according as, just as.*

καθαίρω, καθαρῶ, ἐκάθηρα (καθαρός, *clean; cf.* Lat. *castus, chaste,* Eng. *cathartic*), *cleanse, purify.*

καθάπερ, adv. (καθ' ἅπερ), *just as =* ὥσπερ.

καθαρμός, -οῦ, ὁ (καθαίρω), *purification.*

καθέζομαι, ἐκαθεζόμην, καθεδοῦμαι (simple ἕζομαι, *sit,* rare), *sit down; halt, encamp,* I, 5, 9.

καθέλκω (ἕλκω), *drag* or *draw down.* of ships, *launch.*

καθέντας, see καθίημι.

καθεύδω, impf. ἐκάθευδον (εὕδω, poetic *sleep*), *lie down, sleep, lie idle.*

καθηγέομαι (ἡγέομαι), *lead, conduct, carry out.*

καθηδυπαθέω, aor. καθηδυπάθησα (ἡδυπαθέω, from ἡδύς+πάσχω), *squander in luxury.*

καθήκω (ἥκω), *come down, reach down to;* impers. *it behooves, is the duty of,* with dat., I, 9, 7.

κάθημαι, impf. ἐκαθήμην (ἧμαι, poetic, *sit*), *sit, be seated, be encamped.*

καθῆραι, see καθαίρω.

καθίζω, καθιῶ, ἐκάθισα (ἵζω, *seat*), *make sit down, seat, set.*

καθίημι (ἵημι), *send down;* of spears καθιέναι εἰς προβολήν, *lower for attack,* VI, 5, 25.

καθίστημι (ἵστημι), *place* or *set down, station, establish,* but to be variously rendered; *arrange,* II, 3, 3; *bring,* I, 4, 13; *set in office, appoint,* III, 2, 5; intrans. (in 2 aor., pf. and plpf. act. and the mid., except the 1 aor., *come to, be established in;* 1 aor. mid. trans., *appoint,* III. 1, 39; ὡς καταστησομένων τούτων εἰς τὸ δέον, *since this business would turn out all right,* I, 3, 8.

καθοράω (ὁράω), *look down on from above, observe.*

καί, conj., copulative or intensive, *and, even, also.* As a copula it connects words or clauses; in enumerations it is regularly expressed with each item, not before the last only, as in Eng., although it may be omitted altogether (asyndeton); after πολύς it may be left untranslated, II, 3, 18; after words expressing sameness it may be rendered *as* (cf. Lat. *ac.*), II, 2, 10. As an intensive it is common with concessive partics., I, 9, 31 (cf. καίπερ); with relatives, marking the parallelism, where *and* or *also* is unnatural in Eng., ὅπου ἂν καὶ ὑμεῖς, I, 3, 6; cf. ὥς τις καὶ ἄλλος, I, 3, 15; εἴ τις καὶ ἄλλος, I, 4, 15; καὶ αὐτοί, *they too*, III, 4, 37. καί is often correlated with τε or καί, *both ... and;* for καὶ γάρ, see γάρ.

Κάικος, -ου, ὁ, *the Caicus,* a river of Mysia; Κάικου πεδίον, the adjacent plain.

Καιναί, -ῶν, αἱ, *Caenae,* a city in Mesopotamia on the Tigris.

καίνω, *slay, kill,* III, 2, 39; cf. κατακαίνω.

καίπερ, concessive conj. (καί+περ), *although,* with partic.

καιρός, -οῦ, ὁ, *right* or *fitting time, opportunity, crisis;* ἐν καιρῷ, *opportunely,* III, 1, 39; προσωτέρω τοῦ καιροῦ, *further than was proper* or *wise,* IV, 3, 34.

καίτοι, conj. (καί+τοι), *and yet.*

καίω or **κάω,** καύσω, ἔκαυσα, -κέκαυκα, κέκαυμαι, ἐκαύθην, *burn, burn up;* πῦρ καίειν, *keep a fire burning,* IV, 1, 11; of surgeons, *cauterize,* V, 8, 18; pass. *be on fire.*

κἀκεῖνος, for καὶ ἐκεῖνος.

κακόνοια, -ας ἡ (κακός+νοῦς), *ill will, malice.*

κακόνους, -ουν (κακός+νοῦς), *of evil mind, ill-disposed, hostile.*

κακός, -ή, -όν, comp. κακίων, sup. κάκιστος, *bad, wicked, base, harmful,* of persons or things, esp. of soldiers, *cowardly;* as subst. τὸ κακόν, *evil, harm, mischief,* III, 1, 25; κακόν (κακά) τινα ποιεῖν, *do harm to, injure,* I, 9, 11; cf. κακῶς.

κακουργέω (κακός+ √εργ), *do harm to, maltreat.*

κακοῦργος, -ου, ὁ, (κακός+ √εργ), *an evil-doer, criminal.*

κακόω, κακώσω, etc. (κακός), *hurt, injure.*

κακῶς, adv. (κακός), *badly, ill, wrongly, wretchedly;* κακῶς ποιεῖν, *do harm to, injure,* I, 4, 8; as pass. κακῶς πάσχειν, *be ill treated,* III, 3, 7; κακῶς ἔχειν, *be badly off, in evil case,* I, 5, 16, κακίον πράττειν, *fare worse, be worse off,* I, 9, 10.

κάκωσις, -εως, ἡ (κακόω), *ill treatment.*

καλάμη, -ης, ἡ (cf. κάλαμος), *straw.*

κάλαμος, -ου, ὁ, *reed, straw.*

καλέω (καλῶ, ἐκάλεσα, κέκληκα, κέκλημαι, ἐκλήθην), *call, summon, invite; call, name,* with two accs., VII, 6, 38; so in pass. I, 2, 8; partic. καλούμενος, often, *so-called,* I, 2, 8; I, 8, 10.

καλινδέομαι (cf. κυλινδέω), *roll.*

καλλιερέω, καλλιερήσω, ἐκαλλιέρησα (καλός+ἱερός), *obtain favorable omens in sacrificing.*

Καλλίμαχος, -ου, ὁ, *Callimachus,* of Parrhasia in Arcadia, a Greek captain, noted for his bravery.

καλλίων (κάλλιστος), see καλός.

Vocabulary

κάλλος, -ους, τό (καλός), *beauty*.

καλλωπισμός, -οῦ, ὁ (καλλωπίζω, *adorn*; καλός+ὤψ, *face*), *adornment*.

καλός, -ή, -όν (*cf.* Eng. *whole*), comp. καλλίων, sup. κάλλιστος, *beautiful, fair, noble, honorable*; of omens or sacrifices, *propitious*; as subst. τὸ καλόν, *honor*, II, 6, 18; καλοὶ καὶ ἀγαθοί, *the noble and good* (the Greek phrase for "gentlemen"), II, 6, 19; in military lang., *good and brave*, IV, 1, 19; εἰς καλὸν ἥκετε, *you have come opportunely*, IV, 7, 3.

Κάλπης λιμήν, ὁ, *Calpe haven*, a port in Bithynia. In VI, 3, 24 it is called *Calpe* simply.

Καλχηδονία, -ας, ἡ (Καλχηδών), *Chalcedonia*, the region around Chalcēdon.

Καλχηδών, -όνος, ἡ, *Chalcēdon*, a city in Bithynia opposite Byzantium.

καλῶς, comp. κάλλιον, sup. κάλλιστα (καλός), *beautifully*, but chiefly in a moral sense, *well, honorably, finely, nobly, happily*; καλῶς ἔχειν, *be well, be all right*, I, 8, 13; καλῶς γίγνεσθαι, *turn out well*, IV, 3, 24; καλῶς ποιεῖν, *do well, benefit*, trans. or intrans., II, 6, 20; V, 8, 25; καλῶς ἔχειν δρᾶσθαι, *present a fine appearance*, II, 3, 3.

κάμνω (καμοῦμαι, ἔκαμον, κέκμηκα), *work, toil, be weary, be sick*.

κἀμοί, for καὶ ἐμοί.

κἄν, for καὶ ἐν.

κἄν, for καὶ ἐάν.

κάνδυς, -υος, ὁ (Persian word), a long outer garment worn by Persians, *robe*.

κἀντεῦθεν, for καὶ ἐντεῦθεν.

κἄπειτα, for καὶ ἔπειτα.

καπηλεῖον, -ου, τό (κάπηλος, a *huckster*), *huckster's shop, tavern*.

καπίθη, -ης, ἡ, *capithe*, a Persian dry measure, containing two choinixes, a little less than two quarts.

καπνός, -οῦ, ὁ, *smoke*.

Καππαδοκία, -ας, ἡ, *Cappadocia*, a province of central Asia Minor.

κάπρος, -ου, ὁ (Lat. *caper, he-goat*), *wild boar*.

καρβατίναι, -ῶν, αἱ, *coarse shoes, brogues*.

καρδία, -ας, ἡ (Lat. *cor, heart*, Eng. *heart*), *heart*.

Καρδούχειος, -α, -ον (Καρδοῦχοι), *Carduchian, of the Cardūchi*.

Καρδοῦχοι, -ων, οἱ, *the Cardūchi, Carduchians*, the modern Kurds, a warlike people inhabiting the mountainous region northeast of Mesopotamia.

Κάρκασος, -ου, ὁ, *Carcasus*, a river in Mysia.

καρπαία, -ας, ἡ, *the Carpaea*, a Thessalian pantomimic dance, VI, 1, 7.

καρπόομαι, καρπώσομαι, etc. (καρπός), *reap the fruits of, reap*.

καρπός, -οῦ, ὁ (cf. Lat. *carpo, seize*, Eng. *harvest*), *fruit, crop*.

Κάρσος, -ου, ὁ, *the Carsus*, a small river emptying into the gulf of Issus.

κάρυον, -ου, τό, *nut*; κάρυα πλάτεα οὐκ ἔχοντα δαιφυήν, probably, *chestnuts*, V, 4, 29, 32.

κάρφη, -ης, ἡ (cf. κάρφω, *dry up*), *hay, straw*.

Καστωλός, -οῦ, ἡ, *Castōlus*, a place, presumably near Sardis, where there was a plain (Καστωλοῦ πεδίον), which was the mustering place of the Persian troops under Cyrus, I, 1, 2; I, 9, 7.

κατά (by elision, κατ' or καθ'), prep. with gen. and acc., *down:* (1) with gen., *down along* or *over*, I, 5, 8; *below, under*, VII, 1, 30; (2) with acc., of place, *down, on, at, over, along;* καὶ κατὰ γῆν καὶ κατὰ θάλατταν, *by land and sea*, I, 1, 7; κατὰ ταῦτα, *in these regions*, VII, 5, 13; κατὰ τὰς πύλας, *at the gate*, V, 2, 16; *over against, opposite*, I, 5, 10; I, 8, 21, etc.; with distributive force, κατ' ἴλας καὶ κατὰ τάξεις, *by squadrons and companies*, I, 2, 16; κατ' ἔθνη, *by tribes*, I, 8, 9; καθ' ἕνα, *one by one*, IV, 7, 8; so of time, κατὰ μῆνα, *by the month, monthly*, I, 9, 17; κατ' ἐνιαυτόν, *yearly, annually*, III, 2, 12; in various relations, *according to*, II, 2, 8; καθ' ἡσυχίαν, *in peace and quiet*, II, 3, 8; κατὰ σπουδήν, *in haste*, VII, 6, 28; τὸ κατὰ τοῦτον εἶναι, *as far as this fellow is concerned*, I, 6, 9; κατὰ κράτος, *with all one's might, at full speed*, I, 8, 19 (*cf.* ἀνὰ κράτος, I, 8, 1); in VII, 7, 7 the same phrase means, *by force;* καθ' ἁρπαγήν, *in search of booty*, III, 5, 2; κατὰ ταὐτά, *in the same way*, V, 4, 22.

καταβαίνω (βαίνω), *go down*, esp. from the interior to the coast, II, 5, 22; *descend*, I, 2 22; *dismount*, II, 2, 14; *enter the lists*, IV, 8, 27.

κατάβασις, -εως, ἡ (καταβαίνω), *a going down, descent, march down*, from the interior to the coast; *cf.* ἀνάβασις, IV, 1, 10; V, 5, 4; *place of descent*, III, 4, 37.

καταβλακεύω (βλακεύω), *neglect* or *shrink from through sloth*.

καταγγέλλω (ἀγγέλλω), *report against, denounce*.

κατάγειος, -ον (κατά + γῆ), *under ground*.

καταγελάω (γελάω), *laugh at, mock, laugh to scorn*, abs. or with gen.

κατάγνυμι (ἄγνυμι, -άξω, -έαξα, ἔαγα, -εάγην, *break*), *break, shatter*.

κατάγω (ἄγω), *lead down*, esp. of ships, *bring to land, to port;* also, *bring home, bring back, restore*, esp. of exiles, I, 1, 7; in mid., *arrive at, reach*, III, 4, 26.

καταδαπανάω (δαπανάω), *spend entirely, use up*.

καταδειλιάω, aor. κατεδειλίασα (δειλός), *shrink from through cowardice*.

καταδικάζω (δικάζω, δικάσω, ἐδίκασα, *judge*), *give judgment against* (gen.), VI, 6, 15; *declare one's opinion* (ὅτι), V, 8, 21.

καταδιώκω (διώκω), *pursue hard, drive off*.

καταδοξάζω (δοξάζω, δοξάσω, etc., *believe*), *form an adverse opinion, think to one's discredit*, VII, 7, 30.

καταδραμών, see κατατρέχω.

καταδύω (δύω), *make to go down, sink;* intr. in mid. and 2 aor. act., *sink, sink down*.

καταθεάομαι (θεάομαι), *look down on, survey*.

καταθέω (θέω), *run down*.

καταθήσεσθαι, see κατατίθημι.

καταθύω (θύω), *sacrifice; dedicate*, V, 3, 13.

καταισχύνω (αἰσχύνω), *put to shame, disgrace*.

κατακαίνω (καίνω), a poetic vb. used freely by Xenophon but by no other prose author, *kill, cut down*. In the *Anabasis*, besides the pres. and impf., the 2 aor. ἔκανον occurs and once the 2 fut. pf. κατακεκονότες ἔσεσθε, VII, 6, 36.

κατακαίω or **κατακάω** (καίω), *burn down, destroy by fire*.

κατάκειμαι (κεῖμαι), lie down (for the night), recline (at table), lie idle.
κατακλείω (κλείω), shut in, enclose, hem in.
κατακοντίζω (ἀκοντίζω), shoot down, with a javelin.
κατακόπτω (κόπτω), cut down, slay.
κατακτείνω (κτείνω), slay, kill.
κατακωλύω (κωλύω), hinder, check, keep back.
καταλαμβάνω (λαμβάνω), take, seize, catch; of positions, occupy; overtake, II, 2, 12; find, III, 1, 8; surprise, IV, 2, 5; of motion, arrive at, reach, VII, 8, 8.
καταλέγω (λέγω), reckon, count, II, 6, 27.
καταλείπω (λείπω), leave behind, leave in the lurch, abandon; leave over, III, 5, 5.
καταλεύω (λεύω, -λεύσω, ἐλεύσθην; cf. λᾶας, stone), stone to death, I, 5, 14.
καταλήψομαι, see καταλαμβάνω.
καταλιπεῖν, καταλιπών, see καταλείπω.
καταλλάττω (ἀλλάττω, ἀλλάξω, ἤλλαξα, -ἤλλαχα, -ἤλλαγμαι, -ηλλάχθην or ἠλλάγην, from ἄλλος), change; in mid. and pass., become reconciled, I, 6, 1.
καταλογίζομαι (λογίζομαι), reckon up.
καταλύω (λύω), unloose, dissolve, bring to an end, esp. with πόλεμον expressed or understood, make peace, I, 1, 10; V, 7, 27; unloose or unyoke animals, hence, halt, I, 8, 1.
καταμανθάνω, (μανθάνω) learn thoroughly, understand.
καταμείγνυμι (μείγνυμι, mix), in pass., mingle with, VII, 2, 3.
καταμελέω (ἀμελέω), neglect, be neglectful.
καταμένω (μένω), stay behind.

καταμερίζω (μερίζω), divide or distribute.
κατανοέω (νοέω), observe, mark, perceive.
καταπέμπω (πέμπω), send down.
καταπετρόω (πετρόω, from πέτρος, stone), stone to death.
καταπηδάω (πηδάω, πηδήσω, etc., leap), leap or spring down.
καταπίπτω (πίπτω), fall down or off.
καταπλήττω (πλήττω), strike down; then, daze, terrify; with βροντῇ, III, 4, 12.
καταπολεμέω (πολεμέω), vanquish in war.
καταπράττω (πράττω), accomplish, achieve, bring to an end.
καταράομαι (ἀράομαι, pray, from ἀρά, prayer), imprecate, curse.
κατασβέννυμι (σβέννυμι, ἔσβεσα, quench; cf. Eng. asbestos), put out, of fires.
κατασκέπτομαι (σκέπτομαι), view closely, inspect.
κατασκευάζω (σκευάζω), fit out, equip, furnish; develop, improve, I, 9, 19; mid., make (one's own) preparations.
κατασκηνέω (σκηνέω), pitch one's tent, encamp.
κατασκηνόω (σκηνόω), pitch one's tent, encamp, II, 2, 16.
κατασκοπή, -ῆς, ἡ (cf. κατασκέπτομαι), spying, reconnoissance.
κατασπάω (σπάω), drag or drag down.
κατάστασις, -εως, ἡ (στάσις), state, condition, V, 7, 26.
καταστρατοπεδεύομαι (στρατοπεδεύω), encamp.
καταστρέφω (στρέφω), overturn, overthrow; mid. subject to one's self, subdue.
κατασφάττω (σφάττω), cut down, kill.

κατασχεῖν, see κατέχω.
κατασχίζω (σχίζω), split to pieces; of gates, break down, VII, 1, 16.
κατατείνω (τείνω), stretch taut, strain, strive, insist.
κατατέμνω (τέμνω), cut to pieces, destroy by cutting; pass., of ditches, be cut, dug, II, 4, 13.
κατατίθημι (τίθημι), put down; mid., put away, deposit, lay up; θεοί, παρ' οὓς ἡμεῖς τὴν φιλίαν συνθέμενοι κατεθέμεθα, the gods, to whose keeping we consigned the friendship which we contracted, II, 5, 8.
κατατιτρώσκω (τιτρώσκω), wound severely.
κατατρέχω (τρέχω), run down.
καταυλίζομαι (αὐλίζομαι), encamp.
καταφαγεῖν, see κατέφαγον.
καταφανής, -ές (φαίνω), in sight.
καταφεύγω (φεύγω), flee for refuge.
καταφρονέω (φρονέω), look down on, despise.
καταχωρίζω (χωρίζω), station, arrange.
κατέαξαν, see κατάγνυμι.
κατέβη, see καταβαίνω.
κατεθέμην, see κατατίθημι.
κατεῖδον (εἶδον), as 2 aor. of καθοράω, q. v.
κατειλῆφθαι, κατειληφότες, see καταλαμβάνω.
κάτειμι (εἶμι), go or come down.
κατεργάζομαι (ἐργάζομαι), work out to fulfilment, accomplish, achieve.
κατέρχομαι, aor. κατῆλθον, go or come down; esp. return to one's home, VII, 2, 2.
κατεσφάγη, see κατασφάττω.
κατετέτμηντο, see κατατέμνω.
κατέτρωσαν, see κατατιτρώσκω.
κατέφαγον (ἔφαγον), devour, only in 2 aor.
κατέχω (ἔχω), hold down, hold fast, restrain, check; possess, occupy; of mariners, put into port, land, V, 6, 20; τοσοῦτον χωρίον κατασχεῖν, to cover so much ground, IV, 8, 12.
κατηγορέω, κατηγορήσω, etc. (κατά+ ἀγορά), accuse, charge, with gen of pers.
κατηγορία, -ας, ἡ (cf. κατηγορέω)-charge, accusation.
κατηρεμίζω (ἠρεμίζω, -ηρέμισα, -ηρεμί, σθην, make still; cf. ἠρέμα, quietly), make still, calm, appease.
κατιδόντας, see κατεῖδον.
κατοικέω (οἰκέω), live, dwell.
κατοικίζω (οἰκίζω), settle, colonize, found.
κατορύττω (ὀρύττω), bury in the ground, bury.
κάτω, adv. (κατά), down, downwards, below, underneath; τὸ κάτω, the lower part, IV, 2, 28.
καῦμα, -ατος, τό (καίω), heat.
καύσιμος, -ον (καίω), that may be burnt, combustible.
Καΰστρου πεδίον, -ου, τό, Caÿster Plain, a city in Phrygia.
κέγχρος, -ου, ὁ, millet, a kind of grain; cf. μελίνη.
κεῖμαι, κείσομαι, lie, lie dead, be situated, be stationed, frequently a passive of τίθημι; hence for τὰ ὅπλα ἔκειτο see the phrase θέσθαι τὰ ὅπλα.
κεκραγότων, see κράζω.
κέκτησθε, see κτάομαι.
Κελαιναί, -ῶν, αἱ, Celaenae, a city of Phrygia.
κελεύω, κελεύσω, etc., order, bid, command; less often, urge, advise.
κενός, -ή, -όν, empty, void, vain groundless; πολὺ τῆς φάλαγγος κενὸν ἐποίησαν, they made a great gap in the phalanx, IV, 8, 17.

κενοτάφιον, -ου, τό (κενός+τάφος), *a cenotaph*, i. e., *a mound or tomb erected in honor of those whose dead bodies could not be recovered*, VI, 4, 9.

κεντέω, κεντήσω (cf. κέντρον, *goad, point*, Eng. *centre*), *goad, torment.*

Κεντρίτης, -ου, ὁ, *the Centrītes*, a river flowing into the Tigris.

κεραμεοῦς, -ᾶ, -οῦν (κέραμος, *clay*), *earthen.*

κεράμιον, -ου, τό (κέραμος, *clay*), *earthern jar* for wine, holding about six gallons.

Κεράμων ἀγορά, *Ceramon Agora* (*tile-market*), a town in Phrygia.

κεράννυμι (κεράσω, ἐκέρασα, κέκραμαι, ἐκεράσθην, ἐκράθην), *mix,* esp. of water and wine.

κέρας, κέρατος or κέρως, τό (Lat. *cornu,* Eng. *horn*): (1) *horn* of an animal, then, *bugle, horn;* e. g., II, 2, 4; (2) *a drinking-horn* (Thracian), VII, 2, 23; (3) *the wing, flank* of an army, e. g., I, 7, 1; τὰ δεξιὰ τοῦ κέρατος, *the right of the wing,* i. e., *the extreme right,* I, 8, 4; κατὰ κέρας, *in column,* i. e., *in order of march,* IV, 6, 6; τὴν οὐρὰν τοῦ κέρατος, *the rear of the column,* VI, 5, 5.

Κερασούντιοι, -ων, οἱ (Κερασοῦς), *the people of Cerasus, Cerasuntians.*

Κερασοῦς, -οῦντος, ἡ (cf. Eng. *cherry,* imported from this place to Rome by Lucullus), *Cerasus*, a city in Pontus.

κεράτινος, -η, -ον (κέρας), *of horn.*

Κέρβερος, -ου, ὁ, *Cerberus,* the watch-dog of the lower world, brought to the upper world by Heracles, VI, 2, 2.

κερδαίνω (κερδανῶ, ἐκέρδανα), *gain, acquire.*

κερδαλέος, -α, -ον (κέρδος), *fraught with gain, profitable.*

κέρδος, -ους, τό, *gain, profit,* then, *pay.*

κεφαλαλγής, -ές (κεφαλή + ἄλγος, *pain*), *causing headache.*

κεφαλή, -ῆς, ἡ (Lat. *caput,* Eng. *head*), *head.*

κηδεμών, -όνος, ὁ (cf. κήδομαι), *guardian, protector.*

κήδομαι, *care for,* with gen.

κηρίον, -ου, τό (dim. of κηρός, *wax,* cf. Lat. *cera*), *honeycomb.*

κηρύκειον, -ου, τό (κῆρυξ), *herald's staff.*

κῆρυξ, -υκος, ὁ (καλέω), *herald.*

κηρύττω, κηρύξω, etc. (κῆρυξ), *proclaim as herald, announce;* with σιγήν, *command,* II, 2, 20. impers. ἐκήρυξε, *the herald proclaimed,* III, 4, 36.

Κηφισόδωρος, -ου, ὁ, *Cephisodōrus* an Athenian, captain in the Greek army.

Κηφισοφῶν, -ῶντος, ὁ, *Cephisophon,* father of Cephisodōrus.

κιβώτιον, -ου, τό (dim. of κιβωτός, ἡ, *chest*), *box, chest.*

Κιλικία, -ας, ἡ (Κίλιξ), *Cilicia,* a country on the southeastern coast of Asia Minor.

Κίλιξ, -ικος, *an inhabitant of Cilicia, a Cilician.*

Κίλισσα, -ης, ἡ (Κίλιξ), *a Cilician woman.*

κινδυνεύω, κινδυνεύσω, etc. (κίνδυνος), *incur danger, run a risk, expose oneself;* with infin. expressing likelihood, ἐκινδύνευσεν ἂν, διαφθαρῆναι, *would have come near being killed, would very probably have been killed,* IV, 1, 11.

κίνδυνος, -ου, ὁ, *danger, risk;* κίνδυνός (ἐστι) with infin. or clause with μή, II, 5, 17; IV 1, 6.

κινέω, κινήσω, etc. (cf. Lat. *cieo, cause to go*, Eng. *hie, kinetic*), *set in motion, move, stir.*

κιττός, -οῦ, ὁ, *ivy.*

Κλεαγόρας, -ου, ὁ, *Cleagoras*, a painter from Phlius.

Κλεαίνετος, -ου, ὁ, *Cleaenetus*, a captain in the Greek army.

Κλέανδρος, -ου, ὁ, *Cleander*, a Spartan, governor of Byzantium.

Κλεάνωρ, -ορος, ὁ, *Cleanor*, a Greek general from Orchomenos in Arcadia. See the Introd., § 38.

Κλεάρετος, -ου, ὁ, *Clearetus*, a captain in the Greek army.

Κλέαρχος, -ου, ὁ, *Clearchus*, the most prominent of Cyrus' Greek generals. See the Introd., § 38, and II, 6, 1 ff.

κλεῖθρον, -ου, τό (κλείω), *bar* or *bolt* of a gate; generally pl., *fastenings*, VII, 1, 17.

κλείω, κλείσω, etc. (cf. Lat. *clavis, claudio*), *shut, close.*

κλέπτω, κλέψω, ἔκλεψα, κέκλοφα, κέκλεμμαι, ἐκλάπην (cf. Lat. *clepo, steal*), *steal, embezzle;* hence of various stealthy acts, *conceal, smuggle*, IV, 1, 14; *seize secretly*, IV, 6, 11.

κλῖμαξ, -ακος, ἡ (cf. κλίνη, Eng. *climax*), *ladder.*

κλίνη, -ης, ἡ (κλίνω, *lean*, Lat. *inclino*, Eng. *lean*), *bed, couch.*

κλοπή, -ῆς, ἡ (κλέπτω), *theft, stealing.*

κλωπεύω (κλώψ), *rob, waylay.*

κλώψ, κλωπός, ὁ (κλέπτω), *thief, marauder.*

κνέφας, -ους, τό, *darkness.*

κνημίς, -ῖδος, ἡ (κνήμη, *leg*), *greave*, generally pl.

κόγχη, -ης, ἡ (cf. Eng. *conch*), *mussel, shellfish.*

κογχυλιάτης, -ου, adj. (κογχύλη, *shell;* cf. κόγχη), *shelly*, of stone.

κοῖλος, -η, -ον (cf. Lat. *cavus*, Eng. *hole, hollow*), *hollow;* of a country, *cut up by valleys*, V, 4, 31.

κοιμάω, κοιμήσω, etc. (κεῖμαι), *put to sleep;* mid. and pass., *go to bed, go to sleep.*

κοινός, -ή, -όν (cf. Eng. *epicene*), *common, public;* τὸ κοινόν, *the common good, treasury, authority;* hence ἀπὸ κοινοῦ, *at the public expense*, IV, 7, 27; *by public authority*, V, 7, 18; πρὸς τὸ κοινὸν ἐλθεῖν, *come before the public council* or *assembly*, V, 7, 17; dat. fem. sing., as adv. κοινῇ, *in common, together*, abs. or with μετά or σύν.

κοινόω, κοινώσω, etc. (κοινός), *make common*, mid., *communicate with, consult.*

κοινωνέω, -ήσω, etc. (κοινωνός), *have a share in* (gen.), VII, 6, 28.

κοινωνός, -ου, ὁ (κοινός), *sharer, partner.*

Κοιρατάδας, -ου, ὁ, *Coeratadas*, a Theban adventurer.

Κοῖτοι, -ων, οἱ, *the Coeti*, an autonomous tribe not elsewhere mentioned, VII, 8, 25.

κολάζω, κολάσω, ἐκόλασα, *chastise, punish.*

Κολοσσαί, -ῶν, αἱ, *Colossae*, a city of Phrygia.

Κολχίς, -ίδος, ἡ, *Colchis*, the district east of the Euxine.

Κόλχοι, -ων, οἱ (cf. Κολχίς), *the Colchians*, inhabitants of Colchis.

κολωνός, -οῦ, ὁ (Lat. *collis*, Eng. *hill*), *hill, mound.*

Κομανία, -ας, ἡ, *Comania*, a fortress in Mysia.

κομιδή, -ῆς, ἡ (κομίζω), *conveyance, means of transportation.*

κομίζω, κομιῶ, etc. (cf. κομέω, care for), care for, carry away (to safety), convey, bring; mid., convey oneself or one's own, fetch, III, 2, 26; pass. travel, proceed, V, 4, 1.

κονιατός, -ή, -όν (verbal of κονιάω, plaster, from κονία, dust, ashes; cf. κόνις, dust, Lat. cinis, ashes), plastered, cemented.

κονιορτός, -οῦ, ὁ (κόνις, dust; ὄρνυμι, stir up), cloud of dust.

κόπος, -ου, ὁ (κόπτω), toil, fatigue.

κόπρος, -ου, ἡ, dung.

κόπτω, κόψω, ἔκοψα, κέκοφα, κέκομμαι, ἐκόπην (Eng. chop), cut, cut down, hew; of animals, slaughter; of a door, knock at.

κόρη, -ης, ἡ, girl.

Κορσωτή, -ῆς, ἡ, Corsōte, a city of Mesopotamia, on the Euphrates.

Κορύλας, -α, ὁ, Corylas, ruler of the Paphlagonians.

κορυφή, -ῆς, ἡ, top, peak, summit.

κοσμέω, κοσμήσω, etc. (κόσμος), set in order, array; of troops, marshal, III, 2, 36; adorn, dress, I, 9, 23.

κόσμιος, -α, -ον (κόσμος), orderly, well disciplined.

κόσμος, -ου, ὁ (cf. Eng. cosmic), order, good order; ornament, dress.

Κοτύωρα, -ων, τά, Cotyōra, a city on the Euxine in the country of the Tibareni.

Κοτυωρῖται, -ων, οἱ (Κοτύωρα), the people of Cotyora.

κοῦφος, -η, -ον, light; χόρτος κοῦφος, hay, I, 5, 10.

κούφως, adv. (κοῦφος), lightly.

κράζω, only in 2 perf. κέκραγα, in pres. sense (imitative, like Eng. creak; cf. κραυγή), cry out, shout, VII, 8, 15.

κράνος, -ους, τό (κάρα, head?; cf. Eng. cranium), helmet.

κρατέω, κρατήσω, etc. (κράτος), be strong, be master, rule, be victorious, conquer, subdue (abs., with gen. or acc.).

κρατήρ, -ῆρος, ὁ (κεράννυμι), mixing bowl.

κράτιστος, -η, -ον (κράτος), used as sup. of ἀγαθός, best, strongest, bravest, noblest; κράτιστον (sc. ἐστί), it is best, abs., or with infin.; neut. pl. as adv., best, most bravely; cf. κρείττων.

κράτος, -ους, τό, strength, force, only in the phrases ἀνὰ κράτος and κατὰ κράτος, at full speed; see ἀνά and κατά.

κραυγή, -ῆς, ἡ (κράζω), outcry, shout, tumult.

κρέας, κρέως, pl. κρέα, τό (cf. Lat. caro, flesh), flesh, meat.

κρείττων, -ον, gen. -ονος (κράτος), used as comp. of ἀγαθός, better, stronger, braver, superior to; κρεῖττον (ἐστι), it is better, with infin.; cf. κράτιστος.

κρέμαμαι, ἐκρεμάμην, hang, be suspended.

κρεμάννυμι, κρεμῶ, ἐκρέμασα, ἐκρεμάσθην (κρέμαμαι), hang, hang up.

κρήνη, -ης, ἡ, spring, fountain.

κρηπίς, -ῖδος, ἡ (cf. Lat. crepida), shoe, hence, foundation.

Κρής, Κρητός, ὁ, a Cretan, inhabitant of Crete, the largest of the Greek islands. The Cretans were famous archers.

κριθαί, -ῶν, αἱ, barley; for the pl. cf. πυροί.

κρίθινος, -η, -ον (κριθή), of barley, of bread, IV, 5, 31; οἶνος κρίθινος, beer, IV, 5, 26.

κρίνω, κρινῶ, ἔκρινα, etc. (Lat. cerno, Eng. critic), divide, distinguish.

choose; decide, judge, determine; try (as a judge), VI, 6, 16; so in pass., V, 6, 33.

κριός, -οῦ, ὁ, *ram*.

κρίσις, -εως, ἡ (κρίνω, Eng. *crisis*), *a separating*, then, *judgment, decision, trial*.

κρόμμυον, -ου, τό, *onion*.

κρότος, -ου, ὁ (*cf.* κρούω), *a clapping, applause*.

κρούω, κρούσω, etc., *strike, knock, rattle*.

κρύπτω, κρύψω, ἔκρυψα, etc., *hide, conceal;* with two accs. *hide something from someone*, I, 9, 19·

κρωβύλος, -ου, ὁ, *tuft of hair, top-knot, crest*.

κτάομαι, κτήσομαι, etc., *acquire, gain, procure for oneself;* in the perf., *possess;* with pred. adj. τοὺς Καρδούχους πολεμίους ἐκτησάμεθα, *we made enemies of the Carduchi*, V, 5, 17.

κτείνω (κτενῶ, ἔκτεινα, ἔκτανον, -έκτονα), *kill*, II, 5, 32 n. The simple vb. is rare; see ἀποκτείνω.

κτῆμα, -ατος, τό (κτάομαι), *possession;* in pl., *property*.

κτῆνος, -ους, τό (κτάομαι), *piece of property;* esp. *domestic animal*, generally pl., *cattle*.

Κτησίας, -ου, ὁ, *Ctesias*, a Greek physician living at the court of Artaxerxes. He wrote a history of Persia. See the Introd. § 30.

κυβερνήτης, -ου, ὁ (κυβερνάω, *steer; cf.* Lat. *gubernator*, Eng. *governor*), *helmsman*.

Κύδνος, -ου, ὁ, *the Cydnus*, a river of Cilicia.

Κυζικηνός, -οῦ, ὁ (Κύζικος), *a Cyzicene* a gold coin of Cyzicus with about the value of a Daric. The word is properly an adj. with στατήρ, *stater*, understood.

Κύζικος, -ου, ἡ, *Cyzicus*, an important city of the Propontis, a colony of the Milesians.

κύκλος, -ου, ὁ (*cf.* Lat. *curvus*, bent. *circus, circle*, Eng. *cycle*), *circle;* dat. as adv. κύκλῳ, *in a circle, all around;* pl. *groups* (of men), V, 7, 2.

κυκλόω, κυκλώσω, etc. (κύκλος), *surround;* mid., *form a circle, gather around*, VI, 4, 20.

κύκλωσις, -εως, ἡ, *an encircling, surrounding;* ὡς εἰς κύκλωσιν, *as if to surround*, I, 8, 23.

κυλίνδω, or in pres. system, which alone occurs in the *Anabasis*, κυλινδέω, other tenses as if from κυλίω (*cf.* καλινδέομαι, Eng. *cylinder*), *roll, roll down;* in pass. intr., *roll*.

Κυνίσκος, -ου, ὁ, *Cyniscus*, a Spartan general, warring in the Chersonese.

κυπαρίττινος, -η, -ον (κυπάριττος, *cypress tree*), *of cypress wood*.

Κύρειος, -α, -ον (Κῦρος) *pertaining to Cyrus, Cyrus'*. For οἱ Κύρειοι, III, 2, 17, see the note.

κύριος, -α, -ον (κῦρος, τό, *power*), *empowered, having authority*.

Κῦρος, ὁ, *Cyrus:* (1) *Cyrus the Great*, founder of the Persian empire, ruled 559–529 B. C.; he is called ὁ ἀρχαῖος in I, 9, 1; (2) *Cyrus the Younger*, son of Darius Nothus and Parysatis and younger brother of Artaxerxes Mnemon. Book I gives an account of his ill-fated expedition against Artaxerxes. For a sketch of his character see I, 9; for an account of his death I, 8, 26 ff. See the Introd. § 24.

Κυτώνιον, -ου, τό, *Cytonium*, a town in Mysia, VII, 8, 8. (The text is uncertain, the Paris MS having κερτωνοῦ, whence some assume a town *Certōnus*.)

κύων, κυνός, ὁ or ἡ (*cf*. Lat. *canis, dog*, Eng. *hound, cynic,* etc.), *dog, bitch.*

κωλύω, κωλύσω, etc., *hinder, prevent, check,* abs., with acc., with infin., and (I, 6, 2) with τοῦ and infin.; τὸ κωλῦον, *the hindrance, obstacle,* IV, 5, 20.

κώμαρχης, -ου, ὁ (κώμη+ἄρχω), *village chief.*

κώμη, -ης, ἡ (κεῖμαι), *village.*

κωμήτης, -ου, ὁ (κώμη), *villager.*

κώπη, -ης, ἡ (*cf*. Lat. *capio*, Eng. *haft*), *handle,* esp. of an oar, hence, *oar,* VI, 4, 2.

Λ

λαβεῖν, see λαμβάνω.

λαγχάνω, λήξομαι, ἔλαχον, εἴληχα, εἴληγμαι, ἐλήχθην (λάχος), *get or obtain by lot, get, obtain,* with acc. or part. gen.

λαγώς, -ώ, ὁ, *hare.*

λαθεῖν, see λανθάνω.

λάθρᾳ, adv. (λανθάνω), *secretly;* with gen., *without the knowledge of.*

Λακεδαιμόνιος, -ου, ὁ (Λακεδαίμων), *a citizen of Lacedaemon, a Lacedaemonian.*

Λακεδαίμων, -ονος, ἡ, *Lacedaemon or Sparta,* capital of Laconia, the southeastern state of Peloponnesus.

λάκκος, -ου, ὁ (*cf*. Lat. *lacus*, Eng. *lake, loch*), *cistern, vat,* IV, 2, 22.

λακτίζω, λακτιῶ, etc. (λάξ, *with the foot*), *kick.*

Λάκων, -ωνος, ὁ, *a Laconian;* less exactly, *Spartan.*

Λακωνικός, -ή, -όν (Λάκων), *Lacedaemonian.*

λαμβάνω (λήψομαι, ἔλαβον, εἴληφα, εἴλημμαι, ἐλήφθην), *take,* with various shades of meaning; *seize, capture,* I, 4, 7; *get,* I, 5, 10; *receive,* I, 2, 26; *enlist,* I, 1, 6; *come upon, befall,* I, 10, 18; *find,* I, 1, 6; sometimes with part. gen., I, 5, 7; *cf*. I, 6, 10 The partic. λαβών, like ἔχων, is often rendered *with,* but the meaning is fuller, I, 1, 2, etc.

λαμπρός, -ά, -όν (λάμπω), *shining, splendid, noble.*

λαμπρότης, -ητος, ἡ (λαμπρός), *brilliancy, splendor.*

λάμπω, λάμψω, ἔλαμψα (*cf*. Eng. *lamp*), *be bright, shine, blaze.*

Λαμψακηνοί, -ῶν, οἱ (Λάμψακος), *inhabitants of Lampsacus.*

Λάμψακος, -ου, ἡ, *Lampsacus,* a city in the Troad, on the Hellespont.

λανθάνω (λήσω, ἔλαθον, λέληθα, λέλησμαι), *be hid* or *concealed, be unseen;* with acc., *escape the notice of;* often with supplementary partic., containing the main idea, ἐλάνθανεν τρεφόμενον, *was secretly maintained,* I, 1, 9; so with acc., λαθεῖν αὐτὸν ἀπιών, *get off without his knowledge,* I, 3, 17.

Λάρισα, -ης, ἡ, *Larisa,* commonly spelt Larissa, an Assyrian city, III, 4, 7 n.

λάσιος, -α, -ον, *hairy, shaggy; bushy,* V, 2, 29; τὰ λάσια, *thickets,* VI, 4, 26.

λαφυροπωλέω (λαφυροπώλης), *sell booty.*

λαφυροπώλης, -ου, ὁ (λάφυρον, *spoil,* +πωλέω), *seller of booty.*

λάχος, -ους, τό (*cf*. λαγχάνω), *portion, share, part.*

λαχών, see λαγχάνω.

λέγω (λέξω, ἔλεξα, λέλεγμαι, ἐλέχθην); the perf. is supplied by εἴρηκα (see εἴρω) and the aor. often by εἶπον (see the word); in compounds oftener -αγορεύω, -ερῶ -εῖπον), orig., *count, reckon, tell* (in its older use = *count*), I, 6, 1; then, *say, speak, tell, mention*, etc.; *be spokesman*, II, 5, 39. λέγω has regularly ὅτι or ὡς with a clause, but in the pass. the infin. is preferred and the construction is usually personal (impers. in pass. I, 2, 12, etc.); see I, 2, 8 n. The infin. occurs with the act., V, 4, 34, VII, 5, 13, and the partic. I, 3, 15. When however λέγω means *bid* or *vote*, the infin. is regular, I, 3, 8.

λεία, -ας, ἡ, *booty, plunder*.

λειμών, -ῶνος, ὁ (cf. λείβω, *pour*, λιμήν), *a moist place, meadow*.

λεῖος, -α, -ον (cf. Lat. *levis*), *smooth*; of hills, *gently sloping*.

λείπω (λείψω, ἔλιπον, λέλοιπα, λέλειμμαι, ἐλείφθην), *leave, leave behind, forsake, abandon; leave alive, spare*, VI, 3, 5; pass., *be inferior to*, VII, 7, 31.

λεκτέος, -α, -ον (verbal of λέγω), *must be said or told*.

λελείψεται, see λείπω.

λεξάτω, see λέγω.

Λεοντῖνος, -ον, ὁ, *a Leontine*, native of Leontini, in Sicily.

λευκοθώραξ, -ακος, ὁ, ἡ (λευκός+θώραξ), *with white* (linen?), *cuirass*, I, 8, 9; cf. IV, 7, 15.

λευκός, -ή, -όν (cf. Lat. *lux, light*), *white*.

Λέων, -οντος, ὁ, *Leon*, of Thurii, a soldier in the Greek army.

Λεώνυμος, -ον, ὁ, *Leonymus*, a Spartan in the Greek army, IV, 1, 18.

λήγω, λήξω, ἔληξα, *cease, come to an end; of the wind, abate*, IV, 5, 4.

λήζομαι, ἐλησάμην (λεία), *plunder, pillage, rob*.

λῆρος, -ον, ὁ, *nonsense*.

λήσομεν, see λανθάνω.

ληστεία, -ας, ἡ (λῃστής), *pillaging, plundering*.

ληστής, -ον, ὁ (λῄζομαι), *plunderer, robber*.

ληφθησόμεθα, λήψεσθε, see λαμβάνω.

λίαν, adv., *very*.

λίθινος, -η, -ον (λίθος), *of stone*.

λίθος, -ον, ὁ (cf. Eng. *litho-*), *stone, a stone*.

λιμήν, -ένος, ὁ, *port, harbor*.

λιμός, -οῦ, ὁ, *hunger, famine*.

λινοῦς, -ῆ, -οῦν (λίνον, *linen*, Lat. *linum, flax*), *of flax, of linen*.

λογίζομαι, λογιοῦμαι, etc. (λόγος), *calculate, consider*.

λόγος, -ον, ὁ (λέγω), *word, speech, saying, rumor, narrative, discussion, debate*; εἰς λόγους ἐλθεῖν, dat., *have an interview with*, II, 5, 4.

λόγχη, -ης, ἡ, *spear head, spear point, spear*.

λοιδορέω, λοιδορήσω, etc., *revile, abuse, upbraid*.

λοιπός, -ή, -όν (λείπω), *left, remaining*; with art., *the rest of*; τὸ λοιπόν, *from now on, from then on*, with gen., *for the rest of*, II, 2, 5; τοῦ λοιποῦ, *in the future*, V, 7, 34; τὴν λοιπήν (sc. ὁδόν), *the rest of the way*, III, 4, 46.

Λοκρός, -οῦ, ὁ, *a Locrian, a native of Locris*, a name given to two districts in central Greece, one on the Gulf of Corinth, VII, 4, 18.

Λουσιάτης, -ον, ὁ, = the following.

Λουσιεύς, -έως, ὁ (Λουσοί, *Lusi*) a *Lusian*, native of Lusi in Arcadia. In VII, 6, 40, we have the form Λουσιάτης.

λόφος, -ου, ὁ, *ridge or crest;* then, of land, *hill, ridge.*

λοχαγέω (λοχαγός), *be captain.*

λοχαγία, -ας, ἡ (λοχαγός), *captaincy.*

λοχαγός, -οῦ, ὁ (λόχος+ἄγω), *captain.*

λοχίτης, -ου, ὁ (λόχος), *one of the same* λόχος, *comrade,* VI, 6, 7.

λόχος, -ου, ὁ (*cf.* λέχος, *bed*), properly, *ambush, lying in wait;* then, *body of armed men,* esp. *company,* as a military unit. The λόχος numbered as a rule 100 men, and was divided into two πεντηκοστύες or four ἐνωμοτίαι; ὄρθιοι λόχοι, see ὄρθιος.

Λυδία, -ας, ἡ (Λυδός), *Lydia,* a province of Western Asia Minor, formerly an independent kingdom.

Λύδιος, -α -ον (Λυδός), *Lydian.*

Λυδός, -οῦ, ὁ, *a Lydian.*

Λύκαια, -ων, τά, *the Lycaea,* a festival of Zeus, Λυκαῖος, so called from Mt. Lycaeus in Arcadia.

Λυκάονες, -ων, οἱ, *inhabitants of Lycaonia, Lycaonians.*

Λυκαονία, -ας, ἡ, *Lycaonia,* a country in central Asia Minor.

Λύκειον, -ου, τό (Eng. *lycēum*), *the Lycēum,* a gymnasium at Athens, near the temple of Apollo Lycaeus.

Λύκιος, -ου, ὁ, *Lycius:* (1) an Athenian, in command of the Greek cavalry; (2) a Syracusan of the same name.

Λύκος, -ου, ὁ, *Lycus,* a river flowing into the Euxine near Heraclēa.

λύκος, -ου, ὁ (Lat. *lupus*), *wolf.*

Λύκων, -ωνος, ὁ, *Lycon,* an Achaean in the Greek army.

λυμαίνομαι, λυμανοῦμαι, etc. (λύμη *outrage*), *destroy, ruin, spoil.*

λυπέω, -ήσω, etc. (λύπη), *grieve, pain, vex, molest, annoy.*

λύπη, -ης, ἡ, *pain, grief.*

λυπηρός, -ά, -όν (λύπη), *painful, troublesome, annoying.*

λύττα, -ης, ἡ, *madness.*

λύω (λύσω, ἔλυσα, λέλυκα, λέλυμαι. ἐλύθην; *cf.* Lat. *luo, loose,* Eng, *loose*), *loose, set free, unyoke;* of a bridge or obstacle, *break down, destroy, do away with,* II, 4, 17; of oaths, *break,* II, 5, 38; mid., *ransom,* VII, 8, 6. For III, 4, 36, see the note.

λωτοφάγοι, -ων, οἱ (λωτός, *lotus*+ ἔφαγον), *lotus-eaters,* III, 2, 25 n. The lotus grows in northern Africa. Its fruit, called the jujube, is about the size of an olive and is said to be of delicious flavor. The legend told that whoso ate of it lost all remembrance of his home.

λωφάω (λωφήσω, ἐλώφησα), *cease.*

λῴων, λῷον, gen. -ονος, *preferable, better,* used as comp. of ἀγαθός, chiefly in the phrase λῷόν ἐστι.

M

μά, adv. of swearing, *by,* with acc.; regularly neg., μὰ τοὺς θεούς, *no, by heaven,* I, 4, 8, unless ναί precedes, ναὶ μὰ Δία, *yes, by Zeus,* V, 8, 6.

μάγαδις, -ιδος, ἡ, *magadis,* a harp-like musical instrument of twenty strings.

Μάγνητες, -ων, οἱ, *Magnesians. people of Magnesia,* a district in Thessaly.

μάθε, μάθῃς, μάθοι, see μανθάνω.

Μαίανδρος, -ου, ὁ, *the Maeander*, a large river in western Asia Minor. Its winding course gives us our word *meander*.

μαίνομαι, μανοῦμαι, μέμηνα, ἐμάνην, *be mad;* aor., *go mad*.

Μαισάδης, -ου, ὁ, *Maesades*, father of Seuthes.

μακαρίζω, ἐμακάρισα, ἐμακαρίσθην (μάκαρ, *blessed*), *deem happy*.

μακαριστός, -ή, -όν (μακαρίζω), *to be thought happy, enviable*.

Μακίστιος, -ου, ὁ (Μάκιστος), *a Macistian, inhabitant of Macistas*, a city in southern Elis.

μακρός, -ά, -όν, *long* (of space or time); μακράν (sc. ὁδόν [?]), *a long distance*, III, 4, 17; so μακροτέραν, II, 2, 11; μακροτάτην, VII, 8, 20; μακρὰ πλοῖα, *war-ships*, V, 1, 11; μακρότερον, as adv., *further*, III, 4, 16.

Μάκρωνες, -ων, οἱ, *the Macrōnes, Macronians*, a warlike people of Pontus.

μάλα, by elision μαλ', adv. (*cf*. Lat. *multus?, melior?*), *very*, used with adjs. and advs.; but also with vbs. (V, 4, 18) and with nouns having an adjectival value, μάλα χαιρός ἐστιν, *it's just the time*, IV, 6, 15; αὐτίκα μάλα, *on the spot, immediately*. III, 5, 11; οὐ μάλα, *not very much*, i. e. (by litotes) *not at all*, II, 6, 15; often with intensive καί, I, 5, 8; comp. μᾶλλον, *more, rather*, regularly followed by ἤ, *than;* οὐδὲν μᾶλλον, *none the more*, III, 3, 11; sup. μάλιστα, *most, especially, in the highest degree;* with numerals, *about*, V, 4, 12; often with ὡς, ὅτι, ᾗ, ὅσον, either with or without a vb. of ability, *e.g.*, ὡς μάλιστα ἐδύνατο ἐπικρυπτόμενος, *with all possible secrecy*, I, 1, 6.

μαλακίζομαι (μαλακός, *soft*), *be effeminate* or *lazy, be a coward*.

μάλιστα, see μάλα.

μᾶλλον, see μάλα.

μανέντες, see μαίνομαι.

μανθάνω, μαθήσομαι, ἔμαθον, μεμάθηκα, *learn, find out, understand*.

μαντεία, -ας, ἡ (μαντεύω, *prophesy*, μάντις, *prophet*), *prophecy, response of an oracle*.

μαντευτός, -ή, -όν (verbal of μαντεύομαι), *directed by an oracle, named by an oracle*.

Μαντινεῖς, -ῶν, οἱ, *Mantineans*, people of Mantinēa, in Arcadia.

μάντις, -εως, ὁ (μαίνομαι), *one possessed* or *inspired, a prophet, diviner, soothsayer*.

Μάρδοι, -ων, οἱ, *the Mardi*, a warlike tribe in southern Armenia.

Μαριανδυνοί, -ῶν, οἱ, *the Mariandȳni*, a people near Heraclēa on the Euxine.

μάρσιπος, -ου, ὁ (*cf*. Eng. *marsupial*), *bag, pouch*.

Μαρσύας, -ου, ὁ, *Marsyas*, a satyr famous in legend, I, 2, 8 n.; also a river in Phrygia, named after him, *ibid*.

μαρτυρέω, μαρτυρήσω, etc. (μάρτυς), *bear witness, testify*.

μαρτύριον, -ου, τό (μάρτυς), *evidence, proof*.

μάρτυς, μάρτυρος, ὁ (*cf*. Eng. *martyr*), *witness*.

Μαρωνείτης, -ου, ὁ (Μαρώνεια, Maronēa), *a Maronite*, a native of Maronēa, a city on the southern coast of Thrace.

Μάσκας, Dor. gen. Μάσκα, ὁ, *Mascas*, a stream flowing into the Euphrates, perhaps not a river but a canal.

μαστεύω (poetic), *seek, search after;* with infin., *strive,* III, 1, 43.

μαστιγόω, μαστιγώσω, *etc.* (μάστιξ), *scourge, whip.*

μάστιξ, -ιγος, ἡ, *whip, lash.*

μαστός, -οῦ, ὁ, *breast, one of the breasts;* then, *hill, hillock,* IV, 2, 6, 18.

μάταιος, -α, -ον (μάτη, *folly*) *foolish, vain.*

μάχαιρα, -ας, ἡ (μάχομαι), *sword, sabre* (properly a short sword with single edge; the ξίφος was long and two-edged).

μαχαίριον, -ου, τό (dim. of μάχαιρα), *dagger.*

μάχη, -ης, ἡ (μάχομαι), *fight, battle, engagement; battlefield,* II, 2, 6.

μάχιμος, -ον (μάχομαι), *fit for fighting, warlike.*

μάχομαι (μαχοῦμαι, ἐμαχεσάμην, μεμάχημαι), *fight, fight against,* with dat. or (rarely) πρός and acc.; *quarrel,* IV, 5, 12.

με, see ἐγώ.

Μεγάβυζος, -ου, ὁ, *Megabyzus,* guardian of the temple of Artemis at Ephesus.

μεγάλην, see μέγας.

μεγαληγορέω, aor. ἐμεγαληγόρησα (μέγας+ἀγορά), *talk big, boast.*

μεγαλοπρεπῶς, adv. (μέγας+πρέπω), *in magnificent or princely fashion, magnificently, munificently,* I, 4, 17; sup. μεγαλοπρεπέστατα, VII, 3, 19.

μεγάλως, adv. (μέγας), *greatly.*

Μεγαρεύς, -έως, ὁ (Μέγαρα), *a native of Megara, a Megarian.*

μέγας, μεγάλη, μέγα (*cf.* μακρός, Lat. *magnus,* Eng. *much*), comp. μείζων, sup. μέγιστος, *large, great,* in varying senses; *famous,* II, 6, 17, so μέγας βασιλεύς, as the title of the Persian king (*cf. Great Mogul*); of sound, *loud,* IV, 5, 18; of the sea, *heavy,* V, 8, 20; μέγα, as adv. (inner obj.); *greatly,* III, 1, 38; so μεγάλα, I, 9, 24, III, 3, 14; μέγιστον, *chiefly,* I, 3, 10; οἱ μέγιστα δυνάμενοι, *the most powerful,* II, 6, 21; μέγα φρονεῖν, *be elated, proud,* III, 1, 27.

Μεγαφέρνης, -ου, ὁ, *Megaphernes,* a Persian noble, put to death by Cyrus.

μέγεθος, -ους, τό (μέγας), *size, width,* IV, 1, 2.

μέγιστος, see μέγας.

μέδιμνος, -ου, ὁ, *medimnus,* an Attic dry measure, about 1½ bushels.

μεθ', see μετά.

μεθίημι (ἵημι), *let go.*

μεθίστημι (ἵστημι), *set in a different place, remove;* aor. mid., *remove apart from oneself,* II, 3, 8; 2 aor. act., *go aside or apart,* II, 3, 21.

Μεθυδριεύς, -έως, ὁ (Μεθύδριον, *Methydrium*), *a Methydrian, native of Methydrium,* a town in Arcadia.

μεθύω (μέθυ, *wine; cf.* Eng. *mead*), *be drunk.*

μείζων, see μέγας.

μειλίχιος, -α, -ον, *mild, gentle,* epithet of Zeus, VII, 8, 4.

μεῖναι μείναντες, μείνειαν, μείνῃ, see μένω.

μεῖον, see μείων.

μειράκιον, τό (μεῖραξ, *girl*), *lad, youth,* from 14 to 20 years old.

μείωμα, -ατος, τό (μειόω, *make smaller,* from μείων), *shortage of money.*

μείων, -ον, irreg. comp. of μικρός (*cf.* Lat. *minor*), *smaller, weaker, fewer;* neut. μεῖον, as adv., *less;*

μεῖον ἔχειν, *have the worst of it*, I, 10, 8; *cf*. III, 2, 17.

Μελανδῖται, -ῶν, οἱ, *Melandītae*, a Thracian tribe.

μελανία, -ας, ἡ (μέλας), *blackness*.

μέλας, μέλαινα, μέλαν, gen. μέλανος, etc. (*cf*. Lat. *malus*, Eng. *melancholy*), *black, dark*.

μέλει, μελήσει, ἐμέλησε, μεμέληκε, impers., *it is a care, it concerns;* ἐμοὶ μελήσει, *I will take care,* I, 4, 16; *cf*. I, 8, 13; τῇ θεῷ μελήσει, *the goddess will see to him, i. e., will punish him,* V, 3, 13.

μελετάω, μελετήσω, etc. (μέλει), *practice*.

μελετηρός, -ά, -όν (μελετάω) *diligent in practice*.

μελίνη, -ης, ἡ (Lat. *milium, millet*), *millet*, a kind of grain, in sing. or pl., *cf*. κέγχρος; pl. *millet fields,* II, 4, 13.

Μελινοφάγοι, -ων, οἱ (μελίνη+ἔφαγον), *Melinophagi, Millet-eaters,* a Thracian tribe, living near Byzantium.

μέλλω, μελλήσω, ἐμέλλησα, *be about to, be going to do something;* often with infin. (generally fut.) as a periphrastic fut.; *delay* (*be always on the point of doing*), abs., III, 1, 46; in pass., III, 1, 47 n.; *intend*, II, 5, 5; τὸ μέλλον, *the future,* VI, 1, 21.

μεμνῇο, μέμνησαι, μεμνήσεσθαι, see *μιμνήσκω*.

μέμφομαι, μέμψομαι, ἐμεμψάμην or ἐμέμφθην, *find fault with, blame*.

μέν (a weaker form of μήν), a postpos. particle, rarely admitting of translation. Often it emphasizes a preceding word, ἐγὼ μέν, *I, for my part,* I, 9, 28, but oftener serves to denote that the word or clause is correlated with a following one, which is normally coupled with δέ (I, 1, 1), although ἀλλά, μέντοι, and καί also occur. Frequent are ὁ μέν ... ὁ δέ, *the one ... the other,* in pl. *some ... others* (I, 1, 7). Because of this correlating force μέν often serves to mark the conclusion of an episode or topic, I, 3, 4; I, 10, 18; so μὲν δή, I, 1, 4. μέν is frequently joined with other parts., ἀλλὰ ... μέν, *but ... verily,* I, 7, 6; Ξενίας μὲν δή, *Xenias on his part,* I, 2, 3; οὐ μὲν δή, *not, you may be sure,* I, 9, 13; μὲν τοίνυν (only at the beginning of a speech), *well then,* II, 5, 41.

μέντοι, adv. and conj. (μέν+τοί): (1) confirmative, *certainly, in truth, moreover,* I, 9, 6; (2) adversative, *yet, still, however,* I, 3, 10.

μένω, μενῶ, ἔμεινα, μεμένηκα, *remain, wait, stay; last, hold good,* II, 3, 24; trans., *wait for,* IV, 4, 20.

Μένων, -ωνος, ὁ, *Menon,* a Thessalian, general under Cyrus; see the Introd., § 38, and II, 6, 21 ff.

μέρος, -ους, τό (*cf*. Lat. *mereo, deserve*), *part, portion, share;* μέρος τι τῆς εὐταξίας, *an instance of their discipline,* I, 5, 8; ἐν τῷ μέρει, *each in his turn,* III, 4, 23; κατὰ μέρος, *in turn, by relays,* V, 1, 9; κατὰ τὸ Χειρισόφου μέρος, *in the place of Chirisophus,* VI, 4, 23; καὶ ἐν τῷ μέρει καὶ παρὰ τὸ μέρος, *both in and out of turn (all and more than was my duty),* VII, 6, 36.

μεσημβρία, (μέσος+ἡμέρα), *midday, noon;* hence, *the south,* I, 7, 6; III, 5, 15.

μεσόγεια, -ας, ἡ (μέσας+γῆ), *midland, interior of a country,* VI, 2, 19; 4, 5.

μέσος, -η, -ον (Lat. *medius*, Eng. *mid*), *in the middle, the middle of*; gen. in pred. posit.; neut. (τό) μέσον, *the middle, the center,* I, 2, 15; διὰ μέσου τούτων, *between these,* I, 4, 4; cf. I, 7, 6; μέσαι νύκτες, *midnight,* I, 7, 1; μέσον ἡμέρας, *midday, noon,* I, 8, 8.

μεσόω (μέσος), *be in the middle;* ἤδη πέρα μεσούσης τῆς ἡμέρας, *when it was past midday,* VI, 5, 7.

Μέσπιλα, -ης, ἡ (?), *Mespila,* an Assyrian city, III, 4, 10 n.

μεστός, -ή, -όν, *full of, abounding in* (gen.); abs., *full,* VII, 3, 26.

μετά, by elision μετ' or μεθ', prep. with gen. and acc.; with gen., *with, together with,* in various uses, (for Xen.'s preference for σύν, see σύν); rarely, *by means of,* II, 6, 18; with acc., *after, next,* of place, order, or time; μετὰ τοῦτο (ταῦτα), *after this, thereupon,* I, 3, 9; μεθ' ἡμέραν, *by day (after daybreak),* IV, 6, 12; in composition, μετα- signifies participation, or succession, but oftenest change.

μεταβάλλω (βάλλω), *throw into a different place;* mid., *shift, e. g.,* the shield so that it covered the back in retreat, VI, 5, 16.

μεταγιγνώσκω (γιγνώσκω), *change one's mind.*

μεταδίδωμι (δίδωμι), *give among, distribute to,* dat., *give a share of,* gen. III, 3, 1.

μεταμέλει (μέλει), *it is a care afterward, it repents one* (dat.); best rendered personally, *I repent, am sorry,* I, 6, 7.

μεταξύ, adv. or prep. with gen. (μετά+ξύν), *in the midst, between;* with partic. μεταξὺ ὑπολαβών, *interrupting him in the midst of his talk,* III, 1, 27; οὐ πολλοῦ χρόνου μεταξὺ γενομένου, *after no long interval,* V, 2, 17.

μεταπέμπομαι (πέμπω), *send for, summon.*

μετάπεμπτος, -ον (μεταπέμπομαι), *sent for, summoned.*

μετάσχοι, see μετέχω.

μεταχωρέω (χωρέω), *change one's position, remove,* VII, 2, 18.

μέτειμι (εἰμί), *be among,* but in prose only impers. μέτεστι, etc., *there is a share,* with dat. of possessor and part. gen., III, 1, 20.

μετέχω (ἔχω), *have a share in, take part in.*

μετέωρος (μετά+αἴρω), *raised aloft;* μετεώρους ἐξεκόμισαν, *they raised up and carried out,* I, 5, 8.

μετρέω (μέτρον), *measure.*

μετρίως, adv. (μέτριος, *moderate*), *with moderation,* II, 3, 20.

μέτρον, -ου, τό (cf. Lat. *metior*, *measure,* Eng. *meter*, etc.), *measure.*

μέχρι, adv. *even to;* μέχρι εἰς or ἐπί, *as far as, even to,* V, 1, 1; as improp. prep. with gen., *up to, until, as far as;* μέχρι οὗ, *to a point where,* I, 7, 6; as conj., *until,* like ἕως, I, 4, 13.

μή, adv., *not,* the neg. of will, as οὐ is the neg. of statement; hence used (*a*) in prohibitions with pres. imv. (rarely aor. imv.), or aor. subj., II, 1, 12, etc.; (*b*) with hortatory subj., III, 1, 24; (*c*) in final and obj. clauses after ἵνα, ὅπως, ὡς, I, 4, 18, etc.; (*d*) in condit. clauses, II, 1, 4; (*e*) in rel. clauses with indef. antec.; (*f*) with partics. in generic sense, IV, 4, 15; (*g*) with infin. not in indir. disc., II, 3, 10, etc.; (in indir. disc. after vbs. of swearing and others implying will, II, 2, 8, *etc*.); (*h*) with subj. after vbs., *etc*., expressing fear (Lat. *ne*), I, 3, 10, *etc*.; often redundant after vbs. of hindering, III, 5, 11, εἰ μή, except, II, 1, 12; εἰ δὲ μή, otherwise, II, 2, 1 n. Cpds. of μή are similarly used.

The double neg. οὐ μή is used with the subj. in strong denial of the fut., οὐκέτι μή, II, 2, 12, *etc*. μὴ οὐ is used (*a*) after words expressing fear in the sense of *lest not, that not*, I, 7, 7; (*b*) with infins. and partics., which would in any case have μή, when they follow a neg. expressed or implied, II, 3, 11, *etc*.

μηδαμῇ, adv. (fem. dat. of μηδαμός), *in no way, nowhere*, VII, 6, 29.

μηδαμῶς, adv. (*cf*. μηδαμῇ), *by no means, in no wise*.

μηδέ (μή+δέ), *and not, but not, nor;* when no neg. precedes regularly, *not even*, (*cf*. οὐδέ).

Μήδεια, -ας, ἡ, *Medēa*, wife of Astyages, the last king of the Medes.

μηδείς, μηδεμία, μηδέν (μηδέ+εἷς), *not one, no one, no;* μηδέν, as adv. (inner obj.), *not at all*, V, 4, 19.

μηδέποτε, adv. (μηδέ+ποτέ), *never*.

μηδέτερος, -α, -ον (μηδέ+ἕτερος), *neither* (of two), VII, 4, 10.

Μηδία, -ας, ἡ, *Media*, properly, the country between Assyria and the Caspian Sea, but in the *Anabasis* used loosely of Assyria itself. Μηδίας τεῖχος, *the Median wall*, I, 7, 15 n.

Μῆδοι, -ων, οἱ, *the Medes*, people of Media.

Μήδοκος, -ου, ὁ, *Medocus*, king of the Odrysae in Thrace.

Μηδοσάδης, -ου, ὁ, *Medosades*, ambassador of Seuthes.

μήθ', see μήτε.

μηκέτι (μή+ἔτι, the κ due to the analogy of οὐκέτι) *no longer, not again*.

μῆκος, -ους, τό (*cf*. μακρός), *length*.

μήν, post-pos. particle of asseveration, *in truth, verily, certainly;* καὶ μήν, *and in truth, and yet*, I, 7, 5; ἀλλὰ μήν, *nay truly*, I, 9, 18; ἦ μήν, in oaths, *in very truth*, II, 3, 26.

μήν, μηνός, ὁ (Lat. *mensis*, Eng. *moon, month*), *month*.

μηνοειδής, -ές (μήνη, moon [*cf*. μήν] +εἶδος), *moon-shaped, crescent-shaped*.

μηνύω, μηνύσω, *etc*., *make known, give information*.

μήποτε (μή+ποτέ), *never*.

μήπω, adv. (μή+πώ), *not yet*.

μηρός, -οῦ, ὁ, *thigh*.

μήτε, neg. conj. (μή+τέ; *cf*. οὔτε), *and not, nor;* generally μήτε ... μήτε, *neither ... nor*, I, 3, 14; also followed by τέ, *not ... but*, II, 2, 8 n.

μήτηρ, μητρός, ἡ (Lat. *mater*, Eng. *mother*), *mother*.

μητρόπολις, -εως, ἡ (μήτηρ+πόλις), *mother-city, capital*.

μηχανάομαι, μηχανήσομαι, *etc*. (μηχανή, *device*), *contrive, devise*.

μηχανή, -ῆς, ἡ (*cf*. Eng. *machine*), **μία**, see εἷς.

Μίδας, -ου, ὁ, *Midas*, a legendary king of Phrygia, I, 2, 13 n.

Μιθραδάτης, -ου, ὁ, *Mithradātes* (so spelled in Xen.), satrap of Lycaonia and Cappadocia, VII, 8, 25. He was on the side of Cyrus but after the battle of Cunaxa proved faithless to the Greeks.

μικρός, -ά, -όν (cf. Eng. microscope), small, little, unimportant; neut. μικρόν, as subst., a little (of space or time), II, 1, 6; as adv., barely, hardly, I, 3, 2; κατὰ μικρόν, in small divisions, V, 6, 32; κατὰ μικρά, in bits or morsels, VII, 3, 22.

Μιλήσιος, -α, -ον (Μίλητος), Milesian; commonly as masc. noun, a Milesian, inhabitant of Milētus; fem. ἡ Μιλησία, the Milesian (woman), I, 10, 3.

Μίλητος, -ου, ἡ, Milētus, an important Greek city in Ionia, captured by the Persians, 494 B. C.

Μιλτοκύθης, -ου, ὁ, Miltocythes, in command of Cyrus' Thracian troops; deserted to the king, II, 2, 7.

μιμέομαι, μιμήσομαι, etc. (μῖμος, actor, mime, Eng. mimic, pantomime), imitate; μιμούμενος ὠρχεῖτο, danced a mimetic dance, a dance with pantomime, VI, 1, 9.

μιμνῄσκω, -μνήσω, ἔμνησα, μέμνημαι, ἐμνήσθην, act. remind; mid. and pass. remember (the perf. tenses having the force of pres.; cf. Lat. memini), abs. or with gen.; make mention of, VII, 5, 8; suggest, with infin., VI, 4, 11.

μισέω, μισήσω, etc. (cf. Eng. misanthrope), hate.

μισθοδοσία, -ας, ἡ (μισθός+δίδωμι), giving of pay.

μιθοδοτέω (μισθός+δίδωμι), pay wages to, hire, with dat.

μισθοδότης, -ου, ὁ (μισθός+δίδωμι), paymaster, employer.

μισθός, -οῦ, ὁ (cf. Eng. meed), pay, wages, esp. of soldiers. This was ordinarily a daric a month for privates, two for a captain, and four for a general, VII, 6, 1.

μισθοφορά, -ᾶς, ἡ (μισθός+φέρω), receipt of wages, mercenary service, pay.

μισθοφόρος, -ον (μισθός+φέρω), receiving pay, or wages; οἱ μισθοφόροι, as subst., mercenary troops, mercenaries.

μισθόω, μισθώσω, etc. (μισθός), let out for hire; mid., hire for oneself; pass., be hired.

μνᾶ, -ᾶς, ἡ, mina, one-sixtieth of a talent, or one hundred drachmae (about $18.00; but see the note on δέκα τάλαντα, I, 7, 18).

μνήμη, -ης, ἡ, (μιμνῄσκω), memory, remembrance.

μνημονεύω (μνήμων, mindful; cf. μιμνῄσκω), call to mind, remember.

μνημονικός, -ή -όν (μνήμων, mindful; cf. μιμνῄσκω), having a good memory.

μνησθῇ, see μιμνῄσκω.

μνησικακέω, μνησικακήσω, etc. (μιμνῄσκω+κακός), remember wrongs, cherish ill-will, bear a grudge (with dat. of pers. and gen. of cause).

μόλις, adv., with difficulty, hardly, barely.

μολυβδίς, -ίδος, ἡ (μόλυβδος), leaden ball or bullet.

μόλυβδος, -ου, ὁ, lead.

μόλωσιν, see βλώσκω.

μοναρχία, -ας, ἡ (μόνος+ἄρχω; cf. Eng. monarchy), command vested in one person, sole or chief command.

μοναχῇ, adv. (μοναχός, solitary, from μόνος), alone, only.

μονή, -ῆς, ἡ (μένω), a stay, halt.

μονόξυλος, -ον (μόνος+ξύλον), made of a single log, of canoes, V, 4, 11.

μόνος, -η, -ον (cf. Eng. monk, etc.), alone, only, by oneself; with gen., II, 3, 19; neut. μόνον as adv.; III, 2, 19, and often.

μόσσυν, -ος, irreg. dat. pl. μοσσύνοις, ὁ, *wooden tower*, V, 4, 26.

Μοσσύνοικοι, -ων, οἱ (μόσσυν+οἰκέω), *the Mossynoeci (tower-dwellers), the name of a tribe dwelling on the southeastern shore of the Euxine. Their manners are described in the Anabasis,* V, 4.

μόσχειος, -α, -ον (μόσχος, *calf*), *of a calf;* with κρέα, *veal,* IV, 5, 31.

μοχθέω, μοχθήσω, etc. (μόχθος, *labor*), *labor, toil.*

μοχλός, -οῦ, ὁ, *bar* or *bolt* of a gate or door.

μύζω, *suck.*

Μυρίανδος, -ον, ἡ, *Myriandus,* a city in Syria on the gulf of Iasus.

μυριάς, -άδος, ἡ (μυρίος; cf. Eng. *myriad*), *ten thousand, myriad.*

μυρίος, -α -ον, *countless, infinite,* VII, 1, 30; pl., with changed accent, μύριοι, -αι, -α, *ten thousand;* so in the sing. with a collective noun, I, 7, 10.

μύρον, -ου, τό, *a fragrant oil* or *unguent.*

Μυσία, -ᾶς, ἡ, *Mysia,* a country in the northwestern part of Asia Minor.

Μύσιος, -α, -ον (Μυσός), *Mysian.*

Μυσός, -οῦ, ὁ, *a native of Mysia, a Mysian.*

Μυσός, -οῦ, ὁ (=the foregoing), *Mysus,* the name of a brave Mysian, V, 2, 29.

μυχός, -οῦ, ὁ, *innermost part, nook, recess.*

μῶρος, -α, -ον (cf. Lat. *morus, a fool,* Eng. *sophomore*), *stupid, foolish.*

μώρως, adv. (μῶρος), *stupidly.*

N

ναί, intensive particle (cf. νή, Lat. *ne, nae*), *yea, verily,* in oaths, *yea by,* with acc. with or without μά.

ναός, -οῦ, ὁ, Attic νεώς, -ώ (ναίω, *dwell*), *temple.*

νάπη, -ης, ἡ and νάπος, -ους, τό, *woody glen, valley, vale.*

ναυαρχέω (ναῦς+ἄρχω), *be in command of a fleet, be admiral.*

ναύαρχος, -ου, ὁ (ναῦς+ἄρχω), *commander,* of a fleet, *admiral.*

ναύκληρος, -ου, ὁ (ναῦς+κλῆρος, *lot*), *ship-owner, ship-master, captain.*

ναῦλον, -ου, τό (ναῦς), *passage money, fare.*

ναυπηγήσιμος, -ον (ναῦς+πήγνυμι), *fit for shipbuilding,* of timber.

ναῦς, νεώς, ἡ (Lat. *navis*), *ship,* chiefly, *man-of-war.*

Ναυσικλείδης, -ου, ὁ, *Nausiclīdes,* an envoy who brought pay from Thibron to the Greeks, VII, 8, 6.

ναυσίπορος, -ον (ναῦς+ √περ), *navigable.*

ναυτικός, -ή -όν (ναῦς, cf. Eng. *nautical*), *naval.*

νεανίσκος, -ου, ὁ (νεανίας, *young man*), *young man, youth.*

νεῖμαι, see νέμω.

νεκρός, -οῦ, ὁ, cf. Lat. *nex, death, neco, slay*), *dead body, corpse.*

νέμω, νεμῶ, ἔνειμα, -νενέμηκα, νενέμημαι, ἐνεμήθην, *portion out, award,* of meat, *carve,* VII, 3, 21; of cattle, *drive to pasture;* in mid., *graze, feed,* II, 2, 15.

νενεμημένων, see νέμω.

νενημένων, see νέω.

νεόδαρτος, -ον (νέος+δέρω), *freshly flayed.*

Νέον Τεῖχος, -ους, τό, *New Fort,* a Thracian city on the Propontis.

νέος, a, -ον (cf. Lat. *novus*, Eng. *new*), *new; often, young;* so νεώτερος, I, 1, 1; of things, *fresh,* νέος σῖτος, *this year's grain,* V, 4, 27.

νεῦμα, -ατος, τό (νεύω, *nod*), *nod.*

νευρά, -ᾶς, ἡ (cf. νεῦρον), *sinew;* hence, *bowstring.*

νεῦρον, -ου, τό (Lat. *nervus, sinew*), *sinew, cord.*

νευσόμενοι, see νέω, *swim.*

νεφέλη, -ης, ἡ (τό νέφος, *cloud,* Lat. *nebula*), *cloud.*

νέω, νήσω, νένημαι, *heap* or *pile up.*

νέω, νεύσομαι (cf. ναῦς), *swim.*

νεωκόρος, -ου, ὁ (ναός+κορέω, *sweep*), *keeper of a temple, warder, sacristan.*

Νέων, -ωνος, ὁ, *Neon,* a Spartan from Asine, in the Greek army.

νεώριον, -ου, τό (ναῦς), *navy yard, dockyard,* VII, 1, 27.

νεῶν, see ναῦς.

νεώς, -ώ, ὁ, *temple,* V, 3, 8; see ναός.

νεωστί, adv. (νέος), *newly, lately.*

νή, intensive particle (cf. ναί) used in oaths with affirmative force, *yes by,* with acc., νὴ Δία, I, 7, 9.

νῆες, see ναῦς.

νῆσος, -ου, ἡ (ναῦς), *island.*

Νίκανδρος, -ου, ὁ, *Nicander,* a Laconian.

Νίκαρχος, -ου, ὁ, *Nicarchus,* an Arcadian. He brought the Greeks news of the seizure of their generals, II, 5, 33. A captain of this name deserts, III, 3, 5.

νικάω, νικήσω, etc. (νίκη), *conquer, excel, surpass;* the pres. often has the sense of a perf., *be victorious, have conquered,* I, 8, 21; τὰ πάντα νικᾶν, *be completely victorious,* II, 1, 1; ἐκ τῆς νικώσης (sc. γνώμης), *in accordance with a majority vote,* VI, 1, 18.

νίκη, ης, ἡ, *victory.*

Νικόμαχος, -ου, ὁ, *Nicomachus,* from the region near Mt. Oeta in Thessaly serving with the Greek light armed troops.

νοέω, νοήσω, etc. (cf. νοῦς), *perceive, observe, plan.*

νόθος, -η, -ον, or -ος, -ον, *illegitimate, bastard.*

νομή, -ῆς, ἡ (νέμω), *pasture, grazing herd, herd.*

νομίζω, νομιῶ, etc. (νόμος), *regard as customary* or *proper;* pass., *be the custom, be held right;* so τὰ νομιζόμενα, *the customary* or *regular wages,* VII, 3, 10; *think, believe, consider; suppose,* generally with infin., in VI, 6, 24 with partic.

νόμιμος, -η, -ον (νόμος), *customary, lawful.*

νόμος, -ου, ὁ (νέμω, *assign*), *custom, fashion, usage, law;* in music, *mode, strain,* V, 4, 17.

νοσέω, ἐνόσησα, *be sick;* met. of a country, *be in disorder,* VII, 2, 32.

νόσος, -ου, ἡ, *sickness, disease.*

νότος, -ου, ὁ, *the south wind.*

νουμηνία, -ας, ἡ (νέος+μήν), *new moon, first day of the month.*

νοῦς, νοῦ, ὁ (γιγνώσκω), *mind, sense;* τὸν νοῦν προσέχειν, see the vb.; ἐν νῷ ἔχειν, *purpose, plan,* III, 3, 2; 5, 13.

νυκτερεύω, νυκτερεύσω, ἐνυκτέρευσα (νύξ), *spend the night.*

νύκτα, νυκτί, νυκτός, see νύξ.

νυκτοφύλαξ, -ακος, ὁ (νύξ+φύλαξ), *night-watch, sentinel.*

νύκτωρ, adv. (νύξ), *by night, at night.*

νῦν, adv. of time (cf. Lat. *nunc,* Eng. *now*), *now, at present;* τὸ νῦν εἶναι, *for the present,*

III, 2, 37; τὸν νῦν χρόνον, at present, VI, 6, 13.

νύν, enclitic post-pos. part. (νῦν, less emphasized), *now, then,* of inference.

νυνί, adv., strengthened form of νῦν, *now.*

νύξ, νυκτός, ἡ (cf. Lat. *nox,* Eng. *night*), *night;* νυκτός, *by night,* II, 6, 7; τῆς νυκτός, *during the night,* II, 2, 1; διὰ νυκτός, *all night long,* IV, 6, 22; μέσαι νύκτες, *midnight,* I, 7, 1 n.; III, 1, 33.

νῷ, see *νοῦς.*

νῶτον, -ου, τό, *back.*

Ξ

Ξανθικλῆς, -έους, ὁ, *Xanthicles,* of Achaea, elected general in the place of Socrates, III, 1, 47.

ξενία, -ας, ἡ (ξένος), *a bond of hospitality* or *friendship,* VI, 6, 35.

Ξενίας, -ου, ὁ, *Xenias,* of Parrhasia in Arcadia, a general under Cyrus. He deserted, angered, because some of his troops had gone over to Clearchus, I, 3, 7.

ξενίζω, (ξένος), *entertain, receive hospitably.*

ξενικός, -ή, -όν (ξένος), *belonging to a foreigner, foreign;* τὸ ξενικόν, *mercenary force,* I, 2, 1; II, 5, 22.

ξένιος, -α, -ον (ξένος), *belonging to a stranger,* hence *hospitable;* τὰ ξένια, *gifts* or *pledges of friendship,* IV, 8, 23; Ζεὺς ξένιος, *Zeus, the god of hospitality, the god who protects strangers,* III, 2, 4.

ξενόομαι (ξένος), *be entertained by* (dat.), VII, 8, 6, 8.

ξένος, -ου, ὁ, *stranger,* esp. *one bound by ties of hospitality,* whether guest or host, *guest-friend;* also frequently, *foreign soldier, mercenary.*

Ξενοφών, -ῶντος, ὁ, *Xenophon,* an Athenian, author of the *Anabasis,* see the Introd.

Ξέρξης, -ου, ὁ, *Xerxes,* son of Darius Hystaspes, king of Persia from 485 to 465 B. C.; invaded Greece and was defeated at Salamis, 480 B. C.

ξεστός, -ή, -όν (verbal of ξέω, *scrape*), *scraped, polished.*

ξηραίνω, ξηρανῶ, etc. (ξηρός), *dry.*

ξηρός, -ά, -όν, *dry.*

ξίφος, -ους, τό, *sword.*

ξόανον, -ου, τό (ξέω, *polish;* cf. ξεστός), *wooden image* or *statue.*

ξυήλη, -ης, ἡ (ξύω, = ξέω, *scrape, polish*), *tool for scraping;* hence *curved* or *sickle-shaped dagger,* used by the Spartans.

ξυλίζομαι (ξύλον), *gather wood.*

ξύλινος, -η, -ον (ξύλον), *wooden.*

ξύλον, -ου, τό, *wood,* in the widest sense, *piece of wood; pole,* I, 10, 12; in pl. *wood, fuel, beams* (of a house).

ξυν-, see *συν-.*

Ο

ὁ, ἡ, τό, definite art., *the.*

1) As a demonstrative pron. (its original force), chiefly with μέν and δέ; ὁ μὲν ... ὁ δὲ, *the one ... the other, he ... he,* sing. or pl.; often without a balancing ὁ μέν, ὁ δέ, *and he* (*they*), *but he* (*they*), regularly with change of subj. τὰ μὲν ... τὰ δέ, *partly ... partly,* IV, 1, 14; τῇ μὲν ... τῇ δέ, *in this respect ... in that,* III, 1, 12; τὰ μὲν ... τέλος δέ, *at first ... finally,* I, 9, 6. In this use the nom. is properly accented.

2) As the def. art., much as in Eng.; often with proper names, I, 1, 2 n.; with possessive force, I, 1, 3 n.; often, with ellipsis of the noun, with gens., οἱ ἐκείνου, *his men*, I, 2, 15; with prepositional phrases, τῶν παρὰ βασιλέως, *those (the men) from the king*, I, 1, 5; or with advs., τοὺς οἴκοι, *those at home*, I, 2, 1. In such cases the context shows what (if anything) is to be supplied.

The art. is regularly used with round numbers ἀμφὶ τοὺς δισχιλίους, *about 2,000*, I, 2, 10; very frequently with partics., τοὺς φεύγοντας, *the exiles*, I, 1, 7; sometimes with distrib. force, τοῦ μηνὸς τῷ στρατιώτῃ, *per month per man*, I, 3, 21.

ὅ, see ὅς.

ὀβελίσκος, -ου, ὁ (ὀβελός, ὁ, *spit*), *little spit, spit*.

ὀβολός, -οῦ, ὁ, *obol*, an Attic coin, worth about three cents.

ὀγδοήκοντα, indecl. (ὀκτώ), *eighty*.

ὄγδοος, -η, -ον (ὀκτώ), *eighth*.

ὅδε, ἥδε, τόδε, dem. pron. (ὁ+δέ), *this, the following*, referring usually to what is near the speaker (Lat. *hic*) and often suggesting a gesture, II, 3, 19; τάδε, often, *as follows*, I, 5, 15; τῷδε, as adv., *in the following way* (cf. ὧδε), II, 3, 1; so τῇδε, *here*, VII, 2, 13.

ὁδεύω (ὁδός), *march*.

ὁδοιπορέω (ὁδός + √περ), *go by land*.

ὁδοποιέω, ὁδοποιήσω, etc. (ὁδός+ποιέω), *make a road, repair a road*.

ὁδός, -οῦ, ἡ, *way, road, march, journey*; hence, *way, means*, II, 6, 22.

᾿Οδρύσης, -ου, ὁ, *an Odrysian*; pl. *the Odrysae*, a Thracian tribe.

᾿Οδυσσεύς, -έως, ὁ, *Odysseus*, Lat. *Ulysses*, the hero of the *Odyssey*.

ὅθεν, adv. (ὅς), *whence, from which*; of persons, *from whom*, II, 5, 26.

ὅθενπερ, adv., strengthened form of ὅθεν, *from which very place, just whence*.

οἱ, see ὁ.

οἵ, see ὅς.

οἷ, see οὗ.

οἶδα, 2 pf. with pres. sense (subj. etc. εἰδῶ, εἰδείην, ἴσθι, εἰδέναι, εἰδώς), plpf. ᾔδη or ᾔδειν, fut. εἴσομαι (εἶδον), *know, understand, be acquainted with*, abs., with acc., with ὅτι, infin., partic. (nom. or acc.), or εἰ; χάριν εἰδέναι, *be grateful*, I, 4, 15; οἶδ᾽ ὅτι, parenthetic, *I know well; certainly*, V, 7, 33; cf. δῆλον ὅτι.

οἴει, see οἴομαι.

οἴκαδε, adv. (οἶκος), *homeward, to one's country*; ἡ οἴκαδε ὁδός, *the homeward way*, III, 1, 2.

οἰκεῖος, -α, -ον (οἶκος), *belonging to one's home, familiar, intimate*; οἱ οἰκεῖοι, *one's family, relatives*, or *intimate friends*, III, 2, 26.

οἰκείως, adv. (οἰκεῖος), *familiarly, kindly*.

οἰκέτης, -ου, ὁ (οἰκέω), *member of a household*, esp. *slave*; in pl. *household*, IV, 5, 35.

οἰκέω, οἰκήσω, etc., *dwell, live*; trans. *inhabit, live in*, III, 2, 23; of cities, etc., *be situated, lie*, V, 1, 13; in this sense oftener pass., I, 4, 1.

οἴκημα, -ατος, τό (οἰκέω), *house*.

οἴκησις, -εως, ἡ, *dwelling, residence*.

οἰκία, -ας, ἡ (οἶκος), *house*.

οἰκίζω, οἰκιῶ, ᾤκισα, ᾤκισμαι, ᾠκίσθην, *settle, found, colonize*.

οἰκοδομέω, οἰκοδομήσω, etc. (οἶκος + δέμω, *build*), *build a house*, then gen., *build, construct*.

οἴκοθεν, adv. (οἶκος), *from home*.

οἴκοι, adv. (οἶκος), *at home;* οἱ οἴκοι, *those at home,* I, 2, 1.

οἰκονόμος, -ου, ὁ (οἶκος+νέμω), *housekeeper, steward, manager.*

οἶκος, -ου, ὁ, *house, home.*

οἰκτίρω, οἰκτιρῶ, etc. (οἶκτος, *pity*), *pity.*

οἶμαι, see οἴομαι.

οἶνος, -ου, ὁ (Lat. *vinum*, Eng. *wine*), *wine;* οἶνος φοινίκων, *palm wine,* II, 3, 14; οἶνος κρίθινος, beer, IV, 5, 26.

οἰνοχόος, -ου, ὁ (οἶνος+χέω, *pour*), *wine-pourer, cup-bearer.*

οἴομαι or οἶμαι, οἰήσομαι, ᾠήθην, *suppose, think, believe;* often parenthetic, *methinks,* esp. in the shorter forms οἶμαι and ᾤμην.

οἷος, -α, -ον, rel. pron., *of what sort or size, how great,* frequent in indir. ques., ὁρῶν ἐν οἵοις ἐσμέν, *seeing in what straits we are,* III, 1, 15; properly preceded by a word like τοιοῦτος, but this is often omitted, so that οἷος, alone, may be rendered, *such as;* with infin., οὐ γὰρ ἦν ὥρα οἵα ἄρδειν, *it was not the proper season for watering,* II, 3, 13 n.; οἷοί τ' ἔσεσθε, *you will be able,* V, 4, 9; οὐχ οἷόν τε ἦν, *it was impossible,* III, 3, 9. In these phrases the vb. is often omitted, II, 2, 3, *etc.; cf.* οἷόν τε μάλιστα πεφυλαγμένως, *as guardedly as possible,* II, 4, 24. οἷον, adv., *as for example,* IV, 1, 14; with sup., intensive, like ὡς, IV, 8, 2.

οἷόσπερ, -απερ, -όνπερ, a strengthened form of οἷος, *just such as;* παραπλησία οἷάπερ, freely, *precisely like the one for which, just such a one as,* I, 3, 18.

οἴου, see οἴομαι.

οἷς, οἰός, acc. pl. οἶς, ἡ (*cf.* Lat. *ovis,* Eng. *ewe*), *sheep.*

οἴσει, see φέρω.

οἶσθα, see οἶδα.

οἰστός, -οῦ, ὁ, *arrow.* The common word is τόξευμα.

Οἰταῖος, -ου, ὁ (Οἴτη, Oeta), *an Oetaean,* from the region near Mt. Oeta in Thessaly.

οἴχομαι, οἰχήσομαι, pres. with perf. force, *be gone, have gone;* often with partic. expressing the means of motion, ᾤχετο ἀπελαύνων, *he rode off,* II, 4, 24; euphemistic of the dead, *be missing, be gone,* III, 1, 32.

οἰωνός, -οῦ, ὁ (for ὀϝιωνός [?], *cf.* Lat. *avis*), *bird,* esp. *bird of prey;* then, since eagles, vultures, etc., were observed in augury, *omen, sign,* III, 2, 9.

ὀκέλλω, ὤκειλα, *run ashore,* of ships.

ὀκλάζω, aor. ὤκλασα, *crouch down.*

ὀκνέω, ὀκνήσω, etc. (ὄκνος), *hesitate, shrink from,* with infin., I, 3, 17; *dread, fear,* with μή and subv. or opt.

ὀκνηρῶς, adv. (ὄκνος), *reluctantly.*

ὄκνος, -ου, ὁ, *hesitation, reluctance.*

ὀκτακισχίλιοι (ὀκτώ+χίλιοι), *eight thousand.*

ὀκτακόσιοι, -αι, -α (ὀκτώ+ἑκατόν), *eight hundred.*

ὀκτώ, indecl. (Lat. *octo*), *eight.*

ὀκτωκαίδεκα, indecl. (ὀκτώ+δέκα), *eighteen.*

ὄλεθρος, -ου, ὁ (ὄλλυμι, *destroy*), *destruction, death.*

ὀλίγος, -η, -ον (*cf.* Eng. *oligarchy*), *small, little;* of time, *short;* of number, *few;* neut. as adv., ὀλίγον, *a little;* αὐτοῦ ὀλίγον δεήσαντος καταλευσθῆναι, *though he had come near being stoned to death,* I, 5, 14 (*cf.* δέω); ἐπ᾽ ὀλίγων, *few deep*, IV, 8, 11; ὀλίγας (sc. πληγάς) παίειν, *inflict (too) few blows*, V, 8, 12; παρ' ὀλίγον ποιεῖσθαι, *esteem of little worth*, VI, 6, 11; κατ' ὀλίγους, *in small parties*, VII, 6, 29.

ὀλισθάνω, *slip*.

ὀλισθηρός, -ά, -όν (ὀλισθάνω), *slippery*.

ὁλκάς, -άδος, ἡ (ἕλκω), *a merchantman, trading vessel* (properly *a vessel that is towed*).

ὀλοίτροχος, -ον, ὁ (√ ελ [cf. Lat. volvo]+τρέχω), *a rolling stone, round stone*.

ὁλοκαυτέω (ὅλος+καίω), *offer a whole burnt offering* (instead of certain portions only).

ὅλος, -η, -ον (old Lat. *sollus, solidus*), *whole* (not akin to the Greek word), *all, entire*.

Ὀλυμπία, -ας, ἡ (Ὄλυμπος, ὁ, *Olympus*), *Olympia*, a district in Elis on the Alphēus, where the great games were held.

Ὀλύνθιος, -ον, ὁ (Ὄλυνθος), *an Olynthian, native of Olynthus*, the chief city of Chalcidice.

ὁμαλής, -ές (ἅμα), *even, level*; ὁμαλὲς ἰέναι, *march over level ground*, IV, 6, 12.

ὁμαλός, -ή, -όν (ἅμα), *even, level*; ἐν τῷ ὁμαλῷ, *on level ground*, IV, 2, 16.

ὁμαλῶς, adv. (ὁμαλός), *evenly*.

ὅμηρος, -ον, ὁ (ὁμοῦ+ √ ἀρ), *hostage*.

ὁμιλέω, ὁμιλήσω, etc. (ὅμιλος, *throng*), *associate with, consort with*.

ὁμίχλη, -ης, ἡ (cf. Eng. *mist*), *mist, fog*.

ὄμμα, -ατος, τό (cf. ὄψομαι), *eye*; hence, *look*.

ὄμνυμι or ὀμνύω, ὀμοῦμαι, ὤμοσα, ὀμώμοκα, ὀμώμο(σ)μαι, ὠμό(σ)θην, *swear, take an oath*, with infin., generally fut.; *give an oath to* (dat.), *swear by* (acc.).

ὅμοιος, -α, -ον (ἅμα), *like, resembling, similar*; οἱ ὅμοιοι, *equals in rank, peers*, IV, 6, 14 n.; ἐν τῷ ὁμοίῳ, *on the same footing*, IV, 6, 18; ὅμοιοι ἦσαν θαυμάζουσιν, *were like persons wondering*, i. e., *seemed lost in wonder*, III, 5, 13.

ὁμοίως (ὅμοιος), *in like manner, alike*; ὁμοίως ὥσπερ, *just as if*, VI, 5, 31.

ὁμολογέω, ὁμολογήσω, etc. (ἅμα+λέγω), *think the same as, agree, grant, admit, confess*.

ὁμολογουμένως (ὁμολογέω), *confessedly, with the consent of all*.

ὁμομήτριος, -α, -ον (ἅμα+μήτηρ), *born of the same mother*.

ὀμόσαι, see ὄμνυμι.

ὁμόσε, adv. (ἅμα), *to the same place, to close quarters*.

ὁμοτράπεζος, -ον (ἅμα+τράπεζα), *at the same table with, a table companion*, I, 8, 25 n.; cf. συντράπεζος.

ὁμοῦ, adv. (ἅμα), *together, at the same time, with*; ὁμοῦ εἶναι, with gen., *be near, meet*, IV, 6, 24.

ὀμφαλός, -οῦ, ὁ, *navel*.

ὅμως, adv. (ἅμα), *all the same, nevertheless, yet, however*.

ἔν, see εἰμί.

ὅν, see ὅς.

ὄναρ, τό, only nom. and acc., *dream*.

ὀνῆσαι, see ὀνίνημι.

ὀνίνημι, ὀνήσω, ὤνησα, 2 aor. mid. ὠνήμην, ὠνήθην, *benefit, help, aid*.

ὄνομα, -ατος, τό (γιγνώσκω; cf. Lat. *nomen*), *name*; acc. as adv., *by name*; also, *fame, reputation*, II, 6, 17.

ὀνομαστί, adv. (ὄνομα), *by name*.

ὄνος, -ου, ὁ (Lat. *asinus*, Eng. *ass*), *ass*; ὄνος ἀλέτης, *the upper* (grinding) *mill-stone* (turned by an ass), I, 5, 5.

ὄξος, -ους, τό (ὀξύς), *sour wine.*

ὀξύς, -εῖα, -ύ, *sharp,* of taste, *sour.*

ὅπερ, see ὅσπερ.

ὅπῃ, rel. adv., *where, in what way, how;* loosely, *whither.*

ὄπισθεν, adv., *from behind, from the rear, behind;* οἱ ὄπισθεν, *those in the rear,* IV, 2, 26; τὰ ὄπισθεν, *the rear,* III, 4, 40; εἰς τοὔπισθεν, *backwards,* III, 3, 10.

ὀπισθοφυλακέω, ὠπισθοφυλάκησα (ὄπισθεν+φυλάττω), *guard the rear, form the rear guard.*

ὀπισθοφυλακία, -ας, ἡ (ὄπισθεν+φυλάττω), *command the rear.*

ὀπισθοφύλαξ, -ακος, ὁ (ὄπισθεν+φυλάττω), *one guarding the rear;* pl. *the rear guard.*

ὀπίσω, adv., *back, behind one's back,* VI, 1, 8.

ὁπλίζω, ὥπλισα, ὥπλισμαι, ὡπλίσθην (ὅπλον), *make ready, equip, arm;* mid., *arm oneself;* pf. pass., *be armed.*

ὅπλισις, -εως, ἡ (ὁπλίζω), *equipment, arms.*

ὁπλιτεύω (ὁπλίτης), *serve as hoplite.*

ὁπλίτης, -ου, ὁ (ὅπλον), *hoplite, heavy armed soldier.*

ὁπλιτικός, -ή, -όν (ὁπλίτης), *of* or *for heavy armed troops;* τὸ ὁπλιτικόν, *the hoplite force.*

ὁπλομαχία, -ας, ἡ (ὅπλον+μάχομαι), *fighting in armor, infantry tactics.*

ὅπλον, -ου, τό (ἕπομαι, *handle, be busy with*), *implement, tool;* esp. in pl. *arms, weapons, armor;* τὰ ὅπλα by metonymy = ὁπλῖται, II, 2, 4, or *the place where the arms were stacked, the camp,* II, 4, 15; ἐν τοῖς ὅπλοις *under arms,* IV, 3, 7; εἰς τὰ ὅπλα, *to arms,* I, 5, 13; τίθεσθαι τὰ ὅπλα, *take up a position under arms,* I, 5, 14; II, 2, 21; or *ground* or *rest arms,* I, 10, 16; προβάλλεσθαι τὰ ὅπλα, *advance arms* (for the charge), I, 2, 17.

ὁπόθεν, rel. adv., *from whence, wheneesoever.*

ὅποι, rel. adv., *whither, where.*

ὁποῖος, -α, -ον, rel. pron. (ποῖος), *of what sort* or *kind, of such a sort as, whatsoever.*

ὁπόσος, -η, -ον, rel. pron. (πόσος), *as great as, as many as;* in indir. ques., *how large, how much, how many;* ὁπόσον, as adv., *as far as,* III, 3, 10.

ὁπόταν (ὁπότε+ἄν), rel. adv., *whenever, when,* with subj.

ὁπότε, rel. adv., of time, *when, whenever, as often as,* with indic. or opt.; of cause, *since, because,* VII, 6, 11.

ὁπότερος, -α, -ον, rel. pron., *which of two.*

ὅπου, rel. adv., *where, wherever;* ὅπου μή, *except where,* I, 5, 9.

ὀπτάω, ὀπτήσω, etc., *bake, roast.*

ὀπτός, -ή, -όν, *roasted;* of bricks, *baked,* II, 4, 12.

ὅπως, rel. adv., *in what way, how, as;* οὐκ ἔστιν ὅπως οὐκ, *it is not possible that not,* i.e., *certainly,* II, 4, 6; often in indir. ques.; in obj. clauses, *that,* I, 1, 4; in final clauses, *that, in order that;* in exhortations with fut. indic., ὅπως ἔσεσθε ἄνδρες, *see that ye be men,* I, 7, 3; οὐκ ὅπως, *not only not,* VII, 7, 8.

ὁράω, ἑώρων, ὄψομαι, ἑώρακα, ἑώραμαι or ὦμμαι, ὤφθην, aor. supplied by εἶδον (see the word), *see, look,* *observe, perceive, etc.*; abs., with acc., with acc. and partic., or with ὅτι and a clause, II, 2, 5; with rel. clause, IV, 7, 11; VI, 4, 23; with indir. ques., II, 5, 13; with acc. and infin. (following a partic.), VII, 7, 30. The infin. ὁρᾶν may depend upon an adj. or adv. στυγνὸς ὁρᾶν, *stern to look upon*, II, 6, 9; *cf.* III, 4, 5; so ὁρᾶσθαι, II, 3, 3 n.

ὀργή, -ῆς, ἡ, *temper*, esp. *anger*; as adv. ὀργῇ, *angrily, in a passion*, I, 5, 8; II, 6, 9.

ὀργίζομαι, ὀργιοῦμαι, etc. (ὀργή), *be angry, be enraged*.

ὀργυιά, -ᾶς, ἡ (ὀρέγω), *length of the arms outstretched, fathom*, 6 Greek feet, 5 ft. 10 in., Eng.

ὀρέγω, ὀρέξω, ὤρεξα, ὠρέχθην (*cf.* Lat. *rego*, Eng. *reach*), *reach, reach out*, VII, 3, 29.

ὀρεινός, -ή, -όν (ὄρος), *mountainous*.

ὄρειος, -α, -ον (ὄρος), *belonging to mountains;* of countries, *mountainous;* of persons, *dwelling in the mountains;* as subst., οἱ ὄρειοι, *mountaineers*.

ὄρθιος, -α, -ον (ὀρθός), *steep;* τὸ ὄρθιον, *ascent*, IV, 2, 3; ὄρθιον ἰέναι, *march up hill*, IV, 6, 12; ὄρθιοι λόχοι, *companies in column*, IV, 2, 11 n.

ὀρθός, -ή, όν (*cf.* Eng. *orthodox*), *straight, direct, erect*.

ὄρθρος, -ου, ὁ, *daybreak, dawn*.

ὀρθῶς (ὀρθός), *rightly, justly, with reason;* ὀρθῶς ἔχειν, *be proper*, III, 2, 7.

ὅρια, -ων, τά (ὅρος, *boundary*), *borders of a country, frontier, boundary*.

ὁρίζω, -οριῶ, ὥρισα, etc. (ὅρος, *boundary; cf.* Eng. *horizon*), *be a boundary, bound; determine*, VII, 7, 36; in mid., *set up as one's boundary*, VII, 5, 13.

ὅρκος, -ου, ὁ (εἴργω, *shut in, restrain*, ἕρκος, *fence*), *oath*.

ὁρμάω, ὁρμήσω, etc. (ὁρμή), *start, hasten, rush, set out* (τὴν ὁδόν, *on his march*, III, 1, 8); so mid., I, 1, 9.

ὁρμέω, ὁρμήσω, etc. (ὅρμος, *anchorage*), *lie at anchor*.

ὁρμή, -ῆς, ἡ, *start, motion, attack impulse;* ἐν ὁρμῇ εἶναι, *be on the point of starting*, II, 1, 3; μιᾷ ὁρμῇ, *with one impulse*, III, 2, 9.

ὁρμίζω, ὁρμιοῦμαι, ὥρμισα, ὥρμισμαι, ὡρμίσθην (*cf.* ὁρμέω), *bring to anchor, anchor;* mid., *come to anchor*.

ὄρνεον, -ου, τό (*cf.* ὄρνις), *bird*.

ὀρνίθειος, -α, -ον (ὄρνις), *of a bird or fowl;* with κρέα, *chicken*, IV, 5, 31.

ὄρνις, -ιθος, ὁ, ἡ (*cf.* Eng. *ornithology*), *bird;* esp. *fowl, hen*.

Ὀρόντας, -α, ὁ, *Orontas*, the name of two Persian nobles mentioned in the Anabasis, one a traitor, put to death by Cyrus, I, 6, 1 ff., the other a satrap of Armenia, a son-in-law of the king, and in command of a division of the royal army, II, 4, 8.

ὄρος, -ους, τό, *mountain*.

ὄροφος, -ου, ὁ (*cf.* ἐρέφω, *roof over*) *roof*.

ὀρυκτός, -ή, -όν (verbal of ὀρύττω) *made by digging, dug, artificial*.

ὀρύττω, -ορύξω, ὤρυξα, -ορώρυχα, ὀρώρυγμαι, ὠρύχθην, *dig, quarry*.

ὀρφανός, ή, -όν, *orphan, fatherless*.

ὀρχέομαι, ὀρχήσομαι, ὠρχησάμην, *dance*.

ὄρχησις, -εως, ἡ (ὀρχέομαι), *dance*.

ὀρχηστρίς, -ίδος, ἡ (ὀρχέομαι), *dancing girl*.

Ὀρχομένιος, -ου, ὁ (Ὀρχομενός, Orchomenus), *an Orchomenian, citizen of Orchomenus* in Arcadia.

ὅς, ἥ, ὅ, rel. pron., *who, which, what*; Lat. *qui*.

The antec. is often omitted, πλὴν ὁπόσοι ἱκανοὶ ἦσαν, I, 2, 2; ἔχων οὓς εἴρηκα, I, 2, 5; the rel. is often attracted to the case of the antec., whether expressed or not, ἀνθ' ὧν = ἀντὶ τούτων ἅ, I, 3, 4; *cf.* I, 7, 3; yet ἡγεμόνι ὅν, I, 3, 17; τῆς χάριτος ἥν, II, 5, 14. Rarely the antec. is attr. to the case of the rel. (inverse attr.), I, 4, 15(?) (*cf.* V, 5, 12), θεοῖς οἷς, III, 1, 6. The rel. clause may precede (I, 8, 11), in which case the antec. resumes the rel. with emphasis. Often the antec. is incorporated in the rel. clause, I, 2, 1; I, 9, 14; IV, 4, 2.

The rel. has often causal force, *e.g.*, III, 1, 17.

Rel. clauses have regularly the indic. or the opt. with ἄν when the antec. is definite; the subj. with ἄν, or after secondary tenses the opt., when it is conditional. Rarely in indir. disc. we find the infin. (by attraction), II, 2, 1. The rel. is occasionally used as an indir. interrog. It often stands at the head of a sentence, like the Lat. *quod, as to the fact that*, II, 3, 1; occasionally it has demonstrative force, but only in phrases, καὶ ὅς, *and he*, I, 8, 16, and, less commonly, καὶ οἵ, *and they*, VII, 6, 4.

ἐν ᾧ, *while* (even after a pl.), I, 2, 20; ἀφ' οὗ, *since* (also after a pl.), III, 2, 14; οὗ or ᾗ, as advs., *where*, see the words. μέχρι οὗ, *to a point where*, I, 7, 6; δι' ὅ, *wherefore*; see διό. ἐφ' ᾧ, *on condition that*, with infin., IV, 2, 19.

ὅσιος, -α, -ον, *holy, pious*.

ὅσος, -η, -ον, rel. pron., *how great, how much, how many* (Lat. *quantus*), generally to be rendered, *as much as, as many as, etc.*; properly correlative to τοσοῦτος, τοσοῦτοι ὄντες ὅσους σὺ ὁρᾷς, II, 1, 16; *cf.* I, 5, 9; IV, 8, 12; oftener, however, some form of πᾶς, *all*, is expressed, or felt, as the antec., πάντων ὅσοι, I, 1, 2; ὅσον ἦν αὐτῷ στράτευμα, *his entire army*, I, 2, 1; in indir. ques., II, 5, 10; sometimes with infin., like ὥστε, IV, 1, 5; IV, 8, 12; neut. ὅσον as adv., *as much as*, V, 5, 14; *as far as*, III, 3, 15; with numerals, *about*, I, 8, 6; with superlatives with intensifying force like ὅτι or ὡς, IV, 5, 18; ὅσον οὐ, *almost*, VII, 2, 5; ὅσῳ . . . τοσούτῳ, with comparatives; *cf. quanto . . . tanto*, I, 5, 9.

ὅσοσπερ, ὅσηπερ, ὅσονπερ, strengthened form of ὅσος, *just as great, much*, or *many as*; of time, *just as long as*.

ὅσπερ, ἥπερ, ὅπερ, strengthened form of ὅς, generally more explicit, *who, the very one who*, or *which*.

ὄσπριον, -ου, τό, *pulse*; in pl., *peas beans, etc.*, IV, 4, 9.

ὅστις, ἥτις, ὅ,τι (gen. and dat. ὅτου, ὅτῳ, ὅτων), indef. rel. pron. (ὅς + τις), *whoever, whichever, whatever*; sometimes best rendered, *who, which, what*; with pl. antec., I, 1, 5; III, 3, 1; in indir. ques., I, 3, 11; serving to characterize, *a man who*, III, 2, 4; hence sometimes used after οὕτω, where ὥστε is looked for, II, 5, 12; cf. II, 5, 21; often with fut. indic. in final sense, I, 3, 14; ὅτου δὴ παρεγγυήσαντος, some one or other having given the word, IV, 7, 25; cf. V, 2, 24; ἐξ ὅτου, since, VII, 8, 4.

ὁστισοῦν, ἡτισοῦν, ὁτιοῦν (ὅστις+οῦν), who- or whatsoever.

ὀσφραίνομαι (cf. ὄζω, smell), smell, get a smell of.

ὅταν, rel. adv. (ὅτε+ἄν), whenever, when, with subj., referring to fut., or else in a generalized sense.

ὅτε, rel. adv. (ὅ+τε), by elision ὅτ᾿ or ὅθ᾿, when, as, I, 2, 9; with opt., whenever, as often as, II, 6, 12; cf. ὅταν.

ὅτι, conj. (neut. of ὅστις): (1) that, introducing indir. disc., or sometimes dir. speech, in which case it is to be omitted in translating, e.g., I, 6, 8; (2) causal, because, since, I, 2, 21; (3) intensifying a superlative, ὅτι ἀπαρασκευότατον, as unprepared as possible, I, 1, 6.

ὅτου, ὅτῳ, see ὅστις.

οὐ (before vowels οὐκ or οὐχ), neg. adv., not; accented at the end of a clause, e.g., IV, 8, 3; in questions, expecting the answer, yes, III, 1, 29; for οὐ μή, see μή.

οὗ, dat. οἷ (which is the only singular form in the Anabasis), pl. σφεῖς, σφῶν, σφίσι, σφᾶς, pers. pron. of 3d pers. (orig σϝοῦ; cf. Lat. se, suus), of him, etc.; but in Attic used only as reflexive, and generally indir. reflexive, I, 1, 8; pl. they, themselves, I, 7, 8.

οὗ, rel. adv. (ὅς), where; μέχρι οὗ, to a point where, I, 7, 6.

οὐδαμῇ, adv., in no way, by no means.

οὐδαμόθεν, adv. (cf. οὐδαμῇ), from no place or quarter.

οὐδαμοῖ, adv. (cf. οὐδαμῇ), to no place, nowhere.

οὐδαμοῦ (cf. οὐδαμῇ), nowhere.

οὐδέ (οὐ+δέ), after a neg., and not, but not, nor; but when there is no preceding neg., not even, I, 3, 21; οὐδ᾿ ὥς, not even so, I, 8, 21; οὐ μέντοι οὐδὲ ἀπέκλινε, however, you may be sure he did not turn aside, II, 2, 16.

οὐδείς, οὐδεμία, οὐδέν, gen. οὐδενός, οὐδεμιᾶς, οὐδενός (οὐδέ+εἷς; cf. οὐδέ μιᾶς, VI, 3, 16), not even one, not one, none, II, 5, 1; οὐδείς and οὐδέν often as nouns, nobody, nothing, I, 2, 22; I, 8, 20; οὐδέν, as adv., not at all, I, 1, 8.

οὐδέποτε, adv. (οὐδέ+ποτέ), never.

οὐδέπω, adv. (οὐδέ+πώ), not yet; separated, οὐδὲ νῦν πώ, VII, 6, 35.

οὐθ᾿, see οὔτε.

οὐκ, see οὐ.

οὐκέτι, adv. (οὐ+ἔτι), no longer. For οὐκέτι μή, see οὐ μή, under μή.

οὔκουν, inferential part. (οὐ+οὖν), therefore not, by no means, III, 5, 6.

οὐκοῦν, interr. part. (οὐ+οὖν), not therefore? expecting an affirmative answer as Lat. nonne, I, 6, 7, etc.; also as inferential part., then, therefore, well then, III, 2, 19.

οὖν, a post-pos. part.: (1) confirmatory, certainly; often coupled with other particles, μέν, γάρ, πάνυ, for which Eng. has no equivalents; δ᾿ οὖν (stating a fact and dismissing a hypothesis), be that as it may, I, 2, 12; (2) inferential, now, I, 1, 2; accordingly, then

οὗπερ, strengthened form of οὗ, just where.

οὔποτε, adv. (οὐ+ποτέ), *never*.
οὔπω, adv. (οὐ+πώ), *not yet*.
οὐπώποτε, adv.(οὐ+πώ+ποτέ), *never yet, never before*.
οὐρά, -ᾶς, ἡ, *tail*, of an army, *rear*.
οὐραγός, -οῦ, ὁ (οὐρά+ἄγω), *rear leader, rearmost man* in a column, who became the leader when the file faced about, IV, 3, 26, 29.
οὐρανός, -οῦ, ὁ, *heaven, the sky*.
οὖς, ὠτός, τό (*cf.* Eng. *par-otid*), *ear*.
οὔτε, neg. conj. (οὐ+τέ), *and not*; οὔτε ... οὔτε, *neither ... nor*, I, 2, 26, etc.; οὔτε ... τε, *not ... but*, II, 5, 4, n.
οὔτοι, adv. (οὐ+τοί), *not indeed, certainly not*.
οὗτος, αὕτη, τοῦτο, dem. pron., *this, these;* often as pers. pron., *he, she, it, they*, etc. With the art. it regularly stands in the pred. posit., I, 1, 9, unless used with an attrib. adj., IV, 2, 6; sometimes attracted to the gender of the pred. noun, I, 1, 7; generally οὗτος refers to what precedes, but it sometimes looks forward, especially to a clause with ὅτι, III, 2, 17, or ὅπως, III, 1, 7; καὶ οὗτος, *he too*, III, 2, 5; ταῦτα is often used where Eng. more naturally uses the sing., μετὰ ταῦτα, *after this*, I, 3, 9; καὶ ταῦτα, *and that too*, with partic. I, 4, 12; so καὶ τούτων, II, 5, 21; ταύτῃ, as adv., see the word. οὗτος often refers to something near the person addressed, and thus corresponds to Lat. *iste*, as ὅδε to *hic*. It has sometimes a contemptuous tone, *this fellow*, I, 6, 9; III, 1, 31.
οὑτοσί, αὑτηί, τουτί, a strengthened form of οὗτος, the suffix having the force of a gesture, *this man (fellow) here*, etc.

οὕτω (before a vowel, οὕτως), adv. (οὗτος), *thus, in this way, so, to such a degree;* referring as a rule to what precedes.
οὐχ, see οὐ.
οὐχί, adv., strengthened form of οὐ, *q.v.*
ὀφείλω, ὀφειλήσω, etc., 2 aor., ὤφελον (ὄφελος), *owe*; in pass. of pay, *be due*, I, 2, 11; with infin., *ought;* hence ὤφελον Κῦρος ζῆν in an unattainable wish, *would that Cyrus were living*, II, 1, 4.
ὄφελος, τό, only found in nom. and acc., *help, advantage, use*.
ὀφθαλμός, -οῦ, ὁ (√ὀπ), *eye*; ἔχοντες ἐν ὀφθαλμοῖς, *keeping in sight*, IV, 5, 29.
ὀφλισκάνω, ὀφλήσω, ὦφλον, *owe, be fined*, V, 8, 1.
Ὀφρύνιον, -ου, τό, *Ophrynium*, a city in the Troad.
ὀχετός, -οῦ, ὁ (ἔχω), *channel, ditch*.
ὀχέω, ὀχήσω (ἔχω), *carry;* pass., *be carried, ride*.
ὄχημα, -ατος τό (ὀχέω), *that which carries, vehicle*, III, 2, 19.
ὄχθη, -ης, ἡ, *bank, bluff*.
ὄχλος, -ου, ὁ, *crowd, throng;* often of camp followers, as contrasted with fighting men, ὁ πολὺς ὄχλος, III, 2, 36; ὄχλον παρέχουσιν, *are a nuisance*, III, 2, 27.
ὀχυρός, -ά, -όν (ἔχω), *that may be held, strong, fortified;* τὰ ὀχυρά, *strongholds*, IV, 7, 17.
ὀψέ, adv., *late*.
ὄψεσθαι, see ὁράω.
ὀψίζω (ὀψέ), *be* or *come late*.
ὄψις, -εως, ἡ (√ὀπ), *look, appearance, sight, spectacle*.

Π

παγκράτιον, -ου, τό (πᾶs+κράτοs), the pancratium, an athletic contest combining boxing with wrestling, IV, 8, 27.

παγχαλέπως, adv. (πᾶs + χαλεπόs), very hardly, with very great difficulty; παγχαλέπως εἶχον πρόs, were highly incensed against, VII, 5, 16.

παθεῖν, see πάσχω.

πάθημα, -ατοs, τό (πάσχω), suffering, misfortune.

πάθος, -ουs, τό (πάσχω), experience, trouble, misfortune.

παιανίζω, aor. ἐπαιάνισα (παιάν, paean), sing the paean, properly a prayer for help, or of thanksgiving for deliverance, hence chanted as a war song before attacking, I, 8, 17, and at feasts and sacred ceremonies, III, 2, 9; VI, 1, 5.

παιδεία, -αs, ἡ (παῖs), bringing up, education.

παιδεραστής, -οῦ, ὁ (παῖs + ἔραμαι), lover of boys.

παιδεύω, παιδεύσω, etc. (παῖs), train a child, educate.

παιδικά, -ῶν, τά (παῖs), favorite, darling.

παιδίον, -ου, τό (dim. of παῖs), infant, child.

παιδίσκη, -ηs, ἡ (παῖs), young girl.

παῖς, παιδόs, ὁ, ἡ, child, boy, pl., children. In the Anabasis always masc. in sing. ἐκ παίδων, from boyhood, IV, 6, 14.

παίω, παίσω, ἔπαισα (for πάϝιω, Lat. pavio, strike with fear), strike, strike at, smite, wound.

πάλαι, long ago, long since.

παλαιός, -ά, -όν (πάλαι; cf. Eng. palaeography, etc.), old, ancient; τὸ παλαιόν, in ancient times, III, 4, 7, cf. τὸ ἀρχαῖον; comp. παλαίτεροs, oldish, rather old, IV, 5, 35.

παλαίω (πάλη), wrestle.

πάλη, -ηs, ἡ, wrestling.

πάλιν, adv., back, back again, again, of place or time.

παλλακίς, -ίδοs, ἡ, concubine.

παλτόν, -οῦ, τό (neut. of the verbal of πάλλω, brandish), javelin, spear (not used by the Greeks).

παμπληθής, -ές (πᾶs+πλῆθοs), very numerous, vast.

πάμπολυς, -πόλλη, -πολυ (πᾶs+πολύs), very much, very great; in pl., very many; ἐπὶ παμπολύ, over a vast extent (cf. ἐπὶ πολύ), VII, 5, 12.

παμπόνηρος, -ον (πᾶs+πονηρόs), utterly bad or villainous.

πανουργία, -αs, ἡ (πανοῦργοs), villainy.

πανοῦργος, -ον (πᾶs+ἔργον), doing anything; in a bad sense, villainous.

παντάπασι(ν), adv. (πᾶs), all in all, utterly, wholly; after a neg., at all, II, 5, 18.

πανταχοῦ, adv. (πᾶs), everywhere.

παντελῶς, adv. (πᾶs+τέλοs), utterly, wholly.

πάντῃ, adv. (πᾶs), in every way, on all sides.

παντοδαπός, -ή, -όν (πᾶs), of every sort, of all sorts.

πάντοθεν, adv. (πᾶs), from every side, on all sides.

παντοῖος, -α, -ον (πᾶs), of all sorts or kinds.

πάντοσε, adv. (πᾶs), in all directions, everywhere.

πάντως, adv. (πᾶs), altogether, at any rate.

πάνυ, adv. (πᾶs), very, quite, altogether; with neg., not at all,

I, 8, 14; VI, 1, 26; πάνυ μὲν οὖν, *certainly*, VII, 6, 4.

πάομαι, an unused pres., πάσομαι, ἐπασάμην, πέπαμαι, poetic vb., used by Xen., *acquire*, pf. as pres., *possess*, I, 9, 19; III, 3, 18; VI, 1, 12; VII, 6, 41.

παρά, prep. with gen., dat., and acc., *beside*, generally of persons, and as a rule giving the characteristic locality. With gen., *from beside, from the presence of, from;* of the agent with pass. vb., *on the part of, by*, I, 9, 1; with dat., *beside, at, with, near;* with acc., *to the side of, to, towards; beside, along*, I, 2, 13; of time, *during*, II, 3, 15; *contrary to*, II, 1, 18; of comparison, παρ' ὀλίγον ποιεῖσθαι, *treat as of no account*, VI, 6, 11.

παραβαίνω (βαίνω), *transgress, break* (of a treaty).

παραβοηθέω (βοηθέω), *go to bear aid.*

παραγγέλλω (ἀγγέλλω), *pass the word, command, order, direct;* impers. pass., παρήγγελτο, *commands had been given*, III, 4, 3; VI, 5, 25; κατὰ τὰ παρηγγελμένα, *according to orders*, II, 2, 8.

παράγγελσις, -εως, ἡ (παραγγέλλω), *word of command.*

παραγίγνομαι (γίγνομαι), *be beside, be present, arrive, come.*

παράγω (ἄγω), *lead along* or *beside, lead past, bring forward, bring into line*, IV, 6, 6.

παραγωγή, -ῆς, ἡ (παράγω), *transportation.*

παράδεισος, -ου, ὁ (a Persian word, whence Eng. *paradise*), *park, game-preserve.*

παραδίδωμι (δίδωμι), *give over, deliver, surrender;* of the watchword, *give out*, VII, 3, 34; of the gods, *grant*, VI, 6, 34.

παραδραμεῖν, see παρατρέχω.

παραθαρρύνω (θαρρύνω), *encourage, cheer.*

παραθέω (θέω), *run past.*

παραινέω (αἰνέω, αἰνέσω, *etc., praise*), *advise, exhort.*

παραιτέομαι (αἰτέω), *intercede for*, περί, VI, 6, 29.

παρακαλέω (καλέω), *call to one's side, invite, summon; exhort, encourage.*

παρακαταθήκη, -ης, ἡ (τίθημι), *a deposit* (intrusted to one's care), V, 3, 7.

παράκειμαι (κεῖμαι), *lie before* or *near, be placed before.*

παρακελεύομαι (κελεύω), *exhort, urge, encourage*, with dat.

παρακέλευσις, -εως, ἡ (παρακελεύω), *exhortation, cheering on.*

παρακολουθέω (ἀκολουθέω), *follow along with, accompany.*

παραλαμβάνω (λαμβάνω), *receive* or *take from; take along;* of office, *succeed to*, VI, 4, 11; VII, 8, 24.

παραλείπω (λείπω), *leave at one side, omit, pass by.*

παραλυπέω (λυπέω), *give* or *cause trouble.*

παραλύω (λύω), *loose from*, of a rudder, *unship*, V, 1, 11.

παραμείβομαι (ἀμείβω, ἀμείψω, *change*), dep. mid. and pass., *change one's position*, I, 10, 10.

παραμελέω (ἀμελέω), *neglect, disregard*, abs. or with gen.

παραμένω (μένω), *stay beside* or *by, remain loyal.*

παραμηρίδια, τά (μηρός, *thigh*), *thigh-pieces* (of armor), I, 8, 6.

παραπέμπω (πέμπω), *send along the line, despatch.*

παραπλέω (πλέω), *sail along* or *by.*

παραπλήσιος, -α, -ον (πλησίος), *close beside;* then, *like, resembling.*

παραρρέω, aor. παρερρύην (ῥέω), *flow by,* V, 3, 8; of snow, *run or slip off,* IV, 4, 11.

παρασάγγης, -ου, ὁ, *parasang,* a Persian measure of distance, about 30 stades or 3½ miles, but rather a measure of time, in traveling, than actual distance, and so varying in length with the character of the country traversed.

παρασκευάζω (σκευάζω), *get ready, prepare;* mid., *make one's own preparations, get ready, arrange, provide;* in perf. tenses, *be ready,* abs. or with acc.

παρασκευή, -ῆς, ἡ, *preparation;* in a military sense, *armament, force,* I, 2, 4.

παρασκηνέω (σκηνέω), *encamp beside or near.*

παρασχήσω, see παρέχω.

παρατάττω (τάττω), *draw up side by side;* in the *Anabasis* always pass., *be drawn up in battle array.*

παρατείνω (τείνω), *stretch out, extend.*

παρατίθημι (τίθημι), *put beside or before;* especially of food, *set before, serve.*

παρατρέχω (τρέχω), *run along, run by, run across.*

παραχρῆμα, adv., *immediately, on the spot, in cash,* VII, 7, 24.

παρεγγυάω (παρεγγύη), *pass the word, order, exhort;* ὅτε παρεγγυῷτο, *whenever word was passed,* IV, 1, 17.

παρεγγύη, -ης, ἡ (ἐγγύη, *pledge*), *word passed along the ranks, command,* VI, 5, 13.

παρεδεδραμήκεσαν, see παρατρέχω.

πάρειμι (εἰμί), *be beside, be present, be at hand;* with dat. of possessor, II, 3, 9; III, 2, 18; often as a vb. of motion, *arrive, come;* παρῆν, impers., *it was possible,* IV, 5, 6; *cf.* the acc. abs., παρόν, V, 8, 3. τὰ παρόντα, *the present state of things,* III, 1, 34; so, with πράγματα added, I, 3, 3. ἐν τῷ παρόντι, *in our present straits,* II, 5, 8.

πάρειμι (εἶμι), *go or pass by or along; come forward* (as a speaker), V, 1, 3.

παρελαύνω (ἐλαύνω), *drive or ride past; review,* abs. or with acc.

παρέρχομαι (ἔρχομαι), *pass by or through;* of speakers, *come forward,* V, 5, 24; of time, *go by, pass, elapse,* I, 7, 18.

παρεσχημένος, see παρέχω.

παρέχω (ἔχω), *have at hand or ready, furnish, supply, give, provide,* πράγματα, I, 1, 11, see πρᾶγμα; ἀγοράν, II, 4, 5; *render, make,* II, 5, 13; mid., *contribute,* VI, 2, 10; *show, display,* VII, 6, 11.

παρῆσθα, see πάρειμι (εἰμί).

Παρθένιον, -ου, τό, *Parthenium,* a town in Mysia.

Παρθένιος, -ου, ὁ, *the Parthenius,* a river dividing Paphlagonia from Bithynia and flowing into the Euxine.

παρθένος, -ου, ἡ, *maiden, virgin.*

Παριανοί, -ῶν, οἱ (Πάριον), *natives of Parium, Parians.*

παρίημι (ἵημι), *let pass by, give way, yield.*

Πάριον, -ου, τό, *Parium,* a city on the Propontis.

παρίστημι (ἵστημι), *set near, bring forward, produce,* mid. VI, 1,

22; 2 aor. and 2 pf. act. (as pres.) intrans., *stand by* or *beside*, V, 8, 10, 21.

πάροδος, -ου, ἡ (ὁδός), *way by, passage, pass*.

παροινέω, aor. ἐπαρῴνησα (πάροινος, *given to wine*, παρά+οἶνος), *be drunken, act insolently* or *abusively*, V, 8, 4.

παροίχομαι, (οἴχομαι), *be gone* or *past;* τὰ παροιχόμενα, as subst., *the past*, II, 4, 1.

Παρράσιος, ὁ, *a Parrhasian, a native* or *inhabitant of Parrhasia in Arcadia*.

Παρύσατις, -ιδος, ἡ, *Parysatis*, daughter of Artaxerxes I, half-sister and wife of Darius II, king of Persia, mother of Artaxerxes II and of Cyrus the younger, I, 1, 1; 7, 9; II, 4, 27; saves Cyrus' life, I, 1, 3. For a sketch of her character, see the Introd. § 26.

πᾶς, πᾶσα, πᾶν, gen. παντός, πάσης, παντός, *all, the whole of, entire;* in sing., *every;* rarely = παντοῖος, *of all sorts*, VI, 4, 6; with art. generally in pred. posit.; in attrib. posit., denoting totality, οἱ πάντες ἄνθρωποι, *all human-kind* V, 6, 7; as noun, πᾶν, πάντα, *everything;* πάντες, *everybody;* πάντα as adv., *utterly, in all respects*, I, 3, 10; ἐπὶ πᾶν ἐλθεῖν, *make every effort*, III, 1, 18; περὶ παντὸς ποιεῖσθαι, *count above everything, of all importance*, I, 9, 16; διὰ παντὸς πολέμου ἰέναι, *be on terms of absolute hostility*, III, 2, 8; διὰ παντός, *ever, always*, VII, 8, 11.

Πασίων, -ωνος, ὁ, *Pasion*, a Megarian, general under Cyrus; he deserts, I, 3, 7.

πάσχω, πείσομαι, ἔπαθον, πέπονθα, *experience, suffer, undergo, be treated;* παθεῖν τι, euphemistic for *die*, V, 3, 6; esp. common are the phrases εὖ and κακῶς παθεῖν, *receive benefits* or *injury*, I, 3, 5; III, 3, 7; ἀνθ' ὧν εὖ ἔπαθον, *in return for the favors I had received*, I, 3, 4.

πατάσσω, only in aor. ἐπάταξα, etc., *strike, thrust*.

Πατηγύας, -α, ὁ, *Pategyas*, a Persian in the army of Cyrus.

πατήρ, -τρός, ὁ, (Lat. *pater*, Eng. *father*), *father*.

πάτριος, -α, -ον (πατήρ), *hereditary, ancestral*.

πατρίς, -ίδος, ἡ (πατήρ), *fatherland, native land*.

πατρῷος, -α -ον (πατήρ), *belonging to one's father, inherited, ancestral*.

παῦλα, -ης, ἡ (παύω), *stopping place, stopping, prevention*.

παύω, παύσω, etc. (Lat. *paucus*, Eng. *few*), *stop, bring to an end;* mid., *cease, stop, leave off, rest; be rid of*, V, 1, 2; abs., with gen., or with nom. partic.

Παφλαγονία, -ας, ἡ (Παφλαγών), *Paphlagonia*, a district of Asia Minor on the south shore of the Euxine.

Παφλαγονικός, -ή, -όν (Παφλαγών) *Paphlagonian*, ἡ Παφλαγονική (sc. χώρα), *Paphlagonia*, VI, 1, 15.

Παφλαγών, -όνος, ὁ, *a Paphlagonian, native of Paphlagonia*.

πάχος, ους, τό (cf. παχύς), *thickness*.

παχύς, -εῖα, -ύ (cf. Lat. *pinguis*, Eng. *pachyderm*), *thick, stout, large*.

πέδη, -ης, ἡ (πούς, cf. Lat. *pes*), *fetter*, in pl. IV, 3, 8.

πεδινός, -ή, -όν (cf. πεδίον), *flat, level*.

πεδίον, -ου, τό (cf. πούς), plain, level land; as a final element of a city name (like Fr. -champ, Eng. -field), 1, 2, 11.

πεζεύω, aor. ἐπέζευσα (cf. πεζός), travel on foot or by land.

πεζῇ, adv. (πεζός), on foot, I, 4, 18; by land, V, 4, 5.

πεζός, -ή, -όν (cf. πέδη, πούς), on foot; δύναμις πεζή, infantry force, I, 3, 12; ὁ πεζός, foot soldier; pl. infantry.

πείθω, πείσω, ἔπεισα, πέπεικα, πέποιθα, πέπεισμαι, ἐπείσθην, persuade, induce, win over, bribe; mid. and pass., be convinced, won over, hence, obey, believe.

πεινάω, πεινήσω, etc. (πεῖνα, hunger; πένομαι, toil, be poor, Lat. penuria, poverty), be hungry.

πεῖρα, -ας, ἡ (√περ, go through), a going through, trial, proof; acquaintance with, I, 9, 1.

πειράομαι, πειράσομαι, etc. (πεῖρα; cf. Lat. experior), try, attempt, make trial of, abs., with infin., with obj. clause, III, 2, 3; or with gen., III, 2, 38.

πείσας, πεισθῆτε, see πείθω.

πείσει, πείσομαι, see πάσχω.

πειστέον, verbal of πείθω, one must obey.

πελάζω, aor. ἐπέλασα, approach, draw near (a poetic vb.).

Πελοποννήσιος, -α, -ον (Πελόννησος), of or belonging to the Peloponnesus, Peloponnesian pl. as subst., Peloponnesians, VI, 2, 10.

Πελοπόννησος, -ου, ἡ (Πέλοψ, Pelops +νῆσος), Peloponnēsus, the isle of Pelops, the southern peninsula of Greece.

πελτάζω (πέλτη), serve as a peltast.

Πέλται, -ῶν, αἱ, Peltae, a city of Phrygia.

πελταστής, -οῦ, ὁ (πέλτη), peltast, targeteer, carrying the light shield, πέλτη.

πελταστικός, -ή, -όν (πελταστής), belonging to peltasts; τὸ πελταστικόν, the peltasts, the light-armed troops.

πέλτη, -ης, ἡ, small shield, generally crescent-shaped, in I, 10, 12 it appears to mean pole; see the note.

πεμπταῖος, -α, -ον (πέντε), on the fifth day; of corpses, five days unburied, VI, 4, 9.

πέμπτος, -η, -ον (πέντε), fifth.

πέμπω, πέμψω, ἔπεμψα, πέπομφα, πέπεμμαι, ἐπέμφθην, send, despatch, escort, send word.

πένης, -ητος, ὁ (cf. πένομαι), laborer, poor man.

πενία, -ας, ἡ (πένομαι), poverty.

πένομαι, only in pres. system, toil, labor, be poor.

πεντακόσιοι, -αι, -α, five hundred.

πέντε, indecl., five.

πεντεκαίδεκα, indecl. (πέντε+δέκα), fifteen.

πεντήκοντα, indecl. (πέντε), fifty.

πεντηκοντήρ, -ῆρος, ὁ (πεντήκοντα), commander of fifty men.

πεντηκόντορος, -ου, ἡ (πεντήκοντα), a ship with fifty oars, penteconter.

πεντηκοστύς, -ύος, ἡ (πεντήκοντα), a company of fifty men.

πέπανται, πέπαται, see πάομαι.

πεπόνθασιν, πεπονθώς, see πάσχω.

πεπρακέναι, πεπράσεται, see πιπράσκω.

πεπτωκότα, see πίπτω.

πέρ, post-pos. enclitic part. with intensive force. In Attic prose found only in composition with rels. and parts., ἐάνπερ, εἴπερ, ὅσπερ, ὥσπερ, etc.

πέρα, adv. (√περ), beyond, further.

περαίνω, περανῶ, ἐπέρανα, πεπέρασμαι, ἐπεράνθην (πέρας, end), bring to an end, carry out, accomplish.

περαιόω, -ώσω, etc. (√ περ), carry over, transport; mid. and pass., pass over, cross.

πέραν, adv. (cf. περάω), on the farther side, across, I, 5, 10 (with gen.); τὸ πέραν, the farther bank, III, 5, 2; πέραν (or ἐν τῷ πέραν) γενέσθαι, get across, VI, 5, 22.

περάω, περάσω, etc. (√ περ, cf. πέραν, πέρα), cross.

Πέργαμος, -ου, ἡ, or Πέργαμον, -ου, τό, Pergamus, an important city of Mysia.

πέρδιξ, -ικος, ὁ, ἡ (cf. Eng. partridge), partridge.

περί, prep. with gen., dat., and acc., around, about: (1) with gen. (never local), about, concerning; of value, above, περὶ παντὸς ποιεῖσθαι, to consider all-important, I, 9, 16; so in comp. V, 6, 22; in sup. I, 9, 7 n.; (2) with dat. (rare), round, I, 5, 8; VII, 4, 4; (3) with acc., of place, around, about, often of an important personage and his suite, οἱ περὶ Ἀριαῖον, Ariaeus and his men, II, 4, 2 (cf. ἀμφί, and see the note on οἱ μετὰ Ἀριαῖον, I, 10, 1); of time, I, 7, 1; of things, περὶ τὰ ἐπιτήδεια ἦσαν, were busied with the provisions, III, 5, 7; of actions, etc., concerning, toward, to, I, 4, 8. In comp. beside the lit. meaning, περι- often denotes superiority (e. g., περιγίγνομαι).

περιβάλλω (βάλλω), throw around, embrace; mid., throw oneself around, surround; ὄπισθεν περιβαλλόμενοι τὰς πέλτας, shifting their shields so as to cover their backs, VII, 4, 17.

περιγίγνομαι (γίγνομαι), be superior to, get the better of, conquer, with gen.; result, with ὥστε and infin., V, 8, 26.

περιειλέω (εἰλέω, wrap), wrap around.

περίειμι (εἰμί), be superior to, excel, abs. or with gen.

περίειμι (εἶμι), go around, abs. or with acc.

περιέλκω (ἕλκω), drag around.

περιεστῶτας, see περιίστημι.

περιέχω (ἔχω), surround.

περιιδεῖν, see περιοράω.

περιίστημι (ἵστημι), place around; in mid., 2 aor., and 2 perf. act., intrans., stand around.

περικυκλόομαι (κυκλόω), surround.

περιλαμβάνω (λαμβάνω), seize round, embrace.

περιμένω (μένω), wait around, remain, wait for, expect.

Περίνθιος, -ου, ὁ (Πέρινθος), a Perinthian, native of Perinthus.

Πέρινθος, -ου, ἡ, Perinthus, a city in Thrace on the Propontis.

πέριξ, adv. (περί), round about; as prep. with gen., round, VII, 8, 12.

περίοδος, -ου, ἡ (περί+ὁδός), circuit, circumference.

περιοικέω (οἰκέω), dwell around.

περίοικος, -ον (περί+οἰκέω), lit., dwelling around; as subst., a Perioecus, V, 1, 15. The Perioeci in Laconia were provincials, standing midway between the Spartans and the Helots, or serfs.

περιοράω (ὁράω), overlook, allow, permit, with acc. and partic.

περίπατος, -ον (περί+πάτος, path; cf. Lat. passus, step, Eng. path, peripatetic), place for walking, walk, II, 4, 15.

περιπήγνυμαι (πήγνυμι), in pass., be frozen on, IV, 5, 14.

περιπίπτω (πίπτω), *fall around, fling oneself upon, embrace*, I, 8, 28; *fall in with*, VII, 3, 38.

περιπλέω (πλέω), *sail around*.

περιποιέω (ποιέω), *make remain over;* mid., *acquire, gain*, V, 6, 17.

περιπτύσσω (πτύσσω, πτύξω, etc.), *fold around, outflank*.

περιρρέω (ῥέω), *flow around*, I, 5, 4; *flow* or *slip off* (of fetters), IV, 3, 8.

περισταυρόω, perf. pass. περιεσταύρωμα (σταυρόω, -ώσω, etc., *fence in with stakes; cf*. σταυρός), *surround with a fence of stakes, enclose with a stockade*.

περιστερά, -ᾶς, ἡ, *dove, pigeon*.

περιττεύω, περιττεύσω (περιττός), *be over and above, outnumber, outflank*, IV, 8, 11.

περιττός, -ή, -όν (περί), *over and above, superfluous;* οἱ περιττοί, *outnumbering* or *extra men*, IV, 8, 11; τὸ περιττόν, *surplus*, V, 3, 13.

περιτυγχάνω (τυγχάνω), *fall in with*.

περιφανῶς, adv. (περί+φαίνω), *manifestly*.

περιφέρω (φέρω), *bear* or *carry around*.

περίφοβος, -ον (περί+φόβος), *in great fear* or *alarm*.

Πέρσης, -ου, ὁ, *a Persian*, in a wide sense including all subjects of the king.

περσίζω (Πέρσης), *speak Persian*.

Περσικός, -ή, -όν (Πέρσης), *Persian;* τὸ Περσικόν, *the Persian*, a kind of dance, VI, 1, 10.

περσιστί, adv. (περσίζω), *in Persian*.

πέταλον, -ου, τό (πετάννυμι; *cf.* Eng. *petal*), *leaf*.

πέτομαι, -πτήσομαι, ἐπτόμην, *fly*.

πέτρα, -ας, ἡ (*cf.* πέτρος), *rock, mass of rock, cliff*.

πετροβολία, -ας, ἡ (πέτρος+βάλλω), *a throwing of stones, stoning*.

πέτρος, -ου, ὁ (*cf.* Eng. *petrify, etc.*), *stone*.

πεφυλαγμένως, adv. (from perf. pass. partic. of φυλάττω), *on one's guard, cautiously*.

πῄ, indef. adv., enclitic, *in any way, anyhow*.

πηγή, -ῆς, ἡ, *spring;* of rivers, *source*, always pl. in the *Anabasis*.

πήγνυμι, παγήσομαι, ἔπηξα, πέπηγα, ἐπάγην, *make firm, congeal, freeze*.

πηδάλιον, -ου, τό, *steering oar, rudder*.

πηλός, -οῦ, ὁ (*cf.* Lat. *palus, swamp*), *clay, mire*.

πῆχυς, -εως, ὁ, *forearm;* as a measure of length, the distance from the elbow to the tip of the middle finger, *a cubit*, one and a half Greek feet or about 1 ft. 5½ in.

Πίγρης, -ητος, ὁ, *Pigres*, interpreter to Cyrus.

πιέζω, πιέσω, etc., *press hard, weigh down;* in the *Anabasis* only in pass., *be weighed down*, III, 4, 48; *be hard pressed*, I, 1, 10; *be crowded*, III, 4, 19.

πικρός, -ά, -όν, *bitter*.

πίμπλημι, πλήσω, ἔπλησα, -πέπληκα, -πέπλη(σ)μαι, ἐπλήσθην (γ/.πλα; *cf.* πολύς, πλήρης, Eng. *full*), *fill*, I, 5, 10.

πίνω, πίομαι, ἔπιον, πέπωκα, -πέπομαι, -ἐπόθην, *drink*.

πιπράσκω, πέπρακα, πέπραμαι, ἐπράθην, fut. pf. πεπράσομαι (*cf.* Lat. *pretium, price*), *sell*. In Attic used only in the pf. tenses; *cf.* πωλέω and ἀποδίδομαι.

πίπτω, πεσοῦμαι, ἔπεσον, πέπτωκα, fall, be slain; with εἰς, fall upon, be involved in, II, 3, 18.

Πισίδαι, -ῶν, οἱ, the Pisidians, natives of Pisidia, a mountainous country south of Cyrus' satrapy in Asia Minor.

πιστεύω, πιστεύσω, etc., trust, have confidence in, rely on, believe, with dat., with infin., I, 9, 8.

πίστις, -εως, ἡ (πείθω), trust, confidence, good faith, pledge, assurance; διὰ πίστεως, relying on good faith, III, 2, 8; πίστεως ἕνεκα, to insure his loyalty, III, 3, 4.

πιστός, -ή, -όν (πείθω), trusty, faithful, sure, trustworthy, οἱ πιστοί, "the faithful," title of the counsellors of the Persian king; τὰ πιστά, pledges; ἐπεὶ τὰ πιστὰ ἐγένετο, after pledges had been exchanged, II, 2, 10; cf. II, 4, 7.

πιστότης, -ητος, ἡ (πιστός), fidelity.

πίτυς, -υος, ἡ (cf. Lat. pinus, Eng. pine), pine-tree.

πλάγιος, -α, -ον (πλάγος, τό, side), sideways, oblique; τά πλάγια, flanks, of an army, III, 4, 14; VI, 3, 15; εἰς πλάγιον, as adv., sideways, obliquely, I, 8, 10.

πλαίσιον, -ου, τό, a rectangle; πλαίσιον ἰσόπλευρον, a square, III, 4, 19.

πλανάομαι, πλανήσομαι, etc. (πλανή, wandering), wander; met., of words, wander, be idly spoken, VII, 7, 24.

πλάτος, -ους, τό (πλατύς), breadth.

πλάττω, πλάσω, ἔπλασα, πέπλασμαι, ἐπλάσθην (cf. Eng. plastic), mould, fashion, shape.

πλατύς, -εῖα, -ύ (cf. Eng. place, plateau, etc.), broad, wide.

πλεθριαῖος, -α, -ον, of the length of a plethrum.

πλέθρον, -ου, -τό, plethrum, measure of length, 100 Greek ft. or 97 Eng. ft.

Πλεισθένης, -ους, ὁ, Pleisthenes, an Amphipolitan in the Greek army.

πλεῖστος, -η, -ον, see πολύς.

πλείων, πλεῖον, see πολύς.

πλέκω, πλέξω, etc. (Lat. plico, fold), twist, plait.

πλέον, see πολύς.

πλεονεκτέω, πλεονεκτήσω (πλέον + ἔχω), have more than, have the advantage over (gen.), in (dat.).

πλευρά, -ᾶς, ἡ (cf. Eng. pleurisy), rib, side, flank, generally in pl.

πλέω, πλεύσομαι or πλευσοῦμαι, ἔπλευσα, πέπλευκα, πέπλευσμαι, sail, go by sea.

πληγή, -ῆς, ἡ (πλήττω), blow, in the Anabasis only pl.

πλῆθος, -ους, τό (cf. πλήθω), multitude, crowd, number, amount, extent; τὸ πλῆθος, the rank and file, common soldiers, III, 1, 37.

πλήθω, poetic vb., be full; in the Anabasis only in the phrase ἀμφὶ πλήθουσαν ἀγοράν, about full market time, I, 8, 1; II, 1, 7.

πλήν, adv. or conj., except, save that; also prep. with gen.

πλήρης, -ες (πίμπλημι), full, full of, with gen.; of pay, in full, VII, 5, 5.

πλησιάζω, πλησιάσω, etc. approach, draw near, abs. or with dat.

πλησίος, -α, -ον, near. The pos. is found in prose only in the adv. πλησίον, near, close by; πλησιαίτατος, I, 10, 5; VII, 3, 29.

πλήττω, πλήξω, 2 pf. πέπληγα, 2 aor. pass. ἐπλήγην (cf. Lat. plango, strike, plaga, blow, Eng. apoplexy), strike. The act. is little used in prose.

πλίνθινος, -η, -ον (πλίνθος), of brick, brick.

πλίνθος, -ου, ἡ (cf. Eng. plinth, flint?), brick.

πλοῖον, -ου, τό (πλέω), boat, vessel, of any sort from a canoe (πλοῖον μονόξυλον, V, 4, 11) to a warship (μακρὸν πλοῖον, V, 1, 11). Generally, however, πλοῖον means transport or merchantman, contrasted with ναῦς or τριήρης; see I, 3, 17 n.

πλοῦς, πλοῦ, ὁ (πλέω), a sailing, voyage.

πλούσιος, -α, -ον (πλοῦτος, wealth), rich.

πλουσίως, adv. (πλούσιος), in wealth, richly; comp. πλουσιωτέρως, I, 9, 16.

πλουτέω, πλουτήσω, etc. (πλοῦτος), be rich.

πλουτίζω, perf. πεπλούτικα (πλοῦτος), enrich.

πνεῦμα, -ατος, τό (πνέω; cf. Eng. pneumatic), wind.

πνέω, πνεύσομαι, ἔπνευσα, blow, breathe.

πνίγω, choke; pass., be drowned, V, 7, 25.

ποδαπός, -ή, -όν, from what country, whence.

ποδήρης, -ες (πούς+√αρ), reaching to the feet (of shields).

ποδίζω, only in perf. pass. partic., πεποδισμένοι, fetter, hobble, III, 4, 35.

ποδῶν, see πούς.

πόθεν, adv., whence, from what source, how.

ποθέν, indef. adv., enclitic, from somewhere or other.

ποθέω, ποθήσω, etc. (πόθος), long, yearn.

πόθος, -ου, ὁ, longing.

ποί, indef. adv., enclitic, somewhither, somewhere.

ποιέω, ποιήσω, etc., make, do, perform, render; often with two accs., both nouns, or noun and adj., I, 1, 2; I, 9, 6; bring about, cause, with acc. and infin., I, 7, 4, or with ὥστε and infin., I, 6, 2; imagine, assume, with acc. and infin., V, 7, 9; very commonly εὖ or κακῶς ποιεῖν, to benefit, injure, with acc. of person, I, 4, 8; also ἀγαθόν, κακὸν ποιεῖν, with acc., I, 9, 11; rarely with dat., IV, 2, 23; with ἐκκλησίαν, convene, I, 4, 12; often with advs., I, 1, 11. Mid. similarly used; also frequently with verbal nouns, forming one idea, τὴν πορείαν ἐποιεῖτο = ἐπορεύετο, I, 7, 20; often to be rendered count, esteem, περὶ παντός, πολλοῦ, πλείστου, I, 9, 16, etc.; εὕρημα ἐποιησάμην, I counted it a piece of good luck, II, 3, 18; in V, 3, 5, have made for oneself, ἀνάθημα.

ποιητέος, -α, -ον (verbal of ποιέω), to be done, that must be done, with or without dat. of agent.

ποικίλος, -η, -ον (cf. Lat. pingo, paint), variegated, of many colors; tattooed, V, 4, 32.

ποῖος, -α, -ον, interrog. pron., of what sort or kind, what.

πολεμέω, πολεμήσω, etc. (πόλεμος), make war, carry on war, abs., with dat., or with πρός and acc.

πολεμικός, -ή, -όν (πόλεμος; cf. Eng. polemic), fitted for war, skilled in war, warlike; τὸ πολεμικόν, signal or shout for battle, IV, 3, 29; VII, 3, 33; τὰ πολεμικά, military affairs, III, 1, 38, 43.

πολεμικῶς, adv. (πολεμικός), in a hostile manner; sup. πολεμικώτατα, VI, 1, 1.

πολέμιος, -α, -ον (πόλεμος), *pertaining to war, the enemy's, hostile;* τὰ πολέμια, *military matters,* I, 6, 1; οἱ πολέμιοι, *the enemy;* ἡ πολεμία, *the enemy's country,* III, 3, 5.

πόλεμος, -ου, ὁ, *war.*

πολίζω (πόλις), *found a city;* with χωρίον, *colonize,* VI, 6, 4.

πολιορκέω, πολιορκήσω, *etc.* (πόλις + εἴργω), *besiege, invest.*

πόλις, -εως, ἡ (akin to πολύς), *city, state;* at Athens, *the city proper, the acropolis,* VII, 1, 27.

πόλισμα, -ατος, τό (πολίζω), *town.*

πολιτεύω, πολιτεύσω, *etc.* (πολίτης), *be a citizen;* freely, *live,* III, 2, 26.

πολίτης, -ου, ὁ (πόλις), *citizen.*

πολλάκις, adv. (πολύς), *often.*

πολλαπλάσιος, -α, -ον (πολύς), *many times as much or many.*

πολλαχῇ, adv. (πολύς), *in many places, often,* VII, 3, 12.

πολλαχοῦ, adv. (πολύς), *in many places, often,* IV, 1, 28.

πολυάνθρωπος, -ον (πολύς+ἄνθρωπος), *populous, thickly populated.*

πολυαρχία, -ας, ἡ (πολύς+ἄρχω), *rule or command vested in many,* VI, 1, 18.

Πολυκράτης, -ους, ὁ, *Polycrates,* an Athenian, captain in the Greek army.

Πολύνικος, -ου, ὁ, *Polynīcus,* ambassador from Thibron to the Greek army.

πολυπραγμονέω (πολύς+πράττω), *be a busybody or meddler.*

πολύς, πολλή, πολύ (cf. πλῆθος, πίμπλημι, Lat. *plus* and *plurimus,* Eng. *full*), *much, many,* often to be rendered *great, far, long, mighty, full,* etc. Often joined to another adj. by καί, where Eng. omits the connective, πολλὰ καὶ ἀμήχανα, *many difficulties,* II, 3, 18; τὸ πολύ, *the greater part, the most,* I, 4, 13; οἱ πολλοί, *the most,* II, 3, 16; adv. expressions, πολύ, *much, very, far,* chiefly with comp. and sup. adjs.; so πολλῷ, with comp., II, 5, 32; πολλά, *in many respects, often,* IV, 3, 2; ἐπὶ πολύ and ὡς ἐπὶ τὸ πολύ; see ἐπί. περὶ πολλοῦ (πλέονος, πλείστου) ποιεῖσθαι, see ποιέω. Comp. πλείων, πλεῖον, *more, greater,* with similar range of meanings; neut., as adv., πλεῖον or πλέον; ἐκ πλέονος ... ἔφευγον, *took flight when at a greater distance,* I, 10, 11; sup. πλεῖστος, -η, -ον, *most,* often with ὥς or ὅτι, *the most possible,* I, 1, 6; often as noun, οἱ πλεῖστοι, *most, the most,* I, 5, 13; πλεῖστον, πλεῖστα, as adv., *mostly, generally,* III, 2, 31; VII, 6, 35; ὡς πλεῖστον, *as far as possible,* II, 2, 12.

Πολύστρατος, -ου, ὁ, *Polystratus,* an Athenian, father of Lycius.

πολυτελής, -ές (πολύς + τέλος), *of great price, costly.*

πομπή, -ῆς, ἡ (πέμπω), *escort;* generally solemn procession, in honor of a god, V, 5, 5.

πονέω, πονήσω, etc. (πόνος), *work, toil, labor;* with acc., *earn by labor,* VII, 6, 41; τὰ πεπονημένα, *hardships undergone,* VII, 6, 10.

πονηρός, -ά, -όν (πόνος), properly, *toilsome, laborious;* then, *poor, worthless, bad;* πονηρόν, *a wretched affair,* III, 4, 35; ὁ πονηρός, *a villain,* II, 6, 29; cf. II, 5, 21; in VII, 1, 39, *hostile.*

πονήρως, adv. (πονηρός), *with difficulty.*

πόνος, -ου, ὁ (πένομαι), *toil, labor, work, hardship.*

πόντος, -ου, ὁ, *sea;* generally as a proper name, *the Euxine* or *Black Sea;* hence *Pontus*, the region about the Euxine, V, 6, 15.

πορεία, -ας, ἡ (*cf.* πορεύομαι), *a going, journey, march, road.*

πορευτέος, -α, -ον (verbal of πορεύομαι), *that must be traversed,* II, 5, 18; impers. πορευτέον ἡμῖν, *we must march,* II, 3, 13 n.

πορεύομαι, πορεύσομαι, etc., pass. dep., *go, travel, march;* with acc. of region traversed, IV, 4, 1; *cf.* II, 4, 13.

πορθέω, πορθήσω, etc. (πέρθω, *sack*), *plunder, ravage, lay waste.*

πορίζω, ποριῶ, ἐπόρισα, πεπόρικα, πεπόρισμαι, ἐπορίσθην, *bring to, furnish, supply, provide;* mid., *supply oneself with, obtain.*

πόρος, -ου, ὁ (√περ), *way through* or *across;* of a river, *ford,* IV, 3, 13, 20; in general, *way, means,* II, 5, 20.

πόρρω (πρό), *far off, far from* (gen.).

πορφυροῦς, -ᾶ, -οῦν (πορφύρα, the murex, the shellfish from which purple dye was obtained), *purple.*

ποσί, see πούς.

πόσος, -η, -ον, interrog. pron., *how great, how large, how much;* pl., *how many.*

ποταμός, -οῦ, ὁ (*cf. hippopotamus, Mesopotamia*), *river, stream,* I, 2, 23, etc. The name of the river stands regularly in attrib. position.

ποτέ, indef. adv., enclitic, *at any time, once, ever;* ὅποι ποτε, *where in the world,* III, 5, 13; εἴ ποτε καὶ ἄλλοτε, *now, if ever,* VI, 4, 12.

πότερος, -α, -ον, interrog. pron., *which of two;* hence πότερον, interrog. adv., *whether,* introducing simple questions; πότερον (πότερα) . . . ἤ, *whether . . . or,* introducing alternative questions, direct or indirect.

ποτέρως, interrog. adv. (πότερος), *in which of two ways.*

ποτήριον, -ου, τό (πίνω), *drinking cup.*

ποτός, -ή, -όν (verbal of πίνω), *drinkable;* neut. τὸ ποτόν, *drink,* I, 10, 18; σῖτα καὶ ποτά, *food and drink,* II, 3, 27.

πότος, -ου, ὁ (πίνω), *a drinking bout, banquet.*

ποῦ, interr. adv., *where.*

πού, indef. adv., enclitic, *somewhere, anywhere;* with gen., III, 4, 23; *perhaps, of course,* V, 7, 13.

πούς, ποδός, ὁ (Lat. *pes*, Eng. *foot*), *foot,* in the lit. sense and as a unit of measure, 11⅔ in.; ἐπὶ πόδα ἀναχωρεῖν, *retreat while facing the foe,* V, 2, 32.

πρᾶγμα, -ατος, τό (πράττω), *thing done, thing, act, deed, affair; trouble,* IV, 1, 17; in this sense commonly pl.; πράγματα παρέχειν, with dat., *annoy, give trouble to,* I, 1, 11.

πραγματεύομαι (πρᾶγμα), *be busy at, seek to bring about,* VII, 6, 35.

πρανής, -ές (πρό), *bent forward, headlong, steep;* εἰς τὸ πρανές, *straight down hill,* III, 4, 25; κατὰ τοῦ πρανοῦς, *down the slope,* IV, 8, 28.

πρᾶξις, -εως, ἡ (πράττω), *business, undertaking, enterprise, scheme.*

πρᾷος, -εῖα, -ον, gen. pl. πραέων, *mild, tame,* I, 4, 9.

πράττω, πράξω, ἔπραξα, πέπραχα, πέπραγμαι, ἐπράχθην, *do, perform, bring to pass, effect, manage, transact, negotiate*, etc.; of money, *exact* (with two accs.), VII, 6, 17; with advs., as εὖ (καλῶς) or κακῶς, intrans., *fare well* or *ill*, I, 9, 10; III, 1, 6.

πρᾴως, adv. (πρᾷος), *mildly, lightly*.

πρέπω, πρέψω, etc., *be fitting; be becoming, suitable*, with dat., III, 2, 7; impers., *it is fitting* or *proper*, with infin., III, 2, 16; *cf*. I, 9, 6.

πρεσβεία, -ας, ἡ (πρεσβεύω), *embassy*.

πρεσβεύω, πρεσβεύσω, etc. (πρέσβυς), *serve as ambassador*.

πρέσβυς, -εως, ὁ (Eng. *presbyter, priest*), *old*, poetic adj. In the *Anabasis* only in comp. and sup. πρεσβύτερος, I, 1, 1, πρεσβύτατος, II, 1, 10. As subst., only in pl., οἱ πρέσβεις, *envoys, ambassadors*, III, 1, 28.

πρεσβύτης, -ου, ὁ (πρέσβυς), *old man*.

πρίασθαι, see ἐπριάμην.

πρίν, temporal conj. (πρό), with infin., *before, rarely, until*, I, 4, 13, etc.; with indic., ἄν, with subj., and opt. (cf. ἕως), *until, before*, chiefly after neg. clauses, I, 1, 10; πρόσθεν ... πρίν, I, 1, 10; πρότερον ... πρίν, III, 1, 16; πρὶν ἤ, with infin., IV, 5, 1 n.

πρό, prep. with gen., of place, *before, in front of;* of time, *before;* also, *in defense of, on behalf of, for;* πρὸ τῶν τοξευμάτων, *a defense against the arrows*, VII, 8, 18.

προαγορεύω (ἀγορεύω), *announce publicly*.

προάγω (ἄγω), *lead forward;* intr., *go forward, advance*, VI, 5, 6, 11.

προαιρέω (αἱρέω), *take before;* mid., *choose, select*, VI, 6, 19.

προαισθάνομαι (αἰσθάνομαι), *find out* or *perceive beforehand*.

προαποτρέπομαι (τρέπω), *turn away before* or *too soon*, VI, 5, 31.

προβαίνω (βαίνω), *step forward, go forward, advance*.

προβάλλω (βάλλω), *throw before, hold in front of*, in mid. τὰ ὅπλα προβαλέσθαι, *advance arms* (cf. "charge bayonets"), I, 2, 17; VI, 5, 16; πρὸ ἀμφοῖν προβεβλημένος (sc. τὴν ἀσπίδα), *with his shield held before them both*, IV, 2, 21; also, *bring forward, nominate*, VI, 1, 25; VI, 2, 6.

πρόβατον, -ου, τό (πρό+βαίνω), generally pl., *cattle;* in Attic regularly of small animals, *sheep* or *goats*, esp. the former.

προβολή, -ῆς, ἡ (προβάλλω), of spears, *a throwing forward* (into position for the charge), VI, 5, 25.

προβουλεύω (βουλεύω), *plan for* or *on behalf of*.

πρόγονος, -ου, ὁ (πρό+√γεν), *forefather*, in pl. *ancestors*.

προδίδωμι (δίδωμι), *give over, surrender, betray*.

προδότης, -ου, ὁ (προδίδωμι), *traitor, betrayer*.

προδραμόντες, see προτρέχω.

προδρομή, -ῆς, ἡ (πρό+δρόμος), *a running forth, sally*, IV, 7, 10.

προεῖδον (εἶδον), *see before* or *in front*, I, 8, 20; in mid., VI, 1, 8.

πρόειμι (εἶμι), *go on, go ahead, advance, proceed;* προϊούσης τῆς νυκτός, *as the night went on, in the course of the night*, II, 2, 19.

προεῖπον (εἶπον), serving as 2 aor. to προλέγω or προαγορεύω, *proclaim, give orders*, I, 2, 17.

προελαύνω (ἐλαύνω), intr., *ride* or *march forward, push on*.

προεργάζομαι (ἔργον), *do before, achieve* or *win before*, VI, 1, 21.,

προέρχομαι (ἔρχομαι), *go before, go forward, advance.*
προερῶ (ἐρῶ), as fut. of προλέγω, *tell in advance, warn,* VII, 7, 13.
προέχω (ἔχω), *have the advantage of.*
προηγέομαι (ἡγέομαι), *lead forward.*
προηγορέω (προήγορος, *spokesman,* πρό+ἀγορά), *be spokesman.*
προῆλθον, see προέρχομαι.
προθέω (θέω), *run forward.*
προθυμέομαι, προθυμήσομαι or προθυμηθήσομαι, ἐπροθυμήθην (πρόθυμος), *be eager* or *zealous, wish earnestly,* abs. or with infin.
προθυμία, -ας, ἡ (πρό+θυμός), *eagerness, zeal.*
πρόθυμος, -ον (πρό+θυμός), *ready, eager, zealous.*
προθύμως, adv. (πρόθυμος), *eagerly, willingly, zealously,* comp. προθυμότερον.
προθύω (θύω), *sacrifice before, offer a preliminary sacrifice,* mid.
προίημι (ἵημι), *send forth;* mid., *let go, give over, surrender, abandon.*
προΐστημι (ἵστημι), *put before;* in perf. tenses, intrans., *stand at the head of, be in command of.*
προκαλέω (καλέω), *call forth;* mid., *to oneself,* VII, 7, 2.
προκαλύπτω (καλύπτω, καλύψω, etc., *hide*), *throw a cover before, hide, conceal.*
προκαταθέω (θέω), *run along in advance.*
προκατακαίω or **-κάω** (καίω), *burn down in advance* or *before someone.*
προκαταλαμβάνω (λαμβάνω), *seize* or *occupy in advance.*
πρόκειμαι (κεῖμαι), *lie before* or *in front, project.*

προκινδυνεύω (κινδυνεύω), *incur danger for* or *in behalf of.*
Προκλῆς, -έους, ὁ, *Procles,* governor of Teuthrania in Mysia.
προκρίνω (κρίνω), *prefer.*
προλέγω, προερῶ, προεῖπον, *declare publicly* or *in advance, give warning.*
προμαχεών, -ῶνος, ὁ (μάχομαι), *battlement.*
προμετωπίδιον, -ου, τό (μέτωπον, *forehead*), *frontlet,* a piece of armor worn by horses, protecting the head, I, 8, 7.
προμνάομαι, impf. προύμνᾶτο (μνάομαι, *court*), *sue for, solicit.*
προνοέομαι (νοέω), *take thought for* (gen.), VII, 7, 33; *provide for* (acc.), VII, 7, 37.
πρόνοια, -ας, ἡ (προνοέομαι), *forethought.*
προνομή, -ῆς, ἡ (πρό+νέμω), *foraging party.*
προξενέω, προξενήσω, etc. (πρόξενος), *be one's πρόξενος, bring about for one;* of danger, *put upon one,* VI, 5, 14.
πρόξενος, -ον, ὁ (πρό+ξένος), *a public ξένος,* one acting as official representative of a foreign state among his own people, *consul,* V, 4, 2.
Πρόξενος, -ου, ὁ, *Proxenus,* a Theban, one of Cyrus' generals; the personal friend of Xenophon, III, 1, 4 ff.; treacherously seized and slain after the battle of Cunaxa, II, 5, 31 ff. For a sketch of his character see II, 6, 16 ff. and the Introd. § 38.
προπέμπω (πέμπω), *send forward; escort,* VI, 1, 23.
προπίνω (πίνω), *drink to one, pledge.*
προπονέω (πονέω), *toil for* or *on behalf of.*

πρός (related to πρό): (1) originally an adv., *furthermore, besides,* III, 2, 2, πρὸς δ' ἔτι; (2) as prep. with gen., dat., and acc.: with gen., *on the side of, towards* (properly *from the direction of;* cf. Lat. *ab,* I, 10, 3; II, 2, 4; sometimes as ὑπό with passives, *by, on the part of,* I, 9, 20; πρὸς θεῶν, *in the sight of,* I, 6, 6; so in oaths, II, 1, 17; τρόπον, *in accordance with,* I, 2, 11; with dat., *before, beside, at, near; besides, in addition to;* with acc. after vbs. of motion or implying motion, *to, towards, before;* more personal than εἰς or ἐπί, but used by no means only of persons, I, 5, 7; often in hostile sense, *against,* I, 3, 21; in a more general sense, expressing various relations, καταλῦσαι πρός, *be reconciled with,* I, 1, 10; πρὸς τὴν ἀνάβασιν, *with reference to, regarding,* I, 4, 9; *in comparison with,* VII, 7, 41; of purpose, πρὸς ἄριστον, *for lunch,* I, 10, 19; of time, *towards,* IV, 5, 21; πρὸς φιλίαν, *in friendship,* I, 3, 19; πρὸς ταῦτα, *in view of this, in answer to this,* I, 3, 19. In composition πρός means *to, against, in addition to.*

προσάγω (ἄγω), *lead to* or *against;* intr., *lead on, advance,* I, 10, 9; *bring to bear, employ,* IV, 1, 23.

προσαιτέω (αἰτέω), *ask in addition, ask for more.*

προσαναλίσκω (ἀναλίσκω), *spend besides* or *in addition.*

προσανεῖπον (εἶπον), *command* or *announce further,* VII, 1, 11.

προσβαίνω (βαίνω), *step up to, plant the foot against,* IV, 2, 28.

προσβάλλω (βάλλω), *throw* or *strike against, make an attack.*

προσβατός, -όν (προσβαίνω), *approachable, accessible.*

προσβολή, -ῆς, ἡ (προσβάλλω), *attack.*

προσγίγνομαι (γίγνομαι), *come to, attach oneself to.*

προσδανείζομαι, προσεδανεισάμην (δανείζομαι, *borrow*), *borrow besides.*

προσδεῖ, impers. (δέω), *there is need of besides* or *in addition,* with gen.; also as middle deponent, προσδέομαι, with gen., *need* or *want besides,* VII, 6, 27; *strive for,* VI, 1, 24.

προσδίδωμι (δίδωμι), *give besides* or *in addition.*

προσδοκάω, προσεδόκων, προσεδόκησα (πρός + √δοκ; cf. δοκέω. The simple δοκάω is not found), *expect,* with acc. and infin.

προσδοκεῖ (δοκέω), *it seems good besides.*

προσέδραμον, see προστρέχω.

πρόσειμι (εἶμι), *come to, approach, advance.*

προσελαύνω (ἐλαύνω), *drive* or *ride towards* or *against, march on.*

προσέρχομαι (ἔρχομαι), *come to, approach, come up.*

προσεύχομαι (εὔχομαι), *pray to,* dat.

προσετάχθη, see προστάττω.

προσέχω (ἔχω), in the *Anabasis* only with νοῦν, *give heed to, pay close attention to,* dat.

προσήκω (ἥκω), pres. with force of a perfect, *come to, reach; be related to,* I, 6, 1; impers., *it is fitting* or *proper;* τούτῳ τῆς Βοιωτίας προσήκει οὐδέν, *this fellow has nothing to do with Boeotia,* III, 1, 31.

προσῆλθον, see προσέρχομαι.

προσῆτε, see πρόσειμι.

πρόσθεν, adv. (πρός), *before*, of place, εἰς τὸ πρόσθεν, *forward, to the front*, I, 10, 5; with gen., III, 1, 33; τὸ πρόσθεν, *the van*, III, 2, 36; of time, *before, formerly;* often as attrib., *former*, I, 4, 8; sometimes simply leading up to πρίν, I, 1, 10; τὸ πρόσθεν, as adv., *before, formerly*, I, 10, 11; of preference, πρόσθεν . . . ἤ, *sooner . . . than*, II, 1, 10.

προσθέω (θέω), *run towards, charge.*

προσίασι, see πρόσειμι.

προσίημι (ἵημι), *let come to, let approach*, IV, 5, 5; mid., *admit, receive*, III, 1, 30; IV, 2, 12; of the gods, *permit, sanction*, V, 5, 3.

προσκαλέω (καλέω), *call up, summon.*

προσκτάομαι (κτάομαι), *acquire besides* or *in addition.*

προσκυνέω, προσκυνήσω, etc. (κυνέω, *kiss*), *do obeisance to, bow down before, worship*, of gods, III, 2, 9, 13; of the oriental salaam before men of high rank, I, 6, 10; I, 8, 21.

προσλαμβάνω (λαμβάνω), *take besides* or *in addition to; lay hold of also, lend a hand*, II, 3, 11.

προσμείγνυμι (μείγνυμι, μείξω, ἔμειξα, μέμειγμαι, ἐμείχθην or ἐμίγην, *mix*), *mingle with, join.*

προσμένω (μένω), *wait, wait for.*

πρόσοδος, -ου, ἡ (πρός+ὁδός), lit. *way to, approach*, in pl., V, 2, 3; *procession*, in honor of a god, VI, 1, 11; *revenue, income*, I, 9, 19; VII, 7, 36.

προσόμνυμι (ὄμνυμι), *swear in addition.*

προσομολογέω (ὁμολογέω), *agree to, surrender.*

προσπερονάω (περονάω, *pierce*), perf. pass. προσπεπερόνημαι, *fasten with a pin* (περόνη) or *skewer*, VII, 3, 21.

προσπίπτω (πίπτω), *fall* or *throw oneself on, run to.*

προσποιέομαι (ποιέω), *profess, pretend.*

προσπολεμέω (πολεμέω), *war against.*

προσχόντες, see προσέχω.

προστατεύω (πρό+√στα), *be at the head* or *in chief charge of*, V, 6, 21.

προστατέω (cf. προστάτης), *preside over, manage*, gen., IV, 8, 25.

προστάτης, -ου, ὁ (προΐστημι), *one who stands before* or *at the head of, leader*, VII, 7, 31.

προστάττω (τάττω), *give orders to*, I, 9, 18; in impers. pass. οἷς προσετάχθη, *those who had been bidden*, I, 6, 10 n.

προστελέω (τέλος), *pay in addition.*

προστερνίδιον, -ου, τό (στέρνον), *breastplate*, of horses, I, 8, 7.

προστίθημι (τίθημι), *add to;* mid., *concur in* (something advanced by another), I, 6, 10.

προστρέχω, aor. προσέδραμον (τρέχω), *run up to.*

προσφέρω (φέρω), *bring up, bring against*, V, 2, 14; mid., *conduct oneself, behave*, V, 5, 19; VII, 1, 6.

προσχωρέω (χωρέω), *go over to, surrender to.*

πρόσχωρος, -ον (πρός+χῶρος), *neighboring;* οἱ πρόσχωροι, *neighbors*, V, 3, 9.

πρόσω, adv., comp. προσωτέρω, sup. προσωτάτω (πρό), *forwards, in advance;* so εἰς τὸ πρόσω, *forward*, V, 4, 30; ἰέναι τοῦ πρόσω, *go forward*, I, 3, 1; with local gen. πρόσω τοῦ ποταμοῦ, *far into the river*, IV, 3, 28; also, *far, at a distance;* with gen., *far from*, III, 2, 22; προσωτέρω τοῦ καιροῦ see καιρός.

πρόσωπον, -ου, τό (πρός+√οπ; cf. ὤψ, face), countenance, face, pl. II, 6, 11 n.

προτάττω (τάττω), station in front.

προτελέω (τελέω), pay beforehand.

προτεραῖος, -α, -ον (πρό), only in the phrase τῇ προτεραίᾳ, on the day before, II, 1, 3; V, 4, 23.

πρότερος, -α, -ον (πρό), former, earlier, the adj. being often used where Eng. requires an adv., I, 2, 25; neut. πρότερον, as adv., before; τὸ πρότερον, the time before, IV, 4, 15; πρότερον, like πρόσθεν (I, 1, 10 n.), may lead up to πρίν; it is then not to be translated.

προτιμάω (τιμάω), honor above, prefer in honor; fut. mid. as pass., I, 4, 14.

προτρέχω (τρέχω), run forward, run ahead of (with gen.)

προφαίνω (φαίνω), mid., come to sight, appear.

προὐ-=προε-.

προφασίζομαι (πρόφασις), set up or allege as an excuse.

πρόφασις, -εως, ἡ (φημί), pretext, excuse.

προφυλακή, -ῆς, ἡ (πρό+φυλακή), in pl., outposts, pickets.

προφύλαξ, -ακος, ὁ (πρό+φύλαξ), outpost, sentinel, picket.

προχωρέω (χωρέω), go forward, go on, progress, prosper; of omens, be favorable, VI, 4, 21; impers., be of advantage, I, 9, 13.

πρύμνα, -ης, ἡ, stern (of a ship).

πρῴ, adv. (πρό), in the morning, early; comp. πρῳαίτερον, III, 4, 1.

πρῷρα, -ας, ἡ (πρό), prow, bow (of a ship).

πρῳρεύς, -έως, ὁ (πρῷρα), prow-officer, lookout, ranking next to the κυβερνήτης, V, 8, 20.

πρωτεύω (πρῶτος), be first, hold the first place.

πρῶτος, -η, -ον (πρό), first, foremost, chief, most eminent; οἱ πρῶτοι, the van, II, 2, 17; often where Eng. uses an adv., I, 3, 1, yet always with personal force, πρῶτος ἤγγειλα, I was the first to announce, II, 3, 19; as adv. πρῶτον or τὸ πρῶτον, first, at first, in the first place, I, 2, 16; ὡς τὸ πρῶτον, cum primum, as soon as, VII, 8, 14.

πτάρνυμαι, ἔπταρον (cf. Lat. sternuo, sneeze), sneeze.

πτέρυξ, -υγος, ἡ (πέτομαι), wing, I, 5, 3; flap (of a corselet), IV, 7, 15.

πυγμή, -ῆς, ἡ (πύξ; cf. Eng. pygmy), fist, boxing, IV, 8, 27. In later Greek as in Roman boxing, the forearms were weighted with the cestus of leathern thongs loaded with metal.

Πυθαγόρας, -ου, ὁ, Pythagoras, a Spartan admiral.

πυθόμενος, see πυνθάνομαι.

πυκνός, -ή, -όν (cf. πύξ), close, compact, thick; neut. πυκνά, as adv., constantly, VI, 1, 8.

πύκτης, -ου, ὁ (πύξ), boxer.

Πύλαι, -ῶν (πύλη), Pylae, i. e., the Gates, a fortress or town in Mesopotamia, on the border of Babylonia.

πύλη, -ης, ἡ, gate, chiefly pl., since gates had two folding wings then, entrance, pass, I, 4, 4.

πυνθάνομαι, πεύσομαι, ἐπυθόμην, πέπυσμαι, inquire, ask, learn, discover.

πύξ, adv. (cf. πυκνός, Lat. pugnus), with the fist.

πῦρ, -ρός, τό (Lat. purus, Eng. fire, pyre, etc.), fire; pl., τὰ πυρά (dat. πυροῖς), watch fires, signal fires.

πυραμίς, -ίδος, ἡ (cf. Eng. *pyramid*), *pyramid*.

Πύραμος, -ου, ὁ, *the Pyramus*, a large river flowing through Cilicia.

πυργομαχέω (πύργος+μάχομαι), *storm a tower or wall*.

πύργος, -ου, ὁ, *tower, walled fort*.

πυρέττω (πῦρ), *have a fever*.

πύρινος, -η, -ον (πυρός), *of wheat, wheaten*.

πυροῖς, see πῦρ.

πυροί, -ῶν, οἱ, *wheat*; for the pl., cf. κριθαί.

Πυρρίας, -ου, ὁ, *Pyrrhias*, an Arcadian commanding a division of the Greek army.

πυρρίχη, -ης, ἡ, *the pyrrich*, a mimetic war dance, VI, 1, 12.

πυρσεύω, aor. ἐπύρσευσα (πυρσός, ὁ, *a torch*; cf. πῦρ), *light beacon fires*.

πώ, indef. adv., enclitic and only after a neg., *yet, up to this time*; cf. οὔπω, μήπω.

πωλέω, πωλήσω, ἐπωλήθην (cf. Eng. *monopoly*), *sell*.

πῶλος, -ου, ὁ (cf. Lat. *pullus*, Eng. *foal*), *colt, foal*.

Πῶλος, -ου, ὁ, *Polus*, a Spartan admiral, succeeding Anaxibius, VII, 2, 5.

πῶμα, -ατος, τό (πίνω), *drink, beverage*.

πώποτε, indef. adv. (πώ+ποτέ), after negatives, *at any time, ever, ever yet*.

πῶς, interrog. adv., *in what way? how?*

πώς, indef. adv. enclitic, *somehow, in some way, in any way*; often serving to modify another word, ὧδέ πως, *somewhat as follows*, I, 7, 9; ἀμφὶ τὴν αὐτήν πως ὥραν, *at about the same hour*, IV, 8, 21; ἄλλως πως . . . ἤ, *any other way than*, III, 1, 20.

P

ῥᾴδιος, -α, -ον, comp. ῥᾴων, sup. ῥᾷστος, *easy*, often in neut. with infin.

ῥᾳδίως, adv., comp. ῥᾷον, sup. ῥᾷστα, *easily*.

Ῥαθίνης, -ου, ὁ, *Rathines*, an officer under Pharnabazus.

ῥᾳθυμέω (ῥᾴθυμος, *easy-going*, ῥᾴδιος +θυμός), *be of an easy-going nature, take things easily*.

ῥᾳθυμία, -ας, ἡ (cf. ῥᾳθυμέω), *easy-going disposition, laziness*.

ῥᾷον, ῥᾷστον, see ῥᾴδιος.

ῥᾳστώνη, -ης, ἡ (ῥᾷστος; cf. ῥᾴδιος), *easiness of character, indolence*.

ῥέω, ῥεύσομαι or ῥυήσομαι, ἐρρύηκα, aor. pass., as act., ἐρρύην, *flow*.

ῥήτρα, -ας, ἡ (cf. εἴρω), *agreement, compact*.

ῥῖγος, -ους, τό (cf. Lat. *frigus*), *cold*.

ῥίπτω (in pres. system also ῥιπτέω), ῥίψω, ἔρριψα, etc., *throw, hurl*; of garments, *throw off*.

ῥίς, ῥινός, ἡ (cf. Eng. *rhinoceros*), *nose*.

Ῥόδιος, -α, -ον (Ῥόδος, *Rhodes*), *Rhodian*; ὁ Ῥόδιος, *a Rhodian, native of Rhodes*, a large island off the S.W. coast of Asia Minor.

ῥοφέω (cf. Lat. *sorbeo*), *suck up*.

ῥυθμός, -οῦ, ὁ (akin to ῥέω, Eng. *rhythm*), *measured motion, time, rhythm*.

ῥῦμα, -ατος, τό (cf. ἐρύω, ῥύομαι, *draw*), properly, *that which is drawn*, only in the phrase ἐκ τόξου ῥύματος, *with a bow-shot the start*, III, 3, 15.

ῥώμη, -ης, ἡ (cf. ῥώννυμι), *strength force*.

Ῥωπάρας, -α, ὁ, *Rhoparas*, satrap of Babylonia.

Σ

σά, see σός.

σᾶ, see σῶς.

σάγαρις, -εως, ἡ, *battle-axe*.

σακίον, -ου, τό (dim. of σάκος, *bag*, Eng. *sack*), *sack, bag, pouch*.

Σαλμυδησσός, -οῦ, ὁ, *Salmydessus*, a town and region in Thrace on the Euxine.

σάλπιγξ, -ιγγος, ἡ, *trumpet*, a long straight tube like the Roman *tuba*.

σαλπίζω, ἐσάλπιξα (σάλπιγξ), *sound the trumpet*, the subj. σαλπικτής being generally omitted, I, 2, 17 n.; with inner obj., ῥυθμούς, *keep time with the trumpet*, VII, 3, 32.

σαλπικτής, -οῦ, ὁ (σάλπιγξ), *trumpeter*.

Σάμιος, -α, -ον (Σάμος, *Samos*), *of Samos, Samian*.

Σαμόλας, -α, ὁ, *Samolas*, an Achaean in the Greek army.

Σάρδεις, -εων, αἱ, *Sardis*, capital of Lydia, and of Cyrus' satrapy.

σατραπεύω (σατράπης), *be satrap* (*of*, gen.), III, 4, 31; *govern as satrap*, acc., I, 7, 6.

σατράπης, -ου, ὁ, *satrap*, a Persian title for the governor of a province, I, 1, 2 n.

Σάτυρος, -ου, ὁ, *a satyr*; I, 2, 13, *Silēnus*, the attendant of Dionysus.

σαυτοῦ, etc., see σεαυτοῦ.

σαφής, -ές (cf. σοφός, Lat. *sapio*), *clear, plain*.

σαφῶς, adv. (σαφής), *clearly, plainly, certainly*.

σέ, see σύ.

-σε, a suffix denoting the place *whither*.

σεαυτοῦ, -ῆς, or contr. **σαυτοῦ,** -ῆς (σέ+αὐτός), pl. ὑμῶν αὐτῶν, etc., *of thyself, yourself*.

Σελινοῦς, -οῦντος, ὁ, *Selīnus*, name of two rivers, one in Elis, the other flowing by the temple of Artemis in Ephesus.

σεσωμένοι, σέσωται, see σῴζω.

Σεύθης, -ου, ὁ, *Seuthes*, king of the Odrysae, a tribe in Asiatic Thrace.

Σηλυμβρία, -ας, ἡ, *Selymbria*, a town near Byzantium, VII, 2, 28.

σημαίνω, σημανῶ, ἐσήμηνα, σεσήμασμαι, ἐσημάνθην (σῆμα, *sign*), *give a sign, give the signal*, IV, 3, 32; often impers., *the signal is given*, II, 2, 4; *make known, inform, declare, order*.

σημεῖον, -ου, τό (σῆμα, *sign*), *sign, mark, token, signal, standard*.

σησάμινος, -η, -ον (σήσαμον), *made of sesame*.

σήσαμον, -ου, τό, *sesame*, a leguminous plant from the seeds of which an oil is made, much used in cookery, medicine, etc., I, 2, 22; in pl., *sesame plants* or *seeds*, VI, 4, 6.

σιγάζω (σιγή), *make keep silent, silence*.

σιγάω, σιγήσομαι, etc. (σιγή), *be silent, say nothing*.

σιγή, -ῆς, ἡ, *silence*; σιγῇ as adv., *silently*.

σίγλος, -ου, ὁ (Hebr. *shekel*), *siglus*, a Semitic coin worth 7½ Attic obols, I, 5, 6.

σιδηρεία, -ας, ἡ (σίδηρος), *working in iron*.

σιδηροῦς, -ᾶ, -οῦν (σίδηρος, *iron*), *made of iron, iron*.

Σικυώνιος, -ου, ὁ (Σικυών, *Sicyon*), *a Sicyonian, native of Sicyon*, a small state in northern Peloponnēsus, west of Corinth.

Σιλανός, -οῦ, ὁ, *Silānus*: (1) soothsayer to Cyrus; (2) another individual of the same name, a trumpeter from Macistus.

σίνομαι, do harm to, hurt, III, 4, 16 n.

Σινωπεύς, -έως, ὁ (Σινώπη), a Sinopean, native of Sinōpe.

Σινώπη, -ης, ἡ, Sinōpe, an important city in Paphlagonia on the Euxine.

σιός, Doric for θεός; ναὶ τὼ σιώ, by the twin gods, i. e., Castor and Pollux, a Spartan oath, VI, 6, 34; VII, 6, 39.

σιταγωγός, -ή, -όν (σῖτος+ἄγω), corn or grain carrying, of ships.

Σιτάλκας, -ου, ὁ: (1) Sitalcas, a Thracian king of the time of Darius the Great; (2) a war song composed in his honor, VI, 1, 6.

σιτευτός, -ή, -όν (verbal of σιτεύω, feed; cf. σῖτος), fed-up, fattened.

σιτηρέσιον, -ου, τό (σῖτος), provision-money, VI, 2, 4.

σιτίον, -ου, τό (σῖτος), food; in pl., provisions.

σῖτος, -ου, ὁ, pl. σῖτα, grain, esp. wheat; food, in general, provisions, supplies; σῖτος μελίνης, millet-bread, I, 5, 10.

Σιττάκη, -ης, ἡ, Sittace, a city in Babylonia on the Tigris.

σιωπάω, impf. ἐσιώπων (σιωπή, silence), be silent.

σκεδάννυμι, σκεδῶ or σκεδάσω, ἐσκέδασα, ἐσκέδασμαι, ἐσκεδάσθην (cf. Eng. scatter, shatter), scatter; mid., intr., disperse, III, 5, 2.

σκέλος, -ους, τό (cf. Eng. isosceles), leg.

σκεπτέος, -α, -ον (verbal of σκέπτομαι), to be considered, must be considered.

σκέπτομαι, σκέψομαι, ἐσκεψάμην, ἔσκεμμαι, the pres. is rare, σκοπέω being used in its place (cf. Lat. species,

Eng. spy, skeptic), look at, look into, observe, consider, reflect.

σκευάζω, σκευάσω (σκευή), make ready; of persons, dress.

σκευή, -ῆς, ἡ, dress, robe.

σκεῦος, -ους, τό, utensil; pl., baggage.

σκευοφορέω, σκευοφορήσω (σκεῦος + φέρω), carry baggage.

σκευοφόρος, -ον (σκεῦος+φέρω), baggage-carrying; as subst., baggage-carrier; τὰ σκευοφόρα, pack animals.

σκηνέω, σκηνήσω, ἐσκήνησα (σκηνή), be in tents or in camp, be quartered; in aor., go into camp, II, 4, 14; take meals, feast in one's quarters, IV, 5, 33.

σκηνή, -ῆς, ἡ, tent; then, loosely, quarters, III, 5, 7.

σκηνόω, σκηνώσω, ἐσκήνωσα (cf. σκηνέω), properly, pitch one's tent, go into camp, IV, 5, 23; also = σκηνέω, be in camp, in quarters, V, 5, 11.

σκήνωμα, -ατος, τό (σκηνόω), tent; pl. quarters.

σκηπτός, -οῦ, ὁ, thunder-bolt.

σκηπτοῦχος, -ου, ὁ (σκῆπτον=σκῆπτρον, scept e, + ἔχω), sceptre-bearer, chamberlain, a high official at the Persian court.

Σκιλλοῦς, -οῦντος, ὁ, Scillus, a town in Elis, near Olympia, where Xenophon had an estate presented to him by the Spartans, V, 3, 7.

σκίμπους, -οδος, ὁ, a low couch.

σκληρός, -ά, -όν, hard, rough; ἐν σκληρῷ, on rough ground, IV, 8, 26.

σκληρῶς, adv. (σκληρός), hardly, in hardship.

σκόλοψ, -οπος, ὁ, stake; in pl., palisade, V, 2, 5.

σκοπέω, only in pres. and impf.; *cf.*
σκέπτομαι (σκοπός), *look out for,
watch for, watch; see, learn,
find out,* III, 1, 13; *consider,
ponder,* V, 6, 30.
σκοπός, -οῦ, ὁ (*cf.* σκέπτομαι, Eng.
scope, microscope, etc.), *spy,
scout.*
σκόροδον, -ου, τό, *garlic;* in pl.,
VII, 1, 37.
σκοταῖος, -α, -ον (σκότος), *in the dark.*
σκότος, -ους, τό, *darkness.*
Σκυθηνοί, -ῶν, οἱ, *the Scythēni,* a
tribe dwelling south of the
Black Sea.
σκυλεύω, ἐσκύλευσα (σκῦλον, *spoil*),
strip, despoil.
σκύταλον, -ου, τό, *stick, club.*
σκύτινος, -η, -ον (σκῦτος, *skin*), *of
leather, leathern.*
σμῆνος, -ους, τό, *swarm* (of bees).
Σμίκρης, -ητος, ὁ, *Smicres,* one of
the generals of the Arcadian
army, VI, 3, 4 f.
Σόλοι, -ων, οἱ, *Soli,* a city on the
coast of Cilicia.
σός, σή, σόν, possess. pron. (*cf.* σύ,
Lat. *tuus,* Eng. *thy*), *thy, thine,
your.*
Σοῦσα, τά (biblical *Shushan,* Neh.
1:1), *Susa,* capital of the province of Susiāne, and one of the
capitals of the Persian empire.
Here the King spent the spring
months, II, 4, 25; III, 5, 15, n.
Σοφαίνετος, -ου, ὁ, *Sophaenetus,* of
Stymphālus in Arcadia, a general
under Cyrus.
σοφία, -ας, ἡ (σοφός), *wisdom;* hence
skill, esp. in music.
σοφός, -ή, -όν (Eng. *philosophy*),
wise, clever, skilled.
σπανίζω, σπανιῶ, ἐσπάνισα, ἐσπάνισμαι
(σπάν.s), *lack, want,* with gen.
σπάνιος, -α, -ον (σπάνις), *scanty, rare.*

σπάνις, -εως, ἡ, *scarcity, lack.*
Σπάρτη, -ης, ἡ, *Sparta,* the capital
of Laconia, II, 6, 4.
Σπαρτιάτης, -ου (Σπάρτη), *a Spartan,* one of genuine Dorian stock.
σπάρτον, -ου, τό (σπεῖρα, *coil*), *rope,
cord.*
σπάω, -σπάσω, etc., perf. mid. ἔσπασμαι, *draw;* mid., of one's sword
I, 8, 29.
σπείρω, σπερῶ, ἔσπειρα (*cf.* Eng
spare, sporadic), *sow,* VI, 1, 8;
pass. *be scattered, dispersed,*
VI, 3, 19.
σπείσας, σπείσεσθαι, see σπένδω.
σπένδω, -σπείσω, ἔσπεισα ἔσπεισμαι
(*cf.* Lat. *spondeo*), *pour a libation, make a drink-offering,*
abs., IV, 3, 13, 14; mid., since libations were offered by the contracting parties, *make a treaty
or truce with,* dat.
σπεύδω, σπεύσω, etc., *urge, urge on;*
intrans., *hasten, press, on,* abs.
or with infin.; ταῦτ' ἐγὼ ἔσπευδον,
this was (*the ground of*) *my
ha‹te,* IV, 1, 21.
Σπιθριδάτης, -ου, ὁ, *Spithradātes,*
an officer under Pharnabazus.
σπολάς, -άδος, ἡ, *leathern jacket* or
cuirass.
σπονδή, -ῆς, ἡ (σπένδω), *libation,
drink-offering;* pl. *treaty, truce,
peace.*
σπουδάζω, σπουδάσω, etc. (σπουδή),
be in haste, in earnest.
σπουδαιολογέω, ἐσπουδαιλόγησα, etc
(σπουδαῖος, *serious,*+λέγω), *talk
earnestly with.*
σπουδή, -ῆς, ἡ (σπεύδω), *haste, hurry;*
dat. σπουδῇ, as adv., *hastily,* VI,
5, 14; κατὰ σπουδήν, *in haste,*
VII, 6, 28.
στάδιον, -ου, τό, pl. στάδιοι and
στάδια, *the stadium, stade,* a

Greek measure of distance, 600 Greek or 581½ Eng. ft.; also, *race course* (for foot races, the oldest of Greek athletic games); ἀγωνίζεσθαι στάδιον (inner obj.), *to contend in the foot race*, IV, 8, 27.

σταθμός, -οῦ, ὁ (ἵστημι), *halting-place, quarters;* commonly the distance between two halts, *a day's journey*.

στάς, see ἵστημι.

στασιάζω, στασιάσω, ἐστασίασα (στάσις), *form a faction, be in revolt, rebel,* abs., with dat., or πρός and acc.

στάσις, -εως, ἡ (ἵστημι), *faction, dissension, discord.*

σταυρός, -οῦ, ὁ (ἵστημι), *stake, palisade.*

σταύρωμα, -ατος, τό (σταυρός), *stockade.*

στέαρ, -ατος, τό, *fat, tallow, suet.*

στέγασμα, -ατος, τό (στεγάζω, *cover;* cf. στέγη), *covering.*

στέγη, -ης, ἡ (στέγω, *cover,* Eng. *deck, thatch*), *roof;* hence, *house.*

στεγνός, -ή, -όν, (cf. στέγη), *covered;* neut. τὰ στεγνά, *houses*, VII, 4, 12.

στείβω, *walk on, tread;* pass. partic., of roads, I, 9, 13.

στέλλω, στελῶ, ἔστειλα, -ἔσταλκα, ἔσταλμαι, ἐστάλην, *set in order, equip, dress,* III, 2, 7, mid. *set forth, proceed, travel,* V, 1, 5.

στενός, -ή, -όν, *narrow;* comp. στενότερος, III, 4, 19; as subst., τὸ στενόν, or τὰ στενά, *defile,* pass.

στενοχωρία, -ας, ἡ (στενός+χῶρος), *narrow pass.*

στέργω, στέρξω, *love.*

στερέω, στερήσω, etc. *deprive of,* with acc. and gen.; in pass., *be deprived of, be without.* The pres. pass. is στέρομαι.

στέρνον, -ου, τό (√ στερ, *spread*), *breast.*

στέρομαι (cf. στερέω), only in pres. (the impf. is very rare), and with the force of a pf., *be deprived of, destitute of, have lost,* with gen.

στερρῶς, adv. (στερρός, *hard, firm;* cf. Eng. *stereotype*), *firmly, steadfastly.*

στέφανος, -ου, ὁ (στέφω, *pack close, encircle*), *crown, garland wreath.*

στεφανόω, -ώσω, etc. (στέφανος), *crown;* mid. *crown oneself, put on a wreath* or *garland.*

στήλη, -ης, ἡ (στέλλω), *pillar, slab* (of stone).

στῆναι, see ἵστημι.

στίβος, -ου, ὁ (στείβω), *beaten track, track.*

στίζω, στίξω, ἔστιξα, ἔστιγμαι (cf. Lat. *instigo,* Eng. *stick, sting, stigma*), *to prick, tattoo.*

στῖφος, -ους, τό (στέφω, *pack close;* cf. Lat. *stipo*), *throng, mass.*

στλεγγίς, -ίδος, ἡ, *scraper, strigil,* used after exercising to remove the dust and dirt from the body, I, 2, 10; according to others, *a kind of headdress* or *tiara.*

στολή, -ῆς, ἡ (στέλλω), *dress, robe;* collective, *raiment.*

στόλος, -ου, ὁ (στέλλω), *equipment, armament, expedition.*

στόμα, -ατος, τό (cf. Eng. *stomach*), *mouth, opening, front, van.*

στρατεία, -ας, ἡ (cf. στρατεύω), *expedition, campaign.*

στράτευμα, -ατος, τό (στρατεύω), *army.*

στρατεύω, στρατεύσω, etc. (στρατός), *make an expedition, make war, take the field,* of commanding officers; more commonly mid., of officers or of troops.

στρατηγέω, στρατηγήσω etc. (στρατηγός), be general, take command, abs. or with gen.; στρατηγεῖν ταύτην τὴν στρατηγίαν, assume this command, I, 3, 15; τοῦτο πρῶτον ἡμῶν στρατηγῆσαι, begin your generalship over us with this, VII, 6, 40.

στρατηγία, -ας, ἡ (στρατηγός), office of general, command; generalship, II, 2, 13.

στρατηγιάω (στρατηγός), wish to be general.

στρατηγός, -οῦ, ὁ (στρατός+ἄγω), general, used of the commanders of the various divisions in Cyrus' Greek army, and also of the Persian military governors.

στρατιά, -ᾶς, ἡ (στρατός), army, troops.

στρατιώτης, -ου, ὁ (στρατιά), soldier; in pl. troops.

Στρατοκλῆς, -έους, ὁ, Stratocles, commander of the Cretan archers.

στρατοπεδεύω, -εύσω, etc. (στρατόπεδον), pitch one's camp, encamp, generally mid. The pres. has sometimes the force of a perf., VI, 3, 6.

στρατόπεδον, -ου, τό (στρατός+πέδον, ground), camp; also army in camp.

στρατός, -οῦ, ὁ (στορέννυμι, spread out), army, force (esp. in camp), I, 5, 7.

στραφέντες, see στρέφω.

στρεπτός, -ή, -όν (στρέφω), twisted; ὁ στρεπτός, collar, necklace, worn by Persians of rank.

στρέφω, στρέψω, ἔστρεψα, ἔστραμμαι, ἐστράφην (cf. Eng. strophe, catastrophe), turn, twist, braid, in pass., IV, 7, 15; intr. and in pass., turn or wheel about, I, 10, 6.

στρουθός, -οῦ, ὁ, ἡ, sparrow; ὁ μέγας στρουθός, ostrich, I, 5, 2, 3.

στρωματόδεσμος, -ου, ὁ (στρώματα, bedclothes,+δεσμός), sack for bedclothes, V, 4, 13,

στυγνός, -ή, -όν (cf. στυγέω, hate), hateful, gloomy, sullen, II, 6, 9; τὸ στυγνόν, sullenness, II, 6, 11.

Στυμφάλιος, -ου, ὁ (Στύμφαλος), a native of Stymphālus, in Arcadia.

σύ, σοῦ, pl. ὑμεῖς, pers. pron. (Dor. τύ, Lat. tu, Eng. thou), thou, you. The nom. is used only when emphatic.

συγ- before palatals=σύν.

συγγένεια, -ας, ἡ (συγγενής), kinship.

συγγενής, -ές (σύν+γίγνομαι), of the same race or family, related; οἱ συγγενεῖς, kinsmen.

συγγίγνομαι (γίγνομαι), be with, associate with, meet; of the relations of student with teacher, II, 6, 17; of sexual intercourse, I, 2, 12.

συγκάθημαι (κάθημαι), sit down, together.

συγκαλέω (καλέω), call together, call a meeting of.

συγκάμπτω (κάμπτω, κάμψω, etc., bend), bend.

συγκατακαίω or -κάω (καίω), burn along with.

συγκατασκεδάννυμι (σκεδάννυμι), sprinkle or scatter along with another, VII, 3, 32.

συγκαταστρέφω (στρέφω), join or help in subduing (mid.), II, 1, 14.

σύγκειμαι (κεῖμαι), lie together, be put together, be agreed on; τὸ συγκείμενον, place agreed on, place of rendezvous, VI, 3, 4; in pl. terms of agreement, VII, 2, 7.

συγκλείω (κλείω), shut to, close.

συγκομίζω (κομίζω), bring or gather together, mid., VI, 6, 37.

συγκύπτω (κύπτω, κύψω, etc., stoop), draw together, converge, III, 4, 19, 21.

συγχωρέω (χωρέω), go with, concur, yield.

σύειος, -α, -ον (σῦς), of swine; with χρῖμα, lard, IV, 4, 13.

Συέννεσις, -ιος, ὁ, Syennesis, hereditary title of the kings of Cilicia, used by Xenophon as a proper name, I, 2, 12, n.

σῦκον, -ου, τό, fig.

συλ- before λ=σύν.

συλλαμβάνω (λαμβάνω), seize, arrest, capture.

συλλέγω, -λέξω, -έλεξα, -είλοχα, -είλεγμαι, -ελέγην (λέγω; cf. Lat. colligo), collect, gather, esp. of troops, collect, levy, raise, I, 1, 7; pass intr., gather together, assemble, IV, 1, 10.

συλλογή, -ῆς, ἡ (συλλέγω), collecting, levy, of troops, I, 1, 6.

σύλλογος, -ου, ὁ (συλλέγω), gathering, meeting.

συμβαίνω (βαίνω), come together, occur, happen, III, 1, 13.

συμβάλλω (βάλλω), throw together, collect; mid. contribute, I, 1, 9; agree upon, VI, 3, 3; contract, ξενίαν, VI, 6, 35; sc. γνώμην or λόγους, give one's ideas, converse, IV, 6, 14.

συμβοάω (βοάω), call together, call to one another, VI, 3, 6.

συμβοηθέω (βοηθέω), join in bearing aid.

συμβολή, -ῆς, ἡ (σύν+βάλλω), encounter, battle.

συμβουλεύω (βουλεύω), advise, counsel; in mid. ask advice of, consult with, I, 1, 10; act. and mid. together, II, 1, 17.

συμβουλή, -ῆς, ἡ (σύν+βουλή), advice, counsel; ἡ ἱερά συμβουλή, V, 6, 4; said with reference to the proverb ἱερὸν ἡ συμβουλή, advice is a holy thing.

σύμβουλος, -ου, ὁ (βουλεύω), adviser.

συμμανθάνω (μανθάνω), learn well or thoroughly, become accustomed to.

συμμαχέω (σύμμαχος), be in alliance with.

συμμαχία, -ας, ἡ (σύμμαχος), alliance.

συμμάχομαι (μάχομαι), fight on one's side, be an ally of.

σύμμαχος, -ον (σύν+μάχομαι), fighting with (i. e., on the side of), allied; as subst. ally; τὰ σύμμαχα, things that help, advantages, II, 4, 7.

συμμείγνυμι (μείγνυμι, μείξω, ἔμειξα, μέμειγμαι, ἐμείχθην and ἐμίγην), mix with, unite, join, engage (in battle), dat.

συμπαρασκευάζω (σκευάζω), join or aid in preparing.

συμπαρέχω (ἔχω), join in causing or affording.

σύμπας, -ασα, -αν (πᾶς), all together, all in a body, the whole, I, 2, 9; τὸ σύμπαν, as adv., on the whole, I, 5, 9.

συμπέμπω (πέμπω), send with.

συμπίπτω (πίπτω), fall together, collapse, V, 2, 24; grapple with, I, 9, 6.

σύμπλεως, -ων, gen. -ω (σύν+√πλα), entirely full of, with gen., I, 2, 22.

συμποδίζω (ποδίζω), shackle; hence, hinder, encumber, IV, 4, 11.

συμπολεμέω (πολεμέω), make war along with, help in war.

συμπορεύομαι (πορεύω), march with, accompany.

συμποσίαρχος, -ου, ὁ (συμπόσιον, drinking bout, feast, symposium [from σύν+πίνω]+ἄρχω), symposiarch, master of a feast, VI, 1, 30.

συμπράττω (πράττω), *do with, aid in doing, co-operate with.*

συμπρέσβεις, -εων, οἱ (σύν+πρέσβυς), *fellow-ambassadors* or *envoys*, V, 5, 24.

συμπροθυμέομαι (προθυμέομαι), *share in one's eagerness, join in urging that*, with infin., or ὅπως.

συμφέρω (φέρω), *bring together, collect, gather; be of use* or *advantage;* συμφέρειν τινι τὴν πενίαν, *endure poverty with one*, VII, 6, 20.

σύμφημι (φημί), *agree, grant.*

σύμφορος, -ον (συμφέρω), *advantageous.*

σύν (in the older Attic ξύν), prep. with dat., far more common in Xenophon than in most prose authors, *with, together with, along with*, common in phrases like Μένων καὶ οἱ σὺν αὐτῷ, *Menon and his troops* (cf. ἀμφί), I, 2, 15; *on the side of*, σὺν ἡμῖν, III, 1, 21; often, *with the help of*, esp. σὺν τοῖς θεοῖς, III, 1, 23; σὺν τοῖς ὅπλοις, *with arms in our hands*, III, 2, 8; of clothing, *in*, IV, 5, 33; of manner, I, 8, 4; of means, II, 6, 18. In composition σύν becomes συμ- before a labial or μ, συγ- before a palatal; before λ and ρ, ν is assimilated, and before σ with following cons. is omitted.

συναγείρω (ἀγείρω), *collect together, assemble.*

συνάγω (ἄγω), *bring together, gather, collect, convoke.*

συναδικέω (ἀδικέω), *be an accomplice in wrong-doing.*

συναθροίζω (ἀθροίζω), *collect together;* mid. intrans. *assemble.*

συναινέω (αἰνέω, αἰνέσω, ᾔνεσα, *praise*), *join* or *agree in praising, grant*, VII, 7, 31.

συναιρέω (αἱρέω), *take together, embrace in one phrase;* ὡς συνελόντι εἰπεῖν, *to put the matter briefly, in a word*, III, 1, 38.

συναίτιος, -ον (σύν+αἴτιος), *involved in guilt with another, implicated.*

συνακολουθέω (ἀκολουθέω), *follow along with, accompany.*

συνακούω (ἀκούω), *hear with* or *at the same time.*

συναλίζω (ἁλίζω), *gather* or *collect together.*

συναλλάττω, 2 aor. pass. συνηλλάγην, lit. *change* (so as to bring) *together, reconcile* (πρός), in pass., I, 2, 1.

συναναβαίνω (βαίνω), *go up* or *inland with.*

συναναπράττω (πράττω), *join in exacting.*

συνανίστημι (ἵστημι), *raise* or *set up with;* 2 aor. intrans. *rise up with*, VII, 3, 35.

συναντάω (ἀντάω, ἀντήσω, etc., *meet;* cf. ἀντί), *meet, meet with.*

συνάπειμι (εἶμι), *go back with.*

συναπολαμβάνω (λαμβάνω), *receive one's dues at the same time.*

συνάπτω (ἅπτω), *join, engage in* (acc.) *with* (dat.).

συνάρχω (ἄρχω), *rule* or *command jointly with* (dat.).

σύνδειπνος, -ον, ὁ (σύν+δεῖπνον), *companion* or *guest at dinner.*

συνδιαβαίνω (βαίνω), *cross over with.*

συνδιαπράττω (πράττω), *accomplish with;* mid., *negotiate with* or *at the same time*, IV, 8, 24.

συνδοκέω (δοκέω), *seem good also.*

σύνδυο (δύο), *two together, two by two.*

συνέδραμον, see συντρέχω.

συνεῖδον (εἶδον), *see at a glance, observe.*

συνειλεγμένοι, see συλλέγω.
συνειλημμένοι, συνειλήφασι, see συλλαμβάνω.
σύνειμι (εἰμί), be with; οἱ συνόντες, one's associates, II, 6, 20, 23.
σύνειμι (εἶμι), come together, assemble, III, 5, 7; in hostile sense, encounter, I, 10, 10.
συνείποντο, see συνέπομαι.
συνεισέρχομαι (ἔρχομαι), go in with or together.
συνεισπίπτω (πίπτω), fall or rush in with.
συνεκβαίνω (βαίνω), go out together or with, IV, 3, 22 n.
συνεκβιβάζω (σύν+ἐκ+βιβάζω, βιβάσω or βιβῶ, etc.), join or aid in forcing out.
συνεκκόπτω (κόπτω), join in cutting down.
συνεκπίνω (πίνω), drink to the dregs with, drain with.
συνεκπορίζω (πορίζω), join in providing.
συνέλαβον, see συλλαμβάνω.
συνεληλύθατε, συνελθόντες, see συνέρχομαι.
συνελόντι, see συναιρέω.
συνενεγκόντες, συνενηνεγμένα, see συμφέρω.
συνεξέρχομαι (ἔρχομαι), go forth with.
συνεπαινέω (ἐπαινέω), join in praising or approving.
συνεπεύχομαι (εὔχομαι), vow besides or in addition.
συνεπιμελέομαι (ἐπιμελέομαι), join in taking charge of.
συνεπισπέσθαι, see συνεφέπομαι.
συνεπισπεύδω (σπεύδω), join or aid in pushing on.
συνεπιτρίβω (τρίβω, τρίψω, etc., rub), destroy or ruin utterly.
συνέπομαι (ἕπομαι), follow with, accompany.

συνεπόμνυμι (ὄμνυμι), swear besides (along with another).
συνεργός, -όν (σύν+ἔργον), working with, as subst., co-worker, helper.
συνερρύησαν, see συρρέω.
συνέρχομαι (ἔρχομαι), come together, assemble, meet.
συνέσπων, see συσπάω.
συνεφέπομαι (ἕπομαι), follow along with, follow hard upon.
συνέχω (ἔχω), hold together.
συνήδομαι (ἥδομαι), be glad or rejoice with, congratulate.
συνθεάομαι (θεάομαι), look at with.
σύνθημα, -ατος, τό (σύν+τίθημι), agreement, IV, 6, 20; signal, watchword, I, 8, 16.
συνθηράω (θηράω), hunt with, join in the hunt.
συνθοῖτο, see συντίθημι.
συνιδεῖν, see συνεῖδον.
συνίημι (ἵημι), understand.
συνίστημι (ἵστημι), make stand or bring together, of persons, introduce, III, 1, 8; intr. in mid. and in perf. and 2 aor. act., stand together, assemble, gather, V, 7, 2; συνεστηκός, of troops, in compact order, VI, 5, 30; VII, 6, 26.
σύνοδος, -ου, ἡ (συν+ὁδός), meeting, encounter.
σύνοιδα, (οἶδα), know with (one), share one's knowledge, VII, 6, 18; chiefly with dat. of reflexive pron. and nom. partic. be conscious of, be conscious that, I, 3, 10.
συνοίσειν, see συμφέρω.
συνολολύζω (ὀλολύζω, cry aloud, cf. ὀλολυγή, a cry, Lat. ulula, screech owl, Eng. owl), shout along with, join in crying out, of women, IV, 3, 19.

συνομολογέω (ὁμολογέω), *agree with one* (dat.), *in something* (acc.), *concur;* either case or both cases may be used.

συνοράω (ὁράω), *see together* or *at the same time, watch, view,* IV, 1, 11; V, 2, 13.

συνουσία, -ας, ἡ (σύν+εἰμί), *a being together, intercourse, interview, conference.*

συντάττω (τάττω), *arrange, set in order, array, marshal, form,* of troops; mid., of the leader, *form one's own troops,* I, 10, 5; of the troops, *fall into line, form,* I, 3, 14.

συντίθημι (τίθημι), *put* or *place together;* mid. *contract, agree on something* (acc.), *with somebody* (dat.), I, 9, 7.

σύντομος, -ον (σύν+τέμνω), *cut short, short.*

συντράπεζος, -ου, ὁ (σύν+τράπεζα), *table companion,* I, 9, 31; *cf.* ὁμοτράπεζος.

συντρέχω (τρέχω), *run together.*

συντρίβω (τρίβω, τρίψω, etc., *rub*), *rub together;* συντετριμμένους ἀνθρώπους σκέλη, *men with their legs crushed,* IV, 7, 4.

συντυγχάνω (τυγχάνω), *happen upon, fall in with.*

συνωφελέω (ὠφελέω), *join in helping.*

Συρακόσιος, -ου, ὁ (Συράκουσαι, *Syracuse*), *a Syracusan, inhabitant of Syracuse,* in Sicily.

Συρία, -ας, ἡ (Σύριος), *Syria,* the district between the Euphrates and the Mediterranean (although the name in I, 4, 4 is used of the region east of the river).

Σύριος, -α, -ον (Σύρος), *Syrian.*

Σύρος, -ου, ὁ, *a Syrian, native of Syria.*

συρρέω (ῥέω), *flow together;* of men, *stream* or *flock together.*

σῦς, συός, ὁ, ἡ (cf. ὗς, Lat. *sus,* Eng. *hog, sow*), *swine, pig, boar.*

συσκευάζω (σκευάζω), *bring effects together;* generally mid., *pack one's effects, pack up.*

σύσκηνος, -ου, ὁ (σύν+σκηνή), *messmate.*

συσπάω (σπάω), *draw* or *sew together.*

συσπειράομαι, pf. pass. συνεσπείραμαι (σπεῖρα, *coil*), of troops, *be massed together, be in close array,* I, 8, 21.

συσπουδάζω (σπουδάζω), *share in one's zeal* or *haste.*

συστρατεύομαι, dep. (στρατεύω), *take the field with, join in a campaign with.*

συστράτηγος, -ου, ὁ (σύν+στρατηγός), *fellow-general.*

συστρατιώτης, -ου, ὁ (σύν+στρατιώτης), *fellow-soldier.*

συστρατοπεδεύομαι (στρατοπεδεύομαι), *encamp together.*

συχνός, -ή, -όν, *much, great,* pl. *many;* of time, *long;* διαλείποντα συχνὸν ἀπ' ἀλλήλων, *some distance apart,* I, 8, 10.

σφαγιάζομαι, aor. ἐσφαγιασάμην (σφάγιον), *slay a victim, offer sacrifice.*

σφάγιον, -ου, τό (σφάττω), *sacrificial victim* pl., *sacrifice,* esp. a propitiatory sacrifice and the omens drawn therefrom (*cf.* ἱερά).

σφαιροειδής, -ές (σφαῖρα, *ball,* Eng. *sphere*+εἶδος), *ball-like, round.*

σφάλλω, σφαλῶ, ἔσφηλα, ἔσφαλμαι, ἐσφάλην, *trip;* mid. and pass., *stumble, fall, meet with misfortune.*

σφᾶς, see οὗ.

σφάττω, σφάξω, ἔσφαξα, ἔσφαγμαι, ἐσφάγην, *slaughter* (properly by cutting the throat), *sacrifice;* then, freely, *kill, slay.*

σφεῖς, see οὗ.

σφενδονάω, ἐσφενδόνησα (σφενδόνη), *sling.*

σφενδόνη, -ης, ἡ, *sling;* also loosely used of the missile, *stone, bullet.*

σφενδονήτης, -ου, ὁ (σφενδονάω), *slinger.*

σφίσι, see οὗ.

σφόδρα, adv. (σφοδρός, *vehement, extreme*), *vehemently, exceedingly, very.* In I, 10, 18 many read σφοδρά as adj., *extreme.*

σχεδία, -ας, ἡ, *a raft.*

σχεδόν, adv. (ἔχω), *almost, nearly, about.*

σχεῖν, see ἔχω.

σχέτλιος, -α, -ον (ἔχω), *holding out, unflinching;* hence, *cruel, dreadful,* VII, 6, 30.

σχῆμα, -ατος, τό (ἔχω), *form* or *shape;* of troops, *formation,* I, 10, 10.

σχίζω, ἔσχισα, ἐσχίσθην (cf. Lat. *scindo,* Eng. *schism*), *split* (of wood), I, 5, 12; IV, 4, 12; pass. of troops, *be separated,* VI, 3, 1.

σχολάζω, ἐσχόλασα (σχολή), *be at leisure, have time.*

σχολαῖος, -α, -ον (σχολή), *leisurely, slow.*

σχολαίως (adv. of σχολαῖος), *slowly, sluggishly,* I, 5, 8; compar. σχολαίτερον, I, 5, 9.

σχολή, -ῆς, ἡ (ἔχω; cf. Lat. *schola,* Eng. *school*), *leisure;* σχολῇ, as adv., *slowly,* III, 4, 27; IV, 1, 16.

σῷ, see σῶος.

σῴζω, σώσω, ἔσωσα, σέσωκα, σέσωμαι, ἐσώθην (σῶς), *save, rescue, preserve, hold, keep;* mid. *save oneself, escape,* II, 1, 19; *return* or *arrive safely,* III, 1, 6; σεσωμένοι, *safe and sound,* V, 5, 8.

Σωκράτης, -ου, ὁ, *Socrates:* (1) the famous Athenian philosopher, friend and adviser of Xenophon; (2) an Achaean, general in the army of Cyrus; a brief sketch of his character, II, 6, 30.

σῶμα, -ατος, τό, *body,* I, 9, 27; τὰ ἑαυτῶν σώματα, *their own persons,* I, 9, 12; σώματα ἀνδρῶν, *men,* IV, 6, 10.

σῶος, -α, -ον, or σῶς, σᾶ, σῶν, *safe and sound.*

Σῶσις, ὁ (Σωσίας), *Sosis,* of Syracuse, general under Cyrus.

σωτήρ, -ῆρος, ὁ (σῴζω), *savior,* as a title of Zeus, I, 8, 16.

σωτηρία, -ας, ἡ (σῴζω), *safety.*

Σωτηρίδας, -ου, ὁ, *Soteridas,* a hoplite of Sicyon.

σωτήριος, -ον (σῴζω), *saving, bringing safety;* τὰ σωτήρια, *thank offerings for deliverance,* III, 2, 9; V, 1, 1.

σωφρονέω, σωφρονήσω, etc. (σῶς+φρήν), *be of sound mind, be prudent, wise, moderate.*

σωφρονίζω, ἐσωφρόνισα, etc., *make wise, bring to one's senses.*

σωφροσύνη, -ης, ἡ (σῶς+φρήν, *mind*), *soundness of mind, prudence, self-control, moderation,* I, 9, 3, n.

T

τ', by elision for τε.

τἀγαθά, crasis for τὰ ἀγαθά.

τάλαντον, -ου, τό (√ταλ, *bear; cf.* Lat. *tollo*), *that which bears* or *supports, balance, scale;* hence, *weight,* then as a fixed weight, *talent,* sixty minas or 57¾ lbs. avoirdupois; most commonly a sum or weight of money (never a coin), amounting to sixty minas or about $1,080.00. See the note on I, 7, 18.

τἆλλα, by crasis for τὰ ἄλλα.

ταμιεύω, ταμιεύσω (ταμίας, steward; cf. τέμνω), act as steward, serve out, parcel out, mid. II, 5, 18.

Ταμώς, -ώ, ὁ, Tamos, an Egyptian in command of Cyrus' fleet.

τἀναντία, by crasis for τὰ ἐναντία.

ταξίαρχος, -ου, ὁ (τάξις+ἄρχω), a tuxiarch, commander of a τάξις.

τάξις, -εως, ἡ (τάττω), arrangement, order; esp in a military sense, array, line of battle, division, company; τὰ ἀμφὶ τάξεις, tactics, II, 1, 7.

Τάοχοι, -ων, οἱ, the Taochi, Taochians, a warlike tribe of Pontus.

ταπεινός, -ή, -όν, humble, submissive, groveling, a strong word, II, 5, 13.

ταπεινόω, ἐταπείνωσα, etc. (ταπεινός), humble, humiliate.

τάπις, -ιδος, ἡ (cf. Eng. tape, tapestry), carpet, rug.

τἀπιτήδεια, by crasis for τὰ ἐπιτήδεια.

ταράττω, ταράξω, ἐτάραξα, τετάραγμαι, ἐταράχθην (cf. τάραχος), trouble, disturb; pass., of troops, be thrown into confusion, III, 4, 19.

τάραχος, -ου, ὁ (ταράττω), confusion.

ταριχεύω, τεταρίχευμαι (τάριχος, smoked meat), preserve, pickle.

Ταρσοί, -ῶν, οἱ, Tarsus, the capital of Cilicia, birthplace of St. Paul.

τάττω, τάξω, ἔταξα, τέτοχα, τέταγμαι, ἐτάχθην, arrange, esp. in a military sense, draw up, form; in mid. and pass., take one's post, be stationed; appoint, order, I, 5, 7; so in pass, ταχθείς, I, 6, 6; ἐν τῷ τεταγμένῳ, in the appointed place, III, 3, 18.

ταῦρος, -ου, ὁ (Lat. taurus, Eng. steer), bull.

ταῦτα, see οὗτος.

ταύτῃ, adv. (dat. fem. of οὗτος), in this way, thus, here, in this respect.

ταφείησαν, see θάπτω.

τάφος, -ου, ὁ (θάπτω; cf. Eng. epitaph), burial, grave.

τάφρος, -ου, ἡ (θάπτω), ditch, trench.

τάχα, adv. (ταχύς), quickly, presently, I, 8, 8; perhaps, haply, V, 2, 17.

ταχέως, adv. (ταχύς), quickly, swiftly.

τάχιστα, see ταχύς.

τάχος, -ους, τό (ταχύς), speed, swiftness.

ταχύς, -εῖα, -ύ, comp. θάττων, sup. τάχιστος, swift, quick, speedy; τὴν ταχίστην ὁδόν, by the quickest road, I, 2, 20; so, without ὁδόν, I, 3, 14; διὰ ταχέων, speedily, I, 5, 9; neut. ταχύ as adv., quickly, speedily, soon, I, 5, 3; comp. θᾶττον, I, 2, 17; sup. τάχιστα, most common in intensive phrases, ὡς τάχιστα, as soon as possible, I, 3, 14; ὅτι τάχιστα, IV, 3, 29. In these phrases forms of δύναμαι are often expressed, ᾗ ἐδύνατο τάχιστα, I, 2, 4; ἐπειδὰν (or ὡς) τάχιστα, as soon as, III, 1, 9.

τε (before an aspirated vowel θ'), enclitic copulative conj. (Lat. que), and, rarely standing alone, I, 5, 14; regularly τε . . . τε, τε . . . καί, or τε καί, both . . . and, I, 8, 3; I, 1, 5; I, 9, 1; sometimes οὔτε (μήτε) . . . τε, not . . . but, where Eng. sacrifices the correlation of clauses, II, 5, 4; rarely continued by δέ, V, 5, 8.

τεθνᾶσι, τεθνάναι, τέθνατον, τεθνεῶτες, τεθνηκότα, see θνῄσκω.

τεθραμμένους, see τρέφω.

τέθριππον, -ου, τό (τέτταρες+ἵππος), a four-horse chariot.

τείνω, τενῶ, ἔτεινα, -τέτακα, τέταμαι, ἐτάθην (Lat. tendo, Eng. thin), stretch; hence, exert oneself, rush.

τειχίζω, τειχιῶ, etc., build a wall, fortify.

τεῖχος, -ους, τό (Eng. dike), wall, esp. city wall, then, walled town, stronghold.

τεκμαίρομαι (τεκμήριον), infer.

τεκμήριον, -ου, τό (τεκμαίρομαι), sign, proof, token.

τέκνον, -ου, τό (τίκτω, bear, give birth to), child.

τελέθω (cf. τέλος), become, be, III, 2, 3; of sacrifices, be favorable, VI, 6, 36; cf. γίγνομαι. A poetic vb.

τελευταῖος, -α, -ον (τελευτή), last, hindmost, rear; οἱ τελευταῖοι, the rear guard, IV, 1, 10.

τελευτάω, τελευτήσω, etc. (τελευτή), end, finish, trans. and intrans.; esp., end one's life, die, I, 1, 3; the partic. τελευτῶν, often like an adv., finally, IV, 5, 16.

τελευτή, -ῆς, ἡ (τέλος), end, esp. the end of life, death, with or without βίον.

τελέω, τελῶ or τελέσω, ἐτέλεσα, τετέλεκα, τετέλεσμαι, ἐτελέσθην (τέλος), bring to an end, complete, pay.

τέλος, -ους, τό, end, completion, issue; often, adv. τέλος, at last, in the end, finally, I, 9, 6; διὰ τέλους, from first to last, VI, 6, 11; τέλος ἔχειν, be at, or approaching, an end, VI, 5, 2; also, supreme authority, magistracy; in pl., of the Spartan Ephors, II, 6, 4; VII, 1, 34.

τέμαχος, -ους, τό (cf. τέμνω), slice.

τέμνω, τεμῶ, ἔτεμον (cf. Eng. atom), cut.

τέναγος, -ους, τό, shoal.

τερμίνθινος, -η, -ον (τέρμινθος, later form, τερέβινθος, ἡ, terebinth or turpentine-tree), of turpentine.

τέταρτος, -η, -ον (τέτταρες), fourth.

τετρακισχίλιοι (τέτταρες + χίλιοι), four thousand.

τετρακόσιοι, -αι, -α (τέτταρες+ἑκατόν), four hundred; in sing. with collective noun, I, 7, 10.

τετραμοιρία, -ας, ἡ (τέτταρες+μοῖρα, portion), a quadruple portion, four times as much.

τετραπλοῦς,-ῆ,-οῦν(τέτταρες+ √ πλα), fourfold, quadruple (cf. ἁπλοῦς, διπλοῦς, etc.).

τετταράκοντα (τέτταρες), forty.

τέτταρες, -α, four.

Τευθρανία, -ας, ἡ, Teuthrania, a district in southwestern Mysia.

τεύξεσθε, see τυγχάνω.

τεῦχος, -ους, τό (τεύχω, make, fashion), tool, vessel, jar, chest.

τεχνάζω (τέχνη), use art or cunning.

τέχνη, -ης, ἡ (cf. Eng. technical), art, skill, means, device.

τεχνικῶς, adv. (τεχνιχός, skilful), skilfully, artfully.

τέως, adv. (cf. ἕως), meanwhile, for a time, hitherto, VII, 5, 8.

τῇ, adv. (dat. fem. of the art.); here; τῇ μὲν ... τῇ δέ, in one place ... in another, IV, 8, 10; in some respects ... in others, III, 1, 12; so τῇ μὲν ... ὁπότε δέ, VI, 1, 20 f.

τῇδε, see ὅδε.

τήκω, perf. τέτηκα (cf. Lat. tabes, decay, Eng. thaw), melt.

Τηλεβόας, ὁ, the Teleboas, a river in Armenia, flowing into the Euphrates.

τήμερον (τ-, mutilated demonstr. pron. stem,+ἡμέρα), *today*.

Τημνίτης, -ου, ὁ, *a native of Temnus*, in Aeolis.

τηνικαῦτα, adv. *at that time, then*, answering to ἡνίκα or ἐπεί.

Τήρης, -ου, ὁ, *Teres*, ancestor of Seuthes, king of the Odrysae.

τιάρα, -ας, ἡ (Eng. *tiara*), *tiara*, a Persian headdress. The upright tiara was a badge of royalty, II, 5, 23.

τιαροειδής, -ες (τιάρα+εἶδος), *tiara-shaped*.

Τιβαρηνοί, -ῶν, οἱ, *the Tibarēni*, a tribe in Pontus.

Τίγρης, -ητος, ὁ, *the Tigris*, one of the two great rivers of Assyria.

τίθημι, θήσω, ἔθηκα, τέθηκα, ἐτέθην, 2 aor. mid. ἐθέμην; the perf. mid. is supplied by κεῖμαι (related to Lat. *dare*, Eng. *do*), *place, put, set, arrange;* of games, *institute*, I, 2, 10; θέσθαι τὰ ὅπλα, a military phrase, meaning most commonly, *halt under arms, i. e.*, in a position of rest, but ready at once to assume the defensive, I, 5, 14; or, *take a position under arms*, II, 2, 21, but sometimes also, *ground arms*, I, 5, 17; I, 10, 16.

Τιμασίων, -ωνος, ὁ, *Timasion*, of Dardanus in the Troad, elected general in the place of Clearchus.

τιμάω, -ήσω, etc. (τιμή), *value, honor*.

τιμή, -ῆς, ἡ (τίω, esteem), *value, price*, VII, 5, 2; VII, 8, 6; *honor, esteem*, I, 9, 29.

Τιμησίθεος, -ου, ὁ, *Timesitheus*, of Trapezus, πρόξενος of the Mossynoeci.

τίμιος, -α, -ον (τιμή), *held in honor, esteemed, precious, valuable*.

τιμωρέω, -ήσω, etc. (τιμωρός, *avenger*, from τιμή+ὁράω), *help, avenge;* mid., *take vengeance on, punish;* pass., *be punished*.

τιμωρία, -ας, ἡ (cf. τιμωρέω), *vengeance, punishment*, II, 6, 14.

Τιρίβαζος, -ου, ὁ, *Tiribazus*, governor of western Armenia.

τις, τι, gen. τινός, indef. pron., enclitic, as subst., *somebody, anybody, something, anything, one*, pl. *some, they, people;* often of a definite person whom one does not choose to name, I, 4, 12; as adj., *a, any, some, a certain, a sort of;* often with limiting force, μία τις, ἐλπίς, *any single hope*, II, 1, 19; σχεδόν τι, *pretty nearly*, VI, 4, 20; πόση τίς, *about how large*, II, 4, 21; ὁποῖόν τι, *what sort of a thing*, III, 1, 13.

τίς, τί, gen. τίνος, interrog. pron., *who, which, what, what kind of*, neut. often as adv., *why*.

Τισσαφέρνης, -ου, ὁ, *Tissaphernes*, a Persian noble, satrap of Caria, Lydia, and Ionia. See the Introd., § 23.

τιτρώσκω, τρώσω, ἔτρωσα, etc. (cf. τραῦμα), *wound*.

τλήμων, -ον, gen. -ονος (τλάω, *endure*), *suffering, wretched*.

τοί, post-pos. intensive particle, enclitic (orig. ethic dat. of τύ=σύ), *in truth, verily*, often best rendered by emphasis.

τοιγαροῦν, inferential conj. (τοί+γάρ+οὖν), *therefore, accordingly*.

τοίνυν, inferential conj., post-positive (τοί+νύν), *therefore, then, accordingly, moreover*.

τοιόσδε, -άδε, -όνδε (τοῖος, *such*+-δε), *such*, referring to what follows; esp., ἔλεξε τοιάδε, *he spoke as follows*.

τοιοῦτος, τοιαύτη, τοιοῦτο(ν), dem. pron., *of such a sort or kind, such*, regularly referring to what precedes (contrast τοιόσδε); ἐν τῷ τοιούτῳ, *at such a crisis*, V, 8, 20; *cf*. I, 7, 5, n.; τούτων τοιούτων ὄντων, *this being the case*, II, 5, 12.

τοῖχος, -ου, ὁ (*cf*. τεῖχος), *wall* (of a building).

τολμάω, τολμήσω, etc. (τόλμα, *daring*), *dare, have the courage, endure*, II, 2, 12; in a bad sense, *have the effrontery*, VI, 4, 14; VII, 7, 46.

Τολμίδης, -ου, ὁ, *Tolmides*, an Elean, herald of the Greek army.

τόξευμα, -ατος, τό (τοξεύω), *arrow*.

τοξεύω, τοξεύσω, etc. (τόξον), *shoot with a bow, shoot arrows*, abs.; pass. *be hit with an arrow*, I, 8, 20; IV, 1, 18.

τοξικός, -ή, -όν (τόξον), *pertaining to the bow;* as subst., ἡ τοξική (sc. τέχνη), *archery*, I, 9, 5.

τόξον, -ου, τό, *bow*.

τοξότης, -ου, ὁ (τόξον), *bowman, archer*.

τόπος, -ου, ὁ (*cf*. Eng. *topic*), *place, spot, district, region*.

τοσόσδε, τοσήδε, τοσόνδε, dem. pron. (τόσος, *so great*,+-δε), *so much*, in pl. *so many*, VI, 5, 19; *only so many, i. e., so few*, II, 4, 4.

τοσοῦτος, τοσαύτη, τοσοῦτο(ν), dem. pron., commoner than τοσόσδε, *of such a size or number, so great, so much*, pl., *so many;* often following ὅσος (*cf. quantus . . . tantus*), ὅσῳ . . . τοσούτῳ, with comps., *the more . . . the more*, I, 5, 9; τοσοῦτον, as adv., *so much*, I, 8, 13; III, 1, 45. εἶπε τοσοῦτον, *said only thus much*, I, 3, 15; II, 1, 9.

τότε, adv., *at that time, then;* τῶν τότε, *of the men of that time*, II, 2, 20.

τοτέ, adv., *at times;* τοτὲ μέν . . . τοτὲ δέ, *now . . . then*, VI, 1, 9.

τοὔμπαλιν, crasis for τὸ ἔμπαλιν.

τράγημα, -ατος, τό (ἔτραγον, *ate*), in pl., *dainties, sweetmeats*.

Τράλλεις, -εων, οἱ, *Tralles*, a city of Caria.

Τρανίψαι, -ῶν, οἱ, *the Tranipsae*, a Thracian tribe.

τράπεζα, -ης, ἡ (τέτταρες+πούς), *table*.

Τραπεζούντιος, -ου, ὁ (Τραπεζοῦς), *a Trapezuntian, native of Trapezus*.

Τραπεζοῦς, -οῦντος, ἡ, *Trapezus*, the modern Trebizond, a city in Pontus.

τράποιτο, see τρέπω.

τραῦμα, -ατος, τό (*cf*. τιτρώσκω), *wound*.

τράχηλος, -ου, ὁ, *throat, neck*.

τραχύς, -εῖα, -ύ, *rough, rugged, harsh;* ἡ τραχεῖα (sc. γῆ), *rough ground*, IV, 6, 12.

τρεῖς, τρία, gen. τριῶν (Lat. *tres*, Eng. *three*), *three*.

τρέπω, τρέψω, ἔτρεψα, ἔτραπον, τέτροφα and τέτραφα, τέτραμμαι, ἐτρέφθην and ἐτράπην (Lat. *torqueo*, Eng. *throw*), *turn, turn back, put to flight* (εἰς φυγήν), I, 8, 24; so in mid., V, 4, 16; mid., *turn oneself to, have recourse to*, II, 6, 5; *take flight*, IV, 8, 19; of places, *be turned toward, face*, III, 5, 15.

τρέφω, θρέψω, ἔθρεψα, τέτροφα, τέθραμμαι, ἐτρέφθην, ἐτράφην, *nourish, support, maintain*, V, 1, 12; oftener in pass., *be maintained*, I, 1, 9; *be reared*, III, 2, 13; τεθραμμένους, *fed up, fattened*, V, 4, 32. ἐλάνθανεν τρεφόμενον, see λανθάνω.

τρέχω, δραμοῦμαι, ἔδραμον, -δεδράμηκα, run.
τρέω, aor. ἔτρεσα (cf. Lat. tremo, shake), tremble; with acc., flee from in terror, 1, 9, 6. A poetic verb.
τρία, see τρεῖς.
τριάκοντα, indecl., thirty.
τριακόντορος, -ου, ἡ (τριάκοντα), a ship with thirty oars, triaconter.
τριακόσιοι, -αι, -α (τρεῖς+ἑκατόν), three hundred.
τριβή, -ῆς, ἡ (τρίβω, rub), a rubbing, wearing away; practice, V, 6, 15.
τριήρης, -ους, ἡ (τρεῖς+ √αρ, fit, or √ερ, row), properly an adj., sc. ναῦς, trireme, a ship with three banks of oars, warship; often contrasted with πλοῖον, transport.
τριηρίτης, -ου, ὁ (τριήρης), one serving on a trireme, sailor, VI, 6, 7.
τρίπηχυς, -υ (τρεῖς+πῆχυς), three cubits long.
τριπλάσιος, -α, -ον (τρεῖς+ √πλα), threefold, three times as large.
τρίπλεθρος, -ον (τρεῖς+πλέθρον), of three plethra, three plethra wide.
τρίπους, -ουν, gen., -οδος, ὁ (τρεῖς+πούς), three-footed; as subst. tripod, table with three legs.
τρίς, adv. (τρεῖς), three times; εἰς τρίς, somewhat stronger, up to three times, VI, 4, 16, 19.
τρισάσμενος, -η, -ον (τρίς+ἄσμενος), thrice-glad, very glad.
τρισκαίδεκα, indecl. (τρεῖς καὶ δέκα), thirteen.
τρισμύριοι, -αι, -α (τρεῖς + μύριοι), thirty thousand.
τρισχίλιοι, -αι, -α (τρεῖς + χίλιοι), three thousand.
τριταῖος, -α, -ον (τρίτος), on the third day.

τρίτος, -η, -ον (τρεῖς) third; τὸ τρίτον, the third time, I, 6, 8; τῇ τρίτῃ, on the third day, I, 7, 20; ἐπὶ τῷ τρίτῳ, at the third signal, II, 2, 4.
τρίχα and τριχῇ, adv. (τρεῖς), threefold, in three divisions.
τρίχινος, -η, -ον (θρίξ, τριχός, hair, Eng. trichina), made of hair.
τριχοίνικος, -ον (τρεῖς+χοῖνιξ), holding or filling three choinices.
τρόπαιον, -ου, τό (τροπή; cf. Eng. trophy), trophy, sometimes merely spoils affixed to a tree or post.
τροπή, -ῆς, ἡ (τρέπω), a turning (of the enemy), rout, flight.
τρόπος, -ου, ὁ (τρέπω), turn, manner, way, fashion; τόνδε τὸν τρόπον, in the following way, I, 1, 9; τρόπῳ τινί, after a fashion, II, 2, 17; ἐκ παντὸς τρόπου, by hook or crook, III, 1, 43; of a person, character, bent, πρὸς τοῦ Κύρου τρόπου, in keeping with Cyrus' character, I, 2, 11.
τροφή, -ῆς, ἡ (τρέφω), support, maintenance.
τροχάζω (cf. τροχός, wheel, Eng. truck), run forward.
τρυπάω, τετρύπημαι (τρύπη, hole), bore, pierce; τὰ ὦτα τετρυπημένον, with his ears bored, III, 1, 31.
Τρῳάς, -άδος, ἡ (Τροία, Troy), the Troad, the district in the north western part of Asia Minor.
τρωκτός, -ή, -όν (verbal of τρώγω, gnaw), that may be eaten, edible.
τρωτός, -ή, -όν (verbal of τιτρώσκω) vulnerable.
τυγχάνω, τεύξομαι, ἔτυχον, τετύχηκα: (1) trans., hit, with gen., III, 2, 19; reach, attain, meet, I, 4, 15; 9, 29; τῆς τελευτῆς, II, 6, 29; with

two gens., V, 7, 33; with acc. of thing and gen. of person, VI, 6, 32; (2) intrans., *happen, chance;* generally construed with a supplementary partic., which expresses the main idea; παρὼν ἐτύγχανε, *was there, as it happened*, I, 1, 2. The partic. is at times omitted (or is to be supplied from the context), II, 2, 17; III, 1, 3. Acc. abs. τυχόν, *perhaps*, VI, 1, 20.

Τυριάειον, -ου, τό, *Tyriaeum*, a city in Phrygia.

τυρός, -οῦ, ὁ, *cheese*, in pl. II, 4, 28.

τύρσις, -ιος, ἡ (*cf.* Lat. *turris, tower*), *tower, turret.*

τύχη, -ης, ἡ (*cf.* τυγχάνω), *fortune, luck.*

τυχών, see τυγχάνω.

Υ

ὑβρίζω, ὑβριῶ, ὕβρισα, ὕβρικα, ὕβρισμαι, ὑβρίσθην (ὕβρις), *treat with indignity* or *outrage, abuse, insult*; abs., *act with insolence.*

ὕβρις, -εως, ἡ (ὑπέρ), *overweeningness, arrogance, insolence, wantonness.*

ὑβριστότερος, -α -ον and sup. ὑβριστότατος, -η -ον, *more* or *most insolent* or *wanton*, V, 8, 3, 22. No positive occurs, but the noun ὑβριστής has adjectival force.

ὑγιαίνω (ὑγιής, *healthy*; *cf.* Eng. *hygiene*), *be well, strong.*

ὑγρότης, -ητος, ἡ (ὑγρός, *wet*), *wetness, suppleness*, V, 8, 15.

ὑδροφορέω (ὑδροφόρος), *carry water.*

ὑδροφόρος, -ον (ὕδωρ+φέρω), *bearing water;* as subst., *water-carrier*, IV, 5, 10.

ὕδωρ, -ατος, τό (Lat. *unda*, Eng. *water; cf. hydraulic, etc.) water;* ὕδωρ ἐξ οὐρανοῦ, *rain*, IV, 2, 2.

υἱϊδοῦς, -οῦ, ὁ (*cf. υἱός*), *grandson.*

υἱός, -οῦ, ὁ (often spelt ὑός), *son.*

ὕλη, -ης, ἡ, (Lat. *silva*), *wood, forest, brush.*

ὑμεῖς, see σύ.

ὑμέτερος, -α, -ον (ὑμεῖς), *your, yours.*

ὑπάγω (ἄγω), *lead on, advance slowly, advance;* mid., *lead on* or *suggest craftily*, II, 1, 18.

ὑπαίθριος, -α, -ον (ὑπό+αἰθρία, *open air*), *in the open air.*

ὑπαίτιος, -ον (ὑπό+αἰτία), *under a charge, censurable*, III, 1, 5, n.

ὑπακούω (ἀκούω), *harken to, heed,* IV, 1, 9; *obey*, VII, 3, 7.

ὑπαντάω (ἀντάω, ἀντήσω, ἤντησα, *meet*), *go to meet.*

ὑπαντιάζω, *go to meet, meet.*

ὕπαρχος, -ου, ὁ (ἄρχω), *subordinate officer, lieutenant;* in a province, *prefect, vice-satrap*, IV, 4, 4.

ὑπάρχω (ἄρχω), properly, *be under, serve as foundation, begin*, with partic., II, 3, 23; *support, favor*, I, 1, 4; with dat. (of possessor) it may often be rendered, *have to begin with, have to count upon*, II, 2, 11; ἐκ τῶν ὑπαρχόντων, *as far as their means permitted*, VI, 4, 9.

ὑπασπιστής, -οῦ, ὁ (ὑπό+ἀσπίς), *shield-bearer, squire.*

ὑπείκω (εἴκω, εἴξω, εἶξα, *yield; cf.* Eng. *weak*), *give way, yield, submit.*

ὕπειμι (εἰμί), *be under.*

ὑπεληλυθέναι, see ὑπέρχομαι.

ὑπέρ, prep. with gen. and acc. (*cf.* Lat, *super*, Eng. *over*): (1) with gen., of place, *over, above*, I, 10, 12; *beyond*, I, 10, 14; II, 6, 2 (*cf.* acc. I, 1, 9); *for, on behalf of*, I, 3, 4; *in the name of*, V, 5, 13; (2) with acc., *over, beyond*, I, 1, 9 (*cf.* gen. II, 6, 2), of numbers, *above, more than*, V, 3, 1

ὑπεράλλομαι (ἄλλομαι), *leap over.*

ὑπερανατείνω (τείνω), *stretch out over.*

ὑπερβαίνω (βαίνω), *go over, cross, scale.*

ὑπερβάλλω (βάλλω), *throw over;* intr. *pass* or *cross over,* IV, 1, 7.

ὑπερβολή, -ῆς, ἡ (βάλλω), *a passing over, crossing, pass.*

ὑπερδέξιος, -ον (ὑπέρ+δεξιός), *above on the right, above,* III, 4, 37; V, 7, 31.

ὑπερέρχομαι, ὑπερῆλθον (ἔρχομαι), *cross* or *pass over.*

ὑπερέχω (ἔχω), *be above, project, overhang.*

ὕπερθεν, adv. (ὑπέρ), *from above, overhead.*

ὑπερκάθημαι (κάθημαι), *be stationed above,* with gen.

ὑπερόριος, -α, -ον, or -ος, -ον (ὑπέρ+ὅρος, *boundary; cf.* ὁρίζω), *over the border, foreign;* ἡ ὑπερορία, *foreign lands,* VII, 1, 27.

ὑπερύψηλος, -ον (ὑπέρ+ὑψηλός), *exceedingly high.*

ὑπέρχομαι (ἔρχομαι), *go under, go secretly, withdraw,* V, 2, 30.

ὑπέσχετο, ὑπεσχημένοι, ὑπέσχον, see ὑπισχνέομαι.

ὑπέχω (ἔχω), *undergo, submit to;* in V, 8, 1, δίκην ὑποσχεῖν, *give an account for* (gen.).

ὑπήκοος, -ον (ὑπακούω), *listening to, obedient, subject to;* as subst., *subject, vassal.*

ὑπηρετέω, ὑπηρετήσω, etc. (ὑπηρέτης), *serve as menial, serve, help,* dat., I, 9, 18; *provide,* III, 5, 8.

ὑπηρέτης, -ου, ὁ (ὑπό+ἐρέτης, *rower*), properly, *under-rower;* then, *underling, menial, servant.*

ὑπισχνέομαι, ὑποσχήσομαι, ὑπεσχόμην, ὑπέσχημαι, *promise, undertake* (abs. or with infin., generally fut.).

ὕπνος, -ου, ὁ, *sleep.*

ὑπό (by elision ὑπ' or ὑφ'), prep. with gen., dat., or acc.; *cf.* Lat. *sub. under:* (1) with gen., lit. *from under,* VI, 4, 22, 25; *under;* ὑπὸ μαστίγων, *under the lash,* III, 4, 25; often of the agent, with passives, *by, through, at the hands of,* I, 1, 10; so with virtual passives, παθεῖν, *etc.*, I, 3, 4; also with things (by a slight personification), ὑπὸ λιμοῦ, I, 5, 5; (2) with dat., *under, at the foot of,* with vbs. of rest, I, 2, 8; *in the power of,* VII, 2, 2; (3) with acc., *under,* with vbs. of motion, I, 8, 27. In composition ὑπο- means *under, secretly,* or has the force of *somewhat, rather.*

ὑποδεέστερος, -α, -ον (ὑπό+δέω, *lack*), comp.; the positive ὑποδεής (*cf.* ἐνδεής) does not occur, *inferior,* I, 9, 5.

ὑποδείκνυμι (δείκνυμι), *show privately, give indications,* V, 7, 12.

ὑποδέχομαι (δέχομαι), *receive under one's protection, welcome.*

ὑποδέω (δέω), *tie under;* mid., *bind one's sandals on;* ὑποδεδημένοι, *with their shoes on,* IV, 5, 14.

ὑπόδημα, -ατος, τό (ὑποδέω), *sandal, shoe.*

ὑποζύγιον, -ου, τό (ὑπό+ζυγόν, *yoke*), *beast of burden, baggage animal.*

ὑποκαταβαίνω (βαίνω), *go down a little,* VII, 4, 11.

ὑπολαμβάνω (λαμβάνω), *take* or *receive under one's protection,* I, 1, 7; *take up* (the discourse, λόγον), *reply, answer,* II, 1, 15; μεταξὺ ὑπολαβών, *interrupting him in the midst of his talk,* III, 1, 27.

ὑπολείπω (λείπω), *leave behind;* pass., *be left behind, fall behind.*
ὑπολόχαγος, -ου, ὁ (ὑπό+λοχαγός), *lieutenant,* probably a captain of fifty =πεντηκοντήρ, V, 2, 13.
ὑπολύω (λύω), *loose beneath;* mid., *untie one's sandals,* IV, 5, 13.
ὑπομαλακίζομαι (μαλακίζομαι), *weaken a little, begin to yield.*
ὑπομένω (μένω), *stay behind, wait, halt; await an attack, stand one's ground; wait for,* IV,1,21.
ὑπόμνημα, -ατος, τό (μιμνήσκω), *reminder, mention,* I, 6, 3.
ὑπόπεμπτος, -ον (verbal of ὑποπέμπω), *sent secretly* or *with covert purpose, sent as a spy.*
ὑποπέμπω (πέμπω), *send secretly, send as a spy.*
ὑποπίνω (πίνω), *drink a little;* perf. partic. ὑποπεπωκώς, *rather drunk,* VII, 3, 29.
ὑποπτεύω, ὑπώπτευον, ὑπώπτευσα, *suspect, apprehend, mistrust,* with acc., infin., or μή.
ὑποστρατηγέω (στρατηγέω), *be lieutenant, be general under* (dat.).
ὑποστράτηγος, -ου, ὁ (ὑπό+στρατηγός), *under-general, lieutenant-general.*
ὑποστρέφω (στρέφω), *turn* or *wheel round, face about,* VI, 6, 38; ὑποστρέψας, *evading the trap,* II, 1, 18, n.
ὑποσχεῖν, see ὑπέχω.
ὑπόσχησθε, ὑπόσχοιτο, ὑποσχόμενος, see ὑπισχνέομαι.
ὑπουργός, -όν (ὑπό+ √ εργ), *conducive to,* V, 8, 15.
ὑποφαίνω (φαίνω), intr., *shine a little;* of the day, *begin to dawn.*
ὑποφείδομαι (φείδομαι, φείσομαι, *spare*), *spare somewhat* or *of set purpose,* IV, 1, 8.

ὑποχείριος, -ον (ὑπό+χείρ), *under the hands of, in the power of* (dat.).
ὕποχος, -ον (ὑπό+ἔχω), *under the control of, subject to* (dat.).
ὑποχωρέω (χωρέω), *make way, give way, withdraw, retreat,* I, 4, 18; *move on,* IV, 5, 19.
ὑποψία, -ας, ἡ (ὑφοράω), *suspicion, distrust, apprehension.*
Ὑρκάνιοι, -ων, οἱ, *the Hyrcanians,* a people living southeast of the Caspian Sea.
ὗς, ὑός, ὁ, ἡ (*cf.* σῦς), *swine, pig.*
ὑστεραῖος, -α, -ον (ὕστερος), *later, following, next;* often with ἡμέρα omitted, *e.g.,* τῇ ὑστεραίᾳ, *on the following day,* I, 2, 21; τὴν ὑστεραίαν, III, 5, 13.
ὑστερέω, -ήσω, etc. (ὕστερος), *be* or *come too late for* (gen.).
ὑστερίζω (ὕστερος), *be behindhand.*
ὕστερος, *later, latter, following, behind;* neut. as adv., ὕστερον, *later, afterward.*
ὑφ', see ὑπό.
ὑφειμένως, adv. (ὑφειμένος, perf. partic. of ὑφίημι), *submissively.*
ὑφεῖτο, see ὑφίημι.
ὑφέξω, see ὑπέχω.
ὑφηγέομαι (ἡγέομαι), *lead on slowly.*
ὑφίημι (ἵημι), *put under, concede, give up,* III, 5, 5; *permit,* with dat. and infin., VI, 6, 31; mid., *put oneself under, yield, surrender,* III, 1, 17.
ὑφίστημι (ἵστημι), *place under, station secretly,* IV, 1, 14, n.; intr. in mid. and 2 aor. act., *undertake, promise, volunteer,* IV, 1, 26; *withstand, resist,* III, 2, 11.
ὑφοράω (ὁράω), *regard with suspicion.*

ὑψηλός, -ή, -όν (cf. ὕψος), high, lofty; τὸ ὑψηλόν, height, III, 4, 25.
ὕψος, -ους, τό (ὑπέρ), height.

Φ

φαγεῖν, φάγωσιν, see ἐσθίω.
φαιδρός, -ά -όν (φάω, shine; cf. φαίνω), bright, beaming.
φαίη, see φημί.
φαίνω, φανῶ, ἔφηνα, -πέφαγκα and πέφηνα, πέφασμαι, ἐφάνην (φάος, φῶς, light), bring to light, show, IV, 3, 13; give light, shine, IV, 4, 9; pass., be shown, appear, seem, with infin. (which may be omitted) of mere semblance, I, 3, 19; with partic. of what is true, οὐ φθονῶν ἐφαίνετο, he plainly did not envy, I, 9, 19.
φάλαγξ, -γγος, ἡ, phalanx, battle-array, generally a close formation, eight men deep, I, 2, 17; without reference to the normal form, the main body, III, 3, 11; ἐπὶ φάλαγγος, in line of battle IV, 3, 26.
Φαλῖνος, -ου, ὁ, Phalīnus, a Greek in the service of Tissaphernes.
φανεῖται, φανέντος see φαίνω.
φανερός, -ά, -όν (φαίνω), in plain sight, clear, evident; ἐν τῷ φανερῷ, openly, I, 3, 21; common with partics. in pers. constr., ἐπιβουλεύων μοι φανερὸς γέγονας, it has become clear that you are plotting against me, I, 6, 8.
φανερῶς, adv. (φανερός) plainly, manifestly.
φαρέτρα, -ας, ἡ, quiver.
φάρμακον, -ου, τό (cf. Eng. pharmacy), drug, poison.
φαρμακοποσία, -ας, ἡ (φάρμακον+πίνω), a taking of physic or poison.

Φαρνάβαζος, -ου, ὁ, Pharnabazus, satrap of Lesser Phrygia and Bithynia.
Φασιανοί, -ῶν, οἱ (φᾶσις), the Phasians, a name given to the people living on the banks of the Phasis river: (1) in Colchis, V, 6, 36; (2) in Armenia, IV, 6, 5.
φασίν, see φημί.
Φᾶσις, -ιος, ὁ, the Phasis, a river: (1) in Colchis, V, 6, 36; (2) in Armenia, IV, 6, 4.
φάσκω (φημί), found only in pres. system, say, assert, allege.
φατέ, see φημί.
φαῦλος, -η, -ον, mean, trifling, of no account.
φέρω, οἴσω, ἤνεγκα, ἤνεγκον, ἐνήνοχα, ἐνήνεγμαι, ἐνέχθην (Lat. fero, Eng. bear), bear, carry, bring; carry off, II, 1, 6; yield, produce, I, 2, 22; of tribute, pay, V, 5, 7; of roads, lead, III, 5, 15; so of winds, V, 7, 7; mid., bear off as one's own, VI, 6, 1; pass., often of violent motion, be borne, be hurled, be dashed, fly, I, 8, 20, n.; χαλεπῶς or βαρέως φέρειν, take it ill, be troubled, I, 3, 3; II, 1, 4; φέρειν καὶ ἄγειν, plunder, ravage, II, 6, 5, n.
φεύγω, φεύξομαι and φευξοῦμαι, ἔφυγον, πέφευγα, flee, take flight; flee one's country, be banished, be an exile, IV, 8, 25; οἱ φεύγοντες, the exiles, I, 1, 7.
φημί, φήσω, ἔφησα, rare save in pres., impf., and 2 aor., the fut. being generally ἐρῶ, the aor. εἶπον and the perf. εἴρηκα, declare, affirm, say, regularly calling for the infin. constr.; an isolated case with ὅτι, VII, 1, 5; frequently parenthetic, said he, said they, etc.; in answers, say yes (I, 6, 7), unless a neg. is added, οὐκ ἔφη,

said no, denied, IV, 1, 23. A neg. which in Eng. is attached to the dependent vb. is in Greek regularly attached to φημί; οὐκ ἔφασαν ἰέναι, *they declared they would not go,* I, 3, 1. φημί is the strongest of the vbs. of saying, meaning, *aver, asseverate;* it may even take the neg. μή, as a vb. of swearing.

φῃς, φήσῃ, φήσω, see φημί.

φθάνω, φθάσω or φθήσομαι, ἔφθασα, *get the start of, anticipate, outstrip, act first,* often followed by πρίν, II, 5, 5; often with suppl. partic. which expresses the main idea; φθάσαι καταλαβόντες, *to seize in advance,* I, 3, 14; *cf.* III, 4, 49; πορευόμενον δ' αὐτὸν φθάνει ἡμέρα γενομένη, *the break of day surprised him on his way,* V, 7, 16.

φθέγγομαι, φθέγξομαι, ἐφθεγξάμην (*cf.* Eng. *diphthong), make* or *utter a sound, cry out, scream, shout.*

φθείρω, φθερῶ, ἔφθειρα, ἔφθαρκα and ἔφθορα, ἔφθαρμαι, ἐφθάρην, *corrupt, spoil;* of a country, *lay waste,* IV, 7, 20.

φθονέω, φθονήσω, *etc.* (φθόνος, ὁ, *envy*), *envy* (dat.).

φιάλη, -ης, ἡ, (*cf.* Eng. *phial, vial*), *a shallow bowl,* for drinking or pouring libations.

φιλαίτερον, see φίλος.

φιλέω, φιλήσω, *etc.* (φίλος), *love.*

Φιλήσιος, -ου, ὁ, *Philēsius,* of Achaea, elected general in the place of Menon, III, 1, 47.

φιλία, -ας, ἡ (φίλος), *friendship;* διὰ φιλίας ἰέναι τινί, see διά; πρὸς φιλίαν ἀφιέναι, *let go in peace,* I, 3, 19.

φιλικός, -ή, -όν (φίλος), *friendly.*

φιλικῶς, adv. (φιλικός), *in a friendly manner;* φιλικῶς διακεῖσθαι, *be on friendly terms with,* II, 5, 27.

φίλιος, -α, -ον (φίλος), *friendly, at peace with;* esp. of countries with or without χώρα.

φίλιππος, -ον (φίλος+ἵππος), *fond of horses,* I, 9, 5, in sup.

φιλόθηρος, -ον (φίλος+θήρα), *fond of hunting,* I, 9, 6, in sup.

φιλοκερδέω (φιλοκερδής, *greedy for gain,* φίλος+κέρδος), *be greedy for gain.*

φιλοκίνδυνος, -ον (φίλος+κίνδυνος), *loving danger, venturesome,* II, 6, 7; sup. I, 9, 6.

φιλομαθής, -ές (φίλος+μανθάνω), *fond of learning, eager to learn.*

φιλονικία, -ας, ἡ (φίλος+νίκη), *rivalry,* IV, 8, 27.

φιλοπόλεμος, -ον (φίλος+πόλεμος), *fond of* or *devoted to war.*

φίλος, -η, -ον, adj., *friendly,* comp. φιλαίτερον, I, 9, 29; commonly as a noun, *friend,* I, 1, 2.

φιλόσοφος, -ου, ὁ (φίλος+σοφός), *lover of wisdom, philosopher.*

φιλοστρατιώτης, -ου, adj. (φίλος+στρατιώτης), *friend of the soldiers,* VII, 6, 4.

φιλοτιμέομαι, φιλοτιμήσομαι, *etc.* (φιλότιμος, *loving honor*), *love* or *seek honor, be ambitious, jealous.*

φιλοφρονέομαι, aor. ἐφιλοφρονησάμην or ἐφιλοφρονήθην (φίλος+φρήν), *be well disposed, show kindness;* with acc., *treat kindly, greet kindly,* II, 5, 27.

Φλειάσιος, -ου, ὁ, *a Phliasian, native of Phlius* in Peloponnēsus.

φλυαρέω (φλύαρος, *nonsense*), *talk nonsense.*

φλυαρία, -ας, ἡ, *nonsense, rubbish;* in pl., I, 3, 17.

φοβερός, -ά, -όν (φόβος), *frightful, terrible,* II, 5, 9; pass., *filled with fear, fearful,* V, 7, 2.

φοβέω, φοβήσω, etc. (φόβος), *frighten, scare,* IV, 5, 17; generally deponent, *fear, be afraid, be frightened,* I, 3, 17.

φόβος, -ου, ὁ, *fear, terror, panic;* τὸν ἐκ τῶν Ἑλλήνων εἰς τοὺς βαρβάρους φόβον, *the fear inspired by the Greeks in the barbarians,* I, 2, 18.

Φοινίκη, -ης, ἡ (Φοῖνιξ), *Phoenicia,* the district on the coast of Syria, between the Lebanon mountains and the sea.

φοινικιστής, -οῦ, ὁ (cf. φοινικοῦς), *a wearer of the purple,* i.e., an officer of rank at the Persian court; according to others, *purple-dyer,* I, 2, 20, n.

φοινικοῦς, -ῆ, -οῦν (Φοῖνιξ, since the Phoenicians discovered the dye), *purple, red, scarlet.*

φοῖνιξ, -ικος, ὁ, *palm tree, palm,* I, 5, 10; οἶνος φοινίκων, *palm wine,* II, 3, 14.

Φοῖνιξ, -ικος, *a Phoenician, native of Phoenicia.*

Φολόη, -ης, ἡ, *Pholoe,* a range of mountains between Arcadia and Elis.

φορέω, φορήσω, etc. (φέρω), *bear habitually, wear.*

φόρος, -ου, ὁ (φέρω), *tribute.*

φορτίον, -ου, τό (φέρω), *burden, load.*

φράζω, φράσω, etc. (Eng. *phrase*), *tell* (in detail), *set forth, explain, bid.*

Φρασίας, -ου, ὁ, *Phrasias,* an Athenian, commanding a division of the Greek army.

φρέαρ, φρέατος, τό (cf. Lat. *ferveo*), *well, cistern.*

φρονέω, φρονήσω, etc. (φρήν, *mind*), *have understanding, be wise, be minded;* μέγα φρονεῖν, *be proud, be elated,* III, 1, 27; μεῖζον φρονεῖν, *be too proud,* V, 6, 8.

φρόνημα, -ατος, τό (φρονέω), *mind, spirit, courage.*

φρόνιμος, -ον (φρήν, *mind*), *prudent, wise, shrewd.*

φροντίζω, φροντιῶ, ἐφρόντισα, πεφρόντικα (φρήν), *take thought, be anxious,* II, 3, 25; also, *devise, plan,* II, 6, 8.

φρούραρχος, -ου, ὁ (φρουρά+ἄρχω), *commander of a garrison.*

φρουρέω, φρουρήσω, etc. (πρό+ὁράω), *watch, guard.*

φρούριον, -ου, τό (φρουρός), *guard, garrison, citadel.*

φρουρός, -οῦ, ὁ (πρό+ὁράω), *guard;* in pl., *garrison,* VII, 1, 20.

φρύγανα, -ων, τά (φρύγω, *roast*), *dry sticks, faggots.*

Φρυγία, -ας, ἡ, *Phrygia,* a large territory in central Asia Minor, I, 2, 6; called Φρυγία ἡ μεγάλη (I, 9, 7) to distinguish it from the district on the Propontis also called Phrygia (V, 6, 24).

Φρυνίσκος, -ου, ὁ, *Phryniscus,* an Achaean, one of the Greek generals.

Φρύξ, Φρυγός, ὁ, *a Phrygian, native of Phrygia.*

φυγάς, -άδος, ὁ (φεύγω), *exile, fugitive.*

φυγή, -ῆς, ἡ (φεύγω), *flight, rout; exile, banishment,* VII, 7, 57.

φυγόντες, see φεύγω.

φυλακή, -ῆς, ἡ (φυλάττω), *watch, guard, guard-duty;* also collective, *body of guards, garrison,* I, 1, 6; of time, *watch,* IV, 1, 5.

φύλαξ, -ακος, ὁ (φυλάττω), *guard, picket;* in pl., *bodyguard,* I, 2, 12.

φυλάττω, φυλάξω, ἐφύλαξα, πεφύλαχα, πεφύλαγμαι, ἐφυλάχθην, intrans., *keep watch* or *guard,* I, 2, 22; trans., *guard, defend, keep,* I, 2, 1; mid., *be on one's guard, take* *care, guard against,* acc., I, 6, 9 so with μή, II, 2, 16; with ὥστε μή, VII, 3, 35.

φυσάω, φυσήσω, ἐφυσήθην (φῦσα, *bellows*), *blow up, inflate.*

Φύσκος, -ου, ὁ, *the Physcus,* a river flowing into the Tigris.

φυτεύω, φυτεύσω, etc. (φυτόν, *plant,* from verbal of φύω), *plant, set out.*

φύω, φύσω, etc. (Lat. *fui,* Eng. *be*), *bring forth, produce.*

Φωκαΐς, -ίδος, ἡ (Φώκαια, *Phocaea*), *a woman of Phocaea, Phocaean woman.*

φωνή, -ῆς, ἡ (φημί), *voice, speech, language, dialect.*

φῶς, φωτός, τό (for φάος; cf. φαίνω), *light, daylight.*

X

χαίρω, χαιρήσῳ κεχάρηκα, ἐχάρην, *rejoice, be glad;* imperat. χαῖρε, often, *farewell,* hence ἐᾶν χαίρειν, *bid farewell to, give up,* VII, 3, 23; partic. χαίρων, often = *with impunity,* οὐ χαίροντες ἂν ἀπαλλάξαιτε, *you wouldn't get off without paying for it,* V, 6, 32.

Χαλδαῖοι, -ων, οἱ, *the Chaldaeans,* a warlike tribe in Armenia.

χαλεπαίνω, χαλεπανῶ, ἐχαλέπανα, ἐχαλεπάνθην (χαλεπός), *be severe, be angry;* so in pass., IV, 6, 2.

χαλεπός, -ή, -όν, *hard, difficult, dangerous, harsh, stern, fierce;* τὸ χαλεπόν, *severity, violence,* II, 6, 11; IV, 5, 4.

χαλεπῶς, adv. (χαλεπός), *hardly, with difficulty;* χαλεπῶς φέρειν, *take it ill, be distressed,* I, 3, 3; χαλεπῶς ἔχειν, *be angry,* VI, 4, 16.

χαλινόω, ἐχαλίνωσα (χαλινός, *bridle*), *bridle.*

χαλκός, -οῦ, ὁ, *copper, bronze.*

χαλκοῦς, -ῆ, -οῦν (χαλκός), *of bronze, bronze.*

χάλκωμα, -ατος, τό (χαλκόω, *make in bronze,* χαλκός), *bronze or copper vessel.*

Χάλος, -ου, ὁ, *the Chalus,* a river in northern Syria.

Χάλυβες, -ων, οἱ, *the Chalybes, Chalybians,* a warlike tribe of Pontus.

χαράδρα, -ας, ἡ, *torrent; gorge or ravine* cut by a torrent.

χαράκωμα, -ατος, τό (χαρακόω, *fence in with stakes;* χάραξ, *stake*), *palisade, stockade.*

χαρίεις, -εσσα, -εν (χάρις), *pretty, clever,* III, 5, 12.

χαρίζομαι, χαριοῦμαι, ἐχαρισάμην, κεχάρισμαι (χάρις), *favor, please, oblige* one (dat.) *in something* (acc.).

χάρις, -ιτος, ἡ (χαίρω), *grace, favor, thanks, gratitude;* χάριν εἰδέναι or χάριν ἔχειν, *feel grateful,* I, 4, 15; II, 5, 14; χάριν ἀποδοῦναι, *requite a favor,* I, 4, 15; τοῖς θεοῖς χάρις, *heaven be praised,* III, 3, 14.

Χαρμάνδη, -ης, ἡ, *Charmande,* a large city on the Euphrates.

Χαρμῖνος, -ου, ὁ, *Charmīnus,* a Spartan, ambassador from Thibron to the Greek army.

χειμών, -ῶνος, ὁ (Lat. *hiems*), *storm, wintry weather, winter, cold.*

χείρ, χειρός, ἡ, *hand;* εἰς χεῖρας ἰέναι, *come to close quarters,* IV, 7, 15 (cf. εἰς χεῖρας δέχεσθαι, IV, 3, 31), but I, 2, 26, εἰς χεῖρας ἐλθεῖν τινι, *come into the power of;* οἱ ἐκ χειρὸς βάλλοντες, see βάλλω; ἐκ χειρός, *hand to hand,* V, 4, 25.

Χειρίσοφος, -ου, ὁ (χείρ+σοφός), *Cherisophus,* a Spartan sent by the ephors to join Cyrus' expedition, I, 4, 3. After the murder of the generals he was elected to that office and with Xenophon conducted the Greek retreat; his death, VI, 4, 11.

χειρόομαι, χειρώσομαι (χείρ), *get into one's power, subdue.*

χειροπληθής, -ές (χείρ+ √ πλα), *filling the hand, as large as the hand.*

χειροποίητος, -ον (χείρ+ποιέω), *made by hand, artificial.*

χείρων, -ον, comp. of κακός, *worse, inferior.*

Χερρόνησος, -ου, ἡ (χέρρος or χέρσος, land+νῆσος), *Chersonēsus, the Thracian peninsula, northwest of the Hellespont.*

χηλή, -ῆς, ἡ, *hoof;* then, *breakwater* (from its shape), VII, 1, 17.

χήν, χηνός, ὁ or ἡ (Lat. *anser*, Eng. *gander, goose*), *goose.*

χθές, adv. (*cf.* Lat. *heri*, Eng. *yester-*), *yesterday.*

χίλιοι, -αι, -α, *thousand.*

χιλός, -οῦ, ὁ, *fodder, grass,* I, 5, 7; with ξηρός, *hay,* IV, 5, 33.

χιλόω (χιλός), *feed, of horses.*

χίμαιρα, -ας, ἡ (*cf.* Eng. *chimaera*), *she-goat.*

Χίος, -ου, ὁ (Χίος, ἡ, *Chios*), *a Chian, native of Chios.*

χιτών, -ῶνος, ὁ, *undergarment, tunic.*

χιτωνίσκος, -ου, ὁ (dim. of χιτών), *short tunic,* V, 4, 13.

χιών, -όνος, ἡ (*cf.* Lat. *hiems, winter*), *snow.*

χλαμύς, -ύδος, ἡ, *cloak* or *mantle.*

χοῖνιξ, -ικος, ἡ, *choenix,* an Attic dry measure containing a little less than a quart.

χοίρειος, -α, -ον (χοῖρος, *pig*), *of a pig, of swine;* with κρέα, *pork,* IV, 5, 31.

χοῖρος, -ου, ὁ, ἡ, *young pig.*

χορεύω (χορός), *dance.*

χορός, -οῦ, ὁ (*cf.* Eng. *chorus, choir*), *chorus, band of dancers, dance.*

χόρτος, -ου, ὁ, *grass, fodder,* I, 5, 5; with κοῦφος, *hay,* I, 5, 10.

χράομαι, χρήσομαι, ἐχρησάμην, κέχρημαι, ἐχρήσθην, *use, enjoy, have, treat, find,* abs. or with dat.; often with inner obj., τί βούλεται ἡμῖν χρῆσθαι, *what use he wishes to make of us,* I, 3, 18; χρῆσθαι ὅ, τι ἂν βούλῃ, *treat as you may see fit,* VI, 6, 20.

χρή (properly a noun, *sc.* ἐστί), *it is necessary, one must,* with acc. and infin., I, 3, 11; χρῆναι, as infin., I, 4, 14.

χρῄζω, only in pres. system (akin to χράομαι), *want, wish, desire.*

χρῆμα, -ατος, τό (χράομαι), *a thing used,* generally pl., *goods, possessions,* esp. *money,* I, 1, 9.

χρηματιστικός, -ή, -όν (χρηματίζω, *do business,* from χρῆμα), *pertaining to business* or *money-making;* of an omen, *portending gain,* VI, 1, 23.

χρῆναι, see χρή.

χρῆσθαι, see χράομαι.

χρήσιμος, -η, -ον, or -ος, -ον (χράομαι), *useful, serviceable.*

χρηστός, -ή, -όν (χράομαι), *serviceable, of use, worthy, trusty,* I, 8, 1.

χρῖμα, -ατος, τό (χρίω), *ointment.*

χρίω, χρίσω, etc. (*cf.* Lat. *frio, frico, rub,* Eng. *grind, Christ*), *rub, anoint.*

χρόνος, -ου, ὁ (*cf.* Eng. *chronology,* etc.), *time;* πολλοῦ χρόνου, *in a long while,* I, 9, 25.

χρυσίον, -ου, τό (dim. of χρυσός), *piece of gold, gold coin.*

Χρυσόπολις, -εως, ἡ, *Chrysopolis,* a city on the Bosporus, opposite Byzantium.

χρυσός, -οῦ, ὁ (cf. Eng. chrysanthemum, etc.), *gold*.

χρυσοῦς, -ῆ, -οῦν (χρυσός), *golden, of gold;* less strictly, *gold-mounted*, I, 2, 27; *gilded*, V, 3, 12.

χρυσοχάλινος, -ον (χρυσός+χαλινός, *bridle*), *with golden (i. e., gold-mounted) bridle*, I, 2, 27.

χώρα, -ας, ἡ (cf. χῶρος), *place;* in military sense, *post, position*, I, 5, 17; I, 8, 17; generally in a wider sense, *country, region, land*, I, 1, 11; ἐν ἀνδραπόδων χώρᾳ εἶναι, *be counted a slave*, V, 6, 13; ἐν οὐδεμιᾷ χώρᾳ εἶναι, *be held in no esteem*, V, 7, 28.

χωρέω, χωρήσω, etc. (χῶρος), *move, march, advance, withdraw;* of missiles, *penetrate*, IV, 2, 28; of measures, *hold, contain*, I, 5, 6.

χωρίζω, ἐχώρισα, κεχώρισμαι (χωρίς), *separate, set apart*, VI, 5, 11; pass. *be separate, be different from*, V, 4, 34.

χωρίον, -ου, τό (dim. of χῶρος), *place, spot, space;* hence, *farm, estate*, V, 3, 7; *town*, I, 4, 6; *stronghold, fort*, I, 2, 24.

χωρίς, adv., *apart*, III, 5, 17; as prep. with gen., *apart from*, I, 4, 13.

χῶρος, -ου, ὁ (cf. χώρα), *place, spot, region*.

Ψ

Ψάρος, -ου, ὁ, *the Psarus*, a river flowing through Cilicia.

ψέγω, *blame*.

ψέλιον, -ου, τό, *bracelet*, worn by Persians of rank.

ψευδενέδρα, -ας, ἡ (ψευδής+ἐνέδρα), *sham ambuscade*.

ψευδής, -ές, (ψεύδω), *false, untrue;* τὰ ψευδῆ, *lies*, II, 6, 26.

ψεύδω, ψεύσω, etc. (cf. Eng. pseudonym), *deceive;* mid., *lie, cheat,*
deceive, act falsely; pass., *be deceived*, abs. or with acc.

ψηφίζομαι, ψηφιοῦμαι, ἐψηφισάμην, etc. (ψῆφος), *vote, resolve, decree*.

ψῆφος, -ου, ἡ (cf. ψάω, *rub*), *pebble, ballot;* hence, *decree*, VII, 7, 57.

ψιλός, -ή, -όν, *stripped, bare;* of a country, *barren*, I, 5, 5; οἱ ψιλοί, *light-armed troops*, V, 2, 16; cf. III, 3, 7.

ψιλόω, ψιλώσω, etc. (ψιλός), *strip bare;* pass., *be cleared of, left bare of, deserted by*, I, 10, 13; IV, 3, 27.

ψοφέω (ψόφος), *make a sound, ring*.

ψόφος, -ου, ὁ, *noise*.

ψυχή, -ῆς, ἡ, *breath of life, spirit, soul, life*.

ψῦχος, -ους, τό (ψύχω, *breathe, blow*), *cold*, in pl., III, 1, 23, n.

Ω

ὦ, exclamation, *O*, used commonly with vocatives in Greek, where it should be left untranslated

ὦ, see εἰμί.

ᾧ, see ὅς.

ὧδε, adv. (ὅδε), *as follows, thus*.

ᾠδή, -ῆς, ἡ (from ἀοιδή; cf. ἀείδω, ᾄδω, Eng. ode), *song*.

ὡδοποιημένη, see ὁδοποιέω.

ᾤετο, ᾠήθησαν, see οἴομαι.

ὠθέω, ὤσω, ἔωσα, ἔωσμαι, ἐώσθην, *push;* mid., *push out of one's way*, III, 4, 48.

ὠθισμός, -οῦ, ὁ (ὠθίζομαι, *push, jostle;* cf. ὠθέω), *a pushing, crowding, struggling*.

ᾠκοδόμητο, see οἰκοδομέω.

ᾤμην, see οἴομαι.

ὠμοβόειος, -α, -ον (ὠμός+βοῦς), *of raw* or *untanned ox-hide*.

ὠμός, -ή -όν, *raw, uncooked*, IV, 8, 14 of persons, *cruel, fierce*, II, 6, 12.

ὦμος, -ου, ὁ, *shoulder.*
ὤμοσαν, see ὄμνυμι.
ὠνέομαι, ὠνήσομαι, ἐώνημαι, ἐωνήθην, with ἐπριάμην as 2 aor. mid. (ὦνος, *price*), *buy, purchase.*
ὠνήσατε, see ὀνίνημι.
ὤνιος, -α, -ον (ὦνος, *price*), *for sale*; τὰ ὤνια, as noun, *wares,* I, 2, 18.
ᾤοντο, see οἴομαι.
Ὦπις, -ιδος, ἡ, *Opis*, a city on the river Physcus in Assyria.
ὥρα, -ας, ἡ (Eng. *hour*), *a fixed time, season, hour,* I, 4, 10; *fit or proper time,* I, 3, 11.
ὡραῖος, -α, -ον (ὥρα), *seasonable; of persons, in the bloom of youth;* τὰ ὡραῖα, *fruits of the season,* V, 3, 9.
ὥρμηντο, see ὁρμάω.
ὡς, rel. adv. (ὅς); (1) *as, how;* often, esp. with partics., marking the action as intended, or avowed by the subj., but not (as ἅτε) making a statement on the responsibility of the speaker or writer; to be variously rendered, *as if, on the ground that, thinking that,* I, 1, 3; with numerals, *about,* I, 2, 4; with sup. it has intensive force (like ὅτι and Lat. *quam*), ὡς τάχιστα, *as quickly as possible,* I, 3, 14, etc.; (2) as improper prep., *to,* only with persons; (3) as conj. (*a*) temporal, *as, when, since,* ὡς τάχιστα (*cum primum*), *as soon as,* IV, 3, 9, (*b*) causal, *as, since, because,* II, 4, 17, (*c*) introducing indir. disc., *how, that,* I, 1, 3, (*d*) final (a use chiefly poetic), *that, in order that,* I, 3, 14; so with obj. clause, I, 1, 5, (*e*) con-
secutive (like ὥστε), *so that,* with infin., II, 3, 10; after comparatives, βραχύτερα ἢ ὡς ἐξικνεῖσθαι, *not far enough to reach,* III, 3, 7; with abs. infin. ὡς συνελόντι εἰπεῖν, *to put the matter briefly,* III, 1, 38.
ὥς, adv., *thus,* so only after intensive καί, or οὐδέ (μηδέ), οὐδ᾿ ὥς, *not even thus,* I, 8, 21; III, 2, 23; VI, 4, 22.
ὡσαύτως, adv. (ὥς+αὐτός), *in the very same way, just so, in like manner.*
ὥσθ᾿, by elision for ὥστε.
ὦσιν, see εἰμί.
ὠσίν, see οὖς.
ὥσπερ, rel. adv. (ὡς+πέρ), *just as, like, just as if;* ὥσπερ ἐξόν, *just as if it were possible,* III, 1, 14; ὥσπερ εἶχεν, *just as he was,* IV, 1, 19.
ὥστε, rel. adv. (ὡς+τε), *so as, so that;* as a rule with indic. of actual result and the infin. of tendency, I, 1, 5, 8; less commonly, *on condition that,* with infin., II, 6, 6.
ὦτα, see οὖς.
ᾧτε, only in the phrase ἐφ᾿ ᾧτε, *on condition that,* with infin.; see ἐπί.
ὠτειλή, -ῆς, ἡ, *wound, scar.*
ὠτίς, -ίδος, ἡ, *bustard.*
ὤφελε, see ὀφείλω.
ὠφελέω, ὠφελήσω, etc. (ὄφελος), *benefit, aid, help, be of use,* abs. or with acc.
ὠφέλιμος, -ον (ὠφελέω), *helpful, useful, serviceable.*
ὤφθημεν, see ὁράω.
ὦφλε, see ὀφλισκάνω.
ᾠχόμην, see οἴχομαι.